ENCYCLOPEDIA OF AMERICAN HISTORICAL DOCUMENTS

VOLUME III

ENCYCLOPEDIA OF AMERICAN HISTORICAL DOCUMENTS

VOLUME III

Edited by Susan Rosenfeld

Facts On File, Inc.

Encyclopedia of American Historical Documents

Facts On File, Inc.
132 West 31st Street
New York NY 10001

Library of Congress Cataloging-in-Publication Data

Encyclopedia of American Historical Documents / edited by Susan Rosenfeld
p. cm.
Includes bibliographical references and index.
ISBN 0-8160-4995-5 (set)—ISBN 0-8160-5993-4 (vol. 1)—
ISBN 0-8160-5994-2 (vol. 2)—ISBN 0-8160-5995-0 (vol. 3)
1. United States—History—Sources—Encyclopedias. I. Rosenfeld, Susan C.
E173.E54 2004
973'.03—dc21 2003051610

Text adaptation by Theresa Montoya and Cathy Rincon
Cover design by Cathy Rincon

Printed in the United States of America

VB FOF 10 9 8 7 6 5 4 3 2 1

This book is printed on acid-free paper.

Contents

Volume I

Volume II

Volume III

ERAS 7 TO 10

ERA 7
The Emergence of Modern America (CA. 1901–1929)

The early 20th century has been characterized as the Progressive Era—a time when Americans turned to their government to solve social and economic as well as diplomatic and military problems and, if that government proved corrupt, to reform it. American idealism was evident during the Progressive Era, and to some, entering World War I to save the world for democracy represented the culmination of Progressive Era thought.

At the same time, reform idealism and progress held some very different meanings for Americans in the early 20th century than they do at the beginning of the 21st. Reformers reacted to the problems in their midst caused by industrialization, big business, urbanization, immigration, and political corruption. Women, African Americans, and some segments of the labor movement found their voice in the years before World War I. However, among the contradictions apparent to the present-day reader is how some Progressive aspirations clashed. For example, a number of Progressives thought immigration from eastern and southern Europe threatened the American ideal; curbing this immigration was considered a progressive reform. Similarly, white Americans ignored or were antagonistic to efforts for blacks to rise out of poverty. Jim Crow, which became legalized and solidified after *Plessy v. Ferguson* in 1896, flourished in the Southern and border states, while de facto (extra-legal) segregation persisted in the North. The rights of working people became identified with the anarchist Industrial Workers of the World, and even the more staid American Federation of Labor was unable to achieve true legitimacy in this period.

In the field of foreign affairs, the United States emerged from the Spanish-American War (1898) an imperial power. Its efforts to stay neutral after World War I broke out in Europe in 1914 finally proved untenable, and the United States declared war on Germany and Austria in 1917, well after many Americans had died when ships they were in were torpedoed by the Germans. American entry into World War I confirmed the United States as a world power, a condition it never lost. The events of World War I, and the futile efforts by President Woodrow Wilson to create a lasting peace afterward, hold many lessons for the conditions of the world today. The United States also refused to join the League of Nations, weakening its ability to prevent Japanese, Italian, and German imperial aspirations.

The postwar period, from 1919 to the beginning of the Great Depression in 1929, represents a reaction to

Progressive Era idealism. The years 1919 and 1920 featured race riots and the first Red Scare. But World War I also gave economic opportunities for African Americans and women a boost. Women also gained the vote and began the long road to achieve a constitutional amendment granting them equal rights, a goal still not attained in the early 21st century.

Marking the end of World War I, President Warren G. Harding promised a return to "normalcy."

The 1920s also reacted to big government. Supreme Court decisions erased some Progressive Era reforms, and the military likewise contracted. Culturally, the movies and radio gained wider audiences. Prosperity encouraged people to buy automobiles, and technological advances also became media events, most notably with Charles A. Lindbergh's solo flight across the Atlantic.

Progressivism

W. E. B. DuBois, *The Souls of Black Folk*, 1903

Landmark 1903 work on the African-American experience by black scholar and civil rights activist W. E. B. DuBois. The preeminent African-American intellectual of his time, DuBois charted the psychological and social toll of historical subjugation on black Americans. His scholarship influenced his militant activism on behalf of black equal rights. *Souls of Black Folk,* a collection of essays detailing the spiritual and psychological underpinnings of black life in turn-of-the-century, segregated America, revealed the main currents of DuBois's thought. In characterizing the aspirations of African Americans, DuBois asserted that what blacks wanted and were entitled to by birth were equal social status and economic opportunity. He spelled out his indictment of rival black leader Booker T. Washington, whose accommodationist strategy to win black social and economic advancement, DuBois asserted, would achieve only illusory gains while perpetuating the institutions and attitudes of segregation.

The Forethought

Herein lie buried many things which if read with patience may show the strange meaning of being black here in the dawning of the Twentieth Century. This meaning is not without interest to you, Gentle Reader; for the problem of the Twentieth Century is the problem of the colorline.

I pray you, then, receive my little book in all charity, studying my words with me, forgiving mistake and foible for sake of the faith and passion that is in me, and seeking the grain of truth hidden there.

I have sought here to sketch, in vague, uncertain outline, the spiritual world in which ten thousand thousand Americans live and strive. First, in two chapters I have tried to show what Emancipation meant to them, and what was its aftermath. In a third chapter I have pointed out the slow rise of personal leadership, and criticised candidly the leader who bears the chief burden of his race to-day. Then, in two other chapters I have sketched in swift outline the two worlds within and without the Veil, and thus have come to the central problem of training men for life. Venturing now into deeper detail, I have in two chapters studied the struggles of the massed millions of the black peasantry, and in another have sought to make clear the present relations of the sons of master and man.

Leaving, then, the world of the white man, I have stepped within the Veil, raising it that you may view faintly its deeper recesses—the meaning of its religion, the passion of its human sorrow, and the struggle of its greater souls. All this I have ended with a tale twice told but seldom written.

Some of these thoughts of mine have seen the light before in other guise. For kindly consenting to their republication here, in altered and extended form, I must thank the publishers of *The Atlantic Monthly, The World's Work, The Dial, The New World, and the Annals of the American Academy of Political and Social Science.*

Before each chapter, as now printed, stands a bar of the Sorrow Songs—some echo of haunting melody from the only American music which welled up from black souls in the dark past. And, finally, need I add that I who speak here am bone of the bone and flesh of the flesh of them that live within the Veil?

W. E. B. DuB.
Atlanta, Ga., Feb. 1, 1903.

Herein Is Written
I

Of Our Spiritual Strivings

O water, voice of my heart, crying in the sand,
All night long crying with a mournful cry,
As I lie and listen, and cannot understand
The voice of my heart in my side or the voice of
the sea,
O water, crying for rest, is it I, is it I?
All night long the water is crying to me.

Unresting water, there shall never be rest
Till the last moon droop and the last tide fail,
And the fire of the end begin to burn in the west;
And the heart shall be weary and wonder and cry
like the sea,
All life long crying without avail,
As the water all night long is crying to me.

ARTHUR SYMONS.

Between me and the other world there is ever an unasked question: unasked by some through feelings of delicacy; by others through the difficulty of rightly framing it. All, nevertheless, flutter round it. They approach me in a half-hesitant sort of way, eye me curiously or compassionately, and then, instead of saying directly, How does it feel to be a problem? they say, I know an excellent colored man in my town; or, I fought at Mechanicsville; or, Do not these Southern outrages make your blood boil? At these I smile, or am interested, or reduce the boiling to a simmer, as the occasion may require. To the real question, How does it feel to be a problem? I answer seldom a word.

And yet, being a problem is a strange experience—peculiar even for one who has never been anything else, save perhaps in babyhood and in Europe. It is in the early days of rollicking boyhood that the revelation first bursts upon one, all in a day, as it were. I remember well when the shadow swept across me. I was a little thing, away up in the hills of New England, where the dark Housatonic winds between Hoosac and Taghkanic to the sea. In a wee wooden schoolhouse, something put it into the boys' and girls' heads to buy gorgeous visiting-cards—ten cents a package—and exchange. The exchange was merry, till one girl, a tall newcomer, refused my card—refused it peremptorily, with a glance. Then it dawned upon me with a certain suddenness that I was different from the others; or like, mayhap, in heart and life and longing, but shut out from their world by a vast veil. I had thereafter no desire to tear down that veil, to creep through; I held all beyond it in common contempt, and lived above it in a region of blue sky and great wandering shadows. That sky was bluest when I could beat my mates at examination-time, or beat them at a foot-race, or even beat their stringy heads. Alas, with the years all this fine contempt began to fade; for the worlds I longed for, and all their dazzling opportunities, were theirs, not mine. But they should not keep these prizes, I said; some, all, I would wrest from them. Just how I would do it I could never decide: by reading law, by healing the sick, by telling the wonderful tales that swam in my head—some way. With other black boys the strife was not so fiercely sunny: their youth shrunk into tasteless sycophancy, or into silent hatred of the pale world about them and mocking distrust of everything white; or wasted itself in a bitter cry, Why did God make me an outcast and a stranger in mine own house? The shades of the prison-house closed round about us all: walls strait and stubborn to the whitest, but relentlessly narrow, tall, and unscalable to sons of night who must plod darkly on in resignation, or beat unavailing palms against the stone, or steadily, half hopelessly, watch the streak of blue above.

After the Egyptian and Indian, the Greek and Roman, the Teuton and Mongolian, the Negro is a sort of seventh son, born with a veil, and gifted with second-sight in this American world—a world which yields him no true self-consciousness, but only lets him see himself through the revelation of the other world. It is a peculiar sensation, this double-consciousness, this sense of always looking at one's self through the eyes of others, of measuring one's soul by the tape of a world that looks on in amused contempt and pity. One ever feels his two-ness—an American, a Negro; two souls, two thoughts, two unreconciled strivings; two warring ideals in one dark body, whose dogged strength alone keeps it from being torn asunder.

The history of the American Negro is the history of this strife—this longing to attain self- conscious manhood, to merge his double self into a better and truer self. In this merging he wishes neither of the older selves to be lost. He would not Africanize America, for America has too much to teach the world and Africa. He would not bleach his Negro soul in a flood of white Americanism, for he knows that Negro blood has a message for the world. He simply wishes to make it possible for a man to be both a Negro and an American, without being cursed and spit upon by his fellows, without having the doors of Opportunity closed roughly in his face.

This, then, is the end of his striving: to be a co-worker in the kingdom of culture, to escape both death and isolation, to husband and use his best powers and his latent genius. These powers of body and mind have in the past been strangely wasted, dispersed, or forgotten. The shadow of a mighty Negro past flits through the tale of Ethiopia the Shadowy and of Egypt the Sphinx. Throughout history, the powers of single black men flash here and there like falling stars, and die sometimes before the world has rightly gauged their brightness. Here in America, in the few days since Emancipation, the black man's turning hither and thither in hesitant and doubtful striving has often made his very strength to lose effectiveness, to seem like absence of power, like weakness. And yet it is not weakness—it is the contradiction of double aims. The double-aimed struggle of the black artisan—on the one hand to escape white contempt for a nation of mere hewers of wood and drawers of water, and on the other hand to plough and nail and dig for a poverty-stricken horde—could only result in making him a poor craftsman, for he had but half a heart in either cause. By the poverty and ignorance of his people, the Negro minister or doctor was tempted toward quackery and demagogy; and by the criticism of the other world, toward ideals that made him ashamed of his lowly tasks. The would-be black *savant* was confronted by the paradox that the knowledge his people needed was a twice-told tale to his white neighbors, while the knowledge which would teach the white world was Greek to his own flesh and blood. The innate love of harmony and beauty that set the ruder souls of his people a-dancing and a-singing raised but confusion and doubt in the soul of the black artist; for the beauty revealed to him was the soul-beauty of a race which his larger audience despised, and he could not articulate the message of another people. This waste of double aims, this seeking to satisfy two unreconciled ideals, has wrought sad havoc with the courage and faith and deeds of ten thousand thousand people—has sent them often wooing false gods and invoking false means of salvation, and at times has even seemed about to make them ashamed of themselves.

Away back in the days of bondage they thought to see in one divine event the end of all doubt and disappointment; few men ever worshipped Freedom with half such unquestioning faith as did the American Negro for two centuries. To him, so far as he thought and dreamed, slavery was indeed the sum of all villainies, the cause of all sorrow, the root of all prejudice; Emancipation was the key to a promised land of sweeter beauty than ever stretched before the eyes of wearied Israelites. In song and exhortation swelled one refrain—Liberty; in his tears and curses the God he implored had Freedom in his right hand. At last it came—suddenly, fearfully, like a dream. With one wild carnival of blood and passion came the message in his own plaintive cadences:

"Shout, O children! Shout, you're free! For God has bought your liberty!"

Years have passed away since then—ten, twenty, forty; forty years of national life, forty years of renewal and development, and yet the swarthy spectre sits in its accustomed seat at the Nation's feast. In vain do we cry to this our vastest social problem:

"Take any shape but that, and my firm nerves Shall never tremble!"

The Nation has not yet found peace from its sins; the freedman has not yet found in freedom his promised land. Whatever of good may have come in these years of change, the shadow of a deep disappointment rests upon the Negro people—a disappointment all the more bitter because the unattained ideal was unbounded save by the simple ignorance of a lowly people.

The first decade was merely a prolongation of the vain search for freedom, the boon that seemed ever barely to elude their grasp—like a tantalizing will-o'-the-wisp, maddening and misleading the headless host. The holocaust of war, the terrors of the Ku-Klux Klan, the lies of carpet-baggers, the disorganization of industry, and the contradictory advice of friends and foes, left the bewildered serf with no new watch-word beyond the old cry for freedom. As the time flew, however, he began to grasp a new idea. The ideal of liberty demanded for its attainment powerful means, and these the Fifteenth Amendment gave him. The ballot, which before he had looked upon as a visible sign of freedom, he now regarded as the chief means of gaining and perfecting the liberty with which war had partially endowed him. And why not? Had not votes made war and emancipated millions? Had not votes enfranchised the freedmen? Was anything impossible to a power that had done all this? A million black men started with renewed zeal to vote themselves into the kingdom. So the decade flew away, the revolution of 1876 came, and left the half-free serf weary, wondering, but still inspired. Slowly but steadily, in the following years, a new vision began gradually to replace the dream of political power,—a powerful movement, the rise of another ideal to guide the unguided, another pillar of fire by night after a clouded day. It was the ideal of "book-learning"; the curiosity, born of compulsory ignorance, to know and test the power of the cabalistic letters of the white man, the longing to know. Here at last seemed to have been discovered the mountain path to Canaan; longer than the highway of Emancipation and law, steep and rugged, but straight, leading to heights high enough to overlook life.

Up the new path the advance guard toiled, slowly, heavily, doggedly; only those who have watched and guided the faltering feet, the misty minds, the dull understandings, of the dark pupils of these schools know how faithfully, how piteously, this people strove to learn. It was weary work. The cold statistician wrote down the inches of progress here and there, noted also where here and there a foot had slipped or some one had fallen. To the tired climbers, the horizon was ever dark, the mists were often cold, the Canaan was always dim and far away. If, however, the vistas disclosed as yet no goal, no resting-place, little but flattery and criticism, the journey at least gave leisure for reflection and self-examination; it changed the child of Emancipation to the youth with dawning self-consciousness, self-realization, self- respect. In those sombre forests of his striving his own soul rose before him, and he saw himself—darkly as through a veil; and yet he saw in himself some faint revelation of his power, of his mission. He began to have a dim feeling that, to attain his place in the world, he must be himself, and not another. For the first time he sought to analyze the burden he bore upon his back, that dead-weight of social degradation partially masked behind a half-named Negro problem. He felt his poverty; without a cent, without a home, without land, tools, or savings, he had entered into competition with rich, landed, skilled neighbors. To be a poor man is hard, but to be a poor race in a land of dollars is the very bottom of hardships. He felt the weight of his ignorance—not simply of letters, but of life, of business, of the humanities; the accumulated sloth and shirking and awkwardness of decades and centuries shackled his hands and feet. Nor was his burden all poverty and ignorance. The red stain of bastardy, which two centuries of systematic legal defilement of Negro women had stamped upon his race, meant not only the loss of ancient African chastity, but also the hereditary weight of a mass of corruption from white adulterers, threatening almost the obliteration of the Negro home.

A people thus handicapped ought not to be asked to race with the world, but rather allowed to give all its time and thought to its own social problems. But alas! while sociologists gleefully count his bastards and his prostitutes, the very soul of the toiling, sweating black man is darkened by the shadow of a vast despair. Men call the shadow prejudice, and learnedly explain it as the natural defence of culture against barbarism, learning against ignorance, purity against crime, the "higher" against the "lower" races. To which the Negro cries Amen! and swears that to so much of this strange prejudice as is founded on just homage to civilization, culture, righteousness, and progress, he humbly bows and meekly does obeisance. But before that nameless prejudice that leaps beyond all this he stands helpless, dismayed, and well-nigh speechless; before that personal disrespect and mockery, the ridicule and systematic humiliation, the distortion of fact and wanton license of fancy, the cynical ignoring of the better and the boisterous welcoming of the worse, the all-pervading desire to inculcate disdain for everything black, from Toussaint to the devil—before this there rises a sickening despair that would disarm and discourage any nation save that black host to whom "discouragement" is an unwritten word.

But the facing of so vast a prejudice could not but bring the inevitable self-questioning, self- disparagement, and lowering of ideals which ever accompany repression and breed in an atmosphere of contempt and hate. Whisperings and portents came borne upon the four winds: Lo! we are diseased and dying, cried the dark hosts; we cannot write, our voting is vain; what need of education, since we must always cook and serve? And the Nation echoed and enforced this self-criticism, saying: Be content to be servants, and nothing more; what need of higher culture for half-men? Away with the black man's ballot, by force or fraud—and behold the suicide of a race! Nevertheless, out of the evil came something of good—the more careful adjustment of education to real life, the clearer perception of the Negroes' social responsibilities, and the sobering realization of the meaning of progress.

So dawned the time of *Sturm und Drang:* storm and stress to-day rocks our little boat on the mad waters of the world-sea; there is within and without the sound of conflict, the burning of body and rending of soul; inspiration strives with doubt, and faith with vain questionings. The bright ideals of the past—physical freedom, political power, the training of brains and the training of hands—all these in turn have waxed and waned, until even the last grows dim and overcast. Are they all wrong—all false? No, not that, but each alone was over-simple and incomplete—the dreams of a credulous race-childhood, or the fond imaginings of the other world which does not know and does not want to know our power. To be really true, all these ideals must be melted and welded into one. The training of the schools we need to-day more than ever—the training of deft hands, quick eyes and ears, and above all the broader, deeper, higher culture of gifted minds and pure hearts. The power of the ballot we need in sheer self-defence—else what shall save us from a second slavery? Freedom, too, the long-sought, we still seek—the freedom of life and limb, the freedom to work and think, the freedom to love and aspire. Work, culture, liberty—all these we need, not singly but together, not successively but together, each growing and aiding each, and all striving toward that vaster ideal that swims before the Negro people, the ideal of human brotherhood, gained through the unifying ideal of Race; the ideal of fostering and developing the traits and talents of the Negro, not in opposition to or contempt for other races, but rather in large conformity to the greater ideals of the American Republic, in order that some day on American soil two world-races may give each to each those characteristics both so sadly lack. We the darker ones come even now not altogether empty-handed: there are to-day no truer exponents of the pure human spirit of the Declaration of Independence than the American Negroes; there is no true American music but the wild sweet melodies of the Negro slave; the American fairy tales and folk-lore are Indian and African; and, all in all, we black men seem the sole oasis of simple faith and reverence in a dusty desert of dollars and smartness. Will America be poorer if she replace her brutal dyspeptic blundering with light-hearted but determined Negro humility? or her coarse and cruel wit with loving jovial good-humor? or her vulgar music with the soul of the Sorrow Songs?

Merely a concrete test of the underlying principles of the great republic is the Negro Problem, and the spiritual striving of the freedmen's sons is the travail of souls whose burden is almost beyond the measure of their strength, but who bear it in the name of an historic race, in the name of this the land of their fathers' fathers, and in the name of human opportunity.

And now what I have briefly sketched in large outline let me on coming pages tell again in many ways, with loving emphasis and deeper detail, that men may listen to the striving in the souls of black folk.

II

Of the Dawn of Freedom

> Careless seems the great Avenger;
> History's lessons but record
> One death-grapple in the darkness
> 'Twixt old systems and the Word;
> Truth forever on the scaffold,
> Wrong forever on the throne;
> Yet that scaffold sways the future,
> And behind the dim unknown
> Standeth God within the shadow
> Keeping watch above His own.
>
> Lowell.

The problem of the twentieth century is the problem of the color-line—the relation of the darker to the lighter races of men in Asia and Africa, in America and the islands of the sea. It was a phase of this problem that caused the Civil War; and however much they who marched South and North in 1861 may have fixed on the technical points of union and local autonomy as a shibboleth, all nevertheless knew, as we know, that the question of Negro slavery was the real cause of the conflict. Curious it was, too, how this deeper question ever forced itself to the surface despite effort and disclaimer. No sooner had Northern armies touched Southern soil than this old question, newly guised, sprang from the earth—What shall be done with Negroes? Peremptory military commands, this way and that, could not answer the query; the Emancipation Proclamation seemed but to broaden and intensify the difficulties; and the War Amendments made the Negro problems of to-day.

It is the aim of this essay to study the period of history from 1861 to 1872 so far as it relates to the American Negro. In effect, this tale of the dawn of Freedom is an account of that government of men called the Freedmen's Bureau—one of the most singular and interesting of the attempts made by a great nation to grapple with vast problems of race and social condition.

The war has naught to do with slaves, cried Congress, the President, and the Nation; and yet no sooner had the armies, East and West, penetrated Virginia and Tennessee than fugitive slaves appeared within their lines. They came at night, when the flickering camp-fires shone like vast unsteady stars along the black horizon: old men and thin, with gray and tufted hair; women, with frightened eyes, dragging whimpering hungry children; men and girls, stalwart and gaunt—a horde of starving vagabonds, homeless, helpless, and pitiable, in their dark distress. Two methods of treating these newcomers seemed equally logical to opposite sorts of minds. Ben Butler, in Virginia, quickly declared slave property contraband of war, and put the fugitives to work; while Fremont, in Missouri, declared the slaves free under martial law. Butler's action was approved, but Fremont's was hastily countermanded, and his successor, Halleck, saw things differently. "Hereafter," he commanded, "no slaves should be allowed to come into your lines at all; if any come without your knowledge, when owners call for them deliver them." Such a policy was difficult to enforce; some of the black refugees declared themselves freemen, others showed that their masters had deserted them, and still others were captured with forts and plantations. Evidently, too, slaves were a source of strength to the Confederacy, and were being used as laborers and producers. "They constitute a military resource," wrote Secretary Cameron, late in 1861; "and being such, that they should not be turned over to the enemy is too plain to discuss." So gradually the tone of the army chiefs changed; Congress forbade the rendition of fugitives, and Butler's "contrabands" were welcomed as military laborers. This complicated rather than solved the problem, for now the scattering fugitives became a steady stream, which flowed faster as the armies marched.

Then the long-headed man with care-chiselled face who sat in the White House saw the inevitable, and emancipated the slaves of rebels on New Year's, 1863. A month later Congress called earnestly for the Negro soldiers whom the act of July, 1862, had half grudgingly allowed to enlist. Thus the barriers were levelled and the deed was done. The stream of fugitives swelled to a flood, and anxious army officers kept inquiring: "What must be done with slaves, arriving almost daily? Are we to find food and shelter for women and children?"

It was a Pierce of Boston who pointed out the way, and thus became in a sense the founder of the Freedmen's Bureau. He was a firm friend of Secretary Chase; and when, in 1861, the care of slaves and abandoned lands devolved upon the Treasury officials, Pierce was specially detailed from the ranks to study the conditions. First, he cared for the refugees at Fortress Monroe; and then, after Sherman had captured Hilton Head, Pierce was sent there to found his Port Royal experiment of making free workingmen out of slaves. Before his experiment was barely started, however, the problem of the fugitives had assumed such proportions that it was taken from the hands of the over-burdened Treasury Department and given to the army officials. Already centres of massed freedmen were forming at Fortress Monroe, Washington, New Orleans, Vicksburg and Corinth, Columbus, Ky., and Cairo, Ill., as well as at Port Royal. Army chaplains found here new and fruitful fields; "superintendents of contrabands" multiplied, and some attempt at systematic work was made by enlisting the able-bodied men and giving work to the others.

Then came the Freedmen's Aid societies, born of the touching appeals from Pierce and from these other centres of distress. There was the American Missionary Association, sprung from the *Amistad,* and now full-grown for work; the various church organizations, the National Freedmen's Relief Association, the American Freedmen's Union, the Western Freedmen's Aid Commission—in all fifty or more active organizations, which sent clothes, money, school-books, and teachers southward. All they did was needed, for the destitution of the freedmen was often reported as "too appalling for belief," and the situation was daily growing worse rather than better.

And daily, too, it seemed more plain that this was no ordinary matter of temporary relief, but a national crisis; for here loomed a labor problem of vast dimensions. Masses of Negroes stood idle, or, if they worked spasmodically, were never sure of pay; and if perchance they received pay, squandered the new thing thoughtlessly. In these and other ways were camp-life and the new liberty demoralizing the freedmen. The broader economic organization thus clearly demanded sprang up here and there as accident and local conditions determined. Here it was that Pierce's Port Royal plan of leased plantations and guided workmen pointed out the rough way. In Washington the military governor, at the urgent appeal of the superintendent, opened confiscated estates to the cultivation of the fugitives, and there in the shadow of the dome gathered black farm villages. General Dix gave over estates to the freedmen of Fortress Monroe, and so on, South and West. The government and benevolent societies furnished the means of cultivation, and the Negro turned again slowly to work. The systems of control, thus started, rapidly grew, here and there, into strange little governments, like that of General Banks in Louisiana, with its ninety thousand black subjects, its fifty thousand guided laborers, and its annual budget of one hundred thousand dollars and more. It made out four thousand pay-rolls a year, registered all freedmen, inquired into grievances and redressed them, laid and collected taxes, and established a system of public schools. So, too, Colonel Eaton, the superintendent of Tennessee and Arkansas, ruled over one hundred thousand freedmen, leased and cultivated seven thousand acres of cotton land, and fed ten thousand paupers a year. In South Carolina was General Saxton, with his deep interest in black folk. He succeeded Pierce and the Treasury officials, and sold forfeited estates, leased abandoned plantations, encouraged schools, and received from Sherman, after that terribly picturesque march to the sea, thousands of the wretched camp followers.

Three characteristic things one might have seen in Sherman's raid through Georgia, which threw the new situation in shadowy relief: the Conqueror, the Conquered, and the Negro. Some see all significance in the grim front of the destroyer, and some in the bitter sufferers of the Lost Cause. But to me neither soldier nor fugitive speaks with so deep a meaning as that dark human cloud that clung like remorse on the rear of those swift columns, swelling at times to half their size, almost engulfing and choking them. In vain were they ordered back, in vain were bridges hewn from beneath their feet; on they trudged and writhed and surged, until they rolled into Savannah, a starved and naked horde of tens of thousands. There too came the characteristic military remedy: "The islands from Charleston south, the abandoned rice-fields along the rivers for thirty miles back from the sea, and the country bordering the St. John's River, Florida, are reserved and set apart for the settlement of Negroes now made free by act of war." So read the celebrated "Field-order Number Fifteen."

All these experiments, orders, and systems were bound to attract and perplex the government and the nation. Directly after the Emancipation Proclamation, Representative Eliot had introduced a bill creating a Bureau of Emancipation; but it was never reported. The following June a committee of inquiry, appointed by the Secretary of War, reported in favor of a temporary bureau for the "improvement, protection, and employment of refugee freedmen," on much the same lines as were afterwards followed. Petitions came in to President Lincoln from distinguished citizens and organizations, strongly urging a comprehensive and unified plan of dealing with the freedmen, under a bureau which should be "charged with the study of plans and execution of measures for easily guiding, and in every way judiciously and humanely aiding, the passage of our emancipated and yet to be emancipated blacks from the old condition of forced labor to their new state of voluntary industry."

Some half-hearted steps were taken to accomplish this, in part, by putting the whole matter again in charge of the special Treasury agents. Laws of 1863 and 1864 directed them to take charge of and lease abandoned lands for periods not exceeding twelve months, and to "provide in such leases, or otherwise, for the employment and general welfare" of the freedmen. Most of the army officers greeted this as a welcome relief from perplexing "Negro affairs," and Secretary Fessenden, July 29, 1864, issued an excellent system of regulations, which were afterward closely followed by General Howard. Under Treasury agents, large quantities of land were leased in the Mississippi Valley, and many Negroes were employed; but in August, 1864, the new regulations were suspended for reasons of "public policy," and the army was again in control.

Meanwhile Congress had turned its attention to the subject; and in March the House passed a bill by a majority of two establishing a Bureau for Freedmen in the War Department. Charles Sumner, who had charge of the bill in the Senate, argued that freedmen and abandoned lands ought to be under the same department, and reported a substitute for the House bill attaching the Bureau to the Treasury Department. This bill passed, but too late for action by the House. The debates wandered over the whole policy of the administration and the general question of slavery, without touching very closely the specific merits of the measure in hand. Then the national election took place; and the administration, with a vote of renewed confidence from the country, addressed itself to the matter more seriously. A conference between the two branches of Congress agreed upon a carefully drawn measure which contained the chief provisions of Sumner's bill, but made the proposed organization a department independent of both the War and the Treasury officials. The bill was conservative, giving the new department "general superintendence of all freedmen." Its purpose was to "establish regulations" for them, protect them, lease them lands, adjust their wages, and appear in civil and military courts as their "next friend." There were many limitations attached to the powers thus granted, and the organization was made permanent. Nevertheless, the Senate defeated the bill, and a new conference committee was appointed. This committee reported a new bill, February 28, which was whirled through just as the session closed, and became the act of 1865 establishing in the War Department a "Bureau of Refugees, Freedmen, and Abandoned Lands."

This last compromise was a hasty bit of legislation, vague and uncertain in outline. A Bureau was created, "to continue during the present War of Rebellion, and for one year thereafter," to which was given "the supervision and management of all abandoned lands and the control of all subjects relating to refugees and freedmen," under "such rules and regulations as may be presented by the head of the Bureau and approved by the President." A Commissioner, appointed by the President and Senate, was to control the Bureau, with an office force not exceeding ten clerks. The President might also appoint assistant commissioners in the seceded States, and to all these offices military officials might be detailed at regular pay. The Secretary of War could issue rations, clothing, and fuel to the destitute, and all abandoned property was placed in the hands of the Bureau for eventual lease and sale to ex-slaves in forty-acre parcels.

Thus did the United States government definitely assume charge of the emancipated Negro as the ward of the nation. It was a tremendous undertaking. Here at a stroke of the pen was erected a government of millions of men—and not ordinary men either, but black men emasculated by a peculiarly complete system of slavery, centuries old; and now, suddenly, violently, they come into a new birthright, at a time of war and passion, in the midst of the stricken and embittered population of their former masters. Any man might well have hesitated to assume charge of such a work, with vast responsibilities, indefinite powers, and limited resources. Probably no one but a soldier would have answered such a call promptly; and, indeed, no one but a soldier could be called, for Congress had appropriated no money for salaries and expenses.

Less than a month after the weary Emancipator passed to his rest, his successor assigned Major-Gen. Oliver O. Howard to duty as Commissioner of the new Bureau. He was a Maine man, then only thirty-five years of age. He had marched with Sherman to the sea, had fought well at Gettysburg, and but the year before had been assigned to the command of the Department of Tennessee. An honest man, with too much faith in human nature, little aptitude for business and intricate detail, he had had large opportunity of becoming acquainted at first hand with much of the work before him. And of that work it has been truly said that "no approximately correct history of civilization can ever be written which does not throw out in bold relief, as one of the great landmarks of political and social progress, the organization and administration of the Freedmen's Bureau."

On May 12, 1865, Howard was appointed; and he assumed the duties of his office promptly on the 15th, and began examining the field of work. A curious mess he looked upon: little despotisms, communistic experiments, slavery, peonage, business speculations, organized charity, unorganized almsgiving—all reeling on under the guise of helping the freedmen, and all enshrined in the smoke and blood of war and the cursing and silence of angry men. On May 19 the new government—for a government it really was—issued its constitution; commissioners were to be appointed in each of the seceded States, who were to take charge of "all subjects relating to refugees and freedmen," and all relief and rations were to be given by their consent alone. The Bureau invited continued cooperation with benevolent societies, and declared: "It will be the object of all commissioners to introduce practicable systems of compensated labor," and to establish schools. Forthwith nine assistant commissioners were appointed. They were to hasten to their fields of work; seek gradually to close relief establishments, and make the destitute self-supporting; act as courts of law where there were no courts, or where Negroes were not recognized in them as free; establish the institution of marriage among ex-slaves, and keep records; see that freedmen were free to choose their employers, and help in making fair contracts for them; and finally, the circular said: "Simple good faith, for which we hope on all hands for those concerned in the passing away of slavery, will especially relieve the assistant commissioners in the discharge of their duties toward the freedmen, as well as promote the general welfare."

No sooner was the work thus started, and the general system and local organization in some measure begun, than two grave difficulties appeared which changed largely the theory and outcome of Bureau work. First, there were the abandoned lands of the South. It had long been the more or less definitely expressed theory of the North that all the chief problems of Emancipation might be settled by establishing the slaves on the forfeited lands of their masters—a sort of poetic justice, said some. But this poetry done into solemn prose meant either wholesale confiscation of private property in the South, or vast appropriations. Now Congress had not appropriated a cent, and no sooner did the proclamations of general amnesty appear than the eight hundred thousand acres of abandoned lands in the hands of the Freedmen's Bureau melted quickly away. The second difficulty lay in perfecting the local organization of the Bureau throughout the wide field of work. Making a new machine and sending out officials of duly ascertained fitness for a great work of social reform is no child's task; but this task was even harder, for a new central organization had to be fitted on a heterogeneous and confused but already existing system of relief and control of ex-slaves; and the agents available for this work must be sought for in an army still busy with war operations—men in the very nature of the case ill fitted for delicate social work—or among the questionable camp followers of an invading host. Thus, after a year's work, vigorously as it was pushed, the problem looked even more difficult to grasp and solve than at the beginning. Nevertheless, three things that year's work did, well worth the doing: it relieved a vast amount of physical suffering; it transported seven thousand fugitives from congested centres back to the farm; and, best of all, it inaugurated the crusade of the New England school-ma'am.

The annals of this Ninth Crusade are yet to be written—the tale of a mission that seemed to our age far more quixotic than the quest of St. Louis seemed to his. Behind the mists of ruin and rapine waved the calico dresses of women who dared, and after the hoarse mouthings of the field guns rang the rhythm of the alphabet. Rich and poor they were, serious and curious. Bereaved now of a father, now of a brother, now of more than these, they came seeking a life work in planting New England schoolhouses among the white and black of the South. They did their work well. In that first year they taught one hundred thousand souls, and more.

Evidently, Congress must soon legislate again on the hastily organized Bureau, which had so quickly grown into wide significance and vast possibilities. An institution such as that was well-nigh as difficult to end as to begin. Early in 1866 Congress took up the matter, when Senator Trumbull, of Illinois, introduced a bill to extend the Bureau and enlarge its powers. This measure received, at the hands of Congress, far more thorough discussion and attention than its predecessor. The war cloud had thinned enough to allow a clearer conception of the work of Emancipation. The champions of the bill argued that the strengthening of the Freedmen's Bureau was still a military necessity; that it was needed for the proper carrying out of the Thirteenth Amendment, and was a work of sheer justice to the ex-slave, at a trifling cost to the government. The opponents of the measure declared that the war was over, and the necessity for war measures past; that the Bureau, by reason of its extraordinary powers, was clearly unconstitutional in time of peace, and was destined to irritate the South and pauperize the freedmen, at a final cost of possibly hundreds of millions. These two arguments were unanswered, and indeed unanswerable: the one that the extraordinary powers of the Bureau threatened the civil rights of all citizens; and the other that the government must have power to do what manifestly must be done, and that present abandonment of the freedmen meant their practical re-enslavement. The bill which finally passed enlarged and made permanent the Freedmen's Bureau. It was promptly vetoed by President Johnson as "unconstitutional," "unnecessary," and "extrajudicial," and failed of passage over the veto. Meantime, however, the breach between Congress and the President began to broaden, and a modified form of the lost bill was finally passed over the President's second veto, July 16.

The act of 1866 gave the Freedmen's Bureau its final form—the form by which it will be known to posterity and judged of men. It extended the existence of the Bureau to July, 1868; it authorized additional assistant commissioners, the retention of army officers mustered out of regular service, the sale of certain forfeited lands to freedmen on nominal terms, the sale of Confederate public property for Negro schools, and a wider field of judicial interpretation and cognizance. The government of the unreconstructed South was thus put very largely in the hands of the Freedmen's Bureau, especially as in many cases the departmental military commander was now made also assistant commissioner. It was thus that the Freedmen's Bureau became a full-fledged government of men. It made laws, executed them and interpreted them; it laid and collected taxes, defined and punished crime, maintained and used military force, and dictated such measures as it thought necessary and proper for the accomplishment of its varied ends. Naturally, all these powers were not exercised continuously nor to their fullest extent; and yet, as General Howard has said, "scarcely any subject that has to be legislated upon in civil society failed, at one time or another, to demand the action of this singular Bureau."

To understand and criticise intelligently so vast a work, one must not forget an instant the drift of things in the later sixties. Lee had surrendered, Lincoln was dead, and Johnson and Congress were at loggerheads; the Thirteenth Amendment was adopted, the Fourteenth pending, and the Fifteenth declared in force in 1870. Guerrilla raiding, the ever-present flickering after-flame of war, was spending its force against the Negroes, and all the Southern land was awakening as from some wild dream to poverty and social revolution. In a time of perfect calm, amid willing neighbors and streaming wealth, the social uplifting of four million slaves to an assured and self-sustaining place in the body politic and economic would have been a herculean task; but when to the inherent difficulties of so delicate and nice a social operation were added the spite and hate of conflict, the hell of war; when suspicion and cruelty were rife, and gaunt Hunger wept beside Bereavement—in such a case, the work of any instrument of social regeneration was in large part foredoomed to failure. The very name of the Bureau stood for a thing in the South which for two centuries and better men had refused even to argue—that life amid free Negroes was simply unthinkable, the maddest of experiments.

The agents that the Bureau could command varied all the way from unselfish philanthropists to narrow-minded busy-bodies and thieves; and even though it be true that the average was far better than the worst, it was the occasional fly that helped spoil the ointment.

Then amid all crouched the freed slave, bewildered between friend and foe. He had emerged from slavery—not the worst slavery in the world, not a slavery that made all life unbearable, rather a slavery that had here and there something of kindliness, fidelity, and happiness—but withal slavery, which, so far as human aspiration and desert were concerned, classed the black man and the ox together. And the Negro knew full well that, whatever their deeper convictions may have been, Southern men had fought with desperate energy to perpetuate this slavery under which the black masses, with half-articulate thought, had writhed and shivered. They welcomed freedom with a cry. They shrank from the master who still strove for their chains; they fled to the friends that had freed them, even though those friends stood ready to use them as a club for driving the recalcitrant South back into loyalty. So the cleft between the white and black South grew. Idle to say it never should have been; it was as inevitable as its results were pitiable. Curiously incongruous elements were left arrayed against each other—the North, the government, the carpet-bagger, and the slave, here; and there, all the South that was white, whether gentleman or vagabond, honest man or rascal, lawless murderer or martyr to duty.

Thus it is doubly difficult to write of this period calmly, so intense was the feeling, so mighty the human passions that swayed and blinded men. Amid it all, two figures ever stand to typify that day to coming ages—the one, a gray-haired gentleman, whose fathers had quit themselves like men, whose sons lay in nameless graves; who bowed to the evil of slavery because its abolition threatened untold ill to all; who stood at last, in the evening of life, a blighted, ruined form, with hate in his eyes—and the other, a form hovering dark and mother-like, her awful face black with the mists of centuries, had aforetime quailed at that white master's command, had bent in love over the cradles of his sons and daughters, and closed in death the sunken eyes of his wife—aye, too, at his behest had laid herself low to his lust, and borne a tawny man-child to the world, only to see her dark boy's limbs scattered to the winds by midnight marauders riding after "cursed Niggers." These were the saddest sights of that woful day; and no man clasped the hands of these two passing figures of the present-past; but, hating, they went to their long home, and, hating, their children's children live to-day.

Here, then, was the field of work for the Freedmen's Bureau; and since, with some hesitation, it was continued by the act of 1868 until 1869, let us look upon four years of its work as a whole. There were, in 1868, nine hundred Bureau officials scattered from Washington to Texas, ruling, directly and indirectly, many millions of men. The deeds of these rulers fall mainly under seven heads: the relief of physical suffering, the overseeing of the beginnings of free labor, the buying and selling of land, the establishment of schools, the paying of bounties, the administration of justice, and the financiering of all these activities.

Up to June, 1869, over half a million patients had been treated by Bureau physicians and surgeons, and sixty hospitals and asylums had been in operation. In fifty months twenty-one million free rations were distributed at a cost of over four million dollars. Next came the difficult question of labor. First, thirty thousand black men were transported from the refuges and relief stations back to the farms, back to the critical trial of a new way of working. Plain instructions went out from Washington: the laborers must be free to choose their employers, no fixed rate of wages was prescribed, and there was to be no peonage or forced labor. So far, so good; but where local agents differed *toto celo* in capacity and character, where the *personnel* was continually changing, the outcome was necessarily varied. The largest element of success lay in the fact that the majority of the freedmen were willing, even eager, to work. So labor contracts were written—fifty thousand in a single State—laborers advised, wages guaranteed, and employers supplied. In truth, the organization became a vast labor bureau—not perfect, indeed, notably defective here and there, but on the whole successful beyond the dreams of thoughtful men. The two great obstacles which confronted the officials were the tyrant and the idler—the slaveholder who was determined to perpetuate slavery under another name; and the freedman who regarded freedom as perpetual rest—the Devil and the Deep Sea.

In the work of establishing the Negroes as peasant proprietors, the Bureau was from the first handicapped and at last absolutely checked. Something was done, and larger things were planned; abandoned lands were leased so long as they remained in the hands of the Bureau, and a total revenue of nearly half a million dollars derived from black tenants. Some other lands to which the nation had gained title were sold on easy terms, and public lands were opened for settlement to the very few freedmen who had tools and capital. But the vision of "forty acres and a mule"—the righteous and reasonable ambition to become a landholder, which the nation had all but categorically promised the freedmen—was destined in most cases to bitter disappointment. And those men of marvellous hindsight who are to-day seeking to preach the Negro back to the present peonage of the soil know well, or ought to know, that the opportunity of binding the Negro peasant willingly to the soil was lost on that day when the Commissioner of the Freedmen's Bureau had to go to South Carolina and tell the weeping freedmen, after their years of toil, that their land was not theirs, that there was a mistake—somewhere. If by 1874 the Georgia Negro alone owned three hundred and fifty thousand acres of land, it was by grace of his thrift rather than by bounty of the government.

The greatest success of the Freedmen's Bureau lay in the planting of the free school among Negroes, and the idea of free elementary education among all classes in the South. It not only called the schoolmistresses through the benevolent agencies and built them schoolhouses, but it helped discover and support such apostles of human culture as Edmund Ware, Samuel Armstrong, and Erastus Cravath. The opposition to Negro education in the South was at first bitter, and showed itself in ashes, insult, and blood; for the South believed an educated Negro to be a dangerous Negro. And the South was not wholly wrong; for education among all kinds of men always has had, and always will have, an element of danger and revolution, of dissatisfaction and discontent. Nevertheless, men strive to know. Perhaps some inkling of this paradox, even in the unquiet days of the Bureau, helped the bayonets allay an opposition to human training which still to-day lies smouldering in the South, but not flaming. Fisk, Atlanta, Howard, and Hampton were founded in these days, and six million dollars were expended for educational work, seven hundred and fifty thousand dollars of which the freedmen themselves gave of their poverty.

Such contributions, together with the buying of land and various other enterprises, showed that the ex-slave was handling some free capital already. The chief initial source of this was labor in the army, and his pay and bounty as a soldier. Payments to Negro soldiers were at first complicated by the ignorance of the recipients, and the fact that the quotas of colored regiments from Northern States were largely filled by recruits from the South, unknown to their fellow soldiers. Consequently, payments were accompanied by such frauds that Congress, by joint resolution in 1867, put the whole matter in the hands of the Freedmen's Bureau. In two years six million dollars was thus distributed to five thousand claimants, and in the end the sum exceeded eight million dollars. Even in this system fraud was frequent; but still the work put needed capital in the hands of practical paupers, and some, at least, was well spent.

The most perplexing and least successful part of the Bureau's work lay in the exercise of its judicial functions. The regular Bureau court consisted of one representative of the employer, one of the Negro, and one of the Bureau. If the Bureau could have maintained a perfectly judicial attitude, this arrangement would have been ideal, and must in time have gained confidence; but the nature of its other activities and the character of its *personnel* prejudiced the Bureau in favor of the black litigants, and led without doubt to much injustice and annoyance. On the other hand, to leave the Negro in the hands of Southern courts was impossible. In a distracted land where slavery had hardly fallen, to keep the strong from wanton abuse of the weak, and the weak from gloating insolently over the half-shorn strength of the strong, was a thankless, hopeless task. The former masters of the land were peremptorily ordered about, seized, and imprisoned, and punished over and again, with scant courtesy from army officers. The former slaves were intimidated, beaten, raped, and butchered by angry and revengeful men. Bureau courts tended to become centres simply for punishing whites, while the regular civil courts tended to become solely institutions for perpetuating the slavery of blacks. Almost every law and method ingenuity could devise was employed by the legislatures to reduce the Negroes to serfdom—to make them the slaves of the State, if not of individual owners; while the Bureau officials too often were found striving to put the "bottom rail on top," and give the freedmen a power and independence which they could not yet use. It is all well enough for us of another generation to wax wise with advice to those who bore the burden in the heat of the day. It is full easy now to see that the man who lost home, fortune, and family at a stroke, and saw his land ruled by "mules and niggers," was really benefited by the passing of slavery. It is not difficult now to say to the young freedman, cheated and cuffed about, who has seen his father's head beaten to a jelly and his own mother namelessly assaulted, that the meek shall inherit the earth. Above all, nothing is more convenient than to heap on the Freedmen's Bureau all the evils of that evil day, and damn it utterly for every mistake and blunder that was made.

All this is easy, but it is neither sensible nor just. Some one had blundered, but that was long before Oliver Howard was born; there was criminal aggression and heedless neglect, but without some system of control there would have been far more than there was. Had that control been from within, the Negro would have been re-enslaved, to all intents and purposes. Coming as the control did from without, perfect men and methods would have bettered all things; and even with imperfect agents and questionable methods, the work accomplished was not undeserving of commendation.

Such was the dawn of Freedom; such was the work of the Freedmen's Bureau, which, summed up in brief, may be epitomized thus: For some fifteen million dollars, beside the sums spent before 1865, and the dole of benevolent societies, this Bureau set going a system of free labor, established a beginning of peasant proprietorship, secured the recognition of black freedmen before courts of law, and founded the free common school in the South. On the other hand, it failed to begin the establishment of good-will between ex-masters and freedmen, to guard its work wholly from paternalistic methods which discouraged self-reliance, and to carry out to any considerable extent its implied promises to furnish the freedmen with land. Its successes were the result of hard work, supplemented by the aid of philanthropists and the eager striving of black men. Its failures were the result of bad local agents, the inherent difficulties of the work, and national neglect.

Such an institution, from its wide powers, great responsibilities, large control of moneys, and generally conspicuous position, was naturally open to repeated and bitter attack. It sustained a searching Congressional investigation at the instance of Fernando Wood in 1870. Its archives and few remaining functions were with blunt discourtesy transferred from Howard's control, in his absence, to the supervision of Secretary of War Belknap in 1872, on the Secretary's recommendation. Finally, in consequence of grave intimations of wrong-doing made by the Secretary and his subordinates, General Howard was court-martialed in 1874. In both of these trials the Commissioner of the Freedmen's Bureau was officially exonerated from any wilful misdoing, and his work commended. Nevertheless, many unpleasant things were brought to light—the methods of transacting the business of the Bureau were faulty; several cases of defalcation were proved, and other frauds strongly suspected; there were some business transactions which savored of dangerous speculation, if not dishonesty; and around it all lay the smirch of the Freedmen's Bank.

Morally and practically, the Freedmen's Bank was part of the Freedmen's Bureau, although it had no legal connection with it. With the prestige of the government back of it, and a directing board of unusual respectability and national reputation, this banking institution had made a remarkable start in the development of that thrift among black folk which slavery had kept them from knowing. Then in one sad day came the crash—all the hard-earned dollars of the freedmen disappeared; but that was the least of the loss—all the faith in saving went too, and much of the faith in men; and that was a loss that a Nation which to-day sneers at Negro shiftlessness has never yet made good. Not even ten additional years of slavery could have done so much to throttle the thrift of the freedmen as the mismanagement and bankruptcy of the series of savings banks chartered by the Nation for their especial aid. Where all the blame should rest, it is hard to say; whether the Bureau and the Bank died chiefly by reason of the blows of its selfish friends or the dark machinations of its foes, perhaps even time will never reveal, for here lies unwritten history.

Of the foes without the Bureau, the bitterest were those who attacked not so much its conduct or policy under the law as the necessity for any such institution at all. Such attacks came primarily from the Border States and the South; and they were summed up by Senator Davis, of Kentucky, when he moved to entitle the act of 1866 a bill "to promote strife and conflict between the white and black races . . . by a grant of unconstitutional power." The argument gathered tremendous strength South and North; but its very strength was its weakness. For, argued the plain common-sense of the nation, if it is unconstitutional, unpractical, and futile for the nation to stand guardian over its helpless wards, then there is left but one alternative—to make those wards their own guardians by arming them with the ballot. Moreover, the path of the practical politician pointed the same way; for, argued this opportunist, if we cannot peacefully reconstruct the South with white votes, we certainly can with black votes. So justice and force joined hands.

The alternative thus offered the nation was not between full and restricted Negro suffrage; else every sensible man, black and white, would easily have chosen the latter. It was rather a choice between suffrage and slavery, after endless blood and gold had flowed to sweep human bondage away. Not a single Southern legislature stood ready to admit a Negro, under any conditions, to the polls; not a single Southern legislature believed free Negro labor was possible without a system of restrictions that took all its freedom away; there was scarcely a white man in the South who did not honestly regard Emancipation as a crime, and its practical nullification as a duty. In such a situation, the granting of the ballot to the black man was a necessity, the very least a guilty nation could grant a wronged race, and the only method of compelling the South to accept the results of the war. Thus Negro suffrage ended a civil war by beginning a race feud. And some felt gratitude toward the race thus sacrificed in its swaddling clothes on the altar of national integrity; and some felt and feel only indifference and contempt.

Had political exigencies been less pressing, the opposition to government guardianship of Negroes less bitter, and the attachment to the slave system less strong, the social seer can well imagine a far better policy—a permanent Freedmen's Bureau, with a national system of Negro schools; a carefully supervised employment and labor office; a system of impartial protection before the regular courts; and such institutions for social betterment as savings-banks, land and building associations, and social settlements. All this vast expenditure of money and brains might have formed a great school of prospective citizenship, and solved in a way we have not yet solved the most perplexing and persistent of the Negro problems.

That such an institution was unthinkable in 1870 was due in part to certain acts of the Freedmen's Bureau itself. It came to regard its work as merely temporary, and Negro suffrage as a final answer to all present perplexities. The political ambition of many of its agents and *proteges* led it far afield into questionable activities, until the South, nursing its own deep prejudices, came easily to ignore all the good deeds of the Bureau and hate its very name with perfect hatred. So the Freedmen's Bureau died, and its child was the Fifteenth Amendment.

The passing of a great human institution before its work is done, like the untimely passing of a single soul, but leaves a legacy of striving for other men. The legacy of the Freedmen's Bureau is the heavy heritage of this generation. To-day, when new and vaster problems are destined to strain every fibre of the national mind and soul, would it not be well to count this legacy honestly and carefully? For this much all men know: despite compromise, war, and struggle, the Negro is not free. In the backwoods of the Gulf States, for miles and miles, he may not leave the plantation of his birth; in well-nigh the whole rural South the black farmers are peons, bound by law and custom to an economic slavery, from which the only escape is death or the penitentiary. In the most cultured sections and cities of the South the Negroes are a segregated servile caste, with restricted rights and privileges. Before the courts, both in law and custom, they stand on a different and peculiar basis. Taxation without representation is the rule of their political life. And the result of all this is, and in nature must have been, lawlessness and crime. That is the large legacy of the Freedmen's Bureau, the work it did not do because it could not.

I have seen a land right merry with the sun, where children sing, and rolling hills lie like passioned women wanton with harvest. And there in the King's Highway sat and sits a figure veiled and bowed, by which the traveller's footsteps hasten as they go. On the tainted air broods fear. Three centuries' thought has been the raising and unveiling of that bowed human heart, and now behold a century new for the duty and the deed. The problem of the Twentieth Century is the problem of the color-line.

III

Of Mr. Booker T. Washington and Others

From birth till death enslaved; in word, in
deed, unmanned!
Hereditary bondsmen! Know ye not Who
would be free themselves must strike the
blow?

BYRON.

Easily the most striking thing in the history of the American Negro since 1876 is the ascendancy of Mr. Booker T. Washington. It began at the time when war memories and ideals were rapidly passing; a day of astonishing commercial development was dawning; a sense of doubt and hesitation overtook the freedmen's sons—then it was that his leading began. Mr. Washington came, with a simple definite programme, at the psychological moment when the nation was a little ashamed of having bestowed so much sentiment on Negroes, and was concentrating its energies on Dollars. His programme of industrial education, conciliation of the South, and submission and silence as to civil and political rights, was not wholly original; the Free Negroes from 1830 up to wartime had striven to build industrial schools, and the American Missionary Association had from the first taught various trades; and Price and others had sought a way of honorable alliance with the best of the Southerners. But Mr. Washington first indissolubly linked these things; he put enthusiasm, unlimited energy, and perfect faith into this programme, and changed it from a by-path into a veritable Way of Life. And the tale of the methods by which he did this is a fascinating study of human life.

It startled the nation to hear a Negro advocating such a programme after many decades of bitter complaint; it startled and won the applause of the South, it interested and won the admiration of the North; and after a confused murmur of protest, it silenced if it did not convert the Negroes themselves.

To gain the sympathy and cooperation of the various elements comprising the white South was Mr. Washington's first task; and this, at the time Tuskegee was founded, seemed, for a black man, well-nigh impossible. And yet ten years later it was done in the word spoken at Atlanta: "In all things purely social we can be as separate as the five fingers, and yet one as the hand in all things essential to mutual progress." This Atlanta Compromise" is by all odds the most notable thing in Mr. Washington's career. The South interpreted it in different ways: the radicals received it as a complete surrender of the demand for civil and political equality; the conservatives, as a generously conceived working basis for mutual understanding. So both approved it, and to-day its author is certainly the most distinguished Southerner since Jefferson Davis, and the one with the largest personal following.

Next to this achievement comes Mr. Washington's work in gaining place and consideration in the North. Others less shrewd and tactful had formerly essayed to sit on these two stools and had fallen between them; but as Mr. Washington knew the heart of the South from birth and training, so by singular insight he intuitively grasped the spirit of the age which was dominating the North. And so thoroughly did he learn the speech and thought of triumphant commercialism, and the ideals of material prosperity, that the picture of a lone black boy poring over a French grammar amid the weeds and dirt of a neglected home soon seemed to him the acme of absurdities. One wonders what Socrates and St. Francis of Assisi would say to this.

And yet this very singleness of vision and thorough oneness with his age is a mark of the successful man. It is as though Nature must needs make men narrow in order to give them force. So Mr. Washington's cult has gained unquestioning followers, his work has wonderfully prospered, his friends are legion, and his enemies are confounded. To-day he stands as the one recognized spokesman of his ten million fellows, and one of the most notable figures in a nation of seventy millions. One hesitates, therefore, to criticise a life which, beginning with so little, has done so much. And yet the time is come when one may speak in all sincerity and utter courtesy of the mistakes and shortcomings of Mr. Washington's career, as well as of his triumphs, without being thought captious or envious, and without forgetting that it is easier to do ill than well in the world.

The criticism that has hitherto met Mr. Washington has not always been of this broad character. In the South especially has he had to walk warily to avoid the harshest judgments—and naturally so, for he is dealing with the one subject of deepest sensitiveness to that section. Twice—once when at the Chicago celebration of the Spanish-American War he alluded to the color-prejudice that is "eating away the vitals of the South," and once when he dined with President Roosevelt—has the resulting Southern criticism been violent enough to threaten seriously his popularity. In the North the feeling has several times forced itself into words, that Mr. Washington's counsels of submission overlooked certain elements of true manhood, and that his educational programme was unnecessarily narrow. Usually, however, such criticism has not found open expression, although, too, the spiritual sons of the Abolitionists have not been prepared to acknowledge that the schools founded before Tuskegee, by men of broad ideals and self-sacrificing spirit, were wholly failures or worth of ridicule. While, then, criticism has not failed to follow Mr. Washington, yet the prevailing public opinion of the land has been but too willing to deliver the solution of a wearisome problem into his hands, and say, "If that is all you and your race ask, take it."

Among his own people, however, Mr. Washington has encountered the strongest and most lasting opposition, amounting at times to bitterness, and even to-day continuing strong and insistent even though largely silenced in outward expression by the public opinion of the nation. Some of this opposition is, of course, mere envy; the disappointment of displaced demagogues and the spite of narrow minds. But aside from this, there is among educated and thoughtful colored men in all parts of the land a feeling of deep regret, sorrow, and apprehension at the wide currency and ascendancy which some of Mr. Washington's theories have gained. These same men admire his sincerity of purpose, and are willing to forgive much to honest endeavor which is doing something worth the doing. They cooperate with Mr. Washington as far as they conscientiously can; and, indeed, it is no ordinary tribute to this man's tact and power that, steering as he must between so many diverse interests and opinions, he so largely retains the respect of all.

But the hushing of the criticism of honest opponents is a dangerous thing. It leads some of the best of the critics to unfortunate silence and paralysis of effort, and others to burst into speech so passionately and intemperately as to lose listeners. Honest and earnest criticism from those whose interests are most nearly touched—criticism of writers by readers, of government by those governed, of leaders by those led—this is the soul of democracy and the safeguard of modern society. If the best of the American Negroes receive by outer pressure a leader whom they had not recognized before, manifestly there is here a certain palpable gain. Yet there is also irreparable loss—a loss of that peculiarly valuable education which a group receives when by search and criticism it finds and commissions its own leaders. The way in which this is done is at once the most elementary and the nicest problem of social growth. History is but the record of such group-leadership; and yet how infinitely changeful is its type and character! And of all types and kinds, what can be more instructive than the leadership of a group within a group?—that curious double movement where real progress may be negative and actual advance be relative retrogression. All this is the social student's inspiration and despair.

Now in the past the American Negro has had instructive experience in the choosing of group leaders, founding thus a peculiar dynasty which in the light of present conditions is worth while studying. When sticks and stones and beasts form the sole environment of a people, their attitude is largely one of determined opposition to and conquest of natural forces. But when to earth and brute is added an environment of men and ideas, then the attitude of the imprisoned group may take three main forms—a feeling of revolt and revenge; an attempt to adjust all thought and action to the will of the greater group; or, finally, a determined effort at self-realization and self-development despite environing opinion. The influence of all of these attitudes at various times can be traced in the history of the American Negro, and in the evolution of his successive leaders.

Before 1750, while the fire of African freedom still burned in the veins of the slaves, there was in all leadership or attempted leadership but the one motive of revolt and revenge—typified in the terrible Maroons, the Danish blacks, and Cato of Stono, and veiling all the Americas in fear of insurrection. The liberalizing tendencies of the latter half of the eighteenth century brought, along with kindlier relations between black and white, thoughts of ultimate adjustment and assimilation. Such aspiration was especially voiced in the earnest songs of Phyllis, in the martyrdom of Attucks, the fighting of Salem and Poor, the intellectual accomplishments of Banneker and Derham, and the political demands of the Cuffes.

Stern financial and social stress after the war cooled much of the previous humanitarian ardor. The disappointment and impatience of the Negroes at the persistence of slavery and serfdom voiced itself in two movements. The slaves in the South, aroused undoubtedly by vague rumors of the Haytian revolt, made three fierce attempts at insurrection—in 1800 under Gabriel in Virginia, in 1822 under Vesey in Carolina, and in 1831 again in Virginia under the terrible Nat Turner. In the Free States, on the other hand, a new and curious attempt at self-development was made. In Philadelphia and New York color-prescription led to a withdrawal of Negro communicants from white churches and the formation of a peculiar socio-religious institution among the Negroes known as the African Church—an organization still living and controlling in its various branches over a million of men.

Walker's wild appeal against the trend of the times showed how the world was changing after the coming of the cotton gin. By 1830 slavery seemed hopelessly fastened on the South, and the slaves thoroughly cowed into submission. The free Negroes of the North, inspired by the mulatto immigrants from the West Indies, began to change the basis of their demands; they recognized the slavery of slaves, but insisted that they themselves were freemen, and sought assimilation and amalgamation with the nation on the same terms with other men. Thus, Forten and Purvis of Philadelphia, Shad of Wilmington, Du Bois of New Haven, Barbadoes of Boston, and others, strove singly and together as men, they said, not as slaves; as "people of color," not as "Negroes." The trend of the times, however, refused them recognition save in individual and exceptional cases, considered them as one with all the despised blacks, and they soon found themselves striving to keep even the rights they formerly had of voting and working and moving as freemen. Schemes of migration and colonization arose among them; but these they refused to entertain, and they eventually turned to the Abolition movement as a final refuge.

Here, led by Remond, Nell, Wells-Brown, and Douglass, a new period of self-assertion and self- development dawned. To be sure, ultimate freedom and assimilation was the ideal before the leaders, but the assertion of the manhood rights of the Negro by himself was the main reliance, and John Brown's raid was the extreme of its logic. After the war and emancipation, the great form of Frederick Douglass, the greatest of American Negro leaders, still led the host. Self-assertion, especially in political lines, was the main programme, and behind Douglass came Elliot, Bruce, and Langston, and the Reconstruction politicians, and, less conspicuous but of greater social significance Alexander Crummell and Bishop Daniel Payne.

Then came the Revolution of 1876, the suppression of the Negro votes, the changing and shifting of ideals, and the seeking of new lights in the great night. Douglass, in his old age, still bravely stood for the ideals of his early manhood—ultimate assimilation *through* self-assertion, and on no other terms. For a time Price arose as a new leader, destined, it seemed, not to give up, but to re-state the old ideals in a form less repugnant to the white South. But he passed away in his prime. Then came the new leader. Nearly all the former ones had become leaders by the silent suffrage of their fellows, had sought to lead their own people alone, and were usually, save Douglass, little known outside their race. But Booker T. Washington arose as essentially the leader not of one race but of two—a compromiser between the South, the North, and the Negro. Naturally the Negroes resented, at first bitterly, signs of compromise which surrendered their civil and political rights, even though this was to be exchanged for larger chances of economic development. The rich and dominating North, however, was not only weary of the race problem, but was investing largely in Southern enterprises, and welcomed any method of peaceful cooperation. Thus, by national opinion, the Negroes began to recognize Mr. Washington's leadership; and the voice of criticism was hushed.

Mr. Washington represents in Negro thought the old attitude of adjustment and submission; but adjustment at such a peculiar time as to make his programme unique. This is an age of unusual economic development, and Mr. Washington's programme naturally takes an economic cast, becoming a gospel of Work and Money to such an extent as apparently almost completely to overshadow the higher aims of life. Moreover, this is an age when the more advanced races are coming in closer contact with the less developed races, and the race-feeling is therefore intensified; and Mr. Washington's programme practically accepts the alleged inferiority of the Negro races. Again, in our own land, the reaction from the sentiment of war time has given impetus to race-prejudice against Negroes, and Mr. Washington withdraws many of the high demands of Negroes as men and American citizens. In other periods of intensified prejudice all the Negro's tendency to self-assertion has been called forth; at this period a policy of submission is advocated. In the history of nearly all other races and peoples the doctrine preached at such crises has been that manly self-respect is worth more than lands and houses, and that a people who voluntarily surrender such respect, or cease striving for it, are not worth civilizing.

In answer to this, it has been claimed that the Negro can survive only through submission. Mr. Washington distinctly asks that black people give up, at least for the present, three things—

First, political power,

Second, insistence on civil rights,

Third, higher education of Negro youth— and concentrate all their energies on industrial education, the accumulation of wealth, and the conciliation of the South. This policy has been courageously and insistently advocated for over fifteen years, and has been triumphant for perhaps ten years. As a result of this tender of the palm-branch, what has been the return? In these years there have occurred:

1. The disfranchisement of the Negro.

2. The legal creation of a distinct status of civil inferiority for the Negro.

3. The steady withdrawal of aid from institutions for the higher training of the Negro.

These movements are not, to be sure, direct results of Mr. Washington's teachings; but his propaganda has, without a shadow of doubt, helped their speedier accomplishment. The question then comes: Is it possible, and probable, that nine millions of men can make effective progress in economic lines if they are deprived of political rights, made a servile caste, and allowed only the most meagre chance for developing their exceptional men? If history and reason give any distinct answer to these questions, it is an emphatic *No.* And Mr. Washington thus faces the triple paradox of his career:

1. He is striving nobly to make Negro artisans business men and property-owners; but it is utterly impossible, under modern competitive methods, for workingmen and property-owners to defend their rights and exist without the right of suffrage.

2. He insists on thrift and self-respect, but at the same time counsels a silent submission to civic inferiority such as is bound to sap the manhood of any race in the long run.

3. He advocates common-school and industrial training, and depreciates institutions of higher learning; but neither the Negro common-schools, nor Tuskegee itself, could remain open a day were it not for teachers trained in Negro colleges, or trained by their graduates.

This triple paradox in Mr. Washington's position is the object of criticism by two classes of colored Americans. One class is spiritually descended from Toussaint the Savior, through Gabriel, Vesey, and Turner, and they represent the attitude of revolt and revenge; they hate the white South blindly and distrust the white race generally, and so far as they agree on definite action, think that the Negro's only hope lies in emigration beyond the borders of the United States. And yet, by the irony of fate, nothing has more effectually made this programme seem hopeless than the recent course of the United States toward weaker and darker peoples in the West Indies, Hawaii, and the Philippines—for where in the world may we go and be safe from lying and brute force?

The other class of Negroes who cannot agree with Mr. Washington has hitherto said little aloud. They deprecate the sight of scattered counsels, of internal disagreement; and especially they dislike making their just criticism of a useful and earnest man an excuse for a general discharge of venom from small-minded opponents. Nevertheless, the questions involved are so fundamental and serious that it is difficult to see how men like the Grimkes, Kelly Miller, J.W.E. Bowen, and other representatives of this group, can much longer be silent. Such men feel in conscience bound to ask of this nation three things:

1. The right to vote.

2. Civic equality.

3. The education of youth according to ability.

They acknowledge Mr. Washington's invaluable service in counselling patience and courtesy in such demands; they do not ask that ignorant black men vote when ignorant whites are debarred, or that any reasonable restrictions in the suffrage should not be applied; they know that the low social level of the mass of the race is responsible for much discrimination against it, but they also know, and the nation knows, that relentless color-prejudice is more often a cause than a result of the Negro's degradation; they seek the abatement of this relic of barbarism, and not its systematic encouragement and pampering by all agencies of social power from the Associated Press to the Church of Christ. They advocate, with Mr. Washington, a broad system of Negro common schools supplemented by thorough industrial training; but they are surprised that a man of Mr. Washington's insight cannot see that no such educational system ever has rested or can rest on any other basis than that of the well-equipped college and university, and they insist that there is a demand for a few such institutions throughout the South to train the best of the Negro youth as teachers, professional men, and leaders.

This group of men honor Mr. Washington for his attitude of conciliation toward the white South; they accept the "Atlanta Compromise" in its broadest interpretation; they recognize, with him, many signs of promise, many men of high purpose and fair judgment, in this section; they know that no easy task has been laid upon a region already tottering under heavy burdens. But, nevertheless, they insist that the way to truth and right lies in straightforward honesty, not in indiscriminate flattery; in praising those of the South who do well and criticising uncompromisingly those who do ill; in taking advantage of the opportunities at hand and urging their fellows to do the same, but at the same time in remembering that only a firm adherence to their higher ideals and aspirations will ever keep those ideals within the realm of possibility. They do not expect that the free right to vote, to enjoy civic rights, and to be educated, will come in a moment; they do not expect to see the bias and prejudices of years disappear at the blast of a trumpet; but they are absolutely certain that the way for a people to gain their reasonable rights is not by voluntarily throwing them away and insisting that they do not want them; that the way for a people to gain respect is not by continually belittling and ridiculing themselves; that, on the contrary, Negroes must insist continually, in season and out of season, that voting is necessary to modern manhood, that color discrimination is barbarism, and that black boys need education as well as white boys.

In failing thus to state plainly and unequivocally the legitimate demands of their people, even at the cost of opposing an honored leader, the thinking classes of American Negroes would shirk a heavy responsibility—a responsibility to themselves, a responsibility to the struggling masses, a responsibility to the darker races of men whose future depends so largely on this American experiment, but especially a responsibility to this nation—this common Fatherland. It is wrong to encourage a man or a people in evil-doing; it is wrong to aid and abet a national crime simply because it is unpopular not to do so. The growing spirit of kindliness and reconciliation between the North and South after the frightful differences of a generation ago ought to be a source of deep congratulation to all, and especially to those whose mistreatment caused the war; but if that reconciliation is to be marked by the industrial slavery and civic death of those same black men, with permanent legislation into a position of inferiority, then those black men, if they are really men, are called upon by every consideration of patriotism and loyalty to oppose such a course by all civilized methods, even though such opposition involves disagreement with Mr. Booker T. Washington. We have no right to sit silently by while the inevitable seeds are sown for a harvest of disaster to our children, black and white.

First, it is the duty of black men to judge the South discriminatingly. The present generation of Southerners are not responsible for the past, and they should not be blindly hated or blamed for it. Furthermore, to no class is the indiscriminate endorsement of the recent course of the South toward Negroes more nauseating than to the best thought of the South. The South is not "solid"; it is a land in the ferment of social change, wherein forces of all kinds are fighting for supremacy; and to praise the ill the South is to-day perpetrating is just as wrong as to condemn the good. Discriminating and broad-minded criticism is what the South needs—needs it for the sake of her own white sons and daughters, and for the insurance of robust, healthy mental and moral development.

To-day even the attitude of the Southern whites toward the blacks is not, as so many assume, in all cases the same; the ignorant Southerner hates the Negro, the workingmen fear his competition, the money- makers wish to use him as a laborer, some of the educated see a menace in his upward development, while others—usually the sons of the masters—wish to help him to rise. National opinion has enabled this last class to maintain the Negro common schools, and to protect the Negro partially in property, life, and limb. Through the pressure of the money-makers, the Negro is in danger of being reduced to semi-slavery, especially in the country districts; the workingmen, and those of the educated who fear the Negro, have united to disfranchise him, and some have urged his deportation; while the passions of the ignorant are easily aroused to lunch and abuse any black man. To praise this intricate whirl of thought and prejudice is nonsense; to inveigh indiscriminately against "the South" is unjust; but to use the same breath in praising Governor Aycock, exposing Senator Morgan, arguing with Mr. Thomas Nelson Page, and denouncing Senator Ben Tillman, is not only sane, but the imperative duty of thinking black men.

It would be unjust to Mr. Washington not to acknowledge that in several instances he has opposed movements in the South which were unjust to the Negro; he sent memorials to the Louisiana and Alabama constitutional conventions, he has spoken against lynching, and in other ways has openly or silently set his influence against sinister schemes and unfortunate happenings. Notwithstanding this, it is equally true to assert that on the whole the distinct impression left by Mr. Washington's propaganda is, first, that the South is justified in its present attitude toward the Negro because of the Negro's degradation; secondly, that the prime cause of the Negro's failure to rise more quickly is his wrong education in the past; and, thirdly, that his future rise depends primarily on his own efforts. Each of these propositions is a dangerous half-truth. The supplementary truths must never be lost sight of: first, slavery and race- prejudice are potent if not sufficient causes of the Negro's position; second, industrial and common-school training were necessarily slow in planting because they had to await the black teachers trained by higher institutions—it being extremely doubtful if any essentially different development was possible, and certainly a Tuskegee was unthinkable before 1880; and, third, while it is a great truth to say that the Negro must strive and strive mightily to help himself, it is equally true that unless his striving be not simply seconded, but rather aroused and encouraged, by the initiative of the richer and wiser environing group, he cannot hope for great success.

In his failure to realize and impress this last point, Mr. Washington is especially to be criticised. His doctrine has tended to make the whites, North and South, shift the burden of the Negro problem to the Negro's shoulders and stand aside as critical and rather pessimistic spectators; when in fact the burden belongs to the nation, and the hands of none of us are clean if we bend not our energies to righting these great wrongs.

The South ought to be led, by candid and honest criticism, to assert her better self and do her full duty to the race she has cruelly wronged and is still wronging. The North—her co-partner in guilt—cannot salve her conscience by plastering it with gold. We cannot settle this problem by diplomacy and suaveness, by "policy" alone. If worse come to worst, can the moral fibre of this country survive the slow throttling and murder of nine millions of men?

The black men of America have a duty to perform, a duty stern and delicate—a forward movement to oppose a part of the work of their greatest leader. So far as Mr. Washington preaches Thrift, Patience, and Industrial Training for the masses, we must hold up his hands and strive with him, rejoicing in his honors and glorying in the strength of this Joshua called of God and of man to lead the headless host. But so far as Mr. Washington apologizes for injustice, North or South, does not rightly value the privilege and duty of voting, belittles the emasculating effects of caste distinctions, and opposes the higher training and ambition of our brighter minds—so far as he, the South, or the Nation, does this—we must unceasingly and firmly oppose them. By every civilized and peaceful method we must strive for the rights which the world accords to men, clinging unwaveringly to those great words which the sons of the Fathers would fain forget: "We hold these truths to be self-evident: That all men are created equal; that they are endowed by their Creator with certain unalienable rights; that among these are life, liberty, and the pursuit of happiness."

XIV

The Sorrow Songs

I walk through the churchyard
To lay this body down;
I know moon-rise, I know star-rise;
I walk in the moonlight, I walk in the starlight;
I'll lie in the grave and stretch out my arms,
I'll go to judgment in the evening of the day,
And my soul and thy soul shall meet that day,
When I lay this body down.

Negro Song.

They that walked in darkness sang songs in the olden days—Sorrow Songs—for they were weary at heart. And so before each thought that I have written in this book I have set a phrase, a haunting echo of these weird old songs in which the soul of the black slave spoke to men. Ever since I was a child these songs have stirred me strangely. They came out of the South unknown to me, one by one, and yet at once I knew them as of me and of mine. Then in after years when I came to Nashville I saw the great temple builded of these songs towering over the pale city. To me Jubilee Hall seemed ever made of the songs themselves, and its bricks were red with the blood and dust of toil. Out of them rose for me morning, noon, and night, bursts of wonderful melody, full of the voices of my brothers and sisters, full of the voices of the past.

Little of beauty has America given the world save the rude grandeur God himself stamped on her bosom; the human spirit in this new world has expressed itself in vigor and ingenuity rather than in beauty. And so by fateful chance the Negro folk-song—the rhythmic cry of the slave—stands today not simply as the sole American music, but as the most beautiful expression of human experience born this side the seas. It has been neglected, it has been, and is, half despised, and above all it has been persistently mistaken and misunderstood; but notwithstanding, it still remains as the singular spiritual heritage of the nation and the greatest gift of the Negro people.

Away back in the thirties the melody of these slave songs stirred the nation, but the songs were soon half forgotten. Some, like "Near the lake where drooped the willow," passed into current airs and their source was forgotten; others were caricatured on the "minstrel" stage and their memory died away. Then in war-time came the singular Port Royal experiment after the capture of Hilton Head, and perhaps for the first time the North met the Southern slave face to face and heart to heart with no third witness. The Sea Islands of the Carolinas, where they met, were filled with a black folk of primitive type, touched and moulded less by the world about them than any others outside the Black Belt. Their appearance was uncouth, their language funny, but their hearts were human and their singing stirred men with a mighty power. Thomas Wentworth Higginson hastened to tell of these songs, and Miss McKim and others urged upon the world their rare beauty. But the world listened only half credulously until the Fisk Jubilee Singers sang the slave songs so deeply into the world's heart that it can never wholly forget them again.

There was once a blacksmith's son born at Cadiz, New York, who in the changes of time taught school in Ohio and helped defend Cincinnati from Kirby Smith. Then he fought at Chancellorsville and Gettysburg and finally served in the Freedman's Bureau at Nashville. Here he formed a Sunday-school class of black children in 1866, and sang with them and taught them to sing. And then they taught him to sing, and when once the glory of the Jubilee songs passed into the soul of George L. White, he knew his life-work was to let those Negroes sing to the world as they had sung to him. So in 1871 the pilgrimage of the Fisk Jubilee Singers began. North to Cincinnati they rode—four half-clothed black boys and five girl-women—led by a man with a cause and a purpose. They stopped at Wilberforce, the oldest of Negro schools, where a black bishop blessed them. Then they went, fighting cold and starvation, shut out of hotels, and cheerfully sneered at, ever northward; and ever the magic of their song kept thrilling hearts, until a burst of applause in the Congregational Council at Oberlin revealed them to the world. They came to New York and Henry Ward Beecher dared to welcome them, even though the metropolitan dailies sneered at his "Nigger Minstrels." So their songs conquered till they sang across the land and across the sea, before Queen and Kaiser, in Scotland and Ireland, Holland and Switzerland. Seven years they sang, and brought back a hundred and fifty thousand dollars to found Fisk University.

Since their day they have been imitated—sometimes well, by the singers of Hampton and Atlanta, sometimes ill, by straggling quartettes. Caricature has sought again to spoil the quaint beauty of the music, and has filled the air with many debased melodies which vulgar ears scarce know from the real. But the true Negro folk-song still lives in the hearts of those who have heard them truly sung and in the hearts of the Negro people.

What are these songs, and what do they mean? I know little of music and can say nothing in technical phrase, but I know something of men, and knowing them, I know that these songs are the articulate message of the slave to the world. They tell us in these eager days that life was joyous to the black slave, careless and happy. I can easily believe this of some, of many. But not all the past South, though it rose from the dead, can gainsay the heart-touching witness of these songs. They are the music of an unhappy people, of the children of disappointment; they tell of death and suffering and unvoiced longing toward a truer world, of misty wanderings and hidden ways.

The songs are indeed the siftings of centuries; the music is far more ancient than the words, and in it we can trace here and there signs of development. My grandfather's grandmother was seized by an evil Dutch trader two centuries ago; and coming to the valleys of the Hudson and Housatonic, black, little, and lithe, she shivered and shrank in the harsh north winds, looked longingly at the hills, and often crooned a heathen melody to the child between her knees, thus:

> Do ba-na co-ba, ge-ne me, ge-ne me!
> Do ba-na co-ba, ge-ne me, ge-ne me!
> Ben d' nu-li, nu-li, nu-li, nu-li, ben d' le.

The child sang it to his children and they to their children's children, and so two hundred years it has travelled down to us and we sing it to our children, knowing as little as our fathers what its words may mean, but knowing well the meaning of its music.

This was primitive African music; it may be seen in larger form in the strange chant which heralds "The Coming of John":

> "You may bury me in the East, You may bury
> me in the West, But I'll hear the trumpet
> sound in that morning"

—the voice of exile.

Ten master songs, more or less, one may pluck from this forest of melody—songs of undoubted Negro origin and wide popular currency, and songs peculiarly characteristic of the slave. One of these I have just mentioned. Another whose strains begin this book is "Nobody knows the trouble I've seen." When, struck with a sudden poverty, the United States refused to fulfil its promises of land to the freedmen, a brigadier-general went down to the Sea Islands to carry the news. An old woman on the outskirts of the throng began singing this song; all the mass joined with her, swaying. And the soldier wept.

The third song is the cradle-song of death which all men know—"Swing low, sweet chariot"—whose bars begin the life story of "Alexander Crummell." Then there is the song of many waters, "Roll, Jordan, roll," a mighty chorus with minor cadences. There were many songs of the fugitive like that which opens "The Wings of Atalanta," and the more familiar "Been a-listening." The seventh is the song of the End and the Beginning—"My Lord, what a mourning! when the stars begin to fall"; a strain of this is placed before "The Dawn of Freedom." The song of groping—"My way's cloudy"—begins "The Meaning of Progress"; the ninth is the song of this chapter—"Wrestlin' Jacob, the day is a breaking"—a paean of hopeful strife. The last master song is the song of songs—"Steal away,"—sprung from "The Faith of the Fathers."

There are many others of the Negro folk-songs as striking and characteristic as these, as, for instance, the three strains in the third, eighth, and ninth chapters; and others I am sure could easily make a selection on more scientific principles. There are, too, songs that seem to me a step removed from the more primitive types: there is the maze-like medley, "Bright sparkles," one phrase of which heads "The Black Belt"; the Easter carol, "Dust, dust and ashes"; the dirge, "My mother's took her flight and gone home"; and that burst of melody hovering over "The Passing of the First-Born"—"I hope my mother will be there in that beautiful world on high."

These represent a third step in the development of the slave song, of which "You may bury me in the East" is the first, and songs like "March on" (chapter six) and "Steal away" are the second. The first is African music, the second Afro-American, while the third is a blending of Negro music with the music heard in the foster land. The result is still distinctively Negro and the method of blending original, but the elements are both Negro and Caucasian. One might go further and find a fourth step in this development, where the songs of white America have been distinctively influenced by the slave songs or have incorporated whole phrases of Negro melody, as "Swanee River" and "Old Black Joe." Side by side, too, with the growth has gone the debasements and imitations—the Negro "minstrel" songs, many of the "gospel" hymns, and some of the contemporary "coon" songs—a mass of music in which the novice may easily lose himself and never find the real Negro melodies.

In these songs, I have said, the slave spoke to the world. Such a message is naturally veiled and half articulate. Words and music have lost each other and new and cant phrases of a dimly understood theology have displaced the older sentiment. Once in a while we catch a strange word of an unknown tongue, as the "Mighty Myo," which figures as a river of death; more often slight words or mere doggerel are joined to music of singular sweetness. Purely secular songs are few in number, partly because many of them were turned into hymns by a change of words, partly because the frolics were seldom heard by the stranger, and the music less often caught. Of nearly all the songs, however, the music is distinctly sorrowful. The ten master songs I have mentioned tell in word and music of trouble and exile, of strife and hiding; they grope toward some unseen power and sigh for rest in the End.

The words that are left to us are not without interest, and, cleared of evident dross, they conceal much of real poetry and meaning beneath conventional theology and unmeaning rhapsody. Like all primitive folk, the slave stood near to Nature's heart. Life was a "rough and rolling sea" like the brown Atlantic of the Sea Islands; the "Wilderness" was the home of God, and the "lonesome valley" led to the way of life. "Winter'll soon be over," was the picture of life and death to a tropical imagination. The sudden wild thunderstorms of the South awed and impressed the Negroes—at times the rumbling seemed to them "mournful," at times imperious:

"My Lord calls me, He calls me by the thunder, The trumpet sounds it in my soul."

The monotonous toil and exposure is painted in many words. One sees the ploughmen in the hot, moist furrow, singing:

"Dere's no rain to wet you, Dere's no sun to burn you, Oh, push along, believer, I want to go home."

The bowed and bent old man cries, with thrice-repeated wail:

"O Lord, keep me from sinking down," and he rebukes the devil of doubt who can whisper: "Jesus is dead and God's gone away."

Yet the soul-hunger is there, the restlessness of the savage, the wail of the wanderer, and the plaint is put in one little phrase:

My soul wants something that's new, that's new

Over the inner thoughts of the slaves and their relations one with another the shadow of fear ever hung, so that we get but glimpses here and there, and also with them, eloquent omissions and silences. Mother and child are sung, but seldom father; fugitive and weary wanderer call for pity and affection, but there is little of wooing and wedding; the rocks and the mountains are well known, but home is unknown. Strange blending of love and helplessness sings through the refrain:

"Yonder's my ole mudder, Been waggin' at de hill so long; 'Bout time she cross over, Git home bime-by."

Elsewhere comes the cry of the "motherless" and the "Farewell, farewell, my only child."

Love-songs are scarce and fall into two categories—the frivolous and light, and the sad. Of deep successful love there is ominous silence, and in one of the oldest of these songs there is a depth of history and meaning:

> Poor Ro-sy, poor gal; Poor Ro-sy,
> poor gal; Ro-sy break my poor heart.
> Heav'n shall-a-be my home.

A black woman said of the song, "It can't be sung without a full heart and a troubled sperrit." The same voice sings here that sings in the German folk-song:

"Jetz Geh i' an's brunele, trink' aber net."

Of death the Negro showed little fear, but talked of it familiarly and even fondly as simply a crossing of the waters, perhaps—who knows?—back to his ancient forests again. Later days transfigured his fatalism, and amid the dust and dirt the toiler sang:

"Dust, dust and ashes, fly over my grave, But the Lord shall bear my spirit home."

The things evidently borrowed from the surrounding world undergo characteristic change when they enter the mouth of the slave. Especially is this true of Bible phrases. "Weep, O captive daughter of Zion," is quaintly turned into "Zion, weep-a-low," and the wheels of Ezekiel are turned every way in the mystic dreaming of the slave, till he says:

"There's a little wheel a-turnin' in-a-my heart."

As in olden time, the words of these hymns were improvised by some leading minstrel of the religious band. The circumstances of the gathering, however, the rhythm of the songs, and the limitations of allowable thought, confined the poetry for the most part to single or double lines, and they seldom were expanded to quatrains or longer tales, although there are some few examples of sustained efforts, chiefly paraphrases of the Bible. Three short series of verses have always attracted me—the one that heads this chapter, of one line of which Thomas Wentworth Higginson has fittingly said, "Never, it seems to me, since man first lived and suffered was his infinite longing for peace uttered more plaintively." The second and third are descriptions of the Last Judgment—the one a late improvisation, with some traces of outside influence:

> "Oh, the stars in the elements are falling, And the moon drips away into blood, And the ransomed of the Lord are returning unto God, Blessed be the name of the Lord."

And the other earlier and homelier picture from the low coast lands:

> "Michael, haul the boat ashore, Then you'll hear the horn they blow, Then you'll hear the trumpet sound, Trumpet sound the world around, Trumpet sound for rich and poor, Trumpet sound the Jubilee, Trumpet sound for you and me."

Through all the sorrow of the Sorrow Songs there breathes a hope—a faith in the ultimate justice of things. The minor cadences of despair change often to triumph and calm confidence. Sometimes it is faith in life, sometimes a faith in death, sometimes assurance of boundless justice in some fair world beyond. But whichever it is, the meaning is always clear: that sometime, somewhere, men will judge men by their souls and not by their skins. Is such a hope justified? Do the Sorrow Songs sing true?

The silently growing assumption of this age is that the probation of races is past, and that the backward races of to-day are of proven inefficiency and not worth the saving. Such an assumption is the arrogance of peoples irreverent toward Time and ignorant of the deeds of men. A thousand years ago such an assumption, easily possible, would have made it difficult for the Teuton to prove his right to life. Two thousand years ago such dogmatism, readily welcome, would have scouted the idea of blond races ever leading civilization. So wofully unorganized is sociological knowledge that the meaning of progress, the meaning of "swift" and "slow" in human doing, and the limits of human perfectability, are veiled, unanswered sphinxes on the shores of science. Why should AEschylus have sung two thousand years before Shakespeare was born? Why has civilization flourished in Europe, and flickered, flamed, and died in Africa? So long as the world stands meekly dumb before such questions, shall this nation proclaim its ignorance and unhallowed prejudices by denying freedom of opportunity to those who brought the Sorrow Songs to the Seats of the Mighty?

Your country? How came it yours? Before the Pilgrims landed we were here. Here we have brought our three gifts and mingled them with yours: a gift of story and song—soft, stirring melody in an ill-harmonized and unmelodious land; the gift of sweat and brawn to beat back the wilderness, conquer the soil, and lay the foundations of this vast economic empire two hundred years earlier than your weak hands could have done it; the third, a gift of the Spirit. Around us the history of the land has centred for thrice a hundred years; out of the nation's heart we have called all that was best to throttle and subdue all that was worst; fire and blood, prayer and sacrifice, have billowed over this people, and they have found peace only in the altars of the God of Right. Nor has our gift of the Spirit been merely passive. Actively we have woven ourselves with the very wrap and woof of this nation—we fought their battles, shared their sorrow, mingled our blood with theirs, and generation after generation have pleaded with a headstrong, careless people to despise not Justice, Mercy, and Truth, lest the nation be smitten with a curse. Our song, our toil, our cheer, and warning have been given to this nation in blood-brotherhood. Are not these gifts worth the giving? Is not this work and striving? Would America have been America without her Negro people?

Even so is the hope that sang in the songs of my fathers well sung. If somewhere in this whirl and chaos of things there dwells Eternal Good, pitiful yet masterful, then anon in His good time America shall rend the Veil and the prisoned shall go free. Free, free as the sunshine trickling down the morning into these high windows of mine, free as yonder fresh young voices welling up to me from the caverns of brick and mortar below—swelling with song, instinct with life, tremulous treble and darkening bass. My children, my little children, are singing to the sunshine, and thus they sing:

Let us cheer the wea-ry trav-el-ler,
Cheer the wea-ry trav-el-ler, Let us
cheer the wea-ry trav-el-ler
A-long the heav-en-ly way,

And the traveller girds himself, and sets his face toward the Morning, and goes his way.

The After-Thought

Hear my cry, O God the Reader; vouchsafe that this my book fall not still-born into the world-wilderness. Let there spring, Gentle One, from out its leaves vigor of thought and thoughtful deed to reap the harvest wonderful. (Let the ears of a guilty people tingle with truth, and seventy millions sigh for the righteousness which exalteth nations, in this drear day when human brotherhood is mockery and a snare.) Thus in Thy good time may infinite reason turn the tangle straight, and these crooked marks on a fragile leaf be not indeed

Source:

W. E. B. DuBois, *The Souls of Black Folk.* New York: Vintage Books, 1990.

Elkins Act, 1903

Federal U.S. legislation, passed on February 19, 1903, prohibiting railroads from giving rebates to favored shippers engaged in interstate commerce. Supported by antimonopoly reformers and by the railroads, which were being compelled to grant rebates to certain powerful trusts, the act provided for prosecution and punishment of shippers, railroad corporations, agents, and officers who gave or received rebates. It made deviation from the published rates a misdemeanor and gave federal courts the power to issue injunctions against violators. Introduced by Senator Stephen B. Elkins of West Virginia, the act reinforced the Interstate Commerce Act. On June 29, 1906, the government enacted the Hepburn Act, which strengthened the Elkins Act and increased the power of the Interstate Commerce Commission (ICC) to regulate railroads. In strengthening the Interstate Commerce Act, the 1906 act extended the ICC's jurisdiction to include refrigeration and storage facilities, terminals, bridges, and pipelines. It empowered the commission to set reasonable maximum railroad rates to require uniform accounting methods. It also prohibited railroads from carrying commodities—other than certain products needed for railway operations—produced by companies in which they held a financial interest. The Elkins Act prohibiting rebates was also strengthened. The ICC's rulings were made binding without court action, though its decisions could be appealed.

An Act

To further regulate commerce with foreign nations and among the States.

Be it enacted by the Senate and House of Representatives of the United States of America in Congress assembled, That anything done or omitted to be done by a corporation common carrier, subject to the Act to regulate commerce and the Acts amendatory thereof which, if done or omitted to be done by any director or officer thereof, or any receiver, trustee, lessee, agent, or person acting for or employed by such corporation, would constitute a misdemeanor under said Acts or under this Act shall also be held to be a misdemeanor committed by such corporation, and upon conviction thereof it shall be subject to like penalties as are prescribed in said Acts or by this Act with reference to such persons except as such penalties are herein changed. The willful failure upon the part of any carrier subject to said Acts to file and publish the tariffs or rates and charges as required by said Acts or strictly to observe such tariffs until changed according to law, shall be a misdemeanor, and upon conviction thereof the corporation offending shall be subject to a fine not less than one thousand dollars nor more than twenty thousand dollars for each offense; and it shall be unlawful for any person, persons, or corporation to offer, grant, or give or to solicit, accept, or receive any rebate, concession, or discrimination in respect of the transportation of any property in interstate or foreign commerce by any common carrier subject to said Act to regulate commerce and the Acts amendatory thereto whereby any such property shall by any device whatever be transported at a less rate than that named in the tariffs published and filed by such carrier, as is required by said Act to regulate commerce and the Acts amendatory thereto, or whereby any other advantage is given or discrimination is practiced. Every person or corporation who shall offer, grant, or give or solicit, accept or receive any such rebates, concession, or discrimination shall be deemed guilty of a misdemeanor, and on conviction thereof shall be punished by a fine of not less than one thousand dollars nor more than twenty thousand dollars. In all convictions occurring after the passage of this Act for offenses under said Acts to regulate commerce, whether committed before or after the passage of this Act, or for offenses under this section, no penalty shall be imposed on the convicted party other than the fine prescribed by law, imprisonment wherever now prescribed as part of the penalty being hereby abolished. Every violation of this section shall be prosecuted in any court of the United States having jurisdiction of crimes within the district in which such violation was committed or through which the transportation may have been conducted; and whenever the offense is begun in one jurisdiction and completed in another it may be dealt with, inquired of, tried, determined, and punished in either jurisdiction in the same manner as if the offense had been actually and wholly committed therein.

In construing and enforcing the provisions of this section the act, omission, or failure of any officer, agent, or other person acting for or employed by any common carrier acting within the scope of his employment shall in every case be also deemed to be the act, omission, or failure of such carrier as well as that of the person. Whenever any carrier files with the Interstate Commerce Commission or publishes a particular rate under the provisions of the Act regulate commerce or Acts amendatory thereto, or participates in any rates so filed or published, that rate as against such carrier, its officers, or agents in any prosecution begun under this Act shall be conclusively deemed to be the legal rate, and any departure from such rate, or any offer to depart therefrom, shall be deemed to be an offense under this section of this Act.

Sec. 2. That in any proceeding for the enforcement of the provisions of the statutes relating to interstate commerce, whether such proceedings be instituted before the Interstate Commerce Commission or be begun originally in any circuit court of the United States, it shall be lawful to include as parties, in addition to the carrier, all persons interested in or affected by the rate, regulation, or practice under consideration, and inquiries, investigations, orders, and decrees may be made with reference to and against such additional parties in the same manner, to the same extent, and subject to the same provisions as are or shall be authorized by law with respect to carriers.

Sec. 3. That whenever the Interstate Commerce Commission shall have reasonable ground for belief that any common carrier is engaged in the carriage of passengers or freight traffic between given points at less than the published rates on file, or is committing any discriminations forbidden by law, a petition may be presented alleging such facts to the circuit court of the United States sitting in equity having jurisdiction; and when the act complained of is alleged to have been committed or as being committed in part in more than one judicial district or State, it may be dealt with, inquired of, tried, and determined in either such judicial district or State, whereupon it shall be the duty of the court summarily to inquire into the circumstances, upon such notice and in such manner as the court shall direct and without the formal pleadings and proceedings applicable to ordinary suits in equity, and to make such other persons or corporations parties thereto as the court may deem necessary, and upon being satisfied of the truth of the allegations of said petition said court shall enforce an observance of the published tariffs or direct and require a discontinuance of such discrimination by proper orders, writs, and process, which said orders, writs, and process may be enforceable as well against the parties interested in the traffic as against the carrier, subject to the right of appeal as now provided by law. It shall be the duty of the several district attorneys of the United States, whenever the Attorney-General shall direct, either of his own motion or upon the request of the Interstate Commerce Commission, to institute and prosecute such proceedings, and the proceedings provided for by this Act shall not preclude the bringing of suit for the recovery of damages by any party injured, or any other action provided by said Act approved February fourth, eighteen hundred and eighty-seven, entitled An Act to regulate commerce and the Acts amendatory thereof. And in proceedings under this Act and the Acts to regulate commerce the said courts shall have the power to compel the attendance of witnesses, both upon the part of the carrier and the shipper, who shall be required to answer on all subjects relating directly or indirectly to the matter in controversy, and to compel the production of all books and papers, both of the carrier and the shipper, which relate directly or indirectly to such transaction; the claim that such testimony or evidence may tend to criminate the person giving such evidence shall to excuse such person from testifying or such corporation producing its books and papers, but no person shall be prosecuted or subjected to any penalty or forfeiture for or on account of any transaction, matter, or thing concerning which he may testify or produce evidence documentary or otherwise in such proceeding: *Provided,* That the provisions of an Act entitled "An Act to expedite the hearing and determination of suits in equity pending or hereafter brought under the Act of July second, eighteen hundred and ninety, entitled 'An Act to protect trade and commerce against unlawful restraints and monopolies,' 'An Act to regulate commerce,' approved February fourth, eighteen hundred and eighty-seven, or any other Acts having a like purpose that may be hereafter enacted, approved February eleventh, nineteen hundred and three," shall apply to any case prosecuted under the direction of the Attorney-General in the name of the Interstate Commerce Commission.

Sec. 4. That all Acts and parts of Acts in conflict with the provisions of this Act are hereby repealed but such repeal shall not affect causes now pending nor rights which have already accrued, but such causes shall be prosecuted to a conclusion and such rights enforced in a manner heretofore provided by law and as modified by the provisions of this Act.

Sec. 5. That this Act shall take effect from its passage.

Source:
Statutes at Large, Vol. 32, pp. 847–849.

Lochner v. New York, 1905

U.S. Supreme Court decision of April 17, 1905, invalidating an 1897 New York State law that limited the hours of work in bakeries to not more than 60 hours a week or 10 hours a day. Joseph Lochner, a bakery owner who was convicted of violating the law, challenged it in court. The Supreme Court ruled the law unconstitutional—overstepping the state's own police powers to regulate public safety, health, morals, and general welfare—because the law interfered with the right of contract between an employer and employees and because it violated individual liberty under the due process clause of the Fourteenth Amendment. Peckham wrote the opinion for the Court. Justice Oliver Wendell Holmes dissented, as did Justice Harlan with Justices White and Day concurring. The entire decision may be found in In *Landmark Documents in American History.* www.factsonfile.com.

On September 3, 1916, Congress enacted the Adamson Act, which established an eight-hour day for railroad workers operating on interstate lines, without a reduction in their wages. It replaced the 10-hour day and provided time-and-a-half for overtime. The act was passed as an emergency measure to avoid the threatened strike by railway workers that might have hindered U.S. preparations for World War I. The railroads claimed that the act was unconstitutional, effectively raising wages rather than limiting hours, because normal operation required more than eight hours of work. In *Wilson v. New* (243 U.S. 332 [1917]), the Supreme Court upheld the act under the federal government's right to regulate interstate commerce.

Mr. Justice Peckham . . . delivered the opinion of the court:

The indictment, it will be seen, charges that the plaintiff in error violated the 1005h section of article 8, chapter 415, of the Laws of 1897, known as the labor law of the state of New York, in that he wrongfully and unlawfully required and permitted an employee working for him to work more than sixty hours in one week. . . . It is assumed that the word means nothing more than the requirement arising from voluntary contract for such labor in excess of the number of hours specified in the statute. . . .

The statute necessarily interferes with the right of contract between the employer and employees, concerning the number of hours in which the latter may labor in the bakery of the employer. The general right to make a contract in relation to his business is part of the liberty of the individual protected by the 14th Amendment of the Federal Constitution. . . . Under that provision no state can deprive any person to life, liberty, or property without due process of law. The right to purchase or to sell labor is part of the liberty protected by this amendment, unless there are circumstances which exclude the right. There are, however, certain powers, existing in the sovereignty of each state in the Union, somewhat vaguely termed police powers, the exact description and limitation of which have not been attempted by the courts. Those powers, broadly stated, and without at present, any attempt at a more specific limitation, relate to the safety, health, morals, and general welfare of the public. Both property and liberty are held on such reasonable conditions as may be imposed by the governing power of the state in the exercise of those powers, and with such conditions the 14th Amendment was not designed to interfere. . . .

The state, therefore, has power to prevent the individual from making certain kinds of contracts, and in regard to them the Federal Constitution offers no protection. If the contract be one which the state, in the legitimate exercise of its police power, has the right to prohibit, it is not prevented from prohibiting it by the 14th Amendment. Contracts in violation of a statute, either of the Federal or state government, or a contract to let one's property for immoral purposes, or to do any other unlawful act, could obtain no protection from the Federal Constitution, as coming under the liberty of person or of free contract.

Therefore, when the state, by its legislature, in the assumed exercise of its police powers, has passed an act which seriously limits the right to labor or the right of contract in regard to their means of livelihood between persons who are sui juris (both employer and employee), it becomes of great importance to determine which shall prevail—the right of the individual to labor for such time as he may choose, or the right of the state to prevent the individual from laboring, or from entering into any contract to labor, beyond a certain time prescribed by the state.

This court has recognized the existence and upheld the exercise of the police powers of the states in many cases which might fairly by considered as border ones, and it has, in the course of its determination of questions regarding the asserted invalidity of such statutes, on the ground of their violation of the rights secured by the Federal Constitution, been guided by rules of a very liberal nature, the application of which has resulted, in numerous instances, in upholding the validity of state statutes thus assailed. . . .

* * *

It must, of course, be conceded that there is a limit to the valid exercise of the police power by the state. There is no dispute concerning this general proposition. Otherwise the 14th Amendment would have no efficacy and the legislatures of the states would have unbounded power, and it would be enough to say that any piece of legislation was enacted to conserve the morals, the health, or the safety of the people; such legislation would be valid, no matter how absolutely without foundation the claim might be. The claim of the police power would be a mere pretext—become another and delusive name for the supreme sovereignty of the state to be exercised free from constitutional restraint. This is not contended for. In every case that comes before this court, therefore, where legislation of this character is concerned, and where the protection of the Federal Constitution is sought, the question necessarily arises: Is this a fair, reasonable, and appropriate exercise of the police power of the state, or is it an unreasonable, unnecessary, and arbitrary interference with the right of the individual to his personal liberty, or to enter into those contracts in relation to labor which may seem to him appropriate or necessary for the support of himself and his family? Of course the liberty of contract relating to labor includes both parties to it. The one has as much right to purchase as the other to sell labor.

This is not a question of substituting the judgment of the court for that of the legislature. If the act be within the power of the state it is valid, although the judgment of the court might be totally opposed to the enactment of such a law. But the question would still remain: Is it within the police power of the state? and that question must be answered by the court.

The question whether this act is valid as a labor law, pure and simple, may be dismissed in a few words. There is no reasonable ground for interfering with the liberty of person or the right of free contract, by determining the hours of labor, in the occupation of a baker. There is no contention that bakers as a class are not equal in intelligence and capacity to men in other trades or manual occupations, or that they are not able to assert their rights and care for themselves without the protecting arm of the state, interfering with their independence of judgment and of action. They are in no sense wards of the state. Viewed in the light of a purely labor law, with no reference whatever to the question of health, we think that a law like the one before us involves neither the safety, the morals, nor the welfare, of the public, and that the interest of the public is not in the slightest degree affected by such an act. The law must be upheld, if at all, as a law pertaining to the health of the individual engaged in the occupation of a baker. It does not affect any other portion of the public than those who are engaged in that occupation. Clean and wholesome bread does not depend upon whether the baker works but ten hours per day or only sixty hours a week. The limitation of the hours of labor does not come within the police power on that ground.

It is a question of which of two powers or rights shall prevail—the power of the state to legislate or the right of the individual to liberty of person and freedom of contract. The mere assertion that the subject relates, though but in a remote degree, to the public health, does not necessarily render the enactment valid. The act must have a more direct relation, as a means to an end, and the end itself must be appropriate and legitimate, before an act can be held to be valid which interferes with the general right of an individual to be free in his person and in his power to contract in relation to his own labor.

This case has caused much diversity of opinion in the state courts. . . .

We think the limit of the police power has been reached and passed in this case. There is, in our judgment, no reasonable foundation for holding this to be necessary or appropriate as a health law to safeguard the public health, or the health of the individuals who are following the trade of a baker. If this statute be valid, and if, therefore, a proper case is made out in which to deny the right of an individual, sui juris, as employer or employee, to make contracts for the labor of the latter under the protection of the provisions of the Federal Constitution, there would seem to be no length to which legislation of this nature might not go. The case differs widely, as we have already stated, from the expressions of this court in regard to laws of this nature, as stated in *Holden v. Hardy*. . . .

We think that there can be no fair doubt that the trade of a baker, in and of itself, is not an unhealthy one to that degree which would authorize the legislature to interfere with the right to labor, and with the right of free contract on the part of the individual, either as employer or employee. In looking through statistics regarding all trades and occupations, it may be true that the trade of a baker does not appear to be as healthy as some other trades, and is also vastly more healthy than still others. To the common understanding the trade of a baker has never been regarded as an unhealthy one. Very likely physicians would not recommend the exercise of that or of any other trade as a remedy for ill health. Some occupations are more healthy than others, but we think there are none which might not come under the power of the legislature to supervise and control the hours of working therein, if the mere fact that the occupation is not absolutely and perfectly healthy is to confer that right upon the legislative department of the government. It might be safely affirmed that almost all occupations more or less affect the health. There must be more than the mere fact of the possible existence of some small amount of unhealthiness to warrant legislative interference with liberty. It is unfortunately true that labor, even in any department, may possibly carry with it the seeds of unhealthiness. But are we all, on that account, at the mercy of legislative majorities? A printer, a tinsmith, a locksmith, a carpenter, a cabinetmaker, a dry goods clerk, a bank's, a lawyer's, or a physician's clerk, or a clerk in almost any kind of business, would all come under the power of the legislature, on this assumption. No trade, no occupation, no mode of earning one's living, could escape this all-pervading power, and the acts of the legislature in limiting the hours of labor in all employments would be valid, although such limitation might seriously cripple the ability of the laborer to support himself and his family. . . .

It is also urged, pursuing the same line of argument, that it is to the interest of the state that its population should be strong and robust, and therefore any legislation which may be said to tend to make people healthy must be valid as health laws, enacted under the police power. If this be a valid argument and a justification for this kind of legislation, it follows that the protection of the Federal Constitution from undue interference with liberty of person and freedom of contract is visionary, wherever the law is sought to be justified as a valid exercise of the police power. Scarcely any law but might find shelter under such assumptions, and conduct, properly so called, as well as such terms as they may think best, or which they may agree upon with the other parties to such contracts. Statutes of the nature of that under review, limiting the hours in which grown and intelligent men may labor to earn their living, are mere meddlesome interferences with the rights of the individual, and they are not saved from condemnation by the claim that they are passed in the exercise of the police power and upon the subject of the health of the individual whose rights are interfered with, unless there be some fair ground, reasonable in and of itself, to say that there is material danger to the public health, or to the health of the employees, if the hours of labor are not curtailed. . . .

* * *

It is manifest to us that the limitation of the hours of labor as provided for in this section of the statute under which the indictment was found, and the plaintiff in error convicted, has no such direct relation to, and no such substantial effect upon, the health of the employee, as to justify us in regarding the section as really a health law. It seems to us that the real object and purpose were simply to regulate the hours of labor between the master and his employees (all being men, sui juris), in a private business, not dangerous in any degree to morals, or in any real and substantial degree to the health of the employees. Under such circumstances the freedom of master and employee to contract with each other in relation to their employment, and in defining the same, cannot be prohibited or interfered with, without violating the Federal Constitution.

The judgment of the Court of Appeals of New York, as well as that of the Supreme Court and of the County Court of Oneida County, must be reversed and the case remanded to the County Court for further proceedings not inconsistent with this opinion.

Reversed.

Mr. Justice Holmes dissenting:

I regret sincerely that I am unable to agree with the judgment in this case, and that I think it my duty to express my dissent.

This case is decided upon an economic theory which is large part of the country does not entertain. If it were a question whether I agreed with that theory, I should desire to study it further and long before making up my mind. But I do not conceive that to be my duty, because I strongly believe that my agreement or disagreement has nothing to do with the right of a majority to embody their opinions in law. It is settled by various decisions of this court that state constitutions and state laws may regulate life in many ways which we as legislators might think as injudicious, or if you like as tyrannical, as this, and which, equally with this, interfere with the liberty to contract. Sunday laws and usury laws are ancient examples. A more modern one is the prohibition of lotteries. The liberty of the citizen to do as he likes so long as he does not interfere with the liberty of others to do the same, which has been a shibboleth for some well-known writers, is interfered with by school laws, by the Post office, by every state or municipal institution which takes his money for purposes thought desirable, whether he likes it or not. The 14th Amendment does not enact Mr. Herbert Spencer's Social Statics. . . . But a Constitution is not intended to embody a particular economic theory, whether of paternalism and the organic relation of the citizen to the state or of laissez faire. It is made for people of fundamentally differing views, and the accident of our finding certain opinions natural and familiar, or novel, and even shocking, ought not to conclude our judgment upon the question whether statutes embodying them conflict with the Constitution of the United States.

General propositions do not decide concrete cases. The decision will depend on a judgment or intuition more subtle than any articulate major premise. But I think that the proposition just stated, if it is accepted, will carry us far toward the end. Every opinion tends to become a law. I think that the word "liberty," in the 14th Amendment, is perverted when it is held to prevent the natural outcome of a dominant opinion, unless it can be said that a rational and fair man necessarily would admit that the statute proposed would infringe fundamental principles as they have been understood by the traditions of our people and our law. It does not need research to show that no such sweeping condemnation can be passed upon the statute before us. A reasonable man might think it a proper measure on the score of health. Men whom I certainly could not pronounce unreasonable would uphold it as a first installment of a general regulation of the hours of work. Whether in the latter aspect it would be open to the charge of inequality I think it unnecessary to discuss.

Source:

Supreme Court Reporter, Vol. 25, pp. 539–551.

Niagara Movement, Declaration of Principles, 1905

Manifesto issued by the Niagara Movement, militant forerunner of the National Association for the Advancement of Colored People (NAACP), on its formal organization at Niagara Falls, Ontario, in July 1905. African-American intellectuals, led by the sociologist and civil rights activist W. E. B. DuBois, gathered on the Canadian side of Niagara Falls (since no hotel on the U.S. side would let them register) to found the black protest movement. DuBois's 1903 work *Souls of Black Folk* provided the intellectual impetus for the movement. The Niagara initiative was a reaction against both the U.S. Supreme Court's landmark 1896 *Plessy v. Ferguson* ruling, which propounded the segregationist doctrine of "separate but equal," and black leader Booker T. Washington's accommodationist strategies for black social and economic advancement, as expressed in his 1895 Atlanta Compromise address. The Niagara declaration demanded an end in the United States of all forms of racial prejudice and discrimination and called for equality of economic and educational opportunity. Until such demands were met, the declaration warned, the movement would protest publicly to dramatize racial injustice.

Progress

The members of the conference, known as the Niagara Movement, assembled in annual meeting at Buffalo, July 11th, 12th and 13th, 1905, congratulate the Negro-Americans on certain undoubted evidences of progress in the last decade, particularly the increase of intelligence, the buying of property, the checking of crime, the uplift in home life, the advance in literature and art, and the demonstration of constructive and executive ability in the conduct of great religious, economic and educational institutions.

Suffrage

At the same time, we believe that this class of American citizens should protest emphatically and continually against the curtailment of their political rights. We believe in manhood suffrage; we believe that no man is so good, intelligent or wealthy as to be entrusted wholly with the welfare of his neighbor.

Civil Liberty

We believe also in protest against the curtailment of our civil rights. All American citizens have the right to equal treatment in places of public entertainment according to their behavior and deserts.

Economic Opportunity

We especially complain against the denial of equal opportunities to us in economic life; in the rural districts of the South this amounts to peonage and virtual slavery; all over the South it tends to crush labor and small business enterprises; and everywhere American prejudice, helped often by iniquitous laws, is making it more difficult for Negro Americans to earn a decent living.

Education

Common school education should be free to all American children and compulsory. High school training should be adequately provided for all, and college training should be the monopoly of no class or race in any section of our common country. We believe that, in defense of our own institutions, the United States should aid common school education, particularly in the South, and we especially recommend concerted agitation to this end. We urge an increase in public high school facilities in the South, where the Negro-Americans are almost wholly without such provisions. We favor well-equipped trade and technical schools for the training of artisans, and the need of adequate and liberal endowment for a few institutions of higher education must be patent to sincere well-wishers of the race.

Courts
We demand upright judges in courts, juries selected without discrimination on account of color and the same measure of punishment and the same efforts at reformation for black as for white offenders. We need orphanages and farm schools for dependent children, juvenile reformatories for delinquents, and the abolition of the dehumanizing convict-lease system.

Public Opinion
We note with alarm the evident retrogression in this land of sound public opinion on the subject of manhood rights, republican government and human brotherhood, and we pray God that this nation will not degenerate into a mob of boasters and oppressors, but rather will return to the faith of the fathers, that all men were created free and equal, with certain unalienable rights.

Health
We plead for health—for an opportunity to live in decent houses and localities, for a chance to rear our children in physical and moral cleanliness.

Employers and Labor Unions
We hold up for public execration the conduct of two opposite classes of men: The practice among employers of importing ignorant Negro-American laborers in emergencies, and then affording them neither protection nor permanent employment; and the practice of labor unions in proscribing and boycotting and oppressing thousands of their fellow-toilers, simply because they are black. These methods have accentuated and will accentuate the war of labor and capital, and they are disgraceful to both sides.

Protest
We refuse to allow the impression to remain that the Negro-American assents to inferiority, is submissive under oppression and apologetic before insults. Through helplessness we may submit, but the voice of protest of ten million Americans must never cease to assail the ears of their fellows, so long as America is unjust.

Color-Line
Any discrimination based simply on race or color is barbarous, we care not how hallowed it be by custom, expediency, or prejudice. Differences made on account of ignorance, immorality, or disease are legitimate methods of fighting evil, and against them we have no word of protest; but discriminations based simply and solely on physical peculiarities, place of birth, color or skin, are relies of that unreasoning human savagery of which the world is and ought to be thoroughly ashamed.

"Jim Crow" Cars
We protest against the "Jim Crow" car, since its effect is and must be to make us pay first-class fare for third-class accommodations, render us open to insults and discomfort and to crucify wantonly our manhood, womanhood and self-respect.

Soldiers
We regret that this nation has never seen fit adequately to reward the black soldiers who, in its five wars, have defended their country with their blood, and yet have been systematically denied the promotions which their abilities deserve. And we regard as unjust, the exclusion of black boys from the military and navy training schools.

War Amendments
We urge upon Congress the enactment of appropriate legislation for securing the proper enforcement of those articles of freedom, the thirteenth, fourteenth and fifteenth amendments of the Constitution of the United States.

Oppression
We repudiate the monstrous doctrine that the oppressor should be the sole authority as to the rights of the oppressed. The Negro race in America stolen, ravished and degraded, struggling up through difficulties and oppression, needs sympathy and receives criticism; needs help and is given hindrance, needs protection and is given mob-violence, needs justice and is given charity, needs leadership and is given cowardice and apology, needs bread and is given a stone. This nation will never stand justified before God until these things are changed.

The Church
Especially are we surprised and astonished at the recent attitude of the church of Christ—on the increase of a desire to bow to racial prejudice, to narrow the bounds of human brotherhood, and to segregate black men in some outer sanctuary. This is wrong, unchristian and disgraceful to the twentieth century civilization.

Agitation

Of the above grievances we do not hesitate to complain, and to complain loudly and insistently. To ignore, overlook, or apologize for these wrongs is to prove ourselves unworthy of freedom. Persistent manly agitation is the way to liberty, and toward this goal the Niagara Movement has started and asks the co-operation of all men of all races.

Help

At the same time we want to acknowledge with deep thankfulness the help of our fellowmen from the abolitionist down to those who to-day still stand for equal opportunity and who have given and still give of their wealth and of their poverty for our advancement.

Duties

And while we are demanding, and ought to demand, and will continue to demand the rights enumerated above, God forbid that we should ever forget to urge corresponding duties upon our people:

The duty to vote.

The duty to respect the rights of others.

The duty to work.

The duty to obey the laws.

The duty to be clean and orderly.

The duty to be send our children to school.

The duty to respect ourselves, even as we respect others.

This statement, complaint and prayer we submit to the American people, and Almighty God.

See also BOOKER T. WASHINGTON, "ATLANTA COMPROMISE SPEECH," 1895; W. E. B. DUBOIS, *THE SOULS OF BLACK FOLK*, 1903.

Source:

W. E. B. DuBois Papers, 1803 (1877–1963) 1999. Special Collections and Archives, W. E. B. DuBois Library, University of Massachusetts Amherst.

Pure Food and Drug Act, 1906

Federal legislation enacted on June 30, 1906, prohibiting the manufacture, sale, or transportation of adulterated or fraudulently labeled foods and drugs shipped in foreign or interstate commerce. Among the items prohibited were confectionery that contained dangerous colorings or flavorings, food composed of filthy or decomposed animal matter, food containing poisonous ingredients, and food adulterated to conceal inferior goods. Labels of proprietary medicines were required to indicate the percentages of narcotics, stimulants, or other potentially harmful ingredients.

The same day, Congress enacted the Meat Inspection Act, giving the U.S. secretary of agriculture the power to inspect meat and condemn products that are "unsound, unhealthful, unwholesome, or otherwise unfit for human food." The act was intended to correct unsanitary and dangerous practices in the meat-packing industry, such as resulted in the "embalmed beef" scandal, when soldiers in the Spanish-American War (1898) were fed tainted meat. The act allowed for federal inspection of all companies.

Although President Theodore Roosevelt and others had previously backed pure food and drug legislation, the impetus for these acts came from the publication of Upton Sinclair's *The Jungle* the same year. Sinclair, a socialist, meant his expose of conditions in the meat-packing industry to highlight the exploitation of immigrant workers like his book's protagonist. Instead, the public focused on the sections describing the processing of diseased cattle and the fate of workers who fell unreclaimed into open vats "till but the bones of them had gone out to the world as Durham's Pure Leaf Lard."

The 1906 Pure Food and Drug Act was superseded by the Food and Drug Act of June 24, 1938. It prohibited the sale of foods dangerous to health as well as foods, drugs, and cosmetics packaged in insanitary or contaminated containers. It required manufacturers of foods, drugs, and cosmetics to list their ingredients on the labels. It also prohibited the sale of "poisonous" or "deleterious" substances and broadened the definitions of "adulteration" and "misbranding." The Food and Drug Administration was authorized to enforce the act, and inspection stations were established in several large cities. Three months earlier, in the Wheeler-Lea Act, sponsored by Senator Burton K. Wheeler of Montana and Representative Clarence F. Lea of California, individuals and agencies were prohibited from presenting false or misleading statements about "food, drugs, diagnostic and therapeutic devices, and cosmetics" in interstate media. This statute gave the Federal Trade Commission control over such advertising and gave the Food and Drug Administration authority over questions of misbranding.

An Act

For preventing the manufacture, sale, or transportation of adulterated or misbranded or poisonous or deleterious foods, drugs, medicines, and liquors, and for regulating traffic therein, and for other purposes.

Be it enacted by the Senate and House of Representatives of the United States of America in Congress assembled, That is shall be unlawful for Columbia any article of food or drug which is adulterated or misbranded, within the meaning of this Act; and any person who shall violate any of the provisions of this section shall be guilty of a misdemeanor, and for each offense shall, upon conviction thereof, be fined not to exceed five hundred dollars or shall be sentenced to one year's imprisonment, or both such fine and imprisonment, in the discretion of the court, and for each subsequent offense and conviction thereof shall be fined not less than one thousand dollars or sentenced to one year's imprisonment, or both such fine and imprisonment, in the discretion of the court.

Sec. 2. That the introduction into any State or Territory or the District of Columbia from any other State or Territory or the District of Columbia, or from any foreign country, or shipment to any foreign country of any article of food or drugs which is adulterated or misbranded, within the meaning of this Act, is hereby prohibited; and any person who shall ship or deliver for shipment from any State or Territory or the District of Columbia to any other State or Territory or the District of Columbia, or to a foreign country, or who shall receive in any State or Territory or the District of Columbia from any other State or Territory or the District of Columbia, or foreign country, and having so received, shall deliver, in original unbroken packages, for pay or otherwise, or offer to deliver to any other person, any such article so adulterated or misbranded within the meaning of this Act, or any person who shall sell or offer for sale in the District of Columbia or the Territories of the United States any such adulterated or misbranded foods or drugs, or export or offer to export the same to any foreign country, shall be guilty of a misdemeanor, and for such offense be fined not exceeding two hundred dollars for the first offense, and upon conviction for each subsequent offense not exceeding three hundred dollars or be imprisoned not exceeding one year, or both, in the discretion of the court: *Provided,* That no article shall be deemed misbranded or adulterated within the provisions of this Act when intended for except to any foreign country and prepared or packed according to the specifications or directions of the foreign purchaser when no substance is used in the preparation or packing thereof in conflict with the laws of the foreign country to which said article is intended to be shipped; but if said article shall be in fact sold or offered for sale for domestic use or consumption, then this proviso shall not exempt said article from the operation of any of the other provisions of this Act.

Sec. 3. That the Secretary of the Treasury, the Secretary of Agriculture, and the Secretary of Commerce and Labor shall make uniform rules and regulations for carrying out the provisions of this Act, including the collection and examination of specimens of foods and drugs manufactured or offered for sale in the District of Columbia, or in any Territory of the United States, or which shall be offered for sale in unbroken packages in any State other than that in which they shall have been respectively manufactured or produced, or which shall be received from any foreign country, or intended for shipment to any foreign country, or which may be submitted for examination by the chief health, food, or drug officer of any State, Territory, or the District of Columbia, or at any domestic or foreign port through which such product is offered for interstate commerce, or for export or import between the United States and any foreign port or country.

Sec. 4. That the examinations of specimens of foods and drugs shall be made in the Bureau of Chemistry of the Department of Agriculture, or under the direction and supervision of such Bureau, for the purpose of determining from such examinations whether such articles are adulterated or misbranded within the meaning of this Act; and if it shall appear from any such examination that any of such specimens is adulterated or misbranded within the meaning of this Act, the Secretary of Agriculture shall cause notice thereof to be given to the party from whom such sample was obtained. Any party so notified shall be given an opportunity to be heard, under such rules and regulations as may be prescribed as aforesaid, and if it appears that any of the provisions of this Act have been violated by such party, then the Secretary of Agriculture shall at once certify the facts to the proper United States district attorney, with a copy of the results of the analysis or the examination of such article duly authenticated by the analyst or officer making such examination, under the oath of such officer. After judgment of the court, notice shall be given by publication in such manner as may be prescribed by the rules and regulations aforesaid.

Sec. 5. That is shall be the duty of each district attorney to whom the Secretary of Agriculture shall report any violation of this Act, or to whom any health or food or drug officer or agent of any State, Territory, or the District of Columbia shall present satisfactory evidence of any such violation, to cause appropriate proceedings to be commenced and prosecuted in the proper courts of the United States, without delay, for the enforcement of the penalties as in such case herein provided.

Sec. 6. That the term "drug," as used in this Act, shall include all medicines and preparations recognized in the United States Pharmacopoeia or National Formulary for internal or external use, and any substance or mixture of substances intended to be used for the cure, mitigation, or prevention of disease of either man or other animals. The term "food," as used herein, shall include all articles used for food, drink, confectionery, or condiment by man or other animals, whether simple, mixed, or compound.

Sec. 7. That for the purposes of this Act an article shall be deemed to be adulterated:

In case of drugs:

First. If, when a drug is sold under or by a name recognized in the United States Pharmacopoeia or National Formulary, it differs from the standard of strength, quality, or purity, as determined by the test laid down in the

United States Pharmacopoeia or National Formulary official at the time of investigation: *Provided,* That no drug defined in the United States Pharmacopoeia or National Formulary shall be deemed to be adulterated under this provision if the standard of strength, quality, or purity be plainly stated upon the bottle, box, or other container thereof although the standard may differ from that determined by the test laid down in the United States Pharmacopoeia or National Formulary.

Second. If its strength or purity fall below the professed standard or quality under which it is sold.

In the case of confectionery:

If it contain terra alba, barytes, talc, chrome yellow, or other mineral substance or poisonous color or flavor, or other ingredient deleterious or detrimental to health, or any vinous, malt or spirituous liquor or compound or narcotic drug.

In the case of food:

First. If any substance has been mixed and packed with it so as to reduce or lower or injuriously affect its quality or strength.

Second. If any substance has been substituted wholly or in part for the article.

Third. If any valuable constituent of the article has been wholly or in part abstracted.

Fourth. If it be mixed, colored, powdered, coated, or stained in a manner whereby damage or inferiority is concealed.

Fifth. If it contain any added poisonous or other added deleterious ingredient which may render such article injurious to health: *Provided,* That when in the preparation of food products for shipment they are preserved by any external application applied in such manner that the preservative is necessarily removed mechanically, or by maceration in water, or otherwise, and directions for the removal of said preservative shall be printed on the covering or the package, the provisions of this Act shall be construed as applying only when said products are ready for consumption.

Sixth. If it consists in whole or in part of a filthy, decomposed, or putrid animal or vegetable substance, or any portion of an animal unfit for food, whether manufactured or not, or if it is the product of a diseased animal, or one that has died otherwise than by slaughter.

Sec. 8. That the term, "misbranded," as used herein, shall apply to all drugs, or articles of food, or articles which enter into the composition of food, the package or label of which shall bear any statement, design, or device regarding such article, or the ingredients or substances contained therein which shall be false or misleading in any particular, and to any food or drug product which is falsely branded as to the State, Territory, or country in which it is manufactured or produced.

That for the purposes of this Act an article shall also be deemed to be misbranded:

In case of drugs:

First. If it be an imitation of or offered for sale under the name of another article.

Second. If the contents of the package as originally put up shall have been removed, in whole or in part, and other contents shall have been placed in such package, or if the package fail to bear a statement on the label of the quantity or proportion of any alcohol, morphine, opium, cocaine, heroin, alpha or beta eucaine, chloroform, cannabis indica, chloral hydrate, or acetanilide, or any derivative or preparation of any such substances contained therein.

In the case of food:

First. If it be an imitation of or offered for sale under the distinctive name of another article.

Second. If it be labeled or branded so as to deceive or mislead the purchaser, or purport to be a foreign product when not so, or if the contents of the package as originally put up shall have been removed in whole or in part and other contents shall have been placed in such package, or if it fail to bear a statement on the label of the quantity or proportion of any morphine, opium, cocaine, heroin, alpha or beta eucaine, chloroform, cannabis indica, chloral hydrate, or acetanilide, or any derivative or preparation of any such substances contained therein.

Third. If in package form, and the contents are stated in terms of weight or measure, they are not plainly and correctly stated on the outside of the package.

Fourth. If the package containing it or its label shall bear any statement, design, or device regarding the ingredients or the substances contained therein, which statement, design, or device shall be false or misleading in any particular: *Provided*, That an article of food which does not contain any added poisonous or deleterious ingredients shall not be deemed to be adulterated or misbranded in the following cases:

First. In the case of mixtures or compounds which may be now or from time to time hereafter known as articles of food, under their own distinctive names, and not an imitation of or offered for sale under the distinctive name of another article, if the name be accompanied on the same label or brand with a statement of the place where said article has been manufactured or produced.

Second. In the case of articles labeled, branded, or tagged so as to plainly indicate that they are compounds, imitations, or blends, and the word "compound," "imitation," or "blend," as the case may be, is plainly stated on the package in which it is offered for sale: *Provided*, That the term blend as used herein shall be construed to mean a mixture of like substances, not excluding harmless coloring or flavoring ingredients used for the purpose of coloring and flavoring only: *And provided further*, That nothing in this Act shall be construed as requiring or compelling proprietors or manufacturers of proprietary foods which contain no unwholesome added ingredient to disclose their trade formulas, except in so far as the provisions of this Act may require to secure freedom from adulteration or misbranding.

Sec. 9. That no dealer shall be prosecuted under the provisions of this Act when he can establish a guaranty signed by the wholesaler, jobber, manufacturer, or other party residing in the United States, from whom he purchases such articles, to the effect that the same is not adulterated or misbranded within the meaning of this Act, designating it. Said guaranty, to afford protection, shall contain the name and address of the party or parties making the sale of such articles to such dealer, and in such case said party or parties shall be amenable to the prosecutions, fines, and other penalties which would attach, in due course, to the dealer under the provisions of this Act.

Sec. 10. That any article of food, drug, or liquor that is adulterated or misbranded within the meaning of this Act, and is being transported from one State, Territory, District, or insular possession to another for sale, or, having been transported, remains unloaded, unsold, or in original unbroken packages, or if it be sold or offered for sale in the District of Columbia or the Territories, or insular possessions of the United States, or if it be imported from a foreign country for sale, or if it is intended for export to a foreign country, shall be liable to be proceeded against in any district court of the United States within the district where the same is found, and seized for confiscation by a process of libel for condemnation. And if such article is condemned as being adulterated or misbranded, or of a poisonous or deleterious character, within the meaning of this Act, the same shall be disposed of by destruction or sale, as the said court may direct, and the proceeds thereof, if sold, less the legal costs and charges, shall be paid into the Treasury of the United States, but such goods shall not be sold in any jurisdiction contrary to the provisions of this Act or the laws of that jurisdiction: *Provided, however* , That upon the payment of the costs of such libel proceedings and the execution and delivery of a good and sufficient bond to the effect that such articles shall not be sold or otherwise disposed of contrary to the provisions of this Act, or the laws of any State, Territory, District, or insular possession, the court may by order direct that such articles be delivered to the owner thereof. The proceedings of such libel cases shall conform, as near as may be, to the proceedings in admiralty, except that either party may demand trial by jury of any issue of fact joined in any such case, and all such proceedings shall be at the suit of and in the name of the United States.

Sec. 11. The Secretary of the Treasury shall deliver to the Secretary of Agriculture, upon his request from time to time, samples of foods and drugs which are being imported into the United States or offered for import, giving notice thereof to the owner or consignee, who may appear before the Secretary of Agriculture, and have the right to introduce testimony, and if it appear from the examination of such samples that any article of food or drug offered to be imported into the United States is adulterated or misbranded within the meaning of this Act, or is otherwise dangerous to the health of the people of the United States, or is of a kind forbidden entry into, or forbidden to be sold or restricted in sale in the country in which it is made or from which it is exported, or is otherwise falsely labeled in any respect, the said article shall be refused admission, and the Secretary of the Treasury shall refuse delivery to the consignee and shall cause the destruction of any goods refused delivery which shall not be exported by the consignee within three months from the date of notice of such refusal under such regulations as the Secretary of the Treasury may prescribe: *Provided* , That the Secretary of the Treasury may deliver to the consignee such goods pending examination and decision in the matter on execution of a penal bond for the amount of the full invoice value of such goods, together with the duty thereon, and on refusal to return such goods for any cause to the custody of the Secretary of the Treasury, when demanded, for the purpose of excluding them from the country, or for any other purpose, said consignee shall forfeit the full amount of the bond: *And provided further* , That all charges for storage, cartage, and labor on goods which are refused admission or delivery shall be paid by the owner or consignee, and in default of such payment shall constitute a lien against any future importation made by such owner or consignee.

Sec. 12. That the term "Territory" as used in this Act shall include the insular possessions of the United States. The word "person" as used in this Act shall be construed to import both the plural and the singular, as the case demands, and shall include corporations, companies, societies and associations. When construing and enforcing the provisions of this Act, the act, omission, or failure of any officer, agent, or other person acting for or employed by any corporation, company, society, or association, within the scope of his employment or office, shall in every case be also deemed to be the act, omission, or failure of such corporation, company, society, or association as well as that of the person.

Sec. 13. That this Act shall be in force and effect from and after the first day of January, nineteen hundred and seven.

See also MEAT INSPECTION ACT, 1906; WHEELER-LEA ACT, 1938; FOOD AND DRUG ACT, 1938.

Source:
Statutes at Large, Vol. 34, pp. 768–772.

Adair v. United States, 1908

U.S. Supreme Court ruling of January 27, 1908, that declared unconstitutional the Erdman Act of 1898, which was enacted to prevent disruption of interstate commerce by labor disputes. It protected union members in a number of ways, including the discharge or blacklisting of personnel for labor union activities. William Adair, an agent of the railroad, fired a worker because of his union membership. Adair was convicted of violating the Erdman Act. In a 6-to-2 decision, the Supreme Court overruled this conviction, finding that union membership did not fall under congressional authority to regulate interstate commerce. John Marshall Harlan, writing for the majority, used substantive due process to conclude that the law was an unreasonable invasion of personal liberty and property rights under the Fifth Amendment. Harlan's decision posited an equal relationship between employer and wage-earner, and it became the basis for invalidating state laws protecting union membership.

In *Coppage v. Kansas* (236 U.S. 1), January 25, 1915, the Supreme Court declared unconstitutional state laws forbidding "yellow dog" contracts—that is, contracts in which employers require their workers not to join labor unions. The case arose when a Kansas railway worker was fired for refusing to sign a contract that would have compelled him to resign from his union. A state court upheld the Kansas statute, but the U.S. Supreme Court ruled that the law violated the due process clause of the Fourteenth Amendment by denying an employer the right to contract freely with workers. Yellow dog contracts were later outlawed by the Norris-LaGuardia Act.

Mr. Justice Harlan delivered the opinion of the court:

This case involves the constitutionality of certain provisions of the act of Congress of June 1st, 1898 (30 Stat. at L. 424, chap. 370, U.S. Comp. Stat. 1901, p. 3205), concerning carriers engaged in interstate commerce and their employees.

By the 1st section of the act it is provided: "That the provisions of this act shall apply to any common carrier or carriers and their officers, agents, and employees, except masters of vessels and seamen, as defined in section 4612, Revised Statutes of the United States (U.S. Comp. Stat. 1901, p. 3120), engaged in the transportation of passengers or property wholly by railroad, or partly by railroad and partly by water, for a continuous carriage or shipment from one state or territory of the United States, or the District of Columbia, to any other state or territory of the United States, or the District of Columbia, or from any place in the United States to an adjacent foreign country, or from any place in the United States through a foreign country to any other place in the United States. The term 'railroad,' as used in this act, shall include all bridges and ferries used or operated in connection with any railroad, and also all the road in use by any corporation operating a railroad, whether owned or operated under a contract, agreement, or lease; and the term 'transportation' shall include all instrumentalities of shipment or carriage. The term 'employees,' as used in this act, shall include all persons actually engaged in any capacity in train operation or train service of any description, and notwithstanding that the cars upon or in which they are employed may be held and operated by the carrier under lease or other contract: Provided, however, That this act shall not be held to apply to employees of street railroads, and shall apply only to employees engaged in railroad train service. In every such case the carrier shall be responsible for the acts and defaults of such employees in the same manner and to the same extent as if said cars were owned by it and said employees directly employed by it, and any provisions to the contrary of any such lease or other contract shall be binding only as between the parties thereto, and shall not affect the obligations of said carrier either to the public or to the private parties concerned."

The 2d, 3d, 4th, 5th, 6th, 7th, 8th, and 9th sections relate to the settlement, by means of arbitration, of controversies concerning wages, hours of labor, or conditions of employment, arising between a carrier subject to the provisions of the act and its employees, which seriously interrupt, or threaten to interrupt, the business of the carrier. Those sections prescribe the mode in which controversies may be brought under the cognizance of arbitrators, in what way the arbitrators may be designated, and the effect of their decisions. The first subdivision of Section 3 contains a proviso "that no employee shall be compelled to render personal service without his consent."

The 11th section relates to the compensation and expenses of the arbitrators.

By the 12th section the act of Congress of October 1st, 1888 [25 Stat. at L. 501, chap, 1063], creating boards of arbitrators or commissioners for settling controversies and differences between railroad corporations and other common carriers engaged in interstate or territorial transportation of persons or property and their employees, was repealed.

The 10th section, upon which the present prosecution is based, is in these words:

"That any employers subject to the provisions of this act, and any officer, agent, or receiver of such employer, who shall require any employee, or any person seeking employment, as a condition of such employment, to enter into an agreement, either written or verbal, not to become or remain a member of any labor corporation, association, or organization; *or shall threaten any employee with loss of employment, or shall unjustly discriminate against any employee because of his membership in such a labor corporation, association, or organization;* or who shall require any employee or any person seeking employment, as a condition of such employment, to enter into a contract whereby such employee or applicant for employment shall agree to contribute to any fund for charitable, social, or beneficial purposes; to release such employer from legal liability for any personal injury by reason of any benefit received from such fund beyond the proportion of the benefit arising from the employer's contribution to such fund; or who shall, after having discharged an employee, attempt or conspire to prevent such employee from obtaining employment, or who shall, after the quitting of an employee, attempt or conspire to prevent such employee from obtaining employment, is hereby declared to be guilty of a misdemeanor, and, upon conviction thereof in any court of the United States of competent jurisdiction in the district in which such offense was committed, shall be punished for each offense by a fine of not less than one hundred dollars and not more than one thousand dollars."

It may be observed in passing that while that section makes it a crime against the United States to unjustly discriminate against an employee of an interstate carrier because of his being a member of a labor organization, it does not make it a crime to unjustly discriminate against an employee of the carrier because of his *not* being a member of such an organization.

The present indictment was in the district court of the United States for the Eastern district of Kentucky against the defendant, Adair.

The first count alleged "that at and before the time hereinafter named the Louisville & Nashville Railroad Company is and was a railroad corporation, duly organized and existing by law, and a common carrier engaged in the transportation of passengers and property wholly by steam railroad for a continuous carriage and shipment from one state of the United States to another state of the United States of America; that is to say, from the state of Kentucky into the States of Ohio, Indiana, and Tennessee, and from the state of Ohio into the state of Kentucky, and was, at all times aforesaid, and at the time of the commission of the offense hereinafter named, a common carrier of interstate commerce, and an employer, subject to the provisions of a certain act of Congress of the Unites States of America, entitled, 'An Act Concerning Carriers Engaged in Interstate Commerce and Their Employees,' approved June 1st, 1898, and said corporation was not at anytime a street railroad corporation. That before and at the time of the commission of the offense hereinafter named one William Adair was an agent and employee of said common carrier and employer, and was, at all said times, master mechanic of said common carrier and employer in the district aforesaid, and before and at the time hereinafter stated one O. B. Coppage was an employee of said common carrier and employer in the district aforesaid, and as such employee was, at all times hereinafter named, actually engaged in the capacity of locomotive fireman in train operation and train service for said common carrier and employer in the transportation of passengers and property aforesaid, and was an employee of said common carrier and employer actually engaged in said railroad transportation and train service aforesaid, to whom the provisions of said act applied, and at the time of the commission of the offense hereinafter named said O. B. Coppage was a member of a certain labor organization, known as the Order of Locomotive Firemen, as he, the said William Adair, then and there well knew; a more particular description of said organization and the members thereof is to the grand jurors unknown."

The specific charge in that count was "that said William Adair, agent and employee of said common carrier and employer, as aforesaid, in the district aforesaid, on and before the 15th day of October, 1906, did unlawfully and unjustly discriminate against said O. B. Coppage, employee, as aforesaid, by then and there discharging said O. B. Coppage from such employment of said common carrier and employer, *because of his membership in said labor organization, and thereby did unjustly discriminate against an employee of a common carrier and employer engaged in interstate commerce because of his membership in a labor organization,* contrary to the forms of the statute in such cases made and provided, and against the peace and dignity of the United States."

The second count repeated the general allegations of the first count as to the character of the business of the Louisville & Nashville Railroad Company and the relations between that corporation and Adair and Coppage. It charged "that said William Adair, in the district aforesaid, and within the jurisdiction of this court, agent and employee of said common carrier and employer aforesaid, on and before the 15th day of October, 1906, did unlawfully *threaten said O. B. Coppage, employee as aforesaid, with loss of employment, because of his membership in said labor organization,* contrary to the forms of the statute in such cases made and provided, and against the peace and dignity of the United States."

The accused, Adair, demurred to the indictment as insufficient in law, but the demurrer was overruled. After reviewing the authorities, in an elaborate opinion, the court held the 10th section of the act of Congress to be constitutional. 152 Fed. 737. The defendant pleaded not guilty, and after trial a verdict was returned of guilty on the first count and a judgment rendered that he pay to the United States a fine of $100. We shall, therefore, say nothing as to the second count of the indictment.

It thus appears that the criminal offense charged in the count of the indictment upon which the defendant was convicted was, in substance and effect, that, being an agent of a railroad company engaged in interstate commerce, and subject to the provisions of the above act of June 1st, 1898, he discharged one Coppage from its service *because of his membership in a labor organization*—no other ground for such discharge being alleged.

May Congress make it a criminal offense against the United States—as, by the 10th section of the act of 1898, it does—for an agent or officer of an interstate carrier, having full authority in the premises from the carrier, to discharge an employee from service simply because of his membership in a labor organization?

This question is admittedly one of importance, and has been examined with care and deliberation. And the court has reached a conclusion which, in its judgment, is consistent with both the words and spirit of the Constitution, and is sustained as well by sound reason.

The first inquiry is whether the part of the 10th section of the act of 1898 upon which the first count of the indictment was based is repugnant to the 5th Amendment of the Constitution, declaring that no person shall be deprived of liberty or property without due process of law. In our opinion that section, in the particular mentioned, is an invasion of the personal liberty, as well as of the right of property, guaranteed by that Amendment. Such liberty and right embrace the right to make contracts for the purchase of the labor of others, and equally the right to make contracts for the sale of one's own labor; each right, however, being subject to the fundamental condition that no contract, whatever its subject-matter, can be sustained which the law, upon reasonable grounds, forbids as inconsistent with the public interests, or as hurtful to the public order, or as detrimental to the common good. This court has said that "in every well-ordered society, charged with the duty of conserving the safety of its members, the rights of the individual in respect of his liberty may, at times, under the pressure of great dangers, be subjected to such restraint, to be enforced by reasonable regulations, as the safety of the general public may demand." *Jacobson v. Massachusetts,* 197 U. S. 11, 29, 49 L. ed. 643, 651, 25 Sup. Ct. Rep. 358. 362, and authorities there cited. Without stopping to consider what would have been the rights of the railroad company under the 5th Amendment, had it been indicted under the act of Congress, it' is sufficient in this case to say that, as agent of the railroad company, and, as such, responsible for the conduct of the business of one of its departments, it was the defendant Adair's right—and that right inhered in his personal liberty, and was also a right of property—to serve his employer as best he could, so long as he did nothing that was reasonably forbidden by law as injurious to the public interests. It was the right of the defendant to prescribe the terms upon which the services of Coppage would be accepted, and it was the right of Coppage to become or not, as he chose, an employee of the railroad company upon the terms offered to him. Mr. Cooley, in his treatise on Torts, p. 278, well says: "It is a part of every man's civil rights that he be left at liberty to refuse business relations with any person whomsoever, whether the refusal rests upon reason, or is the result of whim, caprice, prejudice, or malice. With his reasons neither the public nor third persons have any legal concern. It is also his right to have business relations with anyone with whom he can make contracts, and, if he is wrongfully deprived of this right by others, he is entitled to redress."

In *Lochner v. New York,* 198 U. S. 45, 53, 56, 49 L. ed. 937, 940, 941, 25 Sup. Ct. Rep. 539, 541, 543, which involved the validity of a state enactment prescribing certain maximum hours for labor in bakeries, and which made it a misdemeanor for an employer to require or permit an employee in such an establishment to work in excess of a given number of hours each day, the court said: "The general right to make a contract in relation to his business is part of the liberty of the individual protected by the 14th Amendment of the Federal Constitution. *Allgeyer v. Louisiana,* 165 U. S. 578, 41 L. ed. 832, 17 Sup. Ct. Rep. 427. Under that provision no state can deprive any person of life, liberty, or property without due process of law. The right to purchase or to sell labor is part of the liberty protected by this Amendment, unless there are circumstances which exclude the right. There are, however, certain powers existing in the sovereignty of each state in the Union, somewhat vaguely termed 'police powers,' the exact description and limitation of which have not been attempted by the courts. Those powers, broadly stated, and without, at present, any attempt at a more specific limitation, relate to the safety, health, morals, and general welfare of the public. Both property and liberty are held on such reasonable conditions as may be imposed by the governing power of the state in the exercise of those powers, and with such conditions the 14th Amendment was not designed to interfere. *Mugler v. Kansas,* 123 U. S. 623, 31 L. ed. 205, 8 Sup. Ct. Rep. 273; Re Kemmler, 136 U. S. 436, 34 L. ed. 519, 10 Sup. Ct. Rep. 930; *Crowley v. Christensen,* 137 U. S. 86, 34 L. ed. 620, 11 Sup. Ct. Rep. 13; Re Converse, 137 U. S. 624, 34 L. ed. 796, 11 Sup. Ct. Rep. 191. . . . In every case that comes before this court, therefore, where legislation of this character is concerned, and where the protection of the Federal Constitution is sought, the question necessarily arises: Is this a fair, reasonable, and appropriate exercise of the police power of the state, or is it an unreasonable, unnecessary, and arbitrary interference with the right of the individual to his personal liberty or to enter into those contracts in relation to labor which may seem to him appropriate or necessary for the support of himself and his family? Of course, the liberty of contract relating to labor includes both parties to it. The one has as much right to purchase as the other to sell labor." Although there was a difference of opinion in that case among the members of the court as to certain propositions, there was no disagreement as to the general proposition that there is a liberty of contract which cannot be unreasonably interfered with by legislation. The minority were of opinion that the business referred to in the New York statute was such as to require regulation, and that, as the statute was not shown plainly and palpably to have imposed an unreasonable restraint upon freedom of contract, it should be regarded by the courts as a valid exercise of the state's power to care for the health and safety of its people.

While, as already suggested, the right of liberty and property guaranteed by the Constitution against deprivation without due process of law is subject to such reasonable restraints as the common good or the general welfare may require, it is not within the functions of government—at least, in the absence of contract between the parties—to compel any person, in the course of his business and against his will, to accept or retain the personal services of another, or to compel any person, against his will, to perform personal services for another. The right of a person to sell his labor upon such terms as he deems proper is, in its essence, the same as the right of the purchaser of labor to prescribe the conditions upon which he will accept such labor from the person offering to sell it. So the right of the employee to quit the service of the employer, for whatever reason, is the same as the right of the employer, for whatever reason, to dispense with the services of such employee. It was the legal right of the defendant, Adair, —however unwise such a course might have been—to discharge Coppage because of his being a member of a labor organization, as it was the legal right of Coppage, if he saw fit to do so—however unwise such a course on his part might have been—to quit the service in which he was engaged, because the defendant employed some persons who were not members of a labor organization. In all such particulars the employer and the employee have equality of right, and any legislation that disturbs that equality is an arbitrary interference with the liberty of contract which no government can legally justify in a free land. These views find support in adjudged cases, some of which are cited in the margin. Of course, if the parties by contract fixed the period of service, and prescribed the condition upon which the contract may be terminated, such contract would control the rights of the parties as between themselves, and for any violation of those provisions the party wronged would have his appropriate civil action. And it may be—but upon that point we express no opinion—that, in the case of a labor contract between an employer engaged in interstate commerce and his employee, Congress could make it a crime for either party, without sufficient or just excuse or notice, to disregard the terms of such contract or to refuse to perform it. In the absence, however, of a valid contract between the parties controlling their conduct towards each other and fixing a period of service, it cannot be, we repeat, that an employer is under any legal obligation, against his will, to retain an employee in his personal service any more than an employee can be compelled, against his will, to remain in the personal service of another. So far as this record discloses the facts the defendant, who seemed to have authority in the premises, did not agree to keep Coppage in service for any particular time, nor did Coppage agree to remain in such services a moment longer than he chose. The later was a liberty to quit the service without assigning any reason for his leaving. And the defendant was at liberty, in his discretion, to discharge Coppage from service without giving any reason for so doing.

As the relations and the conduct of the parties towards each other was not controlled by any contract other than a general employment on one side to accept the services of the employee and a general agreement on the other side to render services to the employer—no term being fixed for the continuance of the employment—Congress could not, consistently with the 5th Amendment, make it a crime against the United States to discharge the employee because of this being a member of a labor organization.

But it is suggested that the authority to make it a crime for an agent or officer of an interstate carrier, having authority in the premises from his principal, to discharge an employee from service to such carrier, simply because of his membership in a labor organization, can be referred to the power of Congress to regulate interstate commerce, without regard to any question of personal liberty or right of property arising under the 5th Amendment. This suggestion can have no bearing in the present discussion unless the statute, in the particular just stated, is, within the meaning of the Constitution, a regulation of commerce among the states. If it be not, then clearly the government cannot invoke the commerce clause of the Constitution as sustaining the indictment against Adair.

Let us inquire what is commerce, the power to regulate which is given to Congress?

This question has been frequently propounded in this court, and the answer has been—and no more specific answer could well have been given—that commerce among the several states comprehends traffic, intercourse, trade, navigation, communication, the transit of persons, and the transmission of messages by telegraph—indeed, every species of commercial intercourse among the several states—but not that commerce "completely internal, which is carried on between man and man, in a state, or between different parts of the same state, and which does not extend to or affect other states." The power to regulate interstate commerce is the power to prescribe rules by which such commerce must be governed. Of course, as has been often said, Congress has a large discretion in the selection or choice of the means to be employed in the regulation of interstate commerce, and such discretion is not to be interfered with except where that which is done is in plain violation of the Constitution. *Northern Securities Co. v. United States,* 193 U. S. 197, 48 L. ed. 679, 24 Sup. Ct. Rep. 436, and authorities there cited. In this connection we may refer to *Johnson v. Southern P. Co.* 196 U. S. 1, 49 L. ed. 363, 25 Sup. Ct. Rep. 158, relied on in argument, which case arose under the act of Congress of March 2d, 1893 (27 Stat. at L. 531, chap. 196, U. S. Comp. Stat. 1901, p. 3174). That act required carriers engaged in interstate commerce to equip their cars used in such commerce with automatic couplers and continuous brakes, and their locomotives with driving-wheel brakes. But the act upon its face showed that its object was to promote the safety of employees and travelers upon railroads; and this court sustained its validity upon the ground that it manifestly had reference to interstate commerce, and was calculated to subserve the interests of such commerce by affording protection to employees and travelers. It was held that there was a substantial connection between the object sought to be attained by the act and the means provided to accomplished that object. So, in regard to *Howard v. Illinois C. R. Co.* decided at the present term. 207 U. S. 463, ante, 141, 28 Sup. Ct. Rep. 141. In that case the court sustained the authority of Congress, under its power to regulate interstate commerce, to prescribe the rule of liability, as between interstate carriers and its employees in such interstate commerce, in cases of personal injuries received by employees while actually engaged in such commerce. The decision on this point was placed on the ground that a rule of that character would have direct reference to the conduct of interstate commerce, and would, therefore, be within the competency of Congress to establish for commerce among the states, but not as to commerce completely internal to a state. Manifestly, any rule prescribed for the conduct of interstate commerce, in order to be within the competency of Congress under its power to regulate commerce among the states, must have some real or substantial relation to or connection with the commerce regulated. But what possible legal or logical connection is there between an employee's membership in a labor organization and the carrying on of interstate commerce? Such relation to a labor organization cannot have, *in itself* and in the eye of the law, any bearing upon the commerce with which the employee is connected by his labor and services. Labor associations, we assume, are organized for the general purpose of improving or bettering the conditions and conserving the interests of its members as wage-earners—an object entirely legitimate and to be commended rather than condemned. But surely those associations, as labor organizations, have nothing to do with interstate commerce, as such. One who engages in the service of an interstate carrier will, it must be assumed, faithfully perform his duty, whether he be a member or not a member of a labor organization. His fitness for the position in which he labors and his diligence in the discharge of his duties cannot, in law or sound reason, depend in any degree upon his being or not being a member of a labor organization. It cannot be assumed that his fitness is assured, or his diligence increased, by such membership, or that he is less fit or less diligent because of his not being a member of such an organization. It is the employee as a man, and not as a member of a labor organization, who labors in the service of an interstate carrier. Will it be said that the provision in question had its origin in the apprehension, on the part of Congress, that, if it did not show more consideration for members of labor organizations than for wage-earners who were not members of such organizations, or if it did not insert in the statute some such provision as the one here in question, members of labor organizations would, by illegal or violent measures, interrupt or impair the freedom of commerce among the states? We will not indulge in any such conjectures, nor make them, in whole or in part, the basis of our decision. We could not do so consistently with the respect due to a coordinate department of the government. We could not do so without imputing to Congress the purpose to accord to one class of wage- earners privileges withheld from another class of wage-earners, engaged, it may be, in the same kind of labor and serving the same employer. Nor will we assume, in our consideration of this case, that members of labor organizations will, in any considerable numbers, resort to illegal methods for accomplishing any particular object they have in view.

Looking alone at the words of the statute for the purpose of ascertaining its scope and effect, and of determining its validity, we hold that there is no such connection between interstate commerce and membership in a labor organization as to authorize Congress to make it a crime against the United States for an agent of an interstate carrier to discharge an employee because of such membership on his part. If such a power exists in Congress it is difficult to perceive why it might not, by absolute regulation, require interstate carriers, under penalties, to employ, in the conduct of its interstate business, *only* members of labor organizations, or *only* those who are *not* members of such organizations—a power which could not be recognized as existing under the Constitution of the United States. No such rule of criminal liability as that to which we have referred can be regarded as, in any just sense, a regulation of interstate commerce. We need scarcely repeat what this court has more than once said, that the power to regulate interstate commerce, great and paramount as that power is, cannot be exerted in violation of any fundamental right secured by other provisions of the Constitution. *Gibbons v. Ogden,* 9 Wheat. 1, 196, 6 L. ed. 23, 70; Lottery Case (*Champion v. Ames*) 188 U. S. 321, 353, 47 L. ed. 492, 500, 23 Sup. Ct. Rep. 321.

It results, on the whole case, that the provision of the statute under which the defendant was convicted must be held to be repugnant to the 5th Amendment, and as not embraced by nor within the power of Congress to regulate interstate commerce, but, under the guise of regulating interstate commerce, and as applied to this case, it arbitrarily sanctions an illegal invasion of the personal liberty as well as the right of property of the defendant, Adair.

We add that since the part of the act of 1898 upon which the first count of the indictment is based, and upon which alone the defendant was convicted, is severable from its other parts, and as what has been said is sufficient to dispose of the present case, we are not called upon to consider other and independent provisions of the act, such, for instance, as the provisions relating to arbitration. This decision is therefore restricted to the question of the validity of the particular provision in the act of Congress making it a crime against the United States for an agent or officer of an interstate carrier to discharge an employee from its service because of his being a member of a labor organization.

The judgment must be reversed, with directions to set aside the verdict and judgment of conviction, sustain the demurrer to the indictment, and dismiss the case.

It is so ordered.

Mr. Justice Moody did not participate in the decision of this case.

Mr. Justice McKenna, dissenting:

The opinion of the court proceeds upon somewhat narrow lines and either omits or does not give adequate prominence to the considerations which, I think, are determinative of the questions in the case. The principle upon which the opinion is grounded is, as I understand it, that a labor organization has no legal or logical connection with interstate commerce, and that the fitness of an employee has no dependence or relation with his membership in such organization. It is hence concluded that to restrain his discharge merely on account of such membership is an invasion of the liberty of the carrier guaranteed by the 5th Amendment of the Constitution of the United States. The conclusion is irresistible if the propositions from which it is deduced may be viewed as abstractly as the opinion views them. May they be so viewed?

A summary of the act is necessary to understand Section 10. Detach that section from the other provisions of the act and it might be open to condemnation.

The 1st section of the act designates the carriers to whom it shall apply. The 2d section makes it the duty of the chairman of the Interstate Commerce Commission and the Commissioner of Labor, in case of a dispute between carriers and their employees which threatens to interrupt the business of the carriers, to put themselves in communication with the parties to the controversy and use efforts to "mediation and conciliation." If the efforts fail, then Section 3 provides for the appointment of a board of arbitration,—one to be named by the carrier, one by the labor organization to which the employees belong, and the two thus chosen shall select a third.

There is a provision that if the employees belong to different organizations they shall concur in the selection of the arbitrator. The board is to give hearings; power is vested in the board to summon witnesses, and provision is made for filing the award in the clerk's office of the circuit court of the United States for the district where the controversy arose. Others sections complete the scheme of arbitration thus outlined, and make, as far as possible, the proceedings of the arbitrators judicial, and, pending them, put restrictions on the parties, and damages for violation of the restrictions.

Even from this meager outline may be perceived the justification and force of Section 10. It prohibits discrimination by a carrier engaged in interstate commerce, in the employment under the circumstances hereafter mentioned, or the discharge from employment of members of labor organizations *because of such membership."* This the opinion condemns. The actions prohibited, it is asserted, are part of the liberty of a carrier, protected by the Constitution of the United States from limitation or regulation. I may observe that the declaration is clear and unembarrassed by any material benefit to the carrier from its exercise. It may be exercised with reason or without reason, though the business of the carrier is of public concern. This, then, is the contention, and I bring its elements into bold relief to submit against them what I deem to be stronger considerations, based on the statute and sustained by authority.

I take for granted that the expression of the opinion of the court, which seems to indicate that the provisions of Section 10 are illegal because their violation is made criminal, are used only for description and incidental emphasis, and not as the essential ground of the objections to those provisions.

I may assume at the outset that the liberty guaranteed by the 5th Amendment is not a liberty free from all restraints and limitations, and this must be so or government could not be beneficially exercised in many cases. Therefore, in judging of any legislation which imposes restraints or limitations, the inquiry must be, What is their purpose, and is the purpose within one of the powers of government? Applying this principle immediately to the present case, without beating about in the abstract, the inquiry must be whether Section 10 of the act of Congress has relation to the purpose which induced the act, and which it was enacted to accomplish, and whether such purpose is in aid of interstate commerce, and not a mere restriction upon the liberty of carriers to employ whom they please, or to have business relations with whom they please. In the inquiry there is necessarily involved a definition of interstate commerce and of what is a regulation of it. As to the first, I may concur with the opinion; as to the second, an immediate and guiding light is afforded by the case of *Howard v. Illinois* C. R. Co., recently decided. 207 U. S. 463, ante, 141, 28 Sup. Ct. Rep. 141. In that case there was a searching scrutiny of the powers of Congress, and it was held to be competent to establish a new rule of liability of the carrier to his employees; in a word, competent to regulate the relation of master and servant—a relation apparently remote from commerce, and one which was earnestly urged by the railroad to be remote from commerce. To the contention the court said: "But we may not test the power of Congress to regulate commerce solely by abstractly considering the particular subject to which a regulation relates, irrespective of whether the regulation in question is one of interstate commerce. On the contrary, the test of power is not merely the matter regulated, but whether the regulation is directly one of interstate commerce, or is embraced within the grant conferred on Congress to use all lawful means necessary and appropriate to the execution of the power to regulate commerce." In other words, that the power is not confined to a regulation of the mere movement of goods or persons.

And there are other examples in our decisions—examples, too, of liberty of contract and liberty of forming business relations (made conspicuous as grounds of decision in the present case)—which were compelled to give way to the power of Congress. *Northern Securities Co. v. United States,* 193 U. S. 200, 48 L. ed. 679, 24 Sup. Ct. Rep. 436. In that case exactly the same definitions were made as made here and the same contentions were pressed as are pressed here. The Northern Securities Company was not a railroad company. Its corporate powers were limited to buying, selling, and holding stock, bonds, and other securities, and it was contended that, as such business was not commerce at all, it could not be within the power of Congress to regulate. The contention was not yielded to, though it had the support of members of this court. Asserting the application of the anti-trust act of 1890 [26 Stat. at L. 209, chap. 647, U. S. Comp. Stat. 1912, p. 3200] to such business, and the power of Congress to regulate it, the court said "that a sound construction of the Constitution allows to Congress a large discretion 'with respect to the means by which the powers it [the commerce clause] confers are to be carried into execution, which enables that body to perform the high duties assigned to it, in the manner most beneficial to the people.'" It was in recognition of this principle that it was declared in *United States v. Joint Traffic Asso.* 171 U. S. 571, 43 L. ed. 288, 19 Sup. Ct. Rep. 25: "The prohibitions of such contracts [contracts fixing rates] may, in the judgment of Congress, be one of the reasonable necessities for the proper regulation of commerce, and Congress is the *judge* of such necessity and propriety, unless, *in case of a possible gross perversion of the principle,* the courts might be applied to for relief." The contentions of the parties in the case invoked the declaration. There, as here, an opposition was asserted between the liberty of the railroads to contract with one another and the power of Congress to regulate commerce. That power was pronounced paramount, and it was not perceived, as it seems to be perceived now, that it was subordinate, and controlled by the provisions of the 5th Amendment. Nor was that relation of the power of Congress to the Amendment overlooked. It was commented upon and reconciled. And there is nothing whatever in *Gibbons v. Ogden,* 9 Wheat. 1, 6 L. ed. 23, or in Lottery Case (*Champion v. Ames*) 188 U. S. 321, 47 L. ed. 492 23 Sup. Ct. Rep. 321, which is to the contrary.

From these considerations we may pass to an inspection of the statute of which Section 10 is a part, and inquire as to its purpose, and if the means which it employs has relation to that purpose and to interstate commerce. The provisions of the act are explicit and present a well co-ordinated plan for the settlement of disputes between carriers and their employees, by bringing the disputes to arbitration and accommodation, and thereby prevent strikes and the public disorder and derangement of business that may be consequent upon them. I submit no worthier purpose can engage legislative attention or be the object of legislative action, and, it might be urged, to attain which the congressional judgment of means should not be brought under a rigid limitation and condemned, if it contribute in any degree to the end, as a "gross perversion of the principle" of regulation, the condition which, it was said in *United States v. Joint Traffic Asso.* supra, might justify an appeal to the courts.

We are told that labor associations are to be commended. May not, then, Congress recognize their existence? yes, and recognize their power as conditions to be counted with in framing its legislation? Of what use would it be to attempt to bring bodies of men to agreement and compromise of controversies if you put out of view the influences which move them or the fellowship which binds them—maybe controls and impels them, whether rightfully or wrongfully, to make the cause of one the cause of all? And this practical wisdom Congress observed—observed, I may say, not in speculation or uncertain prevision of evils, but in experience of evils—an experience which approached to the dimensions of a national calamity. The facts of history should not be overlooked nor the course of legislation. The act involved in the present case was preceded by one enacted in 1888 of similar purport. 25 Stat. at L. 501, chap. 1063. That act did not recognize labor associations, or distinguish between the members of such associations and the other employees of carriers. It failed in its purpose, whether from defect in its provisions or other cause we may only conjecture. At any rate, it did not avert the strike at Chicago in 1894. Investigation followed, and, as a result of it, the act of 1898 was finally passed. Presumably its provisions and remedy were addressed to the mischief which the act of 1888 failed to reach or avert. It was the judgment of Congress that the scheme of arbitration might be helped by engaging in it the labor associations. Those associations unified bodies of employees in every department of the carriers, and this unity could be an obstacle or an aid to arbitration. It was attempted to be made an aid; but how could it be made an aid if, pending the efforts of "mediation and conciliation" of the dispute, as provided in Section 2 of the act, other provisions of the act may be arbitrarily disregarded, which are of concern to the members in the dispute? How can it be an aid, how can controversies which may seriously interrupt or threaten to interrupt the business of carriers (1 paraphrase the words of the statute) be averted or composed if the carrier can bring on the conflict or prevent its amicable settlement by the exercise of mere whim and caprice? I say mere whim or caprice, for this is the liberty which is attempted to be vindicated as the constitutional right of the carriers. And it may be exercised in mere whim and caprice. If ability, the qualities of efficient and faithful workmanship, can be found outside of labor associations, surely they may be found inside of them. Liberty is an attractive theme, but the liberty which is exercised in sheer antipathy does not plead strongly for recognition.

There is no question here of the right of a carrier to mingle in his service "union" and "nonunion" men. If there were, broader considerations might exist. In such a right there would be no discrimination for the "union" and no discrimination against it. The efficiency of an employee would be its impulse and ground of exercise.

I need not stop to conjecture whether Congress could or would limit such right. It is certain that Congress has not done so by any provision of the act under consideration. Its letter, spirit, and purpose are decidedly the other way. It imposes, however, a restraint, which should be noticed. The carriers may not require an applicant for employment or an employee to agree not to become or remain a member of a labor organization. But this does not constrain the employment of anybody, be he what he may.

But it is said it cannot be supposed that labor organizations will, "by illegal or violent measures, interrupt or impair the freedom of commerce," and to so suppose would be disrespect to a co-ordinate branch of the government, and to impute to it a purpose "to accord to one class of wage- earners privileges withheld from another class of wage-earners, engaged, it may be, in the same kind of labor and serving the same employer." Neither the supposition nor the disrespect is necessary, and, it may be urged, they are no more invidious than to impute to Congress a careless or deliberate or purposeless violation of the constitutional rights of the carriers. Besides, the legislation is to be accounted for. It, by its letter, makes a difference between members of labor organizations and other employees of carriers. If it did not, it would not be here for review. What did Congress mean? Had it no purpose? Was it moved by no cause? Was its legislation mere wantonness and an aimless meddling with the commerce of the country? These questions may find their answers in Re Debs, 158 U. S. 564, 39 L. ed. 1092, 15 Sup. Ct. Rep. 900.

I have said that it is not necessary to suppose that labor organizations will violate the law, and it is not. Their power may be effectively exercised without violence or illegality, and it cannot be disrespect to Congress to let a committee of the Senate speak for it and tell the reason and purposes of its legislation. The committee on education, in its report, said of the bill: "The measure under consideration may properly be called a voluntary arbitration bill, having for its object the settlement of disputes between capital and labor, as far as the interstate transportation companies are concerned. The necessity for the bill arises from the calamitous results in the way of ill-considered strikes arising from the tyranny of capital or the unjust demands of labor organizations, whereby the business of the country is brought to a standstill and thousands of employees, with their helpless wives and children, are confronted with starvation." And, concluding the report, said: "It is our opinion that this bill, should it become a law, would reduce to a minimum labor strikes which affect interstate commerce, and we therefore recommend its passage."

With the report was submitted a letter from the secretary of the Interstate Commerce Commission, which expressed the judgment of that body, formed, I may presume, from experience of the factors in the problem. The letter said: "With the corporations as employers, on one side, and the organizations of railway employees, on the other, there will be a measure of equality of power and force which will surely bring about the essential requisites of friendly relation, respect, consideration, and forbearance." And again: "It has been shown before the labor commission of England that, where the associations are strong enough to command the respect of their employers, the relations between employer and employee seem most amicable. For there the employers have learned the practical convenience of treating with one thoroughly representative body instead of with isolated fragments of workmen; and the labor associations have learned the limitations of their powers."

It is urged by plaintiff in error that "there is a marked distinction between a power to regulate commerce and a power to regulate the affairs of an individual or corporation engaged in such commerce"; and how can it be, it is asked, a regulation of commerce to prevent a carrier from selecting his employees or constraining him to keep in his service those whose loyalty to him is "seriously impaired, if not destroyed, by their prior allegiance to their labor unions"? That the power of regulation extends to the persons engaged in interstate commerce is settled by decision. *Howard v. Illinois C. R. Co.* 207 U. S. 463, ante, 141, 28 Sup. Ct. Rep. 141, and the cases cited in Mr. Justice Moody's dissenting opinion. The other proposition points to no evil or hazard of evil. Section 10 does not constrain the employment of incompetent workmen, and gives no encouragement or protection to the disloyalty of an employee or to deficiency in his work or duty. If guilty of either he may be instantly discharged without incurring any penalty under the statute.

Counsel also makes a great deal of the difference between direct and indirect effect upon interstate commerce, and assert that Section 10 is an indirect regulation at best, and not within the power of Congress to enact. Many cases are cited, which, it is insisted, sustain the contention. I cannot take time to review the cases. I have already alluded to the contention, and it is enough to say that it gives too much isolation to Section 10. The section is part of the means to secure and make effective the scheme of arbitration set forth in the statute. The contention, besides, is completely answered by *Howard v. Illinois C. R. Co.* supra. In that case, as we have seen, the power of Congress was exercised to establish a rule of liability of a carrier to his employees for personal injuries received in his service. It is manifest that the kind or extent of such liability is neither traffic nor intercourse, the transit of persons nor the carrying of things. Indeed, such liability may have wider application than to carriers. It may exist in a factory; it may exist on a farm; and, in both places, or in commerce, its direct influence might be hard to find or describe. And yet this court did not hesitate to pronounce it to be within the power of Congress to establish. "The primary object," it was said in *Johnson v. Southern P. Co.* 196 U. S. 1, 49 L. ed. 363, 25 Sup. Ct. Rep. 158, of the safety appliance act, "was to promote *the public welfare* by securing the safety of employees and travelers." The rule of liability for injuries is even more roundabout in its influence on commerce, and as much so as the prohibition of Section 10. To contend otherwise seems to me to be an oversight of the proportion of things. A provision of law which will prevent, or tend to prevent, the stoppage of every wheel in every car of an entire railroad system, certainly has as direct influence on interstate commerce as the way in which one car may be coupled to another, or the rule of liability for personal injuries to an employee. It also seems to me to be an oversight of the proportions of things to contend that, in order to encourage a policy of arbitration between carriers and their employees which may prevent a disastrous interruption of commerce, the derangement of business, and even greater evils to the public welfare, Congress cannot restrain the discharge of an employee, and yet can, to enforce a policy of unrestrained competition between railroads, prohibit reasonable agreements between them as to the rates at which merchandise shall be carried. And mark the contrast of what is prohibited. In the one case the restraint, it may be, of a whim—certainly of nothing that affects the ability of an employee to perform his duties; nothing, therefore, which is of any material interest to the carrier—in the other case, a restraint of a carefully-considered policy which had as its motive great material interests and benefits to the railroads, and, in the opinion of many, to the public. May such action be restricted, must it give way to the public welfare, while the other, moved, it may be, by prejudice and antagonism, is intrenched impregnably in the 5th Amendment of the Constitution against regulation in the public interest?

I would not be misunderstood. I grant that there are rights which can have no material measure. There are rights which, when exercised in a private business, may not be disturbed or limited. With them we are not concerned. We are dealing with rights exercised in a quasi public business, and therefore subject to control in the interest of the public.

I think the judgment should be affirmed.

Mr. Justice Holmes, dissenting:

I also think that the statute is constitutional, and, but for the decision of my brethren, I should have felt pretty clear about it.

As we all know, there are special labor unions of men engaged in the service of carriers. These unions exercise a direct influence upon the employment of labor in that business, upon the terms of such employment, and upon the business itself. Their very existence is directed specifically to the business, and their connection with it is, at least, as intimate and important as that of safety couplers, and, I should think, as the liability of master to servant,—matters which, it is admitted, Congress might regulate, so far as they concern commerce among the states. I suppose that it hardly would be denied that some of the relations of railroads with unions of railroad employees are closely enough connected with commerce to justify legislation by Congress. If so, legislation to prevent the exclusion of such unions from employment is sufficient near.

The ground on which this particular law is held bad is not so much that it deals with matters remote from commerce among the states, as that it interferes with the paramount individual rights secured by the 5th Amendment. The section is, in substance, a very limited interference with freedom of contract, no more. It does not require the carriers to employ anyone. It does not forbid them to refuse to employ anyone, for any reason they deem good, even where the notion of a choice of persons is a fiction and wholesale employment is necessary upon general principles that it might be proper to control. The section simply prohibits the more powerful party to exact certain undertakings, or to threaten dismissal or unjustly discriminate on certain grounds against those already employed. I hardly can suppose that the grounds on which a contract lawfully may be made to end are less open to regulation than other terms. So I turn to the general question whether the employment can be regulated at all. I confess that I think that the right to make contracts at will that has been derived from the word "liberty" in the Amendments has been stretched to its extreme by the decisions; but they agree that sometimes the right may be restrained. Where there is, or generally is believed to be, an important ground of public policy for restraint, the Constitution does not forbid it, whether this court agrees or disagrees with the policy pursued. It cannot be doubted that to prevent strikes, and, so far as possible, to foster its scheme of arbitration, might be deemed by Congress an important point of policy, and I think it impossible to say that Congress might not reasonably think that the provision in question would help a good deal to carry its policy along. But suppose the only effect really were to tend to bring about the complete unionizing of such railroad laborers as Congress can deal with, I think that object alone would justify the act. I quite agree that the question what and how much good labor unions do, is one on which intelligent people may differ; I think that laboring men sometimes attribute to them advantages, as many attribute to combinations of capital disadvantages, that really are due to economic conditions of a far wider and deeper kind; but I could not pronounce it unwarranted if Congress should decide that to foster a strong union was for the best interest, not only of the men, but of the railroads and the country at large.

Source:
Supreme Court Reporter, Vol. 28, pp. 277–287.

Muller v. Oregon, 1908

U.S. Supreme Court decision of February 24, 1908, upholding a 1903 Oregon law limiting the maximum hours women could work in any factory or laundry to 10 hours a day. The Court unanimously denied a claim that the law violated the liberty-of-contract rights under the Fourteenth Amendment. Attorney and future Supreme Court justice Louis Brandeis, representing the state of Oregon, submitted an extensive brief consisting of historical, medical, psychological, and statistical information to support his legal arguments. He did so at the urging of Florence Kelley and Josephine Goldmark of the Consumer's League. This kind of argument, which embodied Progressive Era principles, became known as a "Brandeis Brief." In upholding the state's law, the Court not only ruled that a state could use its police powers in this area, but also set a precedent for considering nonlegal evidence.

Long considered a landmark decision for women's rights, *Muller* took on a very different look with the second wave of feminism in the late 20th century. This type of protective legislation for women was used to keep them in low-paying "pink collar" jobs and out of better paying positions requiring physical labor, such as construction, or long hours, such as bartending. With the drive for equality, any legislation that put limits on a woman simply because of her gender became anathema.

Another significant Supreme Court decision involving women, *Adkins v. Children's Hospital* (261 U.S. 525, [1923]), issued April 9, 1923, invalidated a 1918 congressional act establishing a wage board in Washington, D.C., to fix minimum wages for women adequate to maintain a decent standard of living. In its 5-3 decision, the Court ruled that the act infringed on the due process clause of the Fifth Amendment by interfering with the freedom of an employer and an employee to make a contract. Justice Oliver Wendell Holmes, in dissent, argued that Congress had a right "to remove conditions leading to ill health, immorality, and the deterioration of the race."

Adkins was overturned in *West Coast Hotel Company v. Parrish* (300 U.S. 379) March 29, 1937. This decision upheld the validity of a Washington state law setting a minimum wage for women and minors. Elsie Parrish, a chambermaid, sued her employer when she received less than $14.50 for 48 hours of work. The hotel challenged the minimum-wage statute as a violation of constitutional rights to due process, depriving employers and employees of freedom of contract, as the Supreme Court had held in *Adkins*. The 5-4 ruling in the *West Coast Hotel* case overturned the Adkins decision and declared that minimum-wage statutes were a valid exercise of the police power of the state.

Mr. Justice **Brewer** delivered the opinion of the court:

On February 19, 1903, the legislature of the state of Oregon passed an act (Session Laws 1903, p. 148) the first section of which is in these words:

"Sec. 1. That no female (shall) be employed in any mechanical establishment, or factory, or laundry in this state more than ten hours during any one day. The hours of work may be so arranged as to permit the employment of females at any time so that they shall not work more than ten hours during the twenty-four hours of any one day."

Sec. 3 made a violation of the provisions of the prior sections a misdemeanor subject to a fine of not less than $10 nor more than $25. On September 18, 1905, an information was filed in the circuit court of the state for the county of Multnomah, charging that the defendant "on the 4th day of September, A. D. 1905, in the county of Multnomah and state of Oregon, then and there being the owner of a laundry, known as the Grand Laundry, in the city of Portland, and the employer of females therein, did then and there unlawfully permit and suffer one Joe Haselbock, he, the said Joe Haselbock, then and there being an overseer, superintendent, and agent of said Curt Muller, in the said Grand Laundry, to require a female, to wit, one Mrs. E. Gotcher, to work more than ten hours in said laundry on said 4th day of September, A.D. 1905, contrary to the statutes in such cases made and provided, and against the peace and dignity of the state of Oregon."

A trial resulted in a verdict against the defendant, who was sentenced to pay a fine of $10. The supreme court of the state affirmed the conviction (48 Or. 252, 85 Pac. 855), whereupon the case was brought here on writ of error.

The single question is the constitutionality of the statute under which the defendant was convicted, so far as it affects the work of a female in a laundry. That it does not conflict with any provisions of the state Constitution is settled by the decision of the supreme court of the state. The contentions of the defendant, now plaintiff in error, are thus stated in his brief:

"(1) Because the statute attempts to prevent persons *sui juris* from making their own contracts, and thus violates the provisions of the 14th Amendment, as follows:

"No state shall make or enforce any law which shall abridge the privileges or immunities of citizens of the United States; nor shall any state deprive any person of life, liberty, or property, without due process of law; nor deny to any person within its jurisdiction the equal protection of the laws.'

"(2) Because the statute does not apply equally to all persons similarly situated, and is class legislation.

"(3) The statute is not a valid exercise of the police power. The kinds of work prescribed are not unlawful, nor are they declared to be immoral or dangerous to the public health; nor can such a law be sustained on the ground that it is designed to protect women on account of their sex. There is no necessary or reasonable connection between the limitation prescribed by the act and the public health, safety, or welfare."

It is the law of Oregon that women, whether married or single, have equal contractual and personal rights with men. As said by Chief Justice Wolverton, in *First Nat. Bank v. Leonard*, 36 Or. 390, 396, 59 Pac. 873, 874, after a review of the various statutes of the state upon the subject:

We may therefore say with perfect confidence that, with these three sections upon the statute book, the wife can deal, not only with her separate property, acquired from whatever source, in the same manner as her husband can with property belonging to him, but that she may make contracts and incur liabilities, and the same may be enforced against her, the same as if she were a *female sole*. There is now no residuum of civil disability resting upon her which is not recognized as existing against the husband. The current runs steadily and strongly in the direction of the emancipation of the wife, and the policy, as disclosed by all recent legislation upon the subject in the state, is to place her upon the same footing as if she were a *female sole*, not only with respect to her separate property, but as it affects her right to make binding contracts; and the most natural corollary to the situation is that the remedies for the enforcement of liabilities incurred are made coextensive and coequal with such enlarged conditions."

It thus appears that, putting to one side the elective franchise, in the matter of personal and contractual rights they stand on the same plane as the other sex. Their rights in these respects can no more be infringed than the equal rights of their brothers. We held in *Lochner v. New York*, 198 U.S. 45, 49 L. ed. 937, 25 Sup. Ct. Rep. 539, that a law providing that no laborer shall be required or permitted to work in bakeries more than sixty hours in a week or ten hours in a day was not as to men a legitimate exercise of the police power of the state, but an unreasonable, unnecessary, and arbitrary interference with the right and liberty of the individual to contract in relation to his labor, and as such was in conflict with, and void under, the Federal Constitution. The decision is invoked by plaintiff in error as decisive of the question before us. But this assumes that the difference between the sexes does not justify a different rule respecting a restriction of the hours of labor.

In patent cases counsel are apt to open the argument with a discussion of the state of the art. It may not be amiss, in the present case, before examining the constitutional question, to notice the course of legislation, as well as expressions of opinion from other than judicial sources. In the brief filed by Mr. Louis D. Brandeis for the defendant in error is a very copious collection of all these matters, an epitome of which is found in the margin.

While there have been but few decisions bearing directly upon the question, the following sustain the constitutionality of such legislation: *Com. v. Hamilton Mfg. Co.* 120 Mass. 383; *Wenham v. State,* 65 Neb. 394, 400, 406, 58 L.R.A. 825, 91 N. W. 421; *State v. Buchanan,* 29 Wash. 602, 59 L.R.A. 342, 92 Am. St. Rep. 930, 70 Pac. 52; *Com. v. Beatty,* 15 Pa. Super. Ct. 5, 17; against them is the case of *Ritchie v. People,* 155 Ill. 98, 29 L.R.A. 79, 46 Am. St. Rep. 315, 40 N.E. 454.

The legislation and opinions referred to in the margin may not be, technically speaking, authorities, and in them is little or no discussion of the constitutional question presented to us for determination, yet they are significant of a widespread belief that woman's physical structure, and the functions she performs in consequence thereof, justify special legislation restricting or qualifying the conditions under which she should be permitted to toil. Constitutional questions, it is true, are not settled by even a consensus of present public opinion, for it is the peculiar value of a written constitution that it places in unchanging form limitations upon legislative action, and thus gives a permanence and stability to popular government which otherwise would be lacking. At the same time, when a question of fact is debated and debatable, and the extent to which a special constitutional limitation goes is affected by the truth in respect to that fact, a widespread and long-continued belief concerning it is worthy of consideration. We take judicial cognizance of all matters of general knowledge.

It is undoubtedly true, as more than once declared by this court, that the general right to contract in relation to one's business is part of the liberty of the individual, protected by the 14th Amendment to the Federal Constitution; yet it is equally well settled that this liberty is not absolute and extending to all contracts, and that a state may, without conflicting with the provisions of the 14th Amendment, restrict in many respects the individual's power of contract. Without stopping to discuss at length the extent to which a state may act in this respect, we refer to the following cases in which the question has been considered: *Allgeyer v. Louisiana,* 165 U. S. 578, 41 L. ed. 832, 17 Sup. Ct. Rep. 427; *Holden v. Hardy,* 169 U. S. 366, 42 L. ed. 780, 18 Sup. Rep. 383; *Lochner v. New York,* supra.

That woman's physical structure and the performance of maternal functions place her at a disadvantage in the struggle for subsistence is obvious. This is especially true when the burdens of motherhood are upon her. Even when they are not, by abundant testimony of the medical fraternity continuance for a long time on her feet at work, repeating this from day to day, tends to injurious effects upon the body, and, as healthy mothers are essential to vigorous offspring, the physical well-being of woman becomes an object of public interest and care in order to preserve the strength and vigor of the race.

Still again, history discloses the fact that woman has always been dependent upon man. He established his control at the outset by superior physical strength, and this control in various forms, with diminishing intensity, has continued to the present. As minors, though not to the same extent, she has been looked upon in the courts as needing especial care that her rights may be preserved. Education was long denied her, and while now the doors of the schoolroom are opened and her opportunities for acquiring knowledge are great, yet even with that and the consequent increase of capacity for business affairs it is still true that in the struggle for subsistence she is not an equal competitor with her brother. Though limitations upon personal and contractual rights may be removed by legislation, there is that in her disposition and habits of life which will operate against a full assertion of those rights. She will still be where some legislation to protect her seems necessary to secure a real equality of right. Doubtless there are individual exceptions, and there are many respects in which she has an advantage over him; but looking at it from the viewpoint of the effort to maintain an independent position in life, she is not upon an equality. Differentiated by these matters from the other sex, she is properly placed in a class by herself, and legislation designed for her protection may be sustained, even when like legislation is not necessary for men, and could not be sustained. It is impossible to close one's eyes to the fact that she still looks to her brother and depends upon him. Even though all restrictions on political, personal, and contractual rights were taken away, and she stood, so far as statutes are concerned, upon an absolutely equal plane with him, it would still be true that she is so constituted that she will rest upon and look to him for protection; that her physical structure and a proper discharge of her maternal functions—having in view not merely her own health, but the well-being of the race—justify legislation to protect her from the greed as well as the passion of man. The limitations which this statute places upon her contractual powers, upon her right to agree with her employer as to the time she shall labor, are not imposed solely for her benefit, but also largely for the benefit of all. Many words cannot make this plainer. The two sexes differ in structure of body, in the functions to be performed by each, in the amount of physical strength, in the capacity for long continued labor, particularly when done standing, the influence of vigorous health upon the future well-being of the race, the self-reliance which enables one to assert full rights, and in the capacity to maintain the struggle for subsistence. This difference justifies a difference in legislation, and upholds that which is designed to compensate for some of the burdens which rest upon her.

We have not referred in this discussion to the denial of the elective franchise in the state of Oregon, for while that may disclose a lack of political equality in all things with her brother, that is not of itself decisive. The reason runs deeper, and rests in the inherent difference between the two sexes, and in the different functions in life which they perform.

For these reasons, and without questioning in any respect the decision in Lochner v. New York, we are of the opinion that it cannot be adjudged that the act in question is in conflict with the Federal Constitution, so far as it respects the work of a female in a laundry, and the judgment of the Supreme Court of Oregon is affirmed.

Source:
Supreme Court Reporter, Vol. 43, pp. 394–406.

Jane Addams, "Problems of Poverty," *Twenty Years at Hull-House*, 1910

Memoir by the crusading American social reformer Jane Addams on Hull-House, her innovative turn-of-the-century group settlement project for Chicago's working-class poor. Inspired by the British social reform movement, Addams in 1889, established the philanthropic Hull-House, an experiment in social outreach, in an old mansion in one of Chicago's poor immigrant neighborhoods. Her project responded to the immigrant community's unmet needs for housing, education, public health, and recreation. She publicized her work with her book *Twenty Years at Hull-House*. In the memoir, she called on her society to value the traditions of its immigrants even as it helped the nation's newcomers adjust to American institutions and ways of life. She asserted that a new social ethic of compassion for the underprivileged was needed to stem the conflicts created by the urban ills of industrial capitalism.

In "Why Women Should Vote," an essay in *The Blue Book: Woman Suffrage, History, Arguments and Results*, a collection of essays published by the National American Woman Suffrage Association, Addams encouraged urban women to seek the vote. She especially wanted to reach immigrants living in crowded and unsanitary conditions in cities who believed that their place was in the home rather than in politics. She showed how women, by voting, could effect change in their domestic lives; as voters they could even better fulfill their duties as mothers and housekeepers.

In the excerpt below, Addams discusses poverty in relation to her influential settlement-house philosophy.

Problems of Poverty

That neglected and forlorn old age is daily brought to the attention of a Settlement which undertakes to bear its share of the neighborhood burden imposed by poverty, was pathetically clear to us during our first months of residence at Hull-House. One day a boy of ten led a tottering old lady into the House, saying that she had slept for six weeks in their kitchen on a bed made up next to the stove; that she had come when her son died, although none of them had ever seen her before; but because her son had "once worked in the same shop with Pa she thought of him when she had nowhere to go." The little fellow concluded by saying that our house was so much bigger than theirs that he thought we would have more room for beds. The old woman herself said absolutely nothing, but looking on with that gripping fear of the poorhouse in her eyes, she was a living embodiment of that dread which is so heartbreaking that the occupants of the Country Infirmary themselves seem scarcely less wretched than those who are making their last stand against it.

This look was almost more than I could bear, for only a few days before some frightened women had bidden me come quickly to the house of an old German woman, whom two men from the county agent's office were attempting to remove to the County Infirmary. The poor old creature had thrown herself bodily upon a small and battered chest of drawers and clung there, clutching it so firmly that it would have been impossible to remove her without also taking the piece of furniture. She did not weep nor moan nor indeed make any human sound, but between her broken gasps for breath she squealed shrilly like a frightened animal caught in a trap. The little group of women and children gathered at her door stood aghast at this realization of the black dread which always clouds the lives of the very poor when work is slack, but which constantly grows more imminent and threatening as old age approaches. The neighborhood women and I hastened to make all sorts of promises as to the support of the old woman and the county officials, only too glad to be rid of their unhappy duty, left her to our ministrations. This dread of the poorhouse, the result of centuries of deterrent Poor Law administration, seemed to me not without some justification one summer when I found myself perpetually distressed by the unnecessary idleness and forlornness of the old women in the Cook County Infirmary, many of whom I had known in the years when activity was still a necessity, and when they yet felt bustlingly important. To take away from an old woman whose life has been spent in household cares all the foolish little belongings to which her affections cling and to which her very fingers have become accustomed, is to take away her last incentive to activity, almost to life itself. To give an old woman only a chair and a bed, to leave her no cupboard in which her treasures may be stowed, not only that she may take them out when she desires occupation, but that her mind may dwell upon them in moments of revery, is to reduce living almost beyond the limit of human endurance.

The poor creature who clung so desperately to her chest of drawers was really clinging to the last remnant of normal living—a symbol of all she was asked to renounce. For several years after this summer I invited five or six old women to take a two week's vacation from the poorhouse which they eagerly and even gayly accepted. Almost all the old men in the County Infirmary wander away each summer taking their chances for finding food or shelter and return much refreshed by the little "tramp," but the old women cannot do this unless they have some help from the outside, and yet the expenditure of a very little money secures for them the coveted vacation. I found that a few pennies paid their car fare into town, a dollar a week procured a lodging with an old acquaintance; assured of two good meals a day in the Hull-House coffee-house they could count upon numerous cups of tea among old friends to whom they would airily state that they had "come out for a little change" and hadn't yet made up their minds about "going in again for the winter." They thus enjoyed a two weeks' vacation to the top of their bent and returned with wondrous tales of their adventures, with which they regaled the other paupers during the long winter.

The reminiscences of these old women, their shrewd comments upon life, their sense of having reached a point where they may at last speak freely with nothing to lose because of their frankness, makes them often the most delightful of companions. I recall one of my guests, the mother of many scattered children, whose one bright spot through all the dreary years had been the wedding feast of her son Mike—a feast which had become transformed through long meditation into the nectar and ambrosia of the very gods. As a farewell fling before she went "in" again, we dined together upon chicken pie, but it did not taste like "the chicken pie at Mike's wedding" and she was disappointed after all.

Even death itself sometimes fails to bring the dignity and serenity which one would fain associate with old age. I recall the dying hour of one old Scotchwoman whose long struggle to "keep respectable" had so embittered her, that her last words were gibes and taunts for those who were trying to minister to her. "So you came in yourself this morning, did you? You only sent things yesterday. I guess you knew when the doctor was coming. Don't try to warm my feet with anything but that old jacket that I've got there; it belonged to my boy who was drowned at sea nigh thirty years ago, but it's warmer yet with human feelings than any of your damned charity hot-water bottles." Suddenly the harsh gasping voice as stilled in death and I awaited the doctor's coming shaken and horrified.

The lack of municipal regulation already referred to was, in the early days of Hull-House, paralleled by the inadequacy of the charitable efforts of the city and an unfounded optimism that there was no real poverty among us. Twenty years ago there was no Charity Organization Society in Chicago and the Visiting Nurse Association had not yet begun its beneficent work, while the relief societies, although conscientiously administered, were inadequate in extent and antiquated in method.

As social reformers gave themselves over to discussion of general principles, so the poor invariably accused poverty itself of their destruction. I recall a certain Mrs. Moran, who was returning one rainy day from the office of the county agent with her arms full of paper bags containing beans and flour which alone lay between her children and starvation. Although she had no money she boarded a street car in order to save her booty from complete destruction by the rain, and as the burst bags dropped "flour on the ladies' dresses" and "beans all over the place," she was sharply reprimanded by the conductor, who was further exasperated when he discovered she had no fare. He put her off, as she had hoped he would, almost in front of Hull-House. She related to us her state of mind as she stepped off the car and saw the last of her wares disappearing; she admitted she forgot the proprieties and "cursed a little," but, curiously enough, she pronounced her male-diction, not against the rain nor the conductor, not yet against the worthless husband who had been sent up to the city prison, but, true to the Chicago spirit of the moment, went to the root of the matter and roundly "cursed poverty."

This spirit of generalization and lack of organization among the charitable forces of the city was painfully revealed in that terrible winter after the World's Fair, when the general financial depression throughout the country was much intensified in Chicago by the numbers of unemployed stranded at the close of the exposition. When the first cold weather came the police stations and the very corridors of the City Hall were crowded by men who could afford no other lodging. They made huge demonstrations on the lake front, reminding one of the London gatherings in Trafalgar Square.

It was the winter in which Mr. Stead wrote his indictment of Chicago. I can vividly recall his visits to Hull-House, some of them between eleven and twelve o'clock at night, when he would come in wet and hungry from an investigation of the levee district, and, while he was drinking hot chocolate before an open fire, would relate in one of his curious monologues, his experience as an out-of-door laborer standing in line without an overcoat for two hours in the sleet, that he might have a chance to sweep the streets; or his adventures with a crook, who mistook him for one of his own kind and offered him a place as an agent for a gambling house, which he promptly accepted. Mr. Stead was much impressed with the mixed goodness in Chicago, the lack of rectitude in many high places, the simple kindness of the most wretched to each other. Before he published "If Christ Came to Chicago" he made his attempt to rally the diverse moral forces of the city in a huge mass meeting, which resulted in a temporary organization, later developing into the Civic Federation. I was a member of the committee of five appointed to carry out the suggestions made in this remarkable meeting, and our first concern was to appoint a committee to deal with the unemployed. But when has a committee ever dealt satisfactorily with the unemployed? Relief stations were opened in various parts of the city, temporary lodging houses were established, Hull-House undertaking to lodge the homeless women who could be received nowhere else, employment stations were opened giving sewing to the women, and street sweeping for the men was organized. It was in connection with the latter that the perplexing question of the danger of permanently lowering wages at such a crisis, in the praiseworthy effort to bring speedy relief, was brought home to me. I insisted that it was better to have the men work half a day for seventy-five cents than a whole day for a dollar, better that they should earn three dollars in two days than in three days. I resigned from the street cleaning committee in despair of making the rest of the committee understand that, as our real object was not street cleaning but the help of the unemployed, we must treat the situation in such wise that the men would not be worse off when they returned to their normal occupations. The discussion opened up situations new to me and carried me far afield in perhaps the most serious economic reading I have ever done.

A beginning also was then made toward a Bureau of Organized Charities, the main office being put in charge of a young man recently come from Boston, who lived at Hull-House. But to employ scientific methods for the first time at such a moment involved difficulties, and the most painful episode of the winter for me came from an attempt on my part to conform to carefully received instructions. A shipping clerk whom I had known for a long time had lost his place, as so many people had that year, and came to the relief station established at Hull-House four or five times to secure help for his family. I told him one day of the opportunity for work on the drainage canal and intimated that if any employment were obtainable, he ought to exhaust that possibility before asking for help. The man replied that he had always worked indoors and that he could not endure outside work in winter. I am grateful to remember that I was too uncertain to be severe, although I held to my instructions. He did not come again for relief, but worked for two days digging on the canal, where he contracted pneumonia and died a week later. I have never lost trace of the two little children he left behind him, although I cannot see them without a bitter consciousness that it was at their expense I learned that life cannot be administered by definite rules and regulations; that wisdom to deal with a man's difficulties comes only through some knowledge of his life and habits as a whole; and that to treat an isolated episode is almost sure to invite blundering.

It was also during this winter that I became permanently impressed with the kindness of the poor to each other; the woman who lives upstairs will willingly share her breakfast with the family below because she knows they "are hard up"; the man who boarded with them last winter will give a month's rent because he knows the father of the family is out of work; the baker across the street, who is fast being pushed to the wall by his downtown competitors, will send across three loaves of stale bread because he has seen the children looking longingly into his window and suspects they are hungry. There are also the families who, during times of business depression, are obliged to seek help from the county or some benevolent society, but who are themselves most anxious not to be confounded with the pauper class, with whom indeed they do not in the least belong. Charles Booth, in his brilliant chapter on the unemployed, expresses regret that the problems of the working class are so often confounded with the problems of the inefficient and the idle, that although working people live in the same street with those in need of charity, to thus confound two problems is to render the solution of both impossible.

I remember one family in which the father had been out of work for this same winter, most of the furniture had been pawned, and as the worn-out shoes could not be replaced the children could not go to school. The mother was ill and barely able to come for the supplies and medicines. Two years later she invited me to supper one Sunday evening in the little home which had been completely restored, and she gave as a reason for the invitation that she couldn't bear to have me remember them as they had been during that one winter, which she insisted had been unique in her twelve years of married life. She said that it was as if she had met me, not as I am ordinarily, but as I should appear misshapen with rheumatism or with a face distorted by neuralgic pain; that it was not fair to judge poor people that way. She perhaps unconsciously illustrated the difference between the relief-station relation to the poor and the Settlement relation to its neighbors, the latter wishing to know them through all the varying conditions of life, to stand by when they are in distress, but by no means to drop intercourse with them when normal prosperity has returned, enabling the relation to become more social and free from economic disturbance.

Possibly something of the same effort has to be made within the Settlement itself to keep its own sense of proportion in regard to the relation of the crowded city quarter to the rest of the country. It was in the spring following this terrible winter, during a journey to meet lecture engagements in California, that I found myself amazed at the large stretches of open country and prosperous towns through which we passed day by day, whose existence I had quite forgotten.

In the latter part of the summer of 1895, I served as a member on a commission appointed by the mayor of Chicago, to investigate conditions in the country poorhouse, public attention having become centered on it through one of those distressing stories, which exaggerates the wrong in a public institution while at the same time it reveals conditions which need to be rectified. However necessary publicity is for securing reformed administration, however useful such exposures may be for political purposes, the whole is attended by such a waste of the most precious human emotions, by such a tearing of living tissue, that it can scarcely be endured. Every time I entered Hull-House during the days of the investigation, I would find waiting for me from twenty to thirty people whose friends and relatives were in the suspected institution, all in such acute distress of mind that to see them was to look upon the victims of deliberate torture. In most cases my visitor would state that it seemed impossible to put their invalids in any other place, but if these stories were true, something must be done. Many of the patients were taken out only to be returned after a few days or weeks to meet the sullen hostility of their attendants and with their own attitude changed from confidence to timidity and alarm.

This piteous dependence of the poor upon the good will of public officials was made clear to us in any early experience with a peasant woman straight from the fields of Germany, whom we met during our first six months at Hull-House. Her four years in America had been spent in patiently carrying water up and down two flights of stairs, and in washing the heavy flannel suits of iron foundry workers. For this her pay had averaged thirty-five cents a day. Three of her daughters had fallen victims to the vice of the city. The mother was bewildered and distressed, but understood nothing. We were able to induce the betrayer of one daughter to marry her; the second, after a tedious lawsuit, supported his child; with the third we were able to do nothing. This woman is now living with her family in a little house seventeen miles from the city. She has made two payments on her land and is a lesson to all beholders as she pastures her cow up and down the railroad tracks and makes money from her ten acres. She did not need charity for she had an immense capacity for hard work, but she sadly needed the service of the state's attorney office, enforcing the laws designed for the protection of such girls as her daughters.

We early found ourselves spending many hours in efforts to secure support for deserted women, insurance for bewildered widows, damages for injured operators, furniture from the clutches of the installment store. The Settlement is valuable as an information and interpretation bureau. It constantly acts between the various institutions of the city and the people for whose benefit these institutions were erected. The hospitals, the county agencies, and state asylums are often but vague rumors to the people who need them most. Another function of the Settlement to its neighborhood resembles that of the big brother whose mere presence on the playground protects the little one from bullies.

We early learned to know the children of hard driven mothers who went our to work all day, sometimes leaving the little things in the casual care of a neighbor, but often locking them into their tenement rooms. The first three crippled children we encountered in the neighborhood had all been injured while their mothers were at work: one had fallen out of a third-story window, another had been burned, and the third had a curved spine due to the fact that for three years he had been tied all day long to the leg of the kitchen table, only released at noon by his older brother who hastily ran in from a neighboring factory to share his lunch with him. When the hot weather came the restless children could not brook the confinement of the stuffy rooms, and, as it was not considered safe to leave the doors open because of sneak thieves, many of the children were locked out. During our first summer an increasing number of these poor little mites would wander into the cool hallway of Hull-House. We kept them there and fed them at noon, in return for which we were sometimes offered a hot penny which had been held in a tight little fist "ever since mother left this morning, to buy something to eat with." Out of kindergarten hours our little guests noisily enjoyed the hospitality of our bedrooms under the so-called care of any resident who volunteered to keep an eye on them, but later they were moved into a neighboring apartment under more systematic supervision.

Hull-House was thus committed to a day nursery which we sustained for sixteen years first in a little cottage on a side street and then in a building designed for its use called the Children's House. It is now carried on by the United Charities of Chicago in a finely equipped building on our block, where the immigrant mothers are cared for as well as the children, and where they are taught the things which will make life in America more possible. Our early day nursery brought us into natural relations with the poorest women of the neighborhood, many of whom were bearing the burden of dissolute and incompetent husbands in addition to the support of their children. Some of them presented an impressive manifestation of that miracle of affection which outlives abuse, neglect, and crime—the affection which cannot be plucked from the heart where it has lived, although it may serve only to torture and torment. "Has your husband come back?" you inquire of Mrs. S., whom you have known for eight years as an overworked woman bringing her three delicate children every morning to the nursery; she is bent under the double burden of earning the money which supports them and giving them the tender care which alone keeps them alive. The oldest two children have at last gone to work, and Mrs. S. has allowed herself the luxury of staying at home two days a week. And now the worthless husband is back again—the "gentlemanly gambler" type who, through all vicissitudes, manages to present a white shirtfront and a gold watch to the world, but who is dissolute, idle, and extravagant. You dread to think how much his presence will increase the drain upon the family exchequer, and you know that he stayed away until he was certain that the children were old enough to earn money for his luxuries. Mrs. S. does not pretend to take his return lightly, but she replies in all seriousness and simplicity, "You know my feeling for him has never changed. You may think me foolish, but I was always proud of his good looks and educated appearance. I was lonely and homesick during those eight years when the children were little and needed so much doctoring, but I could never bring myself to feel hard toward him, and I used to pray the good Lord to keep him from harm and bring him back to us; so, of course, I'm thankful now." She passes on with a dignity which gives one a new sense of the security of affection.

I recall a similar case of a woman who had supported her three children for five years, during which time her dissolute husband constantly demanded money for drink and kept her perpetually worried and intimidated. One Saturday, before the "blessed Easter," he came back from a long debauch, ragged and filthy, but in a state of lachrymose repentance. The poor wife received him as a returned prodigal, believed that his remorse would prove lasting, and felt sure that if she and the children went to church with him on Easter Sunday and he could be induced to take the pledge before the priest, all their troubles would be ended. After hours of vigorous effort and the expenditure of all her savings, he finally sat on the front doorstep the morning of Easter Sunday, bathed, shaved, and arrayed in a fine new suit of clothes. She left him sitting there in the reluctant spring sunshine while she finished washing and dressing the children. When she finally opened the front door with the three shining children that they might all set forth together, the returned prodigal had disappeared, and was not seen again until midnight, when he came back in a glorious state of intoxication from the proceeds of his pawned clothes and clad once more in the dingiest attire. She took him in without comment, only to begin again the wretched cycle. There were of course instances of the criminal husband as well as of they merely vicious. I recall one woman who, during seven years, never missed a visiting day at the penitentiary when she might see her husband, and whose little children in the nursery proudly reported the messages from father with no notion that he was in disgrace, so absolutely did they reflect the gallant spirit of their mother.

While one was filled with admiration for these heroic women, something was also to be said for some of the husbands, for the sorry men who, for one reason or another, had failed in the struggle of life. Sometimes this failure was purely economic and the men were competent to give the children, whom they were not able to support, the care and guidance and even education which were of the highest value. Only a few months ago I met upon the street one of the early nursery mothers who for five years had been living in another part of the city, and in response to my query as to the welfare of her five children, she bitterly replied, "All of them except Mary have been arrested at one time or another, thank you." In reply to my remark that I thought her husband had always had such admirable control over them, she burst out, "That has been the whole trouble. I got tried taking care of him and didn't believe that his laziness was all due to his health, as he said, so I left him and said that I would support the children, but not him. From that minute the trouble with the four boys began. I never knew what they were doing, and after every sort of a scrape I finally put Jack and the twins into institutions where I pay for them. Joe has gone to work at last, but with a disgraceful record behind him. I tell you I ain't so sure that because a woman can make big money that she can be both father and mother to her children."

As I walked on, I could but wonder in which particular we are most stupid—to judge a man's worth so solely by his wage-earning capacity that a good wife feels justified in leaving him, or in holding fast to that wretched delusion that a woman can both support and nurture her children.

One of the most piteous revelations of the futility of the latter attempt came to me through the mother of "Goosie," as the children for years called a little boy who, because he was brought to the nursery wrapped up in his mother's shawl, always had his hair filled with the down and small feathers from the feather brush factory where she worked. One March morning, Goosie's mother was hanging out the washing on a shed roof at six o'clock, doing it thus early before she left for the factory. Five-year-old Goosie was trotting at her heels handing her clothespins, when he was suddenly blown off the roof by the high wind into the alley below. His neck was broken by the fall and as he lay piteous and limp on a pile of frozen refuse, his mother cheerily called him to "climb up again," so confident do overworked mothers become that their children cannot get hurt. After the funeral, as the poor mother sat in the nursery postponing the moment when she must go back to her empty rooms, I asked her, in a futile effort to be of comfort, if there was anything more we could do for her. The overworked, sorrow-stricken woman looked up and replied, "If you could give me my wages for to- morrow, I would not go to work in the factory at all. I would like to stay at home all day and hold the baby. Goosie was always asking me to take him and I never had any time." This statement revealed the condition of many nursery mothers who are obliged to forego the joys and solaces which belong to even the most poverty-stricken. The long hours of factory labor necessary for earning the support of a child leave no time for the tender care and caressing which may enrich the life of the most piteous baby.

With all the efforts made by modern society to nurture and educate the young, how stupid it is to permit the mothers of young children to spend themselves in the coarser work of the world! It is curiously inconsistent that with the emphasis which this generation has placed upon the mother and upon the prolongation of infancy, we constantly allow the waste of this most precious material. I cannot recall without indignation a recent experience. I was detained late one evening in an office building by a prolonged committee meeting of the Board of Education. As I came out at eleven o'clock, I met in the corridor of the fourteenth floor a woman whom I knew, on her knees scrubbing the marble tiling. As she straightened up to greet me, she seemed so wet from her feet up to her chin, that I hastily inquired the cause. Her reply was that she left home at five o'clock every night and had no opportunity for six hours to nurse her baby. Her mother's milk mingled with the very water with which she scrubbed the floors until she should return at midnight, heated and exhausted, to feed her screaming child with what remained within her breasts.

These are only a few of the problems connected with the lives of the poorest people with whom the residents in a Settlement are constantly brought in contact.

I cannot close this chapter without a reference to that gallant company of men and women among whom my acquaintance is so large, who are fairly indifferent to starvation itself because of their preoccupation with higher ends. Among them are visionaries and enthusiasts, unsuccessful artists, writers, and reformers. For many years at Hull-House, we knew a well-bred German woman who was completely absorbed in the experiment of expressing musical phrases and melodies by means of colors. Because she was small and deformed, she stowed herself into her trunk every night, where she slept on a canvas stretched hammock-wise from the four corners and her food was of the meagerest; nevertheless if a visitor left an offering upon her table, it was largely spent for apparatus or delicately colored silk floss, with which to pursue the fascinating experiment. Another sadly crippled old woman, the widow of a sea captain, although living almost exclusively upon malted milk tablets as affording a cheap form of prepared food, was always eager to talk of the beautiful illuminated manuscripts she had sought out in her travels and to show specimens of her own work as an illuminator. Still another of these impressive old women was an inveterate inventor. Although she had seen prosperous days in England, when we knew her, she subsisted largely upon the samples given away at the demonstration counters of the department stores, and on bits of food which she cooked on a coal shovel in the furnace of the apartment house whose basement back room she occupied. Although her inventions were not practicable, various experts to whom they were submitted always pronounced them suggestive and ingenious. I once saw her receive this complimentary verdict—"this ribbon to stick in her coat"—with such dignity and gravity, that the words of condolence for her financial disappointment, died upon my lips.

These indomitable souls are but three out of many, whom I might instance to prove that those who are handicapped in the race for life's goods, sometimes play a magnificent trick upon the jade, life herself, by ceasing to know whether or not they possess any of her tawdry goods and chattels.

Source:

Jane Addams, *Twenty Years at Hull-House*, Champaign: University of Illinois Press, 1990.

Mann Act of 1910

Legislation enacted by the U.S. Congress June 25, 1910, prohibiting the interstate transportation of women and girls for "immoral purposes." Named for its sponsor, Representative James Robert Mann of Illinois, the act was intended to curb prostitution and the importation of women for purposes of prostitution. The Mann Act marked an important extension of federal involvement in national social problems, based on Congress's constitutional power to regulate commerce. Although challenged as an unwarranted restriction on interstate commerce, an intrusion into state jurisdiction, and an overstepping of congressional power, the act was upheld by the U.S. Supreme Court.

It also provided an avenue for the Department of Justice to bring individuals it considered criminal or suspect into the federal orbit. Best known of these cases were ones against the black boxer Jack Johnson (who married the white woman he crossed state lines with) and the head of the Louisiana Ku Klux Klan.

An Act

To further regulate interstate and foreign commerce by prohibiting the transportation therein for immoral purposes of women and girls, and for other purposes.

Be it enacted by the Senate and House of Representatives of the United States of America in Congress assembled, That the term "interstate commerce," as used in this Act, shall include transportation from any State or Territory or the District of Columbia to any other State or Territory or the District of Columbia, and the term "foreign commerce," as used in this Act, shall include transportation from any State or Territory or the District of Columbia to any foreign country and from any foreign country to any State or Territory or the District of Columbia.

Sec. 2. That any person who shall knowingly transport or cause to be transported, or aid or assist in obtaining transportation for, or in transporting, in interstate or foreign commerce, or in any Territory or in the District of Columbia, any woman or girl for the purpose of prostitution or debauchery, or for any other immoral purpose, or with the intent and purpose to induce, entice, or compel such woman or girl to become a prostitute or to give herself up to debauchery, or to engage in any other immoral practice; or who shall knowingly procure or obtain, or cause to be procured or obtained, or aid or assist in procuring or obtaining, any ticket or tickets, or any form of transportation or evidence of the right thereto, to be used by any woman or girl in interstate or foreign commerce, or in any Territory or the District of Columbia, in going to any place for the purpose of prostitution or debauchery, or for any other immoral purpose, or with the intent or purpose on the part of such person to induce, entice, or compel her to give herself up to the practice of prostitution, or to give herself up to debauchery, or any other immoral practice, whereby any such woman or girl shall be transported in interstate or foreign commerce, or in any Territory or the District of Columbia, shall be deemed guilty of a felony, and upon conviction thereof shall be punished by a fine not exceeding five thousand dollars, or by imprisonment of not more than five years, or by both such fine and imprisonment, in the discretion of the court.

Sec. 3. That any person who shall knowingly persuade, induce, entice, or coerce, or cause to be persuaded, induced, enticed, or coerced, or aid or assist in persuading, inducing, enticing, or coercing any woman or girl to go from one place to another in interstate or foreign commerce, or in any Territory or the District of Columbia, for the purpose of prostitution or debauchery, or for any other immoral purpose, or with the intent and purpose on the part of such person that such woman or girl shall engage in the practice of prostitution or debauchery, or any other immoral practice, whether with or without her consent, and who shall thereby knowingly cause or aid or assist in causing such woman or girl to go and to be carried or transported as a passenger upon the line or route of any common carrier or carriers in interstate or foreign commerce, or any Territory or the District of Columbia, shall be deemed guilty of a felony and on conviction thereof shall be punished by a fine of not more than five thousand dollars, or by imprisonment for a term not exceeding five years, or by both such fine and imprisonment, in the discretion of the court.

Sec. 4. That any person who shall knowingly persuade, induce, entice, or coerce any woman or girl under the age of eighteen years from any State or Territory or the District of Columbia to any other State or Territory or the District of Columbia, with the purpose and intent to induce or coerce her, or that she shall be induced or coerced to engage in prostitution or debauchery, or any other immoral practice, and shall in furtherance of such purpose knowingly induce or cause her to go and to be carried or transported as a passenger in interstate commerce upon the line or route of any common carrier or carriers, shall be deemed guilty of a felony, and on conviction thereof shall be punished by a fine of not more than ten thousand dollars, or by imprisonment for a term not exceeding ten years, or by both such fine and imprisonment, in the discretion of the court.

Sec. 5. That any violation of any of the above sections two, three and four shall be prosecuted in any court having jurisdiction of crimes within the district in which said violation was committed, or from, through, or into which any such woman or girl may have been carried or transported as a passenger in interstate or foreign commerce, or in any Territory or the District of Columbia, contrary to the provisions of any of said sections.

Sec. 6. That for the purpose of regulating and preventing the transportation in foreign commerce of alien women and girls for purposes of prostitution and debauchery, and in pursuance of and for the purpose of carrying out the terms of the agreement or project of arrangement for the suppression of the white-slave traffic, adopted July twenty-fifth, nineteen hundred and two, for submission to their respective governments by the delegates of various powers represented at the Paris conference and confirmed by a formal agreement signed at Paris on May eighteenth, nineteen hundred and four, and adhered to by the United States on June sixth, nineteen hundred and eight, as shown by the proclamation of the President of the United States, dated June fifteenth, nineteen hundred and eight, the Commissioner-General of Immigration is hereby designated as the authority of the United States to receive and centralize information concerning the procuration of alien women and girls with a view to their debauchery, and to exercise supervision over such alien women and girls, receive their declarations, establish their identity, and ascertain from them who induced them to leave their native countries, respectively; and it shall be the duty of said Commissioner-General of Immigration to receive and keep on file in his office the statements and declarations which may be made by such alien women and girls, and those which are hereinafter required pertaining to such alien women and girls engaged in prostitution or debauchery in this country, and to furnish receipts for such statements and declarations provided for in this act to the persons, respectively, making and filing them.

Every person who shall keep, maintain, control, support, or harbor in any house or place for the purpose of prostitution, or for any other immoral purpose, any alien woman or girl within three years after she shall have entered the United States from any country, party to the said arrangement for the suppression of the white-slave traffic, shall file with the Commissioner-General of Immigration a statement in writing setting forth the name of such alien woman or girl, the place at which she is kept, and all facts as to the date of her entry into the United States, the port through which she entered, her age, nationality, and parentage, and concerning her procuration to come to this country within the knowledge of such person, and any person who shall fail within thirty days after such person shall commence to keep, maintain, control, support, or harbor in any house or place for the purpose of prostitution, or for any other immoral purpose, any alien woman or girl within three years after she shall have entered the United States from any of the countries, party to the said arrangement for the suppression of the white-slave traffic, to file such statement concerning such alien woman or girl with the Commissioner-General of Immigration, or who shall knowingly and willfully state falsely or fail to disclose in such statement any fact within his knowledge or belief with reference to the age, nationality, or parentage of any such alien woman or girl, or concerning her procuration to come to this country, shall be deemed guilty of a misdemeanor, and on conviction shall be punished by a fine of not more than two thousand dollars, or by imprisonment for a term not exceeding two years, or by both such fine and imprisonment, in the discretion of the court.

In any prosecution brought under this section, if it appear that any such statement required is not on file in the office of the Commissioner-General of Immigration, the person whose duty it shall be to file such statement shall be presumed to have failed to file said statement, as herein required, unless such person or persons shall prove otherwise. No person shall be excused from furnishing the statement, as required by this section, on the ground or for the reason that the statement so required by him, or the information therein contained, might tend to criminate him or subject him to a penalty or forfeiture, but no person shall be prosecuted or subjected to any penalty or forfeiture under any law of the United States for or on account of any transaction, matter, or thing, concerning which he may truthfully report in such statement, as required by the provisions of this section.

Sec. 7. That the term "Territory," as used in this Act, shall include the district of Alaska, the insular possessions of the United States, and the Canal Zone. The word "person," as used in this Act, shall be construed to import both the plural and the singular, as the case demands, and shall include corporations, companies, societies, and associations. When construing and enforcing the provisions of this Act, the act, omission, or failure of any officer, agent, or other person, acting for or employed by any other person or by any corporation, company, society, or association within the scope of his employment or office, shall in every case be also deemed to be the act, omission or failure of such other person, or of such company, corporation, society, or association, as well as that of the person himself.

Sec. 8. That this Act shall be known and referred to as the "White-slave traffic Act."

Source:

Statutes at Large, Vol. 36, pp. 825–827.

Theodore Roosevelt, "New Nationalism," 1910

Speech delivered by former U.S. president Theodore Roosevelt at Osawatomie, Kansas, on August 31, 1910, outlining his progressive New Nationalism program. Breaking with conservatives in his own Republican Party, Roosevelt called for a strong national government, federal regulation of the corporate system, and the protection of human rights over property rights. He argued for the Square Deal (a term he had coined in 1904 to stand for his ideas on government's responsibilities as an even-handed mediator between special interest groups), for equal opportunity for all citizens, for fair wages and working conditions, for government free of control by special interests, and for prohibitions on corporate funding of political activity. "The object of government," he said, "is the welfare of the people."

In its August 1912 national nominating convention in Chicago, the Progressive, or Bull Moose, Party adopted a platform that contained much of Roosevelt's New Nationalism. Former president Theodore Roosevelt assumed leadership of the progressive Republicans, who felt politically alienated from Roosevelt's successor, President William H. Taft. They accused Taft of having betrayed the principles of Roosevelt's New Nationalism to assuage Republican conservatives. Roosevelt and his progressive-reformer followers denounced Taft's June renomination and seceded from Republican ranks to form a third party, which gathered at Chicago in early August and nominated Roosevelt as its presidential candidate. The Progressive platform, titled "A Contract with the People," embodied the upstart party's reformist aspirations for social and economic justice and conservation. It advocated tariff reduction, strict regulation of industrial combinations, recall of judicial decisions, woman suffrage, direct election of U.S. senators, abolition of child labor, and a minimum wage for working women. Virtually all of its provisions would eventually be enacted.

We come here to-day to commemorate one of the epoch-making events of the long struggle for the rights of man—the long struggle for the uplift of humanity. Our country—this great republic—means nothing unless it means the triumph of a real democracy, the triumph of popular government, and, in the long run, of an economic system under which each man shall be guaranteed the opportunity to show the best that there is in him. That is why the history of America is now central feature of the history of the world; for the world has set its face hopefully toward our democracy; and, O my fellow citizens, each one of you carries on your shoulders not only the burden of doing well for the sake of your own country, but the burden of doing well and seeing that this nation does well for the sake of mankind.

There have been two great crises in our country's history: first, when it was formed, and then, again, when it was perpetuated; and, in the second of these great crises—in the time of stress and strain which culminated in the Civil War, on the outcome of which depended the justification of what had been done earlier, you men of the Grand Army, you men who fought through the Civil War, not only did you justify your generation, not only did you render life worth living for our generation, but you justified the wisdom of Washington and Washington's colleagues. If this republic had been founded by them only to be split asunder into fragments when the strain came, then the judgment of the world would have been that Washington's work was not worth doing. It was you who crowned Washington's work, as you carried to achievement the high purpose of Abraham Lincoln.

Now, with this second period of our history the name of John Brown will be forever associated; and Kansas was the theater upon which the first act of the second of our great national life dramas was played. It was the result of the struggle in Kansas which determined that our country should be in deed as well as in name devoted to both union and freedom; that the great experiment of democratic government on a national scale should succeed and not fail. In name we had the Declaration of Independence in 1776; but we gave the lie by our acts to the words of the Declaration of Independence until 1865; and words count for nothing except in so far as they represent acts. This is true everywhere; but, O my friends, it should be truest of all in political life. A broken promise is bad enough in private life. It is worse in the field of politics. No man is worth his salt in public life who makes on the stump a pledge which he does not keep after election; and, if he makes such a pledge and does not keep it, hunt him out of public life. I care for the great deeds of the past chiefly as spurs to drive us onward in the present. I speak of the men of the past partly that they may be honored by our praise of them, but more that they may serve as examples for the future.

It was a heroic struggle; and, as is inevitable with all such struggles, it had also a dark and terrible side. Very much was done of good, and much also of evil; and, as was inevitable in such a period of revolution, often the same man did both good and evil. For our great good fortune as a nation, we, the people of the United States as a whole, can now afford to forget the evil, or, at least, to remember it without bitterness, and to fix our eyes with pride only on the good that was accomplished. Even in ordinary times there are very few of us who do not see the problems of life as through a glass, darkly; and when the glass is clouded by the murk of furious popular passion, the vision of the best and the bravest is dimmed. Looking back, we are all of us now able to do justice to the valor and the disinterestedness and the love of the right, as to each it was given to see the right, shown both by the men of the North and the men of the South in that contest which was finally decided by the attitude of the West. We can admire the heroic valor, the sincerity, the self-devotion shown alike by the men who wore the blue and the men who wore the gray; and our sadness that such men should have had to fight one another is tempered by the glad knowledge that ever hereafter their descendants shall be found fighting side by side, struggling in peace as well as in war for the uplift of their common country, all alike resolute to raise to the highest pitch of honor and usefulness the nation to which they all belong. As for the veterans of the Grand Army of the Republic, they deserve honor an recognition such as is paid to no other citizens of the republic; for to them the republic owes its all; for to them it owes its very existence. It is because of what you and your comrades did in the dark years that we of to-day walk, each of us, head erect, and proud that we belong, not to one of a dozen little squabbling contemptible commonwealths, but to the mightiest nation upon which the sun shines.

I do not speak of this struggle of the past merely from the historic standpoint. Our interest is primarily in the application to-day of the lessons taught by the contest of half a century ago. It is of little use for us to pay lip loyalty to the mighty men of the past unless we sincerely endeavor to apply to the problems of the present precisely the qualities which in other crises enabled the men of that day to meet those crises. It is half melancholy and half amusing to see the way in which well-meaning people gather to do honor to the men who, in company with John Brown, and under the lead of Abraham Lincoln, faced and solved the great problems of the nineteenth century, while, at the same time, these same good people nervously shrink from, or frantically denounce, those who are trying to meet the problems of the twentieth century in the spirit which was accountable for the successful solution of the problems of Lincoln's time.

Of that generation of men to whom we owe so much, the man to whom we owe most is, of course, Lincoln. Part of our debt to him is because he forecast our present struggle and saw the way out. He said:

I hold that while man exists it is his duty to improve not only his own condition, but to assist in ameliorating mankind.

And again:

Labor is prior to, and independent of, capital. Capital is only the fruit of labor, and could never have existed if labor had not first existed. Labor is the superior of capital, and deserves much the higher consideration.

If that remark was original with me, I should be even more strongly denounced as a communist agitator than I shall be anyhow. It is Lincoln's. I am only quoting it; and that is one side; that is the side the capitalist should hear. Now, let the workingman hear his side.

Capital has its rights, which are as worthy of protection as any other rights . . . Nor should this lead to a war upon the owners of property. Property is the fruit of labor; . . . property is desirable; is a positive good in the world.

And then comes a thoroughly Lincolnlike sentence:

Let not him who is houseless pull down the house of another, but let him work diligently and build one for himself, thus by example assuring that his own shall be safe from violence when built.

It seems to me that, in these words, Lincoln took substantially the attitude that we ought to take; he showed the proper sense of proportion in his relative estimates of capital and labor, of human rights and property rights. Above all, in this speech, as in many others, he taught a lesson in wise kindliness and charity; an indispensable lesson to us of to-day. But this wise kindliness and charity never weakened his arm or numbed his heart. We cannot afford weakly to blind ourselves to the actual conflict which faces us to-day. The issue is joined, and we must fight or fail.

In every wise struggle for human betterment one of the main objects, and often the only object, has been to achieve in large measure equality of opportunity. In the struggle for this great end, nations rise from barbarism to civilization, and through it people press forward from one stage of enlightenment to the next. One of the chief factors in progress is the destruction of special privilege. The essence of any struggle for healthy liberty has always been, and must always be, to take from some one man or class of men the right to enjoy power, or wealth, or position, or immunity, which has not been earned by service to his or their fellows. That is what you fought for in the Civil War, and that is what we strive for now,

At many stages in the advance of humanity, this conflict between the men who possess more than they have earned and the men who have earned more than they possess is the central condition of progress. In our day it appears as the struggle of free men to gain and hold the right of self-government as against the special interests, who twist the methods of free government into machinery for defeating the popular will. At every stage, and under all circumstances, the essence of the struggle is to equalize opportunity, destroy privilege, and give to the life and citizenship of every individual the highest possible value both to himself and to the commonwealth. That is nothing new. All I ask in civil life is what you fought for in the Civil War. I ask that civil life be carried on according to the spirit in which the army was carried on. You never get perfect justice, but the effort in handling the army was to bring to the front the men who could do the job. Nobody grudged promotion to Grant, or Sherman, or Thomas, or Sheridan, because they earned it. The only complaint was when a man got promotion which he did not earn.

Practical equality of opportunity for all citizens, when we achieve it, will have two great results. First, every man will have a fair chance to make of himself all that in him lies; to reach the highest point to which his capacities, unassisted by special privilege of his own and unhampered by the special privilege of others, can carry him, and to get for himself and his family substantially what he has earned. Second, equality of opportunity means that the commonwealth will get from every citizen the highest service of which he is capable. No man who carries the burden of the special privileges of another can give to the commonwealth that service to which it is fairly entitled.

I stand for the square deal. But when I say that I am for the square deal, I mean not merely that I stand for fair play under the present rules of the game, but that I stand for having those rules changed so as to work for a more substantial equality of opportunity and of reward for equally good service. One word of warning, which, I think, is hardly necessary in Kansas. When I say I want a square deal for the poor man, I do not mean that I want a square deal for the man who remains poor because he has not got the energy to work for himself. If a man who has had a chance will not make good, then he has got to quit. And you men of the Grand Army, you want justice for the brave man who fought, and punishment for the coward who shirked his work. Is not that so?

Now, this means that our government, national and state, must be freed from the sinister influence or control of special interests. Exactly as the special interests of cotton and slavery threatened our political integrity before the Civil War, so now the great special business interests too often control and corrupt the men and methods of government for their own profit. We must drive the special interests out of politics. That is one of our tasks to-day. Every special interest is entitled to justice—full, fair, and complete,—and, now, mind you, if there were any attempt by mob violence to plunder and work harm to the special interest, whatever it may be, that I most dislike, and the wealthy man, whomsoever he may be, for whom I have the greatest contempt, I would fight for him, and you would if you were worth your salt. He should have justice. For every special interest is entitled to justice, but not one is entitled to a vote in Congress, to a voice on the bench, or to representation in any public office. The Constitution guarantees protection to property, and we must make that promise good. But it does not give the right of suffrage to any corporation.

The true friend of property, the true conservative, is he who insists that property shall be the servant and not the master of the commonwealth; who insists that the creature of man's making shall be the servant and not the master of the man who made it. The citizens of the United States must effectively control the mighty commercial forces which they have themselves called into being.

There can be no effective control of corporations while their political activity remains. To put an end to it will be neither a short nor an easy task, but it can be done.

We must have complete and effective publicity of corporate affairs, so that the people may know beyond peradventure whether the corporations obey the law and whether their management entitles them to the confidence of the public. It is necessary the laws should be passed to prohibit the use of corporate funds directly or indirectly for political purposes; it is still more necessary that such laws should be thoroughly enforced. Corporate expenditures for political purposes, and especially such expenditures by public service corporations, have supplied one of the principal sources of corruption in our political affairs.

It has become entirely clear that we must have government supervision of the capitalization, not only of public service corporations, including, particularly, railways, but of all corporations doing an interstate business. I do not wish to see the nation forced into the ownership of the railways if it can possibly be avoided, and the only alternative is thoroughgoing and effective regulation, which shall be based on a full knowledge of all the facts, including a physical valuation of property. This physical valuation is not needed, or, at least, is very rarely needed, for fixing rates; but it is needed as the basis of honest capitalization.

We have come to recognize that franchises should never be granted except for a limited time, and never without proper provision for compensation to the public. It is my personal belief that the same kind and degree of control and supervision which should be exercised over public service corporations should be extended also to combinations which control necessaries of life, such as meat, oil, and coal, or which deal in them on an important scale. I have no doubt that the ordinary man who has control of them is much like ourselves. I have no doubt he would like to do well, but I want to have enough supervision to help him realize that desire to do well.

I believe that the officers, and, especially, the directors, of corporations should be held personally responsible when any corporation breaks the law.

Combinations in industry are the result of an imperative economic law which cannot be repealed by political legislation. The effort at prohibiting all combination has substantially failed. The way out lies, not in attempting to prevent such combinations, but in completely controlling them in the interest of the public welfare. For that purpose the Federal Bureau of Corporations is an agency of first importance. Its powers, and, therefore, its efficiency, as well as that of the Interstate Commerce Commission, should be largely increased. We have a right to expect from the Bureau of Corporations and from the Interstate Commerce Commission a very high grade of public service. We should be as sure of the proper conduct of the interstate railways and the proper management of interstate business as we are now sure of the conduct and management of the national banks, and we should have as effective supervision in one case as in the other. The Hepburn Act, and the amendment to the Act in the shape in which it finally passed Congress at the last session, represent a long step in advance, and we must go yet further.

There is a widespread belief among our people that, under the methods of making tariffs which have hitherto obtained, the special interests are too influential. Probably this is true of both the big special interests and the little special interests. These methods have put a premium on selfishness, and, naturally, the selfish big interests have gotten more than their smaller, though equally selfish, brothers. The duty of Congress is to provide a method by which the interest of the whole people shall be all that receives consideration. To this end there must be an expert tariff commission, wholly removed from the possibility of political pressure or of improper business influence. Such a commission can find the real difference between cost of production, which is mainly the difference of labor cost here and abroad. As fast as its recommendations are made, I believe in revising one schedule at a time. A general revision of the tariff almost inevitably leads to log-rolling and the subordination of the general public interest to local and special interests.

The absence of effective state, and, especially, national, restraint upon unfair money getting has tended to create a small class of enormously wealthy and economically powerful men, whose chief object is to hold and increase their power. The prime need is to change the conditions which enable these men to accumulate power which it is not for the general welfare that they should hold or exercise. We grudge no man a fortune which represents his own power and sagacity, when exercised with entire regard to the welfare of his fellows. Again, comrades over there, take the lesson from your own experience. Not only did you not grudge, but you gloried in the promotion of the great generals who gained their promotion by leading the army to victory. So it is with us. We grudge no man a fortune in civil life if it is honorably obtained and well used. It is not even enough that it should have been gained without doing damage to the community. We should permit it to be gained only so long as the gaining represents benefit to the community. This, I know, implies a policy of a far more active governmental interference with social and economic conditions in this country than we have yet had, but I think we have got to face the fact that such an increase in governmental control is now necessary.

No man should receive a dollar unless that dollar has been fairly earned. Every dollar received should represent a dollar's worth of service rendered—not gambling in stocks, but service rendered. The really big fortune, the swollen fortune, by the mere fact of its size acquires qualities which differentiate it in kind as well as in degree from what is possessed by men of relatively small means. Therefore, I believe in a graduated income tax on big fortunes, and in another tax which is far more easily collected and far more effective—a graduated inheritance tax on big fortunes, properly safeguarded against evasion and increasing rapidly in amount with the size of the estate.

The people of the United States suffer from periodical financial panics to a degree substantially unknown among the other nations which approach us in financial strength. There is no reason why we should suffer what they escape. It is of profound importance that our financial system should be promptly investigated, and so thoroughly and effectively revised as to make it certain that hereafter our currency will no longer fail at critical times to meet our needs.

It is hardly necessary for me to repeat that I believe in an efficient army and a navy large enough to secure for us abroad that respect which is the surest guarantee of peace. A word of special warning to my fellow citizens who are as progressive as I hope I am. I want them to keep up their interest in our internal affairs; and I want them also continually to remember Uncle Sam's interests abroad. Justice and fair dealing among nations rest upon principles identical with those which cannot justice and fair dealing among the individuals of which nations are composed, with the vital exception that each nation must do its own part in international police work. If you get into trouble here, you can call for the police; but if Uncle Sam gets into trouble, he has got to be his own policeman, and I want to see him strong enough to encourage the peaceful aspirations of other peoples in connection with us. I believe in national friendships and heartiest good will to all nations; but national friendships, like those between men, must be founded on respect as well as on liking, on forbearance as well as upon trust. I should be heartily ashamed of any American who did not try to make the American government act as justly toward the other nations in international relations as he himself would act toward any individual in private relations. I should be heartily ashamed to see us wrong a weaker power, and I should hang my head forever if we tamely suffered wrong from a stronger power.

Of conservation I shall speak more at length elsewhere. Conservation means development as much as it does protection. I recognized the right and duty of this generation to develop and use the natural resources of our land; but I do not recognize the right to waste them, or to rob, by wasteful use, the generations that come after us. I ask nothing of the nation except that it so behave as each farmer here behaves with reference to his own children. That farmer is a poor creature who skins the land and leaves it worthless to his children. The farmer is a good farmer who, having enabled the land to support himself and to provide for the education of his children, leaves it to them a little better than he found it himself. I believe the same thing of a nation.

Moreover, I believe that the natural resources must be used for the benefit of all our people, and not monopolized for the benefit of the few, and here again is another case in which I am accused of taking a revolutionary attitude. People forget now that one hundred years ago there were public men of good character who advocated the nation selling its public lands in great quantities, so that the nation could get the most money out of it, and giving it to the men who could cultivate it for their own uses. We took the proper democratic ground that the land should be granted in small sections to the men who were actually to till it and live on it. Now, with the water power, with the forests, with the mines, we are brought face to face with the fact that there are many people who will go with us in conserving the resources only if they are to be allowed to exploit them for their benefit. That is one of the fundamental reasons why the special interests should be driven out of politics. Of all the questions which can come before this nation, short of the actual preservation of its existence in a great war, there is none which compares in importance with the great central task of leaving this land even a better land for our descendants than it is for us, and training them into a better race to inhabit the land and pass it on. Conservation is a great moral issue, for it involves the patriotic duty of insuring the safety and continuance of the nation. Let me add that the health and vitality of our people are at least as well worth conserving as their forests, waters, lands, and minerals, and in this great work the national government must bear a most important part.

I have spoken elsewhere also of the great task which lies before the farmers of the country to get for themselves and their wives and children not only the benefits of better farming, but also those of better business methods and better conditions of life on the farm. The burden of this great task will fall, as it should, mainly upon the great organizations of the farmers themselves. I am glad it will, for I believe they are all well able to handle it. In particular, there are strong reasons why the Departments of Agriculture of the various states, the United States Department of Agriculture, and the agricultural colleges and experiment stations should extend their work to cover all phases of farm life, instead of limiting themselves, as they have far too often limited themselves, in the past, solely to the question of the production of crops. And now a special word to the farmer. I want to see him make the farm as fine a farm as it can be made; and let him remember to see that the improvement goes on indoors as well as out; let him remember that the farmer's wife should have her share of thought and attention just as much as the farmer himself.

Nothing is more true than that excess of every kind is followed by reaction; a fact which should be pondered by reformer and reactionary alike. We are face to face with new conceptions of the relations of property to human welfare, chiefly because certain advocates of the rights of property as against the rights of men have been pushing their claims too far. The man who wrongly holds that every human right is secondary to his profit must now give way to the advocate of human welfare, who rightly maintains that every man holds his property subject to the general right of the community to regulate its use to whatever degree the public welfare may require it.

But I think we may go still further. The right to regulate the use of wealth in the public interest is universally admitted. Let us admit also the right to regulate the terms and conditions of labor, which is the chief element of wealth, directly in the interest of the common good. The fundamental thing to do for every man is to give him a chance to reach a place in which he will make the greatest possible contribution to the public welfare. Understand what I say there. Give him a chance, not push him up if he will not be pushed. Help any man who stumbles; if he lies down, it is a poor job to try to carry him; but if he is a worthy man, try your best to see that he gets a chance to show the worth that is in him. No man can be a good citizen unless he has a wage more than sufficient to cover the bare cost of living, and hours of labor short enough so that after his day's work is done he will have time and energy to bear his share in the management of the community, to help in carrying the general load. We keep countless men from being good citizens by the conditions of life with which we surround them. We need comprehensive workmen's compensation acts, both state and national laws to regulate child labor and work for women, and, especially, we need in our common schools not merely education in book learning, but also practical training for daily life and work. We need to enforce better sanitary conditions for our workers and to extend the use of safety appliances for our workers in industry and commerce, both within and between the states. Also, friends, in the interest of the workingman himself we need to set our faces like flint against mob violence just as against corporate greed; against violence and injustice and lawlessness by wage workers just as much as against lawless cunning and greed and selfish arrogance of employers. If I could ask but one thing of my fellow countrymen, my request would be that, whenever they go in for reform, they remember the two sides, and that they always exact justice from one side as much as from the other. I have small use for the public servant who can always see and denounce the corruption of the capitalist, but who cannot persuade himself, especially before election, to say a word about lawless mob violence. And I have equally small use for the man, be he a judge on the bench, or editor of a great paper, or wealthy and influential private citizen, who can see clearly enough and denounce the lawlessness of mob violence, but whose eyes are closed so that he is blind when the question is one of corruption in business on a gigantic scale. Also remember what I said about excess in reformer and reactionary alike. If the reactionary man, who thinks of nothing but the rights of property, could have his way, he would bring about a revolution; and one of my chief fears in connection with progress comes because I do not want to see our people, for lack of proper leadership, compelled to follow men whose intentions are excellent, but whose eyes are a little too wild to make it really safe to trust them. Here in Kansas there is one paper which habitually denounces me as the tool of Wall Street, and at the same time frantically repudiates the statement that I am a Socialist on the ground that that is an unwarranted slander of the Socialists.

National efficiency has many factors. It is a necessary result of the principle of conservation widely applied. In the end it will determine our failure or success as a nation. National efficiency has to do, not only with natural resources and with men, but it is equally concerned with institutions. The state must be made efficient for the work which concerns only the people of the state; and the nation for that which concerns all the people. There must remain no neutral ground to serve as a refuge for lawbreakers, and especially for lawbreakers of great wealth, who can hire the vulpine legal cunning which will teach them how to avoid both jurisdictions. It is a misfortune when the national legislature fails to do its duty in providing a national remedy, so that the only national activity is the purely negative activity of the judiciary in forbidding the state to exercise power in the premises.

I do not ask for overcentralization; but I do ask that we work in a spirit of broad and far-reaching nationalism when we work for what concerns our people as a whole. We are all Americans. Our common interest are as broad as the continent. I speak to you here in Kansas exactly as I would speak in New York or Georgia, for the most vital problems are those which affect us all alike. The national government belongs to the whole American people, and where the whole American people are interested, that interest can be guarded effectively only by the national government. The betterment which we seek must be accomplished, I believe, mainly through the national government.

The American people are right in demanding that New Nationalism, without which we cannot hope to deal with new problems. The New Nationalism puts the national need before sectional or personal advantage. It is impatient of the utter confusion that results from local legislatures attempting to treat national issues as local issues. It is still more impatient of the impotence which springs from overdivision of governmental powers, the impotence which makes it possible for local selfishness or for legal cunning, hired by wealthy special interests, to bring national activities to a deadlock. This New Nationalism regards the executive power as the steward of the public welfare. It demands of the judiciary that it shall be interested primarily in human welfare rather than in property, just as it demands that the representative body shall represent all the people rather than any one class or section of the people.

I believe in shaping the ends of government to protect property as well as human welfare. Normally, and in the long run, the ends are the same; but whenever the alternative must be faced, I am for men and not for property, as you were in the Civil War. I am far from underestimating the importance of dividends; but I rank dividends below human character. Again, I do not have any sympathy with the reformer who says he does not care for dividends. Of course, economic welfare is necessary, for a man must pull his own weight and be able to support his family. I know well that the reformers must not bring upon the people economic ruin, or the reforms themselves will go down in the ruin. But we must be ready to face temporary disaster, whether or not brought on by those who will war against us to the knife. Those who oppose all reform will do well to remember that ruin in its worst form is inevitable if our national life brings us nothing better than swollen fortunes for the few and the triumph in both politics and business of a sordid and selfish materialism.

If our political institutions were perfect, they would absolutely prevent the political domination of money in any part of our affairs. We need to make our political representatives more quickly and sensitively responsive to the people whose servants they are. More direct action by the people in their own affairs under proper safeguards is vitally necessary. The direct primary is a step in this direction, if it is associated with a corrupt practices act effective to prevent the advantage of the man willing recklessly and unscrupulously to spend money over his more honest competitor. It is particularly important that all moneys received or expended for campaign purposes should be publicly accounted for, not only after election, but before election as well. Political action must be made simpler, easier, and freer from confusion for every citizen. I believe that the prompt removal of unfaithful or incompetent public servants should be made easy and sure in whatever way experience shall show to be most expedient in any give class of cases.

One of the fundamental necessities in a representative government such as ours is to make certain that the men to whom the people delegate their power shall serve the people by whom they are elected, and not the special interests. I believe that every national officer, elected or appointed, should be forbidden to perform and service or receive any compensation, directly or indirectly, from interstate corporations; and a similar provision could not fail to be useful within the states.

The object of government is the welfare of the people. The material progress and prosperity of a nation are desirable chiefly so far as they lead to the moral and material welfare of all good citizens. Just in proportion as the average man and woman are honest, capable of sound judgment and high ideals, active in public affairs—but, first of all, sound in their home life, and the father and mother of healthy children whom they bring up well—just so far, and no farther, we may count our civilization a success. We must have—I believe we have already—a genuine and permanent moral awakening, without which no wisdom of legislation or administration really means anything; and, on the other hand, we must try to secure the social and economic legislation without which any improvement due to purely moral agitation is necessarily evanescent. Let me again illustrate by a reference to the Grand Army You could not have won simply as a disorderly and disorganized mob. You needed generals; you needed careful administration of the most advanced type; and a good commissary—the cracker line. You well remember that success was necessary in many different lines in order to bring about general success. You had to have the administration at Washington good, just as you had to have the administration in the field; and you had to have the work of the generals good. You could not have triumphed without that administration and leadership; but it would all have been worthless if the average soldier had not had the right stuff in him. He had to have the right stuff in him, or you could not get it out of him. In the last analysis, therefore, vitally necessary though it was to have the right kind of organization and the right kind of generalship, it was even more vitally necessary that the average soldier should have the fighting edge, the right character. So it is in our civil life. No matter now honest and decent we are in our private lives, if we do not have the right kind of law and the right kind of administration of the law, we cannot go forward as a nation. That is imperative; but it must be an addition to, and not a substitution for, the qualities that make us good citizens. In the last analysis, the most important elements in any man's career must be the sum of those qualities which, in the aggregate, we speak of as character. If he has not got it, then no law that the wit of man can devise, no administration of the law by the boldest and strongest executive, will avail to help him. We must have the right kind of character—character that makes a man, first of all, a good man in the home, a good father, a good husband—that makes a man a good neighbor. You must have that, and, then, in addition, you must have the kind of law and the kind of administration of the law which will give to those qualities in the private citizen the best possible chance for development. The prime problem of our nation is to get the right type of good citizenship, and, to get it, we must have progress, and our public men must be genuinely progressive.

Source:
Roosevelt Collection, Harvard College.

Standard Oil Company of New Jersey et al. v. United States, 1911

U.S. Supreme Court decision issued on May 15, 1911, upholding the dissolution of the Standard Oil Company, a powerful monopolistic trust, on the grounds that it represented an "unreasonable" restraint of trade under the Sherman Antitrust Act. The decision resulted from a lawsuit initiated by the federal government in 1906, charging Standard Oil and others with conspiring to restrain trade and commerce in petroleum and related products. The Supreme Court, in upholding a 1909 U.S. circuit court ruling that the company had to divest itself of numerous subsidiaries, declared that the Sherman Antitrust Act should be applied according to the "rule of reason."

As Justice White points out, the case file was exceptionally voluminous and the allegations unusually complicated. However, its prosecution was then, and continues to be, a landmark event. The excerpts here include Justice White's use of history to come to his decision.

Chief Justice White delivered the opinion of the court:

The Standard Oil Company of New Jersey and thirty-three other corporations, John D. Rockefeller, William Rockefeller, and five other individual defendants, prosecute this appeal to reverse a decree of the court below. Such decree was entered upon a bill filed by the United States under authority of Section 4 of the act of July 2, 1890 known as the anti-trust act. . . . The record is inordinately voluminous, consisting of twenty-three volumes of printed matter, aggregating about 12,000 pages, containing a vast amount of confusing and conflicting testimony relating to innumerable, complex, and varied business transactions, extending over a period of nearly forty years. In an effort to pave the way to reach the subjects which we are called upon to consider, we propose at the outset, following the order of the bill, to give the merest possible outline of its contents, to summarize the answer, to indicate the course of the trial, and point out briefly the decision below rendered.

The bill and exhibits, covering 170 pages of the printed record, was filed on November 15, 1906. Corporations known as Standard Oil Company of New Jersey, Standard Oil Company of California, Standard Oil Company of Indiana, Standard Oil Company of Iowa, Standard Oil Company of Kansas, Standard Oil Company of Kentucky, Standard Oil Company of Nebraska, Standard Oil Company of New York, Standard Oil Company of Ohio, and sixty-two other corporations and partnerships, as also seven individuals, were named as defendants. The bill was divided into thirty numbered sections, and sought relief upon the theory that the various defendants were engaged in conspiring "to restrain the trade and commerce in petroleum, commonly called 'crude oil,' in refined oil, and in the other products of petroleum, among the several states and territories of the United States and the District of Columbia and with foreign nations, and to monopolize the said commerce." The conspiracy was alleged to have been formed in or about the year 1870 by three of the individual defendants, viz.: John D. Rockefeller, William Rockefeller, and Henry M. Flagler. The detailed averments concerning the alleged conspiracy were arranged with reference to three periods, the first from 1870 to 1882, the second from 1882 to 1899, and the third from 1899 to the time of the filing of the bill.

[Discussions of the bill and jurisdiction are omitted]

We are thus brought face to face with the merits of the controversy.

Both as to the law and as to the facts, the opposing contentions pressed in the argument are numerous, and in all their aspects are so irreconcilable that it is difficult to reduce them to some fundamental generalization, which, by being disposed of, would decide them all. For instance, as to the law. While both sides agree that the determination of the controversy rests upon the correct construction and application of the 1st and 2d sections of the anti-trust act, yet the views as to the meaning of the act are as wide apart as the poles, since there is no real point of agreement on any view of the act. And this also is the case as to the scope and effect of authorities relied upon, even although in some instances one and the same authority is asserted to be controlling.

So also is it as to the facts. Thus, on the one hand, with relentless pertinacity and minuteness of analysis, it is insisted that the facts establish that the assailed combination took its birth in a purpose to unlawfully acquire wealth by oppressing the public and destroying the just rights of others, and that its entire career exemplifies an inexorable carrying out of such wrongful intents, since, it is asserted, the pathway of the combination from the beginning to the time of the filing of the bill is marked with constant proofs of wrong inflicted upon the public, and is strewn with the wrecks resulting from crushing out, without regard to law, the individual rights of others. Indeed, so conclusive, it is urged, is the proof on these subjects, that it is asserted that the existence of the principal corporate defendant,–the Standard Oil Company of New Jersey—with the vast accumulation of property which it owns or controls, because of its infinite potency for harm and the dangerous example which its continued existence affords, is an open and enduring menace to all freedom of trade, and is a byword and reproach to modern economic methods. On the other hand, in a powerful analysis of the facts, it is insisted that they demonstrate that the origin and development of the vast business which the defendants control was but the result of lawful competitive methods, guided by economic genius of the highest order, sustained by courage, by a keen insight into commercial situations, resulting in the acquisition of great wealth, but at the same time serving to stimulate and increase production, to widely extend the distribution of the products of petroleum at a cost largely below that which would have otherwise prevailed, thus proving to be at one and the same time a benefaction to the general public as well as of enormous advantage to individuals. It is not denied that in the enormous volume of proof contained in the record in the period of almost a lifetime, to which that proof is addressed, there may be found acts of wrongdoing, but the insistence is that they were rather the exception than the rule, and in most cases were either the result of too great individual zeal in the keen rivalries of business, or of the methods and habits of dealing which, even if wrong, were commonly practised at the time. And to discover and state the truth concerning these contentions both arguments call for the analysis and weighing, as we have said at the outset, of a jungle of conflicting testimony covering a period of forty years—a duty difficult to rightly perform, and, even if satisfactorily accomplished, almost impossible to state with any reasonable regard to brevity.

Duly appreciating the situation just stated, it is certain that only one point of concord between the parties is discernible, which is, that the controversy in every aspect is controlled by a correct conception of the meaning of the 1st and 2d sections of the anti-trust act. We shall therefor–departing from what otherwise would be the natural order of analysis–make this one point of harmony the initial basis of our examination of the contentions. . . . When we have done this, we shall then approach the facts. . . .

First. The text of the act and its meaning.

We quote the text of the 1st and 2d sections of the act, as follows:

"Section 1. Every contract, combination in the form of trust or otherwise, or conspiracy, in restraint of trade or commerce among the several states or with foreign nations, is hereby declared to be illegal. Every person how shall make any such contract, or engaged in any such combination or conspiracy, shall be deemed guilty of a misdemeanor, and, on conviction thereof, shall be punished by fine not exceeding $5,000, or by imprisonment not exceeding one year, or by both said punishments, in the discretion of the court.

"Sec. 2. Every person who shall monopolize, or attempt to monopolize, or combine or conspire with any other person or persons to monopolize, any part of the trade or commerce among the several states, or with foreign nations, shall be deemed guilty of a misdemeanor, and, on conviction thereof, shall be punished by fine not exceeding $5,000, or by imprisonment not exceeding one year, or by both said punishments, in the discretion of the court." [26 Stat. at L. 209, chap. 647, U.S. Comp. Stat. 1901, p. 3200.]

The debates show that doubt as to whether there was a common law of the United States which governed the subject in the absence of legislation was among the influences leading to the passage of the act. They conclusively show, however, that the main cause which led to the legislation was the thought that it was required by the economic condition of the times; that is, the vast accumulation of wealth in the hands of corporations and individuals, the enormous development of corporate organization, the facility for combination which such organization afforded, the fact that the facility was being used, and that combinations known as trusts were being multiplied, and the widespread impression that their power had been and would be exerted to oppress individual and injure the public generally. Although debates may not be used as a mean for interpreting a statute, that rule, in the nature of things, is not violated by resorting to debates as a means of ascertaining the environment at the time of the enactment of a particular law; that is, the history of the period when it was adopted.

* * *

The evils which led to the public outcry against monopolies [in England] and to the final denial of the power to make them may be thus summarily stated: (1) The power which the monopoly gave to the one who enjoyed it, to fix the price and thereby injure the public; (2) The power which it engendered of enabling a limitation on production; and (3) The danger of deterioration in quality of the monopolized article which it was deemed was the inevitable resultant of the monopolistic control over its production and sale. . . .

* * *

And by operation of the mental process which led to considering as a monopoly acts which, although they did not constitute a monopoly, were thought to produce some of its baneful effects, so also because of the impediment or burden to the due course of trade which they produced, such acts came to be referred to as in restraint of trade. . . .

Generalizing these considerations, the situation is this: 1. That by the common law, monopolies were unlawful because of their restriction upon individual freedom of contract and their injury to the public. 2. That as to necessaries of life, the freedom of the individual to deal was restricted where the nature and character of the dealing was such as to engender the presumption of intent to bring about at least one of the injuries which it was deemed would result from monopoly—that is, an undue enhancement of price. 3. That to protect the freedom of contract of the individual, not only in his own interest, but principally in the interest of the common weal, a contract of an individual by which he put an unreasonable restraint upon himself as to carrying on his trade or business was void. And that at common law the evils consequent upon . . . those things to be treated as coming within monopoly and sometimes to be called monopoly, and the same considerations caused monopoly, because of its operation and effect, to be brought within and spoken of generally as impeding the due course of, or being in restraint of, trade.

* * *

In this country also the acts from which it was deemed there resulted a part, if not all, of the injurious consequences ascribed to monopoly, came to be referred to as a monopoly itself. In other words, here as had been the case in England, practical common sense caused attention to be concentrated not upon the theoretically correct name to be given to the condition or acts which gave rise to a harmful result, but to the result itself and to the remedying of the evils which it produced. . . .

It is also true that while the principles concerning contracts in restraint of trade, that is, voluntary restraint put by a person on his right to pursue his calling, hence only operating subjectively, came generally to be recognized in accordance with the English rule, it came moreover to pass that contracts or acts which it was considered had a monopolistic tendency, especially those which were thought to unduly diminish competition and hence to enhance prices–in other words, to monopolize–came also in a generic sense to be spoken of and treated as they had been in England, as restricting the due course of trade, and therefore as being in restraint of trade.

* * *

In view of the common law and the law in this country as to restraint of trade, which we have reviewed, and the illuminating effect which that history must have under the rule to which we have referred, we think it results:

a. That the context manifests that the statute was drawn in the light of the existing practical conception of the law of restraint of trade. . . .

b. That in view of the many new forms of contracts and combinations which were being evolved from existing economic conditions, it was deemed essential by an all-embracing enumeration to make sure that no form of contract or combination by which an undue restraint of interstate or foreign commerce was brought about could save such restraint from condemnation. . . . .

c. . . . Thus not specifying, but indubitably contemplating and requiring a standard, it follows that it was intended that the standard of reason which had been applied at the common law and in this country in dealing with subjects of the character embraced by the statute was intended to be the measure used for the purpose of determining whether, in a given case, a particular act had or had not brought about the wrong against which the statute provided.

And a consideration of the text of the 2d section serves to establish that it was intended to supplement the 1st, and to make sure that by no possible guise could the public policy embodied in the 1st section be frustrated or evaded. . . . By reference to the terms of Section 8 it is certain that the word "person" clearly implies a corporation as well as an individual.

* * *

Undoubtedly, the words "to monopolize" and "monopolize," as used in the section, reach every act bringing about the prohibited results. . . .

Second. The contentions of the parties as to the meaning of the statute, and the decisions of this court relied upon concerning those contentions. [Omitted]

Third. The facts and the application of the statute to them.

Beyond dispute the proofs establish substantially as alleged in the bill the following facts:

1. The creation of the Standard Oil Company of Ohio.

2. The organization of the Standard Oil Trust of 1882, and also a previous one of 1879, not referred to in the bill, and the proceedings in the supreme court of Ohio, culminating in a decree based upon the finding that the company was unlawfully a party to that trust; the transfer by the trustees of stocks in certain of the companies; the contempt proceedings; and, finally, the increase of the capital of the Standard Oil Company of New Jersey and the acquisition by that company of the shares of the stock of the other corporations in exchange for its certificates.

The vast amount of property and the possibilities of far-reaching control which resulted from the facts last stated are shown by the statement which we have previously annexed concerning the parties to the trust agreement of 1882, and the corporations whose stock was held by the trustees under the trust, and which came therefore to be held by the New Jersey corporation. But these statements do not with accuracy convey an appreciation of the situation as it existed at the time of the entry of the decree below, since, during the more than ten years which elapsed between the acquiring by the New Jersey corporation of the stock and other property which was formerly held by the trustees under the trust agreement, the situation, of course, had somewhat changed—a change which, when analyzed in the light of the proof, we think establishes that the result of enlarging the capital stock of the New Jersey company and giving it the vast power to which we have referred produced its normal consequences; that is, it gave to the corporation, despite enormous dividends and despite the dropping out of certain corporations enumerated in the decree of the court below, an enlarged and more perfect sway and control over the trade and commerce in petroleum and its products. . . .

Giving to the facts just stated the weight which it was deemed they were entitled to, in the light afforded by the proof of other cognate facts and circumstances, the court below held that the acts and dealings established by the proof operated to destroy the "potentiality of competition" which otherwise would have existed to such an extent as to cause the transfer of stock which were made to the New Jersey Corporation and the control which resulted over the many and various subsidiary corporations to be a combination or conspiracy in restraint of trade, in violation of the 1st section of the act, but also to be an attempt to monopolize and monopolization bringing about a perennial violation of the 2d section.

We see no cause to doubt the correctness of these conclusions, considering the subject from every aspect; that is, both in view of the facts established by the record and the necessary operation and effect of the law as we have construed it upon the inferences deducible from the facts, for the following reasons:

a. Because the unification of power and control over petroleum and its products which was the inevitable result of the combining in the New Jersey corporation by the increase of its stock and the transfer to it of the stocks of so many other corporations, aggregating so vast a capital, gives rise, in and of itself, in the absence of countervailing circumstances, to say the least, to the prima facie presumption of intent and purpose to maintain the dominancy over the oil industry, not as a result of normal methods of industrial development, but by new means of combination which were resorted to in order that greater power might be added than would otherwise have arisen had normal methods been followed, the whole with the purpose of excluding others from the trade, and thus centralizing in the combination of a perpetual control of the movements of petroleum and its products in the channels of interstate commerce.

b. Because the prima facie presumption of intent to restrain trade, to monopolize and to bring about monopolization, resulting from the act of expanding the stock of the New Jersey corporation and vesting it with such vast control of the oil industry, is made conclusive by considering (1) the conduct of the persons or corporations who were mainly instrumental in bringing about the extension of power in the New Jersey corporation before the consummation of the result and prior to the formation of that trust agreements of 1879 and 1882; (2) by considering the proof as to what was done under those agreements and the acts which immediately preceded the vesting of power in the New Jersey corporation, as well as by weighing the modes in which the power vested in that corporation has been exerted and the results which have arisen from it.

* * *

Fourth, The remedy to be administered.

* * *

As penalties which are not authorized by law may not be inflicted by judicial authority, it follows that to meet the situation with which we are confronted the application of remedies two-fold in character becomes essential: 1st. To forbid the doing in the future of acts like those which we have found to have been done in the past which would be violative of the statute. 2d. The exertion of such measure of relief as will effectually dissolve the combination found to exist in violation of the statute, and thus neutralize the extension and continually operating force which the possession of the power unlawfully obtained has brought and will continue to bring about.

In applying remedies for this purpose, however, the fact must not be overlooked that injury to the public by the prevention of an undue restraint on, or the monopolization of, trade or commerce, is the foundation upon which the prohibitions of the statute rest, and moreover that one of the fundamental purposes of the statute is to protect, not to destroy, rights of property.

Let us, then, as a means of accurately determining what relief we are to afford, first come to consider what relief was afforded by the court below, in order to fix how far it is necessary to take from or add to that relief, to the end that the prohibitions of the statute may have complete and operative force.

. . . Section 5 of the decree forbade the New Jersey corporation from in any form or manner exercising any ownership or exerting any power directly or indirectly in virtue of its apparent title to the stocks of the subsidiary corporations, and prohibited those subsidiary corporations from paying any dividends to the New Jersey corporations, or doing any act which would recognize further power in that company, except to the extent that it was necessary to enable that company to transfer the stock. So far as the owners of the stock of the subsidiary corporations and the corporations themselves were concerned after the stock had been transferred, Section 6 of the decree enjoined them from in any way conspiring or combining to violate the act, or to monopolize or attempt to monopolize in virtue of their ownership of the stock transferred to them, and prohibited all agreements between the subsidiary corporations or other stockholders in the future, tending to produce or bring about further violations of the act.

By Section 7, pending the accomplishment of the dissolution of the combination by the transfer of stock, and until it was consummated, the defendants . . . were enjoined from engaging in or carrying on interstate commerce. . . . So far as the decree held that the ownership of the stock of the New Jersey corporation constituted a combination in violation of the 1st section and an attempt to create a monopoly or to monopolize under the 2d section, and commanded the dissolution of the combination, the decree was clearly appropriate. And this also is true of Section 5 of the decree, which restrained both the New Jersey corporation and the subsidiary corporations from doing anything which would recognize or give effect to further ownership in the New Jersey corporation of the stocks which were ordered to be retransferred.

* * *

Our conclusion is that the decree below was right and should be affirmed, except as to the minor matters concerning which we have indicated the decree should be modified. Our order will therefore be one of affirmance, with directions, however, to modify the decree in accordance with this opinion. The court below to retain jurisdiction to the extent necessary to compel compliance in every respect with its decree.

And it is so ordered.

Source:

Supreme Court Reporter, Vol. 31, pp. 502–534.

Woodrow Wilson, First Inaugural Address, 1913

Speech delivered by Woodrow Wilson on March 4, 1913, at his inauguration as 28th president of the United States, calling for a series of national reforms. In it Wilson, a Democrat, reaffirmed his commitment to the New Freedom program on which he had campaigned, later elaborated in a book, *The New Freedom* (1913). In his "New Freedom" speeches he maintained that new economic conditions in the United States, notably the growth of large, impersonal corporations and new relations between labor and capital, required a new social organization. He criticized corruption and the control of government by big business and special interests at the expense of individuals and free enterprise. He proposed new rules to protect workers, to define the rights and obligations of employers and employees, to encourage new enterprises, and to regulate corporations.

In his inaugural address, the new president sought "justice, not pity" and argued for reforms in a tariff system that favored private interests, in an obsolete banking and currency system, in an industrial system that exploited labor and natural resources, and in an inefficient agricultural system. He favored the conservation of human and natural resources and the protection of American health through laws regarding sanitation, pure food, and conditions of labor.

There has been a change of government. It began two years ago, when the House of Representatives became Democratic by a decisive majority. It has now been completed. The Senate about to assemble will also be Democratic. The offices of President and Vice-President have been put into the hands of Democrats. What does the change mean? That is the question that is uppermost in our minds to-day. That is the question I am going to try to answer, in order, if I may, to interpret the occasion.

It means much more than the mere success of a party. The success of a party means little except when the Nation is using that party for a large and definite purpose. No one can mistake the purpose for which the Nation now seeks to use the Democratic Party. It seeks to use it to interpret a change in its own plans and point of view. Some old things with which we had grown familiar, and which had begun to creep into the very habit of our thought and of our lives, have altered their aspect as we have latterly looked critically upon them, with fresh, awakened eyes; have dropped their disguises and shown themselves alien and sinister. Some new things, as we look frankly upon them, willing to comprehend their real character, have come to assume the aspect of things long believed in and familiar, stuff of our own convictions. We have been refreshed by a new insight into our own life.

We see that in many things that life is very great. It is incomparably great in its material aspects, in its body of wealth, in the diversity and sweep of its energy, in the industries which have been conceived and built up by the genius of individual men and the limitless enterprise of groups of men. It is great, also, very great, in its moral force. Nowhere else in the world have noble men and women exhibited in more striking forms the beauty and the energy of sympathy and helpfulness and counsel in their efforts to rectify wrong, alleviate suffering, and set the weak in the way of strength and hope. We have built up, moreover, a great system of government, which has stood through a long age as in many respects a model for those who seek to set liberty upon foundations that will endure against fortuitous change, against storm and accident. Our life contains every great thing, and contains it in rich abundance.

But the evil has come with the good, and much fine gold has been corroded. With riches has come inexcusable waste. We have squandered a great part of what we might have used, and have not stopped to conserve the exceeding bounty of nature, without which our genius for enterprise would have been worthless and impotent , scorning to be careful, shamefully prodigal as well as admirably efficient. We have been proud of our industrial achievements, but we have not hitherto stopped thoughtfully enough to count the human cost, the cost of lives snuffed out, of energies overtaxed and broken, the fearful physical and spiritual cost to the men and women and children upon whom the dead weight and burden of it all has fallen pitilessly the year through. The groans and agony of it all had not yet reached our ears, the solemn, moving undertone of our life, coming up out of the mines and factories, and out of every home where the struggle had its intimate and familiar seat. With the great Government went many deep secret things which we too long delayed to look into and scrutinize with candid, fearless eyes. The great Government we loved has too often been made use of for private and selfish purposes, and those who used it had forgotten the people.

At last a vision has been vouchsafed us of our life as a whole. We see the bad with the good, the debased and decadent with the sound and vital. With this vision we approach new affairs. Our duty is to cleanse, to reconsider, to restore, to correct the evil without impairing the good, to purify and humanize every process of our common life without weakening or sentimentalizing it. There has been something crude and heartless and unfeeling in our haste to succeed and be great. Our thought has been "Let every man look out for himself, let every generation look out for itself," while we reared giant machinery which made it impossible that any but those who stood at the levers of control should have a chance to look out for themselves. We had not forgotten our morals. We remembered well enough that we had set up a policy which was meant to serve the humblest as well as the most powerful, with an eye single to the standards of justice and fair play, and remembered it with pride. But we were very heedless and in a hurry to be great.

We have come now to the sober second thought. The scales of heedlessness have fallen from our eyes. We have made up our minds to square every process of our national life again with the standards we so proudly set up at the beginning and have always carried at our hearts. Our work is a work of restoration.

We have itemized with some degree of particularity the things that ought to be altered and here are some of the chief items: A tariff which cuts us off from our proper part in the commerce of the world, violates the just principles of taxation, and makes the Government a facile instrument in the hand of private interests; a banking and currency system based upon the necessity of the Government to sell its bonds fifty years ago and perfectly adapted to concentrating cash and restricting credits; an industrial system which, take it on all its sides, financial as well as administrative, holds capital in leading strings, restricts the liberties and limits the opportunities of labor, and exploits without renewing or conserving the natural resources of the country; a body of agricultural activities never yet given the efficiency of great business undertakings or served as it should be through the instrumentality of science taken directly to the farm, or afforded the facilities of credit best suited to its practical needs; watercourses undeveloped, waste places unreclaimed, forests untended, fast disappearing without plan or prospect of renewal, unregarded waste heaps at every mine. We have studied as perhaps no other nation has the most effective means of production, but we have not studied cost or economy as we should either as organizers of industry, as statesmen, or as individuals.

Nor have we studied and perfected the means by which government may be put at the service of humanity, in safeguarding the health of the Nation, the health of its men and its women and its children, as well as their rights in the struggle for existence. This is no sentimental duty. The firm basis of government is justice, not pity. These are matters of justice. There can be no equality or opportunity, the first essential of justice in the body politic, if men and women and children be not shielded in their lives, their very vitality, from the consequences of great industrial and social processes which they can not alter, control, or singly cope with. Society must see to it that it does not itself crush or weaken or damage its own constituent parts. The first duty of law is to keep sound the society it serves. Sanitary laws, pure food laws, and laws determining conditions of labor which individuals are powerless to determine for themselves are intimate parts of the very business of justice and legal efficiency.

These are some of the things we ought to do, and not leave the others undone, the old-fashioned, never-to-be-neglected, fundamental safeguarding of property and of individual right. This is the high enterprise of the new day: To lift everything that concerns our life as a Nation to the light that shines from the hearthfire of every man's conscience and vision of the right. It is inconceivable that we should do this as partisans; it is inconceivable we should do it in ignorance of the facts as they are or in blind haste. We shall restore, not destroy. We shall deal with our economic system as it is and as it may be modified, not as it might be if we had a clean sheet of paper to write upon; and step by step we shall make it what it should be, in the spirit of those who question their own wisdom and seek counsel and knowledge, not shallow self-satisfaction or the excitement of excursions whither they can not tell. Justice, and only justice, shall always be our motto.

And yet it will be no cool process of mere science. The Nation has been deeply stirred, stirred by a solemn passion, stirred by the knowledge of wrong, of ideals lost, of government too often debauched and made an instrument of evil. The feelings with which we face this new age of right and opportunity sweep across our heartstrings like some air out of God's own presence, where justice and mercy are reconciled and the judge and the brother are one. We know our task to be no mere task of politics but a task which shall search us through and through, whether we be able to understand our time and the need of our people, whether we be indeed their spokesmen and interpreters, whether we have the pure heart to comprehend and the rectified will to choose our high course of action.

This is not a day of triumph; it is a day of dedication. Here muster, not the forces of party, but the forces of humanity. Men's hearts wait upon us; men's lives hang in the balance; men's hopes call upon us to say what we will do. Who shall live up to the great trust? Who dares fail to try? I summon all honest men, all patriotic, all forward-looking men, to my side. God helping me, I will not fail them, if they will but counsel and sustain me!

Source:
Inaugural Addresses of the Presidents of the United States, 1789–1965. Washington, D.C. Government Printing Office, 1965.

Federal Reserve Act, 1913

Also known as the Glass-Owens Act, this legislation drafted by Representative Carter Glass of Virginia and Senator Robert L. Owen of Oklahoma and enacted on December 23, 1913, established the Federal Reserve System. It resulted from a report on the concentration of control of money and credit in the United States issued February 28, 1913, by the House of Representatives Committee on Banking and Currency. The committee, headed by Arsene P. Pujo, found evidence of a "money trust," a "vast and growing concentration of control of money and credit in the hands of a comparatively few men." This concentration was achieved through the consolidation of banks and trusts, the purchase of competitors' stocks, interlocking directorates, extension of control into diverse industries, and joint purchase of security issues.

The Federal Reserve Act significantly reformed the national banking system and its credit procedures, as well as assuring an elastic currency and more effective supervision. Twelve regional Federal Reserve banks, under the central Federal Reserve Board, were established. All national banks were required to join the system, and state banks were allowed to do so if they met certain requirements. The Federal Reserve banks function as bankers' banks, holding deposits and making loans to member banks. The Federal Reserve Board of Governors, consisting of seven members appointed by the president, adjusts the discount rate—the interest rate at which member banks borrow—and thus influences the availability of credit for individual borrowers.

An Act
To provide for the establishment of Federal reserve banks, to furnish an elastic currency, to afford means of rediscounting commercial paper, to establish a more effective supervision of banking in the United States, and for other purposes.

Be it enacted by the Senate and House of Representatives of the United States of America in Congress assembled, That the short title of this Act shall be the "Federal Reserve Act."

Wherever the word "bank" is used in this Act, the word shall be held to include State bank, banking association, and trust company, except where national banks or Federal reserve banks are specifically referred to.

The terms "national bank" and "national banking association" used in this Act shall be held to be synonymous and interchangeable. The term "member bank" shall be held to mean any national bank, State bank, or bank or trust company which has become a member of one of the reserve banks created by this Act. The term "board" shall be held to mean Federal Reserve Board; the term "district" shall be held to mean Federal reserve district; the term "reserve bank" shall be held to mean Federal reserve bank.

Federal Reserve Districts. [omitted]

Federal Reserve Banks

Upon the filing of such certificate with the Comptroller of the Currency as aforesaid, the said Federal reserve bank shall become a body corporate and as such, and in the name designated in such organization certificate, shall have power—

First. To adopt and use a corporate seal.

Second. To have succession for a period of twenty years from its organization unless it is sooner dissolved by an Act of Congress, or unless its franchise becomes forfeited by some violation of law.

Third. To make contracts.

Fourth. To sue and be sued, complain and defend, in any court of law or equity.

Fifth. To appoint by its board of directors, such officers and employees as are not otherwise provided for in this Act, to define their duties, require bonds of them and fix the penalty thereof, and to dismiss at pleasure such officers or employees.

Sixth. To prescribe by its board of directors, by-laws not inconsistent with law, regulating the manner in which its general business may be conducted, and the privileges granted to it by law may be exercised and enjoyed.

Seventh. To exercise by its board of directors, or duly authorized officers or agents, all powers specifically granted by the provisions of this Act and such incidental powers as shall be necessary to carry on the business of banking within the limitations prescribed by this Act.

Eighth. Upon deposit with the Treasurer of the United States of any bonds of the United States in the manner provided by existing law relating to national banks, to receive from the Comptroller of the Currency circulating notes in blank, registered and countersigned as provided by law, equal in amount to the par value of the bonds so deposited, such notes to be issued under the same conditions and provisions of law as relate to the issue of circulating notes of national banks secured by bonds of the United States bearing the circulating privilege, except that the issue of such notes shall not be limited to the capital stock of such Federal reserve bank.

But no Federal reserve bank shall transact any business except such as is incidental and necessarily preliminary to its organization until it has been authorized by the

Comptroller of the Currency to commence business under the provisions of this Act.

Every Federal reserve bank shall be conducted under the supervision and control of a board of directors.

The board of directors shall perform the duties usually appertaining to the office of directors of banking associations and all such duties as are prescribed by law.

Said board shall administer the affairs of said bank fairly and impartially and without discrimination in favor of or against any member bank or banks and shall subject to the provisions of law and the orders of the Federal Reserve Board, extend to each member bank such discounts, advancements, and accommodations as may be safely and reasonably made with due regard for the claims and demands of other member banks.

* * *

No Senator or Representative in Congress shall be a member of the Federal Reserve Board or an officer or a director of a Federal reserve bank.

* * *

Directors of Federal reserve banks shall receive, in addition to any compensation otherwise provided, a reasonable allowance for necessary expenses in attending meetings of their respective boards, which amount shall be paid by the respective Federal reserve banks. Any compensation that may be provided by boards of directors of Federal reserve banks for directors, officers or employees shall be subject to the approval of the Federal Reserve Board.

* * *

Stock Issues and Division of Capital [Omitted]

* * *

Division of Earnings.

Sec. 7. After all necessary expenses of a Federal reserve bank have been paid or provided for, the stockholders shall be entitled to receive an annual dividend of six per centum on the paid-in capital stock, which dividend shall be cumulative. After the aforesaid dividend claims have been fully met, all the net earnings shall be paid to the United States as a franchise tax, except that one-half of such net earnings shall be paid into a surplus fund until it shall amount to forty per centum of the paid-in capital stock of such bank.

The net earnings derived by the United States from Federal reserve banks shall, in the discretion of the Secretary, be used to supplement the gold reserve held against outstanding United States notes, or shall be applied to the reduction of the outstanding bonded indebtedness of the United States under regulations to be prescribed by the Secretary of the Treasury. Should a Federal reserve bank be dissolved or go into liquidation, any surplus remaining, after the payment of all debts, dividend requirements as hereinbefore provided, and the par value of the stock, shall be paid to and become the property of the United States and shall be similarly applied.

Federal reserve banks, including the capital stock and surplus therein, and the income derived therefrom shall be exempt from Federal, State, and local taxation, except taxes upon real estate.

Sec. 8. Section fifty-one hundred and fifty-four, United States Revised Statutes, is hereby amended to read as follows:

Any bank incorporated by special law of any State or of the United States or organized under the general laws of any State or of the United States and having an unimpaired capital sufficient to entitle it to become a national banking association under the provisions of the existing laws may, by the vote of the shareholders owning not less than fifty-one per centum of the capital stock of such bank or banking association, with the approval of the Comptroller of the Currency be converted into a national banking association, with any name approved by the Comptroller of the Currency:

Provided, however, That said conversion shall not be in contravention of the State law. . . .

State Banks as Members [Omitted]

Federal Reserve Board.

Sec. 10. A Federal Reserve Board is hereby created which shall consist of seven members, including the Secretary of the Treasury and the Comptroller of the Currency, who shall be members ex officio, and five members appointed by the President of the United States, by and with the advice and consent of the Senate. In selecting the five appointive members of the Federal Reserve Board, not more than one of whom shall be selected from any one Federal reserve district, the President shall have due regard to a fair representation of the different commercial, industrial and geographical divisions of the country. The five members of the Federal Reserve Board appointed by the President and confirmed as aforesaid shall devote their entire time to the business of the Federal Reserve Board and shall each receive an annual salary of $12,000, payable monthly together with actual necessary traveling expenses, and the Comptroller of the Currency, as ex officio member of the Federal Reserve Board, shall, in addition to the salary now paid him as Comptroller of the Currency, receive the sum of $7,000 annually for his services as a member of said board.

The members of said board, the Secretary of the Treasury, the Assistant Secretaries of the Treasury, and the Comptroller of the Currency shall be ineligible during the time they are in office and for two years thereafter to hold any office, position, or employment in any member bank.

Of the five members thus appointed by the President at least two shall be persons experienced in banking or finance. One shall be designated by the President to serve for two, one for four, one for six, one for eight, and one for ten years, and thereafter each member so appointed shall serve for a term of ten years unless sooner removed for cause by the President. Of the five persons thus appointed, one shall be designated by the President as governor and one as vice governor of the Federal Reserve Board. The governor of the Federal Reserve Board, subject to its supervision, shall be the active executive officer. The Secretary of the Treasury may assign offices in the Department of the Treasury for the use of the Federal Reserve Board. Each member of the Federal Reserve Board shall within fifteen days after notice of appointment make and subscribe to the oath of office.

The Federal Reserve Board shall have power to levy semiannually upon the Federal reserve banks, in proportion to their capital stock and surplus, an assessment sufficient to pay its estimated expenses and the salaries of its members and employees for the half year succeeding the levying of such assessment, together with any deficit carried forward from the preceding half year.

The first meeting of the Federal Reserve Board shall be held in Washington, District of Columbia, as soon as may be after the passage of this Act, at a date to be fixed by the Reserve Bank Organization Committee. The Secretary of the Treasury shall be ex officio chairman of the Federal Reserve Board. No member of the Federal Reserve Board shall be an officer or director of any bank, banking institution, trust company, or Federal reserve bank nor hold stock in any bank, banking institution, or trust company; and before entering upon his duties as a member of the Federal Reserve Board he shall certify under oath to the Secretary of the Treasury that he has complied with this requirement. Whenever a vacancy shall occur, other than by expiration of term, among the five members of the Federal Reserve Board appointed by the President, as above provided, a successor shall be appointed by the President, with the advice and consent of the Senate, to fill such vacancy, and when appointed he shall hold office for the unexpired term of the member whose place he is selected to fill.

The President shall have power to fill all vacancies that may happen on the Federal Reserve Board during the recess of the Senate, by granting commissions which shall expire thirty days after the next session of the Senate convenes.

Nothing in this Act contained shall be construed as taking away any powers heretofore vested by law in the Secretary of the Treasury which relate to the supervision, management, and control of the Treasury Department and bureaus under such department, and wherever any power vested by this Act in the Federal Reserve Board or the Federal reserve agent appears to conflict with the powers of the Secretary of the Treasury, such powers shall be exercised subject to the supervision and control of the Secretary.

The Federal Reserve Board shall annually make a full report of its operation to the Speaker of the House of Representatives, who shall cause the same to be printed for the information of the Congress.

Section three hundred and twenty-four of the Revised Statutes of the United States shall be amended so as to read as follows: There shall be in the Department of the Treasury a bureau charged with the execution of all laws passed by Congress relating to the issue and regulation of national currency secured by United States bonds and, under the general supervision of the Federal Reserve Board, of all Federal reserve notes, the chief officer of which bureau shall be called the Comptroller of the Currency and shall perform his duties under the general directions of the Secretary of the Treasury.

Sec. 11. The Federal Reserve Board shall be authorized and empowered:

(a) To examine at its discretion the accounts, books and affairs of each Federal reserve bank and of each member bank and to require such statements and reports as it may deem necessary. The said board shall publish once each week a statement showing the condition of each Federal reserve bank and a consolidated statement for all Federal reserve banks. Such statements shall show in detail the assets and liabilities of the Federal reserve banks, single and combined, and shall furnish full information regarding the character of the money held as reserve and the amount, nature and maturities of the paper and other investments owned or held by Federal reserve banks.

(b) To permit, or, on the affirmative vote of at least five members of the Reserve Board to require Federal reserve banks to rediscount the discounted paper of other Federal reserve banks at rates of interest to be fixed by the Federal Reserve Board.

(c) To suspend for a period not exceeding thirty days, and from time to time to renew such suspension for periods not exceeding fifteen days, any reserve requirement specified in this Act: Provided, That it shall establish a graduated tax upon the amounts by which the reserve requirements of this Act may be permitted to fall below the level hereinafter specified: And provided further, That when the gold reserve held against Federal reserve notes falls below forty per centum, the Federal Reserve Board shall establish a graduated tax of not more than one per centum per annum upon such deficiency until the reserves fall to thirty-two and one-half per centum, and when said reserve falls below thirty-two and one-half per centum, a tax at the rate increasingly of not less than one and one-half per centum per annum upon each two and one-half per centum or fraction thereof that such reserve falls below thirty-two and one-half per centum. The tax shall be paid by the reserve bank, but the reserve bank shall add an amount equal to said tax to the rates of interest and discount fixed by the Federal Reserve Board.

(d) To supervise and regulate through the bureau under the charge of the Comptroller of the Currency the issue and retirement of Federal reserve notes, and to prescribe rules and regulations under which such notes may be delivered by the Comptroller to the Federal reserve agents applying therefor.

(e) To add to the number of cities classified as reserve and central reserve cities under existing law in which national banking associations are subject to the reserve requirements set forth in section twenty of this Act; or to reclassify existing reserve and central reserve cities or to terminate their designation as such.

(f) To suspend or remove any officer or director of any Federal reserve bank, the cause of such removal to be forthwith communicated in writing by the Federal Reserve Board to the removed officer or director and to said bank.

(g) To require the writing off of doubtful or worthless assets upon the books and balance sheets of Federal reserve banks.

(h) To suspend, for the violation of any of the provisions of this Act, the operations of any Federal reserve bank, to take possession thereof, administer the same during the period of suspension, and, when deemed advisable, to liquidate or reorganize such bank.

(i) To require bonds of Federal reserve agents, to make regulations for the safeguarding of all collateral, bonds, Federal reserve notes, money or property of any kind deposited in the hands of such agents, and said board shall perform the duties, functions, or services specified in this Act, and make all rules and regulations necessary to enable said board effectively to perform the same.

(j) To exercise general supervision over said Federal reserve banks.

(k) To grant by special permit to national banks applying therefor, when not in contravention of State or local law, the right to act as trustee, executor, administrator, or registrar of stocks and bonds under such rules and regulations as the said board may prescribe.

(l) To employ such attorneys, experts, assistants, clerks, or other employees as may be deemed necessary to conduct the business of the board. All salaries and fees shall be fixed in advance by said board and shall be paid in the same manner as the salaries of the members of said board. All such attorneys, experts, assistants, clerks, and other employees shall be appointed without regard to the provisions of the Act of January sixteenth, eighteen hundred and eighty-three (volume twenty-two, United States Statutes at Large, page four hundred and three), and amendments thereto, or any rule or regulation made in pursuance thereof: Provided, That nothing herein shall prevent the President from placing said employees in the classified service.

Federal Advisory Council.

Sec. 12. There is hereby created a Federal Advisory Council, which shall consist of as many members as there are Federal reserve districts. Each Federal reserve bank by its board of directors shall annually select from its own Federal reserve district one member of said council, who shall receive such compensation and allowances as may be fixed by his board of directors subject to the approval of the Federal Reserve Board. The meetings of said advisory council shall be held at Washington, District of Columbia, at least four times each year, and oftener if called by the Federal Reserve Board. The council may in addition to the meetings above provided for hold such other meetings in Washington, District of Columbia, or elsewhere, as it may deem necessary, may select its own officers and adopt its own methods of procedure, and a majority of its members shall constitute a quorum for the transaction of business. Vacancies in the council shall be filled by the respective reserve banks, and members selected to fill vacancies, shall serve for the unexpired term.

The Federal Advisory Council shall have power, by itself or through its officers, (1) to confer directly with the Federal Reserve Board on general business conditions; (2) to make oral or written representations concerning matters within the jurisdiction of said board; (3) to call for information and to make recommendations in regard to discount rates, rediscount business, not issues, reserve conditions in the various districts, the purchase and sale of gold or securities by reserve banks, open-market operations by said banks, and the general affairs of the reserve banking system.

Powers of Federal Reserve Banks.

Sec. 13. Any Federal reserve bank may receive from any of its member banks, and from the United States, deposits of current funds in lawful money, national-bank notes, Federal reserve notes, or checks and drafts upon solvent member banks, payable upon presentation; or, solely for exchange purposes, may receive from other Federal reserve banks deposits of current funds in lawful money, national-bank notes, or checks and drafts upon solvent member or other Federal reserve banks, payable upon presentation.

Upon the indorsement of any of its member banks, with a waiver of demand, notice and protest by such bank, any Federal reserve bank may discount notes, drafts, and bills of exchange arising out of actual commercial transactions; that is, notes, drafts, and bills of exchange issued or drawn for agricultural, industrial, or commercial purposes, or the proceeds of which have been used, or are to be used, for such purposes, the Federal Reserve Board to have the right to determine or define the character of the paper thus eligible for discount, within the meaning of this Act. Nothing in this Act contained shall be construed to prohibit such notes, drafts, and bills of exchange, secured by staple agricultural products, or other goods, wares, or merchandise from being eligible for such discount; but such definition shall not include notes, drafts, or bills covering merely investments or issued or drawn for the purpose of carrying or trading in stocks, bonds, or other investment securities, except bonds and notes of the Government of the United States. Notes, drafts, and bills admitted to discount under the terms of this paragraph must have a maturity at the time of discount of not more than ninety days: Provided, That notes, drafts, and bills drawn or issued for agricultural purposes or based on live stock and having a maturity not exceeding six months may be discounted in an amount to be limited to a percentage of the capital of the Federal reserve bank, to be ascertained and fixed by the Federal Reserve Board.

Any Federal reserve bank may discount acceptances which are based on the importation or exportation of goods and which have a maturity at time of discount of not more than three months, and indorsed by at least one member bank. The amount of acceptances so discounted shall at no time exceed one-half the paid-up capital stock and surplus of the bank for which the rediscounts are made.

The aggregate of such notes and bills bearing the signature or indorsement of any one person, company, firm, or corporation rediscounted for any one bank shall at no time exceed ten per centum of the unimpaired capital and surplus of said bank; but this restriction shall not apply to the discount of bills of exchange drawn in good faith against actually existing values.

Any member bank may accept drafts or bills of exchange drawn upon it and growing out of transactions involving the importation or exportation of goods having not more than six months sight to run; but no bank shall accept such bills to an amount equal at any time in the aggregate to more than one-half its paid-up capital stock and surplus.

* * *

Open-Market Operations.

Sec. 14. Any Federal reserve bank may, under rules and regulations prescribed by the Federal Reserve Board, purchase and sell in the open market, at home or abroad, either from or to domestic or foreign banks, firms, corporations, or individuals, cable transfers and bankers' acceptances and bills of exchange of the kinds and maturities by this Act made eligible for rediscount, with or without the indorsement of a member bank.

Every Federal reserve bank shall have power:

(a) To deal in gold coin and bullion at home or abroad, to make loans thereon, exchange Federal reserve notes for gold, gold coin, or gold certificates, and to contract for loans of gold coin or bullion, giving therefor, when necessary, acceptable security, including the hypothecation of United States bonds or other securities which Federal reserve banks are authorized to hold;

(b) To buy and sell, at home or abroad, bonds and notes of the United States, and bills, notes, revenue bonds, and warrants with a maturity from date of purchase of not exceeding six months, issued in anticipation of the collection of taxes or in anticipation of the receipt of assured revenues by any State, county, district, political subdivision, or municipality in the continental United States, including irrigation, drainage and reclamation districts, such purchases to be made in accordance with rules and regulations prescribed by the Federal Reserve Board;

(c) To purchase from member banks and to sell, with or without its indorsement, bills of exchange arising out of commercial transactions, as hereinbefore defined;

(d) To establish from time to time, subject to review and determination of the Federal Reserve Board, rates of discount to be charged by the Federal reserve bank for each class of paper, which shall be fixed with a view of accommodating commerce and business;

(e) To establish accounts with other Federal reserve banks for exchange purposes and, with the consent of the Federal Reserve Board, to open and maintain banking accounts in foreign countries, appoint correspondents, and establish agencies in such countries wheresoever it may deem best for the purpose of purchasing, selling, and collecting bills of exchange, and to buy and sell with or without its indorsement, through such correspondents or agencies, bills of exchange arising out of actual commercial transactions which have not more than ninety days to run and which bear the signature of two or more responsible parties.

Government Deposits.

Sec. 15. The moneys held in the general fund of the Treasury except the five per centum fund for the redemption of outstanding national-bank notes and the funds provided in this Act for the redemption of Federal reserve notes may, upon the direction of the Secretary of the Treasury, be deposited in Federal reserve banks, which banks, when required by the Secretary of the Treasury, shall act as fiscal agents of the United States; and the revenues of the Government or any part thereof may be deposited in such banks, and disbursements may be made by checks drawn against such deposits.

* * *

Note Issues.

Sec. 16. Federal reserve notes, to be issued at the discretion of the Federal Reserve Board for the purpose of making advances to Federal reserve banks through the Federal reserve agents as hereinafter set forth and for no other purpose, are hereby authorized. The said notes shall be obligations of the United States and shall be receivable by all national and member banks and Federal reserve banks and for all taxes, customs, and other public dues. They shall be redeemed in gold on demand at the Treasury Department of the United States, in the city of Washington, District of Columbia, or in gold or lawful money of any Federal reserve bank.

Any Federal reserve bank may make application to the local Federal reserve agent for such amount of the Federal reserve notes hereinbefore provided for as it may require. . . .

Every Federal reserve bank shall maintain reserves in gold or lawful money of not less than thirty-five per centum against its deposits and reserves in gold of not less than forty per centum against its Federal reserve notes in actual circulation, and not offset by gold or lawful money deposited with the Federal reserve agent. Notes so paid out shall bear upon their faces a distinctive letter and serial number, which shall be assigned by the Federal Reserve Board to each Federal reserve bank. Whenever Federal reserve notes issued through one Federal reserve bank shall be received by another Federal reserve bank they shall be promptly returned for credit or redemption of the Federal reserve bank through which they were originally issued. No Federal reserve bank shall pay out notes issued through another under penalty of a tax of ten per centum upon the face value of notes so paid out. Notes presented for redemption at the Treasury of the United States shall be paid out of the redemption fund and returned to the Federal reserve banks through which they were originally issued, and thereupon such Federal reserve bank shall, upon demand of the Secretary of the Treasury, reimburse such redemption fund in lawful money or, if such Federal reserve notes have been redeemed by the Treasurer in gold or gold certificates, then such funds shall be reimbursed to the extent deemed necessary by the Secretary of the Treasury in gold or gold certificates, and such Federal reserve bank shall, so long as any of its Federal reserve notes remain outstanding, maintain with the Treasurer in gold an amount sufficient in the judgment of the Secretary to provide for all redemptions to be made by the Treasurer. Federal reserve notes received by the Treasury, otherwise than for redemption, may be exchanged for gold out of the redemption fund hereinafter provided and returned to the reserve bank through which they were originally issued, or they may be returned to such bank for the credit of the United States. Federal reserve notes unfit for circulation shall be returned by the Federal reserve agents to the Comptroller of the Currency for cancellation and destruction.

The Federal Reserve Board shall require each Federal reserve bank to maintain on deposit in the Treasury of the United States a sum in gold sufficient in the judgment of the Secretary of the Treasury for the redemption of the Federal reserve notes issued to such bank, but in no event less than five per centum; but such deposit of gold shall be counted and included as part of the forty per centum reserve hereinbefore required. The board shall have the right, acting through the Federal reserve agent, to grant in whole or in part or to reject entirely the application of any Federal reserve bank for Federal reserve notes; but to the extent that such application may be granted the Federal Reserve Board shall, through its local Federal reserve agent, supply Federal reserve notes to the bank so applying, and such bank shall be charged with the amount of such notes and shall pay such rate of interest on said amount as may be established by the Federal Reserve Board, and the amount of such Federal reserve notes so issued to any such bank shall, upon delivery, together with such notes of such Federal reserve bank as may be issued under section eighteen of this Act upon security of United States two per centum Government bonds, become a first and paramount lien on all the assets of such bank.

Any Federal reserve bank may at any time reduce its liability for outstanding Federal reserve notes by depositing, with the Federal reserve agent, its Federal reserve notes, gold, gold certificates, or lawful money of the United States. Federal reserve notes so deposited shall not be reissued, except upon compliance with the conditions of an original issue.

The Federal reserve agent shall hold such gold, gold certificates, or lawful money available exclusively for exchange for the outstanding Federal reserve notes when offered by the reserve bank of which he is a director. Upon the request of the Secretary of the Treasury the Federal Reserve Board shall require the Federal reserve agent to transmit so much of said gold to the Treasury of the United States as may be required for the exclusive purpose of the redemption of such notes.

Any Federal reserve bank may at its discretion withdraw collateral deposited with the local Federal reserve agent for the protection of its Federal reserve notes deposited with it and shall at the same time substitute therefor other like collateral of equal amount with the approval of the Federal reserve agent under regulations to be prescribed by the Federal Reserve Board.

In order to furnish suitable notes for circulation as Federal reserve notes, the Comptroller of the Currency shall, under the direction of the Secretary of the Treasury, cause plates and dies to be engraved in the best manner to guard against counterfeits and fraudulent alterations, and shall have printed therefrom and numbered such quantities of such notes of the denominations of $5, $10, $20, $50, $100, as may be required to supply the Federal reserve banks. Such notes shall be in form and tenors as directed by the Secretary of the Treasury under the provisions of this Act and shall bear the distinctive numbers of the several Federal reserve banks through which they are issued.

When such notes have been prepared, they shall be deposited in the Treasury, or in the subtreasury or mint of the United States nearest the place of business of each Federal reserve bank and shall be held for the use of such bank subject to the order of the Comptroller of the Currency for their delivery, as provided by this Act.

The plates and dies to be procured by the Comptroller of the Currency for the printing of such circulating notes shall remain under his control and direction. . . .

* * *

Every Federal reserve bank shall receive on deposit at par from member banks or from Federal reserve banks checks and drafts drawn upon any of its depositors, and when remitted by a Federal reserve bank, checks and drafts drawn by any depositor in any other Federal reserve bank or member bank upon funds to the credit of said depositor in said reserve bank or member bank. Nothing herein contained shall be construed as prohibiting a member bank from charging its actual expense incurred in collecting and remitting funds, or for exchange sold to its patrons. The Federal Reserve Board shall, by rule, fix the charges to be collected by the member banks from its patrons whose checks are cleared through the Federal reserve bank and the charge which may be imposed for the service of clearing or collection rendered by the Federal reserve bank.

The Federal Reserve Board shall make and promulgate from time to time regulations governing the transfer of funds and charges therefor among Federal reserve banks and their branches, and may at its discretion exercise the functions of a clearing house for such Federal reserve banks, or may designate a Federal reserve bank to exercise such functions, and may also require each such bank to exercise the functions of a clearing house for its member banks.

* * *

Refunding Bonds [Omitted]
Bank Reserves [Omitted]
Bank Examinations.

The Comptroller of the Currency, with the approval of the Secretary of the Treasury, shall appoint examiners who shall examine every member bank at least twice in each calendar year and oftener if considered necessary: *Provided, however,* That the Federal Reserve Board may authorize examination by the State authorities to be accepted in the case of State banks and trust companies and may at any time direct the holding of a special examination of State banks or trust companies that are stockholders in any Federal reserve bank. The examiner making the examination of any national bank, or of any other member bank, shall have power to make a thorough examination of all the affairs of the bank and in doing so he shall have power to administer oaths and to examine any of the officers and agents thereof under oath and shall make a full and detailed report of the condition of said bank to the Comptroller of the Currency.

* * *

No bank shall be subject to any visitatorial powers other than such as are authorized by law, or vested in the courts of justice or such as shall be or shall have been exercised or directed by Congress, or by either House thereof or by any committee of Congress or of either House duly authorized.

The Federal Reserve Board shall, at least once each year, order an examination of each Federal reserve bank, and upon joint application of ten member banks the Federal Reserve Board shall order a special examination and report of the condition of any Federal reserve bank. Sec. 22. No member bank or any officer, director, or employee thereof shall hereafter make any loan or grant any gratuity to any bank examiner. . . .

* * *

Sec. 23. The stockholders of every national banking association shall be held individually responsible for all contracts, debts, and engagements of such association, each to the amount of his stock therein, at the par value thereof in addition to the amount invested in such stock. The stockholders in any national banking association who shall have transferred their shares or registered the transfer thereof within sixty days next before the date of the failure of such association to meet its obligations, or with knowledge of such impending failure, shall be liable to the same extent as if they had made no such transfer, to the extent that the subsequent transferee fails to meet such liability; but this provision shall not be construed to affect in any way any recourse which such shareholders might otherwise have against those in whose names such shares are registered at the time of such failure.

Loans on Farm Lands.

Sec. 24. Any national banking association not situated in a central reserve city may make loans secured by improved and unencumbered farm land, situated within its Federal reserve district, but no such loan shall be made for a longer time than five years, nor for an amount exceeding fifty per centum of the actual value of the property offered as security. Any such bank may make such loans in an aggregate sum equal to twenty-five per centum of its capital and surplus or to one-third of its time deposits and such banks may continue hereafter as heretofore to receive time deposits and to pay interest on the same.

* * *

Foreign Branches

Sec. 25. Any national banking association possessing a capital and surplus of $1,000,000 or more may file application with the Federal Reserve Board, upon such conditions and under such regulations as may be prescribed by the said board, for the purpose of securing authority to establish branches in foreign countries or dependencies of the United States for the furtherance of the foreign commerce of the United States, and to act, if required to do so, as fiscal agents of the United States. Such application shall specify, in addition to the name and capital of the banking association filing it, the place or places where the banking operations proposed are to be carried on, and the amount of capital set aside for the conduct of its foreign business. The Federal Reserve Board shall have power to approve or to reject such application if, in its judgment, the amount of capital proposed to be set aside for the conduct of foreign business is inadequate, or if for other reasons the granting of such application is deemed inexpedient.

* * *

Sec. 29. If any clause, sentence, paragraph, or part of this Act shall for any reason be adjudged by any court of competent jurisdiction to be invalid, such judgment shall not affect, impair, or invalidate the remainder of this Act, but shall be confined in its operation to the clause, sentence, paragraph, part thereof directly involved in the controversy in which such judgment shall have been rendered.

Sec. 30. The right to amend, alter, or repeal this Act is hereby expressly reserved.

Approved, December 23, 1913.

Source:
Statutes at Large, Vol. 35, pp. 251–275.

Smith-Lever Act, 1914

Federal U.S. legislation enacted on May 8, 1914, that established a national agricultural extension system under the Department of Agriculture, in cooperation with the land-grant colleges. The system provided county agents and demonstrators to teach farmers and their families the latest agricultural and home economics techniques. Federal grants-in-aid were to be matched by equal state contributions to support the program. The goal was to extend the benefits offered by the land-grant colleges and the agricultural experiment stations. Later, the act helped to increase food production during World War I.

Also known as the U.S. Cooperative Marketing Act, the Capper-Volstead Act, enacted February 18, 1922, exempted various agricultural associations, producers, and cooperatives from antitrust laws. It permitted farmers to buy and sell cooperatively in interstate commerce and established a system of agricultural credit. The secretary of agriculture was empowered to administer the act and to prevent these agricultural associations from developing into monopolies. The act was sponsored by Senator Arthur Capper of Kansas and Representative Andrew Joseph Volstead of Minnesota to provide relief to distressed farmers following World War I.

On June 15, 1929, Congress replaced the subsidy and price-fixing proposals of the McNary-Haugen Bill that President Calvin Coolidge had twice vetoed. That bill, enacted in 1927 and 1928, was designed to control American agricultural surplus and stabilize prices. Its sponsors, Senator Charles L. McNary of Oregon and Representative Gilbert N. Haugen of Iowa, called for dual pricing of agricultural products—a fixed domestic price and a free international price for goods sold abroad. It would have established a federal farm board similar to one in the Agricultural Marketing Act of 1929, to purchase surpluses at the domestic price and sell them abroad at the prevailing world price. Any government losses through such sales were to be made up by equalization fees, paid by the farmers.

An Act

To provide for cooperative agricultural extension work between the agricultural colleges in the several States receiving the benefits of an Act of Congress approved July second, eighteen hundred and sixty-two, and of Acts supplementary thereto, and the United States Department of Agriculture.

Be it enacted by the Senate and House of Representatives of the United States of America in Congress assembled, That in order to aid in diffusing among the people of the United States useful and practical information on subjects relating to agriculture and home economics, and to encourage the application of the same, there may be inaugurated in connection with the college or colleges in each State now receiving, or which may hereafter receive, the benefits of the Act of Congress approved July second, eighteen hundred and sixty-two, entitled "An Act donating public lands to the several States and Territories which may provide colleges for the benefit of agriculture and the mechanic arts" (Twelfth Statutes at Large, page five hundred and three), and of the Act of Congress approved August thirtieth, eighteen hundred and ninety (Twenty-sixth Statutes at Large, page four hundred and seventeen and chapter eight hundred and forty-one), agricultural extension work which shall be carried on in cooperation with the United States Department of Agriculture: *Provided,* That in any State in which two or more such colleges have been or hereafter may be established the appropriations hereinafter made to such State shall be administered by such college or colleges as the legislature of such State may direct: *Provided further,* That, pending the inauguration and development of the cooperative extension work herein authorized, nothing in this Act shall be construed to discontinue either the farm management work or the farmers' cooperative demonstration work as now conducted by the Bureau of Plant Industry of the Department of Agriculture.

Sec. 2. That cooperative agricultural extension work shall consist of the giving of instruction and practical demonstrations in agriculture and home economics to persons not attending or resident in said colleges in the several communities, and imparting to such persons information on said subjects through field demonstrations, publications, and otherwise; and this work shall be carried on in such manner as may be mutually agreed upon by the Secretary of Agriculture and the State agricultural college or colleges receiving the benefits of this Act.

Sec. 3. That for the purpose of paying the expenses of said cooperative agricultural extension work and the necessary printing and distributing of information in connection with the same, there is permanently appropriated, out of any money in the Treasury not otherwise appropriated, the sum of $480,000 for each year, $10,000 of which shall be paid annually, in the manner hereinafter provided, to each State which shall by action of its legislature assent to the provisions of this Act: *Provided,* That payment of such installments of the appropriation hereinbefore made as shall become due to any State before the adjournment of the regular session of the legislature meeting next after the passage of this Act may, in the absence of prior legislative assent, be made upon the assent of the governor thereof, duly certified to the Secretary of the Treasury: *Provided further,* That there is also appropriated an additional sum of $600,000 for the fiscal year following that in which the foregoing appropriation first becomes available, and for each year thereafter for seven years a sum exceeding by $500,000 the sum appropriated for each preceding year, and for each year thereafter there is permanently appropriated for each year the sum of $4,100,000 in addition to the sum of $480,000 hereinbefore provided: *Provided further,* That before the funds herein appropriated shall become available to any college for any fiscal year plans for the work to be carried on under this Act shall be submitted by the proper officials of each college and approved by the Secretary of Agriculture. Such additional sums shall be used only for the purposes hereinbefore stated, and shall be allotted annually to each State by the Secretary of Agriculture and paid in the manner hereinbefore provided, in the proportion which the rural population of each State bears to the total rural population of all the States as determined by the next preceding Federal census: *Provided further,* That no payment out of the additional appropriations herein provided shall be made in any year to any State until an equal sum has been appropriated for that year by the legislature of such State, or provided by State, county, college, local authority, or individual contributions from within the State, for the maintenance of the cooperative agricultural extension work provided for in this Act.

Sec. 4. That the sums hereby appropriated for extension work shall be paid in equal semiannual payments on the first day of January and July of each year by the Secretary of the Treasury upon the warrant of the Secretary of Agriculture, out of the Treasury of the United States, to the treasurer or other officer of the State duly authorized by the laws of the State to receive the same; and such officer shall be required to report to the Secretary of Agriculture, on or before the first day of September of each year, a detailed statement of the amount so received during the previous fiscal year, and of its disbursement, on forms prescribed by the Secretary of Agriculture.

Sec. 5. That if any portion of the moneys received by the designated officer of any State for the support and maintenance of cooperative agricultural extension work, as provided in this Act, shall by any action or contingency be diminished or lost, or be misapplied, it shall be replaced by said State to which it belongs, and until so replaced no subsequent appropriation shall be apportioned or paid to said State, and no portion of said moneys shall be applied, directly or indirectly, to the purchase, erection, preservation, or repair of any building or buildings, or the purchase or rental of land, or in college-course teaching, lectures in colleges, promoting agricultural trains, or any other purpose not specified in this Act, and not more than five per centum of each annual appropriation shall be applied to the printing and distribution of publications. It shall be the duty of each of said colleges annually, on or before the first day of January, to make to the governor of the State in which it is located a full and detailed report of its operations in the direction of extension work as defined in this Act, including a detailed statement of receipts and expenditures from all sources for this purpose, a copy of which report shall be sent to the Secretary of Agriculture and to the Secretary of the Treasury of the United States.

Sec. 6. That on or before the first day of July in each year after the passage of this Act the Secretary or Agriculture shall ascertain and certify to the Secretary of the Treasury as to each State whether it is entitled to receive its share of the annual appropriation for cooperative agricultural extension work under this Act, and the amount which it is entitled to receive. If the Secretary of Agriculture shall withhold a certificate from any State of its appropriation, the facts and reasons therefor shall be reported to the President, and the amount involved shall be kept separate in the Treasury until the expiration of the Congress next succeeding a session of the legislature of any State from which a certificate has been withheld, in order that the State may, if it should so desire, appeal to Congress from the determination of the Secretary of Agriculture. If the next Congress shall not direct such sum to be paid, it shall be covered into the Treasury.

Sec. 7. That the Secretary of Agriculture shall make an annual report to Congress of the receipts, expenditures, and results of the cooperative agricultural extension work in all of the States receiving the benefits of this Act, and also whether the appropriation of any State has been withheld; and if so, the reasons therefor.

Sec. 8. That Congress may at any time alter, amend, or repeal any or all of the provisions of this Act.

Source:
Statutes at Large, Vol. 38, pp. 372–374.

Federal Trade Commission Act, 1914

National U.S. legislation enacted September 26, 1914, designed to prohibit "unfair methods of competition" in interstate commerce. It established the bipartisan Federal Trade Commission (FTC), consisting of five members appointed by the president and approved by the Senate. The FTC was authorized to investigate possible violations of antitrust legislation by all interstate businesses (excepting banks and common carriers, which were governed by other regulations) and to issue cease-and-desist orders subject to federal judicial review to eliminate unfair business practices. The act gave the FTC the power to gather information, to require annual or special reports from corporations, and to ensure compliance with federal court rulings on such matters.

An Act
To create a Federal Trade Commission, to define its powers and duties, and for other purposes.

Be it enacted by the Senate and House of Representatives of the United States of America in Congress assembled, That a commission is hereby created and established, to be known as the Federal Trade Commission (hereinafter referred to as the commission), which shall be composed of five commissioners, who shall be appointed by the President, by and with the advice and consent of the Senate. Not more than three of the commissioners shall be members of the same political party. The first commissioners appointed shall continue in office for terms of three, four, five, six, and seven years, respectively, from the date of the taking effect of this Act, the term of each to be designated by the President, but their successors shall be appointed for terms of seven years, except that any person chosen to fill a vacancy shall be appointed only for the unexpired term of the commissioner whom he shall succeed. The commission shall choose a chairman from its own membership. No commissioner shall engage in any other business, vocation, or employment. Any commissioner may be removed by the President for inefficiency, neglect of duty, or malfeasance in office. A vacancy in the commission shall not impair the right of the remaining commissioners to exercise all the powers of the commission.

The commission shall have an official seal, which shall be judicially noticed.

Sec. 2. That each commissioner shall receive a salary of $10,000 a year, payable in the same manner as the salaries of the judges of the courts of the United States. The commission shall appoint a secretary, who shall receive a salary of $5,000 a year, payable in like manner, and it shall have authority to employ and fix the compensation of such attorneys, special experts, examiners, clerks, and other employees as it may from time to time find necessary for the proper performance of its duties and as may be from time to time appropriated for by Congress.

With the exception of the secretary, a clerk to each commissioner, the attorneys, and such special experts and examiners as the commission may from time to time find necessary for the conduct of its work, all employees of the commission shall be a part of the classified civil service, and shall enter the service under such rules and regulations as may be prescribed by the commission and by the Civil Service Commission.

All of the expenses of the commission, including all necessary expenses for transportation incurred by the commissioners or by their employees under their orders, in making any investigation, or upon official business in any other places than in the city of Washington, shall be allowed and paid on the presentation of itemized vouchers therefor approved by the commission.

Until otherwise provided by law, the commission may rent suitable offices for its use.

The Auditor for the State and Other Departments shall receive and examine all accounts of expenditures of the commission.

Sec. 3. That upon the organization of the commission and election of its chairman, the Bureau of Corporations and the offices of Commissioner and Deputy Commissioner of Corporations shall cease to exist; and all pending investigations and proceedings of the Bureau of Corporations shall be continued by the commission.

All clerks and employees of the said bureau shall be transferred to and become clerks and employees of the commission at their present grades and salaries. All records, papers, and property of the said bureau shall become records, papers, and property of the commission, and all unexpended funds and appropriations for the use and maintenance of the said bureau, including any allotment already made to it by the Secretary of Commerce from the contingent appropriation for the Department of Commerce for the fiscal year nineteen hundred and fifteen, or from the departmental printing fund for the fiscal year nineteen hundred and fifteen, shall become funds and appropriations available to be expended by the commission in the exercise of the powers, authority, and duties conferred on it by this Act.

The principal office of the commission shall be in the city of Washington, but it may meet and exercise all its powers at any other place. The commission may, by one or more of its members, or by such examiners as it may designate, prosecute any inquiry necessary to its duties in any part of the United States.

Sec. 4. That the words defined in this section shall have the following meaning when found in this Act, to wit:

"Commerce" means commerce among the several States or with foreign nations, or in any Territory of the United States or in the District of Columbia, or between any such Territory and another, or between any such Territory and any State or foreign nation, or between the District of Columbia and any State or Territory or foreign nation.

"Corporation" means any company or association incorporated or unincorporated, which is organized to carry on business for profit and has shares of capital or capital stock, and any company or association, incorporated or unincorporated, without shares of capital or capital stock, except partnerships, which is organized to carry on business for its own profit or that of its members.

"Documentary evidence" means all documents, papers and correspondence in existence at and after the passage of this Act.

"Acts to regulate commerce" means the Act entitled "An Act to regulate commerce," approved February Fourteenth, eighteen hundred and eighty-seven, and all Acts amendatory thereof and supplementary thereto.

"Antitrust acts" means the Act entitled "An act to protect trade and commerce against unlawful restraints and monopolies," approved July second, eighteen hundred and ninety; also the sections seventy-three to seventy-seven, inclusive, of an Act entitled "An act to reduce taxation, to provide revenue for the Government, and for other purposes," approved August twenty-seventh, eighteen hundred and ninety-four; and also the Act entitled "An act to amend sections seventy-three and seventy-six of the Act of August twenty-seventh, eighteen hundred and ninety- four, entitled 'An act to reduce taxation, to provide revenue for the Government, and for other purposes,'" approved February twelfth, nineteen hundred and thirteen.

Sec. 5. That unfair methods of competition in commerce are hereby declared unlawful.

The commission is hereby empowered and directed to prevent persons, partnerships, or corporations, except banks, and common carriers subject to the Acts to regulate commerce, from using unfair methods of competition in commerce.

Whenever the commission shall have reason to believe that any such person, partnership, or corporation has been or is using any unfair method of competition in commerce, and if it shall appear to the commission that a proceeding by it in respect thereof would be to the interest of the public, it shall issue and serve upon such person, partnership, or corporation a complaint stating its changes in that respect, and containing a notice of a hearing upon a day and at a place therein fixed at least thirty days after the service of said complaint. The person, partnership, or corporation so complained of shall have the right to appear at the place and time so fixed and show cause why an order should not be entered by the commission requiring such person, partnership, or corporation to cease and desist from the violation of the law so charged in said complaint. Any person, partnership, or corporation may make application, and upon good cause shown may be allowed by the commission, to intervene and appear in said proceeding by counsel or in person. The testimony in any such proceeding shall be reduced to writing and filed in the office of the commission. If upon such hearing the commission shall be of the opinion that the method of competition in question is prohibited by this Act, it shall make a report in writing in which it shall state its findings as to the facts, and shall issue and cause to be served on such person, partnership, or corporation an order requiring such person, partnership, or corporation or cease and desist from using such method of competition. Until a transcript of the record in such hearing shall have been filed in a circuit court of appeals of the United States, as hereinafter provided, the commission may at any time, upon such notice and in such manner as it shall deem proper, modify of set aside, in whole or in part, any report or any order made or issued by it under this section.

If such person, partnership, or corporation fails to neglects to obey such order of the commission while the same is in effect, the commission may apply to the circuit court of appeals of the United States, within any circuit where the method of competition in question was used or where such person, partnership, or corporation resides or carries on business, for the enforcement of its order, and shall certify and file with its application a transcript of the entire record in the proceeding, including all the testimony taken and the report and order of the commission. Upon such filing of the application and transcript the court shall cause notice thereof to be served upon such person, partnership, or corporation and thereupon shall have jurisdiction of the proceeding and of the question determined therein, and shall have power to make and enter upon the pleadings, testimony, and proceedings set forth in such transcript a decree affirming, modifying, or setting aside the order of the commission. The findings of the commission as to the facts, if supported by testimony, shall be conclusive. If either party shall apply to the court for leave to adduce additional evidence, and shall show to the satisfaction of the court that such additional evidence is material and that there were reasonable grounds for the failure to adduce such evidence in the proceeding before the commission, the court may order such additional evidence to be taken before the commission and to be adduced upon the hearing in such manner and upon such terms and conditions as to the court may seem proper. The commission may modify its findings as to the facts or make new findings, by reason of the additional evidence so taken, and it shall file such modified or new findings, which, if supported by testimony, shall be conclusive, and its recommendation, if any, for the modification or setting aside of its original order, with the return of such additional evidence. The judgment and decree of the court shall be final, except that the same shall be subject to review by the Supreme Court upon certiorari as provided in section two hundred and forty of the Judicial Code.

Any party required by such order of the commission to cease and desist from using such method of competition may obtain a review of such order in said circuit court of appeals by filing in the court a written petition praying that the order of the commission be set aside. A copy of such petition shall be forthwith served upon the commission, and thereupon the commission forthwith shall certify and file in the court a transcript of the record as hereinbefore provided. Upon the filing of the transcript the court shall have the same jurisdiction to affirm, set aside, or modify the order of the commission as in the case of an application by the commission for the enforcement of its order, and the findings of the commission as to the facts, if supported by testimony, shall in like manner be conclusive.

The jurisdiction of the circuit court of appeals of the United States to enforce, set aside, or modify orders of the commission shall be exclusive.

Such proceedings in the circuit court of appeals shall be given precedence over other cases pending therein, and shall be in every way expedited. No order of the commission or judgment of the court to enforce the same shall in any wise relieve or absolve any person, partnership, or corporation from any liability under the antitrust acts.

Complaints, orders, and other processes of the commission under this section may be served by anyone duly authorized by the commission, either (a) by delivering a copy thereof to the person to be served, or to a member of the partnership to be served, or to the president, secretary, or other executive officer or a director of the corporation to be served; or (b) by leaving a copy thereof at the principal office or place of business of such person, partnership, or corporation; or (c) by registering and mailing a copy thereof addressed to such person, partnership, or corporation at his or its principal office or place of business. The verified return by the person so serving said complaint, order, or other process setting forth the manner of said service shall be proof of the same, and the return, post-office receipt for said complaint, order, or other process registered and mailed as aforesaid shall be proof of the service of the same.

Sec. 6. That the commission shall also have power—

(a) To gather and compile information concerning, and to investigate from time to time the organization, business, conduct, practices, and management of any corporation engaged in commerce, excepting banks and common carriers subject to the Act to regulate commerce, and its relation to other corporations and to individuals, associations, and partnerships.

(b) To require, by general or special orders, corporations engaged in commerce, excepting banks, and common carriers subject to the Act to regulate commerce, or any class of them, or any of them, respectively, to file with the commission in such form as the commission may prescribe annual or special, or both annual and special, reports or answers in writing to specific questions, furnishing to the commission such information as it may require as to the organization business, conduct, practices, management, and relation to other corporations, partnerships, and individuals of the respective corporations filing such reports or answers in writing. Such reports and answers shall be made under oath, or otherwise, as the commission may prescribe, and shall be filed with the commission within such reasonable period as the commission may prescribe, unless additional time be granted in any case by the commission.

(c) Whenever a final decree has been entered against any defendant corporation in any suit brought by the United States to prevent and restrain any violation of the antitrust Acts, to make investigation, upon its own initiative, of the manner in which the decree has been or is being carried out, and upon the application of the Attorney General it shall be its duty to make such investigation. It shall transmit to the Attorney General a report embodying its findings and recommendations as a result of any such investigation, and the report shall be made public in the discretion of the commission.

(d) Upon the direction of the President or either House of Congress to investigate and report the facts relating to any alleged violations of the antitrust Acts by any corporation.

(e) Upon the application of the Attorney General to investigate and make recommendations for the readjustment of the business of any corporation alleged to be violating the antitrust Acts in order that the corporation may thereafter maintain its organization, management, and conduct of business in accordance with law.

(f) To make public from time to time such portions of the information obtained by it hereunder, except trade secrets and names of customers, as it shall deem expedient in the public interest; and to make annual and special reports to the Congress and to submit therewith recommendations for additional legislation; and to provide for the publication of its reports and decisions in such form and manner as may be best adapted for public information and use.

(g) From time to time to classify corporations and to make rules and regulations for the purpose of carrying out the provisions of this Act.

(h) To investigate, from time to time, trade conditions in and with foreign countries where associations, combinations, or practices of manufacturers, merchants, or traders, or other conditions, may affect the foreign trade of the United States, and to report to Congress thereon, with such recommendations as it deems advisable.

Sec. 7. That in any suit in equity brought by or under the direction of the Attorney General as provided in the antitrust Acts, the court may, upon the conclusion of the testimony therein, if it shall be then of opinion that the complainant is entitled to relief, refer said suit to the commission, as a master in chancery, to ascertain and report an appropriate form of decree therein. The commission shall proceed upon such notice to the parties and under such rules of procedure as the court may prescribe, and upon the coming in of such report such exceptions may be filed and such proceedings had in relation thereto as upon the report of a master in other equity causes, but the court may adopt or reject such report, in whole or in part, and enter such decree as the nature of the case may in its judgment require.

Sec. 8. That the several departments and bureaus of the Government when directed by the President shall furnish the commission, upon its request, all records, papers, and information in their possession relating to any corporation subject to any of the provisions of this Act, and shall detail from time to time such officials and employees to the commission as he may direct.

Sec. 9. That for the purposes of this Act the commission, or its duly authorized agent or agents, shall at all reasonable times have access to, for the purpose of examination, and the right to copy any documentary evidence of any corporation being investigated or proceeded against; and the commission shall have power to require by subpoena the attendance and testimony of witnesses and the production of all such documentary evidence relating to any matter under investigation. Any member of the commission may sign subpoenas, and members and examiners of the commission may administer oaths and affirmations, examine witnesses, and receive evidence.

Such attendance of witnesses, and the production of such documentary evidence, may be required from any place in the United States, at any designated place of hearing. And in case of disobedience to a subpoena the commission may invoke the aid of any court of the United States in requiring the attendance and testimony of witnesses and the production of documentary evidence.

Any of the district courts of the United States within the jurisdiction of which such inquiry is carried on may, in case of contumacy or refusal to obey a subpoena issued to any corporation or other person, issue an order requiring such corporation or other person to appear before the commission, or to produce documentary evidence if so ordered, or to give evidence touching the matter in question; and any failure to obey such order of the court may be punished by such court as a contempt thereof.

Upon the application of the Attorney General of the United States, at the request of the commission, the district courts of the United States shall have jurisdiction to issue writs of mandamus commanding any person or corporation to comply with the provisions of this Act or any order of the commission made in pursuance thereof.

The commission may order testimony to be taken by deposition in any proceeding or investigation pending under this Act at any stage of such proceeding or investigation. Such depositions may be taken before any person designated by the commission and having power to administer oaths. Such testimony shall be reduced to writing by the person taking the deposition, or under his direction, and shall then be subscribed by the deponent. Any person may be compelled to appear and depose and to produce documentary evidence in the same manner as witnesses may be compelled to appear and testify and produce documentary evidence before the commission as hereinbefore provided.

Witnesses summoned before the commission shall be paid the same fees and mileage that are paid witnesses in the courts of the United States, and witnesses whose depositions are taken and the persons taking the same shall severally be entitled to the same fees as are paid for like services in the courts of the United States.

No person shall be excused from attending and testifying or from producing documentary evidence before the commission or in obedience to the subpoena of the commission on the ground or for the reason that the testimony or evidence, documentary or otherwise, required of him may tend to criminate him or subject him to a penalty or forfeiture. But no natural person shall be prosecuted or subjected to any penalty or forfeiture for or on account of any transaction, matter, or thing concerning which he may testify, or produce evidence, documentary or otherwise, before the commission in obedience to a subpoena issued by it: *Provided,* That no natural person so testifying shall be exempt from prosecution and punishment for perjury committed in so testifying.

Sec. 10. That any person who shall neglect or refuse to attend and testify, or to answer any lawful inquiry, or to produce documentary evidence, if in his power to do so, in obedience to the subpoena or lawful requirement of the commission, shall be guilty of an offense and upon conviction thereof by a court of competent jurisdiction shall be punished by a fine of not less than $1,000 nor more than $5,000, or by imprisonment for not more than one year, or by both such fine and imprisonment.

Any person who shall willfully make, or cause to be made, any false entry or statement of fact in any report required to be made under this Act, or who shall willfully make, or cause to be made, any false entry in any account, record, or memorandum kept by the corporation subject to this Act, or who shall willfully neglect or fail to make, or to cause to be made, full, true, and correct entries in such accounts, records, or memoranda of all facts and transactions appertaining to the business of such corporation, or who shall willfully remove out of the jurisdiction of the United States, or willfully mutilate, alter, or by any other means falsify and documentary evidence of such corporation, or who shall willfully refuse to submit to the commission or to any of its authorized agents, for the purpose of inspection and taking copies, any documentary evidence of such corporation in his possession or within his control, shall be deemed guilty of an offense against the United States, and shall be subject, upon conviction in any court of the United States of competent jurisdiction, to a fine of not less than $1,000 nor more than $5,000, or to imprisonment for a term of not more than three years, or to both such fine and imprisonment.

If any corporation required by this Act to file any annual or special report shall fail so to do within the time fixed by the commission for filing the same, and such failure shall continue for thirty days after notice of such default, the corporation shall forfeit to the United States the sum of $100 for each and every day of the continuance of such failure, which forfeiture shall be payable into the Treasury of the United States, and shall be recoverable in a civil suit in the name of the United States brought in the district where the corporation has its principal office or in any district in which it shall do business. It shall be the duty of the various district attorneys, under the direction of the Attorney General of the United States, to prosecute for the recovery of forfeitures. The costs and expenses of such prosecution shall be paid out of the appropriation for the expenses of the courts of the United States.

Any officer or employee of the commission who shall make public any information obtained by the commission without its authority, unless directed by a court, shall be deemed guilty of a misdemeanor, and, upon conviction thereof, shall be punished by a fine not exceeding $5,000, or by imprisonment not exceeding one year, or by fine and imprisonment, in the discretion of the court.

Sec. 11. Nothing contained in this Act shall be construed to prevent or interfere with the enforcement of the provisions of the antitrust Acts or the Acts to regulate commerce, nor shall anything contained in the Act be construed to alter, modify, or repeal the said antitrust Acts or the Acts to regulate commerce or any part or parts thereof.

Source:
Statutes at Large, Vol. 38, pp. 717–724.

Clayton Antitrust Act, 1914

Federal legislation enacted on October 15, 1914, that supplemented the Sherman Antitrust Act and outlawed specific practices that would "substantially lessen competition or tend to create a monopoly in any line of commerce." It prohibited exclusive sales contracts, discrimination in prices among different producers, interlocking directorates in large corporations engaged in the same business, rebates, and the acquisition of stock by one company in another. Labor unions and agricultural cooperatives were exempted from the act on the grounds that "the labor of a human being is not a commodity or article of commerce." As a result, the Clayton Act sought to overcome impediments to collective action by labor, such as the 1908 U.S. Supreme Court decision *Loewe v. Lawlor* (208

U.S. 274). In this case, the first applying the Sherman Antitrust Act against organized labor, the Court held that a union boycott constituted a conspiracy in restraint of trade.

An Act

An Act To supplement existing laws against unlawful restraints and monopolies, and for other purposes.

Be it enacted by the Senate and House of Representatives of the United States of America in Congress assembled, That "antitrust laws," as used herein, includes the Act entitled "An Act to protect trade and commerce against unlawful restraints and monopolies," approved July second, eighteen hundred and ninety; sections seventy-three to seventy-seven, inclusive, of an Act entitled "An Act to reduce taxation, to provide revenue for the Government, and for other purposes," of August twenty-seventh, eighteen hundred and ninety-four; and Act entitled "An Act to amend sections seventy-three and seventy-six of the Act of August twenty-seventh, eighteen hundred and ninety-four, entitled 'An Act to reduce taxation, to provide revenue for the Government, and for other purposes,'" approved February twelfth, nineteen hundred and thirteen, and also this Act.

"Commerce," as used herein, means trade or commerce among the several States and with foreign nations, or between the District of Columbia or any Territory of the United States and any State, Territory, or foreign nation, or between any insular possessions or other places under the jurisdiction of the United States, or between any such possession or place and any State or Territory of the United States or the District of Columbia or any foreign nation, or within the District of Columbia or any Territory or any insular possession or other place under the jurisdiction of the United States: *Provided,* That nothing in this Act contained shall apply to the Philippine Islands.

The word "person" or "persons" wherever used in this Act shall be deemed to include corporations and associations existing under or authorized by the laws of either the United States, the laws of any of the Territories, the laws of any State, or the laws of any foreign country.

Sec. 2. That it shall be unlawful for any person engaged in commerce, in the course of such commerce, either directly or indirectly to discriminate in price between different purchasers of commodities, which commodities are sold for use, consumption, or resale within the United States or any Territory thereof or the District of Columbia or any insular possession or other place under the jurisdiction of the United States, where the effect of such discrimination may be to substantially lessen competition or tend to create a monopoly in any line of commerce: *Provided,* That nothing herein contained shall prevent discrimination in price between purchasers of commodities on account of differences in the grade, quality, or quantity of the commodity sold, or that makes only due allowance for difference in the cost of selling or transportation, or discrimination in price in the same or different communities made in good faith to meet competition: *And provided further,* That nothing herein contained shall prevent persons engaged in selling goods, wares, or merchandise in commerce from selecting their own customers in bona fide transactions and not in restraint of trade.

Sec. 3. That it shall be unlawful for any person engaged in commerce, in the course of such commerce, to lease or make a sale or contract for sale of goods, wares, merchandise, machinery, supplies or other commodities, whether patented or unpatented, for use, consumption or resale within the United States or and Territory thereof or the District of Columbia or any insular possession or other place under the jurisdiction of the United States, or fix a price charged therefor, or discount from, or rebate upon, such price, or the condition, agreement or understanding that the lessee or purchaser thereof shall not use or deal in the goods wares, merchandise, machinery, supplies or other commodities of a competitor or competitors of the lessor or seller, where the effect of such lease, sale, or contract for sale or such condition, agreement or understanding may be to substantially lessen competition or tend to create a monopoly in any line of commerce.

Sec. 4. That any person who shall be injured in his business or property by reason of anything forbidden in the antitrust laws may sue therefor in any district court of the United States in the district in which the defendant resides or is found or has an agent, without respect to the amount in controversy, and shall recover threefold the damages by him sustained, and the cost of suit, including a reasonable attorney's fee.

Sec. 5. That a final judgment or decree hereafter rendered in any criminal prosecution or in any suit or proceeding in equity brought by or on behalf of the United States under the antitrust laws to the effect that a defendant has violated said laws shall be prima facie evidence against such defendant in any suit or proceeding brought by any other party against such defendant under said laws as to all matters respecting which said judgment or decree would be an estoppel as between the parties thereto: *Provided,* This section shall not apply to consent judgments or decrees entered before any testimony has been taken: *Provided further,* This section shall not apply to consent judgments or decrees rendered in criminal proceedings or suits in equity, now pending, in which the taking of testimony has been commenced but has not been concluded, provided such judgments or decrees are rendered before any further testimony is taken.

Whenever any suit or proceeding in equity or criminal prosecution is instituted by the United States to prevent, restrain or punish violations of any of the antitrust laws, to running of the statute of limitations in respect of each and every private right of action arising under said laws and based in whole or in part on any matter complained of in said suit or proceeding shall be suspended during the pendency thereof.

Sec. 6. That the labor of a human being is not a commodity or article of commerce. Nothing contained in the antitrust laws shall be construed to forbid the existence and operation of labor, agricultural, or horticultural organizations, instituted for the purposes of mutual help, and not having capital stock of conducted for profit, or to forbid or restrain individual members of such organizations from lawfully carrying out the legitimate objects thereof; nor shall such organizations, or the members thereof, be held or construed to be illegal combinations or conspiracies in restraint of trade, under the antitrust law.

Sec. 7. That no corporation engaged in commerce shall acquire, directly or indirectly, the whole or any part of the stock or other share capital of another corporation engaged also in commerce, where the effect of such acquisition may be to substantially lessen competition between the corporation whose stock is so acquired and the corporation making the acquisition, or to restrain such commerce in any section or community, or tend to create a monopoly of any line of commerce.

No corporation shall acquire, directly or indirectly, the whole or any part of the stock or other share capital of two or more corporations engaged in commerce where the effect of such acquisition, or the use of such stock by the voting or granting of proxies or otherwise, may be to substantially lessen competition between such corporations, or any of them, whose stock or other share capital is so acquired, or to restrain such commerce in any section or community, or tend to create a monopoly of any line of commerce.

This section shall not apply to corporations purchasing such stock solely for investment and not using the same by voting or otherwise to bring about, or in attempting to bring about, the substantial lessening of competition. Nor shall anything contained in this section prevent a corporation engaged in commerce from causing the formation of subsidiary corporations for the actual carrying on of their immediate lawful business, or the natural and legitimate branches or extensions thereof, or from owning and holding all or a part of the stock of such subsidiary corporations, when the effect of such formation is not to substantially lessen competition.

Nor shall anything herein contained be construed to prohibit any common carrier subject to the laws to regulate commerce from aiding in the construction of branches or short lines so located as to become feeders to the main line of the company so aiding in such construction or from acquiring or owning all or any part of the stock of such branch lines, nor to prevent any such common carrier from acquiring and owning all or any part of the stock of a branch or short line constructed by an independent company where there is no substantial competition between the company owning the branch line so constructed and the company owning the main line acquiring the property or an interest therein, nor to prevent such common carrier from extending any of its lines through the medium of the acquisition of stock or otherwise of any other such common carrier where there is no substantial competition between the company extending its lines and the company whose stock, property, or an interest therein is so acquired.

Nothing contained in this section shall be held to affect or impair any right heretofore legally acquired: *Provided*, That nothing in this section shall be held or construed to authorize or make lawful anything heretofore prohibited or made illegal by the antitrust laws, nor to exempt any person from the penal provisions thereof or the civil remedies therein provided.

Sec. 8. That from and after two years from the date of the approval of this Act no person shall at the same time be a director or other officer or employee of more than one bank, banking association or trust company, organized or operating under the laws of the United States, either of which has deposits, capital, surplus, and undivided profits aggregating more than $5,000,000; and no private banker or person who is a director in any bank or trust company, organized and operating under the laws of a State, having deposits, capital, surplus, and undivided profits aggregating more than $5,000,000 shall be eligible to be a director in any bank or banking association organized or operating under the laws of the United States. The eligibility of a director, officer, or employee under the foregoing provisions shall be determined by the average amount of deposits, capital, surplus, and undivided profits as shown in the official statements of such bank, banking association, or trust company filed provided by law during the fiscal year next preceding the date set for the annual election of directors, and when a director, officer, or employee has been elected or selected in accordance with the provisions of this Act it shall be lawful for him to continue as such for one year thereafter under said election or employment.

No bank, banking association or trust company, organized or operating under the laws of the United States, in any city or incorporated town or village of more than two hundred thousand inhabitants, as shown by the last preceding decennial census of the United States, shall have as a director or other officer or employee any private banker or any director or other officer or employee of any other bank, banking association or trust company located in the same place: *Provided*, That nothing in this section shall apply to mutual savings banks not having a capital stock represented by shares: *Provided further,* That a director or other officer or employee of such bank, banking association or trust company may be a director or other officer or employee of not more than one other bank or trust company organized under the laws of the United States or any State where the entire capital stock of one is owned by stockholders in the other: *And provided further,* That nothing contained in this section shall forbid a director of class A of a Federal reserve bank, as defined in the Federal Reserve Act, from being an officer or director or both an officer and director in one member bank.

That from and after two years from the date of approval of this Act no person at the same time shall be a director in any two or more corporations, any one of which has capital, surplus, and undivided profits aggregating more than $1,000,000, engaged in whole or in part in commerce, other than banks, banking associations, trust companies and common carriers subject to the Act to regulate commerce, approved February fourth, eighteen hundred and eighty-seven, if such corporations are or shall have been theretofore, by virtue of their business and location of operation, competitors, so that the elimination of competition by agreement between them would constitute a violation of any of the provisions of any of the antitrust laws. The eligibility of a director under the foregoing provision shall be determined by the aggregate amount of capital, surplus, and undivided profits, exclusive of dividends declared but not paid to stockholders, at the end of the fiscal year of said corporation next preceding the election of directors, and when a director has been elected in accordance with the provisions of this Act it shall be lawful for him to continue as such for one year thereafter.

When any person elected or chosen as a director or officer or selected as an employee of any bank or other corporation subject to the provisions of this Act is eligible at the time of his election or selection to act for such bank or other corporation in such capacity his eligibility to act in such capacity shall not be affected and he shall not become or be deemed amenable to any of the provisions hereof by reason of any change in the affairs of such bank or other corporation from whatsoever cause, whether specifically excepted by any of the provisions hereof or not, until the expiration of one year from the date of his election or employment.

Sec. 9. Every president, director, officer or manager of any firm, association or corporation engaged in commerce as a common carrier, who embezzles, steals, abstracts or willfully misapplies, or willfully permits to be misapplied, any of the moneys, funds, credits, securities, property or assets of such firm, association or corporation, arising or accruing from, or used in, such commerce, in whole or in part, or willfully or knowingly converts the same to his own use or to the use of another, shall be deemed guilty of a felony and upon conviction shall be fined not less than $500 or confined in the penitentiary not less than one year nor more than ten years, or both, in the discretion of the court.

Prosecutions hereunder may be in the district court of the United States for the district wherein the offense may have been committed.

That nothing in this section shall be held to take away or impair the jurisdiction of the courts of the several States under the laws thereof; and a judgment of conviction or acquittal on the merits under the laws of any State shall be a bar to any prosecution hereunder for the same act or acts.

Sec. 10. That after two years from the approval of this Act no common carrier engaged in commerce shall have any dealings in securities, supplies or other articles of commerce, or shall make or have any contracts for construction or maintenance of any kind, to the amount of more than $50,000, in the aggregate, in any one year, with another corporation, firm, partnership or association when the said common carrier shall have upon its board of directors or as its president, manager or as its purchasing or selling officer, or agent in the particular transaction, any person who is at the same time a director, manager, or purchasing or selling officer of, or who has any substantial interest in, such other corporation, firm, partnership or association, unless and except such purchases shall be made from, or such dealings shall be with, the bidder whose bid is the most favorable to such common carrier, to be ascertained by competitive bidding under regulations to be prescribed by rule or otherwise by the Interstate Commerce Commission. No bid shall be received unless the name and address of the bidder or the names and addresses of the officers, directors and general managers thereof, if the bidder be a corporation, or of the members, if it be a partnership or firm, be given with the bid.

Any person who shall, directly or indirectly, do or attempt to do anything to prevent anyone from bidding or shall do any act to prevent free and fair competition among the bidders or those desiring to bid shall be punished as prescribed in this section in the case of an officer or director.

Every such common carrier having any such transactions or making any such purchases shall within thirty days after making the same file with the Interstate Commerce Commission a full and detailed statement of the transaction showing the manner of the competitive bidding, who were the bidders, and the names and addresses of the directors and officers of the corporations and the members of the firm or partnership bidding; and whenever the said commission shall, after investigation or hearing, have reason to believe that the law has been violated in and about the said purchases or transactions it shall transmit all papers and documents and its own views or findings regarding the transaction to the Attorney General.

If any common carrier shall violate this section it shall be fined not exceeding $25,000; and every such director, agent, manager or officer thereof who shall have knowingly voted for or directed the act constituting such violation or who shall have aided or abetted in such violation shall be deemed guilty of a misdemeanor and shall be fined not exceeding $5,000, or confined in jail not exceeding one year, or both, in the discretion of the court.

Sec. 11. That authority to enforce compliance with sections two, three, seven and eight of this Act by the persons respectively subject thereto is hereby vested: in the Interstate Commerce Commission where applicable to common carriers, in the Federal Reserve Board where applicable to banks, banking associations and trust companies, and in the Federal Trade Commission where applicable to all other character of commerce, to be exercised as follows:

Whenever the commission or board vested with jurisdiction thereof shall have reason to believe that any person is violating or has violated any of the provisions of sections two, three, seven and eight of this Act, it shall issue and serve upon such person a complaint stating its charges in that respect, and containing a notice of a hearing upon a day and at a place therein fixed at least thirty days after the service of said compliant. The person so complained of shall have the right to appear at the place and time so fixed and show cause why an order should not be entered by the commission or board requiring such person to cease and desist from the violation of the law so charged in said complaint. Any person may make application, and upon good cause shown may be allowed by the commission or board, to intervene and appear in said proceeding by counsel or in person. The testimony in any such proceeding shall be reduced to writing and filed in the office of the commission or board. If upon such hearing the commission or board, as the case may be, shall be of the opinion that any of the provisions of said section have been or are being violated, it shall make a report in writing in which it shall state its findings as to the facts, and shall issue and cause to be served on such person an order requiring such person to cease and desist from such violations, and divest itself of the stock held or rid itself of the directors chosen contrary to the provisions of sections seven and eight of this Act, if any there be, in the manner and within the time fixed by said order. Until a transcript of the record in such hearing shall have been filed in a circuit court of appeals of the United States, as hereinafter provided, the commission or board may at any time, upon such notice and in such manner as it shall deem proper, modify or set aside, in whole or in part, any report or any order made or issued by it under this section.

If such person fails or neglects to obey such order of the commission or board while the same is in effect, the commission or board may apply to the circuit court of appeals of the United States, within any circuit where the violation complained of was or is being committed or where such person resides or carries on business, for the enforcement of its order, and shall certify and file with its application a transcript of the entire record in the proceeding, including all the testimony taken and the report and order of the commission or board. Upon such filing of the application and transcript the court shall cause notice thereof to be served upon such person and thereupon shall have jurisdiction of the proceeding and of the question determined therein, and shall have power to make and enter upon the pleadings, testimony, and proceedings set forth in such transcript a decree affirming, modifying, or setting aside the order of the commission or board. The findings of the commission or board as to the facts, if supported by testimony, shall be conclusive. If either party shall apply to the court for leave to adduce additional evidence, and shall show to the satisfaction of the court that such additional evidence is material and that there were reasonable grounds for the failure to adduce such evidence in the proceeding before the commission or board, the court may order such additional evidence to be taken before the commission or board and to be adduced upon the hearing in such manner and upon such terms and conditions as to the court may seem proper. The commission or board may modify its findings as to the facts, or make new findings, by reason of the additional evidence so taken, and it shall file such modified or new findings, which, if supported by testimony, shall be conclusive, and its recommendation, if any, for the modification or setting aside of its original order, with the return of such additional evidence. The judgment and decree of the court shall be final, except that the same shall be subject to review by the Supreme Court upon certiorari as provided in section two hundred and forty of the Judicial Code.

Any party required by such order of the commission or board to cease and desist from a violation charged may obtain a review of such order in said circuit of appeals by filing in the court a written petition praying that the order of the commission or board be set aside. A copy of such petition shall be forthwith served upon the commission or board, and thereupon the commission or board forthwith shall certify and file in the court a transcript of the record as hereinbefore provided. Upon the filing of the transcript the court shall have the same jurisdiction to affirm, set aside, or modify the order of the commission or board as in the case of an application by the commission or board for the enforcement of its order, and the findings of the commission or board as to the facts, if supported by testimony, shall in like manner be conclusive.

The jurisdiction of the circuit court of appeals of the United States to enforce, set aside, or modify orders of the commission or board shall be exclusive.

Such proceedings in the circuit court of appeals shall be given precedence over other cases pending therein, and shall be in every way expedited. No order of the commission or board or the judgment of the court to enforce the same shall in any wise relieve or absolve any person from any liability under the antitrust Acts.

Complaints, orders, and other processes of the commission or board under this section may be served by anyone duly authorized by the commission or board, either (a) by delivering a copy thereof to the person to be served, or to a member of the partnership to be served, or to the president, secretary, or other executive officer or a director of the corporation to be served; or (b) by leaving a copy thereof at the principal office or place of business of such person; or (c) by registering and mailing a copy thereof addressed to such person at his principal office of place of business. The verified return by the person so serving said complaint, order, or other process setting forth the manner of said service shall be proof of the same, and the return post-office receipt for said complaint, order, or other process registered and mailed as aforesaid shall be proof of the service of the same.

Sec. 12. That any suit, action, or proceeding under the antitrust laws against a corporation may be brought not only in the judicial district whereof it is an inhabitant, but also in any district wherein it may be found or transacts business; and all process in such cases may be served in the district of which it is an inhabitant, or wherever it may be found.

Sec. 13. That in any suit, action, or proceeding brought by or on behalf of the United States subpoenas for witnesses who are required to attend a court of the United States in any judicial district in any case, civil or criminal, arising under the antitrust laws may run into any other district: *Provided,* That in civil cases no writ of subpoena shall issue for witnesses living out of the district in which the court is held at a greater distance than one hundred miles from the place of holding the same without the permission of the trial court being first had upon proper application and cause shown.

Sec. 14. That whenever a corporation shall violate any of the penal provisions of the antitrust laws, such violation shall be deemed to be also that of the individual directors, officers, or agents of such corporation who shall have authorized, ordered, or done any of the acts constituting in whole or in part such violation, and such violation shall be deemed a misdemeanor, and upon conviction therefor of any such director, officer, or agent he shall be punished by a fine of not exceeding $5,000 or by imprisonment for not exceeding one year, or by both, in the discretion of the court.

Sec. 15. That the several district courts of the United States are hereby invested with jurisdiction to prevent and restrain violations of this Act, and it shall be the duty of the several district attorneys of the United States, in their respective districts, under the direction of the Attorney General, to institute proceedings in equity to prevent and restrain such violations. Such proceedings may be by way of petition setting forth the case and praying that such violation shall be enjoined or otherwise prohibited. When the parties complained of shall have been duly notified of such petition, the court shall proceed, as soon as may be, to the hearing and determination of the case; and pending such petition, and before final decree, the court may at any time make such temporary restraining order or prohibition as shall be deemed just in the premises. Whenever it shall appear to the court before which any such proceeding may be pending that the ends of justice require that other parties should be brought before the court, the court may cause them to be summoned, whether they reside in the district in which the court is held or not, and subpoenas to that end may be served in any district by the marshal thereof.

Sec. 16. That any person, firm, corporation, or association shall be entitled to sue for and have injunctive relief, in any court of the United States having jurisdiction over the parties, against threatened loss or damage by a violation of the antitrust laws, including sections two, three, seven and eight of this Act, when and under the same conditions and principles as injunctive relief against threatened conduct that will cause loss or damage is granted by courts of equity, under the rules governing such proceedings, and upon the execution of proper bond against damages for an injunction improvidently granted and a showing that the danger of irreparable loss or damage is immediate, a preliminary injunction may issue: *Provided,* That nothing herein contained shall be construed to entitle any person, firm, corporation, or association, except the United States, to bring suit in equity for injunctive relief against any common carrier subject to the provisions of the Act to regulate commerce, approved February fourth, eighteen hundred and eighty-seven, in respect of any matter subject to the regulation, supervision, or other jurisdiction of the Interstate Commerce Commission.

Sec. 17. That no preliminary injunction shall be issued without notice to the opposite party.

No temporary restraining order shall be granted without notice to the opposite party unless it shall clearly appear from specific facts shown by affidavit or by the verified bill that immediate and irreparable injury, loss, or damage will result to the applicant before notice can be served and a hearing had thereon. Every such temporary restraining order shall be indorsed with the date and hour of issuance, shall be forthwith filed in the clerk's office and entered of record, shall define the injury and state why it is irreparable and why the order was granted without notice, and shall by its terms expire within such time after entry, not to exceed ten days, as the court or judge may fix, unless within the time so fixed the order is extended for a like period for good cause shown, and the reasons for such extension shall be entered of record. In case a temporary restraining order shall be granted without notice in the contingency specified, the matter of the issuance of a preliminary injunction shall be set down for a hearing at the earliest possible time and shall take precedence of all matters except older matters of the same character; and when the same comes up for hearing the party obtaining the temporary restraining order shall proceed with the application for a preliminary injunction, and if he does not do so the court shall dissolve the temporary restraining order. Upon two days' notice to the party obtaining such temporary restraining order the opposite party may appear and move the dissolution or modification of the order, and in that event the court or judge shall proceed to hear and determine the motion as expeditiously as the ends of justice may require.

Section two hundred and sixty-three of an Act entitled "An Act to codify, revise, and amend the laws relating to the judiciary," approved March third, nineteen hundred and eleven, is hereby repealed.

Nothing in this section contained shall be deemed to alter, repeal, or amend section two hundred and sixty-six of an Act entitled "An Act to codify, revise, and amend the laws relating to the judiciary," approved March third, nineteen hundred and eleven.

Sec. 18. That, except as otherwise provided in section 16 of this Act, no restraining order or interlocutory order of injunction shall issue, except upon the giving of security by the applicant in such sum as the court or judge may deem proper, conditioned upon the payment of such costs and damages as may be incurred or suffered by any party who may be found to have been wrongfully enjoined or restrained thereby.

Sec. 19. That every order of injunction or restraining order shall set forth the reasons for the issuance of the same, shall be specific in terms, and shall describe in reasonable detail, and not by reference to the bill of complaint or other document, the act or acts sought to be restrained, and shall be binding only upon the parties to the suit, their officers, agents, servants, employees, and attorneys, or those in active concert or participating with them, and who shall, by personal service or otherwise, have received actual notice of the same.

Sec. 20. That no restraining order or injunction shall be granted by any court of the United States, or a judge or the judges thereof, in any case between an employer and employees, or between employers and employees, or between employees, or between persons employed and persons seeking employment, involving, or growing out of, a dispute concerning terms or conditions of employment, unless necessary to prevent irreparable injury to property, or to a property right, of the party making the application, for which injury there is no adequate remedy at law, and such property or property right must be described with particularity in the application, which must be in writing and sworn to by the applicant or by his agent or attorney.

And no such restraining order or injunction shall prohibit any person or persons, whether singly or in concert, from terminating any relation of employment, or from ceasing to perform any work or labor, or from recommending, advising, or persuading others by peaceful means so to do; or from attending at any place where any such person or persons may lawfully be, for the purpose of peacefully obtaining or communicating information, or from peacefully persuading any person to work or to abstain from working; or from ceasing to patronize or to employ any party to such dispute, or from recommending, advising, or persuading others by peaceful and lawful means so to do; or from paying or giving to, or withholding from, any person engaged in such dispute, any strike benefits or other moneys or things of value; or from peaceably assembling in a lawful manner, and for lawful purposes; or from doing any act or thing which might lawfully be done in the absence of such dispute by any party thereto; nor shall any of the acts specified in this paragraph be considered or held to be violations of any law of the United States.

Sec. 21. That any person who shall willfully disobey any lawful writ, process, order, rule, decree, or command of any district court of the United States or any court of the District of Columbia by doing any act or thing therein, or thereby forbidden to be done by him, if the act or thing so done by him be of such character as to constitute also a criminal offense under any statute of the United States, or under the laws of any State in which the act was committed, shall be proceeded against for his said contempt as hereinafter provided.

Sec. 22. That whenever it shall be made to appear to any district court of judge thereof, or to any judge therein sitting, by the return of a proper officer on lawful process, or upon the affidavit of some credible person, or by information filed by any district attorney, that there is reasonable ground to believe that any person has been guilty of such contempt, the court or judge thereof, or any judge therein sitting, may issue a rule requiring the said person so charged to show cause upon a day certain why he should not be punished therefor, which rule, together with a copy of the affidavit or information, shall be served upon the person charged, with sufficient promptness to enable him to prepare for and make return to the order at the time fixed therein. If upon or by such return, in the judgment of the court, the alleged contempt be not sufficiently purged, a trial shall be directed at a time and place fixed by the court: *Provided, however,* That if the accused, being a natural person, fail or refuse to make return to the rule to show cause, an attachment may issue against his person to compel an answer, and in case of his continued failure or refusal, or if for any reason it be impracticable to dispose of the matter on the return day, he may be required to give reasonable bail for his attendance at the trial and his submission to the final judgment of the court. Where the accused is a body corporate, an attachment for the sequestration of its property may be issued upon like refusal or failure to answer.

In all cases within the purview of this Act such trial may be by the court, or, upon demand of the accused, by a injury; in which latter event the court may impanel a jury from the jurors then in attendance, or the court or the judge thereof in chambers may cause a sufficient number of jurors to be selected and summoned, as provided by law, to attend at the time and place of trial, at which time a jury shall be selected and impaneled as upon a trial for misdemeanor; and such trial shall conform, as near as may be, to the practice in criminal cases prosecuted by indictment or upon information.

If the accused be found guilty, judgment shall be entered accordingly, prescribing the punishment, either by fine or imprisonment, or both, in the discretion of the court. Such fine shall be paid to the United States or to the complainant or other party injured by the act constituting the contempt, or may, where more than one is so damaged, be divided or apportioned among them as the court may direct, but in no case shall the fine to be paid to the United States exceed, in case the accused is a natural person, the sum of $1,000, nor shall such imprisonment exceed the term of six months: *Provided,* That in any case the court or a judge thereof may, for good cause shown, by affidavit or proof taken in open court or before such judge and filed with the papers in the case, dispense with the rule to show cause, and may issue an attachment for the arrest of the person charged with contempt; in which event such person, when arrested, shall be brought before such court or a judge thereof without unnecessary delay and shall be admitted to bail in a reasonable penalty for his appearance to answer to the charge or for trial for the contempt; and thereafter the proceedings shall be the same as provided herein in case the rule had issued in the first instance.

Sec. 23. That the evidence taken upon the trial of any persons so accused may be preserved by bill of exceptions, and any judgment of conviction may be reviewed upon writ of error in all respects as now provided by law in criminal cases, and may be affirmed, reversed, or modified as justice may require. Upon the granting of such writ of error, execution of judgment shall be stayed, and the accused, if thereby sentenced to imprisonment, shall be admitted to bail in such reasonable sum as may be required by the court, or by any justice, or any judge of any district court of the United States or any court of the District of Columbia.

Sec. 24. That nothing herein contained shall be construed to relate to contempts committed in the presence of the court, or so near thereto as to obstruct the administration of justice, nor to contempts committed in disobedience of any lawful writ, process, order, rule, decree, or command entered in any suit or action brought or prosecuted in the name of, or on behalf of, the United States, but the same, and all other cases of contempt not specifically embraced within section twenty-one of this Act, may be punished in conformity to the usages at law and in equity now prevailing.

Sec. 25. That no proceeding for contempt shall be instituted against any person unless begun within one year from the date of the act complained of; nor shall any such proceeding be a bar to any criminal prosecution for the same act or acts; but nothing herein contained shall affect any proceedings in contempt pending at the time of the passage of this Act.

Sec. 26. If any clause, sentence, paragraph, or part of this Act shall, for any reason, be adjudged by any court of competent jurisdiction to be invalid, such judgment shall not affect, impair, or invalidate the remainder thereof, but shall be confined in its operation to the clause, sentence, paragraph, or part thereof directly involved in the controversy in which such judgment shall have been rendered.

Source:

Statutes at Large, Vol. 38, pp. 730–740.

Harrison Act, 1914

Federal revenue legislation enacted on December 17, 1914, and effective April 1, 1915; it restricted the legal use of narcotics in the United States. The act, as amended, required everyone who imported, manufactured, sold, or dispensed narcotics to register and pay an occupational tax, to render returns, and to sell and exchange all narcotics in accordance with government recording requirements. All narcotics entering into domestic trade had to be tax-stamped. The Treasury Department was charged with enforcement responsibility. In effect, the act prohibited the legal use of narcotics, particularly opium and its derivatives, and encouraged the growth of the black market in drugs.

An Act

To provide for the registration of, with collectors of internal revenue, and to impose a special tax upon all persons who produce, import, manufacture, compound, deal in, dispense, sell, distribute, or give away opium or coca leaves, their salts, derivatives, or preparations, and for other purposes.

Be it enacted by the Senate and House of Representatives of the United States of America in Congress assembled, That on and after the first day of March, nineteen hundred and fifteen, every person who produces, imports, manufactures, compounds, deals in, dispenses, sells, distributes, or gives away opium or coca leaves or any compound, manufacture, salt, derivative, or preparation thereof, shall register with the collector of internal revenue of the district his name or style, place of business, and place or places where such business is to be carried on: *Provided,* That the office, or if none, then the residence of any person shall be considered for the purposes of this Act to be his place of business. At the time of such registry and on or before the first day of July, annually thereafter, every person who produces, imports, manufactures, compounds, deals in, dispenses, sells, distributes, or gives away any of the aforesaid drugs shall pay to the said collector a special tax at the rate of $1 per annum: *Provided,* That no employee of any person who produces, imports, manufactures, compounds, deals in, dispenses, sells, distributes, or gives away any of the aforesaid drugs, acting within the scope of his employment, shall be required to register or to pay the special tax provided by this section: *Provided further,* That the person who employs him shall have registered and paid the special tax as required by this section: *Provided further,* That officers of the United States Government who are lawfully engaged in making purchases of the above-named drugs for the various departments of the Army and Navy, the Public Health Service, and for Government hospitals and prisons, and officers of any State government, or of any county or municipality therein, who are lawfully engaged in making purchases of the above-named drugs for State, county, or municipal hospitals or prisons, and officials of any Territory or insular possession or the District of Columbia or of the United States who are lawfully engaged in making purchases of the above-named drugs for hospitals or prisons therein shall not be required to register and pay the special tax as herein required.

It shall be unlawful for any person required to register under the terms of this Act to produce, import, manufacture, compound, deal in, dispense, sell, distribute, or give away any of the aforesaid drugs without having registered and paid the special tax provided for in this section.

That the word "person" as used in this Act shall be construed to mean and include a partnership, association, company, or corporation, as well as a natural person; and all provisions of existing law relating to special taxes, so far as applicable, including the provisions of section thirty-two hundred and forty of the Revised Statutes of the United States are hereby extended to the special tax herein imposed.

That the Commissioner of Internal Revenue, with the approval of the Secretary of the Treasury, shall make all needful rules and regulations for carrying the provisions of this Act into effect.

Sec. 2. That it shall be unlawful for any person to sell, barter, exchange, or give away any of the aforesaid drugs except in pursuance of a written order of the person to whom such article is sold, bartered, exchanged, or given, on a form to be issued in blank for that purpose by the Commissioner of Internal Revenue. Every person who shall accept any such order, and in pursuance thereof shall sell, barter, exchange, or give away any of the aforesaid drugs, shall preserve such order for a period of two years in such a way as to be readily accessible to inspection by any officer, agent, or employee of the Treasury Department duly authorized for that purpose, and the State, Territorial, District, municipal, and insular officials named in section five of this Act. Every person who shall give an order as herein provided to any other person for any of the aforesaid drugs shall, at or before the time of giving such order, make or cause to be made a duplicate thereof on a form to be issued in blank for that purpose by the Commissioner of Internal Revenue, and in case of the acceptance of such order, shall preserve such duplicate for said period of two years in such a way as to be readily accessible to inspection by the officers, agents, employees, and officials hereinbefore mentioned. Nothing contained in this section shall apply—

(a) To the dispensing or distribution of any of the aforesaid drugs to a patient by a physician, dentist, or veterinary surgeon registered under this Act in the course of his professional practice only: *Provided,* That such physician, dentist, or veterinary surgeon shall keep a record of all such drugs dispensed or distributed, showing the amount dispensed or distributed, the date, and the name and address of the patient to whom such drugs are dispensed or distributed, except such as may be dispensed or distributed to a patient upon whom such physician, dentist or veterinary surgeon shall personally attend; and such record shall be kept for a period of two years from the date of dispensing or distributing such drugs, subject to inspection, as provided in this Act.

(b) To the sale, dispensing, or distribution of any of the aforesaid drugs by a dealer to a consumer under and in pursuance of a written prescription issued by a physician, dentist, or veterinary surgeon registered under this Act: *Provided, however,* That such prescription shall be dated as of the day on which signed and shall be signed by the physician, dentist, or veterinary surgeon who shall have issued the same: *And provided further,* That such dealer shall preserve such prescription for a period of two years from the day on which such prescription is filled in such a way as to be readily accessible to inspection by the officers, agents, employees, and officials hereinbefore mentioned.

(c) To the sale, exportation, shipment, or delivery of any of the aforesaid drugs by any person within the United States or any Territory or the District of Columbia or any of the insular possessions of the United States to any person in any foreign country, regulating their entry in accordance with such regulations for importation thereof into such foreign country as are prescribed by said country, such regulations to be promulgated from time to time by the Secretary of State of the United States.

(d) To the sale, barter, exchange, or giving away of any of the aforesaid drugs to any officer of the United States Government or of any State, territorial, district, county, or municipal or insular government lawfully engaged in making purchases thereof for the various departments of the Army and Navy, the Public Health Service, and for Government, State, territorial district, county, or municipal or insular hospitals or prisons.

The Commissioner of Internal Revenue, with the approval of the Secretary of the Treasury, shall cause suitable forms to be prepared for the purposes above mentioned, and shall cause the same to be distributed to collectors of internal revenue for sale by them to those persons who shall have registered and paid the special tax as required by section one of this Act in their districts, respectively; and no collector shall sell any of such forms to any persons other than a person who has registered and paid the special tax as required by section one of this Act in his district. The price at which such forms shall be sold by said collectors shall be fixed by the Commissioner of Internal Revenue, with the approval of the Secretary of the Treasury, but shall not exceed the sum of $1 per hundred. Every collector shall keep an account of the number of such forms sold by him, the names of the purchasers, and the number of such forms sold to each of such purchasers. Whenever any collector shall sell any of such forms, he shall cause the name of the purchaser thereof to be plainly written or stamped thereon before delivering the same; and no person other than such purchaser shall use any of said forms bearing the name of such purchaser for the purpose of procuring any of the aforesaid drugs, or furnish any of the forms bearing the name of such purchaser to any person with intent thereby to procure the shipment or delivery of any of the aforesaid drugs. It shall be unlawful for any person to obtain by means of said order forms any of the aforesaid drugs for any purpose other than the use, sale, or distribution thereof by him in the conduct of a lawful business in said drugs or in the legitimate practice of his profession.

The provisions of this Act shall apply to the United States, the District of Columbia, the Territory of Alaska, the Territory of Hawaii, the insular possessions of the United States, and the Canal Zone. In Porto Rico and the Philippine Islands the administration of this Act, the collection of the said special tax, and the issuance of the order forms specified in section two shall be performed by the appropriate internal-revenue officers of those governments, and all revenues collected hereunder in Porto Rico and the Philippine Islands shall accrue intact to the general governments thereof, respectively. The courts of first instance in the Philippine Islands shall possess and exercise jurisdiction in all cases arising under this Act in said islands. The President is authorized and directed to issue such Executive orders as will carry into effect in the Canal Zone the intent and purpose of this Act by providing for the registration and the imposition of a special tax upon all persons in the Canal Zone who produce, import, compound, deal in, dispense, sell, distribute, or give away opium or coca leaves, their salts, derivatives, or preparations.

Sec. 3. That any person who shall be registered in any internal-revenue district under the provisions of section one of this Act shall, whenever required so to do by the collector of the district, render to the said collector a true and correct statement or return, verified by affidavit, setting forth the quantity of the aforesaid drugs received by him in said internal-revenue district during such period immediately preceding the demand of the collector, not exceeding three months, as the said collector may fix and determine; the names of the persons from whom the said drugs were received; the quantity in each instance received from each of such persons, and the date when received.

Sec. 4. That it shall be unlawful for any person who shall not have registered and paid the special tax as required by section one of this Act to send, ship, carry, or deliver any of the aforesaid drugs from any State or Territory or the District of Columbia, or any insular possession of the United States, to any person in any other State or Territory or the District of Columbia or any insular possession of the United States: *Provided,* That nothing contained in this section shall apply to common carriers engaged in transporting the aforesaid drugs, or to any employee acting within the scope of his employment, of any person who shall have registered and paid the special tax as required by section one of this Act, or to any person who shall deliver any such drug which has been prescribed or dispensed by a physician, dentist, or veterinarian required to register under the terms of this Act, who has been employed to prescribe for the particular patient receiving such drug, or to any United States, State, county, municipal, District, Territorial, or insular officer or official acting within the scope of his official duties.

Sec. 5. That the duplicate-order forms and the prescriptions required to be preserved under the provisions of section two of this Act, and the statements or returns filed in the office of the collector of the district, under the provisions of section three of this Act, shall be open to inspection by officers, agents, and employees of the Treasury Department duly authorized for that purpose; and such officials of any State or Territory, or of any organized municipality therein, or of the District of Columbia, or any insular possession of the United States, as shall be charged with the enforcement of any law or municipal ordinance regulating the sale, prescribing, dispensing, dealing in, or distribution of the aforesaid drugs. Each collector of internal revenue is hereby authorized to furnish, upon written request, certified copies of any of the said statements or returns filed in his office to any of such officials of any State or Territory or organized municipality therein, or the District of Columbia, or any insular possession of the United States, as shall be entitled to inspect the said statements or returns filed in the office of the said collector, upon the payment of a fee of $1 for each one hundred words or fraction thereof in the copy or copies so requested. Any person who shall disclose the information contained in the said statements or returns or in the said duplicate-order forms, except as herein expressly provided, and except for the purpose of enforcing the provisions of this Act, or for the purpose of enforcing any law of any State or Territory or the District of Columbia, or any insular possession of the United States, or ordinance of any organized municipality therein, regulating the sale, prescribing, dispensing, dealing in, or distribution of the aforesaid drugs, shall, on conviction, be fined or imprisoned as provided by section nine of this Act. And collectors of internal revenue are hereby authorized to furnish upon written request, to any person, a certified copy of the names of any or all persons who may be listed in their respective collection districts as special-tax payers under the provisions of this Act, upon payment of a fee of $1 for each one hundred names or fraction thereof in the copy so requested.

Sec. 6. That the provisions of this Act shall not be construed to apply to the sale, distribution, giving away, dispensing, or possession of preparations and remedies which do not contain more than two grains of opium, or more than one-fourth of a grain of morphine, or more than one-eight of a grain of heroin, or more than one grain of codeine, or any salt or derivative of any of them in one fluid ounce, or, if a solid or semisolid preparation, in one avoirdupois ounce,; or to liniments, ointments, or other preparations which are prepared for external use only, except liniments, ointments, and other preparations which contain cocaine or any of its salts or alpha or beta eucaine or any of their salts or any synthetic substitute for them: *Provided,* That such remedies and preparations are sold, distributed, given away, dispensed, or possessed as medicines and not for the purpose of evading the intentions and provisions of this Act. The provisions of this Act shall not apply to decocainized coca leaves or preparations made therefrom, or to other preparations of coca leaves which do not contain cocaine.

Sec. 7. That all laws relating to the assessment, collection, remission, and refund of internal-revenue taxes, including section thirty-two hundred and twenty-nine of the Revised Statutes of the United States, so far as applicable to and not inconsistent with the provisions of this Act, are hereby extended and made applicable to the special taxes imposed by this Act.

Sec. 8. That it shall be unlawful for any person not registered under the provisions of this Act, and who has not paid the special tax provided for by this Act, to have in his possession or under his control any of the aforesaid drugs; and such possession or control shall be presumptive evidence of a violation of this section, and also of a violation of the provisions of section one of this Act: *Provided,* That this section shall not apply to any employee of a registered person, or to a nurse under the supervision of a physician, dentist, or veterinary surgeon registered under this Act, having such possession or control by virtue of his employment or occupation and not on his own account; or to the possession of any of the aforesaid drugs which has or have been prescribed in good faith by a physician, dentist, or veterinary surgeon registered under this Act; or to any United States, State, county, municipal, District, Territorial, or insular officer or official who has possession of any said drugs, by reason of his official duties, or to a warehouseman holding possession for a person registered and who has paid the taxes under this Act; or to common carriers engaged in transporting such drugs: *Provided further,* That it shall not be necessary to negative any of the aforesaid exemptions in any complaint, information, indictment, or other writ or proceeding laid or brought under this Act; and the burden of proof of any such exemption shall be upon the defendant.

Sec. 9. That any person who violates or fails to comply with any of the requirements of this Act shall, on conviction, be fined not more than $2,000 or be imprisoned not more than five years, or both, in the discretion of the court.

Sec. 10. That the Commissioner of Internal Revenue, with the approval of the Secretary of the Treasury, is authorized to appoint such agents, deputy collectors, inspectors, chemists, assistant chemists, clerks, and messengers in the field and in the Bureau of Internal Revenue in the District of Columbia as may be necessary to enforce the provisions of this Act.

Sec. 11. That the sum of $150,000, or so much thereof as may be necessary, be, and hereby is, appropriated, out of any moneys in the Treasury not otherwise appropriated, for the purpose of carrying into effect the provisions of this Act.

Sec. 12. That nothing contained in this Act shall be construed to impair, alter, amend, or repeal any of the provisions of the Act of Congress approved June thirtieth, nineteen hundred and six, entitled "An Act for preventing the manufacture, sale, or transportation of adulterated or misbranded, or poisonous, or deleterious foods, drugs, medicines, and liquors, and for regulating traffic therein, and for other purposes," and any amendment thereof, or of the Act approved February ninth, nineteen hundred and nine, entitled "An Act to prohibit the importation and use of opium for other than medicinal purposes," and any amendment thereof.

Source:

Statutes at Large, Vol. 38, pp. 785–790.

Adamson Act, 1916

Legislation enacted by the U.S. Congress September 3, 1916, which established an eight-hour day for railroad workers operating on interstate lines, without a reduction in their wages. It replaced the 10-hour day and provided time-and-a-half for overtime. The act was passed as an emergency measure to avoid the threatened strike by railway workers that might have hindered U.S. preparations for World War I. The railroads claimed that the act was unconstitutional, effectively raising wages rather than limiting hours, because normal operation required more than eight hours of work. In *Wilson v. New* (1917) the Supreme Court upheld the act under the federal government's right to regulate interstate commerce.

Congress enacted the Mann-Elkins Act, June 18, 1910. It placed the growing, and previously unregulated, communications industry—including telephone, telegraph, cable, and wireless companies—under the jurisdiction of the Interstate Commerce Commission (ICC). The act, sponsored by Senator Stephen B. Elkins of West Virginia and Representative James Robert Mann of Illinois, also strengthened federal control over railroad rates by giving the ICC power to act on its own initiative, rather than merely in response to formal complaints. The ICC could suspend rate increases pending court decisions and could more effectively enforce provisions preventing carriers from charging more for short hauls than for long ones.

Also known as the Transportation Act of 1920, the Esch-Cummins Act of February 28, 1920, authored by Representative John J. Esch of Wisconsin and Senator Albert B. Cummins of Iowa returned the railroads to private control. Two years earlier, during World War I, the U.S. Congress had passed the Railway Administration Act which provided for the operation of the nation's railroads by the federal government for the duration of the war and a reasonable period thereafter and for just compensation to the owners. The U.S. government had taken control of railroads in December 1917 to prevent a rail crisis following the outbreak of the war. The act guaranteed stockholders and bondholders compensation equal to the average annual net operating income between 1914 and 1917. It also established a regional system of administration.

As significant, the Esch-Cummins Act broadened the powers of the ICC. The act authorized the ICC to consolidate railroads for greater efficiency, exempting the groups from antitrust legislation; to evaluate railroad properties; to set minimum and maximum rates and a fair return to stockholders; and to establish a fund supported by carriers to benefit financially troubled rail lines. The act also created the Railroad Labor Board, composed of employees, company members, and the public, to resolve wage disputes.

May 20, 1926, the Watson-Parker Act (after sponsors Senator James E. Watson of Indiana and Representative James S. Parker of New York), or the U.S. Railway Labor Act, was passed, superseding Esch-Cummins. This act established the U.S. Board of Mediation to settle railroad labor disputes and to replace the Railroad Labor Board. The new, independent agency contained five members appointed by the president and could enter disputes on its own initiative. In the event of an impasse, the board could ask the president to authorize an investigation and to declare a 30-day "cooling-off" period, during which no strike could occur. The act was amended by the Railway Labor Act of 1934, which covered workers' rights to organize and bargain collectively on railroads and airlines and created a board to hear disputes about existing labor contracts.

An Act

To establish an eight-hour day for employees of carriers engaged in interstate and foreign commerce, and for other purposes.

Be it enacted by the Senate and House of Representatives of the United States of America in Congress assembled, That beginning January first, nineteen hundred and seventeen, eight hours shall, in contracts for labor and service, be deemed a day's work and the measure or standard of a day's work for the purpose of reckoning the compensation for services of all employees who are now or may hereafter be employed by any common carrier by railroad, except railroads independently owned and operated not exceeding one hundred miles in length, electric street railroads, and electric interurban railroads, which is subject to the provisions of the Act of February fourth, eighteen hundred and eighty-seven, entitled "An Act to regulate commerce," as amended, and who are now or may hereafter be actually engaged in any capacity in the operation of trains used for the transportation of persons or property on railroads, except railroads independently owned and operated not exceeding one hundred miles in length, electric street railroads, and electric interurban railroads, from any State or Territory of the United States or the District of Columbia to any other State or Territory of the United States or the District of Columbia, or from one place in a Territory to another place in the same Territory, or from any place in the United States to an adjacent foreign country, or from any place in the United States through a foreign country to any other place in the United States: *Provided,* That the above exceptions shall not apply to railroads though less than one hundred miles in length whose principal business is leasing or furnishing terminal or transfer facilities to other railroads, or are themselves engaged in transfers of freight between railroads or between railroads and industrial plants.

Sec. 2. That the President shall appoint a commission of three, which shall observe the operation and effects of the institution of the eight-hour standard workday as above defined and the facts and conditions affecting the relations between such common carriers and employees during a period of not less than six months nor more than nine months, in the discretion of the commission, and within thirty days thereafter such commission shall report its findings to the President and Congress; that each member of the commission created under the provisions of this Act shall receive such compensation as may be fixed by the President. That the sum of $25,000, or so much thereof as may be necessary, be, and hereby is, appropriated, out of any money in the United States Treasury not otherwise appropriated, for the necessary and proper expenses incurred in connection with the work of such commission, including salaries, per diem, traveling expenses of members and employees, and rent, furniture, office fixtures and supplies, books, salaries, and other necessary expenses, the same to be approved by the chairman of said commission and audited by the proper accounting officers of the Treasury.

Sec. 3. That pending the report of the commission herein provided for and for a period of thirty days thereafter the compensation of railway employees subject to this Act for a standard eight-hour workday shall not be reduced below the present standard day's wage, and for all necessary time in excess of eight hours such employees shall be paid at a rate not less than the pro rata rate for such standard eight-hour workday.

Sec. 4. That any person violating any provision of this Act shall be guilty of a misdemeanor and upon conviction shall be fined not less than $100 and not more than $1,000, or imprisoned not to exceed one year, or both.

Source:
Statutes at Large, Vol. 39, pp. 721–722.

Role of the United States in World Affairs in the Early 20th Century

Hay-Pauncefote Treaty, 1901

The second of two treaties concluded between U.S. secretary of state John M. Hay and Lord (Julian) Pauncefote of Preston, Great Britain's ambassador to the United States, on February 5, 1900, which the British Parliament rejected, and again on November 18, 1901, providing for exclusive control by the United States over the construction and management of any future isthmian canal in Central America, which was to be open to ships of all countries on equal terms, under a general principle of its neutrality. The second treaty differed from the first in that it contained an added provision granting the United States the right to fortify and defend any such future canal. The treaty thus abrogated the previous British-U.S. agreement through which both Great Britain and the United States were to share control over the canal.

On June 28, 1902, Congress enacted legislation introduced by Senator John C. Spooner of Wisconsin authorizing President Theodore Roosevelt to purchase from the French the New Panama Canal Company for $40 million, a concession to build a canal across the Isthmus of Panama, a part of Colombia at the time. The act stipulated that Colombia grant to the United States perpetual control over the right of way. If Colombia refused, Congress authorized the U.S. president to initiate negotiations with Nicaragua for the construction of a canal. When Colombia refused to accept the U.S. terms, the province of Panama revolted and declared its independence. The United States recognized the new Republic of Panama in November and negotiated the Hay–Bunau-Varilla Treaty, granting the United States sovereignty over the Panama Canal Zone.

In the Hay–Bunau-Varilla Treaty signed in Washington, D.C., November 18, 1903, by U.S. secretary of state John Hay and Philippe Bunau-Varilla, a French engineer associated with the New Panama Canal Company and the Republic of Panama's appointed minister to Washington, the United States acquired the right to build a canal across the Isthmus of Panama; to perpetually use, occupy, and control a zone 10 miles wide; and the right to acquire additional lands as might be needed for the construction, maintenance, sanitation, operation, and protection of the canal. Panama was to receive $10 million, along with $250,000 annually, beginning nine years after the day the treaty went into effect.

U.S. secretary of state Cordell Hull and Panama's foreign minister Ricardo J. Alfaro agreed to amend the Hay–Bunau-Varilla Treaty in 1939. Hull made substantial concessions to Panama: The United States renounced its guarantee of the independence of Panama, the right to expropriate additional land for Panama Canal use without restrictions, the right of eminent domain in the cities of Panama and Colón, and the unlimited right to defend the canal. Panama's annuity of $250,000 was also increased to $430,000. The U.S. Senate approved the treaty in July 1939, only after the United States was assured the freedom to act without consultation in defense emergencies.

The United States of America and His Majesty Edward the Seventh, of the United Kingdom of Great Britain and Ireland, and of the British Dominions beyond the Seas, King, and Emperor of India, being desirous to facilitate the construction of a ship canal to connect the Atlantic and Pacific Oceans, by whatever route may be considered expedient, and to that end to remove any objection which may arise out of the Convention of the 19th April, 1850, commonly called the Clayton-Bulwer Treaty, to the construction of such canal under the auspices of the Government of the United States, without impairing the "general principle" of neutralization established in Article VIII of that Convention, have for that purpose appointed as their Plenipotentiaries:

The President of the United States, John Hay, Secretary of State of the United States of America;

And His Majesty Edward the Seventh, of the United Kingdom of Great Britain and Ireland, and of the British Dominions beyond the Seas, King, and Emperor of India, the Right Honorable Lord Pauncefote, G. C. B., G. C. M. G., His Majesty's Ambassador Extraordinary and Plenipotentiary to the United States;

Who, having communicated to each other their full powers which were found to be in due and proper form, have agreed upon the following Articles:

Article I

The High Contracting Parties agree that the present Treaty shall supersede the aforementioned Convention of the 19th April, 1850.

Article II

It is agreed that the canal may be constructed under the auspices of the Government of the United States, either directly at its own cost, or by gift or loan of money to individuals or Corporations, or through subscription to or purchase of stock or shares, and that, subject to the provisions of the present Treaty, the said Government shall have and enjoy all the rights incident to such construction, as well as the exclusive right of providing for the regulation and management of the canal.

Article III

The United States adopts, as the basis of the neutralization of such ship canal, the following Rules, substantially as embodied in the Convention of Constantinople, signed the 28th [29th] October, 1888, for the free navigation of the Suez Canal, that is to say:

1. The canal shall be free and open to the vessels of commerce and of war of all nations observing these Rules, on terms of entire equality, so that there shall be no discrimination against any such nation, or its citizens or subjects, in respect of the conditions or changes of traffic, or otherwise. Such conditions and charges of traffic shall be just and equitable.

2. The canal shall never be blockaded, nor shall any right of war be exercised nor any act of hostility be committed within it. The United States, however, shall be at liberty to maintain such military police along the canal as may be necessary to protect it against lawlessness and disorder.

3. Vessels of war of a belligerent shall not revictual nor take any stores in the canal except so far as may be strictly necessary; and the transit of such vessels through the canal shall be effected with the least possible delay in accordance with the Regulations in force, and with only such intermission as may result from the necessities of the service.

Prizes shall be in all respects subject to the same Rules as vessels of war of the belligerents.

4. No belligerent shall embark or disembark troops, munitions of war, or warlike materials in the canal, except

in case of accidental hindrance of the transit, and in such case the transit shall be resumed with all possible dispatch.

5. The provisions of this Article shall apply to waters adjacent to the canal, within 3 marine miles of either end. Vessels of war of a belligerent shall not remain in such waters longer than twenty-four hours at any one time, except in case of distress, and in such case shall depart as soon as possible; but a vessel of war of one belligerent shall not depart within twenty-four hours from the departure of a vessel of war of the other belligerent.

6. The plant, establishments, buildings, and all works necessary to the construction, maintenance, and operation of the canal shall be deemed to be part thereof, for the purposes of this Treaty, and in time of war, as in time of peace, shall enjoy complete immunity from attack or injury by belligerents, and from acts calculated to impair their usefulness as part of the canal.

Article IV

It is agreed that no change of territorial sovereignty or of the international relations of the country or countries traversed by the before-mentioned canal shall affect the general principle of neutralization or the obligation of the High Contracting Parties under the present Treaty.

Article V

The present Treaty shall be ratified by the President of the United States, by and with the advice and consent of the Senate thereof, and by His Britannic Majesty; and the ratifications shall be exchanged at Washington or at London at the earliest possible time within six months from the date hereof.

Source:

Charles I.Bevan, *Treaties and Other Agreements of the United States of America, 1776–1949*, Washington, D.C.: Government Printing Office, 1968–76.

The Platt Amendment, 1901

Amendment designed to regulate the relations between the United States and Cuba and originally attached to the Army Appropriations Bill of 1901. Named after Senator Orville H. Platt of Connecticut, chairman of the Committee on Relations with Cuba, the amendment prohibited Cuba from signing any treaties that might jeopardize its independence; it stipulated that Cuba would leave naval bases to the United States; and it sanctioned United States intervention in Cuba whenever there existed a danger to life, property, or individual freedom. Under pressure from the United States, Cuba reluctantly incorporated the amendment into its 1901 constitution. In effect until 1934, the amendment was finally abrogated under Franklin D. Roosevelt's Good Neighbor Policy.

The Platt Amendment

I

The government of Cuba shall never enter into any treaty or other compact with any foreign power or powers which will impair or tend to impair the independence of Cuba, nor in any manner authorize or permit any foreign power or powers to obtain by colonization or for military or naval purposes or otherwise, lodgment in or control over any portion of said island.

II

Said government shall not assume or contract any public debt, to pay the interest upon which, and to make reasonable sinking fund provision for the ultimate discharge of which, the ordinary revenues of the island, after defraying the current expenses of government, shall be inadequate.

III

The government of Cuba consents that the United States may exercise the right to intervene for the preservation of Cuban independence, the maintenance of a government adequate for the protection of life, property, and individual liberty, and for discharging the obligations with respect to Cuba imposed by the Treaty of Paris on the United States, now to be assumed and undertaken by the government of Cuba.

IV

All acts of the United States in Cuba during its military occupancy thereof are ratified and validated, and all lawful rights acquired thereunder shall be maintained and protected.

V

The government of Cuba will execute, and as far as necessary extend, the plans already devised or other plans to be mutually agreed upon, for the sanitation of the cities of the island, to the end that a recurrence of epidemic and infectious diseases may be prevented, thereby assuring protection to the people and commerce of Cuba, as well as to the commerce of the southern ports of the United States and the people residing therein.

VI

The Isle of Pines shall be omitted from the proposed constitutional boundaries of Cuba, the title thereto being left to future adjustment by treaty.

VII

To enable the United States to maintain the independence of Cuba, and to protect the people thereof, as well as for its own defense, the government of Cuba will sell or lease to the United States lands necessary for coaling or naval stations at certain specified points, to be agreed upon with the President of the United States.

VIII

By way of further assurance the government of Cuba will embody the foregoing provisions in a permanent treaty with the United States.

Source:

Scott, John A., ed. *Living Documents in American History*. New York: Washington Square Press, 1964–68, pp. 615–616.

Lodge Corollary to the Monroe Doctrine, 1912

Statement of U.S. policy related to the Monroe Doctrine that was prepared by Senator Henry Cabot Lodge of Massachusetts and adopted by the Senate on August 2, 1912. The resolution was occasioned by American concern that a Japanese syndicate was trying to obtain control of land on Magdalena Bay in lower California. It declared that any land in the American continents situated where foreign military or naval occupation "might threaten the communications or safety of the United States" could not pass into possession by a corporation or association controlled by a foreign power. The corollary was the first application of the Monroe Doctrine to an Asian power. Previously, the Monroe Doctrine applied only to Latin America. In 1895, Secretary of State Richard Olney intervened in a dispute between Great Britain and Venezuela over a boundary in British Guiana. Olney demanded that Britain submit the dispute to arbitration. In a broad interpretation of the Monroe Doctrine, he argued that British pressure on Venezuela would constitute an unacceptable extension of European colonization in the Americas. His dispatch read: "Today the United States is practically sovereign on this continent, and its fiat is law upon the subjects to which it confines its interposition." To avoid the possibility of war with the United States, Britain agreed to arbitration. The dispute was settled in 1899.

Resolved, That when any harbor or other place in the American continents is so situated that the occupation thereof for naval or military purposes might threaten the communications or the safety of the United States, the Government of the United States could not see without grave concern the possession of such harbor or other place by any corporation or association which has such a relation to another Government, not American, as to give that Government practical power of control for national purposes.

Source:

Congressional Record, Washington, D.C., 1912.

Jones Act, 1917

Legislation enacted by the U.S. Congress on March 2, 1917, that made Puerto Rico a U.S. territory, granted U.S. citizenship to its inhabitants, and broadened self-government in the island. The act incorporated a bill of rights that gave Puerto Ricans most of the civil rights enunciated in the U.S. Constitution, except the right to demand a trial by jury. Male suffrage was granted, and the Puerto Rican senate was made an elective body. Legislative acts were nonetheless subject to veto by the U.S. president, who also retained the power to appoint the governor, the supreme court, and most executive department heads in Puerto Rico.

Jesus M. Balzac, an editor, appealed a Puerto Rican criminal libel conviction on the ground that he had been denied a jury trial, a right guaranteed by the Sixth Amendment. The Supreme Court ruled in *Balzac v. Puerto Rico* (1922) that the right to a jury trial does not apply in unincorporated territories because it is not a "fundamental right which goes wherever the jurisdiction of the United States extends." Puerto Rico was a territory of the United States that was not incorporated into the Union; its residents, though they had been made U.S. citizens by the Jones Act of 1917, did not automatically enjoy all of the rights protected by the U.S. Constitution.

An Act

To provide a civil government for Porto Rico, and for other purposes.

Be it enacted by the Senate and House of Representatives of the United States of America in Congress assembled, That the provisions of this Act shall apply to the island of Porto Rico and to the adjacent islands belonging to the United States, and waters of those islands; and the name Porto Rico as used in this Act shall be held to include not only the island of that name but all the adjacent island as aforesaid.

Bill of Rights.

Sec. 2. That no law shall be enacted in Porto Rico which shall deprive any person of life, liberty, or property without due process of law, or deny to any person therein the equal protection of the laws.

That in all criminal prosecutions the accused shall enjoy the right to have the assistance of counsel for his defense, to be informed of the nature and cause of the accusation, to have a copy thereof, to have a speedy and public trial, to be confronted with the witnesses against him, and to have compulsory process for obtaining witnesses in his favor.

That no person shall be held to answer for a criminal offense without due process of law; and no person for the same offense shall be twice put in jeopardy of punishment, nor shall be compelled in any criminal case to be a witness against himself.

That all persons shall before conviction be bailable by sufficient sureties, except for capital offenses when the proof is evident or the presumption great.

That no law impairing the obligation of contracts shall be enacted.

That no person shall be imprisoned for debt.

That the privilege of the writ of habeas corpus shall not be suspended, unless when in case of rebellion, insurrection, or invasion the public safety may require it, in either of which events the same may be suspended by the President, or by the governor, whenever during such period the necessity for such suspension shall exist.

That no ex post facto law or bill of attainder shall be enacted.

Private property shall not be taken or damaged for public use except upon payment of just compensation ascertained in the manner provided by law.

Nothing contained in this Act shall be construed to limit the power of the legislature to enact laws for the protection of the lives, health, or safety of employees.

That no law granting a title of nobility shall be enacted, and no person holding any office of profit or trust under the government of Porto Rico shall, without the consent of the Congress of the United States, accept any present, emolument, office, or title of any kind whatever from any king, queen, prince, or foreign State, or any officer thereof.

That excessive bail shall not be required, nor excessive fines imposed, nor cruel and unusual punishments inflicted.

That the right to be secured against unreasonable searches and seizures shall not be violated.

That no warrant for arrest or search shall issue but upon probable cause, supported by oath or affirmation, and particularly describing the place to be searched and the persons or things to be seized.

That slavery shall not exist in Porto Rico.

That involuntary servitude, except as a punishment for crime, whereof the party shall have been duly convicted, shall not exist in Porto Rico.

That no law shall be passed abridging the freedom of speech or of the press, or the right of the people peaceably to assemble and petition the Government for redress of grievances.

That no law shall be made respecting an establishment of religion or prohibiting the free exercise thereof, and that the free exercise and enjoyment of religious profession and worship without discrimination or preference shall forever be allowed, and that no political or religious test other than an oath to support the Constitution of the United States and the laws of Porto Rico shall be required as a qualification to any office or public trust under the government of Porto Rico.

That no public money or property shall ever be appropriated, applied, donated, used, directly or indirectly, for the use, benefit, or support of any sect, church, denomination, sectarian institution or association, or system of religion, or for the use, benefit, or support of any priest, preacher, minister, or other religious teacher or dignitary as such, or for charitable, industrial, educational, or benevolent purposes to any person, corporation, or community not under the absolute control of Porto Rico.

Contracting of polygamous or plural marriages hereafter is prohibited . . . .

Source:
Statutes at Large, Vol. 39, pp. 951–968.

Pact of Paris, 1928

Multinational treaty, also known as the Kellogg-Briand Peace Pact, signed by 15 nations at Paris on August 27, 1928, that aimed to outlaw war as an instrument of national policy and to settle international disputes through peaceful means. The treaty, first proposed by French foreign minister Aristide Briand and supported by U.S. secretary of state Frank B. Kellogg, was eventually signed by 62 countries. The treaty condemned "recourse to war for the solution of international controversies." It was ineffective, however, because most nations reserved the right to engage in war in self-defense and because the pact contained no sanctions against violators other than the moral force of international opinion.

Whereas a Treaty between the President of the United States of America, the President of the German Reich, His Majesty the King of the Belgians, the President of the French Republic, His Majesty the King of Great Britain, Ireland and the British Dominions beyond the Seas, Emperor of India, His Majesty the King of Italy, His Majesty the Emperor of Japan, the President of the

Republic of Poland, and the President of the Czechoslovak Republic, providing for the renunciation of war as an instrument of national policy, was concluded and signed by their respective Plenipotentiaries at Paris on the twenty-seventh day of August, one thousand nine hundred and twenty-eight, the original of which Treaty, being in the English and French languages, is word for word as follows:

The President of the German Reich, the President of the United States of America, His Majesty the King of the Belgians, the President of the French Republic, His Majesty the King of Great Britain, Ireland and the British Dominions beyond the Seas, Emperor of India, His Majesty the King of Italy His Majesty the Emperor of Japan, the President of the Republic of Poland, the President of the Czechoslovak Republic.

Deeply sensible of their solemn duty to promote the welfare of mankind;

Persuaded that the time has come when a frank renunciation of war as an instrument of national policy should be made to the end that the peaceful and friendly relations now existing between their peoples may be perpetuated;

Convinced that all changes in their relations with one another should be sought only by pacific means and be the result of a peaceful and orderly process, and that any signatory Power which shall hereafter seek to promote its national interests by resort to war should be denied the benefits furnished by this Treaty;

Hopeful that, encouraged by their example, all the other nations of the world will join in this humane endeavor and by adhering to the present Treaty as soon as it comes into force bring their peoples within the scope of its beneficent provisions, thus uniting the civilized nations of the world in a common renunciation of war as an instrument of their national policy;

Have decided to conclude a Treaty and for that purpose have appointed as their respective Plenipotentiaries:

The President of the German Reich: Dr. Gustav Stresemann, Minister for Foreign Affairs;

The President of the United States of America: The Honorable Frank B. Kellogg, Secretary of State;

His Majesty the King of the Belgians: Mr. Paul Hymans, Minister for Foreign Affairs, Minister of State;

The President of the French Republic: Mr. Aristide Briand, Minister for Foreign Affairs;

His Majesty the King of Great Britain, Ireland and the British Dominions beyond the Seas, Emperor of India:

For Great Britain and Northern Ireland and all parts of the British Empire which are not separate Members of the League of Nations:

The Right Honourable Lord Cushendun, Chancellor of the Duchy of Lancaster, Acting Secretary of State for Foreign Affairs;

For the Dominion of Canada: The Right Honourable William Lyon Mackenzie King, Prime Minister and Minister for External Affairs;

For the Commonwealth of Australia: The Honourable Alexander John McLachlan, Member of the Executive Federal Council;

For the Dominion of New Zealand: The Honourable Sir Christopher James Parr, High Commissioner for New Zealand in Great Britain;

For the Union of South Africa: The Honourable Jacobus Stephanus Smit, High Commissioner for the Union of South Africa in Great Britain;

For the Irish Free State: Mr. William Thomas Cosgrave, President of the Executive Council;

For India: The Right Honourable Lord Cushendun, Chancellor of the Duchy of Lancaster, Acting Secretary of State for Foreign Affairs;

His Majesty the King of Italy: Count Gaetano Manzoni, his Ambassador Extraordinary and Plenipotentiary at Paris;

His Majesty the Emperor of Japan: Count Uchida, Privy Councillor;

The President of the Republic of Poland: Mr. A. Zaleski, Minister for Foreign Affairs;

The President of the Czechoslovak Republic: Dr. Eduard Benes, Minister for Foreign Affairs;

who, having communicated to one another their full powers found in good and due form have agreed upon the following articles:

Article I

The High Contracting Parties solemnly declare in the names of their respective peoples that they condemn recourse to war for the solution of international controversies, and renounce it as an instrument of national policy in their relations with one another.

Article II

The High Contracting Parties agree that the settlement or solution of all disputes or conflicts of whatever nature or of whatever origin they may be, which may arise among them, shall never be sought except by pacific means.

Article III

The present Treaty shall be ratified by the High Contracting Parties named in the Preamble in accordance with their respective constitutional requirements, and shall take effect as between them as soon as all their several instruments of ratification shall have been deposited at Washington.

This Treaty shall, when it has come into effect as prescribed in the preceding paragraph, remain open as long as may be necessary for adherence by all the other Powers of the world. Every instrument evidencing the adherence of a Power shall be deposited at Washington and the Treaty shall immediately upon such deposit become effective as between the Power thus adhering and the other Powers parties hereto.

It shall be the duty of the Government of the United States to furnish each Government named in the Preamble and every Government subsequently adhering to this Treaty with a certified copy of the Treaty and of every instrument of ratification or adherence. It shall also be the duty of the Government of the United States telegraphically to notify such Governments immediately upon the deposit with it of each instrument of ratification or adherence.

In Faith Whereof the respective Plenipotentiaries have signed this Treaty in the French and English languages both texts having equal force, and hereunto affix their seals.

Done at Paris, the twenty-seventh day of August in the year one thousand nine hundred and twenty-eight.

Source:

Charles I. Bevan, *Treaties and Other Agreements of the United States of America, 1776–1949*. Washington, D.C.: Government Printing Office, 1968–76.

Causes and Consequences of World War I

Woodrow Wilson, "Make the World Safe for Democracy," 1917

Address delivered at a joint session of Congress on April 2, 1917, by President Woodrow Wilson, asking Congress to declare war against Germany. Wilson charged that Germany's policy of unrestricted submarine warfare constituted "a warfare against mankind," in which American ships had been sunk and American lives lost.

Only a month before, on March 4, 1917, in his second inaugural address, the president had restated America's commitments to neutrality and to military preparedness, declaring, "We stand firm in armed neutrality. . . . We desire neither conquest nor advantage." Anticipating the possibility of a more active American role, however, he pointed out, "We are provincials no longer. The tragic events of the thirty months of vital turmoil through which we have just passed have made us citizens of the world. There can be no turning back."

In his war address, Wilson admitted that his previous policy of neutrality was impracticable in view of the German threat to international peace and justice: "The world must be made safe for democracy. Its peace must be planted upon the tested foundations of political liberty." Congress declared war four days later, and the United States joined England, France, and Italy in their war against Germany, Japan, and Austria.

Although the resumption of submarine warfare by Germany in late January 1917 was the stated reason for the war, two other events influenced the decision for the United States to finally go to war. Late in February, the British Secret Service gave the State Department a copy of the "Zimmermann telegram," in which the German government proposed that if Mexico allied with it, the Mexicans would regain Texas, New Mexico, and Arizona after the United States was defeated. The note's publication helped overcome the public's aversion to war. Secondly, the czar of Russia (then allied with England) was overthrown March 17 and replaced with a republican government. (The Communists would not take over for several months.) Now Wilson could bring the United States into the war on the side of democracy.

Gentlemen of the Congress: I have called the Congress into extraordinary session because there are serious, very serious, choices of policy to be made, and made immediately, which it was neither right nor constitutionally permissible that I should assume the responsibility of making.

On the third of February last I officially laid before you the extraordinary announcement of the Imperial German Government that on and after the first day of February it was its purpose to put aside all restraints of law or of humanity and use its submarines to sink every vessel that sought to approach either the ports of Great Britain and Ireland or the western coasts of Europe or any of the ports controlled by the enemies of Germany within the Mediterranean. That had seemed to be the object of the German submarine warfare earlier in the war, but since April of last year the Imperial Government had somewhat restrained the commanders of its undersea craft in conformity with its promise then given to us that passenger boats should not be sunk and that due warning would be given to all other vessels which its submarines might seek to destroy, when no resistance was offered or escape attempted, and care taken that their crews were given at least a fair chance to save their lives in their open boats. The precautions taken were meagre and haphazard enough, as was proved in distressing instance after instance in the progress of the cruel and unmanly business, but a certain degree of restraint was observed. The new policy has swept every restriction aside. Vessels of every kind, whatever their flag, their character, their cargo, their destination, their errand, have been ruthlessly sent to the bottom without warning and without thought of help or mercy for those on board, the vessels of friendly neutrals along with those of belligerents. Even hospitals ships and ships carrying relief to the sorely bereaved and stricken people of Belgium, though the latter were provided with safe conduct through the proscribed areas by the German Government itself and were distinguished by unmistakable marks of identity, have been sunk with the same reckless lack of compassion or of principles.

I was for a little while unable to believe that such things would in fact be done by any government that had hitherto subscribed to the humane practices of civilized nations. International law had its origin in the attempt to set up some law which would be respected and observed upon the seas, where no nation had right of dominion and where lay the free highways of the world. By painful stage after stage has that law been built up, with meagre enough results, indeed, after all was accomplished that could be accomplished, but always with a clear view, at least, of what the heart and conscience of mankind demanded. This minimum of right the German Government has swept aside under the plea of retaliation and necessity and because it had no weapons which it could use at sea except these which it is impossible to employ as it is employing them without throwing to the winds all scruples of humanity or of respect for the understandings that were supposed to underlie the intercourse of the world. I am not now thinking of the loss of property involved, immense and serious as that is, but only of the wanton and wholesale destruction of the lives of non-combatants, men, women, and children, engaged in pursuits which have always, even in the darkest periods of modern history, been deemed innocent and legitimate. Property can be paid for; the lives of peaceful and innocent people cannot be. The present German submarine warfare against commerce is a warfare against mankind.

It is a war against all nations. American ships have been sunk, American lives taken, in ways which it has stirred us very deeply to learn of, but the ships and people of other neutral and friendly nations have been sunk and overwhelmed in the waters in the same way. There has been no discrimination. The challenge is to all mankind. Each nation must decide for itself how it will meet it. The choice we make for ourselves must be made with a moderation of counsel and a temperateness of judgment befitting our character and our motives as a nation. We must put excited feeling away. Our motive will not be revenge or the victorious assertion of the physical might of the nation, but only the vindication of right, of human right, of which we are only a single champion.

When I addressed the Congress on the twenty-sixth of February last I thought that it would suffice to assert our neutral rights with arms, our right to use the seas against unlawful interference, our right to keep our people safe against unlawful violence. But armed neutrality, it now appears, is impracticable. Because submarines are in effect outlaws when used as the German submarines have been used against merchant shipping, it is impossible to defend ships against their attacks as the law of nations has assumed that merchantmen would defend themselves against privateers or cruisers, visible craft giving chase upon the open sea. It is common prudence in such circumstances, grim necessity, indeed, to endeavour to destroy them before they have shown their own intention. They must be dealt with upon sight, if dealt with at all. The German Government denies the right of neutrals to use arms at all within the areas of the sea which it has proscribed, even in the defense or rights which no modern publicist has ever before questioned their right to defend. The intimation is conveyed that the armed guards which we have placed on our merchant ships will be treated as beyond the pale of law and subject to be dealt with as pirates would be. Armed neutrality is ineffectual enough at best; in such circumstances and in the face of such pretensions it is worse than ineffectual: it is likely only to produce what it was meant to prevent; it is practically certain to draw us into the war without either the rights or the effectiveness of belligerents. There is one choice we cannot make, we are incapable of making: we will not choose the path of submission and suffer the most sacred rights of our nation and our people to be ignored or violated. The wrongs against which we now array ourselves are no common wrongs; they cut to the very roots of human life.

With a profound sense of the solemn and even tragical character of the step I am taking and of the grave responsibilities which it involves, but in unhesitating obedience to what I deem my constitutional duty, I advise that the Congress declare the recent course of the Imperial German Government to be in fact nothing less than war against the government and people of the United States;

that it formally accept the status of belligerent which has thus been thrust upon it; and that it take immediate steps not only to put the country in a more thorough state of defense but also to exert all its power and employ all its resources to bring the Government of the German Empire to terms and end the war.

What this will involve is clear. It will involve the utmost practicable cooperation in counsel and action with the governments now at war with Germany, and, as incident to that, the extension to those governments of the most liberal financial credits, in order that our resources may so far as possible be added to theirs. It will involve the organization and mobilization of all the material resources of the country to supply the materials of war and serve the incidental needs of the nation in the most abundant and yet the most economical and efficient way possible. It will involve the immediate full equipment of the navy in all respects but particularly in supplying it with the best means of dealing with the enemy's submarines. It will involve the immediate addition to the armed forces of the United States already provided for by law in case of war at least five hundred thousand men, who should, in my opinion, be chosen upon the principle of universal liability to service, and also the authorization of subsequent additional increments of equal force so soon as they may be needed and can be handled in training. It will involve also, of course, the granting of adequate credits to the Government, sustained, I hope, so far as they can equitably be sustained by the present generation, by well conceived taxation.

I say sustained so far as may be equitable by taxation because it seems to me that it would be most unwise to base the credits which will now be necessary entirely on money borrowed. It is our duty, I most respectfully urge, to protect our people so far as we may against the very serious hardships and evils which would be likely to arise out of the inflation which would be produced by vast loans.

In carrying out the measures by which these things are to be accomplished we should keep constantly in mind the wisdom of interfering as little as possible in our own preparation and in the equipment of our own military forces with the duty,—for it will be a very practical duty,—of supplying the nations already at war with Germany with the materials which they can obtain only from us or by our assistance. They are in the field and we should help them in every way to be effective there.

I shall take the liberty of suggesting, through the several executive departments of the Government, for the consideration of your committees, measures for the accomplishment of the several objects I have mentioned. I hope that it will be your pleasure to deal with them as having been framed after very careful thought by the branch of the Government upon which the responsibility of conducting the war and safeguarding the nation will most directly fall.

While we do these things, these deeply momentous things, let us be very clear, and make very clear to all the world what our motives and our objects are. My own thought has not been driven from its habitual and normal course by the unhappy events of the last two months, and I do not believe that the thought of the nation has been altered or clouded by them. I have exactly the same things in mind now that I had in mind when I addressed the Senate on the twenty-second of January last; the same that I had in mind when I addressed the Congress on the third of February and on the twenty-sixth of February. Our object now, as then, is to vindicate the principles of peace and justice in the life of the world as against selfish and autocratic power and to set up amongst the really free and self-governed peoples of the world such a concert of purpose and of action as will henceforth ensure the observance of those principles. Neutrality is no longer feasible or desirable where the peace of the world is involved and the freedom of its peoples, and the menace to that peace and freedom lies in the existence of autocratic governments backed by organized force which is controlled wholly by their will, not by the will of their people. We have seen the last of neutrality in such circumstances. We are at the beginning of an age in which it will be insisted that the same standards of conduct and of responsibility for wrong done shall be observed among nations and their governments that are observed among the individual citizens of civilized states.

We have no quarrel with the German people. We have no feeling towards them but one of sympathy and friendship. It was not upon their impulse that their government acted in entering this war. It was not with their previous knowledge or approval. It was a war determined upon as wars used to be determined upon in the old, unhappy days when peoples were nowhere consulted by their rulers and wars were provoked and waged in the interest of dynasties or of little groups of ambitious men who were accustomed to use their fellow men as pawns and tools. Self-governed nations do not fill their neighbour states with spies or set the course of intrigue to bring about some critical posture of affairs which will give them an opportunity to strike and make conquest. Such designs can be successfully worked out only under cover and where no one has the right to ask questions. Cunningly contrived plans of deception or aggression, carried, it may be, from generation to generation, can be worked out and kept from the light only within the privacy of courts or behind the carefully guarded confidences of a narrow and privileged class. They are happily impossible where public opinion commands and insists upon full information concerning all the nation's affairs.

A steadfast concert for peace can never be maintained except by a partnership of democratic nations. No autocratic government could be trusted to keep faith within it or observe its covenants. It must be a league of honour, a partnership of opinion. Intrigue would eat its vitals away; the plottings of inner circles who could plan what they would and render account to no one would be a corruption seated at its very heart. Only free peoples can hold their purpose and their honour steady to a common end and prefer the interests of mankind to any narrow interest of their own.

Does not every American feel that assurance has been added to our hope for the future peace of the world by the wonderful and heartening things that have been happening within the last few weeks in Russia? Russia was known by those who knew it best to have been always in fact democratic at heart, in all the vital habits of her thought, in all the intimate relationships of her people that spoke their natural instinct, their habitual attitude towards life. The autocracy that crowned the summit of her political structure, long as it had stood and terrible as was the reality of its power, was not in fact Russian in origin, character, or purpose; and now it has been shaken off and the great, generous Russian people have been added in all their naive majesty and might to the forces that are fighting for freedom in the world, for justice, and for peace. Here is a fit partner for a League of Honour.

One of the things that has served to convince us that the Prussian autocracy was not and could never be our friend is that from the very outset of the present war it has filled our unsuspecting communities and even our offices of government with spies and set criminal intrigues everywhere afoot against our national unity of counsel, our peace within and without, our industries and our commerce. Indeed it is now evident that its spies were here even before the war began; and it is unhappily not a matter of conjecture but a fact proved in our court of justice that the intrigues which have more than once come perilously near to disturbing the peace and dislocating the industries of the country have been carried on at the instigation, with the support, and even under the personal direction of official agents of the Imperial Government accredited to the Government of the United States. Even in checking these things and trying to extirpate them we have sought to put the most generous interpretation possible upon them because we knew that their source lay, not in any hostile feeling or purpose of the German people towards us (who were, no doubt as ignorant of them as we ourselves were), but only in the selfish designs of a Government that did what it pleased and told its people nothing. But they have played their part in serving to convince us at last that that Government entertains no real friendship for us and means to act against our peace and security at its convenience. That it means to stir up enemies against us at our very doors the intercepted note to the German Minister at Mexico City is eloquent evidence.

We are accepting this challenge of hostile purpose because we know that in such a government, following such methods, we can never have a friend; and that in the presence of its organized power, always lying in wait to accomplish we know not what purpose, there can be no assured security for the democratic governments of the world. We are now about to accept gauge of battle with this natural foe to liberty and shall, if necessary, spend the whole force of the nation to check and nullify its pretensions and its power. We are glad, now that we see the facts with no veil of false pretence about them, to fight thus for the ultimate peace of the world and for the liberation of its peoples, the German peoples included: for the rights of nations great and small and the privilege of men everywhere to choose their way of life and of obedience. The world must be made safe for democracy. Its peace must be planted upon the tested foundations of political liberty. We have no selfish ends to serve. We desire no conquest, no dominion. We seek no indemnities for ourselves, no material compensation for the sacrifices we shall freely make. We are but one of the champions of the rights of mankind. We shall be satisfied when those rights have been made as secure as the faith and the freedom of nations can make them.

Just because we fight without rancour and without selfish object, seeking nothing for ourselves but what we shall wish to share with all free peoples, we shall, I feel confident, conduct our operations as belligerents without passion and ourselves observe with proud punctilio the principles of right and of fair play we profess to be fighting for.

I have said nothing of the governments allied with the Imperial Government of Germany because they have not made war upon us or challenged us to defend our right and our honour. The Austro-Hungarian Government has, indeed, avowed its unqualified endorsement and acceptance of the reckless and lawless submarine warfare adopted now without disguise by the Imperial German Government, and it has therefore not been possible for this Government to receive Count Tarnowski, the Ambassador recently accredited to this Government by the Imperial and Royal Government of Austria-Hungary; but that Government has not actually engaged in warfare against citizens of the United States on the seas, and I take the liberty, for the present at least, of postponing a discussion of our relations with the authorities at Vienna. We enter this war only where we are clearly forced into it because there are no other means of defending our rights.

It will be all the easier for us to conduct ourselves as belligerents in a high spirit of right and fairness because we act without animus, not in enmity towards a people or with the desire to bring any injury or disadvantage upon them, but only in armed opposition to an irresponsible government which has thrown aside all considerations of humanity and of right and is running amuck. We are, let me say again, the sincere friends of the German people, and shall desire nothing so much as the early re-establishment of intimate relations of mutual advantage between us,—however hard it may be for them, for the time being, to believe that this is spoken from our hearts. We have borne with their present government through all these bitter months because of that friendship,—exercising a patience and forbearance which would otherwise have been impossible. We shall, happily, still have an opportunity to prove that friendship in our daily attitude and actions towards the millions of men and women of German birth and native sympathy who live amongst us and share our life, and we shall be proud to prove it towards all who are in fact loyal to their neighbours and to the Government in the hour of test. They are, most of them, as true and loyal Americans as if they had never known any other fealty or allegiance. They will be prompt to stand with us in rebuking and restraining the few who may be of a different mind and purpose. If there should be disloyalty, it will be dealt with with a firm hand of stern repression; but, if it lifts its head at all, it will lift it only here and there and without countenance except from a lawless and malignant few.

It is a distressing and oppressive duty, Gentlemen of the Congress, which I have performed in thus addressing you. There are, it may be, many months of fiery trial and sacrifice ahead of us. It is a fearful thing to lead this great peaceful people into war, into the most terrible and disastrous of all wars, civilization itself seeming to be in the balance. But the right is more precious than peace, and we shall fight for the things which we have always carried nearest our hearts,—for democracy, for the right of those who submit to authority to have a voice in their own governments, for the rights and liberties of small nations, for a universal dominion of right by such a concert of free peoples as shall bring peace and safety to all nations and make the world itself at last free. To such a task we can dedicate our lives and our fortunes, everything that we are and everything that we have, with the pride of those who know that the day has come when America is privileged to spend her blood and her might for the principles that gave her birth and happiness and the peace which she has treasured. God helping her, she can do no other.

Source:

Link, Arthur S., *The Papers of Woodrow Wilson*. Princeton, N.J.: Princeton University Press, 1966–94.

Selective Service Act, 1917

Federal legislation enacted on May 18, 1917, establishing registration and classification for military service of all men between the ages of 21 and 30, inclusive. Local civilian draft boards were given responsibility for administering the draft. Exemptions were allowed for alienage, physical unfitness, and conscientious objections on religious grounds. The act was amended by the Man Power Act, passed on August 31, 1918, which required registration of all men from age 18 to 45. More than 24 million men were registered over the course of World War I (1914–18). Conscription was halted after the war.

An Act

To authorize the President to increase temporarily the Military Establishment of the United States.

Be it enacted by the Senate and House of Representatives of the United States of America in Congress assembled, That in view of the existing emergency, which demands the raising of troops in addition to those now available, the President be, and he is hereby, authorized—

First. Immediately to raise, organize, officer, and equip all or such number of increments of the Regular Army provided by the national defense Act approved June third, nineteen hundred and sixteen, or such parts thereof as he may deem necessary; to raise all organizations of the Regular Army, including those added by such increments, to the maximum enlisted strength authorized by law. Vacancies in the Regular Army created or caused by the addition of increments as herein authorized which can not be filled by promotion may be filled by temporary appointment for the period of the emergency or until replaced by permanent appointments or by provisional appointments made under the provisions of section twenty-three of the national defense Act, approved June third, nineteen hundred and sixteen, and hereafter provisional appointments under said section may be terminated whenever it is determined, in the manner prescribed by the President, that the officer has not the suitability and fitness requisite for permanent appointment.

Second. To draft into the military service of the United States, organize, and officer, in accordance with the provisions of section one hundred and eleven of said national defense Act, so far as the provisions of said section may be applicable and not inconsistent with the terms of this Act, any or all members of the National Guard and of the National Guard Reserves, and said members so drafted into the military service of the United States shall serve therein for the period of the existing emergency unless sooner discharged: *Provided,* That when so drafted the organizations or units of the National Guard shall, so far as practicable, retain the State designations of their respective organizations.

Third. To raise by draft as herein provided, organize and equip an additional force of five hundred thousand enlisted men, or such part or parts thereof as he may at any time deem necessary, and to provide the necessary officers, line and staff, for said force and for organizations of the other forces hereby authorized, or by combining organizations of said other forces, by ordering members of the Officers' Reserve Corps to temporary duty in accordance with the provisions of section thirty-eight of the national defense Act approved June third, nineteen hundred and sixteen; by appointment from the Regular Army, the Officers' Reserve Corps, from those duly qualified and registered pursuant to section twenty-three of the Act of Congress approved January twenty-first, nineteen hundred and three (Thirty-second Statutes at Large, page seven hundred and seventy-five), from the members of the National Guard drafted into the service of the United States, from those who have been graduated from educational institutions at which military instruction is compulsory, or from those who have had honorable service in the Regular Army, the National Guard, or in the volunteer forces, or from the country at large; by assigning retired officers of the Regular Army to active duty with such force with their rank on the retired list and the full pay and allowances of their grade; or by the appointment of retired officers and enlisted men, active or retired, of the Regular Army as commissioned officers in such forces: *Provided,* That the organization of said force shall be the same as that of the corresponding organizations of the Regular Army: *Provided, further,* That the President is authorized to increase or decrease the number of organizations prescribed for the typical brigades, divisions, or army corps of the Regular Army, and to prescribe such new and different organizations and personnel for army corps, divisions, brigades, regiments, battalions, squadrons, companies, troops, and batteries as the efficiency of the service may require: *Provided further,* That number of organizations in a regiment shall not be increased nor shall the number of regiments be decreased: *Provided further,* That the President in his discretion may organize, officer, and equip for each Infantry and Cavalry brigade three machine-gun companies, and for each Infantry and Cavalry division four machine-gun companies, all in addition to the machine-gun companies comprised in organizations included in such brigades and divisions: *Provided further,* That the President in his discretion may organize for each division one armored motor-car machine-gun company. The machine-gun companies organized under this section shall consist of such commissioned and enlisted personnel and be equipped in such manner as the President may prescribe: *And Provided further,* That officers with rank not above that of colonel shall be appointed by the President alone, and officers above that grade by the President by and with the advice and consent of the Senate: *Provided further,* That the President may in his discretion recommission in the Coast Guard persons who have heretofore held commissions in the Revenue-Cutter Service or the Coast Guard and have left the service honorably, after ascertaining that they are qualified for service physically, morally, and as to age and military fitness.

Fourth. The President is further authorized, in his discretion and at such time as he may determine, to raise and begin the training of an additional force of five hundred thousand men organized, officered, and equipped, as provided for the force first mentioned in the preceding paragraph of this section.

Fifth. To raise by draft, organize, equip, and officer, as provided in the third paragraph of this section, in addition to and for each of the above forces, such recruit training units as he may deem necessary for the maintenance of such forces at the maximum strength.

Sixth. To raise, organize, officer, and maintain during the emergency such number of ammunition batteries and battalions, depot batteries and battalions, and such artillery parks, with such numbers and grades of personnel as he may deem necessary. Such organizations shall be officered in the manner provided in the third paragraph of this section, and enlisted men may be assigned to said organizations from any of the forces herein provided for or raised by selective draft as by this Act provided.

Seventh. The President is further authorized to raise and maintain by voluntary enlistment, to organize, and equip, not to exceed four infantry divisions, the officers of which shall be selected in the manner provided by paragraph three of section one of this Act: *Provided,* That the organization of said force shall be the same as that of the corresponding organization of the Regular Army: *And provided further,* That there shall be no enlistments in said force of men under twenty-five years of age at time of enlisting: *And provided further,* That no such volunteer force shall be accepted in any unit smaller than a division.

Sec. 2. That the enlisted men required to raise and maintain the organizations of the Regular Army and to complete and maintain the organizations embodying the members of the National Guard drafted into the service of the United States, at the maximum legal strength as by this Act provided, shall be raised by voluntary enlistment, or if and whenever the President decides that they can not effectually be so raised or maintained, then by selective draft; and all other forces hereby authorized, except as provided in the seventh paragraph of section one, shall be raised and maintained by selective draft exclusively; but this provision shall not prevent the transfer to any force of training cadres from other forces. Such draft as herein provided shall be based upon liability to military, service of all male citizens, or male persons not alien enemies who have declared their intention to become citizens, between the ages of twenty-one and thirty-years, both inclusive, and shall take place and be maintained under such regulations as the President may prescribe not inconsistent with the terms of this Act. Quotas for the several States, Territories, and the District of Columbia, or subdivisions thereof, shall be determined in proportion to the population thereof, and credit shall be given to any State, Territory, District, or subdivision thereof, for the number of men who were in the military service of the United States as members of the National Guard on April first, nineteen hundred and seventeen, or who have since said date entered the military service of the United States from any such State, Territory, District, or subdivision, either as members of the Regular Army or the National Guard. All persons drafted into the service of the United States and all officers accepting commissions in the forces herein provided for shall, from the date of said draft or acceptance, be subject to the laws and regulations governing the Regular Army, except as to promotions, so far as such laws and regulations are applicable to persons whose permanent retention in the military service on the active or retired list is not contemplated by existing law, and those drafted shall be required to serve for the period of the existing emergency unless sooner discharged: *Provided,* That the President is authorized to raise and maintain by voluntary enlistment or draft, as herein provided, special and technical troops as he may deem necessary, and to embody them into organizations and to officer them as provided in the third paragraph of section one and section nine of this Act. Organizations of the forces herein provided for, except the Regular Army and the divisions authorized in the seventh paragraph of section one, shall, as far as the interests of the service permit, be composed of men who come, and of officers who are appointed from, the same State or locality.

Sec. 3. No bounty shall be paid to induce any person to enlist in the military service of the United States; and no person liable to military service shall hereafter be permitted or allowed to furnish a substitute for such service; nor shall any substitute be received, enlisted, or enrolled in the military service of the United States; and no such person shall be permitted to escape such service or to be discharged therefrom prior to the expiration of his term of service by the payment of money or any other valuable thing whatsoever as consideration for his release from military service or liability thereto.

Sec. 4. That the Vice President of the United States, the officers, legislative, executive, and judicial, of the United States and of the several States, Territories, and the District of Columbia, regular or duly ordained ministers of religion, students who at the time of the approval of this Act are preparing for the ministry in recognized theological or divinity schools, and all persons in the military and naval service of the United States shall be exempt from the selective draft herein prescribed; and nothing in this Act contained shall be construed to require or compel any person to serve in any of the forces herein provided for who is found to be a member of any well-recognized religious sect or organization at present organized and existing and whose existing creed or principles forbid its members to participate in war in any form and whose religious convictions are against war or participation therein in accordance with the creed or principles of said religious organizations, but no person so exempted shall be exempted from service in any capacity that the President shall declare to be noncombatant; and the President is hereby authorized to exclude or discharge from said selective draft and from the draft under the second paragraph of section one hereof, or to draft for partial military service only from those liable to draft as in this Act provided, persons of the following classes: County and municipal officials; customhouse clerks; persons employed by the United States in the transmission of the mails; artificers and workmen employed in the armories, arsenals, and navy yards of the United States, and such other persons employed in the service of the United States as the President may designate; pilots; mariners actually employed in the sea service of any citizen or merchant within the United States; persons engaged in industries, including agriculture, found to be necessary to the maintenance of the Military Establishment or the effective operation of the military forces or the maintenance of national interest during the emergency; those in a status with respect to persons dependent upon them for support which renders their exclusion or discharge advisable; and those found to be physically or morally deficient. No exemption or exclusion shall continue when a cause therefor no longer exists: *Provided,* That notwithstanding the exemptions enumerated herein, each State, Territory, and the District of Columbia shall be required to supply its quota in the proportion that its population bears to the total population of the United States.

The President is hereby authorized, in his discretion, to create and establish throughout the several States and subdivisions thereof and in the Territories and the District of Columbia local boards, and where, in his discretion, practicable and desirable, there shall be created and established one such local board in each county or similar subdivision in each State, and one for approximately each thirty thousand of population in each city of thirty thousand population or over, according to the last census taken or estimates furnished by the Bureau of Census of the Department of Commerce. Such boards shall be appointed by the President, and shall consist of three or more members, none of whom shall be connected with the Military Establishment, to be chosen from among the local authorities of such subdivisions or from other citizens residing in the subdivision or area in which the respective boards will have jurisdiction under the rules and regulations prescribed by the President. Such boards shall have power within their respective jurisdictions to hear and determine, subject to review as hereinafter provided, all questions of exemption under this Act, and all questions of or claims for including or discharging individuals or classes of individuals from the selective draft, which shall be made under rules and regulations prescribed by the President, except any and every question or claim for including or excluding or discharging persons or classes of persons from the selective draft under the provisions of this Act authorizing the President to exclude or discharge from the selective draft "Persons engaged in industries, including agriculture, found to be necessary to the maintenance of the Military Establishment, or the effective operation of the military forces, or the maintenance of national interest during the emergency."

The President is hereby authorized to establish additional boards, one in each Federal judicial district of the United States, consisting of such number of citizens, not connected with the Military Establishment, as the President may determine, who shall be appointed by the President. The President is hereby authorized, in his discretion, to establish more than one such board in any Federal judicial district of the United States, or to establish one such board having jurisdiction of an area extending into more than one Federal judicial district.

Such district boards shall have review on appeal and affirm, modify, or reverse any decision of any local board having jurisdiction in the area in which any such district board has jurisdiction under the rules and regulations prescribed by the President. Such district boards shall have exclusive original jurisdiction within their respective areas to hear and determine all questions or claims for including or excluding or discharging persons or classes of persons from the selective draft, under the provisions of this Act, not included within the original jurisdiction of such local boards.

The decisions of such district boards shall be final except that, in accordance with such rules and regulations as the President may prescribe, he may affirm, modify or reverse any such decision.

Any vacancy in any such local board or district board shall be filled by the President, and any member of any such local board or district board may be removed and another appointed in his place by the President, whenever he considers that the interest of the nation demands it.

The President shall make rules and regulations governing the organization and procedure of such local boards and district boards, and providing for and governing appeals from such local boards to such district boards, and reviews of the decisions of any local board by the district board having jurisdiction, and determining and prescribing the several areas in which the respective local boards and district boards shall have jurisdiction, and all other rules and regulations necessary to carry out the terms and provisions of this section, and shall provide for the issuance of certificates of exemption, or partial or limited exemptions, and for a system to exclude and discharge individuals from selective draft.

Sec. 5. That all male persons between the ages of twenty-one and thirty, both inclusive, shall be subject to registration in accordance with regulations to be prescribed by the President; and upon proclamation by the President or other public notice given by him or by his direction stating the time and place of such registration it shall be the duty of all persons of the designated ages, except officers and enlisted men of the Regular Army, the Navy, and the National Guard and Naval Militia while in the service of the United States, to present themselves for and submit to registration under the provisions of this Act; and every such person shall be deemed to have notice of the requirements of this Act upon the publication of said proclamation or other notice as aforesaid given by the President or by his direction; and any person who shall willfully fail or refuse to present himself for registration or to submit thereto as herein provided, shall be guilty of a misdemeanor and shall, upon conviction in the district court of the United States having jurisdiction thereof, be punished by imprisonment for not more than one year, and shall thereupon be duly registered: *Provided,* That in the call of the docket precedence shall be given, in courts trying the same, to the trial of criminal proceedings under this Act: *Provided further,* That persons shall be subject to registration as herein provided who shall have attained their twenty-first birthday and who shall not have attained their thirty-first birthday on or before the day set for the registration, and all persons so registered shall be and remain subject to draft into the forces hereby authorized, unless exempted or excused therefrom as in this Act provided: *Provided further,* That in the case of temporary absence from actual place of legal residence of any person liable to registration as provided herein such registration may be made by mail under regulations to be prescribed by the President.

Sec. 6. That the President is hereby authorized to utilize the service of any or all departments and any or all officers or agents of the United States and of the several States, Territories, and the District of Columbia, and subdivisions thereof, in the execution of this Act, and all officers and agents of the United States and of the several States, Territories, and subdivisions thereof, and of the District of Columbia, and all persons designated or appointed under regulations prescribed by the President whether such appointments are made by the President himself or by the governor or other officer of any State or Territory to perform any duty in the execution of this Act, are hereby required to perform such duty as the President shall order or direct, and all such officers and agents and persons so designated or appointed shall hereby have full authority for all acts done by them in the execution of this Act by the direction of the President. Correspondence in the execution of this Act may be carried in penalty envelopes bearing the frank of the War Department. Any person charged as herein provided with the duty of carrying into effect any of the provisions of this Act or the regulations made or directions given thereunder who shall fail or neglect to perform such duty; and any person charged with such duty or having and exercising any authority under said Act, regulations, or directions, who shall knowingly make or be a party to the making of any false or incorrect registration, physical examination, exemption, enlistment, enrollment, or muster; and any person who shall make or be a party to the making of any false statement or certificate as to the fitness or liability of himself or any other person for service under the provisions of this Act, or regulations made by the President thereunder, or otherwise evades or aids another to evade the requirements of this Act or of said regulations, or who, in any manner, shall fail or neglect fully to perform any duty required of him in the execution of this Act, shall, if not subject to military law, be guilty of a misdemeanor, and upon conviction in the district court of the United States having jurisdiction thereof, be punished by imprisonment for not more than one year, or, if subject to military law, shall be tried by court-martial and suffer such punishment as a court-martial may direct.

Sec. 7. That the qualifications and conditions for voluntary enlistment as herein provided shall be the same as those prescribed by existing law for enlistments in the Regular Army, except that recruits must be between the ages of eighteen and forty years, both inclusive, at the time of their enlistment; and such enlistments shall be for the period of the emergency unless sooner discharged. All enlistments, including those in the Regular Army Reserve, which are in force on the date of the approval of this Act and which would terminate during the emergency shall continue in force during the emergency unless sooner discharged; but nothing herein contained shall be construed to shorten the period of any existing enlistment: *Provided*, That all persons enlisted or drafted under any of the provisions of this Act shall as far as practicable be grouped into units by States and the political subdivisions of the same: *Provided further*, That all persons who have enlisted since April first, nineteen hundred and seventeen, either in the Regular Army or in the National Guard, and all persons who have enlisted in the National Guard since June third, nineteen hundred and sixteen, upon their application, shall be discharged upon the termination of the existing emergency.

The President may provide for the discharge of any of all enlisted men whose status with respect to dependents renders such discharge advisable; and he may also authorize the employment on any active duty of retired enlisted men of the Regular Army, either with their rank on the retired list or in higher enlisted grades, and such retired enlisted men shall receive the full pay and allowances of the grades in which they are actively employed.

Sec. 8. That the President, by and with the advice and consent of the Senate is authorized to appoint for the period of the existing emergency such general officers of appropriate grades as may be necessary for duty with brigades, divisions, and higher units in which the forces provided for herein may be organized by the President, and general officers of appropriate grade for the several Coast Artillery districts. In so far as such appointments may be made from any of the forces herein provided for, the appointees may be selected irrespective of the grades held by them in such forces. Vacancies in all grades in Regular Army resulting from the appointment of officers thereof to higher grades in the forces other than the Regular Army herein provided for shall be filled by temporary promotions and appointments in the manner prescribed for filling temporary vacancies by section one hundred and fourteen of the national defense Act approved June third, nineteen hundred and sixteen; and officers appointed under the provisions of this Act to higher grades in the forces other than the Regular Army herein provided for shall not vacate their permanent commissions nor be prejudiced in their relative or lineal standing in the Regular Army.

Sec. 9. That the appointments authorized and made as provided by the second, third, fourth, fifth, sixth, and seventh paragraphs of section one and by section eight of this Act, and the temporary appointments in the Regular Army authorized by the first paragraph of section one of this Act, shall be for the period of the emergency, unless sooner terminated by discharge or otherwise. The President is hereby authorized to discharge any officer from the office held by him under such appointment for any cause which, in the judgment of the President, would promote the public service; and the general commanding any division and higher tactical organization or territorial department is authorized to appoint from time to time military boards of not less than three nor more than five officers of the forces herein provided for to examine into and report upon the capacity, qualification, conduct, and efficiency of any commissioned officer within his command other than officers of the Regular Army holding permanent or provisional commissions therein. Each member of such board shall be superior in rank to the officer whose qualifications are to be inquired into, and if the report of such board be adverse to the continuance of any such officer and be approved by the President, such officer shall be discharged from the service at the discretion of the President with one month's pay and allowances.

Sec. 10. That all officers and enlisted men of the forces herein provided for other than the Regular Army shall be in all respects on the same footing as to pay, allowances, and pensions as officers and enlisted men of corresponding grades and length of service in the Regular Army; and commencing June one, nineteen hundred and seventeen, and continuing until the termination of the emergency, all enlisted men of the Army of the United States in active service whose base pay does not exceed $21 per month shall receive an increase of $15 per month; those whose base pay is $24, an increase of $12 per month; those whose base pay is $30, $36, or $40, an increase of $8 per month; and those whose base pay is $45 or more, an increase of $6 per month: *Provided,* That the increases of pay herein authorized shall not enter into the computation of continuous-service pay.

Sec. 11. That all existing restrictions upon the detail, detachment, and employment of officers and enlisted men of the Regular Army are hereby suspended for the period of the present emergency.

Sec. 12. That the President of the United States, as Commander in Chief of the Army, is authorized to make such regulations governing the prohibition of alcoholic liquors in or near military camps and to the officers and enlisted men of the Army as he may from time to time deem necessary or advisable: *Provided,* That no person, corporation, partnership, or association shall sell, supply, or have in his or its possession any intoxicating or spirituous liquors at any military station, cantonment, camp, fort, post, officers' or enlisted men's club, which is being used at the time for military purposes under this Act, but the Secretary of War may make regulations permitting the sale and use of intoxicating liquors for medicinal purposes. It shall be unlawful to sell any intoxicating liquor, including beer, ale, or wine, to any officer or member of the military forces while in uniform, except herein provided. Any person, corporation, partnership, or association violating the provisions of this section of the regulations made thereunder shall, unless otherwise punishable under the Articles of War, be deemed guilty of a misdemeanor and be punished by a fine of not more than $1,000 or imprisonment for not more than twelve months, or both.

Sec. 13. That the Secretary of War is hereby authorized, empowered, and directed during the present war to do everything by him deemed necessary to suppress and prevent the keeping or setting up of houses of ill fame, brothels, or bawdy houses within such distance as he may deem needful of any military camp, station, fort, post, cantonment, training, or mobilization place, and any person, corporation, partnership, or association receiving or permitting to be received for immoral purposes any person into any place, structure, or building used for the purpose of lewdness, assignation, or prostitution within such distance of said places as may be designated, or shall permit any such person to remain for immoral purposes in any such place, structure, or building as aforesaid, or who shall violate any order, rule, or regulation issued to carry out the object and purpose of this section shall, unless otherwise punishable under the Articles of War, be deemed guilty of a misdemeanor and be punished by a fine of not more than $1,000, or imprisonment for not more than twelve months, or both.

Sec. 14. That all laws and parts of laws in conflict with the provisions of this Act are hereby suspended during the period of this emergency.

Source:

Statutes at Large, Vol. 39, pp. 76–83.

Espionage Act, 1917

Federal legislation enacted on June 15, 1917, aimed at suppressing treasonable and disloyal activities after Americans entered World War I. It provided that individuals could be fined up to $10,000 and imprisoned for 20 years for such offenses as aiding the enemy, obstructing recruitment, and causing insubordination, disloyalty, or refusal of duty in the military. The U.S. postmaster general was given the power to exclude from the mails newspapers, magazines, and other items deemed treasonable or seditious. The act was extended by the Espionage (or Sedition) Act of 1918. The constitutionality of the Espionage Act and the Sedition Act was upheld by the U.S. Supreme Court in *Schenck v. United States* and *Abrams v. United States* (1919). Many of the Espionage Act provisions required a state of war to be in effect.

An Act

To punish acts of interference with the foreign relations, the neutrality, and the foreign commerce of the United States, to punish espionage, and better to enforce the criminal laws of the United States, and for other purposes.

Be it enacted by the Senate and House of Representatives of the United States of America in Congress assembled:

Title I

Espionage.

Section 1. That (a) whoever, for the purpose of obtaining information respecting the national defense with intent or reason to believe that the information to be obtained is to be used to the injury of the United States, or to the advantage of any foreign nation, goes upon, enters, flies over, or otherwise obtains information concerning any vessel, aircraft, work of defense, navy yard, naval station, submarine base, coaling station, fort, battery, torpedo station, dockyard, canal, railroad, arsenal, camp, factory, mine, telegraph, telephone, wireless, or signal station, building, office, or other place connected with the national defense, owned or constructed, or in progress of construction by the United States or under the control of the United States, or of any of its officers or agents, or within the exclusive jurisdiction of the United States, or any place in which any vessel, aircraft, arms, munitions, or other materials or instruments for use in time of war are being made, prepared, repaired or stored under any contract or agreement with the United States, or with any person on behalf of the United States, or otherwise on behalf of the United States, or any prohibited place . . . or (b) whoever for the purpose aforesaid, and with like intent or reason to believe, copies, takes, makes, or obtains, or attempts, or induces or aids another to copy, take, make, or obtain, any sketch, photograph, photographic negative, blue print, plan, map, model, instrument, appliance, document, writing, or note of anything connected with the national defense; or (c) whoever, for the purpose aforesaid, receives or obtains or agrees or attempts or induces or aids another to receive or obtain from any person, or from any source whatever, any document, writing, code book, signal book, sketch, photograph, photographic negative, blue print, plan, map, model, instrument, appliance, or note, of anything connected with the national defense, knowing or having reason to believe, at the time he receives or obtains, or agrees or attempts or induces or aids another to receive or obtain it, that it has been or will be obtained, taken, made or disposed of by any person contrary to the provisions of this title; or (d) whoever, lawfully or unlawfully having possession of, access to, control over, or being intrusted with any [of the above listed items] relating to the national defense, willfully communicates or transmits or attempts to communicate or transmit the same to any person not entitled to receive it, or willfully retains the same and fails to deliver it on demand to the officer or employee of the United States entitled to receive it; or (e) whoever, being intrusted with or having lawful possession or control of any document, writing, code book, signal book, sketch, photograph, photographic negative, blue print, plan, map, model, note, or information, relating to the national defense, through gross negligence permits the same to be removed from its proper place of custody or delivered to anyone in violation of his trust, or to be lost, stolen, abstracted, or destroyed, shall be punished by a fine of not more than $10,000, or by imprisonment for not more than two years, or both.

Sec. 2. (a) Whoever, with the intent or reason to believe that it is to be used to the injury of the United States or the advantage of a foreign nation, communicates, delivers, or transmits, or attempts to, or aids or induces another to, communicate, deliver, or transmit, to any foreign government, or to any faction or party or military or naval force within a foreign country, whether recognized or unrecognized by the United States, or to any representative, officer, agent, employee, subject to citizen thereof, either directly or indirectly [of the above listed items] relating to the national defense, shall be punished by imprisonment for not more than twenty years: Provided, That whoever shall violate the provisions of subsection (a) of this section in time of war shall be punished by death or by imprisonment for not more than thirty years; and (b) whoever, in time of war, with intent that the same shall be communicated to the enemy, shall collect, record, publish, or communicate, or attempt to elicit any information with respect to the movement, numbers, description, condition, or disposition of any of the armed forces, ships, aircraft, or war materials of the United States, or with respect to the plans or conduct, or supposed plans or conduct of any naval or military operations, or with respect to any works or measures undertaken for or connected with, or intended for the fortification or defense of any place, or any other information relating to the public defense, which might be useful to the enemy, shall be punished by death or by imprisonment for not more than thirty years.

Sec. 3. Whoever, when the United States is at war, shall willfully make or convey false reports or false statements with intent to interfere with the operation or success of the military or naval forces of the United States or to promote the success of its enemies and whoever when the United States is at war, shall willfully cause or attempt to cause insubordination, disloyalty, mutiny, or refusal of duty, in the military or naval forces of the United States, or shall willfully obstruct the recruiting or enlistment service of the United States, to the injury of the service or of the United States, shall be punished by a fine of not more than $10,000 or imprisonment for not more than twenty years or both.

Sec. 4. If two or more persons conspire to violate the provisions of sections two or three of this title, and one or more of such persons does any act to effect the object of the conspiracy, each of the parties to such conspiracy shall be punished as in paid sections provided in the case of the doing of the act the accomplishment of which is the object of such conspiracy. Except as above provided conspiracies to commit offenses under this title shall be punished as provided by section thirty-seven of the Act to codify, revise, and amend the penal laws of the United States approved March fourth, nineteen hundred and nine.

Sec. 5. Whoever harbors or conceals any person who he knows, or has reasonable grounds to believe or suspect, has committed, or is about to commit, an offense under this title shall be punished by a fine of not more than $10,000 or by imprisonment for not more than two years, or both.

* * *

Sec. 7. Nothing contained in this title shall be deemed to limit the jurisdiction of the general courts-martial, military commissions, or naval courts-martial. . . .

Sec. 8. The provisions of this title shall extend to all Territories, possessions, and places subject to the jurisdiction of the United States whether or not contiguous thereto, and offenses under this title when committed upon the high seas or elsewhere with in the admiralty and maritime jurisdiction of the United States and outside the territorial limits thereof shall be punishable hereunder.

Sec. 9. The Act entitled "An Act to prevent the disclosure of national defense secrets," approved March third, nineteen hundred and eleven, is hereby repealed.

* * *

Title III

Injuring Vessels Engaged in Foreign Commerce.

Section 1. Whoever shall set fire to any vessel of foreign registry or any vessel of American registry entitled to engage in commerce with foreign nations, or to any vessel of the United States as defined in section three hundred and ten of the Act of March fourth, nineteen hundred and nine, entitled "An Act to codify, revise, and amend the penal laws of the United States," or to the cargo of the same, or shall tamper with the motive power or instrumentalities of navigation of such vessel, or shall place bombs or explosives in or upon such vessel, or shall do any other act to or upon such vessel while within the jurisdiction of the United States, or, if such vessel is of American registry, while she is on the high sea, with intent to injure or endanger the safety of the vessel or of her cargo, or of persons on board, whether the injury or danger is to intended to take place within the jurisdiction of the United States, or after the vessel shall have departed therefrom; or whoever shall attempt or conspire to do any such acts with such intent, shall be fined not more than $10,000 or imprisoned not more than twenty years, or both.

Title IV

Interference with Foreign Commerce by Violent Means.

Section 1. Whoever, with intent to prevent, interfere with, or obstruct or attempt to prevent, interfere with, or obstruct the exportation to foreign countries of articles from the United States shall injure or destroy, by fire or explosives, such articles or the places where they may be while in such foreign commerce, shall be fined not more than $10,000, or imprisoned not more that ten years, or both.

* * *

Title VIII

Disturbance of Foreign Relations.

Section 1. Whoever, in relation to any dispute or controversy between a foreign government and the United States, shall willfully and knowingly make any untrue statement, either orally or in writing, under oath before any person authorized and empowered to administer oaths, which the affiant has knowledge or reason to believe will, or may be used to influence the measures or conduct of any foreign government, or of any officer or agent of any foreign government, to the injury of the United States, or with a view or intent to influence any measure of or action by the Government of the United States, or any branch thereof, to the injury of the United States, shall be fined not more than $5,000 or imprisoned not more than five years, or both.

Sec. 2. Whoever within the jurisdiction of the United States shall falsely assume or pretend to be a diplomatic or consular, or other official of a foreign government duly accredited as such to the Government of the United States with intent to defraud such foreign government or any person, and shall take upon himself to act as such, or in such pretended character shall demand or obtain, or attempt to obtain from any person or from said foreign government, or from any officer thereof, any money, paper, document, or other thing of value, shall be fined not more than $5,000, or imprisoned not more than five years, or both.

Sec. 3. Whoever, other than a diplomatic or consular officer of attache, shall act in the United States as an agent of a foreign government without prior notification to the Secretary of State shall be fined not more than $5,000, or imprisoned not more than five years, or both.

Sec. 4. The words "foreign government" . . . shall be deemed to include any Government, faction, or body of insurgents within a country with which the United States is at peace, which Government, faction, or body of insurgents may or may not have been recognized by the United States as a Government.

Sec. 5. If two or more persons within the jurisdiction of the United States conspire to injure or destroy specific property situated within a foreign country and belonging to a foreign Government or to any political subdivision thereof with which the United States is at peace, or any railroad, canal, bridge, or other public utility so situated, and if one or more of such persons commits an act within the jurisdiction of the United States to effect the object of the conspiracy, each of the parties to the conspiracy shall be fined not more than $5,000, or imprisoned not more than three years, or both. Any indictment or information under this section shall describe the specific property which it was the object of the conspiracy to injure or destroy.

Title IX

Passports.

Section 1. Before a passport is issued to any person by or under authority of the United States such person shall subscribe to and submit a written application duly verified by his oath before a person authorized and empowered to administer oaths, which said application shall contain a true recital of each and every matter of fact which may be required by law or by any rules authorized by law to be stated as a prerequisite to the issuance of any such passport. Clerks of United States courts, agents of the Department of State, or other Federal officials authorized, or who may be authorized, to take passport applications and administer oaths thereon, shall collect, for all services in connection therewith, a fee of $1, and no more, in lieu of all fees prescribed by any statute of the United States, whether the application is executed singly, in duplicate, or in triplicate.

Sec. 2. Whoever shall willfully and knowingly make any false statement in an application for passport with intent to induce or secure the issuance of a passport under the authority of the United States, either for his own use or the use of another, contrary to the laws regulating the issuance of passports or the rules prescribed pursuant to such laws, or whoever shall willfully and knowingly use or attempt to use, or furnish to another for use, any passport the issue of which was secured in any way by reason of any false statement, shall be fined not more than $2,000 or imprisoned not more than five years or both.

Sec. 3. Whoever shall willfully and knowingly use, or attempt to use, any passport issued or designed for the use of another than himself, or whoever shall willfully and knowingly use or attempt to use any passport in violation of the conditions or restrictions therein contained, or of the rules prescribed pursuant to the laws regulating the issuance of passports, which said rules shall be printed on the passport; or whoever shall willfully and knowingly furnish, dispose of, or deliver a passport to any person, for use by another than the person for whose use it was originally issued and designed, shall be fined not more than $2,000 or imprisoned not more than five years, or both.

Sec. 4. Whoever shall falsely make, forge, counterfeit, mutilate, or alter, or cause or procure to be falsely made, forged, counterfeited, mutilated, or altered any passport or instrument purporting to be a passport, with intent to use the same, or with intent that the same may be used by another; or whoever shall willfully or knowingly use, or attempt to use, or furnish to another for use and such false, forged, counterfeited, mutilated, or altered passport or instrument purporting to be a passport, or any passport validly issued which has become void by the occurrence of any condition therein prescribed invalidating the same, shall be fined not more than $2,000 or imprisoned not more than five years, or both.

* * *

Title XI

Search Warrants.

Section 1. A search warrant authorized by this title may be issued by a judge of a United States district court, or by a judge or a State or Territorial court of record, or by a United States commissioner for the district wherein the property sought is located.

Sec. 2. A search warrant may be issued under this title upon either of the following grounds:

1. When the property was stolen or embezzled in violation of a law of the United States; in which case it may be taken on the warrant from any house or other place in which it is concealed, or from the possession of the person by whom it was stolen or embezzled, of from any person in whose possession it may be.

2. When the property was used as the means of committing a felony; in which case it may be taken on the warrant from any house or other place in which it is concealed, or from the possession of the person by whom it was used in the commission of the offense, or from any person in whose possession it may be.

* * *

Sec. 3. A search warrant can not be issued but upon probable cause, supported by affidavit, naming or describing the person and particularly describing the property and the place to be searched.

Sec. 4. The judge or commissioner must, before issuing the warrant, examine on oath the complainant and any witness he may produce, and require their affidavits or take their depositions in writing and cause them to be subscribed by the parties making them.

Sec. 5. The affidavits or depositions must set forth the facts tending to establish the grounds of the application or probable cause for believing that they exist.

* * *

Sec. 8. The officer may break open any outer or inner door or window of a house, or any part of a house, or anything therein, to execute the warrant, if, after notice of his authority and purpose, he is refused admittance.

Sec. 9. He may break open any outer or inner door or window of a house for the purpose of liberating a person who, having entered to aid him in the execution of the warrant, is detained therein, or when necessary for his own liberation.

Sec. 10. The judge or commissioner must insert a direction in the warrant that it be served in the daytime, unless the affidavits are positive that the property is on the person or in the place to be searched, in which case he may insert a direction that it be served at any time of the day or night.

Sec. 11. A search warrant must be executed and returned to the judge or commissioner who issued it within ten days after its date; after the expiration of this time the warrant, unless executed, is void.

Sec. 12. When the officer takes property under the warrant, he must give a copy of the warrant together with a receipt for the property taken (specifying it in detail) to the person from whom it was taken by him, or in whose possession it was found; or, in the absence of any person, he must leave it in the place where he found the property.

* * *

Sec. 14. The judge or commissioner must thereupon, if required, deliver a copy of the inventory to the person from whose possession the property was taken and to the applicant for the warrant.

* * *

Sec. 17. The judge or commissioner must annex the affidavits, search warrant, return, inventory, and evidence, and if he has not power to inquire into the offense in respect to which the warrant was issued he must at once file the same, together with a copy of the record of his proceedings, with the clerk of the court having power to so inquire.

Sec. 18. Whoever shall knowingly and willfully obstruct, resist, or oppose any such officer or person in serving or attempting to serve or execute any such search warrant, or shall assault, beat, or wound any such officer or person, knowing him to be an officer or person so authorized, shall be fined not more than $1,000 or imprisoned not more than two years.

Sec. 19. Sections one hundred and twenty-five and one hundred and twenty-six of the Criminal Code of the United States shall apply to and embrace all persons making oath or affirmation or procuring the same under the provisions of this title, and such persons shall be subject to all the pains and penalties of said sections.

Sec. 20. A person who maliciously and without probable cause procures as search warrant to be issued and executed shall be fined not more than $1,000 or imprisoned not more than one year.

Sec. 21. An officer who in executing a search warrant willfully exceeds his authority, or exercises it with unnecessary severity, shall be fined not more than $1,000 or imprisoned not more than one year.

Sec. 22. Whoever, in aid of any foreign Government, shall knowingly and willfully have possession of or control over any property or papers designed or intended for use or which is used as the means of violating any penal statute, or any of the rights or obligations of the United States under any treaty or the law of nations, shall be fined not more than $1,000 or imprisoned not more than two years, or both.

Sec. 23. Nothing contained in this title shall be held to repeal or impair any existing provisions of law regulating search and the issue of search warrants.

Title XII

Use of Mails.

Section 1. Every letter, writing, circular, postal card, picture, print, engraving, photograph, newspaper, pamphlet, book, or other publication, matter, or thing, of any kind, in violation of any of the provisions of this Act is hereby declared to be nonmailable matter and shall not be conveyed in the mails or delivered from any post office or by any letter carrier: *Provided,* That nothing in this Act shall be so construed as to authorize any person other than an employee of the Dead Letter Office, duly authorized thereto, or other person upon a search warrant authorized by law, to open any letter not addressed to himself.

Sec. 2. Every letter, writing, circular, postal card, picture, print, engraving, photograph, newspaper, pamphlet, book, or other publication, matter or thing, of any kind, containing any matter advocating or urging treason, insurrection, or forcible resistance to any law of the United States, is hereby declared to be nonmailable.

Sec. 3. Whoever shall use or attempt to use the mails or Postal Service of the United States for the transmission of any matter declared by this title to be nonmailable, shall be fined not more than $5,000 or imprisoned not more than five years, or both. Any person violating any provision of this title may be tried and punished either in the district in which the unlawful matter or publication was mailed, or to which it was carried by mail for delivery according to the direction thereon, or in which it was caused to be delivered by mail to the person to whom it was addressed.

Title XIII

General Provisions.

Section 1. The term "United States" as used in this Act includes the Canal Zone and all territory and waters, continental or insular, subject to the jurisdiction of the United States.

Sec. 2. The several courts of first instance in the Philippine Islands and the district court of the Canal Zone shall have jurisdiction of offenses under this Act committed within their respective districts, and concurrent jurisdiction with the district courts of the United States of offenses under this Act committed upon the high seas, and of conspiracies to commit such offenses, as defined by section thirty-seven of the Act entitled "An Act to codify, revise, and amend the penal laws of the United States," approved March fourth, nineteen hundred and nine, and the provisions of said section, for the purpose of this Act, are hereby extended to the Philippine Islands, and to the Canal Zone. In such cases the district attorneys of the Philippine Islands and of the Canal Zone shall have the powers and perform the duties provided in this Act for United States attorneys.

Sec. 3. Offenses committed and penalties, forfeitures, or liabilities incurred prior to the taking effect hereof under any law embraced in or changed, modified, or repealed by any chapter of this Act may be prosecuted and punished, and suits and proceedings for causes arising or acts done or committed prior to the taking effect hereof may be commenced and prosecuted in the same manner and with the same effect as if this Act had not been passed.

Sec. 4. If any clause, sentence, paragraph, or part of this Act shall for any reason be adjudged by any court of competent jurisdiction to be invalid, such judgment shall not affect, impair, or invalidate the remainder thereof but shall be confined in its operation to the clause, sentence, paragraph, or part thereof directly involved in the controversy in which such judgment shall have been rendered.

Source:

Statutes at Large, Vol. 40, pp. 217–231; Vol. 40, pp. 533–534.

Woodrow Wilson, Fourteen Points, 1918

Address delivered to Congress on January 8, 1918, by President Woodrow Wilson, setting forth his program for a just and enduring world peace. These points became the basis for negotiating an end to World War I. A year earlier, the president had addressed the U.S. Senate, calling for an end to the war and outlining his ideas for the basis of an enduring world peace. In the speech, Wilson sought a peace that would protect the rights of both sides, a "peace without victory" between nations equal in rights, if not in power. This peace had to be guaranteed by an international organization, "the organized major force of mankind." He argued that peace must be based on the principle of government by the consent of the governed, that all nations must have free access to the seas and the paths of commerce, that no nation should seek to extend its powers over another, that nations should avoid entangling alliances, and that armaments must be limited.

These points were developed further in Wilson's Fourteen Points speech. Wilson called for "open covenants of peace, openly arrived at"; absolute freedom of the seas, in peace and war; equality of trade conditions among nations; reductions of national armaments; impartial adjustment of colonial claims; self-determination for Russia and the peoples of the former Austria-Hungary; restoration or adjustments of Belgian, French, Italian, Rumanian, Serbian, and Montenegrin borders; autonomy for nationalities formerly under Turkish rule, but sovereignty for Turkey; opening of the Dardanelles to all nations; establishment of an independent Poland; and formation of an association of nations to guarantee "political independence and territorial integrity to great and small states alike."

Gentlemen of the Congress: Once more, as repeatedly before, the spokesmen of the Central Empires have indicated their desire to discuss the objects of the war and the possible bases of a general peace. Parleys have been in progress at Brest-Litovsk between representatives of the Central Powers, to which the attention of all the belligerents has been invited for the purpose of ascertaining whether it may be possible to extend these parleys into a general conference with regard to terms of peace and settlement. The Russian representatives presented not only a perfectly definite statement of the principles upon which they would be willing to conclude peace, but also an equally definite programme of the concrete application of those principles. The representatives of the Central Powers, on their part, presented an outline of settlement which, if much less definite, seemed susceptible of liberal interpretation until their specific programme of practical terms was added. That programme proposed no concessions at all either to the sovereignty of Russia or to the preferences of the populations with whose fortunes it dealt, but meant, in a word, that the Central Empires were to keep every foot of territory their armed forces had occupied,—every province, every city, every point of vantage,—as a permanent addition to their territories and their power. It is a reasonable conjecture that the general principles of settlement which they at first suggested originated with the more liberal statesmen of Germany and Austria, the men who have begun to feel the force of their own peoples' thought and purpose, while the concrete terms of actual settlement came from the military leaders who have no thought but to keep what they have got. The negotiations have been broken off. The Russian representatives were sincere and in earnest. They cannot entertain such proposals of conquest and domination.

The whole incident is full of significance. It is also full of perplexity. With whom are the Russian representatives dealing? For whom are the representatives of the Central Empires speaking? Are they speaking for the majorities of their respective parliaments or for the minority parties, that military and imperialistic minority which has so far dominated their whole policy and controlled the affairs of Turkey and of the Balkan states which have felt obliged to become their associates in this war? The Russian representatives have insisted, very justly, very wisely, and in the true spirit of modern democracy, that the conferences they have been holding with the Teutonic and Turkish statesmen should be held within open, not closed doors, and all the world has been audience, as was desired. To whom have we been listening, then? To those who speak the spirit and intention of the Resolutions of the German Reichstag of the ninth of July last, the spirit and intention of the liberal leaders and parties of Germany, or to those who resist and defy that spirit and intention and insist upon conquest and subjugation? Or are we listening, in fact, to both, unreconciled and in open and hopeless contradiction? These are very serious and pregnant questions. Upon the answer to them depends the peace of the world.

But, whatever the results of the parleys at Brest-Litovsk, whatever the confusions of counsel and of purpose in the utterances of the spokesmen of the Central Empires, they have again attempted to acquaint the world with their objects in the war and have again challenged their adversaries to say what their objects are and what sort of settlement they would deem just and satisfactory. There is no good reason why that challenge should not be responded to, and responded to with the utmost candor. We did not wait for it. Not once, but again and again, we have laid our whole thought and purpose before the world, not in general terms only, but each time with sufficient definition to make it clear what sort of definitive terms of settlement must necessarily spring out of them. Within the last week Mr. Lloyd George has spoken with admirable candor and in admirable spirit for the people and Government of Great Britain. There is no confusion of counsel among the adversaries of the Central Powers, no uncertainty of principle, no vagueness of detail. The only secrecy of counsel, the only lack of fearless frankness, the only failure to make definite statement of the objects of the war, lies with Germany and her Allies. The issues of life and death hang upon these definitions. No statesman who has the least conception of his responsibility ought for a moment to permit himself to continue this tragical and appalling outpouring of blood and treasure unless he is sure beyond a peradventure that the objects of the vital sacrifice are part and parcel of the very life of Society and that the people for whom he speaks think them right and imperative as he does.

There is, moreover, a voice calling for these definitions of principle and of purpose which is, it seems to me, more thrilling and more compelling than any of the many moving voices with which the troubled air of the world is filled. It is the voice of the Russian people. They are prostrate and all but helpless, it would seem, before the grim power of Germany, which has hitherto known no relenting and no pity. Their power, apparently, is shattered. And yet their soul is not subservient. They will not yield either in principle or in action. Their conception of what is right, of what is humane and honorable for them to accept, has been stated with a frankness, a largeness of view, a generosity of spirit, and a universal human sympathy which must challenge the admiration of every friend of mankind; and they have refused to compound their ideals or desert others that they themselves may be safe. They call to us to say what it is that we desire, in what, if in anything, our purpose and our spirit differ from theirs; and I believe that the people of the United States would wish me to respond, with utter simplicity and frankness. Whether their present leaders believe it or not, it is our heartfelt desire and hope that some way may be opened whereby we may be privileged to assist the people of Russia to attain their utmost hope of liberty and ordered peace.

It will be our wish and purpose that the processes of peace, when they are begun, shall be absolutely open and that they shall involve and permit henceforth no secret understandings of any kind. The day of conquest and aggrandizement is gone by; so is also the day of secret covenants entered into the interest of particular governments and likely at some unlooked-for moment to upset the peace of the world. It is this happy fact, now clear to the view of every public man whose thoughts do not still linger in an age that is dead and gone, which makes it possible for every nation whose purposes are consistent with justice and the peace of the world to avow now or at any other time the objects it has in view.

We entered this war because violations of right had occurred which touched us to the quick and made the life of our own people impossible unless they were corrected and the world secured once for all against their recurrence. What we demand in this war, therefore, is nothing peculiar to ourselves. It is that the world be made fit and safe to live in; and particularly that it be made safe for every peace-loving nation which, like our own, wishes to live its own life, determine its own institutions, be assured of justice and fair dealing by the other peoples of the world as against force and selfish aggression. All the peoples of the world are in effect partners in this interest, and for our own part we see very clearly that unless justice be done to others it will not be done to us. The programme of the world's peace, therefore, is our programme; and that programme, the only possible programme, as we see it, is this:

I. Open covenants of peace, openly arrived at, after which there shall be no private international understandings of any kind but diplomacy shall proceed always frankly and in the public view.

II. Absolute freedom of navigation upon the seas, outside territorial waters, alike in peace and in war, except as the seas may be closed in whole or in part by international action for the enforcement of international covenants.

III. The removal, so far as possible, of all economic barriers and the establishment of an equality of trade conditions among all the nations consenting to the peace and associating themselves for its maintenance.

IV. Adequate guarantees given and taken that national armaments will be reduced to the lowest point consistent with domestic safety.

V. A free, open-minded, and absolutely impartial adjustment of all colonial claims, based upon a strict observance of the principle that in determining all such questions of sovereignty the interests of the populations concerned must have equal weight with the equitable claims of the government whose title is to be determined.

VI. The evacuation of all Russian territory and such a settlement of all questions affecting Russia as will secure the best and freest and cooperation of the other nations of the world in obtaining for her an unhampered and unembarrassed opportunity for the independent determination of her own political development and national policy and assure her of a sincere welcome into the society of free nations under institutions of her own choosing; and, more than a welcome, assistance also of every kind that she may need and may herself desire. The treatment accorded Russia by her sister nations in the months to come will be the acid test of their good will, of their comprehension of her needs as distinguished from their own interests, and of their intelligent and unselfish sympathy.

VII. Belgium, the whole world will agree, must be evacuated and restored, without any attempt to limit the sovereignty which she enjoys in common with all other free nations. No other single act will serve as this will serve to restore confidence among the nations in the laws which they have themselves set and determined for the government of their relations with one another. Without this healing act the whole structure and validity of international law is forever impaired.

VIII. All French territory should be freed and the invaded portions restored, and the wrong done to France by Prussia in 1871 in the matter of Alsace-Lorraine, which has unsettled the peace of the world for nearly fifty years, should be righted, in order that peace may once more be made secure in the interests of all.

IX. A readjustment of the frontiers of Italy should be effected along clearly recognizable lines of nationality.

X. The peoples of Austria-Hungary, whose place among the nations we wish to see safeguarded and assured, should be accorded the freest opportunity of autonomous development.

XI. Rumania, Serbia, and Montenegro should be evacuated; occupied territories restored; Serbia accorded free and secure access to the sea; and the relations of the several Balkan states to one another determined by friendly counsel along historically established lines of allegiance and nationality; and international guarantees of the political and economic independence and territorial integrity of the several Balkan states should be entered into.

XII. The Turkish portions of the present Ottoman Empire should be assured a secure sovereignty but the other nationalities which are now under Turkish rule should be assured an undoubted security of life and an absolutely unmolested opportunity of autonomous development, and the Dardanelles should be permanently opened as a free passage to the ships and commerce of all nations under international guarantees.

XIII. An independent Polish state should be erected which should include the territories inhabited by indisputably Polish populations, which should be assured a free and secure access to the sea, and whose political and economic independence and territorial integrity should be guaranteed by international covenant.

XIV. A general association of nations must be formed under specific covenants for the purpose of affording mutual guarantees of political independence and territorial integrity to great and small states alike.

In regard to these essential rectifications of wrong and assertions of right we feel ourselves to be intimate partners of all the governments and peoples associated together against the Imperialists. We cannot be separated in interest or divided in purpose. We stand together until the end.

For such arrangements and covenants we are willing to fight and to continue to fight until they are achieved; but only because we wish the right to prevail and desire a just and stable peace such as can be secured only by removing the chief provocations to war, which this programme does remove. We have no jealousy of German greatness, and there is nothing in this programme that impairs it. We grudge her no achievement or distinction of learning or of pacific enterprise such as have made her record very bright and very enviable. We do not wish to injure her or to block in any way her legitimate influence or power. We do not wish to fight her either with arms or with hostile arrangements of trade if she is willing to associate herself with us and the other peace-loving nations of the world in covenants of justice and law and fair dealing. We wish her only to accept a place of equality among the peoples of the world,—the new world in which we now live,—instead of a place of mastery.

Neither do we presume to suggest to her any alteration or modification of her institutions. But it is necessary, we must frankly say, and necessary as a preliminary to any intelligent dealings with her on our part, that we should know whom her spokesmen speak for when they speak to us, whether for the Reichstag majority or for the military party and the men whose creed is imperial domination.

We have spoken now, surely, in terms too concrete to admit of any further doubt or question. An evident principle runs through the whole programme I have outlined. It is the principle of justice to all peoples and nationalities, and their right to live on equal terms of liberty and safely with one another, whether they be strong or weak. Unless this principle be made its foundation no part of the structure of international justice can stand. The people of the United States could act upon no other principle; and to the vindication of this principle they are ready to devote their lives, their honor, and everything that they possess. The normal climax of this the culminating and final war for human liberty has come, and they are ready to put their own strength, their own highest purpose, their own integrity and devotion to the test.

See also WOODROW WILSON, "MAKE THE WORLD SAFE FOR DEMOCRACY," 1917.

Source:

Link, Arthur S., et al., eds. *The Papers of Woodrow Wilson*. Princeton, N.J.: Princeton University Press, 1966–94.

Sedition Act, 1918

Legislation enacted by the U.S. Congress on May 16, 1918, amending the Espionage Act of 1917 and drastically curtailing freedom of speech and the press during World War I. The act established severe penalties for making or conveying false statements that interfered with military or naval operations, promoted enemy successes, obstructed military recruitment or the sale of U.S. bonds, or that incited military insubordination, disloyalty, or refusal of duty. It prohibited "disloyal, profane, scurrilous, or abusive language" about the form of the U.S. government, the U.S. Constitution, the flag, and the military and naval forces, and it outlawed urging the curtailment of essential war production. It also punished the advocating, teaching, defending, or suggesting of any of these actions. The constitutionality of the Espionage Act and the Sedition Act were upheld by the U.S. Supreme Court in *Schenck v. United States* and *Abrams v. United States* both in 1919.

Significantly, this act made sedition a federal crime only in wartime. When the war was over, the U.S. Department of Justice (DOJ) lost its ability to arrest radicals for sedition. Instead, it had to rely on state sedition laws to punish American citizens, or on the Immigration and Naturalization authorities, then the Department of Labor to deport seditious individuals. Despite the efforts of the attorney general, backed by J. Edgar Hoover, who became the effective head of DOJ's Radical Division in 1919, no peacetime federal sedition law was passed. Although affected in part by *Brandenburg v. Ohio* (395 U.S. 444 [1969]), state sedition laws still exist.

An Act

To amend section three, title one, of the Act entitled "An Act to punish acts of interference with the foreign relations, the neutrality, and the foreign commerce of the United States, to punish espionage, and better to enforce the criminal laws of the United States, and for other purposes," approved June fifteenth, nineteen hundred and seventeen, and for other purposes.

Be it enacted by the Senate and House of Representatives of the United States of America in Congress assembled, That section three of title one of the Act entitled "An Act to punish acts of interference with the foreign relations, the neutrality, and the foreign commerce of the United States, to punish espionage, and better to enforce the criminal laws of the United States, and for other purposes," approved June fifteenth, nineteen hundred and seventeen, be, and the same is hereby, amended so as to read as follows:

"Sec. 3. Whoever, when the United States is at war, shall willfully make or convey false reports or false statements with intent to interfere with the operation or success of the military or naval forces of the United States, or to promote the success of its enemies, or shall willfully make or convey false reports or false statements, or say or do anything except by way of bona fide and not disloyal advice to an investor or investors, with intent to obstruct the sale by the United States of bonds or other securities of the United States or the making of loans by or to the United States, and whoever, when the United States is at war, shall willfully cause or attempt to cause, or incite or attempt to incite, insubordination, disloyalty, mutiny, or refusal of duty, in the military or naval forces of the United States, or shall willfully obstruct or attempt to obstruct the recruiting or enlistment service of the United States, and whoever, when the United States is at war, shall willfully utter, print, write, or publish any disloyal, profane, scurrilous, or abusive language about the form of government of the United States, or the Constitution of the United States, or the military or naval forces of the United States, or the flag of the United States, or the uniform of the Army of Navy of the United States, or any language intended to bring the form of government of the United States, or the Constitution of the United States, or the military or naval forces of the United States, or the flag of the United States, or the uniform of the Army or Navy of the United States into contempt, scorn, contumely, or disrepute, or shall willfully utter, print, write, or publish any language intended to incite, provoke, or encourage resistance to the United States, or to promote the cause of its enemies, or shall willfully display the flag of any foreign enemy, or shall willfully by utterance, writing, printing, publication, or language spoken, urge, incite, or advocate any curtailment of production in this country of any thing or things, product or products, necessary or essential to the prosecution of the war in which the United States may be engaged, with intent by such curtailment to cripple or hinder the United States in the prosecution of the war, and whoever shall willfully advocate, teach, defend, or suggest the doing of any of the acts or things in this section enumerated, and whoever shall by word or act support or favor the cause of any country with which the United States is at war or by word or act oppose the cause of the United States therein, shall be punished by a fine of not more than $10,000 or imprisonment for not more than twenty years, or both: *Provided,* That any employee or official of the United States Government who commits any disloyal act or utters any unpatriotic or disloyal language, or who, in an abusive and violent manner criticizes the Army or Navy or the flag of the United States shall be at once dismissed from the service. Any such employee shall be dismissed by the head of the department in which the employee may be engaged, and any such official shall be dismissed by the authority having power to appoint a successor to the dismissed official."

Sec. 2. That section one of Title XII and all other provisions of the Act entitled "An Act to punish acts of interference with the foreign relations, the neutrality, and the foreign commerce of the United States, to punish espionage, and better to enforce the criminal laws of the United States, and for other purposes," approved June fifteenth, nineteen hundred and seventeen, which apply to section three of Title I thereof shall apply with equal force and effect to said section three as amended.

Title XII of the said Act of June fifteenth, nineteen hundred and seventeen, be, and the same is hereby, amended by adding thereto the following section:

"Sec. 4. When the United States is at war, the Postmaster General may, upon evidence satisfactory to him that any person or concern is using the mails in violation of any of the provisions of this Act, instruct the postmaster at any post office at which mail is received addressed to such person or concern to return to the postmaster at the office at which they were originally mailed all letters or other matter so addressed, with the words 'Mail to this address undeliverable under Espionage Act' plainly written or stamped upon the outside thereof, and all such letters or other matter so returned to such postmasters shall be by them returned to the senders thereof under such regulations as the Postmaster General may prescribe."

See also ESPIONAGE ACT, 1917.

Source:
Statutes at Large, Vol. 40, pp. 553–554.

League of Nations Covenant, 1919

Part one of the Treaty of Versailles, the Allies' "dictated peace" with Germany, was signed June 28, 1919, at Versailles, France. This part enunciated the goals and the organizational framework of the proposed new international body, the League of Nations.

The Treaty of Versailles finalized by an Allied committee on April 28, 1919, became effective January 10, 1920. It followed the Armistice of November 11, 1918. In the Armistice, signed at Rethondes, in the forest of Compiègne in northern France, the hostilities of World War I ended. Following the first peace overtures made by Germany on October 6, the Allies agreed that Germany was to evacuate all occupied territory as well as to ground its submarines and naval fleet and destroy its tanks, aircraft, and heavy artillery. All prisoners and deported civilians were to be returned, while the Allies reserved the right to press for monetary compensation for losses sustained during the war. Germany was to nullify the Treaties of Bucharest and Brest-Litovsk and cede to the Allies 150,000 railroad wagons, 5,000 locomotives, and 5,000 trucks. The Allied troops would remain until the peace treaty was signed. The Treaty of Versailles conferred more severe terms than the Armistice had indicated.

The covenant signatories agreed to protect each other against aggression and to accept mediation in settling their disputes. It was to consist of a general assembly (one representative from each member state), a council (representatives from the five main Allied powers, plus four others chosen by rotation), and a permanent Geneva-based secretariat, headed by a secretary-general. A permanent court of international justice was to be established. Disarmament, labor, and health reforms and international cooperation were other key concerns. In 1946, after World War II, its activities were taken over by the United Nations.

The rest of the Treaty of Versailles involved war reparations, by which Germany was required to cede some of its territory to neighboring nations and abolish its air force and curtail its army and navy. The concessions Germany was forced to make produced conditions that led to the rise of the Nazi Party.

The High Contracting Parties,

In order to promote international co-operation and to achieve international peace and security

by the acceptance of obligations not to resort to war,

by the prescription of open, just and honourable relations between nations,

by the firm establishment of the understandings of international law as the actual rule of conduct among Governments, and

by the maintenance of justice and a scrupulous respect for all treaty obligations in the dealings of organised peoples with one another,

Agree to this Covenant of the League of Nations.

Article 1

The original Members of the League of Nations shall be those of the Signatories which are named in the Annex to this Covenant and also such of those other States named in the Annex as shall accede without reservation to this Covenant. Such accession shall be effected by a Declaration deposited with the Secretariat within two months of the coming into force of the Covenant. Notice thereof shall be sent to all other Members of the League.

Any fully self-governing State, Dominion or Colony not named in the Annex may become a Member of the League if its admission is agreed to by two-thirds of the Assembly, provided that it shall give effective guarantees of its sincere intention to observe its international obligations, and shall accept such regulations as may be prescribed by the League in regard to its military, naval and air forces and armaments.

Any Member of the League may, after two years notice of its intention so to do, withdraw from the League, provided that all its international obligations and all its obligations under this Covenant shall have been fulfilled at the time of its withdrawal.

Article 2

The action of the league under this Covenant shall be effected through the instrumentality of an Assembly and of a Council, with a permanent Secretariat.

Article 3

The Assembly shall consist of Representatives of the Members of the League.

The Assembly shall meet at stated intervals and from time to time as occasion may require at the Seat of the League or at such other place as may be decided upon.

The Assembly may deal at its meetings with any matter within the sphere of action of the League or affecting the peace of the world.

At meetings of the Assembly each Member of the League shall have one vote, and may have not more than three Representatives.

Article 4

The Council shall consist of Representatives of the Principal Allied and Associated Powers, together with Representatives of four other Members of the League. These four Members of the League shall be selected by the Assembly from time to time in its discretion. Until the appointment of the Representatives of the four Members of the League first selected by the Assembly, Representatives of Belgium, Brazil, Spain and Greece shall be members of the Council.

With the approval of the majority of the Assembly, the Council may name additional Members of the League whose Representatives shall always be members of the Council; the Council with like approval may increase the number of Members of the League to be selected by the Assembly for representation on the Council.

The Council shall meet from time to time as occasion may require, and at least once a year, at the Seat of the League, or at such other place as may be decided upon.

The Council may deal at its meetings with any matter within the sphere of action of the League or affecting the peace of the world.

Any Member of the League not represented on the Council shall be invited to send a Representative to sit as a member at any meeting of the Council during the consideration of matters specially affecting the interests of that Member of the League.

At meetings of the Council, each Member of the League represented on the Council shall have one vote, and may have not more than one Representative.

Article 5

Except where otherwise expressly provided in this Covenant or by the terms of the present Treaty, decisions at any meeting of the Assembly or of the Council shall require the agreement of all the Members of the League represented at the meeting.

All matters of procedure at meetings of the Assembly or of the Council, including the appointment of Committees to investigate particular matters, shall be regulated by the Assembly or by the Council and may be decided by a majority of the Members of the League represented at the meeting.

The first meeting of the Assembly and the first meeting of the Council shall be summoned by the President of the United States of America.

Article 6

The permanent Secretariat shall be established at the Seat of the League. The Secretariat shall comprise a Secretary General and such secretaries and staff as may be required.

The first Secretary General shall be the person named in the Annex; thereafter the Secretary General shall be appointed by the Council with the approval of the majority Assembly.

The secretaries and staff of that Secretariat shall be appointed by the Secretary General with the approval of the Council.

The Secretary General shall act in the capacity at all meetings of the Assembly and of the Council.

The expenses of the Secretariat shall be borne by the Members of the League in accordance with the apportionment of the expenses of the International Bureau of the Universal Postal Union.

Article 7

The Seat of the League is established at Geneva.

The Council may at any time decide that the Seat of the League shall be established elsewhere.

All positions under or in connection with the League, including the Secretariat, shall be open equally to men and women.

Representatives of the Members of the League and officials of the League when engaged on the business of the League shall enjoy diplomatic privileges and immunities.

The buildings and other property occupied by the League or its officials or by Representatives attending its meetings shall be inviolable.

Article 8

The Members of the League recognise that the maintenance of peace requires the reduction of national armaments to the lowest point consistent with national safety and the enforcement by common action of international obligations.

The Council, taking account of the geographical situation and circumstances of each State, shall formulate plans for such reduction for the consideration and action of the several Governments.

Such plans shall be subject to reconsideration and revision at least every ten years.

After these plans shall have been adopted by the several Governments, the limits of armaments therein fixed shall not be exceeded without the concurrence of the Council.

The Members of the League agree that the manufacture by private enterprise of munitions and implements of war is open to grave objections. The Council shall advise how the evil effects attendant upon such manufacture can be prevented, due regard being had to the necessities of those Members of the League which are not able to manufacture the munitions and implements of war necessary for their safety.

The Members of the League undertake to interchange full and frank information as to the scale of their armaments, their military, naval and air programmes and the condition of such of their industries as are adaptable to war-like purposes.

Article 9

A permanent Commission shall be constituted to advise the Council on the execution of the provision of Articles 1 and 8 and on military, naval and air questions generally.

Article 10

The Members of the League undertake to respect and preserve as against external aggression the territorial integrity and existing political independence of all Members of the League. In case of any such aggression or in case of any threat or danger of such aggression the Council shall advise upon the means by which this obligation shall be fulfilled.

Article 11

Any war or threat of war, whether immediately affecting any of the Members of the League or not, is hereby declared a matter of concern to the whole League, and the League shall take any action that may be deemed wise and effectual to safeguard the peace of nations. In case any such emergency should arise the Secretary General shall on the request of any Member of the League forthwith summon a meeting of the Council.

It is also declared to be the friendly right of each Member of the League to bring to the attention of the Assembly or of the Council any circumstance whatever affecting international relations which threatens to disturb international peace or the good understanding between nations upon which peace depends.

Article 12

The Members of the League agree that if there should arise between them any dispute likely to lead to a rupture, they will submit the matter either to arbitration or to inquiry by the Council, and they agree in no case to resort to war until three months after the award by the arbitrators or the report by the Council.

In any case under this Article the award of the arbitrators shall be made within a reasonable time, and the report of the Council shall be made within six months after the submission of the dispute.

Article 13

The Members of the League agree that whenever any dispute shall arise between them which they recognise to be suitable for submission to arbitration and which cannot be satisfactorily settled by diplomacy, they will submit the whole subject-matter to arbitration.

Disputes as to the interpretation of a treaty, as to any question of international law, as to the existence of any fact which if established would constitute a breach of any international obligation, or as to the extent and nature of the reparation to be made for any such breach, are declared to be among those which are generally suitable for submission to arbitration.

For the consideration of any such dispute the court of arbitration to which the case is referred shall be the Court agreed on by the parties to the dispute or stipulated in any convention existing between them.

The Members of the League agree that they will carry out in full good faith any award that may be rendered, and that they will not resort to war against a Member of the League which complies therewith. In the event of any failure to carry out such an award, the Council shall propose what steps should be taken to give effect thereto.

Article 14

The Council shall formulate and submit to the Members of the League for adoption plans for the establishment of a Permanent Court of International Justice. The Court shall be competent to hear and determine any dispute of an international character which the parties thereto submit to it. The Court may also give an advisory opinion upon any dispute or question referred to it by the Council or by the Assembly.

Article 15

If there should arise between Members of the League any dispute likely to lead to a rupture, which is not submitted to arbitration in accordance with Article 13, the Members of the League agree that they will submit the matter to the Council. Any party to the dispute may effect such submission by giving notice of the existence of the dispute to the Secretary General, who will make all necessary arrangements for a full investigation and consideration thereof.

For this purpose the parties to the dispute will communicate to the Secretary General, as promptly as possible, statements of their case with all the relevant facts and papers, and the Council may forthwith direct the publication thereof.

The Council shall endeavour to effect a settlement of the dispute, and if such efforts are successful, a statement shall be made public giving such facts and explanations regarding the dispute and the terms of settlement thereof as the Council may deem appropriate.

If the dispute is not thus settled, the Council either unanimously or by a majority vote shall make and publish a report containing a statement of the facts of the dispute and the recommendations which are deemed just and proper in regard thereto.

Any Member of the League represented on the Council may make public a statement of the facts of the dispute and of its conclusions regarding the same.

If a report by the Council is unanimously agreed to by the members thereof other than the Representatives of one or more of the parties to the dispute, the Members of the League agree that they will not go to war with any party to the dispute which complies with the recommendations of the report.

If the Council fails to reach a report which is unanimously agreed to by the members thereof, other than the Representatives of one or more of the parties to the dispute, the Members of the League reserve to themselves the right to take such action as they shall consider necessary for the maintenance of right and justice.

If the dispute between the parties is claimed by one of them, and is found by the Council, to arise out of a matter which by international law is solely within the domestic jurisdiction of that party, the Council shall so report, and shall make no recommendation as to its settlement.

The Council may in any case under this Article refer the dispute to the Assembly. The dispute shall be so referred at the request of either party to the dispute, provided that such request be made within fourteen days after the submission of the dispute to the Council.

In any case referred to the Assembly, all the provisions of this Article and of Article 12 relating to the action and powers of the Council shall apply to the action and powers of the Assembly, provided that a report made by the

Assembly, if concurred in by the Representatives of those Members of the League represented on the Council and of a majority of the other Members of the League, exclusive in each case of the Representatives of the parties to the dispute, shall have the same force as a report by the Council concurred in by all the members thereof other than the Representatives of one or more of the parties to the dispute.

Article 16

Should any Member of the League resort to war in disregard of its covenants under Articles 12, 13 or 15, it shall *ipso facto* be deemed to have committed an act of war against all other Members of the League, which hereby undertake immediately to subject it to the severance of all trade or financial relations, the prohibition of all intercourse between their nationals and the nationals of the covenants-breaking State, and the prevention of all financial, commercial or personal intercourse between the nationals of the covenant-breaking State and the nationals of any other State, whether a Member of the League or not.

It shall be the duty of the Council in such case to recommend to the several Governments concerned what effective military naval or air force the Members of the League shall severally contribute to the armed forces to be used to protect the covenants of the League.

The Members of the League agree, further, that they will mutually support one another in the financial and economic measures which are taken under this Article, in order to minimise the loss and inconvenience resulting from the above measures, and that they will mutually support one another in resisting any special measures aimed at one of their number by the covenant-breaking State, and that they will take the necessary steps to afford passage through their territory to the forces of any of the Members of the League which are co-operating to protect the covenants of the League.

Any Member of the League which has violated any covenant of the League may be declared to be no longer a Member of the League by a vote of the Council concurred in by the Representatives of all the other Members of the League represented thereon.

Article 17

In the event of a dispute between a Member of the League and a State which is not a Member of the League, or between States not Members of the League, the State or States not Members of the League shall be invited to accept the obligations of membership in the League for the purposes of such dispute, upon such conditions as the Council may deem just. If such invitation is accepted, the provisions of Articles 12 to 16 inclusive shall be applied with such modifications as may be deemed necessary by the Council.

Upon such invitation being given the Council shall immediately institute an inquiry into the circumstances of the dispute and recommend such action as may seem best and most effectual in the circumstances.

If a State so invited shall refuse to accept the obligations of membership in the League for the purposes of such dispute, and shall resort to war against a Member of the League, the provisions of Article 16 shall be applicable as against the State taking such action.

If both parties to the dispute when so invited refuse to accept the obligations of membership in the League for the purposes of such dispute, the Council may take such measures and make such recommendations as will prevent hostilities and will result in the settlement of the dispute.

Article 18

Every treaty or international engagement entered into hereafter by any Member of the League shall be forthwith registered with the Secretariat and shall as soon as possible be published by it. No such treaty or international engagement shall be binding until so registered.

Article 19

The Assembly may from time to time advise the reconsideration by Members of the League of treaties which have become inapplicable and the consideration of international conditions whose continuance might endanger the peace of the world.

Article 20

The Members of the League severally agree that this Covenant is accepted as abrogating all obligations or understandings *inter se* which are inconsistent with the terms thereof, and solemnly undertake that they will not hereafter enter into any engagements inconsistent with the terms thereof.

In case any Member of the League shall, before becoming a Member of the League, have undertaken any obligations inconsistent with the terms of this Covenant, it shall be the duty of such Member to take immediate steps to procure its release from such obligations.

Article 21

Nothing in this Covenant shall be deemed to affect the validity of international engagements, such as treaties of arbitration or regional understanding like the Monroe doctrine, for securing the maintenance of peace.

Article 22

To those colonies and territories which as a consequence of the late war have ceased to be under the sovereignty of the States which formerly governed them and which are inhabited by peoples not yet able to stand by themselves under the strenuous conditions of the modern world, there should be applied the principle that the will-being and development of such peoples form a sacred trust of civilisation and that securities for the performance of this trust should be embodied in this Covenant.

The best method of giving practical effect to this principle is that the tutelage of such peoples should be entrusted to advanced nations who by reason of their resources, their experience or their geographical position can best undertake this responsibility, and who are willing to accept it, and that this tutelage should be exercised by them as Mandatories on behalf of the League.

The character of the mandate must differ according to the stage of the development of the people, the geographical situation of the territory, its economic conditions and other similar circumstances.

Certain communities formerly belonging to the Turkish Empire have reached a stage of development where their existence as independent nations can be provisionally recognised subject to the rendering of administrative advice and assistance by a Mandatory until such time as they are able to stand alone. The wishes of these communities must be a principal consideration in the selection of the Mandatory.

Other peoples, especially those of Central Africa, are at such a stage that the Mandatory must be responsible for the administration of the territory under conditions which will guarantee freedom of conscience and religion, subject only to the maintenance of public order and morals , the prohibition of abuses such as the slave trade, the arms traffic and the liquor traffic, and the prevention of the establishment of fortifications or military and naval bases and of military training of the natives for other than police purposes and the defence of territory, and will also secure equal opportunities for the trade and commerce of other Members of the League.

There are territories, such as South-West Africa and certain of the South Pacific Islands, which, owing to the sparseness of their population, or their small size, or their remoteness from the centres of civilisation, or their geographical contiguity to the territory of the Mandatory, and other circumstances, can be best administered under the laws of the Mandatory as integral portions of its territory, subject to the safeguards above mentioned in the interests of the indigenous population.

In every case of mandate, the Mandatory shall render to the Council an annual report in reference to the territory committed to its charge.

The degree of authority, control, or administration to be exercised by the Mandatory shall, if not previously agreed upon by the Members of the League, be explicitly defined in each case by the Council.

A permanent Commission shall be constituted to receive and examine the annual reports of the Mandatories and to advise the Council on all matters relating to the observance of the mandates.

Article 23

Subject to and in accordance with the provisions of international conventions existing or hereafter to be agreed upon, the Members of the League:

(a) will endeavour to secure and maintain fair and humane conditions of labour for men, women, and children, both in their own countries and in all countries to which their commercial and industrial relations extend, and for that purpose will establish and maintain the necessary international organisations;

(b) undertake to secure just treatment of the native inhabitants of territories under their control;

(c) will entrust the League with the general supervision over the execution of agreements with regard to the traffic in women and children, and the traffic in opium and other dangerous drugs;

(d) will entrust the League with the general supervision of the trade in arms and ammunition with the countries in which the control of this traffic is necessary in the common interest;

(e) will make provision to secure and maintain freedom of communications and of transit and equitable treatment for the commerce of all Members of the League. In this connection, the special necessities of the regions devastated during the war 1914–1918 shall be borne in mind;

(f) will endeavour to take steps in matters of international concern for the prevention and control of disease.

Article 24

There shall be placed under the direction of the League all international bureaux already established by general treaties if the parties to such treaties consent. All such international bureaux and all commissions for regulation of matters of international interest hereafter constituted shall be placed under the direction of the League.

In all matters of international interest which are regulated by general conventions but which are not placed under the control of international bureaux or commissions, the Secretariat of the League shall, subject to the consent of the Council and if desired by the parties, collect and distribute all relevant information and shall render any other assistance which may be necessary or desirable.

The Council may include as part of the expenses of the Secretariat the expenses of any bureau or commission which is placed under the direction of the League.

Article 25
The Members of the League agree to encourage and promote the establishment and co-operation of duly authorized voluntary national Red Cross organizations having as purposes the improvement of health, the prevention of disease and the mitigation of suffering throughout the world.

Article 26
Amendments to this Covenant will take effect when ratified by the Members of the League whose Representatives compose the Council and by a majority of the Members of the League whose Representative compose the Assembly.

No such amendment shall bind any Member of the League which signifies its dissent therefrom, but in that case it shall cease to be a Member of the League.

Source:
Landmark Documents in American History, Facts On File, Inc..

Schenck v. United States, 1919

U.S. Supreme Court decision issued on March 3, 1919, upholding the Espionage Act of 1917 and ruling that freedom of speech, though guaranteed by the First Amendment, may be suppressed if it creates a "clear and present danger" of bringing about "substantive evils." Charles T. Schenck, a member of the American Socialist Party, had been convicted under the Espionage Act of distributing a pamphlet urging draft resistance during World War I. The Supreme Court unanimously held that the pamphlet might cause insubordination and obstruction to military service, which represented a "clear and present danger." In arguing the limits of free speech, Justice Oliver Wendell Holmes wrote: "The most stringent protection of free speech would not protect a man in falsely shouting fire in a theater and causing a panic."

The same year, the U.S. Supreme Court decision in *Abrams v. United States* (250 U.S. 616) upheld the U.S. Sedition Act of 1918. At issue were leaflets in Yiddish and English opposing the U.S. expeditionary force to Siberia (Russia). Using Holmes's arguments in *Schenck,* Justice John H. Clark concluded that the leaflets constituted a clear and present danger and were not protected by the First Amendment. Holmes, however, had modified his position and, without repudiating *Schenck,* dissented. Writing for himself and Justice Louis D. Brandeis, he argued for the protection of free speech, even of unpopular opinions, unless such ideas pose an imminent threat to national safety: "The ultimate good desired is better reached by free trade in ideas. . . . The best test of truth is the power of the thought to get itself accepted in the competition of the market."

Mr. JUSTICE HOLMES delivered the opinion of the Court.

This is an indictment in three counts. The first charges a conspiracy to violate the Espionage Act of June 15, 1917, c.30, tit. 1, Section 3, 40 Stat. 217, 219 (Comp. St. 1918, Section 10212c), by causing and attempting to cause insubordination, &c., in the military and naval forces of the United States, and to obstruct the recruiting and enlistment service of the United States, when the United States was at war with the German Empire, to-wit, that the defendant willfully conspired to have printed and circulated to men who had been called and accepted for military service under the Act of May 18, 1917, c. 15, 40 Stat. 76 (Comp. St. 1918, Sections 2044a–2044k), a document set forth and alleged to be calculated to cause such insubordination and obstruction. The count alleges overt acts in pursuance of the conspiracy, ending in the distribution of the document set forth. The second count alleges a conspiracy to commit an offense against the United States, to-wit, to use the mails for the transmission of matter declared to be non-mailable by title 12, Section 2, of the Act of June 15, 1917 (Comp. St. 1918, Section 10401b), to-wit, the above mentioned document, with an averment of the same overt acts. The third count charges an unlawful use of the mails for the transmission of the same matter and otherwise as above. The defendants were found guilty on all the counts. They set up the First Amendment to the Constitution forbidding Congress to make any law abridging the freedom of speech, or of the press, and bringing the case here on that ground have argued some other points also of which we must dispose.

[1] It is argued that the evidence, if admissible, was not sufficient to prove that the defendant Schenck was concerned in sending the documents. According to the testimony Schenck said he was general secretary of the Socialist party and had charge of the Socialist headquarters from which the documents were sent. He identified a book bound there as the minutes of the Executive Committee of the party. The book showed a resolution of August 13, 1917, that 15,000 leaflets should be printed on the other side of one of them is use, to be mailed to men who had passed exemption boards, and for distribution. Schenck personally attended to the printing. On August 20 the general secretary's report said "Obtained new leaflets from printer and started work addressing envelopes" &c.; and there was a resolve that Comrade Schenck be allowed $125 for sending leaflets through the mail. He said that he had about fifteen or sixteen thousand printed. There were files of the circular in question in the inner office which he said were printed on the other side of the one sided circular and

were there for distribution. Other copies were proved to have been sent through the mails to drafted men. Without going into confirmatory details that were proved, no reasonable man could doubt that the defendant Schenck was largely instrumental in sending the circulars about. As to the defendant Baer there was evidence that she was a member of the Executive Board and that the minutes of its transactions were hers. The argument as to the sufficiency of the evidence that the defendants conspired to send the documents only impairs the seriousness of the real defense.

[2–4] It is objected that the documentary evidence was not admissible because obtained upon a search warrant, valid so far as appears. The contrary is established. *Adams v. New York,* 192 U. S. 585, 24 Sup. Ct. 372, 48 L. Ed. 575; *Weeks v. United States,* 232 U. S. 383, 395, 396, 34 Sup. Ct. 341, 58 L. Ed. 652, L. R. A. 1915B, 834, Ann. Cas. 1915C, 1177. The search warrant did not issue against the defendant but against the Socialist headquarters at 1326 Arch street and it would seem that the documents technically were not even in the defendants' possession. See *Johnson v. United States,* 228 U. S. 457, 33 Sup. Ct. 572, 57 L. Ed. 919, 47 L. R. A. (N. S.) 263. Notwithstanding some protest in argument the notion that evidence even directly proceeding from the defendant in a criminal proceeding is excluded in all cases by the Fifth Amendment is plainly unsound. *Holt v. United States,* 218 U. S. 245, 252, 253, 31 Sup. Ct. 2, 54 L. Ed. 1021.

[5] The document in question upon its first printed side recited the first section of the Thirteenth Amendment, said that the idea embodied in it was violated by the conscription act and that a conscript is little better than a convict. In impassioned language it intimated that conscription was despotism in its worst form and a monstrous wrong against humanity in the interest of Wall Street's chosen few. If said, "Do not submit to intimidation," but in form at least confined itself to peaceful measures such as a petition for the repeal of the act. The other and later printed side of the sheet was headed "Assert Your Rights." It stated reasons for alleging that any one violated the Constitution when he refused to recognize "your right to assert your opposition to the draft," and went on, "If you do not assert and support your rights, you are helping to deny or disparage rights which it is the solemn duty of all citizens and residents of the United States to retain." It described the arguments on the other side as coming from cunning politicians and a mercenary capitalist press, and even silent consent to the conscription law as helping to support an infamous conspiracy. If denied the power to send our citizens away to foreign shores to shoot up the people of other lands, and added that words could not express the condemnation such cold-blooded ruthlessness deserves, &c., &c., winding up, "You must do your share to maintain, support and uphold the rights of the people of this country." Of course the document would not have been sent unless it had been intended to have some effect, and we do not see what effect it could be expected to have upon persons subject to the draft except to influence them to obstruct the carrying of it out. The defendants do not deny that the jury might find against them on this point.

[6] But it is said, suppose that that was the tendency of this circular, it is protected by the First Amendment to the Constitution. Two of the strongest expressions are said to be quoted respectively from well-known public men. It well may be that the prohibition of laws abridging the freedom of speech is not confined to previous restraints, although to prevent them may have been the main purpose, as intimated in *Patterson v. Colorado,* 205 U. S. 454, 462, 27 Sup. Ct. 556, 51 L. Ed. 879, 10 Ann. Cas. 689. We admit that in many places and in ordinary times the defendants in saying all that was said in the circular would have been within their constitutional rights. But the character of every act depends upon the circumstances in which it is done. *Aikens v. Wisconsin,* 195 U. S. 194, 205, 206, 25 Sup. Ct. 3, 49 L. Ed. 154. The most stringent protection of free speech would not protect a man in falsely shouting fire in a theatre and causing a panic. It does not even protect a man from an injunction against uttering words that may have all the effect of force. *Gompers v. Buck's Stove & Range Co.*, 221 U. S. 418, 439, 31 Sup. Ct. 492, 55 L. Ed. 797, 34 L. R. A. (N. S.) 874. The question in every case in whether the words used are used in such circumstances and are of such a nature as to create a clear and present danger that they will bring about the substantive evils that Congress has a right to prevent. It is a question of proximity and degree. When a nation is at war many things that might be said in time of peace are such a hindrance to its effort that their utterance will not be endured so long as men fight and that no Court could regard them as protected by any constitutional right. It seems to be admitted that if an actual obstruction of the recruiting service were proved, liability for words that produced that effect might be enforced. The statute of 1917 in section 4 (Comp. St. 1918, Section 10212d) punishes conspiracies to obstruct as well as actual obstruction. If the act, (speaking, or circulating a paper,) its tendency and the intent with which it is done are the same, we perceive no ground for saying that success alone warrants making the act a crime. *Goldman v. United States,* 245 U. S. 474, 477, 88 Sup. Ct. 166, 62 L. Ed. 410. Indeed that case might be said to dispose of the present contention if the precedent covers all media concludendi. But as the right to free speech was not referred to specially, we have thought fit to add a few words.

[7, 8] It was not argued that a conspiracy to obstruct the draft was not within the words of the Act of 1917. The words are "obstruct the recruiting or enlistment service," and it might be suggested that they refer only to making it

hard to get volunteers. Recruiting heretofore usually having been accomplished by getting volunteers the word is apt to call up that method only in our minds. But recruiting is gaining fresh supplies for the forces, as well by draft as otherwise. It is put as an alternative to enlistment or voluntary enrollment in this act. The fact that the Act of 1917 was enlarged by the amending Act of May 16, 1918, c. 75, 40 Stat. 553, of course, does not affect the present indictment and would not, even if the former act had been repealed. Rev. St. Section 13 (Comp. St. Section 14).

Source:
Supreme Court Reporter, Vol. 39, pp. 247–249.

Woodrow Wilson, Exposition of the League of Nations, 1919

Address delivered by U.S. president Woodrow Wilson before the Senate Committee on Foreign Relations on August 19, 1919, in an unsuccessful attempt to persuade the Senate to ratify the Covenant of the League of Nations, which had been included in the Treaty of Versailles (1919) that ended World War I. Wilson's exposition answered earlier concerns about the covenant, stating that it respected the Monroe Doctrine, gave the league no authority to act in domestic matters, recognized the right of nations to withdraw from the league, and safeguarded the congressional right to determine all questions of war and peace.

Republican Henry Cabot Lodge of Massachusetts, chairman of the Foreign Relations Committee and the league's primary opponent in the Senate, proposed 14 resolutions to modify the covenant, which had been presented to the Senate for ratification as part of the Treaty of Versailles. The proposed amendments, designed to protect American interests and national sovereignty, included a key provision for Congress to retain the right to decide the conditions under which the U.S. would join the league in collective security measures. President Woodrow Wilson rejected the reservations, claiming that they would nullify rather than ratify the treaty. He especially disliked the Lodge reservation about the permanent territorial borders agreed upon at Versailles.

Wilson conducted a national tour to gather support for ratification of the Covenant of the League of Nations. The "heart of the covenant," according to his speech, was Article Ten, in which Wilson stated, "that no member of the League . . . shall impair the territorial integrity or the political independence of any other member of the League" and that the covenant was essential for the preservation of international peace and to give meaning to the sacrifices made by American soldiers in World War I. Shortly after delivering a speech in Pueblo, Colorado, Wilson collapsed, suffering a stroke that ended his tour and effectively ended all hopes for ratification. The Lodge reservations were defeated in the Senate, as was treaty ratification, in March 1920.

Although the league was established, the United States never became a full member. Because the United States emerged from the World War as a major power, its absence compromised the league's effectiveness.

Mr. Chairman, I have taken the liberty of writing out a little statement in the hope that it might facilitate discussion by speaking directly on some points that I know have been points of controversy and upon which I thought an expression of opinion would not be unwelcome. I am sincerely glad that the committee should have responded in this way to my intimation that I would like to be of service to it. I welcome the opportunity for a frank and full interchange of views.

I hope, too, that this conference will serve to expedite your consideration of the treaty of peace. I beg that you will pardon and indulge me if I again urge that practically the whole task of bringing the country back to normal conditions of life and industry waits upon the decision of the Senate with regard to the terms of the peace.

I venture thus again to urge my advice that the action of the Senate with regard to the treaty be taken at the earliest practicable moment because the problems with which we are face to face in the readjustment of our national life are of the most pressing and critical character, will require for their proper solution the most intimate and disinterested cooperation of all parties and all interests, and can not be postponed without manifest peril to our people and to all the national advantages we hold most dear. May I mention a few of the matters which can not be handled with intelligence until the country knows the character of the peace it is to have? I do so only by a very few samples.

The copper mines of Montana, Arizona, and Alaska, for example, are being kept open and in operation only at a great cost and loss, in part upon borrowed money; the zinc mines of Missouri, Tennessee, and Wisconsin are being operated at about one-half their capacity; the lead of Idaho, Illinois, and Missouri reaches only a portion of its former market; there is an immediate need for cotton belting, and also for lubricating oil, which can not be met—all because the channels of trade are barred by war when there is no war. The same is true of raw cotton, of which the Central Empires alone formerly purchased nearly 4,000,000 bales. And these are only examples. There is hardly a single raw material, a single important foodstuff, a single class of manufactured goods which is not in the same case. Our full, normal profitable production waits on peace.

Our military plans of course wait upon it. We can not intelligently or wisely decide how large a naval or military force we shall maintain or what our policy with regard to military training is to be until we have peace not only, but also until we know how peace is to be sustained, whether by the arms of single nations or by the concert of all the great peoples. And there is more than that difficulty involved. The vast surplus properties of the Army include not food and clothing merely, whose sale will affect normal production, but great manufacturing establishments also which should be restored to their former uses, great stores of machine tools, and all sorts of merchandise which must lie idle until peace and military policy are definitively determined. By the same token there can be no properly studied national budget until then.

The nations that ratify the treaty, such as Great Britain, Belgium, and France, will be in a position to lay their plans for controlling the markets of central Europe without competition from us if we do not presently act. We have no consular agents, no trade representatives there to look after our interests.

There are large areas of Europe whose future will lie uncertain and questionable until their people know the final settlements of peace and the forces which are to administer and sustain it. Without determinate markets our production can not proceed with intelligence or confidence. There can be no stabilization of wages because there can be no settled conditions of employment. There can be no easy or normal industrial credits because there can be no confident or permanent revival of business.

But I will not weary you with obvious examples. I will only venture to repeat that every element of normal life amongst us depends upon and awaits the ratification of the treaty of peace; and also that we can not afford to lose a single summer's day by not doing all that we can to mitigate the winter's suffering, which, unless we find means to prevent it, may prove disastrous to a large portion of the world, and may, at its worst, bring upon Europe conditions even more terrible than those wrought by the war itself.

Nothing, I am led to believe, stands in the way of the ratification of the treaty except certain doubts with regard to the meaning and implication of certain articles of the covenant of the league of nations; and I must frankly say that I am unable to understand why such doubts should be entertained. You will recall that when I had the pleasure of a conference with your committee and with the Committee of the House of Representatives on Foreign Affairs at the White House in March last the questions now most frequently asked about the league of nations were all canvassed with a view to their immediate clarification. The covenant of the league was then in its first draft and subject to revision. It was pointed out that no express recognition was given to the Monroe doctrine; that it was not expressly provided that the league should have no authority to act or to express a judgement on matters of domestic policy; that the right to withdraw from the league was not expressly recognized; and that the constitutional right of the Congress to determine all questions of peace and war was not sufficiently safeguarded. On my return to Paris all these matters were taken up again by the commission on the league of nations and every suggestion of the United States was accepted.

The views of the United States with regard to the questions I have mentioned had, in fact, already been accepted by the commission and there was supposed to be nothing inconsistent with them in the draft of the covenant first adopted—the draft which was the subject of our discussion in March—but no objection was made to saying explicitly in the text what all had supposed to be implicit in it. There was absolutely no doubt as to the meaning of any one of the resulting provisions of the covenant in the minds of those who participated in drafting them, and I respectfully submit that there is nothing vague or doubtful in their wording.

The Monroe doctrine is expressly mentioned as an understanding which is in no way to be impaired or interfered with by anything contained in the covenant and the expression "regional understandings like the Monroe doctrine" was used, not because anyone of the conferees thought there was any comparable agreement anywhere else in existence or in contemplation, but only because it was thought best to avoid the appearance of dealing in such a document with the policy of a single nation. Absolutely nothing is concealed in the phrase.

With regard to domestic questions article 16 of the covenant expressly provides that, if in case of any dispute arising between members of the league the matter involved is claimed by one of the parties "and is found by the council to arise out of a matter which by international law is solely within the domestic jurisdiction of that party, the council shall so report, and shall make no recommendation as to its settlement." The United States was by no means the only Government interested in the explicit adoption of this provision, and there is no doubt in the mind of any authoritative student of international law that such matters as immigration, tariffs, and naturalization are incontestably domestic questions with which no international body could deal without express authority to do so. No enumeration of domestic questions was undertaken because to undertake it, even by sample, would have involved the danger of seeming to exclude those not mentioned.

The right of any sovereign State to withdraw had been taken for granted, but no objection was made to making it explicit. Indeed, so soon as the views expressed at the White House conference were laid before the commission it was at once conceded that it was best not to leave the answer to so important a question to inference. No proposal was made to set up any tribunal to pass judgment upon the question whether a withdrawing nation had in fact fulfilled "all its international obligations and all its obligations under the covenant." It was recognized that that question must be left to be resolved by the conscience of the nation proposing to withdraw; and I must say that it did not seem to me worth while to propose that the article be made more explicit, because I knew that the United States would never itself propose to withdraw from the league if its conscience was not entirely clear as to the fulfillment of all its international obligations. It has never failed to fulfill them and never will.

Article 10 is in no respect of doubtful meaning when read in the light of the covenant as a whole. The council of the league can only "advise upon" the means by which the obligations of that great article are to be given effect to. Unless the United States is a party to the policy or action in question, her own affirmative vote in the council is necessary before any advice can be given, for a unanimous vote of the council is required. If she is a party, the trouble is hers anyhow. And the unanimous vote of the council is only advice in any case. Each Government is free to reject it if it pleases. Nothing could have been made more clear to the conference than the right of our Congress under our Constitution to exercise its independent judgment in all matters of peace and war. No attempt was made to question or limit that right. The United States will, indeed, undertake under article 10 to "respect and preserve as against external aggression the territorial integrity and existing political independence of all members of the league," and that engagement constitutes a very grave and solemn moral obligation. But it is a moral, not a legal, obligation, and leaves our Congress absolutely free to put its own interpretation upon it in all cases that call for action. It is binding in conscience only, not in law.

Article 10 seems to me to constitute the very backbone of the whole covenant. Without it the league would be hardly more than an influential debating society.

It has several times been suggested, in public debate and in private conference, that interpretations of the sense in which the United States accepts the engagements of the covenant should be embodied in the instrument of ratification. There can be no reasonable objection to such interpretations accompanying the act of ratification provided they do not form a part of the formal ratification itself. Most of the interpretations which have been suggested to me embody what seems to me the plain meaning of the instrument itself. But if such interpretations should constitute a part of the formal resolution of ratification, long delays would be the inevitable consequence, inasmuch as all the many governments concerned would have to accept, in effect, the language of the Senate as the language of the treaty before ratification would be complete. The assent of the German Assembly at Weimar would have to be obtained, among the rest, and I must frankly say that I could only with the greatest reluctance approach that assembly for permission to read the treaty as we understand it and as those who framed it quite certainly understood it. If the United States were to qualify the document in any way, moreover, I am confident from what I know of the many conferences and debates which accompanied the formulation of the treaty that our example would immediately be followed in many quarters, in some instances with very serious reservations, and that the meaning and operative force of the treaty would presently be clouded from one end of its clauses to the other…

Source:

Link, Arthur S., et al. eds., *The Papers of Woodrow Wilson.* Princeton, N.J.: Princeton University Press, 1966–94.

Postwar Society

Emma Goldman, "Anarchism: What It Really Stands For," 1917

This 1917 article by Emma Goldman seeks to define the philosophy of anarchism. She identifies the three major forces that stand in the way of its fulfillment: religion, property, and government. An advocate of total personal freedom, Goldman felt that the human mind, body, and soul needed to be "liberated" in order to obtain freedom. "Enslavement" to religion puts God before man and takes away man's power to think and reason for himself. Property enslaves the needs of workers by blocking their ability to fulfill themselves through meaningful work and forcing them to produce goods that do not inspire them mentally, spiritually, or physically. Government imposes a tyranny over people's daily conduct, steals from them in the form of taxes, and kills them through forced participation in war (the draft) and capital punishment.

Goldman was a controversial figure who was frequently maligned by the media of her day, which portrayed her as a bomb-throwing terrorist. She was often at odds with the authorities as well: She was imprisoned six times between 1893 and 1921 on charges ranging from attempted murder to speaking on birth control to inciting a riot. In 1919, after serving a two-year sentence for opposing the draft during World War I, she was deported to Russia. There she quickly became disillusioned with the Bolshevik Revolution after witnessing the increasing bureaucracy of the Russian government and the eroding personal freedoms of the people. She left Russia and lived in exile in Europe for the remainder of her life, returning only once to the United States for a brief visit in 1934.

Goldman was the first person to bring sexual politics into the discussion of anarchism, arguing that the demolition of traditional sex roles, not political action, was the only way to bring about real equality for women. She opposed suffrage for women and advocated free love. Emma Goldman was a powerful personality who brought a great deal of fame and even notoriety to her cause. Her writings stand as a testament to her idealism and dedication.

THE history of human growth and development is at the same time the history of the terrible struggle of every new idea heralding the approach of a brighter dawn. In its tenacious hold on tradition, the Old has never hesitated to make use of the foulest and cruelest means to stay the advent of the New, in whatever form or period the latter may have asserted itself. Nor need we retrace our steps into the distant past to realize the enormity of opposition, difficulties, and hardships placed in the path of every progressive idea. The rack, the thumbscrew, and the knout are still with us; so are the convict's garb and the social wrath, all conspiring against the spirit that is serenely marching on.

Anarchism could not hope to escape the fate of all other ideas of innovation. Indeed, as the most revolutionary and uncompromising innovator, Anarchism must needs meet with the combined ignorance and venom of the world it aims to reconstruct.

To deal even remotely with all that is being said and done against Anarchism would necessitate the writing of a whole volume. I shall therefore meet only two of the principal objections. In so doing, I shall attempt to elucidate what Anarchism really stands for.

The strange phenomenon of the opposition to Anarchism is that it brings to light the relation between so-called intelligence and ignorance. And yet this is not so very strange when we consider the relativity of all things. The ignorant mass has in its favor that it makes no pretense of knowledge or tolerance. Acting, as it always does, by mere impulse, its reasons are like those of a child. "Why?" "Because." Yet the opposition of the uneducated to Anarchism deserves the same consideration as that of the intelligent man.

What, then, are the objections? First, Anarchism is impractical, though a beautiful ideal. Second, Anarchism stands for violence and destruction, hence it must be repudiated as vile and dangerous. Both the intelligent man and the ignorant mass judge not from a thorough knowledge of the subject, but either from hearsay or false interpretation.

A practical scheme, says Oscar Wilde, is either one already in existence, or a scheme that could be carried out under the existing conditions; but it is exactly the existing conditions that one objects to, and any scheme that could accept these conditions is wrong and foolish. The true criterion of the practical, therefore, is not whether the latter can keep intact the wrong or foolish; rather is it whether the scheme has vitality enough to leave the stagnant waters of the old, and build, as well as sustain, new life. In the light of this conception, Anarchism is indeed practical. More than any other idea, it is helping to do away with the wrong and foolish; more than any other idea, it is building and sustaining new life.

The emotions of the ignorant man are continuously kept at a pitch by the most blood-curdling stories about Anarchism. Not a thing too outrageous to be employed against this philosophy and its exponents. Therefore Anarchism represents to the unthinking what the proverbial bad man does to the child,—a black monster bent on swallowing everything; in short, destruction and violence.

Destruction and violence! How is the ordinary man to know that the most violent element in society is ignorance; that its power of destruction is the very thing Anarchism is combating? Nor is he aware that Anarchism, whose roots, as it were, are part of nature's forces, destroys, not healthful tissue, but parasitic growths that feed on the life's essence of society. It is merely clearing the soil from weeds and sagebrush, that it may eventually bear healthy fruit.

Someone has said that it requires less mental effort to condemn than to think. The widespread mental indolence, so prevalent in society, proves this to be only too true. Rather than to go to the bottom of any given idea, to examine into its origin and meaning, most people will either condemn it altogether, or rely on some superficial or prejudicial definition of non-essentials.

Anarchism urges man to think, to investigate, to analyze every proposition; but that the brain capacity of the average reader be not taxed too much, I also shall begin with a definition, and then elaborate on the latter.

ANARCHISM:—The philosophy of a new social order based on liberty unrestricted by man-made law; the theory that all forms of government rest on violence, and are therefore wrong and harmful, as well as unnecessary.

The new social order rests, of course, on the materialistic basis of life; but while all Anarchists agree that the main evil today is an economic one, they maintain that the solution of that evil can be brought about only through the consideration of *every phase* of life,—individual, as well as the collective; the internal, as well as the external phases.

A thorough perusal of the history of human development will disclose two elements in bitter conflict with each other; elements that are only now beginning to be understood, not as foreign to each other, but as closely related and truly harmonious, if only placed in proper environment: the individual and social instincts. The individual and society have waged a relentless and bloody battle for ages, each striving for supremacy, because each was blind to the value and importance of the other. The individual and social instincts,—the one a most potent factor for individual endeavor, for growth, aspiration, self-realization; the other an equally potent factor for mutual helpfulness and social well-being.

The explanation of the storm raging within the individual, and between him and his surroundings, is not far to seek. The primitive man, unable to understand his being, much less the unity of all life, felt himself absolutely dependent on blind, hidden forces ever ready to mock and taunt him. Out of that attitude grew the religious concepts of man as a mere speck of dust dependent on superior powers on high, who can only be appeased by complete surrender. All the early sagas rest on that idea, which continues to be the *Leitmotiv* of the biblical tales dealing with the relation of man to God, to the State, to society. Again and again the same motif, *man is nothing, the powers are everything*. Thus Jehovah would only endure man on condition of complete surrender. Man can have all the glories of the earth, but he must not become conscious of himself. The State, society, and moral laws all sing the same refrain: Man can have all the glories of the earth, but he must not become conscious of himself.

Anarchism is the only philosophy which brings to man the consciousness of himself; which maintains that God, the State, and society are non-existent, that their promises are null and void, since they can be fulfilled only through man's subordination. Anarchism is therefore the teacher of the unity of life; not merely in nature, but in man. There is no conflict between the individual and the social instincts, any more than there is between the heart and the lungs: the one the receptacle of a precious life essence, the other the repository of the element that keeps the essence pure and strong. The individual is the heart of society, conserving the essence of social life; society is the lungs which are distributing the element to keep the life essence—that is, the individual—pure and strong.

"The one thing of value in the world," says Emerson, "is the active soul; this every man contains within him. The soul active sees absolute truth and utters truth and creates." In other words, the individual instinct is the thing of value in the world. It is the true soul that sees and creates the truth alive, out of which is to come a still greater truth, the re-born social soul.

Anarchism is the great liberator of man from the phantoms that have held him captive; it is the arbiter and pacifier of the two forces for individual and social harmony. To accomplish that unity, Anarchism has declared war on the pernicious influences which have so far prevented the harmonious blending of individual and social instincts, the individual and society.

Religion, the dominion of the human mind; Property, the dominion of human needs; and Government, the dominion of human conduct, represent the stronghold of man's enslavement and all the horrors it entails. Religion! How it dominates man's mind, how it humiliates and degrades his soul. God is everything, man is nothing, says religion. But out of that nothing God has created a kingdom so despotic, so tyrannical, so cruel, so terribly exacting that naught but gloom and tears and blood have ruled the world since gods began. Anarchism rouses man to rebellion against this black monster. Break your mental fetters, says Anarchism to man, for not until you think and judge for yourself will you get rid of the dominion of darkness, the greatest obstacle to all progress.

Property, the dominion of man's needs, the denial of the right to satisfy his needs. Time was when property claimed a divine right, when it came to man with the same refrain, even as religion, "Sacrifice! Abnegate! Submit!" The spirit of Anarchism has lifted man from his prostrate position. He now stands erect, with his face toward the light. He has learned to see the insatiable, devouring, devastating nature of property, and he is preparing to strike the monster dead.

"Property is robbery," said the great French Anarchist Proudhon. Yes, but without risk and danger to the robber. Monopolizing the accumulated efforts of man, property has robbed him of his birthright, and has turned him loose a pauper and an outcast. Property has not even the time-worn excuse that man does not create enough to satisfy all needs. The A B C student of economics knows that the productivity of labor within the last few decades far exceeds normal demand. But what are normal demands to an abnormal institution? The only demand that property recognizes is its own gluttonous appetite for greater wealth, because wealth means power; the power to subdue, to crush, to exploit, the power to enslave, to outrage, to degrade. America is particularly boastful of her great power, her enormous national wealth. Poor America, of what avail is all her wealth, if the individuals comprising the nation are wretchedly poor? If they live in squalor, in filth, in crime, with hope and joy gone, a homeless, soilless army of human prey.

It is generally conceded that unless the returns of any business venture exceed the cost, bankruptcy is inevitable. But those engaged in the business of producing wealth have not yet learned even this simple lesson. Every year the cost of production in human life is growing larger (50,000 killed, 100,000 wounded in America last year); the returns to the masses, who help to create wealth, are ever getting smaller. Yet America continues to be blind to the inevitable bankruptcy of our business of production. Nor is this the only crime of the latter. Still more fatal is the crime of turning the producer into a mere particle of a machine, with less will and decision than his master of steel and iron. Man is being robbed not merely of the products of his labor, but of the power of free initiative, of originality, and the interest in, or desire for, the things he is making.

Real wealth consists in things of utility and beauty, in things that help to create strong, beautiful bodies and surroundings inspiring to live in. But if man is doomed to wind cotton around a spool, or dig coal, or build roads for thirty years of his life, there can be no talk of wealth. What he gives to the world is only gray and hideous things, reflecting a dull and hideous existence,—too weak to live, too cowardly to die. Strange to say, there are people who extol this deadening method of centralized production as the proudest achievement of our age. They fail utterly to realize that if we are to continue in machine subserviency, our slavery is more complete than was our bondage to the King. They do not want to know that centralization is not only the death-knell of liberty, but also of health and beauty, of art and science, all these being impossible in a clock-like, mechanical atmosphere.

Anarchism cannot but repudiate such a method of production: its goal is the freest possible expression of all the latent powers of the individual. Oscar Wilde defines a perfect personality as "one who develops under perfect conditions, who is not wounded, maimed, or in danger." A perfect personality, then, is only possible in a state of society where man is free to choose the mode of work, the conditions of work, and the freedom to work. One to whom the making of a table, the building of a house, or the tilling of the soil, is what the painting is to the artist and the discovery to the scientist,—the result of inspiration, of intense longing, and deep interest in work as a creative force. That being the ideal of Anarchism, its economic arrangements must consist of voluntary productive and distributive associations, gradually developing into free communism, as the best means of producing with the least waste of human energy. Anarchism, however, also recognizes the right of the individual, or numbers of individuals, to arrange at all times for other forms of work, in harmony with their tastes and desires.

Such free display of human energy being possible only under complete individual and social freedom, Anarchism directs its forces against the third and greatest foe of all social equality; namely, the State, organized authority, or statutory law,—the dominion of human conduct.

Just as religion has fettered the human mind, and as property, or the monopoly of things, has subdued and stifled man's needs, so has the State enslaved his spirit, dictating every phase of conduct. "All government in essence," says Emerson, "is tyranny." It matters not whether it is government by divine right or majority rule. In every instance its aim is the absolute subordination of the individual.

Referring to the American government, the greatest American Anarchist, David Thoreau, said: "Government, what is it but a tradition, though a recent one, endeavoring to transmit itself unimpaired to posterity, but each instance losing its integrity; it has not the vitality and force of a single living man. Law never made man a whit more just; and by means of their respect for it, even the well disposed are daily made agents of injustice."

Indeed, the keynote of government is injustice. With the arrogance and self-sufficiency of the King who could do no wrong, governments ordain, judge, condemn, and punish the most insignificant offenses, while maintaining themselves by the greatest of all offenses, the annihilation of individual liberty. Thus Ouida is right when she maintains that "the State only aims at instilling those qualities in its public by which its demands are obeyed, and its exchequer is filled. Its highest attainment is the reduction of mankind to clockwork. In its atmosphere all those finer and more delicate liberties, which require treatment and spacious expansion, inevitably dry up and perish. The State requires a taxpaying machine in which there is no hitch, an exchequer in which there is never a deficit, and a public, monotonous, obedient, colorless, spiritless, moving humbly like a flock of sheep along a straight high road between two walls."

Yet even a flock of sheep would resist the chicanery of the State, if it were not for the corruptive, tyrannical, and oppressive methods it employs to serve its purposes. Therefore Bakunin repudiates the State as synonymous with the surrender of the liberty of the individual or small minorities,—the destruction of social relationship, the curtailment, or complete denial even, of life itself, for its own aggrandizement. The State is the altar of political freedom and, like the religious altar, it is maintained for the purpose of human sacrifice.

In fact, there is hardly a modern thinker who does not agree that government, organized authority, or the State, is necessary *only* to maintain or protect property and monopoly. It has proven efficient in that function only.

Even George Bernard Shaw, who hopes for the miraculous from the State under Fabianism, nevertheless admits that "it is at present a huge machine for robbing and slave-driving of the poor by brute force." This being the case, it is hard to see why the clever prefacer wishes to uphold the State after poverty shall have ceased to exist.

Unfortunately, there are still a number of people who continue in the fatal belief that government rests on natural laws, that it maintains social order and harmony, that it diminishes crime, and that it prevents the lazy man from fleecing his fellows. I shall therefore examine these contentions.

A natural law is that factor in man which asserts itself freely and spontaneously without any external force, in harmony with the requirements of nature. For instance, the demand for nutrition, for sex gratification, for light, air, and exercise, is a natural law. But its expression needs not the machinery of government, needs not the club, the gun, the handcuff, or the prison. To obey such laws, if we may call it obedience, requires only spontaneity and free opportunity. That governments do not maintain themselves through such harmonious factors is proven by the terrible array of violence, force, and coercion all governments use in order to live. Thus Blackstone is right when he says, "Human laws are invalid, because they are contrary to the laws of nature."

Unless it be the order of Warsaw after the slaughter of thousands of people, it is difficult to ascribe to governments any capacity for order or social harmony. Order derived through submission and maintained by terror is not much of a safe guaranty; yet that is the only "order" that governments have ever maintained. True social harmony grows naturally out of solidarity of interests. In a society where those who always work never have anything, while those who never work enjoy everything, solidarity of interests is non-existent; hence social harmony is but a myth. The only way organized authority meets this grave situation is by extending still greater privileges to those who have already monopolized the earth, and by still further enslaving the disinherited masses. Thus the entire arsenal of government—laws, police, soldiers, the courts, legislatures, prisons,—is strenuously engaged in "harmonizing" the most antagonistic elements in society.

The most absurd apology for authority and law is that they serve to diminish crime. Aside from the fact that the State is itself the greatest criminal, breaking every written and natural law, stealing in the form of taxes, killing in the form of war and capital punishment, it has come to an absolute standstill in coping with crime. It has failed utterly to destroy or even minimize the horrible scourge of its own creation.

Crime is naught but misdirected energy. So long as every institution of today, economic, political, social, and moral, conspires to misdirect human energy into wrong channels; so long as most people are out of place doing the things they hate to do, living a life they loathe to live, crime will be inevitable, and all the laws on the statutes can only increase, but never do away with, crime. What does society, as it exists today, know of the process of despair, the poverty, the horrors, the fearful struggle the human soul must pass on its way to crime and degradation. Who that knows this terrible process can fail to see the truth in these words of Peter Kropotkin:

> Those who will hold the balance between the benefits thus attributed to law and punishment and the degrading effect of the latter on humanity; those who will estimate the torrent of depravity poured abroad in human society by the informer, favored by the Judge even, and paid for in clinking cash by governments, under the pretext of aiding to unmask crime; those who will go within prison walls and there see what human beings become when deprived of liberty, when subjected to the care of brutal keepers, to coarse, cruel words, to a thousand stinging, piercing humiliations, will agree with us that the entire apparatus of prison and punishment is an abomination which ought to be brought to an end.

The deterrent influence of law on the lazy man is too absurd to merit consideration. If society were only relieved of the waste and expense of keeping a lazy class, and the equally great expense of the paraphernalia of protection this lazy class requires, the social tables would contain an abundance for all, including even the occasional lazy individual. Besides, it is well to consider that laziness results either from special privileges, or physical and mental abnormalities. Our present insane system of production fosters both, and the most astounding phenomenon is that people should want to work at all now. Anarchism aims to strip labor of its deadening, dulling aspect, of its gloom and compulsion. It aims to make work an instrument of joy, of strength, of color, of real harmony, so that the poorest sort of a man should find in work both recreation and hope.

To achieve such an arrangement of life, government, with its unjust, arbitrary, repressive measures, must be done away with. At best it has but imposed one single mode of life upon all, without regard to individual and social variations and needs. In destroying government and statutory laws, Anarchism proposes to rescue the self-respect and independence of the individual from all restraint and invasion by authority. Only in freedom can man grow to his full stature. Only in freedom will he learn to think and move, and give the very best in him. Only in freedom will he realize the true force of the social bonds which knit men together, and which are the true foundation of a normal social life.

But what about human nature? Can it be changed? And if not, will it endure under Anarchism?

Poor human nature, what horrible crimes have been committed in thy name! Every fool, from king to policeman, from the flatheaded parson to the visionless dabbler in science, presumes to speak authoritatively of human nature. The greater the mental charlatan, the more definite his insistence on the wickedness and weaknesses of human nature. Yet, how can any one speak of it today, with every soul in a prison, with every heart fettered, wounded, and maimed?

John Burroughs has stated that experimental study of animals in captivity is absolutely useless. Their character, their habits, their appetites undergo a complete transformation when torn from their soil in field and forest. With human nature caged in a narrow space, whipped daily into submission, how can we speak of its potentialities?

Freedom, expansion, opportunity, and, above all, peace and repose, alone can teach us the real dominant factors of human nature and all its wonderful possibilities.

Anarchism, then, really stands for the liberation of the human mind from the dominion of religion; the liberation of the human body from the dominion of property; liberation from the shackles and restraint of government. Anarchism stands for a social order based on the free grouping of individuals for the purpose of producing real social wealth; an order that will guarantee to every human being free access to the earth and full enjoyment of the necessities of life, according to individual desires, tastes, and inclinations.

This is not a wild fancy or an aberration of the mind. It is the conclusion arrived at by hosts of intellectual men and women the world over; a conclusion resulting from the close and studious observation of the tendencies of modern society: individual liberty and economic equality, the twin forces for the birth of what is fine and true in man.

As to methods, Anarchism is not, as some may suppose, a theory of the future to be realized through divine inspiration. It is a living force in the affairs of our life, constantly creating new conditions. The methods of Anarchism therefore do not comprise an iron-clad program to be carried out under all circumstances. Methods must grow out of the economic needs of each place and clime, and of the intellectual and temperamental requirements of the individual. The serene, calm character of a Tolstoy will wish different methods for social reconstruction than the intense, overflowing personality of a Michael Bakunin or a Peter Kropotkin. Equally so it must be apparent that the economic and political needs of Russia will dictate more drastic measures than would England or America. Anarchism does not stand for military drill and uniformity; it does, however, stand for the spirit of revolt, in whatever form, against everything that hinders human growth. All Anarchists agree in that, as they also agree in their opposition to the political machinery as a means of bringing about the great social change.

"All voting," says Thoreau, "is a sort of gaming, like checkers, or backgammon, a playing with right and wrong; its obligation never exceeds that of expediency. Even voting for the right thing is doing nothing for it. A wise man will not leave the right to the mercy of chance, nor wish it to prevail through the power of the majority." A close examination of the machinery of politics and its achievements will bear out the logic of Thoreau.

What does the history of parliamentarism show? Nothing but failure and defeat, not even a single reform to ameliorate the economic and social stress of the people. Laws have been passed and enactments made for the improvement and protection of labor. Thus it was proven only last year that Illinois, with the most rigid laws for mine protection, had the greatest mine disasters. In States where child labor laws prevail, child exploitation is at its highest, and though with us the workers enjoy full political opportunities, capitalism has reached the most brazen zenith.

Even were the workers able to have their own representatives, for which our good Socialist politicians are clamoring, what chances are there for their honesty and good faith? One has but to bear in mind the process of politics to realize that its path of good intentions is full of pitfalls: wire-pulling, intriguing, flattering, lying, cheating; in fact, chicanery of every description, whereby the political aspirant can achieve success. Added to that is a complete demoralization of character and conviction, until nothing is left that would make one hope for anything from such a human derelict. Time and time again the people were foolish enough to trust, believe, and support with their last farthing aspiring politicians, only to find themselves betrayed and cheated.

It may be claimed that men of integrity would not become corrupt in the political grinding mill. Perhaps not; but such men would be absolutely helpless to exert the slightest influence in behalf of labor, as indeed has been shown in numerous instances. The State is the economic master of its servants. Good men, if such there be, would either remain true to their political faith and lose their economic support, or they would cling to their economic master and be utterly unable to do the slightest good. The political arena leaves one no alternative, one must either be a dunce or a rogue.

The political superstition is still holding sway over the hearts and minds of the masses, but the true lovers of liberty will have no more to do with it. Instead, they believe with Stirner that man has as much liberty as he is willing to take. Anarchism therefore stands for direct action, the open defiance of, and resistance to, all laws and restrictions, economic, social, and moral. But defiance and resistance are illegal. Therein lies the salvation of man. Everything illegal necessitates integrity, self-reliance, and courage. In short, it calls for free, independent spirits, for "men who are men, and who have a bone in their backs which you cannot pass your hand through."

Universal suffrage itself owes its existence to direct action. If not for the spirit of rebellion, of the defiance on the part of the American revolutionary fathers, their posterity would still wear the King's coat. If not for the direct action of a John Brown and his comrades, America would still trade in the flesh of the black man. True, the trade in white flesh is still going on; but that, too, will have to be abolished by direct action. Trade-unionism, the economic arena of the modern gladiator, owes its existence to direct action. It is but recently that law and government have attempted to crush the trade-union movement, and condemned the exponents of man's right to organize to prison as conspirators. Had they sought to assert their cause through begging, pleading, and compromise, trade-unionism would today be a negligible quantity. In France, in Spain, in Italy, in Russia, nay even in England (witness the growing rebellion of English labor unions), direct, revolutionary, economic action has become so strong a force in the battle for industrial liberty as to make the world realize the tremendous importance of labor's power. The General Strike, the supreme expression of the economic consciousness of the workers, was ridiculed in America but a short time ago. Today every great strike, in order to win, must realize the importance of the solidaric general protest.

Direct action, having proven effective along economic lines, is equally potent in the environment of the individual. There a hundred forces encroach upon his being, and only persistent resistance to them will finally set him free. Direct action against the authority in the shop, direct action against the authority of the law, direct action against the invasive, meddlesome authority of our moral code, is the logical, consistent method of Anarchism.

Will it not lead to a revolution? Indeed, it will. No real social change has ever come about without a revolution. People are either not familiar with their history, or they have not yet learned that revolution is but thought carried into action.

Anarchism, the great leaven of thought, is today permeating every phase of human endeavor. Science, art, literature, the drama, the effort for economic betterment, in fact every individual and social opposition to the existing disorder of things, is illumined by the spiritual light of Anarchism. It is the philosophy of the sovereignty of the individual. It is the theory of social harmony. It is the great, surging, living truth that is reconstructing the world, and that will usher in the Dawn.

Source:

Berkeley Digital Library SunSITE. The Emma Goldman Papers. Available on-line. URL: http://sunsite. berkeley.edu/goldman/writing/anarchism.html. Accessed November 2003.

Carrie Chapman Catt, *Woman Voter's Manual*, 1918

Introduction by Carrie Chapman Catt to *the Woman Voter's Manual* by S. E. Forman and Marjorie Shuler. The document notes that more than a third of the women in the United States had either partial or full voting rights at the time of publication in 1918. According to Catt, these women, even more so than men, who did not have to fight for their right to vote, wanted to inform themselves about contemporary issues and the workings of government.

Catt contrasts the state of woman suffrage in the United States with that in Europe. She notes that one of the effects of World War I, which was then being waged, was that it forced countries, such as France and Italy, to accept woman suffrage; out of sheer necessity, restrictions against women fell away. Regarding the status of suffrage for women in the United States, she provides answers to the question of what women would do with the vote once they had it. She considers the extent to which women voters have brought about social change by initiating legislation to establish an eight-hour working day for women, a minimum wage, a mothers' pension, and a child welfare department. Finally, Catt allays fears that women would organize politically in opposition to men, a situation that the strength of women's "nature and personal affections" would not allow.

Of the 27,011,330 women of voting age in the United States, more than one-third are now enfranchised, either as voters for presidential electors, or as fully as our present national laws permit women to be enfranchised. No woman in the United States is yet enfranchised as is her husband or her father or her son or her brother, and will not be until woman suffrage is incorporated in the national constitution. Not even then, unless she can come to hold her naturalization in her own person instead of as a cloak to be put on and off as she marries, unmarries or is widowed.

Whatever the voting strength of these more than 900,000 women of voting age may be, the fact of practical value for such a book as the present one is that a large and ever increasing number of women citizen are avid for information on the new questions of local, State and national government which women and men must now decided together. They are coming up to these questions with a vivid new personal interest that bids fair to lift "civil government" out of the cold aloofness of academic discussion on the one side, and the "mire of politics" on the other. To be bromidic, women are going to humanize questions of government. That will not be, I think, because only to woman is given the human outlook on life, but because the human is composite of men and women and the human in the outlook of both is stirred and developed through cooperative rather than segregated work.

As emergent voters the women of America are to-day facing the same fundamental questions as to the new responsibility as are the young American man of twenty-one and the immigrant. The enfranchisement of woman, the coming of age of the young man, and the naturalization of the immigrant-there you have the three agencies through which the electorate of America is to be kept in a sate of inquiry and action instead of in a condition of acquiescence and being.

A prime difference in the three cases is that the woman is asking all the questions that the other two ought to ask but do not. Of course it would be the woman who would ask the questions. For one thing, it does not go so hard with women to admit their ignorance as it does with men. For another, woman was had to fight for suffrage while the young man was acquiring it as he acquired his moustache, by the simple expedient of getting older, and the immigrant man was acquiring it by the simple expedient of living in America long enough to take on some of those American ideals and commitments into which the woman, if native, was born; and having fought for the suffrage, the fight has informed woman with a special sense of the value in the thing fought for, and a special desire fully to understand it. Suffragists alone would start the questions, but it is not suffragists alone among women who want the answers. The antis mean to vote, the indifferent mean to vote.

In the result, texts on civil government become at one leap of intimate value. Instead of remote summaries of the function of the "judiciary, the legislative, the administrative," that of which they treat is identified as breakfast table talk-the mayor's appointments, home rule for cities, what the legislature is doing with the child labor bill, what Washington will do with bills defining the authority of the government in its war control of this, that, or the other. There is an acute recognition of "the government" as a matter of close contact and an immediate intention to understand it better. And conversely, from now on, thanks to woman's enfranchisement, achieved or impending, it will be necessary for the government to understand woman better, so that the give-and-take, the reflex from woman suffrage into the body politic, and out again upon the community, may be better assimilated.

Woman Suffrage a War Measure

When the world war began shaking the existing ideas of government about, it had the effect upon them that is produced by shaking a barrel of apples, the little ones went to the bottom and the big ones came to the top. Consider some of the first little apples to go out of sight. In Italy and in France women had distinct civil disabilities such as the necessity of getting their husbands' authorization before they could act in legal matters. These ideas have not only sunk to the bottom of the barrel, but have apparently shrunk to a size which has permitted them to fall through cracks and disappear. In a cataclysm which has destroyed class distinctions by demanding leadership from all classes, sex discrimination could no longer endure in the light of the complete sacrifice for service shown by both sexes. In Italy and France municipal suffrage is in process of establishment. It is urged by statesmen as much as by woman suffragists. In France it is indeed a necessity, since in many communities the only people left to protect the standards of life are loyal women who have served their country no less ably than the front line soldiers who have given their lives for France.

The fiercest opponents of woman suffrage in England have demonstrated no little ingenuity in their lightning changes from adamantine hostility to suffrage to fervid acceptance of it.

Democracy has become a password. Every state paper and suggested basis of peace drives home, as with bayonet thrusts, the basic fact that for the word democracy, one may now substitute the phrase "government derives its just powers from the consent of the governed."

Outside of Germany it would be hard to find a statesman with the temerity to gainsay this. Up to date Germany is the only great country which has failed to grasp the fact that this is the real issue of the war. Outside of Germany there are few political leaders-and those few mainly men advanced in years-who do not now know that women are among the "governed." By its recent Franchise Reform Bill, Hungary has demonstrated that the two vital issues, "government by the people" and "women are people," are recognized as fundamental to the life of that nation.

What She Does with the Vote When She Gets It

In the United States the great suffrage victories of the year 1917 have urged the question on beyond interest in its merits or the abstract justice involved in it, to the practical application of it. Whether women vote when they can; what they do with their votes when they get them; and the effects of their enfranchisement upon home and community are, fortunately, demonstrable propositions. In every full voting State in which the records are sufficiently complete to form a basis of judgment, three things have been established: women register and vote in about the same proportion as men; they show an intelligent interest in elections, and they double the voting strength of their states with a comparatively small increase in voting paraphernalia.

Knowledge of the kinds of legislation attempted or achieved by voting women likewise rests upon facts. The legislation accomplished follows the psychology of women; it follows the matters in which they are most vitally interested. If there is truth in the theory that men and women in political life. In New Zealand, where woman have voted for twenty-five years, the infant death rate is lower than in any other part of the world. And the New Zealand methods of caring for the health of women and children are cited as models by authorities. A burning grievance of mothers for countless years was the fact that in the eyes of the law the children they had borne did not belong to them; they belonged to the fathers. When a controversy arose over the disposition of the child, or its religious education, or the right to inherit from it, the advantage has always lain with the father. As soon as woman began to emerge as a social entity, even before she had the vote, this deep suffering of mothers found voice. For seventy years mothers have struggled for an equal share with fathers in the control of their own children. In almost every full suffrage state in the Union this matter has received a first consideration and equal guardianship obtains in every State where women vote on the same terms as men. It does not obtain to any such extent where fathers only vote, as only twenty-five per cent. Of the thirty-six male suffrage States have this law. The District of Columbia's equal guardianship law is the result of the hard work of a woman lawyer.

Six of the woman voting States have secured an eight-hour day for women. Sixty-three per cent. of the full suffrage States (New York not included) have a minimum wage law, less than fourteen per cent. of the man-suffrage States have one. Every full suffrage State has a mothers' pension law. Ninety per cent. of the full suffrage States (New York not included) have the injunction and abatement law.

Recently the Chicago Chief of Police sent out a call for a woman protective police force as a war measure. Behind this recognition of the fact that women can be relied upon as a rear guard, lies an interesting history of a movement to use women as police even in normal times of peace. This movement, both in England and the United States, was initiated by women, urged by women, and steadfastly defeated in America until women got the vote. The mere possession of the franchise by the women of Chicago, before they had a chance to put it in practice, acted as a lever to set the Chicago women police idea on its feet. What the women police have meant in time of war is a momentous chapter not yet written.

Women voters in Illinois, California, Colorado, Washington, and Montana are on record as having achieved such domestic legislation as state-wide laws concerning food inspection. Earl Barnes reports that he has seen "nowhere else such statutes as fearlessly and vigorously enforced as in Idaho."

Montana is, next to New York, one of the youngest children in the suffrage group. It gained enfranchisement in 1914, yet by 1916, the first political campaign in which the women voters participated, old political wheel horses were astonished at the concentration of effort of and energy exhibited by the whole woman electorate of Montana. A woman State Superintendent of Public Instruction, Who ran entirely upon her special qualifications and was supported by the women because of her fitness was elected by an overwhelming majority. Other legislation worked for by women in their first campaign in Montana included an eight-hour day for women, improvements in the mothers' pension law, establishment of a child welfare division of the Department of Public Health and an expert survey of the feebleminded of the State. Colorado's Juvenile Court Law has been called by the head of the National Child Labor Committee "one of the best, if not the best."

As she has become possessed of the vote, the female of the species has proved herself rather fundamentally averse to office-seeking. The practice of women in full suffrage States has been to occupy such public positions as logically develop out of their special training. Women, who make up eighty per cent. of the teaching profession and who as parents are vitally in touch with the needs of childhood, have in all full suffrage States acceptably filled local and state positions as superintendents of public instruction or as members of school boards or as commissioners of Public Welfare in connection with the labor of women and children. In some instances marked ability or experience in these lines has led them into legislative positions. In full suffrage States the woman lawyer is naturally less impeded in her advance from post to post in her own profession than her professional sister in non-suffrage States. The woman doctor mounts the rungs of her ladder less weighed down with artificial burdens. The point in all this is the reassuring fact that the state undergoes no volcanic wrench when women participate in its political career. What women are bound to do anyway, whether because of natural abilities or personal inclinations or because of economic and industrial pressure, they do with fewer handicaps when they have the franchise than when they haven't it. Experience also shows that the large social movements by which all mankind is affected predetermine these matters for women as well as for men. When vast numbers of women are needed in industry they go into it. If such a situation arises, justice and expediency both demand that women should be protected by their own ballots, not by so-called representative ballots, as on the face of it no one ballot can be counted upon to express two persons' "consent" in government.

An obsession exists among some men lest women begin at once to untie all the neat packages into which political parties have tied their inherited traditions. A few men are still shuddering lest women will want to revolutionize banking legislation, throw the tariff overboard and run amuck amongst stocks and bonds. In the first place, they never have done anything of the sort in any State where women vote, and in the second place, women are conservative spenders. A reproach against them has been their timidity in thinking in the gross. They have so long thought in littles.

No Sex Segregation in Politics

Woman, the voter, disproves too, all along the line, the contention that there will ever be a distinct woman's party in the history of the United States. Human interests find few such vertical lines of cleavage between the sexes. It is inconceivable that the thousands of homes in the country could ever be split apart longitudinally. If the extraordinary injustices against women permitted by men in past generations have never yet bred up a group of women combined for attack, is it likely that, as those grievances are more and more removed and men's and women's interests become more and more identical, there will ever be a collective strife of women against men? Human needs are normally group needs, family needs, or needs of industrial units. Society may split apart in horizontal sections with whole groups of men and women will be found valiant in supporting the measures they espouse. But because of the very structure of human society it will never happen that masses of women will have desire to cohere in opposition to masses of men. Nature and personal affections would soon prove too strong for such political differentiations. It is together, as human beings, not as men and not as women that the voters of the United States are moving forward into the new democracy with its larger questions and its finer and surer answers.

Source:

Catt, Carrie Chapman. Introduction to *Woman Voter's Manual*, by S. E. Forman and Marjorie Shuler. National American Woman Suffrage Association Collection, Rare Book and Special Collections. Library of Congress, Washington, D.C.

Woodrow Wilson, Appeal to the U.S. Senate to Submit the Federal Amendment for Woman Suffrage, 1918

Speech delivered in person by President Woodrow Wilson to the U.S. Senate, asking that the Senate vote to submit the Nineteenth Amendment to the states for ratification. At the time of this appeal, World War I raged in Europe, and the cost of U.S. involvement had been severe. Although President Wilson had previously opposed women's suffrage, in 1918 his stance on the issue changed, in large part due to the enormous contributions American women had made to the war effort. This shift helped tip the balance of political sentiment in favor of women's suffrage. In his speech, Wilson states repeatedly that granting women the right to vote is essential to winning the war, and even goes so far as to say, "this war could not have been fought . . . if it had not been for the services of women." He notes that the principle behind granting suffrage to women is indisputable and that both parties had pledged to support it; only the method by which it would be granted remained in question. Wilson raises the issue of national credibility. Even Great Britain, he notes, has granted women the vote; how can the United States lead the rest of the world in democracy if it continues to refuse the vote to women? Since Wilson argues that women deserve the vote due to their service in the war, rather than as a right of citizenship, he needs to supply a reason for suffrage when the war ends. Again avoiding the political implications of woman suffrage, he stresses "the sympathy, and insight and clear moral instinct of the women of the world."

In her 1917 book of essays, *Woman Suffrage by Federal Constitutional Amendment*, with contributions by Mary Summer Boyd and Henry Wade Rogers, suffragist Carrie Chapman Catt argued that a constitutional amendment was the best course of action for achieving woman suffrage. Many suffrage organizations were seeking to amend their state constitutions. In response, Catt and her colleagues published this volume in order to redirect the movement's focus toward the passage of an amendment to the federal Constitution. It was their belief that a constitutional amendment would be easier to achieve and would ultimately prove to be a more powerful measure, and it was the course that, with Wilson's help, eventually succeeded.

Gentlemen of the Senate: The unusual circumstances of a World War in which we stand and are judged in the view not only of our own people and our own consciences but also in the view of all nations and peoples, will, I hope, justify in your thought, as it does in mine, the message I have come to bring you.

I regard the concurrence of the Senate in the constitutional amendment proposing the extension of the suffrage to women as vitally essential to the successful prosecution of the great war of humanity in which we are engaged. I have come to urge upon you the considerations which have led me to that conclusion. It is not only my privilege, it is also my duty to apprise you of every circumstance and element involved in this momentous struggle which seems to me to affect its very processes and its outcome. It is my duty to win the war and to ask you to remove every obstacle that stands in the way of winning it.

I had assumed that the Senate would concur in the amendment, because no disputable principle is involved but only a question of the method by which the suffrage is to be now extended to women. There is and can be no party issue involved in it. Both of our great national parties are pledged, explicitly pledged, to equality of suffrage for the women of the country.

Neither party, therefore, it seems to me, can justify hesitation as to the method of obtaining it, can rightfully hesitate to substitute Federal initiative for State initiative if the early adoption of this measure is necessary to the successful prosecution of the war, and if the method of State action proposed in the party platforms of 1916 is impracticable within any reasonable length of time, if practical at all. And its adoption is, in my judgment, clearly necessary to the successful prosecution of the war and the successful realization of the objects for which the war is being fought.

That judgment I take the liberty of urging upon you with solemn earnestness for reasons which I shall state very frankly and which I shall hope will seem as conclusive to you as they seem to me.

This is a people's war and the people's thinking constitutes its atmosphere and morale, not the predilections of the drawing room or the political considerations of the caucus. If we be indeed democrats and wish to lead the world to democracy, we can ask other peoples to accept in proof of our sincerity and our ability to lead them whither they wish to be led, nothing less persuasive and convincing than our actions.

Our professions will not suffice. Verification must be forthcoming when verification is asked for. And in this case verification is asked for—asked for in this particular matter. You ask by whom? Not through diplomatic channels; not by foreign ministers; not by the intimations of parliaments. It is asked for by the anxious, expectant, suffering peoples with whom we are dealing and who are willing to put their destinies in some measure in our hands, if they are sure that we wish the same things that they do.

I do not speak by conjecture. It is not alone that the voices of statesmen and of newspapers reach me, and that the voices of foolish and intemperate agitators do not reach me at all. Through many, many channels I have been made aware what the plain, struggling, workaday folk are thinking, upon whom the chief terror and suffering of this tragic war fall. They are looking to the great, powerful, famous democracy of the West to lead them to the new day for which they have so long waited; and they think, in their logical simplicity, that democracy means that women shall play their part in affairs alongside men and upon an equal footing with them.

If we reject measures like this, in ignorant defiance of what a new age has brought forth, of what they have seen but we have not, they will cease to believe in us; they will cease to follow or to trust us. They have seen their own governments accept this interpretation of democracy—seen old governments like that of Great Britain, which did not profess to be democratic, promise readily and as of course this justice to women, though they had before refused it; the strange revelations of this war having made many things new and plain to governments as well as to peoples.

Are we alone to refuse to learn the lesson? Are we alone to ask and take the utmost that our women can give—service and sacrifice of every kind—and still say we do not see what title that gives them to stand by our side in the guidance of the affairs of their nation and ours? We have made partners of the women in this war. Shall we admit them only to a partnership of suffering and sacrifice and toil and not to a partnership of privilege and right? This war could not have been fought, either by the other nations engaged or by America, if it had not been for the services of the women—services rendered in every sphere—not merely in the fields of efforts in which we have been accustomed to see them work but wherever men have worked and upon the very skirts and edges of the battle itself.

We shall not only be distrusted, but shall deserve to be distrusted if we do not enfranchise women with the fullest possible enfranchisement, as it is now certain that the other great free nations will enfranchise them. We cannot isolate our thought or action in such a matter from the thought of the rest of the world. We must either conform or deliberately reject what they approve and resign the leadership of liberal minds to others.

The women of America are too intelligent and too devoted to be slackers whether you give or withhold this thing that is mere justice; but I know the magic it will work in their thoughts and spirits if you give it to them. I propose it as I would propose to admit soldiers to the suffrage—the men fighting in the field of our liberties of the world—were they excluded.

The tasks of the women lie at the very heart of the war and I know how much stronger that heart will beat if you do this just thing and show our women that you trust them as much as you in fact and of necessity depend upon them.

I have said that the passage of this amendment is a vitally necessary war measure and do you need further proof? Do you stand in need of the trust of other peoples and of the trust of our own women? Is that trust an asset or is it not? I tell you plainly, as the commander-in-chief of our armies and of the gallant men in our fleets; as the present spokesman of this people in our dealings with the men and women throughout the world who are now our partners; as the responsible head of a great government which stands and is questioned day by day as to its purpose, its principles, its hope. . . . I tell you plainly that this measure which I urge upon you is vital to the winning of the war and to the energies alike of preparation and of battle.

And not to the winning of the war only. It is vital to the right solution of the great problems which we must settle, and settle immediately, when the war is over. We shall need in our vision of affairs, as we have never needed them before, the sympathy and insight and clear moral instinct of the women of the world. The problems of that time will strike to the roots of many things that we have hitherto questioned, and I for one believe that our safety in those questioning days, as well as our comprehension of matters that touch society to the quick, will depend upon the direct and authoritative participation of women in our counsels. We shall need their moral sense to preserve what is right and fine and worthy in our system of life as well as to discover just what it is that ought to be purified and reformed. Without their counsellings we shall be only half wise.

That is my case. This is my appeal. Many may deny its validity, if they choose, but no one can brush aside or answer the arguments upon which it is based. The executive tasks of this war rest upon me. I ask that you lighten them and place in my hands instruments, spiritual instruments, which I have daily to apologize for not being able to employ.

Source:

Elizabeth Frost and Kathryn Cullen-DuPont, *Women's Suffrage in America: An Eyewitness History*. New York: Facts On File, 1992.

Seattle General Strike, 1919

1919 was a year of great unrest, fed by racism and fear of anarchy. With the Great War over, Americans turned from anathemizing Germans to suspicion of Bolsheviks. (Two American Communist Parties began in 1919.) On February 6, 1919, workers in Seattle fed those fears by staging a citywide general strike, the first such strike in the United States. After working under strict wage controls during World War I, shipyard workers were refused a promised postwar raise, and on January 21 more than 35,000 of them went out on strike. An additional 25,000 union members staged a sympathy walkout at the urging of Seattle's Central Labor Council, and the city was effectively shut down, except for essential services. Mayor Ole Hanson called the strikers "Bolshevik" revolutionaries and threatened to impose martial law. By February 11, when the Labor Council officially ended the strike, most workers had already returned to their jobs.

The Seattle strike demonstrated the potential power of labor unions, but it also worked against the unions by focusing public attention on the more radical elements of the labor movement, such as the Industrial Workers of the World (IWW, or Wobblies). According to the preamble to its constitution, the "working class and the employing class have nothing in common," and the mission of the working class is to eliminate capitalism. It stated that the workers must organize to overthrow the capitalists and to form the structure of a new, socialist society. At the organization's fourth convention, in 1908, the preamble was revised by the IWW's radical members in favor of more direct, physical action at the point of production, rather than political effort.

The IWW considered itself a better friend to the worker than the more conservative American Federation of Labor (AFL), which consisted primarily of skilled craftspeople. While never large in numbers, the IWW was most successful among western miners, northwestern lumberjacks, and northeastern textile workers. The IWW accepted all wage-earners, regardless of race, age, gender, or ethnicity. Especially in the Far West, its organizers challenged free speech curbs. They were not only imprisoned but allegedly tortured. Because some Wobblies not only went on strike but burned farms and sabotaged mine and lumber operations, the general public, already inclined to oppose organized labor, supported government and private efforts against the IWW. Corporation-labor clashes became so violent that President Theodore Roosevelt, at management urging, sent troops to keep the peace in Goldfield, Nevada, site of one of the IWW's most successful campaigns.

The IWW reached its height around 1907–08. Although its opposition to World War I hurt the Wobblies, it played a significant role in Seattle's general strike, leading to the government's extreme reaction—more than 1,000 additional police and another 1,000 armed deputies were sworn in to prevent a possible Bolshevik revolution. However, the strike passed without violence. Union members had arranged for milk delivery and ambulance service, and unarmed union veterans patrolled the streets to keep the peace.

Although the strikers failed to win their demands from the shipyard owners, the Seattle general strike showed the power of union solidarity, but it also paved the way for extreme and often violent strike suppression by employers and government officials.

Anna Louise Strong, "No One Knows Where," 1919

There will be many cheering, and there will be some who fear.

Both these emotions are useful, but not too much of either.

We are undertaking the most tremendous move ever made by LABOR in this country, a move which will lead—NO ONE KNOWS WHERE!

We do not need hysteria.

We need the iron march of labor.

* * *

LABOR WILL FEED THE PEOPLE.

Twelve great kitchens have been offered, and from them food will be distributed by the provision trades at low cost to all.

LABOR WILL CARE FOR THE BABIES AND THE SICK.

The milk-wagon drivers and the laundry drivers are arranging plans for supplying milk to babies, invalids and hospitals, and taking care of the cleaning of linen for hospitals.

LABOR WILL PRESERVE ORDER.

The strike committee is arranging for guards, and it is expected that the stopping of the cars will keep people at home.

* * *

A few hot-headed enthusiasts have complained that strikers only should be fed, and the general public left to endure severe discomfort. Aside from the inhumanitarian character of such suggestions, let them get this straight—

NOT THE WITHDRAWAL OF LABOR POWER, BUT THE POWER OF THE WORKERS TO MANAGE WILL WIN THIS STRIKE.

What does Mr. Piez of the Shipping Board care about the closing down of Seattle's shipyards, or even of all the industries of the northwest. Will it not merely strengthen the yards at Hog Island, in which he is more interested?

When the shipyard owners of Seattle were on the point of agreeing with the workers, it was Mr. Piez who wired them that, if they so agreed—

HE WOULD NOT LET THEM HAVE STEEL.

Whether this is camouflage we have no means of knowing. But we do know that the great eastern combinations of capitalists COULD AFFORD to offer privately to Mr. Skinner, Mr. Ames and Mr. Duthie a few millions apiece in eastern shipyard stock.

RATHER THAN LET THE WORKERS WIN.

The closing down of Seattle's industries, as a MERE SHUTDOWN, will not affect these eastern gentlemen much. They could let the whole northwest go to pieces, as far as money alone is concerned.

BUT, the closing down of the capitalistically controlled industries of Seattle, while the WORKERS ORGANIZE to feed the people, to care for the babies and the sick, to preserve order—THIS will move them, for this looks too much like the taking over of POWER by the workers.

* * *

Labor will not only SHUT DOWN the industries, but Labor will REOPEN, under the management of the appropriate trades, such activities as are needed to preserve public health and public peace. If the strike continues, Labor may feel led to avoid public suffering by reopening more and more activities.

UNDER ITS OWN MANAGEMENT.

And that is why we say that we are starting on a road that leads—NO ONE KNOWS WHERE!

Ole Hansen, Mayoral Statement on the General Strike, 1919

Two years ago 15,000 workmen were employed in the industries of Seattle. There are now 65,000. The unions have admitted to their ranks under the stress of war conditions every Bolsheviki and I.W.W. who desired to join. These men have secured control of many labor organizations. The conservative membership have shown their yellow streak by allowing the foes of organized government to run their unions and their affairs.

When the shipyard strike was called, the men went out unwillingly in most instances, although these is a feeling that the lower paid men were not getting sufficient wage when figured on the present cost of living.

Then the radicals, having read of the revolution in Petrograd, tried to duplicate the initial steps of the same here. They wanted to run our light plant and all industries, believing that we would surrender because of economic pressure and suffering of our people. They had forgotten the lesson Germany acquired when they tried the policy of ruthlessness. The city government told them to go to hell; that all things would run as long as there was a government and made no concession to the revolutionists. They closed down the newspapers. Business, always cowardly, hunted its hole for a little time until I announced that all people would be protected to the last man and that we had 1,500 men armed with rifles to kill on sight anyone that caused disorder. Yesterday I notified the strike committee that at 8 o'clock this morning everything would operate. Everything is activity in Seattle this morning. Every municipal car is running. Our light plant has never shut down one minute. Neither has our water plant. Gathered together in Seattle are Joe Ettar of Lawrence, Mass., fame: Mucky

McDonald and men of his stripe from all over the union. Gathered here are hundreds and thousands of Russian Bolsheviki who have arrived here during the past two years. These scoundrels want to take possession of our American government and try to duplicate the anarchy of Russia.

The seat of government is the city hall. We swore in 1,000 extra police and hold in reserve citizens armed with rifles and shotguns. I gave orders to shoot on sight any disturber of the peace. They knew from the experience they had at the riot a few weeks ago that we meant business and believe me, we did.

I wanted a showdown. If there is a majority of these (unprintable) in the United States I don't want to live here. They told me the troops were disloyal and would not help us. I told them that was a lie but even if it was so we would fight until we were dead before we even allowed them to turn out one eight-candlepower light.

Chief of Police Joe Warren is a real man who loves his country. We decided that we would not call in the federal troops. We won't be here. The great body of union men saw the light. Today they are bitterly resenting their false leadership and will overthrow their officers in many unions.

This is a test of unionism or I.W.W.'ism. If anyone owes a higher allegiance to any organization that they do to this country, they are traitors and should be treated as such. That is all there is to it. This is a time when every American must forget all other allegiance and stand by the government.

The unions of the nation are on trial. They are either American Federation of Labor loyalists or Bolsheviki traitors.

This morning the strike is broken. Business is resuming. Strikers are returning to work. Our city no longer lies prostrate. Ninety per cent of Seattle stands firm for Americanism. The other 10 per cent will be driven from this community.

IWW, "General Strike, Or . . . ," 1919

The profiteers have made millions out of the ships the workers built. Now they refuse these workers a living wage. They have forced thirty-thousand men to go on strike.

All the profiteering employers of Seattle are banded together in their Employers' Association. All have a common interest in driving the shipyard workers back to slave conditions and smashing their labor organization, The Metal Trades.

The allied bosses want to smash the shipyard workers now so that they can have a free hand to smash the rest of the union men of Seattle later on.

These profiteers hate all unionism. They hate the longshoremen, the street car men, the electrical workers, the men of the building trades, the restaurant workers and all others as much as they hate the Metal Trades organization that is conducting this strike.

They want to eat labor piece meal. First the shipyard workers, then the others. So they can make this an open shop town and cut wages.

DIVIDE AND CONQUER is the motto of the bosses.

But we have a better motto. It is TOGETHER WE WIN!

If sixty thousand union men and women of Seattle go out on a general strike the bosses will cry for mercy. Capital is helpless without labor. The business interests cannot afford a general strike. And we cannot afford to see our shipyard brothers beaten, because our turn would come next.

A million workers on the Pacific Coast are ready to fall in line behind Seattle. We will show them a magnificent example of solidarity.

All together in the GENERAL STRIKE.

TOGETHER WE WIN! By Solidarity.

Source:

Strong, Anna Louise. "No One Knows Where." American Public Address, Department of Speech and Communication, the University of Washington. Available on-line. URL: http://courses.washington.edu/spcmu/425. Accessed November 2003.

Volstead Act, 1919

Federal U.S. legislation passed on October 28, 1919, to enforce the Eighteenth Amendment, establishing Prohibition, which forbade the sale of intoxicating beverages. Previously, a number of states had anti-liquor laws, and in 1917 Congress, over President William Howard Taft's veto, passed the Webb-Kenyon Act, named for sponsors Representative Edwin Y. Webb of North Carolina and Senator William S. Kenyon of Iowa. It prohibited the interstate shipment of intoxicating liquor into states where its sale or use was illegal. The U.S. Supreme Court upheld the law January 8, 1917. It represented the first federal victory of the Anti-Saloon League.

The Volstead Act, introduced by Representative Andrew J. Volstead of Minnesota and passed over the veto of President Woodrow Wilson, defined intoxicating liquor as containing more than 0.5 percent alcohol by volume. It went into effect on January 16, 1920, and gave federal agents, under the Bureau of Internal Revenue in the Treasury Department, the power to investigate violations. It also prescribed penalties.

Strict enforcement proved impossible, however, and the act became void after the Twenty-first Amendment repealed the Eighteenth. Its failure is often cited by opponents of antinarcotic legislation.

An Act

To prohibit intoxicating beverages, and to regulate the manufacture, production, use, and sale of high-proof spirits for other than beverage purposes, and to insure an ample supply of alcohol and promote its use in scientific research and in the development of fuel, dye, and other lawful industries.

Be it enacted by the Senate and House of Representatives of the United States of America in Congress assembled, That the short title of this Act shall be the "National Prohibition Act."

Title I.

To Provide for the Enforcement of War Prohibition.

The term "War Prohibition Act" used in this Act shall mean the provisions of any Act or Acts prohibiting the sale and manufacture of intoxicating liquors until the conclusion of the present war and thereafter until the termination of demobilization, the date of which shall be determined and proclaimed by the President of the United States. . . .

Sec. 2. The Commissioner of Internal Revenue, his assistants, agents, and inspectors, shall investigate and report violations of the War Prohibition Act to the United States attorney for the district in which committed, who shall be charged with the duty of prosecuting, subject to the direction of the Attorney General. . .

* * *

Sec. 5. The Commissioner of Internal Revenue, his assistants, agents, and inspectors, and all other officers of the United States whose duty it is to enforce criminal laws, shall have all the power for the enforcement of the War Prohibition Act or any provisions thereof which is conferred by law for the enforcement of existing laws relating to the manufacture or sale of intoxicating liquors under the laws of the United States.

Title II.

Prohibition of Intoxicating Beverages.

Sec. 1. When used in Title II and Title III of this Act (1) The word "liquor" or the phrase "intoxicating liquor" shall be construed to include alcohol, brandy, whisky, rum, gin, beer, ale, porter, and wine, and in addition thereto any spirituous, vinous, malt or fermented liquor, liquids, and compounds, whether medicated, proprietary, patented, or not, and by whatever name called, containing one-half of 1 per centum or more of alcohol by volume which are fit for use for beverage purposes. . . .

(2) The word "person" shall mean and include natural persons, associations, copartnerships, and corporations.

(3) The word "commissioner" shall mean Commissioner of Internal Revenue.

* * *

Sec. 2. The Commissioner of Internal Revenue, his assistants, agents, and inspectors shall investigate and report violations of this Act to the United States attorney for the district in which committed, who is hereby charged with the duty of prosecuting the offenders, subject to the direction of the Attorney General, as in the case of other offenses against the laws of the United States; and such Commissioner of Internal Revenue, his assistants, agents, and inspectors may swear out warrants before United States commissioners or other officers or courts authorized to issue the same for the apprehension of such offenders, and may, subject to the control of the said United States attorney, conduct the prosecution at the committing trial for the purpose of having the offenders held for the action of a grand jury. . . .

Sec. 6. No one shall manufacture, sell, purchase, transport, or prescribe any liquor without first obtaining a permit from the commissioner so to do, except that a person may, without a permit, purchase and use liquor for medicinal purposes when prescribed by a physician. . . .

* * *

Source:

Statutes At Large, Vol. 41, pp. 305–323.

Marcus Garvey, Declaration of Rights of the Negro Peoples of the World, 1920

Statement drawn up in 1920 in New York City by delegates at an international convention of the Universal Negro Improvement Association (UNIA). Black nationalist leader Marcus Garvey founded UNIA in London in 1914 to "promote the spirit of race pride." He rejected the concept of integration and started a "back to Africa" movement.

His 1920 declaration points out that blacks have suffered injustices, discrimination, and "inhuman, unchristian, and uncivilized treatment" in most every part of the world and that European nations had taken control of nearly all of Africa, "the Motherland of all Negroes." All blacks were "free citizens of Africa," it states, and they have the right "to reclaim the treasures and possession of the vast continent of [their] forefathers."

Garvey's influential newspaper, *Negro World,* made him the most prominent black leader of the 1920s. The federal government, however, considered him a dangerous radical and tried for years to get him deported. In 1925 the government succeeded. Garvey was convicted of postal fraud associated with his Black Star steamship company. He was jailed and, in 1927, deported to Jamaica.

Preamble

Be It Resolved, That the Negro people of the world, through their chosen representatives in convention assembled in Liberty Hall, in the City of New York and United States of America, from August 1 to August 31, in the year of Our Lord one thousand nine hundred and twenty, protest against the wrongs and injustices they are suffering at the hands of their white brethren, and state what they deem their fair and just rights, as well as the treatment they propose to demand of all men in the future.

We complain:

1. That nowhere in the world, with few exceptions, are black men accorded equal treatment with white men, although in the same situation and circumstances, but, on the contrary, are discriminated against the denied and common rights due to human beings for no other reason than their race and color.

We are not willingly accepted as guests in the public hotels and inns of the world for no other reason than our race and color.

2. In certain parts of the United States of America our race is denied the right of public trial accorded to other races when accused of crime, but are lynched and burned by mobs, and such brutal and inhuman treatment is even practiced upon our women.

3. That European nations have parcelled out among them and taken possession of nearly all of the continent of Africa, and the natives are compelled to surrender their lands to aliens and are treated in most instances like slaves.

4. In the southern portion of the United States of America, although citizens under the Federal Constitution, and in some States almost equal to the whites in population and are qualified land owners and taxpayers, we are, nevertheless, denied all voice in the making and administration of the laws and are taxed without representation by the State governments, and at the same time compelled to do military service in defense of the country.

5. On the public conveyances and common carriers in the southern portion of the United States we are jim-crowed and compelled to accept separate and inferior accommodations and made to pay the same fare charged for first-class accommodations, and our families are often humiliated and insulted by drunken white men who habitually pass through the jim-cow cars going to the smoking car.

6. The physicians of our race are denied the right to attend their patients while in the public hospitals of the cities and States where they reside in certain parts of the United States.

Our children are forced to attend inferior separate schools for shorter terms than white children, and the public school funds are unequally divided between the white and colored schools.

7. We are discriminated against and denied an equal chance to earn wages for the support of our families, and in many instances are refused admission into labor unions and nearly everywhere are paid smaller wages than white men.

8. In the Civil Service and departmental offices we are everywhere discriminated against and made to feel that to be a black man in Europe, America and the West Indies is equivalent to being an outcast and a leper among the races of men, no matter what the character attainments of the black men may be.

9. In the British and other West Indian islands and colonies Negroes are secretly and cunningly discriminated against and denied those fuller rights of government to which white citizens are appointed, nominated and elected.

10. That our people in those parts are forced to work for lower wages than the average standard of white men are kept in conditions repugnant to good civilized tastes and customs.

11. That the many acts of injustices against members of our race before the courts of law in the respective islands and colonies are of such nature as to create disgust and disrespect for the white man's sense of justice.

12. Against all such inhuman, unchristian and uncivilized treatment we here and now emphatically protest, and invoke the condemnation of all mankind.

In order to encourage our race all over the world and to stimulate it to overcome the handicaps and difficulties surrounding it, and to push forward to a higher and grander destiny, we demand and insist on the following Declaration of Rights:

1. Be it known to all men that whereas all men are created equal and entitled to the rights of life, liberty and the pursuit of happiness, and because of this we, the duly elected representatives of the Negro peoples of the world, invoking the aid of the just and Almighty God, do declare all men, women and children of our blood throughout the world free denizens, and do claim them as free citizens of Africa, the Motherland of all Negroes.

[2.] That we believe in the supreme authority of our race in all things racial; that all things are created and given to man as a common possession; that there should be an equitable distribution and apportionment of all such things, and in consideration of the fact that as a race we are now deprived of those things that are morally and legally ours, we believed it right that all such things should be acquired and held by whatsoever means possible.

3. That we believe the Negro, like any other race, should be governed by the ethics of civilization, and therefore should not be deprived of any of those rights or privileges common to order human beings.

4. We declare that Negroes, wheresoever they from a community among themselves should be given the right to elect their own representatives to represent them in Legislatures, courts of law, or such institutions as may exercise control over that particular community.

5. We assert that the Negro is entitled to even-handed justice before all courts of law and equity in whatever country he may be found, and when this is denied him on account of his race or color such denial is an insult to the race as a whole and should be resented by the entire body of Negroes.

6. We declare it unfair and prejudicial to the rights of Negroes in communities where they exist in considerable numbers to be tried by a judge and jury composed entirely of an alien race, but in all such cases members of our race are entitled to representation on the jury.

7. We believe that any law or practice that tends to deprive any African of his land or the privileges of free citizenship within his country is unjust and immoral, and no native should respect any such law or practice.

8. We declare taxation without representation unjust and tyran[n]ous, and there should be no obligation on the part of the Negro to obey the levy of a tax by any law-making body from which he is excluded and denied representation on account of his race and color.

9. We believe that any law especially directed against the Negro to his detriment and singling him out because of his race or color is unfair and immoral, and should not be respected.

10. We believe all men entitled to common human respect and that our race should in no way tolerate any insults that may be interpreted to mean disrespect to our race or color.

11. We deprecate the use of the term "nigger" as applied to Negroes, and demand that the word "Negro" be written with a capital "N."

12. We believe hat the Negro should adopt every means to protect himself against barbarous practices inflicted upon him because of color.

13. We believe in the freedom of Africa for the Negro people of the world, and by the principle of Europe for the Europeans and Asia for the Asiatics, we also demand Africa for the Africans at home and abroad.

14. We believe in the inherent right of the Negro to possess himself of Africa and that his possession of same shall not be regarded as an infringement on any claim or purchase made by any race or nation.

15. We strongly condemn the cupidity of those nations of the world who, by open aggression or secret schemes, have seized the territories and inexhaustible natural wealth of Africa, and we place on record our most solemn determination to reclaim the treasures and possession of the vast continent of our forefathers.

16. We believe all men should live in peace one with the other, but when races and nations provoke the ire of other races and nations by attempting to infringe upon their rights[,] war becomes inevitable, and the attempt in any way to free one's self or protect one's rights or heritage becomes justifiable.

17. Whereas the lynching, by burning, hanging or any other means, of human beings is a barbarous practice and a shame and disgrace to civilization, we therefore declare any country guilty of such atrocities outside the pale of civilization.

18. We protest against the atrocious crime of whipping, flogging and overworking of the native tribes of Africa and Negroes everywhere. These are methods that should be abolished and all means should be taken to prevent a continuance of such brutal practices.

19. We protest against the atrocious practice of shaving the heads of Africans, especially of African women or individuals of Negro blood, when placed in prison as a punishment for crime by an alien race.

20. We protest against segregated districts, separate public conveyances, industrial discrimination, lynchings and limitations of political privileges of any Negro citizen in any part of the world on account of race, color or creed, and will exert our full influence and power against all such.

21. We protest against any punishment inflicted upon a Negro with severity, as against lighter punishment inflicted upon another of an alien race for like offense, as an act of prejudice and injustice, and should be resented by the entire race.

22. We protest against the system of education in any country where Negroes are denied the same privileges and advantages as other races.

23. We declare it inhuman and unfair to boycott Negroes from industries and labor in any part of the world.

24. We believe in the doctrine of the freedom of the press, and we therefore emphatically protest against the suppression of Negro newspapers and periodicals in various parts of the world, and call upon Negroes everywhere to employ all available means to prevent such suppression.

25. We further demand free speech universally for all men.

26. We hereby protest against the publication of scandalous and inflammatory articles by an alien press tending to create racial strife and the exhibition of picture films showing the Negro as a cannibal.

27. We believe in the self-determination of all peoples.

28. We declare for the freedom of religious worship.

29. With the help of Almighty God we declare ourselves the sworn protectors of the honor and virtue of our women and children, and pledge our lives for their protection and defense everywhere and under all circumstances from wrongs and outrages.

30. We demand the right of an unlimited and unprejudiced education for ourselves and our posterity forever[.]

31. We declare that the teaching in any school by alien teachers to our boys and girls, that the alien race is superior to the Negro race, is an insult to the Negro people of the world.

32. Where Negroes form a part of the citizenry of any country, and pass the civil service examination of such country, we declare them entitled to the same consideration as other citizens as to appointments in such civil service.

33. We vigorously protest against the increasingly unfair and unjust treatment accorded Negro travelers on land and sea by the agents and employees of railroad and steamship companies, and insist that for equal fare we receive equal privileges with travelers of other races.

34. We declare it unjust for any country, State or nation to enact laws tending to hinder and obstruct the free immigration of Negroes on account of their race and color.

35. That the right of the Negro to travel unmolested throughout the world be not abridged by any person or persons, and all Negroes are called upon to give aid to a fellow Negro when thus molested.

36. We declare that all Negroes are entitled to the same right to travel over the world as other men.

37. We hereby demand that the governments of the world recognize our leader and his representatives chosen by the race to look after the welfare of our people under such governments.

38. We demand complete control of our social institutions without interference by any alien race or races.

39. That the colors, Red, Black and Green, be the colors of the Negro race.

40. Resolved, That the anthem "Ethiopia, Thou Land of Our Fathers etc.," shall be the anthem of the Negro race. (Copy anthem appended.)

The Universal Ethiopian Anthem
Poem by Burrell and Ford

I

Ethiopia, thou land of our fathers,
Thou land where the gods loved to be,
As storm cloud at night sudden gathers
Our armies come rushing to thee.
We must in the fight be victorious
When swords are thrust outward to glean;
For us will the vict'ry be glorious
When led by the red, black and green

Chorus

Advance, advance to victory,
Let Africa be free;
Advance to meet the foe
With the might
Of the red, the black and the green.

II

Ethiopia, the tyrant's falling,
Who smote thee upon thy knees
And thy children are lustily calling
From over the distant seas.
Jehovah the Great One has heard us,
Has noted our sighs and our tears,
With His spirit of Love he has stirred us
To be One through the coming years.
Chorus—Advance, advance, etc.

III

O, Jehovah, thou God of the ages
Grant unto our sons that lead
The wisdom Thou gave to Thy sages
When Israel was sore in need.
Thy voice thro' the dim past has spoken,
Ethiopia shall stretch forth her hand,
By Thee shall all fetters be broken
And Heav'n bless our dear fatherland.
Chorus—Advance, advance, etc.

41. We believe that any limited liberty which deprives one of the complete rights and prerogatives of full citizenship is but a modified form of slavery.

42. We declare it an injustice to our people and a serious impediment to the health of the race to deny to competent licensed Negro physicians the right to practice in

the public hospitals of the communities in which they reside, for no other reason than their race and color.

43. We call upon the various government[s] of the world to accept and acknowledge Negro representatives who shall be sent to the said governments to represent the general welfare of the Negro peoples of the world.

44. We deplore and protest against the practice of confining juvenile prisoners in prisons with adults, and we recommend that such youthful prisoners be taught gainful trades under human[e] supervision.

45. Be it further resolved, That we as a race of people declare the League of Nations null and void as far as the Negro is concerned, in that it seeks to deprive Negroes of their liberty.

46. We demand of all men to do unto us as we would do unto them, in the name of justice; and we cheerfully accord to all men all the rights we claim herein for ourselves.

47. We declare that no Negro shall engage himself in battle for an alien race without first obtaining the consent of the leader of the Negro people of the world, except in a matter of national self-defense.

48. We protest against the practice of drafting Negroes and sending them to war with alien forces without proper training, and demand in all cases that Negro soldiers be given the same training as the aliens.

49. We demand that instructions given Negro children in schools include the subject of "Negro History," to their benefit.

50. We demand a free and unfettered commercial intercourse with all the Negro people of the world.

51. We declare for the absolute freedom of the seas for all peoples.

52. We demand that our duly accredited representatives be given proper recognition in all leagues, conferences, conventions or courts of international arbitration wherever human rights are discussed.

53. We proclaim the 31st day of August of each year to be an international holiday to be observed by all Negroes.

54. We want all men to know that we shall maintain and contend for the freedom and equality of every man, woman and child for our race, with our lives, our fortunes and our sacred honor.

These rights we believe to be justly ours and proper for the protection of the Negro race at large, and because of this belief we, on behalf of the four hundred million Negroes of the world, do pledge herein the sacred blood of the race in defense, and we hereby subscribe our names as a guarantee of the truthfulness and faithfulness hereof, in the presence of Almighty God, on this 13th day of August, in the year of our Lord one thousand nine hundred and twenty.

Source:

Hill, Robert A., ed. *The Marcus Garvey and Universal Negro Improvement Association Papers.* Vol. 2. Berkeley: University of California Press, 1983–95, pp. 571–580.

Emergency Quota Act, 1921

Emergency legislation enacted by Congress on May 19, 1921, establishing the first quota for immigrants to the United States. It supplanted the Immigration Act of 1917, which passed over President Woodrow Wilson's veto and increased classifications for denying admission, the most significant being a literacy test that lawmakers hoped would deter non-English-speaking immigration, particularly Chinese. The 1921 law reflected fears of a flood of immigration following World War I. Wilson had refused to sign the original bill in 1920, but President Warren Harding signed the act at the beginning of his administration.

Sponsored by Senator William P. Dillingham of Vermont, the 1921 act set a quota, based on the 1910 census, of 357,000 places (aliens); immigrants from a given nation (nationality) were restricted yearly to 3 percent of the population of that nation residing in the United States. Immigrants from Asia—already largely excluded by other agreements—and from the Western Hemisphere were exempt from this act. The act also showed evidence of a bias against people from southern and central Europe, while favoring immigrants from the British Isles and northwestern Europe. This national origins quota system set the pattern for American immigration laws for the first half of the 20th century.

Congress next enacted U.S. immigration legislation on May 26, 1924. It amended the U.S. Emergency Quota Act by halving the 1921 quota (placing the number of immigrants at 164,447) and by limiting annual immigration for any group to 2 percent of that group's U.S. population according to the census of 1890. This quota was to apply until 1927, when the limit on immigrants was to be set at 150,000, apportioned by national origin according to the 1920 census. Sponsored by Senator Hiram W. Johnson of California (Roosevelt's Progressive Party running mate in 1912) and Senator James A. Reed of Missouri, the act continued to favor immigrants from northern and western Europe. It aroused so much hostility that it was not implemented until 1929.

An Act

To limit the immigration of aliens into the United States.

Be it enacted by the Senate and House of Representatives of the United States of America in Congress assembled, That as used in this Act—

The term "United States" means the United States, and any waters, territory, or other place subject to the jurisdiction thereof except the Canal Zone and the Philippine Islands; but if any alien leaves the Canal Zone or any insular possession of the United States and attempts to enter any other place under the jurisdiction of the United States nothing contained in this Act shall be construed as permitting him to enter under any other conditions than those applicable to all aliens.

The word "alien" includes any person not a native-born or naturalized citizen of the United States, but this definition shall not be held to include Indians of the United States not taxed nor citizens of the islands under the jurisdiction of the United States.

The term "Immigration Act" means the Act of February 5, 1917, entitled "An Act to regulate the immigration of aliens to, and the residence of aliens in, the United States"; and the term "immigration laws" includes such Act and all laws, conventions, and treaties of the United States relating to the immigration, exclusion, or expulsion of aliens.

Sec. 2. (a) That the number of aliens of any nationality who may be admitted under the immigration laws to the United States in any fiscal year shall be limited to 3 per centum of the number of foreign born persons of such nationality resident in the United States as determined by the United States census of 1910. This provision shall not apply to the following, and they shall not be counted in reckoning any of the percentage limits provided in this Act: (1) Government officials, their families, attendants, servants, and employees; (2) aliens in continuous transit through the United States; (3) aliens lawfully admitted to the United States who later go in transit from one part of the United States to another through foreign contiguous territory; (4) aliens visiting the United States as tourists or temporarily for business or pleasure; (5) aliens from countries immigration from which is regulated in accordance with treaties or agreements relating solely to immigration; (6) aliens from the so-called Asiatic barred zone, as described in section 3 of the Immigration Act; (7) aliens who have resided continuously for at least one year immediately preceding the time of their admission to the United States in the Dominion of Canada, Newfoundland, the Republic of Cuba, the Republic of Mexico, countries of Central or South America, or adjacent islands; or (8) aliens under the age of eighteen who are children of citizens of the United States.

(b) For the purposes of this Act nationality shall be determined by country of birth, treating as separate countries the colonies or dependencies for which separate enumeration was made in the United States census of 1910.

(c) The Secretary of State, the Secretary of Commerce, and the Secretary of Labor, jointly, shall, as soon as feasible after the enactment of this Act, prepare a statement showing the number of persons of the various nationalities resident in the United States as determined by the United States census of 1910, which statement shall be the population basis for the purposes of this Act. In case of changes in political boundaries in foreign countries occurring subsequent to 1910 and resulting (1) in the creation of new countries, the Governments of which are recognized by the United States, or (2) in the transfer of territory from one country to another, such transfer being recognized by the United States, such officials, jointly, shall estimate the number of persons resident in the United States in 1910 who were born within the area included in such new countries or in such territory so transferred, and revise the population basis as to each country involved in such change of political boundary. For the purpose of such revision and for the purposes of this Act generally aliens born in the area included in any such new country shall be considered as having been born in such country, and aliens born in any territory so transferred shall be considered as having been born in the country to which such territory was transferred.

(d) When the maximum number of aliens of any nationality who may be admitted in any fiscal year under this Act shall have been admitted all other aliens of such nationality, except as otherwise provided in this Act, who may apply for admission during the same fiscal year shall be excluded: *Provided*, That the number of aliens of any nationality who may be admitted in any month shall not exceed 20 per centum of the total number of aliens of such nationality who are admissible in that fiscal year: *Provided further*, That aliens returning from a temporary visit abroad, aliens who are professional actors, artists, lecturers, singers, nurses, ministers of any religious denomination, professors for colleges or seminaries, aliens belonging to any recognized learned profession, or aliens employed as domestic servants, may, if otherwise admissible, be admitted notwithstanding the maximum number of aliens of the same nationality admissible in the same month or fiscal year, as the case may be, shall have entered the United States; but aliens of the classes included in this proviso who enter the United States before such maximum number shall have entered shall (unless excluded by subdivision (a) from being counted) be counted in reckoning the percentage limits provided in this Act: *Provided further*, That in the enforcement of this Act preference shall be given so far as possible to the wives, parents, brothers, sisters, children under eighteen years of age, and fiancees, (1) of citizens of the United States, (2) of aliens now in the United States who have applied for citizenship in the manner provided by law, or (3) of persons eligible to United States citizenship who served in the military or naval forces of the United States at any time between April 6, 1917, and November 11, 1918, both dates inclusive, and have been separated from such forces under honorable conditions.

Sec. 3. That the Commissioner General of Immigration, with the approval of the Secretary of Labor, shall, as soon as feasible after the enactment of this Act, and from time to time thereafter, prescribe rules and regulations necessary to carry the provisions of this Act into effect. He shall, as soon as feasible after the enactment of this Act, publish a statement showing the number of aliens of the various nationalities who may be admitted to the United States between the date this Act becomes effective and the end of the current fiscal year, and on June 30 thereafter he shall publish a statement showing the number of aliens of the various nationalities who may be admitted during the ensuing fiscal year. He shall also publish monthly statements during the time this Act remains in force showing the number of aliens of each nationality already admitted during the then current fiscal year and the number who may be admitted under the provisions of this Act during the remainder of such year, but when 75 per centum of the maximum number of any nationality admissible during the fiscal year shall have been admitted such statements shall be issued weekly thereafter. All statements shall be made available for general publication and shall be mailed to all transportation companies bringing aliens to the United States who shall request the same and shall file with the Department of Labor the address to which such statements shall be sent. The Secretary of Labor shall also submit such statements to the Secretary of State, who shall transmit the information contained therein to the proper diplomatic and consular officials of the United States, which officials shall make the same available to persons intending to emigrate to the United States and to others who may apply.

Sec. 4. That the provisions of this Act are in addition to and not in substitution for the provisions of the immigration laws.

Sec. 5. That this Act shall take effect and be enforced 15 days after its enactment (except sections 1 and 3 and subdivisions (b) and (c) of section 2, which shall take effect immediately upon the enactment of this Act), and shall continue in force until June 30, 1922, and the number of aliens of any nationality who may be admitted during the remaining period of the current fiscal year, from the date when this Act becomes effective to June 30, shall be limited in proportion to the number admissible during the fiscal year 1922.

Source:
Statutes at Large, Vol. 41, pp. 5–7.

Sheppard-Towner Act, 1921

First federal welfare legislation in the United States, cosponsored by Senator John Morris Sheppard of Texas and Representative Horace M. Towner of Iowa and enacted on November 23, 1921. Responding to new woman voters after the passage of the Nineteenth Amendment, it provided federal money to the states for maternal and infant health care and hygiene. Although firmly in the Progressive tradition, it reflected postwar emphasis on local governments by authorizing its annual federal appropriations of $1 million in matching funds to be apportioned among the states. Nevertheless, opponents considered it an unwarranted intrusion on state jurisdiction, and some states refused to accept its provisions. Although it helped mothers and children where it was in effect, the act lapsed in June 1929.

An Act
For the promotion of the welfare and hygiene of maternity and infancy, and for other purposes.

Be it enacted by the Senate and House of Representatives of the United States of America in Congress assembled, That there is hereby authorized to be appropriated annually, out of any money in the Treasury not otherwise appropriated, the sums specified in section 2 of this Act, to be paid to the several States for the purpose of cooperating with them in promoting the welfare and hygiene of maternity and infancy as hereinafter provided.

Sec. 2. For the purpose of carrying out the provisions of this Act, there is authorized to be appropriated, out of any money in the Treasury not otherwise appropriated, for the current fiscal year $480,000, to be equally apportioned among the several States, and for each subsequent year, for the period of five years, $240,000, to be equally apportioned among the several States in the manner hereinafter provided: *Provided,* That there is hereby authorized to be appropriated for the use of the States, subject to the provisions of this Act, for the fiscal year ending June 30, 1922, an additional sum of $1,000,000, and annually thereafter, for the period of five years, an additional sum not to exceed $1,000,000: *Provided further,* That the additional appropriations herein authorized shall be apportioned $5,000 to each State and the balance among the States in the proportion which their population bears to the total population of the States of the United States, according to the last preceding United States census: *And provided further,* That no payment out of the additional appropriation herein authorized shall be made in any year to any State until an equal sum has been appropriated for that year by the legislature of such State for the maintenance of the services and facilities provided for in this Act.

So much of the amount apportioned to any State for any fiscal year as remains unpaid to such State at the close thereof shall be available for expenditures in that State until the close of the succeeding fiscal year.

Sec. 3. There is hereby created a Board of Maternity and Infant Hygiene, which shall consist of the Chief of the Children's Bureau, the Surgeon General of the United States Public Health Service, and the United States Commissioner of Education, and which is hereafter designated in this Act as the Board. The Board shall elect its own chairman and perform the duties provided for in this Act.

The Children's Bureau of the Department of Labor shall be charged with the administration of this Act, except as herein otherwise provided, and the Chief of the Children's Bureau shall be the executive officer. It shall be the duty of the Children's Bureau to make or cause to be made such studies, investigations, and reports as will promote the efficient administration of this Act.

Sec. 4. In order to secure the benefits of the appropriations authorized in section 2 of this Act, any State shall, through the legislative authority thereof, accept the provisions of this Act and designate or authorize the creation of a State agency with which the Children's Bureau shall have all necessary powers to cooperate as herein provided in the administration of the provisions of this Act: *Provided,* That in any State having a child-welfare or child-hygiene division in its State agency of health, the said State agency of health shall administer the provisions of this Act through such divisions. If the legislature of any State has not made provision for accepting the provisions of this Act the governor of such State may in so far as he is authorized to do so by the laws of such State accept the provisions of this Act and designate or create a State agency to cooperate with the Children's Bureau until six months after the adjournment of the first regular session of the legislature in such State following the passage of this Act.

Sec. 5. So much, not to exceed 5 per centum, of the additional appropriations authorized for any fiscal year under section 2 of this Act, as the Children's Bureau may estimate to be necessary for administering the provisions of this Act, as herein provided, shall be deducted for that purpose, to be available until expended.

Sec. 6. Out of the amounts authorized under section 5 of this Act the Children's Bureau is authorized to employ such assistants, clerks, and other persons in the District of Columbia and elsewhere, to be taken from the eligible lists of the Civil Service Commission, and to purchase such supplies, material, equipment, office fixtures, and apparatus, and to incur such travel and other expense as it may deem necessary for carrying out the purposes of this Act.

Sec. 7. Within sixty days after any appropriation authorized by this Act has been made, the Children's Bureau shall make the apportionment herein provided for and shall certify to the Secretary of the Treasury the amount estimated by the bureau to be necessary for administering the provisions of this Act, and shall certify to the Secretary of the Treasury and to the treasurers of the various States the amount which has been apportioned to each State for the fiscal year for which such appropriation has been made.

Sec. 8. Any State desiring to receive the benefits of this Act shall, by its agency described in section 4, submit to the Children's Bureau detailed plans for carrying out the provisions of this Act within such State, which plans shall be subject to the approval of the board: *Provided,* That the plans of the States under this Act shall provide that no official, or agent, or representative in carrying out the provisions of this Act shall enter any home or take charge of any child over the objection of the parents, or either of them, or the person standing in loco parentis or having custody of such child. If these plans shall be in conformity with the provisions of this Act and reasonably appropriate and adequate to carry out its purposes they shall be approved by the board and due notice of such approval shall be sent to the State agency by the chief of the Children's Bureau.

Sec. 9. No official, agent, or representative of the Children's Bureau shall by virtue of this Act have any right to enter any home over the objection of the owner thereof, or to take charge of any child over the objection of the parents, or either of them, or of the person standing in loco parentis or having custody of such child. Nothing in this Act shall be construed as limiting the power of a parent or guardian or person standing in loco parentis to determine what treatment or correction shall be provided for a child or the agency or agencies to be employed for such purpose.

Sec. 10. Within sixty days after any appropriation authorized by this Act has been made, and as often thereafter while such appropriation remains unexpended as changed conditions may warrant, the Children's Bureau shall ascertain the amounts that have been appropriated by the legislatures of the several States accepting the provisions of this Act and shall certify to the Secretary of the Treasury the amount to which each State is entitled under the provisions of this Act. Such certificate shall state (1) that the State has, through its legislative authority, accepted the provisions of this Act and designated or authorized the creation of an agency to cooperate with the Children's Bureau, or that the State has otherwise accepted this Act, as provided in section 4 hereof; (2) the fact that the proper agency of the State has submitted to the Children's Bureau detailed plans for carrying out the provisions of this Act, and that such plans have been approved by the board; (3) the amount, if any, that has been appropriated by the legislature of the State for the maintenance of the services and facilities of this Act, as provided in section 2 hereof; and (4) the amount to which the State is entitled under the provisions of this Act. Such certificate, when in conformity with the provisions hereof, shall, until revoked as provided in section 12 hereof, be sufficient authority to the Secretary of the Treasury to make payment to the State in accordance therewith.

Sec. 11. Each State agency cooperating with the Children's Bureau under this Act shall make such reports concerning its operations and expenditures as shall be prescribed or requested by the bureau. The Children's Bureau may, with the approval of the board, and shall, upon request of a majority of the board, withhold any further certificate provided for in section 10 hereof whenever it shall be determined as to any State that the agency thereof has not properly expended the money paid to it or the moneys herein required to be appropriated by such State for the purposes and in accordance with the provisions of this Act. Such certificate may be withheld until such time or upon such conditions as the Children's Bureau, with the approval of the board, may determine; when so withheld the State agency may appeal to the President of the United States who may either affirm or reverse the action of the Bureau with such directions as he shall consider proper: *Provided*, That before any such certificate shall be withheld from any State, the chairman of the board shall give notice in writing to the authority designated to represent the State, stating specifically wherein said State has failed to comply with the provisions of this Act.

Sec. 12. No portion of any moneys apportioned under this Act for the benefit of the States shall be applied, directly or indirectly, to the purchase, erection, preservation, or repair of any building or buildings or equipment, or for the purchase or rental of any buildings or lands, nor shall any such moneys or moneys required to be appropriated by any State for the purposes and in accordance with the provisions of this Act be used for the payment of any maternity or infancy pension, stipend, or gratuity.

Sec. 13. The Children's Bureau shall perform the duties assigned to it by this Act under the supervision of the Secretary of Labor, and he shall include in his annual report to Congress a full account of the administration of this Act and expenditures of the moneys herein authorized.

Sec. 14. This Act shall be construed as intending to secure to the various States control of the administration of this Act within their respective States, subject only to the provisions and purposes of this Act.

Source:
Statutes at Large, Vol. 42, pp. 224–226.

H. L. Mencken, "The Monkey Trial": A Reporter's Account, 1925

Tennessee v. John Scopes, the so-called Monkey Trial, challenged state laws prohibiting the teaching of Charles Darwin's theory of evolution in public schools. Evolution is defined as a change in the gene pool of a species. According to Darwin, all species, including humans, evolved from a common biological ancestor. Although Darwin's theory of evolution has been refined over the past century and a half, its general outline has been demonstrated through scientific method, and it is accepted by almost all reputable biologists. However, to those who adhere to a literal interpretation of creation as occurring within six 24-hour days, Darwin's theory appears to refute the Bible. His theory was popularly—and according to the latest discoveries, erroneously—characterized as saying that humans evolved directly from monkeys or apes.

In Chapter 27 of the Acts of 1925 (also known as the Butler Law), Tennessee forbade publicly funded schools from teaching theories that denied the biblical account of human origins. The American Civil Liberties Union (ACLU) wanted to challenge this law and recruited John Scopes, a public high school teacher in Dayton, Tennessee, for the purpose. In the resulting trial, which took place in Dayton from July 10 to July 25, 1925, the fundamentalist William Jennings Bryan (former presidential candidate and secretary of state) argued for the prosecution, and the famous, if controversial, Clarence Darrow argued for the defense. The jury found Scopes guilty, and the judge fined him $100.

The trial became a cause célèbre and a media circus. For the northern press, it became an opportunity to ridicule southern Bible-Belt culture. The most scathing articles came from the acerbic but influential *Baltimore Sun* journalist H. L. Mencken. With colorful language and an irreverent tone, Mencken provides a dramatic account of the proceedings and the main players, capturing aspects of the trial beyond the debate between science, religion, and the First Amendment. Characterizing Dayton as a small, zealously Christian town, and Daytonians as ignorant and unsophisticated, he mocks their desire for the publicity the trial will bring them.

In 1955 the trial reentered American culture through *Inherit the Wind,* a play written by Jerome Lawrence and Robert E. Lee; it was shortly thereafter made into a movie. The play has been revived countless times on Broadway and in regional, community, and even high-school theaters. Its continued resonance reflects a revival of the debate over "creationism," which purports to use scientific evidence to refute Darwin. Most, but not all, scientists dispute creationism because, they contend, it is not based on scientific method. Nevertheless, Christian fundamentalists in many parts of the country, not just the South, continue to lobby school boards to give at least equal weight to either creationism or "intelligent design," a theory that supposedly takes religion out of creationism.

The Supreme Court of Tennessee overturned the guilty verdict in 1927. In the opinion of Chief Justice Green, the Acts of 1925 did not violate the First Amendment prohibition against established religion. Instead, the Court found that only the jury, not the judge, could impose a fine of more than $50. The decision was not appealed any further.

July 9

On the eve of the great contest Dayton is full of sickening surges and tremors of doubt. Five or six weeks ago, when the infidel Scopes was first laid by the heels, there was no uncertainty in all this smiling valley. The town bloomers leaped to the assault as one man. Here was an unexampled, almost a miraculous chance to get Dayton upon the front pages, to make it talked about, to put it upon the map. But how now?

Today, with the curtain barely rung up and the worst buffooneries to come, it is obvious to even town boomers that getting upon the map, like patriotism, is not enough. The getting there must be managed discreetly, adroitly, with careful regard to psychological niceties. The boomers of Dayton, alas, had no skill at such things, and the experts they called in were all quacks. The result now turns the communal liver to water. Two months ago the town was obscure and happy. Today it is a universal joke.

I have been attending the permanent town meeting that goes on in Robinson's drug store, trying to find out what the town optimists have saved from the wreck. All I can find is a sort of mystical confidence that God will somehow come to the rescue to reward His old and faithful partisans as they deserve—that good will flow eventually out of what now seems to be heavily evil. More specifically, it is believed that settlers will be attracted to the town as to some refuge from the atheism of the great urban Sodoms and Gomorrah.

But will these refugees bring any money with them? Will they buy lots and build houses? Will they light the fires of the cold and silent blast furnace down the railroad tracks? On these points, I regret to report, optimism has to call in theology to aid it. Prayer can accomplish a lot. It can cure diabetes, find lost pocketbooks and retain husbands from beating their wives. But is prayer made any more officious by giving a circus first? Coming to this thought, Dayton begins to sweat.

The town, I confess, greatly surprised me. I expected to find a squalid Southern village, with darkies snoozing on the horse blocks, pigs rooting under the houses and the inhabitants full of hookworm and malaria. What I found was a country town of charm and even beauty. . . .

July 10 (The First Day)

The town boomers have banqueted Darrow as well as Bryan, but there is no mistaking which of the two has the crowd, which means the venire of tried and true men. Bryan has been oozing around the country since his first day here, addressing this organization and that, presenting the indubitable Word of God in his caressing, ingratiating way, and so making unanimity doubly unanimous. From the defense yesterday came hints that he was making hay before the sun had legally begun to shine—even that it was a sort of contempt of court. But no Daytonian believes anything of the sort. What Bryan says doesn't seem to these congenial Baptists and Methodists to be argument; it seems to be a mere graceful statement to the obvious. . . .

July 11

The selection of a jury to try Scopes, which went on all yesterday afternoon in the atmosphere of a blast furnace, showed to what extreme lengths the salvation of the local primates has been pushed. It was obvious after a few rounds that the jury would be unanimously hot for Genesis. The most that Mr. Darrow could hope for was to sneak in a few bold enough to declare publicly that they would have to hear the evidence against Scopes before condemning him. The slightest sign of anything further brought forth a peremptory challenge from the State. Once a man was challenged without examination for simply admitting that he did not belong formally to any church. Another time a panel man who confessed that he was prejudiced against evolution got a hearty round of applause from the crowd. . . .

In brief this is a strictly Christian community, and such is its notion of fairness, justice and due process of law. Try to picture a town made up wholly of Dr. Crabbes and Dr. Kellys, and you will have a reasonably accurate image of it. Its people are simply unable to imagine a man who rejects the literal authority of the Bible. The most they can conjure up, straining until they are red in the face, is a man who is in error about the meaning of this or that text. Thus one accused of heresy among them is like one accused of boiling his grandmother to make soap in Maryland. . . .

July 13 (The Second Day)

It would be hard to imagine a more moral town than Dayton. If it has any bootleggers, no visitor has heard of them. Ten minutes after I arrived a leading citizen offered me a drink made up half of white mule and half of coca cola, but he seems to have been simply indulging himself in a naughty gesture. No fancy woman has been seen in the town since the end of the McKinley administration. There is no gambling. There is no place to dance. The relatively wicked, when they would indulge themselves, go to Robinson's drug store and debate theology. . . .

July 14 (The Third Day)

The net effect of Clarence Darrow's great speech yesterday seems to be preciously the same as if he had bawled it up a rainspout in the interior of Afghanistan. That is, locally, upon the process against the infidel Scopes, upon the so-called minds of these fundamentalists of upland Tennessee. You have but a dim notice of it who have only read it. It was not designed for reading, but for hearing. The clangtint of it was as important as the logic. It rose like a wind and ended like a flourish of bugles. The very judge on the bench, toward the end of it, began to look uneasy. But the morons in the audience, when it was over, simply hissed it.

During the whole time of its delivery the old mountebank, Bryan, sat tight-lipped and unmoved. There is, of course, no reason why it should have shaken him. He has these hillbillies locked up in his pen and he knows it. His brand is on them. He is at home among them. Since his earliest days, indeed, his chief strength has been among the folk of remote hills and forlorn and lonely farms. Now with his political aspirations all gone to pot, he turns to them for religious consolations. They understand his peculiar imbecilities. His nonsense is their ideal of sense. When he deluges them with his theologic bilge they rejoice like pilgrims disporting in the river Jordan. . . .

July 15 (The Fourth Day)

A preacher of any sect that admit the literal authenticity of Genesis is free to gather a crowd at any time and talk all he wants. More, he may engage in a disputation with any expert. I have heard at least a hundred such discussions, and some of them have been very acrimonious. But the instant a speaker utters a word against divine revelation he begin to disturb the peace and is liable to immediate arrest and confinement in the calaboose beside the railroad tracks. . . .

July 16 (The Fifth Day)

In view of the fact that everyone here looks for the jury to bring in a verdict of guilty, it might be expected that the prosecution would show a considerable amiability and allow the defense a rather free play. Instead, it is contesting every point very vigorously and taking every advantage of its greatly superior familiarity with local procedure. There is, in fact, a considerable heat in the trial. Bryan and the local lawyers for the State sit glaring at the defense all day and even the Attorney-General, A. T. Stewart, who is supposed to have secret doubts about fundamentalism, has shown such pugnacity that it has already brought him to forced apologies.

The high point of yesterday's proceedings was reached with the appearance of Dr. Maynard M. Metcalf of the John Hopkins. The doctor is a somewhat chubby man of bland mien, and during the first part of his testimony, with the jury present, the prosecution apparently viewed his with great equanimity. But the instant he was asked a question bearing directly upon the case at bar there was a flurry in the Bryan pen and Stewart was on his feet with protests. Another question followed, with more and hotter protests. The judge then excluded the jury and the show began.

What ensued was, on the surface, a harmless enough dialogue between Dr. Metcalf and Darrow, but underneath there was tense drama. At the first question Bryan came out from behind the State's table and planted himself directly in front of Dr. Metcalf, and not ten feet away. The two McKenzies followed, with young Sue Hicks at their heels.

Then began one of the clearest, most succinct and withal most eloquent presentations of the case for the evolutionists that I have ever heard. The doctor was never at a loss for a word, and his ideas flowed freely and smoothly. Darrow steered him magnificently. A word or two and he was howling down the wind. Another and he hauled up to discharge a broadside. There was no cocksureness in him. Instead he was rather cautious and deprecatory and sometimes he halted and confessed his ignorance. But what he got over before he finished was a superb counterblast to the fundamentalist buncombe. The jury, at least, in theory heard nothing of it, but it went whooping into the radio and it went banging into the face of Bryan. . . .

This old buzzard, having failed to raise the mob against its rulers, now prepares to raise it against its teachers. He can never be the peasants' President, but there is still a chance to be the peasants' Pope. He leads a new crusade, his bald head glistening, his face streaming with sweat, his chest heaving beneath his rumpled alpaca coat. One somehow pities him, despite his so palpable imbecilities. It is a tragedy, indeed, to begin life as a hero and to end it as a buffoon. But let no one, laughing at him, underestimate the magic that lies in his black, malignant eye, his frayed but still eloquent voice. He can shake and inflame these poor ignoramuses as no other man among us can shake and inflame them, and he is desperately eager to order the charge.

In Tennessee he is drilling his army. The big battles, he believes, will be fought elsewhere.

July 17 (The Sixth Day)

Malone was in good voice. It was a great day for Ireland. And for the defense. For Malone not only out-yelled Bryan, he also plainly out-generaled and out-argued him. His speech, indeed, was one of the best presentations of the case against the fundamentalist rubbish that I have ever heard.

It was simple in structure, it was clear in reasoning, and at its high points it was overwhelmingly eloquent. It was not long, but it covered the whole ground and it let off many a gaudy skyrocket, and so it conquered even the fundamentalist. At its end they gave it a tremendous cheer—a cheer at least four times as hearty as that given to Bryan. For these rustics delight in speechifying, and know when it is good. The devil's logic cannot fetch them, but they are not above taking a voluptuous pleasure in his lascivious phrases. . . .

July 18

All that remains of the great cause of the State of Tennessee against the infidel Scopes is the formal business of bumping off the defendant. There may be some legal jousting on Monday and some gaudy oratory on Tuesday, but the main battle is over, with Genesis completely triumphant. Judge Raulston finished the benign business yesterday morning by leaping with soft judicial hosannas into the arms of the prosecution. The sole commentary of the sardonic Darrow consisted of bringing down a metaphorical custard pie upon the occiput of the learned jurist.

"I hope," said the latter nervously, "that counsel intends no reflection upon this court."

Darrow hunched his shoulders and looked out of the window dreamily.

"Your honor," he said, "is, of course, entitled to hope.". . .

The Scopes trial, from the start, has been carried on in a manner exactly fitted to the anti-evolution law and the simian imbecility under it. There hasn't been the slightest pretense to decorum. The rustic judge, a candidate for reelection, has postured the yokels like a clown in a ten-cent side show, and almost every word he has uttered has been an undisguised appeal to their prejudices and superstitions. The chief prosecuting attorney, beginning like a competent lawyer and a man of self-respect, ended like a convert at a Billy Sunday revival. It fell to him, finally, to make a clear and astounding statement of theory of justice prevailing under fundamentalism. What he said, in brief, was that a man accused of infidelity had no rights whatever under Tennessee law. . . .

Darrow has lost this case. It was lost long before he came to Dayton. But it seems to me that he has nevertheless performed a great public service by fighting it to a finish and in a perfectly serious way. Let no one mistake it for comedy, farcical though it may be in all its details. It serves notice on the country that Neanderthal man is organizing in these forlorn backwaters of the land, led by a fanatic, rid of sense and devoid of conscience. Tennessee, challenging him too timorously and too late, now sees its courts converted into camp meetings and its Bill of Rights made a mock of by its sworn officers of the law. There are other States that had better look to their arsenals before the Hun is at their gates.

See also CHARLES DARWIN, *ON THE ORIGIN OF SPECIES*, 1859.

Source:

Linder, Doug. Famous Trials, University of Missouri–Kansas City Law School Faculty Projects. Available on-line. URL: www.law.umkc.edu/faculty/projects/ftrials/scopes/menk.htm. Accessed November 2003.

Gitlow v. People of New York, 1925

This decision, issued on June 8, 1925, for the first time incorporated First Amendment freedom of speech as a limitation of state as well as federal government. Benjamin Gitlow was a socialist and, with three associates, was convicted for violation of the New York Criminal Anarchy Act of 1902. Because his 1920 pamphlet was found to advocate the overthrow of the government by force, violence, or other unlawful means, the lower court ruled against them, and the Supreme Court majority, in Justice Edward Terry Sanford's opinion, agreed. It held that the state was justified in prohibiting the pamphlet in order to preserve the public peace. But the Court also established that the due process protections of liberty in the Fourteenth Amendment "incorporated the First Amendment." However, not until *Stromberg v. California* (283 U.S. 359 [1931]) did the Court actually strike down a state law on free speech grounds. Justice Oliver Wendell Holmes, with Justice Louis Brandeis concurring, dissented. He asserted that only action, not advocacy, could be punished under Holmes's "clear and present danger" doctrine.

Mr. Justice Sanford delivered the opinion of the Court.

Benjamin Gitlow was indicted in the Supreme Court of New York, with three others, for the statutory crime of criminal anarchy. New York Penal Law, Sections 160, 161. He was separately tried, convicted, and sentenced to imprisonment. The judgment was affirmed by the Appellate Division and by the Court of Appeals. *People v. Gitlow,* 195 App. Div. 773, 187 N. Y. S. 783; 234 N.Y. 132, 136 N.E. 317; and 234 N. Y. 539, 138 N.E. 438. The case is here on writ of error to the Supreme Court, to which the record was remitted. 260 U.S. 703, 43 S. Ct. 163, 67 L. Ed. 472.

The contention here is that the statute, by its terms and as applied in this case, is repugnant to the due process clause of the Fourteenth Amendment. Its material provisions are:

"Sec. 160. *Criminal Anarchy Defined.* Criminal anarchy is the doctrine that organized government should be overthrown by force or violence, or by assassination of the executive head or of any of the executive officials of government, or by any unlawful means. The advocacy of such doctrine either by word of mouth or writing is a felony.

"Sec. 161. *Advocacy of Criminal Anarchy.* Any person who:

"1. By word of mouth or writing advocates, advises or teaches the duty, necessity or propriety of overthrowing or overturning organized government by force or violence, or by assassination of the executive head or of any of the executive officials of government, or by any unlawful means; or,

"2. Prints, publishes, edits, issues or knowingly circulates, sells, distributes or publicly displays any book, paper, document, or written or printed matter in any form, containing or advocating, advising or teaching the doctrine that organized government should be overthrown by force, violence or any unlawful means, . . .

"Is guilty of a felony and punishable" by imprisonment or fine, or both.

The indictment was in two counts. The first charged that the defendant had advocated, advised and taught the duty, necessity and propriety of overthrowing and overturning organized government by force, violence and unlawful means, by certain writings therein set forth entitled "The Left Wing Manifesto"; the second that he had printed, published and knowingly circulated and distributed a certain paper called "The Revolutionary Age," containing the writings set forth in the first count advocating, advising and teaching and doctrine that organized government should be overthrown by force, violence and unlawful means.

The following facts were established on the trial by undisputed evidence and admissions: The defendant is a member of the Left Wing Section of the Socialist Party, a dissenting branch or faction of that party formed in opposition to its dominant policy of "moderate Socialism." Membership in both is open to aliens as well as citizens. The Left Wing Section was organized nationally at a conference in New York City in June, 1919, attended by ninety delegates from twenty different States. The conference elected a National Council, of which the defendant was a member, and left to it the adoption of a "Manifesto." This was published in the Revolutionary Age, the official organ of the Left Wing. The defendant was on the board of managers of the paper and was its business manager. He arranged for the printing of the paper and took to the printer the manuscript of the first issue which contained the Left Wing Manifesto, and also a Communist Program and a Program of the Left Wing that had been adopted by the conference. Sixteen thousand copies were printed, which were delivered at the premises in New York City used as the office of the Revolutionary Age and the headquarters of the Left Wing, and occupied by the defendant and other officials. These copies were paid for by the defendant, as business manager of the paper. Employees at this office wrapped and mailed out copies of the paper under the defendant's direction; and copies were sold from this office. It was admitted that the defendant signed a card subscribing to the Manifesto and Program of the Left Wing, which all applicants were required to sign before being admitted to membership; that he went to different parts of the State to speak to branches of the Socialist Party about the principles of the Left Wing and advocated their adoption; and that he was responsible for the Manifesto as it appeared, that "he knew of the publication, in a general way and he knew of its publication afterwards, and is responsible for the circulation."

There was no evidence of any effect resulting from the publication and circulation of the Manifesto.

No witnesses were offered in behalf of the defendant.

Extracts from the Manifesto are set forth in the margin. Coupled with a review of the rise of Socialism, it condemned the dominant "moderate Socialism" for its recognition of the necessity of the democratic parliamentary state; repudiated its policy of introducing Socialism by legislative measures; and advocated, in plain and unequivocal language, the necessity of accomplishing the "Communist Revolution" by a militant and "revolutionary Socialism," based on "the class struggle" and mobilizing the "power of the proletariat in action," through mass industrial revolts developing into mass political strikes and "revolutionary mass action," for the purpose of conquering and destroying the parliamentary state and establishing in its place, through a "revolutionary dictatorship of the proletariat," the system of Communist Socialism. The then recent strikes in Seattle and Winnipeg were cited as instances of a development already verging on revolutionary action and suggestive of proletarian dictatorship, in which the strike- workers were "trying to usurp the functions of municipal government"; and revolutionary Socialism, it was urged, must use these mass industrial revolts to broaden the strike, make it general and militant, and develop it into mass political strikes and revolutionary mass action for the annihilation of the parliamentary state.

At the outset of the trial the defendant's counsel objected to the introduction of any evidence under the indictment on the grounds that, as a matter of law, the Manifesto "is not in contravention of the statute," and that "the statute is in contravention of" the due process clause of the Fourteenth Amendment. This objection was denied. They also moved, at the close of the evidence, to dismiss the indictment and direct an acquittal "on the grounds stated in the first objection to evidence," and again on the grounds that "the indictment does not charge an offense" and the evidence "does not show an offense." These motions were also denied.

The court, among other things, charged the jury, in substance, that they must determine what was the intent, purpose and fair meaning of the Manifesto; that its words must be taken in their ordinary meaning, as they would be understood by people whom it might reach; that a mere statement or analysis of social and economic facts and historical incidents, in the nature of an essay, accompanied by prophecy as to the future course of events, but with no teaching, advice or advocacy of action, would not constitute the advocacy, advice or teaching of a doctrine for the overthrow of government within the meaning of the statute; that a mere statement that unlawful acts might accomplish such a purpose would be insufficient, unless there was a teaching, advising and advocacy of employing such unlawful acts for the purpose of overthrowing government; and that if the jury had a reasonable doubt that the Manifesto did teach, advocate or advise the duty, necessity or propriety of using unlawful means for the overthrowing of organized government, the defendant was entitled to an acquittal.

The defendant's counsel submitted two requests to charge which embodied in substance the statement that to constitute criminal anarchy within the meaning of the statute it was necessary that the language used or published should advocate, teach or advise the duty, necessity or propriety of doing "some definite or immediate act or acts" of force, violence or unlawfulness directed toward the overthrowing of organized government. These were denied further than had been charged. Two other requests to charge embodied in substance the statement that to constitute guilt the language used or published must be "reasonably and ordinarily calculated to incite certain persons" to acts of force, violence or unlawfulness, with the object of overthrowing organized government. These were also denied.

The Appellate Division, after setting forth extracts from the Manifesto and referring to the Left Wing and Communist Programs published in the same issue of the Revolutionary Age, said:

"It is perfectly plain that the plan and purpose advocated to contemplate the overthrow and destruction of the governments of the United States and of all the States, not by the free action of the majority of the people through the ballot box in electing representatives to authorize a change of government by amending or charging the Constitution, . . . but by immediately organizing the industrial proletariat into militant Socialist unions and at the earliest opportunity through mass strike and force and violence, if necessary, compelling the government to cease to function, and then through a proletarian dictatorship, taking charge of and appropriating all property and administering it and governing through such dictatorship until such time as the proletariat is permitted to administer and govern it. . . . The articles in question are not a discussion of ideas and theories. They advocate a doctrine deliberately determined upon and planned for militantly disseminating a propaganda advocating that it is the duty and necessity of the proletariat engaged in industrial pursuits to organize to such an extent that, by massed strike, the wheels of government may ultimately be stopped and the government overthrown. . . ."

The Court of Appeals held that the Manifesto "advocated the overthrow of this government by violence, or by unlawful means." In one of the opinions representing the views of a majority of the court, it was said:

"It will be seen . . . that this defendant through the Manifesto . . . advocated the destruction of the state and the establishment of the dictatorship of the proletariat. . . . To advocate . . . the commission of this conspiracy or action by mass strike whereby government is crippled, the administration of justice paralyzed, and the health, morals and welfare of a community endangered, and this for the purpose of bringing about a revolution in the state, is to advocate the overthrow of organized government by unlawful means."

In the other it was said:

"As we read this Manifesto . . . we feel entirely clear that the jury were justified in rejecting the view that it was a mere academic and harmless discussion of the advantages of communism and advanced socialism" and "in regarding it as a justification and advocacy of action by one class which would destroy the rights of all other classes and overthrow the state itself by use of revolutionary mass strikes. It is true that there is no advocacy in specific terms of the use of . . . force or violence. There was no need to be. Some things are so commonly incident to others that they do not need to be mentioned when the underlying purpose is described."

And both the Appellate Division and the Court of Appeals held the statute constitutional.

The specification of the errors relied on relates solely to the specific rulings of the trial court in the matters hereinbefore set out. The correctness of the verdict is not questioned, as the case was submitted to the jury. The sole contention here is, essentially, that as there was no evidence of any concrete result flowing from the publication of the Manifesto or of circumstances showing the likelihood of such result, the statute as construed and applied by the trial court penalizes the mere utterance, as such, of "doctrine" having no quality of incitement, without regard either to the circumstances of its utterance or to the likelihood of unlawful sequences; and that, as the exercise of the right of free expression with relation to government is only punishable "in circumstances involving likelihood of substantive evil," the statute contravenes the due process clause of the Fourteenth Amendment. The argument in support of this contention rests primarily upon the following propositions: 1st, That the "liberty" protected by the Fourteenth Amendment includes the liberty of speech and of the press; and 2d, That while liberty of expression "is not absolute," it may be restrained "only in circumstances where its exercise bears a causal relation with some substantive evil, consummated, attempted or likely," and as the statute "takes no account of circumstances," it unduly restrains this liberty and is therefore unconstitutional. . . .

Source:
Supreme Court Reporter, Vol. 45. pp. 625–632.

Margaret Sanger, "Children's Era," 1926

Speech given by Margaret Sanger in 1926 at the sixth International Birth Control Conference. Sanger began advocating women's right to choose contraception in 1914, when she set up the National Birth Control League and started circulating magazines, such as the *Woman Rebel* and *Birth Control Review*. In this speech, Sanger argued for the rights of unborn children as well as of the women who bring them into the world. She asked the conference to understand that not all children are wanted or planned. She pleaded for the freedom of women from "unwilling motherhood" and for help to stop poverty and the unsanitary conditions that accompanied it. Margaret Sanger's activities raised the issue of birth control into the public's eye and helped doctors provide birth control information to their patients.

Mr. Chairman, Ladies and Gentlemen: My subject is "The Children's Era." The Children's Era! This makes me think of Ellen Key's book—The Century of the Child. Ellen Key hoped that this twentieth century was to be the century of the child. The twentieth century, she said, would see this old world of ours converted into a beautiful garden of children. Well, we have already lived through a quarter of this twentieth century. What steps have we taken toward making it the century of the child? So far, very, very few.

Why does the Children's Era still remain a dream of the dim and the distant future? Why has so little been accomplished?—in spite of all our acknowledged love of children, all our generosity, all our good-will, all the enormous sending of millions on philanthropy and charities, all our warm-hearted sentiment, all our incessant activity and social consciousness? Why?

Before you can cultivate a garden, you must know something about gardening. You have got to give your seeds a proper soil in which to grow. You have got to give them sunlight and fresh air. You have got to give them space and the opportunity (if they are to lift their flowers to the sun), to strike their roots deep into that soil. And always—do not forget this—you have got to fight weeds. You cannot have a garden, if you let weeds overrun it. So, if we want to make this world a garden for children, we must first of all learn the lesson of the gardener.

So far we have not been gardeners. We have only been a sort of silly reception committee. A reception committee at the Grand Central Station of life. Trainload after trainload of children are coming in, day and night—nameless refugees arriving out of the Nowhere into the Here. Trainload after trainload—many unwelcome, unwanted, unprepared for, unknown, without baggage, without passports, most of them without pedigrees. These unlimited hordes of refugees arrive in such numbers that the reception committee is thrown into a panic—a panic of activity. The reception committee arouses itself heroically, establishes emergency measures: milk stations, maternity centers, settlement houses, playgrounds, orphanages, welfare leagues and every conceivable kind of charitable effort. But still trainloads of children keep on coming—human weeds crop up that spread so fast in this sinister struggle for existence, that the overworked committee becomes exhausted, inefficient and can think of no way out.

When we protest against this immeasurable, meaningless waste of motherhood and child-life; when we protest against the ever-mounting cost to the world of asylums, prisons, homes for the feeble-minded and such institutions for the unfit, when we protest against the disorder and chaos and tragedy of modern life, when we point out the biological corruption that is destroying the very heart of American life, we are told that we are making merely an "emotional" appeal. When we point the one immediate practical way toward order and beauty in society, the only way to lay the foundations of a society composed of happy children, happy women and happy men, they call this idea indecent and immoral.

It is not enough to clean up the filth and disorder of our overcrowded cities. It is not enough to stop the evil of Child Labor—even if we could! It is not enough to decrease the rate of infantile mortality. It is not enough to open playgrounds, and build more public schools in which we can standardize the minds of the young. It is not enough, to throw millions upon millions of dollars into charities and philanthropies. Don't deceive ourselves that by so doing we are making the world "Safe for Children."

Those of you who have followed the sessions of this Conference must, I am sure, agree with me that the first real step toward the creation of a Children's Era must lie in providing the conditions of healthy life for children not only before birth but even more imperatively before conception. Human society must protect its children—yes, but prenatal care is most essential! The child-to-be, as yet not called into being, has rights no less imperative.

We have learned in the preceding sessions of this Conference that, if we wish to produce strong and sturdy children, the embryo must grow in a chemically healthy medium. The blood stream of the mother must be chemically normal. Worry, strain, shock, unhappiness, enforced maternity, may all poison the blood of the enslaved mother. This chemically poisoned blood may produce a defective baby—a child foredoomed to idiocy, or feeble-mindedness, crime, or failure.

Do I exaggerate? Am I taking a rare exception and making it a general rule? Our opponents declare that children are conceived in love, and that every new-born baby converts its parents to love and unselfishness. My answer is to point to the asylums, the hospitals, the ever-growing institutions for the unfit. Look into the family history of those who are feeble-minded; or behind the bars of jails and prisons. Trace the family histories; find out the conditions under which they were conceived and born, before you attempt to persuade us that reckless breeding has nothing to do with these grave questions.

There is only one way out. We have got to fight for the health and happiness of the Unborn Child. And to do that in a practical, tangible way, we have got to free women from enforced, enslaved maternity. There can be no hope for the future of civilization, no certainty of racial salvation, until every woman can decide for herself whether she will or will not become a mother and when and how many children she cares to bring into the world. That is the first step.

I would like to suggest Civil Service examinations for parenthood! Prospective parents after such an examination would be given a parenthood license, proving that they are physically and mentally fit to be the fathers and mothers of the next generation.

This is an interesting idea—but then arises the questions "Who is to decide?" "Would there be a jury, like a play jury?" Would a Republican administration give parenthood permits only to Republicans—or perhaps only to Democrats? The more you think of governmental interference, the less it works out. Take this plan of civil service examination for parenthood. It suggests Prohibition: there might even be bootlegging in babies!

No, I doubt the advisability of governmental sanction. The problem of bringing children into the world ought to be decided by those most seriously involved—those who run the greatest risks; in the last analysis—by the mother and the child. If there is going to be any Civil Service examination, let it be conducted by the Unborn Child, the Child-to-be.

Just try for a moment to picture the possibilities of such an examination.

When you want a cook or housemaid, you go to an employment bureau. You have to answer questions. You have to exchange references. You have to persuade the talented cook that you conduct a proper well-run household. Children ought to have at least the same privilege as cooks.

Sometimes in idle moments I like to think it would be a very good scheme to have a bureau of the Child-to-be.

At such a bureau of the unborn, the wise child might be able to find out a few things about its father—and its mother. Just think for a moment of this bureau where prospective parents might apply for a baby. Think of the questions they would be asked by the agent of the unborn or by the baby itself.

First: "Mr. Father, a baby is an expensive luxury. Can you really afford one?"

"Have you paid for your last baby yet?"

"How many children have you already? Six? You must have your hands full. Can you take care of so many?"

"Do you look upon children as a reward—or a penalty?"

"How are your ductless glands—well balanced?"

"Can you provide a happy home for one! A sunny nursery? Proper food?"

"What's that you say? Ten children already? Two dark rooms in the slums?"

"No, thank you! I don't care to be born at all if I cannot be well-born. Good-bye!"

And if we could organize a society for the prevention of cruelty to unborn children, we would make it a law that children should be brought into the world only when they were welcome, invited and wanted; that they would arrive with a clean bill of health and heritage; that they would possess healthy, happy, well-mated and mature parents.

And there would be certain conditions of circumstances which would preclude parenthood. These conditions, the presence of which would make parenthood a crime, are the following:

1 Transmissible disease
2 Temporary disease
3 Subnormal children already in the family
4 Space out between births
5 Twenty-three years as a minimum age for parents
6 Economic circumstances adequate
7 Spiritual harmony between parents.

In conclusion, let me repeat:

We are not trying to establish a dictatorship over parents. We want to free women from enslavery and unwilling motherhood. We are fighting for the emancipation of the mothers of the world, of the children of the world, and the children to be. We want to create a real Century of the Child—usher in a Children's Era. We can do this by handing the terrific gift of life in bodies fit and perfect as can be fashioned. Help us to make this Conference which has aroused so much interest the turning point toward this era. Only so can you help in the creation of the future.

Source:

James Andrews and David Zarefsky, eds., *American Voices: Significant Speeches in American History, 1640–1945*. White Plains, N.Y.: Longman, 1989.

Nicola Sacco and Bartolomeo Vanzetti, Final Statements to the Court, 1927

Last formal statement made by Italian immigrant anarchists Nicola Sacco and Bartolomeo Vanzetti, on April 9, 1927, shortly before his execution (along with fellow Italian immigrant anarchist Nicola Sacco) for the 1920 murder of two shoe-factory employees in the course of a robbery. Maintaining his innocence, Vanzetti restated a belief—widely held by liberals about this cause célèbre—that he and Sacco had been judged guilty at their 1921 trial, not because of the evidence against them, but because they were foreign-born and avowed anarchists: "I am suffering because I am a radical and . . . because I [am] an Italian." After numerous appeals, a blue-ribbon panel sustained the verdict, and Sacco and Vanzetti were electrocuted on August 23, 1927. The case has continued to attract scholarly and legal attention. Virtually all commentators found the trial unfair by modern standards. However, forensic and other evidence points to the guilt of at least Sacco for the murders, although a number of researchers consider Vanzetti innocent.

Statement by Nicola Sacco

Yes, sir. I am not an orator. It is not very familiar with me the English language, and as I know, as my friend has told me, my comrade Vanzetti will speak more long, so I thought to give him the chance.

I never know, never heard, even read in history anything so cruel as this Court. After seven years prosecuting they still consider us guilty. And these gentle people here are arrayed with us in this court today.

I know the sentence will be between two class, the oppressed class and the rich class, and there will be always collision between one and the other. We fraternize the people with the books, with the literature. You persecute the people, tyrannize over them and kill them. We try the education of people always. You try to put a path between us and some other nationality that hates each other. That is why I am here today on this bench, for having been the oppressed class. Well, you are the oppressor.

You know it, Judge Thayer,—you know all my life, you know why I have been here, and after seven years that you have been persecuting me and my poor wife, and you still today sentence us to death. I would like to tell all my life, but what is the use? You know all about what I say before, and my friend—that is, my comrade—will be talking, because he is more familiar with the language, and I will give him a chance. My comrade, the man kind, the kind man to all the children, you sentence him two times, in the Bridgewater case and the Dedham case, connected with me, and you know he is innocent. You forget all the population that has been with us for seven years, to sympathize and give us all their energy and all their kindness. You do not care for them. Among that peoples and the comrades and the working class there is a big legion of intellectual people which have been with us for seven years, but to not commit the iniquitous sentence, but still the Court goes ahead. And I think I thank you all, you peoples, my comrades who have been with me for seven years, with the Sacco-Vanzetti case, and I will give my friend a chance.

I forget one thing which my comrade remember me. As I said before, Judge Thayer know all my life, and he know that I am never been guilty, never,—not yesterday nor today nor forever.

Clerk Worthington: "Bartolomeo Vanzetti, have you anything to say why sentence of death should not be passed upon you?"

Statement by Bartolomeo Vanzetti

Yes. What I say is that I am innocent, not only of the Braintree crime, but also of the Bridgewater crime. That I am not only innocent of these two crimes, but in all my life I have never stole and I have never killed and I have never spilled blood. That is what I want to say. And it is not all. Not only am I innocent of these two crimes, not only in all my life I have never stole, never killed, never spilled blood, but I have struggled all my life, since I began to reason, to eliminate crime from the earth.

Everybody that knows these two arms knows very well that I did not need to go in between the street and kill a man to take the money. I can live with my two arms and live well. But besides that, I can live even without work with my arm for other people. I have had plenty of chance to live independently and to live what the world conceives to be a higher life than not to gain our bread with the sweat of our brow.

My father in Italy is in a good condition. I could have come back in Italy and he would have welcomed me every time with open arms. Even if I come back there with not a cent in my pocket, my father could have give me a possession, not to work but to make business, or to oversee upon the land that he owns. He has wrote me many letters in that sense, and other well to do relatives have wrote me many letters in that sense that I can produce.

Well, it may be a boast. My father and my uncle can boast themselves and say things that people may not be compelled to believe. People may say they may be poor when I say that they are to consider to give me a position every time that I want to settle down and form a family and start a settled life. Well, but there are people maybe in this same court that could testify to what I have say and what my father and my uncle have say to me is not a lie, that really they have the means to give me position every time that I want.

Well, I want to reach a little point farther, and it is this—that not only have I not been trying to steal in Bridgewater, not only have I not been in Braintree to steal and kill and have never steal or kill or spilt blood in all my life, not only have I struggled hard against crimes, but I have refused myself the commodity or glory of life, the pride of life of a good position, because in my consideration it is not right to exploit man. I have refused to go in business because I understand that business is a speculation on profit upon certain people that must depend upon the business man, and I do not consider that that is right and therefore I refuse to do that.

Now, I should say that I am not only innocent of all these things, not only have I never committed a real crime in my life—though some sins but not crimes—not only have I struggled all my life to eliminate crimes, the crimes that the official law and the official moral condemns, but also the crime that the official moral and the official law sanctions and sanctifies,—the exploitation and the oppression of the man by the man, and if there is a reason why I am here as a guilty man, if there is a reason why you in a few minutes can doom me, it is this reason and none else.

I beg your pardon. [Referring to paper.] There is the more good man I ever cast my eyes upon since I lived, a man that will last and will grow always more near and more dear to the people, as far as into the heart of the people, so long as admiration for goodness and for sacrifice will last. I mean Eugene Debs. I will say that even a dog that killed the chickens would not have found an American jury to convict it with the proof that the Commonwealth produced against us. That man was not with me in Plymouth or with Sacco where he was on the day of the crime. You can say that it is arbitrary, what we are saying, that he is good and he applied to the other his own goodness, that he is incapable of crime, and he believed that everybody is incapable of crime.

Well, it may be like that but it is not, it could be like that but it is not, and that man has a real experience of court, of prison and of jury. Just because he want the world a little better he was persecuted and slandered from his boyhood to his old age, and indeed he was murdered by the prison. He know, and not only he but every man of understanding in the world, not only in this country but also in the other countries, men that we have provided a certain amount of a record of the times, they all still stick with us, the flower of mankind of Europe, the better writers, the greatest thinkers of Europe, have pleaded in our favor. The scientists, the greatest scientists, the greatest statesmen of Europe, have pleaded in our favor. The people of foreign nations have pleaded in our favor.

Is it possible that only a few on the jury, only two or three men, who would condemn their mother for worldly honor and for earthly fortune; is it possible that they are right against what the world, the whole world has say it is wrong and that I know that it is wrong? If there is one that I should know it, if it is right or if it is wrong, it is I and this man. You see it is seven years that we are in jail. What we have suffered during these seven years no human tongue can say, and yet you see me before you, not trembling, you see me looking you in your eyes straight, not blushing, not changing color, not ashamed or in fear.

Eugene Debs say that not even a dog—something like that—not even a dog that kill the chickens would have been found guilty by American jury with the evidence that the Commonwealth have produced against us. I say that not even a leprous dog would have his appeal refused two times by the Supreme Court of Massachusetts—not even a leprous dog. . . .

Well, I have already say that I not only am not guilty of these two crimes, but I never commit a crime in my life,—I have never steal and I have never kill and I have never spilt blood, and I have fought against the crime, and I have fought and I have sacrificed myself even to eliminate the crimes that the law and the church legitimate and sanctify.

This is what I say: I would not wish to a dog or to a snake, to the most low and misfortunate creature of the earth—I would not wish to any of them what I have had to suffer for things that I am not guilty of. But my conviction is that I have suffered for things that I am guilty of. I am suffering because I am a radical and indeed I am a radical; I have suffered because I was an Italian, and indeed I am an Italian; I have suffered more for my family and for my beloved than for myself; but I am so convinced to be right that if you could execute me two times, and if I could be reborn two other times, I would live again to do what I have done already.

I have finished. Thank you.

Source:

Massachusetts Supreme Judicial Court Archives and Records Preservation. Boston, Massachusetts. Sacco-Vanzetti Case. Vol. 5, pp. 4,895–4,905.

Buck v. Bell, 1927

This 1927 Supreme Court decision upheld a Virginia law permitting the government to order the compulsory sterilization of young women it believed were "unfit to continue their kind." The law was an example of the type of Progressive Era "reform" that would be considered regressive today. Carrie Buck, who was withdrawn from school at the end of fifth grade, lived with a foster Virginia family. Carrie became pregnant at 17 during what she said was a rape by a family member. The family responded by having their own and a second doctor testify to Charlottesville justice of the peace Charles D. Shackleford that Carrie was feebleminded, thereby securing an order committing her to the Virginia State Colony for Epileptics and Feebleminded, in Lynchburg, on January 24, 1924. (The family kept Carrie Buck's infant daughter.) The superintendent of the state colony, Dr. Albert Priddy, believed he could help society limit the number of what he called "mental defectives" by controlling the reproduction of his patients. Dr. Priddy, claiming that he operated only to cure "pelvic disease," had sterilized between 75 and 100 young women without their consent before seeing Carrie Buck. The Virginia assembly in 1924 adopted a bill permitting compulsory sterilization of "feeble-minded" or "socially inadequate person[s]." The colony decided to use Carrie Buck as a test case that eventually reached the Supreme Court.

On May 2, 1927, Justice Oliver Wendell Holmes delivered the Court's opinion and Carrie Buck was sterilized by Dr. Bell on October 16, 1927. *Buck v. Bell*'s implications reached far past Carrie Buck, however. In the United States, more than 50,000 people were sterilized in 30 states in accordance with laws modeled on Virginia's. In Europe, following World War II, Nazi lawyers defended the forced sterilization of 2 million people by citing that the U.S. Supreme Court had declared such laws constitutional in *Buck v. Bell,* which has yet to be reversed specifically.

Mr. JUSTICE HOLMES delivered the opinion of the Court.

This is a writ of error to review a judgment of the Supreme Court of Appeals of the State of Virginia affirming a judgment of the Circuit Court of Amherst County by which the defendant in error, the superintendent of the State Colony for Epileptics and Feeble Minded, was ordered to perform the operation of salpingectomy upon Carrie Buck, the plaintiff in error, for the purpose of making her sterile. 143 Va. 310. The case comes here upon the contention that the statute authorizing the judgment is void under the Fourteenth Amendment as denying to the plaintiff in error due process of law and the equal protection of the laws.

Carrie Buck is a feeble minded white woman who was committed to the State Colony above mentioned in due form. She is the daughter of a feeble minded mother in the same institution, and the mother of an illegitimate feeble minded child. She was eighteen years old at the time of the trial of her case in the Circuit Court, in the latter part of 1924. An Act of Virginia, approved March 20, 1924, recites that the health of the patient and the welfare of society may be promoted in certain cases by the sterilization of mental defectives, under careful safeguard, &c.; that the sterilization may be effected in males by vasectomy and in females by salpingectomy, without serious pain or substantial danger to life; that the Commonwealth is supporting in various institutions many defective persons who, if now discharged, would become a menace, but, if incapable of procreating, might be discharged with safety and become self-supporting with benefit to themselves and to society, and that experience has shown that heredity plays an important part in the transmission of insanity, imbecility, &c. The statute then enacts that, whenever the superintendent of certain institutions, including the above-named State Colony, shall be of opinion that it is for the best interests of the patients and of society that an inmate under his care should be sexually sterilized, he may have the operation performed upon any patient afflicted with hereditary forms of insanity, imbecility, &c., on complying with the very careful provisions by which the act protects the patients from possible abuse.

The superintendent first presents a petition to the special board of directors of his hospital or colony, stating the facts and the grounds for his opinion, verified by affidavit. Notice of the petition and of the time and place of the hearing in the institution is to be served upon the inmate, and also upon his guardian, and if there is no guardian, the superintendent is to apply to the Circuit Court of the County to appoint one. If the inmate is a minor, notice also is to be given to his parents, if any, with a copy of the petition. The board is to see to it that the inmate may attend the hearings if desired by him or his guardian. The evidence is all to be reduced to writing, and, after the board has made its order for or against the operation, the superintendent, or the inmate, or his guardian, may appeal to the Circuit Court of the County. The Circuit Court may consider the record of the board and the evidence before it and such other admissible evidence as may be offered, and may affirm, revise, or reverse the order of the board and enter such order as it deems just. Finally any party may apply to the Supreme Court of Appeals, which, if it grants the appeal, is to hear the case upon the record of the trial in the Circuit Court, and may enter such order as it thinks the Circuit Court should have entered. There can be no doubt that, so far as procedure is concerned, the rights of the patient are most carefully considered, and, as every step in this case was taken in scrupulous compliance with the statute and after months of observation, there is no doubt that, in that respect, the plaintiff in error has had due process of law.

The attack is not upon the procedure, but upon the substantive law. It seems to be contended that in no circumstances could such an order be justified. It certainly is contended that the order cannot be justified upon the existing grounds. The judgment finds the facts that have been recited, and that Carrie Buck is the probable potential parent of socially inadequate offspring, likewise afflicted, that she may be sexually sterilized without detriment to her general health, and that her welfare and that of society will be promoted by her sterilization, and thereupon makes the order. In view of the general declarations of the legislature and the specific findings of the Court, obviously we cannot say as matter of law that the grounds do not exist, and, if they exist, they justify the result. We have seen more than once that the public welfare may call upon the best citizens for their lives. It would be strange if it could not call upon those who already sap the strength of the State for these lesser sacrifices, often not felt to be such by those concerned, in order to prevent our being swamped with incompetence. It is better for all the world if, instead of waiting to execute degenerate offspring for crime or to let them starve for their imbecility, society can prevent those who are manifestly unfit from continuing their kind. The principle that sustains compulsory vaccination is broad enough to cover cutting the Fallopian tubes. *Jacobson v. Massachusetts,* 197 U.S. 11. Three generations of imbeciles are enough.

But, it is said, however it might be if this reasoning were applied generally, it fails when it is confined to the small number who are in the institutions named and is not applied to the multitudes outside. It is the usual last resort of constitutional arguments to point out shortcomings of this sort. But the answer is that the law does all that is needed when it does all that it can, indicates a policy, applies it to all within the lines, and seeks to bring within the lines all similarly situated so far and so fast as its means allow. Of course, so far as the operations enable those who otherwise must be kept confined to be returned to the world, and thus open the asylum to others, the equality aimed at will be more nearly reached.

Judgment affirmed.

Source:

Tom Russell. American Legal History. Available on-line. URL: www.law.du.edu/russell/lh/alh/docs/buckvbell.html. Accessed November 2003.

Olmstead v. United States, 1928

U.S. Supreme Court decision, issued on June 4, 1928, that allowed the admission of wiretapping evidence in court. Federal agents had used recorded conversations obtained from wiretapping to secure convictions of suspected bootleggers during Prohibition. The case was appealed on the grounds that wiretapping constituted an unreasonable search and seizure, prohibited by the Fourth Amendment to the U.S. Constitution. In a 5-4 decision, the Court stated that wiretapping was permitted because it was not physical entry; even though wiretapping was illegal in the state of Washington, where the acts occurred, the evidence was admissible in federal court. The decision stood, and, in fact, was widened to exclude microphones from Fourth Amendment protections, until 1967, despite the passage in 1934 of Section 605 from the Federal Communications Act, which outlawed federal government wiretapping but was interpreted only to exclude overhears from the courtroom. (States continued to govern their own wiretapping policies.) This case is remembered far better for the dissents than for Olmstead's confirming the government's ability to eavesdrop. Justice Louis Brandeis held that the Fourth and Fifth Amendments conferred a right to privacy and famously wrote, "The makers of our Constitution undertook to secure conditions favorable to the pursuit of happiness. . . . They conferred, as against the Government, the right to be let alone—the most comprehensive of rights and the right most valued by civilized men." Also in dissent, Justice Oliver Wendell Holmes called wiretapping a "dirty business" in which the government should not engage. A "right to privacy" was not recognized by the Court majority until Justice William O. Douglas incorporated it into his decision in *Griswold v. Connecticut* (381 U.S. 479 [1965]).

Mr. Chief Justice Taft delivered the opinion of the Court.

* * *

The petitioners were convicted in the District Court for the Western District of Washington of a conspiracy to violate the National Prohibition Act (27 USCA) by unlawfully possessing, transporting and importing intoxicating liquors and maintaining nuisances, and by selling intoxicating liquors. Seventy-two others, in addition to the petitioners, were indicted. Some were not apprehended, some were acquitted, and others pleaded guilty. The evidence in the records discloses a conspiracy of amazing magnitude to import, possess, and sell liquor unlawfully. It involved the employment of not less than 50 persons, of two sea-going vessels for the transportation of liquor to British Columbia, of smaller vessels for coastwise transportation to the state of Washington, the purchase and use of a branch beyond the suburban limits of Seattle, with a large underground cache for storage and a number of smaller caches in that city, the maintenance of a central office manned with operators, and the employment of executives, salesmen, deliverymen dispatchers, scouts, bookkeepers, collectors, and an attorney. In a bad month sales amounted to $176,000; the aggregate for a year must have exceeded $2,000,000. Olmstead was the leading conspirator and the general manager of the business. . . . The information which led to the discovery of the conspiracy and its nature and extent was largely obtained by intercepting messages on the telephones of the conspirators by four federal prohibition officers. Small wires were inserted along the ordinary telephone wires from the residences of four of the petitioners and those leading from the chief office. The insertions were made without trespass upon any property of the defendants. They were made in the basement of the large office building. The taps from house lines were made in the streets near the houses. The gathering of evidence continued for many months. Conversations of the conspirators, of which refreshing stenographic notes were currently made, were testified to by the government witnesses. They revealed the large business transactions of the partners and their subordinates. Men at the wires heard the orders given for liquor by customers and the acceptances; they became auditors of the conversations between the partners. All this disclosed the conspiracy charged in the indictment. Many of the intercepted conversations were not merely reports, but parts of the criminal acts. . . . The Fourth Amendment provides: "The right of the people to be secure in their persons, houses, papers, and effects, against unreasonable searches and seizures, shall not be violated, and no warrants shall issue, but upon probable cause, supported by oath or affirmation, and particularly describing the place to be searched, and the persons or things to be seized." And the Fifth: "No person . . . shall be compelled in any criminal case to be a witness against himself."

* * *

The well-known historical purpose of the Fourth Amendment, directed against general warrants and writs of assistance, was to prevent the use of governmental force to search a man's house, his person, his papers, and his effects, and to prevent their seizure against his will. . . .

* * *

The amendment itself shows that the search is to be of material things—the person, the house, his papers, or his effects. The description of the warrant necessary to make the proceeding lawful is that it must specify the place to be searched and the person or things to be seized. . . . The Fourth Amendment may have proper application to a sealed letter in the mail, because of the constitutional provision for the Postoffice Department and the relations between the government and those who pay to secure protection of their sealed letters. . . . The United States takes no such care of telegraph or telephone messages as of mailed sealed letters. The amendment does not forbid what was done here. There was no searching. There was no seizure. The evidence was secured by the use of the sense of hearing and that only. There was no entry of the houses or offices of the defendants. By the invention of the telephone 50 years ago, and its application for the purpose of extending communications, one can talk with another at a far distant place. The language of the amendment cannot be extended and expanded to include telephone wires, reaching to the whole world from the defendant's house or office. The intervening wires are not part of his house or office, any more than are the highways along which they are stretched. This court, in *Carroll v. United States,* 267 U.S. 132, 149, 45 S. Ct. 280, 284 (69 L. Ed. 543, 39 A.L.R. 790), declared: "The Fourth Amendment is to be construed in the light of what was deemed an unreasonable search and seizure when it was adopted, and in a manner which will conserve public interests, as well as the interest and rights of individual citizens." Justice Bradley, in the Boyd Case, and Justice Clarke, in the Gouled Case, said that the Fifth Amendment and the Fourth Amendment were to be liberally construed to effect the purpose of the framers of the Constitution in the interest of liberty. But that cannot justify enlargement of the language employed beyond the possible practical meaning of houses, persons, papers, and effects, or so to apply the words search and seizure as to forbid hearing or sight. . . . Congress may, of course, protect the secrecy of telephone messages by making them, when intercepted, inadmissible in evidence in federal criminal trials, by direct legislation, and thus depart from the common law of evidence. But the courts may not adopt such a policy by attributing an enlarged and unusual meaning to the Fourth Amendment. The reasonable view is that one who installs in his house a telephone instrument with connecting wires intends to project his voice to those quite outside, and that the wires beyond his house, and messages while passing over them, are not within the protection of the Fourth Amendment. Here those who intercepted the projected voices were not in the house of either party to the conversation. Neither the cases we have cited nor any of the many federal decisions brought to our attention hold the Fourth Amendment to have been violated as against a defendant, unless there has been an official search and seizure of his person or such a seizure of his papers or his tangible material effects or an actual physical invasion of his house "or curtilage" for the purpose of making a seizure. We think, therefore, that the wire tapping here disclosed did not amount to a search or seizure within the meaning of the Fourth Amendment. What has been said disposes of the only question that comes within the terms of our order granting certiorari in these cases. But some of our number, departing from that order, have concluded that there is merit in the twofold objection, overruled in both courts below, that evidence obtained through intercepting of telephone messages by government agents was inadmissible, because the mode of obtaining it was unethical and a misdemeanor under the law of Washington. To avoid any misapprehension of our views of that objection we shall deal with it in both of its phases.

* * *

The common-law rule is that the admissibility of evidence is not affected by the illegality of the means by which it was obtained.

* * *

Nor can we, without the sanction of congressional enactment, subscribe to the suggestion that the courts have a discretion to exclude evidence, the admission of which is not unconstitutional, because unethically secured. This would be at variance with the common-law doctrine generally supported by authority. There is no case that sustains, nor any recognized text-book that gives color to, such a view. Our general experience shows that much evidence has always been receivable, although not obtained by conformity to the highest ethics. . . . A standard which would forbid the reception of evidence, if obtained by other than nice ethical conduct by government officials, would made society suffer and give criminals greater immunity than has been known heretofore. In the absence of controlling legislation by Congress, those who realize the difficulties in bringing offenders to justice may well deem it wise that the exclusion of evidence should be confined to cases where rights under the Constitution would be violated by admitting it. . . .

* * *

The judgments of the Circuit Court of Appeals are affirmed. The mandates will go down forthwith under rule 31. Affirmed.

Mr. Justice Brandeis (dissenting). The defendants were convicted of conspiring to violate the National Prohibition Act (27 USCA). Before any of the persons now charged had been arrested or indicted, the telephones by means of which they habitually communicated with one another and with others had been tapped by federal officers. To this end, a lineman of long experience in wire tapping was employed, on behalf of the government and at its expense. He tapped eight telephones, some in the homes of the persons charged, some in their offices. Acting on behalf of the government and in their official capacity, at least six other prohibition agents listened over the tapped wires and reported the messages taken. Their operations extended over a period of nearly five months. The typewritten record of the notes of conversations overheard occupies 775 typewritten pages. By objections seasonably made and persistently renewed, the defendants objected to the admission of the evidence obtained by wire tapping, on the ground that the government's wire tapping constituted an unreasonable search and seizure, in violation of the Fourth Amendment, and that the use as evidence of the conversations overheard compelled the defendants to be witnesses against themselves, in violation of the Fifth Amendment. The government makes no attempt to defend the methods employed by its officers. . . .

* * *

Moreover, "in the application of a Constitution, our contemplation cannot be only of what has been, but of what may be." The progress of science in furnishing the government with means of espionage is not likely to stop with wire tapping. Ways may some day be developed by which the government, without removing papers from secret drawers, can reproduce them in court, and by which it will be enabled to expose to a jury the most intimate occurrences of the home. Advances in the psychic and related sciences may bring means of exploring unexpressed beliefs, thoughts and emotions. "That places the liberty of every man in the hands of every petty officer" was said by James Otis of much lesser intrusions than these. To Lord Camden a far slighter intrusion seemed "subversive of all the comforts of society. Can it be that the Constitution affords no protection against such invasions of individual security?

* * *

Whenever a telephone line is tapped, the privacy of the persons at both ends of the line is invaded, and all conversations between them upon any subject, and although proper, confidential, and privileged, may be overheard. Moreover, the tapping of one man's telephone line involves the tapping of the telephone of every other person whom he may call, or who may call him. As a means of espionage, writs of assistance and general warrants are but puny instruments of tyranny and oppression when compared with wire tapping.

* * *

Decisions of this court . . . have settled these things. Unjustified search and seizure violates the Fourth Amendment, whatever the character of the paper; whether the paper when taken by the federal officers was in the home, in an office, or elsewhere; whether the taking was effected by force, by fraud, or in the orderly process of a court's procedure. From these decisions, it follows necessarily that the amendment is violated by the officer's reading the paper without a physical seizure, without his even touching it, and that use, in any criminal proceeding, of the contents of the paper so examined—as where they are testified to by a federal officer who thus saw the document or where, through knowledge so obtained, a copy has been procured elsewhere—any such use constitutes a violation of the Fifth Amendment. The protection guaranteed by the amendments is much broader in scope. The makers of our Constitution undertook to secure conditions favorable to the pursuit of happiness. They recognized the significance of man's spiritual nature, of his feelings and of his intellect. They knew that only a part of the pain, pleasure and satisfactions of life are to be found in material things. They sought to protect Americans in their beliefs, their thoughts, their emotions and their sensations. They conferred, as against the government, the right to be let alone—the most comprehensive of rights and the right most valued by civilized men. To protect, that right, every unjustifiable intrusion by the government upon the privacy of the individual, whatever the means employed, must be deemed a violation of the Fourth Amendment. And the use, as evidence in a criminal proceeding, of facts ascertained by such intrusion must be deemed a violation of the Fifth. Applying to the Fourth and Fifth Amendments the established rule of construction, the defendants' objections to the evidence obtained by wire tapping must, in my opinion, be sustained. It is, of course, immaterial where the physical connection with the telephone wires leading into the defendants' premises was made. And it is also immaterial that the intrusion was in aid of law enforcement. Experience should teach us to be most on our guard to protect liberty when the government's purposes are beneficent. Men born to freedom are naturally alert to repel invasion of their liberty by evil-minded rulers. The greatest dangers to liberty lurk in insidious encroachment by men of zeal, well-meaning but without understanding.

* * *

Decency, security, and liberty alike demand that government officials shall be subjected to the same rules of conduct that are commands to the citizen. In a government of laws, existence of the government will be imperiled if it fails to observe the law scrupulously. Our government is the potent, the omnipresent teacher. For good or for ill, it teaches the whole people by its example. Crime is contagious. If the government becomes a lawbreaker, it breeds contempt for law; it invites every man to become a law unto himself; it invites anarchy. To declare that in the administration of the criminal law the end justifies the means—to declare that the government may commit crimes in order to secure the conviction of a private criminal—would bring terrible retribution. Against that pernicious doctrine this court should resolutely set its face Mr. Justice Holmes [dissenting]. My brother Brandeis has given this case so exhaustive an examination that I desire to add but a few words. While I do not deny it I am not prepared to say that the penumbra of the Fourth and Fifth Amendments covers the defendant, although I fully agree that courts are apt to err by sticking too closely to the words of a law where those words import a policy that goes beyond them. . . . But I think, as Mr. Justice Brandeis says, that apart from the Constitution the government ought not to use evidence obtained and only obtainable by a criminal act. There is no body of precedents by which we are bound, and which confines us to logical deduction from established rules. Therefore we must consider the two objects of desire both of which we cannot have and make up our minds which to choose. It is desirable that criminals should be detected, and to that end that all available evidence should be used. It also is desirable that the government should not itself foster and pay for other crimes, when they are the means by which the evidence is to obtained. If it pays its officers for having got evidence by crime I do not see why it may not as well pay them for getting it in the same way, and I can attach no importance to protestations of disapproval if it knowingly accepts and pays and announces that in future it will pay for the fruits. We have to choose, and for my part I think it a less evil that some criminals should escape than that the government should play an ignoble part. For those who agree with me no distinction can be taken between the government as prosecutor and the government as judge. If the existing code does not permit district attorneys to have a hand in such dirty business it does not permit the judge to allow such iniquities to succeed. . . . And if all that I have said so far be accepted it makes no difference that in this case wire tapping is made a crime by the law of the state, not by the law of the United States. It is true that a state cannot make rules of evidence for courts of the United States, but the state has authority over the conduct in question, and I hardly think that the United States would appear to greater advantage when paying for an odious crime against state law than when inciting to the disregard of its own. . . I have said that we are free to choose between two principles of policy. But if we are to confine ourselves to precedent and logic the reason for excluding evidence obtained by violating the Constitution seems to me logically to lead to excluding evidence obtained by a crime of the officers of the law.

Source:
Supreme Court Reporter, Vol. 48, pp. 564–576.

Postwar Economy

Water Power Act, 1920

Federal legislation enacted on June 10, 1920, that established the Federal Power Commission to conserve water power reserves on U.S. public lands and on navigable streams. To improve navigation and develop power, the commission, consisting of the secretaries of war, interior, and agriculture, was authorized to issue licenses for the construction and operation of facilities, such as powerhouses, dams, and reservoirs. Leases were limited to 50 years, with the U.S. government maintaining the right to take over the facilities when the leases expired. The commission was empowered to regulate rates. The act also stated that neighboring states or cities would have the first opportunity to use power sites.

An Act

To create a Federal Power Commission; to provide for the improvement of navigation; the development of water power; the use of the public lands in relation thereto, and to repeal section 18 of the River and Harbor Appropriation Act, approved August 8, 1917, and for other purposes.

Be it enacted by the Senate and House of Representatives of the United States of America in Congress assembled, That a commission is hereby created and established, to be known as the Federal Power Commission (hereinafter referred to as the commission), which shall be composed of the Secretary of War, the Secretary of the Interior, and the Secretary of Agriculture. Two members of the commission shall constitute a quorum for the transaction of business, and the commission shall have an official seal, which shall be judicially noticed. The President shall designate the chairman of the commission.

Sec. 2. That the commission shall appoint an executive secretary, who shall receive a salary of $5,000 a year, and prescribe his duties, and the commission may request the President of the United States to detail an officer from the United States Engineer Corps to serve the commission as engineer officer, his duties to be prescribed by the commission.

The work of the commission shall be performed by and through the Departments of War, Interior, and Agriculture and their engineering, technical, clerical, and other personnel except as may be otherwise provided by law.

All the expenses of the commission, including rent in the District of Columbia, all necessary expenses for transportation and subsistence, including, in the discretion of the commission, a per diem of not exceeding $4 in lieu of subsistence incurred by its employees under its orders in making any investigation, or conducting field work, or upon official business outside of the District of Columbia and away from their designated points of duty, shall be allowed and paid on the presentation of itemized vouchers therefor approved by a member or officer of the commission duly authorized for that purpose; and in order to defray the expenses made necessary by the provisions of this Act there is hereby authorized to be appropriated such sums as Congress may hereafter determine, and the sum of $100,000 is hereby appropriate, out of any moneys in the Treasury not otherwise appropriated, available until expended, to be paid out upon warrants drawn on the Secretary of the Treasury upon order of the commission.

Sec. 3. That the words defined in this section shall have the following meanings for the purposes of this Act, to wit:

"Public lands" means such lands and interest in lands owned by the United States as are subject to private appropriation and disposal under public-land laws. It shall not include "reservations," as hereinafter defined.

"Reservations" means national monuments, national parks, national forests, tribal lands embraced within Indian reservations, military reservations, and other lands and interests in lands owned by the United States, and withdrawn, reserved, or withheld from private appropriation and disposal under the public-land laws; also lands and interests in lands acquired and held for any public purpose.

"Corporation" means a corporation organized under the laws of any State or of the United States empowered to develop, transmit, distribute, sell, lease, or utilize power in addition to such other powers as it may possess, and authorized to transact in the State or States in which its project is located all business necessary to effect the purposes of a license under this Act. It shall not include "municipalities" as hereinafter defined.

"State" means a State admitted to the Union, the District of Columbia, and any organized Territory of the United States.

"Municipality" means a city, county, irrigation district, drainage district, or other political subdivision or agency of a State competent under the laws thereof to carry on the business of developing, transmitting, utilizing, or distributing power.

"Navigable waters" means those parts of streams or other bodies of water over which Congress has jurisdiction under its authority to regulate commerce with foreign nations and among the several States, and which either in their natural or improved condition, notwithstanding interruptions between the navigable parts of such streams or waters by falls, shallows, or rapids compelling land carriage, are used or suitable for use for the transportation of persons or property in interstate or foreign commerce, including therein all such interrupting falls, shallows, or rapids; together with such other parts of streams as shall have been authorized by Congress for improvement by the United States or shall have been recommended to Congress for such improvement after investigation under its authority.

"Municipal purposes" means and includes all purposes within municipal powers as defined by the constitution or laws of the State or by the charter of the municipality.

"Government dam" means a dam or other work, constructed or owned by the United States for Government purposes, with or without contribution from others.

"Project" means complete unit of improvement or development, consisting of a power house, all water conduits, all dams and appurtenant works and structures (including navigation structures) which are a part of said unit, and all storage, diverting, or forebay reservoirs directly connected therewith, the primary line or lines transmitting power therefrom to the point of junction with the distribution system or with the interconnected primary transmission system, all miscellaneous structures used and useful in connection with said unit or any part thereof, and all water rights, rights of way, ditches, dams, reservoirs, lands, or interest in lands, the use and occupancy of which are necessary or appropriate in the maintenance and operation of such unit.

"Project works" means the physical structures of a project.

"Net investment" in a project means the actual legitimate original cost thereof as defined and interpreted in the "classification of investment in road and equipment of steam roads, issue of 1914, Interstate Commerce Commission," plus similar costs of additions thereto and betterments thereof, minus the sum of the following items properly allocated thereto, if and to the extent that such items have been accumulated during the period of the license from earnings in excess of a fair return on such investment: (a) Unappropriated surplus, (b) aggregate credit balances of current depreciation accounts, and (c) aggregate appropriations of surplus or income held in amortization, sinking fund, or similar reserves, or expended for additions or betterments or used for the purposes for which such reserves were created. The term "cost" shall include, in so far as applicable, the elements thereof prescribed in said classification, but shall not include expenditures from funds obtained through donations by States, municipalities, individuals, or others, and said classification of investment of the Interstate Commerce Commission shall in so far as applicable be published and promulgated as a part of the rules and regulations of the commission.

Sec. 4. That the commission is hereby authorized and empowered—

(a) To make investigations and to collect and record data concerning the utilization of the water resources of any region to be developed, the water power industry and its relation to other industries and to interstate or foreign commerce, and concerning the location, capacity, development costs, and relation to markets of power sites, and whether the power from Government dams can be advantageously used by the United States for its public purposes, and what is a fair value of such power, to the extent the commission may deem necessary or useful for the purposes of this Act.

In order to aid the commission in determining the net investment of a licensee in any project, the licensee shall, upon oath, within a reasonable period of time, to be fixed by the commission, after the construction of the original project or any addition thereto or betterment thereof, file with the commission, in such detail as the commission may require, a statement in duplicate showing the actual legitimate cost of construction of such project, addition, or betterment, and the price paid for water rights, rights of way, lands, or interest in lands. The commission shall deposit one of said statements with the Secretary of the Treasury. The licensee shall grant to the commission or to its duly authorized agent or agents, at all reasonable times, free access to such project, addition, or betterment, and to all maps, profiles, contracts, reports of engineers, accounts, books, records, and all other papers and documents relating thereto.

(b) To cooperate with the executive departments and other agencies of State or National Governments in such investigations; and for such purpose the several departments and agencies of the National Government are authorized and directed upon the request of the commission, to furnish such records, papers, and information in their possession as may be requested by the commission, and temporarily to detail to the commission such officers or experts as may be necessary in such investigations.

(c) To make public from time to time the information secured hereunder, and to provide for the publication of its reports and investigations in such form and manner as may be best adapted for public information and use. The commission, on or before the first Monday in December of each year, shall submit to Congress for the fiscal year preceding a classified report showing the permits and licenses issued under this Act, and in each case the parties thereto, the terms prescribed, and the moneys received, if any, on account thereof.

(d) To issue licenses to citizens of the United States, or to any association of such citizens, or to any corporation organized under the laws of the United States or any State thereof, or to any State, or municipality for the purpose of constructing, operating, and maintaining dams, water conduits, reservoirs, power houses, transmission lines, or other project works necessary or convenient for the development and improvement of navigation, and for the development, transmission, and utilization of power across, along, from or in any of the navigable waters of the United States, or upon any part of the public lands and reservations of the United States (including the Territories), or for the purpose of utilizing the surplus water or water power from any Government dam, except as herein provided: *Provided,* That licenses shall be issued within any reservation only after a finding by the commission that the license will not interfere or be inconsistent with the purpose for which such reservation was created or acquired, and shall be subject to and contain such conditions as the Secretary of the department under whose supervision such reservation falls shall deem necessary for the adequate protection and utilization of such reservation: *Provided further,* That no license affecting the navigable capacity of any navigable waters of the United States shall be issued until the plans of the dam or other structures affecting navigation have been approved by the Chief of Engineers and the Secretary of War. Whenever the contemplated improvement is, in the judgment of the commission, desirable and justified in the public interest for the purpose of improving or developing a waterway or waterways for the use or benefit of interstate of foreign commerce, a finding to that effect shall be made by the commission and shall become a part of the records of the commission: *Provided further,* That in case the commission shall find that any Government dam may be advantageously used by the United States for public purposes in addition to navigation, no license therefor shall be issued until two years after it shall have reported to Congress the facts and conditions relating thereto, except that this provision shall not apply to any Government dam constructed prior to the passage of this Act: *And provided further,* That upon the filing of any application for a license which has not been preceded by a preliminary permit under subsection (e) of this section, notice shall be given and published as required by the proviso of said subsection.

(e) To issue preliminary permits for the purpose of enabling applicants for a license hereunder to secure the data and to perform the acts required by section 9 hereof: *Provided, however,* That upon the filing of any application for a preliminary permit by any person, association, or corporation the commission, before granting such application, shall at once give notice of such application in writing to any State or municipality likely to be interested in or affected by such application; and shall also publish notice of such application for eight weeks in a daily or weekly newspaper published in the county or counties in which the project or any part thereof or the lands affected thereby are situated.

(f) To prescribe rules and regulations for the establishment of a system of accounts and for the maintenance thereof of licensees hereunder; to examine all books and accounts of such licensees at any time; to require them to submit at such time or times as the commission may require statements and reports, including full information as to assets and liabilities, capitalization, net investment and reduction thereof, gross receipts, interest due and paid, depreciation and other reserves, cost of project, cost of maintenance and operation of the project, cost of renewals and replacements of the project works, and as to depreciation of the project works and as to production, transmission, use and sale of power; also to require any licensee to make adequate provision for currently determining said costs and other facts. All such statements and reports shall be made upon oath, unless otherwise specified, and in such form and on such blanks as the commission may require. Any person who, for the purpose of deceiving, makes or causes to be made any false entry in the books or the accounts of such licensee, and any person who, for the purpose of deceiving, makes or causes to be made any false statement or report in response to a request or order or direction from the commission for the statements and report herein referred to shall, upon conviction, be fined not more than $2,000 or imprisoned not more than five years, or both.

(g) To hold hearings and to order testimony to be taken by deposition at any designated place in connection with the application for any permit or license, or the regulation of rates, service, or securities, or the making of any investigation, as provided in this Act; and to require by subpoena, signed by any member of the commission, the attendance and testimony of witnesses and the production of documentary evidence from any place in the United States, and in case of disobedience to a subpoena the commission may invoke the aid of any court of the United States in requiring the attendance and testimony of witnesses and the production of documentary evidence. Any member, expert, or examiner of the commission may, when duly designated by the commission for such purposes, administer oaths and affirmations, examine witnesses and receive evidence. Depositions may be taken before any person designated by the commission or by its executive secretary and empowered to administer oaths, shall be reduced to writing by such person or under his direction, and subscribed by the deponent. Witnesses summoned before the commission shall be paid the same fees and mileage that are paid witnesses in the courts of the United States, and witnesses whose depositions are taken and persons taking the same shall severally be entitled to the same fees as are paid for like services in the courts of the United States.

(h) To perform any and all acts, to make such rules and regulations, and to issue such orders not inconsistent with this Act as may be necessary and proper for the purpose of carrying out the provisions of this Act.

Sec. 5. That each preliminary permit issued under this Act shall be for the sole purpose of maintaining priority of application for a license under the terms of this Act for such period or periods, not exceeding a total of three years, as in the discretion of the commission may be necessary for making examinations and surveys, for preparing maps, plans, specifications, and estimates, and for making financial arrangements. Each such permit shall set forth the conditions under which priority shall be maintained and a license issued. Such permits shall not be transferable, and may be canceled by order of the commission upon failure of permittees to comply with the conditions thereof.

Sec. 6. That licenses under this Act shall be issued for a period not exceeding fifty years. Each such license shall be conditioned upon acceptance by the licensee of all the terms and conditions of this Act and such further conditions, if any, as the commission shall prescribe in conformity with this Act, which said terms and conditions and the acceptance thereof shall be expressed in said license. Licenses may be revoked only for the reasons and in the manner prescribed under the provisions of this Act, and may be altered or surrendered only upon mutual agreement between the licensee and the commission after ninety days' public notice.

Sec. 7. That in issuing preliminary permits hereunder or licenses where no preliminary permit has been issued and in issuing licenses to new licensees under section 15 hereof the commission shall give preference to applications therefor by States and municipalities, provided the plans for the same are deemed by the commission equally well adapted, or shall within a reasonable time to be fixed by the commission be made equally well adapted, to conserve and utilize in the public interest the navigation and water resources of the region; and as between other applicants, the commission may give preference to the applicant the plans of which it finds and determines are best adapted to develop, conserve, and utilize in the public interest the navigation and water resources of the region, if it be satisfied as to the ability of the applicant to carry out such plans.

That whenever, in the judgment of the commission, the development of any project should be undertaken by the United States itself, the commission shall not approve any application for such project by any citizen, association, corporation, State, or municipality, but shall cause to be made such examinations, surveys, reports, plans and estimates of the cost of the project as it may deem necessary, and shall submit its findings to Congress with such recommendations as it may deem appropriate concerning the construction of such project or completion of any project upon any Government dam by the United States.

The commission is hereby authorized and directed to investigate and, on or before the 1st day of January, 1921, report to Congress the cost and, in detail, the economic value of the power plant outlined in project numbered 3, House Document numbered 1400, Sixty-second Congress, third session, in view of existing conditions, utilizing such study as may heretofore have been made by any department of the Government; also in connection with such project to submit plans and estimates of cost necessary to secure an increased and adequate water supply for the District of Columbia. For this purpose the sum of $25,000, or so much thereof as may be necessary, is hereby appropriated.

Sec. 8. That no voluntary transfer of any license, or of the rights thereunder granted, shall be made without the written approval of the commission; and any successor or assign of the rights of such licensee, whether by voluntary transfer, judicial sale, foreclosure sale, or otherwise, shall be subject to all the conditions of the license under which such rights are held by such licensee and also subject to all the provisions and conditions of this Act to the same extent as though such successor or assign were the original licensee hereunder: *Provided,* That a mortgage or trust deed or judicial sales made thereunder or under tax sales shall not be deemed voluntary transfers within the meaning of this section.

Sec. 9. That each applicant for a license hereunder shall submit to the commission—

(a) Such maps, plans, specifications, and estimates of cost as may be required for a full understanding of the proposed project. Such maps, plans, and specifications when approved by the commission shall be made a part of the license; and thereafter no change shall be made in said maps, plans, or specifications until such changes shall have been approved and made a part of such license by the commission.

(b) Satisfactory evidence that the applicant has complied with the requirements of the laws of the State or States within which the proposed project is to be located with respect to bed and banks and to the appropriation, diversion, and use of water for power purposes and with respect to the right to engage in the business of developing, transmitting, and distributing power, and in any other business necessary to effect the purposes of a license under this Act.

(c) Such additional information as the commission may require.

Sec. 10. That all licenses issued under this Act shall be on the following conditions:

(a) That the project adopted, including the maps, plans, and specifications, shall be such as in the judgment of the commission will be best adapted to a comprehensive scheme of improvement and utilization for the purposes of navigation, of water-power development, and of other beneficial public uses; and if necessary in order to secure such scheme the commission shall have authority to require the modification of any project and of the plans and specifications of the project works before approval.

(b) That except when emergency shall require for the protection of navigation, life, health, or property, no substantial alteration or addition not in conformity with the approved plans shall be made to any dam or other project works constructed hereunder of a capacity in excess of one hundred horsepower without the prior approval of the commission; and any emergency alteration or addition so made shall thereafter be subject to such modification and change as the commission may direct.

(c) That the licensee shall maintain the project works in a condition of repair adequate for the purposes of navigation and for the efficient operation of said works in the development and transmission of power, shall make all necessary renewals and replacements, shall establish and maintain adequate depreciation reserves for such purposes, shall so maintain and operate said works as not to impair navigation, and shall conform to such rules and regulations as the commission may from time to time prescribe for the protection of life, health, and property. Each licensee hereunder shall be liable for all damages occasioned to the property of others by the construction, maintenance, or operation of the project works or of the works appurtenant or accessory thereto, constructed under the license, and in no event shall the United States be liable therefor.

(d) That after the first twenty years of operation out of surplus earned thereafter, if any, accumulated in excess of a specified reasonable rate of return upon the actual, legitimate investment of a licensee in any project or projects under license the licensee shall establish and maintain amortization reserves, which reserves shall, in the discretion of the commission, be held until the termination of the license or be applied from time to time in reduction of the net investment. Such specified rate of return and the proportion of such surplus earnings to be paid into and held in such reserves shall be set forth in the license.

(e) That the licensee shall pay to the United States reasonable annual charges in an amount to be fixed by the commission for the purpose of reimbursing the United States for the costs of the administration of this Act; for recompensing it for the use, occupancy, and enjoyment of its lands or other property; and for the expropriation to the Government of excessive profits until the respective States shall make provision for preventing excessive profits or for the expropriation thereof to themselves, or until the period of amortization as herein provided is reached, and in fixing such charges the commission shall seek to avoid increasing the price to the consumers of power by such charges, and charges for the expropriation of excessive profits may be adjusted from time to time by the commission as conditions may require: *Provided,* That when licenses are issued involving the use of Government dams or other structures owned by the United States or tribal lands embraced within Indian reservations the commission shall fix a reasonable annual charge for the use thereof, and such charges may be readjusted at the end of twenty years after the beginning of operations and at periods of not less than ten years thereafter in a manner to be described in each license: *Provided,* That licenses for the development, transmission, or distribution of power by States or municipalities shall be issued and enjoyed without charge to the extent such power is sold to the public without profit or is used by such State or municipality for State or municipal purposes, except that as to projects constructed or to be constructed by States or municipalities primarily designed to provide or improve navigation licenses therefor shall be issued without charge; and that licenses for the development, transmission, or distribution of power for domestic, mining, or other beneficial use in projects of not more than one hundred horsepower capacity may be issued without charge, except on tribal lands within Indian reservations; but in no case shall a license be issued free of charge for the development and utilization of power created by any Government dam and that the amount charged therefor in any license shall be such as determined by the commission.

(f) That whenever any licensee hereunder is directly benefited by the construction work of another licensee, a permittee, or of the United States of a storage reservoir or other headwater improvement, the commission shall require as a condition of the license that the licensee so benefited shall reimburse the owner of such reservoir or other improvements for such part of the annual charges for interest, maintenance, and depreciation thereon as the commission may deem equitable. The proportion of such charges to be paid by any licensee shall be determined by the commission.

Whenever such reservoir or other improvement is constructed by the United States the commission shall assess similar charges against any licensee directly benefited thereby, and any amount so assessed shall be paid into the Treasury of the United States, to be reserved and appropriated as a part of the special fund for headwater improvements as provided in section 17 hereof.

(g) Such further conditions not inconsistent with the provisions of this Act as the commission may require.

(h) That combinations, agreements, arrangements, or understandings, express or implied, to limit the output of electrical energy, to restrain trade, or to fix, maintain, or increase prices for electrical energy or service are hereby prohibited.

(i) In issuing licenses for a minor part only of a complete project, or for a complete project of not more than one hundred horsepower capacity, the commission may in its discretion waive such conditions, provisions, and requirements of this Act, except the license period of fifty years, as it may deem to be to the public interest to waive under the circumstances: *Provided,* That the provisions hereof shall not apply to lands within Indian reservations.

Sec. 11. That if the dam or other project works are to be constructed across, along, or in any of the navigable waters of the United States, the commission may, in so far as it deems the same reasonably necessary to promote the present and future needs of navigation and consistent with a reasonable investment cost to the licensee, include in the license any one or more of the following provisions or requirements:

(a) That such licensee shall, to the extent necessary to preserve and improve navigation facilities, construct, in whole or in part, without expense to the United States, in connection with such dam, a lock or locks, booms, sluices, or other structures for navigation purposes, in accordance with plans and specifications approved by the Chief of Engineers and the Secretary of War and made part of such license.

(b) That in case such structures for navigation purposes are not made a part of the original construction at the expense of the licensee, then whenever the United States shall desire to complete such navigation facilities the licensee shall convey to the United States, free of cost, such of its land and its rights of way and such right of passage through its dams or other structures, and permit such control of pools as may be required to complete such navigation facilities.

(c) That such licensee shall furnish free of cost to the United States power for the operation of such navigation facilities, whether constructed by the licensee or by the United States.

Sec. 12. That whenever application is filed for a project hereunder involving navigable waters of the United States, and the commission shall find upon investigation that the needs of navigation require the construction of a lock or locks or other navigation structures, and that such structures can not, consistent with a reasonable investment cost to the applicant, be provided in the manner specified in section 11, subsection (a) hereof, the commission may grant the application with the provision to be expressed in the license that the licensee will install the necessary navigation structures if the Government fails to make provision therefor within a time to be fixed in the license and cause a report upon such project to be prepared, with estimates of cost of the power development and of the navigation structures, and shall submit such report to Congress with such recommendations as it deems appropriate concerning the participation of the United States in the cost of construction of such navigation structures.

Sec. 13. That the licensee shall commence the construction of the project works within the time fixed in the license, which shall not be more than two years from the date thereof, shall thereafter in good faith and with due diligence prosecute such construction, and shall within the time fixed in the license complete and put into operation such part of the ultimate development as the commission shall deem necessary to supply the reasonable needs of the then available market, and shall from time to time thereafter construct such portion of the balance of such development as the commission may direct, so as to supply adequately the reasonable market demands until such development shall have been completed. The periods for the commencement of construction may be extended once but not longer than two additional years and the period for the completion of construction carried on in good faith and will reasonable diligence may be extended by the commission when not incompatible with the public interests. In case the licensee shall not commence actual construction of the project works, or of any specified part thereof, within the time prescribed in the license or as extended by the commission, then, after due notice given, the license shall, as to such project works or part thereof, be terminated upon written order of the commission. In case the construction of the project works, or of any specified part thereof, have been begun but not completed within the time prescribed in the license, or as extended by the commission, then the Attorney General, upon the request of the commission, shall institute proceedings in equity in the district court of the United States for the district in which any part of the project is situated for the revocation of said license, the sale of the works constructed, and such other equitable relief as the case may demand, as provided for in section 26 hereof.

Sec. 14. That upon not less than two years' notice in writing from the commission the United States shall have the right upon or after the expiration of any license to take over and thereafter to maintain and operate any project or projects as defined in section 3 hereof, and covered in whole or in part by the license, or the right to take over upon mutual agreement with the license all property owned and held by the licensee then valuable and serviceable in the development, transmission, or distribution of power and which is then dependent for its usefulness upon the continuance of the license, together with any lock or locks or other aids to navigation constructed at the expense of the licensee, upon the condition that before taking possession it shall pay the net investment of the licensee in the project or projects taken, not to exceed the fair value of the property taken, plus such reasonable damages, if any, to property of the licensee valuable, serviceable, and dependent as above set forth but not taken, as may be caused by the severance therefrom of property taken, and shall assume all contracts entered into by the licensee with the approval of the commission. The net investment of the licensee in the project or projects so taken and the amount of such severance damages, if any, shall be determined by agreement between the commission and the licensee, and in case they can not agree, by proceedings in equity instituted by the United States in the district court of the United States in the district within which any such property may be located: *Provided,* That such net investment shall not include or be affected by the value of any lands, rights of way, or other property of the United States licensed by the commission under this Act, by the license, or by good will, going value, or prospective revenues: *Provided further,* That the values allowed for water rights, rights of way, lands, or interest in lands shall not be in excess of the actual reasonable costs thereof at the time of acquisition by the licensee: *Provided,* That the right of the United States or any State or municipality to take over, maintain, and operate any project licensed under this Act at any time by condemnation proceedings upon payment of just compensation is hereby expressly reserved.

Sec. 15. That if the United States does not, at the expiration of the original license, exercise its right to take over, maintain, and operate any project or projects of the licensee, as provided in section 14 hereof, the commission is authorized to issue a new license to the original licensee upon such terms and conditions as may be authorized or required under the then existing laws and regulations, or to issue a new license under said terms and conditions to a new licensee, which license may cover any project or projects covered by the original license, and shall be issued on the condition that the new licensee, shall, before taking possession of such project or projects, pay such amount, and assume such contracts as the United States is required to do, in the manner specified in section 14 hereof: *Provided,* That in the event the United States does not exercise the right to take over or does not issue a license to a new license, or issue a new license to the original licensee, upon reasonable terms, then the commission shall issue from year to year an annual license to the then licensee under the terms and conditions of the original license until the property is take over or a new license is issued as aforesaid.

Sec. 16. That when in the opinion of the President of the United States, evidenced by a written order addressed to the holder of any license hereunder, the safety of the United States demands it, the United States shall have the right to enter upon and take possession of any project, or part thereof, constructed, maintained, or operated under said license, for the purpose of manufacturing nitrates, explosives, or munitions of war, or for any other purpose involving the safety of the United States, to retain possession, management, and control thereof for such length of time as may appear to the President to be necessary to accomplish said purposes, and then to restore possession and control to the party or parties entitled thereto; and in the event that the United States shall exercise such right it shall pay to the party or parties entitled thereto just and fair compensation for the use of said property as may be fixed by the commission upon the basis of a reasonable profit in time of peace, and the cost of restoring said property to as good condition as existed at the time of the taking over thereof, less the reasonable value of any improvements that may be made thereto by the United States and which are valuable and serviceable to the licensee.

Sec. 17. That all proceeds from any Indian reservation shall be placed to the credit of the Indians of such reservation. All other charges arising from licenses hereunder shall be paid into the Treasury of the United States, subject to the following distribution: Twelve and one-half per centum thereof is hereby appropriated to be paid into the Treasury of the United States and credited to "Miscellaneous receipts"; 50 per centum of the charges arising from licenses hereunder for the occupancy and use of public lands, national monuments, national forests, and national parks shall be paid into, reserved, and appropriated as a part of the reclamation fund created by the Act of Congress known as the Reclamation Act, approved June 17, 1902; and 37 1/2 per centum of the charges arising from licenses hereunder for the occupancy and use of national forests, national parks, public lands, and national monuments, from development within the boundaries of any State shall be paid by the Secretary of the Treasury to such State; and 50 per centum of the charges arising from all other licenses hereunder is hereby reserved and appropriated as a special fund in the Treasury to be expended under the direction of the Secretary of War in the maintenance and operation of dams and other navigation structures owned by the United States or in the construction, maintenance, or operation of headwater or other improvements of navigable waters of the United States.

Sec. 18. That the operation of any navigation facilities which may be constructed as a part of or in connection with any dam or diversion structure built under the provisions of this Act, whether at the expense of a licensee hereunder or of the United States, shall at all times be controlled by such reasonable rules and regulations in the interest of navigation, including the control of the level of the pool caused by such dam or diversion structure as may be made from time to time by the Secretary of War. Such rules and regulations may include the maintenance and operation by such licensee at its own expense of such lights and signals as may be directed by the Secretary of War, and such fishways as may be prescribed by the Secretary of Commerce; and for willful failure to comply with any such rules or regulation such licensee shall be deemed guilty of a misdemeanor, and upon conviction thereof shall be punished as provided in section 25 hereof.

Sec. 19. That as a condition of the license, every licensee hereunder which is a public-service corporation, or a person, association, or corporation owning or operating any project and developing, transmitting, or distributing power for sale or use in public service, shall abide by such reasonable regulation of the services to be rendered to customers or consumers of power, and of rates and charges of payment therefor, as may from time to time be prescribed by any duly constituted agency of the State in which the service is rendered or the rate charged. That in case of the development, transmission, or distribution, or use in public service of power by any licensee hereunder or by its customer engaged in public service within a State which has not authorized and empowered a commission or other agency or agencies within said State to regulate and control the services to be rendered by such licensee or by its customer engaged in public service, or the rates and charges of payment therefor, or the amount or character of securities to be issued by any of said parties, it is agreed as a condition of such license that jurisdiction is hereby conferred upon the commission, upon complaint of any person aggrieved or upon its own initiative, to exercise such regulation and control until such time as the State shall have provided a commission or other authority for such regulation and control: *Provided,* That the jurisdiction of the commission shall cease and determine as to each specific matter of regulation and control prescribed in this section as soon as the State shall have provided a commission or other authority for the regulation and control of that specific matter.

Sec. 20. That when said power or any part thereof shall enter into interstate or foreign commerce the rates charged and the service rendered by any such licensee, or by any subsidiary corporation, the stock of which is owned or controlled directly or indirectly by such licensee, or by any person, corporation, or association purchasing power from such licensee for sale and distribution or use in public service shall be reasonable, nondiscriminatory, and just to the customer and all unreasonable discriminatory and unjust rates or services are hereby prohibited and declared to be unlawful; and whenever any of the States directly concerned has not provided a commission or other authority to enforce the requirements of this section within such State or to regulate and control the amount and character of securities to be issued by any of such parties or such States are unable to agree through their properly constituted authorities on the services to be rendered or on the rates or charges of payment therefor, or on the amount or character of securities to be issued by any of said parties, jurisdiction is hereby conferred upon the commission, upon complaint of any person aggrieved, upon the request of any State concerned, or upon its own initiative to enforce the provisions of this section, to regulate and control so much of the services rendered, and of the rates and charges of payment therefor as constitute interstate or foreign commerce and to regulate the issuance of securities by the parties included within this section, and securities issued by the licensee subject to such regulations shall be allowed only for the bona fide purpose of financing and conducting the business of such licensee.

The administration of the provisions of this section, so far as applicable, shall be according to the procedure and practice in fixing and regulating the rates, charges, and practices of railroad companies as provided in the Act to regulate commerce, approved February 4, 1887, as amended, and that the parties subject to such regulation shall have the same rights of hearing, defense, and review as said companies in such cases.

In any valuation of the property of any licensee hereunder for purposes of rate making, no value shall be claimed by the licensee or allowed by the commission for any project or projects under license in excess of the value or values prescribed in section 14 hereof for the purposes of purchase by the United States, but there shall be included the cost to such licensee of the construction of the lock or locks or other aids of navigation and all other capital expenditures required by the United States, and no value shall be claimed or allowed for the rights granted by the commission or by this Act.

Sec. 21. That when any licensee can not acquire by contract or pledges an unimproved dam site or the right to use or damage the lands or property of others necessary to the construction, maintenance, or operation of any dam, reservoir, diversion structure, or the works appurtenant or accessory thereto, in conjunction with an improvement which in the judgment of the commission is desirable and justified in the public interest for the purpose of improving or developing a waterway or waterways for the use or benefit of interstate or foreign commerce, it may acquire the same by the exercise of the right of eminent domain in the district court of the United States for the district in which such land or other property may be located, or in the State courts. The practice and procedure in any action or proceeding for that purpose in the district court of the United States shall conform as nearly as may be with the practice and procedure in similar action or proceeding in the courts of the State where the property is situated: *Provided,* That United States district courts shall only have jurisdiction of cases when the amount claimed by the owner of the property to be condemned exceeds $3,000.

Sec. 22. That whenever the public interest requires or justifies the execution by the licensee of contracts for the sale and delivery of power for periods extending beyond the date of termination of the license, such contracts may be entered into upon the joint approval of the commission and of the public-service commission or other similar authority in the State in which the sale or delivery of power is made, or if sold or delivered in a State which has no such public-service commission, then upon the approval of the commission, and thereafter, in the event of failure to issue a new license to the original licensee at the termination of the license, the United States or the new licensee, as the case may be, shall assume and fulfill all such contracts.

Sec. 23. That the provisions of this Act shall not be construed as affecting any permit or valid existing right of way heretofore granted, or as confirming or otherwise affecting any claim, or as affecting any authority heretofore given pursuant to law, but any person, association, corporation, State, or municipality, holding or possessing such permit, right of way, or authority may apply for a license hereunder, and upon such application the commission may issue to any such applicant a license in accordance with the provisions of this Act, and in such case the provisions of this Act shall apply to such applicant as a licensee hereunder: *Provided,* That when application is made for a license under this section for a project or projects already constructed, the fair value of said project or projects, determined as provided in this section, shall for the purposes of this Act and of said license be deemed to be the amount to be allowed as the net investment of the applicant in such project or projects as of the date of such license, or as of the date of such determination, if license has not been issued. Such fair value may, in the discretion of the commission, be determined by mutual agreement between the commission and the applicant or, in case they can not agree, jurisdiction is hereby conferred upon the district court of the United States in the district within which such project or projects may be located, upon the application of either party, to hear and determine the amount of such fair value.

That any person, association, corporation, State, or municipality intending to construct a dam or other project works across, along, over, or in any stream or part thereof, other than those defined herein as navigable waters, and over which Congress has jurisdiction under its authority to regulate commerce between foreign nations and among the several States, may in their discretion file declaration of such intention with the commission, whereupon the commission shall cause immediate investigation of such proposed construction to be made, and if upon investigation it shall find that the interests of interstate or foreign commerce would be affected by such proposed construction, such person, association, corporation, State, or municipality shall not proceed with such construction until it shall have applied for and shall have received a license under the provisions of this Act. If the commission shall not so find, and if no public lands or reservations are affected, permission is hereby granted to construct such dam or other project works in such stream upon compliance with State laws.

Sec. 24. That any lands of the United States included in any proposed project under the provisions of this Act shall from the date of filing of application therefor be reserved from entry, location, or other disposal under the laws of the United States until otherwise directed by the commission or by Congress. Notice that such application has been made, together with the date of filing thereof and a description of the lands of the United States affected thereby, shall be filed in the local land office for the district in which such lands are located. Whenever the commission shall determine that the value of any lands of the United States so applied for, or heretofore or hereafter reserved or classified as power sites, will not be injured or destroyed for the purposes of power development by location, entry, or selection under the public-land laws, the Secretary of the Interior, upon notice of such determination, shall declare such lands open to location, entry, or selection, subject to and with a reservation of the right of the United States or its permittees or licensees to enter upon, occupy, and use any part or all of said lands necessary, in the judgment of the commission, for the purposes of this Act, which right shall be expressly reserved in every patent issued for such lands; and no claim or right to compensation shall accrue from the occupation or use of any of said lands for said purposes. The United States or any licensee for any such lands hereunder may enter thereupon for the purposes of this Act, upon payment of any damages to crops, buildings, or other improvements caused thereby to the owner thereof, or upon giving a good and sufficient bond to the United States for the use and benefit of the owner to secure the payment of such damages as may be determined and fixed in an action brought upon the bond in a court of competent jurisdiction, said bond to be in the form prescribed by the commission: *Provided,* That locations, entries, selections, or filings heretofore made for lands reserved as water-power sites or in connection with water-power development or electrical transmission may proceed to approval or patent under and subject to the limitations and conditions in this section contained.

Sec. 25. That any licensee, or any person, who shall willfully fail or who shall refuse to comply with any of the provisions of this Act, or with any of the conditions made a part of any license issued hereunder, or with any subpoena of the commission, or with any regulation or lawful order of the commission, or of the Secretary of War, or of the Secretary of Commerce as to fishways, issued or made in accordance with the provisions of this Act, shall be deemed guilty of a misdemeanor, and on conviction thereof shall, in the discretion of the court, be punished by a fine of not exceeding $1,000, in addition to other penalties herein prescribed or provided by law; and every month any such license or any such person shall remain in default after written notice from the commission, or from the Secretary of War, or from the Secretary of Commerce, shall be deemed a new and separate offense punishable as aforesaid.

Sec. 26. That the Attorney General may, on request of the commission or of the Secretary of War, institute proceedings in equity in the district court of the United States in the district in which any project or part thereof is situated for the purpose of revoking for violation of its terms any permit or license issued hereunder, or for the purpose of remedying or correcting by injunction, mandamus, or other process any act of commission or omission in violation of the provisions of this Act or of any lawful regulation or order promulgated hereunder. The district courts shall have jurisdiction over all of the above-mentioned proceedings and shall have power to issue and execute all necessary process and to make and enforce all writs, orders, and decrees to compel compliance with the lawful orders and regulations of the commission and of the Secretary of War, and to compel the performance of any condition imposed under the provisions of this Act. In the event a decree revoking a license is entered, the court is empowered to sell the whole or any part of the project or projects under license, to wind up the business of such licensee conducted in connection with such project or projects, to distribute the proceeds to the parties entitled to the same, and to make and enforce such further orders and decrees as equity and justice may require. At such sale or sales the vendee shall take the rights and privileges belonging to the licensee and shall perform the duties of such licensee and assume all outstanding obligations and liabilities of the licensee which the court may deem equitable in the premises; and at such sale or sales the United States may become a purchaser, but it shall not be required to pay a greater amount than it would be required to pay under the provisions of section 14 hereof at the termination of the license.

Sec. 27. That nothing herein contained shall be construed as affecting or intending to affect or in any way to interfere with the laws of the respective States relating to the control, appropriation, use, or distribution of water used in irrigation or for municipal or other uses, or any vested right acquired therein.

Sec. 28. That the right to alter, amend, or repeal this Act is hereby expressly reserved; but no such alteration, amendment, or repeal shall affect any license theretofore issued under the provisions of this Act, or the rights of any licensee thereunder.

Sec. 29. That all Acts or parts of Acts inconsistent with this Act are hereby repealed: *Provided,* That nothing herein contained shall be held or construed to modify or repeal any of the provisions of the Act of Congress approved December 19, 1913, granting certain rights of way to the city and county of San Francisco, in the State of California: *Provided further,* That section 18 of an Act making appropriations for the construction, repair, and preservation of certain public works on rivers and harbors, and for other purposes, approved August 8, 1917, is hereby repealed.

Sec. 30. That the short title of this Act shall be "The Federal Water Power Act."

Source:

Statutes at Large, Vol. 41, pp. 1,063–1,077.

Bailey v. Drexel Furniture Company, 1922

U.S. Supreme Court ruling issued on May 15, 1922, that invalidated the U.S. Child Labor Act of 1919. This section of the general federal taxation bill enacted on February 24, 1919, was designed to control child labor by assessing an excise tax of 10 percent on the net profits of mines that employed children under the age of 16, factories that employed children under the age of 14, or that allowed children between 14 and 16 to work more than eight hours a day or six days a week or after 7:00 P.M. or before 6:00 A.M. (In 1900, about 17 percent of all children between 10 and 15 worked full time.)

Chief Justice William Howard Taft, writing for the majority, argued that the tax was intended not to raise revenue but to regulate the employment of children, a right that was reserved to the states by the Tenth Amendment. He stated that the act imposed a penalty, not a true excise tax, and therefore violated constitutional limitations on congressional power. This case demonstrates the reaction to Progressive Era legislation that characterized the 1920s. Previously, the Court had overturned an anti–child labor act based on the interstate commerce clause. In *Hammer v. Dagenhart* (247 U.S. 251), issued on June 3, 1918, the 5-4 majority invalidated the Keating-Owen Act, which forbade interstate shipment of products of child labor. In its 5-4 decision, the Supreme Court ruled that the statute was an unwarranted infringement on state power, "repugnant to the Constitution," an attempt to extend federal authority over a "purely local matter." In dissent, Justice Oliver Wendell Holmes deplored the "evil of premature and excessive child labor," upheld the federal right to regulate interstate commerce, and noted that the states lacked the power to control child labor.

The Court vindicated Holmes in 1937 by overturning *Hammer* in *United States v. Darby Lumber Company.*

Mr. Chief Justice Taft delivered the opinion of the Court.

This case presents the question of the constitutional validity of the Child Labor Tax Law. The plaintiff below, the Drexel Furniture Company, is engaged in the manufacture of furniture in the Western district of North Carolina. On September 20, 1921, it received a notice from Bailey, United States collector of internal revenue for the district, that it had been assessed $6,312.79 for having during the taxable year 1919 employed and permitted to work in its factory a boy under 14 years of age, thus incurring the tax of 10 per cent, on its net profits for that year. The company paid the tax under protest, and, after rejection of its claim for a refund, brought this suit. On demurrer to an amended complaint, judgment was entered for the company against the collector for the full amount, with interest. The writ of error is prosecuted by the collector direct from the District Court under section 238 of the Judicial Code (Comp. St. Section 1215).

The Child Labor Tax Law is title No. XII of an act entitled "An act to provide revenue and for other purposes," approved February 24, 1919, 40 Stat. 1057, 1138 (Comp. St. Ann. Supp. 1919, Sections 6336 7/8a to 6336 7/8h). The heading of the title is "Tax on Employment of Child Labor." It begins with section 1200 and includes eight sections. Section 1200 is as follows:

"Sec. 1200. That every person (other than a bona fide boys' or girls' canning club recognized by the agricultural department of a state and of the United States) operating (a) any mine or quarry situated in the United States in which children under the age of sixteen years have been employed or permitted to work during any portion of the taxable year; or (b) any mill, cannery, workshop, factory, or manufacturing establishment situated in the United States in which children under the age of fourteen years have been employed or permitted to work, or children between the ages of fourteen and sixteen have been employed or permitted to work more than eight hours in any day or more than six days in any week, or after the hour of seven o'clock post meridian, or before the hour of six o'clock ante meridian, during any portion of the taxable year, shall pay for each taxable year, in addition to all other taxes imposed by law, an excise tax equivalent to 10 per centum of the entire net profits received or accrued for such year from the sale or disposition of the product of such mine, quarry, mill, cannery, workshop, factory, or manufacturing establishment."

Section 1203 relieves from liability to the tax any one who employs a child, believing him to be of proper age relying on a certificate to this effect issued by persons prescribed by a board consisting of the Secretary of the Treasury, the Commissioner of Internal Revenue, and the Secretary of Labor, or issued by state authorities. The section also provides in paragraph (b) that—

"The tax imposed by this title shall not be imposed in the case of any person who proves to the satisfaction of the Secretary that the only employment or permission to work which but for this section would subject him to the tax, has been of a child employed or permitted to work under a mistake of fact as to the age of such child and without intention to evade the tax."

Section 1206 gives authority to the Commissioner of Internal Revenue, or any other person authorized by him "to enter and inspect at any time any mine, quarry, mill, cannery, workshop, factory or manufacturing establishment." The Secretary of Labor, or any person whom he authorizes, is given like authority in order to comply with a request of the Commissioner to make such inspection and report the same. Any person who refuses entry or obstructs inspection is made subject to fine or imprisonment or both.

[1] The law is attacked on the ground that it is a regulation of the employment of child labor in the states—an exclusively state function under the federal Constitution and within the reservations of the Tenth Amendment. It is defended on the ground that it is a mere excise tax levied by the Congress of the United States under its broad power of taxation conferred by section 8, article 1, of the federal Constitution. We must construe the law and interpret the intent and meaning of Congress from the language of the act. The words are to be given their ordinary meaning unless the context shows that they are differently used. Does this law impose a tax with only that incidental restraint and regulation which a tax must inevitably involve? Or does it regulate by the use of the so-called tax as a penalty? If a tax, it is clearly an excise. If it were an excise on a commodity or other thing of value, we might not be permitted under previous decisions of this court to infer solely from its heavy burden that the act intends a prohibition instead of a tax. But this act is more. It provides a heavy exaction for a departure from a detailed and specified course of conduct in business. That course of business is that employers shall employ in mines and quarries, children of an age greater than 16 years; in mills and factories, children or an age greater than 14 years, and shall prevent children of less than 16 years in mills and factories from working more than 8 hours a day or 6 days in the week. If an employer departs from this prescribed course of business, he is to pay to the government one-tenth of his entire net income in the business for a full year. The amount is not to be proportioned in any degree to the extent or frequency of the departures, but is to be paid by the employer in full measure whether he employs 500 children for a year, or employs only one for a day. Moreover, if he does not know the child is within the named age limit, he is not to pay; that is to say, it is only where he knowingly departs from the prescribed course that payment is to be exacted. Scienters are associated with penalties, not with taxes. The employer's factory is to be subject to inspection at any time not only by the taxing officers of the Treasury, the Department normally charged with the collection of taxes, but also by the Secretary of Labor and his subordinates, whose normal function is the advancement and protection of the welfare of the workers. In the light of these features of the act, a court must be blind not to see that the so-called tax is imposed to stop the employment of children within the age limits prescribed. Its prohibitory and regulatory effect and purpose are palpable. All others can see and understand this. How can we properly shut our minds to it?

It is the high duty and function of this court in cases regularly brought to its bar to decline to recognize or enforce seeming laws of Congress, dealing with subjects not intrusted to Congress, but left or committed by the supreme law of the land to the control of the states. We cannot avoid the duty, even though it require us to refuse to give effect to legislation designed to promote the highest good. The good sought in unconstitutional legislation is an insidious feature, because it leads citizens and legislators of good purpose to promote it, without thought of the serious breach it will make in the ark of our covenant, or the harm which will come from breaking down recognized standards. In the maintenance of local self-government, on the one hand, and the national power, on the other, our country has been able to endure and prosper for near a century and a half.

[2] Out of proper respect for the acts of a co-ordinate branch of the government, this court has gone far to sustain taxing acts as such, even though there has been ground for suspecting, from the weight of the tax, it was intended to destroy its subject. But in the act before us the presumption of validity cannot prevail, because the proof of the contrary is found on the very face of its provisions. Grant the validity of this law, and all that Congress would need to do, hereafter, in seeking to take over to its control any one of the great number of subjects of public interest, jurisdiction of which the states have never parted with, and which are reserved to them by the Tenth Amendment, would be to enact a detailed measure of complete regulation of the subject and enforce it by a so-called tax upon departures from it. To give such magic to the word "tax" would be to break down all constitutional limitation of the powers of Congress and completely wipe out the sovereignty of the states.

The difference between a tax and a penalty is sometimes difficult to define, and yet the consequences of the distinction in the required method of their collection often are important. Where the sovereign enacting the law has power to impose both tax and penalty, the difference between revenue production and mere regulation may be immaterial, but not so when one sovereign can impose a tax only, and the power of regulation rests in another. Taxes are occasionally imposed in the discretion of the Legislature on proper subjects within the primary motive of obtaining revenue from them and with the incidental motive of discouraging them by making their continuance onerous. They do not lose their character as taxes because of the incidental motive. But there comes a time in the extension of the penalizing features of the so-called tax when it loses its character as such and becomes a mere penalty; with the characteristics of regulation and punishment. Such is the case in the law before us. Although Congress does not invalidate the contract of employment or expressly declare that the employment within the mentioned ages is illegal, it does exhibit its intent practically to achieve the latter result by adopting the criteria of wrongdoing and imposing its principal consequence on those who transgress its standard.

The case before us cannot be distinguished from that of *Hammer v. Dagenhart,* 247 U.S. 251, 38 Sup. Ct. 529, 62 L. Ed. 1101, 3 A. L. R. A. 649, Ann, Cas. 1918 E, 724. Congress there enacted a law to prohibit transportation in interstate commerce of goods made at a factory in which there was employment of children within the same ages and for the same number of hours a day and days in a week as are penalized by the act in this case. This court held the law in that case to be void. It said:

"In our view the necessary effect of this act is, by means of a prohibition against the movement in interstate commerce of ordinary commercial commodities, to regulate the hours of labor of children in factories and mines within the states, a purely state authority."

In the case at the bar, Congress in the name of a tax which on the face of the act is a penalty seeks to do the same thing, and the effort must be equally futile.

The analogy of the Dagenhart Case is clear. The congressional power over interstate commerce is, within its proper scope, just as complete and unlimited as the congressional power to tax, and the legislative motive in its exercise is just as free from judicial suspicion and inquiry. Yet when Congress threatened to stop interstate commerce in ordinary and necessary commodities, unobjectionable as subjects of transportation, and to deny the same to the people of a state in order to coerce them into compliance with Congress' regulation of state concerns, the court said this was not in fact regulation of interstate commerce, but rather that of state concerns and was invalid. So here the so-called tax is a penalty to coerce people of a state to act as Congress wishes them to act in respect of a matter completely the business of the state government under the federal Constitution. This case requires as did the Department Case the application of the principle announced by Chief Justice Marshall in *McCulloch v. Maryland,* 4 Wheat. 316, 423 (4 L. Ed. 579), in a much-quoted passage:

"Should Congress, in the execution of its powers, adopt measures which are prohibited by the Constitution; or should Congress, under the pretext of executing its powers, pass laws for the accomplishment of objects not intrusted to the government; it would become the painful duty of this tribunal, should a case requiring such a decision come before it, to say that such an act was not the law of the land."

But it is pressed upon us that this court has gone so far in sustaining taxing measures the effect and tendency of which was to accomplish purposes not directly within congressional power that we are bound by authority to maintain this law.

The first of these is *Veazie Bank v. Fenno,* 8 Wall. 533, 19 L. Ed. 482. In that case, the validity of a law which increased a tax on the circulating notes of persons and state banks from one per centum to 10 per centum was in question. The main question was whether this was a direct tax to be apportioned among the several states "according to their respective numbers." This was answered in the negative. The second objection was stated by the court:

"It is insisted, however, that the tax in the case before us is excessive, and so excessive as to indicate a purpose on the part of Congress to destroy the franchise of the bank, and is, therefore, beyond the constitutional power of Congress." To this the court answered:

"The first answer to this is that the judicial cannot prescribe to the legislative departments to the environment limitations upon the exercise of its acknowledged powers. The power to tax may be exercised oppressively upon persons, but the responsibility of the Legislature is not to the courts, but to the people by whom its members are elected. So if a particular tax bears heavily upon a corporation, or a class of corporations, it cannot, for that reason only, be pronounced contrary to the Constitution."

It will be observed that the sole objection to the tax here was its excessive character. Nothing else appeared on the face of the act. It was an increase of a tax admittedly legal to a higher rate and that was all. There were no elaborate specifications on the face of the act, as here, indicating the purpose to regulate matters of state concern and jurisdiction through an exaction so applied as to give it the qualities of a penalty for violation of law rather than a tax.

It should be noted, too, that the court, speaking of the extent of the taxing power, used these cautionary words (8 Wall. 541, 19 L. Ed. 482):

"There are, indeed, certain virtual limitations, arising from the principles of the Constitution itself. It would undoubtedly be an abuse of the power if so exercised as to impair the separate existence and independent self-government of the states, or if exercised for ends inconsistent with the limited grants of power in the Constitution."

But more than this, what charged to be the object of the excessive tax was within the congressional authority, as appears from the second answer which the court gave to the objection. After having pointed out the legitimate means taken by Congress to secure a national medium or currency, the court said (8 Wall. 549, 19 L. Ed. 482):

"Having thus, in the exercise of undisputed constitutional powers, undertaken to provide a currency for the whole country, it cannot be questioned that Congress may, constitutionally, secure the benefit of it to the people by appropriate legislation. To this end, Congress has denied the quality of legal tender to foreign coins, and has provided by law against the imposition of counterfeit and base coin on the community. To the same end, Congress may restrain, by suitable enactments, the circulation as money of any notes not issued under its own authority. Without this power, indeed, its attempts to secure a sound and uniform currency for the country must be futile."

The next case is that of *McCray v. United States,* 195 U.S. 27, 24 Sup. Ct. 769, 49 L. Ed. 78, 1 Ann. Cas. 561. That, like the Veazie Bank Case, was the increase of an excise tax upon a subject properly taxable in which the taxpayers claimed that the tax had become invalid because the increase was excessive. It was a tax on oleomargarine, a substitute for butter. The tax on the white Oleomargarine was one-quarter of a cent a pound, and on the yellow oleomargarine was first 2 cents and was then by the act in question increased to 10 cents per pound. This court held that the discretion of Congress in the exercise of its constitutional powers to levy excise taxes could not be controlled or limited by the courts because the latter might deem the incidence of the tax oppressive or even destructive. It was the same principle as that applied in the Veazie Bank Case. This was that Congress, in selecting its subjects for taxation, might impose the burden where and as it would, and that a motive disclosed in its selection to discourage sale or manufacture of an article by a higher tax than on some other did not invalidate the tax. In neither of these cases did the law objected to show on its face as does the law before us the detailed specifications of a regulation of a state concern and business with a heavy exaction to promote the efficacy of such regulation.

The third case is that of *Flint v. Stone Tracy Co.*, 220 U.S. 107, 31 Sup. Ct. 342, 55 L. Ed. 389, Ann. Cas. 1912B, 1312. It involved the validity of an excise tax levied on the doing of business by all corporations, joint-stock companies, associations organized for profit having a capital stock represented by shares, and insurance companies, and measured the excise by the net income of the corporations. There was not in that case the slightest doubt that the tax was a tax, and a tax for revenue, but it was attacked on the ground that such a tax could be made excessive and thus used by Congress to destroy the existence of state corporations. To this, this court gave the same answer as in the Veazie Bank and McCray Cases. It is not so strong an authority for the government's contention as they are.

The fourth case is *United States v. Doremus*, 249 U.S. 86, 39 Sup. Ct. 214, 63 L. Ed. 493. Thus involved the validity of the Narcotic Drug Act (38 Stat. 785 [Comp. St. Section 6287g et seq.]), which imposed a special tax on the manufacture, importation and sale or gift of opium or cocoa leaves or their compounds or derivatives. It required every person subject to the special tax, to register with the collector of internal revenue his name and place of business and forbade him to sell except upon the written order of the person to whom the sale was made on a form prescribed by the Commissioner of Internal Revenue. The vendor was required to keep the order for two years, and the purchaser to keep a duplicate for the same time and all were to be subject to official inspection. Similar requirements were made as to sales upon prescriptions of a physician and as to the dispensing of such drugs directly to a patient by a physician. The validity of a special tax in the nature of an excise tax on the manufacture, importation, and sale of such drugs was, of course, unquestioned. The provisions for subjecting the sale and distribution of the drugs to official supervision and inspection were held to have a reasonable relation to the enforcement of the tax and were therefore held valid.

The court said that the act could not be declared invalid just because another motive than taxation, not shown on the face of the act, might have contributed to its passage. This case does not militate against the conclusion we have reached in respect to the law now before us. The court, there, made manifest its view that the provisions of the so-called taxing act must be naturally and reasonably adapted to the collection of the tax and not solely to the achievement of some other purpose plainly within state power.

For the reasons given, we must hold the Child Labor Tax invalid and the judgment of the District Court is Affirmed.

Source:

Supreme Court Reporter, Vol. 42. pp. 449–459.

Fordney-McCumber Act, 1922

Federal U.S. legislation, also known as the Tariff Act of 1922, enacted on September 21, 1922, that established high tariff rates to protect farmers and infant industries. It set high duties on grains, meats, sugar, wool, and other farm products and raised rates on textiles, dyes, ferro alloys, china, and other manufactured goods. Sponsored by Representative Joseph W. Fordney of Indiana and Senator Porter J. McCumber of North Dakota, the act also made the tariff flexible, giving the U.S. president the power to raise or lower rates by 50 percent in order to equalize American and foreign costs of production.

Prior to World War I, Congress passed two other major tariff acts. The Payne-Aldrich Tariff Act, enacted by Congress on August 5, 1909, reduced overall rates from the high levels of the Dingley Tariff to about 38 percent but raised the levies on coal and iron ore. The act, a compromise between protectionism and the 1908 Republican Party platform promise to lower tariffs, was cosponsored by Senator Nelson W. Aldrich of Rhode Island and Representative Sereno Elisha Payne of New York. It left more than 1,000 tariff schedules unchanged, lowered 650, and raised 220. Its largely protectionist features became a major political issue, resulting in Republican defeat in the election of 1910.

Representative Oscar W. Underwood of Alabama and Senator Furnifold M. Simmons of North Carolina sponsored a tariff bearing their names that passed October 3, 1913. It lowered the average tariff duties from about 40 percent of the value of an imported item to 26 percent. The act also put iron, steel, and raw wool on the free list (sugar was added to the free list in 1916) and imposed the first income tax under the Sixteenth Amendment. Succeeding the Payne-Aldrich Tariff was the Underwood-Simmons Act, called a "competitive tariff" supported by the Democratic Party. Its benefits, however, were swamped by the economic effects of World War I.

The Fordney-McCumber tariff was succeeded by the Smoot-Hawley Tariff Act, which was signed June 17, 1930, by President Herbert Hoover near the beginning of the Great Depression. It raised import duties to the highest level in U.S. history. Sponsored by Republican senator Reed Smoot of Utah and Republican representative Willis C. Hawley of Oregon, this protective tariff represented a congressional compromise, raising rates on both agricultural products, as favored by the Senate, and manufactured goods, as supported by the House of Representatives. Foreign nations passed retaliatory legislation, which damaged U.S. foreign trade and worsened the worldwide depression.

An Act

To provide revenue, to regulate commerce with foreign countries, to encourage the industries of the United States, and for other purposes.

Be it enacted by the Senate and House of Representatives of the United States of America in Congress assembled,

Title I

Dutiable List.

Section 1. That on and after the day following the passage of this Act, except as otherwise specially provided for in this Act, there shall be levied, collected, and paid upon all articles when imported from any foreign country into the United States or into any of its possessions (except the Philippine Islands, the Virgin Islands, and the islands of Guam and Tutuila) the rates of duty which are prescribed by the schedules and paragraphs of the dutiable list of this title, namely:

[Schedule of items taxed follows.]

* * *

Sec. 588. Transportation between ports.—If any merchandise is laden at any port or place in the United States upon any vessel belonging wholly or in part to a subject of a foreign country, and is taken thence to a foreign port or place to be reladen and reshipped to any other port in the United States, either by the same or by another vessel, foreign or American, with intent to evade the provisions relating to the transportation of merchandise from one port or place of the United States to another port or place of the United States in a vessel belonging wholly or in part to a subject of any foreign power, the merchandise shall, on its arrival at such last-named port or place, be seized and forfeited to the United States, and the vessel shall pay a tonnage duty of 50 cents per net ton.

* * *

Sec. 591. Fraud—Penalty—Personal.—If any consignor, seller, owner, importer, consignee, agent, or other person or persons enters or introduces, or attempts to enter or introduce, into the commerce of the United States any imported merchandise by means of any fraudulent or false invoice, declaration, affidavit, letter, paper, or by means of any false statement, written or verbal, or by means of any false or fraudulent practice or appliance whatsoever, or makes any false statement in any declaration under the provisions of section 485 of this Act without reasonable cause to believe the truth of such statement, or aids or procures the making of any such false statement as to any matter material thereto without reasonable cause to believe the truth of such statement, or is guilty of any willful act or omission by means whereof the United States shall or may be deprived of the lawful duties, or any portion thereof, accruing upon the merchandise, or any portion thereof, embraced or referred to in such invoice, declaration, affidavit, letter, paper, or statement, or affected by such act or omission, such person or persons shall upon conviction be fined for each offense a sum not exceeding $5,000, or be imprisoned for a time not exceeding two years, or both, in the discretion of the court: Provided, That nothing in this section shall be construed to relieve imported merchandise from forfeiture by reason of such false statement or for any cause elsewhere provided by law.

Sec. 592. Same—Penalty against goods [Applies to same individuals and causes as Sec. 591] shall be subject to forfeiture, which forfeiture shall only apply to the whole of the merchandise or the value thereof in the case or package containing the particular article or articles of merchandise to which such fraud or false paper or statement relates. The arrival within the territorial limits of the United States of any merchandise consigned for sale and remaining the property of the shipper or consignor, and the acceptance of a false or fraudulent invoice thereof by the consignee or the agent of the consignor, or the existence of any other facts constituting an attempted fraud, shall be deemed, for the purposes of this paragraph, to be an attempt to enter such merchandise notwithstanding no actual entry has been made or offered.

Sec. 593. Smuggling and clandestine importations.—(a) If any person knowingly and willfully, with intent to defraud the revenue of the United States, smuggles, or clandestinely introduces, into the United States any merchandise which should have been invoiced, or makes out or passes, or attempts to pass, through the customhouse any false, forged, or fraudulent invoice, every such person, his, her, or their aiders an abettors, shall be deemed guilty of a misdemeanor, and on conviction thereof shall be fined in any sum not exceeding $5,000, or imprisoned for any term of time not exceeding two years, or both, at the discretion of the court.

(b) If any person fraudulently or knowingly imports or brings into the United States, or assists in so doing, any merchandise, contrary to law, or receives, conceals, buys, sells, or in any manner facilitates the transportation, concealment, or sale of such merchandise after importation, knowing the same to have been imported or brought into the United States contrary to law, such merchandise shall be forfeited and the offender shall be fined in any sum not exceeding $5,000 nor less than $50, or be imprisoned for any time not exceeding two years, or both. Whenever, on trial for a violation of this section, the defendant is shown to have or to have had possession of such goods, such possession shall be deemed evidence sufficient to authorize conviction, unless the defendant shall explain the possession to the satisfaction of the jury.

Sec. 594. Seizure of vessels and vehicles.—Whenever a vessel or vehicle, or the owner or master, conductor, driver, or other person in charge thereof, has become subject to a penalty for violation of the customs-revenue laws of the United States, such vessel or vehicle shall be held for the payment of such penalty and may be seized and proceeded against summarily by libel to recover the same: Provided, That no vessel or vehicle used by any person as a common carrier in the transaction of business as such common carrier shall be so held or subject to seizure or forfeiture under the customs laws, unless it shall appear that the owner or master of such vessel or the conductor, driver, or other person in charge of such vehicle was at the time of the alleged illegal act a consenting party or privy thereto.

Sec. 595. Warrant.—If any collector of customs or other officer or person authorized to make searches and seizures shall have cause to suspect the presence in any dwelling house, store, or other building or place of any merchandise upon which the duties have not been paid, or which has been otherwise brought into the United States contrary to law, he may make application, under oath, to any justice of the peace, to any municipal, county, State, or Federal judge, or to any United States commissioner, and shall thereupon be entitled to a warrant to enter such dwelling house in the daytime only, or such store or other place at night or by day, and to search for and seize such merchandise: Provided, That if any such house, store, or other building, or place in which such merchandise shall be found, is upon or within ten feet of the boundary line between the United States and a foreign country, such portion thereof as is within the United States may forthwith be taken down or removed.

Sec. 596. Buildings on boundary.—Any person who receives or deposits in such building upon the boundary line between the United States and any foreign country, or carries any merchandise through the same, or aids therein, in violation of law, shall be punishable by a fine of not more than $5,000, or by imprisonment for not more than two years, or both.

Sec. 597. Concealment.—If any merchandise is fraudulently concealed in, removed from, or repacked in any bonded warehouse, or if any marks or numbers placed upon packages deposited in such a warehouse be fraudulently altered, defaced, or obliterated, such merchandise and packages shall be subject to forfeiture, and all persons convicted of the fraudulent concealment, repacking, or removal of such merchandise, or of altering, defacing, or obliterating such marks and numbers thereon, and all persons aiding and abetting therein shall be liable to the same penalties as are imposed by section 593 of this Act.

Sec. 598. False seals.—If any unauthorized person affixes or attaches or in any way willfully assists or encourage the affixing or attaching of a customs seal or other fastening to any vessel or vehicle, or of any seal, fastening, or mark purporting to be a customs seal, fastening, or mark; or if any unauthorized person willfully or maliciously removes, breaks, injures, or defaces any customs seal or other fastening placed upon any vessel, vehicle, warehouse, or package containing merchandise or baggage in bond or in customs custody, or willfully aids, abets, or encourages any other person to remove, break, injure, or deface such seal, fastening, or mark; or if any person maliciously enters any bonded warehouse or any vessel or vehicle laden with or containing bonded merchandise with intent unlawfully to remove or cause to be removed therefrom any merchandise or baggage therein, or unlawfully removes or causes to be removed any merchandise or baggage in such vessel, vehicle, or bonded warehouse or otherwise in customs custody or control, or aids or assists therein; or if any person receives or transports any merchandise or baggage unlawfully removed from any such vessel, vehicle, or warehouse, knowing the same to have been unlawfully removed, he shall be guilty of a felony and liable to the same penalties as are imposed by section 593 of this Act.

Sec. 599. Interested officers.—No person employed under the authority of the United States, in the collection of duties on imports or tonnage, shall own, either in whole or in part, any vessel, or act as agent, attorney, or consignee for the owner or owners of any vessel, or of any cargo or lading on board the same; nor shall any such person import, or be concerned directly or indirectly in the importation, of any merchandise for sale into the United States. Every person who violates this section shall be liable to a penalty of $500.

Sec. 600. Gratuity.—Any officer or employee of the United States who, except in payment of the duties or exactions fixed by law, solicits, demands, exacts, or receives from any person, directly or indirectly, any gratuity, money, or thing of value, for any service performed under the customs laws, or in consideration of any official act to be performed by him, or of the omission of performance of any such act, in connection with or pertaining to the importation, entry, inspection or examination, or appraisement of merchandise or baggage, shall be guilty of a misdemeanor and on conviction thereof shall be punished by a fine not exceeding $5,000, or by imprisonment for not more than two years, or both, and evidence, satisfactory to the court in which the trial is had, of such soliciting, demanding, exacting, or receiving shall be prima facie evidence that the same was contrary to law.

Sec. 601. Bribery.—Any person who gives, or offers to give, or promises to give, any money or thing of value, directly or indirectly, to any officer or employee of the United States in consideration of or for any act or omission contrary to law in connection with or pertaining to the importation, appraisement, entry, examination, or inspection of merchandise or baggage, or of the liquidation of the entry thereof, or by threats or demands or promises of any character attempts to improperly influence or control any such officer or employee of the United States as to the performance of his official duties, shall be guilty of a misdemeanor and on conviction thereof shall be punished by a fine not exceeding $5,000 or by imprisonment for a term not exceeding two years, or both, and evidence of such giving, offering or promising to give, or attempting to influence or control, satisfactory to the court in which such trial is had, shall be prima facie evidence that the same was contrary to law.

Sec. 602. Seizure procedure—Report.—It shall be the duty of any officer, agent, or other person authorized by law to make seizures of merchandise or baggage subject to seizure for violation of the customs laws, to report every such seizure immediately to the collector for the district in which such violation occurred, and to turn over and deliver to such collector any vessel, vehicle, merchandise, or baggage seized by him, and to report immediately to such collector every violation of the customs laws.

* * *

Sec. 604. Same—Prosecution.—It shall be the duty of every United States district attorney immediately to inquire into the facts of cases reported to him by collectors and the laws applicable thereto, and, if it appears probable that any fine, penalty, or forfeiture has been incurred by reason of such violation, for the recovery of which the institution of proceedings in the united States district court is necessary, forthwith to cause the proper proceedings to be commenced and prosecuted, without delay, for the recovery of such fine, penalty, or forfeiture in such case provided, unless, upon inquiry and examination, such district attorney decides that such proceedings can not probably be sustained. . . .

* * *

Sec. 608. Same—Claims.—Any person claiming such vessel, vehicle, merchandise, or baggage may at any time within twenty days from the date of the first publication of the notice of seizure file with the collector a claim stating his interest therein. . . .

Sec. 609. Same—Sale.—If no such claims is filed or bond given within the twenty days herein before specified, the collector shall declare the vessel, vehicle, merchandise, or baggage forfeited, and shall sell the same at public auction in the same manner as merchandise abandoned to the United States is sold, and shall deposit the proceeds of sale, after deducting the actual expenses of seizure, publication and sale, in the Treasury of the United States.

* * *

Sec. 615. Burden of proof.—In all suits or actions brought for the forfeiture of any vessel, vehicle, merchandise, or baggage seized under the provisions of any law relating to the collection of duties on imports or tonnage, where the property is claimed by any person, the burden of proof shall lie upon such claimant; and in all suits or actions brought for the recovery of the value of any vessel, vehicle, merchandise or baggage seized for violation of any such law, the burden of proof shall be upon the defendant: Provided, That probable cause shall be first shown for the institution of such suit or action, to be judged of by the court.

* * *

Sec. 619. Award of compensation.—Any person not an officer of the United States who detects and seizes any vessel, vehicle merchandise, or baggage subject to seizure and forfeiture under the customs laws and who reports the same to an officer of the customs, or who furnishes to a district attorney, to the Secretary of the Treasury, or to any customs officer original information.

* * *

Sec. 622. Emergency of war.—Whenever the President shall by proclamation declare an emergency to exist by reason of a state of war, or otherwise, he may authorize the Secretary of the Treasury to extend during the continuance of such emergency the time herein prescribed for the performance of any act.

Sec. 623. General regulations.—In addition to the specific powers conferred by this Act, the Secretary of the Treasury is authorized to make such rules and regulations as may be necessary to carry out the provisions of this Act.

* * *

Sec. 647. This Act may be cited as the "Tariff Act of 1922."

Source:
Statutes at Large, Vol. 42, pp. 858–990.

Herbert Hoover, "Rugged Individualism" Speech, 1928

Speech delivered in New York City by Republican presidential candidate Herbert Hoover October 22, 1928, toward the close of the election campaign. The phrase *rugged individualism* entered American culture as a way to describe conservative economic philosophy. In this speech, Hoover condemned the Democratic platform as a misguided attempt to solve the problems of Prohibition, farm relief, and electrical power through state socialism; he extolled free, private enterprise and initiative—i.e., "rugged individualism"—as the foundation of America's "unparalleled greatness." Government entry into commercial business, he argued, would destroy political equality, increase corruption, stifle initiative, undermine the development of leadership, extinguish opportunity, and "dry up the spirit of liberty and progress."

This campaign now draws near to a close. The platforms of the two parties defining principles and offering solutions of various national problems have been presented and are being earnestly considered by our people.

After four months' debate it is not the Republican Party which finds reason for abandonment of any of the principles it has laid down or of the views it has expressed for solution of the problems before the country. The principles to which it adheres are rooted deeply in the foundations of our national life and the solutions which it proposed are based on experience with government and a consciousness that it may have the responsibility for placing those solutions into action.

In my acceptance speech I endeavored to outline the spirit and ideals with which I would propose to carry that platform into administration. Tonight, I will not deal with the multitude of issues which have been already well canvassed, I propose rather to discuss some of those more fundamental principles and ideals upon which I believe the Government of the United States should be conducted.

Before I enter upon that discussion of principles I wish to lay before you the proof of progress under Republican rule. In doing this I do not need to review its seventy years of constructive history. That history shows that the Republican party has ever been a party of progress. It has reflected the spirit of the American people. We are a progressive people. Our history of 150 years in the greatest epic of human progress. Tonight to demonstrate the constructive character of our Party, I need only briefly picture the advance of fundamental progress during the past seven and a half years since we took over the Government amidst the ruin of war.

First of all, let me deal with the material side. I do this because upon the well-being, comfort and security of the American home do we build up the moral and spiritual virtues as well as the finer flowers of civilization and the wider satisfactions of life.

As a nation we came out of the war with great losses. We made no profits from it. The apparent increases in wages were fictitious. We were poorer as a nation when we emerged from it. Yet during these last eight years we have recovered from these losses and increased our national income by over one-third even if we discount the inflation of the dollar. While some individuals have grown rich, yet that there has been a wide diffusion of our gain in wealth and income is marked by a hundred proofs. I know of no better test of the improved conditions of the average family than the combined increase of life and industrial insurance, building and loan assets, and savings deposits. These are the financial agents of the average man. These alone have in seven years increased by nearly 100 per cent to the gigantic sum of over 50 billions of dollars, or nearly one-six of our whole national wealth. In addition to these evidences of larger savings our people are steadily increasing their spending for higher standards of living. Today there are almost 9 automobiles for each 10 families, where seven and a half years ago only enough automobiles were running to average less than 4 for each 10 families. The slogan of progress is changing from the full dinner pail to the full garage. Our people have more to eat, better things to wear, and better homes. We have even gained in elbow room in our homes, for the increase of residential floor space is over 25 per cent with less than 10 per cent increase in our number of people. We have increased the security of his job to every man and woman. We have decreased the fear of old age, the fear of poverty, the fear of unemployment and these are fears which have always been amongst the greatest calamities of human kind.

All this progress means far more than greater creature comforts. It finds a thousand interpretations into a greater and fuller life. In all this we have steadily reduced the sweat in human labor. A score of new helps save the drudgery of the home. In seven years we have added 25 per cent more electric power to the elbow of every worker, and farther promoted him from a carrier of burdens to a director of machines. Our hours of labor are lessened; our leisure has increased. We have expanded our parks and playgrounds. We have nearly doubled our attendance at games. We pour into outdoor recreation in every direction. The visitors at our national parks have trebled and we have so increased the number of sportsmen fishing in our streams and lakes that the longer time between bites is becoming a political issue. In these seven and one- half years the radio has brought music and laughter, education and political discussion to almost every fireside.

Springing from our prosperity with its greater freedom, its vast endowment of scientific research and the greater resources with which to care for public health, we have according to our insurance actuaries during this short period since the war lengthened the span of life by nearly eight years. We have reduced infant mortality, we have vastly decreased the days of illness and suffering in the life of every man and woman. We have improved the facilities for the care of the crippled and helpless and deranged.

From our increasing resources we have expanded our educational system in eight years from an outlay of 1,200 millions to 2,700 millions of dollars. The education of our youth has become almost the largest and certainly our most important activity. From our ability to free youth from toil we have increased the attendance in our grade schools by 14 per cent, in our high schools by 80 per cent, and in institutions of higher learning by 95 per cent. Today we have more youth in these institutions of higher learning twice over than all the rest of the world put together. We have made progress in literature, art and in public taste.

I do not need to recite more figures and more evidence. There is not a person within the sound of my voice that does not know the profound progress which our country has made in this period. Every man and woman knows that their comfort, their hopes and their confidence for the future are higher this day than they were seven and one-half years ago.

Your city has been an outstanding beneficiary of this great progress. With its suburbs it has, during the last seven and a half years grown by over a million and a half of people, until it has become the largest metropolitan district of all the world. Here you have made abundant opportunity not only for the youth of the land but for the immigrant from foreign shores. This city is the commercial center of the United States. It is the commercial agent of the American people. It is a great organism of specialized skill and leadership in finance, industry and commerce, which reaches every spot in our country. Its progress and its beauty are the pride of the whole American people. It leads our nation in the largest size of its benevolences, in art, in music, literature and drama. It has come to have a greater voice, than any other city in the United States.

But when all is said and done the very life, progress and prosperity of this city is wholly dependent on the prosperity of the 110,000,000 people who dwell in our mountains and valleys across the 3,000 miles to the Pacific Ocean. Every activity of this city is sensitive to every evil and every favorable tide that sweeps this great nation of ours. Be there a slackening of industry in any part of the country it affects New York far more than the rest of the country. In a time of depression one-quarter of all the unemployed in the United States can be numbered in this city. In a time of prosperity the citizens of the great interior of our country pour into your city for business and entertainment at the rate of 200,000 a day. In fact so much is this city the reflex of the varied interests of our country that the concern of every one of your citizens for national stability, for national prosperity and for national progress is far greater than any other single part of our country.

Contributions to Progress

It detracts nothing from the character and energy of the American people, it minimizes in no degree the quality of their accomplishments to say that the policies of the Republican Party have played a large part in the building of this progress of these last seven and one-half years. I can say with emphasis that without the wise policies which the Republican Party has brought into action in this period, no such progress would have been possible.

The first responsibility of the Republican Administration was to renew the march of progress from its collapse by the war. That task involved the restoration of confidence in the future and the liberation and stimulation of the constructive energies of our people. It is not my purpose to enter upon a detailed recitation of the history of the great constructive measures of the past seven and a half years.

It is sufficient to remind you of the restoration of employment to the millions who walked your streets in idleness to remind you of the creation of the budget system; the reduction of six billions of national debt which gave the impulse of that vast sum returned to industry and commerce; the four sequent reductions of taxes and thereby the lift to the living of every family; the enactment of an adequate protective tariff and immigration laws which have raised and safeguarded our wages from floods of goods or labor from foreign countries; the creation of credit facilities and many aids to agriculture; the building up of foreign trade; the care of veterans, the development of aviation, of radio, of our inland waterways, our highways; the expansion of scientific research, of welfare activities, safer highways, safer mines, outdoor recreation, in better homes, in public health and the care of children. Nor do I need remind you that Government today deals with an economic and social system vastly more intricate and delicately adjusted than ever before. It now must be kept in perfect tune if we would not, through dislocation, have a breakdown in employment and in standards of living of our people. The Government has come to more and more touch this delicate web at a thousand points. Yearly the relations of Government to national prosperity becomes more and more intimate. It has only by keen large vision and cooperation by the Government that stability in business and stability in employment has been maintained during this past seven and a half years. Never has there been a period when the Federal Government has given such aid and impulse to the progress of our people, not alone to economic progress but to development of those agencies which make for moral and spiritual progress.

But in addition to this great record of contributions of the Republican Party to progress, there has been a further fundamental contribution—a contribution perhaps more important than all the others—and that is the resistance of the Republican Party to every attempt to inject the Government into business in competition with its citizens.

After the war, when the Republican Party assumed administration of the country, we were faced with the problem of determination of the very nature of our national life. Over 150 years we have builded up a form of self-government and we had builded up a social system which is peculiarly our own. It differs fundamentally from all others in the world. It is the American system. It is just as definite and positive a political and social system as has ever been developed on earth. It is founded upon the conception that self-government can be preserved only by decentralization of Government in the State and by fixing local responsibility; but further than this, it is founded upon the social conception that only through ordered liberty, freedom and equal opportunity to the individual will his initiative and enterprise drive the march of progress.

During the war we necessarily turned to the Government to solve every difficult economic problem—the Government having absorbed every energy of our people to war there was no other solution. For the preservation of the State the Government became a centralized despotism which undertook responsibilities, assumed powers, exercised rights, and took over the business of citizens. To large degree we regimented our whole people temporarily into a socialistic state. However justified it was in time of war if continued in peace time it would destroy not only our system but progress and freedom in our own country and throughout the world. When the war closed the most vital of all issues was whether Governments should continue war ownership and operation of many instrumentalities of production and distribution. We were challenged with the choice of the American system rugged individualism or the choice of a European system of diametrically opposed doctrines—doctrines of paternalism and state socialism. The acceptance of these ideas meant the destruction of self-government through centralization of government; it meant the undermining of initiative and enterprise upon which our people have grown to unparalleled greatness.

The Democratic administration cooperated with the Republican Party to demobilize many of her activities and the Republican Party from the beginning of its period of power resolutely turned its face away from these ideas and these war practices, back to our fundamental conception of the state and the rights and responsibilities of the individual. Thereby it restored confidence and hope in the American people, it freed and stimulated enterprise, it restored the Government to its position as an umpire instead of a player in the economic game. For these reasons the American people have gone forward in progress while the rest of the world is halting and some countries have even gone backwards. If anyone will study the causes which retarded recuperation of Europe, he will find much of it due to the stifling of private initiative on one hand, and overloading of the Government with business on the other.

I regret, however, to say that there has been revived in this campaign a proposal which would be a long step to the abandonment of our American system, to turn to the idea of government in business. Because we are faced with difficulty and doubt over certain national problems which we are faced—that is prohibition, farm relief and electrical power—our opponents propose that we must to some degree thrust government into these businesses and in effect adopt state socialism as a solution.

There is, therefore submitted to the American people the question—Shall we depart from the American system and start upon a new road. And I wish to emphasize this question on this occasion. I wish to make clear my position on the principles involved for they go to the very roots of American life in every act of our Government. I should like to state to you the effect of the extension of government into business upon our system of self government and our economic system. But even more important is the effect upon the average man. That is the effect on the very basis of liberty and freedom not only to those left outside the fold of expanded bureaucracy but to those embraced within it.

When the Federal Government undertakes a business, the state governments are at once deprived of control and taxation of that business; when the state government undertakes a business it at once deprived the municipalities of taxation and control of that business. Business requires centralization; self government requires decentralization. Our government to succeed in business must become in effect a despotism. There is thus at once an insidious destruction of self government.

Moreover there is a limit to human capacity in administration. Particularly is there a limit to the capacity of legislative bodies to supervise governmental activities. Every time the Federal Government goes into business 530 Senators and Congressmen become the Board of Directors of that business. Every time a state government goes into business 100 or 200 state senators and assemblymen become directors of that business. Even if they were supermen, no bodies of such numbers can competently direct that type of human activities which requires instant decision and action. No such body can deal adequately with all sections of the country. And yet if we would preserve government by the people we must preserve the authority of our legislators over the activities of our Government. We have trouble enough with log rolling in legislative bodies today. It originates naturally from desires of citizens to advance their particular section or to secure some necessary service. It would be multiplied a thousandfold were the Federal and state governments in these businesses.

The effect upon our economic progress would be even worse. Business progressiveness is dependent on competition. New methods and new ideas are the outgrowth of the spirit of adventure of individual initiative and of individual enterprise. Without adventure there is no progress. No government administration can rightly speculate and take risks with taxpayers' money. But even more important than this—leadership in business must be through the sheer rise of ability and character. That rise can take place only in the free atmosphere of competition. Competition is closed by bureaucracy. Certainly political choice is a feeble basis for choice of leaders to conduct a business.

There is no better example of the practical incompetence of government to conduct business than the history of our railways. Our railways in the year before being freed from Government operation were not able to meet the demands for transportation. Eight years later we find our them under private enterprise, transporting 15 per cent more goods and meeting every demand for service. Rates have been reduced by 15 per cent and net earnings increased from less than 1 per cent on their valuation to about 5 per cent. Wages of employees have improved by 13 per cent. The wages of railway employees are 2 per cent above pre-war. The wages of Government employees are today . . . will check their figure definitely tomorrow but probably about 70% per cent above pre-war. That should be a sufficient sermon upon the efficiency of Government operation.

But we can examine this question from the point of view of the person who gets a Government job and is admitted into the new bureaucracy. Upon that subject let me quote from a speech of that great leader of labor, Samuel Gompers, delivered in Montreal in 1920, a few years before his death. He said:

"I believe there is no man to whom I would take second position in my loyalty to the Republic of the United States, and yet I would not give it more power over the individual citizenship of our country. . . .

"It is a question of whether it shall be Government ownership or private ownership under control. . . . If I were in the minority of one in this convention, I would want to cast my vote so that the men of labor shall not willingly enslave themselves to Government authority in their industrial effort for freedom. . . .

"Let the future tell the story of who is right or who is wrong; who has stood for freedom and who has been willing to submit their fate industrially to the Government."

I would amplify Mr. Gompers' statement. These great bodies of Government employees would either comprise political machines at the disposal of the party in power, or alternatively to prevent this the Government by stringent civil-service rules must debar its employees from their full rights as free men. If it would keep employees out of politics, its rules must strip them of all right to expression of opinion. It is easy to conceive that they might become so large a body as by their votes to dictate to the Government and their political rights need be further reduced. It must strip them of the liberty to bargain for their own wages, for no Government employee can strike against his Government and thus the whole people. It makes a legislative body with all its political currents their final employer. That bargaining does not rest upon economic need or economic strength but on political potency.

But what of those who are outside the bureaucracy? What is the effect upon their lives of the Government on business and these hundreds of thousands more officials?

At once their opportunities in life are limited because a large area of activities are removed from their participation. Further the Government does not tolerate amongst its customers the freedom of competitive reprisals to which private corporations are subject. Bureaucracy does not spread the spirit of independence; it spreads the spirit of submission into our daily life, penetrates the temper of our people; not with the habit of powerful resistance to wrong, but with the habit of timid acceptance of the irresistible might.

Bureaucracy is ever desirous of spreading its influence and its power. You cannot give to a government the mastery of the daily working life of a people without at the same time giving it mastery of the peoples' souls and thoughts. Every expansion of government means that government in order to protect itself from political consequences of its errors and wrongs is driven onward and onward without peace to greater and greater control of the country's press and platform. Free speech does not live many hours after free industry and free commerce die.

It is false liberalism that interprets itself into the Government operation of business. The bureaucratization of our country would poison the very roots of liberalism that is free speech, free assembly, free press, political equality and equality of opportunity. It is the road, not to more liberty, but to less liberty. Liberalism should be found not striving to spread bureaucracy, but striving to set bounds to it. True liberalism seeks freedom first in the confident belief that without freedom the pursuit of all other blessings and benefits is vain. That belief is the foundation of all American progress, political as well as economic.

Liberalism is a force truly of the spirit, a force proceeding from the deep realization that economic freedom cannot be sacrificed if political freedom is to be preserved. Even if governmental conduct of business could give us more efficiency instead of giving us decreased efficiency, the fundamental objection to it would remain unaltered and unabated. It would destroy political equality. It would cramp and cripple mental and spiritual energies of our people. It would dry up the spirit of liberty and progress. It would extinguish equality of opportunity, and for these reasons fundamentally and primarily it must be resisted. For a hundred and fifty years liberalism has found its true spirit in the American system, not in the European systems.

I do not wish to be misunderstood in this statement. I am defining a general policy! It does not mean that our government is to part with one iota of its national resources without complete protection to the public interest. I have already stated that where the government is engaged in public works for purposes of flood control, of navigation, of irrigation, of scientific research or national defense that, or in pioneering a new art, it will at times necessarily produce power or commodities as a by-product. But they must be by-products, not the major purpose.

Nor do I wish to be misinterpreted as believing that the United States is free-for-all and the devil- take-the-hindmost. The very essence of equality of opportunity is that there shall be no domination by any group or trust or combination in this republic, whether it be business or political. It demands economic justice as well as political and social justice. It is no system to laissez faire.

There is but one consideration in testing these proposals—that is public interest. I do not doubt the sincerity of those who advocate these methods of solving our problems. I believe they will give equal credit to our honesty. If I believed that the adoption of such proposals would decrease taxes, cure abuses or corruption, would produce better service, decrease rates or benefit employees; If I believed they would bring economic equality, would stimulate endeavor, would encourage invention and support individual initiative, would provide equality of opportunity; If I believed that these proposals would not wreck our democracy but would strengthen the foundations of social and spiritual progress in America—or if they would do a few of these things—then I would not hesitate to accept these proposals, stupendous as they are, even though such acceptance would result in the governmental operation of all our power and the buying and selling of the products of our farms or any other product. But it is not true that such benefits would result to the public. The contrary would be true.

I feel deeply on this subject because during the war I had some practical experience with governmental operation and control. I have witnessed not only at home but abroad the many failures of government in business. I have seen its tyrannies, its injustices, its undermining of the very instincts which carry our people forward to progress. I have witnessed the lack of advance, the lowered standards of living, the depressed spirits of people working under such a system. My objection is based not upon theory or upon a failure to recognize wrong or abuse but because I know that the adoption of such methods would strike at the very roots of American life and would destroy the very basis of American progress.

Our people have the right to know whether we can continue to solve our great problems without abandonment of our American system. I know we can. We have demonstrated that our system is responsive enough to meet any new and intricate development in our economic and business life. We have demonstrated that we can maintain our democracy as master in its own house and that we can preserve equality of opportunity and individual freedom.

In the last fifty years we have discovered that mass production will produce articles for us at half the cost that obtained previously. We have seen the resultant growth of large units of production and distribution. This is big business. Business must be bigger for our tools are bigger, our country is bigger. We build a single dynamo of a hundred thousand horsepower. Even fifteen years ago that would have been a big business all by itself. Yet today advance in production requires that we set ten of these units together.

Our great problem is to make certain that while we maintain the fullest use of the large units of business yet that they shall be held subordinate to the public interest. The American people from bitter experience have a rightful fear that these great units might be used to dominate our industrial life and by illegal and unethical practices destroy equality of opportunity. Years ago the Republican Administration established the principle that such evils could be corrected by regulation. It developed methods by which abuses could be prevented and yet the full value of economic advance retained for the public. It insisted that when great public utilities were clothed with the security of part monopoly, whether it be railways, power plants, telephones or what not, then there must be the fullest and most complete control of rates, services, and finances by governmental agencies. These businesses must be conducted with glass pockets. In the development of our great production industry, the Republican Party insisted upon the enactment of a law that not only would maintain competition but would destroy conspiracies to dominate and limit the equality of opportunity amongst our people.

One of the great problems of government is to determine to what extent the Government itself shall interfere with commerce and industry and how much it shall leave to individual exertion. It is just as important that business keep out of government as that government keep out of business. No system is perfect. We have had abuses in the conduct of business that every good citizen resents. But I insist that the results show our system better than any other and retains the essentials of freedom.

As a result of our distinctly American system our country has become the land of opportunity to those born without inheritance not merely because of the wealth of its resources and industry but because of this freedom of initiative and enterprise. Russia has natural resources equal to ours. Her people are equally industrious but she has not had the blessings of 150 years of our form of government and of our social system. The wisdom of our forefathers in their conception that progress must be the sum of the progress of free individuals has been reenforced by all of the great leaders of the country since that day. Jackson, Lincoln, Cleveland, McKinley, Roosevelt, Wilson, and Coolidge have stood unalterably for these principles. By adherence to the principles of decentralization, self-government, ordered liberty, and opportunity and freedom to the individual our American experiment has yielded a degree of well-being unparalleled in all the world. It has come nearer to the abolition of poverty, to the abolition of fear of want that humanity has ever reached before. Progress of the past seven years is the proof of it. It furnishes an answer to those who would ask us to abandon the system by which this has been accomplished.

There is a still further road to progress which is consonant with our American system—a method that reinforces our individualism by reducing, not increasing, Government interference in business.

In this country we have developed a higher sense of cooperation than has ever been known before. This has come partly as the result of stimulation during the war, partly from the impulses of industry itself. We have ten thousand examples of this cooperative tendency in the enormous growth of the associational activities during recent years. Chambers of commerce, trade associations, professional associations, labor unions, trade councils, civic associations, farm cooperatives—these are all so embracing that there is scarcely an individual in our country who does not belong to one or more of them. They represent every phase of our national life both on the economic and the welfare side. They represent a vast ferment toward conscious cooperation. While some of them are selfish and narrow, the majority of them recognize a responsibility to the public as well as to their own interest.

The government in its obligation to the public can through skilled specialists cooperate with these various associations for the accomplishment of high public purposes. And this cooperation can take two distinct directions. The first is in the promotion of constructive projects of public interest, such as the elimination of waste in industry, the stabilization of business and development of scientific research. It can contribute to reducing unemployment and seasonal employment. It can by organized cooperation assist and promote great movements for better homes, for child welfare and for recreation.

The second form that this cooperation can take is in the cure of abuses and the establishment of a higher code of ethics and a more strict standard in its conduct of business. One test of our economic and social system is its capacity to cure its own abuses. New abuses and new relationships to the public interest will occur as long as we continue to progress. If we are to be wholly dependent upon government to cure every evil we shall by this very method have created an enlarged and deadening abuse through the extension of bureaucracy and the clumsy and incapable handling of delicate economic forces. And much abuse has been and can be cured by inspiration and cooperation, rather than by regulation of the government.

Nor is this any idealistic proposal. For the last seven years the Department of Commerce has carried this into practice in hundreds of directions and every single accomplishment of this character minimizes the necessity for government interference with business.

All this is possible because of the cooperative spirit and ability at team play in the American people. There is here a fundamental relief from the necessity of extension of the government into every avenue of business and welfare and therefore a powerful implement for the promotion of progress.

I wish to say something more on what I believe is the outstanding ideal in our whole political, economic and social system—that is equality of opportunity. We have carried this ideal farther into our life than has any other nation in the world. Equality of opportunity is the right of every American, rich or poor, foreign or native born, without respect to race or faith or color, to attain that position in life to which his ability and character entitle him. We must carry this ideal further than to economic and political fields alone. The first steps to equality of opportunity are that there should be no child in America that has not been born and does not live under sound conditions of health, that does not have full opportunity for education from the beginning to the end of our institutions, that is not free from injurious labor, that does not have stimulation to accomplish to the fullest of its capacities.

It is a matter for concern to our Government that we shall strengthen the safeguards to health, that we shall strengthen the bureaus given to research, that we shall strengthen our educational system at every point, that we shall develop cooperation by our Federal Government with state governments and with the voluntary bodies of the country that we may bring not only better understanding but action in these matters.

Furthermore, equality of opportunity in my vision requires an equal opportunity to the people in every section of our country. In these past few years some groups in our country have lagged behind others in the march of progress. They have not had the same opportunity. I refer more particularly to those engaged in the textile, coal and in the agricultural industries. We can assist in solving these problems by cooperation of our Government. To the agricultural industry we shall need advance initial capital to assist them, to stabilize and conduct their own industry. But this proposal is that they shall conduct it themselves, not by the Government. It is in the interest of our cities that we shall bring agriculture into full stability and prosperity. I know you will cooperate gladly in the faith that in the common prosperity of our country lies its future.

Source:

Herbert Hoover. *Public Papers of the Presidents of the United States: Herbert Hoover, 1929–33.* 4 vols. Washington, D.C.: Government Printing Office, 1974–77.

Suggested Reading

Progressivism

Nancy F. Cott, *The Grounding of Modern Feminism*. New Haven, Conn.: Yale University Press, 1987.

Lewis L. Gould, *The Presidency of Theodore Roosevelt*, Lawrence: University Press of Kansas, 1991.

John Higham, *Strangers in the Land: Patterns of American Nativism, 1860–1925*. New Brunswick, N.J.: Rutgers University Press, 2002.

David Montgomery, *The Fall of the House of Labor: The Workplace, the State, and American Labor Activism 1865–1925*. New York: Cambridge University Press, 1987.

Role of the United States in World Affairs in the Early 20th Century

Emily Rosenberg, *Spreading the American Dream: American Economic and Cultural Expansion, 1890–1945*. New York: Hill and Wang, 1982.

Michael Shaller, *The United States and China in the Twentieth Century*. New York: Oxford University Press, 1994.

Causes and Consequences of World War I

Ellis W. Hawley, *The Great War and the Search for a Modern Order: A History of the American People and Their Institutions, 1917–1933*. New York: St. Martin's Press: 1992.

David Kennedy, *Over Here: The First World War and American Society*. New York: Oxford University Press, 1980.

Thomas Krock, *To End All Wars: Woodrow Wilson and the Quest for a New World Order.* Princeton, N.J.: Princeton University Press, 1995.

Paul Murphy. *World War I and the Origin of Civil Liberties in the United States.* New York: W.W. Norton, 1979.

Richard Polenberg, *Fighting Faiths*. Ithaca, N.Y.: Cornell University Press, 1987.

Postwar Society

Kenneth T. Jackson, *Crabgrass Frontier: The Suburbanization of the United States*. New York: Oxford University Press, 1985.

Nancy MacLean, *Behind the Mask of Chivalry: The Making of the Second Ku Klux Klan*. New York: Oxford University Press, 1994.

Robert K. Murray. *Red Scare: A Study of National Hysteria, 1919–1920*. Westport, Conn.: Greenwood Publishing Group, 1980.

Richard Gid Powers. *Secrecy and Power: The Life of J. Edgar Hoover*. New York: The Free Press, 1987.

William Preston. *Aliens and Dissenters: Federal Repression of Radicals, 1903–1933*. Urbana: University of Illinois Press, 1995.

Rosalind Rosenberg, *Divided Lives: American Women in the Twentieth Century*. New York: Hill and Wang, 1992.

Postwar Economy

William Leuchtenberg, *The Perils of Prosperity, 1914–1932*. 2d ed. Chicago: University of Chicago Press, 1958.

Richard Tedlow, *New and Improved: The Story of Mass Marketing in America*. New York: Basic Books, 1990.

Postwar Culture

Lynn Dumeil, *Modern Temper: American Culture and Society in the 1920s*. New York: Hill and Wang, 1995.

Lewis Erenberg, *Steppin' Out: New York Nightlife and the Transformation of American Culture, 1890–1930*. Chicago: University of Chicago Press, 1984.

Warren Goldstein, *A Brief History of American Sports*. New York: Hill and Wang, 1993.

ERA 8
The Great Depression and World War II (1930–1945)

Superlatives abound in discussing the period from 1930 to 1945. The Great Depression was the worst economic crisis the United States ever suffered; the response, the New Deal, produced a resurgence and flourishing of government ventures. Although many of the problems were alleviated through New Deal programs, the economy did not recover until Americans began reacting to World War II, which began in Europe in 1939. The United States remained neutral until the Japanese attacked Pearl Harbor, Hawaii, December 7, 1941. Today, we refer to those who fought the Axis powers (Japan, Germany, and Italy) as the "greatest generation" for their sacrifices and heroism in conquering fascism.

The New Deal philosophy emphasized the ways that big government could alleviate the rampant social problems created by the depression. It brought idealistic Americans from all over the country to Washington, D.C., to help combat poverty. Legislation passed during that time, ironically, may well have saved capitalism in the United States. By underpinning and elevating labor it enabled workers to buy into the American dream that they, too, could become prosperous, and it obviated the need for the kind of workers' revolution advocated by communists. Nevertheless, the 1930s were, in the words of one historian of the period, "the heyday of American communism." Not only did communism attract Americans by its vision of a future without poverty. The American Communist Party (CPUSA) also advocated racial equality, something neither the business-dominated Republicans nor the Democratic Party, with its strong white Southern influence, promoted. In fact, an anti-lynching bill could never get through Congress, and violence against African Americans remained a local issue (and usually went unpunished) until the 1960s. The communist Soviet Union also supported the Spanish Loyalist government against Fascist rebels backed by Hitler and Mussolini during the Spanish civil war (1936–1939), while the United States, along with France and Great Britain, remained neutral. This, too, attracted anti-fascist Americans to communism.

By entering the war, the United States became an ally of the Soviet Union as well as Great Britain. (France had been conquered by Germany in 1940). World War II brought the United States out of its 1930s isolationism and it consolidated the nation's global stature.

As in every war, civil liberties took their toll, but on no one more than American citizens of Japanese descent and

Japanese aliens living on the West Coast. They were put into internment camps under harsh conditions. The Supreme Court upheld the government's argument that this was a military necessity (a decision that has not been overturned). Not until the 1980s did the American government admit that this action was wrong and pay reparations to the former internees. Also ironic, since the hallmark of Nazism was racism, American armed forces remained racially segregated, and even anti-Semitism persisted in many quarters. Neither African Americans nor the famous "code-talking" Navajo Indians were awarded Medals of Honor during or immediately after World War II. Presidents Clinton and George W. Bush rectified this in ceremonies during their administrations after many of the recipients were deceased.

Despite persistent prejudice and discrimination, minorities and women ultimately benefited from their experiences during World War II, when everyone was needed in the labor pool. African Americans won the backing of the government for "fair labor standards," and women commanded nontraditional jobs. Although the postwar economy, with its returning veterans, forced women out of the workplace and the postwar culture discouraged women from holding paying positions, their experience with economic independence would eventually foster the second wave of feminism beginning in the 1960s.

The Great Depression and American Life in the 1930s

Near v. Minnesota, 1930

U.S. Supreme Court decision, issued on June 1, 1931, that upheld the right of the press to criticize public officials. It invalidated a Minnesota statute known as the "gag law," which allowed the courts to suppress a "malicious, scandalous, and defamatory" periodical as a public nuisance. Under this statute, the state had banned further publication of the weekly *Saturday Press* (edited by J. M. Near) because it had published a series of articles charging corruption among law enforcement officers. In its 5-4 decision, the Court ruled the law unconstitutional, maintaining that the state could not exercise prior restraint by closing down a newspaper, although it could prosecute for criminal libel after publication of objectionable material. Subsequent decisions, notably *New York Times v. United States* (403 U.S. 713 [1971]) and *United States v. Progressive* (F. Supp. 990 [W.D. Wisconsin], 1979), however, appeared to allow prior restraint if national security was threatened.

Mr. Chief Justice Hughes delivered the opinion of the Court.

Chapter 285 of the Session Laws of Minnesota for the year 1925 provides for the abatement, as a public nuisance, of a "malicious, scandalous and defamatory newspaper, magazine or other periodical." Section 1 of the act is as follows:

"Section 1. Any person who, as an individual, or as a member or employee of a firm, or association or organization, or as an officer, director, member or employee of a corporation, shall be engaged in the business of regularly or customarily producing, publishing or circulating, having in possession, selling or giving away.

"(a) an obscene, lewd and lascivious newspaper, magazine, or other periodical, or

"(b) a malicious, scandalous and defamatory newspaper, magazine or other periodical,

—is guilty of a nuisance, and all persons guilty of such nuisance may be enjoined, as hereinafter provided.

"Participation in such business shall constitute a commission of such nuisance and render the participant liable and subject to the proceedings, orders and judgments provided for in this Act. Ownership, in whole or in part, directly or indirectly, of any such periodical, or of any stock or interest in any corporation or organization which owns the same in whole or in part, or which publishes the same, shall constitute such participation.

"In actions brought under (b) above, there shall be available the defense that the truth was published with good motives and for justifiable ends and in such actions the plaintiff shall not have the right to report (sic) to issues or editions of periodicals taking place more than three months before the commencement of the action."

Section 2 provides that, whenever any such nuisance is committed or exists . . . a temporary injunction may be granted. . . .

Under this statute (section 1, clause (b), the county attorney of Hennepin county brought this action to enjoin the publication of what was described as a "malicious, scandalous and defamatory newspaper, magazine or other periodical," known as The Saturday Press, published by the defendants in the city of Minneapolis. The complaint alleged that the defendants . . . published and circulated editions of that periodical which were "largely devoted to malicious, scandalous and defamatory articles. . . .Without attempting to summarize the contents of the voluminous exhibits attached to the complaint, we deem it sufficient to say that the articles charged, in substance, that a Jewish gangster was in control of gambling, bootlegging, and racketeering in Minneapolis, and that law enforcing officers and agencies were not energetically performing their duties. Most of the charges were directed against the chief of police; he was charged with gross neglect of duty, illicit relations with gangsters, and with participation in graft. The county attorney was charged with knowing the existing conditions and with failure to take adequate measures to remedy them. The mayor was accused of inefficiency and dereliction. One member of the grand jury was stated to be in sympathy with the gangsters. A special grand jury and a special prosecutor were demanded to deal with the situation in general, and, in particular, to investigate an attempt to assassinate one Guilford, one of the original defendants, who, it appears from the articles, was shot by gangsters after the first issue of the periodical had been published. There is no question but that the articles made serious accusations against the public officers named and others in connection with the prevalence of crimes and the failure to expose and punish them.

At the beginning of the action on November 22, 1927, and upon the verified complaint, an order was made directing the defendants to show cause why a temporary injunction should not issue and meanwhile forbidding the defendants to publish, circulate, or have in their possession any editions of the periodical from September 24, 1927, to November 19, 1927, inclusive, and from publishing, circulating or having in their possession, "any future editions to said The Saturday Press" and "any publication, known by any other name whatsoever containing malicious, scandalous and defamatory matter of the kind alleged in plaintiff's complaint herein or otherwise."

The defendants demurred to the complaint upon the ground that it did not state facts sufficient to constitute a cause of action, and on this demurrer challenged the constitutionality of the statute. The district court overruled the demurrer and certified the question of constitutionality to the Supreme Court of the state. The Supreme Court sustained the statute . . . and it is conceded by the appellee that the act was thus held to be valid over the objection that it violated not only the State Constitution, but also the Fourteenth Amendment of the Constitution of the United States.

Thereupon the defendant Near, the present appellant, answered the complaint. He averred that he was the sole owner and proprietor of the publication in question. He admitted the publication of the articles in the issues described in the complaint, but denied that they were malicious, scandalous, or defamatory as alleged. He expressly invoked the protection of the due process clause of the Fourteenth Amendment. The case then came on for trial. . . . .

The district court made findings of fact, which . . . found in general terms that the editions in question were "chiefly devoted to malicious, scandalous and defamatory articles" concerning the individuals named. The court further found that the defendants through these publications "did engage in the business of regularly and customarily producing, publishing and circulating a malicious, scandalous and defamatory newspaper," and that "the said publication". . . constitutes a public nuisance under the laws of the State." Judgment was thereupon entered adjudging that "the newspaper, magazine and periodical known as The Saturday Press," as a public nuisance, "be and is hereby abated." The judgment perpetually enjoined the defendants "from producing, editing, publishing, circulating, having in their possession, selling or giving away any publication whatsoever which is a malicious, scandalous or defamatory newspaper, as defined by law," and also "from further conducting said nuisance under the name and title of said The Saturday Press or any other name or title."

The defendant Near appealed from this judgment to the Supreme Court of the State, again asserting his right under the Federal Constitution, and the judgment was affirmed. . . .

From the judgment as thus affirmed, the defendant Near appeals to this Court.

[1-3] This statute, for the suppression as a public nuisance of a newspaper of periodical, is unusual, if not unique, and raises questions of grave importance transcending the local interests involved in the particular action. It is no longer open to doubt that the liberty of the press and of speech is within the liberty safeguarded by the due process clause of the Fourteenth Amendment from invasion by state action. It was found impossible to conclude that this essential personal liberty of the citizen was left unprotected by the general guaranty of fundamental rights of person and property. . . . In maintaining this guaranty, the authority of the state to enact laws to promote the

health, safety, morals, and general welfare of its people is necessarily admitted. The limits of this sovereign power must always be determined with appropriate regard to the particular subject of its exercise. . . . Liberty of speech and of the press is also not an absolute right, and the state may punish its abuse. . . . Liberty, in each of its phases, has its history and connotation, and, in the present instance, the inquiry is as to the historic conception of the liberty of the press and whether the statute under review violates the essential attributes of that liberty.

The appellee insists that the questions of the application of the statute to appellant's periodical, and of the construction of the judgment of the trial court, are not presented for review; that appellant's sole attack was upon the constitutionality of the statute, however it might be applied. The appellee contends that no question either of motive in the publication, or whether the decree goes beyond the direction of the statute, is before us. The appellant replies that, in his view, the plain terms of the statute were not departed from in this case, and that, even if they were, the statute is nevertheless unconstitutional under any reasonable construction of its terms. The appellant states that he has not argued that the temporary and permanent injunctions were broader than were warranted by the statute; he insists that what was done was properly done if the statute is valid, and that the action taken under the statute is a fair indication of its scope.

* * *

First. That statute is not aimed at the redress of individual or private wrongs. Remedies for libel remain available and unaffected. . . . In order to obtain an injunction to suppress the future publication of the newspaper or periodical, it is not necessary to prove the falsity of the charges that have been made in the publication condemned. In the present action there was no allegation that the matter published was not true. It is alleged, and the statute requires the allegation that the publication was "malicious." But, as in prosecutions for libel, there is no requirement of proof by the state of malice in fact as distinguished from malice inferred from the mere publication of the defamatory matter. The judgment in this case proceeded upon the mere proof of publication. The statute permits the defense, not of the truth alone, but only that the truth was published with good motives and for justifiable ends. It is apparent that under the statute the publication is to be regarded as defamatory if it injures reputation, and that it is scandalous if it circulates charges of reprehensible conduct, whether criminal or otherwise, and the publication is thus deemed to invite public reprobation and to constitute a public scandal. The court sharply defined the purpose of the statute, bringing out the precise point, in these words: "There is no constitutional right to publish a fact merely because it is true. It is a matter of common knowledge that prosecutions under the criminal libel statutes do not result in efficient repression or suppression of the evils of scandal. Men who are the victims of such assaults seldom resort to the courts. This is especially true if their sins are exposed and the only question relates to whether it was done with good motive and for justifiable ends. This law is not for the protection of the person attacked nor to punish the wrong doer. It is for the protection of the public welfare."

[5] Second. The statute is directed not simply at the circulation of scandalous and defamatory statements with regard to private citizens, but at the continued publication by newspapers and periodicals of charges against public officers of corruption, malfeasance in office, or serious neglect of duty. Such charges by their very nature create a public scandal. They are scandalous and defamatory within the meaning of the statute, which has its normal operation in relation to publications dealing prominently and chiefly with the alleged derelictions of public officers.

Third. The object of the statute is not punishment, in the ordinary sense, but suppression of the offending newspaper or periodical. The reason for the enactment, as the state court has said, is that prosecutions to enforce penal statutes for libel do not result in "efficient repression or suppression of the evils of scandal." . . .Under this statute, a publisher of a newspaper or periodical, undertaking to conduct a campaign to expose and to censure official derelictions, and devoting his publication principally to that purpose, must face not simply the possibility of a verdict against him in a suit or prosecution for libel, but a determination that his newspaper or periodical is a public nuisance to be abated, and that this abatement and suppression will follow unless he is prepared with legal evidence to prove the truth of the charges and also to satisfy the court that, in addition to being true, the matter was published with good motives and for justifiable ends.

This suppression is accomplished by enjoining publication, and that restraint is the object and effect of the statute.

Fourth. The statute not only operates to suppress the offending newspaper or periodical, but to put the publisher under an effective censorship. When a newspaper or periodical is found to be "malicious, scandalous and defamatory," and is suppressed as such, resumption of publication is punishable as a contempt of court by fine or imprisonment. Thus, where a newspaper or periodical has been suppressed because of the circulation of charges against public officers of official misconduct, it would seem to be clear that the renewal of the publication of such charges would constitute a contempt, and that the judgment would lay a permanent restraint upon the publisher, to escape which he must satisfy the court as to the character of a new publication. Whether he would be permitted again to publish matter deemed to be derogatory to the same or other public officers would depend upon the court's ruling. In the present instance the judgment restrained the defendants from "publishing, circulating, having in their possession, selling or giving away any publication whatsoever which is a malicious, scandalous or defamatory newspaper, as defined by law." The law gives no definition except that covered by the words "scandalous and defamatory," and publications charging official misconduct are of that class. While the court, answering the objection that the judgment was too broad, saw no reason for construing it as restraining the defendants "from operating a newspaper in harmony with the public welfare to which all must yield," and said that the defendants had not indicated "any desire to conduct their business in the usual and legitimate manner," the manifest inference is that, at least with respect to a new publication directed against official misconduct, the defendant would be held, under penalty of punishment for contempt as provided in the statute, to a manner of publication which the court considered to be "usual and legitimate" and consistent with the public welfare.

[6] If we cut through mere details of procedure, the operation and effect of the statute in substance is that public authorities may bring the owner or publisher of a newspaper or periodical before a judge upon a charge of conducting a business of publishing scandalous and defamatory matter—in particular that the matter consists of charges against public officers of official dereliction—and, unless the owner or publisher is able and disposed to bring competent evidence to satisfy the judge that the charges are true and are published with good motives and for justifiable ends, his newspaper or periodical is suppressed and further publication is made punishable as a contempt. This is of the essence of censorship.

[7] The question is whether a statute authorizing such proceedings in restraint of publication is consistent with the conception of the liberty of the press as historically conceived and guaranteed. In determining the extent of the constitutional protection, it has been generally, if not universally, considered that it is the chief purpose of the guaranty to prevent previous restraints upon publication.

. . .For whatever wrong the appellant has committed or may commit, by his publications, the state appropriately affords, both public and private redress by its libel laws. As has been noted, the statute in question does not deal with punishments; it provides for no punishment, except in case of contempt for violation of the court's order, but for suppression and injunction—that is, for restraint upon publication.

The objection has also been made that the principle as to immunity from previous restraint is stated too broadly, if every such restraint is deemed to be prohibited. That is undoubtedly true; the protection even as to previous restraint is not absolutely unlimited. But the limitation has been recognized only in exceptional cases. . . .

The exceptional nature of its limitations places in a strong light the general conception that liberty of the press, historically considered and taken up by the Federal Constitution, has meant, principally although not exclusively, immunity from previous restraints or censorship.

* * *

The fact that for approximately one hundred and fifty years there has been almost an entire absence of attempts to impose previous restraints upon publications relating to the malfeasance of public officers is significant of the deep-seated conviction that such restraints would violate constitutional right. . . .

. . . The fact that the liberty of the press may be abused by miscreant purveyors of scandal does not make any the less necessary the immunity of the press from previous restraint in dealing with official misconduct. Subsequent punishment for such abuses as may exist is the appropriate remedy, consistent with constitutional privilege.

* * *

[14] For these reasons we hold the statute, so far as it authorized the proceedings in this action under clause (b) of section 1, to be an infringement of the liberty of the press guaranteed by the Fourteenth Amendment. We should add that this decision rests upon the operation and effect of the statute, without regard to the question of the truth of the charges contained in the particular periodical. The fact that the public officers named in this case, and those associated with the charges of official dereliction, may be deemed to be impeccable, cannot affect the conclusion that the statute imposes an unconstitutional restraint upon publication.

Judgment reversed.

Source:

Supreme Court Reporter, Vol. 51, pp. 625–639.

Franklin Roosevelt, "Forgotten Man," Radio Speech, 1932

National radio address delivered by Franklin D. Roosevelt, then Democratic governor of New York, on April 7, 1932, in which he argued that hope for national economic recovery from the Great Depression resided with the ordinary farmer and industrial worker—"the forgotten man at the bottom of the economic pyramid." Roosevelt spoke from Albany under the auspices of the Democratic National Committee. An emerging presidential candidate, he used the speech to present his alternative to the Republican Hoover administration's economic reform effort. Roosevelt likened the nation's economic crisis in 1932 to the grave emergency America faced in 1916 as it entered World War I. Just as America had mobilized economically for war from "bottom to top," he asserted, so it now must do to survive the depression. An economic reform program, he said, must rest upon the "forgotten man," who represented the indispensable unit of economic power. Roosevelt advocated federal measures to restore the farmer's purchasing power, provide mortgage relief to small banks and home owners, and lower tariffs to promote export markets for American goods.

Although I understand that I am talking under the auspices of the Democratic National Committee, I do not want to limit myself to politics. I do not want to feel that I am addressing an audience of Democrats, nor that I speak merely as a Democrat myself. The present condition for our national affairs is too serious to be viewed through partisan eyes for partisan purposes.

Fifteen years ago my public duty called me to an active part in a great national emergency—the World War. Success then was due to a leadership whose vision carried beyond the timorous and futile gesture of sending a tiny army of 150,000 trained soldiers and the regular Navy to the aid of our Allies.

The generalship of that moment conceived of a whole nation mobilized for war, economic, industrial, social and military resources gathered into a vast unit, capable of and actually in the process of throwing into the scales 10,000,000 men equipped with physical needs and sustained by the realization that behind them were the united efforts of 110,000,000 human beings. It was a great plan because it was build from bottom to top and not from top to bottom.

In my calm judgment, the nation faces today a more grave emergency than in 1917.

It is said that Napoleon lost the Battle of Waterloo because he forgot his infantry. He staked too much upon the more spectacular but less substantial cavalry.

The present Administration in Washington provides a close parallel. It has either forgotten or it does not want to remember the infantry of our economic army.

These unhappy times call for the building of plans that rest upon the forgotten, the unorganized but the indispensable units of economic power, for plans like those of 1917 that build from the bottom up and not from the top down, that put their faith once more in the forgotten man at the bottom of the economic pyramid.

Obviously, these few minutes tonight permit no opportunity to lay down the ten or a dozen closely related objectives of a plan to meet our present emergency, but I can draw a few essentials, a beginning, in fact, of a planned program.

It is the habit of the unthinking to turn in times like this to the illusions of economic magic. People suggest that a huge expenditures of public funds by the Federal Government and by State and local governments will completely solve the unemployment problem. But it is clear that even if we could raise many billions of dollars and find definitely useful public works to spend these billions on, even all that money would not give employment to the 7,000,000 or 10,000,000 people who are out of work.

Let us admit frankly that it would be only a stopgap. A real economic cure must go to the killing of bacteria in the system rather than to the treatment of external symptoms.

How much do the shallow thinkers realize, for example, that approximately one-half of our population, fifty or sixty million people, earn their living by farming or in small towns where existence immediately depends on farms. They have today lost their purchasing power. Why? They are receiving for farm products less than the cost to them of growing these farm products.

The result of this loss of purchasing power is that many other millions of people engaged in industry in the cities cannot sell industrial products to the farming half of the nation. This brings home to every city worker that his own employment is directly tied up with the farmer's dollar. No nation can long continue half bankrupt. Main Street, Broadway, the mills, the mines will close if half of the buyers are broke.

I cannot escape the conclusion that one of the essentials of a national program of restoration must be to restore purchasing power to the farming half of the country. Without this the wheels of railroads and of factories will not turn.

Closely associated with this first objective is the problem of keeping the home-owner and the farm-owner where he is, without being dispossessed through the foreclosure of his mortgage.

His relationship to the great banks of Chicago and New York is pretty remote. The two billion dollar fund which President Hoover and the Congress have put at the disposal at the big banks, the railroads and the corporations of the nation is not for him.

His is a relationship to his little local bank or local loan company. It is a sad fact that even though the local lender in many cases does not want to evict the farmer or home-owner by foreclosure proceedings, he is forced to do so in order to keep his bank or company solvent. Here should be an objective of government itself, to provide at least as much assistance to the little fellow as it is now giving to the large banks and corporations. That is another example of building from the bottom up.

One other objective closely related to the problem of selling American products is to provide a tariff policy based upon economic common sense rather than upon politics—hot air—pull.

This country during the past few years, culminating with the Hawley-Smoot Tariff of 1929, has compelled the world to build tariff fences so high that world trade is decreasing to the vanishing point. The value of goods internationally exchanged is today less than half of what it was three or four years ago.

Every man and woman who gives any thought to the subject knows that if our factories run even 80 per cent of capability they will turn out more products that we as a nation can possibly use ourselves.

The answer is that if they are to run on 80 per cent of capacity we must sell some goods abroad. How can we do that if the outside nations cannot pay us in cash—and we know by sad experience that they cannot do that. The only way they can pay us is in their own goods or raw materials, but this foolish tariff of ours makes that impossible.

What we must do is this: To revise our tariff on the basis of a reciprocal exchange of goods, allowing other nations to buy and to pay for our goods by sending us such of their goods as will not seriously throw any of our industries out of balance, and, incidentally, making impossible in this county the continuance of pure monopolies which cause us to pay excessive prices for many of the necessities of life.

Such objectives as these three—restoring farmers' buying power, relief to the small banks and homeowners and a reconstructed tariff policy—these are only a part of ten or dozen vital factors.

But they seem to be beyond the concern of a National Administration which can think in terms only of the top of the social and economic structure. They have sought temporary relief from the top down rather than permanent relief from the bottom up. They have totally failed to plan ahead in a comprehensive way. They have waited until something has cracked and then at the last moment have sought to prevent total collapse.

It is high time to get back to fundamentals. It is high time to admit with courage that we are in the midst of an emergency at least equal to that of war. Let us mobilize to meet it.

Source:
Landmark Documents in American History, Facts On File, Inc.

The Bonus March, 1932

A press release of July 28, 1932, from the White House to justify sending in troops to oust World War I veterans calling for an immediate release of their "bonus." President Herbert Hoover was about to launch his presidential campaign, and his controversial act, called "One of the blackest pages in our history," by California senator Hiram Johnson, was being severely criticized.

A bonus had been offered in the World War Adjusted Compensation Act of 1924, which was passed over the veto of President Calvin Coolidge. This legislation provided "adjusted compensation" for veterans of World War I, with payment to be deferred until 1945. Each veteran was to receive a dollar a day for service within the United States and $1.25 a day for service abroad, payable in endowment insurance policy certificates. Certificates valued at $3.5 billion were issued, averaging about $1,000 per veteran. However, unemployed and desperately poor veterans, suffering in the Great Depression, marched to Washington, D.C., with their families in 1932 to demand the entire bonus immediately. This Bonus Expeditionary Force, consisted of between 17,000 and 25,000 people who erected a giant "Hooverville" shantytown not far from the U.S. Capitol. When Congress failed to pass a new bonus bill, 5,000 to 6,000 of the marchers accepted President Hoover's offer of return fares and left. (Accurate statistics are hard to develop in this controversial and politically charged episode.) Others refused to leave their tent city, and rioting broke out resulting in two deaths and many injuries to both marchers and police. The president, on July 28, 1932, sent General Douglas MacArthur to evict the remaining veterans. Ignoring orders neither to arm his soldiers nor to move into the shantytown, MacArthur used tanks and ordered his bayonet-carrying troops to burn down the Hooverville. A number of injuries resulted. The brutality of the soldiers added to President Hoover's growing unpopularity due to the Great Depression, and has overshadowed the riot that preceded it, in which the marchers acted violently.

To justify sending in troops, President Hoover claimed that radicals and communists, not veterans, had taken over the leadership of the marchers. After the fact, he asked FBI (then U.S. Bureau of Investigation) director J. Edgar Hoover to confirm the presence of communists. After checking his fingerprint files, J. E. Hoover acknowledged only that the presence of tanks may have prevented violence from the marchers. In 1936, over the veto of President Franklin D. Roosevelt, Congress approved immediate payment.

July 28, 1932.

The President said: "For some days police authorities and Treasury officials have been endeavoring to persuade the so-called bonus marchers to evacuate certain buildings which they were occupying without permission. These buildings are on sites where government construction is in progress and their demolition was necessary in order to extend employment in the district and to carry forward the government's construction program.

"This morning the occupants of these buildings were notified to evacuate and at the request of the police did evacuate the buildings concerned. Thereafter, however, several thousand men from different camps marched in and attacked the police with brickbats and otherwise injuring several policemen, one probably fatally.

"I have received the attached letter from the Commissioners of the District of Columbia stating that they can no longer preserve law and order in the District.

"In order to put an end to this rioting and defiance of civil authority, I have asked the Army to assist the District authorities to restore order.

"Congress made provision for the return home of the so-called bonus marchers who have for many weeks been given every opportunity of free assembly, free speech and free petition to the Congress. Some 5,000 took advantage of this arrangement and have returned to their homes. An examination of a large number of names disclosed the fact that a considerable part of those remaining are not veterans; many are communists and persons with criminal records.

"The veterans amongst these numbers are no doubt unaware of the character of their companions and are being led into violance [sic] which no government can tolerate.

"I have asked the Attorney General to investigate the whole incident and to cooperate with the District civil authorities in such measures against leaders and rioters as may be necessary."

Source:

Herbert Hoover Presidential Library and Museum. Hoover Online Digital Archives. "Press Releases." Available on-line. URL: www.ecommcode.com/hoover/hooveronline/hoover_and_the_depression/bonus_march/group_index.cfm?GroupID=18. Accessed November 2003.

The New Deal

Franklin D. Roosevelt, First Inaugural Address, 1933

Speech delivered by Franklin Delano Roosevelt on March 4, 1933, at his inauguration as the 32nd president of the United States. His address, delivered at the height of the Great Depression, offered reassurance to the nation and the promise of prompt, vigorous action. Stating that "the only thing we have to fear is fear itself," Roosevelt castigated the nation's bankers for their "stubbornness and . . . incompetence" in the face of the economic crisis, and broadly outlined his plan for recovery. The greatest task, he stated, was to put people to work; this he would accomplish in part by direct government employment. He called for strict supervision of banking, credit, and investment; a sound currency; and an end to speculation. Regarding hemispheric relations, he proposed the "good neighbor" policy.

The depression continued through Roosevelt's first term. In his Second Inaugural Address he noted that the nation faced the challenge of "tens of millions of its citizens [who] are denied the greater part of what the very lowest standards of today call the necessities of life. . . . I see one-third of a nation ill-housed, ill-clad, ill-nourished." The president spoke, he said, not in despair but in hope, "because the Nation, seeing and understanding the injustice in it, proposes to paint it out." The address was delivered on January 20, 1937, the first time a president was inaugurated on this day, which was set by the Twentieth Amendment.

I am certain that my fellow Americans expect that on my induction into the Presidency I will address them with a candor and a decision which the present situation of our Nation impels. This is preeminently the time to speak the truth, the whole truth, frankly and boldly. Nor need we shrink from honestly facing conditions in our country today. This great Nation will endure as it has endured, will revive and will prosper. So, first of all, let me assert my firm belief that the only thing we have to fear is fear itself—nameless, unreasoning, unjustified terror which paralyzes needed efforts to convert retreat into advance. In every dark hour of our national life a leadership of frankness and vigor has met with that understanding and support of the people themselves which is essential to victory. I am convinced that you will again give that support to leadership in these critical days.

In such a spirit on my part and on yours we face our common difficulties. They concern, thank God, only material things. Values have shrunken to fantastic levels; taxes have risen; our ability to pay has fallen; government of all kinds is faced by serious curtailment of income; the means of exchange are frozen in the currents of trade; the withered leaves of industrial enterprise lie on every side; farmers find no markets for their produce; the savings of many years in thousands of families are gone.

More important, a host of unemployed citizens face the grim problem of existence, and an equally great number toil with little return. Only a foolish optimist can deny the dark realities of the moment.

Yet our distress comes from no failure of substance. We are stricken by no plague of locusts. Compared with the perils which our forefathers conquered because they believed and were not afraid, we have still much to be thankful for. Nature still offers her bounty and human efforts have multiplied it. Plenty is at our doorstep, but a generous use of it languishes in the very sight of the supply. Primarily this is because the rulers of the exchange of mankind's goods have failed, through their own stubbornness and their own incompetence, have admitted their failure, and abdicated. Practices of the unscrupulous money changers stand indicated in the court of public opinion, rejected by the hearts and minds of men.

True they have tried, but their efforts have been cast in the pattern of an outworn tradition. Faced by failure of credit they have proposed only the lending of more money. Stripped of the lure of profit by which to induce our people to follow their false leadership, they have resorted to exhortations, pleading tearfully for restored confidence. They know only the rules of a generation of self-seekers. They have no vision, and when there is no vision the people perish.

The money changers have fled from their high seats in the temple of our civilization. We may now restore that temple to the ancient truths. The measure of the restoration lies in the extent to which we apply social values more noble than mere monetary profit.

Happiness lies not in the mere possession of money; it lies in the joy of achievement, in the thrill of creative effort. The joy and moral stimulation of work no longer must be forgotten in the mad chase of evanescent profits. These dark days will be worth all they cost us if they teach us that our true destiny is not to be ministered unto but to minister to ourselves and to our fellow men.

Recognition of the falsity of material wealth as the standard of success goes hand in hand with the abandonment of the false belief that public office and high political position are to be valued only by the standards of pride of place and personal profit; and there must be an end to a conduct in banking and in business which too often has given to a sacred trust the likeness of callous and selfish wrongdoing. Small wonder that confidence languishes, for it thrives only on honesty, on honor, on the sacredness of obligations, on faithful protection, on unselfish performance; without them it cannot live.

Restoration calls, however, not for changes in ethics alone. This Nation asks for action, and action now.

Our greatest primary task is to put people to work. This is no unsolvable problem if we face it wisely and courageously. It can be accomplished in part by direct recruiting by the Government itself, treating the task as we would treat the emergency of a war, but at the same time, through this employment, accomplishing greatly needed projects to stimulate and reorganize the use of our natural resources.

Hand in hand with this we must frankly recognize the overbalance of population in our industrial centers and, by engaging on a national scale in a redistribution, endeavor to provide a better use of the land for those best fitted for the land. The task can be helped by definite efforts to raise the values of agricultural products and with this the power to purchase the output of our cities. It can be helped by preventing realistically the tragedy of the growing loss through foreclosure of our small homes and our farms. It can be helped by insistence that the Federal, State, and local governments act forthwith on the demand that their cost be drastically reduced. It can be helped by the unifying of relief activities which to-day are often scattered, uneconomical, and unequal. It can be helped by national planning for and supervision of all forms of transportation and of communications and other utilities which have a definitely public character. There are many ways in which it can be helped, but it can never be helped merely by talking about it. We must act and act quickly.

Finally, in our progress toward a resumption of work we require two safeguards against a return of the evils of the old order; there must be a strict supervision of all banking and credits and investments; there must be an end to speculation with other people's money, and there must be provision for an adequate but sound currency.

There are the lines of attack. I shall presently urge upon a new Congress in special session detailed measures for their fulfillment, and I shall seek the immediate assistance of the several States.

Through this program of action we address ourselves to putting our own national house in order and making income balance outgo. Our international trade relations, though vastly important, are in point of time and necessity secondary to the establishment of a sound national economy. I favor as a practical policy the putting of first things first. I shall spare no effort to restore world trade by international economic readjustment, but the emergency at home cannot wait on that accomplishment.

The basic thought that guides these specific means of national recovery is not narrowly nationalistic. It is the insistence, as a first consideration, upon the interdependence of the various elements in all parts of the United States—a recognition of the old and permanently important manifestation of the American spirit of the pioneer. It is the way to recovery. It is the immediate way. It is the strongest assurance that the recovery will endure.

In the field of world policy I would dedicate this Nation to the policy of the good neighbor—the neighbor who resolutely respects himself and, because he does so, respects the rights of others—the neighbor who respects his obligations and respects the sanctity of his agreements in and with a world of neighbors.

If I read the temper of our people correctly, we now realize as we have never realized before our interdependence on each other; that we can not merely take but we must give as well; that if we are to go forward, we must move as a trained and loyal army willing to sacrifice for the good of a common discipline, because without such discipline no progress is made, no leadership becomes effective. We are, I know, ready and willing to submit our lives and property to such discipline, because it makes possible a leadership which aims at a larger good. This I propose to offer, pledging that the larger purposes will bind upon us all as a sacred obligation with a unity of duty hitherto evoked only in time of armed strife.

With this pledge taken, I assume unhesitatingly the leadership of this great army of our people dedicated to a disciplined attack upon our common problems.

Action in this image and to this end is feasible under the form of government which we have inherited from our ancestors. Our Constitution is so simple and practical that it is possible always to meet extraordinary needs by changes in emphasis and arrangement without loss of essential form. That is why our constitutional system has proved itself the most superbly enduring political mechanism the modern world has produced. It has met every stress of vast expansion of territory, of foreign wars, of bitter internal strife, of world relations.

It is to be hoped that the normal balance of executive and legislative authority may be wholly adequate to meet the unprecedented task before us. But it may be that an unprecedented demand and need for undelayed action may call for temporary departure from that normal balance of public procedure.

I am prepared under my constitutional duty to recommend the measures that a stricken nation in the midst of a stricken world may require. These measures, or such other measures as the Congress may built out of its experience and wisdom, I shall seek, within my constitutional authority to bring to speedy adoption.

But in the event that the Congress shall fail to take one of these two courses, and in the event that the national emergency is still critical, I shall not evade the clear course of duty that will then confront me. I shall ask the Congress for the one remaining instrument to meet the crisis—broad Executive power to wage a war against the emergency, as great as the power that would be given to me if we were in fact invaded by a foreign foe.

For the trust reposed in me I will return the courage and the devotion that befit the time. I can do no less.

We face the arduous days that lie before us in the warm courage of the national unity; with the clear consciousness of seeking old and precious moral values; with the clean satisfaction that comes from the stern performance of duty by old and young alike. We aim at the assurance of a rounded and permanent national life.

We do not distrust the future of essential democracy. The people of the United States have not failed. In their need they have registered a mandate that they want direct, vigorous action. They have asked for discipline and direction under leadership. They have made me the present instrument of their wishes. In the spirit of the gift I take it.

In this dedication of a Nation we humbly ask the blessing of God. May He protect each and every one of us. May He guide me in the days to come.

Source:

Inaugural Addresses of the Presidents of the United States, 1789–1965. Washington, D.C.: Government Printing Office, 1965.

Franklin Roosevelt, Bank Holiday Declaration, 1933

Edict issued by President Franklin D. Roosevelt on March 5, 1933, and effective the following day, declaring a four-day national banking holiday, halting all transactions in banks (including Federal Reserve banks), trust companies, credit unions, and other financial institutions. It also placed an embargo on the export of silver, gold, and currency. Roosevelt, claiming authority under the Trading with the Enemy Act of 1917, intended the emergency measure to allow time to prepare legislation to handle the national crisis of bank failures and to protect the nation's diminishing gold reserves. The edict allowed the use of scrip so that businesses might continue.

Four days later a special session of Congress gave the president broad powers over the national banking and monetary systems. The quickly passed Emergency Bank Relief Act validating the Bank Holiday Declaration gave the president control over gold transactions, authorized the issuance of new Federal Reserve bank notes, forbade gold hoarding and export, and authorized the Treasury Department to grant or withhold licenses to reopen banks and to appoint conservators for those of questionable soundness. Qualified banks were permitted to begin reopening on March 13.

On January 30, 1934, the Gold Reserve Act of 1934 was enacted. It removed the United States from a full gold standard and placed it on a modified one. The act empowered the president to reduce the gold content of the dollar to between 50 and 60 percent of its former weight and to change that value within those limits as necessary. It made the government the sole legal owner of monetary gold, prohibiting the domestic use of gold as money, the redemption of dollars in gold, and individual gold holdings (except under federal license for specified purposes). While gold remained the currency reserve, every dollar had to be fully backed by that metal. The act also established a stabilization fund to balance international payments. On January 31, President Franklin D. Roosevelt used the authority.

Whereas there have been heavy and unwarranted withdrawals of gold and currency from our banking institutions for the purpose of hoarding; and

Whereas continuous and increasingly extensive speculative activity abroad in foreign exchange has resulted in severe drains on the Nation's stocks of gold; and

Whereas those conditions have created a national emergency; and

Whereas it is in the best interests of all bank depositors that a period of respite be provided with a view to preventing further hoarding of coin, bullion or currency or speculation in foreign exchange and permitting the application of appropriate measures to protect the interests for our people; and

Whereas it is provided in Section 5 (b) of the Act of October 6, 1917 (40 Stat. L. 411), as amended, "That the President may investigate, regulate, or prohibit, under such rules and regulations as he may prescribe, by means of licenses or otherwise, any transactions in foreign exchange and the export, hoarding, melting, or earmarkings of gold or silver coin or bullion or currency. . ."; and

Whereas it is provided in Section 16 of the said Act "That whoever shall willfully violate any of the provisions of this Act or of any license, rule, or regulation issued thereunder, and whoever shall willfully violate, neglect, or refuse to comply with any order of the President issued in compliance with the provisions of this Act, shall, upon conviction, be fined not more than $10,000, or, if a natural person, imprisoned for not more than ten years, or both. . .";

Now, therefore, I, Franklin D. Roosevelt, President of the United States of America, in view of such national emergency and by virtue of the authority vested in me by said Act and in order to prevent the export, hoarding, or earmarking of gold or silver coin or bullion or currency, do hereby proclaim, order, direct and declare that from Monday, the Sixth day of March, to Thursday, the Ninth day of March, Nineteen Hundred and Thirty-three, both dates inclusive, there shall be maintained and observed by all banking institutions and all branches thereof located in the United States of America, including the territories and insular possessions, a bank holiday, and that during said period all banking transactions shall be suspended. During such holiday, excepting as hereinafter provided, no such banking institution or branch shall pay out, export, earmark, or permit the withdrawal or transfer in any manner or by any device whatsoever, of any gold or silver coin or bullion or currency or take any other action which might facilitate the hoarding thereof; nor shall any such banking institution or branch pay out deposits, make loans or discounts, deal in foreign exchange, transfer credits from the United States to any place abroad, or transact any other banking business whatsoever.

During such holiday, the Secretary of the Treasury, with the approval of the President and under such regulations as he may prescribe, is authorized and empowered (a) to permit any or all of such banking institutions to perform any or all of the usual banking functions, (b) to direct, require or permit the issuance of clearing house certificates or other evidences of claims against assets of banking institutions, and (c) to authorize and direct the creation in such banking institutions of special trust accounts for the receipt of new deposits which shall be subject to withdrawal on demand without any restriction or limitation and shall be kept separately in cash or on deposit in Federal Reserve Banks or invested in obligations of the United States.

As used in this order the term "banking institutions" shall include all Federal Reserve Banks, national banking associations, banks, trust companies, savings banks, building and loan associations, credit unions, or other corporations, partnerships, associations or persons, engaged in the business of receiving deposits, making loans, discounting business paper, or transacting any other form of banking business.

Source:

Franklin D. Roosevelt, *The Public Papers and Addresses of Franklin D. Roosevelt*. New York: Random House, 1938–1950.

Franklin Roosevelt, Message to Congress on the Tennessee Valley Authority, 1933

Message of April 10, 1933, to Congress accompanying President Franklin D. Roosevelt's proposal for legislation to create the Tennessee Valley Authority (TVA). The Roosevelt administration sought to expand the federally owned project at Muscle Shoals on the Tennessee River in Alabama into an ambitious program for the economic and social development of the Tennessee River Valley, an area covering seven states that was frequently ravaged by floods. The TVA envisioned in FDR's message was to be a publicly owned corporation charged with directing the development of the Tennessee River drainage basin for the region's social and economic benefit. The regional planning authority's mandate included rural electrification, flood control, reforestation, fertilizer production, agricultural development, and soil preservation. Roosevelt asserted that the welfare of millions of Americans depended on the enactment of his bold proposal. Congress passed legislation creating the TVA on May 18, 1933. TVA brought full employment, cheap electric power, low-cost housing, soil restoration, and reforestation to the area.

The continued idleness of a great national investment in the Tennessee Valley leads me to ask the Congress for legislation necessary to enlist this project in the service of the people.

It is clear that the Muscle Shoals development is but a small part of the potential public usefulness of the entire Tennessee River. Such use, if envisioned in its entirety, transcends mere power development: it enters the wide fields of flood control, soil erosion, afforestation, elimination from agricultural use of marginal lands, and distribution and diversification of industry. In short, this power development of war days leads logically to national planning for a complete river water shed involving many States and the future lives and welfare of millions. It touches and gives life to all forms of human concerns.

I, therefore, suggest to the Congress legislation to create a Tennessee Valley Authority—a corporation clothed with the power of government but possessed of the flexibility and initiative of a private enterprise. It should be charged with the broadest duty of planning for the proper use, conservation and development of the natural resources of the Tennessee River drainage basin and its adjoining territory for the general social and economic welfare of the nation. This Authority should also be clothed with the necessary power to carry these plans into effect. Its duty should be the rehabilitation of the Muscle Shoals development and the coordination of it with the wider plan.

Many hard lessons have taught us the human waste that results from lack of planning. Here and there a few wise cities and counties have looked ahead and planned. But our nation has "just grown." It is time to extend planning to a wider field, in this instance comprehending in one great project many States directly concerned with the basin of one of our greatest rivers.

This in a true sense is a return to the spirit and vision of the pioneer. If we are successful here we can march on, step by step, in a like development of other great natural territorial units within our borders.

Source:
Landmark Documents in American History, Facts On File, Inc.

Agricultural Adjustment Act (AAA), 1933

New Deal legislation enacted by the U.S. Congress on May 12, 1933, to raise farm income and commodity prices—and to reduce surpluses of basic commodities—by curtailing production. This act replaced the Federal Farm Board created by the Agricultural Marketing Act of June 15, 1929, that implemented the farm relief policy of President Herbert Hoover's administration. The board consisted of eight members and the U.S. secretary of agriculture and was to promote the marketing of agricultural products through cooperatives and stabilization corporations. The act replaced the subsidy and price-fixing proposals of the McNary-Haugen Bill.

Its efforts proved unsuccessful and was replaced in 1933 by the Agricultural Adjustment Act. Farmers who voluntarily reduced their production of various staples were to receive payments derived from taxes levied on the processors of certain farm products. Restricted commodities included hogs, corn, wheat, cotton, rice, dairy items, and tobacco. In 1934 the list was enlarged to include cattle, sugar, flax, grain sorghums, peanuts, barley, and rye. The act established the Agricultural Adjustment Administration to oversee the program. In 1936, in *United States v. Butler* (297 U.S. 1), the Supreme Court declared parts of the act invalid.

Shortly after the AAA was enacted, June 16, 1933, the Farm Credit Act was passed. It centralized all farm credit services into the Farm Credit Administration, allowing American farmers to refinance their mortgages on long terms at low interest rates. The legislation completed action begun by President Franklin D. Roosevelt's executive order of March 27, which had consolidated several federal agencies—among them the Federal Farm Board and the Federal Farm Loan Board—dealing with farm credit. It established production credit corporations in 12 regional districts to provide long-term financing for farmers. This act was followed January 31, 1934, by the Farm Mortgage Refinancing Act, which established the Federal Farm Mortgage Corporation (FFMC) to assist in the refinancing of farm debts. The FFMC was to advance the loan operations of the federal land banks by issuing fully guaranteed tax-exempt bonds and exchanging the proceeds for land-bank bonds. The FFMC, set up under the Farm Credit Corporation, was authorized to issue up to $2 million in bonds, whose principal and interest were guaranteed.

On June 28, 1934, a bill was enacted sponsored by Senator Lynn Frazier and Representative William Lemke to assist farmers threatened with foreclosures on their mortgages by enabling them to get credit extensions. This act allowed bankrupt farmers to repurchase their properties at a lower appraised value, with an interest rate of 1 percent paid over a five-year period. Where creditors refused a settlement, the act allowed farmers to retain possession of the properties, at reasonable rents, by suspending bankruptcy proceedings for five years in certain cases. The Supreme Court, in *Louisville Joint Stock Land Bank v. Radford* (May 27, 1935), declared the act unconstitutional, but similar legislation was enacted later that year.

On February 29, 1936, Congress enacted the Soil Conservation and Domestic Allotment Act to control not only soil erosion but also agricultural production, in order to prevent the accumulation of unmarketable surpluses. After the judicial invalidation of the U.S. Agricultural Adjustment Act of 1933, the 1936 act used indirect control of production, by authorizing benefit payments to farmers who practiced soil conservation under government programs. The programs shifted millions of acres from the cultivation of soil-depleting crops (such as corn, cotton, tobacco, wheat, and oats, which had also contributed to the production surpluses) to soil-conserving crops (such as clover and soybeans), or to soil-building efforts.

On February 16, 1938, after the Supreme Court began to affirm New Deal legislation, Congress passed a new Agricultural Adjustment Act that authorized the Agricultural Adjustment Administration to fix national acreage allotments for staple crops in order to reduce farm surpluses and stabilize farm prices. It established an "ever-normal granary" plan to store surpluses for use in bad years. The U.S. government encouraged farmers to operate within the allotments by offering them loans based on the "parity" price (a figure based on the 1909–14 farm purchasing power) of the stored surpluses; these surpluses would be sold in lean years and the loans repaid. If two-thirds of participating farmers agreed, the secretary of agriculture was authorized to fix marketing quotas when a surplus of an export commodity threatened price levels. The act also established a permanent soil conservation program.

An Act

To relieve the existing national economic emergency by increasing agricultural purchasing power, to raise revenue for extraordinary expenses incurred by reason of such emergency, to provide emergency relief with respect to agricultural indebtedness, to provide for the orderly liquidation of joint-stock land banks, and for other purposes.

Be it enacted by the Senate and House of Representatives of the United States of America in Congress assembled,

Title I—Agricultural Adjustment

Declaration of Emergency

That the present acute economic emergency being in part the consequence of a severe and increasing disparity between the prices of agricultural and other commodities, which disparity has largely destroyed the purchasing power of farmers for industrial products, has broken down the orderly exchange of commodities, and has seriously impaired the agricultural assets supporting the national credit structure, it is hereby declared that these conditions in the basic industry of agriculture have affected transactions in agricultural commodities with a national public interest, have burdened and obstructed the normal currents of commerce in such commodities, and render imperative the immediate enactment of title I of this Act.

Declaration of Policy

Sec. 2. It is hereby declared to be the policy of Congress—

(1) To establish and maintain such balance between the production and consumption of agricultural commodities, and such marketing conditions therefor, as will reestablish prices to farmers at a level that will give agricultural commodities a purchasing power with respect to articles that farmers buy, equivalent to the purchasing power of agricultural commodities in the base period. The base period in the case of all agricultural commodities except tobacco shall be the prewar period, August 1909-July 1914. In the case of tobacco, the base period shall be the postwar period, August 1919-July 1929.

(2) To approach such equality of purchasing power by gradual correction of the present inequalities therein at as rapid a rate as is deemed feasible in view of the current consumptive demand in domestic and foreign markets.

(3) To protect the consumers' interest by readjusting farm production at such level as will not increase the percentage of the consumers' retail expenditures for agricultural commodities, or products derived therefrom, which is returned to the farmer, above the percentage which was returned to the farmer in the prewar period, August 1909-July 1914.

Part 1—Cotton Option Contracts

Sec. 3. The Federal Farm Board and all departments and other agencies of the Government, not including the Federal intermediate credit banks, are hereby directed—

(a) To sell to the Secretary of Agriculture at such price as may be agreed upon, not in excess of the market price, all cotton now owned by them.

* * *

Sec 5. The Reconstruction Finance Corporation is hereby authorized and directed to advance money and to make loans to the Secretary of Agriculture to acquire such cotton and to pay the classing, carrying, and merchandising costs thereon, in such amounts and upon such terms as may be agreed upon by the Secretary and the Reconstruction Finance Corporation, with such warehouse receipts as collateral security. . . .

* * *

Sec. 6. (a) The Secretary of Agriculture is hereby authorized to enter into option contracts with the producers of cotton to sell to any such producer an amount of cotton to be agreed upon not in excess of the amount of reduction in production of cotton by such producer below the amount produced by him in the preceding crop year, in all cases where such producer agrees in writing to reduce the amount of cotton produced by him in 1933, below his production in the previous year, by not less than 30 per centum, without increase in commercial fertilization per acre.

(b) To any such producer so agreeing to reduce production the Secretary of Agriculture shall deliver a nontransferable-option contract agreeing to sell to said producer an amount, equivalent to the amount of his agreed reduction, of the cotton in the possession and control of the Secretary.

(c) The producer is to have the option to buy said cotton at the average price paid by the Secretary for the cotton procured under section 3, and is to have the right at any time up to January 1, 1934, to exercise his option, upon proof that he has complied with his contract and with all the rules and regulations of the Secretary of Agriculture with respect thereto, by taking said cotton upon payment by him of his option price and all actual carrying charges on such cotton; or the Secretary may sell such cotton for the account of such producer, paying him the excess of the market price at the date of sale over the average price above referred to after deducting all actual and necessary carrying charges: Provided, That in no event shall the producer be held responsible or liable for financial loss incurred in the holding of such cotton or on account of the carrying charges therein: Provided further, That such agreement to curtail cotton production shall contain a further provision that such cotton producer shall not use the land taken out of cotton production for the production for sale, directly or indirectly, of any other nationally produced agricultural commodity or product.

(d) If any cotton held by the Secretary of Agriculture is not disposed of under subsection (c), the Secretary is authorized to enter into similar option contracts with respect to such cotton, conditioned upon a like reduction of production in 1934, and permitting the producer in each case to exercise his option at any time up to January 1, 1935.

Sec. 7. The Secretary shall sell the cotton held by him at his discretion, but subject to the foregoing provisions: Provided, That he shall dispose of all cotton held by him by March 1, 1936: Provided further, That the Secretary shall have authority to enter into additional option contracts for so much of such cotton as is not necessary to comply with the provisions of section 6, in combination with benefit payments as provided for in part 2 of this title.

Part 2—Commodity Benefits

General Powers

Sec. 8. In order to effectuate (1) the declared policy, the Secretary of Agriculture shall have power—

(1) To provide for reduction in the acreage or reduction in the production for market, or both, of any basic agricultural commodity, through agreements with producers or by other voluntary methods, and to provide for rental or benefit payments in connection therewith or upon that part of the production of any basic agricultural commodity required for domestic consumption, in such amounts as the Secretary deems fair and reasonable, to be paid out of any moneys available for such payments. Under regulations of the Secretary of Agriculture requiring adequate facilities for the storage of any non-perishable agricultural commodity on the farm, inspection and measurement of any such commodity so stored, and the locking and sealing thereof, and such other regulations as may be prescribed by the Secretary of Agriculture for the protection of such commodity and for the marketing thereof, a reasonable percentage of any benefit payment may be advanced on any such commodity so stored. In any such case, such deduction may be made from the amount of the benefit payment as the Secretary of Agriculture determines will reasonably compensate for the cost of inspection and sealing, but no deduction may be made for interest.

1 So in original.

(2) To enter into marketing agreements with processors, associations of producers, and others engaged in the handling, in the current of interstate or foreign commerce of any agricultural commodity or product thereof, after due notice and opportunity for hearing to interested parties. The making of any such agreement shall not be held to be in violation of any of the antitrust laws of the United States, and any such agreement shall be deemed to be law-

ful: Provided, That no such agreement shall remain in force after the termination of this Act. For the purpose of carrying out any such agreement the parties thereto shall be eligible for loans from the Reconstruction Finance Corporation under section 5 of the Reconstruction Finance Corporation Act. Such loans shall not be in excess of such amounts as may be authorized by the agreements.

(3) To issue licenses permitting processors, associations of producers, and others to engage in the handling, in the current of interstate or foreign commerce, of any agricultural commodity or product thereof, or any competing commodity or product thereof. Such licenses shall be subject to such terms and conditions, not in conflict with existing Acts of Congress or regulations pursuant thereto, as may be necessary to eliminate unfair practices or charges that prevent or tend to prevent the effectuation of the declared policy and the restoration of normal economic conditions in the marketing of such commodities or products and the financing thereof. The Secretary of Agriculture may suspend or revoke any such license, after due notice and opportunity for hearing, for violations of the terms or conditions thereof. Any order of the Secretary suspending or revoking any such license shall be final if in accordance with law. Any such person engaged in such handling without a license as required by the Secretary under this section shall be subject to a fine of not more than $1,000 for each day during which the violation continues.

(4) To require any licensee under this section to furnish such reports as to quantities of agricultural commodities or products thereof bought and sold and the prices thereof, and as to trade practices and charges, and to keep such systems of accounts, as may be necessary for the purpose of part 2 of this title.

(5) No person engaged in the storage in a public warehouse of any basic agricultural commodity in the current interstate or foreign commerce, shall deliver any such commodity upon which a warehouse receipt has been issued and is outstanding, without prior surrender and cancellation of such warehouse receipt. Any person violating any of the provisions of this subsection shall, upon conviction, be punished by a fine of not more than $5,000, or by imprisonment for not more than two years, or both. The Secretary of Agriculture may revoke any license issued under subsection (3) of this section, if he finds, after due notice and opportunity for hearing, that the licensee has violated the provisions of this subsection.

Processing Tax

Sec. 9. (a) To obtain revenue for extraordinary expenses incurred by reason of the national economic emergency, there shall be levied processing taxes as hereinafter provided. When the Secretary of Agriculture determines that rental or benefit payments are to be made with respect to any basic agricultural commodity, he shall proclaim such determination, and a processing tax shall be in effect with respect to such commodity from the beginning of the marketing year therefor next following the date of such proclamation. The processing tax shall be levied, assessed, and collected upon the first domestic processing of the commodity, whether of domestic production or imported, and shall be paid by the processor. The rate of tax shall conform to the requirements of subsection (b). Such rate shall be determined by the Secretary of Agriculture as of the date the tax first takes effect, and the rate so determined shall, at such intervals as the Secretary finds necessary to effectuate the declared policy, be adjusted by him to conform to such requirements. The processing tax shall terminate at the end of the marketing year current at the time the Secretary proclaims that rental or benefit payments are to be discontinued with respect to such commodity. The marketing year for each commodity shall be ascertained and prescribed by regulations of the Secretary of Agriculture: Provided, That upon any article upon which a manufacturers' sales tax is levied under the authority of the Revenue Act of 1932 and which manufacturers' sales tax is computed on the basis of weight, such manufacturers' sales tax shall be computed on the basis of the weight of said finished article less the weight of the processed cotton contained therein on which a processing tax has been paid.

(b) The processing tax shall be at such rate as equals the difference between the current average farm price for the commodity and the fair exchange value of the commodity. . . .

c) For the purposes of part 2 of this title, the fair exchange value of a commodity shall be the price therefor that will give the commodity the same purchasing power, with respect to articles farmers buy, as such commodity had during the base period specified in section 2; and the current average farm price and the fair exchange value shall be ascertained by the Secretary of Agriculture from available statistics of the Department of Agriculture.

* * *

Appropriation

Sec. 12. (a) There is hereby appropriated, out of any money in the Treasury not otherwise appropriated, the sum of $100,000,000 to be available to the Secretary of Agriculture for administrative expenses under this title and for rental and benefit payments made with respect to reduction in acreage or reduction in production for market under part 2 of this title. Such sum shall remain available until expended.

(b) In addition to the foregoing, the proceeds derived from all taxes imposed under this title are hereby appropriated to be available to the Secretary of Agriculture for expansion of markets and removal of surplus agricultural products and [various administrative] purposes. . . .

* * *

Termination of Act

Sec. 13. This title shall cease to be in effect whenever the President finds and proclaims that the national economic emergency in relation to agriculture has been ended; and pending such time the President shall by proclamation terminate with respect to any basic agricultural commodity such provisions of this title as he finds are not requisite to carrying out the declared policy with respect to such commodity. The Secretary of Agriculture shall make such investigations and reports thereon to the President as may be necessary to aid him in executing this section.

Separability of Provisions

Sec. 14. If any provision of this title is declared unconstitutional, or the applicability thereof to any person, circumstance, or commodity is held invalid the validity of the remainder of this title and the applicability thereof to other persons, circumstances, or commodities shall not be affected thereby.

* * *

Title II—Agricultural Credits

Part 1—Amendments to Federal Farm Loan Act

Issuance of Bonds by Land Banks

Section 21. Section 32 of the Federal Farm Loan Act, as amended (U.S.C., title 12, sec. 991), is amended by adding at the end thereof the following new paragraph:

"Until such time as the Farm Loan Commissioner determines that Federal farm-loan bonds (other than those issued under this paragraph) are readily salable in the open market at a yield not in excess of 4 per centum per annum, but in no case more than two years after this paragraph takes effect, Federal land banks may issue farm-loan bonds as authorized under this Act, for the purpose of making new loans, or for purchasing mortgages or exchanging bonds for mortgages. . . .

* * *

Reduction of Interest on Loans and Deferment of Principal

Sec. 24. Section 12 of the Federal Farm Loan Act, as amended (U.S.C., title 12, secs. 771-772), is amended by adding at the end thereof the following new paragraph:

"Twelfth. Notwithstanding the provisions of paragraph Second,' the rate of interest on any loans on mortgage made through national farm-loan associations or through agents as provided in section 15, or purchased from joint-stock land banks, by any Federal land bank, outstanding on the date this paragraph takes effect or made through national farm-loan associations within two years after such date, shall not exceed 4 1/2 per centum per annum for all interest payable on installment dates occurring within a period of five years commencing sixty days after the date this paragraph takes effect; and no payment of the principal portion of any installment of any such loan shall be required during such five-year period if the borrower shall not be in default with respect to any other condition or covenant of his mortgage. The foregoing provisions shall apply to loans made by Federal land banks through branches, except that the rate of interest on such loans for such five-year period shall be 5 per centum in lieu of 4 1/2 per centum. The Secretary of the Treasury shall pay each Federal land bank, as soon as practicable after October 1, 1933, and after the end of each quarter thereafter, such amount as the Farm Loan Commissioner certifies to the Secretary of the Treasury is equal to the amount by which interest payments on mortgages held by such bank have been reduced, during the preceding quarter. . . .

* * *

Direct Loans

Sec. 26. Section 7 of the Federal Farm Loan Act, as amended, is amended by striking out the last paragraph and inserting in lieu thereof the following new paragraphs:

"Whenever it shall appear to the Farm Loan Commissioner that national farm-loan associations have not been formed in any locality in the continental United States, or that the farmers residing in the territory covered by the charter of a national farm-loan association are unable to apply to the Federal land bank of the district for loans on account of the inability of the bank to accept applications from such association, the Farm Loan Commissioner shall authorize said bank to make direct loans to borrowers secured by first mortgages on farm lands situated within any such locality or territory. Except as herein otherwise specifically provided, all provisions of this Act applicable with respect to loans made through national farm-loan associations shall, insofar as practicable, apply with respect to such direct loans, and the Farm Loan Commissioner is authorized to make such rules and regulations as he may deem necessary with respect to such direct loans.

* * *

Part 2—Joint-Stock Land Banks

* * *

Loans to Joint-Stock Land Banks to Provide for Orderly Liquidation

Sec. 30. (a) The Reconstruction Finance Corporation is authorized and directed to make available to the Farm

Loan Commissioner, out of the funds of the Corporation, the sum of $100,000,000, to be used, for a period not exceeding two years from the date of enactment of this Act, for the purpose of making loans to the joint-stock land banks organized and doing business under the Federal Farm Loan Act, as amended, at a rate of interest not to exceed 4 per centum per annum, payable annually. Such loans shall be made upon application therefor by such banks and upon compliance with the requirements of this section. The amount which may be loaned hereunder to any such bank shall not exceed an amount having the same proportion to the said $100,000,000 as the unpaid principal of the mortgages held by such bank on the date of enactment of this Act bears to the total amount of the unpaid principal of the mortgages held by all the joint-stock land banks on such date.

* * *

Part 3—Loans to Farmers by Farm Loan Commissioner

Reduction of Debts and Redemption of Foreclosed Farms

Sec. 32. The Reconstruction Finance Corporation is authorized and directed to allocate and make available to the Farm Loan Commissioner the sum of $200,000,000, or so much thereof as may be necessary, to be used for the purpose of making loans as hereinafter provided to any farmer, secured by a first or second mortgage upon the whole or any part of the farm property, real or personal, including crops, of the farmer. . . .

* * *

Part 8: Short Title

Sec. 42. This title may be cited as the "Emergency Farm Mortgage Act of 1933."

Title III—Financing—And Exercising Power Conferred by Section 8 of Article I of the Constitution: To Coin Money and to Regulate the Value Thereof

Sec. 43. Whenever the President finds, upon investigation, that (1) the foreign commerce of the United States is adversely affected by reason of the depreciation in the value of the currency of any other government or governments in relation to the Present standard value of gold, or (2) action under this section is necessary in order to regulate and maintain the parity of currency issues of the United States, or (3) an economic emergency requires an expansion of credit, or (4) an expansion of credit is necessary to secure by international agreement a stabilization at proper levels of the currencies of various governments, the President is authorized, in his discretion—

(a) To direct the Secretary of the Treasury to enter into agreements with the several Federal Reserve banks and with the Federal Reserve Board whereby the Federal Reserve Board will, and it is hereby authorized to, notwithstanding any provisions of law or rules and regulations to the contrary, permit such reserve banks to agree that they will, (1) conduct, pursuant to existing law, throughout specified periods, open market operations in obligations of the United States Government or corporations in which the United States is the majority stockholder, and (2) purchase directly and hold in portfolio for an agreed period or periods of time Treasury bills or other obligations of the United States Government in an aggregate sum of $3,000,000,000 in addition to those they may then hold, unless prior to the termination of such period or periods the Secretary shall consent to their sale. No suspension of reserve requirements of the Federal Reserve banks, under the terms of section 11(c) of the Federal Reserve Act, necessitated by reason of operations under this section, shall require the imposition of the graduated tax upon any deficiency in reserves as provided in said section 11(c). Nor shall it require any automatic increase in the rates of interest or discount charged by any Federal Reserve bank, as otherwise specified in that section. The Federal Reserve Board, with the approval of the Secretary of the Treasury, may require the Federal Reserve banks to take such action as may be necessary, in the judgment of the Board and of the Secretary of the Treasury, to prevent undue credit expansion.

(b) If the Secretary, when directed by the President, is unable to secure the assent of the several Federal Reserve banks and the Federal Reserve Board to the agreements authorized in this section, or if operations under the above provisions prove to be inadequate to meet the purposes of this section, or if for any other reason additional measures are required in the judgment of the President to meet such purpose, then the President is authorized—

(1) To direct the Secretary of the Treasury to cause to be issued in such amount or amounts as he may from time to time order, United States notes, as provided in the Act entitled "An Act to authorize the issue of United States notes and for the redemption of funding thereof and for funding the floating debt of the United States," approved February 25, 1862, and Acts supplementary thereto and amendatory thereof, in the same size and of similar color to the Federal Reserve notes heretofore issued and in denominations of $1, $5, $10, $20, $50, $100, $500, $1,000, and $10,000; but notes issued under this subsection shall be issued only for the purpose of meeting maturing Federal obligations to repay sums borrowed by the United States and for purchasing United States bonds and other interest-bearing obligations of

the United States: Provided, That when any such notes are used for such purpose the bond or other obligation so acquired or taken up shall be retired and canceled. Such notes shall be issued at such times and in such amounts as the President may approve but the aggregate amount of such notes outstanding at any time shall not exceed $3,000,000,000. . . .

(2) By proclamation to fix the weight of the gold dollar in grains nine tenths fine and also to fix the weight of the silver dollar in grains nine tenths fine at a definite fixed ratio in relation to the gold dollar at such amounts as he finds necessary from his investigation to stabilize domestic prices or to protect the foreign commerce against the adverse effect of depreciated foreign currencies, and to provide for the unlimited coinage of such gold and silver at the ratio so fixed. . . .

(c) The silver accepted and received under the provisions of this section shall be deposited in the Treasury of the United States, to be held, used, and disposed of as in this section provided.

(d) The Secretary of the Treasury shall cause silver certificates to be issued in such denominations as he deems advisable to the total number of dollars for which such silver was accepted in payment of debts. Such silver certificates shall be used by the Treasurer of the United States in payment of any obligations of the United States.

(e) The silver so accepted and received under this section shall be coined into standard silver dollars and subsidiary coins sufficient, in the opinion of the Secretary of the Treasury, to meet any demands for redemption of such silver certificates issued under the provisions of this section, and such coins shall be retained in the Treasury for the payment of such certificates on demand. . . .

* * *

Sec. 46. Section 19 of the Federal Reserve Act, as amended, is amended by inserting immediately after paragraph (c) thereof the following new paragraph:

"Notwithstanding the foregoing provisions of this section, the Federal Reserve Board, upon the affirmative vote of not less than five of its members and with the approval of the President, may declare that an emergency exists by reason of credit expansion, and may by regulation during such emergency increase or decrease from time to time, in its discretion, the reserve balances required to be maintained against either demand or time deposits."

Approved, May 12, 1933.

Source:

Statutes at Large, Vol. 47, pp. 31–54.

National Industrial Recovery Act (NIRA), 1933

Federal legislation enacted on June 16, 1933, intended to encourage industrial and business recovery, reduce unemployment, foster fair competition, and provide for the construction of public works. The centerpiece of President Franklin D. Roosevelt's New Deal legislation, the NIRA created the National Recovery Administration (NRA) to supervise industrial self-regulation under codes of fair competition. The codes, which had the force of law, gave workers the right to organize and bargain collectively and, thus, have a direct influence on minimum wages, maximum hours, and other working conditions. It also created the Public Works Administration to increase employment and business activity by building roads, public buildings, and similar projects. The NRA's sign was a blue eagle, and businesses that subscribed to NRA codes displayed it. By 1935 more than 750 NRA codes had been adopted, affecting some 23 million people. However, they were hastily drawn and often favored business over the workers.

The act gave the president broad powers to manage the national economy based on the president's declared national emergency. On May 27, 1935, the Supreme Court unanimously declared the NIRA unconstitutional in *Schecter Poultry Corporation v. United States* (295 U.S. 495). The case arose from alleged violations by a New York slaughterhouse of the city's code for fair competition for the live poultry industry. In his decision, Chief Justice Charles Evans Hughes declared that the NIRA improperly delegated legislative power to the executive branch lacked constitutional authority and regulated purely intrastate (not interstate) commerce, which was outside the authority of Congress. "Extraordinary conditions [the Great Depression] do not create or enlarge constitutional powers." This decision, though unanimous, set the stage for the many 5-4 rulings that would occur in the next two years against New Deal legislation.

AN ACT to encourage national industrial recovery, to foster fair competition, and to provide for the construction of certain useful public works, and for other purposes.

Be it enacted by the Senate and House of Representatives of the United States of America in Congress assembled,

Title I—Industrial Recovery

Declaration of Policy

Section 1. A national emergency productive of widespread unemployment and disorganization of industry, which burdens interstate and foreign commerce, affects the public welfare, and undermines the standards of living of the American people, is hereby declared to exist. It is hereby declared to be the policy of Congress to remove obstructions to the free flow of interstate and foreign commerce which tend to diminish the amount thereof; and to provide for the general welfare by promoting the organization of industry for the purpose of cooperative action among trade groups, to induce and maintain united action of labor and management under adequate governmental sanctions and supervision, to eliminate unfair competitive practices, to promote the fullest possible utilization of the present protective capacity of industries, to avoid undue restriction of production (except as may be temporarily required), to increase the consumption of industrial and agricultural products by increasing purchasing power, to reduce and relieve unemployment, to improve standards of labor, and otherwise to rehabilitate industry and to conserve natural resources.

Source:
United States Statutes at Large, Vol. 47, pp. 195–211.

Indian Reorganization Act, 1934

Federal legislation enacted on June 18, 1934, that restored some Native American lands to tribal ownership and authorized federal funds to encourage Native American businesses. Sponsored by Senator Burton K. Wheeler of Montana and Representative Edgar Howard of Nebraska, the act gave Native Americans residing on reservations the right to adopt constitutions for self-government or to petition the secretary of the interior for a charter of incorporation. The Bureau of Indian Affairs retained a veto power over tribal decisions. To conserve and develop tribal lands, the act ended land allotments in severalty and restored to tribal ownership "surplus lands" that had previously been open for sale to homesteaders. The act also authorized funds to enlarge tribal land holdings, to support Native American education, and to encourage economic development through federal loans.

An Act
To conserve and develop Indian lands and resources; to extend to Indians the right to form business and other organizations; to establish a credit system for Indians; to grant certain rights of home rule to Indians; to provide for vocational education for Indians; and for other purposes.

Be it enacted by the Senate and House of Representative of the United States of America in Congress assembled, That hereafter no land of any Indian reservation, created or set apart by treaty or agreement with the Indians, Act of Congress, Executive order, purchase, or otherwise, shall be allotted in severalty to any Indian.

Sec. 2. The existing periods of trust placed upon any Indian lands and any restriction on alienation thereof are hereby extended and continued until otherwise directed by Congress.

Sec. 3. The Secretary of the Interior, if he shall find it to be in the public interest, is hereby authorized to restore to tribal ownership the remaining surplus lands of any Indian reservation heretofore opened, or authorized to be opened, to sale, or any other form of disposal by Presidential proclamation, or by any of the public-land laws of the United States: *Provided, however,* That valid rights or claims of any persons to any lands so withdrawn existing on the date of the withdrawal shall not be affected by this Act: *Provided further,* That this section shall not apply to lands within any reclamation project heretofore authorized in any Indian reservation: *Provided further,* That the order of the Department of the Interior signed, dated, and approved by Honorable Ray Lyman Wilbur, as Secretary of the Interior, on October 28, 1932, temporarily withdrawing lands of the Papago Indian Reservation in Arizona from all forms of mineral entry or claim under the public land mining laws, is hereby revoked and rescinded, and the lands of the said Papago Indian Reservation are hereby restored to exploration and location, under the existing mining laws of the United States, in accordance with the express terms and provisions declared and set forth in the Executive orders establishing said Papago Indian Reservation: *Provided further,* That damages shall be paid to the Papago Tribe for loss of any improvements on any land located for mining in such a sum as may be determined by the Secretary of the Interior but not to exceed the cost of said improvements: *Provided further,* That a yearly rental not to exceed five cents per acre shall be paid to the Papago Tribe for loss of the use or occupancy of any land withdrawn by the requirements of mining operations, and payments derived from damages or rentals shall be deposited in the Treasury of the United States to the credit of the Papago Tribe: *Provided further,* That in the event any person or persons, partnership, corporation, or association, desires a mineral patent, according to the mining laws of the United States, he or they shall first deposit in the Treasury of the United States to the credit of the Papago Tribe the sum of $1.00 per acre in lieu of annual rental, as hereinbefore provided, to compensate for the loss or occupancy of the lands withdrawn by the requirements of mining operations: *Provided further,* That patentee shall also pay into the Treasury of the United States to the credit of the Papago Tribe damages for the loss of improvements not heretofore paid in such a sum as may be determined by the Secretary of the Interior, but not to exceed the cost thereof; the payment of $1.00 per acre for surface use to be refunded to patentee in the event that patent is not acquired.

Nothing herein contained shall restrict the granting or use of permits for easements or rights-of-way; or ingress or egress over the lands for all proper and lawful purposes; and nothing contained herein, except as expressly provided, shall be construed as authority for the Secretary of the Interior, or any other person, to issue or promulgate a rule or regulation in conflict with the Executive order of February 1, 1917, creating the Papago Indian Reservation in Arizona or the Act of February 21, 1931 (46 Stat. 1202).

Sec. 4. Except as herein provided, no sale, devise, gift, exchange or other transfer of restricted Indian lands or of shares in the assets of any Indian tribe or corporation organized hereunder, shall be made or approved: *Provided, however,* That such lands or interests may, with the approval of the Secretary of the Interior, be sold, devised, or otherwise transferred to the Indian tribe in which the lands or shares are located or from which the shares were derived or to a successor corporation; and in all instances such lands or interests shall descend or be devised, in accordance with the then existing laws of the State or Federal laws where applicable, in which said lands are located or in which the subject matter of the corporation is located, to any member of such tribe or of such corporation or any heirs of such member: *Provided further,* That the Secretary of the Interior may authorize voluntary exchanges of lands of equal value and the voluntary exchange of shares of equal value whenever such exchange, in his judgment, is expedient and beneficial for a compatible with the proper consolidation of Indian lands and for the benefit of cooperative organizations.

Sec. 5. The Secretary of the Interior is hereby authorized, in his discretion, to acquire through purchase, relinquishment, gift, exchange, or assignment, any interest in lands, water rights or surface rights to lands, within or without existing reservations, including trust or otherwise restricted allotments whether the allottee be living or decreased, for the purpose of providing land for Indians.

For the acquisition of such lands, interests in lands, water rights, and surface rights, and for expenses incident to such acquisition, there is hereby authorized to be appropriated, out of any funds in the Treasury not otherwise appropriated, a sum not to exceed $2,000,000 in any one fiscal year: *Provided,* That no part of such funds shall be used to acquire additional land outside of the exterior boundaries of Navajo Indian Reservation for the Navajo Indians in Arizona and New Mexico, in the event that the proposed Navajo boundary extension measures now pending in Congress and embodied in the bills (S. 2499 and H.R. 8927) to define the exterior boundaries of the Navajo Indian Reservation in Arizona, and for other purposes, and the bills (S. 2531 and H.R. 8982) to define the exterior boundaries of the Navajo Indian Reservation in New Mexico and for other purposes, or similar legislation, become law.

The unexpended balances of any appropriations made pursuant to this section shall remain available until expended.

Title to any lands or rights acquired pursuant to this Act shall be taken in the name of the United States in trust for the Indian tribe or individual Indian for which the land is acquired, and such lands or rights shall be exempt from State and local taxation.

Sec. 6. The Secretary of the Interior is directed to make rules and regulations for the operation and management of Indian forestry units on the principle of sustained-yield management, to restrict the number of livestock grazed on Indian range units to the estimated carrying capacity of such ranges, and to promulgate such other rules and regulations as may be necessary to protect the range from deterioration, to prevent soil erosion, to assure full utilization of the range, and like purposes.

Sec. 7. The Secretary of the Interior is hereby authorized to proclaim new Indian reservations on lands acquired pursuant to any authority conferred by this Act, or to add such lands to existing reservations: *Provided,* That lands added to existing reservations shall be designated for the exclusive use of Indians entitled by enrollment or by tribal membership to residence at such reservations.

Sec. 8. Nothing contained in this Act shall be construed to relate to Indian holdings of allotments or homesteads upon the public domain outside of the geographic boundaries of any Indian reservation now existing or established hereafter.

Sec. 9. There is hereby authorized to be appropriated, out of any funds in the Treasury not otherwise appropriated, such sums as may be necessary, but not to exceed $250,000 in any fiscal year, to be expended at the order of the Secretary of the Interior, in defraying the expenses of organizing Indian chartered corporations or other organizations created under this Act.

Sec. 10. There is hereby authorized to be appropriated, out of any funds in the Treasury not otherwise appropriated, the sum of $10,000,000 to be established as a revolving fund from which the Secretary of the Interior, under such rules and regulations as he may prescribe, may make loans to Indian chartered corporations for the purpose of promoting the economic development of such tribes and of their members, and may defray the expenses of administering such loans. Repayment of amounts loaned under this authorization shall be credited to the revolving fund and shall be available for the purposes for which the fund is established. A report shall be made annually to Congress to transactions under this authorization.

Sec. 11. There is hereby authorized to be appropriated, out of any funds in the United States Treasury not otherwise appropriated, a sum not to exceed $250,000 annually, together with any unexpended balances of previous appropriations made pursuant to this section, for loans to Indians for the payment of tuition and other expenses in recognized vocational and trade schools: *Provided,* That not more than $50,000 of such sum shall be available for loans to Indian students in high schools and colleges. Such loans shall be reimbursable under rules established by the Commissioner of Indian Affairs.

Sec. 12. The Secretary of the Interior is directed to establish standards of health, age, character, experience, knowledge, and ability for Indians who may be appointed, without regard to civil-service laws, to the various positions maintained, now or hereafter, by the Indian Office, in the administration of functions or services affecting any Indian tribe. Such qualified Indians shall hereafter have the preference to appointment to vacancies in any such positions.

Sec. 13. The provisions of this Act shall not apply to any of the Territories, colonies, or insular possessions of the United States, except that sections 9, 10, 11, 12, and 16, shall apply to the Territory of Alaska: *Provided,* That Sections 2, 4, 7, 16, 17 and 18 of this Act shall not apply to the following-named Indian tribes, the members of such Indian tribes, together with members of other tribes affiliated with such named tribes located in the State of Oklahoma, as follows: Cheyenne, Arapaho, Apache, Comanche, Kiowa, Caddo, Delaware, Wichita, Osage, Kaw, Otoe, Tonkawa, Pawnee, Ponca, Shawnee, Ottawa, Quapaw, Seneca, Wyandotte, Iowa, Sac and Fox, Kickapoo, Pottawatomi, Cherokee, Chickasaw, Choctaw, Creek, and Seminole. Section 4 of this Act shall not apply to the Indians of the Klamath Reservation in Oregon.

Sec. 14. The Secretary of the Interior is hereby directed to continue the allowance of the articles enumerated in section 17, of the Act of March 2, 1889 (23 Stat. L. 894), or their commuted cash value under the Act of June 10, 1896 (29 Stat. L. 334), to all Sioux Indians who would be eligible, but for the provisions of this Act, to receive allotments of lands in severalty under section 19 of the Act of May 29, 1908 (25 Stat.L. 451), or under any prior Act, and who have the prescribed status of the head of a family or single person over the age of eighteen years, and his approval shall be final and conclusive, claims therefor to be paid as formerly from the permanent appropriation made by said section 17 and carried on the books of the Treasury for this purpose. No person shall receive in his own right more than one allowance of the benefits, and application must be made and approved during the lifetime of the allottee or the right shall lapse. Such benefits shall continue to be paid upon such reservation until such time as the lands available therein for allotment at the time of the passage of this Act would have been exhausted by the award to each person receiving such benefits of an allotment of eighty acres of such land.

Sec. 15. Nothing in this Act shall be construed to impair or prejudice any claim or suit of any Indian tribe against the United States. It is hereby declared to be the intent of Congress that no expenditures for the benefit of Indians made out of appropriations authorized by this Act shall be considered as offsets in any suit brought to recover upon any claim of such Indians against the United States.

Sec. 16. Any Indian tribe, or tribes, residing on the same reservation, shall have the right to organize for its common welfare, and may adopt an appropriate constitution and bylaws, which shall become effective when ratified by a majority vote of the adult members of the tribe, or of the adult Indians residing on such reservation, as the case may be, at a special election authorized and called by the Secretary of the Interior under such rules and regulations as he may prescribe. Such constitution and bylaws when ratified as aforesaid and approved by the Secretary of the Interior shall be revocable by an election open to the same voters and conducted in the same manner as hereinabove provided. Amendments to the constitution and bylaws may be ratified and approved by the Secretary in the same manner as the original constitution and bylaws.

In additions to all powers vested in any Indian tribe or tribal council by existing law, the constitution adopted by said tribe shall also vest in such tribe or its tribal council the following rights and powers: To employ legal counsel, the choice of counsel and fixing of fees to be subject to the approval of the Secretary of the Interior; to prevent the sale, disposition, lease, or encumbrance of tribal lands, interests in lands, or other tribal assets without the consent of the tribe; and to negotiate with the Federal, State, and local Governments. The Secretary of the Interior shall advise such tribe or its tribal council of all appropriation estimates or Federal projects for the benefit of the tribe prior to the submission of such estimates to the Bureau of the Budget and the Congress.

Sec. 17. The Secretary of the Interior may, upon petition by at least one-third of the adult Indians, issue a charter of incorporation to such tribe: *Provided,* That such charter shall not become operative until ratified at a special election by a majority vote of the adult Indians living on the reservation. Such charter may convey to the incorporated tribe the power to purchase, take by gift, or bequest, or otherwise, own, hold, manage, operate, and dispose of property of every description, real and personal, including the power to purchase restricted Indian lands and to issue in exchange therefor interests in corporate property, and such further powers as may be incidental to the conduct of corporate business, not inconsistent with law, but no authority shall be granted to sell, mortgage, or lease for a period exceeding ten years any of the land included in the limits of the reservation. Any charter so issued shall not be revoked or surrendered except by Act of Congress.

Sec. 18. This Act shall not apply to any reservation wherein a majority of the adult Indians, voting at a special election duly called by the Secretary of the Interior, shall vote against its application. It shall be the duty of the Secretary of the Interior, within one year after the passage and approval of this Act, to call such an election, which election shall be held by secret ballot upon thirty days' notice.

Sec. 19. The term "Indian" as used in this Act shall include all persons of Indian descent who are members of any recognized Indian tribe now under Federal jurisdiction, and all persons who are descendants of such members who were, on June 1, 1934, residing within the present boundaries of any Indian reservation, and shall further include all other persons of one-half or more Indian blood. For the purposes of this Act, Eskimos and other aboriginal peoples of Alaska shall be considered Indians. The term "tribe" wherever used in this Act shall be construed to refer to any Indian tribe, organized band, pueblo, or the Indians residing on one reservation. The words "adult Indians" wherever used in this Act shall be construed to refer to Indians who have attained the age of twenty-one years.

Source:
United States Statutes at Large, Vol. 48, pp. 984–988.

Federal Communications Act, 1934

Federal legislation enacted on June 19, 1934, creating the Federal Communications Commission (FCC) to regulate interstate and foreign communications by telegraph, cable, and radio. The FCC replaced the Federal Radio Commission and consolidated regulatory powers formerly vested in the Interstate Commerce Commission and the Postal and Commerce Departments. The commission was to consist of seven members appointed by the president, with the consent of the Senate. The act authorized new regulations to control the radio broadcasting industry. The act eventually also applied to television but was considered inadequate regarding electronic computer transmissions. As a result, the Communications Act of 1986 was passed to cover these newer methods of communication.

Note the provisions concerning free and obscene speech (Section 326) and that foreshadowing the establishment of the Emergency Broadcast System (Section 606), used during the cold war in case of a nuclear attack but today it primarily warns of impending tornadoes or floods.

Of special significance for the future of law enforcement and counterintelligence was Section 605 that apparently outlawed federal eavesdropping on telephone communications. It responded to the 1928 *Olmstead* decision, which did not consider off-sight eavesdropping a violation of the Fourth Amendment, by restricting law enforcement use of wiretaps. Civil libertarians at the time and thereafter have emphasized the "unauthorized use" provisions that appear to require the sender's permission. At the time the Federal Communications Act was passed, the FBI permitted wiretaps only in life-threatening instances like kidnappings, and only with director J. Edgar Hoover's personal authorization. In 1937, in the case of *Nardone v. United States* (302 U.S. 379), the Supreme Court held that evidence from interstate wiretaps could not be used in court. The Department of Justice advised Hoover that it considered interstate wiretaps permissible as long as the evidence was not "divulged" in federal court; intrastate wiretaps, however, could be used without violating the act. Nevertheless, Hoover advised that the FBI's policy would remain the same: He had to approve all wiretaps, and they could be used only for intelligence purposes. Hoover continued thereafter to approve wiretaps as long as the results were not used in court. This policy prevailed until 1966.

An Act
To provide for the regulation of interstate and foreign communication by wire or radio, and for other purposes.

Be it enacted by the Senate and House of Representatives of the United States of America in Congress assembled,

Title I—General Provisions
Purposes of Act; Creation of Federal Communications Commission

Section 1. For the purpose of regulating interstate and foreign commerce in communication by wire and radio so as to make available, so far as possible, to all the people of the United States a rapid, efficient, Nation-wide, and world-wide wire and radio communication service with adequate facilities at reasonable charges, for the purpose of the national defense, and for the purpose of securing a more effective execution of this policy by centralizing authority heretofore granted by law to several agencies and by granting additional authority with respect to interstate and foreign commerce in wire and radio communication, there is hereby created a commission to be known as the "Federal Communications Commission," which shall be constituted as hereinafter provided, and which shall execute and enforce the provisions of this Act.

Application of Act

Sec. 2. (a) The provisions of this Act shall apply to all interstate and foreign communication by wire or radio and all interstate and foreign transmission of energy by radio, which originates and/or is received within the United States, and to all persons engaged within the United States in such communication or such transmission of energy by radio, and to the licensing and regulating of all radio stations as hereinafter provided. . . .

(b) Subject to the provisions of section 301, nothing in this Act shall be construed to apply or to give the Commission jurisdiction with respect to (1) charges, classifications, practices, services, facilities, or regulations for or in connection with intrastate communication service of any carrier, or (2) any carrier engaged in interstate or foreign communication solely through physical connection with the facilities of another carrier not directly or indirectly controlling or controlled by, or under direct or indirect common control with, such carrier; [with exceptions].

Definitions

Sec. 3. For the purposes of this Act, unless the context otherwise requires—

(a) "Wire communication" or "communication by wire" means the transmission of writing, signs, signals, pictures, and sounds of all kinds by aid of wire, cable, or other like connection between the points of origin and reception of such transmission, including all instrumentalities, facilities, apparatus, and services (among other things, the receipt, forwarding, and delivery of communications) incidental to such transmission.

(b) "Radio communication" or "communication by radio" means the transmission by radio of writing, signs, signals, pictures, and sounds of all kinds, including all instrumentalities, facilities, apparatus, and services (among other things, the receipt, forwarding, and delivery of communications) incidental to such transmission.

(c) "Licensee" means the holder of a ratio station license granted or continued in force under authority of this Act.

* * *

(e) "Interstate communication" or "interstate transmission" means communication or transmission (1) from any State, Territory, or possession of the United States (other than the Philippine Islands and the Canal Zone), or the District of Columbia, to any other State, Territory, or possession of the United States (other than the Philippine Islands and the Canal Zone), or the District of Columbia, (2) from or to the United States to or from the Philippine Islands or the Canal Zone, insofar as such communication or transmission takes place within the United States, or (3) between points within the United States but through a foreign country; but shall not include wire communication between points within the same State, Territory, or possession of the United States, or the District of Columbia, through any place outside thereof, if such communication is regulated by a State commission.

(f) "Foreign communication" or "foreign transmission" means communication or transmission from or to any place in the United States to or from a foreign country, or between a station in the United States and a mobile station located outside the United States.

(g) "United States" means the several States and Territories, the District of Columbia, and the possessions of the United States, but does not include the Philippine Islands or the Canal Zone.

* * *

(k) "Radio station" or "station" means a station equipped to engage in radio communication or radio transmission of energy.

* * *

(o) "Broadcasting" means the dissemination of radio communications intended to be received by the public, directly or by the intermediary of relay stations.

* * *

(v) "State" includes the District of Columbia and the Territories and possessions.

Provisions Relating to the Commission

Sec. 4. (a) The Federal Communications Commission (in this Act referred to as the "Commission") shall be composed of seven commissioners appointed by the President, by and with the advice and consent of the Senate, one of whom the President shall designate as chairman.

(b) Each member of the Commission shall be a citizen of the United States. No member of the Commission or person in its employ shall be financially interested in the manufacture or sale of radio apparatus or of apparatus for wire or radio communication; in communication by wire or radio or in radio transmission of energy; in any company furnishing services or such apparatus to any company engaged in communication by wire or radio or to any company manufacturing or selling apparatus used for communication by wire or radio; or in any company owning stocks, bonds, or other securities of any such company; nor be in the employ of or hold any official relation to any person subject to any of the provisions of this Act, nor own stocks, bonds, or other securities of any corporation subject to any of the provisions of this Act. Such commissioners shall not engage in any other business, vocation, or employment. Not more than four commissioners shall be members of the same political party.

(c) The commissioners first appointed under this Act shall continue in office for the terms of one, two, three, four, five, six, and seven years, respectively, from the date of the taking effect of this Act, the term of each to be designated by the President, but their successors shall be appointed for terms of seven years; except that any person chosen to fill a vacancy shall be appointed only for the unexpired term of the commissioner whom he succeeds. No vacancy in the Commission shall impair the right of the remaining commissioners to exercise all the powers of the Commission.

(d) Each commissioner shall receive an annual salary of $10,000, payable in monthly installments.

* * *

(i) The Commission may perform any and all acts, make such rules and regulations, and issue such orders, not inconsistent with this Act, as may be necessary in the execution of its functions.

* * *

Title III—Special Provisions Relating to Radio

License for Radio Communication or Transmission of Energy

Section 301. It is the purpose of this Act, among other things, to maintain the control of the United States over all the channels of interstate and foreign radio transmission; and to provide for the use of such channels, but not the ownership thereof, by persons for limited periods of time, under licenses granted by Federal authority, and no such license shall be construed to create any right, beyond the terms, conditions, and periods of the license. No person shall use or operate any apparatus for the transmission of energy or communications or signals by radio (a) from one place in any Territory or possession of the United States or in the District of Columbia to another place in the same Territory, possession, or District; or (b) from any State, Territory, possession of the United States, or from the District of Columbia to any other State, Territory, or possession of the United States; or (c) from any place in any State, Territory, or possession of the United States, or in the District of Columbia, to any place in any foreign country or to any vessel; or (d) within any State when the effects of such use extend beyond the borders of said State, or when interference is caused by such use or operation with the transmission of such energy, communications, or signals from within said State to any place beyond its borders, or from any place beyond its borders to any place within said State, or with the transmission or reception of such energy, communications, or signals from and/or to places beyond the borders of said State; or (e) upon any vessel or aircraft of the United States; or (f) upon any other mobile stations within the jurisdiction of the United States, except under and in accordance with this Act and with a license in that behalf granted under the provisions of this Act.

* * *

General Powers of Commission

Sec. 303. Except as otherwise provided in this Act, the Commission from time to time, as public convenience, interest, or necessity requires, shall—

(a) Classify radio stations;

(b) Prescribe the nature of the service to be rendered by each class of licensed stations and each station within any class;

(c) Assign bands of frequencies to the various classes of stations, and assign frequencies for each individual station and determine the power which each station shall use and the time during which it may operate;

(d) Determine the location of classes of stations or individual stations;

(e) Regulate the kind of apparatus to be used with respect to its external effects and the purity and sharpness of the emissions from each station and from the apparatus therein;

(f) Make such regulations not inconsistent with law as it may deem necessary to prevent interference between stations and to carry out the provisions of this Act: Provided, however, That changes in the frequencies, authorized power, or in the times of operation of any station, shall not be made without the consent of the station licensee unless, after a public hearing, the Commission shall determine that such changes will promote public convenience or interest or will serve public necessity, or the provisions of this Act will be more fully complied with;

(g) Study new uses for radio, provide for experimental uses of frequencies, and generally encourage the larger and more effective use of radio in the public interest;

* * *

Censorship; Indecent Language

Sec. 326. Nothing in this Act shall be understood or construed to give the Commission the power of censorship over the radio communications or signals transmitted by any radio station, and no regulation or condition shall be promulgated or fixed by the Commission which shall interfere with the right of free speech by means of radio communication. No person within the jurisdiction of the United States shall utter any obscene, indecent, or profane language by means of radio communication.

* * *

Title VI—Miscellaneous Provisions

Transfer to Commission of Duties, Powers, and Functions under Existing Law

Section 601. (a) All duties, powers, and functions of the Interstate Commerce Commission under the Act of August 7, 1888 (25 Stat. 382), relating to operation of telegraph lines by railroad and telegraph companies granted Government aid in the construction of their lines, are hereby imposed upon and vested in the Commission: Provided, That such transfer of duties, powers, and functions shall not be construed to affect the duties, powers, functions, or jurisdiction of the Interstate Commerce Commission under, or to interfere with or prevent the enforcement of, the Interstate Commerce Act and all Acts amendatory thereof or supplemental thereto.

(b) All duties, powers, and functions of the Postmaster General with respect to telegraph companies and telegraph lines under any existing provision of law are hereby imposed upon and vested in the Commission.

Repeals and Amendments

Sec. 602. (a) The Radio Act of 1927, as amended, is hereby repealed.

(b) The provisions of the Interstate Commerce Act, as amended, insofar as they relate to communication by wire or wireless, or to telegraph, telephone, or cable companies operating by wire or wireless, except the last proviso of section 1(5) and the provisions of this section 1(7), are hereby repealed.

* * *

(c) All appropriations and unexpended balances of appropriations available for expenditure by the Federal Radio Commission shall be available for expenditure by the Commission for any and all objects of expenditure authorized by this Act in the discretion of the Commission, without regard to the requirement of apportionment under the Antideficiency Act of February 27, 1906.

Effect of Transfer, Repeals, and Amendments

Sec. 604. (a) All orders, determinations, rules, regulations, permits, contracts, licenses, and privileges which have been issued, made, or granted by the Interstate Commerce Commission, the Federal Radio Commission, or the Postmaster General, under any provision of law repealed or amended by this Act or in the exercise of duties, powers, or functions transferred to the Commission by this Act, and which are in effect at the time this section takes effect, shall continue in effect until modified, terminated, superseded, or repealed by the Commission or by operation of law.

* * *

Unauthorized Publication of Communications

Sec. 605. No person receiving or assisting in receiving, or transmitting, or assisting in transmitting, any interstate or foreign communication by wire or radio shall divulge or publish the existence, contents, substance, purport, effect, or meaning thereof, except through authorized channels of transmission or reception, to any person other than the addressee, his agent, or attorney, or to a person employed or authorized to forward such communication to its destination, or to proper accounting or distributing officers of the various communicating centers over which the communication may be passed, or to the master of a ship under whom he is serving, or in response to a subpena issued by a court of competent jurisdiction, or on demand of other lawful authority; and no person not being authorized by the sender shall intercept any communication and divulge or publish the existence, contents, substance, purport, effect, or meaning of such intercepted communication to any person; and no person not being entitled thereto shall receive or assist in receiving any interstate or foreign communication by wire or radio and use the same or any information therein contained for his own benefit or for the benefit or another not entitled thereto; and no person having received such intercepted communication or having become acquainted with the contents, substance, purport, effect, or meaning of the same or any part thereof, knowing that such information was so obtained, shall divulge or publish the existence, contents, substance, purport, effect, or meaning of the same or any part thereof, or use the same or any information therein contained for his own benefit or for the benefit or another not entitled thereto: Provided, That this section shall not apply to the receiving divulging, publishing, or utilizing the contents of any radio communication broadcast, or transmitted by amateurs or others for the use of the general public, or relating to ships in distress.

War Emergency—Powers of President

Sec. 606. (a) During the continuance of a war in which the United States is engaged, the President is authorized, if he finds it necessary for the national defense and security, to direct that such communications as in his judgment may be essential to the national defense and security shall have preference or priority with any carrier subject to this Act. He may give these directions at and for such times as he may determine, and may modify, change, suspend, or annual them and for any such purpose he is hereby authorized to issue orders directly, or through such person or persons as he designates for the purpose, or through the Commission. Any carrier complying with any such order or direction for preference or priority herein authorized shall be exempt from any and all provisions in existing law imposing civil or criminal penalties, obligations, or liabilities upon carriers by reason of giving preference or priority in compliance with such order or direction.

* * *

Short Title

Sec. 609. This Act may be cited as the "Communications Act of 1934."

Approved, June 19, 1934.

Source:

United States Statutes at Large, Vol. 48, pp. 1,064–1,105.

Securities Exchange Act, 1934

Federal legislation enacted on June 6, 1934, that established the Securities and Exchange Commission (SEC) to regulate American stock exchanges and to enforce the U.S. Securities Act enacted May 27, 1933. The latter act was designed to ensure full disclosure to purchasers of all stocks and bonds offered for public sale (with the exception of certain government bonds, railroad securities, and securities of some nonprofit institutions). The securities were to be registered with the U.S. Federal Trade Commission, and such registration had to include accurate and complete financial and other relevant information, as well as a prospectus. The prospectus was required to be given to every potential investor. The act imposed stiff penalties for the sale of misrepresented or unregistered securities.

The SEC, consisting of five members appointed by the president and approved by the Senate, was authorized to license stock exchanges and regulate securities trading. To prevent unfair and deceptive practices, the act required that current information about corporations whose securities were traded be made available to investors and that each security traded be registered with the SEC. The Federal Reserve Board was authorized to regulate margin requirements in securities trading so as to reduce speculation. Roosevelt appointed financier and speculator Joseph P. Kennedy, father of the future president, as the SEC's first chair, because "he knew the tricks of the trade."

Congress designed both acts to curb the problems that led to the stock market crash of 1929. While recessions occurred periodically after the 1930s, the country did not suffer a major depression again in the 20th century. However, a number of securities regulations were modified or abrogated during the prosperity of the 1990s. By taking advantage of loopholes the changes had opened, and through downright corruption, corporate executives contributed to a severe downturn in the stock markets of the first years of the 21st century.

An Act

To provide for the regulation of securities exchanges and of over-the-counter markets operating in interstate and foreign commerce and through the mails, to prevent inequitable and unfair practices on such exchanges and markets, and for other purposes.

Be it enacted by the Senate and House of Representatives of the United States of America in Congress assembled,

Title I—Regulation of Securities Exchanges

Short Title

Section 1. This Act may be cited as the "Securities Exchange Act of 1934."

Necessity for Regulation as Provided in This Title

Sec. 2. For the reasons hereinafter enumerated, transactions in securities as commonly conducted upon securities exchanges and over-the-counter markets are affected with a national public interest which makes it necessary to provide for regulation and control of such transactions and of practices and matters related thereto, including transactions by officers, directors, and principal security holders, to require appropriate reports, and to impose requirements necessary to make such regulation and control reasonably complete and effective, in order to protect interstate commerce, the national credit, the Federal taxing power, to protect and make more effective the national banking system and Federal Reserve System, and to insure the maintenance of fair and honest markets in such transactions:

(1) Such transactions (a) are carried on in large volume by the public generally and in large part originate outside the States in which the exchanges and over-the-counter markets are located and/or are effected by means of the mails and instrumentalities of interstate commerce; (b) constitute an important part of the current of interstate commerce; (c) involve in large part the securities of issuers engaged in interstate commerce; (d) involve the use of credit, directly affect the financing of trade, industry, and transportation in interstate commerce, and directly affect and influence the volume of interstate commerce; and affect the national credit.

(2) The prices established and offered in such transactions are generally disseminated and quoted throughout the United States and foreign countries and constitute a basis for determining and establishing the prices at which securities are bought and sold, the amount of certain taxes owning to the United States and to the several States by owners, buyers, and sellers of securities, and the value of collateral for bank loans.

(3) Frequently the prices of securities on such exchanges and markets are susceptible to manipulation and control, and the dissemination of such prices gives rise to excessive speculation, resulting in sudden and unrea-

sonable fluctuations in the prices of securities which (a) cause alternately unreasonable expansion and unreasonable contraction of the volume of credit available for trade, transportation, and industry in interstate commerce, (b) hinder the proper appraisal of the value of securities and thus prevent a fair calculation of taxes owing to the United States and to the several States by owners, buyers, and sellers of securities, and (c) prevent the fair valuation of collateral for bank loans and/or obstruct the effective operation of the national banking system and Federal Reserve System.

(4) National emergencies, which produce widespread unemployment and the dislocation of trade, transportation, and industry, and which burden interstate commerce and adversely affect the general welfare, are precipitated, intensified, and prolonged by manipulation and sudden and unreasonable fluctuations of security prices and by excessive speculation on such exchanges and markets, and to meet such emergencies the Federal Government is put to such great expense as to burden the national credit.

Source:

United States Statutes at Large, Vol. 48, pp. 881–909.

National Labor Relations Act, 1935

New Deal legislation, enacted on July 5, 1935, that created the National Labor Relations Board (NLRB) and guaranteed workers the right to organize and to bargain collectively through their chosen representatives. It represented a major landmark in the history of the labor movement.

Previously, in an act of March 23, 1932, Congress forbade the use of federal court injunctions to preserve antiunion employment contracts or to restrain strikes, boycotts, or picketing, except where such strikes affected the public safety. Sponsored by Senator George W. Norris of Nebraska and Representative Fiorello LaGuardia of New York, it protected workers' rights to join a union by prohibiting "yellow dog" contracts (agreements by which employers required their workers not to join unions and not to participate in any strike against the employers).

The National Labor Relations Act was also sponsored by Senator Wagner joined by Representative William P. Connery Jr. of Massachusetts. It authorized the NLRB to investigate complaints, issue cease-and-desist orders against unfair labor practices in interstate commerce, protect the right to collective bargaining, and arbitrate labor disputes. It prohibited employers from interfering with workers' rights to organize or to join independent unions, from promoting company unions, from discriminating in employment because of union membership, from punishing employees who file charges or testify under the act, and from refusing to negotiate with an elected union.

Its constitutionality was upheld 5-4 on April 12, 1937 in *NLRB v. Jones and Laughlin Steel Corporation* (301 U.S. 1).

An Act

To diminish the causes of labor disputes burdening or obstructing interstate and foreign commerce, to create a National Labor Relations Board, and for other purposes.

Be it enacted by the Senate and House of Representatives of the United States of America in Congress assembled,

Findings and Policy

Section 1. The denial by employers of the right of employees to organize and the refusal by employers to accept the procedure of collective bargaining lead to strikes and other forms of industrial strife or unrest, which have the intent or the necessary effect of burdening or obstructing commerce by (a) impairing the efficiency, safety, or operation of the instrumentalities of commerce; (b) occurring in the current of commerce; (c) materially affecting, restraining, or controlling the flow of raw materials or manufactured or processed goods from or into the channels of commerce, or the prices of such materials or goods in commerce; or (d) causing diminution of employment and wages in such volume as substantially to impair or disrupt the market for goods flowing from or into the channels of commerce.

The inequality of bargaining power between employees who do not possess full freedom of association or actual liberty of contract, and employers who are organized in the corporate or other forms of ownership association substantially burdens and affects the flow of commerce, and tends to aggravate recurrent business depressions, by depressing wage rates and the purchasing power of wage earners in industry and by preventing the stabilization of competitive wage rates and working conditions within and between industries.

Experience has proved that protection by law of the right of employees to organize and bargain collectively safeguards commerce from injury, impairment, or interruption, and promotes the flow of commerce by removing certain recognized sources of industrial strife and unrest, by encouraging practices fundamental to the friendly adjustment of industrial disputes arising out of differences as to wages, hours, or other working conditions, and by restoring equality of bargaining power between employers and employees.

It is hereby declared to be the policy of the United States to eliminate the causes of certain substantial obstructions to the free flow of commerce and to mitigate and eliminate these obstructions when they have occurred by encouraging the practice and procedure of collective bargaining and by protecting the exercise by workers of full freedom of association, self-organization, and designation of representatives of their own choosing, for the purpose of negotiating the terms and conditions of their employment or other mutual aid or protection...

Rights of Employees

Sec. 7. Employees shall have the right to self-organization, to form, join, or assist labor organizations, to bargain collectively through representatives of their own choosing, and to engage in concerted activities, for the purpose of collective bargaining or other mutual aid or protection.

Sec. 8. It shall be an unfair labor practice for an employer—

(1) To interfere with, restrain, or coerce employees in the exercise of the rights guaranteed in section 7.

(2) To dominate or interfere with the formation or administration of any labor organization or contribute financial or other support to it: *Provided,* That subject to rules and regulations made and published by the Board pursuant to section 6(a), an employer shall not be prohibited from permitting employees to confer with him during working hours without loss of time or pay.

(3) By discrimination in regard to hire or tenure of employment or any term or condition of employment to encourage or discourage membership in any labor organization: *Provided,* That nothing in this Act, or in the National Industrial Recovery Act (U.S.C., Supp. VII, title 15, secs. 701-712), as amended from time to time, or in any code or agreement approved or prescribed thereunder, or in any other statute of the United States, shall preclude an employer from making an agreement with a labor organization (not established, maintained, or assisted by any action defined in this Act as an unfair labor practice) to require as a condition of employment membership therein, if such labor organization is the representative of the employees as provided in section 9(a), in the appropriate collective bargaining unit covered by such agreement when made.

(4) To discharge or otherwise discriminate against an employee because he has filed charges or given testimony under this Act.

(5) To refuse to bargain collectively with the representatives of his employees, subject to the provisions of Section 9(a).

Source:

Statutes at Large, Vol. 48, pp. 449–457.

Social Security Act, 1935

New Deal legislation enacted by Congress on August 14, 1935, to provide old-age retirement insurance as an entitlement (i.e., it was for everyone over a designated age regardless of their means), unemployment insurance, survivors' and disability insurance, and public assistance. It created the Social Security Board to administer these programs. The act granted federal subsidies to state assistance programs that aided the needy elderly; it also created a federally administered annuity for retired workers aged 65 and over, based on previous wages and funded by payroll taxes paid by employers and employees. It set up a cooperative state-federal unemployment insurance program financed by a payroll tax on employers. The act also furnished grants to states for aid to dependent children, maternal and child welfare, the blind, projects for vocational rehabilitation, and public health work. The act originally covered only industrial and commercial workers, but it has been amended many times to extend coverage and include new programs.

On May 24, 1937, in *Steward Machine Company v. Davis* (301 U.S. 548), the Supreme Court upheld the tax provisions of the Social Security Act. The case challenged provisions in the unemployment compensation section of the act that established a federal payroll tax on employers, to be paid into the federal treasury. The act allowed a credit, up to 90 percent, for any amount paid into a federally approved state unemployment compensation system. The Steward Machine Company paid the tax but sued for a refund. In its 5-4 decision, the Supreme Court denied the company's claim that the tax provisions were an unconstitutional attempt by Congress to coerce the states or to usurp their powers; it declared that the provisions merely gave the states a compelling "inducement" to establish unemployment compensation.

Note the occupations not covered by the Act (Title II: Definitions, Section 210b). Amendments to the act over the years have brought domestic and some agricultural workers under it. Employees of the federal government who joined the federal retirement system before 1983 were given a choice whether or not to come under Social Security; for those hired after that year, it was mandatory. The Social Security account has been used to pay other federal expenses and keep down the federal debt. Below are excerpts from the act.

An Act

To provide for the general welfare by establishing a system of Federal old-age benefits, and by enabling the several States to make more adequate provision for aged persons, blind persons, dependent and crippled children, maternal and child welfare, public health, and the administration of their unemployment compensation laws; to establish a Social Security Board; to raise revenue; and for other purposes.

Title I—Grants to States for Old-Age Assistance

Appropriation

Section 1. For the purpose of enabling each State to furnish financial assistance, as far as practicable under the conditions in such State, to aged needy individuals, there is hereby authorized to be appropriated for the fiscal year ending June 30, 1936, the sum of $49,750,000, and there is hereby authorized to be appropriated for each fiscal year thereafter a sum sufficient to carry out the purposes of this title. . . .

State Old-Age Assistance Plans

Sec. 2.

* * *

(b)The Board shall approve any plan which fulfills the conditions specified in subsection (a), except that it shall not approved any plan which imposes, as a condition of eligibility for old-age assistance under the plan—

(1) An age requirement of more than sixty-five years, except that the plan may impose, effective until January 1, 1940, an age requirement of as much as seventy years; or

(2) Any residence requirement which excludes any resident of the State who has resided therein five years during the nine years immediately preceding the application for old-age assistance and has resided therein continuously for one year immediately preceding the application; or

(3) Any citizenship requirement which excludes any citizen of the United States.

* * *

Definition

Sec. 6. When used in this title the term "old-age assistance" means money payments to aged individuals.

Title II—Federal Old-Age Benefits

Old-Age Reserve Account

Section 201. (a) There is hereby created an account in the Treasury of the United States to be known as the "Oil-Age Reserve Account" hereinafter in this title called the "Account." There is hereby authorized to be appropriated to the Account for each fiscal year, beginning with the fiscal year ending June 30, 1937, an amount sufficient as an annual premium to provide for the payments required under this title, such amount to be determined on a reserve basis in accordance with accepted actuarial principles, and based upon such tables of mortality as the Secretary of the Treasury shall from time to time adopt, and upon an interest rate of 3 per centum per annum compounded annually. The Secretary of the Treasury shall submit annually to the Bureau of the Budget an estimate of the appropriations to be made to the Account.

(b) It shall be the duty of the Secretary of the Treasury to invest such portion of the amounts credited to the Account as is not, in his judgment, required to meet current withdrawals. Such investment may be made only in interest-bearing obligations of the United States or in obligations guaranteed as to both principal and interest by the United States. . . .

* * *

Old-Age Benefit Payments

Sec. 202. (a) Every qualified individual (as defined in section 210) shall be entitled to receive, with respect to the period beginning on the date he attains the age of sixty-five, or on January 1, 1942, whichever is the later, and ending on the date of his death, an old-age benefit (payable as nearly as practicable in equal monthly installments). . .

* * *

(d) Whenever the Board finds that any qualified individual has received wages with respect to regular employment after he attained the age of sixty-five, the old-age benefit payable to such individual shall be reduced, for each calendar month in any part of which such regular employment occurred, by an amount equal to one month's benefit. Such reduction shall be made, under regulations prescribed by the Board, by deductions from one or more payments of old-age benefit to such individual.

Payments Upon Death

Sec. 203. (a) If any individual dies before attaining the age of sixty-five, there shall be paid to his estate an amount equal to 3 1/2 per centum of the total wages determined by the Board to have been paid to him, with respect to employment after December 31, 1936.

Payments to Aged Individuals not Qualified for Benefits

Sec. 204. (a) There shall be paid in a lump sum to any individual who, upon attaining the age of sixty-five, is not a qualified individual, an amount equal to 3 1/2 per centum of the total wages determined by the Board to have been paid to him, with respect to employment after December 31, 1936, and before he attained the age of sixty-five.

(b) After any individual becomes entitled to any payment under subsection (a), no other payment shall be made under this title in any manner measured by wages paid to him, except that any part of any payment under subsection (a) which is not paid to him before his death shall be paid to his estate.

* * *

Definitions

Sec. 210. When used in this title—

(a) The term "wages" means all remuneration for employment, including the cash value of all remuneration paid in any medium other than cash; except that such term shall not include that part of the remuneration which, after remuneration equal to $3,000 has been paid to an individual by an employer with respect to employment during any calendar year, is paid to such individual to such employer with respect to employment during such calendar year.

(b) The term "employment" means any service, of whatever nature, performed within the United States by an employee for his employer, except—

(1) Agricultural labor;

(2) Domestic service in a private home;

(3) Casual labor not in the course of the employer's trade or business;

(4) Service performed as an officer or member of the crew of a vessel documented under the laws of the United States or of any foreign country;

(5) Service performed in the employ of the United States Government or of an instrumentality of the United States;

(6) Service performed in the employ of a State, a political subdivision thereof, or an instrumentality of one or more States or political subdivisions;

(7) Service performed in the employ of a corporation, community chest, fund, or foundation, organized and operated exclusively for religious, charitable, scientific, literary, or educational purposes, or for the prevention of cruelty to children or animals, no part of the net earnings of which inures to the benefit of any private shareholder or individual.

(c) The term "qualified individual" means any individual with respect to whom it appears to the satisfaction of the Board that—

(1) He is at least sixty-five years of age. . . .

Title III—Grants to States for Unemployment Compensation Administration

Appropriation

Section 301. For the purpose of assisting the States in the administration of their unemployment compensation laws, there is hereby authorized to be appropriated, for the fiscal year ending June 30, 1936, the sum of $4,000,000, and for each fiscal year thereafter the sum of $49,000,000, to be used as hereinafter provided.

* * *

Title IV—Grants to States for Aid to Dependent Children

Appropriation

Section 401. For the purpose of enabling each State to furnish financial assistance, as far as practicable under the conditions in such State, to needy dependent children, there is hereby authorized to be appropriated for the fiscal year ending June 30, 1936, the sum of $24,750,000, and there is hereby authorized to be appropriated for each fiscal year thereafter a sum sufficient to carry out the purposes of this title. The sums made available under this section shall be used for making payments to States which have submitted, and had approved by the Board, State plans for aid to dependent children.

* * *

Definitions

Sec. 406. When used in this title—

(a) The term "dependent child" means a child under the age of sixteen who has been deprived of parental support or care by reason of the death, continued absence from the home, or physical or mental incapacity of a parent, and who is living with his father, mother, grandfather, grandmother, brother, sister, stepfather, stepmother, stepbrother, stepsister, uncle, or aunt, in a place of residence maintained by one or more of such relatives as his or their own home;

* * *

Title V—Grants to States for Maternal and Child Welfare

Part 1—Maternal and Child Health Services

Appropriation

Section 501. For the purpose of enabling each State to extend and improve, as far as practicable under the conditions in such State, services for promoting the health of mothers and children, especially in rural areas and in areas suffering from severe economic distress, there is hereby authorized to be appropriated for each fiscal year, beginning with the fiscal year ending June 30, 1936, the sum of $3,800,000. The sums made available under this section shall be used for making payments to States which have submitted, and had approved by the Chief of the Children's Bureau, State plans for such services.

* * *

Part 2—Services for Crippled Children

Appropriation

Sec. 511. For the purpose of enabling each State to extend and improve (especially in rural areas and in areas suffering from severe economic distress), as far as practicable under the conditions in such State, services for locating crippled children, and for providing medical, surgical, corrective, and other services and care, and facilities for diagnosis, hospitalization, and aftercare, for children who are crippled or who are suffering from conditions which lead to crippling, there is hereby authorized to be appropriated for each fiscal year, beginning with the fiscal year ending June 30, 1936, the sum of $2,850,000. The sums made available under this section shall be used for making payments to States which have submitted, and had approved by the Chief of the Children's Bureau, State plans for such services.

* * *

Part 3—Child-Welfare Services

Sec. 521. (a) For the purpose of enabling the United States, through the Children's Bureau, to cooperate with State public-welfare agencies in establishing, extending, and strengthening, especially in predominantly rural areas, public-welfare services (hereinafter in this section referred to as "child-welfare services") for the protection and care of homeless, dependent, and neglected children, and children in danger of becoming delinquent, there is hereby authorized to be appropriated for each fiscal year, beginning with the fiscal year ending June 30, 1936, the sum of $1,500,000. Such amount shall be allotted by the Secretary of Labor for use by cooperating State public-welfare agencies on the basis of plans developed jointly by the State agency and the Children's Bureau. . . . The amount so allotted shall be expended for payment of part of the cost of district, county or other local child-welfare services in areas predominantly rural, and for developing State services for the encouragement and assistance of adequate methods of community child-welfare organization in areas predominantly rural and other areas of special need. . . .

Part 4—Vocational Rehabilitation

Sec. 531. (a) In order to enable the United States to cooperate with the States and Hawaii in extending and strengthening their programs of vocational rehabilitation of the physically disabled, and to continue to carry out the provisions and purposes of . . . "An Act to provide for the promotion of vocational rehabilitation of persons disabled in industry or otherwise and their return to civil employment". . . there is hereby authorized to be appropriated for the fiscal years ending June 30, 1936, and June 30, 1937, the sum of $841,000 for each such fiscal year in addition to the amount of the existing authorization, and for each fiscal year thereafter the sum of $1,938,000. . . .

Title VI—Public Health Work

Appropriation

Section 601. For the purpose of assisting States, counties, health districts, and other political subdivisions of the States in establishing and maintaining adequate public-health services, including the training or personnel for State and local health work, there is hereby authorized to be appropriated for each fiscal year, beginning with the fiscal year ending June 30, 1936, the sum of $8,000,000 to be used as hereinafter provided.

* * *

Investigations

Sec. 603. (a) There is hereby authorized to be appropriated for each fiscal year, beginning with the fiscal year ending June 30, 1936, the sum of $2,000,000 for expenditure by the Public Health Service for investigation of disease and problems of sanitation (including the printing and binding of the findings of such investigations), and for the pay and allowances and traveling expenses of personnel of the Public Health Service, including commissioned officers, engaged in such investigations or detailed to cooperate with the health authorities of any State in carrying out the purposes specified in section 601: Provided, That no personnel of the Public Health Service shall be detailed to cooperate with the health authorities of any State except at the request of the proper authorities of such State.

* * *

Title VII—Social Security Board

Establishment

Section 701. There is hereby established a Social Security Board (in this Act referred to as the "Board") to be composed of three members to be appointed by the President, by and with the advice and consent of the Senate. . . . The President shall designate one of the members as the chairman of the Board.

Duties of Social Security Board

Sec. 702. The Board shall perform the duties imposed upon it by this Act and shall also have the duty of studying and making recommendations as to the most effective methods of providing economic security through social insurance, and as to legislation and matters of administrative policy concerning old-age pensions, unemployment compensation, accident compensation, and related subjects.

* * *

Sec. 704. The Board shall make a full report to Congress, at the beginning of each regular session, of the administration of the functions with which it is charged.

Title VIII—Taxes with Respect to Employment

Income Tax on Employees

Section 801. In addition to other taxes, there shall be levied, collected, and paid upon the income of every individual. . . .

Sec. 802. (a) The tax imposed by section 801 shall be collected by the employer of the taxpayer, by deducting the amount of the tax from the wages as and when paid. Every employer required so to deduct the tax is hereby made liable for the payment of such tax, and is hereby indemnified against the claims and demands of any person for the amount of any such payment made by such employer.

Deductibility from Income Tax

Sec. 803. For the purposes of the income tax imposed by Title I of the Revenue Act of 1934 or by any Act of Congress in substitution therefor, the tax imposed by section 801 shall not be allowed as a deduction to the taxpayer in computing his net income for the year in which such tax is deducted from his wages.

Excise Tax on Employers

Sec. 804. In addition to other taxes, every employer shall pay an excise tax, with respect to having individuals in his employ. . . .

Collection and Payment of Taxes

Sec. 807. (a) The taxes imposed by this title shall be collected by the Bureau of Internal Revenue under the direction of the Secretary of the Treasury and shall be paid into the Treasury of the United States as internal-revenue collections. . . .

* * *

Title IX—Tax on Employers of Eight or More

* * *

Unemployment Trust Fund

Sec. 904. (a) There is hereby established in the Treasury of the United States a trust fund to be known as the "Unemployment Trust Fund," hereinafter in this title called the "Fund." The Secretary of the Treasury is authorized and directed to receive and hold in the Fund all moneys deposited therein by a State agency from a State unemployment fund. Such deposit may be made directly with the Secretary of the Treasury or with any Federal reserve bank or member bank of the Federal Reserve System designated by him for such purpose.

(b) It shall be the duty of the Secretary of the Treasury to invest such portion of the Fund as is not, in his judgment, required to meet current withdrawals. Such investment may be made only in interest bearing obligations of the United States or in obligations guaranteed as to both principal and interest by the United States. . . .

* * *

Title X—Grants to States for Aid to the Blind

Appropriation

Section 1001. For the purpose of enabling each State to furnish financial assistance, as far as practicable under the conditions in such State, to needy individuals who are blind, there is hereby authorized to be appropriated for the fiscal year ending June 30, 1936, the sum of $3,000.000, and there is hereby authorized to be appropriated for each fiscal year thereafter a sum sufficient to carry out the purposes of this title. The sums made available under this section shall be used for making payments to States which have submitted, and had approved by the Social Security Board, State plans for aid to the blind.

* * *

Title XI—General Provisions

Definitions

Section 1101. (a) When used in this Act—

(1) The term "State" (except then used in section 531) includes Alaska, Hawaii, and the District of Columbia.

(2) The term "United States" when used in a geographical sense means the States, Alaska, Hawaii, and the District of Columbia.

(3) The term "person" means an individual, a trust or estate, a partnership, or a corporation.

(4) The term "corporation" includes associations, joint-stock companies, and insurance companies.

(5) The term "shareholder" includes a member in an association, joint-stock company, or insurance company.

(6) The term "employee" includes an officer of a corporation.

(b) The terms "includes" and "including" when used in a definition contained in this Act shall not be deemed to exclude other things otherwise within the meaning of the term defined.

(c) Whenever under this Act or any Act of Congress, or under the law of any State, an employer is required or permitted to deduct any amount from the remuneration of an employee and to pay the amount deducted to the United States, a State, or any political subdivision thereof, then for the purposes of this Act the amount so deducted shall be considered to have been paid to the employee at the time of such deduction.

(d) Nothing in this Act shall be construed as authorizing any Federal official, agent, or representative, in carrying out any of the provisions of this Act, to take charge of any child over the objection of either of the parents of such child, or of the person standing in loco parentis to such child.

Rules and Regulations

Sec. 1102. The Secretary of the Treasury, the Secretary of Labor, and the Social Security Board, respectively, shall make and publish such rules and regulations, not inconsistent with this Act, as may be necessary to the efficient administration of the functions with which each is charged under this Act.

Source:
United States Statutes at Large, Vol. 48, pp. 620–647.

Revenue Act, 1935

New Deal legislation enacted on August 30, 1935, that increased estate, gift, and capital stock tax rates, levied an excess profits tax, and raised the surtax rate on individual incomes over $50,000 to the highest rates in U.S. history. It established a modest graduated tax on corporations in place of the existing uniform tax, lowering the rate for small corporations and raising the rates for corporations with incomes above $50,000. It raised federal taxes by $250 million. The act represented a watered-down version of President Franklin D. Roosevelt's controversial proposed program to redistribute wealth and economic power.

An Act
To provide revenue, equalize taxation, and for other purposes.

Be it enacted by the Senate and House of Representatives of the United States of America in Congress assembled, That this Act may be cited as the "Revenue Act of 1935."

Title I—Income and Excess-Profits Taxes
Sec. 101. Surtaxes on Individuals

* * *

"$7,700 upon surtax net incomes of $50,000; and upon surtax net incomes in excess of $50,000 and not in excess of $56,000, 31 per centum in addition of such excess.

"$9,560 upon surtax net incomes of $56,000; and upon surtax net incomes in excess of $56,000 and not in excess of $62,000, 35 per centum in addition of such excess.

"$11,660 upon surtax net incomes of $62,000; and upon surtax net incomes in excess of $62,000 and not in excess of $68,000, 39 per centum in addition of such excess.

"$14,000 upon surtax net incomes of $68,000; and upon surtax net incomes in excess of $68,000 and not in excess of $74,000, 43 per centum in addition of such excess.

"$16,580 upon surtax net incomes of $74,000; and upon surtax net incomes in excess of $74,000 and not in excess of $80,000, 47 per centum in addition of such excess.

"$19,400 upon surtax net incomes of $80,000; and upon surtax net incomes in excess of $80,000 and not in excess of $90,000, 51 per centum in addition of such excess.

"$24,500 upon surtax net incomes of $90,000; and upon surtax net incomes in excess of $90,000 and not in excess of $100,000, 55 per centum in addition of such excess.

* * *

"$286,000 upon surtax net incomes of $500,000; and upon surtax net incomes in excess of $500,000 and not in excess of $750,000, 70 per centum in addition of such excess.

"$461,000 upon surtax net incomes of $750,000; and upon surtax net incomes in excess of $750,000 and not in excess of $1,000,000, 72 per centum in addition of such excess.

"$641,000 upon surtax net incomes of $1,000,000; and upon surtax net incomes in excess of $1,000,000 and not in excess of $2,000,000, 73 per centum in addition of such excess.

"$1,371,000 upon surtax net incomes of $2,000,000; and upon surtax net incomes in excess of $2,000,000 and not in excess of $5,000,000, 74 per centum in addition of such excess.

"$3,591,000 upon surtax net incomes of $5,000,000; and upon surtax net incomes in excess of $5,000,000, 75 per centum in addition of such excess."

Sec. 102. Income Taxes on Corporations

(a) Section 13(a) of the Revenue Act of 1934 is amended to read as follows:

"(a) Rate of Tax.—There shall be levied, collected, and paid for each taxable year upon the net income (in excess of the credit against net income provided in section 26) of every corporation, a tax as follows:

"Upon net incomes not in excess of $2,000, 12 1/2 per centum.

"$250 upon net incomes of $2,000; and upon net incomes in excess of $2,000 and not in excess of $15,000, 13 per centum in addition of such excess.

"$1,940 upon net incomes of $15,000; and upon net incomes in excess of $15,000 and not in excess of $40,000, 14 per centum in addition of such excess.

"$5,440 upon net incomes of $40,000; and upon net incomes in excess of $40,000, 15 per centum in addition of such excess."

* * *

(c) Section 23 of the Revenue Act of 1934 (relating to deductions from gross income) is amended by adding at the end thereof a new subsection as follows:

"(r) Charitable and Other Contributions by Corporations.— In the case of a corporation, contributions or gifts made within the taxable year to or for the use of a domestic corporation, or domestic trust, or domestic community chest, fund, or foundation, organized and operated exclusively for religious, charitable, scientific, literary, or educational purposes or the prevention of cruelty to children. . . no part of the net earnings of which inures to the benefit of any private shareholder or individual, and no substantial part of the activities of which is carrying on propaganda, or otherwise attempting, to influence legislation; to an amount which does not exceed 5 per centum of the taxpayer's net income as computed without the benefit of this subsection. Such contributions or gifts shall be allowable as deductions only if verified under rules and regulations prescribed by the Commissioner, with the approval of the Secretary."

* * *

Sec. 105. Capital Stock Tax

(a) For each year ending June 30, beginning with the year ending June 30, 1936, there is hereby imposed upon every domestic corporation with respect to carrying on or doing business for any part of such year an excise tax of $1.40 for each $1,000 of the adjusted declared value of its capital stock.

(b) For each year ending June 30, beginning with the year ending June 30, 1936, there is hereby imposed upon every foreign corporation with respect to carrying on or doing business in the United States for any part of such year an excise tax equivalent to $1.40 for each $1,000 of the adjusted declared value of capital employed in the transaction of its business in the United States.

* * *

Sec. 106. Excess-Profits Tax

(a) There is hereby imposed upon the net income of every corporation for each income-tax taxable year ending after the close of the first year in respect of which it is taxable under section 105, an excess-profits tax equal to the sum of the following:

6 per centum of such portion of its net income for such income-tax taxable year as is in excess of 10 per centum and not in excess of 15 per centum of the adjusted declared value;

12 per centum of such portion of its net income for such income-tax taxable year as is in excess of 15 per centum of the adjusted declared value.

* * *

Sec. 109. Personal Holding Companies

"(a) Imposition of Tax.—There shall be levied, collected, and paid, for each taxable year, upon the undistributed adjusted net income of every personal holding company a surtax equal to the sum of the following:

"(1) 20 per centum of the amount thereof not in excess of $2,000; plus

"(2) 30 per centum of the amount thereof in excess of $2,000 and not in excess of $100,000; plus

"(3) 40 per centum of the amount thereof in excess of $100.000 and not in excess of $500,000; plus

"(4) 50 per centum of the amount thereof in excess of $500,000 and not in excess of $1,000,0000; plus

"(5) 60 per centum of the amount thereof in excess of 1,000,000."

* * *

Title II—Amendments to Estate Tax

Sec. 201. Estate Tax Rates

"Upon net estates not in excess of $10,000, 2 per centum.

"$200 upon net estates of $10,000; and upon net estates in excess of $10,000 and not in excess of $20,000, 4 per centum in addition of such excess.

"$600 upon net estates of $20,000; and upon net estates in excess of $20,000 and not in excess of $30,000, 6 per centum in addition of such excess.

"$1,200 upon net estates of $30,000; and upon net estates in excess of $30,000 and not in excess of $40,000, 8 per centum in addition of such excess.

"$2,000 upon net estates of $40,000; and upon net estates in excess of $40,000 and not in excess of $50,000, 10 per centum in addition of such excess.

"$3,000 upon net estates of $50,000; and upon net estates in excess of $50,000 and not in excess of $70,000, 12 per centum in addition of such excess.

* * *

"$112,600 upon net estates of $600,000; and upon net estates in excess of $600,000 and not in excess of $800,000, 26 per centum in addition of such excess.

* * *

"$222,600 upon net estates of $1,000,000; and upon net estates in excess of $1,000,000 and not in excess of $1,500,000, 32 per centum in addition of such excess.

* * *

"$1,922,600 upon net estates of $5,000,000; and upon net estates in excess of $5,000,000 and not in excess of $6,000,000, 56 per centum in addition of such excess.

* * *

"$4,962,600 upon net estates of $10,000,000; and upon net estates in excess of $10,000,000 and not in excess of $20,000,000, 67 per centum in addition of such excess.

* * *

"$32,362,600 upon net estates of $50,000,000; and upon net estates in excess of $50,000,000, 70 per centum in addition of such excess."

* * *

Title III—Amendments to Gift Tax

Sec. 301. Gift Tax Rates

"Upon net gifts not in excess of $10,000, 1 1/2 per centum.

* * *

"$1,500 upon net gifts of $40,000; and upon net gifts in excess of $40,000 and not in excess of $50,000, 7 1/2 per centum in addition of such excess.

"$2,250 upon net gifts of $50,000; and upon net gifts in excess of $50,000 and not in excess of $70,000, 9 per centum in addition of such excess.

* * *

"$7,200 upon net gifts of $100,000; and upon net gifts in excess of $100,000 and not in excess of $200,000, 12 3/4 per centum in addition of such excess.

* * *

"$84,450 upon net gifts of $600,000; and upon net gifts in excess of $600,000 and not in excess of $800,000, 19 1/2 per centum in addition of such excess.

* * *

"$166,950 upon net gifts of $1,000,000; and upon net gifts in excess of $1,000,000 and not in excess of $1,500,000, 24 per centum in addition of such excess.

* * *

"$1,441,950 upon net gifts of $5,000,000; and upon net gifts in excess of $5,000,000 and not in excess of $6,000,000, 42 per centum in addition of such excess.

* * *

"$3,721,950 upon net gifts of $10,000,000; and upon net gifts in excess of $10,000,000 and not in excess of $20,000,000, 50 1/4 per centum in addition of such excess.

* * *

"$24,271,950 upon net gifts of $50,000,000; and upon net gifts in excess of $50,000,000, 52 1/2 per centum in addition of such excess."

* * *

Title IV—Miscellaneous Provisions

* * *

Sec. 406. Failure to File Returns

In the case of a failure to make and file an internal-revenue tax return required by law, within the time prescribed by law or prescribed by the Commissioner in pursuance of law, if the last date so prescribed for filing the return is after the date of the enactment of this Act, if a 25 per centum addition to the tax is prescribed by existing law, then there shall be added to the tax, in lieu of such 25 per centum; 5 per centum if the failure is for not more than 30 days, with an additional 5 per centum for each additional 30 days or fraction thereof during which failure continues, not to exceed 25 per centum in the aggregate.

* * *

Title V—General Provisions

Sec. 501. Definitions

(a) When used in this Act—

(1) The term "person" means an individual, a trust or estate, a partnership, or a corporation.

(2) The term "corporation" includes associations, joint-stock companies, and insurance companies.

(3) The term "domestic" when applied to a corporation or partnership means created or organized in the United States or under the law of the United States or of any State or Territory.

(4) The term "foreign" when applied to a corporation or partnership means a corporation or partner which is not domestic.

(5) The term "stock" includes the share in an association, joint-stock company, or insurance company.

(6) The term "shareholder" includes a member in an association, joint-stock company, or insurance company.

(7) The term "United States" when used in a geographical sense includes only the States, the Territories of Alaska and Hawaii, and the District of Columbia.

* * *

Sec. 502. Separability Clause

If any provision of this Act, or the application thereof to any person or circumstances, is held invalid, the remainder of the Act, and the application of such provisions to other persons or circumstances, shall not be affected thereby.

Sec. 503. Effective Date of Act

Except as otherwise provided, this Act shall take effect upon its enactment.

Approved, August 30, 1935, at 6 p.m.

Source:

United States Statutes at Large, vol. 48, pp. 1,014–1,028.

Neutrality Act of 1937

Federal legislation enacted on May 1, 1937, to keep the United States from becoming embroiled in international conflicts, particularly the Spanish civil war (1936–39). That war pitted the government loyalists against rebel fascists under Francisco Franco. Because Nazi leader Adolf Hitler and Italian dictator Benito Mussolini supported Franco, many North Americans and Europeans considered the war an opportunity to stop fascism from spreading. However, Great Britain, France, and the United States refused to get involved. Only the Soviet Union sent troops against Franco, assisted by several "international brigades," which were under communist leadership. A number of American antifascists, regardless of whether they were party members, joined the Abraham Lincoln Brigade. During the cold war, their participation in the Spanish civil war would brand them as communists or communist sympathizers.

The act strengthened earlier congressional resolutions (1935–37) by placing an embargo on the export of arms, ammunition, and other war materials to belligerents in civil wars or wars between two or more foreign powers; by prohibiting loans or credit to belligerents; by forbidding American vessels to carry arms to belligerents; and by restricting the use of U.S. ports as a base of supply by such nations. American merchant vessels were prohibited from being armed. The act created the National Munitions Control Board to enforce its provisions.

The U.S. Neutrality Act of November 4, 1939, repealed the arms embargo. Passed after the eruption of World War II in Europe, the act restated a U.S. policy of neutrality but allowed Great Britain and France to buy arms and munitions on a "cash and carry" basis; they would have to pay cash and transport the war materials themselves. The act prohibited U.S. citizens from sailing on belligerent ships and U.S. ships from sailing to belligerent ports; it authorized the president to forbid ships to enter combat zones. It also prohibited the arming of merchant vessels. In November 1941 Congress repealed the restrictions on the arming of merchant vessels and allowed such ships to carry cargoes to belligerent ports.

Joint Resolution

To amend the joint resolution entitled "Joint resolution providing for the prohibition of the export of arms, ammunition, and implements of war to belligerent countries; the prohibition of the transportation of arms, ammunition, and implements of war by vessels of the United States for the use of belligerent states; for the registration and licensing of persons engaged in the business of manufacturing, exporting, or importing arms, ammunition, or implements of war; and restricting travel by American citizens on belligerent ships during war," approved August 31, 1935, as amended.

Resolved by the Senate and House of Representatives of the United States of America in Congress assembled, That the joint resolution entitled "Joint resolution providing for the prohibition of the export or arms, ammunition, and implements of war to belligerent countries; the prohibition of the transportation of arms, ammunition, and implements of war by vessels of the United States for the use of belligerent states; for the registration and licensing of persons engaged in the business of manufacturing, exporting, or importing arms, ammunition, or implements of war; and restricting travel by American citizens on belligerent ships during war," approved August 31, 1935, as amended, is amended to read as follows:

"Export of Arms, Ammunition, and Implements of War

"Section 1. (a) Whenever the President shall find that there exists a state of war between, or among, two or more foreign states, the President shall proclaim such fact, and it shall thereafter be unlawful to export, or attempt to export, or cause to be exported, arms, ammunition, or implements of war from any place in the United States to any belligerent state named in such proclamation, or to any neutral state for transshipment to, or for the use of, any such belligerent state.

"(b) The President shall, from time to time, by proclamation, extend such embargo upon the export of arms, ammunition, or implements of war to other states as and when they may become involved in such war.

"(c) Whenever the President shall find that a state of civil strife exists in a foreign state and that such civil strife is of a magnitude or is being conducted under such conditions that the export of arms, ammunition, or implements of war from the United States to such foreign state would threaten or endanger the peace of the United States, the President shall proclaim such fact, and it shall thereafter be unlawful to export, or attempt to export, or cause to be exported, arms, ammunition, or implements of war from any place in the United States to such foreign state, or to any neutral state for transshipment to, or for the use of, such foreign state.

"(d) The President shall, from time to time by proclamation, definitely enumerate the arms, ammunition, and implements of war, the export of which is prohibited by this section. The arms, ammunition, and implements of war so enumerated shall include those enumerated in the President's proclamation Numbered 2163, of April 10, 1936, but shall not include raw materials or any other articles or materials not of the same general character as those enumerated in the said proclamation, and in the Convention for the Supervision of the International Trade in Arms and Ammunition and in Implements of War, signed at Geneva June 17, 1925.

"(e) Whoever, in violation of any of the provisions of this Act, shall export, or attempt to export, or cause to be exported, arms, ammunition, or implements of war from the United States shall be fined not more than $10,000, or imprisoned not more than five years, or both, and the property, vessel, or vehicle containing the same shall be subject to the provisions of sections 1 to 8, inclusive, title 6, chapter 30, of the Act approved June 15, 1917 (40 Stat. 223-225; U.S.C., 1934 ed., title 22, secs. 238-245).

"(f) In the case of the forfeiture of any arms, ammunition, or implements of war by reason of a violation of this Act, no public or private sale shall be required; but such arms, ammunition, or implements of war shall be delivered to the Secretary of War for such use or disposal thereof as shall be approved by the President of the United States.

"(g) Whenever, in the judgment of the President, the conditions which have cause him to issue any proclamation under the authority of this section have ceased to exist, he shall revoke the same, and the provisions of this section shall thereupon cease to apply with respect to the state or states named in such proclamation, except with respect to offenses committed, or forfeitures incurred, prior to such revocation...

"Financial Transactions

"Sec. 3. (a) Whenever the President shall have issued a proclamation under the authority of section 1 of this Act, it shall thereafter be unlawful for any person within the United States to purchase, sell, or exchange bonds, securities, or other obligations of the government of any belligerent state or of any state wherein civil strife exists, named in such proclamation, or of any political subdivision of any such state, or of any person acting for or on behalf of the government of any such state, or of any faction or asserted government within any such state wherein civil strife exists, or of any person acting for or on behalf of any faction or asserted government within any such state wherein civil strife exists, issued after the date of such proclamation, or to make any loan or extend any credit to any such government, political subdivision, faction, asserted government, or person, or to solicit or receive any contribution for any such government, political subdivision, faction, asserted government, or person: *Provided*, That if the President shall find that such action will serve to protect the commercial or other interests of the United States or its citizens, he may, in his discretion, and to such extent and under such regulations as he may prescribe, except from the operation of this section ordinary commercial credits and short-time obligations in aid of legal transactions and of a character customarily used in normal peacetime commercial transactions. Nothing in this subsection shall be construed to prohibit the solicitation or collection of funds to be used for medical aid and assistance, or for food and clothing to relieve human suffering, when such solicitation or collection of funds is made on behalf of and for use by any person or organization which is not acting for or on behalf of any such government, political subdivision, faction, or asserted government, but all such solicitations and collections of funds shall be subject to the approval of the President and shall be made under such rules and regulations as he shall prescribe.

"(b) The provisions of this section shall not apply to a renewal or adjustment of such indebtedness as may exist on the date of the President's proclamation.

"(c) Whoever shall violate the provisions of this section or of any regulations issued hereunder shall, upon conviction thereof, be fined not more than $50,000 or imprisoned for not more than five years, or both. Should the violation be by a corporation, organization, or association, each officer or agent thereof participating in the violation may be liable to the penalty herein prescribed.

"(d) Whenever the President shall have revoked any such proclamation issued under the authority of section 1 of this Act, the provisions of this section and of any regulations issued by the President hereunder shall thereupon cease to apply with respect to the state or states named in such proclamation, except with respect to offenses committed prior to such revocation.

Exceptions—American Republics

"Sec. 4. This Act shall not apply to an American republic or republics engaged in war against a non-American state or states, provided the American republic is not cooperating with a non-American state or states in such war.

"National Munitions Control Board

"Sec. 5. (a) There is hereby established a National Munitions Control Board (hereinafter referred to as the 'Board') to carry out the provisions of this Act. The Board shall consist of the Secretary of State, who shall be chairman and executive officer of the Board, the Secretary of the Treasury, the Secretary of War, the Secretary of the Navy, and the Secretary of Commerce. Except as otherwise provided in this Act, or by other law, the administration of this Act is vested in the Department of State. The Secretary of State shall promulgate such rules and regulations with regard to the enforcement of this section as he may deem necessary to carry out its provisions. The Board shall be convened by the chairman and shall hold at least one meeting a year.

"(b) Every person who engages in the business of manufacturing, exporting, or importing any of the arms, ammunition, or implements of war referred to in this Act, whether as an exporter, importer, manufacturer, or dealer, shall register with the Secretary of State his name, or business name, principal place of business, and places of business in the United States, and a list of the arms, ammunition, and implements of war which he manufactures, imports, or exports.

"(c) Every person required to register under this section shall notify the Secretary of State of any change in the arms, ammunition, or implements of war which he exports, imports, or manufactures; and upon such notification the Secretary of State shall issue to such person an amended certificate of registration, free of charge, which shall remain valid until the date of expiration of the original certificate. Every person required to register under the provisions of this section shall pay a registration fee of $500, unless he manufactured, exported, or imported arms, ammunition, and implements of war to a total sales value of less than $50,000 during the twelve months immediately preceding his registration, in which case he shall pay a registration fee of $100. Upon receipt of the required registration fee, the Secretary of State shall issue a registration certificate valid for five years, which shall be renewable for further periods of five years upon the payment for each renewal of a fee of $500 in the case of persons who manufactured, exported, or imported arms, ammunition, and implements of war to a total sales value of more than $50,000 during the twelve months immediately preceding the renewal, or a fee of $100 in the case of persons who manufactured, exported, or imported arms, ammunition, and implements of war to a total sales value of less than $50,000 during the twelve months immediately preceding the renewal. The Secretary of the Treasury is hereby directed to refund, out of any moneys in the Treasury not otherwise appropriated, the sum of $400 to every person who shall have paid a registration fee of $500 pursuant to this Act, who manufactured, exported, or imported arms, ammunition, and implements of war to a total sales value of less than $50,000 during the twelve months immediately preceding his registration.

"(d) It shall be unlawful for any person to export, or attempt to export, from the United States to any other state, any of the arms, ammunition, or implements of war referred to in this Act, or to import, or attempt to import, to the United States from any other state, any of the arms, ammunition, or implements of war referred to in this Act, without first having obtained a license therefor.

"(e) All persons required to register under this section shall maintain, subject to the inspection of the Secretary of State, or any person or persons designated by him, such permanent records of manufacture for export, importation, and exportation of arms, ammunition, and implements of war as the Secretary of State shall prescribe.

"(f) Licenses shall be issued to persons who have registered as herein provided for, except in cases of export or import licenses where the export of arms, ammunition, or implements of war would be in violation of this Act or any other law of the United States, or of a treaty to which the United States is a party, in which cases such licenses shall not be issued.

"(g) Whenever the President shall have issued a proclamation under the authority of section 1 of this Act, all licenses theretofore issued under this Act shall ipso facto and immediately upon the issuance of such proclamation, cease to grant authority to export arms, ammunition, or implements of war from any place in the United States to any belligerent state, or to any state wherein civil strife exists, named in such proclamation, or to any neutral state for transshipment to, or for the use of, any such belligerent state or any such state wherein civil strife exists; and said licenses, insofar as the grant of authority to export to the state or states named in such proclamation is concerned, shall be null and void.

"(h) No purchase of arms, ammunition, or implements of war shall be made on behalf of the United States by any officer, executive department, or independent establishment of the Government from any person who shall have failed to register under the provisions of this Act.

"(i) The provisions of the Act of August 29, 1916, relating to the sale of ordnance and stores to the Government of Cuba (39 Stat. 619, 643; U.S.C., 1934 ed., title 50, sec. 72), are hereby repealed as of December 31, 1937.

"(j) The Board shall make an annual report to Congress, copies of which shall be distributed as are other reports transmitted to Congress. Such reports shall contain such information and data collected by the Board as may be considered of value in the determination of questions connected with the control of trade in arms, ammunition, and implements of war. The Board shall include in such reports a list of all persons required to register under the provisions of this Act, and full information concerning the licenses issued hereunder

"(k) The President is hereby authorized to proclaim upon recommendation of the Board from time to time a list of articles which shall be considered arms, ammunition, and implements of war for the purposes of this section.

"American Vessels Prohibited from Carrying Arms to Belligerent States

"Sec. 6. (a) Whenever the President shall have issued a proclamation under the authority of section 1 of this Act, it shall thereafter be unlawful, until such proclamation is revoked, for any American vessel to carry any arms, ammunition, or implements of war to any belligerent state, or to any state wherein civil strife exists, named in such proclamations, or to any neutral state for transshipment to, or for the use of, any such belligerent state or any such state wherein civil strife exists.

"(b) Whoever, in violation of the provisions of this section, shall take, or attempt to take, or shall authorize, hire, or solicit another to take, any American vessel carrying such cargo out of port or from the jurisdiction of the United States shall be fined not more than $10,000, or imprisoned not more than five years, or both; and, in addition, such vessel, and her tackle, apparel, furniture, and equipment, and the arms, ammunition, and implements of war on board, shall be forfeited to the United States.

"Use of American Ports as Base of Supply

"Sec. 7. (a) Whenever, during any war in which the United States is neutral, the President, or any person thereunto authorized by him, shall have cause to believe that any vessel, domestic or foreign, whether requiring clearance or not, is about to carry out of a port of the United States, fuel, men, arms, ammunition, implements of war, or other supplies to any warship, tender, or supply ship of a belligerent state, but the evidence is not deemed sufficient to justify forbidding the departure of the vessel as provided for by section 1, title V, chapter 30, of the Act approved June 15, 1917 (40 Stat. 217, 221; U.S.C., 1934 ed., title 18, sec. 31), and if, in the President's judgment; such action will serve to maintain peace between the United States and foreign states, or to protect the commercial interests of the United States and its citizens, or to promote the security or neutrality of the United States, he shall have the power and it shall be his duty to require the owner, master, or person in command thereof, before departing from a port of the United States, to give a bond to the United States, with sufficient sureties, in such amount as he shall deem proper, conditioned that the vessel will not deliver the men, or any part of the cargo, to any warship, tender, or supply ship of a belligerent state.

"(b) If the President, or any person thereunto authorized by him, shall find that a vessel, domestic or foreign, in a port of the United States, has previously cleared from a port of the United States during such war and delivered its cargo or any part thereof to a warship, tender, or supply ship of a belligerent state, he may prohibit the departure of such vessel during the duration of the war.

"Submarines and Armed Merchant Vessels

"Sec. 8. Whenever, during any war in which the United States is neutral, the President shall find that special restrictions placed on the use of the ports and territorial waters of the United States by the submarines or armed merchant vessels of a foreign state, will serve to maintain peace between the United States and foreign states, or to protect the commercial interests of the United States and its citizens, or to promote the security of the United States, and shall make proclamation thereof, it shall thereafter be unlawful for any such submarine or armed merchant vessel to enter a port or the territorial waters of the United States or to depart therefrom, except under such conditions and subject to such limitations as the President may prescribe. Whenever, in his judgment, the conditions which have caused him to issue his proclamation have ceased to exist, he shall revoke his proclamation and the provisions of this section shall thereupon cease to apply.

"Travel on Vessels of Belligerent States

"Sec. 9. Whenever the President shall have issued a proclamation under the authority of section 1 of this Act it shall thereafter be unlawful for any citizen of the United States to travel on any vessel of the state or states named in such proclamation, except in accordance with such rules and regulations as the President shall prescribe: *Provided, however,* That the provisions of this section shall not apply to a citizen of the United States traveling on a vessel whose voyage was begun in advance of the date of the President's proclamation, and who had no opportunity to discontinue his voyage after that date: *And provided further,* That they shall not apply under ninety days after the date of the President's proclamation to a citizen of the United States returning from a foreign state to the United States. Whenever, in the President's judgment, the conditions which have caused him to issue his proclamation have ceased to exist, he shall revoke his proclamation and the provisions of this section shall thereupon cease to apply with respect to the state or states named in such proclamation, except with respect to offenses committed prior to such revocation.

"Arming of American Merchant Vessels Prohibited

"Sec. 10. Whenever the President shall have issued a proclamation under the authority of section 1, it shall thereafter be unlawful, until such proclamation is revoked, for any American vessel engaged in commerce with any belligerent state, or any state wherein civil strife exists, named in such proclamation, to be armed or to carry any armament, arms, ammunition, or implements of war, except small arms and ammunition therefor which the President may deem necessary and shall publicly designate for the preservation of discipline aboard such vessels.

Source:
United States Statutes at Large, Vol. 49, pp. 121–128.

Franklin Roosevelt, Court-Packing Bill, Fireside Chat, 1937

National radio address by President Franklin D. Roosevelt on March 9, 1937, promoting his controversial legislative proposal to reorganize the federal judiciary.

Beginning early in his first term, Roosevelt used these radio lectures, dubbed "fireside chats," to give them a homey, personal air, to address and reassure the nation concerning current problems during the Great Depression.

Roosevelt was frustrated by the Supreme Court's declaration of emergency New Deal legislation as unconstitutional. The Court's invalidation of early New Deal measures persuaded FDR that the federal judiciary, unless tamed, would derail his program for saving the country from the economic and social ruin of the depression. Emboldened by his landslide reelection in 1936, Roosevelt moved legislatively to rein in the courts. He used a fireside chat to present to the American people his plan, which he had formally presented to Congress on February 5. It called for adding a justice for each one who, having served at least 10 years, remained on the bench for more than six months after he (they were all men) turned 70. Dubbed "court-packing" by his critics, the plan, according to them, reinforced by the message in the fireside chat, simply sought to increase the Supreme Court's membership in order to pack it with sympathetic justices who would uphold the New Deal. In the address, FDR suggested that the federal courts in the previous generation had aggrandized power at the expense of Congress and the president, wielding such power to frustrate the popular will. The Supreme Court, he asserted, imperiled the national interest by blocking his crisis program for restoring and stabilizing the U.S. economic system. He masked his overt political purpose by offering the plan as a necessary reform initiative for the overburdened and inefficient federal judiciary.

My friends, last Thursday I described in detail certain economic problems which everyone admits now face the Nation. For the many messages which have come to me after that speech, and which it is physically impossible to answer individually, I take this means of saying "Thank you."

Tonight, sitting at my desk in the White House, I make my first radio report to the people in my second term of office.

I am reminded of that evening in March, four years ago, when I made my first radio report to you. We were then in the midst of the great banking crisis.

Soon after, with the authority of the Congress, we asked the Nation to turn over all of its privately held gold, dollar for dollar, to the Government of the United States.

Today's recovery proves how right that policy was.

But when, almost two years later, it came before the Supreme Court, its constitutionality was upheld only by a five-to-four vote. The change of one vote would have thrown all the affairs of this great Nation back into hopeless chaos. In effect, four Justices ruled that the right under a private contract to exact a pound of flesh was more sacred than the main objectives of the Constitution to establish an enduring Nation.

In 1933 you and I knew that we must never let our economic system get completely out of joint again—that we could not afford to take the risk of another great depression.

We also became convinced that the only way to avoid a repetition of those dark days was to have a government with power to prevent and to cure the abuses and the inequalities which had thrown that system out of joint.

We then began a program of remedying those abuses and inequalities—to give balance and stability to our economic system—to make it bomb-proof against the causes of 1929.

Today we are only part-way through that program—and recovery is speeding up to a point where the dangers of 1929 are again becoming possible, not this week or month perhaps, but within a year or two.

National laws are needed to complete that program. Individual or local or state effort alone cannot protect us in 1937 any better than ten years ago.

It will take time—and plenty of time—to work out our remedies administratively even after legislation is passed. To complete our program of protection in time, therefore, we cannot delay one moment in making certain that our National Government has power to carry through.

Four years ago action did not come until the eleventh hour. It was almost too late.

If we learned anything from the depression we will not allow ourselves to run around in new circles of futile discussion and debate, always postponing the day of decision.

The American people have learned from the depression. For in the last three national elections an overwhelming majority of them voted a mandate that the Congress and the President begin the task of providing that protection—not after long years of debate, but now.

The Courts, however, have cast doubts on the ability of the elected Congress to protect us against catastrophe by meeting squarely our modern social and economic conditions.

We are at a crisis, a crisis in our ability to proceed with that protection. It is a quiet crisis. There are no lines of depositors outside closed banks. But to the far-sighted it is far-reaching in its possibilities of injury to America.

I want to talk with you very simply tonight about the need for present action in this crisis—the need to meet the unanswered challenge of one-third of a Nation ill-nourished, ill-clad, ill-housed.

Last Thursday I described the American form of Government as a three-horse team provided by the Constitution to the American people so that their field might be plowed. The three horses are, of course, the Congress, the Executive and the Courts. Two of the horses, the Congress and the Executive, are pulling in unison today; the third is not. Those who have intimated that the President of the United States is trying to drive that team, overlook the simple fact that the President, as Chief Executive, is himself one of the three horses.

It is the American people themselves who are in the driver's seat. It is the American people themselves who want the furrow plowed.

It is the American people themselves who expect the third horse to pull in unison with the other two.

I hope that you have re-read the Constitution of the United States in these past few weeks. Like the Bible, it ought to be read again and again.

It is an easy document to understand when you remember that it was called into being because the Articles of Confederation under which the original thirteen States tried to operate after the Revolution showed the need of a National Government with power enough to handle national problems. In its Preamble, the Constitution states that it was intended to form a more perfect Union and promote the general welfare; and the powers given to the Congress to carry out those purposes can best be described by saying that they were all the powers needed to meet each and every problem which then had a national character and which could not be met by merely local action.

But the framers went further. Having in mind that in succeeding generations many other problems then undreamed of would become national problems, they gave to the Congress the ample broad powers "to levy taxes . . . and provide for the common defense and general welfare of the United States."

That, may friends, is what I honestly believe to have been the clear and underlying purpose of the patriots who wrote a Federal Constitution to create a National Government with national power, intended as they said, "to form a more perfect union . . . for ourselves and our posterity."

For nearly twenty years there was no conflict between the Congress and the Court. Then, in 1803, Congress passed a statute which the Court said violated an express provision of the Constitution. The Court claimed the power to declare it unconstitutional and did so declare it. But a little later the Court itself admitted that it was an extraordinary power to exercise and through Mr. Justice Washington laid down this limitation upon it. He said: "It is but a decent respect due to the wisdom, the integrity and the patriotism of the Legislative body, by which any law is passed, to presume in favor of its validity until its violation of the Constitution is proved beyond all reasonable doubt."

But since the rise of the modern movement for social and economic progress through legislation, the Court has more and more often and more and more boldly asserted a power to veto laws passed by the Congress and by State Legislatures in complete disregard of this original limitation, which I have just read.

In the last four years the sound rule of giving statutes the benefit of all reasonable doubt has been cast aside. The Court has been acting not as a judicial body, but as a policy-making body.

When the Congress has sought to stabilize national agriculture, to improve the conditions of labor, to safeguard business against unfair competition, to protect our national resources, and in many other ways to serve our clearly national needs, the majority of the Court has been assuming the power to pass on the wisdom of these Acts of the Congress—and to approve or disapprove the public policy written into these laws.

That is not only my accusation. It is the accusation of most distinguished Justices of the present Supreme Court. I have not the time to quote to you all the language used by dissenting Justices in many of these cases. But in the case holding the Railroad Retirement Act unconstitutional, for instance, Chief Justice Hughes said in a dissenting opinion that the majority opinion was "a departure from sound principles," and placed "an unwarranted limitation upon the commerce clause." And three other Justices agreed with him.

In the case holding the Triple A unconstitutional, Justice Stone said of the majority opinion that it was a "tortured construction of the Constitution." And two other Justices agreed with him.

In the case holding the New York Minimum Wage Law unconstitutional, Justice Stone said that the majority were actually reading into the Constitution their own "personal economic predilections," and that if the legislative power is not left free to choose the methods of solving the problems of poverty, subsistence and health of large numbers in the community, then "government is to be rendered impotent." And two other Justices agreed with him.

In the face of these dissenting opinions, there is no basis for the claim made by some members of the Court that something in the Constitution has compelled them regretfully to thwart the will of the people.

In the face of such dissenting opinions, it is perfectly clear that, as Chief Justice Hughes has said: "We are under a Constitution but the Constitution is what the Judges say it is."

The Court, in addition to the proper use of its judicial functions, has improperly set itself up as a third House of the Congress—a super-legislature, as one of the Justices has called it— reading into the Constitution words and implications which are not there, and which were never intended to be there.

We have, therefore, reached the point as a Nation where we must take action to save the Constitution from the Court and the Court from itself. We must find a way to take an appeal from the Supreme Court to the Constitution itself. We want a Supreme Court which will do justice under the Constitution—not over it. In our Courts we want a government of laws and not of men.

I want—as all Americans want—an independent judiciary as proposed by the framers of the Constitution. That means a Supreme Court that will enforce the Constitution as written—that will refuse to amend the Constitution by the arbitrary exercise of judicial power—amendment, in other words, by judicial say-so. It does not mean a judiciary so independent that it can deny the existence of facts which are universally recognized.

How then could we proceed to perform the mandate given us? It was said in last year's Democratic platform, and here are the words, "If these problems cannot be effectively solved within the Constitution, we shall seek such clarifying amendment as will assure the power to enact those laws, adequately to regulate commerce, protect public health and safety, and safeguard economic security." In other words, we said we would seek an amendment only if every other possible means by legislation were to fail.

When I commenced to review the situation with the problem squarely before me, I came by a process of elimination to the conclusion that short of amendments the only method which was clearly constitutional, and would at the same time carry out other much needed reforms, was to infuse new blood into all our Courts. We must have men worthy and equipped to carry out impartial justice. But, at the same time, we must have Judges who will bring to the Courts a present-day sense of the Constitution—Judges who will retain in the Courts the judicial functions of a court, and reject the legislative powers which the Courts have today assumed.

It is well for us to remember that in forty-five out of the forty-eight States of the Union Judges are chosen not for life but for a period of years. In many states Judges must retire at the age of seventy. Congress has provided financial security by offering life pensions at full pay for Federal Judges on all Courts who are willing to retire at seventy. In the case of Supreme Court Justices that pension is $20,000. a year. But all Federal Judges, once appointed, can, if they choose, hold office for life, no matter how old they may get to be.

What is my proposal? It is simply this: Whenever a Judge or Justice of any Federal Court has reached the age of seventy and does not avail himself of the opportunity to retire on a pension, a new member shall be appointed by the President then in office, with the approval, as required by the Constitution, of the Senate of the United States.

That plan has two chief purposes. By bringing into the Judicial system a steady and continuing stream of new and younger blood, I hope, first, to make the administration of all Federal justice, from the bottom to the top, speedier and, therefore, less costly; secondly, to bring to the decision of social and economic problems younger men who have had personal experience and contact with modern facts and circumstances under which average men have to live and work. This plan will save our national Constitution from hardening of the judicial arteries.

The number of Judges to be appointed would depend wholly on the decision of present Judges now over seventy, or those who would subsequently reach the age of seventy.

If, for instance, any one of the six Justices of the Supreme Court now over the age of seventy should retire as provided under the plan, no additional place would be created. Consequently, although there never can be more than fifteen, there may be only fourteen, or thirteen, or twelve. And there may be only nine.

There is nothing novel or radical about this idea. It seeks to maintain the Federal bench in full vigor. It has been discussed and approved by many persons of high authority ever since a similar proposal passed the House of Representatives in 1869.

Why was the age fixed at seventy? Because the laws of many states, and the practice of the Civil Service, the regulations of the Army and Navy, and the rules of many of our universities and of almost every great private business enterprise, commonly fix the retirement age at seventy years or less.

The statute would apply to all the Courts in the Federal system. There is general approval so far as the lower Federal courts are concerned. The plan has met opposition only so far as the Supreme Court of the United States itself is concerned. But, my friends, if such a plan is good for the lower courts it certainly ought to be equally good for the highest Court from which there is no appeal.

Those opposing this plan have sought to arouse prejudice and fear by crying that I am seeking to "pack" the Supreme Court and that a baneful precedent will be established.

What do they mean by the words "packing the Supreme Court"?

Let me answer this question with a bluntness that will end all honest misunderstanding of my purposes.

If by that phrase "packing the Court" it is charged that I wish to place on the bench spineless puppets who would disregard the law and would decide specific cases as I wished them to be decided, I make this answer—that no President fit for his office would appoint, and no Senate of honorable men fit for their office would confirm, that kind of appointees to the Supreme Court.

But if by that phrase the charge is made that I would appoint and the Senate would confirm Justices worthy to sit beside present members of the Court who understand modern conditions—that I will appoint Justices who will not undertake to override the judgment of the Congress on legislative policy—that I will appoint Justices who will act as Justices and not as legislators—if the appointment of such Justices can be called "packing the Court," then I say that I, and with me the vast majority of the American people, favor doing just that thing—now.

Is it a dangerous precedent for the Congress to change the number of the Justices? The Congress has always had, and will have, that power. The number of Justices has been changed several times before—in the Administrations of John Adams and Thomas Jefferson—both of them signers of the Declaration of Independence—in the Administrations of Andrew Jackson, Abraham Lincoln and Ulysses S. Grant.

I suggest only the addition of Justices to the bench in accordance with a clearly defined principle relating to a clearly defined age limit. Fundamentally, if in the future, America cannot trust the Congress it elects to refrain from abuse of our Constitutional usages, democracy will have failed far beyond the importance to democracy of any kind of precedent concerning the Judiciary.

We think it so much in the public interest to maintain a vigorous judiciary that we encourage the retirement of elderly Judges by offering them a life pension at full salary. Why then should we leave the fulfillment of this public policy to chance or make it dependent upon the desire or prejudice of any individual Justice?

It is the clear intention of our public policy to provide for a constant flow of new and younger blood into the Judiciary. Normally every President appoints a large number of District and Circuit Judges and a few members of the Supreme Court. Until my first term practically every President of the United States in our history had appointed at least one member of the Supreme Court. President Taft appointed five members and named a Chief Justice—President Wilson three—President Harding four including a Chief Justice—President Coolidge one—President Hoover three including a Chief Justice.

Such a succession of appointments should have provided a Court well-balanced as to age. But chance and the disinclination of individuals to leave the Supreme bench have now given us a Court in which five Justices will be over seventy-five years of age before next June and one over seventy. Thus a sound public policy has been defeated.

So, I now propose that we establish by law an assurance against any such ill-balanced Court in the future. I propose that hereafter, when a Judge reaches the age of seventy, a new and younger Judge shall be added to the Court automatically. In this way I propose to enforce a sound public policy by law instead of leaving the composition of our Federal Courts, including the highest, to be determined by chance or the personal decision of individuals.

If such a law as I propose is regarded as establishing a new precedent—is it not a most desirable precedent?

Like all lawyers, like all Americans, I regret the necessity of this controversy. But the welfare of the United States, and indeed of the Constitution itself, is what we all must think about first. Our difficulty with the Court today rises not from the Court as an institution but from human beings within it. But we cannot yield our constitutional destiny to the personal judgment of a few men who, being fearful of the future, would deny us the necessary means of dealing with the present.

This plan of mine is no attack on the Court; it seeks to restore the Court to its rightful and historic place in our system of Constitutional Government and to have it resume its high task of building anew on the Constitution "a system of living law." The Court itself can best undo what the Court has done . . .

Source:

Franklin D. Roosevelt, *The Public Papers and Addresses of Franklin D. Roosevelt.* New York: Random House, 1938–1950.

Bankhead-Jones Farm Tenant Act, 1937

U.S. legislation sponsored by Senator John Hollis Bankhead II of Alabama and Representative John M. Jones of Texas and enacted on July 22, 1937, to stop the decline in farm ownership and to check the growth of tenant farming and sharecropping. This federal act established the Farm Security Administration (FSA) and authorized it to grant low-interest, long-term loans to farm tenants, sharecroppers, and farm workers who wished to purchase their own farms. It encouraged the retirement of worn-out land and provided rehabilitation loans, educational assistance, and technical aid. The FSA also regulated the wages and hours of migrant workers and provided them with sanitary medical facilities. As part of its work, FSA sent photographers around the country to document the plight of farm workers. Their pictures influenced contemporary public opinion and endure in books and exhibits as a graphic reminder of the Great Depression.

An Act

To create the Farmers' Home Corporation, to promote more secure occupancy of farms and farm homes, to correct the economic instability resulting from some present forms of farm tenancy, and for other purposes.

Be it enacted by the Senate and House of Representatives of the United States of America in Congress assembled, That this Act may be cited as "The Bankhead-Jones Farm Tenant Act."

Title I—Farm Tenant Provisions

Power of Secretary

Section 1. (a) The Secretary of Agriculture (hereinafter referred to as the "Secretary") is authorized to make loans in the United States and in the Territories of Alaska and Hawaii and in Puerto Rico to persons eligible to receive the benefits of this title to enable such persons to acquire farms.

(b) Only farm tenants, farm laborers, sharecroppers, and other individuals who obtain, or who recently obtained, the major portion of their income from farming operations shall be eligible to receive the benefits of this title. In making available the benefits of this title, the Secretary shall give preference to persons who are married, or who have dependent families, or, wherever practicable, to persons who are able to make an initial down payment, or who are owners of livestock and farm implements necessary successfully to carry on farming operations. No person shall be eligible who is not a citizen of the United States.

(c) No loan shall be made for the acquisition of any farm unless it is of such size as the Secretary determines to be sufficient to constitute an efficient farm-management unit and to enable a diligent farm family to carry on successful farming of a type which the Secretary deems can be successfully carried on in the locality in which the farm is situated.

County Committees and Loans

Sec. 2. (a) The County Committee. . .shall—

(1) Examine applications (filed with the county agent in the county, or with such other person as the Secretary may designate) of persons desiring to finance the acquisition of farms in the county by means of a loan from the Secretary under this title.

(2) Examine and appraise farms in the county with respect to which an application for a loan is made.

(b) If the committee finds that an applicant is eligible to receive the benefits of this title, that by reason of his character, ability, and experience he is likely successfully to carry out undertakings required of him under a loan which may be made under this title, and that the farm with respect to which the application is made is of such character that there is a reasonable likelihood that the making of a loan with respect thereto will carry out the purposes of this title, it shall so certify to the Secretary. The committee shall also certify to the Secretary the amount which the committee finds is the reasonable value of the farm.

(c) No certification under this section shall be made with respect to any farm in which any member of the committee or any person related to such member within the third degree of consanguinity or affinity has any property interest, direct or indirect, or in which they or either of them have had such interest within one year prior to the date of certification.

(d) No loan shall be made to any person or with respect to any farm unless certification as required under this section has been made with respect to such person and such farm by the committee.

Terms of Loans

Sec. 3. (a) Loans made under this title shall be in such amount (not in excess of the amount certified by the County Committee to be the value of the farm) as may be necessary to enable the borrower to acquire the farm and for necessary repairs and improvements thereon, and shall be secured by a first mortgage or deed of trust on the farm.

(b) The instruments under which the loan is made and security given therefor shall—

(1) Provide for the repayment of the loan within an agreed period of not more than forty years from the making of the loan.

(2) Provide for the payment of interest on the unpaid balance of the loan at the rate of 3 per centum per annum.

* * *

(5) Provide that the borrower shall pay taxes and assessments on the farm to the proper authorities, and insure and pay for insurance on farm buildings.

(6) Provide that upon the borrower's assigning, selling, or otherwise transferring the farm, or any interest therein, without the consent of the Secretary, or upon default in the performance of, or upon any failure to comply with, any covenant or condition contained in such instruments, or upon involuntary transfer or sale, the Secretary may declare the amount unpaid immediately due and payable, and that, without the consent of the Secretary, no final payment shall be accepted, or release of the Secretary's interest be made, less than five years after the making of the loan.

* * *

Avoidance of Production Expansion

Sec. 5. In carrying out this title, the Secretary shall give due consideration to the desirability of avoiding the expansion of production for market for basic commodities where such expansion would defeat the policy of Congress . . . and shall, so far as practicable, assist beneficiaries of the program under this title to become established upon lands now in cultivation.

Appropriation

Sec. 6. To carry out the provisions of this title, there is authorized to be appropriated not to exceed $10,000,000 for the fiscal year ending June 30, 1938, not to exceed $25,000,000 for the fiscal year ending June 30, 1939, and not exceed $50,000,000 for each fiscal year thereafter. Not more than 5 per centum of the sums appropriated for any fiscal year in pursuance of this section shall be available for administrative expenses in carrying out this title during such fiscal year.

Title II—Rehabilitation Loans

Borrowers and Terms

Sec. 21. (a) Out of the funds made available under section 23, the Secretary shall have power to make loans to eligible individuals for the purchase of livestock, farm equipment, supplies, and for other farm needs (including minor improvements and minor repairs to real property), and for the refinancing of indebtedness, and for family subsistence.

(b) Loans made under this section shall bear interest at a rate not in excess of 3 per centum per annum, and shall have maturities not in excess of five years, and may be renewed. . . .

(c) Only farm owners, farm tenants, farm laborers, sharecroppers, and other individuals who obtain, or who recently obtained, the major portion of their income from farming operations, and who cannot obtain credit on reasonable terms from any federally incorporated lending institution, shall be eligible for loans under this section.

Debt Adjustment

Sec. 22. The Secretary shall have power to assist in the voluntary adjustment of indebtedness between farm debtors and their creditors and may cooperate with any pay the whole or part of the expenses of State, Territorial, and local agencies and committees engaged in such debt adjustment. He is also authorized to continue and carry out undertakings with respect to farm debt adjustment uncompleted at the time when appropriations for the purpose of this section are first available. Services finished by the Secretary under this section shall be without charge to the debtor or creditor.

Appropriation

* * *

(b) The President is authorized to allot to the Secretary, out of appropriations made for relief or work relief for any fiscal year ending prior to July 1, 1939, such sums as he determines to be necessary to carry out the provisions of this title and to enable the Secretary to carry out such other forms and rehabilitation of individuals eligible under this title to receive loans as may be authorized by law and designated in the Executive order directing the allotment.

Title III—Retirement of Submarginal Land

Program

Sec. 31. The Secretary is authorized and directed to develop a program of land conservation and land utilization, including the retirement of lands which are submarginal or not primarily suitable for cultivation, in order thereby to correct maladjustments in land use, and thus assist in controlling soil erosion, reforestation, preserving natural resources, mitigating floods, preventing impairment of dams and reservoirs, conserving surface and subsurface moisture, protecting the watersheds of navigable streams, and protecting the public lands, health, safety, and welfare.

Powers under Land Program

Sec. 32. To effectuate the program provided for in section 31, the Secretary is authorized—

(a) To acquire by purchase, gift, or devise, or by transfer from any agency of the United States or from any State, Territory, or political subdivision, submarginal land and land not primarily suitable for cultivation, and interests in and options on such land. . . .

(b) To protect, improve, develop, and administer any property so acquired and to construct such structures thereon as may be necessary to adapt it to its most beneficial use.

(c) To sell, exchange, lease, or otherwise dispose of, with or without a consideration, any property so acquired, under such terms and conditions as he deems will best accomplish the purposes of this title, but any sale, exchange, or grant shall be made only to public authorities and agencies and only on condition that the property is used for public purposes. The Secretary may recommend to the President other Federal, State, or Territorial agencies to administer such property, together with the conditions of use and administration which will best serve the purposes of a land-conservation and land-utilization program, and the President is authorized to transfer such property to such agencies.

(d) With respect to any land, or any interest therein, acquired by, or transferred to, the Secretary for the purposes of this title, to make dedications or grants, in his discretion, for any public purpose, and to grant licenses and easements upon such terms as he deems reasonable.

(e) To cooperate with Federal, State, Territorial, and other public agencies in developing plans for a program of land conservation and land utilization, to conduct surveys and investigations relating to conditions and factors affecting, and the methods of accomplishing most effectively, the purposes of this title, and to disseminate information concerning these activities.

(f) To make such rules and regulations as he deems necessary to prevent trespasses and otherwise regulate the use and occupancy of property acquired by, or transferred to, the Secretary for the purposes of this title, in order to conserve and utilize it or advance the purposes of this title. Any violation of such rules and regulations shall be punished. . . .

* * *

Title IV—General Provisions

Farmer's Home Corporation

Sec. 40. (a) There is hereby created as an agency, of and within the Department of Agriculture, a body corporate with the name "Farmers' Home Corporation" (in this Act called the Corporation).The principal office of the Corporation shall be located in the District of Columbia, but there may be established agencies or branch offices elsewhere in the United States under rules and regulations prescribed by the Board of Directors.

(b) The Secretary shall have power to delegate to the Corporation such powers and duties conferred upon him under title I or title II, or both, and such powers under title IV as relate to the exercise of the powers and duties so delegated, as he deems may be necessary to the efficient carrying out of the purposes of such titles and may be executed by the Corporation, and to transfer to the Corporation such funds available for such purposes as he deems necessary. In connection with and in the exercise of such powers and duties so delegated, all provisions of this Act relating to the powers and duties of, and limitations upon, the Secretary shall apply to the Corporation in the same manner as to the Secretary, and the term "Secretary" shall be construed to include "Corporation".

(c) The Corporation shall have a nominal capital stock in an amount determined and subscribed for by the Secretary. Receipts for payments for or on account of such stock shall be issued by the Corporation to the Secretary and shall be evidence of the stock ownership of the United States.

(d) The management of the Corporation shall be vested in a board of directors (in this Act called the Board) subject to the general supervision of the Secretary. The Board shall consist of three persons employed in the Department of Agriculture who shall be designated by the Secretary. Vacancies in the Board, so long as there are two members in office, shall not impair the powers of the Board to execute its functions and two of the members in office shall constitute a quorum for the transaction of business. The directors, appointed as hereinbefore provided, shall receive no additional compensation for their services as such directors but may be allowed travel and subsistence expenses when engaged in business of the Corporation outside of the District of Columbia.

* * *

(f) The Corporation—

* * *

(3) May sue and be sued in its corporate name in any court of a competent jurisdiction, State or Federal: Provided , That the prosecution and defense of all litigation to which the Corporation may be a party shall be conducted under the supervision of the Attorney General, and the Corporation shall be represented by the United States Attorneys for the districts, respectively, in which such litigation may arise, or by such other attorney or attorneys as may, under the law, be designated by the Attorney General: And provided further, That no attachment, injunction, garnishment, or other similar process, mesne or final, shall be issued against the Corporation or its property;

(4) May adopt, amend, and repeal bylaws, rules, and regulations governing the manner in which its business may be conducted and the powers vested in it may be exercised and enjoyed;

* * *

(6) Shall have such powers as may be necessary or appropriate for the exercise of the powers vested in the Corporation (including, but subject to the limitations of this Act, the power to make contracts, and to purchase or lease, and to hold or dispose of, such real and personal property as it deems necessary) and all such incidental powers as are customary in corporations generally. The Board shall define the authority and duties of the officers and employees of the Corporation, delegate to them such of the powers vested in the Corporation as it may determine, and require bonds of such of them as it may designate and fix the penalties and pay the premiums of such bonds.

* * *

County Committee

Sec. 42. (a) The Secretary is authorized and directed to appoint in each county in which activities are carried on under title I a county committee composed of three farmers residing in the county.

* * *

(c) The committee shall meet on the call of the county agent in the county, or on the call of such other person as the Secretary may designate.

* * *

Surveys and Research

Sec. 47. The Secretary is authorized to conduct surveys, investigations, and research relating to the conditions and factors affecting, and the methods of accomplishing most effectively, the purposes of this Act, and may publish and disseminate information pertinent to the various aspects of his activities.

* * *

Separability

Sec. 55. If any provision of this Act, or the application thereof to any person or circumstances, is held invalid, the remainder of the Act, and the application of such provisions to other persons or circumstances, shall not be affected thereby.

Approved, July 22, 1937.

Source:

Statutes at Large, Vol. 49, pp. 522–533.

Fair Labor Standards Act, 1938

Federal U.S. legislation enacted on June 25, 1938, that established a minimum wage of 25 cents per hour (to be increased gradually to 40 cents) and a maximum work week of 44 hours (to be reduced gradually to 40 hours), with time and a half for overtime. It also prohibited labor by children under age 16, and protected children under 18 from hazardous occupations. The act applied only to businesses engaged in interstate commerce and exempted such occupations as farm, domestic, and professional workers and fishermen. The constitutionality of the act was upheld in *United States v. Darby Lumber Company* (312 U.S. 100 [1941]). The act has been amended many times to raise the minimum wage and extend coverage to more workers.

(excerpt)

An Act

To provide for the establishment of fair labor standards in employments in and affecting interstate commerce, and for other purposes.

Be it enacted by the Senate and House of Representatives of the United States of America in Congress assembled , That this Act may be cited as the "Fair Labor Standards Act of 1938."

Finding and Declaration of Policy

Sec. 2. (a) The Congress hereby finds that the existence, in industries engaged in commerce or in the production of goods for commerce, of labor conditions detrimental to the maintenance of the minimum standard of living necessary for health, efficiency, and general well-being of workers (1) causes commerce and the channels and instrumentalities of commerce to be used to spread and perpetuate such labor conditions among the workers of the several States; (2) burdens commerce and the free flow of goods in commerce; (3) constitutes an unfair method of competition in commerce; (4) leads to labor disputes burdening and obstructing commerce and the free flow of goods in commerce; and (5) interferes with the orderly and fair marketing of goods in commerce.

(b) It is hereby declared to be the policy of this Act, through the exercise by Congress of its power to regulate commerce among the several States, to correct and as rapidly as practicable to eliminate the conditions above referred to in such industries without substantially curtailing employment or earning power . . .

Minimum Wages

Sec. 6. (a) Every employer shall pay to each of his employees who is engaged in commerce or in the production of goods for commerce wages at the following rates—

(1) during the first year from the effective date of this section, not less than 25 cents an hour,

(2) during the next six years from such date, not less than 30 cents an hour,

(3) after the expiration of seven years from such date, not less than 40 cents an hour, or the rate (not less than 30 cents an hour) prescribed in the applicable order of the Administrator issued under section 8, whichever is lower, and

(4) at any time after the effective date of this section, not less than the rate (not in excess of 40 cents an hour) prescribed in the applicable order of the Administrator issued under section 8.

(b) This section shall take effect upon the expiration of one hundred and twenty days from the date of enactment of this Act.

Maximum Hours

Sec. 7. (a) No employer shall, except as otherwise provided in this section, employ any of his employees who is engaged in commerce or in the production of goods for commerce—

(1) for a workweek longer than forty-four hours during the first year from the effective date of this section,

(2) for a workweek longer than forty-two hours during the second year from such date, or

(3) for a workweek longer than forty hours after the expiration of the second year from such date, unless such employee receives compensation for his employment in excess of the hours above specified at a rate not less than one and one-half times the regular rate at which he is employed.

(b) No employer shall be deemed to have violated subsection (a) by employing any employee for a workweek in excess of that specified in such subsection without paying the compensation for overtime employment prescribed therein if such employee is so employed—

(1) in pursuance of an agreement, made as a result of collective bargaining by representatives of employees certified as bona fide by the National Labor Relations Board, which provides that no employee shall be employed more than one thousand hours during any period of twenty-six consecutive weeks,

(2) on an annual basis in pursuance of an agreement with his employer, made as a result of collective bargaining by representatives of employees certified as bona fide by the National Labor Relations Board, which provides that the employee shall not be employed more than two thousand hours during any period of fifty-two consecutive weeks, or

(3) for a period or periods of not more than fourteen workweeks in the aggregate in any calendar year in an industry found by the Administrator to be of a seasonal nature, and if such employee receives compensation for employment in excess of 12 hours in any workday, or for employment in excess of 56 hours in any workweek, as the case may be, at a rate not less than one and one-half times the regular at which he is employed.

(c) In the case of an employer engaged in the first processing of milk, whey, skimmed milk, or cream into dairy products, or in the ginning and compressing of cotton, or in the processing of cottonseed, or in the processing of sugar beets, sugar beet molasses, sugarcane, or maple sap, into sugar (but not refined sugar) or into syrup, the provisions of subsection (a) shall not apply to his employees in any place of employment where he is so engaged; and in the case of an employer engaged in the first processing of, or in canning or packing, perishable or seasonal fresh fruits or vegetables, or in the first processing, within the area of production (as defined by the Administrator), of any agricultural or horticultural commodity during seasonal operations, or in handling, slaughtering, or dressing poultry or livestock, the provisions of subsection (a), during a period or periods of not more than fourteen workweeks in the aggregate in any calendar year, shall not apply to his employees in any place of employment where he is so engaged.

(d) This section shall take effect upon the expiration of one hundred and twenty days from the date of enactment of this Act.

Source:

Statutes at Large, Vol. 49, pp. 1,060–1,069.

Between the Wars

Stimson Doctrine, 1931

Doctrine of nonrecognition formulated by U.S. secretary of state Henry L. Stimson in response to Japan's invasion of Chinese Manchuria in 1931. The noninterventionist Hoover administration, while deploring Japan's seizure of Manchuria, was determined to keep the United States from direct involvement in the Far East crisis, favoring a negotiated Japanese-Chinese settlement. Faced with expanding Japanese aggression and the threat to U.S. interests in Asia it posed, Secretary Stimson expounded the nonrecognition doctrine through a pair of diplomatic notes sent to both China and Japan in January 1932. The notes stated that the United States would refuse to recognize any territorial gains or other privileges brought about by use of armed force in violation of international law. The declaration of U.S. intentions carried no threat of armed intervention and amounted basically to a moral sanction against aggression.

. . . The practice of this country as to the recognition of new governments has been substantially uniform from the days of the administration of Secretary of State Jefferson in 1792 to the days of Secretary of State Bryan in 1913. There were certain slight departures from this policy during the Civil War, but they were manifestly due to the exigencies of warfare and were abandoned immediately afterward. This general policy, as thus observed, was to base the act of recognition not upon the question of the constitutional legitimacy of the new government but upon its de facto capacity to fulfill its obligations as a member of the family of nations. This country recognized the right of other nations to regulate their own internal affairs of government and disclaimed any attempt to base its recognition upon the correctness of their constitutional action.

Said Mr. Jefferson in 1792:

"We certainly cannot deny to other nations that principle whereon our own government is founded, that every nation has a right to govern itself internally under what forms it pleases, and to change these forms at its own will; and externally to transact business with other nations through whatever organ it chooses, whether that be a king, convention, assembly, committee, president, or whatever it be."

In these essentials our practice corresponded with the practice of the other nations of the world.

The particular considerations upon which our action was regularly based were well stated by Mr. Adee, long the trusted Assistant Secretary of State of this government, as follows:

"Ever since the American Revolution entrance upon diplomatic intercourse with foreign States has been de facto, dependent upon the existence of three conditions of fact: the control of the administrative machinery of the State; the general acquiescence of its people; and the ability and willingness of their government to discharge international and conventional obligations. The form of government has not been a conditional factor in such recognition; in other words, the de jure element of legitimacy of title has been left aside."

With the advent of President Wilson's administration this policy of over a century was radically departed from in respect to the Republic of Mexico, and, by a public declaration on March 11, 1913, it was announced that—

"Cooperation (with our sister republics of Central and South America) is possible only when supported at every turn by the orderly processes of just government based upon law, not upon arbitrary or irregular force.

"We hold, as I am sure that all thoughtful leaders of republican government everywhere hold, that just government rests always upon the consent of the governed, and that there can be no freedom without order based upon law and upon the public conscience and approval.

"We shall look to make these principles the basis, of mutual intercourse, respect and helpfulness between our sister republics and ourselves."

Mr. Wilson's government sought to put this new policy into effect in respect to the recognition of the then Government of Mexico held by President Victoriano Huerta. Although Huerta's government was in de facto possession, Mr. Wilson refused to recognize it, and he sought through the influence and pressure of his great office, to force it from power. Armed conflict followed with the forces of Mexico, and disturbed relations between us and that republic lasted until a comparatively few years ago.

In his sympathy for the development of free constitutional institutions among the people of our Latin American neighbors, Mr. Wilson did not differ from the feelings of the great mass of his countrymen in the United States, including Mr. Jefferson and Mr. Adams, whose statements I have quoted; but he differed from the practice of his predecessors in seeking actively to propagate these institutions in a foreign country by the direct influence of this government and to do this against the desire of the authorities and people of Mexico.

The present administration has declined to follow the policy of Mr. Wilson and has followed consistently the former practice of this government since the days of Jefferson.

As soon as it was reported to us, through our diplomatic representatives, that the new governments in Bolivia, Peru, Argentina, Brazil and Panama were in control of the administrative machinery of the State, with the apparent general acquiescence of their people, and that they were willing and apparently able to discharge their international and conventional obligations, they were recognized by our government.

And, in view of the economic depression, with the consequent need for prompt measures of financial stabilization, we did this with as little delay as possible in order to give those sorely pressed countries the quickest possible opportunities for recovering their economic poise...

Source:

New York Times, February 7, 1931.

Recognition of the Soviet Union, 1933

Notes exchanged in 1933 that established formal diplomatic relations between the United States and the Soviet Union. Following the Bolshevik victory in the 1917 Russian Revolution, U.S. presidents from Woodrow Wilson to Herbert Hoover refused to recognize the Soviet communist government, owing to its repudiation of former Russian debts, confiscation of private property, and promotion of worldwide communist revolution. The Roosevelt administration pursued formal U.S.-Soviet ties as a cooperative front against Japanese aggression in the Far East and as a step toward improved trade relations, which would help boost an American economy mired in the depression. On November 16, 1933, at Washington, D.C., President Franklin D. Roosevelt and Soviet foreign minister Maxim Litvinov concluded a series of notes normalizing U.S.-Soviet relations. The Soviet Union pledged to settle Russian debts, refrain from supporting subversive activities in the United States, and protect the religious freedom of Americans in the USSR. Roosevelt faced harsh criticism when Joseph Stalin's Soviet regime failed to abide by the 1933 agreement.

Franklin Roosevelt, Letter to Kalinin
Washington, October 10, 1993

My dear Mr. President:

Since the beginning of my administration, I have contemplated the desirability of an effort to end the present abnormal relations between the hundred and twenty-five million people of the United States and the hundred and sixty million people of Russia.

It is most regrettable that these great peoples, between whom a happy tradition of friendship existed for more than a century to their mutual advantage, should now be without a practical method of communicating directly with each other.

The difficulties that have created this anomalous situation are serious but not, in my opinion, insoluble; and difficulties between great nations can be removed only by frank, friendly conversations. If you are of similar mind, I should be glad to receive my representative you may designate to explore with me personally all questions outstanding between our countries.

Participation in such a discussion would, of course, not commit either nation to any future course of action, but would indicate a sincere desire to reach a satisfactory solution of the problems involved. It is my hope that such conversations might result in good to the people of both our countries.

I am, my dear Mr. President,
Very sincerely yours,
Franklin D. Roosevelt.

Mikhail Kalinin, Letter to President Franklin Roosevelt
Moscow, October 17th, 1933.

My dear Mr. President:

I have received your message of October tenth.

I have always considered most abnormal and regrettable a situation wherein, during the past sixteen years, two great republics—the United States of America and the Union of Soviet Socialist Republics—have lacked the usual methods of communication and have been deprived of the benefits which such communication could give. I am glad to note that you also reached the same conclusion.

There is no doubt that difficulties, present or arising, between two countries, can be solved only when direct relations exist between them; and that, on the other hand, they have no chance for solution in the absence of such relations. I shall take the liberty further to express the opinion that the abnormal situation, to which you correctly refer in your message, has an unfavorable effect not only on the interests of the two states concerned, but also on the general international situation, increasing the element of disquiet, complicating the process of consolidating world peace and encouraging forces tending to disturb that peace.

In accordance with the above, I gladly accept your proposal to send to the United States a representative of the Soviet Government to discuss with you the questions of interest to our countries. The Soviet Government will be represented by Mr. M. M. Litvinov, People's Commissar for Foreign Affairs, who will come to Washington at a time to be mutually agreed upon.

I am, my dear Mr. President,
Very sincerely yours,
Mikhail Kalinin.

Source:

Franklin D. Roosevelt Library, President's Secretary's Files (PSF), Box 48, Russia.

World War II at Home and Abroad

Cantwell v. Connecticut, 1940

U.S. Supreme Court decision issued on May 20, 1940, upholding the First Amendment right to the free exercise of religion. Newton Cantwell, a Jehovah's Witness, was convicted of a breach of the peace for publicly playing a recording that attacked organized religion and for soliciting funds without a state certificate. In its unanimous decision, the Supreme Court ruled that Cantwell had a constitutional right "peacefully to impart his views to others," even when such views were offensive to some citizens. The Court also ruled that the First Amendment "embraces two concepts—freedom to believe and freedom to act. The first is absolute but . . . the second cannot be." While the state has the right to regulate conduct to preserve public peace and safety, it may not use that right to censor a religion.

Mr. Justice Roberts, delivered the opinion of the Court.

Newton Cantwell and his two sons, Jesse and Russell, members of a group known as Jehovah's witnesses, and claiming to be ordained ministers, were arrested in New Haven, Connecticut, and each was charged by information in five counts, with statutory and common law offenses. After trial in the Court of Common Pleas of New Haven County each of them was convicted on the third count, which charged a violation of Section 6294 of the General Statutes of Connecticut, and on the fifth count, which charged commission of the common law offense of inciting a breach of the peace. On appeal to the Supreme Court the conviction of all three on the third count was affirmed. The conviction of Jesse Cantwell, on the fifth count, was also affirmed, but the conviction of Newton and Russell on that count was reversed and a new trial ordered as to them.

By demurrers to the information, by requests for rulings of law at the trial, and by their assignments of error in the State Supreme Court, the appellants pressed the contention that the statute under which the third count was drawn was offensive to the due process clause of the Fourteenth Amendment because, on its face and as construed and applied, it denied them freedom of speech and prohibited their free exercise of religion. In like manner they made the point that they could not be found guilty on the fifth count, without violation of the Amendment.

We have jurisdiction on appeal from the judgments on the third count, as there was drawn in question the validity of a state statute under the federal Constitution, and the decision was in favor of validity. Since the conviction on the fifth count was not based upon a statute, but presents a substantial question under the federal Constitution, we granted the writ of certiorari in respect of it.

The facts adduced to sustain the convictions on the third count follow. On the day of their arrest the appellants were engaged in going singly from house to house on Cassius Street in New Haven. They were individually equipped with a bag containing books and pamphlets on religious subjects, a portable phonograph and a set of records, each of which, when played, introduced, and was a description of, one of the books. Each appellant asked the person who responded to his call for permission to play one of the records. If permission was granted he asked the person to buy the book described and, upon refusal, he solicited such contribution towards the publication of the pamphlets as the listener was willing to make. If a contribution was received a pamphlet was delivered upon condition that it would be read.

Cassius Street is in a thickly populated neighborhood, where about ninety per cent of the residents are Roman Catholics. A phonograph record, describing a book entitled "Enemies," included an attack on the Catholic religion. None of the persons interviewed were members of Jehovah's witnesses.

The statute under which the appellants were charged provides:

"No person shall solicit money, services, subscriptions or any valuable thing for any alleged religious, charitable or philanthropic cause, from other than a member of the organization for whose benefit such person is soliciting or within the county in which such person or organization is located unless such cause shall have been approved by the secretary of the public welfare council. Upon application of any person in behalf of such cause, the secretary shall determine whether such cause is a religious one or is a bona fide object of charity or philanthropy and conforms to reasonable standards of efficiency and integrity, and, if he shall so find, shall approve the same and issue to the authority in charge a certificate to that effect. Such certificate may be revoked at any time. Any person violating any provision of this section shall be fined not more than one hundred dollars or imprisoned not more than thirty days or both."

The appellants claimed that their activities were not within the statute but consisted only of distribution of books, pamphlets, and periodicals. The State Supreme Court construed the finding of the trial court to be that "in addition to the sale of the books and the distribution of the pamphlets the defendants were also soliciting contributions or donations of money for an alleged religious cause, and thereby came within the purview of the statute." [126 Conn. 1, 8 A.2d 535.] It overruled the contention that the Act, as applied to the appellants, offends the due process clause of the Fourteenth Amendment, because it abridges or denies religious freedom and liberty of speech and press. The court stated that it was the solicitation that brought the appellants within the sweep of the Act and not their other activities in the dissemination of literature. It declared the legislation constitutional as an effort by the State to protect the public against fraud and imposition in the solicitation of funds for what purported to be religious, charitable, or philanthropic causes.

The facts which were held to support the conviction of Jesse Cantwell on the fifth count were that he stopped two men in the street, asked, and received, permission to play a phonograph record, and played the record "Enemies," which attacked the religion and church of the two men, who were Catholics. Both were incensed by the contents of the record and were tempted to strike Cantwell unless he went away. On being told to be on his way he left their presence. There was no evidence that he was personally offensive or entered into any argument with those he interviewed.

The court held that the charge was not assault or breach of the peace or threats on Cantwell's part, but invoking or inciting others to breach of the peace, and that the facts supported the conviction of that offense.

[1-8] *First.* We hold that the statute, as construed and applied to the appellants, deprives them of their liberty without due process of law in contravention of the Fourteenth Amendment. The fundamental concept of liberty embodied in that Amendment embraces the liberties guaranteed by the First Amendment. The First Amendment declares that Congress shall make no law respecting an establishment of religion or prohibiting the free exercise thereof. The Fourteenth Amendment has rendered the legislatures of the states as incompetent as Congress to enact such laws. The constitutional inhibition of legislation on the subject of religion has a double aspect. On the one hand, it forestalls compulsion by law of the acceptance of any creed or the practice of any form of worship. Freedom of conscience and freedom to adhere to such religious organization or form of worship as the individual may choose cannot be restricted by law. On the other hand, it safeguards the free exercise of the chosen form of religion. Thus the Amendment embraces two concepts,—freedom to believe and freedom to act. The first is absolute but, in the nature of things, the second cannot be. Conduct remains subject to regulation for the protection of society. The freedom to act must have appropriate definition to preserve the enforcement of that protection. In every case the power to regulate must be so exercised as not, in attaining a permissible end, unduly to infringe the protected freedom. No one would contest the proposition that a state may not, by statute, wholly deny the right to preach or to disseminate religious views. Plainly such a previous and absolute restraint would violate the terms of the guarantee. It is equally clear that a state may by general and non-discriminatory legislation regulate the times, the places, and the manner of soliciting upon its streets, and of holding meetings thereon; and may in other respects safeguard the peace, good order and comfort of the community, without unconstitutionally invading the liberties protected by the Fourteenth Amendment. The appellants are right in their insistence that the Act in question is not such a regulation. If a certificate is procured, solicitation is permitted without restraint but, in the absence of a certificate, solicitation is altogether prohibited.

The appellants urge that to require them to obtain a certificate as a condition of soliciting support for their views amounts to a prior restraint on the exercise of their religion within the meaning of the Constitution. The State insists that the Act, as construed by the Supreme Court of Connecticut, imposes no previous restraint upon the dissemination of religious views or teaching but merely safeguards against the perpetration of frauds under the cloak of religion. Conceding that this is so, the question remains whether the method adopted by Connecticut to that end transgresses the liberty safeguarded by the Constitution.

[9] The general regulation, in the public interest, of solicitation, which does not involve any religious test and does not unreasonably obstruct or delay the collection of funds, is not open to any constitutional objection, even though the collection be for a religious purpose. Such regulation would not constitute a prohibited previous restraint on the free exercise of religion or interpose an inadmissible obstacle to its exercise.

[10] It will be noted, however, that the Act requires an application to the secretary of the public welfare council of the State; that he is empowered to determine whether the cause is a religious one, and that the issue of a certificate depends upon his affirmative action. If he finds that the cause is not that of religion, to solicit for it becomes a crime. He is not to issue a certificate as a matter of course. His decision to issue or refuse it involves appraisal of facts the exercise of judgment, and the formation of an opinion. He is authorized to withhold his approval if he determines that the cause is not a religious one. Such a censorship of religion as the means of determining its right to survive is a denial of liberty protected by the First Amendment and

included in the liberty which is within the protection of the Fourteenth.

[11, 12] The State asserts that if the licensing officer acts arbitrarily, capriciously, or corruptly, his action is subject to judicial correction. Counsel refer to the rule prevailing in Connecticut that the decision of a commission or an administrative official will be reviewed upon a claim that "it works material damage to individual or corporate rights, or invades or threatens such rights, or is so unreasonable as to justify judicial intervention, or is not consonant with justice, or that a legal duty has not been performed." It is suggested that the statute is to be read as requiring the officer to issue a certificate unless the cause in question is clearly not a religious one; and that if he violates his duty his action will be corrected by a court.

To this suggestion there are several sufficient answers. The line between a discretionary and a ministerial act is not always easy to mark and statute has not been construed by the State court to impose a mere ministerial duty on the secretary of the welfare council. Upon his decision as to the nature of the cause, the right to solicit depends. Moreover, the availability of a judicial remedy for abuses in the system of licensing still leaves that system one of previous restraint which, in the field of free speech and press, we have held inadmissible. A statute authorizing previous restraint upon the exercise of the guaranteed freedom by judicial decision after trial is as obnoxious to the Constitution as one providing for like restraint by administrative action.

[13] Nothing we have said is intended even remotely to imply that, under the cloak of religion, persons may, with impunity, commit frauds upon the public. Certainly penal laws are available to punish such conduct. Even the exercise of religion may be at some slight inconvenience in order that the state may protect its citizens from injury. Without doubt a state may protect its citizens from fraudulent solicitation by requiring a stranger in the community, before permitting him publicly to solicit funds for any purpose, to establish his identity and his authority to act for the cause which he purports to represent. The state is likewise free to regulate the time and manner of solicitation generally, in the interest of public safety, peace, comfort or convenience. But to condition the solicitation of aid for the perpetuation of religious views or systems upon a license, the grant of which rests in the exercise of a determination by state authority as to what is a religious cause, is to lay a forbidden burden upon the exercise of liberty protected by the Constitution.

[14, 15] *Second.* We hold that, in the circumstances disclosed, the conviction of Jesse Cantwell on the fifth count must be set aside. Decision as to the lawfulness of the conviction demands the weighing of two conflicting interests. The fundamental law declares the interest of the United States that the free exercise of religion be not prohibited and that freedom to communicate information and opinion be not abridged. The state of Connecticut has an obvious interest in the preservation and protection of peace and good order within her borders. We must determine whether the alleged protection of the State's interest, means to which end would, in the absence of limitation by the federal Constitution, lie wholly within the State's discretion, has been pressed, in this instance, to a point where it has come into fatal collision with the overriding interest protected by the federal compact.

Conviction on the fifth count was not pursuant to a statute evincing a legislative judgment that street discussion of religious affairs, because of its tendency to provoke disorder, should be regulated, or a judgment that the playing of a phonograph on the streets should in the interest of comfort or privacy be limited or prevented. Violation of an Act exhibiting such a legislative judgment and narrowly drawn to prevent the supposed evil, would pose a question differing from that we must here answer. Such a declaration of the State's policy would weigh heavily in any challenge of the law as infringing constitutional limitations. Here, however, the judgment is based on a common law concept of the most general and undefined nature. The court below has held that the petitioner's conduct constituted the commission of an offense under the State law, and we accept its decision as binding upon us to that extent.

The offense known as breach of the peace embraces a great variety of conduct destroying or menacing public order and tranquility. It includes not only violent acts but acts and words likely to produce violence in others. No one would have the hardihood to suggest that the principle of freedom of speech sanctions incitement to riot or that religious liberty connotes the privilege to exhort others to physical attack upon those belonging to another sect. When clear and present danger of riot, disorder, interference with traffic upon the public streets, or other immediate threat to public safety, peace, or order, appears, the power of the state to prevent or punish is obvious. Equally obvious is it that a state may not unduly suppress free communication of views, religious or other, under the guise of conserving desirable conditions. Here we have a situation analogous to a conviction under a statute sweeping in a great variety of conduct under a general and indefinite characterization, and leaving to the executive and judicial branches too wide a discretion in its application.

Having these considerations in mind, we note that Jesse Cantwell, on April 26, 1938, was upon a public street, where he had a right to be, and where he had a right peacefully to impart his views to others. There is no showing that his deportment was noisy, truculent, overbearing or offensive. He requested of two pedestrians permission to play to them a phonograph record. The permission was granted. It is not claimed that he intended to insult or affront the hearers by playing the record. It is plain that he wished only to interest them in his propaganda. The sound of the phonograph is not shown to have disturbed residents of the street, to have drawn a crowd, or to have impeded traffic. Thus far he had invaded no right or interest of the public or of the men accosted.

The record played by Cantwell embodies a general attack on all organized religious systems as instruments of Satan and injurious to man; it then singles out the Roman Catholic Church for strictures couched in terms which naturally would offend not only persons of that persuasion, but all others who respect the honestly held religious faith of their fellows. The hearers were in fact highly offended. One of them said he felt like hitting Cantwell and the other that he was tempted to throw Cantwell off the street. The one who testified he felt like hitting Cantwell said, in answer to the question "Did you do anything else or have any other reaction?" "No, sir, because he said he would take the victrola and he went." The other witness testified that he told Cantwell he had better get off the street before something happened to him and that was the end of the matter as Cantwell picked up his books and walked up the street.

[16] Cantwell's conduct, in the view of the court below, considered apart from the effect of his communication upon his hearers, did not amount to a breach of the peace. One may, however, be guilty of the offense if he commit acts or make statements likely to provoke violence and disturbance of good order, even though no such eventuality be intended. Decisions to this effect are many, but examination discloses that, in practically all, the provocative language which was held to amount to a breach of the peace consisted of profane, indecent, or abusive remarks directed to the person of the hearer. Resort to epithets or personal abuse is not in any proper sense communication of information or opinion safeguarded by the Constitution, and its punishment as a criminal act would raise no question under that instrument.

[17] We find in the instant case no assault or threatening of bodily harm, no truculent bearing, no intentional discourtesy, no personal abuse. On the contrary, we find only an effort to persuade a willing listener to buy a book or to contribute money in the interest of what Cantwell, however misguided others may think him, conceived to be true religion.

In the realm of religious faith, and in that of political belief, sharp differences arise. In both fields the tenets of one man may seem the rankest error to his neighbor. To persuade others to his own point of view, the pleader, as we know, at times, resorts to exaggeration, to vilification of men who have been, or are, prominent in church or state, and even no false statement. But the people of this nation have ordained in the light of history, that, in spite of the probability of excesses and abuses, these liberties are, in the long view, essential to enlightened opinion and right conduct on the part of the citizens of a democracy.

The essential characteristic of these liberties is, that under their shield many types of life, character, opinion and belief can develop unmolested and unobstructed. Nowhere is this shield more necessary than in our own country for a people composed of many races and of many creeds. There are limits to the exercise of these liberties. The danger in these times from the coercive activities of those who in the delusion of racial or religious conceit would incite violence and breaches of the peace in order to deprive others of their equal right to the exercise of their liberties, is emphasized by events familiar to all. These and other transgressions of those limits the states appropriately may punish.

Although the contents of the record not unnaturally aroused animosity, we think that, in the absence of a statute narrowly drawn to define and punish specific conduct as constituting a clear and present danger to a substantial interest of the State, the petitioner's communication, considered in the light of the constitutional guarantees, raised no such clear and present menace to public peace and order as to render him liable to conviction of the common law offense in question.

The judgment affirming the convictions on the third and fifth counts is reversed and the cause is remanded for further proceedings not inconsistent with this opinion. So ordered.

Reversed and remanded.

Source:

Supreme Court Reporter, Vol. 60, pp. 900–906.

Franklin Roosevelt, Address at University of Virginia, 1940

Commencement address delivered at the University of Virginia in June 1940 by President Franklin D. Roosevelt in which he pledged U.S. domestic mobilization against the threat of national security posed by fascist aggression abroad. FDR spoke against the backdrop of the German and Japanese military onslaught in World War II, in which the United States remained officially neutral. Shortly before, May 26, 1940, the president had addressed the same subject in a fireside chat. The isolationist goal of complete U.S. detachment from World War II—a goal underscored by a belief that a neutral United States could enjoy unmolested peace within its hemisphere by minding its own business—was being exposed as folly by the course of the conflict in Europe, FDR argued. He warned that a defense policy based on a false sense of security would leave the nation dangerously susceptible. Roosevelt announced the program his administration had sent to Congress for improving the nation's defensive readiness by strengthening its military. He described a partnership of private industry and the federal government to carry out the emergency defense buildup most speedily and efficiently. Common decency, he asserted, demanded that no arms maker profit unduly from the war. He urged a continuation of his New Deal policies, contending that America's military viability hinged ultimately on the strength of the nation's domestic economic and social fabric, and on public morale.

In the University of Virginia Address, FDR warned that the war's widening scope raised fresh and serious perils to U.S. security. He said that the philosophy of force embodied by Nazi Germany and Imperial Japan threatened the survival of free and democratic institutions everywhere. With its heritage of liberty, he asserted, the United States must not be indifferent to the global assault on freedom. He assailed the isolationist desire for American insularity as a deluded aspiration in a world increasingly governed by force. American moral support in the world war, he said, lay squarely with the nations opposing Germany and Japan. He declared that the United States would, within the limits of neutrality, offer material assistance to nations aligned against fascism and upgrade its defensive military preparedness.

President Newcomb, my friends of the University of Virginia:

I notice by the program that I am asked to address the class of 1940. I avail myself of that privilege. But I also take this very apt occasion to speak to many other classes that have graduated through all the years, classes that are still in the period of study, not alone in the schools of learning of the Nation, but classes that have come up through the great schools of experience; in other words a cross section of the country, just as you who graduate today are a cross section of the Nation as a whole.

Every generation of young men and women in America has questions to ask the world. Most of the time they are the simple but nevertheless difficult questions, questions of work to do, opportunities to find, ambitions to satisfy.

But every now and again in the history of the Republic a different kind of question presents itself—a question that asks, not about the future of an individual or even of a generation, but about the future of the country, the future of the American people.

There was such a time at the beginning of our history as a Nation. Young people asked themselves in those days what lay ahead, not for themselves, but for the new United States.

There was such a time again in the seemingly endless years of the War Between the States. Young men and young women on both sides of the line asked themselves, not what trades or professions they would enter, what lives they would make, but what was to become of the country they had known.

There is such a time again today. Again today the young men and the young women of America ask themselves with earnestness and with deep concern this same question: "What is to become of the country we know?"

Now they ask it with even greater anxiety than before. They ask, not only what the future holds for this Republic, but what the future holds for all peoples and all nations that have been living under democratic forms of Government—under the free institutions of a free people.

It is understandable to all of us that they should ask this question. They read the words of those who are telling them that the ideal of individual liberty, the ideal of free franchise, the ideal of peace through justice, are decadent ideals. They read the word and hear the boast of those who say that a belief in force—force directed by self-chosen leaders—is the new and vigorous system which will overrun the earth. They have seen the ascendancy of this philosophy of force in nation after nation where free institutions and individual liberties were once maintained.

It is natural and understandable that the younger generation should first ask itself what the extension of the philosophy of force to all the world would lead to ultimately. We see today in stark reality some of the consequences of what we call the machine age.

Where control of machines has been retained in the hands of mankind as a whole, untold benefits have accrued to mankind. For mankind was then the master; and the machine was the servant.

But in this new system of force the mastery of the machine is not in the hands of mankind. It is in the control of infinitely small groups of individuals who rule without a single one of the democratic sanctions that we have known. The machine in hands of irresponsible conquerors becomes the master; mankind is not only the servant; it is the victim, too. Such mastery abandons with deliberate contempt all the moral values to which even this young country for more than three hundred years has been accustomed and dedicated.

Surely the new philosophy proves from month to month that it could have no possible conception of the way of life or the way of thought of a nation whose origins go back to Jamestown and Plymouth Rock.

Conversely, neither those who spring from that ancient stock nor those who have come hither in later years can be indifferent to the destruction of freedom in their ancestral lands across the sea.

Perception of danger to our institutions may come slowly or it may come with a rush and a shock as it has to the people of the United States in the past few months. This perception of danger has come to us clearly and overwhelmingly; and we perceive the peril in a world-wide arena—an arena that may become so narrowed that only the Americas will retain the ancient faiths.

Some indeed still hold to the now somewhat obvious delusion that we of the United States can safely permit the United States to become a lone island, a lone island in a world dominated by the philosophy of force.

Such an island may be the dream of those who still talk and vote as isolationists. Such an island represents to me and to the overwhelming majority of Americans today a helpless nightmare of a people without freedom—the nightmare of a people lodged in prison, handcuffed, hungry, and fed through the bars from day to day by the contemptuous, unpitying masters of other continents.

It is natural also that we should ask ourselves how now we can prevent the building of that prison and the placing of ourselves in the midst of it.

Let us not hesitate—all of us—to proclaim certain truths. Overwhelmingly we, as a nation—and this applies to all the other American nations—are convinced that military and naval victory for the gods of force and hate would endanger the institutions of democracy in the western world, and that equally, therefore, the whole of our sympathies lies with those nations that are giving their life blood in combat against these forces.

The people and the Government of the United States have seen with the utmost regret and with grave disquiet the decision of the Italian Government to engage in the hostilities now raging in Europe.

More than three months ago the Chief of the Italian Government sent me word that because of the determination of Italy to limit, so far as might be possible, the spread of the European conflict, more than two hundred millions of people in the region of the Mediterranean had been enabled to escape the suffering and the devastation of war.

I informed the Chief of the Italian Government that this desire on the part of Italy to prevent the war from spreading met with full sympathy and response on the part of the Government and the people of the United States, and I expressed the earnest hope of this Government and of this people that this policy on the part of Italy might be continued. I made it clear that in the opinion of the Government of the United States any extension of hostilities in the region of the Mediterranean might result in a still greater enlargement of the scene of the conflict, the conflict in the Near East and in Africa and that if this came to pass no one could foretell how much greater the theater of the war eventually might become.

Again on a subsequent occasion, not so long ago, recognizing that certain aspirations of Italy might form the basis of discussions among the powers most specifically concerned, I offered, in a message addressed to the Chief of the Italian Government, to send to the Governments of France and of Great Britain such specific indications of the desires of Italy to obtain readjustments with regard to her position as the Chief of the Italian Government might desire to transmit through me. While making it clear that the Government of the United States in such an event could not and would not assume responsibility for the nature of the proposals submitted nor for agreements which might thereafter be reached, I proposed that if Italy would refrain from entering the war I would be willing to ask assurances from the other powers concerned that they would faithfully execute any agreement so reached and that Italy's voice in any future peace conference would have the same authority as if Italy had actually taken part in the war, as a belligerent.

Unfortunately to the regret of all of us and the regret of humanity, the Chief of the Italian Government was unwilling to accept the procedure suggested and he has made no counter proposal.

This Government directed its efforts to doing what it could to work for the preservation of peace in the Mediterranean area, and it likewise expressed its willingness to endeavor to cooperate with the Government of Italy when the appropriate occasion arose for the creation of a more stable world order, through the reduction of armaments, and through the construction of a more liberal international economic system which would assure to all powers equality of opportunity in the world's markets and in the securing of raw materials on equal terms.

I have likewise, of course, felt it necessary in my communications to Signor Mussolini to express the concern of the Government of the United States because of the fact that any extension of the war in the region of the Mediterranean would inevitably result in great prejudice to the ways of life and Government and to the trade and commerce of all the American Republics.

The Government of Italy has now chosen to preserve what it terms its "freedom of action" and to fulfill what it states are its promises to Germany. In so doing it has manifested disregard for the rights and security of other nations, disregard for the lives of the peoples of those nations which are directly threatened by this spread of the war; and has evidenced its unwillingness to find the means through pacific negotiations for the satisfaction of what it believes are its legitimate aspirations.

On this tenth day of June, 1940, the hand that held the dagger has struck it into the back of its neighbor.

On this tenth day of June 1940, in this University founded by the first great American teacher of democracy, we send forth our prayers and our hopes to those beyond the seas who are maintaining with magnificent valor their battle for freedom.

In our American unity, we will pursue two obvious and simultaneous courses; we will extend to the opponents of force the material resources of this nation; and, at the same time, we will harness and speed up the use of those resources in order that we ourselves in the Americas may have equipment and training equal to the task of any emergency and every defense.

All roads leading to the accomplishment of these objectives must be kept clear of obstructions. We will not slow down or detour. Signs and signals call for speed—full speed ahead.

It is right that each new generation should ask questions. But in recent months the principal question has been somewhat simplified. Once more the future of the nation and of the American people is at stake.

We need not and we will not, in any way, abandon our continuing effort to make democracy work within our borders. We still insist on the need for vast improvements in our own social and economic life.

But that is a component part of national defense itself.

The program unfolds swiftly and into that program will fit the responsibility and the opportunity of every man and woman in the land to preserve his and her heritage in days of peril.

I call for effort, courage, sacrifice, devotion. Granting the love of freedom, all of these are possible.

And the love of freedom is still fierce and steady in the nation today.

Source:

Franklin F. Roosevelt, *The Public Papers and Addresses of Franklin D. Roosevelt*. New York: Random House, 1938–1950.

Alien Registration Act (Smith Act), 1940

U.S. legislation, best known as the Smith Act after its primary sponsor, Representative Howard W. Smith of Virginia, was enacted June 28, 1940. It strengthened existing laws concerning the admission and deportation of aliens and required the registration and fingerprinting of all aliens living in the United States. Its primary purpose, however, as the United States was being drawn into World War II, was to reduce subversive activities, particularly communist-led strikes that might injure the American defense industry. The act declared it illegal to advocate or teach the forceful overthrow of the U.S. government or knowingly to join a group that did so. In 1951 the Supreme Court upheld the constitutionality of the act in *Dennis et al. v. United States* (341 U.S. 494).

An Act

To prohibit certain subversive activities; to amend certain provisions of law with respect to the admission and deportation of aliens; to require the fingerprinting and registration of aliens; and for other purposes.

Be it enacted by the Senate and House of Representatives of the United States of America in Congress assembled,

Title I

Section 1. (a) It shall be unlawful for any person, with intent to interfere with, impair, or influence the loyalty, morale, or discipline of the military or naval forces of the United States—

(1) to advise, counsel, urge, or in any manner cause insubordination, disloyalty, mutiny, or refusal of duty by any member of the military or naval forces of the United States; or

(2) to distribute any written or printed matter which advises, counsels, or urges insubordination, disloyalty, mutiny, or refusal of duty by any member of the military or naval forces of the United States.

(b) For the purposes of this section, the term "military or naval forces of the United States" includes the Army of the United States, as defined in section 1 of the National Defense Act of June 3, 1916, as amended (48 Stat. 153; U.S.C., title 10, sec. 2), the Navy, Marine Corps, Coast Guard, Naval Reserve, and Marine Corps Reserve of the United States; and, when any merchant vessel is commissioned in the Navy or is in the service of the Army or the Navy, includes the master, officers, and crew of such vessel.

Sec. 2. (a) It shall be unlawful for any person—

(1) to knowingly or willfully advocate, abet, advise, or teach the duty, necessity, desirability, or propriety of overthrowing or destroying any government in the United States by force or violence, or by the assassination of any officer of any such government;

(2) with the intent to cause the overthrow or destruction of any government in the United States, to print, publish, edit, issue, circulate, sell, distribute, or publicly display any written or printed matter advocating, advising, or teaching the duty, necessity, desirability, or propriety of overthrowing or destroying any government in the United States by force or violence.

(3) to organize or help to organize any society, group, or assembly of persons who teach, advocate, or encourage the overthrow or destruction of any government in the

United States by force or violence; or to be or become a member of, or affiliate with, any such society, group, or assembly of persons, knowing the purposes thereof.

(b) For the purposes of this section, the term "government in the United States" means the Government of the United States, the government of any State, Territory, or possession of the United States, the government of the District of Columbia, or the government of any political subdivision of any of them.

Sec. 3. It shall be unlawful for any person to attempt to commit, or to conspire to commit, any of the acts prohibited by the provisions of this title.

Sec. 4. Any written or printed matter of the character described in section 1 or section 2 of this Act, which is intended for use in violation of this Act, may be taken from any house or other place in which it may be found, or from any person in whose possession it may be, under a search warrant issued pursuant to the provisions of title XI of the Act entitled "An Act to punish acts of interference with the foreign relations, the neutrality and the foreign commerce of the United States, to punish espionage, and better to enforce the criminal laws of the United States, and for other purposes", approved June 15, 1917 (40 Stat. 228; U.S.C., title 18, ch. 18).

Sec. 5. (a) Any person who violates any of the provisions of this title shall, upon conviction thereof, be fined not more than $10,000 or imprisoned for not more than ten years, or both.

(b) No person convicted of violating any of the provisions of this title shall, during the five years next following his conviction, be eligible for employment by the United States, or by any department or agency thereof (including any corporation the Stock of which is wholly owned by the United States).

Title II

Sec. 20. Section 19 of the Immigration Act of February 5, 1917 (39 Stat. 889; U.S.C., title 8, sec. 155), as amended, is amended by inserting, after "Sec. 19.," the letter "(a)," and by adding at the end of such section the following new subsections:

"(b) Any alien of any of the classes specified in this subsection, in addition to aliens who are deportable under other provisions of law, shall, upon warrant of the Attorney General, be taken into custody and deported:

"(1) Any alien who, at any time within five years after entry, shall have, knowingly and for gain, encouraged, induced, assisted, abetted, or aided any other alien to enter or to try to enter the United States in violation of law.

"(2) Any alien who, at any time after entry, shall have on more than one occasion, knowingly and for gain, encouraged, induced, assisted, abetted, or aided any other alien or aliens to enter or to try to enter the United States in violation of law.

"(3) Any alien who, at any time after entry, shall have been convicted of possessing or carrying in violation of any law any weapon which shoots or is designed to shoot automatically or semi-automatically more than one shot without manual reloading, by a single function of the trigger, or a weapon commonly called a sawed-off shotgun.

"(4) Any alien who, at any time within five years after entry, shall have been convicted of violating the provisions of title I of the Alien Registration Act, 1940.

"(5) Any alien who, at any time after entry, shall have been convicted more than once of violating the provisions of title I of the Alien Registration Act, 1940.

"No alien who is deportable under the provisions of paragraph (3), (4), or (5) of this subsection shall be deported until the termination of his imprisonment or the entry of an order releasing him on probation or parole.

"(c) In the same of any alien (other than one to whom subsection (d) is applicable) who is deportable under any law of the United States and who has proved good moral character for the preceding five years, the Attorney General may (1) permit such alien to depart the United States to any country of his choice at his own expense, in lieu of deportation, or (2) suspend deportation of such alien if not racially inadmissible or ineligible to naturalization in the United States if he finds that such deportation would result in serious economic detriment to a citizen or legally resident alien who is the spouse, parent, or minor child of such deportable alien. If the deportation of any alien is suspended under the provisions of this subsection for more than six months, all of the facts and pertinent provisions of law in the case shall be reported to the Congress within ten days after the beginning of its next regular session, with the reasons for such suspension. The Clerk of the House shall have such report printed as a public document. If during that session the two Houses pass a concurrent resolution stating in substance that the Congress does not favor the suspension of such deportation, the Attorney General shall thereupon deport such alien in the manner provided by law. If during the session the two Houses do not pass such a resolution, the Attorney General shall cancel deportation proceedings upon the termination of such session, except that such proceedings shall not be canceled in the case of any alien who was not legally admitted for permanent residence at the time of his last entry into the United States, unless such alien pays to the Commissioner of Immigration and Naturalization a fee of $18 (which fee shall be deposited in the Treasury of the United States as miscellaneous receipts). Upon the cancelation of such proceedings in any case in which such fee has been paid, the Commissioner shall record the alien's admission for permanent residence as of the date of his last entry into the United States and the Secretary of State shall, if the alien was a quota immigrant at the time of entry and was not charged to the appropriate quota, reduce by one the immigration quota of the country of the alien's nationality as defined in section 12 of the Act of May 26, 1924 (U. S. C., title 8, sec. 212), for the fiscal year then current or next following.

"(d) The provisions of subsection (c) shall not be applicable in the case of any alien who is deportable under (1) the Act of October 16, 1918 (40 Stat. 1008; U. S. C., title 8, sec. 137), entitled 'An Act to exclude and expel from the United States aliens who are members of the anarchist and similar classes', as amended; (2) the Act of May 26, 1922, entitled 'An Act to amend the Act entitled "An Act to prohibit the importation and use of opium for other than medicinal purposes", approved February 9, 1909, as amended' (42 Stat. 596; U. S. C., title 21, sec. 175); (3) the Act of February 18, 1931, entitled 'An Act to provide for the deportation of aliens convicted and sentenced for violation of any law regulating traffic in narcotics', as amended (46 Stat. 1171; U. S. C., title 8, sec. 156a); (4) any of the provisions of so much of subsection (a) of this section as relates to criminals, prostitutes, procurers, or other immoral persons, the mentally and physically deficient, anarchists, and similar classes; or (5) subsection (b) of this section."

Sec. 21. The Act entitled "An Act to provide for the deportation of aliens convicted and sentenced for violation of any law regulating traffic in narcotics," approved February 18, 1931, is amended—

(1) By striking out the words "and sentenced";

(2) By inserting after the words "any statute of the United States" the following: "or of any State, Territory, possession, or of the District of Columbia,"; and

(3) By inserting after the word "heroin" a comma and the word "marihuana."

Sec. 22. No alien shall be deportable by reason of the amendments made by section 20 or 21 on account of any act committed prior to the date of enactment of this Act.

Sec. 23. (a) The first paragraph of section 1 of the Act entitled "An Act to exclude and expel from the United States aliens who are members of the anarchistic and similar classes," approved October 16, 1918, as amended, is amended to read as follows:

"That any alien who, at any time, shall be or shall have been a member of any one of the following classes shall be excluded from admission into the United States:".

(b) Section 2 of such Act of October 16, 1918, as amended, is amended to read as follows:

"Sec. 2. Any alien who was at the time of entering the United States, or has been at any time thereafter, a member of any one of the classes of aliens enumerated in section 1 of this Act, shall, upon the warrant of the Attorney General, be taken into custody and deported in the manner provided in the Immigration Act of February 5, 1917. The provisions of this section shall be applicable to the classes of aliens mentioned in this Act, irrespective of the time of their entry into the United States."

Title III

Sec. 30. No visa shall hereafter be issued to any alien seeking to enter the United States unless said alien has been registered and fingerprinted in duplicate. One copy of the registration and fingerprint record shall be retained by the consul. The second copy shall be attached to the alien's visa and shall be taken up by the examining immigrant inspector at the port of arrival of the alien in the United States and forwarded to the Department of Justice, at Washington, District of Columbia.

Any alien seeking to enter the United States who does not present a visa (except in emergency cases defined by the Secretary of State), a reentry permit, or a border-crossing identification card shall be excluded from admission to the United States.

Sec. 31. (a) It shall be the duty of every alien now or hereafter in the United States, who (1) is fourteen years of age or older, (2) has not been registered and fingerprinted under section 30, and (3) remains in the United States for thirty days or longer, to apply for registration and to be fingerprinted before the expiration of such thirty days.

(b) It shall be the duty of every parent or legal guardian of any alien now or hereafter in the United States, who (1) is less than fourteen years of age, (2) has not been registered under section 30, and (3) remains in the United States for thirty days or longer, to apply for the registration of such alien before the expiration of such thirty days. Whenever any alien attains his fourteenth birthday in the United States he shall, within thirty days thereafter, apply in person for registration and to be fingerprinted.

Sec. 32. Notwithstanding the provisions of sections 30 and 31—

(a) The application for the registration and fingerprinting, or for the registration, of any alien who is in the United States on the effective date of such sections may be made at any time within four months after such date.

(b) No foreign government official, or member of his family, shall be required to be registered or fingerprinted under this title.

(c) The Commissioner is authorized to prescribe, with the approval of the Attorney General, special regulations for the registration and fingerprinting of (1) alien seamen, (2) holders of border-crossing identification cards, (3) aliens confined in institutions within the United States, (4) aliens under order or deportation, and (5) aliens of any other class not lawfully admitted to the United States for permanent residence.

Sec. 33. (a) All applications for registration and fingerprinting under section 31 shall be made at post offices or such other places as may be designated by the Commissioner.

(b) It shall be the duty of every postmaster, with such assistance as shall be provided by the Commissioner, to register and fingerprint any applicant for registration and fingerprinting under such section, and for such purposes to designate appropriate space in the local post office for such registration and fingerprinting. Every postmaster shall forward promptly to the Department of Justice, at Washington, District of Columbia, the registration and fingerprint record of every alien registered and fingerprinted by him. The Commissioner may designate such other places for registration and fingerprinting as may be necessary for carrying out the provisions of this Act, and provide for registration and fingerprinting of aliens at such places by officers or employees of the Immigration and Naturalization Service designated by the Commissioner. The duties imposed upon any postmaster under this Act shall also be performed by any employees at the post office of such postmaster who are designated by the postmaster for such purpose.

Sec. 34. (a) The Commissioner is authorized and directed to prepare forms for the registration and fingerprinting of aliens under this title. Such forms shall contain inquiries with respect to (1) the date and place of entry of the alien into the United States; (2) activities in which he has been and intends to be engaged; (3) the length of time he expects to remain in the United States; (4) the criminal record, if any, of such alien; and (5) such additional matters as may be prescribed by the Commissioner, with the approval of the Attorney General.

(b) All registration and fingerprint records made under the provisions of this title shall be secret and confidential, and shall be made available only to such persons or agencies as may be designated by the Commissioner, with the approval of the Attorney General.

(c) Every person required to apply for the registration of himself or another under this title shall submit under oath the information required for such registration. Any person authorized to register aliens under this title shall be authorized to administer oaths for such purpose.

Sec. 35. Any alien required to be registered under this title who is a resident of the United States shall notify the Commissioner in writing of each change of residence and new address within five days from the date of such change. Any other alien required to be registered under this title shall notify the Commissioner in writing of his address at the expiration of each three months' period of residence in the United States. In the case of an alien for whom a parent or legal guardian is required to apply for registration, the notices required by this section shall be given by such parent or legal guardian.

Sec. 36. (a) Any alien required to apply for registration and to be fingerprinted who willfully fails to refuses to make such application or to be fingerprinted, and any parent or legal guardian required to apply for the registration of any alien who willfully fails or refuses to file application for the registration of such alien shall, upon conviction thereof be fined not to exceed $1,000 or be imprisoned not more than six months, or both.

(b) Any alien, or any parent or legal guardian of any alien, who fails to give written notice to the Commissioner of change of address as required by section 35 of this Act shall, upon conviction thereof, be fined not to exceed $100, or be imprisoned not more than thirty days, or both.

(c) Any alien or any parent or legal guardian of any alien, who files an application for registration containing statements known by him to be false, or who procures or attempts to procure registration of himself or another person through fraud, shall, upon conviction thereof, be fined not to exceed $1,000, or be imprisoned not more than six months, or both; and any alien so convicted within five years after entry into the United States shall, upon the warrant of the Attorney General, be taken into custody and be deported in the manner provided in sections 19 and 20 of the Immigration Act of February 5, 1917, as amended.

Sec. 37. (a) The Commissioner, with the approval of the Attorney General, is authorized and empowered to make the prescribe, and from time to time to change and amend, such rules and regulations not in conflict with this Act as he may deem necessary and proper in aid of the administration and enforcement of this title (including provisions for the identification of aliens registered under this title); except that all such rules and regulations, insofar as they relate to the performance of functions by consular officers or officers or employees in the Postal Service, shall be prescribed by the Secretary of State and the Postmaster General, respectively, upon recommendation of the Attorney General. The powers conferred upon the Attorney General by this Act and all other powers of the Attorney General relating to the administration of the Immigration and Naturalization Service may be exercised by the Attorney General through such officers of the Department of Justice, including officers of the Immigration and Naturalization Service, attorneys, special attorneys, and special assistants to the Attorney General, as he may designate specifically for such purposes.

(b) The Commissioner is authorized to make such expenditures, to employ such additional temporary and permanent employees, and to rent such quarters outside the District of Columbia as may be necessary for carrying out the provisions of this title.

Sec. 38. (a) For the purposes of this title—

(1) the term "United States", when used in a geographical sense, means the States, the Territories of Alaska and Hawaii, the District of Columbia, Puerto Rico, and the Virgin Islands;

(2) the term "Commissioner" means the Commissioner of Immigration and Naturalization.

(b) The provisions of this title shall take effect upon the date of enactment of this Act; except that sections 30 and 31 shall take effect sixty days after the date of its enactment.

Sec. 39. The President is authorized to provide, by Executive order, for the registration and fingerprinting, in a manner as nearly similar to that provided in this title as he deems practicable, of aliens in the Panama Canal Zone.

Title IV

Sec. 40. If any provision of this Act, or the application thereof to any person or circumstance, is held invalid, the remainder of the Act, and the application of such provision to other persons or circumstances, shall not be affected thereby.

Sec. 41. This Act may be cited as the "Alien Registration Act, 1940".

Source:

Statutes at Large, Vol. 54, pp. 670–676.

Ogdensburg Declaration, 1940

Statement issued by U.S. president Franklin D. Roosevelt and Canadian prime minister W. L. Mackenzie King at Ogdensburg, New York, on August 18, 1940, announcing the establishment of the Permanent Joint Board of Defense, to plan for the cooperative defense of North America in case of any foreign attack. The board, with members from both Canada and the United States, was to investigate mutual personnel and material sea, land, and air defense problems. Soon after the declaration, Canada served as a mediator between the United States and Great Britain for the Destroyers-for-Bases Agreement.

Continuing the pattern of friendship and cooperative defense established by the Ogdensburg Declaration, on April 20, 1941, Roosevelt and King met at Roosevelt's estate at Hyde Park, New York, and signed an agreement that provided for shared defense production and for greater U.S. purchases of war materials from Canada, thus creating closer economic ties between the two nations.

August 24, 1940

The Prime Minister and the President have discussed the mutual problems of defense in relation to the safety of Canada and the United States.

It has been agreed that a Permanent Joint Board on Defense shall be set up at once by the two countries.

This Permanent Joint Board on Defense shall commence immediate studies relating to sea, land, and air problems including personnel and materiel.

It will consider in the broad sense the defense of the north half of the Western Hemisphere.

The Permanent Joint Board on Defense will consist of four or five members from each country, most of them from the services. It will meet shortly.

Source:

Charles I. Bevans, comp. *Treaties and Other Agreements of the United States of America, 1776–1949,* Washington, D.C.: Government Printing Office, 1968–76.

Destroyers-for-Bases Agreement, 1940

Although the United States, until December 8, 1941, was technically neutral in World War II, which began in 1939, President Franklin D. Roosevelt considered an Allied victory to be an American interest. He therefore found various ways to help Great Britain and the Soviet Union against the Axis powers. The destroyer deal was one of them. In this mutual defense agreement announced by Roosevelt on September 2, 1940, the United States transferred 50 "overage" World War I destroyers to Great Britain (then engaged in the aerial Battle of Britain) in exchange for 99-year leases on British naval and air bases in the Western Hemisphere. The destroyers, used to escort convoys, helped Britain protect its sea lanes. Linking British survival with American security, Roosevelt called the exchange the "most important action in the reinforcement of our national defense . . . since the Louisiana Purchase."

The technique used in the destroyer deal was strengthened March 11, 1941, by the Lend-Lease legislation. It authorized the president to sell, transfer, exchange, lease, or lend arms or other war supplies to any country whose defense he deemed vital to U.S. security. Opposed by those who feared direct U.S. involvement in World War II, the controversial legislation enabled the United States to aid the hard-pressed Allies despite U.S. neutrality laws. Congress promptly appropriated $7 billion for the first installment of the program. By the time the program was terminated, on August 21, 1945, total Lend-Lease aid had exceeded $50 billion.

Friday, August 2, 1940
9:37 P.M.

Memorandum:
At Cabinet meeting, in afternoon, long discussion in regard to devising ways and means to sell directly or indirectly fifty or sixty World War old destroyers to Great Britain. It was the general opinion, without any dissenting voice, that the survival of the British Isles under German attack might very possibly depend on their getting these destroyers.

It was agreed that legislation to accomplish this is necessary.

It was agreed that such legislation if asked for by me without any preliminaries would meet with defect or interminable delay in reaching a vote.

It was agreed that the British be approached through Lord Lothian to find out if they would agree to give positive assurance that the British Navy, in the event of German success in Great Britain, would not under any conceivable circumstances fall into the hands of the Germans and that if such assurances could be received and made public, the opposition in the Congress would be greatly lessened. I suggested that we try to get further assurance from the British that the ships of their Navy would not be sunk, but would sail for North America or British Empire ports where they would remain afloat and available.

It was agreed that I would call up William Allen White, who has recently talked with Willkie on this subject; ask White to come to Washington at once to see Hull, Knox and Stimson and after that to see me; then returning to see Willkie and seek to get, with Willkie's approval, the support of Joe Martin and Charlie McNary for such a plan. It was agreed that if this procedure went through successfully that I would, at once, send a definite request to the Congress for the necessary legislation.

I stressed the point that in all probability the legislation would fail if it had substantially unanimous Republican opposition—and that the crux of the matter lay in the vote of the Republican minority in each house. I stressed the importance of having the issue acted on without regard to party politics in any way.

At 8:30 p.m., I talked with William Allen White, who was in Estes Park, Colorado; explained the above to him and asked him to come East.

He told me that he was sure that Willkie's attitude in the matter was the same as mine. I explained to him that that was wholly insufficient, and that Willkie's attitude was not what counted but that the Republican policy in Congress was the one essential.

White told me he would get in touch with Willkie and let me know at the earliest possible moment.

F.D.R

Source:
Franklin D. Roosevelt Library.

Franklin Roosevelt, Radio Address on Selective Service Registration Day, 1940

National radio address delivered by President Franklin D. Roosevelt on October 16, 1940, marking Selective Service Registration Day. With the outbreak of World War II in Europe in September 1939, FDR declared a national emergency, calling for increases in troop levels to bolster the nation's inadequate defenses. Volunteer enlistments, while boosting army strength, failed to satisfy the Roosevelt administration's troop-level goals and led FDR to propose the politically risky military draft. The nation had never had a peacetime draft, and strong isolationist sentiment in Congress figured to fight its implementation. But the worsening international crisis built support for the Selective Service Act, sponsored by Senator Edward R. Burke of Nebraska and Representative James W. Wadsworth, Jr., of New York and enacted on September 16, 1940. It required the registration of all men between ages 21 and 35. It prohibited the use of bounties and substitutes and limited service to a 12-month period. The order of call-up was to be based on the drawing of lots. By its terms, 16 million American men registered for the military draft on October 16. In his radio address, FDR stressed that military service in the national defense was a free citizen's first duty. He asserted that his scheme for increasing U.S. forces was warranted by threats of aggression from abroad and commensurate with such threats. The draft was to be administered by a network of local boards under the national Selective Service System.

On this day more than sixteen million young Americans are reviving the three hundred year old American custom of the Muster. They are obeying that first duty of free citizenship by which, from the earliest Colonial times, every able-bodied citizen was subject to the call for service in the national defense.

It is a day of deep and purposeful meaning in the lives of all of us. For on this day we Americans proclaim the vitality of our history, the singleness of our will and the unity of our nation.

We prepare to keep the peace in this New World which free men have built for free men to live in. The United States, a nation of one hundred and thirty million people, has today only about five hundred thousand—half a million—officers and men in Army and National Guard. Other nations, smaller in population, have four and five and six million trained men in their armies. Our present program will train eight hundred thousand additional men this coming year and somewhat less than one million men each year thereafter. It is a program obviously of defensive preparation and of defensive preparation only.

Calmly, without fear and without hysteria, but with clear determination, we are building guns and planes and tanks and ships—and all the other tools which modern defense requires. We are mobilizing our citizenship, for we are calling on men and women and property and money to join in making our defense effective. Today's registration for training and service is the key-stone in the arch of our national defense.

In the days when our forefathers laid the foundation of our democracy, every American family had to have its gun and know how to use it. Today we live under threats, threats of aggression from abroad, which call again for the same readiness, the same vigilance. Ours must one again be the spirit of those who were prepared to defend as they built, to defend as they worked, to defend as they worshipped.

The duty of this day has been imposed upon us from without. Those who have dared to threaten the whole world with war—those who have created the name and deed of Total War—have imposed upon us and upon all free peoples the necessity of preparation for total defense.

But this day not only imposes a duty; it provides also an opportunity—an opportunity for united action in the cause of liberty—an opportunity for the continuing creation on this continent of a country where the people alone shall be master, where the people shall be truly free.

To the sixteen million young men who register today, I say that democracy is your cause—the cause of youth.

Democracy is the one form of society which guarantees to every new generation of men the right to imagine and to attempt to bring to pass a better world. Under the despotisms the imagination of a better world and its achievement are alike forbidden.

Your act today affirms not only your loyalty to your country, but your will to build your future for yourselves.

We of today, with God's help, can bequeath to Americans of tomorrow a nation in which the ways of liberty and justice will survive and be secure. Such a nation must be devoted to the cause of peace. And it is for that cause that American arms itself.

It is to that cause—the cause of peace—that we Americans today devote our national will and our national spirit and our national strength.

See also SELECTIVE SERVICE AND TRAINING ACT (BURKE-WADSWORTH) ACT, 1940.

Source:

Franklin D. Roosevelt, *The Public Papers and Addresses of Franklin D. Roosevelt*. New York: Random House, 1938–50.

Franklin Roosevelt, "Four Freedoms," 1941

Address delivered by President Franklin D. Roosevelt on January 6, 1941, in his annual message to Congress. Roosevelt called for a world founded on "four essential human freedoms": freedom of speech and expression, freedom of worship, freedom from want, and freedom from fear. Urging citizens to relinquish the false security of isolationism, he described a national policy committed to all-inclusive national defense, full support of other nations trying to preserve democracy, and refusal to buy peace at the cost of other people's freedom. He urged the United States to serve as an arsenal—providing ships, planes, tanks, and guns—for those countries already struggling against international aggression during World War II.

Mr. President, Mr. Speaker, Members of the Seventy-seventh Congress:

I address you, the Members of the Seventy-seventh Congress, at a moment unprecedented in the history of the Union. I use the word "unprecedented," because at no previous time has American security been as seriously threatened from without as it is today.

Since the permanent formation of our Government under the Constitution, in 1789, most of the periods of crisis in our history have related to our domestic affairs. Fortunately, only one of these—the four-year War Between the States—ever threatened our national unity. Today, thank God, one hundred and thirty million Americans, in forty-eight States, have forgotten points of the compass in our national unity.

It is true that prior to 1914 the United States often had been disturbed by events in other Continents. We had even engaged in two wars with European nations and in a number of undeclared wars in the West Indies, in the Mediterranean and in the Pacific for the maintenance of American rights and for the principles of peaceful commerce. But in no case had a serious threat been raised against our national safety or our continued independence.

What I seek to convey is the historic truth that the United States as a nation has at all times maintained clear, definite opposition, to any attempt to lock us in behind an ancient Chinese wall while the procession of civilization went past. Today, thinking of our children and of their children, we oppose enforced isolation for ourselves or for any other part of the Americas.

That determination of ours, extending over all these years. was proved, for example, during the quarter century of wars following the French Revolution.

While the Napoleonic struggles did threaten interests of the United States because of the French foothold in the West Indies and in Louisiana, and while we engaged in the War of 1812 to vindicate our right to peaceful trade, it is nevertheless clear that neither France nor Great Britain, nor any other nation, was aiming at domination of the whole world.

In like fashion from 1815 to 1914—ninety-nine years—no single war in Europe or in Asia constituted a real threat against our future or against the future of any other American nation.

Except in the Maximilian interlude in Mexico, no foreign power sought to establish itself in this Hemisphere; and the strength of the British fleet in the Atlantic has been a friendly strength. It is still a friendly strength.

Even when the World War broke out in 1914, it seemed to contain only small threat of danger to our own American future. But, as time went on, the American people began to visualize what the downfall of democratic nations might mean to our own democracy.

We need not overemphasize imperfections in the Peace of Versailles. We need not harp on failure of the democracies to deal with problems of world reconstruction. We should remember that the Peace of 1919 was far less unjust than the kind of "pacification" which began even before Munich, and which is being carried on under the new order of tyranny that seeks to spread over every continent today. The American people have unalterably set their faces against that tyranny.

Every realist knows that the democratic way of life is at this moment being directly assailed in every part of the world—assailed either by arms, or by secret spreading of poisonous propaganda by those who seek to destroy unity and promote discord in nations that are still at peace.

During sixteen long months this assault has blotted out the whole pattern of democratic life in an appalling number of independent nations, great and small. The assailants are still on the march, threatening other nations, great and small.

Therefore, as your President, performing my constitutional duty to "give to the Congress information of the state of the Union," I find it, unhappily, necessary to report that the future and the safety of our country and of our democracy are overwhelmingly involved in events far beyond our borders.

Armed defense of democratic existence is now being gallantly waged in four continents. If that defense fails, all the population and all the resources of Europe, Asia, Africa and Australasia will be dominated by the conquerors. Let us remember that the total of those populations and their resources in those four continents greatly exceeds the sum total of the population and the resources of the whole of the Western Hemisphere—many times over.

In times like these it is immature—and incidentally, untrue— for anybody to brag that an unprepared America, single-handed, and with one hand tied behind its back, can hold off the whole world.

No realistic American can expect from a dictator's peace international generosity, or return of true independence, or world disarmament, or freedom of expression, or freedom of religion— or even good business.

Such a peace would bring no security for us or for our neighbors. "Those, who would give up essential liberty to purchase a little temporary safety, deserve neither liberty nor safety."

As a nation, we may take pride in the fact that we are soft-hearted; but we cannot afford to be soft-headed.

We must always be wary of those who with sounding brass and a tinkling cymbal preach the "ism" of appeasement.

We must especially beware of that small group of selfish men who would clip the wings of the American eagle in order to feather their own nests.

I have recently pointed out how quickly the tempo of modern warfare could bring into our very midst the physical attack which we must eventually expect if the dictator nations win this war.

There is much loose talk of our immunity from immediate and direct invasion from across the seas. Obviously, as long as the British Navy retains its power, no such danger exists. Even if there were no British Navy, it is not probable that any enemy would be stupid enough to attack us by landing troops in the United States from across thousands of miles of ocean, until it had acquired strategic bases from which to operate.

But we learn much from the lessons of the past years in Europe—particularly the lesson of Norway, whose essential seaports were captured by treachery and surprise built up over a series of years.

The first phase of the invasion of this Hemisphere would not be the landing of regular troops. The necessary strategic points would be occupied by secret agents and their dupes—and great numbers of them are already here, and in Latin America.

As long as the aggressor nations maintain the offensive, they—not we—will choose the time and the place and the method of their attack.

That is why the future of all the American Republics is today in serious danger.

That is why this Annual Message to the Congress is unique in our history.

That is why every member of the Executive Branch of the Government and every member of the Congress faces great responsibility and great accountability.

The need of the moment is that our actions and our policy should be devoted primarily—almost exclusively—to meeting this foreign peril. For all our domestic problems are now a part of the great emergency.

Just as our national policy in internal affairs has been based upon a decent respect for the rights and the dignity of all our fellow men within our gates, so our national policy in foreign affairs has been based on a decent respect for the rights and dignity of all nations, large and small. And the justice of morality must and will win in the end.

Our national policy is this:

First, by an impressive expression of the public will and without regard to partisanship, we are committed to all-inclusive national defense.

Second, by an impressive expression of the public will and without regard to partisanship, we are committed to full support of all those resolute peoples, everywhere, who are resisting aggression and are thereby keeping war away from our Hemisphere. By this support, we express our determination that the democratic cause shall prevail; and we strengthen the defense and the security of our own nation.

Third, by an impressive expression of the public will and without regard to partisanship, we are committed to the proposition that principles of morality and considerations for our own security will never permit us to acquiesce in a peace dictated by aggressors and sponsored by appeasers. We know that enduring peace cannot be bought at the cost of other people's freedom.

In the recent national election there was no substantial difference between the two great parties in respect to that national policy. No issue was fought out on this line before the American electorate. Today it is abundantly evident that American citizens everywhere are demanding and supporting speedy and complete action in recognition of obvious danger.

Therefore, the immediate need is a swift and driving increase in our armament production.

Leaders of industry and labor have responded to our summons. Goals of speed have been set. In some cases these goals are being reached ahead of time; in some cases we are on schedule; in other cases there are slight but not serious delays; and in some cases—and I am sorry to say very important cases—we are all concerned by the slowness of the accomplishment of our plans.

The Army and Navy, however, have made substantial progress during the past year. Actual experience is improving and speeding up our methods of production with every passing day. And today's best is not good enough for tomorrow.

I am not satisfied with the progress thus far made. The men in charge of the program represent the best in training, in ability, and in patriotism. They are not satisfied with the progress thus far made. None of us will be satisfied until the job is done.

No matter whether the original goal was set too high or too low, our objective is quicker and better results.

To give you two illustrations:

We are behind schedule in turning out finished airplanes; we are working day and night to solve the innumerable problems and to catch up.

We are ahead of schedule in building warships but we are working to get even further ahead of that schedule.

To change a whole nation from a basis of peacetime production of implements of peace to a basis of wartime production of implements of war is no small task. And the greatest difficulty comes at the beginning of the program, when new tools, new plant facilities, new assembly lines, and new ship ways must first be constructed before the actual materiel begins to flow steadily and speedily from them.

The Congress, of course, must rightly keep itself informed at all times of the progress of the program. However, there is certain information, as the Congress itself will readily recognize, which, in the interests of our own security and those of the nations that we are supporting, must of needs be kept in confidence.

New circumstances are constantly begetting new needs for our safety. I shall ask this Congress for greatly increased new appropriations and authorizations to carry on what we have begun.

I also ask this Congress for authority and for funds sufficient to manufacture additional munitions and war supplies of many kinds, to be turned over to those nations which are now in actual war with aggressor nations.

Our most useful and immediate role is to act as an arsenal for them as well as for ourselves. They do not need man power, but they do need billions of dollars worth of the weapons of defense.

The time is near when they will not be able to pay for them all in ready cash. We cannot, and we will not, tell them that they must surrender, merely because of present inability to pay for the weapons which we know they must have.

I do not recommend that we make them a loan of dollars with which to pay for these weapons—a loan to be repaid in dollars.

I recommend that we make it possible for those nations to continue to obtain war materials in the United States, fitting their orders into our own program. Nearly all their materiel would, if the time ever came, be useful for our own defense.

Taking counsel of expert military and naval authorities, considering what is best for our own security, we are free to decide how much should be kept here and how much should be sent abroad to our friends who by their determined and heroic resistance are giving us time in which to make ready our own defense.

For what we send abroad, we shall be repaid within a reasonable time following the close of hostilities, in similar materials, or, at our option, in other goods of many kinds, which they can produce and which we need.

Let us say to the democracies: "We Americans are vitally concerned in your defense of freedom. We are putting forth our energies, our resources and our organizing powers to give you the strength to regain and maintain a free world. We shall send you, in ever-increasing numbers, ships, planes, tanks, guns. This is our purpose and our pledge."

In fulfillment of this purpose we will not be intimidated by the threats of dictators that they will regard as a breach of international law or as an act of war our aid to the democracies which dare to resist their aggression. Such aid is not an act of war, even if a dictator should unilaterally proclaim it so to be.

When the dictators, if the dictators, are ready to make war upon us, they will not wait for an act of war on our part. They did not wait for Norway or Belgium or the Netherlands to commit an act of war.

Their only interest is in a new one-way international law, which lacks mutuality in its observance, and, therefore, becomes an instrument of oppression.

The happiness of future generations of Americans may well depend upon how effective and how immediate we can make our aid felt. No one can tell the exact character of the emergency situations that we may be called upon to meet. The Nation's hands must not be tied when the Nation's life is in danger.

We must all prepare to make the sacrifices that the emergency—almost as serious as war itself—demands. Whatever stands in the way of speed and efficiency in defense preparations must give way to the national need.

A free nation has the right to expect full cooperation from all groups. A free nation has the right to look to the leaders of business, of labor, and of agriculture to take the lead in stimulating effort, not among other groups but within their own groups.

The best way of dealing with the few slackers or trouble makers in our midst is, first, to shame them by patriotic example, and, if that fails, to use the sovereignty of Government to save Government.

As men do not live by bread alone, they do not fight by armaments alone. Those who man our defenses, and those behind them who build our defenses, must have the stamina and the courage which come from unshakable belief in the manner of life which they are defending. The mighty action that we are calling for cannot be based on a disregard of all things worth fighting for.

The Nation takes great satisfaction and much strength from the things which have been done to make its people conscious of their individual stake in the preservation of democratic life in America. Those things have toughened the fiber of our people, have renewed their faith and strengthened their devotion to the institutions we make ready to protect.

Certainly this is no time for any of us to stop thinking about the social and economic problems which are the root cause of the social revolution which is today a supreme factor in the world.

For there is nothing mysterious about the foundations of a healthy and strong democracy. The basic things expected by our people of their political and economic systems are simple. They are:

Equality of opportunity for youth and for others.

Jobs for those who can work.

Security for those who need it.

The ending of special privilege for the few.

The preservation of civil liberties for all.

The enjoyment of the fruits of scientific progress in a wider and constantly rising standard of living.

These are the simple, basic things that must never be lost sight of in the turmoil and unbelievable complexity of our modern world. The inner and abiding strength of our economic and political systems is dependent upon the degree to which they fulfill these expectations.

Many subjects connected with our social economy call for immediate improvement.

As examples:

We should bring more citizens under the coverage of old-age pensions and unemployment insurance.

We should widen the opportunities for adequate medical care.

We should plan a better system by which persons deserving or needing gainful employment may obtain it.

I have called for personal sacrifice. I am assured of the willingness of almost all Americans to respond to that call.

A part of the sacrifice means the payment of more money in taxes. In my Budget Message I shall recommend that a greater portion of this great defense program be paid for from taxation than we are paying today. No person should try, or be allowed, to get rich out of this program; and the principle of tax payments in accordance with ability to pay should be constantly before our eyes to guide our legislation.

If the Congress maintains these principles, the voters, putting patriotism ahead of pocketbooks, will give you their applause.

In the future days, which we seek to make secure, we look forward to a world founded upon four essential human freedoms.

The first is freedom of speech and expression—everywhere in the world.

The second is freedom of every person to worship God in his own way—everywhere in the world.

The third is freedom from want—which, translated into world terms, means economic understandings which will secure to every nation a healthy peacetime life for its inhabitants— everywhere in the world.

The fourth is freedom from fear—which, translated into world terms, means a world-wide reduction of armaments to such a point and in such a thorough fashion that no nation will be in a position to commit an act of physical aggression against any neighbor—anywhere in the world.

That is no vision of a distant millennium. It is a definite basis for a kind of world attainable in our own time and generation. That kind of world is the very antithesis of the so-called new order to tyranny which the dictators seek to create with the crash of a bomb.

To that new order we oppose the greater conception—the moral order. A good society is able to face schemes of world domination and foreign revolutions alike without fear.

Since the beginning of our American history, we have been engaged in change—in a perpetual peaceful revolution—a revolution which goes on steadily, quietly adjusting itself to changing conditions—without the concentration camp or the quick-lime in the ditch. The world order which we seek is the cooperation of free countries, working together in a friendly, civilized society.

This nation has placed its destiny in the hands and heads and hearts of its millions of free men and women; and its faith in freedom under the guidance of God. Freedom means the supremacy of human rights everywhere. Our support goes to those who struggle to gain those rights or keep them. Our strength is our unity of purpose.

To that high concept there can be no end save victory.

Source:

Franklin D. Roosevelt. *The Public Papers and Addresses of Franklin D. Roosevelt*. New York: Random House, 1938–50.

Franklin Roosevelt, Executive Order 8802, 1941

In Executive Order (EO) 8802 issued June 25, 1941, President Franklin D. Roosevelt reaffirmed the administration's policy "of full participation in the defense program by all persons, regardless of race, creed, color, or national origin." The armed forces, however, remained strictly segregated by race; the approximately 1 million African Americans who served in World War II were usually employed as noncombatants, and the few black combat units that were created most often had white officers. One of the best known of the black units was the Tuskegee Airmen (the 99th Pursuit Squadron), which trained at the Tuskegee Institute in Alabama and flew sorties in North Africa, Italy, and Germany. One of the most decorated units, the 442nd Regimental Combat Team, consisted of Nisei (first-generation Americans of Japanese descent) who fought in Italy.

On July 26, 1948, President Harry S. Truman, announced EO 9081, which desegregated the military and created the President's Committee on Equality of Treatment and Opportunity in the Armed Services. In response to pressure from A. Philip Randolph and other civil rights leaders, President Truman ordered the desegregation of the armed services "as rapidly as possible." Three years later, the last all-black regiment—the 24th Infantry—was disbanded.

A general climate of racism had kept some blacks from getting proper recognition for their "extraordinary bravery"during World War II according to a 1993 Department of the Army inquiry into why no African Americans had been awarded the Medal of Honor for heroism. Six of the veterans received the honor posthumously. The lone living member of the group, Joseph V. Baker of Idaho, received his medal from President Bill Clinton at the White House ceremony honoring all seven recipients. "History has been made whole today," the president declared, "and our nation is bestowing honor on those who have long deserved it."

Reaffirming Policy of Full Participation in the Defense Programs by All Persons, Regardless of Race, Creed, Color, or National Origin, and Directing Certain Action in Furtherance of Said Policy.

Whereas it is the policy of the United States to encourage full participation in the national defense program by all citizens of the United States, regardless of race, creed, color, or national origin, in the firm belief that the democratic way of life within the Nation can be defended successfully only with the help and support of all groups within its borders; and

Whereas there is evidence that available and needed workers have been barred from employment in industries engaged in defense production solely because of considerations of race, creed, color, or national origin, to the detriment of workers' morale and of national unity:

Now, therefore, by virtue of the authority vested in me by the Constitution and the statutes, and as a prerequisite to the successful conduct of our national defense production effort, I do hereby reaffirm the policy of the United States that there shall be no discrimination in the employment of workers in defense industries or government because of race, creed, color, or national origin, and I do hereby declare that it is the duty of employers and of labor organizations, in furtherance of said policy and of this order, to provide for the full and equitable participation of all workers in defense industries, without discrimination because of race, creed, color, or national origin;

And it is hereby ordered as follows:

1. All departments and agencies of the Government of the United States concerned with vocational and training programs for defense production shall take special measures appropriate to assure that such programs are administered without discrimination because of race, creed, color, or national origin;

2. All contracting agencies of the Government of the United States shall include in all defense contracts hereafter negotiated by them a provision obligating the contractor not to discriminate against any worker because of race, creed, color or national origin;

3. There is established in the Office of Production Management a Committee on Fair Employment Practice, which shall consist to a chairman and four other members to be appointed by the President. The chairman and members of the Committee shall serve as such without compensation but shall be entitled to actual and necessary transportation, subsistence and other expenses incidental to performance of their duties. The Committee shall receive and investigate complaints of discrimination in violation of the provisions of this order and shall take appropriate steps to redress grievances which it finds to be valid. The Committee shall also recommend to the several departments and agencies of the Government of the United States and to the President all measures which may be deemed by it necessary or proper to effectuate the provisions of this order.

Franklin D. Roosevelt
The White House,
June 25, 1941.

Source:

Franklin D. Roosevelt Presidential Library and Museum. Available on-line. URL: http://www.fdrlibrary.marist.edu/odex8802.html. Accessed January 2004.

Franklin Roosevelt and Winston Churchill, Atlantic Charter, 1941

Joint British and American statement of principles for world peace issued on August 14, 1941, by British prime minister Winston Churchill and U.S. president Franklin D. Roosevelt at the conclusion of their shipboard meeting off the coast of Newfoundland during World War II. It expressed their hopes for peace "after the final destruction of the Nazi tyranny" so that people could travel freely and live "in freedom from fear and want." Their countries, it clarified, were neither interested in territorial gains nor in gains made against the wishes of their peoples. They affirmed their respect for the sovereign rights of all nationalities and promised help in restoring self-government where it had been denied. Additional provisions called for equal access to trade and raw materials for all countries, for international cooperation to improve economic and labor conditions, and for social security. Finally, Churchill and FDR reiterated their commitment to disarmament "pending the establishment of a wider and permanent system of general security," an idea that led to the formation of the United Nations. Ten of the Allied nations endorsed the Atlantic Charter.

The U.S. destroyer *Greer* was attacked on September 4, 1941, off the coast of Newfoundland when a German U-boat fired two torpedoes at it; the missiles, however, missed the ship. Roosevelt, in his speech, called the German action "piracy." He denounced the Nazi's attempt to "control the seas," and said that their ultimate goal was the "domination of the United States and domination of the Western Hemisphere by force of arms." Therefore, he ordered the navy to "shoot on sight" any German vessels.

The President of the United States of America and the Prime Minister, Mr. Churchill, representing His Majesty's Government in the United Kingdom, being met together, deem it right to make known certain common principles in the national policies of their respective countries on which they base their hopes for a better future for the world.

First, their countries seek no aggrandizement, territorial or other;

Second, they desire to see no territorial changes that do not accord with the freely expressed wishes of the peoples concerned;

Third, they respect the right of all peoples to choose the form of government under which they will live; and they wish to see sovereign rights and self government restored to those who have been forcibly deprived of them;

Fourth, they will endeavor, with due respect for their existing obligations, to further the enjoyment by all States, great or small, victor or vanquished, of access, on equal terms, to the trade and to the raw materials of the world which are needed for their economic prosperity;

Fifth, they desire to bring about the fullest collaboration between all nations in the economic field with the object of securing, for all, improved labor standards, economic advancement and social security;

Sixth, after the final destruction of the Nazi tyranny, they hope to see established a peace which will afford to all nations the means of dwelling in safety within their own boundaries, and which will afford assurance that all the men in all the lands may live out their lives in freedom from fear and want;

Seventh, such a peace should enable all men to traverse the high seas and oceans without hindrance;

Eighth, they believe that all of the nations of the world, for realistic as well as spiritual reasons must come to the abandonment of the use of force. Since no future peace can be maintained if land, sea or air armaments continue to be employed by nations which threaten, or may threaten, aggression outside of their frontiers, they believe, pending the establishment of a wider and permanent system of general security, that the disarmament of such nations is essential. They will likewise aid and encourage all other practicable measures which will lighten for peace-loving peoples the crushing burden of armaments.

SIGNED **Franklin D. Roosevelt**
Winston S. Churchill

Source:

Henry Steele Commager, ed. *Documents of American History*. 9th ed. New York: Appleton-Century-Crofts, 1973.

Franklin Roosevelt, "Day of Infamy" Speech, 1941

Address to a joint session of the U.S. Congress delivered by President Franklin D. Roosevelt on December 8, 1941, the day after Japan's surprise naval air attack on the U.S. naval base at Pearl Harbor, Hawaii. Although American intelligence knew an attack was planned, it did not know exactly where or when. In fact, Roosevelt, had sent a letter to Japanese emperor Hirohito on December 6 in an attempt to revive negotiations between the two countries that had broken off December 1.

Naval battleships were moored close together in Pearl Harbor, and eight were sunk or immobilized. Numerous smaller boats were destroyed, with more than 3,000 casualties. (Fortunately, three aircraft carriers normally docked at Pearl Harbor happened to be outside that day.)

Calling December 7 "a date which will live in infamy," Roosevelt announced that Japanese forces had also attacked other Pacific targets: Malaya, Hong Kong, Guam, the Philippines, Wake Island, and Midway Island. He asked Congress to declare war on Japan because of this "unprovoked and dastardly attack." Within an hour Congress complied, with only one dissenting vote, and the United States entered World War II. On December 11, 1941, Germany and Italy, Japan's allies, declared war on the United States. Congress responded with separate declarations of war against these Axis nations.

Yesterday, December 7, 1941—a date which will live in infamy—the United States of America was suddenly and deliberately attacked by naval and air forces of the Empire of Japan.

The United States was at peace with that nation and, at the solicitation of Japan, was still in conversation with its Government and its Emperor looking toward the maintenance of peace in the Pacific. Indeed, one hour after Japanese air squadrons had commenced bombing in the American Island of Oahu, the Japanese Ambassador to the United States and his colleague delivered to our Secretary of State a formal reply to a recent American message. And while this reply stated that it seemed useless to continue the existing diplomatic negotiations, it contained no threat or hint of war or armed attack.

It will be recorded that the distance of Hawaii from Japan makes it obvious that the attack was deliberately planned many days or even weeks ago. During the intervening time the Japanese Government has deliberately sought to deceive the United States by false statements and expressions of hope for continued peace.

The attack yesterday on the Hawaiian Islands has caused severe damage to American naval and military forces, I regret to tell you that very many American lives have been lost. In addition American ships have been reported torpedoed on the high seas between San Francisco and Honolulu.

Yesterday the Japanese Government also launched an attack against Malaya.

Last night Japanese forces attacked Hong Kong.

Last night Japanese forces attacked Guam.

Last night Japanese forces attacked the Philippine Islands.

Last night the Japanese attacked Wake Island.

And this morning the Japanese attacked Midway Island.

Japan has, therefore, undertaken a surprise offensive extending throughout the Pacific area. The facts of yesterday and today speak for themselves. The people of the United States have already formed their opinions and well understand the implications to the very life and safety of our nation.

As Commander-in-Chief of the Army and Navy I have directed that all measures be taken for our defense.

But always will our whole nation remember the character of the onslaught against us.

No matter how long it may take us to overcome this premeditated invasion, the American people in their righteous might will win through to absolute victory.

I believe that I interpret the will of the Congress and of the people when I assert that we will not only defend ourselves to the uttermost but will make it very certain that this form of treachery shall never again endanger us.

Hostilities exist. There is no blinking at the fact that our people, our territory and our interests are in grave danger.

With confidence in our armed forces—with the unbounding determination of our people—we will gain the inevitable triumph—so help us God.

I ask that the Congress declare that since the unprovoked and dastardly attack by Japan on Sunday, December seventh, 1941, a state of war has existed between the United States and the Japanese Empire.

Source:

Franklin D. Roosevelt. *The Public Papers of the Presidents of the United States*. New York: Random House, 1938–50.

Franklin Roosevelt, Executive Order 9066: The Japanese Relocation Act, 1942

Order issued by President Franklin D. Roosevelt on February 19, 1942, authorizing military commanders to establish special zones from which "any or all persons" might be excluded. The order, prompted by fears of sabotage and espionage following the Japanese attack on Pearl Harbor, allowed the U.S. Army to evacuate persons of Japanese ancestry living on the U.S. West Coast to inland "relocation centers." A number of Italians living on the East Coast were also interned. The Order was popular among white Californians and was supported by the governor, future Supreme Court chief justice Earl Warren. Opposing it was FBI director J. Edgar Hoover, who argued that before the Pearl Harbor attack the bureau had identified the people of Japanese, German, and Italian descent who posed a danger, and they were arrested on December 7 and 8, 1941.

On March 21, Congress enacted legislation in support of this order. Some 112,000 people—most of them native-born U.S. citizens—were forced to sell or abandon their homes and businesses and remove to bleak internment camps, where most remained until 1945. The U.S. Supreme Court, in *Korematsu v. United States* (323 U.S. 214), upheld the internment, but in 1983 a federal commission called the program "a grave injustice." In 1988 Congress authorized reparations for Japanese Americans interned during World War II, and the following year provided funding for payments of $20,000 for each surviving internee.

Executive Order
Authorizing the Secretary of War to Prescribe Military Areas

Whereas the successful prosecution of the war requires every possible protection against espionage and against sabotage to national-defense material, national-defense premises, and national-defense utilities as defined in Section 4, Act of April 20, 1918, 40 Stat. 533, as amended by the Act of November 30, 1940, 54 Stat. 1220, and the Act of August 21, 1941, 55 Stat. 655 (U.S., Title 50, Sec. 104):

Now therefore, by virtue of the authority vested in me as President of the United States, and Commander in Chief of the Army and Navy, I hereby authorize and direct the Secretary of War, and the Military Commanders whom he may from time to time designate, whenever he or any designated Commander deems such action necessary or desirable, to prescribe military areas in such places and of such extent as the or the appropriate Military Commander may determine, from which any or all persons may be excluded, and with respect to which, the right of any person to enter, remain in, or leave shall be subject to whatever restrictions the Secretary of War or the appropriate Military Commander may impose in his discretion. The Secretary of War is hereby authorized to provide for residents of any such area who are excluded therefrom, such transportation, food, shelter, and other accommodations as may be necessary, in the judgment of the Secretary of War or the said Military Commander, and until other arrangements are made, to accomplish the purpose of this order. The designation of military areas in any region or locality shall supersede designations of prohibited and restricted areas by the Attorney General under the Proclamations of December 7 and 8, 1941, and shall supersede the responsibility and authority of the Attorney General under the said Proclamations in respect of such prohibited and restricted areas.

I hereby further authorize and direct the Secretary of War and the said Military Commanders to take such other steps as he or the appropriate Military Commander may deem advisable to enforce compliance with the restrictions applicable to each Military area hereinabove authorized to be designated, including the use of Federal troops and other Federal Agencies, with authority to accept assistance of state and local agencies.

I hereby further authorize and direct all Executive Departments, independent establishments and other Federal Agencies, to assist the Secretary of War or the said Military Commanders in carrying out this Executive Order, including the furnishing of medical aid, hospitalization, food, clothing, transportation, use of land, shelter, and other supplies, equipment, utilities, facilities, and services.

This order shall not be construed as modifying or limiting in any way the authority heretofore granted under Executive Order No. 8972, dated December 12, 1941, nor shall it be construed as limiting or modifying the duty and responsibility of the Federal Bureau of Investigation, with respect to the investigation of alleged acts of sabotage or the duty and responsibility of the Attorney General and the Department of Justice under the Proclamations of December 7 and 8, 1941, prescribing regulations for the conduct and control of alien enemies, except as such duty and responsibility is superseded by the designation of military areas hereunder.

Franklin D Roosevelt
The White House,
February 19, 1942.

Source:
Federal Register, Vol. 7, no. 38, (February 25, 1942): 1,407.

Ex Parte Quirin, 1942

This decision upheld the power of the president of the United States to convene military tribunals for unlawful combatants. It involved eight men of German descent who had previously lived in the United States, including one who claimed U.S. citizenship through his parents. In June 1942 these men came into the United States from German submarines, four in Amagansett, Long Island, New York, and four at Ponte Vedra Beach in Florida. Their intention was to blow up industrial plants and transportation facilities. After landing, they buried their German uniforms and donned civilian clothes. A suspicious Coast Guardsman patrolling the Long Island beach stopped them. Although he didn't detain anyone, he may have sufficiently frightened one, George Dasch, that he telephoned the FBI. The Coast Guard, meanwhile, located the buried uniforms and also called the FBI. Several days later, Dasch turned himself in to the bureau in Washington and pointed out the other seven saboteurs. Within two weeks they were all in custody. After their secret two-day trial, July 29–30, they were sentenced to death. President Roosevelt, however, commuted the sentences of Dasch and Ernest Burger, who also helped, to 30 years. The others were executed August 8, 1942. President Truman granted Dasch and Burger clemency in 1948 and then deported them.

The details of the incident remained secret throughout the war, enabling the public (and the Germans) to believe that it was the quick investigative work of the FBI that solved the case so expeditiously. In fact, no other documented instance of German sabotage occurred after their arrests.

The opinion, written by Chief Justice Harlan Fiske Stone, could be considered "after the fact." President Franklin D. Roosevelt wanted it to be resolved quickly, and the courts expedited the saboteurs' petitions for habeas corpus. He wanted them tried out of the public eye by military tribunal and that is what the Court's decision, on narrow grounds, gave him. It issued an unsigned, paragraph-long per curiam opinion on July 31, 1942, denying the petitioners their writ and affirming that they could be tried by military commission. However, the full decision, backed up with references to the constitution, statutes, and case law, was not handed down until October 29, months after six saboteurs had been hanged.

Nevertheless, it has not been overturned. President George W. Bush referred to *Quirin* in his decision to establish military tribunals for potential terrorists after the events of September 11, 2001. The decision also appeared to bolster Bush's contention that detainees, including American citizens, who fought with the Taliban in Afghanistan should be considered unlawful combatants rather than prisoners of war.

Justice Murphy took no part in the consideration or decision of these cases.

Mr. Chief Justice STONE delivered the opinion of the Court.

These cases are brought here by petitioners' several applications for leave to file petitions for habeas corpus in this Court, and by their petitions for certiorari to review orders of the District Court for the District of Columbia, which denied their applications for leave to file petitions for habeas corpus in that court.

The question for decision is whether the detention of petitioners by respondent for trial by Military Commission, appointed by Order of the President of July 2, 1942, [317 U.S. 1, 19] on charges preferred against them purporting to set out their violations of the law of war and of the Articles of War, is in conformity to the laws and Constitution of the United States.

. . . In view of the public importance of the questions raised by their petitions and of the duty which rests on the courts, in time of war as well as in time of peace, to preserve unimpaired the constitutional safeguards of civil liberty, and because in our opinion the public interest required that we consider and decide those questions without any avoidable delay, we directed that petitioners' applications be set down for full oral argument at a special term of this Court, convened on July 29, 1942. . . .

On July 31, 1942, after hearing argument of counsel and after full consideration of all questions raised, this Court affirmed the orders of the District Court and denied petitioners' applications for leave to file petitions for habeas corpus. . . .

The following facts appear from the petitions or are stipulated. Except as noted they are undisputed.

All the petitioners were born in Germany; all have lived in the United States. All returned to Germany between 1933 and 1941. All except petitioner Haupt are admittedly citizens of the German Reich, with which the United States is at war. Haupt came to this country with his parents when he was five years old; it is contended that he became a citizen of the United States by virtue of the naturalization of his parents during his minority and that he has not since lost his citizenship. The Government, however, takes the position that on attaining his majority he elected to maintain German allegiance and citizenship or in any case that he has by his conduct renounced or abandoned his United States citizenship. For reasons presently to be stated we do not find it necessary to resolve these contentions. After the declaration of war between the United States and the German Reich, petitioners received training at a sabotage school near Berlin, Germany, where they were instructed in the use of explosives and in methods of secret writing. Thereafter petitioners, with a German citizen, Dasch, proceeded from Germany to a seaport in Occupied France, where petitioners Burger, Heinck and Quirin, together with Dasch, boarded a German submarine which proceeded across the Atlantic to Amagansett Beach on Long Island, New York. The four were there landed from the submarine in the hours of darkness, on or about June 13, 1942, carrying with them a supply of explosives, fuses and incendiary and timing devices. While landing they wore German Marine Infantry uniforms or parts of uniforms. Immediately after landing they buried their uniforms and the other articles mentioned and proceeded in civilian dress to New York City.

The remaining four petitioners at the same French port boarded another German submarine, which carried them across the Atlantic to Ponte Vedra Beach, Florida. On or about June 17, 1942, they came ashore during the hours of darkness wearing caps of the German Marine Infantry and carrying with them a supply of explosives, fuses, and incendiary and timing devices. They immediately buried their caps and the other articles mentioned and proceeded in civilian dress to Jacksonville, Florida, and thence to various points in the United States. All were taken into custody in New York or Chicago by agents of the Federal Bureau of Investigation. All had received instructions in Germany from an officer of the German High Command to destroy war industries and war facilities in the United States, for which they or their relatives in Germany were to receive salary payments from the German Government. They also had been paid by the German Government during their course of training at the sabotage school and had received substantial sums in United States currency, which were in their possession when arrested. The currency had been handed to them by an officer of the German High Command, who had instructed them to wear their German uniforms while landing in the United States.

The President, as President and Commander in Chief of the Army and Navy, by Order of July 2, 1942, appointed a Military Commission and directed it to try petitioners for offenses against the law of war and the Articles of War, and prescribed regulations for the procedure on the trial and for review of the record of the trial and of any judgment or sentence of the Commission. On the same day, by Proclamation, the President declared that 'all persons who are subjects, citizens or residents of any nation at war with the United States or who give obedience to or act under the direction of any such nation, and who during time of war enter or attempt to enter the United States . . . through coastal or boundary defenses, and are charged with committing or attempting or preparing to commit sabotage, espionage, hostile or warlike acts, or violations of the law of war, shall be subject to the law of war and to the jurisdiction of military tribunals'.

The Proclamation also stated in terms that all such persons were denied access to the courts.

Pursuant to direction of the Attorney General, the Federal Bureau of Investigation surrendered custody of petitioners to respondent, Provost Marshal of the Military District of Washington, who was directed by the Secretary of War to receive and keep them in custody, and who thereafter held petitioners for trial before the Commission.

On July 3, 1942, the Judge Advocate General's Department of the Army prepared and lodged with the Commission the following charges against petitioners, supported by specifications:

1. Violation of the law of war.

2. Violation of Article 81 of the Articles of War, defining the offense of relieving or attempting to relieve, or corresponding with or giving intelligence to, the enemy.

3. Violation of Article 82, defining the offense of spying.

4. Conspiracy to commit the offenses alleged in charges 1, 2 and 3.

The Commission met on July 8, 1942, and proceeded with the trial, which continued in progress while the causes were pending in this Court. On July 27th, before petitioners' applications to the District Court, all the evidence for the prosecution and the defense had been taken by the Commission and the case had been closed except for arguments of counsel. It is conceded that ever since petitioners' arrest the state and federal courts in Florida, New York, and the District of Columbia, and in the states in which each of the petitioners was arrested or detained, have been open and functioning normally.

While it is the usual procedure on an application for a writ of habeas corpus in the federal courts for the court to issue the writ and on the return to hear and dispose of the case, it may without issuing the writ consider and determine whether the facts alleged by the petition, if proved, would warrant discharge of the prisoner. Presentation of the petition for judicial action is the institution of a suit. Hence denial by the district court of leave to file the petitions in these causes was the judicial determination of a case or controversy, reviewable on appeal to the Court of Appeals and reviewable here by certiorari.

Petitioners' main contention is that the President is without any statutory or constitutional authority to order the petitioners to be tried by military tribunal for offenses with which they are charged; that in consequence they are entitled to be tried in the civil courts with the safeguards, including trial by jury, which the Fifth and Sixth Amendments guarantee to all persons charged in such courts with criminal offenses. In any case it is urged that the President's Order, in prescribing the procedure of the Commission and the method for review of its findings and sentence, and the proceedings of the Commission under the Order, conflict with Articles of War adopted by Congress . . . are illegal and void.

The Government challenges each of these propositions. But regardless of their merits, it also insists that petitioners must be denied access to the courts, both because they are enemy aliens or have entered our territory as enemy belligerents, and because the President's Proclamation undertakes in terms to deny such access to the class of persons defined by the Proclamation, which aptly describes the character and conduct of petitioners. It is urged that if they are enemy aliens or if the Proclamation has force no court may afford the petitioners a hearing. But there is certainly nothing in the Proclamation to preclude access to the courts for determining its applicability to the particular case. And neither the Proclamation nor the fact that they are enemy aliens forecloses consideration by the courts of petitioners' contentions that the Constitution and laws of the United States constitutionally enacted forbid their trial by military commission. As announced in our per curiam opinion we have resolved those questions by our conclusion that the Commission has jurisdiction to try the charge preferred against petitioners. There is therefore no occasion to decide contentions of the parties unrelated to this issue. We pass at once to the consideration of the basis of the Commission's authority.

We are not here concerned with any question of the guilt or innocence of petitioners. Constitutional safeguards for the protection of all who are charged with offenses are not to be disregarded in order to inflict merited punishment on some who are guilty. But the detention and trial of petitioners—ordered by the President in the declared exercise of his powers as Commander in Chief of the Army in time of war and of grave public danger—are not to be set aside by the courts without the clear conviction that they are in conflict with the Constitution or laws of Congress constitutionally enacted.

Congress and the President, like the courts, possess no power not derived from the Constitution. But one of the objects of the Constitution, as declared by its preamble, is to 'provide for the common defence.' As a means to that end the Constitution gives to Congress the power to 'provide for the common Defence', [List of specific clauses in Art. I, 8.]

The Constitution confers on the President the 'executive Power,' Art II [list of sections and clauses in Article II.]

The Constitution thus invests the President as Commander in Chief with the power to wage war which Congress has declared, and to carry into effect all laws passed by Congress for the conduct of war and for the government and regulation of the Armed Forces, and all laws defining and punishing offences against the law of nations, including those which pertain to the conduct of war.

By the Articles of War, Congress has provided rules for the government of the Army. The Articles . . . recognize the 'military commission' appointed by military command as an appropriate tribunal for the trial and punishment of offenses against the law of war not ordinarily tried by court martial. . . .

Similarly the Espionage Act of 1917, which authorizes trial in the district courts of certain offenses that tend to interfere with the prosecution of war, provides that nothing contained in the act 'shall be deemed to limit the jurisdiction of the general courts-martial, military commissions, or naval courts-martial.'

From the very beginning of its history this Court has recognized and applied the law of war as including that part of the law of nations which prescribes, for the conduct of war, the status, rights and duties of enemy nations as well as of enemy individuals. By the Articles of War, Congress has explicitly provided, so far as it may constitutionally do so, that military tribunals shall have jurisdiction to try offenders or offenses against the law of war in appropriate cases. Congress . . . has thus exercised its authority to define and punish offenses against the law of nations by sanctioning, within constitutional limitations, the jurisdiction of military commissions to try persons for offenses which, according to the rules and precepts of the law of nations, and more particularly the law of war, are cognizable by such tribunals. And the President, as Commander in Chief, by his Proclamation in time of war has invoked that law. By his Order creating the present Commission he has undertaken to exercise the authority conferred upon him by Congress, and also such authority as the Constitution itself gives the Commander in Chief, to direct the performance of those functions which may constitutionally be performed by the military arm of the nation in time of war.

An important incident to the conduct of war is the adoption of measures by the military command not only to repel and defeat the enemy, but to seize and subject to disciplinary measures those enemies who in their attempt to thwart or impede our military effort have violated the law of war. It is unnecessary for present purposes to determine to what extent the President as Commander in Chief has constitutional power to create military commissions without the support of Congressional legislation. For here Congress has authorized trial of offenses against the law of war before such commissions. We are concerned only with the question whether it is within the constitutional power of the national government to place petitioners upon trial before a military commission for the offenses with which they are charged. We must therefore first inquire whether any of the acts charged is an offense against the law of war cognizable before a military tribunal, and if so whether the Constitution prohibits the trial. . . . As we shall show, these petitioners were charged with an offense against the law of war which the Constitution does not require to be tried by jury.

It is no objection that Congress in providing for the trial of such offenses has not itself undertaken to codify that branch of international law or to mark its precise boundaries, or to enumerate or define by statute all the acts which that law condemns. . . . By the reference in the 15th Article of War to 'offenders or offenses that . . . by the law of war may be triable by such military commissions', Congress has incorporated by reference, as within the jurisdiction of military commissions, all offenses which are defined as such by the law of war and which may constitutionally be included within that jurisdiction. . . .

By universal agreement and practice the law of war draws a distinction between . . . between those who are lawful and unlawful combatants. Lawful combatants are subject to capture and detention as prisoners of war by opposing military forces. Unlawful combatants are likewise subject to capture and detention, but in addition they are subject to trial and punishment by military tribunals for acts which render their belligerency unlawful. The spy who secretly and without uniform passes the military lines of a belligerent in time of war, seeking to gather military information and communicate it to the enemy, or an enemy combatant who without uniform comes secretly through the lines for the purpose of waging war by destruction of life or property, are familiar examples of belligerents who are generally deemed not to be entitled to the status of prisoners of war, but to be offenders against the law of war subject to trial and punishment by military tribunals.

Such was the practice of our own military authorities before the adoption of the Constitution, and during the Mexican and Civil Wars. . . These and related provisions have been continued in substance by the Rules of Land Warfare promulgated by the War Department for the guidance of the Army. . . .

* * *

By a long course of practical administrative construction by its military authorities, our Government has likewise recognized that those who during time of war pass surreptitiously from enemy territory into our own, discarding their uniforms upon entry, for the commission of hostile acts involving destruction of life or property, have the status of unlawful combatants punishable as such by military commission. . . .

Specification 1 of the First charge is sufficient to charge all the petitioners with the offense of unlawful belligerency. . . .

* * *

Citizenship in the United States of an enemy belligerent does not relieve him from the consequences of a belligerency which is unlawful because in violation of the law of war. Citizens who associate themselves with the military arm of the enemy government, and with its aid, guidance and direction enter this country bent on hostile acts are enemy belligerents within the meaning of the Hague Convention and the law of war. It is as an enemy belligerent that petitioner Haupt is charged with entering the United States, and unlawful belligerency is the gravamen of the offense of which he is accused.

Nor are petitioners any the less belligerents if, as they argue, they have not actually committed or attempted to commit any act of depredation or entered the theatre or zone of active military operations. . . . It is that each petitioner, in circumstances which gave him the status of an enemy belligerent, passed our military and naval lines and defenses or went behind those lines, in civilian dress and with hostile purpose. . . .

But petitioners insist that even if the offenses with which they are charged are offenses against the law of war, their trial is subject to the requirement of the Fifth Amendment that no person shall be held to answer for a capital or otherwise infamous crime unless on a presentment or indictment of a grand jury, and that such trials. . . must be by jury in a civil court. . . .

. . . Military tribunals . . . are not courts in the sense of the Judiciary Article, and which in the natural course of events are usually called upon to function under conditions precluding resort to such procedures. . . .

* * *

. . . We must conclude that §2 of Article III and the Fifth and Sixth Amendments cannot be taken to have extended the right to demand a jury to trials by military commission, or to have required that offenses against the law of war not triable by jury at common law be tried only in the civil courts.

* * *

Petitioners, and especially petitioner Haupt, stress the pronouncement of this Court in the *Milligan* case [71 U.S. 2], that the law of war 'can never be applied to citizens in states which have upheld the authority of the government, and where the courts are open and their process unobstructed.' Elsewhere in its opinion, the Court was at pains to point out that Milligan . . . was a non-belligerent, not subject to the law of war. . . .

. . . It is enough that petitioners here, upon the conceded facts, were plainly within those boundaries, and were held in good faith for trial by military commission, charged with being enemies who, with the purpose of destroying war materials and utilities, entered or after entry remained in our territory without uniform—an offense against the law of war. We hold only that those particular acts constitute an offense against the law of war which the Constitution authorizes to be tried by military commission.

There remains the contention that the President's Order of July 2, 1942, so far as it lays down the procedure to be followed on the trial before the Commission and on the review of its findings and sentence, and the procedure in fact followed by the Commission, are in conflict with Articles of War. Petitioners argue that their trial by the Commission, by a procedure which Congress has prohibited would invalidate any conviction which could be obtained against them and renders their detention for trial likewise unlawful; that the President's Order prescribes such an unlawful procedure; and that the secrecy surrounding the trial and all proceedings before the Commission, as well as any review of the decision, will preclude a later opportunity to test the lawfulness of the detention.

Accordingly, we conclude that Charge I, on which petitioners were detained for trial by the Military Commission, alleged an offense which the President is authorized to order tried by military commission; that his Order convening the Commission was a lawful order and that the Commission was lawfully constituted; that the petitioners were held in lawful custody and did not show cause for their discharge. It follows that the orders of the District Court should be affirmed, and that leave to file petitions for habeas corpus in this Court should be denied.

* * *

Source:

U.S. Reports, The University of Chicago. D'Angelo Law Library. Available on-line. URL: www.law.uchicago.edu.tribunals/docs/usvcox.pdf. Accessed January 2004.

West Virginia State Board of Education v. Barnette (319 U.S. 624), 1943

U.S. Supreme Court decision issued on June 14, 1943, while Americans were fighting in World War II, invalidating—as a violation of First Amendment rights—a state requirement that public school children salute and pledge allegiance to the flag. The majority opinion by Justice Robert Jackson is one of the most spirited defenses of the First Amendment in the history of the Supreme Court. Similarly, the dissenting opinion of Justice Felix Frankfurter is one of the most personal. It also contains an affirmation of his theory of strict constitutional interpretation and what is termed "original intent," trying to discern how the drafters of the Constitution would have interpreted the situation at question.

Before U.S. entry into the war, *Minersville School District v. Gobitis,* (310 U.S. 586), had tested the constitutionality of a similar law passed by the Pennsylvania legislature. The petitioner, a member of the Jehovah's Witnesses and the parent of a student, objected to the Pledge of Allegiance on religious grounds. Like Walter Barnette, also a Jehovah's Witness, he challenged the constitutionality of the law as a violation of his First Amendment rights. The Supreme Court, however, decided by a vote of 8 to 1, with only Associate Justice Stone dissenting, that the state law should be upheld. Associate Justice Frankfurter, writing for the majority, held that in light of the impending world war, it was important for a "unifying sentiment" to be instilled in the children of the country and that for the Supreme Court to question the means by which that sentiment should be instilled "would in effect make us the school board for the country." Interestingly, the salute at that time was not placing the hand over the heart but holding out the right arm in a form similar to that used by the Nazis.

The West Virginia regulation stated that children who refused to salute could be expelled and their parents fined. In its 6-3 decision, the Supreme Court ruled that the state cannot compel students to declare a belief, stating that "no official . . . can prescribe what shall be orthodox in politics, nationalism, religion, or other matters of opinion or force citizens to confess by word or act their faith therein."

Mr. Justice Jackson delivered the opinion of the Court.

Following the decision by this Court on June 3, 1940, in *Minersville School District v. Gobitis*. . ., the West Virginia legislature amended its statutes to require all schools therein to conduct courses of instruction in history, civics, and in the Constitutions of the United States and of the State "for the purpose of teaching, fostering and perpetuating the ideals, principles and spirit of Americanism, and increasing the knowledge of the organization and machinery of the government." . . .

The Board of Education on January 9, 1942, adopted a resolution containing recitals taken largely from the Court's *Gobitis* opinion and ordering that the salute to the flag become "a regular part of the program of activities in the public schools," that all teachers and pupils "shall be required to participate in the salute honoring the Nation represented by the Flag; provided, however, that refusal to salute the Flag be regarded as an Act of insubordination, and shall be dealt with accordingly."

The resolution originally required the "commonly accepted salute to the Flag" which it defined. Objections to the salute as "being too much like Hitler's" were raised by the Parent and Teachers Association, the Boy and Girl Scouts, the Red Cross, and the Federation of Women's Clubs. Some modification appears to have been made in deference to these objections, but no concession was made to Jehovah's Witnesses. What is now required is the "stiff-arm" salute, the saluter to keep the right hand raised with palm turned up while the following is repeated: "I pledge allegiance to the Flag of the United States of America and to the Republic for which it stands; one Nation, indivisible, with liberty and justice for all."

Failure to conform is "insubordination" dealt with by expulsion. Readmission is denied by statute until compliance. Meanwhile the expelled child is "unlawfully absent" and may be proceeded against as a delinquent. His parents or guardians are liable to prosecution, and if convicted are subject to fine not exceeding $50 and jail term not exceeding thirty days.

Appellees, citizens of the United States and of West Virginia, brought suit in the United States District Court for themselves and others similarly situated asking its injunction to restrain enforcement of these laws and regulation against Jehovah's Witnesses. The Witnesses are an unincorporated body teaching that the obligation imposed by law of God is superior to that of laws enacted by temporal government. Their religious beliefs include a literal version of Exodus, Chapter 20, verses 4 and 5, which says: "Thou shalt not make unto thee any graven image, or any likeness of anything that is in heaven above, or that is in the earth beneath, or that is in the water under the earth; thou shalt not bow down thyself to them nor serve them." They consider that the flag is an "image" within this command. For this reason they refuse to salute it.

Children of this faith have been expelled from school and are threatened with exclusion for no other cause. Officials threaten to send them to reformatories maintained for criminally inclined juveniles. Parents of such children have been prosecuted and are threatened with prosecutions for causing delinquency.

The Board of Education moved to dismiss the complaint setting forth these facts and alleging that the law and regulations are an unconstitutional denial of religious freedom, and of freedom of speech, and are invalid under the "due process" and "equal protection" clauses of the Fourteenth Amendment to the Federal Constitution. The cause was submitted on the pleadings to a District Court of three judges. It restrained enforcement as to the plaintiffs and those of that class. The Board of Education brought the case here by direct appeal.

This case calls upon us to reconsider a precedent decision, at the Court throughout its history often has been required to do. Before turning to the *Gobitis* case, however, it is desirable to notice certain characteristics by which this controversy is distinguished.

. . . The refusal of these persons to participate in the ceremony does not interfere with or deny rights of others to do so. Nor is there any question in this case that their behavior is peaceable and orderly. The sole conflict is between authority and rights of the individual. . . .

[1] As the present Chief Justice said in dissent in the *Gobitis* case, the State may "require teaching by instruction and study of all in our history and in the structure and organization of our government, including the guaranties of civil liberty which tend to inspire patriotism and love of country.". . . Here, however, we are dealing with a compulsion of students to declare a belief. They are not merely made acquainted with the flag salute so that they may be informed as to what it is or even what it means. The issue here is whether this slow and easily neglected route to aroused loyalties constitutionally may be short- cut by substituting a compulsory salute and slogan. . . .

There is no doubt that, in connection with the pledges, the flag salute is a form of utterance. Symbolism is a primitive but effective way of communicating ideas. The use of an emblem or flag to symbolize some system, idea, institution, or personality, is a short cut from mind to mind. Causes and nations, political parties, lodges and ecclesiastical groups seek to knit the loyalty of their followings to a flag or banner, a color or design. The State announces rank, function, and authority through crowns and maces, uniforms and black robes; the church speaks through the Cross, the Crucifix, the altar and shrine, and clerical raiment. Symbols of State often convey political ideas just as religious symbols come to convey theological ones. Associated with many of these symbols are appropriate gestures of acceptance or respect: a salute, a bowed or bared head, a bended knee. A person gets from a symbol the meaning he puts into it, and what is one man's comfort and inspiration is another's jest and scorn.

. . . Here it is the State that employs a flag as a symbol of adherence to government as presently organized. It requires the individual to communicate by word and sign his acceptance of the political ideas it thus bespeaks. Objection to this form of communication when coerced is an old one, well known to the framers of the Bill of Rights.

. . . It is now a commonplace the censorship or suppression of expression of opinion is tolerated by our Constitution only when the expression presents a clear and present danger of action of a kind that State is empowered to prevent and punish. It would seem that involuntary affirmation could be commanded only on even more immediate and urgent grounds than silence. But here the power of compulsion is invoked without any allegation that remaining passive during a flag salute ritual creates a clear and present danger that would justify an effort even to muffle expression. To sustain the compulsory flag salute we are required to say that a Bill of Rights which guards the individual's right to speak his own mind, left it open to public authorities to compel him to utter what is not in his mind.

Whether the First Amendment to the Constitution will permit officials to order observance of ritual of this nature does not depend upon whether as a voluntary exercise we would think it to be good, bad or merely innocuous. Any credo of nationalism is likely to include what some disapprove or to omit what others think essential, and to give off different overtones as it takes on different accents or interpretations. If official power exists to coerce acceptance of any patriotic creed, what it shall contain cannot be decided by courts, but must be largely discretionary with the ordaining authority, whose power to prescribe would no doubt include power to amend. Hence validity of the asserted power to force an American citizen publicly to profess any statement of belief or to engage in any ceremony of assent to one presents questions of power that must be considered independently of any idea we may have as to the utility of the ceremony in question.

Nor does the issue as we see it turn on one's possession of particular religious views or the sincerity with which they are held. . . . Many citizens who do not share these religious views hold such a compulsory rite to infringe constitutional liberty of the individual. It is not necessary to inquire whether non-conformist beliefs will exempt from the duty to salute unless we first find power to make the salute a legal duty.

The *Gobitis* decision, however, assumed, as did the argument in that case and in this, that power exists in the State to impose the flag salute discipline upon school children in general. . . . The question which underlies the flag salute controversy is whether such a ceremony so touching matters of opinion and political attitude may be imposed upon the individual by official authority under powers committed to any political organization under our Constitution. We examine rather than assume existence of this power and, against this broader definition of issues in this case, re-examine specific grounds assigned for the *Gobitis* decision.

* * *

Government of limited power need not be anemic government. Assurance that rights are secure tends to diminish fear and jealousy of strong government, and by making us feel safe to live under it makes for its better support. Without promise of a limiting Bill of Rights it is doubtful if our Constitution could have mustered enough strength to enable its ratification. To enforce those rights today is not to choose weak government over strong government. It is only to adhere as a means of strength to individual freedom of mind in preference to officially disciplined uniformity for which history indicates a disappointing and disastrous end.

The subject now before us exemplifies this principle. Free public education, if faithful to the ideal of secular instruction and political neutrality, will not be partisan or enemy of any class, creed, party, or faction. . . .

3. . . . The very purpose of a Bill of Rights was to withdraw certain subjects from the vicissitudes of political controversy, to place them beyond the reach of majorities and officials and to establish them as legal principles to be applied by the courts. One's right to life, liberty, and property, to free speech, a free press, freedom of worship and assembly, and other fundamental rights may not be submitted to vote; they depend on the outcome of no elections.

* * *

4. Lastly, and this is the very heart of the *Gobitis* opinion, it reasons that "National unity is the basis of national security," that the authorities have "the right to select appropriate means for its attainment," and hence reaches the conclusion that such compulsory measures toward "national unity" are constitutional. . . . Upon the verity of this assumption depends our answer in this case.

National unity as an end which officials may foster by persuasion and example is not in question. The problem is whether under our Constitution compulsion as here employed is a permissible means for its achievement.

Struggles to coerce uniformity of sentiment in support of some end thought essential to their time and country have been waged by many good as well as by evil men. Nationalism is a relatively recent phenomenon but at other times and places the ends have been racial or territorial security, support of a dynasty or regime, and particular plans for saving souls. As first and moderate methods to attain unity have failed, those bent on its accomplishment must resort to an ever-increasing severity.

As governmental pressure toward unity becomes greater, so strife becomes more bitter as to whose unity it shall be. Probably no deeper division of our people could proceed from any provocation than from finding it necessary to choose what doctrine and whose program public educational officials shall compel youth to unite in embracing. Ultimate futility of such attempts to compel coherence is the lesson of every such effort from the Roman drive to stamp out Christianity as a disturber of its pagan unity, the Inquisition, as a means to religious and dynastic unity, the Siberian exiles as a means to Russian unity, down to the fast failing efforts to our present totalitarian enemies. Those who begin coercive elimination of dissent soon find themselves exterminating dissenters. Compulsory unification of opinion achieves only the unanimity of the graveyard.

[8] It seems trite but necessary to say that the First Amendment to our Constitution was designed to avoid these ends by avoiding these beginnings. There is no mysticism in the American concept of the State or of the nature or origin of its authority. We set up government by consent of the governed, and the Bill of Rights denies those in power any legal opportunity to coerce that consent. Authority here is to be controlled by public opinion, not public opinion by authority.

[9] The case is made difficult not because the principles of its decision are obscure but because the flag involved is our own. Nevertheless, we apply the limitations of the Constitution with no fear that freedom to be intellectually and spiritually diverse or even contrary will disintegrate the social organization. To believe that patriotism will not flourish if patriotic ceremonies are voluntary and spontaneous instead of a compulsory routine is to make an unflattering estimate of the appeal of our institutions to free minds. We can have intellectual individualism and the rich cultural diversities that we owe to exceptional minds only at the price of occasional eccentricity and abnormal attitudes. When they are so harmless to others or to the States as those we deal with here, the price is not too great. But freedom to differ is not limited to things that do not matter much. That would be a mere shadow of freedom. The test of its substance is the right to differ as to things that touch the heart of the existing order.

[10] If there is any fixed star in our constitutional constellation, it is that no official, high or petty, can prescribe what shall be orthodox in politics, nationalism, religion, or other matters of opinion or force citizens to confess by word or act their faith therein. If there are any circumstances which permit an exception, they do not now occur to us.

[11] We think the action of the local authorities in compelling the flag salute and pledge transcends constitutional limitations on their power and invades the sphere of intellect and spirit which it is the purpose of the First Amendment to our Constitution to reverse from all official control.

The decision of this Court in *Minersville School District v. Gobitis* and the holdings of those few *per curiam* decisions which preceded and foreshadowed it are overruled, and the judgment enjoining enforcement of the West Virginia Regulation is affirmed.

Affirmed.

* * *

Mr. Justice Frankfurter, dissenting.

One who belongs to the most vilified and persecuted minority in history is not likely to be insensible to the freedoms guaranteed by our Constitution. Were my purely personal attitude relevant I should wholeheartedly associate myself with the general libertarian views in the Court's opinion, representing as they do the thought and action of a lifetime. But as judges we are neither Jew nor Gentile, neither Catholic nor agnostic. We owe equal attachment to the Constitution and are equally bound by our judicial obligations whether we derive our citizenship from the earliest or the latest immigrants to these shores. As a member of this Court I am not justified in writing my private notions of policy into the Constitution, no matter how deeply I may cherish them or how mischievous I may deem their disregard. The duty of a judge who must decide which of two claims before the Court shall prevail, that of a State to enact and enforce laws within its general competence or that of an individual to refuse obedience because of the demands of his conscience, is not that of the ordinary person. It can never be emphasized too much that one's own opinion about the wisdom or evil of a law should be excluded altogether when one is doing one's duty on the bench. The only opinion of our own even looking in that direction that is material is our opinion whether legislators could in reason have enacted such a law. In the light of all the circumstances, including the history of this question in this Court, it would require more daring than I possess to deny that reasonable legislators could have taken the action which is before us for review. Most unwillingly, therefore, I must differ from my brethren with regard to legislation like this. I cannot bring my mind to believe that the "liberty" secured by the Due Process Clause gives this Court authority to deny to the State of West Virginia the attainment of that which we all recognize as a legitimate legislative end, namely, the promotion of good citizenship, by employment of the means here chosen.

Not so long ago we were admonished that "the only check upon our own exercise of power is our own sense of self-restraint. For the removal of unwise laws from the statute books appeal lies, not to the courts, but to the ballot and to the processes of democratic government." . . .We have been told that generalities do not decide concrete cases. But the intensity with which a general principle is held may determine a particular issue, and whether we put first things first may decide a specific controversy.

The admonition that judicial self-restraint alone limits arbitrary exercise of our authority is relevant every time we are asked to nullify legislation. The Constitution does not give us greater veto power when dealing with one phase of "liberty" than with another, or when dealing with grade school regulations than with college regulations that offend conscience. . . . Judicial self-restraint is equally necessary whenever an exercise of political or legislative power is challenged. There is no warrant in the constitutional basis of this Court's authority for attributing different roles to it depending upon the nature of the challenge to the legislation. Our power does not vary according to the particular provision of the Bill of Rights which is invoked. The right not to have property taken without just compensation has, so far as the scope of judicial power is concerned, the same constitutional dignity as the right to be protected against unreasonable searches and seizures, and the latter has no less claim than freedom of the press or freedom of speech or religious freedom. In no instance is this Court the primary protector of the particular liberty that is invoked. This Court has recognized, what hardly could be denied, that all the provisions of the first ten Amendments are "specific" prohibitions. . . . But each specific Amendment, in so far as embraced within the Fourteenth Amendment, must be equally respected, and the function of this Court does not differ in passing on the constitutionality of legislation challenged under different Amendments.

When Mr. Justice Holmes, speaking for this Court, wrote that "it must be remembered that legislature are ultimate guardians of the liberties and welfare of the people in quite as great a degree as the courts". . . he went to the very essence of our constitutional system and the democratic conception of our society. . . . He was stating the comprehensive judicial duty and role of this Court in our constitutional scheme whenever legislation is sought to be nullified on any ground, namely, that responsibility for legislation lies with legislatures, answerable as they are directly to the people, and this Court's only and very narrow function is to determine whether within the broad grant of authority vested in legislatures they have exercised a judgment for which reasonable justification can be offered.

The framers of the federal Constitution might have chosen to assign an active share in the process of legislation to this Court. . . . But the framers of the Constitution denied such legislative powers to the federal judiciary. They chose instead to insulate the judiciary from the legislative function. They did not grant to this Court supervision over legislation.

* * *

The precise scope of the question before us defines the limits of the constitutional power that is in issue. The State of West Virginia requires all pupils to share in the salute to the flag as part of school training in citizenship. The present action is one to enjoin the enforcement of this requirement by those in school attendance. We have not before us any attempt by the State to punish disobedient children or visit penal consequences on their parents. All that is in question is the right of the state to compel participation in this exercise by those who choose to attend the public schools.

We are not reviewing merely the action of a local school board. The flag salute requirement in this case comes before us with the full authority of the State of West Virginia. We are in fact passing judgment on "the power of the State as a whole". . . .To suggest that we are here concerned with the heedless action of some village tyrants is to distort the augustness of the constitutional issue and the reach of the consequences of our decision.

Under our constitutional system the legislature is charged solely with civil concerns of society. If the avowed or intrinsic legislative purpose is either to promote or to discourage some religious community or creed, it is clearly within the constitutional restrictions imposed on legislatures and cannot stand. But it by no means follows that legislative power is wanting whenever a general nondiscriminatory civil regulation in fact touches conscientious scruples or religious beliefs of an individual or a group. Regard for such scruples or beliefs undoubtedly presents one of the most reasonable claims for the exertion of legislative accommodation. It is, of course, beyond our power to rewrite the state's requirement, by providing exemptions for those who do not wish to participate in the flag salute or by making some other accommodations to meet their scruples. That wisdom might suggest the making of such accommodations and that school administration would not find it too difficult to make them and yet maintain the ceremony for those not refusing to conform, is outside our province to suggest. Tact, respect, and generosity toward variant views will always commend themselves to those charged with the duties of legislation so as to achieve a maximum of good will and to require a minimum of unwilling submission to a general law. But the real question is, who is to make such accommodations, the courts or the legislature?

This is no dry, technical matter. It cuts deep into one's conception of the democratic process. . . . A court . . . can only say "This or that law is void." It cannot modify or qualify, it cannot make exceptions to a general requirement. And it strikes down not merely for a day. . . . When we are dealing with the Constitution of the United States, and more particularly with the great safeguards of the Bill of Rights, we are dealing with principles of liberty and justice "so rooted in the traditions and conscience of our people as to be ranked as fundamental"—something without which "a fair and enlightened system of justice would be impossible". . .We have been told that such compulsions [conscientious scruples] override religious scruples only as to major concerns of the state. But the determination of what is major and what is minor itself raises questions of policy. . . . Judges should be very diffident in setting their judgment against that of a state in determining what is and what is not a major concern, what means are appropriate to proper ends, and what is the total social cost in striking the balance of imponderables.

What one can say with assurance is that the history out of which grew constitutional provisions for religious equality and the writings of the great exponents of religious freedom—Jefferson, Madison, John Adams, Benjamin Franklin—are totally wanting in justification for a claim by dissidents of exceptional immunity from civic measures of general applicability, measures not in fact disguised assaults upon such dissident views. The great leaders of the American Revolution were determined to remove political support from every religious establishment. . . . But Jefferson and the others also knew that minorities may disrupt society. It never would have occurred to them to write into the Constitution the subordination of the general civil authority of the state to sectarian scruples.

The constitutional protection of religious freedom terminated disabilities, it did not create new privileges. It gave religious equality, not civil immunity. . . .

* * *

The essence of the religious freedom guaranteed by our Constitution is therefore this: no religion shall either receive the state's support or incur its hostility. Religion is outside the sphere of political government . . . . The validity of secular laws cannot be measured by their conformity to religious doctrines. It is only in a theocratic state that ecclesiastical doctrines measure legal right or wrong.

An act compelling profession of allegiance to a religion, no matter how subtly or tenuously promoted, is bad. But an act promoting good citizenship and national allegiance is within the domain of governmental authority and is therefore to be judged by the same considerations of power and of constitutionality as those involved in the many claims of immunity from civil obedience because of religious scruples.

That claims are pressed on behalf of sincere religious convictions does not of itself establish their constitutional validity. Nor does waving the banner of religious freedom relieve us from examining into the power we are asked to deny the states. Otherwise the doctrine of separation of church and state, so cardinal in the history of this nation and for the liberty of our people, would mean not the disestablishment of a state church but the establishment of all churches and of all religious groups.

* * *

That which to the majority may seem essential for the welfare of the state may offend the consciences of a minority. But, so long as no inroads are made upon the actual exercise of religion by the minority, to deny the political power of the majority to enact laws concerned with civil matters, simply because they may offend the consciences of a minority, really means that the consciences of a minority are more sacred and more enshrined in the Constitution that the consciences of a majority.

We are told that symbolism is a dramatic but primitive way of communicating ideas. Symbolism is inescapable. Even the most sophisticated live by symbols. But it is not for this Court to make psychological judgments as to the effectiveness of a particular symbol in inculcating concededly indispensable feelings, particularly if the state happens to see fit to utilize the symbol that represents our heritage and our hopes. . . .

* * *

Of course patriotism cannot be enforced by the flag salute. But neither can the liberal spirit be enforced by judicial invalidation of illiberal legislation. Our constant preoccupation with the constitutionality of legislation rather than with its wisdom tends to preoccupation of the American mind with a false value. The tendency of focusing attention on constitutionality is to make constitutionality synonymous with wisdom, to regard a law as all right if it is constitutional. Such an attitude is a great enemy of liberalism. Particularly in legislation affecting freedom of thought and freedom of speech much which should offend a free-spirited society is constitutional. Reliance for the most precious interests of civilization, therefore, must be found outside of their vindication in courts of law. Only a persistent positive translation of the faith of a free society into the convictions and habits and actions of a community is the ultimate reliance against unabated temptations to fetter the human spirit.

Source:
Supreme Court Reporter, Vol. 63, pp. 1,178–1,200.

Smith-Connally Anti-Strike Act, 1943

U.S. legislation sponsored by Representative Howard W. Smith of Virginia and Senator Thomas T. Connally of Texas and enacted on June 25, 1943, that authorized the president to seize any plant or industry in which a labor dispute might interfere with war production. Anyone promoting a strike after such seizure was subject to criminal prosecution, and unions were liable to damage suits if they failed to give 30 days' notice of intention to strike in war industries. The act was opposed by organized labor and was vetoed by President Franklin D. Roosevelt, but Congress overrode the veto. The president used the act in December 1943 to take temporary possession of U.S. railroads threatened by a strike. The law expired in 1947.

An Act
Relating to the use and operation by the United States of certain plants, mines, and facilities in the prosecution of the war, and preventing strikes, lock-outs, and stoppages of production, and for other purposes.

Be it enacted by the Senate and House of Representatives of the United States of America in Congress assembled, That this Act may be cited as the "War Labor Disputes Act" . . .

Power of President to Take Possession of Plants
Sec. 3. Section 9 of the Selective Training and Service Act of 1940 is hereby amended by adding at the end thereof the following new paragraph:

"The power of the President under the foregoing provisions of this section to take immediate possession of any plant upon a failure to comply with any such provisions, and the authority granted by this section for the use and operation by the United States or in its interests of any plant of which possession is so taken, shall also apply as hereinafter provided to any plant, mine, or facility equipped for the manufacture, production, or mining of any articles or materials which may be required for the war effort or which may be useful in connection therewith. Such power and authority may be exercised by the President through such department or agency of the Government as he may designate, and may be exercised with respect to any such plant, mine, or facility whenever the President finds, after investigation, and proclaims that there is an interruption of the operation of such plant, mine, or facility as a result of a strike or other labor disturbance, that the war effort will be unduly impeded or delayed by such interruption, and that the exercise of such power and authority is necessary to insure the operation of such plant, mine, or facility in the interest of the war effort: *Provided,* That whenever any such plant, mine, or facility has been or is hereafter so taken by reason of a strike, lock-out, threatened strike, threatened lock-out, work stoppage, or other cause, such plant, mine, or facility shall be returned to the owners thereof as soon as practicable, but in no event more than sixty days after the restoration of the productive efficiency thereof prevailing prior to the taking of possession thereof: *Provided further,* That possession of any plant, mine, or facility shall not be taken under authority of this section after the termination of hostilities in the present war, as proclaimed by the President, or after the termination of the War Labor Disputes Act; and the authority to operate any such plant, mine, or facility under the provisions of this section shall terminate at the end of six months after the termination of such hostilities as so proclaimed." . . .

Interference with Government Operation of Plants
Sec. 6. (a) Whenever any plant, mine, or facility is in the possession of the United States, it shall be unlawful for any person (1) to coerce, instigate, induce, conspire with, or encourage any person, to interfere, by lock-out, strike, slow-down, or other interruption, with the operation of such plant, mine, or facility, or (2) to aid any such lock-out, strike, slow-down, or other interruption interfering with the operation of such plant, mine, or facility by giving direction or guidance in the conduct of such interruption, or by providing funds for the conduct or direction thereof or for the payment of strike, unemployment, or other benefits to those participating therein. No individual shall be deemed to have violated the provisions of this section by reason only of his having ceased work or having refused to continue to work or to accept employment.

(b) Any person who willfully violates any provision of this section shall be subject to a fine of not more than $5,000, or to imprisonment for not more than one year, or both.

Source:
Statutes at Large, Vol. 57, pp. 163–169.

Teheran Conference Communiqué, 1943

Communiqué that was issued at the conclusion of the first war conference held by the leaders of the three major Allied forces in the capital of Iran from November 28 to December 1, 1943. The conference was attended by President Franklin D. Roosevelt of the United States, Prime Minister Winston Churchill of Great Britain, and Premier Joseph Stalin of the Soviet Union. The Teheran Declaration stated that the Allies reached "complete agreement as to the scope and timing of operations" that would defeat Nazi Germany. The three leaders promised to "express our determination that our nations shall work together in war and in the peace that will follow." Their common goal was to make a peace, which would "banish the scourge and terror of war for many generations." However, the grand words of the final communiqué told almost nothing about the actual agreements that were made by the Big Three at Teheran (Tehran). The second front would finally be opened by an Anglo-American invasion of western France (Operation Overlord) in the late spring of 1944. The USSR agreed to enter the war against Japan once Germany was defeated.

Declaration of the Three Powers:
We, the President of the United States, the Prime Minister of Great Britain, and the Premier of the Soviet Union, have met these four days past, in this, the Capital of our ally, Iran, and have shaped and confirmed our common policy.

We express our determination that our Nations shall work together in war and in the peace that will follow.

As to war—our military staffs have joined in our round-table discussions, and we have concerted our plans for the destruction of the German forces. We have reached complete agreement as to the scope and timing of the operations to be undertaken from the east, west, and south.

The common understanding which we have here reached guarantees that victory will be ours.

And as to peace—we are sure that our concord will win an enduring peace. We recognize fully the supreme responsibility resting upon us and all the United Nations to make a peace which will command the good will of the overwhelming mass of the peoples of the world and banish the scourge and terror of war for many generations.

With our diplomatic advisers we have surveyed the problems of the future. We shall seek the cooperation and active participation of all Nations, large and small, whose peoples in heart and mind are dedicated, as are our own peoples, to the elimination of tyranny and slavery, oppression and intolerance. We will welcome them, as they may choose to come, into a world family of democratic Nations.

No power on earth can prevent our destroying the German armies by land, their U-boats by sea, and their war plants from the air.

Our attack will be relentless and increasing.

Emerging from these cordial conferences we look with confidence to the day when all peoples of the world may live free lives, untouched by tyranny, and according to their varying desires and their own consciences.

We came here with hope and determination. We leave here, friends in fact, in spirit, and in purpose.

Signed: Roosevelt, Churchill, and Stalin.

Source:
Franklin D. Roosevelt. *The Public Papers and Addresses of Franklin D. Roosevelt*. New York: Random House, 1938–50.

Smith v. Allwright, 1944

U.S. Supreme Court decision issued on April 3, 1944, overturning a Texas Democratic Party policy that excluded black citizens from membership in the party and therefore prevented them from voting in the primary elections.

Previously, in *Guinn and Beal v. United States* (238 U.S. 347, [1915]) issued June 21, 1915, the U.S. Supreme Court declared the "grandfather clause" unconstitutional. The grandfather clause, a legal device used extensively in the South, exempted from various financial and educational voting requirements those whose fathers or grandfathers had voted before 1867; it effectively disenfranchised most blacks, whose ancestors had then been slaves. The test case arose from an attempt to include such a clause in the Oklahoma Constitution and was brought before the Supreme Court by the National Association for the Advancement of Colored People. The Court ruled that the clause violated the purpose and intent of the Fifteenth Amendment, which was to assure equal voting rights regardless of race, color, or previous condition of servitude. However, other laws, standards imposed by registrars, and economic and terrorist coercion continued to keep southern blacks from voting in significant numbers until the late 1960s.

The "white primary" was one such device. In Texas, as in all the former Confederate states, the Democratic primary was tantamount to election. Lonnie E. Smith, a black, challenged the policy, suing election judge S. E. Allwright on the grounds that Smith was excluded from voting in the primaries because of his race. Reversing its 1935 decision in *Grovey v. Townsend* (295 U.S. 45), the Supreme Court ruled that party primaries could not be considered private matters and that the party was acting as an agency of the state. The use of white primaries was therefore prohibited by the Fifteenth Amendment. The broader significance of the case comes from the Court's placing substance over form in determining voting rights, a concept that led directly to overturning other discriminatory legislation.

Future Supreme Court Justice Thurgood Marshall argued the case for the NAACP Legal and Education Fund. Although he is better known for arguing the landmark *Brown v. Board of Education* (347 U.S. 483 [1954]), Marshall considered *Smith v. Allwright* the most important case he argued. After *Allwright* legal actions to deny blacks the franchise had to be directed against individuals such as poll taxes (outlawed by the Twenty-fourth Amendment) and literacy tests (outlawed by the Voting Rights Act of 1965). By bringing primaries under federal aegis, it enabled the Department of Justice through the FBI to investigate primary voting rights violations.

Mr. Justice Reed delivered the opinion of the Court.

This writ of certiorari brings here for review a claim for damages in the sum of $5,000 on the part of petitioner, a Negro citizen of the 48th precinct of Harris County, Texas, for the refusal of respondents, election and associate election judges respectively of that precinct, to give petitioner a ballot or to permit him to cast a ballot in the primary election of July 27, 1940, for the nomination of Democratic candidates for the United States Senate and House of Representatives, and Governor and other state officers. The refusal is alleged to have been solely because of the race and color of the proposed voter.

The actions of respondents are said to violate Sections 31 and 43 of Title 8 of the United States Code, 8 U.S.C.A. Section 31 and 43, in that petitioner was deprived of rights secured by Sections 2 and 4 of Article I and the Fourteenth, Fifteenth and Seventeenth Amendments to the United States Constitution. The suit was filed in the District Court of the United States for the Southern District of Texas, which had jurisdiction under Judicial Code Section 24, subsection 14, 28 U.S.C.A. Section 41 (14).

The District Court denied the relief sought and the Circuit Court of Appeals quite properly affirmed its action on the authority of *Grovey v. Townsend*, 295 U.S. 45. . . . We granted the petition for certiorari to resolve a claimed inconsistency between the decision in the *Grovey* case and that of *United States v. Classic*, 313 U.S. 299. . . .

The State of Texas by its Constitution and statutes provides that every person, if certain other requirements are met which are not here in issue, qualified by residence in the district or county "shall be deemed a qualified elector." . . . Primary elections for United States Senators, Congressmen and state officers are provided for by Chapters Twelve and Thirteen of the statutes. Under these chapters, the Democratic Party was required to hold the primary which was the occasion of the alleged wrong to petitioner. . . .

The Democratic Party of Texas is held by the Supreme Court of that state to be a "voluntary association" . . .

* * *

The Democratic party on May 24, 1932, in a State Convention adopted the following resolution, which has not since been "amended, abrogated, annulled or avoided":

"Be it resolved that all white citizens of the State of Texas who are qualified to vote under the Constitution and laws of the State shall be eligible to membership in the Democratic party and, as such, entitled to participate in its deliberations." It was by virtue of this resolution that the respondents refused to permit the petitioner to vote.

[1] Texas is free to conduct her elections and limit her electorate as she may deem wise, save only as her action may be affected by the prohibitions of the United States Constitution or in conflict with powers delegated to and exercised by the National Government. The Fourteenth Amendment forbids a state from making or enforcing any law which abridges the privileges or immunities of citizens of the United States and the Fifteenth Amendment specifically interdicts any denial or abridgment by a state of the right of citizens to vote on account of color. Respondents appeared in the District Court and the Circuit Court of Appeals and defended on the ground that the Democratic party of Texas is a voluntary organization with members banded together for the purpose of selecting individuals of the group representing the common political beliefs as candidates in the general election. As such a voluntary organization, it was claimed, the Democratic party is free to select its own membership and limit to whites participation in the party primary. Such action, the answer asserted, does not violate the Fourteenth, Fifteenth or Seventeenth Amendment as officers of government cannot be chosen at primaries and the Amendments are applicable only to general elections where governmental officers are actually elected. Primaries, it is said, are political party affairs, handled by party not governmental officers. . . .

The right of a Negro to vote in the Texas primary has been considered heretofore by this Court. The first case was *Nixon v. Herndon*, 273 U.S. 536, . . . declared "in no event shall a Negro be eligible to participate in a Democratic party primary election . . . in the State of Texas." Nixon was refused the right to vote in a Democratic primary and brought a sought for damages against the election officers. . . . Without consideration of the Fifteenth

[Amendment], this Court held that the action of Texas in denying the ballot to Negroes by statute was in violation of the equal protection clause of the Fourteenth Amendment and reversed the dismissal of the suit.

The legislature of Texas reenacted the article but gave the State Executive Committee of a party the power to prescribe the qualifications of its members for voting or other participation. This article remains in the statues. The State Executive Committee of the Democratic party adopted a resolution that white Democrats and none other might participate in the primaries of that party. Nixon was refused again the privilege of voting in a primary and again brought suit for damages. . . . This Court again reversed the dismissal of the suit for the reason that the Committee action was deemed to be State and invalid as discriminatory under the Fourteenth Amendment. The test was said to be whether the Committee operated as representative of the State in the discharge of the State's authority. . . . The question of the inherent power of a political party in Texas "without restraint by any law to determine its own membership" was left open.

In *Grovey v. Townsend* . . . this Court had before it another suit for damages for the refusal in a primary of a county clerk, a Texas officer with only public functions to perform, to furnish petitioner, a Negro, an absentee ballot. The refusal was solely on the ground of race.

This case differed from *Nixon v. Condon,* supra, in that a state convention of the Democratic party had passed the resolution of May 24, 1932, hereinbefore quoted. . . . The managers of the primary election were therefore declare not to be state officials in such sense that their action was state action. A state convention of a party was said not to be an organ of the state. This Court went on to announce that to deny a vote in a primary was a mere refusal of party membership with which "the state need have no concern" . . . Consequently, there was found no ground for holding that the county clerk's refusal of a ballot because of racial ineligibility for party membership denied the petitioner any right under the Fourteenth or Fifteenth Amendments.

Since *Grovey v. Townsend* and prior to the present suit, no case from Texas involving primary elections has been before this Court. We did decide, however, *United States v. Classic*. . . . We there held that Section 4 of Article I of the Constitution authorized Congress to regulate primary as well as general elections. . . . Consequently, in the *Classic* case, we upheld the applicability to frauds in a Louisiana primary of . . . the Criminal Code, 18 U.S.C.A. Sections 51, 52. Thereby corrupt acts of election officers were subjected to Congressional sanctions because that body had power to protect rights to Federal suffrage by the Constitution in primary as in general elections. . . . This decision depended, too, on the determination that under the Louisiana statutes the primary was a part of the procedure for choice of Federal officials. By this decision the doubt as to whether or not such primaries were a part of "elections" subject to Federal control . . . was erased. The Nixon cases were decided under the equal protection clause of the Fourteenth Amendment without a determination of the status of the primary as a part of the electoral process. The exclusion of Negroes from the primaries by action of the State was held invalid under that Amendment. The fusing by the *Classic* case of the primary and general elections, into a single instrumentality for choice of officers has a definite bearing on the permissibility under the Constitution of excluding Negroes from primaries. This is not to say that the *Classic* case cuts directly into the rationale of *Grovey v. Townsend*. This latter case was not mentioned in the opinion. *Classic* bears upon *Grovey v. Townsend* not because exclusion of Negroes from primaries is any more or less state action by reason of the unitary character of the electoral process but because the recognition of the place of the primary in the electoral scheme makes clear that state delegation to party of the power to fix the qualifications of primary elections is delegation of a state function that may make the party's action the action of the state. . . . As the Louisiana statutes for holding primaries are similar to those of Texas, our ruling in *Classic* as to the unitary character of the electoral process calls for a reexamination as to whether or not the exclusion of Negroes from a Texas party primary was state action.

The statutes of Texas relating to primaries and the resolution of the Democratic party of Texas extending the privileges of membership to white citizens only are the same in substance and effect today as they were when *Grovey v. Townsend* was decided by a unanimous Court. The question as to whether the exclusionary action of the party was the action of the State persists as the determinative factor. . . .

[2] It may now be taken as a postulate that the right to vote in such a primary for the nomination of candidates without discrimination by the State, like the right to vote in a general election, is a right secured by the Constitution . . . By the terms of the Fifteenth Amendment that right may not be abridged by any state on account of race. Under our Constitution the great privilege of the ballot may not be denied a man by the State because of his color.

[3] We are thus brought to an examination of the qualifications for Democratic primary electors in Texas, to determine whether state action or private action has excluded Negroes from participation. Despite Texas' decision that the exclusion is produced by private or party action. . . Federal courts must for themselves appraise the facts leading to that conclusion. It is only by the performance of this obligation that a final and uniform interpretation can be given to the Constitution, the "supreme Law of the Land." . . . Texas requires electors in a primary

to pay a poll tax. Every person who does so pay and who has the qualifications of age and residence is an acceptable voter for the primary. . . . No convention may place in platform or resolution any demand for specific legislation without endorsement of such legislation by the voters in a primary. Texas thus directs the selection of all party officers.

Primary elections are conducted by the party under state statutory authority. . . . These party committees or the state convention certify the party's candidates to the appropriate officers for inclusion on the official ballot for the general election. No name which has not been so certified may appear upon the ballot for the general election as a candidate of a political party. No other name may be printed on the ballot which has not been placed in nomination by qualified voters who must take oath that they did not participate in a primary for the selection of a candidate for the office for which the nomination is made.

The state courts are given exclusive original jurisdiction of contested elections and of mandamus proceedings to compel party officers to perform their statutory duties.

[4, 5] We think that this statutory system for the selection of party nominees for inclusion on the general election ballot makes the party which is required to follow these legislative directions an agency of the state in so far as it determines the participants in a primary election. The party takes its character as a state agency from the duties imposed upon it by state statutes; the duties do not become matters of private law because they are performed by a political party. The plan of the Texas primary follows substantially that of Louisiana, with the exception that in Louisiana the state pays the cost of the primary while Texas assesses the cost against candidates. In numerous instances, the Texas statutes fix or limit the fees to be charged. Whether paid directly by the state or through state requirements, it is state action which compels. When primaries become a part of the machinery for choosing officials, state and national, as they have here, the same tests to determine the character of discrimination or abridgement should be applied to the primary as are applied to the general election. If the state requires a certain electoral procedure, prescribes a general election ballot made up of party nominees so chosen and limits the choice of the electorate in general elections for state offices, practically speaking, to those whose names appear on such a ballot, it endorses, adopts and enforces the discrimination against Negroes, practiced by a party entrusted by Texas law with the determination of the qualifications of participants in the primary. This is state action within the meaning of the Fifteenth Amendment. . . .

[6] The United States is a constitutional democracy. Its organic law grants to all citizens a right to participate in the choice of elected officials without restriction by any state because of race. This grant to the people of the opportunity for choice is not to be nullified by a state through casting its electoral process in a form which permits a private organization to practice racial discrimination in the election. Constitutional rights would be of little value if they could be thus indirectly denied. . . . .

[7, 8] The privilege of membership in a party may be, as this Court said in *Grovey v. Townsend*, . . . no concern of a state. But when, as here, that privilege is also the essential qualification for voting in a primary to select nominees for a general election, the state makes the action of the party the action of the state. In reaching this conclusion we are not unmindful of the desirability of continuity of decision in constitutional questions. However, when convinced of former error, this Court has never felt constrained to follow precedent. In constitutional questions, where correction depends upon amendment and not upon legislative action this Court throughout its history has freely exercised its power to reexamine the basis of its constitutional decisions. This has long been accepted practice, and this practice has continued to this day. This is particularly true when the decision believed erroneous is the application of a constitutional principle rather than an interpretation of the Constitution to extract the principle itself. Here we are applying, contrary to the recent decision in *Grovey v. Townsend*, the well established principle of the Fifteenth Amendment, forbidding the abridgement by a state of a citizen's right to vote. *Grovey v. Townsend* is overruled.

Judgment reversed.

Source:

Supreme Court Reporter, Vol. 64, pp. 757–768.

General Dwight D. Eisenhower, If D Day Fails, 1944

One of the most dramatic events of World War II was Operation Overlord, the invasion of western Europe by more than 14,000 Allied troops (mostly Americans) on the beaches near Cherbourg in Normandy beginning June 6, 1944, D Day. The invasion involved more than 5,000 vessels, 11,000 airplanes, and 175,000 men, who left from England the night before. To keep plans for this gigantic invasion from the Germans, who had occupied France, the Allies set up a parallel but totally fictional invasion force that was to land in Calais under the supposed direction of a real general, George Patton. The ruse worked, and the Germans sent their best divisions to Calais. However, they also had a formidable force in Normandy. British and American paratroopers along with several thousand dummy paratroopers preceded the seaborne force, which also served to confuse the Germans. Nevertheless, the Germans met the landing parties with heavy gunfire and artillery. By the end of the first day, the Allies controlled five beaches but casualties included more than 6,000 Americans, 3,000 British, and almost 1,000 Canadians.

Considering the possibility that the invasion would fail, General Dwight D. Eisenhower, who was in charge of Overlord, penned this note a few hours after giving the order to begin the operation. In his haste or trepidation he misdated the document July 5 instead of June 5. Fortunately, the note was not needed. But the European war would continue for another 11 months before the Germans surrendered.

Our landings in the Cherbourg-Havre area have failed to gain a satisfactory foothold and I have withdrawn the troops. My decision to attack at this time and place was based upon the best information available. The troops, the air and the Navy did all that Bravery [sic] and devotion to duty could do. If any blame or fault attaches to the attempt it is mine alone. July 5

Source:

National Archives and Records Administration, Dwight D. Eisenhower Library, Abilene, Kansas. Available on-line. URL: http://www.archives.gov/exhibit_hall/american_originals_iv/images/d_day/eisenhower_note.html. Accessed January 2004.

GI Bill of Rights, 1944

U.S. legislation enacted on June 22, 1944, authorizing economic and educational assistance for veterans of World War II. (A veteran or member of the U.S. armed forces is called a GI, an abbreviation of "government issue.") The law provided low-interest, federally guaranteed mortgages for the purchase of new homes, farms, and businesses; allowed substantial unemployment benefits for up to one year; provided assistance to returning veterans in finding jobs; and gave educational and vocational subsidies for up to four years of college, allowing up to $500 a year for tuition and books and $50 a month as a stipend. It also authorized aid for veterans' hospitals and vocational rehabilitation.

This was possibly the most influential economic and social act of the century. Some 12 million veterans were able to attain college and graduate degrees qualifying them for higher paying jobs and/or to purchase homes giving them a capital base for their future and spurring the move to suburbia. Without detracting from deserving veterans it should be noted that the GI Bill not only helped produce the general prosperity of the 1950s and 1960s, it helped increase the disparity between those who benefited and those who did not. The armed services had racial and gender quotas, and some positions filled primarily or exclusively by women or racial minorities did not qualify for the GI Bill or other veterans' benefits.

An Act

To provide Federal Government aid for the readjustment in civilian life of returning World War II veterans.

Be it enacted by the Senate and House of Representatives of the United States of America in Congress assembled, That this Act may be cited as the "Servicemen's Readjustment Act of 1944."

Title I

Chapter I—Hospitalization, Claims, and Procedures

Sec. 100. The Veterans' Administration is hereby declared to be an essential war agency and entitled, second only to the War and Navy Departments, to priorities in personnel, equipment, supplies, and material under any laws, Executive orders, and regulations pertaining to priorities, and in appointments of personnel from civil-service registers the Administrator of Veterans' Affairs is hereby granted the same authority and discretion as the War and Navy Departments and the United States Public Health Service: Provided, That the provisions of this section as to priorities for materials shall apply to any State institution to be built for the care or hospitalization of veterans.

Sec. 101. The Administrator of Veterans' Affairs and the Federal Board of Hospitalization are hereby authorized and directed to expedite and complete the construction of additional hospital facilities for war veterans, and to enter into agreements and contracts for the use by or transfer to the Veterans' Administration of suitable Army and Navy hospitals after termination of hostilities in the present war or after such institutions are no longer needed by the armed services; and the Administrator of Veterans' Affairs is hereby authorized and directed to establish necessary . . . subordinate offices in centers of population where there is no Veterans' Administration facility, or where such a facility is not readily available or accessible. . .

* * *

Chapter III—Reviewing Authority

* * *

Sec. 301. The Secretary of War and the Secretary of the Navy, after conference with the Administrator of Veterans' Affairs, are authorized and directed to establish in the War and Navy Departments, respectively, boards of review composed of five members each, whose duties shall be to review, the type and nature of [a former officer or enlisted man or woman's] discharge or dismissal, except a discharge or dismissal by reason of the sentence of a general court martial. Such review shall be based upon all available records of the service department relating to the person requesting such review, and such other evidence as may be presented by such person. Witnesses shall be permitted to present testimony either in person or by affidavit and the person requesting review shall be allowed to appear before such board in person or by counsel. . . . Such board shall have authority, except in the case of a discharge or dismissal by reason of the sentence of a general court martial, to change, correct, or modify any discharge or dismissal, and to issue a new discharge in accord with the facts presented to the board . . . . the findings thereof to be final subject only to review by the Secretary of War or the Secretary of the Navy, respectively. . . .

Sec. 302. (a) The Secretary of War, the Secretary of the Navy, and the Secretary of the Treasury are authorized and directed to establish, from time to time, boards of review composed of five commissioned officers, two of whom shall be selected from the Medical Corps of the Army or Navy, or from the Public Health Service, as the case may be. It shall be the duty of any such board to review, at the request of any officer retired or released to inactive service, without pay, for physical disability pursuant to the decision of a retiring board, the findings and decision of such retiring board. Such review shall be based upon all available service records relating to the officer requesting such review, and such other evidence as may be presented by such officer. Witnesses shall be permitted to present testimony. . . . The proceedings and decision of each such board of review . . . shall be transmitted to the Secretary of War, the Secretary of Navy, or the Secretary of the Treasury, as the case may be, and shall be laid by him before the President for his approval or disapproval and orders in the case.

* * *

Title II

Chapter IV—Education of Veterans

* * *

"Part VIII

"1. Any person who served in the active military or naval service on or after September 16, 1940, and prior to the termination of the present war, and who shall have been discharged or released therefrom under conditions other than dishonorable, and whose education or training was impeded, delayed, interrupted, or interfered with by reason of his entrance into the service, or who desires a refresher or retraining course, and who either shall have served ninety days or more, exclusive of any period he was assigned for a course of education or training under the Army specialized training program or the Navy college training program, which course was a continuation of his civilian course and was pursued to completion, or as a cadet or midshipman at one of the service academies, or shall have been discharged or released from active service by reason of an actual service-incurred injury or disability, shall be eligible for and entitled to receive education or training under this part. . . . And provided further, That any such person who was not over 25 years of age at the time he entered the service shall be deemed to have had his education or training impeded, delayed, interrupted, or interfered with.

"2. Any such eligible person shall be entitled to education or training, or a refresher or retraining course, at an approved educational or training institution, for a period of one year (or the equivalent thereof in continuous part-time study), or for such lesser time as may be required for the course of instruction chosen by him. Upon satisfactory completion of such course of education or training, according to the regularly prescribed standards and practices of the institutions, except a refresher or retraining course, such person shall be entitled to an additional period or periods of education or training, not to exceed the time such person was in the active service or on after September 16, 1940, and before the termination of the war, exclusive of any period he was assigned for a course of education or training under the Army specialized training program or the Navy college training program, which course was a continuation of his civilian course and was pursued to completion, or as a cadet or midshipman at one of the service academies, but in no event shall the total period of education or training exceed four years: Provided, That his work continues to be satisfactory throughout the period, according to the regularly prescribed standards and practices of the institution. . . .

"3. Such person shall be eligible for and entitled to such course of education or training as the may elect, and at any approved educational or training institution at which he chooses to enroll, whether or not located in the State in which he resides, which will accept or retain him as a student or trainee in any field or branch of knowledge which such institution finds him qualified to undertake or pursue: Provided, That, for reasons satisfactory to the Administrator, he may change a course of instruction: And provided further, That any such course of education or training may be discontinued at any time, if it is found by the Administrator that, according to the regularly prescribed standards and practices of the institution, the conduct or progress of such person is unsatisfactory.

* * *

5. The Administrator shall pay to the educational or training institution, for each person enrolled in full time or part time course of education or training, the customary

cost of tuition, and such laboratory, library, health, infirmary, and other similar fees as are customarily charged, and may pay for books, supplies, equipment, and other necessary expenses, exclusive of board, lodging, other living expenses, and travel, as are generally required for the successful pursuit and completion of the course by other students in the institution: Provided, That in no event shall such payments, with respect to any person, exceed $500 for an ordinary school year: Provided further, That no payments shall be made to institutions, business or other establishments furnishing apprentice training on the job: And provided further, That if any such institution has no established tuition fee, or if its established tuition fee shall be found by the Administrator to be inadequate compensation to such institution for furnishing such education or training, he is authorized to provide for the payment, with respect to any such person, of such fair and reasonable compensation as will not exceed $500 for an ordinary school year.

"6. While enrolled in and pursuing a course under this part, such person, upon application to the Administrator, shall be paid a subsistence allowance of $50 per month, if without a dependent or dependents, or $75 per month, if he has a dependent or dependents, including regular holidays and leave not exceeding thirty days in a calendar year. Such person attending a course on a part-time basis, and such person receiving compensation for productive labor performed as part of their apprentice or other training on the job at institutions, business or other establishments, shall be entitled to receive such lesser sums, if any, as subsistence or dependency allowances, as may be determined by the Administrator: Provided, That any such person eligible under this part, and within the limitations thereof, may pursue such full time or part-time course or courses as he may elect, without subsistence allowance.

* * *

"8. No department, agency, or officer of the United States, in carrying out the provisions of this part, shall exercise any supervision or control, whatsoever, over any State educational agency, or State apprenticeship agency, or any educational or training institutions: Provided, That nothing in this section shall be deemed to prevent any department, agency, or officer of the United States from exercising any supervision or control which such department, agency, or officer is authorized, by existing provisions of law, to exercise over any Federal educational or training institution, or to prevent the furnishing of education or training under this part in any institution over which supervision or control is exercised by such other department, agency, or officer under authority of existing provisions of law.

* * *

"11. As used in this part, the term 'educational or training institutions' shall include all public or private elementary, secondary, and other schools furnishing education for adults, business schools and colleges, scientific and technical institutions, colleges, vocational schools, junior colleges, teachers colleges, normal schools, professional schools, universities, and other educational institutions, and shall also include business or other establishments providing apprentice or other training on the job, including those under the supervision of an approved college or university or any State department of education, or any State apprenticeship agency or State board of vocational education, or any State apprenticeship council or the Federal Apprentice Training Service established in accordance with Public, Numbered 308, Seventy-fifth Congress, or any agency in the executive branch of the Federal Government authorized under other laws to supervise such training."

* * *

Title III—Loans for the Purchase or Construction of Homes, Farms, and Business Property

Chapter V—General Provisions for Loans

Sec. 500. (a) Any person who shall have served in the active military or naval service of the United States at any time on or after September 16, 1940, and prior to the termination of the present war and who shall have been discharged or released therefrom under conditions other than dishonorable after active service of ninety days or more, or by reason of an injury or disability incurred in service in line of duty, shall be eligible for the benefits of this title. Any such veteran may apply within two years after separation from the military or naval forces, or two years after termination of the war, whichever is the later date, but in no event more than five years after the termination of the war, to the Administrator of Veterans' Affairs for the guaranty by the Administrator of not to exceed 50 per centum of a loan or loans for any of the purposes specified . . . That the aggregate amount guaranteed shall not exceed $2,000. If the Administrator finds that the veteran is eligible for the benefits of this title and that the loan applied for appears practicable, the Administrator shall guarantee the payment of the part thereof as set forth in this title.

* * *

(c) Loans guaranteed by the Administrator under this title shall be payable under such terms and conditions as may be approved by the Administrator: Provided, That the liability under the guaranty, within the limitations of this title, shall decrease or increase pro rata with any decrease or increase of the amount of the unpaid portion of the obligation: Provided further, That loans guaranteed by the Administrator shall bear interest at a rate not exceeding 4 per centum per annum and shall be payable in full in not more than twenty years. The Administrator is authorized and directed to guarantee loans to veterans subject to the provisions of this title on approved applications made to persons, firms, associations, and corporations and to governmental agencies and corporations, either State or Federal.

Purchase or Construction of Homes

Sec. 501. (a) Any application made by a veteran under this title for the guaranty of a loan to be used in purchasing residential property or in constructing a dwelling on unimproved property owned by him to be occupied as his home may be approved by the Administrator of Veterans' Affairs if he finds—

(1) that the proceeds of such loans will be used for payment for such property to be purchased or constructed by the veteran;

(2) that the contemplated terms of payment required in any mortgage to be given in part payment of the purchase price or the construction cost bear a proper relation to the veteran's present and anticipated income and expenses; and that the nature and condition of the property is such as to be suitable for dwelling purposes; and

(3) that the purchase price paid or to be paid by the veteran for such property or the construction cost, including the value of the unimproved lot, does not exceed the reasonable normal value thereof as determined by proper appraisal.

(b) Any application for the guaranty of a loan under this section for the purpose of making repairs, alterations, or improvements in, or paying delinquent indebtedness, taxes, or special assessments on, residential property owned by the veteran and used by him as his home, may be approved by the Administrator if he finds that the proceeds of such loan will be used for such purpose or purposes.

* * *

Purchase of Farms and Farm Equipment

Sec. 502. Any application made under this title for the guaranty of a loan to be used in purchasing any land, buildings, livestock, equipment, machinery, or implements, or in repairing, altering, or improving any buildings or equipment, to be used in farming operations conducted by the applicant, may be approved by the Administrator of Veterans' Affairs if he finds—

(1) that the proceeds for such loan will be used in payment for real or personal property purchased or to be purchased by the veteran, or for repairing, altering, or improving any buildings or equipment, to be used in bona fide farming operations conducted by him;

(2) that such property will be useful in and reasonably necessary for efficiently conducting such operations;

(3) that the ability and experience of the veteran, and the nature of the proposed farming operations to be conducted by him, are such that there is a reasonable likelihood that such operations will be successful; and

(4) that the purchase price paid or to be paid by the veteran for such property does not exceed the reasonable normal value thereof as determined by proper appraisal.

Purchase of Business Property

Sec. 503. Any application made under this title for the guaranty of a loan to be used in purchasing any business, land, buildings, supplies, equipment, machinery, or tools, to be used by the applicant in pursuing a gainful occupation (other than farming) may be approved by the Administrator of Veterans' Affairs if he finds—

(1) that the proceeds of such loan will be used for payment for real or personal property purchased or to be purchased by the veteran and used by him in the bona fide pursuit of such gainful occupation;

(2) that such property will be useful in and reasonably necessary for the efficient and successful pursuit of such occupation;

(3) that the ability and experience of the veteran, and the conditions under which he proposes to pursue such occupation, are such that there is a reasonable likelihood that he will be successful in the pursuit of such occupation; and

(4) that the purchase price paid or to be paid by the veteran for such property does not exceed the reasonable normal value thereof as determined by proper appraisal.

* * *

Title IV

CHAPTER IV—EMPLOYMENT OF VETERANS

Sec. 600. (a) In the enactment of the provisions of this title Congress declares as its intent and purpose that there shall be an effective job counseling and employment placement service for veterans, and that, to this end, policies shall be promulgated and administered, so as to provide for them the maximum of job opportunity in the field of gainful employment. For the purpose there is hereby created to cooperate with and assist the United States Employment Service. . . . a Veterans' Placement Service Board. . . . The Board shall determine all matters of policy relating to the administration of the Veterans' Employment Service of the United States Employment Service.

* * *

Sec. 601. The United States Employment Service shall assign to each of the States a veterans' employment representative, who shall be a veteran of the wars of the United States separated from active service under honorable conditions, who at the time of appointment shall have been a bona fide resident of the State for at least two years, and who shall be appointed, subject to the approval of the Board, in accordance with the civil-service laws. . . . He shall be administratively responsible to the Board, through its executive secretary, for the execution of the Board's veterans' placement policies through the public employment service in the State.

In cooperation with the public employment service staff in the state, he shall—

(a) be functionally responsible for the supervision of the registration of veterans in local employment offices for suitable types of employment and for placement of veterans in employment;

(b) assist in securing and maintaining current information as to the various types of available employment in public works and private industry or business;

(c) promote the interest of employers in employing veterans;

(d) maintain regular contact with employers and veterans' organizations with a view of keeping employers advised of veterans available for employment and veterans advised of opportunities for employment; and

(e) assist in every possible way in improving working conditions and the advancement of employment of veterans.

* * *

Title V

Chapter VII—Readjustment Allowances for Former Members of the Armed Forces Who Are Unemployed

Sec. 700. (a) Any person who shall have served in the active military or naval service of the United States at any time after September 16, 1940, and prior to the termination of the present war, and who shall have been discharged or released from active service under conditions other than dishonorable, after active service of ninety days or more, or by reason of an injury or disability incurred in service in line of duty, shall be entitled, in accordance with the provisions of this title and regulations issued by the Administrator of Veterans' Affairs pursuant thereto, to receive a readjustment allowance as provided herein for each week of unemployment, not to exceed a total of fifty-two weeks. . . .

(b) Such person shall be deemed eligible to receive an allowance for any week of unemployment if claim is made for such allowance and the Administrator finds with respect to such week that—

(1) the person is residing in the United States at the time of such claim;

(2) the person is completely unemployed, having performed no service and received no wages, or is partially unemployed in that services have been performed for less than a full work-week and the wages for the week are less than the allowance under this title plus $3;

(3) the person is registered with and continues to report to a public employment office, in accordance with its regulations;

(4) the person is able to work and available for suitable work

Chapter VIII—Disqualifications

* * *

(2) In determining under subsection (a) of this section the suitability of work, no work shall be deemed suitable for an individual if—

(A) the position offered is vacant due directly to a strike, lock-out, or other labor dispute; or

(B) the wages, hours, or other conditions of the work offered are substantially less favorable to him than those prevailing for similar work in the locality.

* * *

Chapter XI—Administration

Sec. 1100. (a) The Administrator of Veterans' Affairs is authorized to administer this title and shall, insofar as possible, utilize existing facilities and services of Federal and State departments or agencies on the basis of mutual agreements with such departments or agencies. Such agreements shall provide for the filing of claims for readjustment allowances with the Administrator through established public employment offices and State unemployment-compensation agencies. Such agencies, through agreement, shall also be utilized in the processing, adjustment, and determination of such claims and the payment of such allowances. To facilitate the carrying out of agreements with State departments or agencies and to assist in the discharge of the Administrator's duties under this title, a representative of the Administrator, who shall be a war veteran separated from active service under honorable conditions and who at the time of appointment shall have been a bona fide resident of the State for at least two years, shall be located in each participating State department or agency.

(b) The Administrator, consistent with the provisions of this title, shall prescribe such rules and regulations and require such records and reports as he may find necessary to carry out its purposes: Provided, however, That cooperative rules and regulations relating to the performance by Federal or State departments, or agencies, of functions under agreements made therewith may be made by the Administrator after consultation and advisement with representatives of such departments or agencies.

* * *

CHAPTER XIII—PENALTIES

Sec. 1300. Any claimant who knowingly accepts an allowance to which he is not entitled shall be ineligible to receive any further allowance under this title.

Sec. 1301. (a) Whoever, for the purpose of causing an increase in any allowance authorized under this title, or for the purpose of causing any allowance to be paid where none is authorized under this title, shall made or cause to be made any false statement or representation as to any wages paid or received, or whoever makes or causes to be made any false statement of a material fact in any claim for any allowance under this title, or whoever makes or causes to be made any false statement, representation, affidavit, or document in connection with such claim, shall be guilty of a misdemeanor and upon conviction thereof shall be fined not more than $1,000 or imprisoned for not more than one year, or both.

(b) Whoever shall obtain or receive any money, check, or allowance under this title, without being entitled thereto and with intent to defraud the United States, shall be punished by a fine of not more than $1,000 or by imprisonment for not more than one year, or both.

* * *

Title VI

* * *

Sec. 1503. A discharge or release from active service under conditions other than dishonorable shall be a prerequisite to entitlement to veterans' benefits provided by this Act or Public Law Numbered 2, Seventy-third Congress, as amended.

Sec. 1504. The Administrator shall transmit to the Congress annually a report of operations under this Act. If the Senate or the House of Representatives is not in session, such reports shall be transmitted to the Secretary of the Senate or the Clerk of the House of Representatives, as the case may be.

* * *

Approved June 22, 1944.

Source:

Statutes at Large, Vol. 58, pp. 284–301.

Korematsu v. United States, 1944

U.S. Supreme Court decision, issued on December 18, 1944, that upheld the constitutionality of the Japanese evacuation program established under Executive Order 9066 after Pearl Harbor. Fred Korematsu, an American-born citizen of Japanese ancestry, refused to obey the evacuation order on the grounds that it violated his Fifth Amendment rights to due process. In its 6-3 decision, the Court ruled that military authorities were justified in relocating people of Japanese descent without individual hearings because of national security needs. In dissent, Justice Frank Murphy criticized the evacuation program as "legalization of racism." In 1983, when Korematsu sued for vindication on a charge of "prosecutorial misconduct," a federal court vacated his conviction and erased his criminal record. The original decision, which has never been overturned, has resonated within the Arab-American community prior to and during the 1991 Gulf War and after the September 2001 terrorist attacks.

Previously, the U.S. Supreme Court had in *Hirabayashi* v. *United States* (320 U.S. 81) upheld a military curfew established on the West Coast after the Japanese attack on Pearl Harbor. Gordon Hirabayashi, an American-born citizen of Japanese ancestry, refused to obey the 8:00 P.M. to 6:00 A.M. curfew and the evacuation order imposed on Japanese Americans on the grounds that they constituted racial discrimination in violation of his Fifth Amendment right to due process. In its unanimous decision, the Court refused to consider the evacuation issue but justified the curfew as a temporary, emergency war measure. In 1983 Hirabayashi sued for vindication, charging "prosecutorial misconduct." In 1986 a federal district court struck down his conviction for refusing to obey the evacuation order but declined to reverse the curfew violation. The decision also discusses *Hirabayashi.*

The same month as *Korematsu*, the U.S. Supreme Court declared in *Ex Parte Endo* (323 U.S. 283) that the government could not detain in a relocation camp a Japanese American whose loyalty had been established. Misuye Endo, an American citizen of Japanese descent, had reported for internment, then challenged her detention by the War Relocation Authority. In a unanimous opinion, the Court granted her liberty, ruling that Congress had not authorized an indefinite detention program for Japanese Americans declared "loyal"; the Court did not rule on the constitutionality of the program in general.

In both *Hirabayashi* and *Korematsu* the Court noted that "we cannot reject as unfounded the judgment of the military authorities and of Congress that there were disloyal members of that population, whose number and strength could not be precisely and quickly ascertained." Unknown outside of the Department of Justice was a memorandum from FBI director J. Edgar Hoover to the attorney general regarding Executive Order 9066 stating that from its pre–Pearl Harbor investigations, the FBI had identified all those persons of Japanese,

German, and Italian descent it considered probable spies and saboteurs and that they were arrested on December 7 and 8, 1942.

The army ordered the release of all loyal Japanese Americans in January 1945.

Below are excerpts from the majority opinion by Justice Black and dissents by Justices Roberts and Murphy. Justice Frankfurter also concurred, and Justice Jackson also dissented.

Mr. Justice Black delivered the opinion of the Court.

The petitioner, an American citizen of Japanese descent, was convicted in a federal district court for remaining in San Leandro, California, a "Military Area," contrary to Civilian Exclusion Order No. 34 of the Commanding General of the Western Command, U.S. Army, which directed that after May 9, 1942, all persons of Japanese ancestry should be excluded from that area. No question was raised as to petitioner's loyalty to the United States. The Circuit Court of Appeals affirmed, and the importance of the constitutional question involved caused us to grant certiorari.

It should be noted, to begin with, that all legal restrictions which curtail the civil rights of a single racial group are immediately suspect. That is not to say that all such restrictions are unconstitutional. It is to say that courts must subject them to the most rigid scrutiny. Pressing public necessity may sometimes justify the existence of such restrictions; racial antagonism never can.

In the instant case prosecution of the petitioner was begun by information charging violation of an Act of Congress, of March 21, 1942 which provides that ". . . whoever shall enter, remain in, leave, or commit any act in any military area or military zone prescribed, under the authority of an Executive order of the President, by the Secretary of War, or by any military commander designated by the Secretary of War, contrary to the restrictions applicable to any such area or zone or contrary to the order of the Secretary of War or any such military commander, shall . . . be guilty of a misdemeanor and upon conviction shall be liable to a fine of not to exceed $5,000 or to imprisonment for not more than one year, or both, for each offense."

Exclusion Order No. 34, which the petitioner knowingly and admittedly violated was one of a number of military orders and proclamations, all of which were substantially based upon Executive Order No. 9066. That order, issued after we were at war with Japan, declared that "the successful prosecution of the war requires every possible protection against espionage and against sabotage to national-defense material, national-defense premises, and national-defense utilities. . . ."

One of the series of orders and proclamations, a curfew order, which like the exclusion order here was promulgated pursuant to Executive Order 9066, subjected all persons of Japanese ancestry in prescribed West Coast military areas to remain in their residences from 8 p.m. to 6 a.m. As is the case with the exclusion order here, that prior curfew order was designed as a "protection against espionage and against sabotage." In *Kiyoshi Hirabayashi v. United States* [320 U.S. 81] we sustained a conviction obtained for violation of the curfew order. The *Hirabayashi* conviction and this one thus rest on the same 1942 Congressional Act and the same basic executive and military orders, all of which orders were aimed at the twin dangers of espionage and sabotage.

The 1942 Act was attacked in the *Hirabayashi* case as an unconstitutional delegation of power; it was contended that the curfew order and other orders on which it rested were beyond the war powers of the Congress, the military authorities and of the President, as Commander in Chief of the Army; and finally that to apply the curfew order against none but citizens of Japanese ancestry amounted to a constitutionally prohibited discrimination solely on account of race. . . . We upheld the curfew order as an exercise of the power of the government to take steps necessary to prevent espionage and sabotage in an area threatened by Japanese attack.

In the light of the principles we announced in the *Hirabayashi* case, we are unable to conclude that it was beyond the war power of Congress and the Executive to exclude those of Japanese ancestry from the West Coast war area at the time they did. [Prior to this heads of household and single individuals were to report to "Assembly Centers" pursuant to relocation of all those of Japanese descent.] True, exclusion from the area in which one's home is located is a far greater deprivation than constant confinement to the home 8 p.m. to 6 a.m. Nothing short of apprehension by the proper military authorities of the gravest imminent danger to the public safety can constitutionally justify either. But exclusion from a threatened area, no less than curfew, has a definite and close relationship to the prevention of espionage and sabotage. The military authorities, charged with the primary responsibility of defending our shores, concluded that curfew provided inadequate protection and ordered exclusion. They did so . . . in accordance with Congressional authority to the military to say who should, and who should not, remain in the threatened areas.

In this case the petitioner challenges the assumptions upon which we rested our conclusions in the *Hirabayashi* case. He also urges that by May 1942, when Order No. 34 was promulgated, all danger of Japanese invasion of the West Coast had disappeared. After careful consideration of these contentions we are compelled to reject them.

Here, as in the *Hirabayashi* case we cannot reject as unfounded the judgment of the military authorities and of Congress that there were disloyal members of that population, whose number and strength could not be precisely and quickly ascertained. We cannot say that the war-making branches of the Government did not have ground for believing that in a critical hour such persons could not readily be isolated and separately dealt with, and constituted a menace to the national defense and safety, which demanded that prompt and adequate measures be taken to guard against it."

Like curfew, exclusion of those of Japanese origin was deemed necessary because of the presence of an unascertained number of disloyal members of the group, most of whom we have no doubt were loyal to this country. It was because we could not reject the finding of the military authorities that it was impossible to bring about an immediate segregation of the disloyal from the loyal that we sustained the validity of the curfew order as applying to the whole group. In the instant case, temporary exclusion of the entire group was rested by the military on the same ground. The judgment that exclusion of the whole group was for the same reason a military imperative answers the contention that the exclusion was in the nature of group punishment based on antagonism to those of Japanese origin. That there were members of the group who retained loyalties to Japan has been confirmed by investigations made subsequent to the exclusion. Approximately five thousand American citizens of Japanese ancestry refused to swear unqualified allegiance to the United States and to renounce allegiance to the Japanese Emperor, and several thousand evacuees requested repatriation to Japan.

We uphold the exclusion order as of the time it was made and when the petitioner violated it. In doing so, we are not unmindful of the hardships imposed by it upon a large group of American citizens. But hardships are part of war, and war is an aggregation of hardships. All citizens alike, both in and out of uniform, feel the impact of war in greater or lesser measure. Citizenship has its responsibilities as well as its privileges, and in time of war the burden is always heavier. Compulsory exclusion of large groups of citizens from their homes, except under circumstances of direst emergency and peril, is inconsistent with our basic governmental institutions. But when under conditions of modern warfare our shores are threatened by hostile forces, the power to protect must be commensurate with the threatened danger.

* * *

The Assembly Center was conceived as a part of the machinery for group evacuation. The power to exclude includes the power to do it by force if necessary. And any forcible measure must necessarily entail some degree of detention or restraint whatever method of removal is selected. But whichever view is taken, it results in holding that the order under which petitioner was convicted was valid.

. . . Our task would be simple, our duty clear, were this a case involving the imprisonment of a loyal citizen in a concentration camp because of racial prejudice. Regardless of the true nature of the assembly and relocation centers–and we deem it unjustifiable to call them concentration camps with all the ugly connotations that term implies–we are dealing specifically with nothing but an exclusion order. To cast this case into outlines of racial prejudice, without reference to the real military dangers which were presented, merely confuses the issue. Korematsu was not excluded from the Military Area because of hostility to him or his race. He was excluded because we are at war with the Japanese Empire, because the properly constituted military authorities feared an invasion of our West Coast and felt constrained to take proper security measures, because they decided that the military urgency of the situation demanded that all citizens of Japanese ancestry be segregated from the West Coast temporarily, and finally, because Congress, reposing its confidence in this time of war in our military leaders–as inevitably it must–determined that they should have the power to do just this. There was evidence of disloyalty on the part of some, the military authorities considered that the need for action was great, and time was short. We cannot–by availing ourselves of the calm perspective of hindsight–now say that at that time these actions were unjustified.

Affirmed.

Mr. Justice Roberts.

I dissent, because I think the indisputable facts exhibit a clear violation of Constitution rights.

. . . It is the case of convicting a citizen as a punishment for not submitting to imprisonment in a concentration camp, based on his ancestry, and solely because of his ancestry, without evidence or inquiry concerning his loyalty and good disposition towards the United States. If this be a correct statement of the facts disclosed by this record, and facts of which we take judicial notice, I need hardly labor the conclusion that Constitutional rights have been violated.

* * *

The petitioner . . . is a native of the United States of Japanese ancestry who, according to the uncontradicted evidence, is a loyal citizen of the nation.

A chronological recitation of events will make it plain that the petitioner's supposed offense did not, in truth, consist in his refusal voluntarily to leave the area which included his home in obedience to the order excluding him therefrom. . . .

. . . [Chronology]

May 3, 1942, General DeWitt issued Civilian Exclusion Order No. 34 providing that, after 12 o'clock May 8, 1942, all persons of Japanese ancestry, both alien and non-alien, were to be excluded from a described portion of Military Area No. 1, which included the County of Alameda, California. . . . The obvious purpose of the orders made, taken together, was to drive all citizens of Japanese ancestry into Assembly Centers within the zones of their residence, under pain of criminal prosecution.

. . . An Assembly Center was a euphemism for a prison. No person within such a center was permitted to leave except by Military Order.

In the dilemma that he dare not remain in his home, or voluntarily leave the area, without incurring criminal penalties, and that the only way he could avoid punishment was to go to an Assembly Center and submit himself to military imprisonment, the petitioner did nothing.

. . . We further know that, on March 18, 1942, the President had promulgated Executive Order No. 9102 establishing the War Relocation Authority under which so-called Relocation Centers, a euphemism for concentration camps, were established pursuant to cooperation between the military authorities of the Western Defense Command and the Relocation Authority, and that the petitioner has been confined either in an Assembly Center, within the zone in which he had lived or has been removed to a Relocation Center where, as the facts disclosed in *Ex parte Mitsuye Endo* demonstrate, he was illegally held in custody.

. . .The [Government's] opinion refers to the *Hirabayashi* case, supra, to show that this court has sustained the validity of a curfew order in an emergency.

The argument then is that exclusion from a given area of danger, while somewhat more sweeping than a curfew regulation, is of the same nature—a temporary expedient made necessary by a sudden emergency. . . . The liberty of every American citizen freely to come and to go must frequently, in the face of sudden danger, be temporarily limited or suspended. . . . But the facts . . . show that the exclusion was but a part of an over-all plan for forceable detention. This case cannot, therefore, be decided on any such narrow ground as the possible validity of a Temporary Exclusion Order. . . . To make the case turn on any such assumption is to shut our eyes to reality.

* * *

I would reverse the judgement of conviction.

Mr. Justice Murphy, dissenting.

This exclusion of "all persons of Japanese ancestry, both alien and non-alien," from the Pacific Coast area on a plea of military necessity in the absence of martial law ought not to be approved. Such exclusion goes over "the very brink of constitutional power" and falls into the ugly abyss of racism.

In dealing with matters relating to the prosecution and progress of a war, we must accord great respect and consideration to the judgments of the military authorities who are on the scene and who have full knowledge of the military facts. The scope of their discretion must, as a matter of necessity and common sense, be wide. And their judgements ought not to be overruled lightly by those whose training and duties ill-equip them to deal intelligently with matters so vital to the physical security of the nation.

At the same time, however, it is essential that there be definite limits to military discretion, especially where martial law has not been declared. Individuals must not be left impoverished of their constitutional rights on a plea of military necessity that has neither substance nor support. Thus, like other claims conflicting with the asserted constitutional rights of the individual, the military claim must subject itself to the judicial process of having its reasonableness determined and its conflicts with other interest reconciled. . . .

The judicial test of whether the Government, on a plea of military necessity, can validly deprive an individual of any of his constitutional rights is whether the deprivation is reasonably related to a public danger that is so "immediate, imminent, and impending" as not to admit of delay and not to permit the intervention of ordinary constitutional processes to alleviate the danger. Civilian Exclusion Order No. 34 . . . clearly does not meet that test. Being an obvious racial discrimination, the order deprives all those within its scope of the equal protection of the laws as guaranteed by the Fifth Amendment. It further deprives these individuals of their constitutional rights to live and work where they will, to establish a home where they choose and to move about freely. In excommunicating them without benefit of hearings, this order also deprives them of all their constitutional rights to procedural due process. Yet no reasonable relation to an "immediate, imminent, and impending" public danger is evident to support this racial restriction which is one of the most sweeping and complete deprivations of constitutional rights in the history of this nation in the absence of martial law.

It must be conceded that the military and naval situation in the spring of 1942 was such as to generate a very real fear of invasion of the Pacific Coast, accompanied by fears of sabotage and espionage in that area. The military command was therefore justified in adopting all reasonable means necessary to combat these dangers. In adjudging the military action taken in light of the then apparent dangers, we must not erect too high or too meticulous standards; it is necessary only that the action have some reasonable relation to the removal of the dangers of invasion, sabotage and espionage. But the exclusion, either temporarily or permanently, of all persons with Japanese blood in their veins has no such reasonable relation. And that relation is lacking because the exclusion order necessarily must rely for its reasonableness upon the assumption that all persons of Japanese ancestry may have a dangerous tendency to commit sabotage and espionage and to aid our Japanese enemy in other ways. It is difficult to believe that reason, logic of experience could be marshalled in support of such an assumption.

That this forced exclusion was the result in good measure of this erroneous assumption of racial guilt rather than bona fide military necessity is evidenced by the Commanding General's Final Report on the evacuation from the Pacific Coast area. In it he refers to all individuals of Japanese descent as "subversive," as belonging to "an enemy race" whose "racial strains are undiluted," and as constituting "over 112,000 potential enemies . . . at large today" along the Pacific Coast. In support of this blanket condemnation of all persons of Japanese descent, however, no reliable evidence is cited to show that such individuals were generally disloyal, or had generally so conducted themselves in this area as to constitute a special menace to defense installations or war industries, or had otherwise by their behavior furnished reasonable ground for their exclusion as a group.

Justification for the exclusion is sought, instead, mainly upon questionable racial and sociological grounds not ordinarily within the realm of expert military judgment, supplemented by certain semi-military conclusions drawn from an unwarranted use of circumstantial evidence. Individuals of Japanese ancestry are condemned because they are said to be "a large, unassimilated, tightly knit racial group, bound to an enemy nation by strong ties of race, culture, custom and religion." They are claimed to be given to "emperor worshipping ceremonies" and to "dual citizenship." Japanese language schools and allegedly pro-Japanese organizations are cited as evidence of possible group disloyalty, together with facts as to certain persons being educated and residing at length in Japan. It is intimated that many of these individuals deliberately resided "adjacent to strategic points," thus enabling them "to carry into execution a tremendous program of sabotage on a mass scale should any considerable number of them have been inclined to do so." The need for protective custody is also asserted. The report refers without identity to "numerous incidents of violence" as well as to other admittedly unverified or cumulative incidents. From this, plus certain other events not shown to have been connected with the Japanese Americans, it is concluded that the "situation was fraught with danger to the Japanese population itself" and that the general public "was ready to take matters into its own hands." . . .

The main reasons . . . for the forced evacuation, therefore, do not prove a reasonable relation between the group characteristics of Japanese Americans and the dangers of invasion, sabotage and espionage. The reasons appear, instead, to be largely an accumulation of much of the misinformation, half-truths and insinuations that for years have been directed against Japanese Americans by people with racial and economic prejudices–the same people who have been among the foremost advocates of the evacuation. A military judgment based upon such racial and sociological considerations is not entitled to the great weight ordinarily given the judgments based upon strictly military considerations. Especially is this so when every charge relative to race, religion, culture, geographical location, and legal and economic status has been substantially discredited by independent studies made by experts in these matters.

. . . No one denies, of course, that there were some disloyal persons of Japanese descent on the Pacific Coast who did all in their power to aid their ancestral land. Similar disloyal activities have been engaged in by many persons of German, Italian and even more pioneer stock in our country. But to infer that examples of individual disloyalty prove group disloyalty and justify discriminatory action against the entire group is to deny that under our system of law individual guilt is the sole basis for deprivation of rights. Moreover, this inference, which is at the very heart of the evacuation orders, has been used in support of the abhorrent and despicable treatment of minority groups by the dictatorial tyrannies which this nation is now pledged to destroy. To give constitutional sanction to that inference in this case . . . is to adopt one of the cruelest of the rationales used by our enemies to destroy the dignity of the individual and to encourage and open the door to discriminatory actions against other minority groups in the passions of tomorrow.

No adequate reason is given for the failure to treat these Japanese Americans on an individual basis by holding investigations and hearings to separate the loyal from the disloyal, as was done in the case of persons of German and Italian ancestry.

. . . Nearly four months elapsed after Pearl Harbor before the first exclusion order was issued; nearly eight months went by until the last order was issued; and the last of these "subversive" persons was not actually removed until almost eleven months had elapsed. Leisure and deliberation seem to have been more of the essence than speed. And the fact that conditions were not such as to warrant a declaration of martial law adds strength to the belief that the factors of time and military necessity were not as urgent as they have been represented to be.

Moreover, there was no adequate proof that the Federal Bureau of Investigation and the military and naval intelligence services did not have the espionage and sabotage situation well in hand during this long period. Nor is there any denial of the fact that not one person of Japanese ancestry was accused or convicted of espionage or sabotage after Pearl Harbor while they were still free, a fact which is some evidence of the loyalty of the vast majority of these individuals and of the effectiveness of the established methods of combatting these evils. It seems incredible that under these circumstances it would have been impossible to hold loyalty hearings for the mere 112,000 persons involved—or at least for the 70,000 American citizens—especially when a large part of this number represented children and elderly men and women. Any inconvenience that may have accompanied an attempt to conform to procedural due process cannot be said to justify violations of constitutional rights of individuals.

I dissent, therefore, from this legalization of racism. Racial discrimination in any form and in any degree has no justifiable part whatever in our democratic way of life. It is unattractive in any setting but it is utterly revolting among a free people who have embraced the principles set forth in the Constitution of the United States. All residents of this nation are kin in some way by blood or culture to a foreign land. Yet they are primarily and necessarily a part of the new and distinct civilization of the United States. They must accordingly be treated at all times as the heirs of the American experiment and as entitled to all the rights and freedoms guaranteed by the Constitution.

See also FRANKLIN ROOSEVELT, EXECUTIVE ORDER 9066: THE JAPANESE RELOCATION ACT, 1942.

Source:
Supreme Court Reporter, Vol. 65, pp. 193–208.

Franklin Roosevelt, Campaign Speech to the Teamsters Union, 1944

Radio address delivered by President Franklin D. Roosevelt on September 23, 1944, at a Teamsters union dinner in Washington, D.C. This was Roosevelt's first major speech of the 1944 presidential campaign. The president used the speech to show the American public that their "old" wartime commander in chief could still rouse his audience with traditional Rooseveltian campaign oratory. He dealt with the issue of his "advanced age" by saying that it was true that he was actually four years older than in his last campaign; however, he asserted that millions of Americans have aged in the 11 years since the New Deal began "to clean up the mess that was dumped into our laps in 1933." Roosevelt then criticized the Republicans, denouncing their decision to position themselves as "labor's friends" a few months before the election, after having opposed every prolabor legislation enacted during the previous three years and six months. He also defended the administration's war record. The most memorable phrase from this address came when he stated: "These Republican leaders have not been content with attacks on me, or my wife, or my sons. . . . They now include my little dog, Fala."

Mr. Tobin—I should say Dan, I always have—ladies and gentlemen. I am very much touched, and I am very happy in your applause, and very happy at the informalities of this dinner with old friends of mine. You know, this is not the first time that we have met together on this basis, and I am particularly happy that this national campaign opens in your presence as it did four years ago. And I don't mind mentioning the fact that Dan Tobin and I are just a little bit superstitious.

Well, here we are—here we are again—after four years—and what years they have been! You know, I am actually four years older—(laughter)—which is a fact that seems to annoy some people. In fact, in the mathematical field there are millions of Americans who are more than eleven years older than when we started in to clear up the mess that was dumped in our laps in 1933.

We all know that certain people who make it a practice to depreciate the accomplishments of labor—who even attack labor as unpatriotic—they keep this up usually for three years and six months in a row. But then, for some strange reason— (laughter)—they change their tune—every four years—just before election day. When votes are at stake, they suddenly discover that they really love labor—and that they are anxious to protect labor from its old friends.

I got quite a laugh, for example—and I am sure that you did—when I read this plank in the Republican platform adopted at their National Convention in Chicago last July:

"The Republican party accepts the purposes of the National Labor Relations Act, the Wage and Hour Act, the Social Security Act and all other Federal statutes designed to promote and protect the welfare of American working men and women, and we promise a fair and just administration of these laws." (laughter)

You know, many of the Republican leaders and Congressmen and candidates, who shouted enthusiastic approval of that plank in that Convention Hall would not even recognize these progressive laws, if they met them in broad daylight. Indeed, they have personally spent years of effort and energy— and much money—in fighting every one of those laws in the Congress, and in the press, and in the courts, ever since this Administration began to advocate them and enact them into legislation. That is a fair example of their insincerity and of their inconsistency.

The whole purpose of Republican oratory these days seems to be to switch labels. The object is to persuade the American people that the Democratic party was responsible for the 1929 crash and the depression, and that the Republican party was responsible for all social progress under the New Deal. (continued laughter)

Now, imitation may be the sincerest form of flattery—but I am afraid that in this case it is the most obvious common or garden variety of fraud. (more laughter, and applause)

Of course, it is perfectly true that there are enlightened, liberal elements in the Republican party, and they have fought hard and honorably to bring the party up to date and to get it in step with the forward march of American progress. But these liberal elements were not able to drive the Old Guard Republicans from their entrenched positions.

Can the Old Guard pass itself off as the New Deal? (laughter)

I think not.

We have all seen many marvelous stunts in the circus, but no performing elephant could turn a hand-spring without falling flat on his back. (laughter, cheers and applause)

I need not recount to you the centuries of history which have been crowded into these four years since I saw you last.

There were some—in the Congress and out—who raised their voices against our preparations for defense—before and after 1939—objected to them, raised their voices against them as hysterical war mongering, who cried out against our help to the Allies as provocative and dangerous. We remember the voices. They would like to have us forget them now. But in 1940 and 1941—my, it seems a long time ago—they were loud voices. Happily they were a minority and—fortunately for ourselves, and for the world—they could not stop America.

There are some politicians who kept their heads buried deep in the sand while the storms of Europe and Asia were headed our way, who said that the lend-lease bill "would bring an end"—and I am quoting—"to free government in the United States," and who said, and I am quoting, "only hysteria entertains the idea that Germany, Italy or Japan contemplate war on us." These men—these very men are now asking the American people to intrust to them the conduct of our foreign policy and our military policy.

What the Republican leaders are now saying in effect is this: "Oh, just forget what we used to say, we have changed our minds now—we have been reading the public opinion polls about these things—(laughter)—and now we know what the American people want." And they say: "Don't leave the task of making the peace to those old men who first urged it and who have already laid the foundations for it, and who have had to fight all of us inch by inch during the last five years to do it. Why, just turn it all over to us. We'll do it so skillfully—that we won't lose a single isolationist vote or a single isolationist campaign contribution." (laughter, cheers and applause)

I think there is one thing that you know, I am too old for that. I cannot talk out of both sides of my mouth at the same time.

The Government of the United States welcomes all sincere supporters of the cause of effective world collaboration in the making of a lasting peace. Millions of Republicans all over the nation are with us—and have been with us—in our unshakable determination to build the solid structure of peace. And they too will resent this campaign—this campaign talk by those who first woke up to the facts of international life a few short months ago—(laughter)—when they began to study the polls of public opinion. (more laughter, cheers and applause)

Those who today have the military responsibility for waging this war in all parts of the globe are not helped by the statements of men who, without responsibility and without the knowledge of the facts, lecture the Chiefs of Staff of the United States as to the best means of dividing our armed forces and our military resources between the Atlantic and Pacific, between the Army and the Navy, and among the Commanding Generals of the different theatres of war. And I may say that those Commanding Generals are making good in a big way. (cheers and applause)

When I addressed you four years ago, I said this. I said, "I know that America will never be disappointed in its expectation that labor will always continue to do its share of the job—the job we now face, and do it patriotically and effectively and unselfishly."

Today we know that America has not been disappointed. In his Order of the Day when the Allied Armies first landed in Normandy two months ago, General Eisenhower said: "Our home fronts have given us overwhelming superiority in weapons and munitions of war." (cheers and applause)

The country knows that there is a breed of cats, luckily not too numerous, called labor-baiters. I know that those labor-baiters among the opposition are there, who instead of calling attention to the achievements of labor in this war, prefer to pick on the occasional strikes that have occurred—strikes that have been condemned by every responsible national labor leader. I ought to say, parenthetically, all but one [John L. Lewis of the United Mine Workers]. And that one labor leader, incidentally, is not conspicuous among my supporters. (more laughter)

Labor-baiters forget that at our peak American labor and management have turned out airplanes at the rate of 109,000 a year; tanks—57,000 a year; combat vessels—573 a year; landing vessels, to get the troops ashore—31,000 a year; cargo ships—19 million tons a year—(cheers and applause)—and Henry Kaiser is here tonight, I am glad to say—(more cheers and applause); and small arms ammunition—oh, I can't understand it, I don't believe you can, either—23 billion rounds a year.

But a strike is news, and generally appears in shrieking headlines—and, of course, they say labor is always to blame. The fact is that since Pearl Harbor only one-tenth of one percent of manhours have been lost by strikes. Can you beat that? (prolonged cheers and applause)

But, you know, even those candidates who burst out in election-year affection for social legislation and for labor in general, still think that you ought to be good boys and stay out of politics. (laughter) And above all, they hate to see any working man or woman contribute a dollar bill to any wicked political party. (more laughter) Of course, it is all right for large financiers and industrialists and monopolists to contribute tens of thousands of dollars—but their solicitude for that dollar which the men and women in the ranks of labor contribute is always very touching.

They are, of course, perfectly willing to let you vote—unless you happen to be a soldier or a sailor overseas, or a merchant seaman carrying the munitions of war. In that case they have made it pretty hard for you to vote at all—for there are some political candidates who think that they may have a chance of election, if only the total vote is small enough. (laughter and applause)

And while I am on the subject of voting, let me urge every American citizen—man and woman—to use your sacred privilege of voting, no matter which candidate you expect to support. Our millions of soldiers and sailors and merchant seamen have been handicapped or prevented from voting by those politicians, those candidates who think that they stand to lose by such votes. You here at home have the freedom of the ballot. Irrespective of party, you should register and vote this November. I think that is a matter of plain good citizenship.

Words come easily, but they do not change the record. You are, most of you, old enough to remember what things were like for labor in 1932.

You remember the closed banks and the breadlines and the starvation wages; the foreclosures of homes and farms, and the bankruptcies of business; the "Hoovervilles," and the young men and women of the nation facing a hopeless, jobless future; the closed factories and mines and mills; the ruined and abandoned farms; the stalled railroads, the empty docks; the blank despair of a whole nation—and the utter impotence of the Federal Government.

You remember the long hard road, with its gains and its setbacks, which we have traveled together ever since those days.

Now there are some politicians who do not remember that far back—(laughter)—and there are some who remember but find it convenient to forget. No, the record is not to be washed away that easily.

The opposition in this year has already imported into this campaign a very interesting thing, because it is foreign. They have imported the propaganda technique invented by the dictators abroad. Remember, a number of years ago, there was a book *Mein Kampf* written by Hitler himself. The technique was all set out in Hitler's book—and it was copied by the aggressors of Italy and Japan. According to that technique, you should never use a small falsehood; always a big one for its very fantastic nature would make it more credible—if only you keep repeating it over and over and over again.

Well, let us take some simple illustrations that come to mind. For example, although I rubbed my eyes when I read it, we have been told that it was not a Republican depression, but a Democratic depression from which this nation was saved in 1933—that this Administration—this one—today—is responsible for all the suffering and misery that the history books and the American people have always thought had been brought about during the twelve ill-fated years when the Republican party was in power.

Now, there is an old and somewhat lugubrious adage which says: "Never speak of a rope in the house of a man who has been hanged." (laughter) In the same way, if I were a Republican leader speaking to a mixed audience, the last word in the whole dictionary that I think I would use is that word "depression." (more laughter, and applause)

You know, they pop up all the time. For another example, I learned—much to my amazement—that the policy of this Administration was to keep men in the Army when the war was over, because there might be no jobs for them in civil life.

Well, the very day that this fantastic charge was first made, a formal plan for the method of speedy discharge from the Army had already been announced by the War Department—a plan based on the wishes of the soldiers themselves.

This callous and brazen falsehood about demobilization did, of course, a very simple thing, it was an effort to stimulate fear among American mothers and wives and sweethearts. And, incidentally, it was hardly calculated to bolster the morale of our soldiers and sailors and airmen who are fighting our battles all over the world.

But perhaps the most ridiculous of these campaign falsifications is the one that this Administration failed to prepare for the war that was coming. I doubt whether even Goebbels would have tried that one. (laughter and applause) For even he would never have dared hope that the voters of America had already forgotten that many of the Republican leaders in the Congress and outside the Congress tried to thwart and block nearly every attempt that this Administration made to warn our people and arm our nation. (cheers and applause) Some of them called our 50,000 airplane program fantastic. Many of those very same leaders who fought every defense measure that we proposed are still in control of the Republican party—look at their names—were in control of its National Convention in Chicago, and would be in control of the machinery of the Congress and of the Republican party, in the event of a Republican victory this fall.

These Republican leaders have not been content with attacks on me, or my wife, or on my sons. No, not content with that they now include my little dog, Fala. (prolonged laughter, cheers and applause) Well, of course, I don't resent attacks, and my family don't resent attacks, but Fala *does* resent them. (more laughter, cheers and applause) You know—you know, Fala is Scotch, and being a Scottie, as soon as he learned that the Republican fiction-writers in Congress and out had concocted a story that I had left him behind on the Aleutian Islands and had sent a destroyer back to find him—at a cost to the taxpayers of two or three, or eight or twenty million dollars—his Scotch soul was furious. (continued laughter and applause) He has not been the same dog since. (more laughter and applause) I am accustomed to hearing malicious falsehoods about myself—such as that old, worm-eaten chestnut that I have represented myself as indispensable. But I think I have a right to resent, to object to libelous statement about my dog. (more laughter and applause)

Well, I think we all recognize the old technique. The people of this country know the past too well to be deceived into forgetting. Too much is at stake to forget. There are tasks ahead of us which we must now complete with the same will and the same skill and intelligence and devotion that have already led us so far along the road to victory.

There is the task finishing victoriously this most terrible of all wars as speedily as possible and with the least cost in lives.

There is the task of setting up international machinery to assure that the peace, once established, will not again be broken.

And there is the task that we face here at home—the task of reconverting our economy from the purposes of war to the purposes of peace.

These peace-building tasks were faced once before, nearly a generation ago. They were botched by a Republican administration. That must not happen this time. We will not let it happen this time.

Fortunately, we do not begin from scratch. Much has been done. Much more is under way. The fruits of victory this time will not be apples sold on street corners. (cheers and applause)

Many months ago this Administration set up necessary machinery for an orderly peace-time demobilization. The Congress has passed much more legislation continuing the agencies needed for demobilization—with additional powers to carry out their functions.

I know that the American people—business and labor and agriculture—have the same will to do for peace what they have done for war. (cheers and applause) And I know that they can sustain a national income that will assure full production and full employment under our democratic system of private enterprise, with Government encouragement and aid whenever and wherever that is necessary.

The keynote back of all this literature that we read, the keynote of all that we propose to do in reconversion can be found in the one word Jobs.

We shall lease or dispose of our Government-owned plants and facilities and our surplus war property and land, on the basis of how they can best be operated by private enterprise to give jobs to the greatest number. (cheers and applause)

We shall follow a wage policy that will sustain the purchasing power of labor—for that means more production and more jobs.

You and I know that the present policies on wages and prices were conceived to serve the needs of the great masses of the people. They stopped inflation. They kept prices on a relatively stable level. Through the demobilization period, policies will be carried out with the same objective in mind—to serve the needs of the great masses of the people.

This is not the time in which men can be forgotten as they were in the Republican catastrophe that we inherited. The returning soldiers, the workers by their machines, the farmers in the field, the miners, the men and women in offices and shops, do not intend to be forgotten. (cheers and applause)

No, they know that they are not surplus. Because they know that they are America.

We must set targets and objectives for the future which will seem impossible—like the airplanes—to those who live in and are weighted down by the dead past.

And for months—and today and in the future we are working and will continue to put forth the logistics of the peace, just as Marshall and King and Arnold, MacArthur,

Eisenhower and Nimitz are organizing the logistics of this war.

I think that the victory of the American people and their Allies in this war will be for more than a victory against fascism and reaction and the dead hand of despotism of the past. The victory of the American people and their Allies in this war will be a victory for democracy. It will constitute such an affirmation of the strength and power and vitality of government by the people as history has never before witnessed.

And so, my friends, with that affirmation of the vitality of democratic government behind us, that demonstration of its resilience and its capacity for decision and for action—with that knowledge of our own strength and power—we move forward with God's help to the greatest epoch of free achievement by free men that the world has ever known or imagined possible.

Source:

Franklin D. Roosevelt. *The Public Papers of the Presidents of the United States.* New York: Random House, 1938–50.

Report of Decorations Board, 1st Lt. Annie G. Fox, 1944

First Lieutenant Annie G. Fox was one of more than 59,000 American nurses who served in the Army Nurse Corps during World War II. They served under fire in field hospitals and evacuation hospitals, on hospital trains and hospital ships, and as flight nurses on medical transport planes. Because of their contribution, fewer than 4 percent of the American soldiers who received medical care in the field or underwent evacuation died from wounds or disease.

Annie G. Fox served as head nurse at Hickam Field near Pearl Harbor, Hawaii, in 1941. She supervised the treatment of those wounded in the Japanese attack on December 7. Initially awarded the Purple Heart, which was normally reserved for those who were wounded, Fox was later given the Bronze Star medal, one of 565 women to receive that honor, which was considered more appropriate. At least four army nurses received Silver Stars for extraordinary courage in Italy.The Army Nurse Corps was one of several forces in which women served during World War II. As part of the armed services they could join the Women's Army Corps (WACS), as did some 350,000 by the end of the war. Applicants had to be U.S. citizens between the ages of 21 and 45 with no dependents, at least five feet tall, and weigh 100 pounds or more. After Pearl Harbor, more than 35,000 women from all over the country applied for less than 1,000 anticipated positions. In addition, they could become navy WAVES (Women Accepted for Voluntary Emergency Service), Coast Guard SPARS (from the service's motto *Semper Paratus*), marines (who gave no specific name to their women's units), or fly in the Women's Auxiliary Service Pilots (WASPS). Until close to the end of the war, only the WACS and navy nurses were permitted to serve overseas, the navy nurses, limited to ships and planes. After the war, many of the military and naval women had to fight to receive veteran's benefits, but not all succeeded. The WASPs, who flew planes and were among the casualties, were not considered military. The 38 women who died in the line of duty were buried without military honors, and the living WASPs did not share any veterans' privileges such as the G.I. Bill to pay for schooling, low-interest housing loans, or health benefits. In 1977, Congress declared that the WASPs were indeed World War II veterans and the air force formally recognized them as such in 1979. Finally, in 1984, each WASP was awarded the Victory Medal, and those who served for more than one year received the American Theater medal. In the report of the Decorations Board, signed by the board's president, a major general, noted that the pronoun "him" is used by mistake in the last paragraph. Although the board recommends rescinding the Purple Heart, as of March 30, 1945, it had not been acted upon.

1. The board having been properly convened and organized, has considered the record of the case of [Annie G. Fox].

2. By decision of a majority of the board, the abovenamed individual is recommended for the award of the BRONZE STAR MEDAL with citation substantially as follows:

First Lieutenant Annie G. Fox, N 700454, Army Nurse Corps, Station Hospital, United States Army. For heroic and meritorious service in military operations against the enemy during the attack on Hickam Field by Japanese forces (aircraft) on 7 December 1941. During the attack Lieutenant Fox, in an exemplary manner, performed her duties as Head Nurse of the Station Hospital, Hickam Field, T. H. [Territory of Hawaii]. In addition, she administered anaesthesia to patients during the heaviest part of the bombardment, assisted in dressing the wounded, taught civilian volunteer nurses to make and wrap dressings, and worked ceaselessly with coolness and efficiency, and her fine example of calmness, courage and leadership was of great benefit to the morale of all with whom she came in contact. The loyalty and devotion to duty displayed by Lieutenant Fox on this occasion reflected great credit upon herself and the military service.

The Bronze Star Medal is in lieu of the Purple Heart awarded him [sic] in General Orders No. 33, Headquarters Seventh Air Force Base Command, 23 September 1942. Since Lieutenant Fox was not wounded in action. [sic] Cancellation of the award of the Purple Heart is also recommended.

Source:

National Archives and Records Administration. "A People at War." Available on-line. www.archives.gov/exhibit_hall/a_people_at_war/women_who_served/annie_g_fox.html. Accessed November 2003.

Yalta Agreement, 1945

Agreements signed on February 11, 1945, by the "Big Three" Allied leaders: U.S. president Franklin D. Roosevelt, British prime minister Winston Churchill, and Soviet premier Joseph Stalin. The conference took place at Yalta, in the USSR, from February 4 to 11, 1945. (Roosevelt was ill and weak at the time; he died on April 12.) This meeting was convened in the final months of World War II to discuss strategies for the invasion and final defeat of Nazi Germany and the terms of settlement. The three powers agreed to demand Germany's unconditional surrender, and they planned to divide Germany into four zones of occupation; they would each take one zone, and France would be the fourth occupying power. The leaders also finalized the dates of the meeting in San Francisco to draft the United Nations Charter, and the Soviet Union promised to enter the war against Japan after the German surrender.

The Soviets also agreed to allow European countries to settle their political and economic problems by democratic means. Instead, when the war ended, the Soviets dominated the countries of their zone, and they all became communist. Since that time, critics of Roosevelt have accused him of selling out to the Soviets. However, the president considered Soviet help essential in defeating the Japanese, and he had no control over the fate of the areas of eastern Europe already occupied by the Russian army.

The Yalta provisions were discussed further by the new U.S. president, Harry S. Truman, Churchill, and Stalin at Potsdam, outside of Berlin. The Allied powers' declaration of July 26, 1945, contained their plans for the future of Germany. Their intention, they clarified, was not "to destroy or enslave the German people," but to ensure that Germany would never again threaten world peace. Therefore, they sought to abolish Germany's armed forces and prohibit the manufacture of armaments, bring war criminals to trial, destroy Nazism and its institutions, and give German education a new direction. Germany was divided into four zones, administered by France, Germany, Britain, and the United States. Germany had to surrender territory to Poland and the Soviet Union, and its economy would be decentralized and industrial strength severely limited. War reparations payable to the Allies were also discussed. A council of foreign ministers was formed to negotiate settlements with Italy, Bulgaria, Romania, Hungary, and Finland.

YALTA AGREEMENT

The Defeat of Germany

We have considered and determined the military plans of the three Allied powers for the final defeat of the common enemy. The military staffs of the three Allied Nations have met in daily meetings throughout the Conference. These meetings have been most satisfactory from every point of view and have resulted in closer coordination of the military effort of the three Allies than ever before. The fullest information has been interchanged. The timing, scope, and coordination of new and even more powerful blows to be launched by our armies and air forces into the heart of Germany from the East, West, North, and South have been fully agreed and planned in detail.

Our combined military plans will be made known only as we execute them, but we believe that the very close working partnership among the three staffs attained at this Conference will result in shortening the war. Meetings of the three staffs will be continued in the future whenever the need arises.

Nazi Germany is doomed. The German people will only make the cost of their defeat heavier to themselves by attempting to continue a hopeless resistance.

The Occupation and Control of Germany

We have agreed on common policies and plans for enforcing the unconditional surrender terms which we shall impose together on Nazi Germany after German armed resistance has been finally crushed. These terms will not be made known until the final defeat of Germany has been accomplished. Under the agreed plan, the forces of the three powers will each occupy a separate zone of Germany. Coordinated administration and control has been provided for under the plan through a central control commission consisting of the Supreme Commanders of the three powers with headquarters in Berlin. It has been agreed that France should be invited by the three powers, if she should so desire, to take over a zone of occupation, and to participate as a fourth member of the control commission. The limits of the French zone will be agreed by the four Governments concerned through their representatives on the European Advisory Commission.

It is our inflexible purpose to destroy German militarism and Nazism and to ensure that Germany will never again be able to disturb the peace of the world. We are determined to disarm and disband all German armed forces; break up for all time the German General Staff that has repeatedly contrived the resurgence of German militarism; remove or destroy all German military equipment; eliminate or control all German industry that could be used for military production; bring all war criminals to just and swift punishment and exact reparation in kind for the destruction wrought by the Germans; wipe out the Nazi

Party, Nazi laws, organizations and institutions, remove all Nazi and militarist influences from public office and from the cultural and economic life of the German people; and take in harmony such other measures in Germany as may be necessary to the future peace and safety of the world. It is not our purpose to destroy the people of Germany, but only when Nazism and militarism have been extirpated will there be hope for a decent life for Germans, and a place for them in the comity of Nations.

Reparation by Germany

We have considered the question of the damage caused by Germany to the Allied Nations in this war and recognized it as just that Germany be obliged to make compensation for this damage in kind to the greatest extent possible. A commission for the compensation of damage will be established. The commission will be instructed to consider the question of the extent and methods for compensating damage caused by Germany to the Allied countries. The commission will work in Moscow.

United Nations Conference

We are resolved upon the earliest possible establishment with our allies of a general international organization to maintain peace and security. We believe that this is essential, both to prevent aggression and to remove the political, economic, and social causes of war through the close and continuing collaboration of all peace-loving peoples.

The foundations were laid at Dumbarton Oaks. On the important question of voting procedure, however, agreement was not there reached. The present Conference has been able to resolve this difficulty.

We have agreed that a conference of United Nations should be called to meet at San Francisco in the United States on April 25, 1945, to prepare the charter of such an organization, along the lines proposed in the informal conversations at Dumbarton Oaks.

The Government of China and the Provisional Government of France will be immediately consulted and invited to sponsor invitations to the conference jointly with the Governments of the United States, Great Britain, and the Union of Soviet Socialist Republics. As soon as the consultation with China and France has been completed, the next of the proposals on voting procedure will be made public.

Declaration on Liberated Europe

The Premier of the Union of Soviet Socialist Republics, the Prime Minister of the United Kingdom, and the President of the United States of America have consulted with each other in the common interests of the peoples of their countries and those of liberated Europe. They jointly declare their mutual agreement to concert during the temporary period of instability in liberated Europe the policies of their three Governments in assisting the peoples liberated from the domination of Nazi Germany and the peoples of the former Axis satellite states of Europe to solve by democratic means their pressing political and economic problems.

The establishment of order in Europe and the rebuilding of national economic life must be achieved by processes which will enable the liberated peoples to destroy the last vestiges of Nazism and Fascism and to create democratic institutions of their own choice. This is a principle of the Atlantic Charter—the right of all peoples to choose the form of government under which they will live—the restoration of sovereign rights and self-government to those peoples who have been forcibly deprived of them by the aggressor Nations.

To foster the conditions in which the liberated peoples may exercise these rights, the three Governments will jointly assist the people in any European liberated state or former Axis satellite state in Europe where in their judgment conditions require (a) to establish conditions of internal peace; (b) to carry out emergency measures for the relief of distressed peoples; (c) to form interim governmental authorities broadly representative of all democratic elements in the population and pledged to the earliest possible establishment through free elections of governments responsive to the will of the people; and (d) to facilitate where necessary the holding of such elections.

The three Governments will consult the other United Nations and provisional authorities or other Governments in Europe when matters of direct interest to them are under consideration.

When, in the opinion of the three Governments, conditions in any European liberated state or any former Axis satellite state in Europe make such action necessary, they will immediately consult together on the measures necessary to discharge the joint responsibilities set forth in this declaration.

By this declaration we reaffirm our faith in the principles of the Atlantic Charter, our pledge in the declaration by the United Nations, and our determination to build in cooperation with other peace-loving Nations world order under law, dedicated to peace, security, freedom, and general well-being of all mankind.

In issuing this declaration, the three powers express the hope that the Provisional Government of the French Republic may be associated with them in the procedure suggested.

Poland

A new situation has been created in Poland as a result of her complete liberation by the Red Army. This calls for the establishment of a Polish provisional government which can be more broadly based than was possible before the recent liberation of western Poland. The provisional government which is now functioning in Poland should therefore be reorganized on a broader democratic basis with the inclusion of democratic leaders from Poland itself and from Poles abroad. This new government should then be called the Polish Provisional Government of National Unity.

M. Molotov, Mr. Harriman, and Sir A. Clark Kerr are authorized as a commission to consult in the first instance in Moscow with members of the present provisional government and with other Polish democratic leaders from within Poland and from abroad, with a view to the reorganization of the present government along the above lines. This Polish Provisional Government of National Unity shall be pledged to the holding of free and unfettered elections as soon as possible on the basis of universal suffrage and secret ballot. In these elections all democratic anti-Nazi parties shall have the right to take part and to put forward candidates.

When a Polish Provisional Government of National Unity has been properly formed in conformity with the above, the Government of the U.S.S.R., which now maintains diplomatic relations with the present provisional government of Poland, and the Government of the United Kingdom and the Government of the U.S.A. will establish diplomatic relations with the new Polish Provisional Government of National Unity, and will exchange ambassadors by whose reports the respective Governments will be kept informed about the situation in Poland.

The three heads of government consider that the eastern frontier of Poland should follow the Curzon line with digressions from it in some regions of five to eight kilometers in favor of Poland. They recognized that Poland must receive substantial accessions of territory in the North and West. They feel that the opinion of the new Polish Provisional Government of National Unity should be sought in due course on the extent of these accessions and that the final delimitation of the western frontier of Poland should thereafter await the peace conference.

Yugoslavia

We have agreed to recommend to Marshal Tito and Dr. Subasic that the agreement between them should be put into effect immediately, and that a new government should be formed on the basis of that agreement.

We also recommend that as soon as the new government has been formed it should declare that:

1. The anti-Fascist Assembly of National Liberation (Avnoj) should be extended to include members of the last Yugoslav Parliament (Skupschina) who have not compromised themselves by collaboration with the enemy, thus forming a body to be known as a temporary Parliament; and,

2. Legislative acts passed by the anti-Fascist Assembly of National Liberation will be subject to subsequent ratification by a constituent assembly.

There was also a general review of other Balkan questions.

Meetings of Foreign Secretaries

Throughout the Conference, besides the daily meetings of the heads of governments and the Foreign Secretaries, separate meetings of the three Foreign Secretaries, and their advisers have also been held daily.

These meetings have proved of the utmost value and the Conference agreed that permanent machinery should be set up for regular consultation between the three Foreign Secretaries. They will, therefore, meet as often as may be necessary, probably about every three or four months. These meetings will be held in rotation in the three capitals, the first meeting being held in London, after the United Nations Conference on World Organization.

Unity for Peace as for War

Our meeting here in the Crimea has reaffirmed our common determination to maintain and strengthen in the peace to come that unity of purpose and of action which has made victory possible and certain for the United Nations in this war. We believe that this is a sacred obligation which our Governments owe to our peoples and to all the peoples of the world.

Only with the continuing and growing cooperation and understanding among our three countries and among all the peace-loving Nations can the highest aspiration of humanity be realized—a secure and lasting peace which will, in the words of the Atlantic Charter, "afford assurance that all the men in all the lands may live out their lives in freedom from fear and want."

Victory in this war and establishment of the proposed international organization will provide the greatest opportunity in all history to create in the years to come the essential conditions of such a peace.

Source:

Franklin D. Roosevelt. *The Public Papers of the Presidents of the United States*. New York: Random House, 1938–50.

Act of Chapultepec, 1945

Agreement signed by 21 American republics on March 3, 1945, during the Inter-American Conference on Problems of War and Peace held at Chapultepec Castle in Mexico City.

On December 24, 1938, in Lima, Peru, at an Inter-American conference, these American states had agreed to defend American principles against foreign intervention. In case of any threat to their peace, security, or territorial integrity, foreign ministers should meet for consultation. This act reaffirmed decisions already reached in a similar conference at Buenos Aires, Argentina, in 1936. At Lima, the United States had wanted a more potent declaration of unity in the Western Hemisphere, to oppose totalitarian Germany and Italy and others. However, for much of World War II, which began in 1939, some South American countries sympathized with Germany.

On April 14, 1939, Pan-American Day, President Franklin D. Roosevelt proclaimed the solidarity of the American nations against outside attack, whether military or economic, and at the same time recognized the interrelationship between the New World and the Old. Roosevelt declared that the United States was prepared to defend the sovereignty and independence of "the American family of nations." He also stated: "The truest defense of the peace of our hemisphere must always lie in the hope that our sister nations beyond the seas will break the bonds . . . of perpetual warfare." Five months later, a further declaration was issued at the Pan-American Conference on Neutrality, held in Panama from September 23 to October 3, 1939. It stated that the American republics would create a safety zone around the hemisphere, exclusive of Canada (part of the British Empire), which was to present a united front against aggressors. In this zone, varying from 250 miles to 1,250 miles in width, no aggressor would be permitted to commit a hostile act. The area would be policed by the navies of the United States and the Latin American countries. The declaration, however, quickly became ineffective, as it was violated in the fighting between German and British warships. In January 1940 Great Britain and Germany refused to recognize the zone.

The 1945 agreement provided for common action against an aggressor from without or within the Western Hemisphere (World War II was still in progress). The act proclaimed that an attack against any American state would be considered an act of aggression against all, thus calling for collective action against the aggressor. A turning point in the development of inter-American relations, the Act of Chapultepec expanded the Monroe Doctrine's unilateral guarantee against intervention in the hemisphere into a mutual security system, and for the first time it included provisions that would ban aggression by one American state against another.

DECLARATION on Reciprocal Assistance and American Solidarity by the Governments Represented at the Inter-American Conference on War and Peace **Whereas:**

(1) The peoples of the Americas, animated by a profound love of justice, remain sincerely devoted to the principles of international law:

(2) It is their desire that such principles, notwithstanding the present difficult circumstances, may prevail with greater force in future international relations:

(3) The Inter-American Conferences have repeatedly proclaimed certain fundamental principles, but these must be reaffirmed and proclaimed at a time when the juridical bases of the community of nations are being established:

(4) The new situation in the world makes more imperative than ever the union and solidarity of the American peoples, for the defense of their rights and the maintenance of international peace:

(5) The American States have been incorporating in their international law, since 1890, by means of conventions, resolutions and declarations, the following principles:

(a) The prescription of territorial conquest and the non-recognition of all acquisitions made by force (First International Conference of American States, 1890).

(b) The condemnation of intervention by a State in the internal or external affairs of another (Seventh International Conference of American States, 1933, and Inter-American Conference for the Maintenance of Peace, 1936).

(c) The recognition that every war or threat of war affects directly or indirectly all civilized peoples, and endangers the great principles of liberty and justice which constitute the American ideal and the standard of its international policy (Inter-American Conference for the Maintenance of Peace, 1936).

(d) The procedure of mutual consultation in order to find means of peaceful co-operation in the event of war or threat of war between American countries (Inter-American Conference for the Maintenance of Peace, 1936).

(e) The recognition that every act susceptible of disturbing the peace of America affects each and every one of them and justifies the initiation of the procedure of consultation (Inter-American Conference for the Maintenance of Peace, 1936).

(f) That any difference or dispute between the American nations, whatever its nature or origin, shall be settled by the methods of conciliation, or unrestricted arbitration, or through the operation of international justice (Inter-American Conference for the Maintenance of Peace, 1936).

(g) The recognition that respect for the personality, sovereignty and independence of each American State constitutes the essence of international order sustained by continental solidarity, which historically has been expressed and sustained by declarations and treaties in force (Eighth International Conference of American States, 1938).

(h) The affirmation that respect for and the faithful observance of treaties constitutes the indispensable rule for the development of peaceful relations between States, and treaties can only be revised by agreement of the contracting parties (Declaration of American Principles, Eighth International Conference of American States, 1938).

(i) That in case the peace, security or territorial integrity of any American republic is threatened by acts of any nature that may impair them, they proclaim their common concern and their determination to make effective their solidarity, co-ordinating their respective sovereign will by means of the procedure of consultation, using the measures which in each case the circumstances may make advisable (Declaration of Lima, Eighth International Conference of American States, 1938).

(j) That any attempt on the part of a non-American State against the integrity or inviolability of the territory, the sovereignty or the political independence of an American State be considered as an act of aggression against all the American States (Declaration of the Second Meeting of the Ministers of Foreign Affairs, Habana, 1940).

(6) The furtherance of these principles, which the American States have practiced in order to secure peace and solidarity between the nations of the continent, constitutes an effective means of contributing to the general system of world security and of facilitating its establishment: and

(7) The security and solidarity of the continent are affected to the same extent by an act of aggression against of the American States by a non-American State, as by an American State against one or more American States.

Part I. Declaration.

The Government Represented at the Inter-American Conference on War and Peace Declare:

First. That all sovereign States are juridically equal amongst themselves.

Second. That every State has the right to the respect of its individuality and independence, on the part of the other members of the international community.

Third. That every attack of a State against the integrity or the inviolability of territory, or against the sovereignty or political independence of an American State, shall, conformably to Part III hereof, be considered as an act of aggression against the other States which sign this declaration. In any case, invasion by armed forces of one State into the territory of another trespassing boundaries established by treaty and demarcated in accordance there with shall constitute an act of aggression.

Fourth. That in case acts of aggression occur or there may be reasons to believe that an aggression is being prepared by any other State against the integrity and inviolability of territory, or against the sovereignty or political independence of an American State, the States signatory to this declaration will consult amongst themselves in order to agree upon measures it may be advisable to take.

Fifth. That during the war, and until the treaty recommended in Part II hereof is concluded, the signatories of this declaration recognize that such threats and acts of aggression as indicated paragraphs Third and Fourth above constitute an interference with the war effort of the United Nations, calling for such procedures, within the scope of their constitutional powers of a general nature and for war, as may be found necessary, including:

recall of chiefs of diplomatic missions; breaking of diplomatic relations; breaking of consular relations; breaking of postal, telegraphic, telephonic, radiotelephonic relations; interruption of economic, commercial and financial relations; use of armed force to prevent or repeal aggression.

Sixth. That the principles and procedure contained in this declaration shall become effective immediately, inasmuch as any act of aggression or threat of aggression during the present state of war interferes with the war effort of the United Nations to obtain victory. Henceforth, and with the view that the principles and procedure herein stipulated shall conform with the constitutional principles of each republic, the respective Governments shall take the necessary steps to perfect this instrument on order that it shall be in force at all times.

Part II. Recommendation.

The Inter-American Conference on Problems of War and Peace Recommends:

That for the purpose of meeting threats or acts of aggression against any American republic following the establishment of peace, the Governments of the American republics should consider the conclusion, in accordance with their constitutional processes, of a treaty establishing procedures whereby such threats or acts may be met by:

The use, by all or some of the signatories of said treaty of any one or more of the following measures:

recall of chiefs of diplomatic missions; breaking of diplomatic relations; breaking of consular relations; breaking of postal, telegraphic, telephonic, radiotelephonic relations; interruption of economic, commercial and financial relations; use of armed force to prevent or repeal aggression.

Part III.

This declaration and recommendation provide for a regional arrangement for dealing with matters relating to the maintenance of international peace and security as are appropriate for regional action in this hemisphere and said arrangements and the activities and procedures referred to therein shall be consistent with the purposes and principles of the general international organization, when established. This declaration and recommendation shall be known as the Act of Chapultepec.

The regional treaty mentioned in Part III was signed on Sept. 2, 1947 and is known as the Inter-American Treaty of Reciprocal Assistance.

Source:
Landmark Documents in American History, Facts On File, Inc.

Germany's Surrender in World War II, 1945

Instrument of unconditional surrender of Germany signed in Rheims, France, at a little red schoolhouse, the forward command post of SHAEF (Supreme Headquarters of the Allied Expeditionary Force, or AEF), on May 7, 1945, by Colonel General Alfred Jodl, chief of staff of the German army; U.S. lieutenant general Walter B. Smith, for the Supreme Allied Command; General François Savez, for the commander of French forces of the AEF; and General Ivan Susloparov, for the Russian High Command. It provided for an end to German hostilities in World War II. The document specified the unconditional surrender of all German forces to the Supreme Allied Command and the Russian High Command; that all forces remain in their present positions; that the German High Command issue a cease-fire at 12:01 A.M. on May 9, 1945; that the German High Command obey all orders issued by U.S. general Dwight D. Eisenhower (supreme commander of the AEF) or the Russian High Command; and that, in the event of German noncompliance with the terms of surrender, the Allies would "take such punitive or other action as they deem appropriate."

The United States and West Germany formally ended a state of war between them August 2, 1951. However, this document was not a formal peace treaty as long as Germany was divided; the Western Allies agreed that only with a united Germany could there be a true "peaceful settlement." Under the contract, the Allies ended their military occupation, but they reserved their military rights in West Germany. The Bonn government gained almost complete control over its internal affairs. . . . The Allies also pledged to defend West Berlin in a cover letter to the contract.

Act of Military Surrender

1. We the undersigned, acting by authority of the German High Command, hereby surrender unconditionally to the Supreme Commander, Allied Expeditionary Force and simultaneously to the Soviet High Command all forces on land, sea, and in the air who are at this date under German control.

2. The German High Command will at once issue orders to all German military, naval and air authorities and to all forces under German control to cease active operations at 2301 hours Central European time on 8 May and to remain in the positions occupied at that time. No ship, vessel, or aircraft is to be scuttled, or any damage done to their hull, machinery or equipment.

3. The German High Command will at once issue to the appropriate commanders, and ensure the carrying out of any further orders issued by the Supreme Commander, Allied Expeditionary Force and by the Soviet High Command.

4. This act of military surrender is without prejudice to, and will be superseded by any general instrument of surrender imposed by, or on behalf of the United Nations and applicable to Germany and the German armed forces as a whole.

5. In the event of the German High Command or any of the forces under their control failing to act in accordance with this Act of Surrender, the Supreme Commander, Allied Expeditionary Force and the Soviet High Command will take such punitive or other action as they deem appropriate.

Signed at Rheims France at 0241 on the 7th day of May, 1945.

Source:
Harry S. Truman Presidential Library.

Harry S. Truman, Announcement of the Atomic Bombing of Hiroshima, 1945

Statement issued on August 6, 1945, announcing that the United States had dropped a single atomic bomb on the Japanese city of Hiroshima earlier that day. Truman described the bomb as a revolutionary new force for destruction, harnessing the basic power of the universe and having more force than 20,000 tons of TNT. More than 70,000 people were killed. Truman warned that if the Japanese continued to refuse to surrender unconditionally, "they may expect a rain of ruin from the air, the like of which has never been seen on this earth." On August 9, the United States dropped a second atomic bomb, on Nagasaki. In his statement, Truman also promised to establish a commission to control the production and use of atomic power within the United States.

Truman justified using the bomb, to prevent prolonging the war and to save the lives of Americans fighting in the Pacific (the European phase of the war had already ended).

Even at the time, using the bomb was controversial. The atom bomb project had been spurred by a letter written over Albert Einstein's signature but probably drafted by Hungarian-born refugee physicist Leo Szilard. Dated August 2, 1939, the letter warned of the possibility that Germany was trying to construct a new type of extremely powerful bomb derived from nuclear chain reactions in a large mass of uranium. Such a bomb, according to the letter, could destroy an entire port and surrounding territory. It urged the United States to speed up its experimental work. Einstein later considered his recommendation to build an atomic bomb to be "the great mistake" of his life.

On June 11, 1945, seven distinguished scientists, led by German-born American physicist and Nobel laureate James Franck, issued a report to the U.S. secretary of war urging the United States to refrain from using atomic weapons against Japan. Nuclear power, they wrote, "is fraught with infinitely greater dangers than were all the inventions of the past." Warning that use of a new weapon of indiscriminate destruction against civilians would cost the U.S. support of other nations and would precipitate a nuclear arms race, the report urged a demonstration of the atomic bomb, before representatives of the United Nations, on a desert or barren island, to pressure Japan into surrendering during World War II. The report also proposed an international agreement to prevent nuclear warfare.

In recent years a controversy has raged among historians and between historians and veterans over why Truman really used the bomb, and whether either the Hiroshima or Nagasaki bomb was justified. Veterans, especially those who had been stationed in the Pacific, supported the use of the bomb. So did historians who hold that Japan would not have surrendered otherwise. Those opposing Truman's decision believe that his major reason was to demonstrate American power to the Russians, then our ally, but already identified by many in government as a future enemy. The controversy flourished quite publically in response to a proposed exhibit at the Smithsonian Institution about the first atomic bombs. A recapitulation of the controversy with an emphasis on the veteran's arguments is available at <www.afa.org/media/enolagay>.

Sixteen Hours Ago an American airplane dropped one bomb on Hiroshima, an important Japanese Army base. That bomb had more power than 20,000 tons of T.N.T. It had more than two thousand times the blast power of the British "Grand Slam" which is the largest bomb ever yet used in the history of warfare.

The Japanese began the war from the air at Pearl Harbor. They have been repaid many fold. And the end is not yet. With this bomb we have now added a new and revolutionary increase in destruction to supplement the growing power of our armed forces. In their present form these bombs are now in production and even more powerful forms are in development.

It is an atomic bomb. It is a harnessing of the basic power of the universe. The force from which the sun draws its power has been loosed against those who brought war to the Far East.

Before 1939, it was the accepted belief of scientists that it was theoretically possible to release atomic energy. But no one knew any practical method of doing it. By 1942, however, we knew that the Germans were working feverishly to find a way to add atomic energy to the other engines of war with which they hoped to enslave the world. But they failed. We may be grateful to Providence that the Germans got the V-1's and V-2's late and in limited quantities and even more grateful that they did not get the atomic bomb at all.

The battle of the laboratories held fateful risks for us as well as the battles of the air, land and sea, and we have now won the battle of the laboratories as we have won the other battles.

Beginning in 1940, before Pearl Harbor, scientific knowledge useful in war was pooled between the United States and Great Britain, and many priceless helps to our victories have come from that arrangement. Under that general policy the research on the atomic bomb was begun. With American and British scientists working together we entered the race of discovery against the Germans.

The United States had available the large number of scientists of distinction in the many needed areas of knowledge. It had the tremendous industrial and financial resources necessary for the project and they could be devoted to it without undue impairment of other vital war work. In the United States the laboratory work and the production plants, on which a substantial start had already been made, would be out of reach of enemy bombing, while at that time Britain was exposed to constant air attack and was still threatened with the possibility of invasion. For these reasons Prime Minister Churchill and President Roosevelt agreed that it was wise to carry on the project here. We now have two great plants and many lesser works devoted to the production at atomic power. Employment during peak construction numbered 125,000 and 65,000 individuals are even now engaged in operating the plants. Many have worked there for two and a half years. Few know what they have been producing. They see great quantities of material going in and they see nothing coming out of these plants, for the physical size of the explosive charge is exceedingly small. We have spent two billion dollars on the greatest scientific gamble in history—and won.

But the greatest marvel is not the size of the enterprise, its secrecy, nor its cost, but the achievement of scientific brains in putting together infinitely complex pieces of knowledge held by many men in different fields of science into a workable plan. And hardly less marvelous has been the capacity of industry to design, and of labor to operate, the machines and methods to do things never done before so that the brain child of many minds came forth in physical shape and performed as it was supposed to do. Both science and industry worked under the direction of the United States Army, which achieved a unique success in managing so diverse a problem in the advancement of knowledge in an amazingly short time. It is doubtful if such another combination could be got together in the world. What has been done is the greatest achievement of organized science in history. It was done under high pressure and without failure.

We are now prepared to obliterate more rapidly and completely every productive enterprise the Japanese have above ground in any city. We shall destroy their docks, their factories, and their communications. Let there be no mistake; we shall completely destroy Japan's power to make war.

It was to spare the Japanese people from utter destruction that the ultimatum of July 26 was issued at Potsdam. Their leaders promptly rejected that ultimatum. If they do not now accept our terms they may expect a rain of ruin from the air, the like of which has never been seen on this earth. Behind this air attack will follow sea and land forces in such numbers and power as they have not yet seen and with the fighting skill of which they are already well aware.

The Secretary of War, who has kept in personal touch with all phases of the project, will immediately make public a statement giving further details.

His statement will give facts concerning the sites at Oak Ridge near Knoxville, Tennessee, and at Richland near Pasco, Washington, and an installation near Santa Fe, New Mexico. Although the workers at the sites have been making materials to be used in producing the greatest destructive force in history they have not themselves been in danger beyond that of many other occupations, for the utmost care has been taken of their safety.

The fact that we can release atomic energy ushers in a new era in man's understanding of nature's forces. Atomic energy may in the future supplement the power that now comes from coal, oil, and falling water, but at present it cannot be produced on a basis to compete with them commercially. Before that comes there must be a long period of intensive research.

It has never been the habit of the scientists of this country or the policy of this Government to withhold from the world scientific knowledge. Normally, therefore, everything about the work with atomic energy would be made public.

But under present circumstances it is not intended to divulge the technical processes of production or all the military applications, pending further examination of possible methods of protecting us and the rest of the world from the danger of sudden destruction.

I shall recommend that the Congress of the United States consider promptly the establishment of an appropriate commission to control the production and use of atomic power within the United States. I shall give further consideration and make further recommendations to the Congress as to how atomic power can become a powerful and forceful influence towards the maintenance of world peace.

Source:

Public Papers of the Presidents of the United States, Harry S. Truman, 1945–1953. Washington, D.C.: Government Printing Office, 1966.

London Agreement and Charter of the International Military Tribunal, 1945

Signed August 8, 1945, this document established what became known as the Nuremburg Tribunal, named for the place in which German war criminals were tried in 1946.

When the Allies liberated the concentration camps after World War II they were shocked and sickened by what they found. Those still breathing were like barely living skeletons. Worse, some 6,000,000 Jews and hundreds of thousands of Poles, homosexuals, gypsies, and disabled persons had died as a result of disease, starvation, mistreatment as slave labor, and most horrifying of all, the systematic murder of Jews using gas chambers, ovens, and mass executions by shooting. As early as 1942, President Roosevelt and British prime minister Winston Churchill, upon hearing of Hitler's "Final Solution," warned that its perpetrators would be brought to justice for "crimes against humanity." The Japanese received a similar warning. Under Truman and Churchill the European tribunal was established by this agreement. Associate Supreme Court justice Robert H. Jackson served as the American special prosecutor. Eventually 12 Nazis received death sentences and seven others were imprisoned. Public opinion supported the trials and none of the convicted Nazis appealed. Since then some 2,000 other trials have been held throughout Europe, the United States, and Israel, plus an unknown number in the Soviet Union, as Nazis who escaped after the war were located. The Nuremburg trials in effect invented a new category: "crimes against humanity." After special tribunals tried perpetrators of heinous crimes against humanity in Africa and the former Yugoslavia, in 2002 a special court was established in the Hague to try officials that were not punished by their home countries.

AGREEMENT by the Government of the UNITED STATES OF AMERICA, the Provisional Government of the FRENCH REPUBLIC, the Government of the UNITED KINGDOM OF GREAT BRITAIN AND NORTHERN IRELAND and the Government of the UNI0N Of SOVIET SOCIALIST REPUBLICS for the Prosecution and Punishment of the MAJOR WAR CRIMINALS of the EUROPEAN AXIS

WHEREAS the United Nations have from time to time made declarations of their intention that War Criminals shall be brought to justice;

AND WHEREAS the Moscow Declaration of the 30th October 1943 on German atrocities in Occupied Europe stated that those German Officers and men and members of the Nazi Party who have been responsible for or have taken a consenting part in atrocities and crimes will be sent back to the countries in which their abominable deeds were done in order that they may be judged and punished according to the laws of these liberated countries and of the free Governments that will be created therein;

AND WHEREAS this Declaration was stated to be without prejudice to the case of major criminals whose offenses have no particular geographical location and who will be punished by the joint decision of the Governments of the Allies;

Now THEREFORE the Government of the United States of America, the Provisional Government of the French Republic, the Government of the United Kingdom of Great Britain and Northern Ireland and the Government of the Union of Soviet Socialist Republics (hereinafter called "the Signatories") acting in the interests of all the United Nations and by their representatives duly authorized thereto have concluded this Agreement.

Article 1. There shall be established after consultation with the Control Council for Germany an International Military Tribunal for the trial of war criminals whose offenses have no particular geographical location whether they be accused individually or in their capacity as members of organizations or groups or in both capacities.

* * *

Article 7. This Agreement shall come into force on the day of signature and shall remain in force for the period of one year and shall continue thereafter, subject to the right of any Signatory to give, through the diplomatic channel, one month's notice of intention to terminate it. Such termination shall not prejudice any proceedings already taken or any findings already made in pursuance of this Agreement.

IN WITNESS WHEREOF the Undersigned have signed the present Agreement.

DONE in quadruplicate in London this 8th, day of August 1945 each in English, French and Russian, and each text to have equal authenticity.

For the Government of the United States of America R0BERT H. JACKSON. For the Provisional Government of the French Republic ROBERT FALCO. For the Government of the United Kingdom of Great Britain and Northern Ireland JOWITT C. For the Government of the Union of Soviet Socialist Republics I. NIKITCHENKO A. TRAININ

Charter of the International Military Tribunal

1. CONSTITUTION OF THE INTERNATIONAL MILITARY TRIBUNAL Article 1. In pursuance of the Agreement signed on the 8th, day of August 1945 by the Government of the United States of America, the Provisional Government of the French Republic, the Government of the United Kingdom of Great Britain and Northern Ireland and the Government of the Union of Soviet Socialist Republics, there shall be established an International Military Tribunal (hereinafter called "the Tribunal") for the just and prompt trial and punishment of the major war criminals of the European Axis.

Article 2. The Tribunal shall consist of four members, each with an alternate. One member and one alternate shall be appointed by each of the Signatories. The alternates shall, so far as they are able, be present at all sessions of the Tribunal. In case of illness of any member of the Tribunal or his incapacity for some other reason to fulfill his functions, his alternate shall take his place.

* * *

II. JURISDICTION AND GENERAL PRINCIPLES Article 6. The Tribunal established by the Agreement referred to in Article 1 hereof for the trial and punishment of the major war criminals of the European Axis countries shall have the power to try and punish persons who, acting in the interests of the European Axis countries, whether as individuals or as members of organizations, committed any of the following crimes.

The following acts, or any of them, are crimes coming within the jurisdiction of the Tribunal for which, there shall be individual responsibility:

(a) CRIMES AGAINST PEACE: namely, planning, preparation, initiation or waging of a war of aggression, or a war in violation of international treaties, agreements or assurances, or participation in a common plan or conspiracy for the accomplishment of any of the foregoing;

(b) WAR CRIMES: namely, violations of the laws or customs of war. Such violations shall include, but not be limited to, murder, ill-treatment or deportation to slave labor or for any other purpose of civilian population of or in occupied territory, murder or ill-treatment of prisoners of war or persons on the seas, killing of hostages, plunder of public or private property, wanton destruction of cities, towns or villages, or devastation not justified by military necessity;

(c) CRIMES AGAINST HUMANITY: namely, murder, extermination, enslavement, deportation, and other inhumane acts committed against any civilian population, before or during the war; or persecutions on political, racial or religious grounds in execution of or in connection with any crime within the jurisdiction of the Tribunal, whether or not in violation of the domestic law of the country where perpetrated.

Leaders, organizers, instigators and accomplices participating in the formulation or execution of a common plan or conspiracy to commit any of the foregoing crimes are responsible for all acts performed by any persons in execution of such plan.

Article 7. The official position of defendants, whether as Heads of State or responsible officials in Government Departments, shall not be considered as freeing them from responsibility or mitigating punishment.

Article 8. The fact that the Defendant acted pursuant to order of his Government or of a superior shall not free him from responsibility, but may be considered in mitigation of punishment if the Tribunal determines that justice so requires.

Article 9. At the trial of any individual member of any group or organization the Tribunal may declare (in connection with any act of which the individual may be convicted) that the group or organization of which the individual was a member was a criminal organization.

* * *

II. JURISDICTION AND GENERAL PRINCIPLES Article 6. The Tribunal established by the Agreement referred to in Article 1 hereof for the trial and punishment of the major war criminals of the European Axis countries shall have the power to try and punish persons who, acting in the interests of the European Axis countries, whether as individuals or as members of organizations, committed any of the following crimes.

The following acts, or any of them, are crimes coming within the jurisdiction of the Tribunal for which, there shall be individual responsibility:

(a) CRIMES AGAINST PEACE: namely, planning, preparation, initiation or waging of a war of aggression, or a war in violation of international treaties, agreements or assurances, or participation in a common plan or conspiracy for the accomplishment of any of the foregoing;

(b) WAR CRIMES: namely, violations of the laws or customs of war. Such violations shall include, but not be limited to, murder, ill-treatment or deportation to slave labor or for any other purpose of civilian population of or in occupied territory, murder or ill-treatment of prisoners of war or persons on the seas, killing of hostages, plunder of public or private property, wanton destruction of cities, towns or villages, or devastation;

(c) CRIMES AGAINST HUMANITY: namely, murder, extermination, enslavement, deportation, and other inhumane acts committed against any civilian population, before or during the war; or persecutions on political, racial or religious grounds in execution of or in connection with any crime within the jurisdiction of the Tribunal, whether or not in violation of the domestic law of the country where perpetrated.(1)

Leaders, organizers, instigators and accomplices participating in the formulation or execution of a common plan or conspiracy to commit any of the foregoing crimes are responsible for all acts performed by any persons in execution of such plan.

Article 7. The official position of defendants, whether as Heads of State or responsible officials in Government Departments, shall not be considered as freeing them from responsibility or mitigating punishment.

Article 8. The fact that the Defendant acted pursuant to order of his Government or of a superior shall not free him from responsibility, but may be considered in mitigation of punishment if the Tribunal determines that justice so requires.

Article 9. At the trial of any individual member of any group or organization the Tribunal may declare (in connection with any act of which the individual may be convicted) that the group or organization of which the individual was a member was a criminal organization.

* * *

VI. JUDGMENT AND SENTENCE Article 26. The judgment of the Tribunal as to the guilt or the innocence of any Defendant shall give the reasons on which it is based, and shall be final and not subject to review.

Article 27. The Tribunal shall have the right to impose upon a Defendant, on conviction, death or such other punishment as shall be determined by it to be just.

Article 28. In addition to any punishment imposed by it, the Tribunal shall have the right to deprive the convicted person of any stolen property and order its delivery to the Control Council for Germany.

Article 29. In case of guilt, sentences shall be carried out in accordance with the orders of the Control Council for Germany, which may at any time reduce or otherwise alter the sentences, but may not increase the severity thereof. If the Control Council for Germany, after any

Defendant has been convicted and sentenced, discovers fresh evidence which, in its opinion, would found a fresh charge against him, the Council shall report accordingly to the Committee established under Article 14 hereof, for such action as they may consider proper, having regard to the interests of justice.

* * *

Source:

International Conference on Military Trials, Report of Robert H. Jackson, United States Representative to the International Conference on Military Trials, London, 1945.

Japan's Unconditional Surrender, 1945

Instrument of surrender of Japan signed aboard the U.S. battleship *Missouri* in Tokyo Bay on September 2, 1945, by Foreign Minister Shigemitsu Mamoru and General Umezu Yoshijiro and by representatives of Australia, China, France, New Zealand, the Netherlands, Great Britain, the Soviet Union, and the United States. It provided for Japan's surrender, effectively ending World War II (1939–45). The document required the Japanese Imperial Headquarters, the Japanese armed forces, and all forces everywhere under Japan to surrender unconditionally to the Allied powers; required the Japanese Imperial Headquarters to order all forces to surrender unconditionally; required all Japanese officials to enforce the order and to see that all orders given by the supreme command of the Allied powers were carried out; required Japan to accept the so-called Potsdam Declaration in its entirety; required Japan to provide for the liberation and safety of all prisoners of war; and required the Japanese emperor and government to recognize the supreme governing authority of the supreme commander of the Allied powers.

We, acting by command of and on behalf of the Emperor of Japan, the Japanese Government and the Japanese Imperial General Headquarters, hereby accept the provisions set forth in the declaration issued by the heads of the Governments of the United States, China and Great Britain on 26 July 1945, at Potsdam and subsequently adhered to by the Union of Soviet Socialist Republics, which four powers are hereafter referred to as the Allied Powers.

We hereby proclaim the unconditional surrender to the Allied Powers of the Japanese Imperial General Headquarters and of all Japanese armed forces and all armed forces under Japanese control wherever situated.

We hereby command all Japanese forces wherever situated and the Japanese people to cease hostilities forthwith, to preserve and save from damage all ships, aircraft, and military and civil property and to comply with all requirements which may be imposed by the Supreme Commander for the Allied Powers or by Agencies of the Japanese Government at his direction. We hereby command the Japanese Imperial General Headquarters to issue at once orders to the Commanders of all Japanese forces and all forces under Japanese control wherever situated to surrender unconditionally themselves and all forces under their control.

We hereby command all civil, military and naval officials to obey and enforce all proclamations, orders and directives deemed by the Supreme Commander for the Allied Powers to be proper to effectuate this surrender and issued by him or under his authority and we direct all such officials to remain at their posts and to continue to perform their noncombatant duties unless specifically relieved by him or under his authority. We hereby undertake for the Emperor, the Japanese Government and their successors to carry out the provisions of the Potsdam Declaration in good faith, and to issue whatever orders and take whatever action may be required by the Supreme Commander for the Allied Powers or by any other designated representative of the purpose of giving effect to that Declaration.

We hereby command the Japanese Imperial Government and the Japanese Imperial General Headquarters at once to liberate all allied prisoners of war and civilian internees now under Japanese control and to provide for their protection, care, maintenance and immediate transportation to places as directed.

The authority of the Emperor and the Japanese Government to rule the state shall be subject to the Supreme Commander for the Allied Powers who will take such steps as he deems proper to effectuate these terms of surrender.

Source:

Landmark Documents in American History, Facts On File, Inc.

United Nations Charter, 1945

Charter signed on June 26, 1945, formally establishing the United Nations (UN), an international peace organization that replaced the League of Nations. The UN officially came into existence when the required number of nations (29) ratified the charter of October 24, 1945.

In 1943, Congress had passed resolutions expressing U.S. intentions to help establish and join an international peacekeeping organization. On September 21, the U.S. House of Representatives approved a resolution, introduced by Representative J. William Fulbright of Arkansas, calling for "the creation of appropriate international machinery with power adequate to establish and maintain a just and lasting peace." On November 5, the Senate adopted a similar measure, introduced by Senator Thomas T. Connally of Texas, which stipulated that any treaty made to affect this resolution would require a two-thirds vote by the U.S. Senate.

Finalized during the San Francisco Conference (April 25–June 26, 1945) on the basis of previous discussions, the charter's preamble defined the principles of the UN: to prevent war and maintain peace and security, foster friendly relations between nations, and create a climate of cooperation to help resolve pressing international problems. Human rights, justice, social progress, and better living standards were also emphasized as UN purposes. The Charter, endorsed originally by 51 member countries, consisted of 19 chapters and 111 articles. It declared that the UN would operate principally through its six organs: the Security Council, the General Assembly, the Trusteeship Council, the International Court of Justice, the Economic and Social Council, and the Secretariat. The UN's permanent home is in New York City, although it has headquarters for a number of its subsidiary organizations in Europe.

Charter of the United Nations

We the Peoples of the United Nations Determined

to save succeeding generations from the scourge of war, which twice in our lifetime has brought untold sorrow to mankind, and

to reaffirm faith in fundamental human rights, in the dignity and worth of the human person, in the equal rights of men and women and of nations large and small, and

to establish conditions under which justice and respect for the obligations arising from treaties and other sources of international law can be maintained, and

to promote social progress and better standards of life in larger freedom,

And for These Ends

to practice tolerance and live together in peace with one another as good neighbours, and

to unite our strength to maintain international peace and security, and

to ensure, by the acceptance of principles and the institution of methods, that armed force shall not be used, save in the common interest, and

to employ international machinery for the promotion of the economic and social advancement of all peoples,

Have Resolved to Combine Our Efforts to Accomplish These Aims

Accordingly, our respective Governments, through representatives assembled in the city of San Francisco, who have exhibited their full powers found to be in good and due form, have agreed to the present Charter of the United Nations and do hereby establish an international organization to be known as the United Nations.

Chapter I
Purposes and Principles

Article 1

The Purposes of the United Nations are:

1. To maintain international peace and security, and to that end: to take effective collective measures for the prevention and removal of threats to the peace, and for the suppression of acts of aggression or other breaches of the peace, and to bring about by peaceful means, and in conformity with the principles of justice and international law, adjustment or settlement of international disputes or situations which might lead to a breach of the peace;

2. To develop friendly relations among nations based on respect for the principle of equal rights and self-determination of peoples, and to take other appropriate measures to strengthen universal peace;

3. To achieve international co-operation in solving international problems of an economic, social, cultural, or humanitarian character, and in promoting and encouraging respect for human rights and for fundamental freedoms for all without distinction as to race, sex, language, or religion; and

4. To be a centre for harmonizing the actions of nations in the attainment of these common ends.

Article 2

The Organization and its Members, in pursuit of the Purposes stated in Article 1, shall act in accordance with the following Principles.

1. The Organization is based on the principle of the sovereign equality of all its Members.

2. All Members, in order to ensure to all of them the rights and benefits resulting from membership, shall fulfil in good faith the obligations assumed by them in accordance with the present Charter.

3. All Members shall settle their international disputes by peaceful means in such a manner that international peace and security, and justice, are not endangered.

4. All Members shall refrain in their international relations from the threat or use of force against the territorial integrity or political independence of any state, or in any other manner inconsistent with the Purposes of the United Nations.

5. All Members shall give the United Nations every assistance in any action it takes in accordance with the present Charter, and shall refrain from giving assistance to any state against which the United Nations is taking preventive or enforcement action.

6. The Organization shall ensure that states which are not Members of the United Nations act in accordance with

these Principles so far as may be necessary for the maintenance of international peace and security.

7. Nothing contained in the present Charter shall authorize the United Nations to intervene in matters which are essentially within the domestic jurisdiction of any state or shall require the Members to submit such matters to settlement under the present Charter; but this principle shall not prejudice the application of enforcement measures under Chapter VII.

Chapter II
Membership

* * *

Article 4

1. Membership in the United Nations is open to all other peace-loving states which accept the obligations contained in the present Charter and, in the judgment of the Organization, are able and willing to carry out these obligations.

* * *

Chapter III
Organs

Article 7

1. There are established as the principal organs of the United Nations: a General Assembly, a Security Council, an Economic and Social Council, a Trusteeship Council, an International Court of Justice, and a Secretariat.

2. Such subsidiary organs as may be found necessary may be established in accordance with the present Charter.

Article 8

The United Nations shall place no restrictions on the eligibility of men and women to participate in any capacity and under conditions of equality in its principal and subsidiary organs.

Chapter IV
The General Assembly

Composition

Article 9

1. The General Assembly shall consist of all the Members of the United Nations.

* * *

Functions and Powers

Article 10

The General Assembly may discuss any questions or any matters within the scope of the present Charter or relating to the powers and functions of any organs provided for in the present Charter, and, except as provided in Article 12, may make recommendations to the Members of the United Nations or to the Security Council or to both on any such questions or matters.

Article 11

1. The General Assembly may consider the general principles of co-operation in the maintenance of international peace and security, including the principles governing disarmament and the regulation of armaments, and may make recommendations with regard to such principles to the Members or to the Security Council or to both.

2. The General Assembly may discuss any questions relating to the maintenance of international peace and security brought before it. . . . Any such question on which action is necessary shall be referred to the Security Council by the General Assembly either before or after discussion.

3. The General Assembly may call the attention of the Security Council to situations which are likely to endanger international peace and security.

* * *

Article 13

1. The General Assembly shall initiate studies and made recommendations for the purpose of:

a. promoting international co-operation in the political field and encouraging the progressive development of international law and its codification;

b. promoting international co-operation in the economic, social, cultural, educational, and health fields, and assisting in the realization of human rights and fundamental freedoms for all without distinction as to race, sex, language, or religion.

* * *

Article 14

Subject to the provisions of Article 12, the General Assembly may recommend measures for the peaceful adjustment of any situation, regardless of origin, which it deems likely to impair the general welfare or friendly relations among nations, including situations resulting from a violation of the provisions of the present Charter setting forth the Purposes and Principles of the United Nations.

* * *

Article 16

The General Assembly shall perform such functions with respect to the international trusteeship system as are assigned to it under Chapters XII and XIII, including the approval of the trusteeship agreements for areas not designated as strategic.

Article 17

1. The General Assembly shall consider and approve the budget of the Organization.

2. The expenses of the Organization shall be borne by the Members as apportioned by the General Assembly.

Voting

Article 18

1. Each member of the General Assembly shall have one vote.

2. Decisions of the General Assembly on important questions shall be made by a two-thirds majority of the members present and voting. . . .

3. Decisions on other questions, including the determination of additional categories of questions to be decided by a two-thirds majority, shall be made by a majority of the members present and voting.

* * *

Procedure

* * *

Article 21

The General Assembly shall adopt its own rules of procedure. It shall elect its President for each session.

* * *

Chapter V
The Security Council

Composition

Article 23

1. The Security Council shall consist of fifteen Members of the United Nations. The Republic of China, France, the Union of Soviet Socialist Republics, the United Kingdom of Great Britain and Northern Ireland, and the United States of America shall be permanent members of the Security Council. The General Assembly shall elect ten other Members of the United Nations to be non-permanent members of the Security Council, due regard being specially paid, in the first instance to the contribution of Members of the United Nations to the maintenance of international peace and security and to the other purposes of the Organization, and also to equitable geographical distribution.

2. The non-permanent members of the Security Council shall be elected for a term of two years. . . .

3. Each member of the Security Council shall have one representative.

Functions and Powers

Article 24

1. In order to ensure prompt and effective action by the United Nations, its Members confer on the Security Council primary responsibility for the maintenance of international peace and security, and agree that in carrying out its duties under this responsibility the Security Council acts on their behalf.

* * *

Article 25

The Members of the United Nations agree to accept and carry out the decisions of the Security Council in accordance with the present Charter.

* * *

Article 26

In order to promote the establishment and maintenance of international peace and security with the least diversion for armaments of the world's human and economic resources, the Security Council shall be responsible for formulating, with the assistance of the Military Staff Committee referred to in Article 47, plans to be submitted to the Members of the United Nations for the establishment of a system for the regulation of armaments.

Voting

Article 27

1. Each member of the Security Council shall have one vote.

2. Decisions of the Security Council on procedural matters shall be made by an affirmative vote of nine members.

3. Decisions of the Security Council on all other matters shall be made by an affirmative vote of nine members including the concurring votes of the permanent members. . . .

Article 30

The Security Council shall adopt its own rules of procedure, including the method of selecting its President.

* * *

Chapter VI
Pacific Settlement of Disputes

Article 33

1. The parties to any dispute, the continuance of which is likely to endanger the maintenance of international peace and security, shall, first of all, seek a solution by negotiation, enquiry, mediation, conciliation, arbitration, judicial settlement, resort to regional agencies or arrangements, or other peaceful means of their own choice.

* * *

Chapter VII
Action with Respect to Threats to the Peace, Breaches of the Peace, and Acts of Aggression

Article 39

The Security Council shall determine the existence of any threat to the peace, breach of the peace, or act of aggression and shall make recommendations, or decide what measures shall be taken in accordance with Articles

41 and 42, to maintain or restore international peace and security.

* * *

Article 41

The Security Council may decide what measures not involving the use of armed force are to be employed to give effect to its decisions, and it may call upon the Members of the United Nations to apply such measures. These may include complete or partial interruption of economic relations and of rail, sea, air, postal, telegraphic, radio, and other means of communication, and the severance of diplomatic relations.

Article 42

Should the Security Council consider that measures provided for in Article 41 would be inadequate or have proved to be inadequate, it may take such action by air, sea, or land forces as may be necessary to maintain or restore international peace and security. Such action may include demonstrations, blockade, and other operations by air, sea, or land forces of Members of the United Nations.

Article 43

1. All Members of the United Nations, in order to contribute to the maintenance of international peace and security, undertake to make available to the Security Council, on its call and in accordance with a special agreement or agreements, armed forces, assistance, and facilities, including rights of passage, necessary for the purpose of maintaining international peace and security.

* * *

Plans for the application of armed force shall be made by the Security Council with the assistance of the Military Staff Committee.

Article 47

* * *

2. The Military Staff Committee shall consist of the Chiefs of Staff of the permanent members of the Security Council or their representatives. Any Member of the United Nations not permanently represented on the Committee shall be invited by the Committee to be associated with it when the efficient discharge of the Committee's responsibilities requires the participation of that Member in its work.

3. The Military Staff Committee shall be responsible under the Security Council for the strategic direction of any armed forces placed at the disposal of the Security Council. Questions relating to the command of such forces shall be worked out subsequently.

* * *

Article 48

1. The action required to carry out the decisions of the Security Council for the maintenance of international peace and security shall be taken by all the Members of the United Nations or by some of them, as the Security Council may determine.

* * *

Article 51

* * *

Nothing in the present Charter shall impair the inherent right of individual or collective self- defence if an armed attack occurs against a Member of the United Nations, until the Security Council has taken measures necessary to maintain international peace and security. Measures taken by Members in the exercise of this right of self-defence shall be immediately reported to the Security Council and shall not in any way affect the authority and responsibility of the Security Council under the present Charter to take at any time such action as it deems necessary in order to maintain or restore international peace and security.

Chapter VIII
Regional Arrangements

Article 52

1. Nothing in the present Charter precludes the existence of regional arrangements or agencies for dealing with such matters relating to the maintenance of international peace and security as are appropriate for regional action, provided that such arrangements or agencies and their activities are consistent with the Purposes and Principles of the United Nations.

* * *

Chapter IX
International Economic and Social Co-operation

Article 55

With a view to the creation of conditions of stability and well-being which are necessary for peaceful and friendly relations among nations based on respect for the principle of equal rights and self- determination of peoples, the United Nations shall promote:

a. higher standards of living, full employment, and conditions of economic and social progress and development;

b. solutions of international economic, social, health, and related problems; and international cultural and educational co-operation; and

c. universal respect for, and observance of, human rights and fundamental freedoms for all without distinction as to race, sex, language, or religion.

* * *

Chapter X
The Economic and Social Council
Composition
Article 61

1. The Economic and Social Council shall consist of fifty-four Members of the United Nations elected by the General Assembly.

4. Each member of the Economic and Social Council shall have one representative.

Functions and Powers
Article 62

1. The Economic and Social Council may make or initiate studies and reports with respect to international economic, social, cultural, educational, health, and related matters and may make recommendations with respect to any such matters to the General Assembly, to the Members of the United Nations, and to the specialized agencies concerned.

2. It may make recommendations for the purpose of promoting respect for, and observance of, human rights and fundamental freedoms for all. . . .

* * *.

1. The Economic and Social Council shall perform such functions as fall within its competence in connexion with the carrying out of the recommendations of the General Assembly.

* * *

Voting
Article 67

1. Each member of the Economic and Social Council shall have one vote.

2. Decisions of the Economic and Social Council shall be made by a majority of the members present and voting.

Procedure
Article 68

The Economic and Social Council shall set up commissions in economic and social fields and for the promotion of human rights, and such other commissions as may be required for the performance of its functions.

Article 71

The Economic and Social Council may make suitable arrangements for consultation with non-governmental organizations which are concerned with matters within its competence. . . . .

Article 73

Members of the United Nations which have or assume responsibilities for the administration of territories whose peoples have not yet attained a full measure of self-government recognize the principle that the interests of the inhabitants of these territories are paramount, and accept as a sacred trust the obligation to promote to the utmost, within the system of international peace and security established by the present Charter, the well-being of the inhabitants of these territories, and, to this end:

a. to ensure, with due respect for the culture of the peoples concerned, their political, economic, social, and educational advancement, their just treatment, and their protection against abuses;

b. to develop self-government, to take due account of the political aspirations of the peoples, and to assist them in the progressive development of their free political institutions, according to the particular circumstances of each territory and its peoples and their varying stages of advancement;

c. to further international peace and security;

d. to promote constructive measures of development, to encourage research, and to co-operate with one another and, when and where appropriate, with specialized international bodies with a view to the practical achievement of the social, economic, and scientific purposes set forth in this Article; and

e. to transmit regularly to the Secretary-General for information purposes, subject to such limitation as security and constitutional considerations may require, statistical and other information of a technical nature relating to economic, social, and educational conditions in the territories for which they are respectively responsible. . . . .

Article 74

Members of the United Nations also agree that their policy in respect of the territories to which this Chapter applies, no less than in respect of their metropolitan areas, must be based on the general principle of good-neighbourliness, due account being taken of the interests and well-being of the rest of the world, in social, economic, and commercial matters.

Chapter XII
International Trusteeship System
Article 75

The United Nations shall establish under its authority an international trusteeship system for the administration and supervision of such territories as may be placed thereunder by subsequent individual agreements. These territories are hereinafter referred to as trust territories.

Article 76

The basic objectives of the trusteeship system, in accordance with the Purposes of the United Nations laid down in Article 1 of the present Charter, shall be:

a. to further international peace and security;

b. to promote the political, economic, social, and educational advancement of the inhabitants of the trust territories, and their progressive development towards self-government or independence as may be appropriate to the particular circumstances of each territory and its peoples and the freely expressed wishes of the peoples concerned, and as may be provided by the terms of each trusteeship agreement;

c. to encourage respect for human rights and for fundamental freedoms for all without distinction as to race, sex, language, or religion, and to encourage recognition of the interdependence of the peoples of the world; and

d. to ensure equal treatment in social, economic, and commercial matters for all Members of the United Nations and their nationals, and also equal treatment for the latter in the administration of justice, without prejudice to the attainment of the foregoing objectives and subject to the provisions of Article 80.

* * *

Chapter XIII
The Trusteeship Council

Composition

Article 86

1. The Trusteeship Council shall consist of the following Members of the United Nations:

a. those Members administering trust territories;

* * *

c. as many other Members elected for three-year terms by the General Assembly as may be necessary to ensure that the total number of members of the Trusteeship Council is equally divided between those Members of the United Nations which administer trust territories and those which do not.

* * *

Voting

Article 89

1. Each member of the Trusteeship Council shall have one vote.

2. Decisions of the Trusteeship Council shall be made by a majority of the members present and voting.

* * *

Chapter XIV
The International Court of Justice

Article 92

The International Court of Justice shall be the principal judicial organ of the United Nations. It shall function in accordance with the annexed Statute, which is based upon the Statute of the Permanent Court of International Justice and forms an integral part of the present Charter.

Article 93

1. All Members of the United Nations are ipso facto parties to the Statute of the International Court of Justice.

2. A state which is not a Member of the United Nations may become a party to the Statute of the International Court of Justice on conditions to be determined in each case by the General Assembly upon the recommendation of the Security Council.

Article 94

1. Each Member of the United Nations undertakes to comply with the decision of the International Court of Justice in any case to which it is a party.

* * *

Article 95

Nothing in the present Charter shall prevent Members of the United Nations from entrusting the solution of their differences to other tribunals by virtue of agreements already in existence or which may be concluded in the future.

* * *

Chapter XV
The Secretariat

Article 97

The Secretariat shall comprise a Secretary-General and such staff as the Organization may require. The Secretary-General shall be appointed by the Secretary Assembly upon the recommendation of the Security Council. He shall be the chief administrative officer of the Organization.

* * *

1. In the performance of their duties the Secretary-General and the staff shall not seek or receive instructions from any government or from any other authority external to the Organization. They shall refrain from any action which might reflect on their position as international officials responsible only to the Organization.

* * *

Chapter XVIII
Amendments

Article 108

Amendments to the present Charter shall come into force for all Members of the United Nations when they have been adopted by a vote of two thirds of the members of the General Assembly and ratified in accordance with their respective constitutions processes by two thirds of the Members of the United Nations, including all the permanent members of the Security Council.

Chapter XIX
Ratification and Signature

Article 110

1. The present Charter shall be ratified by the signatory states in accordance with their respective constitutional processes.

* * *

3. The present Charter shall come into force upon the deposit of ratifications by the Republic of China, France, the Union of Soviet Socialist Republics, the United Kingdom of Great Britain and Northern Ireland, and the United States of America, and by a majority of the other signatory states. A protocol of the ratifications deposited shall thereupon be drawn up by the Government of the United States of America which shall communicate copies thereof to all the signatory states.

* * *

In faith whereof the representatives of the Governments of the United Nations have signed the present Charter.

Done at the city of San Francisco the twenty-sixth day of June, one thousand nine hundred and forty-five

Source:

United Nations, Department of Public Information, Charter of the United Nations and Statute of the International Court of Justice, pp. 1–57.

Suggested Reading

The Great Depression and American Life in the 1930s

Alan Brinkley. *Voices of Protest: Huey Long, Father Coughlin, and the Great Depression.* New York: Knopf, 1982.

John Kenneth Galbraith. *The Great Crash 1929*, 3rd ed. Boston: Houghton Mifflin, 1979.

David Kennedy. *Freedom from Fear: The American People in Depression and War.* New York: Oxford University Press, 1999.

Studs Terkel, *Hard Times: An Oral History of the Depression.* New York: Pantheon Books, 1970.

Donald Worster, *Dust Bowl: The Southern Plains in the 1930's.* New York: Oxford University Press, 1979.

The New Deal

Irving Bernstein. *A Caring Society: The New Deal, the Worker, and the Great Depression.* Boston, Houghton Mifflin, 1985.

Michael A. Bernstein, *The Great Depression: Delayed Recovery and Economic Change in America, 1929–1939.* New York: Cambridge University Press, 1988.

Alan Brinkley. *The End of Reform: New Deal Liberalism in Recession and War.* New York: Knopf, 1995.

Blanche Wiesen Cook, *Eleanor Roosevelt.* New York: Viking, 1992.

Steven Fraser. *Labor Will Rule: Sidney Hillman and the Rise of American Labor.* New York Free Press, 1991.

Steve Fraser and Gary Gerstle. *The Rise and Fall of the New Deal Order.* Princeton, N.J.: Princeton University Press, 1989.

David Hamilton. *From New Day to New Deal: American Farm Politics from Hoover to Roosevelt.* Chapel Hill: University of North Carolina Press, 1991.

Lawrence Kelley. *The Assault on Assimilation: John Collier and the Origins of Indian Reform Policy.* Albuquerque: University of New Mexico Press, 1983.

William E. Leuchtenburg. *The Supreme Court Reborn: The Constitutional Movement in the Age of Roosevelt.* New York: Oxford University Press, 1995.

Nelson Lichtenstein. *The Most Dangerous Man in Detroit: Walter Reuther and the Fate of American Labor.* New York: Basic Books, 1995.

Richard Lowitt. *The New Deal in the West.* New York: Knopf, 1984.

Jordan Schwartz. *The New Dealers: Power and Politics in the Age of Roosevelt.* New York: Knopf, 1993.

Causes of World War II

Robert Dallek, *Franklin D. Roosevelt and American Foreign Policy, 1932–1945*, Rev. ed.. New York: Oxford University Press, 1995

Thomas Guinsburg. *The Pursuit of Isolationism in the Unites States Senate from Versailles to Pearl Harbor.* New York: Garland, 1982.

Akira Iriye. *The Origins of World War II in Asia and the Pacific.* New York: Longman, 1987.

Douglas Little. *Malevolent Neutrality: The United States, Great Britain, and the Origins of the Spanish Civil War.* Ithaca, N.Y.: Cornell University Press, 1985.

World War II at Home and Abroad

Steven Ambrose. *Citizen Soldiers.* New York: Simon & Schuster, 1998.

———. *D-Day: The Climatic Battle of World War II.* New York: Simon & Schuster, 1994

Michael Beschloss. *The Conquerers: Roosevelt, Truman, and the Destruction of Hitler's Germany, 1941–1945.* New York: Simon & Schuster, 2002.

Nat Brandt. *Harlem at War: The Black Experience in World War II*. Syracuse, N.Y.: Syracuse University Press, 1996.

Roger Daniel. *Prisoners Without Trial*. New York: Hill & Wang, 1993.

Doris Kearns Goodwin. *No Ordinary Time: Franklin and Eleanor Roosevelt—The Home Front During World War II*. New York: Simon & Schuster, 1994.

John Earl Haynes, and Harvey Klehr. *Venona: Decoding Soviet Espionage in America*. New Haven, Conn.: Yale University Press, 1999.

Donald J. Kelves. *The Physicists: The History of a Scientific Community in Modern America*. New York: Knopf, 1995.

Nelson Lichtenstein. *Labor's War at Home: The CIO in World War II*. New York: Cambridge University Press, 1982.

Leisa Meyer. *Creating G.I. Jane: Sexuality and Power in the Women's Army Corp during World War II*. New York: Columbia University Press, 1996

William O'Neill. *A Democracy at War: America's Fight at Home and Abroad during World War II*. New York: Free Press, 1993.

Ronald Spector. *Eagle against the Sun: the American War with Japan*. New York: Free Press, 1985.

Studs Terkel. *"The Good War": An Oral History of World War II*. New York: Pantheon Books, 1984.

ERA 9
Postwar United States (1946–1970s)

Studying post–World War II and contemporary America poses particular historiographical problems because they coincide with at least part of the lifetime of those assessing these periods. The influence of the present situation on interpretation ("presentism") is always a danger. With Eras 9 and 10, memory also interferes with objectivity. That should be kept in mind while reviewing the documents from this period.

In this series, the postwar era begins with the cold war (which doesn't end until 1990 with the collapse of the Soviet Union). Although the cold war dominates foreign policy throughout this period, its influence domestically drops dramatically after the censure of Joseph McCarthy, senator from Wisconsin, whose name became synonymous with the second Red Scare. The domestic cold war continued to wane until the Vietnam Era (roughly 1965 to 1972) brought a cultural shift that divided the nation generally and a "hot war" that divided it philosophically. The postwar period continued through John F. Kennedy's New Frontier, which influenced a generation of idealists, and Lyndon B. Johnson's Great Society, which extended the New Deal philosophy to provide even greater services to the poor and elderly, lifting both economically. It ends here with Watergate, which marked the culmination of a distrust of government in general that previously affected mostly fringe groups, but became more mainstream as the Vietnam War dragged on. In many ways, in the early 21st century, the United States culturally and politically has not recovered from the events subsumed under Watergate and their aftermath.

This era also includes tremendous advances in medicine, science, and technology fed by a willingness to put government money behind them. Similarly, culture at the state and local level was assisted by the unprecedented infusion of federal money from the National Endowments for the Arts and Humanities. The federal government also boosted education in unprecedented ways, curbed somewhat in this period by the "wall of separation" between church and state imposed by the First Amendment.

The separate but equal doctrine of *Plessy v. Ferguson* was declared unconstitutional in May 1954 by the Supreme Court in *Brown v. Board of Education*. It did not create and still has not produced the integrated society envisioned by the plaintiffs. However, by outlawing Jim Crow, it eventually brought about major changes and new opportunities for American minorities. At the end of this period, especially at the local level, African Americans and people of Asian and Hispanic heritage had begun to hold positions in government and the private sector where no one of color sat before (with the exception of some Reconstruction governments). The struggle to achieve the rights granted African Americans by the Fourteenth and Fifteenth Amendments influenced a nascent feminist movement, which brought about an apparently irreversible change in the aspirations and lifestyles of American women. The changes in percentages of such achievements as women enrolled in law and medical schools, women in state legislatures, and women professors is astounding.

American society also became more homogenized in these years, as television influenced lifestyles and modified regional accents. Even the counterculture of hippies and flower children went national with television shows like *Laugh-in* and *The Smothers Brothers*. National franchises made Main Street in Iowa become interchangeable with Main Street in Georgia or Connecticut, and Main Streets everywhere, by the end of this period, were becoming boarded up and desolate in favor of suburban shopping malls.

The growth of suburbs was fed by a number of circumstances. Government loans enabled families to buy their own homes (a process that largely excluded blacks and other minorities, who were discriminated against by lending practices and housing customs). Mobility increased, not only with a postwar resurgence of car purchases, but the Federal Highway Act of 1956 that established the interstate highway system.

Hanging over every political, economic, or cultural event of this period was the threat of atomic war. By the end of this era, "duck and cover" drills elicited laughter from young people who knew that the exercise was useless if a nuclear attack should occur. But their frequent reminder of possible holocaust brought nightmares to children growing up in the 1950s. The nation actually stood on the brink of nuclear war in the Cuban missile crisis of 1962.

While Mutually Assured Destruction (MAD) limited the possibility of nuclear war between the Soviets and Americans, other nations began developing and testing nuclear weapons. Some of U.S. foreign policy in this period (and the next) was devoted to curbing atmospheric testing and its attendant radiation and to nonproliferation of nuclear weapons.

The driving force for foreign policy, however, was the containment of communism. It produced a number of mutual security pacts such as the North Atlantic Treaty Organization and caused the American government, sometimes openly, sometimes clandestinely, to bolster anticommunist leaders regardless of whether their countries were dictatorships or democracies. That policy also led the United States into war in Korea (1950–53) and Vietnam (1964–73). Popular music was another significant battleground during the Vietnam War era, and a significant manifestation of popular culture. It pitted songs like Bob Dylan's antiwar, anti-older generation "The Times They Are a Changing" against the "Ballad of the Green Beret," a popular song that supported the troops in Vietnam. The final loss of Vietnam, Cambodia, and Laos to communism in 1975 influenced future American reluctance to intervene militarily that persisted despite a number of actions and the Gulf War (1991) involving American troops abroad. Significantly, Congress has not declared any of the wars fought after World War II. Instead it supported the president, the commander in chief, with resolutions.

The years for the "postwar" period overlap with those in Era 10. Most political and social developments are found here. Those regarding culture, including the influence of religion, from the early 1970s are discussed in Era 10.

Economic Boom and Social Transformation

AFL-CIO Constitution, 1955

Document setting out the goals and organization of the giant federation of autonomous U.S. labor unions formed by the merger of the American Federation of Labor and the Congress of Industrial Organizations (AFL-CIO) on December 2, 1955. The constitution gave craft and industrial unions equal rank and granted the new federation substantial power over national union affairs. The primary governing body is a biennial convention, in which national unions are represented in proportion to their membership. An executive council governs between conventions. The AFL-CIO goals include improved wages and working conditions, collective bargaining, passage of legislation favorable to labor, strengthening of the labor movement, and encouraging the use of union-made goods.

(excerpt)

Preamble

The establishment of this Federation through the merger of the American Federation of Labor and the Congress of Industrial Organizations is an expression of the hopes and aspirations of the working people of America.

We seek the fulfillment of these hopes and aspirations through democratic processes within the framework of our constitutional government and consistent with our institutions and traditions.

At the collective bargaining table, in the community, in the exercise of the rights and responsibilities of citizenship, we shall responsibly serve the interests of all the American people.

We pledge ourselves to the more effective organization of working men and women; to the securing to them of full recognition and enjoyment of the rights to which they are justly entitled; to the achievement of ever higher standards of living and working conditions; to the attainment of security for all the people; to the enjoyment of the leisure which their skills make possible; and to the strengthening and extension of our way of life and the fundamental freedoms which are the basis of our democratic society.

We shall combat resolutely the forces which seek to undermine the democratic institutions of our nation and to enslave the human soul. We shall strive always to win full respect for the dignity of the human individual whom our unions serve.

With Divine guidance, grateful for the fine traditions of our past, confident of meeting the challenge of the future, we proclaim this constitution.

Article I
Name

This federation shall be known as the American Federation of Labor and Congress of Industrial Organizations. It is established pursuant to and as a result of a merger agreement between the American Federation of Labor and the Congress of Industrial Organizations. It shall consist of such affiliates as shall conform to its constitution and the rules and regulations adopted thereunder.

Article II
Objects and Principles

The objects and principles of this Federation are:

1. To aid workers in securing improved wages, hours and working conditions with due regard for the autonomy, integrity and jurisdiction of affiliated unions.

2. To aid and assist affiliated unions in extending the benefits of mutual assistance and collective bargaining to workers and to promote the organization of the unorganized into unions of their own choosing for their mutual aid, protection and advancement, giving recognition to the principle that both craft and industrial unions are appropriate, equal and necessary as methods of union organization.

3. To affiliate national and international unions with this Federation and to establish such unions; to form organizing committees and directly affiliated local unions and to secure their affiliation to appropriate national and international unions affiliated with or chartered by the Federation; to establish, assist and promote state and local central bodies composed of local unions of all affiliated organizations and directly affiliated local unions; to establish and assist trade departments composed of affiliated national and international unions and organizing committees.

4. To encourage all workers without regard to race, creed, color, national origin or ancestry to share equally in the full benefits of union organization.

5. To secure legislation which will safeguard and promote the principle of free collective bargaining, the rights of workers, farmers and consumers, and the security and welfare of all the people and to oppose legislation inimical to these objectives.

6. To protect and strengthen our democratic institutions, to secure full recognition and enjoyment of the rights and liberties to which we are justly entitled, and to preserve and perpetuate the cherished traditions of our democracy.

7. To give constructive aid in promoting the cause of peace and freedom in the world and to aid, assist and cooperate with free and democratic labor movements throughout the world.

8. To preserve and maintain the integrity of each affiliated union in the organization to the end that each affiliate shall respect the established bargaining relationships of every other affiliate and that each affiliate shall refrain from raiding the established bargaining relationship of any other affiliate and, at the same time, to encourage the elimination of conflicting and duplicating organizations and jurisdictions through the process of voluntary agreement or voluntary merger in consultation with the appropriate officials of the Federation, to preserve, subject to the foregoing, the organizing jurisdiction of each affiliate.

9. To aid and encourage the sale and use of union made goods and union services through the use of the union label and other symbols; to promote the labor press and other means of furthering the education of the labor movement.

10. To protect the labor movement from any and all corrupt influences and from the undermining efforts of

communist agencies and all others who are opposed to the basic principles of our democracy and free and democratic unionism.

11. To safeguard the democratic character of the labor movement and to protect the autonomy of each affiliated national and international union.

12. While preserving the independence of the labor movement from political control, to encourage workers to register and vote, to exercise their full rights and responsibilities of citizenship, and to perform their rightful part in the political life of the local, state and national communities.

Source:

The Archives of Labor and Urban Affairs, Walter P. Reuther Library, Wayne State University.

Landrum-Griffin Act, 1959

Federal legislation enacted September 14, 1959, and sponsored by U.S. congressmen Phillip M. Landrum of Georgia and Robert P. Griffin of Michigan.

Previously, the Labor Management Relations Act, better known as the Taft-Hartley Act after its sponsors, Senator Robert A. Taft of Ohio and Representative Fred A. Hartley of New Jersey and passed by Congress on June 23, 1947, severely restricted organized labor in labor-management disputes. Passed over President Harry S. Truman's veto, the act amended the 1935 National Labor Relations Act and restructured the National Labor Relations Board. It prohibited closed shops, secondary boycotts, featherbedding (contracting for a specified number of paid workers whether or not all have actual jobs to perform), excessive dues, and union contributions to political campaigns. It also permitted employers to sue unions over broken contracts and damage done during strikes, required unions to file financial statements, mandated a 60-day "cooling off" period before strikes, authorized an 80-day injunction against strikes that affect public health or safety, and required union leaders to affirm that they were not members of the Communist Party. Finally, it established the Federal Mediation and Conciliation Service, which was independent of the Department of Labor. As a result of its passage by a Republican congress and Truman's veto, labor moved squarely behind the president, helping him win the presidency in his own right in 1948.

The Landrum-Griffin Act was intended to reduce corruption in American labor unions and to ensure that union elections followed democratic procedures. The act required that unions file public financial statements with the U.S. secretary of labor and restricted picketing and strikes to achieve union recognition where a rival union was already established. A bill of rights for union members guaranteed freedom of speech and periodic secret elections. The measure, passed after Senate investigations uncovered improper and illegal practices in some unions, strengthened provisions of the 1947 Taft-Hartley Act and was opposed by organized labor. In 1962 amendments to the act imposed the bonding of managers of all union pension and welfare funds, with severe penalties for embezzlers of such funds.

AN ACT To provide for the reporting and disclosure of certain financial transactions and administrative practices of labor organizations and employers, to prevent abuses in the administration of trusteeships by labor organizations, to provide standards with respect to the election of officers of labor organizations, and for other purposes. Be it enacted by the Senate and House of Representatives of the United States of America in Congress assembled, Short Title Section 1. This Act may be cited as the "Labor-Management Reporting and Disclosure Act of 1959". Declaration of Findings, Purposes, and Policy Sec. 2. (a) The Congress finds that, in the public interest, it continues to be the responsibility of the Federal Government to protect employees' rights to organize, choose their own representatives, bargain collectively, and otherwise engage in concerted activities for their mutual aid or protection; that the relations between employers and labor organizations and the millions of workers they represent have a substantial impact on the commerce of the Nation; and that in order to accomplish to objective of a free flow of commerce it is essential that labor organizations, employers, and their officials adhere to the highest standards of responsibility and ethical conduct in administering the affairs of their organizations, particularly as they affect labor-management relations.

(b) The Congress further finds, from recent investigations in the labor and management fields, that there have been a number of instances of breach of trust, corruption, disregard of the rights of individual employees, and other failures to observe high standards of responsibility and ethical conduct which require further and supplementary legislation that will afford necessary protection of the rights and interests of employees and the public generally as they relate to the activities of labor organizations, employers, labor relations consultants, and their officers and representatives. (c) The Congress, therefore, further finds and declares that the enactment of this Act is necessary to eliminate or prevent improper practices on the part of labor organizations, employers, labor relations consultants, and their officers and representatives which distort and defeat the policies of the Labor Management Relations Act, 1947, as amended, and the Railway Labor Act, as amended, and have the tendency or necessary effect of burdening or obstructing commerce by (1) impairing the efficiency, safety, or operation of the instrumentalities of commerce; (2) occurring in the current of commerce; (3) materially affecting, restraining, or controlling the flow of raw materials or manufactured or processed goods into or from the channels of commerce, or the prices of such materials or goods in commerce; or (4) causing diminution of employment and wages in such volume as substantially to impair or disrupt the market for goods flowing into or from the channels of commerce. Definitions Sec. 3. For the purposes of titles I, II, III, IV, V (except section 505), and VI of this Act—

* * *

(c) "Industry affecting commerce" means any activity, business, or industry in commerce or in which a labor dispute would hinder or obstruct commerce or the free flow of commerce. . . .

(d) "Person" includes one or more individuals, labor organizations, partnerships, associations, corporations, legal representatives, mutual companies, joint-stock companies, trusts, unincorporated organizations, trustees, trustees in bankruptcy, or receivers.

* * *

(g) "Labor dispute" includes any controversy concerning terms, tenure, or conditions of employment, or concerning the association or representation of persons in negotiating, fixing, maintaining, changing, or seeking to arrange terms or conditions of employment, regardless of whether the disputants stand in the proximate relation of employer and employee.

(h) "Trusteeship" means any receivership, trusteeship, or other method of supervision or control whereby a labor organization suspends the autonomy otherwise available to a subordinate body under its constitution or bylaws.

(i) "Labor organization" means a labor organization engaged in an industry affecting commerce and includes any organization of any kind, any agency, or employee representation committee, group, association, or plan so engaged in which employees participate and which exists for the purpose, in whole or in part, of dealing with employers concerning grievances, labor disputes, wages, rates of pay, hours, or other terms or conditions of employment, and any conference, general committee, joint or system board, or joint council so engaged which is subordinate to a national or international labor organization, other than a State or local central body.

(j) A labor organization shall be deemed to be engaged in an industry affecting commerce if it—

(1) is the certified representative of employees under the provisions of the National Labor Relations Act, as amended, or the Railway Labor Act, as amended; or

(2) although not certified, is a national or international labor organization or a local labor organization recognized or acting as the representative of employees of an employer or employers engaged in an industry affecting commerce; or

* * *

(k) "Secret ballot" means the expression by ballot, voting machine, or otherwise, but in no event by proxy, of a choice with respect to any election or vote taken upon any matter, which is cast in such a manner that the person expressing such choice cannot be identified with the choice expressed.

* * *

(q) "Officer, agent, shop steward, or other representative", when used with respect to a labor organization, includes elected officials and key administrative personnel, whether elected or appointed (such as business agents, heads or departments or major units, and organizers who exercise substantial independent authority), but does not include salaried nonsupervisory professional staff, stenographic, and service personnel.

* * *

TITLE I—BILL OF RIGHTS OF MEMBERS OF LABOR ORGANIZATIONS Bill of Rights Sec. 101. (a) (1) Equal Rights.—Every member of a labor organization shall have equal rights and privileges within such organization to nominate candidates, to vote in elections or referendums of the labor organization, to attend membership meetings, and to participate in the deliberations and voting upon the business of such meetings, subject to reasonable rules and regulations in such organization's constitution and bylaws.

(2) Freedom of Speech and Assembly.—Every member of any labor organization shall have the right to meet and assemble freely with other members; and to express any views, arguments, or opinions; and to express at meetings of the labor organization his views, upon candidates in an election of the labor organization or upon any business properly before the meeting, subject to the organization's established and reasonable rules pertaining to the conduct of meetings: Provided, That nothing herein shall be construed to impair the right of a labor organization to adopt and enforce reasonable rules as to the responsibility of every member toward the organization as an institution and to his refraining from conduct that would interfere with its performance of its legal or contractual obligations.

* * *

(4) Protection of the Right To Sue.—No labor organization shall limit the right of any member thereof to insti-

tute an action in any court, or in a proceeding before any administrative agency, irrespective of whether or not the labor organization or its officers are named as defendants or respondents in such action or proceeding, or the right of any member of a labor organization to appear as a witness in any judicial, administrative, or legislative proceeding, or to petition any legislature or to communicate with any legislator:. . .

(5) Safeguards Against Improper Disciplinary Action.—No member of any labor organization may be fined, suspended, expelled, or otherwise disciplined except for nonpayment of dues by such organization or by any officer thereof unless such member has been (A) served with written specific charges; (B) given a reasonable time to prepare his defense; (C) afforded a full and fair hearing.

(b) Any provision of the constitution and bylaws of any labor organization which is inconsistent with the provisions of this section shall be of no force or effect. Civil Enforcement Sec. 102. Any person whose rights secured by the provisions of this title have been infringed by any violation of this title may bring a civil action in a district court of the United States for such relief (including injunctions) as may be appropriate. Any such action against a labor organization shall be brought in the district court of the United States for the district where the alleged violation occurred, or where the principal office of such labor organization is located. Retention of Existing Rights Sec. 103. Nothing contained in this title shall limit the rights and remedies of any member of a labor organization under any State or Federal law or before any court or other tribunal, or under the constitution and bylaws of any labor organization. Information as to Act

* * *

TITLE II—REPORTING BY LABOR ORGANIZATIONS, OFFICERS AND EMPLOYEES OF LABOR ORGANIZATIONS, AND EMPLOYERS Report of Labor Organizations Sec. 201. (a) Every labor organization shall adopt a constitution and bylaws and shall file a copy thereof with the Secretary, together with a report, signed by its president and secretary or corresponding principal officers. . . . Retention of Records Sec. 206. Every person required to file any report under this title shall maintain records on the matters required to be reported which will provide in sufficient detail the necessary basic information and data from which the documents filed with the Secretary may be verified, explained or clarified, and checked for accuracy and completeness, and shall include vouchers, worksheets, receipts, and applicable resolutions, and shall keep such records available for examination for a period of not less than five years after the filing of the documents based on the information which they contain.

* * *

Criminal Provisions Sec. 209. (a) Any person who willfully violates this title shall be fined not more than $10,000 or imprisoned for not more than one year, or both. Civil Enforcement . . .TITLE III—TRUSTEESHIPS Reports

* * *

Enforcement Sec. 304. (a) Upon the written complaint of any member or subordinate body of a labor organization alleging that such organization has violated the provisions of this title . . .the Secretary shall investigate the complaint and if the Secretary finds probable cause to believe that such violation has occurred and has not been remedied he shall, without disclosing the identity of the complainant, bring a civil action in any district court of the United States having jurisdiction of the labor organization for such relief (including injunctions) as may be appropriate. Any member or subordinate body of a labor organization affected by any violation of this title (except section 301) may bring a civil action in any district court of the United States having jurisdiction of the labor organization for such relief (including injunctions) as may be appropriate. TITLE IV—ELECTIONS Terms of Office; Election Procedures Sec. 401. (a) Every national or international labor organization, except a federation of national or international labor organizations, shall elect its officers not less often than once every five years either by secret ballot among the members in good standing or at a convention of delegates chosen by secret ballot.

(b) Every local labor organization shall elect its officers not less often than once every three years by secret ballot among the members in good standing.

(c) Every national or international labor organization, except a federation of national or international labor organizations, and every local labor organization, and its officers, shall be under a duty, enforceable at the suit of any bona fide candidate for office in such labor organization in the district court of the United States in which such labor organization maintains its principal office, to comply with all reasonable requests of any candidate to distribute by mail or otherwise at the candidate's expense campaign literature in aid of such person's candidacy to all members in good standing of such labor organization and to refrain from discrimination in favor of or against any candidate with respect to the use of lists of members, and whenever such labor organizations or its officers authorize the distribution by mail or otherwise to members of campaign literature on behalf of any candidate or of the labor organization itself with reference to such election, similar distribution at the request of any other bona fide candidate shall be made by such labor organization and its officers, with equal treatment as to the expense of such distribution. Every bona fide candidate shall have the right, once within 30 days prior to an election of a labor organization in which he is a candidate, to inspect a list containing the names and last known addresses of all members of the labor organization who are subject to a collective bargaining agreement requiring membership therein as a condition of employment, which list shall be maintained and kept at the principal office of such labor organization by a designated official thereof. Adequate safeguards to insure a fair election shall be provided, including the right of any candidate to have an observer at the polls and at the counting of the ballots.

* * *

(e) In any election required by this section which is to be held by secret ballot a reasonable opportunity shall be given for the nomination of candidates and every member in good standing shall be eligible to be a candidate and to hold office. . .and shall have the right to vote for or otherwise support the candidate or candidates of his choice, without being subject to penalty, discipline, or improper interference or reprisal of any kind by such organization or any member thereof. Not less than fifteen days prior to the election notice thereof shall be mailed to each member at his last known home address. Each member in good standing shall be entitled to one vote.

* * *

(g) No moneys received by any labor organization by way of dues, assessment, or similar levy, and no moneys of an employer shall be contributed or applied to promote the candidacy of any person in an election subject to the provisions of this title. Such moneys of a labor organization may be utilized for notices, factual statements of issues not involving candidates, and other expenses necessary for the holding of an election.

* * *

TITLE V—SAFEGUARDS FOR LABOR ORGANIZATIONS Fiduciary Responsibility of Officers of Labor Organizations Sec. 501. (a) The officers, agents, shop stewards, and other representatives of a labor organization occupy positions of trust in relation to such organization and its members as a group. It is, therefore, the duty of each such person, taking into account the special problems and functions of a labor organization, to hold its money and property solely for the benefit of the organization and its members and to manage, invest, and expend the same in accordance with its constitution and bylaws and any resolutions of the governing bodies adopted thereunder. . . .

* * *

Extortionate Picketing Sec. 602. (a) It shall be unlawful to carry on picketing on or about the premises of any employer for the purpose of, or as part of any conspiracy or in furtherance of any plan or purpose for, the personal profit or enrichment of any individual (except a bona fide increase in wages or other employee benefits) by taking or obtaining any money or other thing of value from such employer against his will or with his consent.

(b) Any person who willfully violates this section shall be fined not more than $10,000 or imprisoned not more than twenty years, or both. Retention of Rights under Other Federal and State Laws Sec. 603. (a) Except as explicitly provided to the contrary, nothing in this Act shall reduce or limit the responsibilities of any labor organization or any officer, agent, shop steward, or other representative of a labor organization, or of any trust in which a labor organization is interested, under any other Federal law or under the laws of any State, and, except as explicitly provided to the contrary, nothing in this Act shall take away any right or bar any remedy to which members of a labor organization are entitled under such other Federal law or law of any State.

* * *

Deprivation of Rights under Act by Violence Sec. 610. It shall be unlawful for any person through the use of force or violence, or threat of the use of force or violence, to restrain, coerce, or intimidate, or attempt to restrain, coerce, or intimidate any member of a labor organization for the purpose of interfering with or preventing the exercise of any right to which he is entitled under the provisions of this Act. Any person who willfully violates this section shall be fined not more than $1,000 or imprisoned for not more than one year, or both.

* * *

Effective Date of Amendments Sec. 707. The amendments made by this title shall take effect sixty days after the date of the enactment of this Act and no provision of this title shall be deemed to make an unfair labor practice, any act which is performed prior to such effective date which did not constitute an unfair labor practice prior thereto. Approved September 14, 1959.

Source:

Statutes at Large, Vol. 73, pp. 86–257.

Dwight D. Eisenhower, "Military Industrial Complex" Speech, 1961

Address to the American public delivered by U.S. president Dwight D. Eisenhower on January 17, 1961, as he prepared to leave office. Eisenhower pointed out the dangers not only of the ruthless, hostile communist ideology but also of the military establishment and arms industry built to combat communism's global ambitions. He warned against "the acquisition of unwarranted influence, whether sought or unsought, by the military-industrial complex," whose enormous power, if not properly meshed with peaceful methods and goals, could threaten American liberties and the democratic process. He also warned that centralized research could inhibit intellectual curiosity and that public policy could become "the captive of the scientific-technological elite." He urged the nation not to plunder tomorrow's resources for today's comforts and argued that disarmament must be a continuing imperative.

After leaving office, Eisenhower remained an influential voice within the Republican Party and beyond. His warning about the influence of the military-industrial complex proved prescient. It grew stronger in the Kennedy administration, and Eisenhower's phrase describing the marriage of government and private industry dedicated to defense entered the American vocabulary.

My fellow Americans:

Three days from now, after half a century in the service of our country, I shall lay down the responsibilities of office as, in traditional and solemn ceremony, the authority of the Presidency is vested in my successor.

This evening I come to you with a message of leave-taking and farewell, and to share a few final thoughts with you, my countrymen.

Like every other citizen, I wish the new President, and all who will labor with him, Godspeed. I pray that the coming years will be blessed with peace and prosperity for all.

Our people expect their President and the Congress to find essential agreement on issues of great moment, the wise resolution of which will better shape the future of the Nation.

My own relations with the Congress, which began on a remote and tenuous basis when, long ago, a member of the Senate appointed me to West Point, have since ranged to the intimate during the war and immediate post-war period, and, finally, to the mutually interdependent during these past eight years.

In this final relationship, the Congress and the Administration have, on most vital issues, cooperated well, to serve the national good rather than mere partisanship, and so have assured that the business of the Nation should go forward. So, my official relationship with the Congress ends in a feeling, on my part, of gratitude that we have been able to do so much together.

II.

We now stand ten years past the midpoint of a century that has witnessed four major wars among great nations. Three of these involved our own country. Despite these holocausts America is today the strongest, the most influential and most productive nation in the world. Understandably proud of this pre-eminence, we yet realize that America's leadership and prestige depend, not merely upon our unmatched material progress, riches and military strength, but on how we use our power in the interests of world peace and human betterment.

III.

Throughout America's adventure in free government, our basic purposes have been to keep the peace; to foster progress in human achievement, and to enhance liberty, dignity and integrity among people and among nations. To strive for less would be unworthy of a free and religious people. Any failure traceable to arrogance, or our lack of comprehension or readiness to sacrifice would inflict upon us grievous hurt both at home and abroad.

Progress toward these noble goals is persistently threatened by the conflict now engulfing the world. It commands our whole attention, absorbs our very beings. We face a hostile ideology—global in scope, atheistic in character, ruthless in purpose, and insidious in method. Unhappily the danger is poses promises to be of indefinite duration. To meet it successfully, there is called for, not so much the emotional and transitory sacrifices of crisis, but rather those which enable us to carry forward steadily, surely, and without complaint the burdens of a prolonged and complex struggle—with liberty the stake. Only thus shall we remain, despite every provocation, on our charted course toward permanent peace and human betterment.

Crises there will continue to be. In meeting them, whether foreign or domestic, great or small, there is a recurring temptation to feel that some spectacular and costly action could become the miraculous solution to all current difficulties. A huge increase in newer elements of our defense; development of unrealistic programs to cure every ill in agriculture; a dramatic expansion in basic and applied research—these and many other possibilities, each possibly promising in itself, may be suggested as the only way to the road we wish to travel.

But each proposal must be weighed in the light of a broader consideration: the need to maintain balance in and among national programs—balance between the private and the public economy, balance between cost and hoped for advantage—balance between the clearly necessary and the comfortably desirable; balance between our essential requirements as a nation and the duties imposed by the nation upon the individual; balance between actions of the moment and the national welfare of the future. Good judgment seeks balance and progress; lack of it eventually finds imbalance and frustration.

The record of many decades stands as proof that our people and their government have, in the main, understood these truths and have responded to them well, in the face of stress and threat. But threats, new in kind or degree, constantly arise. I mention two only.

IV.

A vital element in keeping the peace is our military establishment. Our arms must be mighty, ready for instant action, so that no potential aggressor may be tempted to risk his own destruction.

Our military organization today bears little relation to that known by any of my predecessors in peacetime, or indeed by the fighting men of World War II or Korea.

Until the latest of our world conflicts, the United States had no armaments industry. American makers of plowshares could, with time and as required, make swords as well. But now we can no longer risk emergency improvisation of national defense; we have been compelled to create a permanent armaments industry of vast proportions. Added to this, three and a half million men and women are directly engaged in the defense establishment. We annually spend on military security more than the net income of all United States corporations.

This conjunction of an immense military establishment and a large arms industry is new in the American experience. The total influence—economic, political, even spiritual—is felt in every city, every State house, every office of the Federal government. We recognize the imperative need for this development. Yet we must not fail to comprehend its grave implications. Our toil, resources and livelihood are all involved; so is the very structure of our society.

In the councils of government, we must guard against the acquisition of unwarranted influence, whether sought or unsought, by the military-industrial complex. The potential for the disastrous rise of misplaced power exists and will persist.

We must never let the weight of this combination endanger our liberties or democratic processes. We should take nothing for granted. Only an alert and knowledgeable citizenry can compel the proper meshing of the huge industrial and military machinery of defense with our peaceful methods and goals, so that security and liberty may prosper together.

Akin to, and largely responsible for the sweeping changes in our industrial-military posture, has been the technological revolution during recent decades.

In this revolution, research has become central; it also becomes more formalized, complex, and costly. A steadily increasing share is conducted for, by, or at the direction of, the Federal government.

Today, the solitary inventor, tinkering in his shop, has been over-shadowed by task forces of scientists in laboratories and testing fields. In the same fashion, the free university, historically the fountainhead of free ideas and scientific discovery, has experienced a revolution in the conduct of research. Partly because of the huge costs involved, a government contract becomes virtually a substitute for intellectual curiosity. For every old blackboard there are now hundreds of new electronic computers.

The prospect of domination of the nation's scholars by Federal employment, project allocations, and the power of money is ever present—and is gravely to be regarded.

Yet, in holding scientific research and discovery in respect, as we should, we must also be alert to the equal and opposite danger that public policy could itself become the captive of a scientific- technological elite.

It is the task of statesmanship to mold, to balance, and to integrate these and other forces, new and old, within the principles of our democratic system—ever aiming toward the supreme goals of our free society.

V.

Another factor in maintaining balance involves the element of time. As we peer into society's future, we—you and I, and our government—must avoid the impulse to live only for today, plundering, for our own ease and convenience, the precious resources of tomorrow. We cannot mortgage the material assets of our grandchildren without risking the loss also of their political and spiritual heritage. We want democracy to survive for all generations to come, not to become the insolvent phantom of tomorrow.

VI.

Down the long lane of the history yet to be written America knows that this world of ours, ever growing smaller, must avoid becoming a community of dreadful fear and hate, and be instead, a proud confederation of mutual trust and respect.

Such a confederation must be one of equals. The weakest must come to the conference table with the same confidence as do we, protected as we are by our moral, economic, and military strength. That table, though scarred by many past frustrations, cannot be abandoned for the certain agony of the battlefield.

Disarmament, with mutual honor and confidence, is a continuing imperative. Together we must learn how to compose differences, not with arms, but with intellect and decent purpose. Because this need is so sharp and apparent I confess that I lay down my official responsibilities in this field with a definite sense of disappointment. As one who has witnessed the horror and the lingering sadness of war—as one who knows that another war could utterly destroy this civilization which has been so slowly and painfully built over thousands of years—I wish I could say tonight that a lasting peace is in sight.

Happily, I can say that war has been avoided. Steady progress toward our ultimate goal has been made. But, so much remains to be done. As a private citizen, I shall never cease to do what little I can to help the world advance along that road.

VII.

So—in this my last good night to you as your President—I thank you for the many opportunities you have given me for public service in war and peace. I trust that in that service you find some things worthy; as for the rest of it, I know you will find ways to improve performance in the future.

You and I—my fellow citizens—need to be strong in our faith that all nations, under God, will reach the goal of peace with justice. May we be ever unswerving in devotion to principle, confident but humble with power, diligent in pursuit of the Nation's great goals.

To all the peoples of the world, I once more give expression to America's prayerful and continuing aspiration:

We pray that peoples of all faiths, all races, all nations, may have their great human needs satisfied; that those now denied opportunity shall come to enjoy it to the full; that all who yearn for freedom may experience its spiritual blessings; that those who have freedom will understand, also, its heavy responsibilities; that all who are insensitive to the needs of others will learn charity; that the scourges of poverty, disease and ignorance will be made to disappear from the earth, and that, in the goodness of time, all peoples will come to live together in a peace guaranteed by the binding force of mutual respect and love.

Source:

Public Papers of the Presidents of the United States: Dwight D. Eisenhower, 1960–1961, Washington, D.C.: Government Printing Office, 1961, pp. 1,035–1,040.

John F. Kennedy, Moon Landing Speech, 1961

Address given by President John F. Kennedy to a special joint session of Congress on May 25, 1961, in which he appealed for a new program that would put a man on the Moon before 1970. Kennedy called the speech his "second State of the Union message of 1961." In it, he called for some $1.8 billion in new federal appropriations for space, military, civil defense, and other programs. He delivered the speech on the eve of a trip to Vienna to meet Soviet premier Nikita Khrushchev. Shortly before, on April 12, Soviet citizen Yuri Gagarin became the first human being in space.

The Soviets had launched the world's first artificial satellite, *Sputnik 1*, on October 4, 1957, whereas America's first attempts to launch satellites, Project Vanguard, starting December 6, 1957, resulted in very public failures until the U.S. Army sent *Explorer 1* into space, January 31, 1958. *Sputnik* also spurred Americans to boost scientific education in order to "beat the Russians." As a result, Congress passed the National Defense Education Act signed into law by President Eisenhower on September 2, 1958. The act established federal loans for college and graduate students and forgave 50 percent of the interest for those who worked as elementary or secondary school teachers for at least five years after graduation. It also set up fellowships for graduate students who were training to become college and university instructors. The legislation provided for buying modern equipment for science, mathematics, and foreign languages and established a number of foreign-language institutes.

The most historically significant result of Kennedy's proposal was his attempt to recover American scientific prestige with an accelerated program to develop new booster rockets, satellites, and unmanned spaceflights aimed at putting a man on the Moon by 1970. Kennedy's dream was realized when Neil Armstrong and Buzz Aldrin walked on the Moon for the first time July 20, 1969. After alighting, Armstrong spoke the words "One small step for a man; one giant leap for mankind." Although space exploration continued, the last moon walk occurred in December 1972.

In other areas, Kennedy requested more than $500 million in foreign economic and military aid, $160 million to allow the U.S. Army and U.S. Marines to increase their combat strength, a new civil defense program, and a new program to train American workers affected by automation in the workplace.

(excerpt)

Mr. Speaker, Mr. Vice President, my co-partners in Government, gentlemen—and ladies:

The Constitution imposes upon me the obligation to "from time to time give to the Congress information of the State of the Union." While this has traditionally been interpreted as an annual affair, this tradition has been broken in extraordinary times.

These are extraordinary times. And we face an extraordinary challenge. Our strength as well as our convictions have imposed upon this nation the role of leader in freedom's cause.

No role in history could be more difficult or more important. We stand for freedom. That is our conviction for ourselves—that is our only commitment to others. No friend, no neutral and no adversary should think otherwise. We are not against any man—or any nation—or any system—except as it is hostile to freedom. Nor am I here to present a new military doctrine, bearing any one name or aimed at any one area. I am here to promote the freedom doctrine.

* * *

IX. Space

Finally, if we are to win the battle that is now going on around the world between freedom and tyranny, the dramatic achievements in space which occurred in recent weeks should have made clear to us all, as did the Sputnik in 1957, the impact of this adventure on the minds of men everywhere, who are attempting to make a determination of which road they should take. Since early in my term, our efforts in space have been under review. With the advice of the Vice President, who is Chairman of the National Space Council, we have examined where we are strong and where we are not, where we may succeed and where we may not. Now it is time to take longer strides—time for a great new American enterprise—time for this nation to take a clearly leading role in space achievement, which in many ways may hold the key to our future on earth.

I believe we possess all the resources and talents necessary. But the facts of the matter are that we have never made the national decisions or marshaled the national resources required for such leadership. We have never specified long-range goals on an urgent time schedule, or managed our resources and our time so as to insure their fulfillment.

Recognizing the head start obtained by the Soviets with their large rocket engines, which gives them many months of lead-time, and recognizing the likelihood that they will exploit this lead for some time to come in still more impressive successes, we nevertheless are required to make new efforts on our own. For while we cannot guarantee that we shall one day be first, we can guarantee that any failure to make this effort will make us last. We take an additional risk by making it in full view of the world, but as shown by the feat of astronaut Shepard, this very risk enhances our stature when we are successful. But this is not merely a race. Space is open to us now; and our eagerness to share its meaning is not governed by the efforts of others. We go into space because whatever mankind must undertake, free men must fully share.

I therefore ask the Congress, above and beyond the increases I have earlier requested for space activities, to provide the funds which are needed to meet the following national goals:

First, I believe that this nation should commit itself to achieving the goal, before this decade is out, of landing a man on the moon and returning him safely to the earth. No single space project in this period will be more impressive to mankind, or more important for the long-range exploration of space; and none will be so difficult or expensive to accomplish. We propose to accelerate the development of the appropriate lunar space craft. We propose to develop alternate liquid and solid fuel boosters, much larger than any now being developed, until certain which is superior. We propose additional funds for other engine development and for unmanned explorations—explorations which are particularly important for one purpose which this nation will never overlook: the survival of the man who first makes this daring flight. But in a very real sense, it will not be one man going to the moon—if we make this judgment affirmatively, it will be an entire nation. For all of us must work to put him there.

Secondly, an additional 23 million dollars, together with 7 million dollars already available, will accelerate development of the Rover nuclear rocket. This gives promise of some day providing a means for even more exciting and ambitious exploration of space, perhaps beyond the moon, perhaps to the very end of the solar system itself.

Third, an additional 50 million dollars will make the most of our present leadership, by accelerating the use of space satellites for world-wide communications.

Fourth, an additional 75 million dollars—of which 53 million dollars is for the Weather Bureau—will help give us at the earliest possible time a satellite system for world-wide weather observation.

Let it be clear—and this is a judgment which the Members of the Congress must finally make—let if be clear that I am asking the Congress and the country to accept a firm commitment to a new course of action—a course which will last for many years and carry very heavy costs: 531 million dollars in fiscal '62—an estimated seven to nine billion dollars additional over the next five years. If we are to go only half way, or reduce our sights in the face of difficulty, in my judgment it would be better not to go at all.

Now this is a choice which this country must make, and I am confident that under the leadership of the Space Committees of the Congress, and the Appropriating Committees, that you will consider the matter carefully.

It is a most important decision that we make as a nation. But all of you have lived through the last four years and have seen the significance of space and the adventures in space, and no one can predict with certainty what the ultimate meaning will be of mastery of space.

I believe we should go to the moon. But I think every citizen of this country as well as the Members of the Congress should consider the matter carefully in making their judgment, to which we have given attention over many weeks and months, because it is a heavy burden, and there is no sense in agreeing or desiring that the United States take an affirmative position in outer space, unless we are prepared to do the work and bear the burdens to make it successful. If we are not, we should decide today and this year.

This decision demands a major national commitment of scientific and technical manpower, materiel and facilities, and the possibility of their diversion from other important activities where they are already thinly spread. It means a degree of dedication, organization and discipline which have not always characterized our research and development efforts. It means we cannot afford undue work stoppages, inflated costs of material or talent, wasteful interagency rivalries, or a high turnover of key personnel.

New objectives and new money cannot solve these problems. They could in fact, aggravate them further—unless every scientist, every engineer, every serviceman, every technician, contractor, and civil servant gives his personal pledge that this nation will move forward, with the full speed of freedom, in the exciting adventure of space.

X. Conclusion

In conclusion, let me emphasize one point. It is not a pleasure for any President of the United States, as I am sure it was not a pleasure for my predecessors, to come before the Congress and ask for new appropriations which place burdens on our people. I came to this conclusion with some reluctance. But in my judgment, this is a most serious time in the life of our country and in the life of freedom around the globe, and it is the obligation, I believe, of the President of the United States to at least make his recommendations to the Members of the Congress, so that they can reach their own conclusions with that judgment before them. You must decide yourselves, as I have decided, and I am confident that whether you finally decide in the way that I have decided or not, that your judgment—as my judgment—is reached on what is in the best interest of our country.

In conclusion, let me emphasize one point: that we are determined, as a nation in 1961 that freedom shall survive and succeed—and whatever the peril and set-backs, we have some very large advantages.

The first is the simple fact that we are on the side of liberty—and since the beginning of history, and particularly since the end of the Second World War, liberty has been winning out all over the globe.

A second great asset is that we are not alone. We have friends and allies all over the world who share our devotion to freedom. May I cite as a symbol of traditional and effective friendship the great ally I am about to visit—France. I look forward to my visit to France, and to my discussion with a great Captain of the Western World, President de Gaulle, as a meeting of particular significance, permitting the kind of close and ranging consultation that will strengthen both our countries and serve the common purposes of world-wide peace and liberty. Such serious conversations do not require a pale unanimity—they are rather the instruments of trust and understanding over a long road.

A third asset is our desire for peace. It is sincere, and I believe the world knows it. We are proving it in our patience at the test-ban table, and we are proving it in the UN where our efforts have been directed to maintaining that organization's usefulness as a protector of the independence of small nations. In these and other instances, the response of our opponents has not been encouraging.

Yet it is important to know that our patience at the bargaining table is nearly inexhaustible, though our credulity is limited—that our hopes for peace are unfailing, while our determination to protect our security is resolute. For these reasons I have long thought it wise to meet with the Soviet Premier for a personal exchange of views. A meeting in Vienna turned out to be convenient for us both; and the Austrian government has kindly made us welcome. No formal agenda is planned and no negotiations will be undertaken; but we will make clear America's enduring concern is for both peace and freedom—that we are anxious to live in harmony with the Russian people—that we seek no conquests, no satellites, no riches—that we seek only the day when "nation shall not lift up sword against nation, neither shall they learn war any more."

Finally, our greatest asset in this struggle is the American people—their willingness to pay the price for these programs—to understand and accept a long struggle—to share their resources with other less fortunate people—to meet the tax levels and close the tax loopholes I have requested—to exercise self-restraint instead of pushing up wages or prices, or over-producing certain crops, or spreading military secrets, or urging unessential expenditures or improper monopolies or harmful work stoppages—to serve in the Peace Corps or the Armed Services or the Federal Civil Service or the Congress—to strive for excellence in their schools, in their cities and in their physical fitness and that of their children—to take part in Civil Defense—to pay higher postal rates, and higher payroll taxes and higher teachers' salaries, in order to strengthen our society—to show friendship to students and visitors from other lands who visit us and go back in many cases to be the future leaders, with an image of America—and I want that image, and I know you do, to be affirmative and positive—and, finally, to practice democracy at home, in all States, with all races, to respect each other and to protect the Constitutional rights of all citizens.

I have not asked for a single program which did not cause one or all Americans some inconvenience, or some hardship, or some sacrifice. But they have responded—and you in the Congress have responded to your duty—and I feel confident in asking today for a similar response to these new and larger demands. It is heartening to know, as I journey abroad, that our country is united in its commitment to freedom—and is ready to do its duty.

Source:

Public Papers of the Presidents of the United States, John F. Kennedy, 1961. Washington, D.C.: Government Printing Office, 1962, pp. 396–406. Also available on-line. URL: www.jfklink.com/speeches/jfk/public_papers/1961/jfk_contents_papers1961.html.

National Foundation on the Arts and the Humanities Act, 1965

Signed by President Lyndon B. Johnson on September 29, 1965, this act represents the first national effort to fund artists, musicians, historians, and literary endeavors since the New Deal. The National Endowment for the Humanities (NEH) resulted from the efforts of the American Council of Learned Societies (ACLS), the Council of Graduate Schools in America, and the United Chapters of Phi Beta Kappa, which co-sponsored the establishment of a National Commission on the Humanities and instructed the Commission to conduct a study of "the state of the humanities in America." Barnaby Keeney, president of Brown University, chaired the commission. Johnson later appointed him first director of NEH.

Preceding the act's passage, the National Council for the Arts was established through the National Arts and Cultural Development Act of 1964. Its first members, appointed by President Lyndon Johnson, included noted artists such as contralto Marian Anderson; violinist Isaac Stern; composer Richard Rogers; conductor-composers Leonard Bernstein and Duke Ellington; choreographer Agnes de Mille; actors Helen Hayes, Charleston Heston, Gregory Peck, Sidney Poitier, and Rosalind Russell; artist David Smith; and authors Harper Lee and John Steinbeck. NEH is the largest single funder of the nonprofit arts sector in the United States. Its work has fostered theater, orchestras, and other artistic endeavors that could never have developed using local resources alone.

Senator Claiborne Pell of Rhode Island introduced the Johnson administration's legislation to establish a National Foundation on the Arts and the Humanities in March 1965. The act, however, separated the two endeavors into independent agencies, NEH and the National Endowment for the Arts (NEA). The final act provided for citizens' advisory committees for both the NEA (the National Council on the Arts), and NEH (the National Council for the Humanities). The two agencies also support state endowments for humanities and arts.

In January 1966 President Johnson appointed the first members of the National Councils on the Arts and Humanities. The first 157 NEH fellowships and 130 summer stipends were awarded in 1967.

The act has been amended several times.

AN ACT To provide for the establishment of the National Foundation on the Arts and the Humanities to promote progress and scholarship in the humanities and the arts in the United States, and for other purposes.

Be it enacted by the Senate and House of Representatives of the United States of America in Congress assembled,

Short Title

Section 1. This Act may be cited as the "National Foundation on the Arts and Humanities Act of 1965".

Declaration of Findings and Purposes

SEC. 2. The Congress finds and declares the following:

(1) The arts and the humanities belong to all the people of the United States.

(2) The encouragement and support of national progress and scholarship in the humanities and the arts, while primarily a matter for private and local initiative, are also appropriate matters of concern to the Federal Government.

(3) An advanced civilization must not limit its efforts to science and technology alone, but must give full value and support to the other great branches of scholarly and cultural activity in order to achieve a better understanding of the past, a better analysis of the present, and a better view of the future.

(4) Democracy demands wisdom and vision in its citizens. It must therefore foster and support a form of education, and access to the arts and the humanities, designed to make people of all backgrounds and wherever located masters of their technology and not its unthinking servants.

(5) It is necessary and appropriate for the Federal Government to complement, assist, and add to programs for the advancement of the humanities and the arts by local, State, regional, and private agencies and their organizations. In doing so, the Government must be sensitive to the nature of public sponsorship. Public funding of the

arts and humanities is subject to the conditions that traditionally govern the use of public money. Such funding should contribute to public support and confidence in the use of taxpayer funds. Public funds provided by the Federal Government must ultimately serve public purposes the Congress defines.

(6) The arts and the humanities reflect the high place accorded by the American people to the nation's rich cultural heritage and to the fostering of mutual respect for the diverse beliefs and values of all persons and groups.

(7) The practice of art and the study of the humanities require constant dedication and devotion. While no government can call a great artist or scholar into existence, it is necessary and appropriate for the Federal Government to help create and sustain not only a climate encouraging freedom of thought, imagination, and inquiry but also the material conditions facilitating the release of this creative talent.

(8) The world leadership which has come to the United States cannot rest solely upon superior power, wealth, and technology, but must be solidly founded upon worldwide respect and admiration for the Nation's high qualities as a leader in the realm of ideas and of the spirit.

(9) Americans should receive in school, background and preparation in the arts and humanities to enable them to recognize and appreciate the aesthetic dimensions of our lives, the diversity of excellence that comprises our cultural heritage, and artistic and scholarly expression.

(10) It is vital to democracy to honor and preserve its multicultural artistic heritage as well as support new ideas, and therefore it is essential to provide financial assistance to its artists and the organizations that support their work.

(11) To fulfill its educational mission, achieve an orderly continuation of free society, and provide models of excellence to the American people, the Federal Government must transmit the achievement and values of civilization from the past via the present to the future, and make widely available the greatest achievements of art.

(12) In order to implement these findings and purposes, it is desirable to Establish a National Foundation on the Arts and the Humanities.

Source:

National Endowment for the Humanities. "National Foundation on the Arts and the Humanities Act of 1965 (P./L. 89-209)" Available on-line. URL: <www.neh.gov/whoweare//legislation.html. Accessed November 2003.

Occupational Safety and Health Act, 1970

Federal legislation enacted on December 29, 1970, that established federal supervision over health and safety in the workplace. The secretary of labor was given authority to establish safety standards for all workers engaged in interstate commerce. A three-member board, appointed by the president, was empowered to enforce the standards. The act called for penalties of up to $1,000 for each violation of the standards, or $10,000 for each "willful" violation. The legislation created a National Institute for Occupational Health and Safety under the Department of Health, Education, and Welfare (later Health and Human Services). It also set up a commission to examine state worker's compensation laws.

An Act

To assure safe and healthful working conditions for working men and women; by authorizing enforcement of the standards developed under the Act; by assisting and encouraging the States in their efforts to assure safe and healthful working condition; by providing for research, information, education, and training in the field of occupational safety and health; and for other purposes.

Be it enacted by the Senate and House of Representatives of the United States of America in Congress assembled, That this Act may be cited as the "Occupational Safety and Health Act of 1970".

Congressional Findings and Purpose

Sec. (2) The Congress finds that personal injuries and illnesses arising out of work situations impose a substantial burden upon, and are a hindrance to, interstate commerce in terms of lost production, wage loss, medical expenses, and disability compensation payments.

(b) The Congress declares it to be its purpose and policy, through the exercise of its powers to regulate commerce among the several States and with foreign nations and to provide for the general welfare, to assure so far as possible every working man and woman in the Nation safe and healthful working conditions and to preserve our human resources—

(1) by encouraging employers and employees in their efforts to reduce the number of occupational safety and health hazards at their places of employment, and to stimulate employers and employees to institute new and to perfect existing programs for providing safe and healthful working conditions;

(2) by providing that employers and employees have separate but dependent responsibilities and rights with respect to achieving safe and healthful working conditions;

(3) by authorizing the Secretary of Labor to set mandatory occupational safety and health standards applicable to businesses affecting interstate commerce, and by creating an Occupational Safety and Health Review Commission for carrying out adjudicatory functions under the Act;

* * *

(5) by providing for research in the field of occupational safety and health, including the psychological factors involved, and by developing innovative methods, techniques, and approaches for dealing with occupational safety and health problems;

(6) by exploring ways to discover latent diseases, establishing causal connections between diseases and work in environmental conditions, and conducting other research relating to health problems, in recognition of the fact that occupational health standards present problems often different from those involved in occupational safety;

(7) by providing medical criteria which will assure insofar as practicable that no employee will suffer diminished health, functional capacity, or life expectancy as a result of his work experience;

(8) by providing for training programs to increase the number and competence of personnel engaged in the field of occupational safety and health;

* * *

(10) by providing an effective enforcement program which shall include a prohibition against giving advance notice of any inspection and sanctions for any individual violating this prohibition;

(11) by encouraging the States to assume the fullest responsibility for the administration and enforcement of their occupational safety and health laws by providing grants to the States to assist in identifying their needs and responsibilities in the area of occupational safety and health, to develop plans in accordance with the provisions of this Act, to improve the administration and enforcement of State occupational safety and health laws, and to conduct experimental and demonstration projects in connection therewith;

* * *

(13) by encouraging joint labor-management efforts to reduce injuries and disease arising out of employment.

Definitions

Sec. 3. For the purposes of this Act—

* * *

(8) The term "occupational safety and health standard" means a standard which requires conditions, or the adoption or use of one or more practices, means, methods, operations, or processes, reasonably necessary or appropriate to provide safe or healthful employment and places of employment.

(9) The term "national consensus standard" means any occupational safety and health standard or modification thereof which (1), has been adopted and promulgated by a nationally recognized standards-producing organization under procedures whereby it can be determined by the Secretary that persons interested and affected by the scope or provisions of the standard have reached substantial agreement on its adoption, (2) was formulated in a manner which afforded an opportunity for diverse views to be considered and (3) has been designated as such a standard by the Secretary, after consultation with other appropriate Federal agencies.

* * *

Applicability of this Act

* * *

(4) Nothing in this Act shall be construed to supersede or in any manner affect any workmen's compensation law or to enlarge or diminish or affect in any other manner the common law or statutory rights, duties, or liabilities of employers and employees under any law with respect to injuries, diseases, or death of employees arising out of, or in the course of, employment.

Duties

Sec. 5. (a) Each employer—

(1) shall furnish to each of his employees employment and a place of employment which are free from recognized hazards that are causing or are likely to cause death or serious physical harm to his employees;

Occupational Safety and Health Standards

* * *

(2) The Secretary shall publish a proposed rule promulgating, modifying, or revoking an occupational safety or health standard in the Federal Register and shall afford interested persons a period of thirty days after publication to submit written data or comments. . . .

* * *

(5) The Secretary, in promulgating standards dealing with toxic materials or harmful physical agents under this subsection, shall set the standard which most adequately assures, to the extent feasible, on the basis of the best available evidence, that no employee will suffer material impairment of health or functional capacity even if such employee has regular exposure to the hazard dealt with by such standard for the period of his working life. Development of standards under this subsection shall be based upon research, demonstrations, experiments, and such other information as may be appropriate. In addition to the attainment of the highest degree of health and safety protection for the employee, other considerations shall be the latest available scientific data in the field, the feasibility of the standards, and experience gained under this and other health and safety laws. Whenever practicable, the standard promulgated shall be expressed in terms of objective criteria and of the performance desired.

(6)(A) Any employer may apply to the Secretary for a temporary order granting a variance from a standard or any provision thereof promulgated under this section. Such temporary order shall be granted only if the employer . . . establishes that (i) he is unable to comply with a standard by its effective date because of unavailability of professional or technical personnel or of materials and equipment needed to come into compliance with the standard or because necessary construction or alteration of facilities cannot be completed by the effective date, (ii) he is taking all available steps to safeguards his employees against the hazards covered by the standard, and (iii) he has an effective program for coming into compliance with the standard as quickly as practicable.

* * *

(g) In determining the priority for establishing standards under this section, the Secretary shall give due regard to the urgency of the need for mandatory safety and health standards for particular industries, trades, crafts, occupations, businesses, workplaces or work environments. The Secretary shall also give due regard to the recommendations of the Secretary of Health, Education, and Welfare regarding the need for mandatory standards in determining the priority for establishing such standards.

Advisory Committees; Administration

Sec. 7. (a)(1) There is hereby established a National Advisory Committee on Occupational Safety and Health consisting of twelve members appointed by the Secretary, four of whom are to be designated by the Secretary of Health, Education, and Welfare, without regard to the provisions of title 5, United States Code, governing appointments in the competitive service, and composed of representatives of management, labor, occupational safety and occupational health professions, and of the public. The Secretary shall designate one of the public members as Chairman. The members shall be selected upon the basis of their experience and competence in the field of occupational safety and health.

(2) The Committee shall advise, consult with, and make recommendations to the Secretary and the Secretary of Health, Education, and Welfare on matters relating to the administration of the Act. The Committee shall hold no fewer than two meetings during each calendar year. All meetings of the Committee shall be open to the public and a transcript shall be kept and made available for public inspection.

* * *

(b) Inspections, Investigations, and Recordkeeping

Sec. 8. (a) In order to carry out the purposes of this Act, the Secretary, upon presenting appropriate credentials to the owner, operator, or agent in charge, is authorized—

(1) to enter without delay and at reasonable times any factory, plant, establishment, construction site, or other area, workplace or environment where work is performed by an employee of an employer; and

(2) to inspect and investigate during regular working hours and at other reasonable times, and within reasonable limits and in a reasonable manner, any such place of employment and all pertinent conditions, structures, machines, apparatus, devices, equipment, and materials therein, and to question privately any such employer, owner, operator, agent or employee.

(b) In making his inspections and investigations under this Act the Secretary may require the attendance and testimony of witnesses and the production of evidence under oath. Witnesses shall be paid the same fees and mileage that are paid witnesses in the courts of the United States. In case of a contumacy, failure, or refusal of any person to obey such an order, any district court of the United States or the United States courts of any territory or possession, within the jurisdiction of which such person is found, or resides or transacts business, upon the application by the Secretary, shall have jurisdiction to issue to such person an order requiring such person to appear to produce evidence if, as, and when so ordered, and to give testimony relating to the matter under investigation or in question, and any failure to obey such order of the court may be punished by said court as a contempt thereof.

(c)(1) Each employer shall make, keep and preserve, and make available to the Secretary or the Secretary of Health, Education, and Welfare, such records regarding his activities relating to this Act as the Secretary, in cooperation with the Secretary of Health, Education, and Welfare, may prescribed by regulation as necessary or appropriate for the enforcement of this Act or for developing information regarding the causes and prevention of occupational accidents and illnesses. In order to carry out the provisions of this paragraph such regulations may include provisions requiring employers to conduct periodic inspections. The Secretary shall also issue regulations requiring that employers, through posting of notices or other appropriate means, keep their employees informed of their protections and obligations under this Act, including the provisions of applicable standards.

(2) The Secretary, in cooperation with the Secretary of Health, Education, and Welfare, shall prescribe regulations requiring employers to maintain accurate records of, and to make periodic reports on, work-related deaths, injuries and illnesses other than minor injuries requiring only first aid treatment and which do not involve medical treatment, loss of consciousness, restriction of work or motion, or transfer to another job.

(3) The Secretary, in cooperation with the Secretary of Health, Education, and Welfare, shall issue regulations requiring employers to maintain accurate records of employee exposures to potentially toxic materials or harmful physical agents which are required to be monitored or measured under section 6. Such regulations shall provide employees or their representatives with an opportunity to observe such monitoring or measuring, and to have access to the records thereof. Such regulations shall also make appropriate provision for each employee or former employee to have access to such records as will indicate his own exposure to toxic materials or harmful physical agents. Each employer shall promptly notify any employee who has been or is being exposed to toxic materials or harmful physical agents in concentrations or at levels which exceed those prescribed by an applicable occupational safety and health standard promulgated under section 6, and shall inform any employee who is being thus exposed of the corrective action being taken.

* * *

(f)(1) Any employees or representative of employees who believe that a violation of a safety or health standard exists that threatens physical harm, or that an imminent danger exists, may request an inspection by giving notice to the Secretary or his authorized representative of such violation or danger.

* * *

(2) The Secretary and the Secretary of Health Education, and Welfare shall each prescribe such rules and regulations as he may deem necessary to carry out their responsibilities under this Act, including rules and regulations dealing with the inspection of an employer's establishment.

* * *

Procedure for Enforcement

* * *

Judicial Review

Sec. 11. (a) Any person adversely affected or aggrieved by an order of the Commission issued under subsection (c) of section 10 may obtain a review of such order in any United States court of appeals for the circuit in which the violation is alleged to have occurred or where the employer has its principal office, or in the Court of Appeals for the District of Columbia Circuit. . . .

(b) The Secretary may also obtain review or enforcement of any final order of the Commission by filing a petition for such relief. . . .

(c)(1) No person shall discharge or in any manner discriminate against any employee because such employee has filed any complaint or instituted or caused to be instituted any proceeding under or related to this Act or has testified or is about to testify in any such proceeding or because of the exercise by such employee on behalf of himself or others of any right afforded by this Act. . . .

The Occupational Safety and Health Review Commission

Sec. 12. (a) The Occupational Safety and Health Review Commission is hereby established. The Commission shall be composed of three members who shall be appointed by the President, by and with the advice and consent of the Senate, from among persons who by reason of training, education, or experience are qualified to carry out the functions of the Commission under this Act. The President shall designate one of the members of the Commission to serve as Chairman. . . .

* * *

Confidentiality of Trade Secrets

Sec. 15. All information reported to or otherwise obtained by the Secretary or his representative in connection with any inspection or proceeding under this Act which contains or which might reveal a trade secret . . . shall be considered confidential for the purpose of that section. . . .

* * *

(e) Any employer who willfully violates any standard, rule, or order promulgated pursuant to section 6 of this Act, or of any regulations prescribed pursuant to this Act, and that violation caused death to any employee, shall, upon conviction, be punished by a fine of not more than $10,000 or by imprisonment for not more than six months, or by both; except that if the conviction is for a violation committed after a first conviction of such person, punishment shall be by a fine of not more than $20,000 or by imprisonment for not more than one year, or by both.

(f) Any person who gives advance notice of any inspection to be conducted under this Act, without authority from the Secretary or his designees, shall, upon conviction, be punished by a fine of not more than $1,000 or by imprisonment for not more than six months, or by both.

* * *

(j) The Commission shall have authority to assess all civil penalties provided in this section, giving due consideration to the appropriateness of the penalty with respect to the size of the business of the employer being charged, the gravity of the violation, the good faith of the employer, and the history of previous violations.

(k) For purposes of this section, a serious violation shall be deemed to exist in a place of employment if there is a substantial probability that death or serious physical harm could result from a condition which exists, or from one or more practices, means, methods, operations, or processes which have been adopted or are in use, in such place of employment unless the employer did not, and could not with the exercise of reasonable diligence, know of the presence of the violation.

State Jurisdiction and State Plans

Sec. 18. (a) Nothing in this Act shall prevent any State agency or court from asserting jurisdiction under State law over any occupational safety or health issue with respect to which no standard is in effect under section thereof, if such plan in his judgment—

* * *

(8) provides that the State agency will make such reports to the Secretary in such form and containing such information, as the Secretary shall from time to time require.

* * *

(g) The State may obtain a review of a decision of the Secretary withdrawing approval of or rejecting its plan by the United States court of appeals for the circuit in which the State is located by filing in such court within thirty days following receipt of notice of such decision a petition to modify or set aside in whole or in part the action of the Secretary.

* * *

Federal Agency Safety Programs and Responsibilities

Sec. 19. (a) It shall be the responsibility of the land of each Federal agency to establish and maintain an effective and comprehensive occupational safety and health program which is consistent with the standards promulgated under section 6. The head of each agency shall (after consultation with representatives of the employees thereof)—

(1) provide safe and healthful places and conditions of employment, consistent with the standards. . . .

(2) acquire, maintain, and require the use of safety equipment, personal protective equipment, and devices reasonably necessary to protect employees;

(3) keep adequate records of all occupational accidents and illnesses for proper evaluation and necessary corrective action;

* * *

(d) The Secretary shall have access to records and reports kept and filed by Federal agencies pursuant to subsections. . . .

Research and Related Activities

Sec. 20. (a)(1) The Secretary of Health, Education, and Welfare, after consultation with the Secretary and with other appropriate Federal departments or agencies, shall conduct (directly or by grants or contracts) research, experiments, and demonstrations relating to occupational safety and health, including studies of psychological factors involved, and relating to innovative methods, techniques, and approaches for dealing with occupational safety and health problems.

(2) The Secretary of Health, Education, and Welfare shall from time to time consult with the Secretary in order to develop specific plans for such research, demonstrations, and experiments as are necessary to produce criteria, including criteria identifying toxic substances, enabling the Secretary to meet his responsibility for the formulation of safety and health standards under this Act; and the Secretary of Health, Education, and Welfare, on the basis of such research, demonstrations, and experiments and any other information available to him, shall develop and publish at least annually such criteria as will effectuate the purposes of this Act.

(3) The Secretary of Health, Education, and Welfare, on the basis of such research, demonstrations, and experiments, and any other information available to him, shall develop criteria dealing with toxic materials and harmful physical agents and substances which will describe exposure levels that are safe for various periods of employment, including but not limited to the exposure levels at which no employee will suffer impaired health or functional capacities or diminished life expectancy as a result of his work experience.

(4) The Secretary of Health, Education, and Welfare shall also conduct special research, experiments, and demonstrations relating to occupational safety and health as are necessary to explore new problems, including those created by new technology in occupational safety and health, which may require ameliorative action beyond that which is otherwise provided for in the operating provisions of this Act. The Secretary of Health, Education, and Welfare shall also conduct research into the motivational and behavioral factors relating to the field of occupational safety and health.

(5) The Secretary of Health, Education, and Welfare, in order to comply with his responsibilities under paragraph (2), and in order to develop needed information regarding potentially toxic substances or harmful physical agents, may prescribe regulations requiring employers to measure, record, and make reports on the exposure of employees to substances or physical agents which the Secretary of Health, Education, and Welfare reasonably believes may endanger the health or safety of employees. The Secretary of Health, Education, and Welfare also is authorized to establish such programs of medical examinations and tests as may be necessary for determining the incidence of occupational illnesses and the susceptibility of employees to such illnesses. Nothing in this or any other

provision of this Act shall be deemed to authorize or require medical examination, immunization, or treatment for those who object thereto on religious grounds, except where such is necessary for the protection of the health or safety of others. Upon the request of any employer who is required to measure and record exposure of employees to substances or physical agents as provided under this subsection, the Secretary of Health, Education, and Welfare shall furnish full financial or other assistance to such employer for the purpose of defraying any additional expense incurred by him in carrying out the measuring and recording as provided in this subsection.

(6) The Secretary of Health, Education, and Welfare shall publish within six months of enactment of this Act and thereafter as needed but at least annually a list of all known toxic substances by generic family or other useful grouping, and the concentrations at which such toxicity is known to occur. He shall determine following a written request by any employer or authorized representative of employees, specifying with reasonable particularity the grounds on which the request is made, whether any substance normally found in the place of employment has potentially toxic effects in such concentrations as used or found; and shall submit such determination both to employers and affected employees as soon as possible. If the Secretary of Health, Education, and Welfare determines that any substance is potentially toxic at the concentrations in which it is used or found in a place of employment, and such substance is not covered by an occupational safety or health standard promulgated under section 6, the Secretary of Health, Education, and Welfare shall immediately submit such determination to the Secretary, together with all pertinent criteria.

(7) Within two years of enactment of this Act, and annually thereafter the Secretary of Health, Education, and Welfare shall conduct and publish industrywide studies of the effect of chronic or low-level exposure to industrial materials, processes, and stresses on the potential for illness, disease, or loss of functional capacity in aging adults.

(b) The Secretary of Health, Education, and Welfare is authorized to make inspections and question employers and employees as provided in section 8 of this Act in order to carry out his functions and responsibilities under this section.

(c) The Secretary is authorized to enter into contracts, agreements, or other arrangements with appropriate public agencies or private organizations for the purpose of conducting studies relating to his responsibilities under this Act. In carrying out his responsibilities under this subsection, the Secretary shall cooperate with the Secretary of Health, Education, and Welfare in order to avoid any duplication of efforts under this section. . . .

* * *

Training and Employee Education

Sec. 21. (a) The Secretary of Health, Education, and Welfare, after consultation with the Secretary and with other appropriate Federal departments and agencies, shall conduct, directly or by grants or contracts (1) education programs to provide an adequate supply of qualified personnel to carry out the purposes of this Act, and (2) informational programs on the importance of and proper use of adequate safety and health equipment.

(b) The Secretary is also authorized to conduct, directly or by grants or contracts, short-term training of personnel engaged in work related to his responsibilities under this Act.

(c) The Secretary, in consultation with the Secretary of Health, Education, and Welfare, shall (1) provide for the establishment and supervision of programs for the education and training of employers and employees in the recognition, avoidance, and prevention of unsafe or unhealthful working conditions in employments covered by this Act, and (2) consult with and advise employers and employees, and organizations representing employers and employees as to effective means of preventing occupational injuries and illnesses.

National Institute for Occupational Safety and Health

Sec. 22. (a) It is the purpose of this section to establish a National Institute for Occupational Safety and Health in the Department of Health, Education, and Welfare. . . .

(b) There is hereby established in the Department of Health, Education, and Welfare a National Institute for Occupational Safety and Health. The Institute shall be headed by a Director who shall be appointed by the Secretary of Health, Education, and Welfare, and who shall serve for a term of six years unless previously removed by the Secretary of Health, Education, and Welfare.

(c) The Institute is authorized to—

(1) develop and establish recommended occupational safety and health standards; and

(2) perform all functions of the Secretary of Health, Education, and Welfare under sections 20 and 21 of this Act.

(d) Upon his own initiative, or upon the request of the Secretary or the Secretary of Health, Education, and Welfare, the Director is authorized (1) to conduct such research and experimental programs as he determines are necessary for the development of criteria for new and improved occupational safety and health standards, and (2) after consideration of the results of such research and experimental programs make recommendations concerning new or improved occupational safety and health standards. Any occupational safety and health standard recommended pursuant to this section shall immediately be forwarded to the Secretary of Labor; and to the Secretary of Health, Education, and Welfare.

* * *

(1) prescribe such regulations as he deems necessary governing the manner in which its functions shall be carried out;

* * *

Grants to the States

Sec. 23. (a) The Secretary is authorized, during the fiscal year ending June 30, 1971, and the two succeeding fiscal years, to make grants to the States which have designated a State agency. . .

* * *

(g) The Workmen's Compensation Commission is authorized to enter into contracts with Federal or State agencies, private firms, institutions, and individuals for the conduct of research or surveys, the preparation of reports, and other activities necessary to the discharge of its duties.

* * *

Effective Date

Sec. 34. This Act shall take effect one hundred and twenty days after the date of its enactment.

Approved December 29, 1970.

Source:

Statutes at Large, Vol. 84, pp. 1,590–1,620.

Cold War: U.S. International Relations

Control of Atomic Energy, 1946

Joint declaration on control of atomic energy issued by U.S. president Harry S. Truman, British prime minister Clement Attlee, and Canadian prime minister W. L. Mackenzie King November 15, 1946. In January 1946 the United Nations Atomic Energy Commission was formed to establish international control over atomic energy and devise a scheme for nuclear disarmament. That June, Bernard M. Baruch, the U.S. representative, presented to the commission America's proposal for relinquishing its atomic weapons monopoly under an international security system. The Baruch Plan called for the United States to stop nuclear weapons production, dispose of its stockpiles, and disclose to a proposed international authority its nuclear secrets. Irreconcilable U.S.-Soviet differences on the issue produced a stalemate in the United Nations. On November 15, after reaching a unified U.S.-Anglo-Canadian position on atomic energy control, the three leaders released their agreed declaration. Warning of the cataclysmic peril of atomic weapons of mass destruction, it asserted that the whole civilized world bore responsibility for seeing that atomic energy be used for beneficial purposes rather than as an instrument of war. The United Nations, it stated, must lead international efforts to prevent nuclear weapons proliferation and promote the peaceful use of atomic energy.

The President of the United States, the Prime Minister of the United Kingdom, and the Prime Minister of Canada have issued the following statement:

1. We recognize that the application of recent scientific discoveries to the methods and practice of war has placed at the disposal of mankind means of destruction hitherto unknown, against which there can be no adequate military defense, and in the employment of which no single nation can in fact have a monopoly.

2. We desire to emphasize that the responsibility for devising means to insure that the new discoveries shall be used for the benefit of mankind, instead of as a means of destruction, rests not on our nations alone, but upon the whole civilized world. Nevertheless, the progress that we have made in the development and use of atomic energy demands that we take an initiative in the matter, and we have accordingly met together to consider the possibility of international action—

(a) to prevent the use of atomic energy for destructive purposes;

(b) to promote the use of recent and future advances in scientific knowledge, particularly in the utilization of atomic energy, for peaceful and humanitarian ends.

3. We are aware that the only complete protection for the civilized world from the destructive use of scientific knowledge lies in the prevention of war. No system of safeguards that can be devised will of itself provide an effective guaranty against production of atomic weapons by a nation bent on aggression. Nor can we ignore the possibility of the development of other weapons or of new methods of warfare which may constitute as great a threat to civilization as the military use of atomic energy.

4. Representing, as we do, the three countries which possess the knowledge essential to the use of atomic energy, we declare at the outset our willingness, as a first contribution, to proceed with the exchange of fundamental scientific information and the interchange of scientists and scientific literature for peaceful ends with any nation that will fully reciprocate.

5. We believe that the fruits of scientific research should be made available to all nations, and that freedom of investigation and free interchange of ideas are essential to the progress of knowledge. In pursuance of this policy, the basic scientific information essential to the development of atomic energy for peaceful purposes has already been made available to the world. It is our intention that all further information of this character that may become available from time to time should be similarly treated. We trust that other nations will adopt the same policy, thereby creating an atmosphere of reciprocal confidence in which political agreement and cooperation will flourish.

6. We have considered the question of the disclosure of detailed information concerning the practical industrial application of atomic energy. The military exploitation of atomic energy depends, in large part, upon the same methods and processes as would be required for industrial uses.

We are not convinced that the spreading of the specialized information regarding the practical application of atomic energy, before it is possible to devise effective, reciprocal, and enforceable safeguards acceptable to all nations, would contribute to a constructive solution of the problem of the atomic bomb. On the contrary, we think it might have the opposite effect. We are, however, prepared to share, on a reciprocal basis with others of the United Nations, detailed information concerning the practical industrial application of atomic energy just as soon as effective enforceable safeguards against its use for destructive purposes can be devised.

7. In order to attain the most effective means of entirely eliminating the use of atomic energy for destructive purposes and promoting its widest use for industrial and humanitarian purposes, we are of the opinion that at the earliest practicable date a commission should be set up under the United Nations Organization to prepare recommendations for submission to the Organization.

The Commission should be instructed to proceed with the utmost dispatch and should be authorized to submit recommendations from time to time dealing with separate phases of its work.

In particular the Commission should make specific proposals—

(a) for extending between all nations the exchange of basic scientific information for peaceful ends;

(b) for control of atomic energy to the extent necessary to insure its use only for peaceful purposes;

(c) for the elimination from national armaments of atomic weapons and of all other major weapons adaptable to mass destruction;

(d) for effective safeguards by way of inspection and other means to protect complying States against the hazards of violations and evasions.

8. The work of the Commission should proceed by separate stages, the successful completion of each one of which will develop the necessary confidence of the world before the next stage is undertaken. Specifically it is considered that Commission might well devote its attention first to the wide exchange of scientists and scientific information, and as a second stage to the development of full knowledge concerning natural resources of raw materials.

9. Faced with the terrible realities of the application of science to destruction, every nation will realize more urgently than before the overwhelming need to maintain the rule of law among nations and to banish the scourge of war from the earth. This can only be brought about by giving wholehearted support to the United Nations Organization, and by consolidating and extending its authority, thus creating conditions of mutual trust in which all peoples will be free to devote themselves to the arts of peace. It is our firm resolve to work without reservation to achieve these ends.

Harry S. Truman,
President of the United States.
C.R. Attlee,
Prime Minister of the United Kingdom.
W.L. Mackenzie King,
Prime Minister of Canada.

Source:

Henry Steele Commager, ed., *Documents of American History*; Vol. 2, *Since 1898*. 9th ed. Englewood Cliffs, N.J.: Prentice Hall, 1973, pp. 516–518.

Truman Doctrine, 1947

Doctrine enunciated by President Harry S. Truman in a speech to Congress March 12, 1947, proclaiming a U.S.

commitment to help noncommunist countries resist Soviet expansion. Truman, announcing this plan for the "containment" of communism, declared that American policy was "to help free peoples to maintain their free institutions and their national integrity against aggressive movements that seek to impose upon them totalitarian regimes." He asked Congress for $400 million to support anticommunist factions fighting in Greece and Turkey. Congress approved the request in May 1947, signaling a return to a policy of involvement in European affairs.

George F. Kennan, head of the State Department Policy Planning Staff, first discussed containment policy in public in an anonymous paper, "Sources of Soviet Conduct," in the July 1947 issue of *Foreign Affairs*. The ambiguous language of the article gave the impression that Kennan saw the USSR as a military threat and advocated "a long term, patient but firm and vigilant containment of Russian expansive tendencies" and "the adroit and vigilant application of counterforce" against the Soviet Union. However, he later insisted that he meant "the political containment of a political threat" in this article. In any case, Kennan became an outspoken dove, making pronouncements against American involvement in Vietnam and, as he approached his hundredth birthday, against President George W. Bush's plan to invade Iraq.

Mr. Vice President, Mr. Speaker, Members of the Congress of the United States:

The gravity of the situation which confronts the world today necessitates my appearance before a joint session of the Congress.

The foreign policy and the national security of this country are involved.

One aspect of the present situation, which I present to you at this time for your consideration and decision, concerns Greece and Turkey.

The United States has received from the Greek Government an urgent appeal for financial and economic assistance. Preliminary reports from the American Economic Mission now in Greece and reports from the American Ambassador in Greece corroborate the statement of the Greek Government that assistance is imperative if Greece is to survive as a free nation.

I do not believe that the American people and the Congress wish to turn a deaf ear to the appeal of the Greek Government.

Greece is not a rich country. Lack of sufficient natural resources has always forced the Greek people to work hard to make both ends meet. Since 1940, this industrious, peace loving country has suffered invasion, four years of cruel enemy occupation, and bitter internal strife.

When forces of liberation entered Greece they found that the retreating Germans had destroyed virtually all the railways, roads, port facilities, communications, and merchant marine. More than a thousand villages had been burned. Eighty-five percent of the children were tubercular. Livestock, poultry, and draft animals had almost disappeared. Inflation had wiped out practically all savings.

As a result of these tragic conditions, a militant minority, exploiting human want and misery, was able to create political chaos which, until now, has made economic recovery impossible.

Greece is today without funds to finance the importation of those goods which are essential to bare subsistence. Under these circumstances the people of Greece cannot make progress in solving their problems of reconstruction. Greece is in desperate need of financial and economic assistance to enable it to resume purchases of food, clothing, fuel and seeds. These are indispensable for the subsistence of its people and are obtainable only from abroad. Greece must have help to import the goods necessary to restore internal order and security so essential for economic and political recovery.

The Greek Government has also asked for the assistance of experienced American administrators, economists and technicians to insure that the financial and other aid given to Greece shall be used effectively in creating a stable and self-sustaining economy and in improving its public administration.

The very existence of the Greek state is today threatened by the terrorist activities of several thousand armed men, led by Communists, who defy the government's authority at a number of points, particularly along the northern boundaries. A Commission appointed by the United Nations Security Council is at present investigating disturbed conditions in northern Greece and alleged border violations along the frontier between Greece on the one hand and Albania, Bulgaria, and Yugoslavia on the other.

Meanwhile, the Greek Government is unable to cope with the situation. The Greek army is small and poorly equipped. It needs supplies and equipment if it is to restore authority to the government throughout Greek territory.

Greece must have assistance if it is to become a self-supporting and self-respecting democracy.

The United States must supply this assistance. We have already extended to Greece certain types of relief and economic aid but these are inadequate.

There is no other country to which democratic Greece can turn.

No other nation is willing and able to provide the necessary support for a democratic Greek government.

The British Government, which has been helping Greece, can give no further financial or economic aid after

March 31. Great Britain finds itself under the necessity of reducing or liquidating its commitments in several parts of the world, including Greece.

We have considered how the United Nations might assist in this crisis. But the situation is an urgent one requiring immediate action, and the United Nations and its related organizations are not in a position to extend help of the kind that is required.

It is important to note that the Greek Government has asked for our aid in utilizing effectively the financial and other assistance we may give to Greece, and in improving its public administration. It is of the utmost importance that we supervise the use of any funds made available to Greece, in such a manner that each dollar spent will count toward making Greece self-supporting, and will help to build an economy in which a healthy democracy can flourish.

No government is perfect. One of the chief virtues of a democracy, however, is that its defects are always visible and under democratic processes can be pointed out and corrected. The government of Greece is not perfect. Nevertheless it represents 85 percent of the members of the Greek Parliament who were chosen in an election last year. Foreign observers, including 692 Americans, considered this election to be a fair expression of the views of the Greek people.

The Greek Government has been operating in an atmosphere of chaos and extremism. It has made mistakes. The extension of aid by this country does not mean that the United States condones everything that the Greek Government has done or will do. We have condemned in the past, and we condemn now, extremist measures of the right or the left. We have in the past advised tolerance, and we advise tolerance now.

Greece's neighbor, Turkey, also deserves our attention.

The future of Turkey as an independent and economically sound state is clearly no less important to the freedom-loving peoples of the world than the future of Greece. The circumstances in which Turkey finds itself today are considerably different from those of Greece. Turkey has been spared the disasters that have beset Greece. And during the war, the United States and Great Britain furnished Turkey with material aid.

Nevertheless, Turkey now needs our support.

Since the war Turkey has sought additional financial assistance from Great Britain and the United States for the purpose of effecting that modernization necessary for the maintenance of its national integrity.

That integrity is essential to the preservation of order in the Middle East.

The British Government has informed us that, owing to its own difficulties, it can no longer extend financial or economic aid to Turkey.

As in the case of Greece, if Turkey is to have the assistance if needs, the United States must supply it. We are the only country able to provide that help.

I am fully aware of the broad implications involved if the United States extends assistance to Greece and Turkey, and I shall discuss these implications with you at this time.

One of the primary objectives of the foreign policy of the United States is the creation of conditions in which we and other nations will be able to work out a way of life free from coercion. This was fundamental issue in the war with Germany and Japan. Our victory was won over countries which sought to impose their will, and their way of life, upon other nations.

To ensure the peaceful development of nations, free from coercion, the United States has taken a leading part in establishing the United Nations. The United Nations is designed to make possible lasting freedom and independence for all its members. We shall not realize our objectives, however, unless we are willing to help free peoples to maintain their free institutions and their national integrity against aggressive movements that seek to impose upon them totalitarian regimes. This is no more than a frank recognition that totalitarian regimes imposed upon free peoples, by direct or indirect aggression, undermine the foundations of international peace and hence the security of the United States.

The peoples of a number of countries of the world have recently had totalitarian regimes forced upon them against their will. The Government of the United States has made frequent protests against coercion and intimidation, in violation of the Yalta agreement, in Poland, Rumania, and Bulgaria. I must also state that in a number of other countries there have been similar developments.

At the present moment in world history nearly every nation must choose between alternative ways of life. The choice is too often not a free one.

One way of life is based upon the will of the majority, and is distinguished by free institutions, representative government, free elections, guarantees of individual liberty, freedom of speech and religion, and freedom from political oppression.

The second way of life is based upon the will of a minority forcibly imposed upon the majority. It relies upon terror and oppression, a controlled press and radio, fixed elections, and the suppression of personal freedoms.

I believe that it must be the policy of the United States to support free peoples who are resisting attempted subjugation by armed minorities or by outside pressures.

I believe that we must assist free peoples to work out their own destinies in their own way.

I believe that our help should be primarily through economic and financial aid which is essential to economic stability and orderly political processes.

The world is not static, and the *status quo* is not sacred. But we cannot allow changes in the *status quo* in violation of the Charter of the United Nations by such methods as coercion, or by such subterfuges as political infiltration. In helping free and independent nations to maintain their freedom, the United States will be giving effect to the principles of the Charter of the United Nations.

It is necessary only to glance at a map to realize that the survival and integrity of the Greek nation are of grave importance in a much wider situation. If Greece should fall under the control of an armed minority, the effect upon its neighbor, Turkey, would be immediate and serious. Confusion and disorder might well spread throughout the entire Middle East.

Moreover, the disappearance of Greece as an independent state would have a profound effect upon those countries in Europe whose peoples are struggling against great difficulties to maintain their freedoms and their independence while they repair the damages of war.

It would be an unspeakable tragedy if these countries, which have struggled so long against overwhelming odds, should lose that victory for which they sacrificed so much. Collapse of free institutions and loss of independence would be disastrous not only for them but for the world. Discouragement and possibly failure would quickly be the lot of neighboring peoples striving to maintain their freedom and independence.

Should we fail to aid Greece and Turkey in this fateful hour, the effect will be far reaching to the West as well as to the East.

We must take immediate and resolute action.

I therefore ask the Congress to provide authority for assistance to Greece and Turkey in the amount of $400,000,000 for the period ending June 30, 1948. In requesting these funds, I have taken into consideration the maximum amount of relief assistance which would be furnished to Greece out of the $350,000,000 which I recently requested that the Congress authorize for the prevention of starvation and suffering in countries devastated by the war.

In addition to funds, I ask the Congress to authorize the detail of American civilian and military personnel to Greece and Turkey, at the request of those countries, to assist in the tasks of reconstruction, and for the purpose of supervising the use of such financial and material assistance as may be furnished. I recommend that authority also be provided for the instruction and training of selected Greek and Turkish personnel.

Finally, I ask that the Congress provide authority which will permit the speediest and most effective use, in terms of needed commodities, supplies, and equipment, of such funds as may be authorized.

If further funds, or further authority, should be needed for the purposes indicated in this message, I shall not hesitate to bring the situation before the Congress. On this subject the Executive and Legislative branches of the Government must work together.

This is a serious course upon which we embark.

I would not recommend it except that the alternative is much more serious.

The United States contributed $341,000,000,000 toward winning World War II. This is an investment in world freedom and world peace.

The assistance that I am recommending to Greece and Turkey amounts to little more than 1/10 of 1 percent of this investment. It is only common sense that we should safeguard this investment and make sure that it was not in vain.

The seeds of totalitarian regimes are nurtured by misery and want. They spread and grow in the evil soil of poverty and strife. They reach their full growth when the hope of a people for a better life has died.

We must keep that hope alive.

The free peoples of the world look to us for support in maintaining their freedoms.

If we falter in our leadership, we may endanger the peace of the world—and we shall surely endanger the welfare of this Nation.

Great responsibilities have been placed upon us by the swift movement of events.

I am confident that the Congress will face these responsibilities squarely.

Source:

Public Papers of the Presidents of the United States: Harry S. Truman, 1945–63. Washington, D.C.: Government Printing Office, 1966, pp. 176–180. Also available on-line from the Truman Presidential Library. URL: http://www.trumanlibrary.org/publicpapers/index.php?pid=2189&st=&st1=.

Marshall Plan, 1947

Plan first proposed by Secretary of State George C. Marshall in an address at Harvard University, June 5, 1947; it established a U.S.-sponsored program to give financial aid to European countries "willing to assist in the task of recovery" from World War II. In Paris, 16 European nations drafted a four-year program costing $22.4 billion. The U.S. Congress in 1948 authorized $5.4 billion the first year; participating European nations then matched the aid they received during the program. Canada and countries in Latin America and other parts of the world also contributed to the plan, some 70 percent of whose cost was paid by the United States. It ended in late 1951, a year ahead of schedule, after an outlay of some $12 billion. Grouped together as the Organization for European Economic Cooperation (OEEC) plus West Germany, these nations restored their economic and agricultural production by completing many projects, including new roads, bridges, hydroelectric plants, land reclamations, irrigation systems, and large-scale housing, among other undertakings. The Soviet Union and its satellites in Eastern Europe refused to join the plan. By helping the economic recovery of Western Europe, the Marshall Plan checked and reduced communist influence there.

Also spreading good will with European nations after World War II, the Fulbright Act of August 1, 1946, financed international educational and cultural exchange programs, using funds derived from the sale to foreign governments of surplus World War II property. The act was submitted by Senator J. William Fulbright of Arkansas as an amendment to the Surplus Property Act of 1944 in order to "increase [American] understanding of others and their understanding of us." It created a large fund that allowed the exchange of thousands of students, teachers, researchers, journalists, government leaders, and others.

I need not tell you gentlemen that the world situation is very serious. That must be apparent to all intelligent people. I think one difficulty is that the problem is one of such enormous complexity that the very mass of facts presented to the public by press and radio make it exceedingly difficult for the man in the street to reach a clear appraisement of the situation. Furthermore, the people of this country are distant from the troubled areas of the earth and it is hard for them to comprehend the plight and consequent reactions of the long-suffering peoples, and the effect of those reactions on their governments in connection with our efforts to promote peace in the world.

In considering the requirements for the rehabilitation of Europe the physical loss of life, the visible destruction of cities, factories, mines, and railroads was correctly estimated, but it has become obvious during recent months that this visible destruction was probably less serious than the dislocation of the entire fabric of European economy. For the past 10 years conditions have been highly abnormal. The feverish preparation for war and the more feverish maintenance of the war effort engulfed all aspects of national economies. Machinery has fallen into disrepair or is entirely obsolete. Under the arbitrary and destructive Nazi rule, virtually every possible enterprise was geared into the German war machine. Long-standing commercial ties, private institutions, banks, insurance companies and shipping companies disappeared, through loss of capital, absorption through nationalization or by simple destruction. In many countries, confidence in the local currency has been severely shaken. The breakdown of the business structure of Europe during the war was complete. Recovery has been seriously retarded by the fact that 2 years after the close of hostilities a peace settlement with Germany and Austria has not been agreed upon. But even given a more prompt solution of these difficult problems, the rehabilitation of the economic structure of Europe quite evidently will require a much longer time and greater effort than had been foreseen.

There is a phase of this matter which is both interesting and serious. The farmer has always produced the foodstuffs to exchange with the city dweller for the other necessities of life. This division of labor is the basis of modern civilization. At the present time it is threatened with breakdown. The town and city industries are not producing adequate goods to exchange with the food-producing farmer. Raw materials and fuel are in short supply. Machinery is lacking or worn out. The farmer or the peasant cannot find the goods for sale which he desires to purchase. So the sale of his farm produce for money which he cannot use seems to him an unprofitable transaction. He, therefore, has withdrawn many fields from crop cultivation and is using them for grazing. He feeds more grain to stock and finds for himself and his family an ample supply of food, however short he may be on clothing and the other ordinary gadgets of civilization. Meanwhile people in the cities are short of food and fuel. So the governments are forced to use their foreign money and credits to procure these necessities abroad. This process exhausts funds which are urgently needed for reconstruction. Thus a very serious situation is rapidly developing which bodes no good for the world. The modern system of the division of labor upon which the exchange of products is based is in danger of breaking down.

The truth of the matter is that Europe's requirements for the next 3 or 4 years of foreign food and other essential products— principally from America—are so much greater than her present ability to pay that she must have substantial additional help, or face economic, social, and political deterioration of a very grave character.

The remedy lies in breaking the vicious circle and restoring the confidence of the European people in the economic future of their own countries and of Europe as a whole. The manufacturer and the farmer throughout wide areas must be able and willing to exchange their products for currencies the continuing value of which is not open to question.

Aside from the demoralizing effect on the world at large and the responsibilities of disturbances arising as a result of the desperation of the people concerned, the consequences to the economy of the United States should be apparent to all. It is logical that the United States should do whatever it is able to do to assist in the return of normal economic health in the world, without which there can be no political stability and no assured peace. Our policy is directed not against any country or doctrine but against hunger, poverty, desperation, and chaos. Its purpose should be the revival of a working economy in the world so as to permit the emergence of political and social conditions in which free institutions can exist. Such assistance, I am convinced, must not be on a piecemeal basis as various crises develop. Any assistance that this Government may render in the future should provide a cure rather than a mere palliative. Any government that is willing to assist in the task of recovery will find full cooperation, I am sure, on the part of the United States Government. Any government which maneuvers to block the recovery of other countries cannot expect help from us. Furthermore, governments, political parties, or groups which seek to perpetuate human misery in order to profit therefrom politically or otherwise will encounter the opposition of the United States.

It is already evident that, before the United States Government can proceed much further in its efforts to alleviate the situation and help start the European world on its way to recovery, there must be some agreement among the countries of Europe as to the requirements of the situation and the part those countries themselves will take in order to give proper effect to whatever action might be undertaken by this Government. It would be neither fitting nor efficacious for this Government to undertake to draw up unilaterally a program designed to place Europe on its feet economically. This is the business of the Europeans. The initiative, I think, must come from Europe. The role of this country should consist of friendly aid in the drafting of a European program and of later support of such a program so far as it may be practical for us to do so. The program should be a joint one, agreed to by a number, if not all European nations.

An essential part of any successful action on the part of the United States is an understanding on the part of the people of America of the character of the problem and the remedies to be applied. Political passion and prejudice should have no part. With foresight, and a willingness on the part of our people to face up to the vast responsibility which history has clearly placed upon our country, the difficulties I have outlined can and will be overcome.

Source:

Henry Steele Commager, ed., *Documents of American History*, Vol. 2, *Since 1898*, 9th ed. Englewood Cliffs, N.J., Prentice Hall, 1973, pp. 532–534.

National Security Act, 1947

Federal legislation enacted July 26, 1947, that coordinated the formerly separate departments of the U.S. Army, Navy, and Air Force within a single, unified command called the National Military Establishment. The agency was headed by a secretary of defense, who was to be a civilian and who became a member of the president's cabinet. The purpose of the act was to eliminate overlapping authority and to make national defense efforts more efficient and effective. In 1949 the department was reorganized, with greater authority for the secretary of defense to enforce cooperation among the services, and was renamed the Department of Defense.

The act also set up the National Security Council to advise the president on security issues and established the Central Intelligence Agency as an independent civilian agency headed by a director of Central Intelligence (DCI) whose job was to coordinate intelligence collection outside of the United States, including military intelligence. (The Federal Bureau of Investigation had charge of intelligence and counterintelligence within the United States.) However, into the 21st century, the DCI was never able to exercise real authority over the military intelligence agencies, including those of the services, the Defense Intelligence Agency, and the National Security Agency.

An Act

To promote the national security by providing for a Secretary of Defense; for a National Military Establishment; for a Department of the Army, a Department of the Navy, and a Department of the Air Force; and for the coordination of the activities of the National Military Establishment with other departments and agencies of the Government concerned with the national security.

Be it enacted by the Senate and House of Representatives of the United States of America in Congress assembled,

Short Title

That this Act may be cited as the "National Security Act of 1947."

* * *

Declaration of Policy

Sec. 2. In enacting this legislation, it is the intent of Congress to provide a comprehensive program for the future security of the United States; to provide for the establishment of integrated policies and procedures for the departments, agencies, and functions of the Government relating to the national security; to provide three military department for the operation and administration of the Army, the Navy (including naval aviation and the

United States Marine Corps), and the Air Force, with their assigned combat and service components; to provide for their authoritative coordination and unified direction under civilian control but not to merge them; to provide for the effective strategic direction of the armed forces and for their operation under unified control and for their integration into an efficient team of land, naval, and air forces.

Title I—Coordination for National Security

National Security Council

Sec. 101. (a) There is hereby established a council to be known as the National Security Council (hereinafter in this section referred to as the "Council").

The President of the United States shall preside over meetings of the Council: Provided, That in his absence he may designate a member of the Council to preside in his place.

The function of the Council shall be to advise the President with respect to the integration of domestic, foreign, and military policies relating to the national security so as to enable the military services and the other departments and agencies of the Government to cooperate more effectively in matters involving the national security.

The Council shall be composed of the President; the Secretary of State; the Secretary of Defense, appointed under section 202; the Secretary of the Army, referred to in section 205; the Secretary of the Navy; the Secretary of the Air Forces, appointed under section 207; the Chairman of the National Security Resources Board, appointed under section 103; and such of the following named officers as the President may designate from time to time: The Secretaries of the executive departments, the Chairman of the Munitions Board appointed under section 213, and the Chairman of the Research and Development Board appointed under section 214; but no such additional member shall be designated until the advice and consent of the Senate has been given to his appointment to the office the holding of which authorizes his designation as a member of the Council.

(b) In addition to performing such other functions as the President may direct, for the purpose of more effectively coordinating the policies and functions of the departments and agencies of the Government relating to the national security, it shall, subject to the direction of the President, be the duty of the Council—

(1) to assess and appraise the objectives, commitments, and risks of the United States in relation to our actual and potential military power, in the interest of national security, for the purpose of making recommendations to the President in connection therewith; and

(2) to consider policies on matters of common interest to the departments and agencies of the Government concerned with the national security, and to make recommendations to the President in connection therewith.

(c) The Council shall have a staff to be headed by a civilian executive secretary who shall be appointed by the President, and who shall receive compensation at the rate of $10,000 a year. The executive secretary, subject to the direction of the Council, is hereby authorized, subject to the civil-service laws and the Classification Act of 1923, as amended, to appoint and fix the compensation of such personnel as may be necessary to perform such duties as may be prescribed by the Council in connection with the performance of its functions.

(d) The Council shall, from time to time, make such recommendations, and such other reports to the President as it deems appropriate or as the President may require.

Central Intelligence Agency

Sec. 102. (a) There is hereby established under the National Security Council a Central Intelligence Agency with a Director of Central Intelligence, who shall be the head thereof. The Director shall be appointed by the President, by and with the advice and consent of the Senate, from among the commissioned officers of the armed services or from among individuals in civilian life. The Director shall receive compensation at the rate of $14,000 a year.

(b) (1) If a commissioned officer of the armed services is appointed as Director then—

(A) in the performance of his duties as Director, he shall be subject to no supervision, control, restriction, or prohibition (military or otherwise) other than would be operative with respect to him if he were a civilian in no way connected with the Department of the Army, the Department of the Navy, the Department of the Air Force, or the armed services or any component thereof; and

(B) he shall not possess or exercise any supervision, control, powers, or functions (other than such as he possesses, or is authorized or directed to exercise, as Director) with respect to the armed services or any component thereof, the Department of the Army, the Department of the Navy, or the Department of the Air Force, or any branch, bureau, unit or division thereof, or with respect to any of the personnel (military or civilian) of any of the foregoing.

(2) Except as provided in paragraph (1), the appointment to the office of Director of a commissioned officer of the armed services, and his acceptance of and service in such office, shall in no way affect any status, office, rank, or grade he may occupy or hold in the armed services, or any emolument, perquisite, right, privilege, or benefit incident to or arising out of any such status, office, rank, or grade. Any such commissioned officer shall, while serving in the office of Director, receive the military pay and allowances (active or retired, as the case may be) payable to a commissioned officer of his grade and length of ser-

vice and shall be paid, from any funds available to defray the expenses of the Agency, annual compensation at a rate equal to the amount by which $14,000 exceeds the amount of his annual military pay and allowances.

(c) Notwithstanding the provisions of section 6 of the Act of August 24, 1912 (37 Stat. 555), or the provisions of any other law, the Director of Central Intelligence may, in his discretion, terminate the employment of any officer or employee of the Agency whenever he shall deem such termination necessary or advisable in the interests of the United States, but such termination shall not affect the right of such officer or employee to seek or accept employment in any other department or agency of the Government if declared eligible for such employment by the United States Civil Service Commission.

(d) For the purpose of coordinating the intelligence activities of the several Government departments and agencies in the interest of national security, it shall be the duty of the Agency, under the direction of the National Security Council—

(1) to advise the National Security Council in matters concerning such intelligence activities of the Government departments and agencies as relate to national security;

(2) to make recommendations to the National Security Council for the coordination of such intelligence activities of the departments and agencies of the Government as relate to the national security;

(3) to correlate and evaluate intelligence relating to the national security, and provide for the appropriate dissemination of such intelligence within the Government using where appropriate existing agencies and facilities: Provided, That the Agency shall have no police, subpena, law-enforcement powers, or internal-security functions: Provided further, That the departments and other agencies of the Government shall continue to collect, evaluate, correlate, and disseminate departmental intelligence: And provided further, That the Director of Central Intelligence shall be responsible for protecting intelligence sources and methods from unauthorized disclosure;

(4) to perform, for the benefit of the existing intelligence agencies, such additional services of common concern as the National Security Council determines can be more efficiently accomplished centrally;

(5) to perform such other functions and duties related to intelligence affecting the national security as the National Security Council may from time to time direct.

(e) To the extent recommended by the National Security Council and approved by the President, such intelligence of the departments and agencies of the Government, except as hereinafter provided, relating to the national security shall be open to the inspection of the Director of Central Intelligence, and such intelligence as relates to the national security and is possessed by such departments and other agencies of the Government, except as hereinafter provided, shall be made available to the Director of Central Intelligence for correlation, evaluation, and dissemination: Provided, however, That upon the written request of the Director of Central Intelligence, the Director of the Federal Bureau of Investigation shall make available to the Director of Central Intelligence such information for correlation, evaluation, and dissemination as may be essential to the national security.

(f) Effective when the Director first appointed under subsection (a) has taken office—

(1) the National Intelligence Authority (11 Fed. Reg. 1337, 1339, February 5, 1946) shall cease to exist; and

(2) the personnel, property, and records of the Central Intelligence Group are transferred to the Central Intelligence Agency, and such Group shall cease to exist. Any unexpended balances of appropriations, allocations, or other funds available or authorized to be made available for such Group shall be available and shall be authorized to be made available in like manner for expenditure by the Agency.

National Security Resources Board

Sec. 103. (a) There is hereby established a National Security Resources Board (hereinafter in this section referred to as the "Board") to be composed of the Chairman of the Board and such heads or representatives of the various executive departments and independent agencies as may from time to time be designated by the President to be members of the Board. The Chairman of the Board shall be appointed from civilian life by the President, by and with the advice and consent of the Senate, and shall receive compensation at the rate of $14,000 a year.

(b) The Chairman of the Board, subject to the direction of the President, is authorized, subject to the civil-service laws and the Classification Act of 1923, as amended, to appoint and fix the compensation of such personnel as may be necessary to assist the Board in carrying out its functions.

(c) It shall be the function of the Board to advise the President concerning the coordination of military, industrial, and civilian mobilization, including—

(1) policies concerning industrial and civilian mobilization in order to assure the most effective mobilization and maximum utilization of the Nation's manpower in the event of war;

(2) programs for the effective use in time of war of the Nation's natural and industrial resources for military and civilian needs, for the maintenance and stabilization of the civilian economy in time of war, and for the adjustment of such economy to war needs and conditions;

(3) policies for unifying, in time of war, the activities of Federal agencies and departments engaged in or concerned with production, procurement, distribution, or

transportation of military or civilian supplies, materials, and products;

(4) the relationship between potential supplies of, and potential requirements for, manpower, resources, and productive facilities in time of war;

(5) policies for establishing adequate reserves of strategic and critical material, and for the conservation of these reserves;

(6) the strategic relocation of industries, services, government, and economic activities, the continuous operation of which is essential to the Nation's security.

(d) In performing its functions, the Board shall utilize to the maximum extent the facilities and resources of the departments and agencies of the Government.

Title II—The National Military Establishment

Establishment of the National Military Establishment

Sec. 201. (a) There is hereby established the National Military Establishment, and the Secretary of Defense shall be the head thereof.

(b) The National Military Establishment shall consist of the Department of the Army, the Department of the Navy, and the Department of the Air Force, together with all other agencies created under title II of this Act.

Secretary of Defense

Sec. 202. (a) There shall be a Secretary of Defense, who shall be appointed from civilian life by the President, by and with the advice and consent of the Senate: Provided, That a person who has within ten years been on active duty as a commissioned officer in a Regular component of the armed services shall not be eligible for appointment as Secretary of Defense. The Secretary of Defense shall be the principal assistant to the President in all matters relating to the national security. Under the direction of the President and subject to the provisions of this Act he shall perform the following duties:

(1) Establish general policies and programs for the National Military Establishment and for all of the departments and agencies therein;

(2) Exercise general direction, authority, and control over such departments and agencies;

(3) Take appropriate steps to eliminate unnecessary duplication or overlapping in the fields of procurement, supply, transportation, storage, health, and research;

(4) Supervise and coordinate the preparation of the budget estimates of the departments and agencies comprising the National Military Establishment; formulate and determine the budget estimates for submittal to the Bureau of the Budget; and supervise the budget programs of such departments and agencies under the applicable appropriation Act:

Provided, That nothing herein contained shall prevent the Secretary of the Army, the Secretary of the Navy, or the Secretary of the Air Force from presenting to the President or to the Director of the Budget, after first so informing the Secretary of Defense, any report or recommendation relating to his department which he may deem necessary: And provided further, That the Department of the Army, the Department of the Navy, and the Department of the Air Force shall be administered as individual executive departments by their respective Secretaries and all powers and duties relating to such departments not specifically conferred upon the Secretary of Defense by this Act shall be retained by each of their respective Secretaries.

(b) The Secretary of Defense shall submit annual written reports to the President and the Congress covering expenditures, work, and accomplishments of the National Military Establishment, together with such recommendations as he shall deem appropriate.

(c) The Secretary of Defense shall cause a seal of office to be made for the National Military Establishment, of such design as the President shall approve, and judicial notice shall be taken thereof.

Military Assistants to the Secretary

Sec. 203. Officers of the armed services may be detailed to duty as assistants and personal aides to the Secretary of Defense, but he shall not establish a military staff.

Civilian Personnel

Sec. 204. (a) The Secretary of Defense is authorized to appoint from civilian life not to exceed three special assistants to advise and assist him in the performance of his duties. Each such special assistant shall receive compensation at the rate of $10,000 a year.

(b) The Secretary of Defense is authorized, subject to the civil-service laws and the Classification Act of 1923, as amended, to appoint and fix the compensation of such other civilian personnel as may be necessary for the performance of the functions of the National Military Establishment other than those of the Departments of the Army, Navy, and Air Force.

Department of the Army

Sec. 205. (a) The Department of War shall hereafter be designated the Department of the Army, and the title of the Secretary of War shall be changed to Secretary of the Army. Changes shall be made in the titles of other officers and activities of the Department of the Army as the Secretary of the Army may determine.

(b) All laws, orders, regulations, and other actions relating to the Department of War or to any officer or activity whose title is changed under this section shall, insofar as they are not inconsistent with the provisions of this Act, be deemed to relate to the Department of the Army within the National Military Establishment or to such officer or activity designated by his or its new title.

(c) The term "Department of the Army" as used in this Act shall be construed to mean the Department of the Army at the seat of government and all field headquarters, forces, reserve components, installations, activities, and functions under the control or supervision of the Department of the Army.

(d) The Secretary of the Army shall cause a seal of office to be made for the Department of the Army, of such design as the President may approve, and judicial notice shall be taken thereof.

(e) In general the United States Army, within the Department of the Army, shall include land combat and service forces and such aviation and water transport as may be organic therein. It shall be organized, trained, and equipped primarily for prompt and sustained combat incident to operations on land. It shall be responsible for the preparation of land forces necessary for the effective prosecution of war except as otherwise assigned and, in accordance with integrated joint mobilization plans, for the expansion of peacetime components of the Army to meet the needs of war.

Department of the Navy

Sec. 206. (a) The term "Department of the Navy" as used in this Act shall be construed to mean the Department of the Navy at the seat of government; the headquarters, United States Marine Corps; the entire operating forces of the United States Navy, including naval aviation, and of the United States Marine Corps, including the reserve components of such forces; all field activities, headquarters, forces, bases, installations, activities, and functions under the control or supervision of the Department of the Navy; and the United States Coast Guard when operating as a part of the Navy pursuant to law.

(b) In general the United States Navy, within the Department of the Navy, shall include naval combat and services forces and such aviation as may be organic therein. It shall be organized, trained, and equipped primarily for prompt and sustained combat incident to operations at sea. It shall be responsible for the preparation of naval forces necessary for the effective prosecution of war except as otherwise assigned, and, in accordance with integrated joint mobilization plans, for the expansion of the peacetime components of the Navy to meet the needs of war.

All naval aviation shall be integrated with the naval service as part thereof within the Department of the Navy. Naval aviation shall consist of combat and service and training forces, and shall include land-based naval aviation, air transport essential for naval operations, all air weapons and air techniques involved in the operations and activities of the United States Navy, and the entire remainder of the aeronautical organization of the United States Navy, together with the personnel necessary therefor.

The Navy shall be generally responsible for naval reconnaissance, antisubmarine warfare, and protection of shipping.

The Navy shall develop aircraft, weapons, tactics, technique, organization and equipment of naval combat and service elements; matters of joint concern as to these functions shall be coordinated between the Army, the Air Force, and the Navy.

(c) The United States Marine Corps, within the Department of the Navy, shall include land combat and service forces and such aviation as may be organic therein. The Marine Corps shall be organized, trained, and equipped to provide fleet marine forces of combined arms, together with supporting air components, for service with the fleet in the seizure or defense of advanced naval bases and for the conduct of such land operations as may be essential to the prosecution of a naval campaign. It shall be the duty of the Marine Corps to develop, in coordination with the Army and the Air Force, those phases of amphibious operations which pertain to the tactics, technique, and equipment employed by landing forces. In addition, the Marine Corps shall provide detachments and organizations for service on armed vessels of the Navy, shall provide security detachments for the protection of naval property at naval stations and bases, and shall perform such other duties as the President may direct: Provided That such additional duties shall not detract from or interfere with the operations for which the Marine Corps is primarily organized. The Marine Corps shall be responsible, in accordance with integrated joint mobilization plans, for the expansion of peacetime components of the Marine Corps to meet the needs of war.

Department of the Air Force

Sec. 207. (a) Within the National Military Establishment there is hereby established an executive department to be known as the Department of the Air Force, and a Secretary of the Air Force, who shall be the head thereof. The Secretary of the Air Force shall be appointed from civilian life by the President, by and with the advice and consent of the Senate.

(b) Section 158 of the Revised Statutes is amended to include the Department of the Air Force and the provisions of so much of title IV of the Revised Statutes as now or hereafter amended as is not inconsistent with this Act shall be applicable to the Department of the Air Force.

(c) The term "Department of the Air Force" as used in this Act shall be construed to mean the Department of the Air Force at the seat of government and all field headquarters, forces, reserve components, installations, activities, and functions under the control or supervision of the Department of the Air Force.

(d) There shall be in the Department of the Air Force an Under Secretary of the Air Force and two Assistant

Secretaries of the Air Force, who shall be appointed from civilian life by the President by and with the advice and consent of the Senate.

(e) The several officers of the Department of the Air Force shall perform such functions as the Secretary of the Air Force may prescribe.

(f) So much of the functions of the Secretary of the Army and of the Department of the Army, including those of any officer of such Department, as are assigned to or under the control of the Commanding General, Army Air Forces, or as are deemed by the Secretary of Defense to be necessary or desirable for the operations of the Department of the Air Force or the United States Air Force, shall be transferred to and vested in the Secretary of the Air Force and the Department of the Air Force: Provided, That the National Guard Bureau shall, in addition to the functions and duties performed by it for the Department of the Army, be charged with similar functions and duties for the Department of the Air Force, and shall be the channel of communication between the Department of the Air Force and the several States on all matters pertaining to the Air National Guard: And provided further, That, in order to permit an orderly transfer, the Secretary of Defense may, during the transfer period hereinafter prescribed, direct that the Department of the Army shall continue for appropriate periods to exercise any of such functions, insofar as they relate to the Department of the Air Force, or the United States Air Force or their property and personnel. Such of the property, personnel, and records of the Department of the Army used in the exercise of functions transferred under this subsection as the Secretary of Defense shall determine shall be transferred or assigned to the Department of the Air Force.

(g) The Secretary of the Air Force shall cause a seal of office to be made for the Department of the Air Force, of such device as the President shall approve, and judicial notice shall be taken thereof.

United States Air Force

Sec. 208. (a) The United States Air Force is hereby established under the Department of the Air Force. The Army Air Forces, the Air Corps, United States Army, and the General Headquarters Air Force (Air Force Combat Command), shall be transferred to the United States Air Force.

(b) There shall be a Chief of Staff, United States Air Force, who shall be appointed by the President, by and with the advice and consent of the Senate, for a term of four years from among the officers of general rank who are assigned to or commissioned in the United States Air Force. Under the direction of the Secretary of the Air Force, the Chief of Staff, United States Air Force, shall exercise command over the United States Air Force and shall be charged with the duty of carrying into execution all lawful orders and directions which may be transmitted to him. The functions of the Commanding General, General Headquarters Air Force (Air Force Combat Command), and of the Chief of the Air Corps and of the Commanding General, Army Air Forces, shall be transferred to the Chief of Staff, United States Air Force. When such transfer becomes effective, the offices of the Chief of the Air Corps, United States Army, and Assistants to the Chief of the Air Corps, United States Army, provided for by the Act of June 4, 1920, as amended (41 Stat. 768), and Commanding General, General Headquarters Air Force, provided for by section 5 of the Act of June 16, 1936 (49 Stat. 1525), shall cease to exist. While holding office as Chief of Staff, United States Air Force, the incumbent shall hold a grade and receive allowances equivalent to those prescribed by law for the Chief of Staff, United States Army. The Chief of Staff, United States Army, the Chief of Naval Operations, and the Chief of Staff, United States Air Force, shall take rank among themselves according to their relative dates of appointment as such, and shall each take rank above all other officers on the active list of the Army, Navy, and Air Force: Provided, That nothing in this Act shall have the effect of changing the relative rank of the present Chief of Staff, United States Army, and the present Chief of Naval operations.

(c) All commissioned officers, warrant officers, and enlisted men, commissioned, holding warrants, or enlisted, in the Air Corps, United States Army, or the Army Air Forces, shall be transferred in branch to the United States Air Force. All other commissioned officers, warrant officers, and enlisted men, who are commissioned, hold warrants, or are enlisted, in any component of the Army of the United States and who are under the authority or command of the Commanding General, Army Air Forces, shall be continued under the authority or command of the Chief of Staff, United States Air Force, and under the jurisdiction of the Department of the Air Force. Personnel whose status is affected by this subsection shall retain their existing commissions, warrants, or enlisted status in existing components of the armed forces unless otherwise altered or terminated in accordance with existing law; and they shall not be deemed to have been appointed to a new or different office or grade, or to have vacated their permanent or temporary appointments in an existing component of the armed forces, solely by virtue of any change in status under this subsection. No such change in status shall alter or prejudice the status of any individual so assigned, so as to deprive him of any right, benefit, or privilege to which he may be entitled under existing law.

(d) Except as otherwise directed by the Secretary of the Air Force, all property, records, installations, agencies, activities, projects, and civilian personnel under the jurisdiction, control, authority, or command of the Commanding General, Army Air Forces, shall be continued to the same extent under the jurisdiction, control, authority, or command, respectively, of the Chief of Staff, United States Air Force, in the Department of the Air Force.

(e) For a period of two years from the date of enactment of this Act, personnel (both military and civilian), property, records, installations, agencies, activities, and projects may be transferred between the Department of the Army and the Department of the Air Force by direction of the Secretary of Defense.

(f) In general the United States Air Force shall include aviation forces both combat and service not otherwise assigned. It shall be organized, trained, and equipped primarily for prompt and sustained offensive and defensive air operations. The Air Force shall be responsible for the preparation of the air forces necessary for the effective prosecution of war except as otherwise assigned and, in accordance with integrated joint mobilization plans, for the expansion of the peacetime components of the Air Force to meet the needs of war.

Effective Date of Transfers

Sec. 209. Each transfer, assignment, or change in status under section 207 or section 208 shall take effect upon such date or dates as may be prescribed by the Secretary of Defense.

War Council

Sec. 210. There shall be within the National Military Establishment a War Council composed of the Secretary of Defense, as Chairman, who shall have power of decision; the Secretary of the Army; the Secretary of the Navy; the Secretary of the Air Force; the Chief of Staff, United States Army; the Chief of Naval Operations; and the Chief of Staff, United States Air Force. The War Council shall advise the Secretary of Defense on matters of broad policy relating to the armed forces, and shall consider and report on such other matters as the Secretary of Defense may direct.

Joint Chiefs of Staff

Sec. 211. (a) There is hereby established within the National Military Establishment the Joint Chiefs of Staff, which shall consist of the Chief of Staff, United States Army; the Chief of Naval Operations; the Chief of Staff, United States Air Force; and the Chief of Staff to the Commander in Chief, if there be one.

(b) Subject to the authority and direction of the President an the Secretary of Defense, it shall be the duty of the Joint Chiefs of Staff—

(1) to prepare strategic plans and to provide for the strategic direction of the military forces;

(2) to prepare joint logistic plans and to assign to the military services logistic responsibilities in accordance with such plans;

(3) to establish unified commands in strategic areas when such unified commands are in the interest of national security;

(4) to formulate policies for joint training of the military forces;

(5) to formulate policies for coordinating the education of members of the military forces;

(6) to review major material and personnel requirements of the military forces, in accordance with strategic and logistic plans; and

(7) to provide United States representation on the Military Staff Committee of the United Nations in accordance with the provisions of the Charter of the United Nations.

(c) The Joint Chiefs of Staff shall act as the principal military advisers to the President and the Secretary of Defense and shall perform such other duties as the President and the Secretary of Defense may direct or as may be prescribed by law.

Joint Staff

Sec. 212. There shall be, under the Joint Chiefs of Staff, a Joint Staff to consist of not to exceed one hundred officers and to be composed of approximately equal numbers of officers from each of the three armed services. The Joint Staff, operating under a Director thereof appointed by the Joint Chiefs of Staff, shall perform such duties as may be directed by the Joint Chiefs of Staff. The Director shall be an officer junior in grade to all members of the Joint Chiefs of Staff.

Munitions Board

Sec. 213. (a) There is hereby established in the National Military Establishment a Munitions Board (hereinafter in this section referred to as the "Board").

(b) The Board shall be composed of a Chairman, who shall be the head thereof, and an Under Secretary or Assistant Secretary from each of the three military departments, to be designated in each case by the Secretaries of their respective departments. The Chairman shall be appointed from civilian life by the President, by and with the advice and consent of the Senate, and shall receive compensation at the rate of $14,000 a year.

(c) It shall be the duty of the Board under the direction of the Secretary of Defense and in support of strategic and logistic plans prepared by the Joint Chiefs of Staff—

(1) to coordinate the appropriate activities within the National Military Establishment with regard to industrial matters, including the procurement, production, and distribution plans of the departments and agencies comprising the Establishment;

(2) to plan for the military aspects of industrial mobilization;

(3) to recommend assignment of procurement responsibilities among the several military services and to plan for

standardization of specifications and for the greatest practicable allocation of purchase authority of technical equipment and common use items on the basis of single procurement;

(4) to prepare estimates of potential production, procurement, and personnel for use in evaluation of the logistic feasibility of strategic operations;

(5) to determine relative priorities of the various segments of the military procurement programs;

(6) to supervise such subordinate agencies as are or may be created to consider the subjects falling within the scope of the Board's responsibilities;

(7) to make recommendations to regroup, combine, or dissolve existing interservice agencies operating in the fields of procurement, production, and distribution in such manner as to promote efficiency and economy;

(8) to maintain liaison with other departments and agencies for the proper correlation of military requirements with the civilian economy, particularly in regard to the procurement or disposition of strategic and critical material and the maintenance of adequate reserves of such material, and to make recommendations as to policies in connection therewith;

(9) to assemble and review material and personnel requirements presented by the Joint Chiefs of Staff and those presented by the production, procurement, and distribution agencies assigned to meet military needs, and to make recommendations thereon to the Secretary of Defense; and

(10) to perform such other duties as the Secretary of Defense may direct.

(d) When the Chairman of the Board first appointed has taken office, the Joint Army and Navy Munitions Board shall cease to exist and all its records and personnel shall be transferred to the Munitions Board.

(e) The Secretary of Defense shall provide the Board with such personnel and facilities as the Secretary may determine to be required by the Board for the performance of its functions.

Research and Development Board

Sec. 214. (a) There is hereby established in the National Military Establishment a Research and Development Board (hereinafter in this section referred to as the "Board"). The Board shall be composed of a Chairman, who shall be the head thereof, and two representatives from each of the Departments of the Army, Navy, and Air Force, to be designated by the Secretaries of their respective Departments. The Chairman shall be appointed from civilian life by the President, by and with the advice and consent of the Senate, and shall receive compensation at the rate of $14,000 a year. The purpose of the Board shall be to advise the Secretary of Defense as to the status of scientific research relative to the national security, and to assist him in assuring adequate provision for research and development on scientific problems relating to the national security.

(b) It shall be the duty of the Board, under the direction of the Secretary of Defense—

(1) to prepare a complete and integrated program of research and development for military purposes;

(2) to advise with regard to trends in scientific research relating to national security and the measures necessary to assure continued and increasing progress;

(3) to recommend measures of coordination of research and development among the military departments, and allocation among them of responsibilities for specific programs of joint interest;

(4) to formulate policy for the National Military Establishment in connection with research and development matters involving agencies outside the National Military Establishment;

(5) to consider the interaction of research and development and strategy, and to advise the Joint Chiefs of Staff in connection therewith; and

(6) to perform such other duties as the Secretary of Defense may direct.

(c) When the Chairman of the Board first appointed has taken office, the Joint Research and Development Board shall cease to exist and all its records and personnel shall be transferred to the Research and Development Board.

(d) The Secretary of Defense shall provide the Board with such personnel and facilities as the Secretary may determine to be required by the Board for the performance of its functions.

Title III—Miscellaneous

Compensation of Secretaries

Sec. 301. (a) The Secretary of Defense shall receive the compensation prescribed by law for heads of executive departments.

(b) The Secretary of the Army, the Secretary of the Navy, and the Secretary of the Air Force shall each receive the compensation prescribed by law for heads of executive departments.

Under Secretaries and Assistant Secretaries

Sec. 302. The Under Secretaries and Assistant Secretaries of the Army, the Navy, and the Air Force shall each receive compensation at the rate of $10,000 a year and shall perform such duties as the Secretaries of their respective departments may prescribe.

Advisory Committees and Personnel

Sec. 303. (a) This Secretary of Defense, the Chairman of the National Security Resources Board, and the Director of Central Intelligence are authorized to appoint such advisory committees and to employ, consistent with other provisions of this Act, such part-time advisory personnel as they may deem necessary in carrying out their respective functions and the functions of agencies under their control. Persons holding other offices or positions under the United States for which they receive compensation while serving as members of such committees shall receive no additional compensation for such service. Other members of such committees and other part-time advisory personnel so employed may serve without compensation or may receive compensation at a rate not to exceed $35 for each day of service, as determined by the appointing authority.

(b) Service of an individual as a member of any such advisory committee, or in any other part-time capacity for a department or agency hereunder, shall not be considered as service bringing such individual within the provisions of section 109 or 113 of the Criminal Code (U.S.C., 1940 edition, title 18, secs. 198 and 203), or section 19(e) of the Contract Settlement Act of 1944, unless the act of such individual, which by such section is made unlawful when performed by an individual referred to in such section, is with respect to any particular matter which directly involves a department or agency which such person is advising or in which such department or agency is directly interested.

Status of Transferred Civilian Personnel

Sec. 304. All transfers of civilian personnel under this Act shall be without change in classification or compensation, but the head of any department or agency to which such a transfer is made is authorized to make such changes in the titles and designations and prescribe such changes in the duties of such personnel commensurate with their classification as he may deem necessary and appropriate.

Saving Provisions

Sec. 305. (a) All laws, orders, regulations, and other actions applicable with respect to any function, activity, personnel, property, records, or other thing transferred under this Act, or with respect to any officer, department, or agency, from which such transfer is made, shall, except to the extent rescinded, modified, superseded, terminated, or made inapplicable by or under authority of law, have the same effect as if such transfer had not been made; but, after any such transfer, any such law, order, regulation, or other action which vested functions in or otherwise related to any officer, department, or agency from which such transfer was made shall, insofar as applicable with respect to the function, activity, personnel, property, records or other thing transferred and to the extent not inconsistent with other provisions of this Act, be deemed to have vested such function in or relate to the officer, department, or agency to which the transfer was made.

(b) No suit, action, or other proceeding lawfully commenced by or against the head of any department or agency or other officer of the United States, in his official capacity or in relation to the discharge of his official duties, shall abate by reason of the taking effect of any transfer or change in title under the provisions of this Act; and, in the case of any such transfer, such suit, action, or other proceeding may be maintained by or against the successor of such head or other officer under the transfer, but only if the court shall allow the same to be maintained on motion or supplemental petition filed within twelve months after such transfer takes effect, showing a necessity for the survival of such suit, action, or other proceeding to obtain settlement of the questions involved.

(c) Notwithstanding the provisions of the second paragraph of section 5 of title I of the First War Powers Act, 1941, the existing organization of the War Department under the provisions of Executive Order Numbered 9082 of February 28, 1942, as modified by Executive Order Numbered 9722 of May 13, 1946, and the existing organization of the Department of the Navy under the provisions of Executive Order Numbered 9635 of September 29, 1945, including the assignment of functions to organizational units within the War and Navy Departments, may, to the extent determined by the Secretary of Defense, continue in force for two years following the date of enactment of this Act except to the extent modified by the provisions of this Act or under the authority of law.

Transfer of Funds

Sec. 306. All unexpended balances of appropriations, allocations, nonappropriated funds, or other funds available or hereafter made available for use by or on behalf of the Army Air Forces or officers thereof, shall be transferred to the Department of the Air Force for use in connection with the exercise of its functions. Such other unexpended balances of appropriations, allocations, nonappropriated funds, or other funds available or hereafter made available for use by the Department of War or the Department of the Army in exercise of functions transferred to the Department of the Air Force under this Act, as the Secretary of Defense shall determine, shall be transferred to the Department of the Air Force for use in connection with the exercise of its functions. Unexpended balances transferred under this section may be used for the purposes for which the appropriations, allocations, or other funds were originally made available, or for new expenditures occasioned by the enactment of this Act. The transfers herein authorized may be made with or without warrant action as may be appropriate from time to time from any appropriation covered by this section to any other such appropriation or to such new accounts established on the books of the Treasury as may be determined to be necessary to carry into effect provisions of this Act.

Authorization for Appropriations

Sec. 307. There are hereby authorized to be appropriated such sums as may be necessary and appropriate to carry out the provisions and purposes of this Act.

Definitions

Sec. 308. (a) As used in this Act, the term "function" includes functions, powers, and duties.

(b) As used in this Act, the term "budget program" refers to recommendations as to the apportionment, to the allocation and to the review of allotments of appropriated funds.

Separability

Sec. 309. If any provision of this Act or the application thereof to any person or circumstances is held invalid, the validity of the remainder of the Act and of the application of such provision to other persons and circumstances shall not be affected thereby.

Effective Date

Sec. 310. (a) The first sentence of section 202(a) and sections 1, 2, 307, 308, 309, and 310 shall take effect immediately upon the enactment of this Act.

(b) Except as provided in subsection (a), the provisions of this Act shall take effect on whichever of the following days is the earlier: The day after the day upon which the Secretary of Defense first appointed takes office, or the sixtieth day after the date of the enactment of this Act.

Succession to the Presidency

Sec. 311. Paragraph (1) of subsection (d) of section 1 of the Act entitled "An Act to provide for the performance of the duties of the office of President in case of the removal, resignation, death, or inability both of the President and Vice President", approved July 18, 1947, is amended by striking out "Secretary of War" and inserting in lieu thereof "Secretary of Defense", and by striking out "Secretary of the Navy,".

Approved July 26, 1947.

Source:

United States Statutes at Large, Vol. 61, pp. 495–510.

President Truman's Recognition of the State of Israel, White House Press Releases, 5/14/48 and 1/31/49

In the aftermath of the Holocaust, most of the remaining European Jews had no country. For religious, economic, and social reasons, Zionists (supporters of a Jewish homeland) had begun to populate and purchase land in Palestine (a British protectorate, and before that under Turkish jurisdiction) since early in the 20th century. Zionists saw their dream realized when the United Nations General Assembly voted in principle to partition Palestine into Jewish and Arab areas. The British announced they would leave May 15, 1948, and on May 14 the Jews proclaimed their state. In order to make certain that the United States rather than the Soviets would have primacy in Israel, Truman recognized the new state within minutes. The next day, Arab forces invaded. A UN-sponsored truce did not last long and Israel and her Arab neighbors have been fighting in one form or another ever since. Truman's initial recognition was de facto because Israel had only a provisional government. On January 31, 1949, after elections, the recognition became de jure, i.e. within the law. Israel may not have survived without U.S. recognition and support, nor would it have been able to join the United Nations.

Statement by President Truman, 1948

This Government has been informed that a Jewish state has been proclaimed in Palestine, and recognition has been requested by the provisional government thereof.

The United States recognizes the provisional government as the *de facto* authority of the new State of Israel.

Statement by President Truman, 1949

On October 24, 1948, the president stated that when a permanent government was elected in Israel, it would promptly be given *de jure* recognition. Elections for such a government were held on January 25th. The votes have now been counted, and this Government has been officially informed of the results. The United States Government is therefore pleased to extend *de jure* recognition to the Government of Israel as of this date.

Source:

White House Press Releases in Henry Steele Commager, ed., *Documents of American History*, 6th ed., New York: Appleton, Century, Crofts, 1958.

George Marshall, Note on Berlin Blockade and Airlift, 1948

Note by U.S. secretary of state George C. Marshall July 6, 1948, to the Soviet Union, protesting that nation's June 24 halting of all land and water traffic between West Germany and the city of West Berlin.

Berlin, the former capital of Germany, although located more than 100 miles into the Soviet-dominated East Germany, was jointly occupied by the United States, France, and the United Kingdom, as well as the USSR. It remained a major source of conflict between the Soviet Union and the West until 1989.

After Germany's surrender, the Allies carved Berlin into four zones of occupation. By June 1948 the French, American, and British zones had merged, and preparations had begun to create what became West Germany (the Federal Republic of Germany–FRG) in 1949. In retaliation, Soviet officials, declaring that Berlin was an integral part of the Soviet zone, refused to permit the Western occupying powers access to the western zones of the city. Marshall, in his note, demanded restoration of free access to Berlin, maintaining the city was an international, not a USSR, zone of occupation. The Soviet blockade, however, lasted until May 12, 1949. During that period, the Western nations airlifted more than 2 million tons of food, clothing, and other necessities into the city.

In 1961, Premier Nikita Khrushchev demanded that British, French, and U.S. troops be removed from West Berlin. In a report to the American people on July 25, President Kennedy called the Soviet proposal a threat to peace and freedom. "We do not want to fight, but we have fought before. . . . We cannot and will not permit the Communists to drive us out of Berlin, either gradually or by force." He asked Congress to appropriate additional funding for the armed forces and for civil defense, to authorize an increase in military personnel, and to increase draft calls. The Soviet response was to build a wall separating East and West Berlin. East Berliners escaping over it risked being shot. The wall stood until 1989 when Germans tore it down in defiance of the Soviets.

On June 3, 1972, the ambassadors of Great Britain, France, and the United States to the FRG, and the Soviet ambassador to the German Democratic Republic (GDR) signed the Four Power Agreement on the status of Berlin. The previous year, they agreed to help ease the tension in the area, to settle disputes by peaceful means, and to respect their individual and common rights and obligations. This agreement eased transit and communications between West Berlin and the FRG. Berlin's legal status, however, remained unchanged, and Great Britain, France, and the United States reiterated their continued and absolute responsibility for West Berlin.

Excellency: I have the honor to acknowledge the receipt of your note No. 51/41/48 of June 18, 1948, protesting on behalf of your Government the recommendations resulting from the Six-Power talks on Germany, recently held in London, on the grounds that the participants were "not competent and not empowered to deal with these problems." You stressed your Government's opposition to many of the recommendations as being contrary to existing international agreements and your Government's belief that all matters involving the future of Germany should be the exclusive concern of the Council of Foreign Ministers. I noted with particular interest your observation that "any possible difficulties in reconciling the positions within the Council cannot be insuperable, if all the Powers will abide by the Potsdam agreements."

I need hardly remind you of my Government's persistent efforts to achieve four-power agreement on Germany on the basis of the Potsdam Agreement. I discussed this point in my note to you of September 30, 1947, in connection with the decision to revise the level of industry in the Anglo-American zone. The record clearly shows that the continuing efforts of my Government to achieve an equitable solution of the German problem in the Council of Foreign Ministers and in the Allied Control Council in Berlin have been fruitless largely as a result of the intransigent attitude of one of the occupying powers. The records of the Control Council as of March 1948 show that the Soviet representative has vetoed the agreed decisions of the other three powers in 69 instances—nearly three times the combined number of vetoes exercised by the other powers. As explained in my note under reference, it is because of the repeated failure over a period of three years to achieve four-power agreement that my Government "feels justified in pursuing objectives which have been commonly agreed and making arrangements for that purpose with any other occupying power willing to work toward the common end."

My Government agrees with your Government that German resources ought to be used for the benefit of the general reconstruction of Europe rather than for the reconstruction of only a part of Europe. The United States has consistently endeavored to implement the clear understanding in the Potsdam Agreement that Germany, including the Soviet Zone, should be treated as an economic whole and it has consistently striven to create those conditions which would lead to the establishment of a democratic German state capable of assisting the reconstruction of all the devastated countries of Europe and yet not constituting a threat to the security of those nations. The assertion that the United States has sought to divide Germany or to divide Europe is without any foundation. The fact that its offer to assist the general European recovery has not been accepted by certain countries, including Poland, has of necessity limited the application of that recovery program to those countries which have accepted it. The apparent division of Germany today after three years of unsuccessful attempts to hold it together is greatly deplored by my Government. Here again the necessity to confine our joint program in Germany to Western Germany is not of our making and certainly not in accordance with our wishes. The fact that the efforts of the United States toward the rehabilitation of Europe now have to be concentrated on the program for Western Europe, including Western Germany, is a direct result of the failure of the other countries of Europe at the instigation of the Soviet

Union to join in a common program looking toward the rehabilitation of all Europe.

With regard to the substance of the London recommendations I must point out that there was no attempt in these talks to cover all aspects of the German problem. Therefore, there is no basis for your protesting the fact that the problem of reparations was omitted in the recommendations of the conference, a conference which you have insisted had no right to discuss any matters relating to Germany.

I must take exception to your comments on the recommendations concerning security and your statement that the fundamental aim of removing Germany's economic basis of aggression has been ignored. It should not be necessary for me to remind you that the United States has twice been engaged in major wars with Germany and that it is vitally interested in preventing a recurrence of German aggression. Security considerations, far from having been relegated to a secondary position, were constantly in mind throughout the London discussions as should be evident from the communique reporting the final recommendations. This problem has of course become more complicated as a result of the unwillingness of the Soviet Union to join the other occupying powers in a long term treaty guaranteeing the disarmament and demilitarization of Germany. The London recommendations on the Ruhr and on general security make specific provision against the rebuilding of German economic power as a means to future aggression.

Your comments on the plan for the control of the Ruhr have, I believe, been answered in the general discussion above with respect to the division of Germany and of Europe. It should be observed that the program for the rehabilitation of Western Germany does not exclude that area from trade relations with Eastern Europe but, on the contrary, seeks to foster such trade in the common interest. If certain countries "who suffered most in consequence of German aggression" claim that their interests are not sufficiently taken into account by the program planned for Western Germany, their complaint should not be addressed to the United States Government but to the Government primarily responsible for preventing these countries from cooperating in the general recovery program for Europe. In the same way it seems to me that your protest against the failure to utilize quadripartite consultative machinery, should more appropriately be addressed to the occupying power responsible for the present deplorable division of Europe and Germany.

Source:

U.S. Department of State, Bulletin, Vol. 19 (July 18, 1948), pp. 86–87.

North Atlantic Treaty, 1949

Security pact established on April 4, 1949, by countries of the North Atlantic region. The treaty created the North Atlantic Treaty Organization (NATO), a military and political alliance intended to counteract the Soviet Union's increasing military presence and expansionist postures in Europe. Successor to the Brussels Treaty of 1948, the North Atlantic Treaty was endorsed by Belgium, Britain, Canada, Denmark, France, Iceland, Italy, Luxembourg, the Netherlands, Norway, Portugal, and the United States, and later joined by Greece, Turkey, and West Germany. The treaty, initiated by the United States, bound its signatories to help each other in the event of aggression (an attack on one was to be regarded as an attack on all) and "to safeguard the freedom, common heritage, and civilization of their peoples founded on the principles of democracy, individual organization, liberty and the rule of law." NATO has standing military forces in Europe and operates chiefly through its council (made up of representatives from the member nations). NATO's major adversary was the Warsaw Pact, consisting of Eastern European Communist countries. However, since the fall of communism and the breakup of the Soviet Union, several former Warsaw Pact nations have joined or are otherwise associated with NATO.

Several pacts also reinforced relationships between the United States and Latin American countries. On September 2, 1947, they signed the Rio Treaty, followed by the formal chartering of the Organization of American States (OAS) in Bogotá, Colombia, April 30, 1948. Signed at the close of the Ninth Pan-American Conference by representatives of the 21 American states (excluding, notably, Canada), the charter laid down fundamental principles for the OAS and described its structure. Through this document the signatories agreed to settle all disputes peacefully; to work together to promote economic, social, and cultural progress among them; and to respect the right of each state to govern itself in its own way. While not explicitly stated, the OAS was anticommunist in its orientation.

On September 1, 1951, Australia, New Zealand, and the United States (ANZUS) signed a mutual security treaty for the preservation of peace and security in the Pacific region. Meeting in San Francisco, they reaffirmed their commitment to the United Nations Charter and agreed to consult and help each other if their "territorial integrity, political independence or security" was threatened in the Pacific. Ratified by the Australian Parliament in 1952, the treaty was considered valid indefinitely. ANZUS located its headquarters in the Australian capital of Canberra.

The Southeast Asia Treaty Organization (SEATO) began September 8, 1954, in Manila, Philippines, to counteract the growing communist influence in the Far East. Signed by Britain, France, the United States, Australia, New Zealand, the Philippines, Pakistan, and Thailand, the treaty became operative on February 19, 1955. Headquartered in Bangkok,

SEATO's role was mainly to provide consultation during an emergency; unlike NATO it did not command standing forces. The absence of India, Indonesia, and Burma (Myanmar) and the exclusion of Vietnam, Laos, and Cambodia undermined SEATO's effectiveness in the region. After losing Pakistan in 1973 (following the creation of Bangladesh) and France in 1974, SEATO's signatories decided in September 1975 to gradually phase out operations in view of the changing regional picture. SEATO was formally dissolved on June 30, 1977.

April 4, 1949

The parties to this Treaty reaffirm their faith in the purposes and principles of the Charter of the United Nations and their desire to live in peace with all peoples and all governments.

They are determined to safeguard the freedom, common heritage and civilization of their peoples, founded on the principles of democracy, individual liberty and the rule of law.

The seek to promote stability and well-being in the North Atlantic area.

They are resolved to unite their efforts for collective defense and for the preservation of peace and security.

They therefore agree to this North Atlantic Treaty

Art. 1. The Parties undertake, as set forth in the Charter of the United Nations to settle any international disputes in which they may be involved by peaceful means in such a manner that international peace and security, and justice, are not endangered, and to refrain in their international relations from the threat or use of force in any manner inconsistent with the purpose of the United Nations.

Art. 2. The Parties will contribute toward the further development of peaceful and friendly international relations by strengthening their free institutions, by bringing about a better understanding of the principles upon which these institutions are founded, and by promoting conditions of stability and well-being. They will seek to eliminate conflict in their international economic policies and will encourage economic collaboration between any or all of them.

Art. 3. In order more effectively to achieve the objectives of this treaty, The Parties, separately and jointly by means of continuous and effective self-help and mutual aid, will maintain and develop their individual and collective capacity to resist armed attack.

Art. 4. The Parties will consult together whenever, in the opinion of any of them, the territorial integrity, political independence or security of any of the Parties is threatened.

Art. 5. The Parties agree that an armed attack against one or more of them in Europe or North America shall be considered an attack against them all and consequently they agree that, if such an armed attack occurs, each of them, in exercise of the right of individual or collective self-defense recognized by article 51 of the Charter of the United Nations, will assist the Party or Parties so attacked by taking forthwith, individually and in concert with the other Parties, such action as it deems necessary, including the use of armed force, to restore and maintain the security of the North Atlantic area. Any such armed attack and all measures taken as a result thereof shall immediately be reported to the Security Council. Such measures shall be terminated when Security Council has taken the measures necessary to restore and maintain international peace and security.

Art. 6. For the purpose of Article 5 an armed attack on one or more of the Parties is deemed to include an armed attack on the territory of any of the Parties in Europe or North America, on the Algerian Departments of France, on the territory of Turkey or on the islands under the jurisdiction of any of the Parties in the North Atlantic area north of the Tropic of Cancer; on the forces, vessels or aircraft of any of the Parties, when in or over these territories or any other area in Europe in which occupation forces of any of the Parties were stationed on the date when the treaty entered into force or the Mediterranean Sea or the North Atlantic area north of the Tropic of Cancer.

Art. 7. This Treaty does not affect, and shall not be interpreted as affecting, in any way the rights and obligations under the Charter of the Parties which are members of the United Nations, or the primary responsibility of the Security Council for the maintenance of international peace and security.

Art. 8. Each Party declares that none of the international engagements now in force between it and any other of the Parties or any third State is in conflict with the provisions of this Treaty, and undertakes not to enter into any international engagement in conflict with this Treaty.

Art. 9. The Parties hereby establish a council, on which each of them shall be represented, to consider matters concerning the implementation of this Treaty. The council shall be so organized as to be able to meet promptly at any time. The council shall set up such subsidiary bodies as may be necessary; in particular it shall establish immediately a defence committee which shall recommend measures for the implementation of Articles 3 and 5.

Art. 10. The Parties may, by unanimous agreement, invite any other European State in a position to further the principles of this Treaty and to contribute to the security of the North Atlantic area to accede to this Treaty. Any state so invited may become a party to the Treaty by depositing its instrument of accession with the Government of the United States of America. The Government of the United

States of America will inform each of the Parties of the deposit of each such instrument of accession.

Art. 11. This Treaty shall be ratified and its provisions carried out by the Parties in accordance with their respective constitutional processes. The instruments of ratification shall be deposited as soon as possible with the Government of the United States of America, which will notify all the other signatories of each deposit. The Treaty shall enter into force between the States which have ratified it as soon as the ratification of the majority of the signatories, including the ratifications of Belgium, Canada, France, Luxembourg, the Netherlands, the United Kingdom and the United States, have been deposited and shall come into effect with respect to other States on the date of the deposit of their ratifications.

Art. 12. After the Treaty has been in force for ten years, or at any time thereafter, the Parties shall, if any of them so requests, consult together for the purpose of reviewing the Treaty, having regard for the factors then affecting peace and security in the North Atlantic area, including the development of universal as well as regional arrangements under the Charter of the United Nations for the maintenance of international peace and security.

Art. 13. After the Treaty has been in force for twenty years, any Party may cease to be a party one year after its notice of denunciation has been given to the Government of the United States of America, which will inform the Governments of the other Parties of the deposit of each notice of denunciation.

Art. 14. This Treaty, of which the English and French texts are equally authentic, shall be deposited in the archives of the Government of the United States of America. Duly certified copies thereof will be transmitted by that Government to the Governments of the other signatories.

See also THE ACT OF CHAPULTEPEC, 1945.

Source:
Landmark Documents in American History, Facts On File, Inc.

President Truman's Statement on the Korean War, 1950

Statement issued by President Harry S. Truman on June 27, 1950, following the outbreak of the Korean War. Because the U.S. Congress never declared war, Truman termed American involvement a police action.

The conflict began June 25, when Communist North Korea launched a full-scale invasion of South Korea. On June 27, the United Nations Security Council approved an American-sponsored resolution calling on all member nations to assist South Korea in repelling the attack and restoring peace. The Soviet Union, which could have exercised a veto, was absent at that time. In his statement, Truman announced that he would immediately order U.S. air and naval forces to provide support to South Korea. Truman asserted that the invasion of the South proved that the forces of communism were prepared to use aggression to achieve global hegemony. His desire to keep the Korean hostilities from escalating into a destabilizing regional conflict, he said, had led him to dispatch the U.S. Seventh Fleet to Taiwan (Formosa) to prevent an outbreak of fighting between Nationalist China and the communist mainland. He also disclosed that he had ordered a strengthening of American forces in the Philippines and an acceleration of military aid to French Indochina.

During the war, in April 1952, Truman, citing national defense needs in the face of an impending strike by the United Steel Workers of America, ordered the secretary of commerce to seize and operate the steel mills. Several weeks later, the U.S. Supreme Court invalidated the seizure in *Youngstown Sheet and Tubing v. Sawyer* (343 U.S. 579). The 6-3 decision rejected Truman's claim to broad inherent powers in the presidency and stated that no constitutional or congressional provision had given him the authority to seize the steel mills.

The war finally ended with an armistice signed at Panmunjom, South Korea, July 27, 1953, by Lieutenant General William K. Harrison, Jr., representing the United Nations Command, and by General Nam Il, representing the Communist Command. The armistice provided for the cessation of hostilities and, within 72 hours of that, for the establishment of a neutral demilitarized zone between the North and South Korean borderline, near the 38th parallel. It also called for the formation of a military armistice commission consisting of representatives from Sweden, Switzerland, Poland, and Czechoslovakia, which would be responsible for seeing that the armistice's terms were not violated. The truce also provided for the repatriation of all prisoners of war who desired it and for the future convocation of representatives of both sides at a conference to bring about a peaceful conclusion to the Korean question. No formal peace treaty has ever been signed. However, North and South Korea began improving relations at the end of the 1990s, which continued into the early 21st century. Even so, President George W. Bush named North Korea as part of an "axis of evil" in his 2002 State of the Union address. Several months later, North Korea, contrary to treaties and pacts, admitted that it was producing components for nuclear weapons; intelligence sources speculated that it already possessed nuclear bombs.

On November 17, 1955, South Korea and the United States ratified a mutual defense treaty that maintained that the United States would militarily defend the Seoul regime only if an "external armed attack" is made against the country. A Treaty of Friendship, Commerce, and Navigation, signed in Seoul November 28, 1956, gave most-favored-nation trading status to South Korea. It enforced freedom of commerce and navigation and provided for the equal treatment of American and South Korean businessmen in either country. In addition it covered religious rights, travel rights, and legal rights, both for individuals and corporations.

In Korea the Government forces, which were armed to prevent border raids and to preserve internal security, were attacked by invading forces from North Korea. The Security Council of the United Nations called upon the invading troops to cease hostilities and to withdraw to the 38th parallel. This they have not done, but on the contrary have pressed the attack. The Security Council called upon all members of the United Nations to render every assistance to the United Nations in the execution of this resolution. In these circumstances I have ordered United States air and sea forces to give the Korean Government troops cover and support.

The attack upon Korea makes it plain beyond all doubt that Communism has passed beyond the use of subversion to conquer independent nations and will now use armed invasion and war. It has defied the orders of the Security Council of the United Nations issued to preserve international peace and security. In these circumstances the occupation of Formosa by Communist forces would be a direct threat to the security of the Pacific area and to the United States forces performing their lawful and necessary functions in that area. Accordingly I have ordered the Seventh Fleet to prevent any attack on Formosa. As a corollary of this action I am calling upon the Chinese Government on Formosa to cease all air and sea operations against the mainland. The Seventh Fleet will see that this is done. The determination of the future status of Formosa must await the restoration of security in the Pacific, a peace settlement with Japan, or consideration by the United Nations.

I have also directed that United States Forces in the Philippines be strengthened and that military assistance to the Philippine Government be accelerated.

I have similarly directed acceleration in the furnishing of military assistance to the forces of France and the Associated States in Indo-China and the dispatch of a military mission to provide close working relations with those forces.

I know that all members of the United Nations will consider carefully the consequences of this latest aggression in Korea in defiance of the Charter of the United Nations. A return to the rule of force in international affairs would have far reaching effects. The United States will continue to uphold the rule of law.

I have instructed Ambassador Austin, as the representative of the United States to the Security Council, to report these steps to the Council.

See also DWIGHT D. EISENHOWER, "I SHALL GO TO KOREA" SPEECH, 1952; KOREAN WAR ARMISTICE, 1953; U.S. KOREA TREATY OF FRIENDSHIP, COMMERCE AND NAVIGATION.

Source:

Henry Steele Commager, ed. *Documents of American History*, Vol. 2, *Since 1898*. 9th ed. Englewood Cliffs, N.J.: Prentice Hall, 1973, pp. 553–554.

Eisenhower Doctrine, 1957

Doctrine proposed by President Dwight D. Eisenhower January 5, 1957, and adopted by Congress on March 9, authorizing military aid for any Middle Eastern nation requesting such assistance in order to resist communist aggression. It was promulgated after the withdrawal of British, French, and Israeli troops from Egypt during the 1956 Suez Canal crisis, which arose after pro-Soviet Egyptian leader Gamal Abdel Nasser nationalize, and, when attacked, blocked the canal. The doctrine was an effort to forestall Soviet attempts to fill the subsequent power vacuum. In July 1958 Eisenhower used the doctrine to send U.S. forces to protect a pro-Western government in Lebanon. Some of the later problems of U.S. relations in the Middle East trace back to American support of anticommunist but otherwise dictatorial or overly Westernized rulers.

To the Congress of the United States:

First may I express to you my deep appreciation of your courtesy in giving me, at some inconvenience to yourselves, this early opportunity of addressing you on a matter I deem to be of grave importance to our country.

In my forthcoming State of the Union Message, I shall review the international situation generally. There are worldwide hopes which we can reasonably entertain, and there are worldwide responsibilities which we must carry to make certain that freedom—including our own—may be secure.

There is, however, a special situation in the Middle East which I feel I should, even now, lay before you.

Before doing so it is well to remind ourselves that our basic national objective in international affairs remains peace—a world peace based on justice. Such a peace must include all areas, all peoples of the world if it is to be enduring. There is no nation, great or small, with which we would refuse to negotiate, in mutual good faith, with patience and in the determination to secure a better understanding between us. Out of such understandings must, and eventually will, grow confidence and trust, indispensable ingredients to a program of peace and to plans for lifting from us all the burdens of expensive armaments. To promote these objectives, our government works tirelessly, day by day, month by month, year by year. But until a degree of success crowns our efforts that will assure to all nations peaceful existence, we must, in the interests of peace itself, remain vigilant, alert and strong.

I.

The Middle East has abruptly reached a new and critical stage in its long and important history. In past decades many of the countries in that area were not fully self-governing. Other nations exercised considerable authority in the area and the security of the region was largely built around their power. But since the First World War there has been a steady evolution toward self-government and independence. This development the United States has welcomed and has encouraged. Our country supports without reservation the full sovereignty and independence of each and every nation of the Middle East.

The evolution to independence has in the main been a peaceful process. But the area has been often troubled. Persistent cross-currents of distrust and fear with raids back and forth across national boundaries have brought about a high degree of instability in much of the Mid East. Just recently there have been hostilities involving Western European nations that once exercised much influence in the area. Also the relatively large attack by Israel in October has intensified the basic differences between that nation and its Arab neighbors. All this instability has been heightened and, at times, manipulated by International Communism.

II.

Russia's rulers have long sought to dominate the Middle East. That was true of the Czars and it is true of the Bolsheviks. The reasons are not hard to find. They do not affect Russia's security, for no one plans to use the Middle East as a base for aggression against Russia. Never for a moment has the United States entertained such a thought.

The Soviet Union has nothing whatsoever to fear from the United States in the Middle East, or anywhere else in the world, so long as its rulers do not themselves first resort to aggression.

That statement I make solemnly and emphatically.

Neither does Russia's desire to dominate the Middle East spring from its own economic interest in the area. Russia does not appreciably use or depend upon the Suez Canal. In 1955 Soviet traffic through the Canal represented only about three fourths of 1% of the total. The Soviets have no need for, and could provide no market for, the petroleum resources which constitute the principal natural wealth of the area. Indeed, the Soviet Union is a substantial exporter of petroleum products.

The reason for Russia's interest in the Middle East is solely that of power politics. Considering her announced purpose of Communizing the world, it is easy to understand her hope of dominating the Middle East.

This region has always been the crossroads of the continents of the Eastern Hemisphere. The Suez Canal enables the nations of Asia and Europe to carry on the commerce that is essential if these countries are to maintain well-rounded and prosperous economies. The Middle East provides a gateway between Eurasia and Africa.

It contains about two thirds of the presently known oil deposits of the world and it normally supplies the petroleum needs of many nations of Europe, Asia and Africa. The nations of Europe are peculiarly dependent upon this supply, and this dependency relates to transportation as well as to production! This has been vividly demonstrated since the closing of the Suez Canal and some of the pipelines. Alternate ways of transportation and, indeed, alternate sources of power can, if necessary, be developed. But these cannot be considered as early prospects.

These things stress the immense importance of the Middle East. If the nations of that area should lose their independence, if they were dominated by alien forces hostile to freedom, that would be both a tragedy for the area and for many other free nations whose economic life would be subject to near strangulation. Western Europe would be endangered just as though there had been no Marshall Plan, no North Atlantic Treaty Organization. The free nations of Asia and Africa, too, would be placed in serious jeopardy. And the countries of the Middle East would lose the markets upon which their economies depend. All this would have the most adverse, if not disastrous, effect upon our own nation's economic life and political prospects.

Then there are other factors which transcend the material. The Middle East is the birthplace of three great religions—Moslem, Christian and Hebrew. Mecca and Jerusalem are more than places on the map. They symbolize religions which teach that the spirit has supremacy over matter and that the individual has a dignity and rights of which no despotic government can rightfully deprive him. It would be intolerable if the holy places of the Middle East should be subjected to a rule that glorifies atheistic materialism.

International Communism, of course, seeks to mask its purposes of domination by expressions of good will and by superficially attractive offers of political, economic and military aid. But any free nation, which is the subject of Soviet enticement, ought, in elementary wisdom, to look behind the mask.

Remember Estonia, Latvia and Lithuania! In 1939 the Soviet Union entered into mutual assistance pacts with these then independent countries; and the Soviet Foreign Minister, addressing the Extraordinary Fifth Session of the Supreme Soviet in October 1939, solemnly and publicly declared that "we stand for the scrupulous and punctilious observance of the pacts on the basis of complete reciprocity, and we declare that all the nonsensical talk about the Sovietization of the Baltic countries is only to the interest of our common enemies and of all anti-Soviet provocateurs." Yet in *1940,* Estonia, Latvia and Lithuania were forcibly incorporated into the Soviet Union.

Soviet control of the satellite nations of Eastern Europe has been forcibly maintained in spite of solemn promises of a contrary intent, made during World War II.

Stalin's death brought hope that this pattern would change. And we read the pledge of the Warsaw Treaty of 1955 that the Soviet Union would follow in satellite countries "the principles of mutual respect for their independence and sovereignty and non-interference in domestic affairs." But we have just seen the subjugation of Hungary by naked armed force. In the aftermath of this Hungarian tragedy, world respect for and belief in Soviet promises have sunk to a new low. International Communism needs and seeks a recognizable success.

Thus, we have these simple and indisputable facts:

1. The Middle East, which has always been coveted by Russia, would today be prized more than ever by International Communism.

2. The Soviet rulers continue to show that they do not scruple to use any means to gain their ends.

3. The free nations of the Middle East need, and for the most part want, added strength to assure their continued independence.

III.

Our thoughts naturally turn to the United Nations as a protector of small nations. Its charter gives it primary responsibility for the maintenance of international peace and security. Our country has given the United Nations its full support in relation to the hostilities in Hungary and in Egypt. The United Nations was able to bring about a cease-fire and withdrawal of hostile forces from Egypt because it was dealing with governments and peoples who had a decent respect for the opinions of mankind as reflected in the United Nations General Assembly. But in the case of Hungary, the situation was different. The Soviet Union vetoed action by the Security Council to require the withdrawal of Soviet armed forces from Hungary. And it has shown callous indifference to the recommendations, even the censure, of the General Assembly. The United Nations can always be helpful, but it cannot be a wholly dependable protector of freedom when the ambitions of the Soviet Union are involved.

IV.

Under all the circumstances I have laid before you, a greater responsibility now devolves upon the United States. We have shown, so that none can doubt, our dedication to the principle that force shall not be used internationally for any aggressive purpose and that the integrity and independence of the nations of the Middle East should be inviolate. Seldom in history has a nation's dedication to principle been tested as severely as ours during recent weeks.

There is general recognition in the Middle East, as elsewhere, that the United States does not seek either political or economic domination over any other people. Our desire is a world environment of freedom, not servitude. On the other hand many, if not all, of the nations of the Middle East are aware of the danger that stems from International Communism and welcome closer cooperation with the United States to realize for themselves the United Nations goals of independence, economic well-being and spiritual growth.

If the Middle East is to continue its geographic role of uniting rather than separating East and West; if its vast economic resources are to serve the well-being of the peoples there, as well as that of others; and if its cultures and religions and their shrines are to be preserved for the uplifting of the spirits of the peoples, then the United States must make more evident its willingness to support the independence of the freedom-loving nations of the area.

V.

Under these circumstances I deem it necessary to seek the cooperation of the Congress. Only with that cooperation can we give the reassurance needed to deter aggression, to give courage and confidence to those who are dedicated to freedom and thus prevent a chain of events which would gravely endanger all of the free world.

There have been several Executive declarations made by the United States in relation to the Middle East. There is the Tripartite Declaration of May 25, 1950, followed by the Presidential assurance of October 31, 1950, to the King of Saudi Arabia. There is the Presidential declaration of April 9, 1956, that the United States will within constitutional means oppose any aggression in the area. There is our Declaration of November 29, 1956, that a threat to the territorial integrity or political independence of Iran, Iraq, Pakistan, or Turkey would be viewed by the United States with the utmost gravity.

Nevertheless, weaknesses in the present situation and the increased danger from International Communism, convince me that basic United States policy should now find expression in joint action by the Congress and the Executive. Furthermore, our joint resolve should be so couched as to make it apparent that if need be our words will be backed by action.

VI.

It is nothing new for the President and the Congress to join to recognize that the national integrity of other free nations is directly related to our own security.

We have joined to create and support the security system of the United Nations. We have reinforced the collective security system of the United Nations by a series of collective defense arrangements. Today we have security treaties with 42 other nations which recognize that our peace and security are intertwined. We have joined to take decisive action in relation to Greece and Turkey and in relation to Taiwan.

Thus, the United States through the joint action of the President and the Congress, or, in the case of treaties, the Senate, has manifested in many endangered areas its purpose to support free and independent governments—and peace—against external menace, notably the menace of International Communism. Thereby we have helped to maintain peace and security during a period of great danger. It is now essential that the United States should manifest through joint action of the President and the Congress our determination to assist those nations of the Mid East area, which desire that assistance.

The action which I propose would have the following features.

It would, first of all, authorize the United States to cooperate with and assist any nation or group of nations in the general area of the Middle East in the development of economic strength dedicated to the maintenance of national independence.

It would, in the second place, authorize the Executive to undertake in the same region programs of military assistance and cooperation with any nation or group of nations which desires such aid.

It would, in the third place, authorize such assistance and cooperation to include the employment of the armed forces of the United States to secure and protect the territorial integrity and political independence of such nations, requesting such aid, against overt armed aggression from any nation controlled by International Communism.

These measures would have to be consonant with the treaty obligations of the United States, including the Charter of the United Nations and with any action or recommendations of the United Nations. They would also, if armed attack occurs, be subject to the overriding authority of the United Nations Security Council in accordance with the Charter.

The present proposal would, in the fourth place, authorize the President to employ, for economic and defensive military purposes, sums available under the Mutual Security Act of 1954, as amended, without regard to existing limitations.

The legislation now requested should not include the authorization or appropriation of funds because I believe that, under the conditions I suggest, presently appropriated funds will be adequate for the balance of the present fiscal year ending June 30. I shall, however, seek in subsequent legislation the authorization of $200,000,000 to be available during each of the fiscal years 1958 and 1959 for discretionary use in the area, in addition to the other mutual security programs for the area hereafter provided for by the Congress.

VII.

This program will not solve all the problems of the Middle East. Neither does it represent the totality of our policies for the area. There are the problems of Palestine and relations between Israel and the Arab States, and the future of the Arab refugees. There is the problem of the future status of the Suez Canal. These difficulties are aggravated by International Communism, but they would exist quite apart from that threat. It is not the purpose of the legislation I propose to deal directly with these problems. The United Nations is actively concerning itself with all these matters, and we are supporting the United Nations. The United States has made clear, notably by Secretary Dulles' address of August 26, 1955, that we are willing to do much to assist the United Nations in solving the basic problems of Palestine.

The proposed legislation is primarily designed to deal with the possibility of Communist aggression, direct and indirect. There is imperative need that any lack of power in the area should be made good, not by external or alien force, but by the increased vigor and security of the independent nations of the area.

Experience shows that indirect aggression rarely if ever succeeds where there is reasonable security against direct aggression; where the government disposes of loyal security forces, and where economic conditions are such as not to make Communism seem an attractive alternative. The program I suggest deals with all three aspects of this matter and thus with the problem of indirect aggression.

It is my hope and belief that if our purpose be proclaimed, as proposed by the requested legislation, that very fact will serve to halt any contemplated aggression. We shall have heartened the patriots who are dedicated to the independence of their nations. They will not feel that they stand alone, under the menace of great power. And I should add that patriotism is, throughout this area, a powerful sentiment. It is true that fear sometimes perverts true patriotism into fanaticism and to the acceptance of dangerous enticements from without. But if that fear can be allayed, then the climate will be more favorable to the attainment of worthy national ambitions.

And as I have indicated, it will also be necessary for us to contribute economically to strengthen those countries, or groups of countries, which have governments manifestly dedicated to the preservation of independence and resistance to subversion. Such measures will provide the greatest insurance against Communist inroads. Words alone are not enough.

VIII.

Let me refer again to the requested authority to employ the armed forces of the United States to assist to defend the territorial integrity and the political independence of any nation in the area against Communist armed aggression. Such authority would not be exercised except at the desire of the nation attacked. Beyond this it is my profound hope that this authority would never have to be exercised at all.

Nothing is more necessary to assure this than that our policy with respect to the defense of the area be promptly and clearly determined and declared. Thus the United Nations and all friendly governments, and indeed governments which are not friendly, will know where we stand.

If, contrary to my hope and expectation, a situation arose which called for the military application of the policy which I ask the Congress to join me in proclaiming, I would of course maintain hour-by-hour contact with the Congress if it were in session. And if the Congress were not in session, and if the situation had grave implications, I would, of course, at once call the Congress into special session.

In the situation now existing, the greatest risk, as is often the case, is that ambitious despots may miscalculate. If power-hungry Communists should either falsely or correctly estimate that the Middle East is inadequately defended, they might be tempted to use open measures of armed attack. If so, that would start a chain of circumstances which would almost surely involve the United States in military action. I am convinced that the best insurance against this dangerous contingency is to make clear now our readiness to cooperate fully and freely with our friends of the Middle East in ways consonant with the purposes and principles of the United Nations. I intend promptly to send a special mission to the Middle East to explain the cooperation we are prepared to give.

IX.

The policy which I outline involves certain burdens and indeed risks for the United States. Those who covet the area will not like what is proposed. Already, they are grossly distorting our purpose. However, before this Americans have seen our nation's vital interests and human freedom in jeopardy, and their fortitude and resolution have been equal to the crisis, regardless of hostile distortion of our words, motives and actions.

Indeed, the sacrifices of the American people in the cause of freedom have, even since the close of World War II, been measured in many billions of dollars and in thousands of the precious lives of our youth. These sacrifices, by which great areas of the world have been preserved to freedom, must not be thrown away.

In those momentous periods of the past, the President and the Congress have united, without partisanship, to serve the vital interests of the United States and of the free world.

The occasion has come for us to manifest again our national unity in support of freedom and to show our deep respect for the rights and independence of every nation—however great, however small. We seek not violence, but peace. To this purpose we must now devote our energies, our determination, ourselves.

Dwight D. Eisenhower

Source:

Public Papers of the Presidents of the United States: Dwight D. Eisenhower, 1957, Washington, D.C.: Government Printing Office, 1953–1961, pp. 6–16.

Proclamation 3504: Interdiction of the Delivery of Offensive Weapons to Cuba, 1962

Presidential proclamation issued by President John F. Kennedy October 23, 1962, imposing a naval blockade of Cuba to prevent further deliveries of weapons from the Soviet Union.

The day before announcing this proclamation, President Kennedy addressed the nation explaining the Soviet Union's secret placement of medium- and intermediate-range ballistic missiles in Cuba and the U.S. response. Calling the Soviet action "an explicit threat to the peace and security of all the Americas," Kennedy announced the blockade. He declared that any nuclear missile launched from Cuba against any nation in the Western Hemisphere would be considered an attack by the Soviet Union against the United States and would elicit a full retaliatory response upon the Soviet Union.

The October 23 proclamation ordered U.S. land, sea, and air forces to prohibit the delivery of all offensive weapons to Cuba. It gave U.S. forces the authority to search any ship heading toward Cuba and to take into custody any ship that failed to comply. It said that force would be used "only to the extent necessary." Copies of the text were given to all foreign ambassadors in Washington, D.C., and were transmitted by the United States to all foreign governments; the Soviet Foreign Ministry refused to accept its copy.

For a week, as the United States turned away several Soviet ships, the threat of a full-fledged nuclear war loomed. But negotiations continued. President Kennedy wrote to Soviet premier Nikita Khrushchev October 27, 1962, responding to terms received from Khrushchev the previous day. Kennedy accepted Moscow's proposal that all Soviet missiles be removed from Cuba under UN supervision if the United States suspended its blockade and gave assurances that it would not invade the island. Regarding a second proposal issued by Khrushchev later on October 26, demanding that the United States remove its nuclear missiles from Turkey, Kennedy noted only that he was "very much interested in reducing tensions and halting the arms race" but resolving the Cuban missiles situation came first. Two days later, Khrushchev agreed to stop building bases in Cuba and to dismantle and remove offensive weapons there.

The Cuban missile crisis of 1962 produced a widespread awareness of the possibility of an accidental nuclear war between the two nations. As a result, the United States and the Soviet Union agreed June 20, 1963, to establish a direct communications link (the so-called hot line) between the two governments for use in times of emergency. The 4,883-mile cable telephone line between the White House and the Kremlin opened August 30, 1963. In 1978 the hot line began operating via satellite.

Whereas the peace of the world and the security of the United States and of all American States are endangered by reason of the establishment by the Sino-Soviet powers of an offensive military capability in Cuba, including bases for ballistic missiles with a potential range covering most of North and South America;

Whereas by a Joint Resolution passed by the Congress of the United States and approved on October 3, 1962, it was declared that the United States is determined to prevent by whatever means may be necessary, including the use of arms, the Marxist-Leninist regime in Cuba from extending, by force or the threat of force, its aggressive or subversive activities to any part of this hemisphere, and to prevent in Cuba the creation or use of an externally supported military capability endangering the security of the United States; and

Whereas the Organ of Consultation of the American Republics meeting in Washington on October 23, 1962, recommended that the Member States, in accordance with Articles 6 and 8 of the Inter-American Treaty of Reciprocal Assistance, take all measures, individually and collectively, including the use of armed force, which they may deem necessary to ensure that the Government of Cuba cannot continue to receive from the Sino-Soviet powers military material and related supplies which may threaten the peace and security of the Continent and to prevent the missiles in Cuba with offensive capability from ever becoming an active threat to the peace and security of the Continent:

Now, Therefore, I, John F. Kennedy, President of the United States of America, acting under and by virtue of the authority conferred upon me by the Constitution and statutes of the United States, in accordance with the aforementioned resolutions of the United States Congress and of the Organ of Consultation of the American Republics, and to defend the security of the United States, do hereby proclaim that the forces under my command are ordered, beginning at 2:00 p.m. Greenwich time October 24, 1962, to interdict, subject to the instructions herein contained, the delivery of offensive weapons and associated materiel to Cuba.

For the purposes of this Proclamation, the following are declared to be prohibited materiel:

Surface-to-surface missiles; bomber aircraft; bombs, air-to-surface rockets and guided missiles; warheads for any of the above weapons; mechanical or electronic equipment to support or operate the above items; and any other classes of materiel hereafter designated by the Secretary of Defense for the purpose of effectuating this Proclamation.

To enforce this order, the Secretary of Defense shall take appropriate measures to prevent the delivery of prohibited materiel to Cuba, employing the land, sea and air forces of the United States in cooperation with any forces that may be made available by other American States.

The Secretary of Defense may make such regulations and issue such directives as he deems necessary to ensure the effectiveness of this order, including the designation, within a reasonable distance of Cuba, of prohibited or restricted zones and of prescribed routes.

Any vessel or craft which may be proceeding toward Cuba may be intercepted and may be directed to identify itself, its cargo, equipment and stores and its ports of call, to stop, to lie to, to submit to visit and search, or to proceed as directed. Any vessel or craft which fails or refuses to respond to or comply with directions shall be subject to being taken into custody. Any vessel or craft which it is believed is en route to Cuba and may be carrying prohibited materiel or may itself constitute such materiel shall, wherever possible, be directed to proceed to another destination of its own choice and shall be taken into custody if it fails or refuses to obey such directions. All vessels or craft taken into custody shall be sent into a port of the United States for appropriate disposition.

In carrying out this order, force shall not be used except in case of failure or refusal to comply with directions, or with regulations or directives of the Secretary of Defense issued hereunder, after reasonable efforts have been made to communicate them to the vessel or craft, or in case of self-defense. In any case, force shall be used only to the extent necessary.

In Witness Whereof, I have hereunto set my hand and cause the seal of the United States of America to be affixed.

Done in the City of Washington this twenty-third day of October in the year of our Lord, nineteen hundred and sixty-two, and of the Independence of the United States of America the one hundred and eighty-seventh.

John F. Kennedy

Source:

Public Papers of the Presidents of the United States, John F. Kennedy, 1962. Washington, D.C.: Government Printing Office, 1962–64. pp. 809–811.

Lyndon Johnson, Tonkin Gulf Incident Message; Gulf of Tonkin Resolution, 1964

Joint resolution passed overwhelmingly by the U.S. Congress on August 7, 1964, giving President Lyndon B. Johnson broad powers to fight communism in Southeast Asia. Two days earlier, Johnson had announced that he had ordered air strikes against North Vietnam in retaliation for alleged North Vietnamese attacks on U.S. destroyers in the Gulf of Tonkin. The resolution gave Johnson congressional approval for "all necessary measures to repel any armed attack" against U.S. forces and for "all necessary steps" to assist any ally in Southeast Asia seeking to defend its freedom. It became the basis for Johnson's escalation of the war in Vietnam. A 1968 U.S. Senate investigation raised serious doubts about the alleged Gulf of Tonkin attacks, and the resolution was repealed in May 1970.

The problems in Southeast Asia trace back to the war of the indigenous, communist-inspired Indochinese (Vietnamese, Cambodian, and Laotian) colonists against the French. The United States refused to assist France, but in 1954, with the war still going on, President Dwight D. Eisenhower told the press in Washington, D.C., that as one Asian country falls to communism its neighbor follows until all are lost. "You would call the 'falling domino' principle. You have a row of dominoes set up, you knock over the first one, and what will happen to the last one is the certainty that it will go over very quickly. So you could have a beginning of a disintegration that would have the most profound influences." This "Domino Theory" influenced Presidents Johnson and Nixon and their advisers to persist in their involvement in the former Indochina, even when, early on, it appeared that a victory for anticommunist forces would require a major expenditure in money, manpower, and loss of life.

Lyndon Johnson, Tonkin Gulf Incident Message, 1964

To the Congress of the United States:

Last night I announced to the American people that the North Vietnamese regime had conducted further deliberate attacks against US naval vessels operating in international waters, and that I had therefore directed air action against gun boats and supporting facilities used in these hostile operations. This air action has now been carried out with substantial damage to the boats and facilities. Two US aircraft were lost in the action.

After consultation with the leaders of both parties in the Congress, I further announced a decision to ask the Congress for a Resolution expressing the unity and determination of the United States in supporting freedom and in protecting peace in Southeast Asia.

These latest actions of the North Vietnamese regime have given new and grave turn to the already serious situation in Southeast Asia. Our commitments in that area are well known to the Congress. They were first made in 1954 by President Eisenhower. They were further defined in the Southeast Asia Collective Defense Treaty approved by the Senate in February 1955.

This Treaty with its accompanying protocol obligates the United States and other members to act in accordance with their Constitutional processes to meet the Communist aggression against any of the parties or protocol states.

Our policy in Southeast Asia has been consistent and unchanged since 1954. I summarized it on June 2 in four simple propositions:

1. *America keeps her word.* Here as elsewhere, we must and shall honor our commitments.

2. *The issue is the future of Southeast Asia as a whole.* A threat to any nation in that region is a threat to all, and a threat to us.

3. *Our purpose is peace.* We have no military, political or territorial ambitions in the area.

4. *This is not just a jungle war, but a struggle for freedom on every front of human activity.* Our military and

economic assistance to South Vietnam and Laos in particular has the purpose of helping these countries to repel aggression and strengthen their independence.

The threat to the free nations of Southeast Asia has long been clear. The North Vietnamese regime has constantly sought to take over South Vietnam and Laos. This Communist regime has violated the Geneva Accords for Vietnam. It has systematically conducted a campaign of subversion, which includes the direction, training, and supply of personnel and arms for the conduct of guerrilla warfare in South Vietnamese territory. In Laos, the North Vietnamese regime has maintained military forces, used Laotian territory for infiltration into South Vietnam, and most recently carried out combat operations—all in direct violation of the Geneva Agreements of 1962.

In recent months, the actions of the North Vietnamese regime have become steadily more threatening. In May, following new acts of Communist aggression in Laos, the United States undertook reconnaissance flights over Laotian territory, at the request of the Government of Laos. These flights had the essential mission of determining the situation in territory where Communist forces were preventing inspection by the International Control Commission. When the Communists attacked these aircraft, I responded by furnishing escort fighters with instructions to fire when fired upon. Thus, these latest North Vietnamese attacks on our naval vessels are not the first direct attack on armed forces of the United States.

As President of the United States I have concluded that I should now ask the Congress, on its part, to join in affirming the national determination that all such attacks will be met, and that the U.S. will continue in its basic policy of assisting the free nations of the area to defend their freedom.

As I have repeatedly made clear, the United States intends no rashness, and seeks no wider war. We must make it clear to all that the United States is united in its determination to bring about the end of Communist subversion and aggression in the area. We seek the full and effective restoration of the international agreements signed in Geneva in 1954, with respect to South Vietnam, and again in Geneva in 1962, with respect to Laos.

I recommend a Resolution expressing the support of the Congress for all necessary action to protect our armed forces and to assist nations covered by the SEATO Treaty. At the same time, I assure the Congress that we shall continue readily to explore any avenues of political solution that will effectively guarantee the removal of Communist subversion and the preservation of the independence of the nations of the area.

The Resolution could well be based upon similar resolutions enacted by the Congress in the past—to meet the threat to Formosa in 1955, to meet the threat to the Middle East in 1957, and to meet the threat in Cuba in 1962. It could state in the simplest terms the resolve and support of the Congress for action to deal appropriately with attacks against our armed forces and to defend freedom and preserve peace in southeast Asia in accordance with the obligations of the United States under the southeast Asia Treaty. I urge the Congress to enact such a Resolution promptly and thus to give convincing evidence to the aggressive Communist nations, and to the world as a whole, that our policy in southeast Asia will be carried forward—and that the peace and security of the area will be preserved.

The events of this week would in any event have made the passage of a Congressional Resolution essential. But there is an additional reason for doing so at a time when we are entering on three months of political campaigning. Hostile nations must understand that in such a period the United States will continue to protect its national interests, and that in these matters there is no division among us.

Lyndon B. Johnson

Gulf of Tonkin Resolution, 1964
JOINT RESOLUTION

To promote the maintenance of international peace and security in southeast Asia.

Whereas naval units of the Communist regime in Vietnam, violation of the principles of the Charter of the United Nations and of international law, have deliberately and repeatedly attacked United States naval vessels lawfully present in international waters, and have thereby created a serious threat to international peace; and

Whereas these attacks are part of a deliberate and systematic campaign of aggression that the Communist regime in North Vietnam has been waging against its neighbors and the nations joined with them in the collective defense of their freedom; and

Whereas the United States is assisting the peoples of southeast Asia to protect their freedom and has no territorial, military or political ambitions in the area, but desires only that these peoples should be left in peace to work out their own destinies in their own way: Now, therefore, be it

Resolved by the Senate and House of Representatives of the United States of America in Congress assembled, That the Congress approves and supports the determination of the President, as Commander in Chief, to take all necessary measures to repel any armed attack against the forces of the United States and to prevent further aggression.

Sec. 2. The United States regards as vital to its national interest and to world peace the maintenance of international peace and security in southeast Asia. Consonant with the Constitution of the United States and the Charter of the United Nations and in accordance with its obligations under the Southeast Asia Collective Defense Treaty, the United States is, therefore, prepared, as the President determines, to take all necessary steps, including the use of armed force, to assist any member or protocol state of the Southeast Asia Collective Defense Treaty requesting assistance in defense of its freedom.

Sec. 3. This resolution shall expire when the President shall determine that the peace and security of the area is reasonably assured by international conditions created by action of the United Nations or otherwise, except that it may be terminated earlier by concurrent resolution of the Congress.

Approved August 10, 1964.

Source:

Gulf of Tonkin Resolution, 1964, *United States Statutes at Large*; Lyndon Johnson, Tonkin Gulf Incident Message, *Public Papers of the Presidents of the United States: Lyndon B. Johnson, 1963–64*. Washington, D.C.: Government Printing Office, 1963–69. Vol. 78, pp. 384, 930–932.

Address on Vietnam before the National Legislative Congress, 1967

Televised speech delivered by President Lyndon B. Johnson to the National Legislative Conference at San Antonio, Texas, September 29, 1967. Johnson used this opportunity to defend his administration's policies in Vietnam. Because Vietnam was "the arena where Communist expansionism is most aggressively at work in the world today," it directly threatens the security of the United States. Johnson invoked the Domino Theory, warning that if South Vietnam fell to the Communists, this would likely "be followed by a Communist conquest of Southeast Asia." Moreover, he insisted that South Vietnam was making progress toward the formation of a "constitutional government." Johnson condemned Hanoi's refusal to accept the U.S. proposals to begin direct talks and blamed continuance of the war squarely on North Vietnam. He maintained that the United States would "continue to press forward" in its commitment to South Vietnam and asserted that the antiwar protests at home would not "produce surrender."

Speaker Barnes, Governor Hughes, Governor Smith, Congressman Kazen, Representative Graham, most distinguished legislators, ladies and gentlemen:

I deeply appreciate this opportunity to appear before an organization whose members contribute every day such important work to the public affairs of our State and of our country.

This evening I came here to speak to you about Vietnam.

I do not have to tell you that our people are profoundly concerned about that struggle.

There are passionate convictions about the wisest course for our Nation to follow. There are many sincere and patriotic Americans who harbor doubts about sustaining the commitment that three Presidents and a half a million of our young men have made.

Doubt and debate are enlarged because the problems of Vietnam are quite complex. They are a mixture of political turmoil—of poverty—of religious and factional strife—of ancient servitude and modern longing for freedom. Vietnam is all of these things.

Vietnam is also the scene of a powerful aggression that is spurred by an appetite for conquest.

It is the arena where Communist expansionism is most aggressively at work in the world today—where it is crossing international frontiers in violation of international agreements; where it is killing and kidnapping; where it is ruthlessly attempting to bend free people to its will.

Into this mixture of subversion and war, of terror and hope, America has entered—with its material power and with its moral commitment.

Why?

Why should three Presidents and the elected representatives of our people have chosen to defend this Asian nation more than 10,000 miles from American shores?

We cherish freedom—yes. We cherish self-determination for all people—yes. We abhor the political murder of any state by another, and the bodily murder of any people by gangsters of whatever ideology. And for 27 years—since the days of lend-lease—we have sought to strengthen free people against domination by aggressive foreign powers.

But the key to all that we have done is really our own security. At times of crisis—before asking Americans to fight and die to resist aggression in a foreign land—every American President has finally had to answer this question:

Is the aggression a threat—not only to the immediate victim—but to the United States of America and to the peace and security of the entire world of which we in America are a very vital part?

That is the question which Dwight Eisenhower and John Kennedy and Lyndon Johnson had to answer in facing the issue in Vietnam.

That is the question that the Senate of the United States answered by a vote of 82 to 1 when it ratified and approved the SEATO treaty in 1955, and to which the Members of the United States Congress responded in a resolution that it passed in 1964 by a vote of 504 to 2, " . . . the United States is, therefore, prepared, as the President determines, to take all necessary steps, including the use of armed force, to assist any member or protocol state of the Southeast Asia Collective Defense Treaty requesting assistance in defense of its freedom."

Those who tell us now that we should abandon our commitment—that securing South Vietnam from armed domination is not worth the price we are paying—must also answer this question. And the test they must meet is this: What would be the consequences of letting armed aggression against South Vietnam succeed? What would follow in the time ahead? What kind of world are they prepared to live in 5 months or 5 years from tonight?

For those who have borne the responsibility for decision during these past 10 years, the stakes to us have seemed clear—and have seemed high.

President Dwight Eisenhower said in 1959:

Strategically, South Vietnam's capture by the Communists would bring their power several hundred miles into a hitherto free region. The remaining countries in Southeast Asia would be menaced by a great flanking movement. The freedom of 12 million people would be lost immediately, and that of 150 million in adjacent lands would be seriously endangered. The loss of South Vietnam would set in motion a crumbling process that could, as it progressed, have grave consequences for us and for freedom. . ."

And President John F. Kennedy said in 1962:

" . . . withdrawal in the case of Vietnam and the case of Thailand might mean a collapse of the entire area."

A year later, he reaffirmed that:

"We are not going to withdraw from that effort. In my opinion, for us to withdraw from that effort would mean a collapse not only of South Vietnam, but Southeast Asia. So we are going to stay there," said President Kennedy.

This is not simply an American viewpoint, I would have you legislative leaders know. I am going to call the roll now of those who live in that part of the world—in the great arc of Asian and Pacific nations—and who bear the responsibility for leading their people, and the responsibility for the fate of their people.

The President of the Philippines had this to say:

"Vietnam is the focus of attention now. . .It may happen to Thailand or the Philippines, or anywhere, wherever there is misery, disease, ignorance . . . For you to renounce your position of leadership in Asia is to allow the Red Chinese to gobble up all of Asia."

The Foreign Minister of Thailand said:

"(The American) decision will go down in history as the move that prevented the world from having to face another major conflagration."

The Prime Minister of Australia said:

"We are there because while Communist aggression persists the whole of Southeast Asia is threatened."

President Park of Korea said:

"For the first time in our history, we decided to dispatch our combat troops overseas. . .because in our belief any aggression against the Republic of Vietnam represented a direct and grave menace against the security and peace of free Asia, and therefore directly jeopardized the very security and freedom of our own people."

The Prime Minister of Malaysia warned his people that if the United States pulled out of South Vietnam, it would go to the Communists, and after that, it would be only a matter of time until they moved against neighboring states.

The Prime Minister of New Zealand said:

"We can thank God that America at least regards aggression in Asia with the same concern as it regards aggression in Europe—and is prepared to back up its concern with action."

The Prime Minister of Singapore said:

"I feel the fate of Asia—South and Southeast Asia—will be decided in the next few years by what happens in Vietnam."

I cannot tell you tonight as your President—with certainty—that a Communist conquest of South Vietnam would be followed by a Communist conquest of Southeast Asia. But I do know there are North Vietnamese troops in Laos. I do know that there are North Vietnamese trained guerrillas tonight in northeast Thailand. I do know that there are Communist-supported guerrilla forces operating in Burma. And a Communist coup was barely averted in Indonesia, the fifth largest nation in the world.

So your American President cannot tell you—with certainty—that a Southeast Asia dominated by Communist power would bring a third world war much closer to terrible reality. One could hope that this would not be so.

But all that we have learned in this tragic century strongly suggests to me that it would be so. As President of the United States, I am not prepared to gamble on the chance that it is not so. I am not prepared to risk the security—indeed, the survival—of this American Nation on mere hope and wishful thinking. I am convinced that by seeing this struggle through now, we are greatly reducing the chances of a much larger war—perhaps a nuclear war. I would rather stand in Vietnam, in our time, and by meeting this danger now, and facing up to it, thereby reduce the danger for our children and for our grandchildren.

I want to turn now to the struggle in Vietnam itself.

There are questions about this difficult war that must trouble every really thoughtful person. I am going to put some of these questions. And I am going to give you the very best answers that I can give you.

First, are the Vietnamese—with our help, and that of their other allies—really making any progress? Is there a forward movement? The reports I see make it clear that there is. Certainly there is a positive movement toward constitutional government. Thus far the Vietnamese have met the political schedule that they laid down in January 1966.

The people wanted an elected, responsive government. They wanted it strongly enough to brave a vicious campaign of Communist terror and assassination to vote for it. It has been said that they killed more civilians in 4 weeks trying to keep them from voting before the election than our American bombers have killed in the big cities of North Vietnam in bombing military targets.

On November 1, subject to the action, of course, of the Constituent Assembly, an elected government will be inaugurated and an elected Senate and Legislature will be installed. Their responsibility is clear: To answer the desires of the South Vietnamese people for self-determination and for peace, for an attack on corruption, for economic development, and for social justice.

There is progress in the war itself, steady progress considering the war that we are fighting; rather dramatic progress considering the situation that actually prevailed when we sent our troops there in 1965; when we intervened to prevent the dismemberment of the country by the Vietcong and the North Vietnamese.

The campaigns of the last year drove the enemy from many of their major interior bases. The military victory almost within Hanoi's grasp in 1965 has now been denied them. The grip of the Vietcong on the people is being broken.

Since our commitment of major forces in July 1965 the proportion of the population living under Communist control has been reduced to well under 20 percent. Tonight the secure proportion of the population has grown from about 45 percent to 65 percent—and in the contested areas, the tide continues to run with us.

But the struggle remains hard. The South Vietnamese have suffered severely, as have we—particularly in the First Corps area in the north, where the enemy has mounted his heaviest attacks, and where his lines of communication to North Vietnam are shortest. Our casualties in the war have reached about 13,500 killed in action, and about 85,000 wounded. Of those 85,000 wounded, we thank God that 79,000 of the 85,000 have been returned, or will return to duty shortly. Thanks to our great American medical science and the helicopter.

I know there are other questions on your minds, and on the minds of many sincere, troubled Americans: "Why not negotiate now?" so many ask me. The answer is that we and our South Vietnamese allies are wholly prepared to negotiate tonight.

I am ready to talk with Ho Chi Minh, and other chiefs of state concerned, tomorrow.

I am ready to have Secretary Rusk meet with their foreign minister tomorrow.

I am ready to send a trusted representative of America to any spot on this earth to talk in public or private with a spokesman of Hanoi.

We have twice sought to have the issue of Vietnam dealt with by the United Nations—and twice Hanoi has refused.

Our desire to negotiate peace—through the United Nations or out—has been made very, very clear to Hanoi—directly and many times through third parties.

As we have told Hanoi time and time and time again, the heart of the matter is really this: The United States is willing to stop all aerial and naval bombardment of North Vietnam when this will lead promptly to productive discussions. We, of course, assume that while discussions proceed, North Vietnam would not take advantage of the bombing cessation or limitation.

But Hanoi has not accepted any of these proposals.

So it is by Hanoi's choice—and not ours, and not the rest of the world's—that the war continues.

Why, in the face of military and political progress in the South, and the burden of our bombing in the North, do they insist and persist with the war?

From many sources the answer is the same. They still hope that the people of the United States will not see this struggle through to the very end. As one Western diplomat reported to me only this week—he had just been in Hanoi—"They believe their staying power is greater than ours and that they can't lose." A visitor from a Communist capital had this to say: "They expect the war to be long, and that the Americans in the end will be defeated by a breakdown in morale, fatigue, and psychological factors." The Premier of North Vietnam said as far back as 1962: "Americans do not like long, inconclusive war. . .Thus we are sure to win in the end."

Are the North Vietnamese right about us?

I think not. No. I think they are wrong. I think it is the common failing of totalitarian regimes that they cannot really understand the nature of our democracy:

—They mistake dissent for disloyalty.

—They mistake restlessness for a rejection of policy.

—They mistake a few committees for a country.

—They misjudge individual speeches for public policy.

They are no better suited to judge the strength and perseverance of America than the Nazi and the Stalinist propagandists were able to judge it. It is a tragedy that they must discover these qualities in the American people, and discover them through a bloody war.

And, soon or late, they will discover them.

In the meantime, it shall be our policy to continue to seek negotiations—confident that reason will some day prevail; that Hanoi will realize that it just can never win; that it will turn away from fighting and start building for its own people.

Since World War II, this Nation has met and has mastered many challenges—challenges in Greece and Turkey, in Berlin, in Korea, in Cuba.

We met them because brave men were willing to risk their lives for their nation's security. And braver men have never lived than those who carry our colors in Vietnam at this very hour.

The price of these efforts, of course, has been heavy. But the price of not having made them at all, not having seen them through, in my judgment would have been vastly greater.

Our goal has been the same—in Europe, in Asia, in our own hemisphere. It has been—and it is now—peace.

And peace cannot be secured by wishes; peace cannot be preserved by noble words and pure intentions. "Enduring peace," Franklin D. Roosevelt said, "cannot be bought at the cost of other people's freedom."

The late President Kennedy put it precisely in November 1961, when he said: "We are neither warmongers nor appeasers, neither hard nor soft. We are Americans determined to defend the frontiers of freedom by an honorable peace if peace is possible but by arms if arms are used against us."

The true peace-keepers in the world tonight are not those who urge us to retire from the field in Vietnam—who tell us to try to find the quickest, cheapest exit from that tormented land, no matter what the consequences to us may be.

The true peace-keepers are those men who stand out there on the DMZ at this very hour, taking the worst that the enemy can give. The true peace-keepers are the soldiers who are breaking the terrorist's grip around the villages of Vietnam—the civilians who are bringing medical care and food and education to people who have already suffered a generation of war.

And so I report to you that we are going to continue to press forward. Two things we must do. Two things we shall do.

First, we must not mislead the enemy. Let him not think that debate and dissent will produce wavering and withdrawal. For I can assure you they won't. Let him not think that protests will produce surrender. Because they won't. Let him not think that he will wait us out. For he won't.

Second, we will provide all that our brave men require to do the job that must be done. And that job is going to be done.

These gallant men have our prayers—have our thanks—have our heart-felt praise—and our deepest gratitude.

Let the world know that the keepers of peace will endure through every trial—and that with the full backing of their countrymen, they are going to prevail.

Source:

The Public Papers of the Presidents of the United States: Lyndon B. Johnson, 1967. Washington, D.C.: Government Printing Office, 1963–69, pp. 876–881.

Selective Service Act, 1967

Federal U.S. legislation enacted on June 20, 1967, that provided for full-time college students to receive deferments from military service. It amended the Selective Service Act of 1948, which reinstituted the draft because of the cold war. The draft was renewed continuously until 1973.

Passed during the Vietnam War, the 1967 act allowed deferments until students in any institute of higher instruction completed their baccalaureate degrees, failed to continue satisfactorily in full-time studies, or reached the age of 24, whichever occurred first. There were also deferments for graduate students in medicine and other fields, as well as for, among others, fathers, extreme hardship cases, sole surviving sons, ministers, some agricultural and industrial workers, and persons with physical, mental, and moral problems (the latter, under the predominant beliefs of the day, included homosexuals). This act, like its predecessors, left many decisions to the discretion of local draft boards.

One draft exemption permitted those with religious scruples to achieve conscientious objector status. In *United States v. Seeger* (860 U.S. 868), issued March 8, 1965, the U.S. Supreme Court denied exemption from military service if conscientious objection relied only on a personal moral code that is in no way related to a supreme being. The case involved three young men who did not belong to any traditional religious groups and did not declare a belief in a supreme being. Interpreting the Burke-Wadsworth Act of 1940, the Supreme Court ruled that the statutory requirement for belief in a supreme being could be met by anyone who had a "sincere and meaningful belief" that occupied in the life of its possessor a place parallel to that filled by the orthodox belief in God." It defined "Supreme Being" as a broad concept of a power "to which all else is subordinate or upon which all else is ultimately dependent."

In *Gillette v. United States* (401 U.S. 437), March 8, 1971, the Supreme Court also limited conscientious-objector status to those who object to all wars, not to those who oppose a particular war. In its decision, the Court declared that the Selective Service Act of 1967, which allowed exemption from service only for those "conscientiously opposed to participation in war in any form," did not violate constitutional protections of the free exercise of religion and prohibitions against the establishment of religion.

On November 1, 1969, a lottery system was introduced based on a registrant's birthday. It removed some of the biases that sent a disproportionate number of minority and poor and working-class whites into the service. Student deferments, however, remained until 1971.

The Selective Service Act expired on June 30, 1971; the Selective Service Act of 1971 supplanted it. The new act's draft-induction authority expired June 30, 1973. Although the draft ended, registration for 18-year-old males continues to be mandatory.

(excerpt)

An Act

To amend the Universal Military Training and Service Act, and for other purposes.

Be it enacted by the Senate and House of Representatives of the United States of America in Congress assembled, That the Universal Military Training and Service Act is amended as follows:

(1) Section 1(a) (50 App. U.S.C. 451(a)) is amended to read as follows:

"(a) This Act may be cited as the 'Military Selective Service Act of 1967.'"

(2) Section 4 (50 App. U.S.C. 454) is amended by:

(a) Inserting after the first proviso of subsection (a) the following: " *Provided further,* That, notwithstanding any other provision of law, any registrant who has failed or refused to report for induction shall continue to remain liable for induction and when available shall be immediately inducted.", and

(b) Adding the following new subsection (g) to read as follows:

"(g) The National Security Council shall periodically advise the Director of the Selective Service System and coordinate with him the work of such State and local volunteer advisory committees which the Director of Selective Service may establish, with respect to the identification, selection, and deferment of needed professional and scientific personnel and those engaged in, and preparing for, critical skills and other essential occupations. In the performance of its duties under this subsection the National Security Council shall consider the needs of both the Armed Forces and the civilian segment of the population."

(3) Section 5(a) (50 App. U.S.C. 455(a)) is amended by inserting "(1)" immediately after "Sec. 5. (a)"; and by adding at the end thereof a new paragraph as follows:

(2) Notwithstanding the provisions of paragraph (1) of this subsection, the President in establishing the order of induction for registrants within the various age groups found qualified for induction shall not effect any change in the method of determining the relative order of induction for such registrants within such age groups as has been heretofore established and in effect on the date of enactment of this paragraph, unless authorized by law enacted after the date of enactment of the Military Selective Service Act of 1967."

(4) Section 6(c)(2)(A) (50 App. U.S.C. 456(c)(2)(A)), is amended to read as follows:

"(2)(A) Any person, other than a person referred to in subsection (d) of this section, who—

"(i) prior to the issuance of orders for him to report for induction; or

"(ii) prior to the date scheduled for his induction and pursuant to a proclamation by the Governor of a State to the effect that the authorized strength of any organized unit of the National Guard of that State cannot be maintained by the enlistment or appointment of persons who have not been issued orders to report for induction under this title; or

"(iii) prior to the date scheduled for his induction and pursuant to a determination by the President that the strength of the Ready Reserve of the Army Reserve, Naval Reserve, Marine Corps Reserve, Air Force Reserve, or Coast Guard Reserve cannot be maintained by the enlistment or appointment of persons who have not been issued orders to report for induction under this title;

enlists or accepts appointment, before attaining the age of 26 years, in the Ready Reserve of any Reserve component of the Armed Forces, the Army National Guard, or the Air National Guard, shall be deferred from training and service under this title so long as he serves satisfactorily as a member of an organized unit of such Reserve or National Guard in accordance with section 270 of title 10 or section 502 of title 32, United States Code, as the case may be, or satisfactorily performs such other Ready Reserve service as may be prescribed by the Secretary of Defense. Enlistments or appointments under subparagraphs (ii) and (iii) of this clause may be accepted notwithstanding the provisions of section 15(d) of this title. Notwithstanding the provisions of subsection (h) of this section, no person deferred under this clause who has completed six years of such satisfactory service as a member of the Ready Reserve or National Guard, and who during such service has performed active duty for training with an armed force for not less than four consecutive months, shall be liable for induction for training and service under this Act, except after a declaration of war or national emergency made by the Congress after August 9, 1955. In no event shall the number of enlistments or appointments made under authority of this paragraph in any fiscal year in any Reserve component of the Armed Forces or in the Army National Guard or the Air National Guard cause the personnel strength of such Reserve component or the Army National Guard or the Air National Guard, as the case may be, to exceed the personnel strength for which funds have been made available by the Congress for such fiscal year.". . .

Source:
Statutes at Large, Vol. 81, pp. 100–106.

Nuclear Non-Proliferation Treaty, 1968

Agreement adopted by the United Nations General Assembly June 12, 1968, to prevent the spread of nuclear weapons.

The move to refrain from testing and increasing the number of nuclear weapons goes back at least to an address on disarmament delivered by President Dwight D. Eisenhower July 21, 1955, at a summit conference in Geneva, Switzerland. In this "open skies" proposal, Eisenhower declared that the United States was prepared to enter a "sound and reliable agreement" for arms reduction with provisions for inspection and proposed that the United States and the Soviet Union give each other "a complete blueprint of our military establishments" and allow mutual aerial photography for reconnaissance purposes. The French and British approved the proposals, but the Russians rejected them.

Eisenhower's proposal was reinforced June 10, 1963, when President John F. Kennedy used his speech at the American University commencement to address world peace. He urged a rapprochement with the Soviet Union and a reexamination of America's cold war policy, arguing that the USSR and the United States have common interests in "a just and genuine peace" and an end to the nuclear arms race. In addition, he announced an American, British, and Soviet agreement to begin negotiations on a comprehensive nuclear test ban treaty. To show good faith, he initiated a U.S. moratorium on atmospheric testing so long as other states also refrained from such testing.

Shortly thereafter, on August 5, 1963, the United Kingdom, the United States, and the Soviet Union signed a treaty in Moscow prohibiting the testing of nuclear weapons in the atmosphere, in outer space, or underwater. Underground testing was allowed because there were no provisions for on-site inspection, control posts, or for international supervision, and offsite seismographic technology was not deemed acceptable. Nor did the treaty address such issues as reduction in nuclear stockpiles, halting the production of nuclear weapons, or limiting their employment during war. The signatories, however, intended it as the first step on the road to complete disarmament. Before enforcement (October 10, 1963), more than 100 countries had endorsed it—France and the People's Republic of China (which detonated its first nuclear weapon in 1964) being the two major exceptions.

The 1968 Non-Proliferation Treaty banned the transfer of nuclear weapons and devices to another country, as was the acquiring of such by non–nuclear weapon countries, whose nuclear systems would be subject to verification. However, the development, manufacture, and use of nuclear energy for peaceful purposes, and international cooperation in this regard—ensuring that any benefits accruing from peaceful applications of nuclear technology could be passed on to nonnuclear weapon states—would be encouraged. The signatories pledged to continue negotiations for ending the nuclear arms race at an early date. Subject then to ratification by the Soviet Union, the United Kingdom, the United States, and 40 other countries, the treaty would be reviewed every five years. In 1995, the treaty was extended permanently. By that time, 178 countries had signed it.

On May 26, 1972, United States president Richard M. Nixon and Soviet general secretary Leonid I. Brezhnev began implementing disarmament with a five-year interim agreement and protocol, Strategic Arms Limitation Treaty (SALT) I, signed in Moscow. No new land-based, intercontinental ballistic missile (ICBM) launchers would be built after July 1, 1972. Submarine-launched ballistic missiles (SLBMs) and other modern ballistic missiles would be restricted to those already in use or under construction, but these could be modernized or replaced. The treaty permitted technical verification and condemned interference in this process. The Standing Consultative Commission (established by the treaty, limiting antiballistic missile systems) would assist in implementing the provisions of this agreement. Negotiations were to continue for further reduction in strategic offensive weapons. The protocol limited the number of SLBM launchers (710, United States; 950, Soviet Union) and ballistic missile submarines (44, United States; 62, Soviet Union) for each country.

At the same time, the two leaders announced the signing of an Anti-Ballistic Missile (ABM) Treaty concerning ballistic (guided) missile defense systems. The intent behind prohibiting the United States and Soviet Union from deploying antiballistic missile defense systems was to ensure that a country with a defense system would not launch an attack knowing that a counterattack would be unsuccessful. In theory, this balance would maintain the cold war defensive policy of mutually assured destruction.

The ABM Treaty's main protocol stated that neither party should deploy a nationwide ABM defense system, although each party could research and develop missile defense systems, as was done in the Ronald Reagan administration in the Strategic Defense Initiative (SDI), dubbed "Star Wars" by its critics. The treaty also allowed limited deployment of an ABM system in two sites, reduced in July 1974 to one, and reduced the total missiles and launchers to 100. Article XV gave each party the right to withdraw from the treaty. President George W. Bush, against the wishes of Russian president Vladimir Putin, abrogated the treaty in 2002.

The States concluding this Treaty, hereinafter referred to as the "Parties to the Treaty",

Considering the devastation that would be visited upon all mankind by a nuclear war and the consequent need to make every effort to avert the danger of such a war and to take measures to safeguard the security of peoples,

Believing that the proliferation of nuclear weapons would seriously enhance the danger of nuclear war,

In conformity with resolutions of the United Nations General Assembly calling for the conclusion of an agreement on the prevention of wider dissemination of nuclear weapons,

Undertaking to cooperate in facilitating the application of International Atomic Energy Agency safeguards on peaceful nuclear activities,

Expressing their support for research, development and other efforts to further the application, within the framework of the International Atomic Energy Agency safeguards system, of the principle of safeguarding effectively the flow of source and special fissionable materials by use of instruments and other techniques at certain strategic points,

Affirming the principle that the benefits of peaceful applications of nuclear technology, including any technological by-products which may be derived by nuclear-weapon States from the development of nuclear explosive devices, should be available for peaceful purposes to all Parties to the Treaty, whether nuclear-weapon or non-nuclear-weapon States,

Convinced that, in furtherance of this principle, all Parties to the Treaty are entitled to participate in the fullest possible exchange of scientific information for, and to contribute alone or in cooperation with other States to, the further development of the applications of atomic energy for peaceful purposes,

Declaring their intention to achieve at the earliest possible date the cessation of the nuclear arms race and to undertake effective measures in the direction of nuclear disarmament,

Urging the cooperation of all States in the attainment of this objective,

Recalling the determination expressed by the Parties to the 1963 Treaty banning nuclear weapon tests in the atmosphere in outer space and under water in its Preamble to seek to achieve the discontinuance of all test explosions of nuclear weapons for all time and to continue negotiations to this end,

Desiring to further the easing of international tension and the strengthening of trust between States in order to facilitate the cessation of the manufacture of nuclear weapons, the liquidation of all their existing stockpiles, and the elimination from national arsenals of nuclear weapons and the means of their delivery pursuant to a treaty on general and complete disarmament under strict and effective international control,

Recalling that, in accordance with the Charter of the United Nations, States must refrain in their international relations from the threat or use of force against the territorial integrity or political independence of any State, or in any other manner inconsistent with the Purposes of the United Nations, and that the establishment and maintenance of international peace and security are to be promoted with the least diversion for armaments of the world's human and economic resources,

Have agreed as follows:

Article I

Each nuclear-weapon State Party to the Treaty undertakes not to transfer to any recipient whatsoever nuclear weapons or other nuclear explosive devices or control over such weapons or explosive devices directly, or indirectly; and not in any way to assist, encourage, or induce any non-nuclear-weapon State to manufacture or otherwise acquire nuclear weapons or other nuclear explosive devices, or control over such weapons or explosive devices.

Article II

Each non-nuclear-weapon State Party to the Treaty undertakes not to receive the transfer from any transferor whatsoever of nuclear weapons or other nuclear explosive devices or of control over such weapons or explosive devices directly, or indirectly; not to manufacture or otherwise acquire nuclear weapons or other nuclear explosive devices; and not to seek or receive any assistance in the manufacture of nuclear weapons or other nuclear explosive devices.

Article III

1. Each non-nuclear-weapon State Party to the Treaty undertakes to accept safeguards, as set forth in an agreement to be negotiated and concluded with the International Atomic Energy Agency in accordance with the Statute of the International Atomic Energy Agency and the Agency's safeguards system, for the exclusive purpose of verification of the fulfillment of its obligations assumed under this Treaty with a view of preventing diversion of nuclear energy from peaceful uses to nuclear weapons to other nuclear explosive devices. Procedures for the safe-

guards required by this article shall be followed with respect to source or special fissionable material whether it is being produced, processed or used in any principal nuclear facility or is outside any such facility. The safeguards required by this article shall be applied on all source or special fissionable material in all peaceful nuclear activities within the territory of such State, under its jurisdiction, or carried out under its control anywhere.

2. Each State Party to the Treaty undertakes not to provide: (a) source or special fissionable material, or (b) equipment or material especially designed or prepared for the processing, use or production of special fissionable material, to non-nuclear-weapon State for peaceful purposes, unless the source or special fissionable material shall be subject to the safeguards required by this article.

3. The safeguards required by this article shall be implemented in a manner designed to comply with article IV of this Treaty, and to avoid hampering the economic or technological development of the Parties or international cooperation in the field of peaceful nuclear activities, including the international exchange of nuclear material and equipment for the processing, use or production of nuclear material for peaceful purposes in accordance with the provisions of this article and the principle of safeguarding set forth in the Preamble of the Treaty.

4. Non-nuclear-weapon States Party to the Treaty shall conclude agreements with the International Atomic Energy Agency to meet the requirements of this article either individually or together with other States in accordance with the Statute of the International Atomic Energy Agency. Negotiation of such agreements shall commence within 180 days from the original entry into force of this Treaty. For States depositing their instruments of ratification or accession after the 180-day period, negotiation of such agreements shall commence not later than the date of such deposit. Such agreements shall enter into force not later than eighteen months after the date of initiation of negotiations.

Article IV

1. Nothing in this Treaty shall be interpreted as affecting the inalienable right of all Parties to the Treaty to develop research, production and use of nuclear energy for peaceful purposes without discrimination and in conformity with articles I and II of this Treaty.

2. All the Parties to the Treaty undertake to facilitate, and have the right to participate in, the fullest possible exchange of equipment, materials and scientific and technological information for the peaceful uses of nuclear energy. Parties to the Treaty in a position to do so shall also cooperate in contributing alone or together with other States or international organizations to the further development of the applications of nuclear energy for peaceful purposes, especially in the territories of non-nuclear-weapon States Party to the Treaty, with due consideration for the needs of the developing areas of the world.

Article V

Each Party to the Treaty undertakes to take appropriate measures to ensure that, in accordance with this Treaty, under appropriate international observation and through appropriate international procedures, potential benefits from any peaceful applications of nuclear explosions will be made available to non-nuclear-weapon States Party to the Treaty on a non-discriminatory basis and that the charge to such Parties for the explosive devices used will be as low as possible and exclude any charge for research and development. Non-nuclear-weapon States Party to the Treaty shall be able to obtain such benefits, pursuant to a special international agreement or agreements, through an appropriate international body with adequate representation of non-nuclear-weapon States. Negotiations on this subject shall commence as soon as possible after the Treaty enters into force. Non-nuclear-weapon States Party to the Treaty so desiring may also obtain such benefits pursuant to bilateral agreements.

Article VI

Each of the Parties to the Treaty undertakes to pursue negotiations in good faith on effective measures relating to cessation of the nuclear arms race at an early date and to nuclear disarmament, and on a treaty on general and complete disarmament under strict and effective international control.

Article VII

Nothing in this Treaty affects the right of any group of States to conclude regional treaties in order to assure the total absence of nuclear weapons in their respective territories.

Article VIII

1. Any Party to the Treaty may propose amendments to this Treaty. The text of any proposed amendment shall be submitted to the Depositary Governments which shall circulate it to all Parties to the Treaty. Thereupon, if requested to do so by one-third or more of the Parties to the Treaty, the Depositary Governments shall convene a conference, to which they shall invite all the Parties to the Treaty, to consider such an amendment.

2. Any amendment to this Treaty must be approved by a majority of the votes of all the Parties to the Treaty, including the votes of all nuclear-weapon States Party to the Treaty and all other Parties which, on the date the

amendment is circulated, are members of the Board of Governors of the International Atomic Energy Agency. The amendment shall enter into force for each Party that deposits its instrument of ratification of the amendment upon the deposit of such instruments of ratification by a majority of all the Parties, including the instruments of ratification of all nuclear-weapon States Party to the Treaty and all other Parties which, on the date the amendment is circulated, are members of the Board of Governors of the International Atomic Energy Agency. Thereafter, it shall enter into force for any other Party upon the deposit of its instrument of ratification of the amendment.

3. Five years after the entry into force of this Treaty, a conference of Parties to the Treaty shall be held in Geneva, Switzerland, in order to review the operation of this Treaty with a view to assuring that the purposes of the Preamble and the provisions of the Treaty are being realized. At intervals of five years thereafter, a majority of the Parties to the Treaty may obtain, by submitting a proposal to this effect to the Depositary Governments, the convening of further conferences with the same objective of reviewing the operation of the Treaty.

Article IX

1. This Treaty shall be open to all States for signature. Any State which does not sign the Treaty before its entry into force in accordance with paragraph 3 of this article may accede to it at any time.

2. This Treaty shall be subject to ratification by signatory States. Instruments of ratification and instruments of accession shall be deposited with the Governments of the United States of America, the United Kingdom of Great Britain and Northern Ireland and the Union of Soviet Socialist Republics, which are hereby designated the Depositary Governments.

3. This Treaty shall enter into force after its ratification by the States, the Governments of which are designated Depositaries of the Treaty, and forty other States signatory to this Treaty and the deposit of their instruments of ratification. For the purposes of this Treaty, a nuclear-weapon State is one which has manufactured and exploded a nuclear weapon or other nuclear explosive device prior to January 1, 1967.

4. For States whose instruments of ratification or accession are deposited subsequent to the entry into force of this Treaty, it shall enter into force on the date of the deposit of their instruments of ratification or accession.

5. The Depositary Governments shall promptly inform all signatory and acceding States of the date of each signature, the date of deposit of each instrument of ratification or of accession, the date of the entry into force of this Treaty, and the date of receipt of any requests for convening a conference or other notices.

6. This Treaty shall be registered by the Depositary Governments pursuant to article 102 of the Charter of the United Nations.

Article X

1. Each Party shall in exercising its national sovereignty have the right to withdraw from the Treaty if it decides that extraordinary events, related to the subject matter of this Treaty, have jeopardized the supreme interests of its country. It shall give notice of such withdrawal to all other Parties to the Treaty and to the United Nations Security Council three months in advance. Such notice shall include a statement of the extraordinary events it regards as having jeopardized its supreme interests.

2. Twenty-five years after the entry into force of the Treaty, a conference shall be convened to decide whether the Treaty shall continue in force indefinitely, or shall be extended for an additional fixed period or periods. This decision shall be taken by a majority of the Parties to the Treaty.

Article XI

This Treaty, the English, Russian, French, Spanish and Chinese texts of which are equally authentic, shall be deposited in the archives of the Depositary Governments. Duly certified copies of this Treaty shall be transmitted by the Depositary Governments to the Governments of the signatory and acceding States.

In Witness Whereof the undersigned, duly authorized, have signed this Treaty.

Done in triplicate, at the cities of Washington, London and Moscow, this first day of July one thousand nine hundred sixty-eight.

Source:

U.S. Department of State, *Treaties and Other International Acts Series,* No. 6839.

Richard M. Nixon, News Conference on Cambodia, 1970

News conference given by President Richard M. Nixon on May 8, 1970, a week after he had ordered U.S. troops into Cambodia in an expansion of the Vietnam War. The move had triggered widespread protests on U.S. college campuses. On several, Reserve Officer Training Corps (ROTC) buildings were burned and the fire fighters called to douse the flames were stoned and their hoses cut. Kent State University in Ohio was one campus where these events occurred, and the next day the governor called out the National Guard to prevent further violence. Instead, during a demonstration, the Guard fired on the students, killing four and wounding others.

In an informal speech at the Pentagon May 1, Nixon had referred to student protesters as "bums" in contrast to their peers who did their duty by fighting in Vietnam. In his May 8 news conference, Nixon defended the Cambodia move, insisting that it would shorten the war in Vietnam. He sought to clarify his May 1 statement, saying the word "bums" applied only to students who engaged in violent acts. He also denied reports that he intended to "censor" Vice President Spiro Agnew, whose criticism of antiwar protesters had been especially virulent.

On June 30, the Senate passed an amendment to the foreign military sales bill drafted by Senators John Sherman Cooper (R-Ky.) and Frank Church (D-Idaho) in response to the invasion of Cambodia. It would have banned the Nixon administration from funding any U.S. military operations in Cambodia without receiving congressional authorization. Opponents managed to delay a vote until after American troops had withdrawn and the House defeated the bill July 9.

At the end of August, four antiwar activists set off the strongest terrorist bomb anywhere until 1983, destroying the Army Math Research Center and damaging many other buildings at the University of Wisconsin in Madison. The explosion killed a graduate student and injured four others. Along with the Kent State shootings, the Wisconsin bombing effectively ended the more violent side of the antiwar movement. The most revolutionary militants continued their antiwar-anticapitalist terrorism through small cells, such as the Weather Underground and the Symbionese Liberation Army.

Protests and the Decision on Cambodia

Q. Mr. President, have you been surprised by the intensity of the protest against your decision to send troops into Cambodia, and will these protests affect your policy in any way?

The President. No, I have not been surprised by the intensity of the protests. I realize that those who are protesting believe that this decision will expand the war, increase American casualties, and increase American involvement. Those who protest want peace. They want to reduce American casualties and they want our boys brought home.

I made the decision, however, for the very reasons that they are protesting. As far as affecting my decision is concerned—their protests I am concerned about. I am concerned because I know how deeply they feel. But I know that what I have done will accomplish the goals that they want. It will shorten this war. It will reduce American casualties. It will allow us to go forward with our withdrawal program. The 150,000 Americans that I announced for withdrawal in the next year will come home on schedule. It will in my opinion serve the cause of a just peace in Vietnam.

Q. Mr. President.

The President. Mr. Cormier.

Communication with the College Communities

Q. Do you believe that you can open up meaningful communications with this college-age generation, and how?

The President. I would like to try as best I can to do that. It is not easy. Sometimes they, as you know, talk so loudly that it is difficult to be heard, as we have learned during the campaigns, and also during the appearances many of the Cabinet officers have made on university campuses. However, on an individual basis, I believe that it is possible to do what I have been doing, to bring representatives of the college and university communities to my office, to talk with them, to have a dialogue. I am very glad that Chancellor Heard, the Chancellor of Vanderbilt, has agreed to take 2 months off from his very important responsibilities in that position to work with us in the administration to see if we cannot develop better lines of communication both to school administrators, but also to school students.

Mr. Kaplow.

The Students' Message

Q. Mr. President, what do you think the students are trying to say in this demonstration?

The President. They are trying to say that they want peace. They are trying to say that they want to stop the killing. They are trying to say that they want to end the draft. They are trying to say that we ought to get out of Vietnam. I agree with everything that they are trying to accomplish.

I believe, however, that the decisions that I have made, and particularly this last terribly difficult decision of going into the Cambodian sanctuaries which were completely occupied by the enemy—I believe that that decision will serve that purpose, because you can be sure that everything that I stand for is what they want.

I would add this: I think I understand what they want. I would hope they would understand somewhat what I want. When I came to the Presidency—I did not send these men to Vietnam—there were 525,000 men there. And since I have been here, I have been working 18 or 20 hours a day, mostly on Vietnam, trying to bring these men home.

We brought home 115,000. Our casualties were the lowest in the first quarter of this year in 5 years. We are going to bring home another 150,000. And, as a result of the greater accomplishments than we expected in even the first week of the Cambodian campaign, I believe that we will have accomplished our goal of reducing American casualties and, also, of hastening the day that we can have a just peace. But above everything else, to continue the withdrawal program that they are for and that I am for.

Yes, sir?

Progress of Vietnamization

Q. On April 20th, you said Vietnamization was going so well that you could pull 150,000 American troops out of Vietnam. Then you turned around only 10 days later and said that Vietnamization was so badly threatened you were sending troops into Cambodia.

Would you explain this apparent contradiction for us?

The President. I explained it in my speech of April 20th, as you will recall, because then I said that Vietnamization was going so well that we could bring 150,000 out by the spring of next year, regardless of the progress in the Paris peace talks and the other criteria that I mentioned.

But I also warned at that time that increased enemy action in Laos, in Cambodia, as well as in Vietnam, was something that we had noted, and that if I had indicated, and if I found, that that increased enemy action would jeopardize the remaining forces who would be in Vietnam after we had withdrawn 150,000, I would take strong action to deal with it. I found that the action that the enemy had taken in Cambodia would leave the 240,000 Americans who would be there a year from now without many combat troops to help defend them, would leave them in an untenable position. That is why I had to act.

The Possibility of Revolution and Repression

Q. Mr. President, some Americans believe this country is heading for revolution, and others believe that crime and dissent and violent demonstrations are leading us to an era of repression. I wonder if you would give us your view of the state of the American society and where it is heading.

The President. That would require rather an extended answer. Briefly, this country is not headed for revolution. The very fact that we do have the safety valves of the right to dissent, the very fact that the President of the United States asked the District Commissioners to waive their rule for 30 days' notice for a demonstration, and also asked that that demonstration occur not just around the Washington Monument but on the Ellipse where I could here it—and you can hear it pretty well from there, I can assure you—that fact is an indication that when you have that kind of safety valve you are not going to have revolution which comes from repression.

The second point, with regard to repression: That is nonsense, in my opinion. I do not see that the critics of my policies, our policies, are repressed. I note from reading the press and from listening to television that criticism is very vigorous and sometimes quite personal. It has every right to be. I have no complaints about it.

Yes, sir?

Paris Peace Talks

Q. One of the consequences of the Cambodian action was the fact that the other side boycotted this week's peace talks in Paris. There is some question as to whether our side will attend next week. Have you made a decision on that?

The President. Our side will attend next week. We expect the talks to go forward. And at the time that we are cleaning out the enemy sanctuaries in Cambodia, we will pursue the path of peace at the negotiating table there and in a number of other forums that we are presently working on.

Mr. Horner?

Response to North Vietnamese Action

Q. Mr. President, Secretary of Defense Laird said last week that if the North Vietnamese troops should move across the DMZ in force, he would recommend resumption of the bombing. What would be your reaction to such a recommendation in those circumstances?

The President: I am not going to speculate as to what the North Vietnamese may do. I will only say that if the North Vietnamese did what some have suggested they might do—move a massive force of 250,000 to 300,000 across the DMZ against our Marine Corps people who are there—I would certainly not allow those men to be massacred without using more force and more effective force against North Vietnam.

I think we have warned the leaders of North Vietnam on this point several times, and because we have warned them I do not believe they will move across the DMZ.

Mrs. Dickerson?

The Vice President's Speech

Q. After you met with the eight university presidents yesterday, they indicated that you had agreed to tone down the criticism in your administration of those who disagree with you. Then tonight Vice President Agnew is quoted all over the news programs as making a speech which includes these words, "That every debate has a cadre of Jeremiahs, normally a gloomy coalition of choleric young intellectuals and tired, embittered elders." Why?

The President. Mrs. Dickerson, I have studied the history of this country over the past 190 years. And, of course, the classic and the most interesting game is to try to drive a wedge between the President and Vice President. Believe me, I had 8 years of that, and I am experienced on that point.

Now, as far as the Vice President is concerned, he will answer for anything that he has said. As far as my attempting to tone him down or my attempting to censor the Secretary of the Interior because he happens to take a different point of view, I shall not do that. I would hope that all of the members of this administration would have in mind the fact, a rule that I have always had, and it is a very simple one: When the action is hot, keep the rhetoric cool.

Schedule for Withdrawal from Cambodia

Q. Mr. President, on April 30 you announced that you, as Commander in Chief, were sending in U.S. units and South Vietnamese units into Cambodia. Do the South Vietnamese abide by the same pull-out deadline as you have laid down for the American forces?

The President. No, they do not. I would expect that the South Vietnamese would come out approximately at the same time that we do because when we come out our logistical support and air support will also come out with them.

I would like also to say that with response to that deadline I can give the members of the press some news with regard to the developments that have occurred. The action actually is going faster than we had anticipated. The middle of next week the first units, American units, will come out. The end of next week the second group of American units will come out. The great majority of all American units will be out by the second week of June, and all Americans of all kinds, including advisers, will be out of Cambodia by the end of June.

I will take you next, Mr. Potter. The writing press gets a break.

Student Dissenters

Q. Mr. President, do you believe that the use of the word "bums" to categorize some of those who are engaged in dissent—and I know you meant it to apply to those who are destructive, but it has been used in a broader context—do you believe that is in keeping with your suggestion that the rhetoric should be kept cool.?

The President. I would certainly regret that my use of the word "bums" was interpreted to apply to those who dissent. All the members of this press corps know that I have for years defended the right of dissent. I have always opposed the use of violence. On university campuses the rule of reason is supposed to prevail over the rule of force. And when students on university campuses burn buildings, when they engage in violence, when they break up furniture, when they terrorize their fellow students and terrorize the faculty, then I think "bums" is perhaps too kind a word to apply to that kind of person. Those are the kind I was referring to.

Mr. Rather? I will get you next, Mr. Bailey.

Accomplishments in Cambodia

Q. Mr. President, you mentioned that you expected the Americans to be out of Cambodia by some time in June. President Thieu was quoted as saying in an interview that he felt the North Vietnamese could reestablish their sanctuaries in Cambodia within 6 months and possibly, he was quoted as saying, within 2 or 3 months.

If that is the case, what have we accomplished in Cambodia? Was it worth the risks, and what do we do when they reestablish those sanctuaries.?

The President. I am planning to give a report to the Nation when our own actions are completed, toward the latter part of June. At that time, I will answer that question in full.

At the present time, I will say that it is my belief, based on what we have accomplished to date, that we have bought at least 6 months and probably 8 months of time for the training of the ARVN, the Army of South Vietnam. We have also saved, I think, hundreds, if not thousands, of Americans, as Frank Reynolds reported tonight on ABC. Rockets by the thousands and small arms ammunition by the millions have already been captured and those rockets and small arms will not be killing Americans in these next few months. And what we have also accomplished is that by buying time, it means that if the enemy does come back into those sanctuaries next time, the South Vietnamese will be strong enough and well trained enough to handle it alone.

I should point out too, that they are handling a majority of the assignment now in terms of manpower.

Mr. Bailey?

Secretary Hickel's Letter to the President

Q. Sir, without asking you to censor the Secretary of the Interior, could you comment on the substantive points that he made in his letter?

The President. I think the Secretary of the Interior is a man who has very strong views. He is outspoken. He is courageous. That is one of the reasons I selected him for the Cabinet, and one of the reasons that I defended him very vigorously before this press corps when he was under attack.

As far as his views are concerned, I will, of course, be interested in his advice. I might say, too, that I hope he gives some advice to the Postmaster General. That was the fastest mail delivery I have had since I have been in the White House. [*Laughter.*]

Mr. Scali?

Reasons for the Cambodian Action

Q. Mr. President, how do you answer the criticism that the justification that you give for going into the Cambodian sanctuaries is hauntingly similar to the reasons that President Lyndon Johnson gave as he moved step by step up the ladder of escalation? He wanted peace, too, sir.

The President: Mr. Scali, President Johnson did want peace, and, if I may use the vernacular, he has taken a bad rap from those who say that he wanted war.

However, the difference is that he did move step by step. This action is a decisive move, and this action also puts the enemy on warning that if it escalates while we are trying to deescalate, we will move decisively and not step by step.

Mr. Healy.

Will the War Prove Worthwhile?

Q. Mr. President, this war was well underway before you came in, as you just said. Considering the toll in lives and in everything else that is happening now, do you think it will have proved to be worthwhile?

The President. It is rather a moot question, Mr. Healy, as to whether it will prove to have been worthwhile. As Commander in Chief, I have found for 525,000 Americans it has been my responsibility to do everything I could to protect their lives and to get them home as quickly as I can. And we have succeeded pretty well. We brought 115,000 home. We are going to bring another 150,000, and this action will assure the continued success of that program.

However, looking at the whole of Southeast Asia, looking at the fact that we have lost lives there, I would say that only history will record whether it was worthwhile.

I do know this: Now that America is there, if we do what many of our very sincere critics think we should do, if we withdraw from Vietnam and allow the enemy to come into Vietnam and massacre the civilians there by the millions, as they would—if we do that, let me say that America is finished insofar as the peacekeeper in the Asian world is concerned.

Police and National Guard Conduct

Q. Mr. President, in the light of the Kent State University incident, could you tell us what, in your judgment, is the proper action and conduct for a police force or a National Guard force when ordered to clear the campus area and faced with a crowd throwing rocks?

The President. We think we have done a rather good job here in Washington in that respect. As you know, we handled the two demonstrations, October 15 and November 15 of last year, without any significant casualties, and that took a lot of doing because there were some pretty rough people involved—a few were rough; most of them were very peaceful.

I would hope that the experience that we have had in that respect could be shared by the National Guards, which, of course, are not under Federal control but under State control.

Now, what I say is not to be interpreted as a criticism in advance of my getting the facts of the National Guard at Kent State. I want to know what the facts are. I have asked for the facts. When I get them, I will have something to say about it. But I do know when you do have a situation of a crowd throwing rocks and the National Guard is called in, that there is always the chance that it will escalate into the kind of a tragedy that happened at Kent State.

If there is one thing I am personally committed to, it is this: I saw the pictures of those four youngsters in the Evening Star the day after that tragedy, and I vowed then that we were going to find methods that would be more effective to deal with these problems of violence, methods that would deal with those who would use force and violence and endanger others, but, at the same time, would not take the lives of innocent people.

Cambodia's Future

Q. After the American troops are removed from Cambodia, there may still be a question as to the future of Cambodia's ability to exist as a neutralist country.

What is your policy toward Cambodia's future?

The President. The United States is, of course, interested in the future of Cambodia, and the future of Laos, both of which, of course, as you know, are neutral countries. However, the United States, as I indicated in what is called the Guam or Nixon Doctrine, cannot take the responsibility and should not take the responsibility in the future to send American men in to defend the neutrality of countries that are unable to defend them themselves.

In this area, what we have to do is to go down the diplomatic trail, and that is why we are exploring with the Soviet Union—with not too much success to date, but we are going to continue to explore it—with Great Britain, with the Asian countries that are meeting in Djakarta, and through every possible channel, methods through which the neutrality of countries like Cambodia and Laos, who cannot possibly defend themselves, to see that that neutrality is guaranteed without having the intervention of foreign forces.

Progress toward Goals

Q. Mr. President, in your Inaugural Address, you said that one of your goals was to bring us together in America. You said that you wanted to move us in international terms from an era of confrontation to an era of negotiation. You said you wanted to bring peace to Vietnam. During the past 2 weeks, it seems that we are farther than ever from the goals. How do you account for this apparent failure?

The President. Don't judge us too quickly. When it comes to negotiation, I would suggest that you recognize the fact that some very important talks are going forward on arms limitation with the Soviet Union. We are still far apart. But I will predict now that there will be an agreement. When that agreement comes, it will have great significance. I say that having in mind the fact that we are far apart from the Soviet Union in our policy toward Southeast Asia, in our policy toward the Mideast; but I say that where the problem of arms is concerned, here is where our interests are together. The Soviet Union has just as great an interest as we have in seeing that there is some limitation on nuclear arms...

Paris Talks and Consideration of a Coalition Government

Q. Mr. President, is the United States prepared to pursue with equal fervor in Paris negotiations to find a political settlement of this war, including the possibility of discussing with the other side a coalition government?

The President. We are prepared to seek not only in Paris but in any other forum a political settlement of this war. We are not prepared, however, to seek any settlement in which we or anyone else imposes upon the people of South Vietnam a government that they do not choose. If the people of South Vietnam choose a coalition government, if they choose to change the leaders they presently have, that is a decision we will accept. President Thieu has indicated he will accept it. But we do not intend to impose at the conference table on the people of South Vietnam a government they do not choose...

The Cambodian Decision

Q. Mr. President, did Secretary of State Rogers oppose your decision to go into Cambodia or did Dr. Kissinger oppose it?

The President. Every one of my advisers, the Secretary of State, the Secretary of Defense, Dr. Kissinger, Director Helms, raised questions about the decision, and, believe me, I raised the most questions, because I knew the stakes that were involved, I knew the division that would be caused in this country. I knew also the problems internationally. I knew the military risks. And then after hearing all of their advice, I made the decision. Decisions, of course, are not made by vote in the National Security Council or in the Cabinet. They are made by the President with the advice of those, and I made this decision. I take the responsibility for it. I believe it was the right decision. I believe it will work out. If it doesn't, then I am to blame. They are not.

Mr. Morgan?

Administration Discourse with Dissenters

Q. Volumes have been written about the loneliness of the Presidency. You, yourself, have said that you were not going to get trapped into an isolation as President. Have you, particularly in recent days, felt isolated? And if you have not, could you explain to us why it was not until yesterday that you, whose voice means more than anybody else's in the administration, whether it be Mr. Agnew or Mr. Hickel, waited until yesterday to tell the educators that the administration was lowering—was modifying its discourse with the dissenters?

The President. Well, first let us understand what I told the educators. The educators came in to discuss their problems, and since they are all presidents I felt a community of interest with them.

I indicated to them that I didn't want to make their job any harder for them and I would appreciate it if they wouldn't make my job any harder for me in their own activities.

They raised questions about the Vice President, and about other people in the administration, about the rhetoric, and I know, of course, questions have been raised about my rhetoric.

Let me say that in terms, however, of the Vice President, in terms of what I told the educators, I did not indicate to them that I was going to muzzle the Vice President, that I was going to censor him.

I believe that the Vice President, the Secretary of the Interior, the Secretary of HEW, everybody in this administration, should have the right, after considering all the factors, to speak out and express his views. This is an open administration. It will continue to be.

I also think that people should have the right to speak out as they do in the House, in the Senate, in the media, and in the universities. The only difference is that, of all these people—and I refer particularly to some of my lively critics in the House and Senate—they have the luxury of criticism.

I was once a Senator and a House Member; I thought back to this when I called Harry Truman today and wished him well on his 86th birthday, to some of the rather rugged criticisms that I directed in his direction.

They have the luxury of criticism because they can criticize and if it doesn't work out then they can gloat over it, or if it does work out, the criticism will be forgotten.

I don't have that luxury. As Commander in Chief, I, alone, am responsible for the lives 425,000 or 430,000 Americans in Vietnam. That is what I have been thinking about. And the decision that I made on Cambodia will save those lives. It will bring the peace that we all want, in my opinion. I could be wrong, but if I am wrong, I am responsible and nobody else.

Troop Withdrawals from Vietnam

Q. Mr. President, early in the news conference, in saying that the troop withdrawals would continue, you said that a year from now there would be 240,000 American soldiers in Vietnam.

The President. Don't hold me to the exact figure. I haven't—

Q. That is 185,000 less. Are you announcing a larger withdrawal tonight?

The President. No, I wasn't. What I was indicating was a range. But don't get the impression that we might not get that low also, because you understand we are going to go forward on the negotiating track at this time, and I am not among those who has given up on that track. I still think there is a possibility of progress there.

Possibility of Meeting with Demonstrators

Q. Mr. President, will you see any of the demonstrators tomorrow in the White House? Will you talk with them?

The President. If arrangements are made by my staff so that they can come in to see me, I will be glad to. I talk to great numbers of people. I will be here all day long. As a matter of fact, I will be here tonight and tomorrow as well. But sometimes it is quite difficult to arrange which groups should come in. I know members of my staff will go out to see them. I have asked all the younger members of my staff to talk to the demonstrators and try to get their views, as we did on November 15 and October 15. I will be glad to see them if some of them are available.

Frank Cormier, Associated Press: Thank you, Mr. President.

See also COOPER CHURCH AMENDMENT, 1970.

Source:

The Richard Nixon Library and Birthplace, Yorba Linda, Calif.

Richard M. Nixon, Announcement on China, 1971

Broadcast address given by President Richard M. Nixon on July 15, 1971, in which he announced that he would become the first U.S. president to visit the People's Republic of China and meet with its leader, Communist Party chairman Mao Zedong (Tse-tung). The announcement came as a complete surprise to the media and almost all government officials. Nixon told viewers that the visit, scheduled to take place before May 1972, had been worked out in a series of secret meetings in Beijing between Chinese premier Chou En-lai and Nixon's National Security Advisor, Henry A. Kissinger. Nixon described the visit as part of his efforts to build a lasting peace in the world.

Mainland China had fallen completely to Communist control in August 1949, when the Nationalist leader Jiang Jieshi (Chiang Kai-shek) fled to Taiwan. China (which has never recognized Taiwan as a separate country) became the People's Republic of China (PRC).

Coming shortly after the detonation of an atomic bomb by the Soviets, the fall of the world's most populous nation to communism profoundly affected U.S. international relations and domestic politics. The Republicans then mounted a politically motivated campaign against China experts in and out of the government who they alleged "lost" China. As it turned out, some of these individuals held communist sympathies, but nothing confirming the accusations has ever turned up regarding the most highly publicized individuals, John Stewart Service and Owen Lattimore. However, the criticism resulted in muzzling dissenting voices and resonated in the loss of expertise regarding Korea and Vietnam.

On December 2, 1954, the United States and the Republic of China (Nationalist China—Taiwan) signed a mutual defense treaty promising U.S. assistance if the PRC attacked it or the nearby Pescadores Islands. It did not, however, apply to the Chinese Nationalist–held islands of Quemoy and Matsu. Jiang agreed not to attack the mainland unilaterally. In January 1955 Congress gave President Dwight Eisenhower the authority to use U.S. armed forces if necessary to defend Taiwan and the Pescadores.

In announcing his visit, President Nixon, in an implicit reference to the Nationalist government on Taiwan, insisted that it would not "come at the expense of our old friends." The "two China policy" of the United States has continued to plague American foreign policy since 1971. President Nixon visited China in 1972, and the PRC and the United States began formal diplomatic relations in 1974 when Nixon named future president George H. W. Bush to head the American liaison office. President Jimmy Carter granted the PRC full diplomatic recognition in December 1978.

Commentators noted at the time that only someone with unquestionable anticommunist credentials like Nixon could have initiated relations with the PRC. Ever since, this action has become a metaphor for politicians who take a major action against the stated policy of their party.

Good evening:

I have requested this television time tonight to announce a major development in our efforts to build a lasting peace in the world.

As I have pointed out on a number of occasions over the past 3 years, there can be no stable and enduring peace without the participation of the People's Republic of China and its 750 million people. That is why I have undertaken initiatives in several areas to open the door for more normal relations between our two countries.

In pursuance of that goal, I sent Dr. Kissinger, my Assistant for National Security Affairs, to Peking during his recent world tour for the purpose of having talks with Premier Chou En-Lai.

The announcement I shall now read is being issued simultaneously in Peking and in the United States:

Premier Chou En-Lai and Dr. Henry Kissinger, President Nixon's Assistant for National Security Affairs, held talks in Peking from July 9 to 11, 1971. Knowing of President Nixon's expressed desire to visit the People's Republic of China, Premier Chou En-Lai, on behalf of the Government of the People's Republic of China, has extended an invitation to President Nixon to visit China at an appropriate date before May 1972. President Nixon has accepted the invitation with pleasure.

The meeting between the leaders of China and the United States is to seek the normalization of relations between the two countries and also to exchange views on questions of concern to the two sides.

In anticipation of the inevitable speculation which will follow this announcement, I want to put our policy in the clearest possible context.

Our action in seeking a new relationship with the People's Republic of China will not be at the expense of our old friends. It is not directed against any other nation. We seek friendly relations with all nations. Any nation can be our friend without being any other nation's enemy.

I have taken this action because of my profound conviction that all nations will gain from a reduction of tensions and a better relationship between the United States and the People's Republic of China.

It is in this spirit that I will undertake what I deeply hope will become a journey for peace, peace not just for our generation but for future generations on this earth we share together.

Thank you and good night.

Source:

Public Papers of the Presidents of the United States: Richard Nixon, 1971. Washington, D.C.: Government Printing Office, 1969–74. pp. 819–820.

Agreement to End the Vietnam War, 1973

Agreement on Ending the War and Restoring Peace in Vietnam, signed on January 27, 1973, in Paris, by representatives of the United States, the Republic of Vietnam (South Vietnam), the Democratic Republic of Vietnam (North Vietnam), and the Provisional Revolutionary Government of South Vietnam (the National Liberation Front, the political representation of the Viet Cong).

Many of those voting for Nixon as president in 1968 had expected him to end the war during his first administration. A year after his election, with the war, now the longest in U.S. history, continuing and protests becoming larger and attracting a more mainstream demonstrator, the president delivered a radio and television address announcing a new policy on the Vietnam War. He revealed his plan "for the complete withdrawal of all U.S. combat ground forces and their replacement by South Vietnamese forces. However, he refused to announce any timetable for total withdrawal, arguing that it would remove any incentive for the Communist side to negotiate a final settlement. He concluded the speech by asking, in a phrase that entered the American cultural vocabulary, for the support of the "great silent majority of my fellow Americans."

At the start of Nixon's second administration, he announced a permanent cease-fire in the war to be monitored by two joint military commissions made up of the parties to the conflict. In the next 60 days, all U.S. prisoners of war were to be released by Hanoi. At the same time, all U.S. military personnel would be withdrawn from South Vietnam. Both the United States and North Vietnam pledged to respect the right of the people of South Vietnam to self-determination. The enforcement of the peace agreement was to be the job of an international control commission.

By March 29, the last of the remaining 23,500 U.S. troops left South Vietnam, and the North released 586 POWs. The longest war in American history seemed to be over. However, the reconciliation between the Viet Cong and the Saigon government, as specified by the agreement, never occurred. Soon, the fighting resumed, with the North Vietnamese emerging victorious. Americans were forced to escape by helicopter from the roof of their embassy, leaving behind many of their South Vietnamese allies. On April 30, 1975, Saigon fell, finally bringing the war to an end. Vietnam was formally reunited the following year and Saigon was renamed Ho Chi Minh City.

(excerpt)

Paris, France
January 27, 1973

The Parties participating in the Paris Conference on Vietnam,

With a view to ending the war and restoring peace in Vietnam on the basis of respect for the Vietnamese people's fundamental national rights and the South Vietnamese people's right to self-determination, and to contributing to the consolidation of peace in Asia and the world,

Have agreed on the following provisions and undertake to respect and to implement them:

Chapter I
The Vietnamese People's Fundamental National Rights

Article 1. The United States and all other countries respect the independence, sovereignty, unity, and territorial integrity of Vietnam as recognized by the 1954 Geneva Agreements on Vietnam.

Chapter II
Cessation of Hostilities—Withdrawal of Troops

Article 2. A ceasefire shall be observed throughout South Vietnam as of 2400 hours G.M.T., on January 27, 1973.

At the same hour, the United States will stop all its military activities against the territory of the Democratic Republic of Vietnam by ground, air and naval forces, wherever they may be based, and end the mining of the territorial waters, ports, harbors, and waterways of the Democratic Republic of Vietnam. The United States will remove, permanently deactivate or destroy all the mines in the territorial waters, ports, harbors, and waterways of North Vietnam as soon as this Agreement goes into effect.

The complete cessation of hostilities mentioned in this Article shall be durable and without limit of time.

Article 3. The parties undertake to maintain the ceasefire and to ensure a lasting and stable peace.

As soon as the ceasefire goes into effect:

(a) The United States forces and those of the other foreign countries allied with the United States and the Republic of Vietnam shall remain in place pending the implementation of the plan of troop withdrawal. The Four-Party Joint Military Commission described in Article 16 shall determine the modalities.

(b) The armed forces of the two South Vietnamese parties shall remain in place. The Two-Party Joint Military Commission described in Article 17 shall determine the areas controlled by each party and the modalities of stationing.

(c) The regular forces of all services and arms and the irregular forces of the parties in South Vietnam shall stop all offensive activities against each other and shall strictly abide by the following stipulations:

—All acts of force on the ground, in the air, and on the sea shall be prohibited;

—All hostile acts, terrorism and reprisals by both sides will be banned.

Article 4. The United States will not continue it military involvement or intervene in the internal affairs of South Vietnam.

Article 5. Within sixty days of the signing of this Agreement, there will be a total withdrawal from South Vietnam of troops, military advisers, and military personnel, including technical military personnel and military personnel associated with the pacification program, armaments, munitions, and war material of the United States and those of the other foreign countries mentioned in Article 3 (a). Advisers from the above-mentioned countries to all paramilitary organizations and the police force will also be withdrawn within the same period of time.

Article 6. The dismantlement of all military bases in South Vietnam of the United States and of the other foreign countries mentioned in Article 3 (a) shall be completed within sixty days of the signing of this Agreement.

Article 7. From the enforcement of the ceasefire to the formation of the government provided for in Articles 9 (b) and 14 of this Agreement, the two South Vietnamese parties shall not accept the introduction of troops, military advisers, and military personnel including technical military personnel, armaments, munitions, and war material into South Vietnam.

The two South Vietnamese parties shall be permitted to make periodic replacement of armaments, munitions and war material which have been destroyed, damaged, worn out or used up after the ceasefire, on the basis of piece-for-piece, of the same characteristics and properties, under the supervision of the Joint Military Commission of the two South Vietnamese parties and of the International Commission of Control and Supervision . . .

Source:

J. A. S. Grenville and Bernard Wasserstein, ed., *The Major International Treaties since 1945: A History and Guide with Texts*, London: Methuen, 1987.

War Powers Act, 1973

The last time Congress declared war was in December 1941 after Japan attacked Pearl Harbor. Frustrated over the conduct of the Vietnam War, Congress passed the War Powers Act November 7, 1973 (over the October 24 veto by President Richard M. Nixon) that restricted the right of the president to use his powers as commander in chief to introduce U.S. armed forces into foreign wars or situations abroad where hostilities were imminent. The act required the president to consult with Congress before and during any direct involvement of U.S. forces in hostilities abroad. It limited the commitment of armed forces by the president to 60 days (plus a possible 30-day extension) unless Congress declared war or authorized the continued use of forces in the situation. In the absence of a declaration of war or statutory authorization, Congress was given the right, by adopting a concurrent resolution, to order the removal of such forces. Every president, including Nixon, has considered the War Powers Act an unconstitutional infringement on the powers of president as commander in chief. However, presidents have received confirming resolutions when they have mobilized a major commitment of troops, as with the Gulf War (1990–91) and war against Iraq (2002).

(excerpt)

Concerning the war powers of Congress and the President.

Resolved by the Senate and House of Representatives of the United States of America in Congress assembled,

Short Title

Section 1. This joint resolution may be cited as the "War Powers Resolution."

Purpose and Policy

Sec. 2. (a) It is the purpose of this joint resolution to fulfill the intent of the framers of the Constitution of the United States and insure that the collective judgment of both the Congress and the President will apply to the introduction of United States Armed Forces into hostilities, or into situations where imminent involvement in hostilities is clearly indicated by the circumstances, and to the continued use of such forces in hostilities or in such situations.

(b) Under article I, section 8, of the Constitution, it is specifically provided that the Congress shall have the power to make all laws necessary and proper for carrying into execution, not only its own powers but also all other powers vested by the Constitution in the Government of the United States, or in any department or officer thereof.

(c) The constitutional powers of the President as Commander-in-Chief to introduce United States Armed Forces into hostilities, or into situations where imminent involvement in hostilities is clearly indicated by the circumstances, are exercised only pursuant to (1) a declaration of war, (2) specific statutory authorization, or (3) a national emergency created by attack upon the United States, its territories or possessions, or its armed forces.

Consultation

Sec. 3. The President in every possible instance shall consult with Congress before introducing United States Armed Forces into hostilities or into situations where imminent involvement in hostilities is clearly indicated by the circumstances, and after every such introduction shall consult regularly with the Congress until United States Armed Forces are no longer engaged in hostilities or have been removed from such situations.

Reporting

Sec. 4. (a) In the absence of a declaration of war, in any case in which United States Armed Forces are introduced—

(1) into hostilities or into situations where imminent involvement in hostilities is clearly indicated by the circumstances;

(2) into the territory, airspace or waters of a foreign nation, while equipped for combat, except for deployments which relate solely to supply, replacement, repair, or training of such forces; or

(3) in numbers which substantially enlarge United States Armed Forces equipped for combat already located in a foreign nation; the President shall submit within 48 hours to the Speaker of the House of Representatives and to the President pro tempore of the Senate a report, in writing, setting forth—

(A) the circumstances necessitating the introduction of United States Armed Forces;

(B) the constitutional and legislative authority under which such introduction took place; and

(C) the estimated scope and duration of the hostilities or involvement.

(b) The President shall provide such other information as the Congress may request in the fulfillment of its constitutional responsibilities with respect to committing the Nation to war and to the use of United States Armed Forces abroad.

(c) Whenever United States Armed Forces are introduced into hostilities or into any situation described in subsection (a) of this section, the President shall, so long as such armed forces continue to be engaged in such hostilities or situation, report to the Congress periodically on the status of such hostilities or situations as well as on the scope and duration of such hostilities or situation, but in no event shall he report to the Congress less often than once every six months.

Congressional Action

Sec. 5. (a) Each report submitted pursuant to section 4(a)(1) shall be transmitted to the Speaker of the House of Representatives and to the President pro tempore of the Senate on the same calendar day. Each report so transmitted shall be referred to the Committee on Foreign Affairs on the House of Representatives and to the Committee on Foreign Relations of the Senate for appropriate action. If, when the report is transmitted, the Congress has adjourned sine die or has adjourned for any period in excess of three calendar days, the Speaker of the House of Representatives and the President pro tempore of the Senate, if they deem it advisable (or if petitioned by at least 30 percent of the membership of their respective Houses) shall jointly request the President to convene Congress in order that it may consider the report and take appropriate action pursuant to this section.

(b) Within sixty calendar days after a report is submitted or is required to be submitted pursuant to section 4(a)(1), whichever is earlier, the President shall terminate any use of United States Armed Forces with respect to which such report was submitted (or required to be submitted), unless the Congress (1) has declared war or has enacted a specific authorization for such use of United States Armed Forces, (2) has extended by law such sixty-day period, or (3) is physically unable to meet as a result of an armed attack upon the United States. Such sixty-day period shall be extended for not more than an additional thirty days if the President determines and certifies to the Congress in writing that unavoidable military necessity respecting the safety of United States Armed Forces requires the continued use of such armed forces in the course of bringing about a prompt removal of such forces.

(c) Notwithstanding subsection (b), at any time that United States Armed Forces are engaged in hostilities outside the territory of the United States, its possessions and territories without a declaration of war or specific statutory authorization, such forces shall be removed by the President if the Congress so directs by concurrent resolution.

Source:
Statutes st Large, Vol. 87, pp. 555–559.

Domestic Policies after World War II

Harry S. Truman, Statement by the President Regarding the Loyalty Program, 1947

President Harry S. Truman used Executive Order (EO) 9835, March 21, 1947, to answer allegations that the U.S. government harbored Communists by tightening the federal government's loyalty procedures. Disloyalty was defined to include espionage, sabotage, disclosure of confidential documents, and "membership in, affiliation with or sympathetic association with" organizations that the attorney general (AG) designated as totalitarian, fascist, communist, subversive, or advocating force, violence, or the use of unconstitutional means to alter the government.

Previously a signed oath asserting that a federal employee had not belonged to an organization advocating violent overthrow of the government was considered sufficient proof of loyalty. In addition to an oath and affidavit, the new program required loyalty investigations by the FBI at an agency's request for all civilian employees of the executive branch and all its job applicants on whom "derogatory" information was alleged. After the investigation, the decision whether to keep or dismiss an employee was the responsibility of the agency. The EO created agency review boards and a policy-making Loyalty Review Board (LRB) within the Civil Service Commission. Regional boards and the LRB could hear disputes, with the LRB decision being final. (Contrary to popular belief, only the requesting agency or a review board, not the FBI, had the power to "clear" someone.) In this statement, delivered November 14, 1947, Truman outlined how he envisioned the loyalty program would work.

Approximately 6,000 individuals resigned their positions rather than undergo a loyalty check, but only about 1,200 of some 5 million civilian and military federal personnel actually lost their jobs as a result of the program. The numbers, however, do not account for the chilling effect the program may have had on potential applicants. Although highly criticized at the time by civil libertarians for implicating "innocent" people, virtually all individuals who came before a loyalty board did so because they had some connection to a suspect organization.

At least during its earliest years, however, the program did not result in automatic expulsions, even if an employee had associations with one or more of the communist, fascist, and other groups prohibited by the AG's List of Subversive Organizations.

Truman's program was criticized for not touching those who were loyal but still posed a security risk. Therefore, President Dwight D. Eisenhower, in EO 10450, made security rather than loyalty, the determination of a person's government employment. Many of those dismissed under its provisions had criminal records or engaged in conduct considered questionable in the 1950s, such as alcoholism or homosexuality, rather than disloyalty.

Prescribing Procedures for the Administration of an Employees Loyalty Program in the Executive Branch of the Government

Whereas each employee of the Government of the United States is endowed with a measure of trusteeship over the democratic processes which are the heart and sinew of the United States; and

Whereas it is of vital importance that persons employed in the Federal service be of complete and unswerving loyalty to the United States; and

Whereas, although the loyalty of by far the overwhelming majority of all Government employees is beyond question, the presence within the Government service of any disloyal or subversive person constitutes a threat to our democratic processes; and

Whereas maximum protection must be afforded the United States against infiltration of disloyal persons into the ranks of its employees, and equal protection from unfounded accusations of disloyalty must be afforded the loyal employees of the Government:

Now, Therefore, by virtue of the authority vested in me by the Constitution and statutes of the United States, including the Civil Service Act of 1883 (22 Stat. 403), as amended, and section 9A of the act approved August 2, 1939 (18 U.S.C. 61i), and as President and Chief Executive of the United States, it is hereby, in the interest of the internal management of the Government, ordered as follows:

Part I—Investigation of Applicants

1. There shall be a loyalty investigation of every person entering the civilian employment of any department or agency of the executive branch of the Federal Government.

a. Investigations of persons entering the competitive service shall be conducted by the Civil Service Commission, except in such cases as are covered by a special agreement between the Commission and any given department or agency.

b. Investigations of persons other than those entering the competitive service shall be conducted by the employing department or agency. Departments and agencies without investigative organizations shall utilize the investigative facilities of the Civil Service Commission.

2. The investigations of persons entering the employ of the executive branch may be conducted after any such person enters upon actual employment therein, but in any such case the appointment of such person shall be conditioned upon a favorable determination with respect to his loyalty.

a. Investigations of persons entering the competitive service shall be conducted as expeditiously as possible; provided, however, that if any such investigation is not completed within 18 months from the date on which a person enters actual employment, the condition that his employment is subject to investigation shall expire, except in a case in which the Civil Service Commission has made an initial adjudication of disloyalty and the case continues to be active by reason of an appeal, and it shall then be the responsibility of the employing department or agency to conclude such investigation and make a final determination concerning the loyalty of such person.

3. An investigation shall be made of all applicants at all available pertinent sources of information and shall include reference to:

a. Federal Bureau of Investigation files.

b. Civil Service Commission files.

c. Military and naval intelligence files.

d. The files of any other appropriate government investigative or intelligence agency.

e. House Committee on un-American Activities files.

f. Local law-enforcement files at the place of residence and employment of the applicant, including municipal, county, and State law-enforcement files.

g. Schools and colleges attended by applicant.

h. Former employers of applicant.

i. References given by applicant.

j. Any other appropriate source.

4. Whenever derogatory information with respect to loyalty of an applicant is revealed a full investigation shall be conducted. A full field investigation shall also be conducted of those applicants, or of applicants for particular positions, as may be designated by the head of the employing department or agency, such designations to be based on the determination by any such head of the best interests of national security.

Part II—Investigation of Employees

1. The head of each department and agency in the executive branch of the Government shall be personally responsible for an effective program to assure that disloyal civilian officers or employees are not retained in employment in his department or agency.

a. He shall be responsible for prescribing and supervising the loyalty determination procedures of his department or agency, in accordance with the provisions of this order, which shall be considered as providing minimum requirements.

b. The head of a department or agency which does not have an investigative organization shall utilize the investigative facilities of the Civil Service Commission.

2. The head of each department and agency shall appoint one or more loyalty boards, each composed of not less than three representatives of the department or agency concerned, for the purpose of hearing loyalty cases arising within such department or agency and making recommendations with respect to the removal of any officer or employee of such department or agency on grounds relating to loyalty, and he shall prescribe regulations for the conduct of the proceedings before such boards.

a. An officer or employee who is charged with being disloyal shall have a right to an administrative hearing before a loyalty board in the employing department or agency. He may appear before such board personally, accompanied by counsel or representative of his own choosing, and present evidence on his own behalf, through witnesses or by affidavit.

b. The officer or employee shall be served with a written notice of such hearing in sufficient time, and shall be informed therein of the nature of the charges against him in sufficient detail, so that he will be enabled to prepare his defense. The charges shall be stated as specifically and completely as, in the discretion of the employing department or agency, security considerations permit, and the officer or employee shall be informed in the notice (1) of his right to reply to such charges in writing within a specified reasonable period of time, (2) of his right to an administrative hearing on such charges before a loyalty board, and (3) of his right to appear before such board personally, to be accompanied by counsel or representative of his own choosing, and to present evidence on his behalf, through witness or by affidavit.

3. A recommendation of removal by a loyalty board shall be subject to appeal by the officer or employee affected, prior to his removal, to the head of the employing department or agency or to such person or persons as may be designated by such head, under such regulations as may be prescribed by him, and the decision of the department or agency concerned shall be subject to appeal to the Civil Service Commission's Loyalty Review Board, hereinafter provided for, for an advisory recommendation.

4. The rights of hearing, notice thereof, and appeal therefrom shall be accorded to every officer or employee prior to his removal on grounds of disloyal'y, irrespective of tenure, or of manner, method, or nature of appointment, but the head of the employing department or agency may suspend any officer or employee at any time pending a determination with respect to loyalty.

5. The loyalty boards of the various departments and agencies shall furnish to the Loyalty Review Board, hereinafter provided for, such reports as may be requested concerning the operation of the loyalty program in any such department or agency.

Part III—Responsibilities of Civil Service Commission

1. There shall be established in the Civil Service Commission a Loyalty Review Board of not less than three impartial persons, the members of which shall be officers or employees of the Commission.

a. The Board shall have authority to review cases involving persons recommended for dismissal on grounds relating to loyalty by the loyalty board of any department or agency and to make advisory recommendations thereon to the head of the employing department or agency. Such cases may be referred to the Board either by the employing department or agency, or by the officer or employee concerned.

b. The Board shall make rules and regulations, not inconsistent with the provisions of this order, deemed necessary to implement statutes and Executive orders relating to employee loyalty.

c. The Loyalty Review Board shall also:

(1) Advise all departments and agencies on all problems relating to employee loyalty.

(2) Disseminate information pertinent to employee loyalty programs.

(3) Coordinate the employee loyalty policies and procedures of the several departments and agencies.

(4) Make reports and submit recommendations to the Civil Service Commission for transmission to the President from time to time as may be necessary to the maintenance of the employee loyalty program.

2. There shall also be established and maintained in the Civil Service Commission a central master index covering all persons on whom loyalty investigations have been made by any department or agency since September 1, 1939. Such master index shall contain the name of each person investigated, adequate identifying information concerning each such person, and a reference to each department and agency which has conducted a loyalty investigation concerning the person involved.

a. All executive departments and agencies are directed to furnish to the Civil Service Commission all information appropriate for the establishment and maintenance of the central master index.

b. The reports and other investigative material and information developed by the investigating department or agency shall be retained by such department or agency in each case.

3. The loyalty Review Board shall currently be furnished by the Department of Justice the name of each

foreign or domestic organization, association, movement, group or combination of persons which the Attorney General, after appropriate investigation and determination, designates as totalitarian, fascist, communist or subversive, or as having adopted a policy of advocating or approving the commission of acts of force or violence to deny others their rights under the Constitution of the United States, or as seeking to alter the form of government of the United States by unconstitutional means.

a. The Loyalty Review Board shall disseminate such information to all departments and agencies.

Part IV—Security Measures in Investigations

1. At the request of the head of any department or agency of the executive branch an investigative agency shall make available to such head, personally, all investigative material and information collected by the investigative agency concerning any employee or prospective employee of the requesting department or agency, or shall make such material and information available to any officer or officers designated by such head and approved by the investigative agency.

2. Notwithstanding the foregoing requirement, however, the investigative agency may refuse to disclose the names of confidential informants, provided it furnishes sufficient information about such informants on the basis of which the requesting department or agency can make an adequate evaluation of the information furnished by them, and provided it advises the requesting department or agency in writing that it is essential to the protection of the informants or to the investigation of other cases that the identity of the informants not be revealed. Investigative agencies shall not use this discretion to decline to reveal sources of information where such action is not essential.

3. Each department and agency of the executive branch should develop and maintain, for the collection and analysis of information relating to the loyalty of its employees and prospective employees, a staff specially trained in security techniques, and an effective security control system for protecting such information generally and for protecting confidential sources of such information particularly.

Part V—Standards

1. The standard for the refusal of employment or the removal from employment in an executive department or agency on grounds relating to loyalty shall be that, on all the evidence, reasonable grounds exist for belief that the person involved is disloyal to the Government of the United States.

2. Activities and associations of an applicant or employee which may be considered in connection with the determination of disloyalty may include one or more of the following:

a. Sabotage, espionage, or attempts or preparations therefor, or knowingly associating with spies or saboteurs;

b. Treason or sedition or advocacy thereof;

c. Advocacy of revolution or force or violence to alter the constitutional form of government of the United States;

d. Intentional, unauthorized disclosure to any person, under circumstances which may indicate disloyalty to the United States, of documents or information of a confidential or non-public character obtained by the person making the disclosure as a result of his employment by the Government of the United States;

e. Performing or attempting to perform his duties, or otherwise acting, so as to serve the interests of another government in preference to the interests of the United States.

f. Membership in, affiliation with or sympathetic association with any foreign or domestic organization, association, movement, group or combination of persons, designated by the Attorney General as totalitarian, fascist, communist, or subversive, or as having adopted a policy of advocating or approving the commission of acts of force or violence to deny other persons their rights under the Constitution of the United States, or as seeking to alter the form of government of the United States by unconstitutional means.

Part VI—Miscellaneous

1. Each department and agency of the executive branch, to the extent that it has not already done so, shall submit, to the Federal Bureau of Investigation of the Department of Justice, either directly or through the Civil Service Commission, the names (and such other necessary identifying material as the Federal Bureau of Investigation may require) of all of its incumbent employees.

a. The Federal Bureau of Investigation shall check such names against its records of persons concerning whom there is substantial evidence of being within the purview of paragraph 2 of Part V hereof, and shall notify each department and agency of such information.

b. Upon receipt of the above-mentioned information from the Federal Bureau of Investigation, each department and agency shall make, or cause to be made by the Civil Service Commission, such investigation of those employees as the head of the department or agency shall deem advisable.

2. The Security Advisory Board of the State-War-Navy Coordinating Committee shall draft rules applicable to the handling and transmission of confidential documents and other documents and information which should not be publicly disclosed, and upon approval by the President

such rules shall constitute the minimum standards for the handling and transmission of such documents and information, and shall be applicable to all departments and agencies of the executive branch.

3. The provisions of this order shall not be applicable to persons summarily removed under the provisions of section 3 of the act of December 17, 1942, 56 Stat. 1053, of the act of July 5, 1946, 60 Stat. 453, or of any other statute conferring the power of summary removal.

4. The Secretary of War and the Secretary of the Navy, and the Secretary of the Treasury with respect to the Coast Guard, are hereby directed to continue to enforce and maintain the highest standards of loyalty within the armed services, pursuant to the applicable statutes, the Articles of War, and the Articles for the Government of the Navy.

5. This order shall be effective immediately, but compliance with such of its provisions as require the expenditure of funds shall be deferred pending the appropriation of such funds.

6. Executive Order No. 9300 of February 5, 1943, is hereby revoked.

Harry S. Truman
The White House, March 21, 1947.

Source:

Harry S. Truman Presidential Library, *Papers of Harry S. Truman,* Official File, Box 102, FBI.

J. Edgar Hoover, Statement before the Committee on Un-American Activities, House of Representatives, 1947

The House Committee on Un-American Activities (HUAC) was one of the most aggressive anticommunist governmental institutions. Federal Bureau of Investigation (FBI) director J. Edgar Hoover outlined his vision of the internal Communist menace to this committee March 26, 1947. From the Gangster era in the 1930s through the capture of German spies and saboteurs in World War II and into the cold war, Hoover was considered an American hero and his pronouncements were influential.

In his testimony, Hoover outlined the FBI's previous role in countering German subversion and espionage and its current role in combating communism. The excerpts here include the reasons why he contends that communism threatens American security and how to recognize communists, their sympathizers, and their propaganda. The statement incorporates arguments Hoover will use the rest of his career to support continued vigilance against American "Marxist-Leninism." It concludes with a refrain that echoes in Congress and in the courts: "Communism . . . is not a political Party. It is . . . an evil and malignant way of life."

A technique Communists often used with congressional committees was a refusal to answer questions on the grounds of the Fifth Amendment. In *Ullmann v. United States* (350 U.S. 452) decided March 26, 1956, the U.S. Supreme Court upheld the Immunity Act of 1954, under which witnesses could be forced to testify in national security cases—in courts and grand juries, as well as congressional committees—by granting them immunity from prosecution for criminal actions they might admit. Ullmann, pleading the Fifth Amendment, had refused to testify about an espionage ring when questioned by a grand jury and a congressional committee. He was later granted immunity but argued that he could lose his job, his union membership, and eligibility for a passport, and could be subjected to public censure, if he admitted any subversive activity. The Supreme Court ruled that the Fifth Amendment did protect against such noncriminal penalties.

(excerpts)

March 26, 1947

My feelings concerning the Communist Party of the United States are well known. I have not hesitated over the years to express my concern and apprehension. As a consequence its professional smear brigades have conducted a relentless assault against the FBI. You who have been members of this committee also know the fury with which the party, its sympathizers and fellow travelers can launch an assault. I do not mind such attacks. What has been disillusioning is the manner in which they have been able to enlist support often from apparently well-meaning but thoroughly duped persons. . . .

The communist movement in the United States began to manifest itself in 1919. Since then it has changed its name and its party line whenever expedient and tactical. But always it comes back to fundamentals and bills itself as the party of Marxism-Leninism. As such, it stands for the destruction of our American form of government; it stands for the destruction of American democracy; it stands for the destruction of free enterprise; and it stands for the creation of a "Soviet of the United States" and ultimate world revolution. . . .

The communist, once he is fully trained and indoctrinated, realizes that he can create his order in the United States only by "bloody revolution." Their chief textbook, "The History of the Communist Party of the Soviet Union," is used as a basis for planning their revolution. Their tactics require that to be successful they must have:

1. The will and sympathy of the people.
2. Military aid and assistance.
3. Plenty of guns and ammunition.

4. A program for extermination of the police as they are the most important enemy and are termed "trained fascists."

5. Seizure of all communications, buses, railroads, radio stations, and other forms of communications and transportation. . . .

One thing is certain. The American progress which all good citizens seek, such as old-age security, houses for veterans, child assistance, and a host of others, is being adopted as window dressing by the communists to conceal their true aims and entrap gullible followers. . . .

The mad march of Red fascism is a cause for concern in America. But the deceit, the trickery, and the lies of the American communists are catching up with them. Whenever the spotlight of truth is focused upon them they cry, "Red-baiting." Now that their aims and objectives are being exposed, they are creating a Committee for the Constitutional Rights of Communists, and are feverishly working to build up what they term a quarter-million-dollar defense fund to place ads in papers, to publish pamphlets, to buy radio time. They know that their backs will soon be to the wall. . . .

What is important is the claim of the communists themselves that for every party member there are 10 others ready, willing and able to do the party's work. Herein lies the greatest menace of communism. For these are the people who infiltrate and corrupt various spheres of American life. So rather than the size of the Communist Party, the way to weigh its true importance is by testing its influence, its ability to infiltrate. . . .

The communists have developed one of the greatest propaganda machines the world has ever known. They have been able to penetrate and infiltrate many respectable public opinion mediums. They capitalize upon ill-founded charges associating known honest progressive liberals with left-wing causes. I have always entertained the view that there are few appellations more degrading than "communist" and hence it should be reserved for those justly deserving the degradation.

The communist propaganda technique is designed to promote emotional response with the hope that the victim will be attracted by what he is told the communist way of life holds in store for him. The objective, of course, is to develop discontent and hasten the day when the communists can gather sufficient support and following to overthrow the American way of life. . . .

Communists and their followers are prolific letter writers, and some of the more energetic ones follow the practice of directing numerous letters of protest to editors but signing a different name to each. Members of Congress are well aware of communists starting their pressure campaigns by an avalanche of mail which follows the party line. . . .

The American communists launched a furtive attack on Hollywood in 1935 by the issuance of a directive calling for a concentration in Hollywood. The orders called for action on two fronts: One, an effort to infiltrate the labor unions; two, infiltrate the so-called intellectual and creative fields.

In movie circles, communists developed an effective defense a few years ago in meeting criticism. They would counter with the question "After all, what is the matter with communism?" It was effective because many persons did not possess adequate knowledge of the subject to give an intelligent answer. . . .

I feel that this committee could render a great service to the nation through its power of exposure in quickly spotlighting existing front organizations and those which will be created in the future. There are easy tests to establish the real character of such organizations:

1. Does the group espouse the cause of Americanism or the cause of Soviet Russia?

2. Does the organization feature as speakers at its meeting known communists, sympathizers, or fellow travelers?

3. Does the organization shift when the party line shifts?

4. Does the organization sponsor causes, campaigns, literature, petitions, or other activities sponsored by the party or other front organizations?

5. Is the organization used as a sounding board by or is it endorsed by communist-controlled labor unions?

6. Does its literature follow the communist line or is it printed by the communist press?

7. Does the organization receive consistent favorable mention in the communist publications?

8. Does the organization present itself to be nonpartisan yet engage in political activities and consistently advocate causes favored by the communists?

9. Does the organization denounce American and British foreign policy while always lauding Soviet policy?

10. Does the organization utilize communist "double-talk" by referring to Soviet dominated countries as democracies, complaining that the United States is imperialistic and constantly denouncing monopoly-capital?

11. Have outstanding leaders in public life openly renounced affiliation with the organization?

12. Does the organization, if espousing liberal progressive causes, attract well-known honest patriotic liberals or does it denounce well-known liberals?

13. Does the organization have a consistent record of supporting the American viewpoint over the years?

14. Does the organization consider matters now directly related to its avowed purposes and objectives?

The Communist Party of the United States is a fifth column if there ever was one. It is far better organized than were the Nazis in occupied countries prior to their capitulation. They are seeking to weaken America just as they did in their era of obstruction when they were aligned with the Nazis. Their goal is the overthrow of our government. There is no doubt as to where a real communist's loyalty rests. Their allegiance is to Russia, not the United States. . . .

What can we do? And what should be our course of action? The best antidote to communism is vigorous, intelligent, old-fashioned Americanism, with eternal vigilance. I do not favor any course of action which would give the communists cause to portray and pity themselves as martyrs. I do favor unrelenting prosecution wherever they are found to be violating our country's laws.

As Americans, our most effective defense is a workable democracy that guarantees and preserves our cherished freedoms.

I would have no fears if more Americans possessed the zeal, the fervor, the persistence and the industry to learn about this menace of Red fascism. I do fear for the liberal and progressive who has been hoodwinked and duped into joining hands with the communists. I confess to a real apprehension so long as communists are able to secure ministers of the gospel to promote their evil work and espouse a cause that is alien to the religion of Christ and Judaism. I do fear so long as school boards and parents tolerate conditions whereby communists and fellow travelers, under the guise of academic freedom, can teach our youth a way of life that eventually will destroy the sanctity of the home, that undermines faith in God, that causes them to scorn respect for constituted authority and sabotage our revered Constitution.

I do fear so long as American labor groups are infiltrated, dominated or saturated with the virus of communism. I do fear the palliation and weasel-worded gestures against communism indulged in by some of our labor leaders who should know better, but who have become pawns in the hands of sinister but astute manipulations for the communist cause.

I fear for ignorance on the part of all our people who may take the poisonous pills of communist propaganda.

Source:

National Archives. Also available on-line at CNN Interactive. URL: http://edition.cnn.com/SPECIALS/cold.war/episodes/06/documents/hoover/. Accessed November 2003.

Internal Security Act, 1950

Also known as the McCarran Act and the Subversive Activities Control Act, this legislation was passed September 23, 1950, over the veto of President Harry S. Truman. Congress intended it to effectively destroy the Communist Party in the United States without actually outlawing it. Sponsored by Senator Patrick A. McCarran of Nevada, the act required all Communist and Communist-front organizations to register with the attorney general. It prohibited Communists from working in defense plants and prevented them from acquiring passports. It allowed the president, during national emergencies, to authorize the seizure and detention of persons who might engage in espionage or sabotage and established a Subversive Activities Control Board to determine who "knowingly" acted in behalf of a foreign individual or entity to establish "a totalitarian dictatorship."

The act was widely criticized as a violation of civil liberties, most prominently by the president in his veto message. President Truman felt so strongly that the McCarran Act would be detrimental to both countersubversion and civil rights that he had copies of his veto message typed on one side of the page only and placed on the desk of every member of Congress. He noted that rather than hinder any dangerous American Communists, who would lie to protect themselves, it was more likely to curb American progressives and dissidents entitled to express their opinions under the First Amendment. The Korean War had been going on for over two months, and the president noted that "when our young men are fighting for freedom . . . it would be tragic to advance the objectives of communism in this country, as this bill would do." Ultimately, the courts overturned so many of its provisions that by the end of the 1950s it was virtually defunct, although the detention provisions remained until Congress removed them in 1971.

On August 24, 1954, Congress strengthened the Internal Security Act by, for the first time, outlawing the Communist Party in the Communist Control Act. The act declared the party an "instrumentality of conspiracy" to overthrow the U.S. government and a clear and present danger to the nation's security. In addition, it provided severe penalties for Communists who did not register, refused collective bargaining powers to Communist-controlled unions, and removed the legal "rights, privileges, and immunities" of the party. Though criticized as repressive, the act was promoted by liberal anticommunist Democrats such as Minnesota senator Hubert H. Humphrey as well as conservatives. This act, like the Internal Security Act, failed to produce any effective prosecutions. In *Pennsylvania v. Nelson* (350 U.S. 497 [1956]) the Supreme Court declared that it and the Smith Act precluded the states from prosecuting anyone for advocating overthrow of the federal government although they might be liable for advocating overthrow of state governments.

(excerpt)

An Act

To protect the United States against certain un-American and subversive activities by requiring registration of Communist organizations, and for other purposes.

Be it enacted by the Senate and House of Representatives of the United States of America in Congress assembled, That this Act may be cited as the "Internal Security Act of 1950."

Title I—Subversive Activities Control

Section 1. (a) This title may be cited as the "Subversive Activities Control Act of 1950."

(b) Nothing in this Act shall be construed to authorize, require, or establish military or civilian censorship or in any way to limit or infringe upon freedom of the press or of speech as guaranteed by the Constitution of the United States and no regulation shall be promulgated hereunder having that effect.

Necessity for Legislation

Sec. 2. As a result of evidence adduced before various committees of the Senate and House of Representatives, the Congress hereby finds that—

(1) There exists a world Communist movement which, in its origins, its development, and its present practice, is a world-wide revolutionary movement whose purpose it is, by treachery, deceit, infiltration into other groups (governmental and otherwise), espionage, sabotage, terrorism, and any other means deemed necessary, to establish a Communist totalitarian dictatorship in the countries throughout the world through the medium of a world-wide Communist organization.

(2) The establishment of a totalitarian dictatorship in any country results in the suppression of all opposition to the party in power, the subordination of the rights of individuals to the state, the denial of fundamental rights and liberties which are characteristic of a representative form of government, such as freedom of speech, of the press, of assembly, and of religious worship, and results in the maintenance of control over the people through fear, terrorism, and brutality.

(3) The system of government known as a totalitarian dictatorship is characterized by the existence of a single political party, organized on a dictatorial basis, and by substantial identity between such party and its policies and the government and governmental policies of the country in which it exists.

(4) The direction and control of the world Communist movement is vested in and exercised by the Communist dictatorship of a foreign country.

(5) The Communist dictatorship of such foreign country, in exercising such direction and control and in furthering the purposes of the world Communist movement, establishes or causes the establishment of, and utilizes, in various countries, action organizations which are not free and independent organizations, but are sections of a world-wide Communist organization and are controlled, directed, and subject to the discipline of the Communist dictatorship of such foreign country.

(6) The Communist action organizations so established and utilized in various countries, acting under such control, direction, and discipline, endeavor to carry out the objectives of the world Communist movement by bringing about the overthrow of existing governments by any available means, including force if necessary, and setting up Communist totalitarian dictatorships which will be subservient to the most powerful existing Communist totalitarian dictatorship. Although such organizations usually designate themselves as political parties, they are in fact constituent elements of the world-wide Communist movement and promote the objectives of such movement by conspiratorial and coercive tactics, instead of through the democratic processes of a free elective system or through the freedom-preserving means employed by a political party which operates as an agency by which people govern themselves.

(7) In carrying on the activities referred to in paragraph (6), such Communist organizations in various countries are organized on a secret, conspiratorial basis and operate to a substantial extent through organizations, commonly known as "Communist fronts," which in most instances are created and maintained, or used, in such manner as to conceal the facts as to their true character and purposes and their membership. One result of this method of operation is that such affiliated organizations are able to obtain financial and other support from persons who would not extend such support if they knew the true purposes of, and the actual nature of the control and influence exerted upon, such "Communist fronts."

(8) Due to the nature and scope of the world Communist movement, with the existence of affiliated constituent elements working toward common objectives in various countries of the world, travel of Communist members, representatives, and agents from country to country facilitates communication and is prerequisite for the carrying on of activities to further the purposes of the Communist movement.

(9) In the United States those individuals who knowingly and willfully participate in the world Communist movement, when they so participate, in effect repudiate their allegiance to the United States, and in effect transfer their allegiance to the foreign country in which is vested the direction and control of the world Communist movement.

(10) In pursuance of communism's stated objectives, the most powerful existing Communist dictatorship has, by the methods referred to above, already caused the estab-

lishment in numerous foreign countries of Communist totalitarian dictatorships, and threatens to establish similar dictatorships in still other countries.

(11) The agents of communism have devised clever and ruthless espionage and sabotage tactics which are carried out in many instances in form or manner successfully evasive of existing law.

(12) The Communist network in the United States is inspired and controlled in large part by foreign agents who are sent into the United States ostensibly as attaches of foreign legations, affiliates of international organizations, members of trading commissions, and in similar capacities, but who use their diplomatic or semidiplomatic status as a shield behind which to engage in activities prejudicial to the public security.

(13) There are, under our present immigration laws, numerous aliens who have been found to be deportable, many of whom are in the subversive, criminal, or immoral classes who are free to roam the country at will without supervision or control.

(14) One device for infiltration by Communists is by procuring naturalization for disloyal aliens who use their citizenship as a badge for admission into the fabric of our society.

(15) The Communist movement in the United States is an organization numbering thousands of adherents, rigidly and ruthlessly disciplined. Awaiting and seeking to advance a moment when the United States may be so far extended by foreign engagements, so far divided in counsel, or so far in industrial or financial straits, that overthrow of the Government of the United States by force and violence may seem possible of achievement, it seeks converts far and wide by an extensive system of schooling and indoctrination. Such preparations by Communist organizations in other countries have aided in supplanting existing governments. The Communist organization in the United States, pursuing its stated objectives, the recent successes of Communist methods in other countries, and the nature and control of the world Communist movement itself, present a clear and present danger to the security of the United States and to the existence of free American institutions, and make it necessary that Congress, in order to provide for the common defense, to preserve the sovereignty of the United States as an independent nation, and to guarantee to each State a republican form of government, enact appropriate legislation recognizing the existence of such worldwide conspiracy and designed to prevent it from accomplishing its purpose in the United States.

Definitions

Sec. 3. For the purposes of this title—

(1) The term "person" means an individual or an organization.

* * *

(3) The term "Communist-action organization" means—

(a) any organization in the United States (other than a diplomatic representative or mission of a foreign government accredited as such by the Department of State) which (i) is substantially directed, dominated, or controlled by the foreign government or foreign organization controlling the world Communist movement referred to in section 2 of this title, and (ii) operates primarily to advance the objectives of such world Communist movement . . . and

(b) any section, branch, fraction, or cell of any organization defined in subparagraph (a) of this paragraph which has not complied with the registration requirements of this title.

(4) The term "Communist-front organization" means any organization in the United States (other than a Communist-action organization as defined in paragraph (3) of this section) which (A) is substantially directed, dominated, or controlled by a Communist-action organization, and (B) is primarily operated for the purpose of giving aid and support to a Communist-action organization, a Communist foreign government, or the world Communist movement referred to in section 2 of this title.

(5) The term "Communist organization" means a Communist-action organization or a Communist-front organization.

(6) The term "to contribute funds or services" includes the rendering of any personal service and the making of any gift, subscription, loan, advance, or deposit, of money or of anything of value, and also the making of any contract, promise, or agreement to contribute funds or services, whether or not legally enforcible.

(7) The term "facility" means any plant, factory or other manufacturing, producing or service establishment, airport, airport facility, vessel, pier, water-front facility, mine, railroad, public utility, laboratory, station, or other establishment or facility, or any part, division, or department of any of the foregoing. The term "defense facility" means any facility designated and proclaimed by the Secretary of Defense pursuant to section 5(b) of this title and included on the list published and currently in effect under such subsection, and which is in compliance with the provisions of such subsection respecting the posting of notice of such designation.

(8) The term "publication" means any circular, newspaper, periodical, pamphlet, book, letter, post card, leaflet, or other publication.

* * *

(13) The term "advocates" includes advises, recommends, furthers by overt act, and admits belief in; and the

giving, loaning, or promising of support or of money or anything of value to be used for advocating any doctrine shall be deemed to constitute the advocating of such doctrine.

(14) The term "world communism" means a revolutionary movement, the purpose of which is to establish eventually a Communist totalitarian dictatorship in any or all the countries of the world through the medium of an internationally coordinated Communist movement.

(15) The terms "totalitarian dictatorship" and "totalitarianism" mean and refer to systems of government not representative in fact, characterized by (A) the existence of a single political party, organized on a dictatorial basis, with so close an identity between such party and its policies and the governmental policies of the country in which it exists, that the party and the government constitute an indistinguishable unit, and (B) the forcible suppression of opposition to such party.

(16) The term "doctrine" includes, but is not limited to, policies, practices, purposes, aims, or procedures.

(17) The giving, loaning, or promising of support or of money or any other thing of value for any purpose to any organization shall be conclusively presumed to constitute affiliation therewith; but nothing in this paragraph shall be construed as an exclusive definition of affiliation.

(18) "Advocating the economic, international, and governmental doctrines of world communism" means advocating the establishment of a totalitarian Communist dictatorship in any or all of the countries of the world through the medium of an internationally coordinated Communist movement.

(19) "Advocating the economic and governmental doctrines of any other form of totalitarianism" means advocating the establishment of totalitarianism (other than world communism) and includes, but is not limited to, advocating the economic and governmental doctrines of fascism and nazism.

Certain Prohibited Acts

Sec. 4. (a) It shall be unlawful for any person knowingly to combine, conspire, or agree, with any other person to perform any act which would substantially contribute to the establishment within the United States of a totalitarian dictatorship, as defined in paragraph (15) of section 3 of this title, the direction and control of which is to be vested in, or exercised by or under the domination or control of, any foreign government, foreign organization, or foreign individual: Provided, however, That this subsection shall not apply to the proposal of a constitutional amendment.

(b) It shall be unlawful for any officer or employee of the United States or of any department or agency thereof, or of any corporation the stock of which is owned in whole or in major part by the United States or any department or agency thereof, to communicate in any manner or by any means, to any other person whom such officer or employee knows or has reason to believe to be an agent or representative of any foreign government or any officer or member of any Communist organization . . . any information of a kind which shall have been classified by the President (or by the head of any such department, agency, or corporation with the approval of the President) as affecting the security of the United States, knowing or having reason to know that such information has been so classified, unless such officer or employees shall have been specifically authorized . . . to make such disclosure of such information.

(c) It shall be unlawful for any agent or representative of any foreign government, or any officer or member of any Communist organization . . . knowingly to obtain or receive, or attempt to obtain or receive, directly or indirectly, from any officer or employee of the United States or of any department or agency thereof or of any corporation the stock of which is owned in whole or in major part by the United States or any department or agency thereof, any information of a kind which shall have been classified . . . as affecting the security of the United States, unless special authorization for such communication shall first have been obtained from the head of the department, agency, or corporation having custody of or control over such information.

(d) Any person who violates any provision of this section shall, upon conviction thereof, be punished by a fine . . . or imprisonment for not more than ten years, or by both such fine and such imprisonment, and shall, moreover, be thereafter ineligible to hold any office, or place of honor, profit, or trust created by the Constitution or laws of the United States.

(e) Any person may be prosecuted, tried, and punished for any violation of this section at any time within ten years after the commission of such offence, notwithstanding the provisions of any other statute of limitations: Provided, That if at the time of the commission of the offense such person is an officer or employee of the United States or of any department or agency thereof, or of any corporation the stock of which is owned in whole or in major part by the United States or any department or agency thereof, such person may be prosecuted, tried, and punished for any violation of this section at any time within ten years after such person has ceased to be employed as such officer or employee.

(f) Neither the holding of office nor membership in any Communist organization by any person shall constitute per se a violation of subsection (a) or subsection (c) of this section or of any other criminal statute. The fact of the registration of any person under. . . this title as an officer or member of any Communist organization shall not be received in evidence against such person in any prosecution for any alleged violation of subsection (a) or subsection (c) of this section or for any alleged violation of any other criminal statute.

Employment of Members of Communist Organizations

Sec. 5. (a) When a Communist organization, as defined in paragraph (5) of section 3 of this title, is registered or there is in effect a final order of the Board requiring such organization to register, it shall be unlawful—

(1) For any member of such organization, with knowledge or notice that such organization is so registered or that such order has become final—

(A) in seeking, accepting, or holding any nonelective office or employment under the United States, to conceal or fail to disclose the fact that he is a member of such organization; or

(B) to hold any nonelective office or employment under the United States; or

(C) in seeking, accepting, or holding employment in any defense facility, to conceal or fail to disclose the fact that he is a member of such organization; or

(D) if such organization is a Communist-action organization, to engage in any employment in any defense facility.

(2) For any officer or employee of the United States or of any defense facility, with knowledge or notice that such organization is so registered or that such order has become final—

(A) to contribute funds or services to such organization; or

(B) to advise, counsel or urge any person, with knowledge or notice that such person is a member of such organization, to perform, or to omit to perform, any act if such act or omission would constitute a violation of any provision of subparagraph (1) of this subsection.

(b) The Secretary of Defense is authorized and directed to designate and proclaim, and from time to time revise, a list of facilities . . . with respect to the operation of which he finds and determines that the security of the United States requires the application of the provisions of subsection (a) of this section. The Secretary shall cause such list as designated and proclaimed, or any revision thereof, to be promptly published in the Federal Register. . .

Denial of Passports to Members of Communist Organizations

Sec. 6. (a) When a Communist organization as defined in paragraph (5) of section 3 of this title is registered, or there is in effect a final order of the Board requiring such organization to register, it shall be unlawful for any member of such organization, with knowledge or notice that such organization is so registered or that such order has become final—

(1) to make application for a passport, or the renewal of a passport, to be issued or renewed by or under the authority of the United States; or

(2) to use or attempt to use any such passport.

* * *

Harry S. Truman, Veto of the Internal Security Act, 1950

I return herewith, without my approval, H.R. 9490, the proposed "Internal Security Act of 1950. . ."

* * *

It would actually weaken our existing internal security measures and would seriously hamper the Federal Bureau of Investigation and our other security agencies.

It would help the Communists in their efforts to create dissension and confusion within our borders.

It would help the Communist propagandists throughout the world who are trying to undermine freedom by discrediting as hypocrisy the efforts of the United States on behalf of freedom.

Specifically, some of the principal objections to the bill are as follows:

1. It would aid potential enemies by requiring the publication of a complete list of vital defense plants, laboratories, and other installations.

2. It would require the Department of Justice and its Federal Bureau of Investigation to waste immense amounts of time and energy attempting to carry out its unworkable registration provisions.

3. It would deprive us of the great assistance of many aliens in intelligence matters.

5. It would put the Government of the United States in the thought-control business.

6. It would make it easier for subversive aliens to become naturalized as United States Citizens.

7. It would make it give Government officials vast powers to harass all of our citizens in the exercise of their right of free speech.

* * *

Fortunately, we already have on the books strong laws, which give us most of the protection we need from the real dangers of treason, espionage, sabotage, and actions looking to the overthrow of our Government by force and violence. Most of the provisions of this bill have no relation to these real dangers.

* * *

Sections 1 through 17 are . . . intended to force Communist organizations to register and to divulge certain information about themselves—information on their officers, their finances, and, in some cases, their membership. These provisions would in practice be ineffective, and would result in obtaining no information about Communists that the FBI and our other security agencies do not already have. But in trying to enforce these sections, we would have to spend a great deal of time, effort, and money–all to no good purpose. Second, these provisions are intended to impose various penalties on Communists and others covered by the terms of the bill. So far as Communists are concerned, all these penalties . . . are already in effect under existing laws and procedures. But the language of the bill is so broad and vague that it might well result in penalizing the legitimate activities of people who are not Communists at all, but loyal citizens.

Thus the net result of these sections of the bill would be: no serious damage to the Communists, must damage to the rest of us. Only the communist movement would gain from such an outcome.

* * *

Sections 100 through 117 of Title II are intended to give the Government power, in the event of invasion, war, or insurrection in the United States in aid of a foreign enemy, to seize and hold persons who could be expected to attempt acts of espionage or sabotage, even though they had as yet committed no crime. It may be that legislation of this type should be on the statute books. But the provisions in H.R. 9490 would very probably prove ineffective to achieve the objective sought, since they would not suspend the write of habeas corpus and under our legal system to detain a man not charged with a crime would raise serious constitutional questions unless the writ of habeas corpus were suspended. . . .

* * *

The idea of requiring Communist organizations to divulge information about themselves. . .is about as practical as requiring thieves to register with the sheriff. Obviously, no such organization as the Communist Party is likely to register voluntarily.

* * *

. . . But under this bill, the Attorney General would have to attempt the . . . difficult task of producing concrete legal evidence [for the Subversive Activities Control Board (SACB)] that men have particular ideas or opinions. This would inevitably require the disclosure of many of the FBI's confidential sources of information and thus would damage our national security.

If [the SACB gave] a favorable decision . . . the Board's decision could be appealed to the courts. The courts would review any questions of law involved, and whether the Board's findings of fact were supported by the preponderance of the evidence.

All these proceedings would require great effort and much time. . . .

* * *

The simple fact is that when the courts at long last found that a particular organization was required to register, all the leaders of the organization would have to do to frustrate the law would be to dissolve the organization and establish a new one with a different name and a new roster of nominal officers. The Communist Party has done this again and again in countries throughout the world. . . .

* * *

. . . To impose these fruitless burdens upon the FBI would divert it from its vital security duties and thus give aid and comfort to the very Communists whom the bill is supposed to control.

Unfortunately, these provisions are not merely ineffective and unworkable. They represent a clear and present danger to our institutions.

. . .The application o the registration requirements to so-called Communist-front organizations can be the greatest danger to freedom of speech, press, and assembly, since the Alien and Sedition Laws of 1798. . . .

. . . The bill would permit such a determination to be based solely upon the extent to which the positions taken or advanced by it from time to time on matters of policy do not deviate from those of the Communist movement.

This provision could easily be used to classify as a Communist-front organization any organization which is advocating a single policy or objective which is also being urged by the Communist Party or by a Communist foreign government. In fact, this may be the intended result, since the bill defines "organization" to include a group of persons permanently or temporarily associated together for joint action on any subject or subjects." Thus, an organization which advocates low-cost housing for sincere humanitarian reasons might be classified as a Communist-front organization because the Communists regularly exploit slum conditions as one of their fifth-column techniques.

* * *

The basic error of these sections is that they move in the direction of suppressing opinion and belief. This would be a very dangerous course to take, not because we have any sympathy for Communsit opinions, but because any governmental stifling of the free expression of opinion is a long step toward totalitarianism.

There is no more fundamental axiom of American freedom than the familiar statement: In a free country, we punish men for the crimes they commit, but never for the opinions they have. And the reason this is so fundamental to freedom is not, as many suppose, that it protects the few unorthodox from suppression by the majority. To permit freedom of expression is primarily for the benefit of the majority because it protects criticism and criticism leads to progress.

We can and we will prevent espionage, sabotage, or other actions endangering our national security. But we would betray our finest traditions if we attempted, as this bill would attempt, to curb the simple expression of opinion. This we should never do, no matter how distasteful the opinion may be to the vast majority of our people. The course proposed by this bill would delight the Communists, for it would make a mockery of the Bill of Rights and of our claims to stand for freedom in the world.

And what kind of effect would these provisions have on the normal expression of political views? Obviously, if this law were on the statute books, the part of prudence would be to avoid saying anything that might be construed by someone as not deviating sufficiently from the current communist propaganda line. And since no one could be sure in advance what views were safe to express, the inevitable tendency would be to express no views on controversial subjects. The result could only be to reduce the vigor and strength of our political life—an outcome that the Communists would happily welcome, but that free men should abhor.

We need not fear the expression of ideas—we do need to fear their suppression.

Our position in the vanguard of freedom rests largely on our demonstration that the free expression of opinion coupled with government by popular consent, leads to national strength and human advancement. Let us not, in cowering and foolish fear, throw away the ideals which are the fundamental basis of our free society.

* * *

This is a time when we must marshal all our resources and all the moral strength of our free system in self-defense against the threat of Communist aggression. We will fail in this, and we will destroy all that we seek to preserve, if we sacrifice the liberties of our citizens in a misguided attempt to achieve national security.

* * *

No consideration of expediency can justify the enactment of such a bill as this, a bill which would so greatly weaken our liberties and give aid and comfort to those who would destroy us. I have, therefore, no alternative but to return this bill without my approval, and I earnestly request the Congress to reconsider its action.

Harry S. Truman

Source:

Statutes at Large, Vol. 68, pp. 987–1031; *Congressional Record,* 81st Cong., 2d Sess., Vol. 96, part 2, 15,629–15,632.

Dennis v. United States, 1951

U.S. Supreme Court decision, issued June 4, 1951, that upheld the provisions of the Smith Alien Registration Act of 1940 prohibiting anyone from advocating the forceful overthrow of the U.S. government. Eleven high-ranking Communist Party leaders had been convicted in New York of conspiring to teach and advocate the violent destruction of the government and conspiring to organize the Communist Party in the United States in order to advance that purpose. No overtly violent acts were charged. In its 6-2 decision, the Supreme Court confirmed the convictions, modifying its previous requirement that the law could prohibit only speech that represented a "clear and present danger." Dissenting opinions argued that the act violated First Amendment guarantees of free speech. Shortly after the Court upheld the Smith Act, the FBI arrested the "second echelon" Communist Party leaders. However, this time when the arrests were appealed, the Court in effect overturned *Dennis* in *Yates v. United States* (355 U.S. 66 [1957]). *Yates* set a standard that was so high it was almost impossible to convict anyone.

Between *Dennis* and *Yates*, on March 3, 1952, the U.S. Supreme Court, in *Adler v. Board of Education* (342 U.S. 485), upheld a New York law requiring the New York Board of Regents to deny employment in the public schools to members of organizations that advocated or taught the doctrine of overthrowing the United States government by force, violence, or any unlawful means. The Board of Regents was instructed to prepare a list of such subversive organizations. Membership in them constituted "prima facie evidence" for disqualification from employment. The 6-2 decision was overturned in *Keyishian v. Board of Regents* in 1967.

Mr. Chief Justice Vinson announced the judgment of the Court and an opinion in which Mr. Justice Reed, Mr. Justice Burton and Mr. Justice Minton join.

Petitioners were indicted in July, 1948, for violation of the conspiracy provisions of the Smith Act, 54 Stat. 671, 18 U.S.C. (1946 ed.) Section 11, during the period of April, 1945, to July, 1948. The pretrial motion to quash the indictment on the grounds, *inter alia,* that the statute was unconstitutional was denied, *United States v. Foster*, D.C., 80 F.Supp. 479, and the case was set for trial on January 17, 1949. A verdict of guilty as to all the petitioners was returned by the jury on October 14, 1949. The Court of Appeals affirmed the convictions. 183 F.2d 201. We granted certiorari, 340 U.S. 863, 71 S.Ct. 91, limited to the following two questions: (1) Whether either Section 2 or Section 3 of the Smith Act, inherently or as construed and applied in the instant case, violates the First Amendment and other provisions of the Bill of Rights; (2) whether either Section 2 or Section 3 of the Act, inherently or as construed and applied in the instant case, violates the First and Fifth Amendments because of indefiniteness.

Sections 2 and 3 of the Smith Act, 54 Stat. 671, 18 U.S.C. (1946 ed.) Sections 10, 11 (see present 18 U.S.C. Section 2385), provide as follows:

"Sec. 2.

"(a) It shall be unlawful for any person—

"(1) to knowingly or willfully advocate, abet, advise, or teach the duty, necessity, desirability, or propriety of overthrowing or destroying any government in the United States by force or violence, or by the assassination of any officer of any such government;

"(2) with intent to cause the overthrow or destruction of any government in the United States, to print, publish, edit, issue, circulate; sell, distribute, or publicly display any written or printed matter advocating, advising, or teaching the duty, necessity, desirability, or propriety of overthrowing or destroying any government in the United States by force or violence;

"(3) to organize or help to organize any society, group, or assembly of persons who teach, advocate, or encourage the overthrow or destruction of any government in the United States by force or violence; or to be or become a member of, or affiliate with, any such society, group, or assembly of persons, knowing the purposes thereof.

"(b) For the purposes of this section, the term 'government in the United States' means the Government of the United States, the government of any State, Territory, or possession of the United States, the government of the District of Columbia, or the government of any political subdivision of any of them.

"Sec. 3. It shall be unlawful for any person to attempt to commit, or to conspire to commit, any of the acts prohibited by the provisions of . . . this title."

The indictment charged the petitioners with wilfully and knowingly conspiring (1) to organize as the Communist Party of the United States of America a society, group and assembly of persons who teach and advocate the overthrow and destruction of the Government of the United States by force and violence, and (2) knowingly and wilfully to advocate and teach the duty and necessity of overthrowing and destroying the Government of the United States by force and violence. The indictment further alleged that Section 2 of the Smith Act proscribes these acts and that any conspiracy to take such action is a violation of Section 3 of the Act.

The trial of the case extended over nine months, six of which were devoted to the taking of evidence, resulting in a record of 16,000 pages. Our limited grant of the writ of certiorari has removed from our consideration any question as to the sufficiency of the evidence to support the jury's determination that petitioners are guilty of the offense charged. Whether on this record petitioners did in fact advocate the overthrow of the Government by force and violence is not before us, and we must base any discussion of this point upon the conclusions stated in the opinion of the Court of Appeals, which treated the issue in great detail. That court held that the record in this case amply supports the necessary finding of the jury that petitioners, the leaders of the Communist Party in this country, were unwilling to work within our framework of democracy, but intended to initiate a violent revolution whenever the propitious occasion appeared. Petitioners dispute the meaning to be drawn from the evidence, contending that the Marxist-Leninist doctrine they advocated taught that force and violence to achieve a Communist form of government in an existing democratic state would be necessary only because the ruling classes of that state would never permit the transformation to be accomplished peacefully, but would use force and violence to defeat any peaceful political and economic gain the Communists could achieve. But the Court of Appeals held that the record supports the following broad conclusions: By virtue of their control over the political apparatus of the Communist Political Association, petitioners were able to transform that organization into the Communist Party; that the policies of the Association were changed from peaceful cooperation with the United States and its economic and political structure to a policy which had existed before the United States and the Soviet Union were fighting a common enemy, namely, a policy which worked for the overthrow of the Government by force and violence; that the Communist Party is a highly disciplined organization, adept at infiltration into strategic positions, use of aliases, and double-meaning language; that the Party is rigidly controlled; that Communists, unlike other political parties, tolerate no dissension from the policy laid down by the guiding forces, but that the approved program is slavishly followed by the members of the Party; that the literature of the Party and the statements and activities of its leaders, petitioners here, advocate, and the general goal of the Party was, during the period in question, to achieve a successful overthrow of the existing order by force and violence.

Source:
Supreme Court Reporter, Vol. 71, pp. 857–909.

U.S. Senate, Censure of Joseph McCarthy, 1954

Action taken by the U.S. Senate to condemn Senator Joseph McCarthy (R-Wis.) on December 2, 1954, for abusing the Senate and the Senate Privileges and Elections Subcommittee. McCarthy became famous after a February 1950 speech in which he charged that the State Department employed 205 members of the Communist Party. (The number changed when he repeated the speech on the Senate floor.) After that, the Wisconsin senator made it his main political objective to investigate alleged Communist Party activities in government. Democrats opposing him were defeated in the 1952 congressional elections, making him virtually invulnerable to public criticism from politicians, including Dwight Eisenhower during his presidential campaign and as president. McCarthy's influence reached its peak when he became chairman of the Senate Permanent Investigating Subcommittee in 1953. Other Senate committees were also looking into Communist penetration into education and the entertainment industry. This period became known as the "McCarthy Era," and the term "McCarthyism," first used by political cartoonist Herblock, is still used today by both the left and right to characterize "witch hunts" against holders of particular political beliefs.

In late 1953, McCarthy's subcommittee began investigating charges of subversive activities at a U.S. army base. The hearings were played live on national television, preempting normal programming and exposing the senator's bullying tactics to an audience estimated at as many as 12 million. His frequent interruptions with "point of order" began to invoke laughter instead of fear. On June 9, 1954, McCarthy named a young lawyer, Fred Fisher, in the firm of army counsel Joseph Welch, as a member of the National Lawyers Guild, an organization that both included and defended Communists. Welch countered: "Little did I dream that you could be so reckless and so cruel as to do an injury to that lad. . . . I fear he shall always bear a scar needlessly inflicted by you." When McCarthy continued to excoriate Fisher, Welch famously dismissed him with "Senator, you have done enough. Have you no sense of decency, sir, at long last? Have you left no sense of decency?" Six months later, no longer afraid of McCarthy personally, his Senate colleagues voted 67 to 22 to censure him, the mildest punishment the Senate could give.

Resolved, That the Senator from Wisconsin, Mr. McCarthy, failed to cooperate with the Subcommittee on Privileges and Elections of the Senate Committee on Rules and Administration in clearing up matters referred to that subcommittee which concerned his conduct as a Senator and affected the honor of the Senate and, instead, repeatedly abused the subcommittee and its members who were trying to carry out assigned duties, thereby obstructing the constitutional processes of the Senate, and that this conduct of the Senator from Wisconsin, Mr. McCarthy, is contrary to senatorial traditions and is hereby condemned.

Sec. 2. The Senator from Wisconsin, Mr. McCarthy, in writing to the chairman of the Select Committee To Study Censure Charges (Mr. Watkins) after the select committee had issued its report and before the report was presented to the Senate charging three members of the select committee with "deliberate deception" and "fraud" for failure to disqualify themselves; in stating to the press on November 4, 1954, that the special Senate session that was to begin November 8, 1954, was a "lynch party"; in repeatedly describing this special Senate session as a "lynch bee" in a nationwide television and radio show on November 7, 1954; in stating to the public press on November 13, 1954, that the chairman of the select committee (Mr. Watkins) was guilty of "the most unusual, most cowardly thing I've heard of" and stating further: "I expected he would be afraid to answer the questions, but didn't think he'd be stupid enough to make a public statement"; and in characterizing the said committee as the "unwitting handmaiden," "involuntary agent," and "attorneys in fact" of the Communist Party and in charging that the said committee in writing its report "imitated Communist methods—that it distorted, misrepresented, and omitted in its effort to manufacture a plausible rationalization" in support of its recommendations to the Senate, which characterizations and charges were contained in a statement released to the press and inserted in the Congressional Record of November 10, 1954, acted contrary to senatorial ethics and tended to bring the Senate into dishonor and disrepute, to obstruct, the constitutional processes of the Senate, and to impair its dignity; and such conduct is hereby condemned.

Source:
Congressional Record, Vol. 100, pt. 12, p. 16,392.

Roth v. United States, 1957

U.S. Supreme Court decision issued June 24, 1957, that upheld the constitutionality of obscenity laws, declaring that obscenity is not a form of free speech protected by the First Amendment, and, therefore, laws prohibiting obscene material were constitutional. The case involved the federal prosecution of American publisher Samuel Roth for sending alleged pornographic and obscene material through the mails. The problem lay in defining exactly what was obscene and differentiating it from nonobscene pornography and erotica. Justice William Brennan's majority decision required obscene material to be totally without redeeming social value. Overturning laws based on excerpts and harm to the most susceptible members of a community (i.e., children), the Court specified that to be obscene the material, "taken as a whole" had to appeal "to the prurient interest" of the average person. Despite its attempt at specificity, definitional problems remained. In *Miller v. California* (413 U.S. 15), decided June 21, 1973, Chief Justice Warren Burger further refined "community standards" to apply to a limited geographical area. As a result, pornography foes attacked nationally distributed sexual material in areas where "community standards" were likely to be offended, therefore potentially threatening their publication nationwide. However, the Supreme Court narrowed the definition of community standards to obviate that threat. The popularity of pornographic material on the Internet was also causing First Amendment problems at the end of the 20th century, because adults were entitled to view pornography (as opposed to anything obviously "obscene"), but many parents objected to its availability to children using computers in schools and libraries. As of the early 21st century, the courts overturned congressional attempts to curb availability to potentially pornographic material on the Internet.

(excerpt)

Mr. Justice Brennan delivered the opinion of the Court.

The constitutionality of a criminal obscenity statute is the question in each of these cases. In *Roth*, the primary constitutional question is whether the federal obscenity statute violates the provision of the First Amendment that "Congress shall make no law . . . abridging the freedom of speech, or of the press. . . ." In *Alberts*, the primary constitutional question is whether the obscenity provisions of the California Penal Code invade the freedoms of speech and press as they may be incorporated in the liberty protected from state action by the Due Process Clause of the Fourteenth Amendment.

Other constitutional questions are: whether these statutes violate due process, because too vague to support conviction for crime; whether power to punish speech and press offensive to decency and morality is in the States alone, so that the federal obscenity statute violates the Ninth and Tenth Amendments (raised in *Roth*); and whether Congress, by enacting the federal obscenity statute, under the power delegated by Art, I Section 8, cl. 7, to establish post offices and post roads, pre-empted the regulation of the subject matter.

Roth conducted a business in New York in the publication and sale of books, photographs and magazines. He used circulars and advertising matter to solicit sales. He was convicted by a jury in the District Court for the Southern District of New York upon 4 counts of a 26-count indictment charging him with mailing obscene circulars and advertising, and an obscene book, in violation of the federal obscenity statute. His conviction was affirmed by the Court of Appeals for the Second Circuit. We granted certiorari.

Alberts conducted a mail-order business from Los Angeles. He was convicted by the Judge of the Municipal Court of the Beverly Hills Judicial District under a misdemeanor complaint which charged him with lewdly keeping for sale obscene and indecent books, and with writing, composing and publishing an obscene advertisement of them, in violation of the California Penal Code. The conviction was affirmed by the Appellate Department of the Superior Court of the State of California in and for the County of Los Angeles. We noted probable jurisdiction.

The dispositive question is whether obscenity is utterance within the area of protected speech and press. Although this is the first time the question has been squarely presented to this Court, either under the First Amendment or under the Fourteenth Amendment, expressions found in numerous opinions indicate that this Court has always assumed that obscenity is not protected by the freedoms of speech and press . . .

. . . The guaranties of freedom of expression in effect in 10 of the 14 States which by 1792 had ratified the Constitution, gave no absolute protection for every utterance. Thirteen of the 14 States provided for the prosecution of libel, and all of those States made either blasphemy or profanity, or both, statutory crimes. As early as 1712, Massachusetts made it criminal to publish "any filthy, obscene, or profane song, pamphlet, libel or mock sermon" in imitation or mimicking of religious services. Acts and Laws of the Province of Mass. Bay, c. CV, Section 8 (1712), Mass. Bay Colony Charters & Laws 399 (1814). Thus, profanity and obscenity were related offenses.

[1] In light of this history, it is apparent that the unconditional phrasing of the First Amendment was not intended to protect every utterance. This phrasing did not prevent this Court from concluding that libelous utterances are not within the area of constitutionally protected speech. *Beauharnais v. People of State of Illinois*, 343 U.S. 250, 266, 72 S.Ct. 725, 735, 96 L.Ed. 919. At the time of the adoption of the First Amendment, obscenity law was not as fully developed as libel law, but there is sufficiently contemporaneous evidence to show that obscenity, too, was outside the protection intended for speech and press.

[2] The protection given speech and press was fashioned to assure unfettered interchange of ideas for the

bringing about of political and social changes desired by the people. This objective was made explicit as early as 1774 in a letter of the Continental Congress to the inhabitants of Quebec:

"The last right we shall mention, regards the freedom of the press. The importance of this consists, besides the advancement of truth, science, morality, and arts in general, in its diffusion of liberal sentiments on the administration of Government, its ready communication of thoughts between subjects, and its consequential promotion of union among them, whereby oppressive officers are shamed or intimidated, into more honourable and just modes of conducting affairs." 1 *Journals of the Continental Congress* 108 (1774).

[3] All ideas having even the slightest redeeming social importance—unorthodox ideas, controversial ideas, even ideas hateful to the prevailing climate of opinion—have the full protection of the guaranties, unless excludable because they encroach upon the limited area of more important interests. But implicit in the history of the First Amendment is the rejection of obscenity as utterly without redeeming social importance. This rejection for that reason is mirrored in the universal judgment that obscenity should be restrained, reflected in the international agreement of over 50 nations, in the obscenity laws of all of the 48 States, and in the 20 obscenity laws enacted by the Congress from 1842 to 1956. This is the same judgment expressed by this Court in *Chaplinsky v. New Hampshire,* 315 U.S. 568, 571-572, 62 S.Ct. 766, 769, 86 L.Ed. 1031:

" . . . There are certain well-defined and narrowly limited classes of speech, the prevention and punishment of which have never been thought to raise any Constitutional problem. *These include the lewd and obscene . . . . It has been well observed that such utterances are no essential part of any exposition of ideas, and are of such slight social value as a step to truth that any benefit that may be derived from them is clearly outweighed by the social interest in order and morality . . . .*"

We hold that obscenity is not within the area of constitutionally protected speech or press.

[4] It is strenuously urged that these obscenity statutes offend the constitutional guaranties because they punish incitation to impure sexual *thoughts,* not shown to be related to any overt antisocial conduct which is or may be incited in the persons stimulated to such *thoughts.* In *Roth,* the trial judge instructed the jury: "The words 'obscene, lewd and lascivious' as used in the law, signify that form of immorality which has relation to sexual impurity and has a tendency to excite lustful *thoughts.*" In *Alberts,* the trial judge applied the test laid down in *People v. Wepplo,* 78 Cal.App.2d Supp. 959, 178 P.2d 853, 855, namely, whether the material has "a substantial tendency to deprave or corrupt its readers by inciting lascivious *thoughts* or arousing lustful desires." (Emphasis added.) It is insisted that the constitutional guaranties are violated because convictions may be had without proof either that obscene material will perceptibly create a clear and present danger of antisocial conduct, or will probably induce its recipients to such conduct. But, in light of our holding that obscenity is not protected speech, the complete answer to this argument is in the holding of this Court in *Beauharnais v. People of State of Illinois,* supra, 343 U.S. at page 266, 72 S.Ct. at page 735:

"Libelous utterances not being within the area of constitutionally protected speech, it is unnecessary, either for us or for the State courts, to consider the issues behind the phrase 'clear and present danger.' Certainly no one would contend that obscene speech, for example, may be punished only upon a showing of such circumstances. Libel, as we have seen, is in the same class."

[5, 6] However, sex and obscenity are not synonymous. Obscene material is material which deals with sex in a manner appealing to prurient interest. The portrayal of sex, *e.g.,* in art, literature and scientific works, is not itself sufficient reason to deny material the constitutional protection of freedom of speech and press. Sex, a great and mysterious motive force in human life, has indisputably been a subject of absorbing interest to mankind through the ages; it is one of the vital problems of human interest and public concern. As to all such problems this Court said in *Thornhill v. State of Alabama,* 310 U.S. 88, 101–102, 60 S.Ct 736, 744, 84 L.Ed. 1093:

"The freedom of speech and of the press guaranteed by the Constitution embraces at the least the liberty to discuss publicly and truth fully *all matters of public concern* without previous restraint or fear of subsequent punishment. The exigencies of the colonial period and the efforts to secure freedom from oppressive administration developed a broadened conception of these liberties as adequate to supply the public need for *information and education with respect to the significant issues of the times.* . . . Freedom of discussion, if it would fulfill its historic function in this nation, must embrace *all issues about which information is needed or appropriate to enable the members of society to cope with the exigencies of their period*".

[7] The fundamental freedoms of speech and press have contributed greatly to the development and well-being of our free society and are indispensable to its continued growth. Ceaseless vigilance is the watchword to prevent their erosion by Congress or by the States. The door barring federal and state intrusion into this area cannot be left ajar; it must be kept tightly closed and opened only the slightest crack necessary to prevent encroachment upon more important interests. It is therefore vital that the standards for judging obscenity safeguard the protection of

freedom of speech and press for material which does not treat sex in a manner appealing to prurient interest . . .

Source:
Supreme Court Reporter, Vol. 77, pp. 1,304–1,324.

John F. Kennedy, Inaugural Address, 1961

Address delivered by John F. Kennedy January 20, 1961, at his inauguration as the 35th president of the United States. Speaking to and for a new generation of Americans, Kennedy pledged loyalty to old allies, support for new ones, and an "alliance for progress" with Latin America. He offered to America's adversaries a new request for peace and cooperation, for arms control and inspection. In the most quoted line of this speech, Kennedy challenged all Americans to join in a struggle against tyranny, poverty, disease, and war: "Ask not what your country can do for you. Ask what you can do for your country."

One lasting legacy of Kennedy's New Frontier that captured the idealism inherent in his inaugural address was the Peace Corps. He began it by executive order and announced it in a message to Congress March 1, 1961, and Congress established it as a permanent agency within the State Department, September 22, 1961. At first, it consisted of mostly young volunteers who went to developing nations to work for social and economic progress. They taught in primary and secondary schools, constructed development projects, demonstrated modern methods of sanitation, instructed farmers in modern agricultural techniques, and performed other tasks. The host countries had to invite them. Later, older adults, including the mother of future president Jimmy Carter, also became Peace Corps Volunteers. After the fall of the Soviet Union, a number of formerly communist Eastern European nations also became host countries.

President Kennedy was assassinated November 22, 1963, in Dallas, Texas, and Vice President Lyndon B. Johnson became president. Lee Harvey Oswald was soon arrested as the assassin; he, in turn, was killed by Dallas bar owner Jack Ruby. President Johnson quickly appointed a seven-member commission, chaired by Chief Justice Earl Warren, to investigate both murders. Its findings were published September 27, 1964. After evaluating thousands of reports from federal and local sources, and questioning hundreds of witnesses, the commission concluded that Oswald had acted alone and that there was no prior connection between Oswald and Ruby. Many critics have attacked the commission's procedures and conclusions, arguing that a conspiracy, either foreign or domestic, was responsible for the assassinations. Since the Warren Report's publication, a great deal of information relating to the assassination has been released that was not known to the public and perhaps not known to the commissioners and staff. This information included assassination attempts sponsored by the CIA on Fidel Castro (Oswald had Cuban and Soviet connections) and suggestions by organized crime figures that the Kennedy brothers should be killed. (Brother Attorney General Robert Kennedy was assassinated by Sirhan Sirhan in 1968.) While many Americans cannot accept that Oswald acted alone, no credible evidence of a wider conspiracy leading to Kennedy's death has surfaced, despite congressional and independent investigations, including examination of the bullets from Oswald's rifle by forensic scientists using modern methods. Congress appointed an Assassination Records Review Board pursuant to a 1992 act. The documents it collected are in the National Archives and Records Administration and almost all are available to the public.

Mr. Chief Justice, President Eisenhower, Vice President Nixon, President Truman, reverend clergy, fellow citizens, we observe today not a victory of party, but a celebration of freedom—symbolizing an end, as well as a beginning—signifying renewal, as well as change. For I have sworn before you and Almighty God the same solemn oath our forebears prescribed nearly a century and three quarters ago.

The world is very different now. For man holds in his mortal hands the power to abolish all forms of human poverty and all forms of human life. And yet the same revolutionary beliefs for which our forebears fought are still at issue around the globe—the belief that the rights of man come not from the generosity of the state, but from the hand of God.

We dare not forget today that we are the heirs of that first revolution. Let the word go forth from this time and place, to friend and foe alike, that the torch has been passed to a new generation of Americans—born in this century, tempered by war, disciplined by a hard and bitter peace, proud of our ancient heritage—and unwilling to witness or permit the slow undoing of those human rights to which this Nation has always been committed, and to which we are committed today at home and around the world.

Let every nation know, whether it wishes us well or ill, that we shall pay any price, bear any burden, meet any hardship, support any friend, oppose any foe, in order to assure the survival and the success of liberty.

This much we pledge—and more.

To those old allies whose cultural and spiritual origins we share, we pledge the loyalty of faithful friends. United, there is little we cannot do in a host of cooperative ventures. Divided, there is little we can do—for we dare not meet a powerful challenge at odds and split asunder.

To those new States whom we welcome to the ranks of the free, we pledge our words that one form of colonial control shall not have passed away merely to be replaced by a far greater iron tyranny. We shall not always expect to find them supporting our view. But we shall always hope to find them strongly supporting their own freedom—and to remember that, in the past, those who foolishly sought power by riding the back of the tiger ended up inside.

To those peoples in the huts and villages across the globe struggling to break the bonds of mass misery, we pledge our best efforts to help them help themselves, for whatever period is required—not because the Communists may be doing it, not because we seek their votes, but because it is right. If a free society cannot help the many who are poor, it cannot save the few who are rich.

To our sister republics south of our border, we offer a special pledge—to convert our good words into good deeds, in a new alliance for progress, to assist free men and free governments in casting off the chains of poverty. But this peaceful revolution of hope cannot become the prey of hostile powers. Let all our neighbors know that we shall join with them to oppose aggression or subversion anywhere in the Americas. And let every other power know that this hemisphere intends to remain the master of its own house.

To that world assembly of sovereign states, the United Nations, our last best hope in an age where the instruments of war have far outpaced the instruments of peace, we renew our pledge of support—to prevent it from becoming merely a forum for invective—to strengthen its shield of the new and the weak—and to enlarge the area in which its writ may run.

Finally, to those nations who would make themselves our adversary, we offer not a pledge but a request: that both sides begin anew the quest for peace, before the dark powers of destruction unleashed by science engulf all humanity in planned or accidental self-destruction.

We dare not tempt them with weakness. For only when our arms are sufficient beyond doubt can we be certain beyond doubt that they will never be employed.

But neither can two great and powerful groups of nations take comfort from our present course—both sides overburdened by the cost of modern weapons, both rightly alarmed by the steady spread of the deadly atom, yet both racing to alter that uncertain balance of terror that stays the hand to mankind's final war.

So let us begin anew—remembering on both sides that civility is not a sign of weakness, and sincerity is always subject to proof. Let us never negotiate out of fear. But let us never fear to negotiate.

Let both sides explore what problems unite us instead of laboring those problems which divide us.

Let both sides, for the first time, formulate serious and precise proposals for the inspection and control of arms—and bring the absolute power to destroy other nations under the absolute control of all nations.

Let both sides seek to invoke the wonders of science instead of its terrors. Together let us explore the stars, conquer the deserts, eradicate disease, tap the ocean depths, and encourage the arts and commerce.

Let both sides unite to heed in all corners of the earth the command of Isaiah—to "undo the heavy burdens and to let the oppressed go free."

And if a beachhead of cooperation may push back the jungle of suspicion, let both sides join in creating a new endeavor, not a new balance of power, but a new world of law, where the strong are just and the weak secure and the peace preserved.

All this will not be finished in the first 100 days. Nor will it be finished in the first 1,000 days, nor in the life of this administration, nor even perhaps in our lifetime on this planet. But let us begin.

In your hands, my fellow citizens, more than in mine, will rest the final success or failure of our course. Since this country was founded, each generation of Americans has been summoned to give testimony to its national loyalty. The graves of young Americans who answered the call to service surround the globe.

Now the trumpet summons us again—not as a call to bear arms, though arms we need; not as a call to battle, though embattled we are; but a call to bear the burden of a long twilight struggle, year in, and year out, "rejoicing in hope, patient in tribulation"—a struggle against the common enemies of man: tyranny, poverty, disease, and war itself.

Can we forge against these enemies a grand and global alliance, North and South, East and West, that can assure a more fruitful life for all mankind? Will you join in that historic effort?

In the long history of the world, only a few generations have been granted the role of defending freedom in its hour of maximum danger. I do not shrink from this responsibility—I welcome it. I do not believe that any of us would exchange places with any other people or any other generation. The energy, the faith, the devotion which we bring to this endeavor will light our country and all who serve it—and the glow from that fire can truly light the world.

And so, my fellow Americans, ask not what your country can do for you: Ask what you can do for your country.

My fellow citizens of the world: Ask not What America will do for you, but what together we can do for the freedom of man.

Finally, whether you are citizens of America or citizens of the world, ask of us the same high standards of strength and sacrifice which we ask of you. With a good conscience our only sure reward, with history the final judge of our deeds, let us go forth to lead the land we love, asking His blessing and His help, but knowing that here on earth God's work must truly be our own.

Source:

Inaugural Addresses of the Presidents of the United States, 1789–1965. Washington, D.C.: Government Printing Office, 1965.

John F. Kennedy, Freedom Riders, 1961

Statement issued by President John F. Kennedy on May 20, 1961, after angry whites in Montgomery, Alabama, attacked a busload of black and white "Freedom Riders" who were attempting to test segregation barriers in interstate buses and terminals.

Theoretically, *Brown v. Board,* bolstered by additional court decisions, should have outlawed separate "colored" and white facilities serving interstate commerce. However, Jim Crow continued throughout the South. The Freedom Riders, under the auspices of the Congress of Racial Equality (CORE), traveled as far as Anniston, Alabama, meeting mostly dirty looks and fist fights with local toughs hanging out in a South Carolina station. At Anniston, an organized mob met the bus and set it on fire. The occupants were beaten with tire irons and pipes as they emerged coughing from the smoke. Finally, state troopers arrived and broke up the mob. More violence greeted them in Birmingham. A second interracial group continued the Freedom Ride.

Until that point, the Kennedy administration had been reluctant to interfere with desegregation efforts because it needed the support of southern congressmen to pass legislation that it considered necessary. Forced by the publicity the violence against the Freedom Riders had received, President Kennedy sent an emissary, John Siegenthaler, Attorney General (AG) Robert Kennedy's administrative assistant, to speak to Alabama governor John Patterson, who promised that the riders would be safe. His troopers escorted the bus to just outside Montgomery, where their jurisdiction ended. The promised protection from Montgomery police promptly disappeared, leaving this group to a mob that seriously injured the riders and Siegenthaler, who was helping one of them.

In 1961 there were only two ways that the federal government could interfere in situations where local law prevailed: As a last resort the president could call out federal troops or federalize the national guard, as President Eisenhower did in Little Rock in 1957. Before that becomes necessary, the Attorney General on the president's orders, can call on the U.S. Marshal Service. Shortly after the president's announcement, Attorney General Kennedy announced that he was sending over 350 U.S. marshals to Montgomery.

In October 1962, the Kennedy administration once again felt forced to call upon federal marshals, and eventually U.S. troops, to quell a riot at the University of Mississippi in Oxford when African-American James Meredith registered. Some 3,000 anti-integration forces armed with pipes, bricks, Molotov cocktails, and guns virtually overwhelmed the town; the Mississippi Highway Patrol refused to stop them. The 500 marshals on scene could not prevent violence, and the troops did not arrive for almost seven hours. In the end, two bystanders were killed, and approximately 160 people were injured. Meredith, guarded the entire year, was able to graduate.

May 20, 1961

The Situation which has developed in Alabama is a source of the deepest concern to me as it must be to the vast majority of the citizens of Alabama and other Americans. I have instructed the Justice Department to take all necessary steps based on their investigations and information. I call upon the Governor and other responsible State officials in Alabama as well as the Mayors of Birmingham and Montgomery to exercise their lawful authority to prevent any further outbreaks of violence. I would also hope that any persons, whether a citizen of Alabama or a visitor there, would refrain from any action which would in any way tend to provoke further outbreaks. I hope that state and local officials in Alabama will meet their responsibilities. The United States Government intends to meet its.

Source:

Public Papers of the Presidents of the United States: John F. Kennedy, 1962. Washington, D.C.: Government Printing Office, 1960–63. Also available on-line at http://www.jfklink.com/speeches/jfk/publicpapers/1961/jfk198_61.html.

Port Huron Statement of the Students for a Democratic Society, 1962

Manifesto of the Students for a Democratic Society (SDS), issued at the organization's national convention in Port Huron, Michigan, June 11–15, 1962. It condemned the American establishment and proclaimed a revolution of social experimentation beginning on university campuses. The Port Huron Statement is considered the founding document of the so-called New Left, as opposed to the communist, fellow-traveling, and socialist "Old Left." (The term "New Left" was a media and academic construct. Its participants never embraced it.)

SDS had its roots in an "Old Left" organization, the League for Industrial Democracy. Initially, its members worked among the urban and rural poor, but by 1968 it became identified with direct, militant action. Its numbers burgeoned nationwide, especially after the riots during the 1968 Democratic Convention in Chicago in which SDS leader and future California state senator Tom Hayden was arrested under the

Anti-Riot Statute. This provision, part of the Civil Rights Act of that year, was originally written to contain black "rabble-rousers" like SNCC leader H. Rap Brown. However, it was most famously used against the "Chicago Seven," white radicals, including Hayden, who were accused of fomenting the convention disorders. The act prohibited interstate travel or communication to participate in or incite a "riot." The constitutionality of the Anti-Riot Act was upheld in *United States v. Dellinger* et al., the Chicago Seven conspiracy trial. (An eighth person, Black Panther Bobby Seale, had his case severed from the others.) Judge Julius Hoffman, in sentencing the five guilty defendants (including Hayden), wrote, "we consider it unreal . . . to suppose that the existence of this obtuse and obscure provision will deter expression." The Seventh U.S. Circuit Court of Appeals, however, disagreed. In *United States v. Dellinger*, issued November 21, 1972, it reversed the convictions, finding that Judge Hoffman improperly prohibited the defense from inquiring into the "background and attitudes" of potential jurors during the jury selection process. According to the appeal ruling, Judge Hoffman also made "a series of judicial remarks deprecating defense counsel and the defense case "that could have caused undue bias among jurors."

The Anti-Riot Act still stands. However, protesters who are arrested are more likely to be charged with local offenses such as parading without a permit, disturbing the peace, or vandalism, than the federal antiriot statute.

Eventually, SDS split, as some of its members espoused terrorist actions such as use of explosives. The most militant called themselves the Weatherman faction and succeeded not only in planting explosives in federal buildings but several blew themselves up in 1970 while making antipersonnel bombs.

(excerpt)

Introduction: Agenda for a Generation

We are people of this generation, bred in at least modest comfort, housed now in universities, looking uncomfortably to the world we inherit.

When we were kids the United States was the wealthiest and strongest country in the world: the only one with the atom bomb, the least scarred by modern war, an initiator of the United Nations that we thought would distribute Western influence throughout the world. Freedom and equality for each individual, government of, by, and for the people—these American values we found good, principles by which we could live as men. Many of us began maturing in complacency.

As we grew, however, our comfort was penetrated by events too troubling to dismiss. First, the permeating and victimizing fact of human degradation, symbolized by the Southern struggle against racial bigotry, compelled most of us from silence to activism. Second, the enclosing fact of the Cold War, symbolized by the presence of the Bomb, brought awareness that we ourselves, and our friends, and millions of abstract "others" we knew more directly because of our common peril, might die at any time. We might deliberately ignore, or avoid, or fail to feel all other human problems, but not these two, for these were too immediate and crushing in their impact, too challenging in the demand that we as individuals take the responsibility for encounter and resolution.

While these and other problems either directly oppressed us or rankled our consciences and became our own subjective concerns, we began to see complicated and disturbing paradoxes in our surrounding America. The declaration "all men are created equal . . . rang hollow before the facts of Negro life in the South and the big cities of the North. The proclaimed peaceful intentions of the United States contradicted its economic and military investments in the Cold War status quo.

We witnessed, and continue to witness, other paradoxes. With nuclear energy whole cities can easily be powered, yet the dominant nation-states seem more likely to unleash destruction greater than that incurred in all wars of human history. Although our own technology is destroying old and creating new forms of social organization, men still tolerate meaningless work and idleness. While two-thirds of mankind suffers undernourishment, our own upper classes revel amidst superfluous abundance. Although world population is expected to double in forty years, the nations still tolerate anarchy as a major principle of international conduct and uncontrolled exploitation governs the sapping of the earth's physical resources. Although mankind desperately needs revolutionary leadership, America rests in national stalemate, its goals ambiguous and tradition-bound instead of informed and clear, its democratic system apathetic and manipulated rather than "of, by, and for the people."

Not only did tarnish appear on our image of American virtue, not only did disillusion occur when the hypocrisy of American ideals was discovered, but we began to sense that what we had originally seen as the American Golden Age was actually the decline of an era. The worldwide outbreak of revolution against colonialism and imperialism, the entrenchment of totalitarian states, the menace of war, overpopulation, international disorder, supertechnology—these trends were testing the tenacity of our own commitment to democracy and freedom and our abilities to visualize their application to a world in upheaval.

Our work is guided by the sense that we may be the last generation in the experiment with living. But we are a minority—the vast majority of our people regard the temporary equilibriums of our society and world as eternally-functional parts. In this is perhaps the outstanding paradox: we ourselves are imbued with urgency, yet the message of our society is that there is no viable alternative to the present. Beneath the reassuring tones of the politicians, beneath the common opinion that America will "muddle through," beneath the stagnation of those who have closed their minds to the future, is the pervading feeling that there simply are no alternatives, that our times have witnessed the exhaustion not only of Utopias, but of any new departures as well. Feeling the press of complexity upon the emptiness of life, people are fearful of the thought that at any moment things might thrust out of control. They fear change itself, since change might smash whatever invisible framework seems to hold back chaos for them now. For most Americans, all crusades are suspect, threatening. The fact that each individual sees apathy in his fellows perpetuates the common reluctance to organize for change. The dominant institutions are complex enough to blunt the minds of their potential critics, and entrenched enough to swiftly dissipate or entirely repel the energies of protest and reform, thus limiting human expectancies. Then, too, we are a materially improved society, and by our own improvements we seem to have weakened the case for further change.

Some would have us believe that Americans feel contentment amidst prosperity—but might it not better be called a glaze above deeply-felt anxieties about their role in the new world? And if these anxieties produce a developed indifference to human affairs, do they not as well produce a yearning to believe there is an alternative to the present, that something can be done to change circumstances in the school, the workplaces, the bureaucracies, the government? It is to this latter yearning, at once the spark and engine of change, that we direct our present appeal. The search for truly democratic alternatives to the present, and a commitment to social experimentation with them, is a worthy and fulfilling human enterprise, one which moves us and, we hope, others today. On such a basis do we offer this document of our convictions and analysis: as an effort in understanding and changing the conditions of humanity in the late twentieth century, an effort rooted in the ancient, still unfulfilled conception of man attaining determining influence over his circumstances of life.

Source:
The Office of California senator Tom Hayden.

Barry Goldwater, "Extremism in the Defense of Liberty," 1964

Address delivered to the Republican National Convention by Senator Barry Goldwater of Arizona July 16, 1964, accepting the party's presidential nomination. Goldwater, an economic conservative and staunch anticommunist, responded to accusations that he was a right-wing extremist by declaring that "extremism in the defense of liberty is no vice" and "moderation in the pursuit of justice is no virtue." He blamed the Democratic Party for communist gains in Cuba, Europe, and Southeast Asia, as well as for violence and corruption in the United States. His uncompromising speech set the tone for his campaign, in which Lyndon B. Johnson soundly defeated him. However, some historians claim that while he lost the battle Goldwater won the war. In 1968 he reentered the Senate where he staunchly defended American involvement in Vietnam. Through his retirement in 1986 and after, Goldwater became a respected voice as conservatism under Ronald Reagan captured the American political mainstream.

My good friend and great Republican, Dick Nixon and your charming wife; Pat; my running mate—that wonderful Republican who has served us so well for so long—Bill Miller and his wife, Stephanie; to Thurston Morton, who's done such a commendable job in chairmaning this convention; to Mr. Herbert Hoover who I hope is watching, and to that great American and his wife, General and Mrs. Eisenhower. To my own wife, fellow Republicans here assembled, and Americans across this great nation:

From this moment, united and determined, we will go forward together dedicated to the ultimate and undeniable greatness of the whole man.

Together we will win.

I accept your nomination with a deep sense of humility. I accept, too, the responsibility that goes with it, and I seek your continued help and your continued guidance. My fellow Republicans, our cause is too great for any man to feel worthy of it. Our task would be too great for any man did he not have with him the heart and the hands of this great Republican party.

And I promise you tonight that every fiber of my being is consecrated to our cause, that nothing shall be lacking from the struggle that can be brought to it by enthusiasm by devotion and plain hard work.

In this world no person, no party can guarantee anything, but what we can do and what we shall do is to deserve victory and victory will be ours. The Good Lord raised this mighty Republican—Republic to be a home for the Brave and to flourish as the land of the free—not to stagnate in the swampland of collectivism, not to cringe before the bully of Communism.

Now my fellow Americans, the tide has been running against freedom. Our people have followed false prophets. We must, and we shall, return to proven ways—not because they are old, but because they are true.

We must, and we shall, set the tide running again in the cause of freedom. And this party, with its every action, every word, every breath and every heart beat, has but a single resolve, and that is freedom.

Freedom made orderly for this nation by our constitutional government. Freedom under a government limited by laws of nature and of nature's God. Freedom balanced so that order lacking liberty will not become the slavery of the prison cell; balanced so that liberty lacking order will not become the license of the mob and of the jungle.

Now, we Americans understand freedom, we have earned it; we have lived for it, and we have died for it. This nation and its people are freedom's models in a searching world. We can be freedom's missionaries in a doubting world.

But, ladies and gentlemen, first we must renew freedom's mission in our own hearts and in our own homes.

During four futile years the Administration which we shall replace has distorted and lost that faith. It has talked and talked and talked and talked the words of freedom but it has failed and failed and failed in the works of freedom.

Now failure cements the wall of shame in Berlin; failures blot the sands of shame at the Bay of Pigs; failures marked the slow death of freedom in Laos; failures infest the jungles of Vietnam, and failures haunt the houses of our once great alliances and undermine the greatest bulwark ever erected by free nations, the NATO community.

Failures proclaim lost leadership, obscure purpose, weakening wills and the risk of inciting our sworn enemies to new aggressions and to new excesses.

And because of this Administration we are tonight a world divided. We are a nation becalmed. We have lost the brisk pace of diversity and the genius of individual creativity. We are plodding along at a pace set by centralized planning, red tape, rules without responsibility and regimentation without recourse.

Rather than useful jobs in our country, people have been offered bureaucratic makework; rather than moral leadership, they have been given bread and circuses; they have been given spectacles, and, yes, they've even been given scandals.

Tonight there is violence in our streets, corruption in our highest offices, aimlessness among our youth, anxiety among our elderly, and there's a virtual despair among the many who look beyond material success toward the inner meaning of their lives. And where examples of morality should be set, the opposite is seen. Small men seeking great wealth or power have too often and too long turned even the highest levels of public service into mere personal opportunity.

Now, certainly simple honesty is not too much to demand of men in government. We find it in most. Republicans demand it from everyone.

They demand it from everyone no matter how exalted or protected his position might be.

The growing menace in our country tonight, to personal safety, to life, to limb and property, in homes, in churches, on the playgrounds and places of business, particularly in our great cities, is the mounting concern or should be of every thoughtful citizen in the United States. Security from domestic violence, no less than from foreign aggression, is the most elementary and fundamental purpose of any government, and a government that cannot fulfill this purpose is one that cannot long command the loyalty of its citizens.

History shows us, demonstrates that nothing, nothing prepares the way for tyranny more than the failure of public officials to keep the streets safe from bullies and marauders.

Now we Republicans see all this as more—much more—than the result of mere political differences, or more political mistakes. We see this as a result of a fundamentally and absolutely wrong view of man, his nature and his destiny.

Those who seek to live your lives for you, to take your liberty in return for relieving you of yours; those who elevate the state and downgrade the citizen, must see ultimately a world in which earthly power can be substituted for Divine Will. And this nation was founded upon the rejection of that notion and upon the acceptance of God as the author of freedom.

Now those who seek absolute power, even though they seek it to do what they regard as good, are simply demanding the right to enforce their own version of heaven on earth, and let me remind you they are the very ones who always create the most hellish tyranny.

Absolute power does corrupt, and those who seek it must be suspect and must be opposed. Their mistaken course stems from false notions, ladies and gentlemen, of equality. Equality, rightly understood as our founding fathers understood it, leads to liberty and to the emancipation of creative differences; wrongly understood, as it has been so tragically in our time, it leads first to conformity and then to despotism.

Fellow Republicans, it is the cause of Republicanism to resist concentrations of power, private or public, which enforce such conformity and inflict such despotism.

It is the cause of Republicanism to insure that power remains in the hands of the people—and, so help us God, that is exactly what a Republican President will do with the help of a Republican Congress.

It is further the cause of Republicanism to restore a clear understanding of the tyranny of man over man in the world at large. It is our cause to dispel the foggy thinking which avoids hard decisions in the delusion that a world of conflict will somehow resolve itself into a world of harmony, if we just don't rock the boat or irritate the forces of aggression—and this is hogwash.

It is, further, the cause of Republicanism to remind ourselves, and the world, that only the strong can remain free; that only the strong can keep the peace.

Now I needn't remind you, or my fellow Americans regardless of party, that Republicans have shouldered this hard responsibility and marched in this cause before. It was Republican leadership under Dwight Eisenhower that kept the peace, and passed along to this Administration the mightiest arsenal for defense the world has ever known.

And I needn't remind you that it was the strength and the believable will of the Eisenhower years that kept the peace by using our strength, by using it in the Formosa Strait, and in Lebanon, and by showing it courageously at all times.

It was during those Republican years that the thrust of Communist imperialism was blunted. It was during those years of Republican leadership that this world moved closer not to war but closer to peace than at any other time in the last three decades.

And I needn't remind you, but I will, that it's been during Democratic years that our strength to deter war has been stilled and even gone into a planned decline. It has been during Democratic years that we have weakly stumbled into conflicts, timidly refusing to draw our own lines against aggression, deceitfully refusing to tell even our own people of our full participation and tragically letting our finest men die on battlefields unmarked by purpose, unmarked by pride or the prospect of victory.

Yesterday it was Korea: tonight it is Vietnam. Make no bones of this. Don't try to sweep this under the rug. We are at war in Vietnam. And yet the President, who is the Commander in Chief of our forces, refuses to say, refuses to say mind you, whether or not the objective over there is victory, and his Secretary of Defense continues to mislead and misinform the American people, and enough of it has gone by.

And I needn't remind you, but I will, it has been during Democratic years that a billion persons were cast into Communist captivity and their fate cynically sealed.

Today—today in our beloved country we have an Administration which seems eager to deal with Communism in every coin known—from gold to wheat; from consulates to confidence, and even human freedom itself.

Now the Republican cause demands that we brand communism as the principal disturber of peace in the world today. Indeed, we should brand it as the only significant disturber of the peace. And we must make clear that until its goals of conquest are absolutely renounced, and its relations with all nations tempered, Communism and the governments it now controls are enemies, of every man on earth who is or wants to be free.

Now, we here in American can keep the peace only if we remain vigilant, and only if we remain strong. Only if we keep our eyes open and keep our guard up can we prevent war.

And I want to make this abundantly clear—I don't intend to let peace or freedom be torn from our grasp because of lack of strength, or lack of will—and that I promise you Americans.

I believe that we must look beyond the defense of freedom today to its extension tomorrow. I believe that the Communism which boasts it will bury us will instead give way to the forces of freedom. And I can see in the distant and yet recognizable future the outlines of a world worthy of our dedication, our every risk, our every effort, our every sacrifice along the way. Yes, a world that will redeem the suffering of those who will be liberated from tyranny.

I can see, and I suggest that all thoughtful men must contemplate, the flowering of an Atlantic civilization, the whole world of Europe reunified and free, trading openly across its borders, communicating openly across the world.

This is a goal far, far more meaningful than a moon shot.

It's a truly inspiring goal for all free men to set for themselves during the latter half of the twentieth century. I can see and all free men must thrill to the events of this Atlantic civilization joined by a straight ocean highway to the United States. What a destiny! What a destiny can be ours to stand as a great central pillar linking Europe, the Americas and the venerable and vital peoples and cultures of the Pacific.

I can see a day when all the Americans—North and South—will be linked in a mighty system—a system in which the errors and misunderstandings of the past will be submerged one by one in a rising tide of prosperity and interdependence.

We know that the misunderstandings of centuries are not to be wiped away in a day or wiped away in an hour. But we pledge, we pledge, that human sympathy—what our neighbors to the South call an attitude of sympatico—no less than enlightened self-interest will be our guide.

And I can see this Atlantic civilization galvanizing and guiding emergent nations everywhere. Now I know this freedom is not the fruit of every soil. I know that our own freedom was achieved through centuries of unremitting efforts by brave and wise men. And I know that the road to freedom is a long and a challenging road, and I know also that some men may walk away from it, that some men resist challenge, accepting the false security of governmental paternalism.

And I pledge that the America I envision in the years ahead will extend its hand in help in teaching and in cultivation so that all new nations will be at least encouraged to go our way; so that they will not wander down the dark alleys of tyranny or to the dead-end streets of collectivism.

My fellow Republicans, we do no man a service by hiding freedom's light under a bushel of mistaken humility.

I seek an America proud of its past, proud of its ways, proud of its dreams and determined actively to proclaim them. But our examples to the world must, like charity, begin at home.

In our vision of a good and decent future, free and peaceful, there must be room, room for the liberation of the energy and the talent of the individual, otherwise our vision is blind at the outset.

We must assure a society here which while never abandoning the needy, or forsaking the helpless, nurtures incentives and opportunity for the creative and the productive.

We must know the whole good is the product of many single contributions. And I cherish the day when our children once again will restore as heroes the sort of men and women who, unafraid, and undaunted, pursue the truth, strive to cure disease, subdue and make fruitful our natural environment, and produce the inventive engines of production, science and technology.

This nation, whose creative people have enhanced this entire span of history, should again thrive upon the greatness of all those things which we—we as individual citizens—can and should do.

During Republican years, this again will be a nation of men and women, of families proud of their role, jealous of their responsibilities, unlimited in their aspirations—a nation where all who can will be self-reliant.

We Republicans see in our constitutional form of government the great framework which assures the orderly but dynamic fulfillment of the whole man, and we see the whole man as the great reason for instituting orderly government in the first place.

We see in private property and in economy based upon and fostering private property the one way to make government a durable ally of the whole man rather than his determined enemy.

We see in the sanctity of private property the only durable foundation for constitutional government in a free society.

And beyond that we see and cherish diversity of ways, diversity of thoughts, of motives, and accomplishments. We don't seek to live anyone's life for him. We only seek to secure his rights, guarantee him opportunity, guarantee him opportunity to strive with government performing only those needed and constitutionally sanctioned tasks which cannot otherwise be performed.

We, Republicans, seek a government that attends to its inherent responsibilities of maintaining a stable monetary and fiscal climate, encouraging a free and competitive economy and enforcing law and order.

Thus do we seek inventiveness, diversity and creative difference within a stable order, for we Republicans define government's role where needed at many, many levels, preferably through the one closest to the people involved: our towns and our cities, then our counties, then our states, then our regional contacts and only then the national government.

That, let me remind you, is the land of liberty built by decentralized power. On it also we must have balance between the branches of government at every level.

Balance, diversity, creative difference—these are the elements of Republican equation. Republicans agree, Republicans agree heartily, to disagree on many, many of their applications. But we have never disagreed on the basic fundamental issues of why you and I are Republicans.

This is a party—this Republican party is a party for free men. Not for blind followers and not for conformists.

Back in 1858 Abraham Lincoln said this of the Republican party, and I quote him because he probably could have said it during the last week or so: It was composed of strained, discordant, and even hostile elements.

Yet all of these elements agreed on one paramount objective: to arrest the progress of slavery, and place it in the course of ultimate extinction.

Today, as then, but more urgently and more broadly than then, the task of preserving and enlarging freedom at home and of safeguarding it from the forces of tyranny abroad is great enough to challenge all our resources and to require all our strength.

Anyone who joins us in all sincerity we welcome. Those, those who do not care for our cause, we don't expect to enter our ranks in any case. And let our Republicanism so focused and so dedicated not be made fuzzy and futile by unthinking and stupid labels.

I would remind you that extremism in the defense of liberty is no vice!

And let me remind you also that moderation in the pursuit of justice is no virtue!

By the—the beauty of the very system we Republicans are pledged to restore and revitalize, the beauty of this Federal system of ours is in its reconciliation of diversity with unity. We must not see malice in honest differences of opinion, and no matter how great, so long as they are not inconsistent with the pledges we have given to each other in and through our Constitution.

Our Republican cause is not to level out the world or make its people conform in computer-regimented sameness. Our Republican cause is to free our people and light the way for liberty throughout the world. Ours is a very human cause for very humane goals. This party, its good people, and its unquestionable devotion to freedom will not fulfill the purposes of this campaign which we launch here now until our cause has won the day, inspired the world, and shown the way to a tomorrow worthy of all our yesteryears.

I repeat, I accept your nomination with humbleness, with pride and you and I are going to fight for the goodness of our land. Thank you.

Source:
Landmark Documents in American History, Facts On File, Inc.

Lyndon B. Johnson, "Great Society" Speech, 1965

Speech given by President Lyndon B. Johnson on May 22, 1965, at the University of Michigan commencement. In his address, Johnson enhanced his war on poverty by proposing a plan to build a "Great Society" in the United States—one which elevated the quality of individual lives and advanced American civilization. To achieve his goal, Johnson declared that the entire urban United States must be rebuilt; pollution, overcrowding, and the disappearance of forests and fields curtailed; every child must have access to adequate schooling; and education must offer a viable escape from poverty. The president noted that such changes required what he termed "a creative federalism" between the government and local community leaders.

Previously, Congress, on August 20, 1964, put teeth into Johnson's war on poverty by enacting the Economic Opportunity Act, which established the Office of Economic Opportunity (OEO) and authorized funding for a variety of programs. The funds established the Job Corps, to provide training for youths aged 16 to 21; a work-study program to aid low-income students; on-the-job training for youths; urban and rural community-action programs designed to ensure "maximum feasible participation" by the poor; adult education programs; the VISTA (Volunteers in Service to America) program of volunteer social service workers and teachers for the disadvantaged; Head Start, to aid poor preschool children; and assistance for migrant workers and their families.

Improving educational opportunities was a major part of Johnson's vision. On April 11, 1965, he signed the Elementary and Secondary Education Act, which provided $1.3 billion in federal aid to schools with large numbers of children from low-income families. The funds helped both private and public schools, and public agencies controlled expenditures. Although the law stated that no direct federal aid would go to church-related institutions, needy children enrolled in their schools could receive "on loan" textbooks and other instructional materials that would remain the property of the public schools. The act also provided funds for supplemental education centers, services, and research; and strengthened state education departments.

President Hatcher, Governor Romney, Senators McNamara and Hart, Congressmen Meader and Staebler, and other members of the fine Michigan delegation, members of the graduating class, my fellow Americans:

It is a great pleasure to be here today. This university has been coeducational since 1870, but I do not believe it was on the basis of your accomplishments that a Detroit high school girl said, "In choosing a college, you first have to decide whether you want a coeducational school or an educational school."

Well, we can find both here at Michigan, although perhaps at different hours.

I came out here today very anxious to meet the Michigan student whose father told a friend of mine that his son's education had been a real value. It stopped his mother from bragging about him.

I have come today from the turmoil of your Capital to the tranquillity of your campus to speak about the future of your country.

The purpose of protecting the life of our Nation and preserving the liberty of our citizens is to pursue the happiness of our people. Our success in that pursuit is the test of our success as a Nation.

For a century we labored to settle and to subdue a continent. For half a century we called upon unbounded invention and untiring industry to create an order of plenty for all of our people.

The challenge of the next half century is whether we have the wisdom to use that wealth to enrich and elevate our national life, and to advance the quality of our American civilization.

Your imagination, your initiative, and your indignation will determine whether we build a society where progress is the servant of our needs, or a society where old values and new visions are buried under unbridled growth. For in your time we have the opportunity to move not only toward the rich society and the powerful society, but upward to the Great Society.

The Great Society rests on abundance and liberty for all. It demands an end to poverty and racial injustice, to which we are totally committed in our time. But that is just the beginning.

The Great Society is a place where every child can find knowledge to enrich his mind and to enlarge his talents. It is a place where leisure is a welcome chance to build and reflect, not a feared cause of boredom and restlessness. It is a place where the city of man serves not only the needs of the body and the demands of commerce but the desire for beauty and the hunger for community.

It is a place where man can renew contact with nature. It is a place which honors creation for its own sake and for what is adds to the understanding of the race. It is a place where men are more concerned with the quality of their goals than the quantity of their goods.

But most of all, the Great Society is not a safe harbor, a resting place, a final objective, a finished work. It is a challenge constantly renewed, beckoning us toward a destiny where the meaning of our lives matches the marvelous products of our labor.

So I want to talk to you today about three places where we begin to build the Great Society—in our cities, in our countryside, and in our classrooms.

Many of you will live to see the day, perhaps 50 years from now, when there will be 400 million Americans—four-fifths of them in urban areas. In the remainder of this century urban population will double, city land will double, and we will have to build homes, highways, and facilities equal to all those built since this country was first settled. So in the next 40 years we must re-build the entire urban United States.

Aristotle said: "Men come together in cities in order to live, but they remain together in order to live the good life." It is harder and harder to live the good life in American cities today.

The catalog of ills is long: there is the decay of the centers and the despoiling of the suburbs. There is not enough housing for our people or transportation for our traffic. Open land is vanishing and old landmarks are violated.

Worst of all expansion is eroding the precious and time honored values of community with neighbors and communion with nature. The loss of these values breeds loneliness and boredom and indifference.

Our society will never be great until our cities are great. Today the frontier of imagination and innovation is inside those cities and not beyond their borders.

New experiments are already going on. It will be the task of your generation to make the American city a place where future generations will come, not only to live but to live the good life.

I understand that if I stayed here tonight I would see that Michigan students are really doing their best to live the good life.

This is the place where the Peace Corps was started. It is inspiring to see how all of you, while you are in this country, are trying so hard to live at the level of the people.

A second place where we begin to build the Great Society is in our countryside. We have always prided ourselves on being not only America the strong and America the free, but America the beautiful. Today that beauty is in danger. The water we drink, the food we eat, the very air that we breathe, are threatened with pollution. Our parks are overcrowded, our seashores overburdened. Green fields and dense forests are disappearing.

A few years ago we were greatly concerned about the "Ugly American." Today we must act to prevent an ugly America.

For once the battle is lost, once our natural splendor is destroyed, it can never be recaptured. And once man can no longer walk with beauty or wonder at nature his spirit will wither and his sustenance be wasted.

A third place to build the Great Society is in the classrooms of America. There your children's lives will be shaped. Our society will not be great until every young mind is set free to scan the farthest reaches of thought and imagination. We are still far from that goal.

Today, 8 million adult Americans, more than the entire population of Michigan, have not finished 5 years of school. Nearly 20 million have not finished 8 years of school. Nearly 54 million—more than one-quarter of all America—have not even finished high school.

Each year more than 100,000 high school graduates, with proved ability, do not enter college because they cannot afford it. And if we cannot educate today's youth, what will we do in 1970 when elementary school enrollment will be 5 million greater than 1960? And high school enrollment will rise by 5 million. College enrollment will increase by more than 3 million.

In many places, classrooms are overcrowded and curricula are outdated. Most of our qualified teachers are underpaid, and many of our paid teachers are unqualified. So we must give every child a place to sit and a teacher to learn from. Poverty must not be a bar to learning, and learning must offer an escape from poverty.

But more classrooms and more teachers are not enough. We must seek an educational system which grows in excellence as it grows in size. This means better training for our teachers. It means preparing youth to enjoy their hours of leisure as well as their hours of labor. It means exploring new techniques of teaching, to find new ways to stimulate the love of learning and the capacity for creation.

These are three of the central issues of the Great Society. While our Government has many programs directed at those issues, I do not pretend that we have the full answer to those problems.

But I do promise this: We are going to assemble the best thought and the broadest knowledge from all over the world to find those answers for America. I intend to establish working groups to prepare a series of White House conferences and meetings—on the cities, on natural beauty, on the quality of education, and on other emerging challenges. And from these meetings and from this inspiration and from these studies we will begin to set our course toward the Great Society.

The solution to these problems does not rest on a massive program in Washington, nor can it rely solely on the strained resources of local authority. They require us to create new concepts of cooperation, a creative federalism, between the National Capital and the leaders of local communities.

Woodrow Wilson once wrote: "Every man sent out from his university should be a man of his Nation as well as a man of his time."

Within your lifetime powerful forces, already loosed, will take us toward a way of life beyond the realm of our experience, almost beyond the bounds of our imagination.

For better or for worse, your generation has been appointed by history to deal with those problems and to lead America toward a new age. You have the chance never before afforded to any people in any age. You can help build a society where the demands of morality, and the needs of the spirit, can be realized in the life of the Nation.

So, will you join in the battle to give every citizen the full equality which God enjoins and the law requires, whatever his belief, or race, or the color of his skin?

Will you join in the battle to give every citizen an escape from the crushing weight of poverty?

Will you join in the battle to make it possible for all nations to live in enduring peace—as neighbors and not as mortal enemies?

Will you join in the battle to build the Great Society, to prove that our material progress is only the foundation on which we will build a richer life of mind and spirit?

There are those timid souls who say this battle cannot be won; that we are condemned to a soulless wealth. I do not agree. We have the power to shape the civilization that we want. But we need your will, your labor, your hearts, if we are to build that kind of society.

Those who came to this land sought to build more than just a new country. They sought a new world. So I have come here today to your campus to say that you can make their vision our reality. So let us from this moment begin our work so that in the future men will look back and say: It was then, after a long and weary way, that man turned the exploits of his genius to the full enrichment of his life.

Thank you. Good-bye.

Source:

Public Papers of the Presidents of the United States, Lyndon B. Johnson, 1965. Washington, D.C.: Government Printing Office, 1963–68. pp. 704–707.

Social Security Amendments Act (Medicare), 1965

Federal legislation enacted July 30, 1965, providing federally funded health insurance for the elderly. President Lyndon Baines Johnson signed the measure into law at a ceremony in Independence, Missouri, honoring former president Harry S. Truman, who had been the first president to propose such a plan. The legislation established both a basic Medicare plan and a supplemental plan. The basic plan provided for limited hospitalization and nursing home care for each Social Security recipient over age 65. The basic plan also covered hospital diagnostic services and limited home health care visits following a hospitalization. The optional supplementary plan, for which enrollees initially paid a $3 monthly premium, provided for a wider range of services, including those provided by physicians, radiologists, anesthesiologists, and psychiatrists, as well as prosthetic devices, ambulance services, and home health care visits without prior hospitalization. The legislation also expanded other federal health and welfare programs and revised the Social Security payroll tax to help pay for the new program.

(excerpt)

An Act

To provide a hospital insurance program for the aged under the Social Security Act with a supplementary medical benefits program and an expanded program of medical assistance, to increase benefits under the Old-Age, Survivors, and Disability Insurance System, to improve the Federal-State public assistance programs, and for other purposes.

Be it enacted by the Senate and House of Representatives of the United States of America in Congress assembled, That this Act, with the following table of contents, may be cited as the "Social Security Amendments of 1965."

* * *

Title I—Health Insurance for the Aged and Medical Assistance

Short Title

Sec. 100. This title may be cited as the "Health Insurance for the Aged Act."

Part 1—Health Insurance Benefits for the Aged

Entitlement to Hospital Insurance Benefits

Sec. 101. Title II of the Social Security Act is amended by adding at the end thereof the following new section:

"Entitlement to Hospital Insurance Benefits

"Sec. 226. (a) Every individual who—

"(1) has attained the age of 65, and

"(2) is entitled to monthly insurance benefits under section 202 or is a qualified railroad retirement beneficiary shall be entitled to hospital insurance benefits under part A of title XVIII for each month for which he meets the condition specified in paragraph (2), beginning with the first month after June 1966 for which he meets the conditions specified in paragraphs (1) and (2).

"(b) For purposes of subsection (a)—

"(1) entitlement of an individual to hospital insurance benefits for a month shall consist of entitlement to have payment made under, and subject to the limitations in, part A of title XVIII on his behalf for inpatient hospital services, post-hospital extended care services, post-hospital home health services, and outpatient hospital diagnostic services (as such terms are defined in part C of title XVIII) furnished him in the United States (or outside the United States in the case of inpatient hospital services furnished under the conditions described in section 1814(f)) during such month; except that (A) no such payment may be made for post-hospital extended care services furnished before January 1967, and (B) no such payment may be made for post-hospital extended care services or post-hospital home health services unless the discharge from the hospital required to qualify such services for payment under part A of title XVIII occurred after June 30, 1966, or on or after the first day of the month in which he attains age 65, whichever is later; and

"(2) an individual shall be deemed entitled to monthly insurance benefits under section 202, or to be a qualified railroad retirement beneficiary, for the month in which he died if he would have been entitled to such benefits, or would have been a qualified railroad retirement beneficiary, for such month had he died in the next month.

"(c) For purposes of this section, the term 'qualified railroad retirement beneficiary' means an individual whose name has been certified to the Secretary by the Railroad Retirement Board under section 21 of the Railroad Retirement Act of 1937. An individual shall cease to be a qualified railroad retirement beneficiary at the close of the month preceding the month which is certified by the Railroad Retirement Board as the month in which he ceased to meet the requirements of section 21 of the Railroad Retirement Act of 1937.

"(d) For entitlement to hospital insurance benefits in the case of certain uninsured individuals, see section 103 of the Social Security Amendments of 1965."

Hospital Insurance Benefits and Supplementary Medical Insurance Benefits

Sec. 102. (a) The Social Security Act is amended by adding after title XVII the following new title:

"Title XVIII—Health Insurance for the Aged

"Prohibition against any Federal Interference

"Sec. 1801. Nothing in this title shall be construed to authorize any Federal officer or employee to exercise any supervision or control over the practice of medicine or the manner in which medical services are provided, or over the selection, tenure, or compensation of any officer or employee of any institution, agency, or person providing health services; or to exercise any supervision or control over the administration or operation of any such institution, agency, or person.

* * *

Source:

Statutes at Large, Vol. 79, pp. 286–423.

Clean Air Act, 1970

Federal U.S. legislation enacted on December 31, 1970, that provided for national ambient air quality standards and set deadlines for the abatement of most mobile and stationary sources of air pollution that adversely affect public health and welfare. It established the principle that clean air must be maintained and placed authority to administer the program under the new Environmental Protection Agency (EPA). The act required that states submit for EPA approval air quality plans to achieve federally mandated goals. The plans had to assure the achievement of primary standards, to protect public health, and secondary standards, to avoid any adverse environmental effects; limit emissions; set compliance schedules; and include land-use and transportation control.

Previously, the National Environmental Policy Act, which became effective on January 1, 1970, required federal agencies to include an environmental impact statement in every recommendation or report on proposed federal action or legislation significantly affecting the U.S. environment. The statement had to identify any unavoidable, adverse environmental effects, alternatives to the proposed action, the relationship between local short-term use of the environment and the maintenance of long-term productivity, and any irreversible commitments of resources that the action would involve. The act declared as national policy "a productive harmony between man and his environment" and established the Council on Environmental Quality to advise the president on environmental issues.

Under the Clean Air Act, the EPA could establish its own emission standards for pollutants deemed hazardous to health and for motor vehicle emissions. The act provided for vehicle testing, maintenance requirements, and recalls. As a result of this act, the air in major cities became demonstrably cleaner. Nevertheless, smog and pollution continued to plague not only metropolitan areas but even sparsely populated places downwind of cities, including major national parks and wilderness areas. In addition, the amount of various elements considered dangerous was revised over time.

Congress, in a law signed by President George H. W. Bush on November 15, 1990, updated and tightened federal air pollution standards in order to curb acid rain, urban smog, and toxic chemicals. Environmental groups praised the regulations, the implementation of which was expected to cost as much as $25 billion a year; industry representatives expressed much less approval. Ironically, under George H. W. Bush's son, George W., clean air standards themselves became endangered as his administration weakened them in favor of industry.

On December 20, 1973, President Richard M. Nixon, signed an environmental law that demonstrated the rule of unintended consequences, the Endangered Species Act. It provided absolute protection for fish and wildlife, including plants, that were in peril of becoming extinct ("endangered species"), and developed a second category with somewhat lesser protections, species "threatened" with extinction. The act increased the penalties on illegal trafficking of endangered species and barred the federal government from funding any programs that "jeopardize the continued existence" of endangered and threatened species, or "result in the destruction or modification of habitat" seen as critical to the survival of the wildlife living there. Environmentalists used the latter provision to stop federal projects such as dams and highways. The act authorized the secretaries of the interior and commerce to provide lands and waters in order to protect and replenish endangered and threatened species. While the courts upheld the letter of the law, most famously in the "snail darter" case in the late 1970s, administrations attempted to mediate between the loss of jobs and corporate income in national forests, as President Bill Clinton did with the spotted owl situation in the Northwest. President Ronald Reagan's and especially George W. Bush's administrations, however, worked to undo a number of previously protected areas and favored industry and recreation enthusiasts over environmental protection.

(excerpt)

An Act

To amend the Clean Air Act to provide for a more effective program to improve the quality of the Nation's air.

Be it enacted by the Senate and House of Representatives of the United States of America in Congress assembled, That this Act may be cited as the "Clean Air Amendments of 1970."

Research

Sec. 2. (a) Section 103 of the Clean Air Act (42 U.S.C. 1857, et seq.) is amended by adding at the end thereof the following new subsection:

"(f)(1) In carrying out research pursuant to this Act, the Administrator shall give special emphasis to research on the short-and long-term effects of air pollutants on public health and welfare. In the furtherance of such research, he shall conduct an accelerated research program—

"(A) to improve knowledge of the contribution of air pollutants to the occurrence of adverse effects on health, including, but not limited to, behavioral, physiological, toxicological, and biochemical effects; and

"(B) to improve knowledge of the short-and long-term effects of air pollutants on welfare.

"(2) In carrying out the provisions of this subsection the Administrator may—

"(A) conduct epidemiological studies of the effects of air pollutants on mortality and morbidity;

"(B) conduct clinical and laboratory studies on the immunologic, biochemical, physiological, and the toxicological effects including carcinogenic, teratogenic, and mutagenic effects of air pollutants;

"(C) utilize, on a reimbursable basis, the facilities of existing Federal scientific laboratories and research centers;

"(D) utilize the authority contained in paragraphs (1) through (4) of subsection (b); and

"(E) consult with other appropriate Federal agencies to assure that research or studies conducted pursuant to this subsection will be coordinated with research and studies of such other Federal agencies.

"(3) In entering into contracts under this subsection, the Administrator is authorized to contract for a term not to exceed 10 years in duration. For the purposes of this paragraph, there are authorized to be appropriated $15,000,000. Such amounts as are appropriated shall remain available until expended and shall be in addition to any other appropriations under this Act."

(b) Section 104(a)(1) of the Clean Air Act is amended to read as follows:

"(1) conduct and accelerate research programs directed toward development of improved, low-cost techniques for—

"(A) control of combustion by products of fuels,

"(B) removal of potential air pollutants from fuels prior to combustion,

"(C) control of emissions from the evaporation of fuels,

"(D) improving the efficiency of fuels combustion so as to decrease atmospheric emissions, and

"(E) producing synthetic or new fuels which, when used, result in decreased atmospheric emissions."

(c) Section 104(a)(2) of the Clean Air Act is amended by striking and (B)" and inserting in lieu thereof the following: "(B) part of the cost of programs to develop low emission alternatives to the present internal combustion engine; (C) the cost to purchase vehicles and vehicle engines, or portions thereof, for research, development, and testing purposes; and (D)."

Source:
Statutes at Large, Vol. 84, pp. 1,676–1,713.

The Meeting of Elvis Presley and President Richard Nixon, 1970

Visit of popular singer and cult figure Elvis Presley (known as "the King") to President Richard M. Nixon, December 21, 1970, at Presley's request. The entertainer offered to influence teenagers against using illegal drugs, which had become popular nationwide during the previous decade. Nixon agreed to see Presley because "he thought he could reach young people." The meeting represented the significance of a youth culture figure like Presley to the president, especially since the Twenty-sixth Amendment to the U.S. Constitution, which would soon be ratified, lowered the voting age to 18. Ironically Presley himself may have died of an overdose of prescription drugs. Representations of "The President and the King" shaking hands on T-shirts, mugs, and other paraphernalia ranging from $3 pens and magnets to a $65 framed poster are best-sellers of the National Archives and the Nixon Birthplace and Library. This continuing enthusiasm for "the King" demonstrates the role of nostalgia in American culture, especially for "baby boomers" (born between 1946 and 1964) and their slightly older brothers and sisters (Elvis's first big hit, *Heartbreak Hotel,* was in 1956).

The meeting opened with pictures taken of the President and Elvis Presley.

Presley immediately began showing the President his law enforcement paraphernalia including badges from police departments in California, Colorado and Tennessee. Presley indicated that he had been playing Las Vegas and the President indicated that he was aware of how difficult it is to perform in Las Vegas.

The President mentioned that he thought Presley could reach young people, and that it was important for Presley to retain his credibility. Presley responded that he did his thing by "just singing." He said that he could not get to the kids if he made a speech on the stage, that he had to reach them in his own way. The President nodded in agreement.

Presley indicated that he thought the Beatles had been a real force for anti-American spirit. He said that the Beatles came to this country, made their money, and then returned to England where they promoted an anti-American theme. The President nodded in agreement and expressed some surprise. The President then indicated that those who use drugs are also those in the vanguard of anti-American protest. Violence, drug usage, dissent, protest all seem to merge in generally the same group of young people.

Presley indicated to the President in a very emotional manner that he was "on your side." Presley kept repeating that he wanted to be helpful, that he wanted to restore some respect for the flag which was being lost. He mentioned that he was just a poor boy from Tennessee who had gotten a lot from his country, which in some way he wanted to repay. He also mentioned that he is studying Communist brainwashing and the drug culture for over ten years. He mentioned that he knew a lot about this and was accepted by the hippies. He said he could go right into a group of young people or hippies and be accepted which he felt could be helpful to him in his drug drive. The President indicated again his concern that Presley retain his credibility.

At the conclusion of the meeting, Presley again told the President how much he supported him, and then, in a surprising, spontaneous gesture, put his left arm around the President and hugged him.

In going out, Presley asked the President if he would see his two associates. The President agreed and they came over and shook hands with the President briefly. At this meeting, the President thanked him for their efforts and again mentioned his concern for Presley's credibility.

—Bud Krogh

Source:
Memorandum for the President's File from Bud Krogh, Nixon Materials Project, National Archives and Records Administration. Available on-line. URL: http://www.archives.gov/exhibit_hall/when_nixon_met_elvis/summary.html.

New York Times v. United States; United States v. Washington Post, 1971

The chain of events that led up to Watergate may be traced to the Nixon administration's attempt to halt publication in 1971 of the *Pentagon Papers,* a classified report about the history of the war in Vietnam in prior administrations that had been copied and given to the *New York Times* and *Washington Post.* In the *New York Times v. United States* and *United States v.*

Washington Post the Supreme Court refused to allow the government to exercise prior restraint of publication in this instance. However, it left open the possibility that the government could prevent publication in the future if it could demonstrate that publication would seriously compromise national security.

(excerpt)

Mr. Justice Black, with whom Mr. Justice Douglas joins, concurring.

I adhere to the view that the Government's case against the *Washington Post* should have been dismissed and that the injunction against the *New York Times* should have been vacated without oral argument when the cases were first presented to this Court. I believe that every moment's continuance of the injunctions against these newspapers amounts to a flagrant, indefensible, and continuing violation of the First Amendment. Furthermore, after oral argument, I agree completely that we must affirm the judgment of the Court of Appeals for the District of Columbia Circuit and reverse the judgment of the Court of Appeals for the Second Circuit for the reasons stated by my Brothers Douglas and Brennan. In my view it is unfortunate that some of my Brethren are apparently willing to hold that the publication of news may sometimes be enjoined. Such a holding would make a shambles of the First Amendment.

Our Government was launched in 1789 with the adoption of the Constitution. The Bill of Rights, including the First Amendment, followed in 1791. Now, for the first time in the 182 years since the founding of the Republic, the federal courts are asked to hold that the First Amendment does not mean what it says, but rather means that the Government can halt the publication of current news of vital importance to the people of this country.

In seeking injunctions against these newspapers and in its presentation to the Court, the Executive Branch seems to have forgotten the essential purpose and history of the First Amendment. When the Constitution was adopted, many people strongly opposed it because the document contained no Bill of Rights to safeguard certain basic freedoms. They especially feared that the new powers granted to a central government might be interpreted to permit the government to curtail freedom of religion, press, assembly, and speech. In response to an overwhelming public clamor, James Madison offered a series of amendments to satisfy citizens that these great liberties would remain safe and beyond the power of government to abridge. Madison proposed what later became the First Amendment in three parts, two of which are set out below, and one of which proclaimed: "The people shall not be deprived or abridged of their right to speak, to write, or to publish their sentiments; and the freedom of the press, as one of the great bulwarks of liberty, shall be inviolable." The amendments were offered to curtail and restrict the general powers granted to the Executive, Legislative, and Judicial Branches two years before in the original Constitution. The Bill of Rights changed the original Constitution into a new charter under which no branch of government could abridge the people's freedoms of press, speech, religion, and assembly. Yet the Solicitor General argues and some members of the Court appear to agree that the general powers of the Government adopted in the original Constitution should be interpreted to limit and restrict the specific and emphatic guarantees of the Bill of Rights adopted later. I can imagine no greater perversion of history. Madison and the other Framers of the First Amendment, able men that they were, wrote in language they earnestly believed could never be misunderstood: "Congress shall make no law . . . abridging the freedom . . . of the press. . . ." Both the history and language of the First Amendment support the view that the press must be left free to publish news, whatever the source, without censorship, injunctions, or prior restraints.

In the First Amendment the Founding Fathers gave the free press the protection it must have to fulfill its essential role in our democracy. The press was to serve the governed, not the governors. The Government's power to censor the press was abolished so that the press would remain forever free to censure the Government. The press was protected so that it could bare the secrets of government and inform the people. Only a free and unrestrained press can effectively expose deception in government. And paramount among the responsibilities of a free press is the duty to prevent any part of the government from deceiving the people and sending them off to distant lands to die of foreign fevers and foreign shot and shell. In my view, far from deserving condemnation for their courageous reporting, the *New York Times*, the *Washington Post*, and other newspapers should be commended for serving the purpose that the Founding Fathers saw so clearly. In revealing the workings of government that led to the Vietnam war, the newspapers nobly did precisely that which the Founders hoped and trusted they would do. . . .

. . . Two federal district courts, two United States courts of appeals, and this Court—within a period of less than three weeks from inception until today—have been pressed into hurried decision of profound constitutional issues on inadequately developed and largely assumed facts without the careful deliberation that, one would hope, should characterize the American judicial process. . . .

With such respect as may be due to the contrary view, this, in my opinion, is not the way to try a lawsuit of this magnitude and asserted importance. It is not the way for federal courts to adjudicate, and to be required to adjudicate, issues that allegedly concern the Nation's vital welfare. The country would be none the worse off were the cases tried quickly, to be sure, but in the customary and properly deliberate manner. The most recent of the material, it is said, dates no later than 1968, already about three years ago, and the *Times* itself took three months to formulate its plan of procedure and, thus, deprived its public for that period.

The First Amendment, after all, is only one part of an entire Constitution. Article II of the great document vests in the Executive Branch primary power over the conduct of foreign affairs and places in that branch the responsibility for the Nation's safety. Each provision of the Constitution is important, and I cannot subscribe to a doctrine of unlimited absolutism for the First Amendment at the cost of downgrading other provisions. First Amendment absolutism has never commanded a majority of this Court . . . . What is needed here is a weighing, upon properly developed standards, of the broad right of the press to print and of the very narrow right of the Government to prevent. Such standards are nor yet developed. The parties here are in disagreement as to what those standards should be. But even the newspapers concede that there are situations where restraint is in order and is constitutional. . . .

I therefore would remand these cases to be developed expeditiously, of course, but on a schedule permitting the orderly presentation of evidence from both sides, with the use if discovery, if necessary, as authorized by the rules, and with the preparation of briefs, oral argument, and court opinions of a quality better than has been seen to this point. In making this last statement, I criticize no lawyer or judge. I know from past personal experience the agony of time pressure in the preparation of litigation. But these cases and the issues involved and the courts, including this one, deserve better than has been produced thus far.

It may well be that if these cases were allowed to develop as they should be developed, and to be tried as lawyers should try them and as courts should hear them, free of pressure and panic and sensationalism, other light would be shed on the situation and contrary consideration, for me, might prevail. But that is not the present posture of the litigation.

The Court, however, decides the cases today the other way. I therefore add one final comment.

I strongly urge, and sincerely hope, that these two newspapers will be fully aware of their ultimate responsibilities to the United States of America. Judge Wilkey, dissenting in the District of Columbia case, after a review of only the affidavits before his court (the basic papers had not then been made available by either party), concluded that there were a number of examples of documents that, if in the possession of the *Post*, and if published, "could clearly result in great harm to the nation," and he defined "harm" to mean "the death of soldiers, the destruction of alliances, the greatly increased difficulty of negotiation with our enemies, the inability of our diplomats to negotiate . . . ." I, for one, have now been able to give at least some cursory study not only to the affidavits, but to the material itself. I regret to say that from this examination I fear that Judge Wilkey's statements have possible foundation. I therefore share his concern. I hope that damage has not already been done. If, however, damage has been done, and if, with the Court's action today, these newspapers proceed to publish the critical documents and there results therefrom "the death of soldiers, the destruction of alliances, the greatly increased difficulty of negotiation with our enemies, the inability of our diplomats to negotiate," to which list I might add the factors of prolongation of the war and of further delay in the freeing of United States prisoners, then the Nation's people will know where the responsibility for these sad consequences rests.

See also *UNITED STATES V. NIXON*, 1974.

Source:

Supreme Court Reporter, Vol. 91, pp. 2,140–2,166.

United States v. Nixon, 1974

In *United States v. Nixon*, a unanimous Court dealt with the constitutional limits of executive privilege. Its forced the president to make public all the White House tape recordings subpoenaed by the Watergate Special Prosecutor. As a result, Nixon was forced to disclose the so-called smoking gun tape of June 23, 1972, in which he attempted to interfere with the investigation of the June 17, 1972, break-in at the Watergate office building, headquarters of the Democratic National Committee. The decision was preceded by the House Judiciary Committee's completion of articles of impeachment against President Richard M. Nixon. Together, the Court decision and the articles of impeachment convinced the president's advisers that his only alternatives were to resign or be convicted by the Senate. He resigned August 9.

The House Judiciary Committee, was composed of 21 Democrats, all of whom approved all three articles, and 19 Republicans. On May 9, 1979, the committee began conducting formal impeachment hearings. It voted to approve the first article, for deliberately engaging in obstruction of justice, 27 to 11 on July 27. Article Two was approved July 29, by a vote of 28 to 10. It charged the president with abuse of powers in violation of the Constitution by using the IRS, the FBI, and other government agencies to spy on American citizens. The third article of impeachment passed 21 to 17, July 30. It charged that Nixon violated the Constitution by ignoring congressional subpoenas of White House documents.

Both the obstruction of justice impeachment article and *United States v. Nixon* resulted from the refusal of the president to hand over the tape recordings he had secretly made in the White House and at Camp David. The investigation, conducted by the Watergate Special Prosecution Force, ended in the indictment of seven officials of the Nixon administration. The president was considered an unindicted co-conspirator. According to Special Prosecutor Leon Jaworsky, the tape recordings of conversations involving the defendants were needed for use in their trial. President Nixon refused to comply, claiming absolute executive privilege over all material requested. At issue was the apparent conflict between legitimate executive privilege and the autonomy of the presidency, on the one hand, and the right of the judicial branch to facilitate criminal proceedings, on the other. On July 24, 1974, the Supreme Court decided by a vote of 8 to 0, with Associate Justice Rehnquist not participating, that the executive privilege claimed by the president was not absolute and that the judiciary had a legitimate right to judge the merits of claims of executive privilege. Since the subpoenaed tapes were directly relevant to an ongoing criminal prosecution, the chief justice ruled that the president's "generalized interest in confidentiality" was subordinate to "the fundamental demands of due process of law in the fair administration of criminal justice."

As a result of the role campaign funding played in the Watergate scandals, Congress passed campaign reform legislation signed by President Gerald Ford on October 15, 1974. The Federal Election Campaign Act provided public financing of presidential primaries and elections and set ceilings on contributions and spending in House, Senate, and presidential campaigns. Designed to eliminate undue influence of large contributors or special interest groups, the act failed by the 1990s because of a loophole. This provision allowed huge sums of money to be donated to federal campaigns through the political parties and by political action committees (PACs) for ads that advocated or criticized political positions without actually mentioning a candidate's name. Use of this so-called soft money was outlawed by the McCain-Feingold bill passed in March 2002, but did not go into effect until after the congressional election of that year.

(excerpt)

In support of his claim of absolute privilege, the President's counsel urges two grounds; one of which is common to all governments and one of which is peculiar to our system of separation of powers. The first ground is the valid need for protection of communications between high Government officials and those who advise and assist them in the performance of their manifold duties; the importance of this confidentiality is too plain to require further discussion. Human experience teaches that those who expect public dissemination of their remarks may well temper candor with a concern for appearances and for their own interests to the detriment of the decision making process. Whatever the nature of the privilege of confidentiality of Presidential communications in the exercises of Art. II powers, the privilege can be said to derive from the supremacy of each branch within its own assigned area of constitutional duties. Certain powers and privileges flow from the nature of enumerated powers; the protection of the confidentiality of Presidential communications has similar constitutional underpinnings.

The second ground asserted by the President's counsel in support of the claim of absolute privilege rests on the doctrine of separation of powers. Here it is argued that the independence of the Executive Branch within its own sphere, *Humphrey's Executor v. United States,* 295 U.S. 602, 692–630, 55 S.Ct. 869, 874–875, 79 L.Ed. 1611 (1935); *Kilbourn v. Thompson,* 103 U.S. 168, 190–191, 26 L.Ed. 377 (1881), insulates a President from a judicial subpoena in an ongoing criminal prosecution, and thereby protects confidential Presidential communications.

[36] However, neither the doctrine of separation of powers, nor the need for confidentiality of high-level communications, without more, can sustain an absolute, unqualified Presidential privilege of immunity from judicial process under all circumstances. The President's need for complete candor and objectivity from advisers calls for great deference from the courts. However, when the privilege depends solely on the broad, undifferentiated claim of public interest in the confidentiality of such conversations, a confrontation with other values arises. Absent a claim of need to protect military, diplomatic, or sensitive national security secrets, we find it difficult to accept the argument that even the very important interest in confidentiality of Presidential communications is significantly diminished by production of such material for *in camera* inspection with all the protection that a district court will be obliged to provide.

The impediment that an absolute, unqualified privilege would place in the way of the primary constitutional duty of the Judicial Branch to do justice in criminal prosecutions would plainly conflict with the function of the courts under Art. III. In designing the structure of our Government and dividing and allocating the sovereign power among three co-equal branches, the Framers of the Constitution sought to provide a comprehensive system, but the separate powers were not intended to operate with absolute independence.

"While the Constitution diffuses power the better to secure liberty, it also contemplates that practice will integrate the dispersed powers into a workable government. It enjoins upon its branches separateness but interdependence. autonomy but reciprocity." *Youngstown Sheet & Tube Co. v. Sawyer,* 343 U.S., at 635, 72 S.Ct., at 870 (Jackson, J., concurring).

See also *NEW YORK TIMES V. UNITED STATES, UNITED STATES V. WASHINGTON POST,* 1971.

Source:

Supreme Court Reporter, Vol. 94, pp. 3,090–3,111.

Struggle for Racial and Gender Equality and for the Extension of Civil Liberties

Brown v. Board of Education of Topeka, Kansas, 1954

Landmark U.S. Supreme Court decision issued on May 17, 1954, declaring that racial segregation in public schools was unconstitutional. Reversing *Plessy v. Ferguson,* which allowed for "separate but equal" facilities, the Court now unanimously ruled that "separate educational facilities are inherently unequal" and violate the equal protection guarantees of the Fourteenth Amendment. The Topeka case was brought before the Court by the National Association for the Advancement of Colored People (NAACP) on behalf of Linda Brown, a student who attended an all-black elementary school. Also included in the decision were several other cases brought on behalf of students in Delaware, Virginia, and South Carolina districts. A separate case handled the segregated District of Columbia system. *Brown* paved the way for prohibiting de jure (i.e., legislated) Jim Crow (segregation) laws in all phases of society, including public accommodations and housing. However, it could not touch de facto segregation, in which, for example, housing patterns rather than ordinances kept schools segregated, as happened frequently in the North. The decision itself, overturning more than a half-century of racial separation, was so difficult for the justices that they took another year to suggest hov. desegregation should take place (*Brown II*). The solution, "with all deliberate speed," resulted in slow and even non-existent desegregation in many areas.

On April 20, 1971, in *Swann v. Mecklenberg Board of Education,* the Supreme Court ruled unanimously that the district courts were justified in ordering compliance with their own desegregation plans when the local school authorities fail to desegregate voluntarily. Chief Justice Burger, writing for the Court, held that the objective of the courts was to eliminate all vestiges of state-imposed segregation in public schools.

Almost a half-century after *Brown,* many major public school systems still have de facto segregation. Attempts to rectify years of discrimination by affirmative action initially appeared effective. However, whites, beginning in the 1970s, brought cases contending that they were being discriminated against because of race, e.g., *Regents of the University of California v. Bakke* (438 U.S. 265 [1978]). Although de jure Jim Crow no longer exists in the United States, the Rehnquist Court has for all intents and purposes removed race from affirmative consideration in all but the most restrictive situations, exacerbating continued separation.

Mr. Chief Justice Warren delivered the opinion of the Court.

These cases come to us from the States of Kansas, South Carolina, Virginia, and Delaware. They are premised on different facts and different local conditions, but a common legal question justifies their consideration together in this consolidated opinion.

In each of the cases, minors of the Negro race, through their legal representatives, seek the aid of the courts in obtaining admission to the public schools of their community on a nonsegregated basis. In each instance, they have been denied admission to schools attended by white children under laws requiring or permitting segregation according to race. This segregation was alleged to deprive the plaintiffs of the equal protection of the laws under the Fourteenth Amendment. In each of the cases other than the Delaware case, a three-judge federal district court denied relief to the plaintiffs on the so-called "separate but equal" doctrine announced by this Court in *Plessy v. Ferguson,* 163 U.S. 537, 16 S.Ct. 1138, 41 L.Ed. 256. Under that doctrine, equality of treatment is accorded when the races are provided substantially equal facilities, even though these facilities be separate. In the Delaware case, the Supreme Court of Delaware adhered to that doctrine, but ordered that the plaintiffs be admitted to the white schools because of their superiority to the Negro schools.

The plaintiffs contend that segregated public schools are not "equal" and cannot be made "equal," and that hence they are deprived of the equal protection of the laws. Because of the obvious importance of the question presented, the Court took jurisdiction. Argument was heard in the 1952 Term, and reargument was heard this Term on certain questions propounded by the Court.

Reargument was largely devoted to the circumstances surrounding the adoption of the Fourteenth Amendment in 1868. It covered exhaustively consideration of the Amendment in Congress, ratification by the states, then existing practices in racial segregation, and the views of proponents and opponents of the Amendment. This discussion and our own investigation convince us that, although these sources cast some light, it is not enough to resolve the problem with which we are faced. At best, they are inconclusive. The most avid proponents of the postwar Amendments undoubtedly intended them to remove all legal distinctions among "all persons born or naturalized in the United States." Their opponents, just as certainly, were antagonistic to both the letter and the spirit of the Amendments and wished them to have the most limited effect. What others in Congress and the state legislatures had in mind cannot be determined with any degree of certainty.

An additional reason for the inconclusive nature of the Amendment's history, with respect to segregated schools, is the status of public education at that time. In the South, the movement toward free common schools, supported by general taxation, had not yet taken hold. Education of white children was largely in the hands of private groups. Education of Negroes was almost nonexistent, and practically all of the race were illiterate. In fact, any education of Negroes was forbidden by law in some states. Today, in contrast, many Negroes have achieved outstanding success in the arts and sciences as well as in the business and professional world. It is true that public school education at the time of the Amendment had advanced further in the North, but the effect of the Amendment on Northern States was generally ignored in the congressional debates. Even in the North, the conditions of public education did not approximate those existing today. The curriculum was usually rudimentary; ungraded schools were common in rural areas; the school term was but three months a year in many states; and compulsory school attendance was virtually unknown. As a consequence, it is not surprising that there should be so little in the history of the Fourteenth Amendment relating to its intended effect on public education.

In the first cases in this Court construing the Fourteenth Amendment, decided shortly after its adoption, the Court interpreted it as proscribing all state-imposed discriminations against the Negro race. The doctrine of "separate but equal" did not make its appearance in this Court until 1896 in the case of *Plessy v. Ferguson,* supra, involving not education but transportation. American courts have since labored with the doctrine for over half a century. In this Court, there have been six cases involving the "separate but equal" doctrine in the field of public education. In *Cumming v. Board of Education of Richmond County,* 175 U.S. 528, 20 S.Ct. 197, 44 L.Ed. 262, and Gong Lum v. Rice, 275 U.S. 78, 48 S.Ct. 91, 72 L.Ed. 172, the validity of the doctrine itself was not challenged. In more recent cases, all on the graduate school level, inequality was found in that specific benefits enjoyed by white students were denied to Negro students of the same educational qualifications. State of Missouri ex rel. *Gaines v. Canada,* 305 U.S. 337, 59 S.Ct. 232, 83 L.Ed. 208; *Sipuel v. Board of Regents of University of Oklahoma,* 332 U.S. 631, 68 S.Ct. 299, 92 L.Ed. 247; *Sweatt v. Painter,* 339 U.S. 629, 70 S.Ct. 848, 94 L.Ed. 1114; *McLaurin v. Oklahoma State Regents,* 339 U.S. 637, 70 S.Ct. 851, 94 L.Ed. 1149. In none of these cases was it necessary to re-examine the doctrine to grant relief to the Negro plaintiff. And in *Sweatt v. Painter,* supra, the Court expressly reserved decision on the question whether *Plessy v. Ferguson* should be held inapplicable to public education.

In the instant cases, that question is directly presented. Here, unlike *Sweatt v. Painter,* there are findings below that the Negro and white schools involved have been equalized, or are being equalized, with respect to buildings, curricula, qualifications and salaries of teachers, and other "tangible" factors. Our decision, therefore, cannot turn on merely a comparison of these tangible factors in the Negro and white schools involved in each of the cases. We must look instead to the effect of segregation itself on public education.

[1] In approaching this problem, we cannot turn the clock back to 1868 when the Amendment was adopted, or even to 1896 when *Plessy v. Ferguson* was written. We must consider public education in the light of its full development and its present place in American life throughout the Nation. Only in this way can it be determined if segregation in public schools deprives these plaintiffs of the equal protection of the laws.

[2] Today, education is perhaps the most important function of state and local governments. Compulsory school attendance laws and the great expenditures for education both demonstrate our recognition of the importance of education to our democratic society. It is required in the performance of our most basic public responsibilities, even service in the armed forces. It is the very foundation of good citizenship. Today it is a principal instrument in awakening the child to cultural values, in preparing him for later professional training, and in helping him to adjust normally to his environment. In these days, it is doubtful that any child may reasonably be expected to succeed in life if he is denied the opportunity of an education. Such an opportunity, where the state has undertaken to provide it, is a right which must be made available to all on equal terms.

[3] We come then to the question presented: Does segregation of children in public schools solely on the basis of race, even though the physical facilities and other "tangible" factors may be equal, deprive the children of the minority group of equal educational opportunities? We believe that it does.

In *Sweatt v. Painter*, supra [339 U.S. 629, 70 S.Ct. 850], in finding that a segregated law school for Negroes could not provide them equal educational opportunities, this Court relied in large part on "those qualities which are incapable of objective measurement but which make for greatness in a law school." In *McLaurin v. Oklahoma State Regents*, supra [339 U.S. 637, 70 S.Ct. 853], the Court, in requiring that a Negro admitted to a white graduate school be treated like all other students, again resorted to intangible considerations: ". . . his ability to study, to engage in discussions and exchange views with other students, and, in general, to learn his profession." Such considerations apply with added force to children in grade and high schools. To separate them from others of similar age and qualifications solely because of their race generates a feeling of inferiority as to their status in the community that may affect their hearts and minds in a way unlikely ever to be undone. The effect of this separation on their educational opportunities was well stated by a finding in the Kansas case by a court which nevertheless felt compelled to rule against the Negro plaintiffs:

"Segregation of white and colored children in public schools has a detrimental effect upon the colored children. The impact is greater when it has the sanction of the law; for the policy of separating the races is usually interpreted as denoting the inferiority of the negro group. A sense of inferiority affects the motivation of a child to learn. Segregation with the sanction of law, therefore, has a tendency to [retard] the educational and [mental] development of Negro children and to deprive them of some of the benefits they would receive in a racial[ly] integrated school system. Whatever may have been the extent of psychological knowledge at the time of *Plessy v. Ferguson*, this finding is amply supported by modern authority. Any language in *Plessy v. Ferguson* contrary to this finding is rejected.

[4] We conclude that in the field of public education the doctrine of "separate but equal" has no place. Separate educational facilities are inherently unequal. Therefore, we hold that the plaintiffs and others similarly situated for whom the actions have been brought are, by reason of the segregation complained of, deprived of the equal protection of the laws guaranteed by the Fourteenth Amendment. This disposition makes unnecessary any discussion whether such segregation also violates the Due Process Clause of the Fourteenth Amendment.

[5] Because these are class actions, because of the wide applicability of this decision, and because of the great variety of local conditions, the formulation of decrees in these cases presents problems of considerable complexity. On reargument, the consideration of appropriate relief was necessarily subordinated to the primary question—the constitutionality of segregation in public education. We have now announced that such segregation is a denial of the equal protection of the laws. In order that we may have the full assistance of the parties in formulating decrees, the cases will be restored to the docket, and the parties are requested to present further argument on Questions 4 and 5 previously propounded by the Court for the reargument this Term. The Attorney General of the United States is again invited to participate. The Attorneys General of the states requiring or permitting segregation in public education will also be permitted to appear as *amici curiae* upon request to do so by September 15, 1954, and submission of briefs of October 1, 1954.

It is so ordered.

Cases ordered restored to docket for further argument on question of appropriate decrees

See also SOUTHERN MANIFESTO ON INTEGRATION, 1956; DWIGHT D. EISENHOWER, STATEMENTS CONCERNING LITTLE ROCK, ARKANSAS, 1957.

Source:
Supreme Court Reporter, Vol. 74, pp. 686–693.

Southern Manifesto on Integration, 1956

Declaration issued March 12, 1956, and signed by 101 southern members of the U.S. Senate and House of Representatives condemning the U.S. Supreme Court decision in *Brown v. Board of Education of Topeka, Kansas* and stating that they would try to overturn it. It called the decision "a clear abuse of judicial power" and urged the use of "all lawful means to bring about a reversal of this decision which is contrary to the Constitution." It encouraged states to resist the Supreme Court's mandate to desegregate public schools, which many southern localities did to the point of closing all public schools and instituting subsidized private ones open to whites only.

Among those resisting desegregation was Governor Orval Faubus of Arkansas. When courts ordered the Little Rock schools to admit black students, the governor resisted. The nine students entering Central High School were met by a hostile mob. When Faubus called out the National Guard, it was not to protect them, but to keep them out. President Dwight D. Eisenhower announced September 24 that he had sent federal troops to preserve order. Declaring that "mob rule cannot be allowed to override the decisions of our courts," Eisenhower, who sympathized with white southerners, justified his action as necessary to preserve peace and order (not to enforce integration) when state and local authorities failed to do so. Though the speech was conciliatory, many white southerners were enraged by Eisenhower's action.

Integration of schools in any state was upheld by the U.S. Supreme Court in *Cooper v. Aaron,* issued September 29, 1958. This unanimous decision stated that the attempts of the legislature and governor of Arkansas to resist court-ordered desegregation were unconstitutional. State regulation of education must be consistent with federal constitutional requirements of equal justice under law. State officials cannot nullify, either directly or indirectly, through "evasive schemes for segregation," the constitutional rights of children to be protected against discrimination.

The unwarranted decision of the Supreme Court in the public school cases is now bearing the fruit always produced when men substitute naked power for established law.

The Founding Fathers gave us a Constitution of checks and balances because they realized the inescapable lesson of history that no man or group of men can be safely entrusted with unlimited power. They framed this Constitution with its provisions for change by amendment in order to secure the fundamentals of government against the dangers of temporary popular passion or the personal predilections of public officeholders.

We regard the decision of the Supreme Court in the school cases as clear abuse of judicial power. It climaxes a trend in the Federal judiciary undertaking to legislate, in derogation of the authority of Congress, and to encroach upon the reserved rights of the states and the people.

The original Constitution does not mention education. Neither does the Fourteenth Amendment nor any other amendment. The debates preceding the submission of the Fourteenth Amendment clearly show that there was no intent that it should affect the systems of education maintained by the states.

The very Congress which proposed the amendment subsequently provided for segregated schools in the District of Columbia.

When the amendment was adopted in 1868, there were thirty-seven states of the Union. Every one of the twenty-six states that had any substantial racial differences among its people either approved the operation of segregated schools already in existence or subsequently established such schools by action of the same law-making body which considered the Fourteenth Amendment.

As admitted by the Supreme Court in the public school case (*Brown v. Board of Education*), the doctrine of separate but equal schools "apparently originated in *Roberts v. City of Boston* (1849), upholding school segregation against attack as being violative of a state constitutional guarantee of equality." This constitutional doctrine began in the North—not in the South—and it was followed not only in Massachusetts but in Connecticut, New York, Illinois, Indiana, Michigan, Minnesota, New Jersey, Ohio, Pennsylvania and other northern states until they, exercising their rights as states through the constitutional processes of local self-government, changed their school systems.

In the case of *Plessy v. Ferguson* in 1896 the Supreme Court expressly declared that under the Fourteenth Amendment no person was denied any of his rights if the states provided separate but equal public facilities. This decision has been followed in many other cases. It is notable that the Supreme Court, speaking through Chief Justice Taft, a former President of the United States, unanimously declared in 1927 in *Lum v. Rice* that the "separate but equal" principle is ". . . within the discretion of the state in regulating its public schools and does not conflict with the Fourteenth Amendment."

This interpretation, restated time and again, became a part of the life of the people of many of the states and confirmed their habits, customs, traditions and way of life. It is founded on elemental humanity and common sense, for parents should not be deprived by Government of the right to direct the lives and education of their own children.

Though there has been no constitutional amendment or act of Congress changing this established legal principle almost a century old, the Supreme Court of the United States, with no legal basis for such action, undertook to exercise their naked judicial power and substituted their personal political and social ideas for the established law of the land.

This unwarranted exercise of power by the court, contrary to the Constitution, is creating chaos and confusion in the states principally affected. It is destroying the amicable relations between the white and Negro races that have been created through ninety years of patient effort by the good people of both races. It has planted hatred and suspicion where there has been heretofore friendship and understanding.

Without regard to the consent of the governed, outside agitators are threatening immediate and revolutionary changes in our public school systems. If done, this is certain to destroy the system of public education in some of the states.

With the gravest concern for the explosive and dangerous condition created by this decision and inflamed by outside meddlers.

We reaffirm our reliance on the Constitution as the fundamental law of the land.

We decry the Supreme Court's encroachments on rights reserved to the states and to the people, contrary to established law and to the Constitution.

We commend the motives of those states which have declared the intention to resist forced integration by any lawful means.

We appeal to the states and people who are not directly affected by these decisions to consider the constitutional principles involved against the time when they too, on issues vital to them, may be the victims of judicial encroachment.

Even though we constitute a minority in the present congress, we have full faith that a majority of the American people believe in the dual system of government which has enabled us to achieve our greatness and will in time demand that the reserved rights of the states and of the people be made secure against judicial usurpation.

We pledge ourselves to use all lawful means to bring about a reversal of this decision which is contrary to the Constitution and to prevent the use of force in its implementation.

In this trying period, as we all seek to right this wrong, we appeal to our people not to be provoked by the agitators and troublemakers invading our states and to scrupulously refrain from disorder and lawless acts.

Signed by:

Members of the United States Senate:

Alabama—John Sparkman and Lister Hill.
Arkansas—J. W. Fulbright and John L. McClellan.
Florida—George A. Smathers and Spessard L. Holland.
Georgia—Walter F. George and Richard B. Russell.
Louisiana—Allen J. Ellender and Russell B. Lono.
Mississippi—John Stennis and James O. Eastland.
North Carolina—Sam J. Ervin Jr. and W. Kerr Scott.
South Carolina—Strom Thurmon and Olin D. Johnston.
Texas—Price Daniel.
Virginia—Harry F. Bird and A. Willis Robertson.

Members of the United States House of Representatives:

Alabama—Frank J. Boykin, George M. Grant, George M. Andrews, Kenneth R. Roberts, Albert Rains, Armistead I. Selden Jr., Carl Elliott, Robert E. Jones and George Huddleston Jr.
Arkansas—E. C. Gathings, Wilbur D. Mills, James W. Trimble, Oren Harris, Brooks Hays, F. W. Norrell.
Florida—Charles E. Bennett Robert L. Sikes, A. S. Her Jr., Paul G. Rogers, James A. Haley, D. R. Matthews.
Georgia—Prince H. Preston, John L. Pilcher, E. L. Forrester, John James Flint Jr., James C. Davis, Carl Vinson, Henderson Lanham, Iris F. Blitch, Phil M. Landrum, Paul Brown.
Louisiana—F. Edward Hebert, Hale Boggs, Edwin E. Willis, Overton Brooks, Otto E. Passman, James H. Morrison, T. Ashton Thompson, George S. Long.
Mississippi—Thomas G. Abernethy, Jamie L. Whitten, Frank E. Smith, John Bell Williams, Arthur Winsted, William M. Colmer.
North Carolina—Herbert C. Bonner, L. H. Fountain, Graham A. Barden, Carl T. Durham, F. Ertel Carlyle, Hugh Q. Alexander, Woodrow W. Jones, George A. Shuford.
South Carolina—L. Mendel Rivers, John J. Riley, W. J. Bryan Dorn, Robert T. Ashmore, James P. Richards, John L. McMillan.
Tennessee—James B. Frazier Jr., Tom Murray, Jere Cooper, Clifford Davis.
Texas—Wright Patman, John Dowdy, Walter Rogers, O. C. Fisher.
Virginia—Edward J. Robeson Jr., Porter Hardy Jr., J. Vaughan Gary, Watkins M. Abbitt, William M. Tuck, Richard H. Poff, Burr P. Harrison, Howard W. Smith, W. Pat Jennings, Joel T. Brothill.

Source:

New York Times, March 12, 1956.

Civil Rights Act, 1957

The first federal civil rights legislation since Reconstruction, this legislation, enacted September 9, 1957, was a step protecting the civil rights of all American citizens, especially blacks. It established the federal Civil Rights Commission, elevated the Department of Justice (DOJ) Civil Rights Section to a division (CRD) headed by an assistant attorney general to prosecute civil rights violators, and permitted the federal government to seek injunctions to protect civil rights. The commission was authorized to investigate violations of voting and equal protection rights under the law and to recommend new legislation to Congress.

Mild as it was, this act provided the underpinnings for civil rights enforcement that later civil rights acts would provide. The next civil rights bill, enacted May 6, 1960, also strengthened civil rights protection by providing criminal penalties for obstruction of court orders for school desegregation, requiring that election records be kept for two years and be available to DOJ, providing for education of children of military personnel where schools were closed to avoid desegregation, and establishing a system of court-appointed voting referees to register black voters who had been denied registration in areas where there was a pattern of racial discrimination. However the federal government did not have the authority to initiate suits regarding registration until 1965, rendering the latter clause ineffective.

The much better known 1964 Civil Rights Act, signed July 2, 1964, and which received strong backing from Presidents John F. Kennedy and Lyndon B. Johnson, prohibited discrimination in all public accommodations serving an interstate clientele or involving interstate commerce, such as hotels, gas stations, restaurants, and theaters, and in any program receiving federal funds. The act prohibited employers from refusing to hire, from firing, or from discriminating against any individual because of race, religion, or sex (Title VII) and established the Equal Employment Opportunity Commission to enforce these provisions. It also required state voting registrars to apply qualification standards equally.

The Civil Rights Act of April 11, 1968, also called the Fair Housing Act, was passed to end discrimination based on race, color, religion, or national origin in housing in the United States. It prohibited discrimination in the sale or rental of housing owned or financed at least in part by the federal government, except for owner-occupied dwellings of four or fewer units, and in single-family houses sold or rented through brokers, and prohibited discrimination in the financing of housing and in brokerage services. Also included in this act was the Anti-riot Act. An amendment enacted October 14, 1972, renewed the Commission on Civil Rights and extended the jurisdiction of the commission to include sexual discrimination. Fair housing was expanded in 1988 with amendments that provided new, more stringent provisions against discrimination in housing. Now discrimination in public and private housing against both the disabled and families with children (except in housing specifically designated as housing for the retired) became illegal. In addition, transgressors would receive substantial fines from the government.

None of these civil rights acts addressed racially motivated violence. (The federal authority for combating those violations is found in the civil rights statutes of 1866 and are now codified as 18 U.S.C. 141 and 142. Federal prosecutions under them remained of questionable constitutionality until 1966, a full century after their original passage.)

No federal civil rights legislation has included sexual orientation in its provisions.

An Act

To provide means of further securing and protecting the civil rights of persons within the jurisdiction of the United States.

Be it enacted by the Senate and House of Representatives of the United States of America in Congress assembled,

Part I—Establishment of the Commission on Civil Rights

Sec. 101. (a) There is created in the executive branch of the Government a Commission on Civil Rights (hereinafter called the "Commission").

(b) The Commission shall be composed of six members who shall be appointed by the President by and with the advice and consent of the Senate. Not more than three of the members shall at any one time be of the same political party.

(c) The President shall designate one of the members of the Commission as Chairman and one as Vice Chairman. The Vice Chairman shall act as Chairman in the absence or disability of the Chairman, or in the event of a vacancy in that office.

(d) Any vacancy in the Commission shall not affect its powers and shall be filled in the same manner, and subject to the same limitation with respect to party affiliations as the original appointment was made.

(e) Four members of the Commission shall constitute a quorum.

Rules of Procedure of the Commission

Sec. 102. (a) The Chairman or one designated by him to act as Chairman at a hearing of the Commission shall announce in an opening statement the subject of the hearing.

(b) A copy of the Commission's rules shall be made available to the witness before the Commission.

(c) Witnesses at the hearings may be accompanied by their own counsel for the purpose of advising them concerning their constitutional rights.

(d) The Chairman or Acting Chairman may punish breaches of order and decorum and unprofessional ethics on the part of counsel, by censure and exclusion from the hearings.

(e) If the Commission determines that evidence or testimony at any hearing may tend to defame, degrade, or incriminate any person, it shall (1) receive such evidence or testimony in executive session; (2) afford such person an opportunity voluntarily to appear as a witness; and (3) receive and dispose of requests from such person to subpena additional witnesses.

(f) Except as provided in sections 102 and 105 (f) of this Act, the Chairman shall receive and the Commission shall dispose of requests to subpena additional witnesses.

(g) No evidence or testimony taken in executive session may be released or used in public sessions without the consent of the Commission. Whoever releases or uses in public without the consent of the Commission evidence or testimony taken in executive session shall be fined not more than $1,000, or imprisoned for not more than one year.

(h) In the discretion of the Commission, witnesses may submit brief and pertinent sworn statements in writing for inclusion in the record. The Commission is the sole judge of the pertinency of testimony and evidence adduced at its hearings.

(i) Upon payment of the cost thereof, a witness may obtain a transcript copy of his testimony given at a public session or, if given at an executive session, when authorized by the Commission.

(j) A witness attending any session of the Commission shall receive $4 for each day's attendance and for the time necessarily occupied in going to and returning from the same, and 8 cents per mile for going from and returning to his place of residence. Witnesses who attend at points so far removed from their respective residences as to prohibit return thereto from day to day shall be entitled to an additional allowance of $12 per day for expenses of subsistence, including the time necessarily occupied in going to and returning from the place of attendance. Mileage payments shall be tendered to the witness upon service of a subpena issued on behalf of the Commission or any subcommittee thereof.

(k) The Commission shall not issue any subpena for the attendance and testimony of witnesses or for the production of written or other matter which would require the presence of the party subpenaed at a hearing to be held outside of the State, wherein the witness is found or resides or transacts business.

Compensation of Members of the Commission

Sec. 103. (a) Each member of the Commission who is not otherwise in the service of the Government of the United States shall receive the sum of $50 per day for each day spent in the work of the Commission, shall be reimbursed for actual and necessary travel expenses, and shall receive a per diem allowance of $12 in lieu of actual expenses for subsistence when away from his usual place of residence, inclusive of fees or tips to porters and stewards.

(b) Each member of the Commission who is otherwise in the service of the Government of the United States shall serve without compensation in addition to that received for such other service, but while engaged in the work of the Commission shall be reimbursed for actual and necessary travel expenses, and shall receive a per diem allowance of $12 in lieu of actual expenses for subsistence when away from his usual place of residence, inclusive of fees or tips to porters and stewards.

Duties of the Commission

Sec. 104. (a) The Commission shall—

(1) investigate allegations in writing under oath or affirmation that certain citizens of the United States are being deprived of their right to vote and have that vote counted by reason of their color, race, religion, or national origin; which writing, under oath or affirmation, shall set forth the facts upon which such belief or beliefs are based;

(2) study and collect information concerning legal developments constituting a denial of equal protection of the laws under the Constitution; and

(3) appraise the laws and policies of the Federal Government with respect to equal protection of the laws under the Constitution.

(b) The Commission shall submit interim reports to the President and to the Congress at such times as either the Commission or the President shall deem desirable, and shall submit to the President and to the Congress a final and comprehensive report of its activities, findings, and recommendations not later than two years from the date of the enactment of this Act.

(c) Sixty days after the submission of its final report and recommendations the Commission shall cease to exist.

Powers of the Commission

Sec. 105. (a) There shall be a full-time staff director for the Commission who shall be appointed by the President by and with the advice and consent of the Senate and who shall receive compensation at a rate, to be fixed by the President, not in excess of $22,500 a year. The President shall consult with the Commission before submitting the nomination of any person for appointment to the position of staff director. Within the limitations of its appropriations, the Commission may appoint such other personnel as it deems advisable, in accordance with the civil service and classification laws, and may procure services as authorized by section 15 of the Act of August 2, 1946 (60 Stat. 810; 5 U.S.C. 55a), but at rates for individuals not in excess of $50 per diem.

(b) The Commission shall not accept or utilize services of voluntary or uncompensated personnel, and the term "whoever" as used in paragraph (g) of section 102 hereof shall be construed to mean a person whose services are compensated by the United States.

(c) The Commission may constitute such advisory committees within States composed of citizens of that State and may consult with governors, attorneys general, and other representatives of State and local governments, and private organizations, as it deems advisable.

(d) Members of the Commission, and members of advisory committees constituted pursuant to subsection (c) of this section, shall be exempt from the operation of sections 281, 283, 284, 434, and 1914 of title 18 of the United States Code, and section 190 of the Revised Statutes (5 U.S.C. 99).

(e) All Federal agencies shall cooperate fully with the Commission to the end that it may effectively carry out its functions and duties.

(f) The Commission, or on the authorization of the Commission any subcommittee of two or more members, at least one of whom shall be of each major political party, may, for the purpose of carrying out the provisions of this Act, hold such hearings and act at such times and places as the Commission or such authorized subcommittee may deem advisable. Subpenas for the attendance and testimony of witnesses or the production of written or other matter may be issued in accordance with the rules of the Commission as contained in section 102(j) and (k) of this Act, over the signature of the Chairman of the Commission or of such subcommittee, and may be served by any person designated by such Chairman.

(g) In case of contumacy or refusal to obey a subpena, any district court of the United States or the United States court of any Territory or possession, or the District Court of the United States for the District of Columbia, within the jurisdiction of which the inquiry is carried on or within the jurisdiction of which said person guilty of contumacy or refusal to obey is found or resides or transacts business, upon application by the Attorney General of the United States shall have jurisdiction to issue to such person an order requiring such person to appear before the Commission or a subcommittee thereof, there to produce evidence if so ordered, or there to give testimony touching the matter under investigation; and any failure to obey such order of the court may be punished by said court as a contempt thereof.

Appropriations

Sec. 106. There is hereby authorized to be appropriated, out of any money in the Treasury not otherwise appropriated, so much as may be necessary to carry out the provisions of this Act.

Part II—To Provide for an Additional Assistant Attorney General

Sec. 111. There shall be in the Department of Justice one additional Assistant Attorney General, who shall be appointed by the President, by and with the advice and consent of the Senate, who shall assist the Attorney General in the performance of his duties, and who shall receive compensation at the rate prescribed by law for other Assistant Attorneys General.

Part III—To Strengthen the Civil Rights Statutes, and for Other Purposes

Sec. 121. Section 1343 of title 28, United States Code, is amended as follows:

(a) Amend the catch line of said section to read, "~~~ 1343. Civil rights and elective franchise"

(b) Delete the period at the end of paragraph (3) and insert in lieu thereof a semicolon.

(c) Add a paragraph as follows:

"(4) To recover damages or to secure equitable or other relief under any Act of Congress providing for the protection of civil rights, including the right to vote."

Sec. 122. Section 1989 of the Revised Statutes (42 U.S.C. 1993) is hereby repealed.

Part IV—To Provide Means of Further Securing and Protecting the Right to Vote

Sec. 131. Section 2004 of the Revised Statutes (42 U.S.C. 1971), is amended as follows:

(a) Amend the catch line of said section to read, "Voting rights."

(b) Designate its present text with the subsection symbol "(a)."

(c) Add, immediately following the present text, four new subsections to read as follows:

"(b) No person, whether acting under color of law or otherwise, shall intimidate, threaten, coerce, or attempt to intimidate, threaten, or coerce any other person for the purpose of interfering with the right of such other person to vote or to vote as he may choose, or of causing such other person to vote for, or not to vote for, any candidate for the office of President, Vice President, presidential elector, Member of the Senate, or Member of the House of Representatives, Delegates or Commissioners from the Territories or possessions, at any general, special, or primary election held solely or in part for the purpose of selecting or electing any such candidate.

"(c) Whenever any person has engaged or there are reasonable grounds to believe that any person is about to engage in any act or practice which would deprive any other person of any right or privilege secured by subsection (a) or (b), the Attorney General may institute for the United States, or in the name of the United States, a civil action or other proper proceeding for preventive relief, including an application for a permanent or temporary injunction, restraining order, or other order. In any proceeding hereunder the United States shall be liable for costs the same as a private person.

"(d) The district courts of the United States shall have jurisdiction of proceedings instituted pursuant to this section and shall exercise the same without regard to whether the party aggrieved shall have exhausted any administrative or other remedies that may be provided by law.

"(e) Any person cited for an alleged contempt under this Act shall be allowed to make his full defense by counsel learned in the law; and the court before which he is cited or tried, or some judge thereof, shall immediately, upon his request, assign to him such counsel, not exceeding two, as he may desire, who shall have free access to him at all reasonable hours. He shall be allowed, in his defense to make any proof that he can produce by lawful witnesses, and shall have the like process of the court to compel his witnesses to appear at his trial or hearing, as is usually granted to compel witnesses to appear on behalf of the prosecution. If such person shall be found by the court to be financially unable to provide for such counsel, it shall be the duty of the court to provide such counsel."

Part V—To Provide Trial by Jury for Proceedings to Punish Criminal Contempts of Court Growing Out of Civil Rights Cases and to Amend the Judicial Code Relating to Federal Jury Qualifications

Sec. 151. In all cases of criminal contempt arising under the provisions of this Act, the accused, upon conviction, shall be punished by fine or imprisonment or both: *Provided however*, That in case the accused is a natural person the fine to be paid shall not exceed the sum of $1,000, nor shall imprisonment exceed the term of six months: *Provided further*, That in any such proceeding for criminal contempt, at the discretion of the judge, the accused may be tried with or without a jury: *Provided further, however,* That in the event such proceeding for criminal contempt be tried before a judge without a jury and the sentence of the court upon conviction is a fine in excess of the sum of $300 or imprisonment in excess of forty-five days, the accused in said proceeding, upon demand therefor, shall be entitled to a trial de novo before a jury, which shall conform as near as may be to the practice in other criminal cases.

This section shall not apply to contempts committed in the presence of the courts or so near thereto as to interfere directly with the administration of justice nor to the misbehavior, misconduct, or disobedience, of any officer of the court in respect to the writs, orders, or process of the court.

Nor shall anything herein or in any other provision of law be construed to deprive courts of their power, by civil contempt proceedings, without a jury, to secure compliance with or to prevent obstruction of, as distinguished from punishment for violations of, any lawful writ, process, order, rule, decree, or command of the court in accordance with the prevailing usages of law and equity, including the power of detention.

Sec. 152. Section 1861, title 28, of the United States Code is hereby amended to read as follows:

"~~~ 1861. Qualifications of Federal jurors

"Any citizen of the United States who has attained the age of twenty-one years and who has resided for a period of one year within the judicial district, is competent to serve as a grand or petit juror unless—

"(1) He has been convicted in a State or Federal court of record of a crime punishable by imprisonment for more than one year and his civil rights have not been restored by pardon or amnesty.

"(2) He is unable to read, write, speak, and understand the English language.

"(3) He is incapable, by reason of mental or physical infirmities to render efficient jury service."

Sec. 161. This Act may be cited as the "Civil Rights Act of 1957."

Approved September 9, 1957.

Source:

Statutes at Large, Vol. 71, pp. 634–638.

Dwight D. Eisenhower, Statements Concerning Little Rock, Arkansas, 1957

The failures of the 1957 Civil Rights Act were underscored by the problems Eisenhower faced when Governor Orval Faubus of Arkansas called out the National Guard to prevent integrating Little Rock's Central High School. Eisenhower, born in Texas and raised in segregated Kansas, served in a segregated army and kept his vacation White House in segregated Georgia. His sympathies lay with white southerners who opposed integration. However, he considered upholding court orders much more important than preserving racial separation. In the end, Eisenhower was forced to use federal troops.

Eisenhower's actions received support in *Cooper v. Aaron* (358 U.S. 1), issued September 29, 1958, which declared that the states were required to obey the Court's mandate to end segregation in the public schools, following *Brown v. Board of Education of Topeka, Kansas*. The unanimous decision stated that the attempts of the legislature and governor of Arkansas to resist court-ordered desegregation were unconstitutional. State regulation of education had to be consistent with federal constitutional requirements of equal justice under law and state officials could not nullify, either directly or indirectly, through "evasive schemes for segregation," the constitutional rights of children to be protected against discrimination.

Good Evening, My Fellow Citizens:

For a few minutes this evening I want to speak to you about the serious situation that has arisen in Little Rock. To make this talk I have come to the President's office in the White House. I could have spoken from Rhode Island, where I have been staying recently, but I felt that, in speaking from the house of Lincoln, of Jackson and of Wilson, my words would better convey both the sadness I feel in the action I was compelled today to take and the firmness with which I intend to pursue this course until the orders of the Federal Court at Little Rock can be executed without unlawful interference.

In that city, under the leadership of demagogic extremists, disorderly mobs have deliberately prevented the carrying out of proper orders from a Federal Court. Local authorities have not eliminated that violent opposition and, under the law, I yesterday issued a Proclamation calling upon the mob to disperse.

This morning the mob again gathered in front of the Central High School of Little Rock, obviously for the purpose of again preventing the carrying out of the Court's order relating to the admission of Negro children to that school.

Whenever normal agencies prove inadequate to the task and it becomes necessary for the Executive Branch of the Federal Government to use its powers and authority to uphold Federal Courts, the President's responsibility is inescapable.

In accordance with that responsibility, I have today issued an Executive Order directing the use of troops under Federal authority to aid in the execution of Federal law at Little Rock, Arkansas. This became necessary when my Proclamation of yesterday was not observed, and the obstruction of justice still continues.

It is important that the reasons for my action be understood by all our citizens.

As you know, the Supreme Court of the United States has decided that separate public educational facilities for the races are inherently unequal and therefore compulsory school segregation laws are unconstitutional.

Our personal opinions about the decision have no bearing on the matter of enforcement; the responsibility and authority of the Supreme Court to interpret the Constitution are very clear. Local Federal Courts were instructed by the Supreme Court to issue such orders and decrees as might be necessary to achieve admission to public schools without regard to race—and with all deliberate speed.

During the past several years, many communities in our Southern States have instituted public school plans for gradual progress in the enrollment and attendance of school children of all races in order to bring themselves into compliance with the law of the land.

They thus demonstrated to the world that we are a nation in which laws, not men, are supreme.

I regret to say that this truth—the cornerstone of our liberties—was not observed in this instance.

It was my hope that this localized situation would be brought under control by city and State authorities. If the use of local police powers had been sufficient, our traditional method of leaving the problems in those hands would have been pursued. But when large gatherings of obstructionists made it impossible for the decrees of the Court to be carried out, both the law and the national interest demanded that the President take action.

Here is the sequence of events in the development of the Little Rock school case.

In May of 1955, the Little Rock School Board approved a moderate plan for the gradual desegregation of the public schools in that city. It provided that a start toward integration would be made at the present term in the high school, and that the plan would be in full operation by 1963. Here I might say that in a number of communities in Arkansas integration in the schools has already started and without violence of any kind. Now this Little Rock plan was challenged in the courts by some who believed that the period of time as proposed in the plan was too long.

The United States Court at Little Rock, which has supervisory responsibility under the law for the plan of desegregation in the public schools, dismissed the challenge, thus approving a gradual rather than an abrupt change from the existing system. The court found that the school board had acted in good faith in planning for a public school system free from racial discrimination.

Since that time, the court has on three separate occasions issued orders directing that the plan be carried out. All persons were instructed to refrain from interfering with the efforts of the school board to comply with the law.

Proper and sensible observance of the law then demanded the respectful obedience which the nation has a right to expect from all its people. This, unfortunately, has not been the case a Little Rock. Certain misguided persons, many of them imported into Little Rock by agitators, have insisted upon defying the law and have sought to bring it into disrepute. The orders of the court have thus been frustrated.

The very basis of our individual rights and freedoms rests upon the certainty that the President and the Executive Branch of Government will support and insure the carrying out of the decisions of the Federal Courts, even, when necessary with all the means at the President's command.

Unless the President did so, anarchy would result.

There would be no security for any except that which each one of us could provide for himself.

The interest of the nation in the proper fulfillment of the law's requirements cannot yield to opposition and demonstrations by some few persons.

Mob rule cannot be allowed to override the decisions of our courts.

Now, let me make it very clear that Federal troops are not being used to relieve local and state authorities of their primary duty to preserve the peace and order of the community. Nor are the troops there for the purpose of taking over the responsibility of the School Board and the other responsible local officials in running Central High School. The running of our school system and the maintenance of peace and order in each of our States are strictly local affairs and the Federal Government does not interfere except in a very few special cases and when requested by one of the several States. In the present case the troops are there, pursuant to law, solely for the purpose of preventing interference with the orders of the Court.

The proper use of the powers of the Executive Branch to enforce the orders of a Federal Court is limited to extraordinary and compelling circumstances. Manifestly, such an extreme situation has been created in Little Rock. This challenge must be met and with such measures as will preserve to the people as a whole their lawfully-protected rights in a climate permitting their free and fair exercise.

The overwhelming majority of our people in every section of the country are united in their respect for observance of the law—even in those cases where they may disagree with that law.

They deplore the call of extremists to violence.

The decision of the Supreme Court concerning school integration, of course, affects the South more seriously than it does other sections of the country. In that region I have many warm friends, some of them in the city of Little Rock. I have deemed it a great personal privilege to spend in our Southland tours of duty while in the military service and enjoyable recreational periods since that time.

So from intimate personal knowledge, I know that the overwhelming majority of the people in the South—including those of Arkansas and of Little Rock—are of good will, united in their efforts to preserve and respect the law even when they disagree with it.

They do not sympathize with mob rule. They, like the rest of our nation, have proved in two great wars their readiness to sacrifice for America.

A foundation of our American way of life is our national respect for law.

In the South, as elsewhere, citizens are keenly aware of the tremendous disservice that has been done to the people of Arkansas in the eyes of the nation, and that has been done to the nation in the eyes of the world.

At a time when we face grave situations abroad because of the hatred that Communism bears toward a system of government based on human rights, it would be difficult to exaggerate the harm that is being done to the prestige and influence, and indeed to the safety, of our nation and the world.

Our enemies are gloating over this incident and using it everywhere to misrepresent our whole nation. We are portrayed as a violator of those standards of conduct which the peoples of the world united to proclaim in the Charter of the United Nations. There they affirmed "faith in fundamental human rights" and "in the dignity and worth of the human person" and they did so "without distinction as to race, sex, language or religion."

And so, with deep confidence, I call upon the citizens of the State of Arkansas to assist in bringing to an immediate end all interference with the law and its processes. If resistance to the Federal Court orders ceases at once, the further presence of Federal troops will be unnecessary and the City of Little Rock will return to its normal habits of peace and order and a blot upon the fair name and high honor of our nation in the world will be removed.

Thus will be restored the image of America and of all its parts as one nation, indivisible, with liberty and justice for all.

Good night, and thank you very much.

Source:

Public Papers of the Presidents of the United States, Dwight D. Eisenhower, 1957. Washington, D.C.: Government Printing Office, 1953–61. pp. 678–679; 689–694.

NAACP v. Alabama, 1958

U.S. Supreme Court's unanimous decision, issued June 30, 1958, protecting the right to privacy of association by ruling that an organization may not be required to divulge its membership lists as a condition of doing business in a state. Alabama, attempting to hamper the civil rights work of the National Association for the Advancement of Colored People (NAACP) through a corporate registration requirement, sought to compel the association to reveal the names and addresses of its members in Alabama. The organization, fearing social, economic, and physical reprisals, refused. The Supreme Court stated that Alabama's requirement would violate the constitutional rights of members to associate lawfully in support of common beliefs.

The following year, in *Uphaus v. Wyman*, the U.S. Supreme Court affirmed the right of a state to investigate possible subversives by questioning their associates. The Court upheld the civil contempt conviction of the Reverend Willard Uphaus for refusing to divulge, to a legislative committee investigating subversive activities in the state, the names of persons who had attended a World Fellowship camp in New Hampshire. In its 5-4 decision, the Court ruled that the state's interest in "self-preservation" outweighed individual rights to privacy in association. The dissenting justices argued that the investigation was "exposure for exposure's sake" and violated constitutional rights to privacy in relation to freedom of speech and association.

Mr. Justice Harlan delivered the opinion of the Court.

We review from the standpoint of its validity under the Federal Constitution a judgment of civil contempt entered against petitioner, the National Association for the Advancement of Colored People, in the courts of Alabama. The question presented is whether Alabama, consistently with the Due Process Clause of the Fourteenth Amendment, can compel petitioner to reveal to the State's Attorney General the names and addresses of all its Alabama members and agents, without regard to their positions or functions in the Association. The judgment of contempt was based upon petitioner's refusal to comply fully with a court order requiring in part the production of membership lists. Petitioner's claim is that the order, in the circumstances shown by this record, violated rights assured to petitioner and its members under the Constitution.

Alabama has a statute similar to those of many other States which requires a foreign corporation, except as exempted, to qualify before doing business by filing its corporate charter with the Secretary of State and designating a place of business and an agent to receive service of process. The statute imposes a fine on a corporation transacting intrastate business before qualifying and provides for criminal prosecution of officers of such a corporation. The National Association for the Advancement of Colored People is a nonprofit membership corporation organized under the laws of New York. Its purposes, fostered on a nationwide basis, are those indicated by its name, and it operates through chartered affiliates which are independent unincorporated associations, with membership therein equivalent to membership in petitioner. The first Alabama affiliates were chartered in 1918. Since that time the aims of the Association have been advanced through activities of its affiliates, and in 1951 the Association itself opened a regional office in Alabama, at which it employed two supervisory persons and one clerical worker. The Association has never complied with the qualification statute, from which it considered itself exempt.

In 1956 the Attorney General of Alabama brought an equity suit in the State Circuit Court, Montgomery County, to enjoin the Association from conducting further activities within, and to oust it from, the State. Among other things the bill in equity alleged that the Association had opened a regional office and had organized various affiliates in Alabama; had recruited members and solicited contributions within the State; had given financial support and furnished legal assistance to Negro students seeking admission to the state university; and had supported a Negro boycott of the bus lines in Montgomery to compel the seating of passengers without regard to race. The bill recited that the Association, by continuing to do business in Alabama without complying with the qualification statute, was "causing irreparable injury to the property and civil rights of the residents and citizens of the State of Alabama for which criminal prosecution and civil actions at law afford no adequate relief" On the day the complaint was filed, the Circuit Court issued ex parte and order restraining the Association, pendente lite, from engaging in further activities within the State and forbidding it to take any steps to qualify itself to do business therein.

Petitioner demurred to the allegations of the bill and moved to dissolved the restraining order. It contended that its activities did not subject it to the qualification requirements of the statute and that in any event what the State sought to accomplish by its suit would violate rights to freedom of speech and assembly guaranteed under the Fourteenth Amendment to the Constitution of the United States. Before the date set for a hearing on this motion, the State moved for the production of a large number of the Association's records and papers, including bank statements, leases, deeds, and records containing the names and addresses of all Alabama "members" and "agents" of the Association. It alleged that all such documents were necessary for adequate preparation for the hearing, in view of petitioner's denial of the conduct of intrastate business within the meaning of the qualification statute. Over petitioner's objections, the court ordered the production of a substantial part of the requested records, including the membership lists, and postponed the hearing on the restraining order to a date later than the time ordered for production.

Thereafter petitioner filed its answer to the bill in equity. It admitted its Alabama activities substantially as alleged in the complaint and that it had not qualified to do business in the State. Although still disclaiming the statute's application to it, petitioner offered to qualify if the bar from qualification made part of the restraining order were lifted, and it submitted with the answer an executed set of the forms required by the statute. However, petitioner did not comply with the production order, and for this failure was adjudged in civil contempt and fined $10,000. The contempt judgment provided that the fine would be subject to reduction or remission if compliance were forthcoming within five days but otherwise would be increased to $100,000.

At the end of the five-day period petitioner produced substantially all the data called for by the production order except its membership lists, as to which it contended that Alabama could not constitutionally compel disclosure, and moved to modify or vacate the contempt judgment, or stay its execution pending appellate review. This motion was denied. While a similar stay application, which was later denied, was pending before the Supreme Court of Alabama, the Circuit Court made a further order adjudging petitioner in continuing contempt and increasing the fine already imposed to $100,000. Under Alabama law, see *Jacoby v. Goetter, Weil & Co.*, 74 Ala. 427, the effect of the contempt adjudication was to foreclose petitioner from obtaining a hearing on the merits of the underlying ouster action, or from taking any steps to dissolve the temporary restraining order which had been issued ex parte, until it purged itself of contempt. . . .The State Supreme Court thereafter twice dismissed petitions for certiorari to review this final contempt judgment, the first time, 265 Ala. 699, 91 So. 2d 221, for insufficiency of the petition's allegations and the second time on procedural grounds. 265 Ala. 349, 91 So. 2d 214. We granted certiorari because of the importance of the constitutional questions presented.

I.

We address ourselves first to respondent's contention that we lack jurisdiction because the denial of certiorari by the Supreme Court of Alabama rests on an independent nonfederal ground, namely, that petitioner in applying for certiorari had pursued the wrong appellate remedy under state law. Respondent recognizes that our jurisdiction is not defeated if the nonfederal ground relied on by the state court is "without any fair or substantial support,". . . It thus becomes our duty to ascertain, "in order that constitutional guaranties may appropriately be enforced, whether the asserted non-federal ground independently and adequately supports the judgment."

The Alabama Supreme Court held that it could not consider the constitutional issues underlying the contempt judgment which related to the power of the State to order production of membership lists because review by certiorari was limited to instances " where the court lacked jurisdiction of the proceeding, or where on the face of its the order disobeyed was void, or where procedural requirements with respect to citation for contempt and the like were not observed, or where the fact or contempt is not sustained." . . . The proper means for petitioner to obtain review of the judgment in light of its constitutional claims, said the court, was by way of mandamus to quash the discovery order prior to the contempt adjudication. Because of petitioner's failure to pursue this remedy, its challenge to the contempt order was restricted to the above grounds. Apparently not deeming the constitutional objections to draw into question whether "on the face of it the order disobeyed was void," the court found no infirmity in the contempt judgment under this limited scope of review. At the same time it did go on to consider petitioner's constitutional challenge to the order to produce membership lists but found it untenable since membership lists were not privileged against disclosure pursuant to reasonable state demands and since the privilege against self-incrimination was not available to corporations.

We are unable to reconcile the procedural holding of the Alabama Supreme Court in the present case with its past unambiguous holdings as to the scope of review available upon a writ of certiorari addressed to a contempt judgment. As early as 1909 that court said in such a case, "Originally, on certiorari, only the question of jurisdiction was inquired into; but this limit has been removed, and now the court 'examines the law questions involved in the case which may affect its merits.' . . . [T]he judgment of this court is that the proper way to review the action of the court in cases of this kind is by certiorari, and not by appeal.

"We think that certiorari is a better remedy than mandamus, because the office of a 'mandamus' is to require the lower court or judge to act, and not 'to correct error or to reverse judicial action,' . . . whereas, in a proceeding by certiorari, errors of law in the judicial action of the lower court may be inquired into and corrected."

This statement was in full accord with the earlier case of *Ex parte Boscowitz,* 84 Ala. 463 So. 279, and the practice in the later Alabama cases, until we reach the present one, appears to have been entirely consistent with this rule. For example, in *Ex parte Morris,* 252 Ala. 551 42 So.2d 17, decided as late as 1949, the petitioner had been held in contempt for his refusal to obey a court order to produce names of members of the Ku Klux Klan. On write of certiorari, constitutional grounds were urged in part for reversal of the contempt conviction. In denying the writ of certiorari, the Supreme Court concluded that petitioner had been accorded due process, and in explaining its denial the court considered and rejected various constitutional claims relating to the validity of the order. There was no intimation that the petitioner had selected an inappropriate form of appellate review to obtain consideration of all questions of law raised by a contempt judgment. The Alabama cases indicate, as was said in the opinion below, that an order requiring production of evidence " . . . may be reviewed on petition for mandamus." . . . But we can discover nothing in the prior state cases which suggests that mandamus is the exclusive remedy for reviewing court orders after disobedience of them had led to contempt judgments. Nor, so far as we can find, do any of these prior decisions indicate that the validity of such orders can be drawn in question by way of certiorari only in instances where a defendant had no opportunity to apply for mandamus. Although the opinion below suggests no such distinction, the State now argues that this was in fact the situation in all of the earlier certiorari cases, because there the contempt adjudications, unlike here, had followed almost immediately the disobedience to the court orders. Even if that is indeed the rationale of the Alabama Supreme Court's present decision, such a local procedural rule, although it may now appear in retrospect to form part of a consistent pattern of procedures to obtain appellate review, cannot avail the State here, because petitioner could not fairly be deemed to have been apprised of its existence. Novelty in procedural requirements cannot be permitted to thwart review in this Court applied for by those who, in justified reliance upon prior decisions, seek vindication in state courts of their federal constitutional rights . . .

That there was justified reliance here is further indicated by what the Alabama Supreme Court said in disposing of petitioner's motion for a stay of the first contempt judgment in this case. This motion, which was filed prior to the final contempt judgment and which stressed constitutional issues, recited that "[t]he only way in which the [Association] can seek a review of the validity of the order upon which the adjudication of contempt is based [is] by filing a petition for Writ of Certiorari in this Court." In denying the motion, 265 Ala. 356, 357, 91 So.2d 220, 221, the Supreme Court stated:

"It is the established rule of this Court that the proper method of reviewing a judgment for civil contempt of the kind here involved is by a petition for common law writ of certiorari. . . .

"But the petitioner here has not applied for writ of certiorari, and we do not feel that the petition [for a stay] presently before us warrants our interference with the judgment of the Circuit Court of Montgomery County here sought to be stayed."

We hold that this Court has jurisdiction to entertain petitioner's federal claims.

II.

The Association both urges that it is constitutionally entitled to resist official inquiry into its membership lists, and that it may assert, on behalf of its members, a right personal to them to be protected from compelled disclosure by the State of their affiliation with the Association as revealed by the membership lists. We think that petitioner argues more appropriately the rights of its members, and that its nexus with them is sufficient to permit that it act as their representative before this Court. In so concluding, we reject respondent's argument that the Association lacks standing to assert here constitutional rights pertaining to the members, who are not of course parties to the litigation.

To limit the breadth of issues which must be dealt with in particular litigation, this Court has generally insisted that parties rely only on constitutional rights which are personal to themselves. . . . This rule is related to the broader doctrine that constitutional adjudication should where possible be avoided. . . . The principle is not disrespected where constitutional rights of persons who are not immediately before the Court could not be effectively vindicated except through an appropriate representative before the Court.

If petitioner's rank-and-file members are constitutionally entitled to withhold their connection with the Association despite the production order, it is manifest that this right is properly assertable by the Association. To require that it be claimed by the members themselves would result in nullification of the right at the very moment of its assertion. Petitioner is the appropriate party to assert these rights, because it and its members are in every practical sense identical. The Association, which provides in its constitution that "[a]ny person who is in accordance with [its] principles and policies . . . " may become a member, is but the medium through which its individual members seek to make more effective the expression of their own views. The reasonable likelihood that the Association itself through diminished financial support and membership may be adversely affected if production is compelled is a further factor pointing towards our holding that petitioner has standing to complain of the production order on behalf of its members.

III.

We thus reach petitioner's claim that the production order in the state litigation trespasses upon fundamental freedoms protected by the Due Process Clause of the Fourteenth Amendment. Petitioner argues that in view of the facts and circumstances shown in the record, the effect of compelled disclosure of the membership lists will be to abridge the rights of it rank-and-file members to engage in lawful association in support of their common beliefs. It contends that governmental action which, although not directly suppressing association, nevertheless carries this consequence, can be justified only upon some overriding valid interest of the State.

Effective advocacy of both public and private points of view, particularly controversial ones, is undeniably enhanced by group association, as this Court has more than once recognized by remarking upon the close nexus between the freedoms of speech and assembly.

It is beyond debate that freedom to engage in association for the advancement of beliefs and ideas is an inseparable aspect to the "liberty" assured by the Due Process Clause of the Fourteenth Amendment, which embraces freedom of speech.

Of course, it is immaterial whether the beliefs sought to be advanced by association pertain to political, economic, religious or cultural matters, and state action which may have the effect of curtailing the freedom of associate is subject to the closest scrutiny.

The fact that Alabama, so far as is relevant to the validity of the contempt judgment presently under review, has taken no direct action, . . . to restrict the right of petitioner's members to associate freely, does not end inquiry into the effect of the production order. . . . In the domain of these indispensable liberties, whether of speech, press, or association, the decisions of this Court recognize that abridgement of such rights, even though unintended, may inevitably follow from varied forms of governmental action. Thus in *Douds,* the Court stressed that the legislation there challenged, which on its face sought to regulate labor unions and to secure stability in interstate commerce, would have the practical effect "of discouraging" the exercise of constitutionally protected political rights, . . . and it upheld the statute only after concluding that the reasons advanced for its enactment were constitutionally sufficient to justify its possible deterrent effect upon such freedoms. Similar recognition of possible unconstitutional intimidation of the free exercise of the right to advocate underlay this Court's narrow construction of the authority of a congressional committee investigating lobbying and of an Act regulating lobbying, although in neither case was there an effort to suppress speech. . . . The governmental action challenged may appear to be totally unrelated to protected liberties. Statutes imposing taxes upon rather than prohibiting particular activity have been struck down when perceived to have the consequence of unduly curtailing the liberty of freedom of press assured under the Fourteenth Amendment. . . .

It is hardly a novel perception that compelled disclosure of affiliation with groups engaged in advocacy may constitute as effective a restraint on freedom of association as the forms of governmental action in the cases above were thought likely to produce upon the particular constitutional rights there involved. This Court has recognized the vital relationship between freedom to associate and privacy in one's associations. When referring to the varied forms of governmental action which might interfere with freedom of assembly, it said "A requirement that adherents of particular religious faiths or political parties wear identifying arm-bands, for example, is obviously of this nature." Compelled disclosure of membership in an organization engaged in advocacy of particular beliefs is of the same order. Inviolability of privacy in group association may in many circumstances be indispensable to preservation of freedom of association, particularly where a group espouses dissident beliefs. . . .

We think that the production order, in the respects here drawn in question, must be regarded as entailing the likelihood of a substantial restraint upon the exercise by petitioner's members of their right to freedom of association. Petitioner has made an uncontroverted showing that on past occasions revelation of the identity of its rank-and-file members has exposed these members to economic reprisal, loss of employment, threat of physical coercion, and other manifestations of public hostility. Under these circumstances, we think it apparent that compelled disclosure of petitioner's Alabama membership is likely to affect adversely the ability of petitioner and its members to pursue their collective effort to foster beliefs which they admittedly have the right to advocate, it that it may induce members to withdraw from the Association and dissuade others from joining it because of fear of exposure of their beliefs shown through their associations and of the consequences of this exposure.

It is not sufficient to answer, as the State does here, that whatever repressive effect compulsory disclosure of names of petitioner's members may have upon participation by Alabama citizens in petitioner's activities follows not from state action but from private community pressures. The crucial factor is the interplay of governmental and private action, for it is only after the initial exertion of state power represented by the production order that private action takes hold.

We turn to the final question whether Alabama has demonstrated an interest in obtaining the disclosures it seeks from petitioner which sufficient to justify the deterrent effect which we have concluded these disclosures may well have on the free exercise by petitioner's members of their constitutionally protected right of association. . . . It is not of moment that the State has here acted solely through its judicial branch, for whether legislative or judicial, it is still the application of state power which we are asked to scrutinize.

It is important to bear in mind that petitioner asserts no right to absolute immunity from state investigation, and no right to disregard Alabama's laws. As shown by its substantial compliance with the production order, petitioner does not deny Alabama's right to obtain from it such information as the State desires concerning the purposes of the Association and its activities within the State. Petitioner has not objected to divulging the identity of its members who are employed by or hold official positions with it. It has urged the rights solely of its ordinary rank-and-file members. This is therefore not analogous to a case involving the interest of a State in protecting its citizens in their dealings with paid solicitors or agents of foreign corporations by requiring identification. . . .

Whether there was "justification" in this instance turns solely on the substantiality of Alabama's interest in obtaining the membership lists. During the course of a hearing before the Alabama Circuit Court on a motion of petitioner to set aside the production order, the State Attorney General presented at length, under examination by petitioner, the State's reason for requesting the membership lists. The exclusive purpose was to determine whether petitioner was conducting intrastate business in violation of the Alabama foreign corporation registration statute, and the membership lists were expected to help resolve this question. The issues in the litigation commenced by Alabama by its bill in equity were whether the character of petitioner and its activities in Alabama had been such as to make petitioner subject to the registration statute, and whether the extent of petitioner's activities without qualifying suggested its permanent ouster from the State. Without intimating the slightest view upon the merits of these issues, we are unable to perceive that the disclosure of the names of petitioner's rank-and-file members has a substantial bearing on either of them. As matters stand in the state court, petitioner (1) has admitted its presence and conduct of activities in Alabama since 1918; (2) has offered to comply in all respects with the state qualification statute, although preserving its contention that the statute does not apply to it; and (3) has apparently complied satisfactorily with the production order, except for the membership lists, by furnishing the Attorney General with varied business records, its charter and statement of purposes, the names of all of its directors and officers, and with the total number of its Alabama members and the amount of their dues. These last items would not on this record appear subject to constitutional challenge and have been furnished, but whatever interest the State may have in obtaining names of ordinary members has not been shown to be sufficient to overcome petitioner's constitutional objections to the production order.

From what has already been said, we think it apparent that *People of State of New York ex rel. Bryant v. Zimmerman,* 278 U.S. 63, 49 S.Ct. 61, 73 L.Ed. 184, cannot be relied on in support of the State's position, for that case involved markedly different considerations in terms of the interest of the State in obtaining disclosure. There, this Court upheld as applied to a member of a local chapter of the Ku Klux Klan, a New York statute requiring any unincorporated association which demanded an oath as a condition to membership to file with state officials copies of its ". . . constitutions by-laws, rules, regulations and oath of membership, together with a roster of its membership and a list of its officers for the current year." . . . In its opinion, the Court took care to emphasize the nature of the organization which New York sought to regulate. The decision was based on the particular character of the Klan's activities, involving acts of unlawful intimidation and violence, which the Court assumed was before the state legislature when it enacted the statute, and of which the Court itself took judicial notice. Furthermore, the situation before us is significantly different from that in *Bryant,* because the organization there had made no effort to comply with any of the requirements of New York's statute but rather had refused to furnish the State with any information as to its local activities.

. . . We hold that the immunity from state scrutiny of membership lists which the Association claims on behalf of its members is here so related to the right of the members to pursue their lawful private interests privately and to associate freely with others in so doing as to come within the protection of the Fourteenth Amendment. And we conclude that Alabama has fallen short of showing a controlling justification for the deterrent effect on the free enjoyment of the right to associate which disclosure of membership lists is likely to have. Accordingly, the judgment of civil contempt and the $100,000 fine which resulted from petitioner's refusal to comply with the production order in this respect must fall.

IV.

Petitioner joins with its attack upon the production order a challenge to the constitutionality of the State's ex parte temporary restraining order preventing it from soliciting support in Alabama, and it asserts that the Fourteenth Amendment precludes such state action. But as noted above, petitioner has never received a hearing on the merits of the ouster suit, and we do not consider these questions properly here. The Supreme Court of Alabama noted in its denial of the petition for certiorari that such petition raised solely a question pertinent to the contempt adjudication. "The ultimate aim and purpose of the litigation is to determine the right of the state to enjoin petitioners from doing business in Alabama. That question, however, is not before us in this proceeding." The proper method for raising questions in the state appellate courts pertinent to the underlying suit for an injunction appears to be by appeal, after a hearing on the merits and final judgment by the lower state court. Only from the disposition of such an appeal can review be sought here.

For the reasons stated, the judgment of the Supreme Court of Alabama must be reversed and the case remanded for proceedings not inconsistent with this opinion.

Source:

Supreme Court Reporter, Vol. 78, pp. 1,163–1,174.

Mapp v. Ohio, 1961

U.S. Supreme Court decision, issued on June 19, 1961, that extended to state courts the federal courts' constitutional protections against unreasonable searches and seizures. In 1957 police officers in Cleveland, Ohio, seeking a fugitive, broke into the home of Doll Ree Mapp without a search warrant. They found no fugitive but did discover some "lewd and lascivious material." Mapp was later convicted of possession of obscene items. In a 5-3 decision, the Supreme Court overturned the conviction on the grounds that the evidence had been seized in violation of Fourth Amendment requirements of a search warrant. Previously, the exclusion of such evidence was binding only in federal court. As a result, federal investigators would sometimes hand over (on a "silver platter," as it was called) evidence inadmissable in federal courts to state authorities. *Mapp* cut off the admissibility of any illegally collected evidence by extending it to state courts through the Fourteenth Amendment. The Burger and Rehnquist courts later modified *Mapp* by permitting the "good faith" collection of evidence pursuant to a warrant later found to be tainted and by allowing it to stand if its exclusion would not have materially affected the outcome of the trial.

Mr. Justice Clark delivered the opinion of the Court.

Appellant stands convicted of knowingly having had in her possession and under her control certain lewd and lascivious books, pictures, and photographs in violation of Section 2905.34 of Ohio's Revised Code. As officially stated in the syllabus to its opinion, the Supreme Court of Ohio found that her conviction was valid though "based primarily upon the introduction in evidence of lewd and lascivious books and pictures unlawfully seized during an unlawful search of defendant's home. . . ."

On May 23, 1957, three Cleveland police officers arrived at appellant's residence in that city pursuant to information that "a person [was] hiding out in the home, who was wanted for questioning in connection with a recent bombing, and that there was a large amount of policy paraphernalia being hidden in the home." Miss Mapp and her daughter by a former marriage lived on the top floor of the two-family dwelling. Upon their arrival at that house, the officers knocked on the door and demanded entrance but appellant, after telephoning her attorney, refused to admit them without a search warrant. They advised their headquarters of the situation and undertook a surveillance of the house.

The officers again sought entrance some three hours later when four or more additional officers arrived on the scene. When Miss Mapp did not come to the door immediately, at least one of the several doors to the house was forcibly opened and the policemen gained admittance. Meanwhile Miss Mapp's attorney arrived, but the officers, having secured their own entry, and continuing in their defiance of the law, would permit him neither to see Miss Mapp nor to enter the house. It appears that Miss Mapp was halfway down the stairs from the upper floor to the front door when the officers, in this highhanded manner, broke into the hall. She demanded to see the search warrant. A paper, claimed to be a warrant, was held up by one of the officers. She grabbed the "warrant" and placed it in her bosom. A struggle ensued in which the officers recovered the piece of paper and as a result of which they handcuffed appellant because she had been "belligerent" in resisting their official rescue of the "warrant" from her person. Running roughshod over appellant, a policeman "grabbed" her, "twisted [her] hand," and she "yelled [and] pleaded with him" because "it was hurting." Appellant, in handcuffs, was then forcibly taken upstairs to her bedroom where the officers searched a dresser, a chest of drawers, a closet and some suitcases. They also looked into a photo album and through personal papers belonging to the appellant. The search spread to the rest of the second floor including the child's bedroom, the living room, the kitchen and a dinette. The basement of the building and a trunk found therein were also searched. The obscene materials for possession of which she was ultimately convicted were discovered in the course of that widespread search.

At the trial no search warrant was produced by the prosecution, nor was the failure to produce one explained or accounted for. At best, "There is, in the record, considerable doubt as to whether there ever was any warrant for the search of defendant's home." . . . The Ohio Supreme Court believed a "reasonable argument" could be made that the conviction should be reversed "because the 'methods' employed to obtain the [evidence] were such as to 'offend '"a sense of justice,"' but the court found determinative the fact that the evidence had not been taken "from defendant's person by the use of brutal or offensive physical force against defendant." . . .

The State says that even if the search were made without authority, or otherwise unreasonably, it is not prevented from using the unconstitutionally seized evidence at trial, citing *Wolf v. People of State of Colorado,* 1949 . . . in which this Court did indeed hold "that in a prosecution in a State court for a State crime the Fourteenth Amendment does not forbid the admission of evidence obtained by an unreasonable search and seizure." On this appeal, of which we have noted probable jurisdiction, . . . it is urged once again that we review that holding.

I.

Seventy-five years ago, on *Boyd v. United States,* 1886 . . . considering the Fourth and Fifth Amendments as running "almost into each other" on the facts before it, this Court held that the doctrines of those Amendments

"apply to all invasions on the part of the government and its employees of the sanctity of a man's home and the privacies of life. It is not the breaking of his doors, and the rummaging of his drawers, that constitutes the essence of the offence; but it is the invasion of his indefeasible right of personal security, personal liberty and private property. . . . Breaking into a house and opening boxes and drawers are circumstances of aggravation; but any forcible and compulsory extortion of man's own testimony or of his private papers to be used as evidence to convict him of crime or to forfeit his goods, is within the condemnation . . . [of those Amendments]."

The Court noted that

"constitutional provisions for the security of person and property should be liberally construed. . . . It is the duty of courts to be watchful for the constitutional rights of the citizen, and against any stealthy encroachments thereon." . . .In this jealous regard for maintaining the integrity of individual rights, the Court gave life to Madison's prediction that "independent tribunals of justice . . . will be naturally led to resist every encroachment upon rights expressly stipulated for in the Constitution by the declaration of rights." Concluding, the Court specifically referred to the use of the evidence there seized as "unconstitutional."

Less than 30 years after *Boyd,* this Court, in *Weeks v. United States,* 1914, stated that

"that 4th Amendment . . . put the courts of the United States and Federal officials, in the exercise of their power and authority, under limitations and restraints [and] . . . forever secure[d] the people, their persons, houses, papers, and effects, against all unreasonable searches and seizures under the guise of law . . . and the duty of giving to it force and effect is obligatory upon all entrusted under our Federal system with the enforcement of the laws."

Specifically dealing with the use of the evidence unconstitutionally seized, the Court concluded:

"If letters and private documents can thus be seized and held and used in evidence against a citizen accused of an offense, the protection of the Fourth Amendment declaring his right to be secure against such searches and seizures is of no value, and, so far as those thus placed are concerned, might as well be stricken from the Constitution. The efforts of the courts and their officials to bring the guilty to punishment, praiseworthy as they are, are not to be aided by the sacrifice of those great principles established by years of endeavor and suffering which have resulted in their embodiment in the fundamental law of the land." . . .

Finally, the Court in that case clearly stated that use of the seized evidence involved "a denial of the constitutional rights of the accused." . . . Thus, in the year 1914, in the *Weeks* case, this Court "for the first time" held that "in a federal prosecution the Fourth Amendment barred the use of evidence secured through an illegal search and seizure." . . . This Court has ever since required of federal law officers a strict adherence to that command which this Court has held to be a clear, specific, and constitutionally required—even if judicially implied—deterrent safeguard without insistence upon which the Fourth Amendment would have been reduced to "a form of words." . . .It meant, quite simply, that "conviction by means of unlawful seizures and enforced confessions . . . should find no sanction in the judgments of the courts . . . ," . . .and that such evidence "shall not be used at all. . . .

There are in the cases of this Court some passing references to the *Weeks* rule as being one of evidence. But the plain and unequivocal language of *Weeks*—and its later paraphrase in *Wolf*—to the effect that the *Weeks* rule is of constitutional origin, remains entirely undisturbed. . . . A unanimous Court declared that "the doctrine [cannot] . . . be tolerated under our constitutional system, that evidences of crime discovered by a federal officer in making a search without lawful warrant may be used against the victim of the unlawful search where a timely challenge has been interposed." The Court, in *Olmstead v. United States,* 1928, in unmistakable language restated the Weeks rule:

"The striking outcome of the *Weeks* case and those which followed it was the sweeping declaration that the Fourth Amendment, although not referring to or limiting the use of evidence in court, really forbade its introduction if obtained by government officers through a violation of the amendment."

In *McNabb v. United States,* 1943, . . . we note this statement:

"[A] conviction in the federal courts, the foundation of which is evidence obtained in disregard of liberties deemed fundamental by the Constitution, cannot stand.

Boyd v. United States . . . *Weeks v. United States*. . . . And this Court has, on Constitutional grounds, set aside convictions, both in the federal and state courts, which were based upon confessions 'secured by protracted and repeated questioning of ignorant and untutored persons, in whose minds the power of officers was greatly magnified' . . . or who have been unlawfully held incommunicado without advice of friends or counsel' . . ."

Significantly, in *McNabb,* the Court did then pass on to formulate a rule of evidence, saying, "[i]n the view we take of the case, however, it becomes unnecessary to reach the Constitutional issue [for] . . . [t]he principles governing the admissibility of evidence in federal criminal trials have not been restricted . . . to those derived solely from the Constitution." . . .

II.

In 1949, 35 years after *Weeks* was announced, this Court, in *Wolf v. People of State of Colorado,* supra, again for the first time, discussed the effect of the Fourth Amendment upon the States through the operation of the Due Process Clause of the Fourteenth Amendment. It said:

"[W]e have no hesitation in saying that were a State affirmatively to sanction such police incursion into privacy it would run counter to the guaranty of the Fourteenth Amendment." . . .

Nevertheless, after declaring that the "security of one's privacy against arbitrary intrusion by the police" is "implicit in 'the concept of ordered liberty' and as such enforceable against the States through the Due Process Clause," . . . and announcing that it "stoutly adhere[d]" to the *Weeks* decision, the Court decided that the *Weeks* exclusionary rule would not then be imposed upon the States as "an essential ingredient of the right." . . . The Court's reasons for not considering essential to the right to privacy, as a curb imposed upon the States by the Due Process Clause, that which decades before had been posited as part and parcel of the Fourth Amendment's limitation upon federal encroachment of individual privacy, were bottomed on factual considerations.

While they are not basically relevant to a decision that the exclusionary rule is an essential ingredient of the Fourth Amendment as the right it embodies is vouchsafed against the States by the Due Process Clause, we will consider the current validity of the factual grounds upon which *Wolf* was based.

The Court in *Wolf* first stated that "[t]he contrariety of views of the States" on the adoption of the exclusionary rule of Weeks was "particularly impressive". . . ; and, in this connection, that it could not "brush aside the experience of States which deem the incidence of such conduct by the police too slight to call for a deterrent remedy . . . by overriding the [States'] relevant rules of evidence." . . . While in 1949, prior to the *Wolf* case, almost two-thirds of the States were opposed to the use of the exclusionary rule, now, despite the *Wolf* case, more than half of those since passing upon it, by their own legislative or judicial decision, have wholly or partly adopted or adhered to the *Weeks* rule. . . . Significantly, among those now following the rule is California, which, according to its highest court, was "compelled to reach that conclusion because other remedies have completely failed to secure compliance with the constitutional provisions. . . ." . . . In connection with this California case, we note that the second basis elaborated in *Wolf* in support of its failure to enforce the exclusionary doctrine against the States was that "other means of protection" have been afforded "the right to privacy." . . . The experience of California that such other remedies have been worthless and futile is buttressed by the experience of other States. The obvious futility of relegating the Fourth Amendment to the protection of other remedies has, moreover, been recognized by this Court since *Wolf.*

Likewise, time has set its face against what *Wolf* called the "weighty testimony" of *People v. Defore,* 1926. . . . There Justice (then Judge) Cardozo, rejecting adoption of the *Weeks* exclusionary rule in New York, had said that "[t]he Federal rule as it stands is either too strict or too lax." . . . However, the force of that reasoning has been largely vitiated by later decision of this Court. These include the recent discarding of the "silver platter" doctrine which allowed federal judicial use of evidence seized in violation of the Constitution by state agents; the relaxation of the formerly strict requirements as to standing to challenge the use of evidence thus seized, so that now the procedure of exclusion, "ultimately referable to constitutional safeguards," is available to anyone even "legitimately on [the] premises" unlawfully searched . . . and finally, the formulation of a method to prevent state use of evidence unconstitutionally seized by federal agents, *Rea v. United States,* 1956. Because there can be no fixed formula, we are admittedly met with "recurring questions of the reasonableness of searches," but less is not to be expected when dealing with a Constitution, and, at any rate, "[r]easonableness is in the first instance for the [trial court] to determine." . . .

It, therefore, plainly appear that the factual considerations supporting the failure of the *Wolf* Court to include the *Weeks* exclusionary rule when it recognized the enforceability of the right to privacy against the States in 1949, while not basically relevant to the constitutional consideration, could not, in any analysis, now be deemed controlling.

III.

Some five years after *Wolf,* in answer to a plea made here Term after Term that we overturn its doctrine on applicability of the *Weeks* exclusionary rule, this court indicated that such should not be done until the States had "adequate opportunity to adopt or reject the [*Weeks*] rule." *Irvine v. People of State of California,* supra, 347 U.S. at page 134, 74 S.Ct. at page 384. There again it was said:

"Never until June of 1949 did this Court hold the basic search-and-seizure prohibition in any way applicable to the states under the Fourteenth Amendment." Ibid.

And only last Term, after again carefully re-examining the *Wolf* doctrine in *Elkins v. United States,* supra, the Court pointed out that "the controlling principles" as to search and seizure and the problem of admissibility "seemed clear" . . . until the announcement in *Wolf* "that the Due Process Clause of the Fourteenth Amendment does not itself require state courts to adopt the exclusionary rule" of the *Weeks* case. . . . At the same time, the Court pointed out, "the underlying constitutional doctrine which *Wolf* established . . . that the Federal Constitution . . . prohibits unreasonable searches and seizures by state officers" had undermined the "foundation upon which the admissibility of state-seized evidence in a federal trial originally rested. . . ." . . . The Court concluded that it was therefore obliged to hold, although it chose the narrower ground on which to do so, that all evidence obtained by an unconstitutional search and seizure was inadmissible in a federal court regardless of its source. Today we once again examine *Wolf's* constitutional documentation of the right to privacy free from unreasonable state intrusion, and, after its dozen years on our books, are led by it to close the only courtroom door remaining open to evidence secured by official lawlessness in flagrant abuse of that basic right, reserved to all persons as a specific guarantee against that very same unlawful conduct. We hold that all evidence obtained by searches and seizures in violation of the Constitution is, by that same authority, inadmissible in a state court.

IV.

Since the Fourth Amendment's right of privacy has been declared enforceable against the States through the Due Process Clause of the Fourteenth, it is enforceable against them by the same sanction of exclusion as is used against the Federal Government. Were it otherwise, then just as without the *Weeks* rule the assurance against unreasonable federal searches and seizures would be "a form of words," valueless and undeserving of mention in a perpetual charter of inestimable human liberties, so too, without that rule the freedom from state invasions of privacy would be so ephemeral and so neatly severed from its conceptual nexus with the freedom from all brutish means of coercing evidence as not to merit this Court's high regard as a freedom "implicit in 'the concept of ordered liberty.'" At the time that the Court held in WOLF that the Amendment was applicable to the States through the Due Process Clause, the cases of this Court, as we have seen, had steadfastly held that as to federal officers the Fourth Amendment included the exclusion of the evidence seized in violation of its provisions. Even *Wolf* "stoutly adhered" to that proposition. The right to privacy, when conceded operatively enforceable against the States, was not susceptible of destruction by avulsion of the sanction upon which its protection and enjoyment had always been deemed dependent under the *Boyd, Weeks* and *Silverthorne* cases. Therefore, in extending the substantive protections of due process to all constitutionally unreasonable searches—state or federal—it was logically and constitutionally necessary that the exclusion doctrine—an essential part of the right to privacy—be also insisted upon as an essential ingredient of the right newly recognized by the *Wolf* case. In short, the admission of the new constitutional right by *Wolf* could not consistently tolerate denial of its most important constitutional privilege, namely, the exclusion of the evidence which an accused had been forced to give by reason of the unlawful seizure. To hold otherwise is to grant the right but in reality to withhold its privilege and enjoyment. Only last year the Court itself recognized that the purpose of the exclusionary rule "is to deter—to compel respect for the constitutional guaranty in the only effectively available way—by removing the incentive to disregard it." . . .

Indeed, we are aware of no restraint, similar to that rejected today, conditioning the enforcement of any other basic constitutional right. The right to privacy, no less important than any other right carefully and particularly reserved to the people, would stand in marked contrast to all other rights declared as "basic to a free society." . . .This Court has not hesitated to enforce as strictly against the States as it does against the Federal Government the rights of free speech and of a free press, the rights to notice and to a fair, public trial, including, as it does, the right not to be convicted by use of a coerced confession, however logically relevant it be, and without regard to its reliability. . . . And nothing could be more certain that that when a coerced confession is involved, "the relevant rules of evidence" are overridden without regard to "the incidence of such conduct by the police," slight or frequent. Why should not the same rule apply to what is tantamount to coerced testimony by way of unconstitutional seizure of goods, papers, effects, documents, etc.? We find that, as to the Federal Government, the Fourth and Fifth Amendments and, as to the States, the freedom from unconscionable invasions of privacy and the freedom from convictions based upon coerced confessions do enjoy an "intimate relation" in their perpetuation of "principles of humanity and civil liberty [secured] . . . only after years of struggle." . . .They express "supplementing phases of the same constitutional purpose—to maintain inviolate large areas of personal privacy." . . . The philosophy of each Amendment and of each freedom is complementary to, although not dependent upon, that of the other in its sphere of influence—the very least that together they assure in either sphere is that no man is to be convicted on unconstitutional evidence. . . .

V.

Moreover, our holding that the exclusionary rule is an essential part of both the Fourth and Fourteenth Amendments is not only the logical dictate of prior cases, but it also makes very good sense. There is no war between the Constitution and common sense. Presently, a federal prosecutor may make no use of evidence illegally seized, but a State's attorney across the street may, although he supposedly is operating under the enforceable prohibitions of the same Amendment. Thus the State, by admitting evidence unlawfully seized, serves to encourage disobedience to the Federal Constitution which it is bound to uphold. Moreover, as was said in *Elkins*, "[t]he very essence of a healthy federalism depends upon the avoidance of needless conflict between state and federal courts." . . . Such a conflict, hereafter needless, arose this very Term, in *Wilson v. Schnettler*, 1961, . . . in which, and in spite of the promise made by Rea, we gave full recognition to our practice in this regard by refusing to restrain a federal officer from testifying in a state court as to evidence unconstitutionally seized by him in the performance of his duties. Yet the double standard recognized until today hardly put such a thesis into practice. In non-exclusionary States, federal officers, being human, were by it invited to and did, as our cases indicate, step across the street to the State's attorney with their unconstitutionally seized evidence. Prosecution on the basis of that evidence was then had in a state court in utter disregard of the enforceable Fourth Amendment. If the fruits of an unconstitutional search had been inadmissible in both state and federal courts, this inducement to evasion would have been sooner eliminated. There would be no need to reconcile such cases as **Rea** and *Schnettler*, each pointing up the hazardous uncertainties of our heretofore ambivalent approach.

Federal-state cooperation in the solution of crime under constitutional standards will be promoted, if only by recognition of their now mutual obligation to respect the same fundamental criteria in their approaches. "However much in a particular case insistence upon such rules may appear as a technically that inures to the benefit of a guilty person, the history of the criminal law proves that tolerance of shortcut methods in law enforcement impairs its enduring effectiveness." *Miller v. United States*, 1958. . . . Denying shortcuts to only one of two cooperating law enforcement agencies tends naturally to breed legitimate suspicion of "working arrangements" whose results are equally tainted. . . .

There are those who say, as did Justice (then Judge) Cardozo, that under our constitutional exclusionary doctrine "[t]he criminal is to go free because the constable has blundered." . . . In some cases this will undoubtedly be the result. But, as was said in *Elkins*, "there is another consideration—the imperative of judicial integrity." . . .The criminal goes free, if he must, but it is the law that sets him free. Nothing can destroy a government more quickly than its failure to observe its own laws, or worse, its disregard of the charter of its own existence. As Mr. Justice Brandeis, dissenting, said in *Olmstead v. United States*, 1928. . . . "Our government is the potent, the omnipresent teacher. For good or for ill, it teaches the whole people by its example . . . If the government becomes a lawbreaker, it breeds contempt for law; it invites every man to become a law unto himself; it invites anarchy." Nor can it lightly be assumed that, as a practical matter, adoption of the exclusionary rule fetters law enforcement. Only last year this Court expressly considered that contention and found that "pragmatic evidence of a sort" to the contrary was not wanting. . . .

"The federal courts themselves have operated under the exclusionary rule of *Weeks* for almost half a century; yet it has not been suggested either that the Federal Bureau of Investigation has thereby been rendered ineffective, or that the administration of criminal justice in the federal courts has thereby been disrupted. Moreover, the experience of the states is impressive. . . . The movement towards the rule of exclusion has been halting but seemingly inexorable." . . .

The ignoble shortcut to conviction left open to the State tends to destroy the entire system of constitutional restraints on which the liberties of the people rest. Having once recognized that the right to privacy embodied in the Fourth Amendment is enforceable against the States, and that the right to be secure against rude invasions of privacy by state officers is, therefore, constitutional in origin, we can no longer permit that right to remain an empty promise. Because it is enforceable in the same manner and to like effect as other basic rights secured by the Due Process Clause, we can no longer permit it to be revocable at the whim of any police officer who, in the name of law enforcement itself, chooses to suspend its enjoyment. Our decision, founded on reason and truth, gives to the individual no more than that which the Constitution guarantees him, to the police officer no less than that to which honest law enforcement is entitled, and, to the courts, that judicial integrity so necessary in the true administration of justice.

The judgment of the Supreme Court of Ohio is reversed and the cause remanded for further proceedings not inconsistent with this opinion.

Reversed and remanded.

Source:
Supreme Court Reporter, Vol. 81, pp. 1,684–1,708.

Baker v. Carr, 1962

U.S. Supreme Court decision issued March 26, 1962, ruling that state legislative apportionment practices were subject to judicial review and control. In 1959 some Tennessee citizens sued state election officials for depriving them of federal constitutional rights because no legislative reapportionment had been made in the state since 1901, despite a state constitutional requirement that the legislature redraw districts for senators and representatives at least every 10 years according to the number of qualified voters in each county or district. The lack of reapportionment had produced inequities in representation. The Supreme Court reversed *Colegrove v. Green* (1946) in deciding that legislative districting controversies could be heard by federal courts.

The U.S. Supreme Court followed *Baker* June 15, 1964, by ruling in *Reynolds v. Sims* (377 U.S. 533) that members of both houses of the state legislatures must be elected from equal population districts. In establishing the principle of "one person/one vote," the Court assumed a basic standard of equality among voters and invoked the principles of representative government, majority rule, and equal protection of the laws. Chief Justice Earl Warren wrote: "Legislators represent people, not trees or acres. Legislators are elected by votes, not farms or cities or economic interests." Unequal districting, he said, debases a citizen's right to vote.

Mr. Justice Whittaker did not participate in the decision of this case.

(excerpt)

Mr. Justice Brennan delivered the opinion of the Court.

This civil action was brought under 42 U.S.C. Sections 1983 and 1988 to redress the alleged deprivation of federal constitutional rights. The complaint, alleging that by means of a 1901 statute of Tennessee apportioning the members of the General Assembly among the State's 95 counties, "these plaintiffs and others similarly situated, are denied the equal protection of the laws accorded them by the Fourteenth Amendment to the Constitution of the United States by virtue of the debasement of their votes," was dismissed by a three-judge court . . . in the Middle District of Tennessee. The court held that it lacked jurisdiction of the subject matter and also that no claim was stated upon which relief could be granted. . . . We hold that the dismissal was error, and remand the cause to the District Court for trial and further proceedings consistent with this opinion.

The General Assembly of Tennessee consists of the Senate with 33 members and the House of Representatives with 99 members. The Tennessee Constitution provides in Art. II as follows:

"Sec. 3. Legislative authority—Term of office.—The Legislative authority of this State shall be vested in a General Assembly, which shall consist of a Senate and House of Representatives, both dependent on the people; who shall hold their offices for two years from the day of the general election.

"Sec. 4. Census.—An enumeration of the qualified voters, and an apportionment of the Representatives in the General Assembly, shall be made in the year one thousand eight hundred and seventy-one, and within every subsequent term of ten years.

"Sec. 5. Apportionment of representatives.—The number of Representatives shall, at the several periods of making the enumeration, be apportioned among the several counties or districts, according to the number of qualified voters in each; and shall not exceed seventy-five, until the population of the State shall be one million and a half, and shall never exceed ninety-nine; Provided, that any county having two-thirds of the ratio shall be entitled to one member.

"Sec 6. Apportionment of senators.—The number of Senators shall, at the several periods of making the enumeration, be apportioned among the several counties or districts according to the number of qualified electors in each, and shall not exceed one-third the number of representatives. In apportioning the Senators among the different counties, the fraction that may be lost by any county or counties, in the apportionment of members to the House of Representatives, shall be made up to such county or counties in the Senate, as near as may be practicable. When a district is composed of two or more counties, they shall be adjoining; and no county shall be divided in forming a district."

Thus, Tennessee's standard for allocating legislative representation among her counties is the total number of qualified voters resident in the respective counties, subject only to minor qualifications. Decennial reapportionment in compliance with the constitutional scheme was effected by the General Assembly each decade from 1871 to 1901. . . . In 1901 the General Assembly abandoned separate enumeration in favor of reliance upon the Federal Census and passed the Apportionment Act here in controversy. In the more than 60 years since that action, all proposals in both Houses of the General Assembly for the reapportionment have failed to pass.

Between 1901 and [1960], Tennessee has experienced substantial growth and redistribution of her population. In 1901 the population was 2,020,616, of whom 487,380 were eligible to vote. The 1960 Federal Census reports the

State's population at 3,567,089, of whom 2,092,891 are eligible to vote. The relative standings of the counties in terms of qualified voters have changed significantly. It is primarily the continued application of the 1901 Apportionment Act to this shifted and enlarged voting population which gives rise to the present controversy.

Indeed, the complaint alleges that the 1901 statute, even as of the time of its passage, "made no apportionment of Representatives and Senators in accordance with the constitutional formula . . . , but instead arbitrarily and capriciously apportioned representatives in the Senate and House without reference . . . to any logical or reasonable formula whatever." It is further alleged that "because of the population changes since 1900, and the failure of the Legislature to reapportion itself since 1901," the 1901 statute became "unconstitutional and obsolete." Appellants also argue that, because of the composition of the legislature effected by the 1901 Apportionment Act, redress in the form of a state constitutional amendment to change the entire mechanism for reapportioning, or any other change short of that, is difficult or impossible. The complaint concludes that "these plaintiffs and others similarly situated, are denied the equal protection of the laws accorded them by the Fourteenth Amendment to the Constitution of the United States by virtue of the debasement of their votes." They seek a declaration that the 1901 statute is unconstitutional and an injunction restraining the appellees from acting to conduct any further elections under it. They also pray that unless and until the General Assembly enacts a valid reapportionment, the District Court should either decree a reapportionment by mathematical application of the Tennessee constitutional formulae to the most recent Federal Census figures, or direct the appellees to conduct legislative elections, primary and general, at large. They also pray for such other and further relief as may be appropriate.

I.

The District Court's Opinion and Order of Dismissal.

Because we deal with this case on appeal from an order of dismissal granted on appellees' motions, precise identification of the issues presently confronting us demands clear exposition of the grounds upon which the District Court rested in dismissing the case. The dismissal order recited that the court sustained the appellees' grounds "(1) that the Court lacks jurisdiction of the subject matter, and (2) that the complaint fails to state a claim upon which relief can be granted . . ."

* * *

The court proceeded to explain its action as turning on the case's presenting a "question of the distribution of political strength for legislative purposes." For,

"From a review of [numerous Supreme Court] . . . decisions there can be no doubt that the federal rule, as enunciated and applied by the Supreme Court, is that the federal courts, whether from a lack of jurisdiction or from the inappropriateness of the subject matter for judicial consideration, will not intervene in cases of this type to compel legislative reapportionment." . . .

The court . . . made clear that its dismissal reflected a view not of doubt that violation of constitutional rights was alleged, but of a court's impotence to correct that violation.

* * *

In light of the District Court's treatment of the case, we hold today only (a) that the court possessed jurisdiction of the subject matter; (b) that a justiciable cause of action is stated upon which appellants would be entitled to appropriate relief; and (c) because appellees raise the issue before this Court, that the appellants have standing to challenge the Tennessee apportionment statutes. Beyond noting that we have no cause at this stage to doubt the District Court will be able to fashion relief if violations of constitutional rights are found, it is improper now to consider what remedy would be most appropriate if appellants prevail at the trial.

II.

Jurisdiction of the Subject Matter.

The District Court was uncertain whether our cases withholding federal judicial relief rested upon a lack of federal jurisdiction or upon the inappropriateness of the subject matter for judicial consideration—what we have designated "nonjusticiability." The distinction between the two grounds is significant. In the instance of nonjusticiability, consideration of the cause is not wholly and immediately foreclosed; rather, the Court's inquiry necessarily proceeds to the point of deciding whether the duty asserted can be judicially identified and its breach judicially determined, and whether protection for the right asserted can be judicially molded. In the instance of lack of jurisdiction the cause either does not "arise under" the Federal Constitution, laws or treaties (or fall within one of the other enumerated categories of Art. III, Section 2), or is not a "case or controversy" within the meaning of that section; or the cause is not one described by any jurisdictional statute. Our conclusion . . . that this cause presents no nonjusticiable "political question" settles the only possible doubt that it is a case or controversy. Under the present heading of "Jurisdiction of the Subject Matter" we hold only that the matter set forth in the complaint does arise under the Constitution and is within 28 U.S.C. Section 1343, 28 U.S.C.A. Section 1343.

Article III, Section 2, of the Federal Constitution provides that "The judicial Power shall extend to all Cases, in

Law and Equity, arising under this Constitution, the Laws of the United States, and Treaties made, or which shall be made, under their Authority . . ." It is clear that the cause of action is one which "arises under" the Federal Constitution. The complaint alleges that the 1901 statute effects on apportionment that deprives the appellants of the equal protection of the laws in violation of the Fourteenth Amendment. Dismissal of the complaint upon the ground of lack of jurisdiction of the subject matter would, therefore, be justified only if that claim were "so attenuated and unsubstantial as to be absolutely devoid of merit," . . . or "frivolous." . . . Since the District Court obviously and correctly did not deem the asserted federal constitutional claim insubstantial and frivolous, it should not have dismissed the complaint for want of jurisdiction of the subject matter. And of course no further consideration of the merits of the claim is relevant to a determination of the court's jurisdiction of the subject matter. We said in an earlier voting case from Tennessee: "It is obvious . . . that the court, in dismissing for want of jurisdiction, was controlled by what it deemed to be the want of merit in the averments which were made in the complaint as to the violation of the Federal right. But as the very nature of the controversy was Federal, and, therefore, jurisdiction existed, whilst the opinion of the court as to the want of merit in the cause of action might have furnished ground for dismissing for that reason, it afforded no sufficient ground for deciding that the action was not one arising under the Constitution and laws of the United States." . . .

Since the complaint plainly sets forth a case arising under the Constitution, the subject matter is within the federal judicial power defined in Art. III, Section 2, and so within the power of Congress to assign to the jurisdiction of the District Courts. . . .

An unbroken line of our precedents sustains the federal courts' jurisdiction of the subject matter of federal constitutional claims of this nature. . . .

* * *

We hold that the District Court has jurisdiction of the subject matter of the federal constitutional claim asserted in the complaint.

III.

Standing.

A federal court cannot "pronounce any statute, either of a state or of the United States, void, because irreconcilable with the constitution, except as it is called upon to adjudge the legal rights of litigants in actual controversies." . . . Have the appellants alleged such a personal stake in the outcome of the controversy as to assure that concrete adverseness which sharpens the presentation of issues upon which the court so largely depends for illumination of difficult constitutional questions? This is the gist of the question of standing. It is, of course, a question of federal law.

The complaint was filed by residents of Davidson, Hamilton, Knox, Montgomery, and Shelby Counties. Each is a person allegedly qualified to vote for members of the General Assembly representing his county. These appellants sued "on their own behalf and on behalf of all qualified voters of their respective counties, and further, on behalf of all voters of the State of Tennessee who are similarly situated. . . ." The appellees are the Tennessee Secretary of State, Attorney General, Coordinator of Elections, and members of the State Board of Elections; the members of the State Board are sued in their own right and also as representatives of the County Election Commissioners whom they appoint.

We hold that the appellants do have standing to maintain this suit. Our decisions plainly support this conclusion. Many of the cases have assumed rather than articulated the premise in deciding the merits of similar claims. And *Colegrove v. Green* . . . squarely held that voters who allege facts showing disadvantage to themselves as individuals have standing to sue. A number of cases decided after *Colegrove* recognized the standing of the voters there involved to bring those actions.

These appellants seek relief in order to protect or vindicate an interest of their own, and of those similarly situated. Their constitutional claim is, in substance, that the 1901 statute constitutes arbitrary and capricious state action, offensive to the Fourteenth Amendment in its irrational disregard of the standard of apportionment prescribed by the State's Constitution or of any standard, effecting a gross disproportion of representation to voting population. The injury which appellants assert is that this classification disfavors the voters in the counties in which they reside, placing them in a position of constitutionally unjustifiable inequality vis-a-vis voters in irrationally favored counties. A citizen's right to a vote free of arbitrary impairment by state action has been judicially recognized as a right secured by the Constitution, when such impairment resulted from dilution by a false tally . . . ; or by a refusal to count votes from arbitrarily selected precincts . . . , or by a stuffing of the ballot box. . . .

It would not be necessary to decide whether appellants' allegations of impairment of their votes by the 1901 apportionment will, ultimately, entitle them to any relief, in order to hold that they have standing to seek it. If such impairment does produce a legally cognizable injury, they are among those who have sustained it. They are asserting "a plain, direct and adequate interest in maintaining the effectiveness of their votes . . ." They are entitled to a hearing and to the District Court's decision on their claims. "The very essence of civil liberty certainly consists in the right of every individual to claim the protection of the laws, whenever he receives an injury." . . .

IV.

Justiciability.

. . . We understand the District Court to have read the cited cases as compelling the conclusion that since the appellants sought to have a legislative apportionment held unconstitutional, their suit presented a "political question" and was therefore nonjusticiable. We hold that this challenge to an apportionment presents no nonjusticiable "political question." . . .

. . . It is argued that apportionment cases, whatever the actual wording of the complaint, can involve no federal constitutional right except one resting on the guaranty of a republican form of government, and that complaints based on that clause have been held to present political questions which are nonjusticiable.

. . . Appellants' claim that they are being denied equal protection is justiciable, and if "discrimination is sufficiently shown, the right to relief under the equal protection clause is not diminished by the fact that the discrimination relates to political rights."

To show why we reject the argument based on the Guaranty Clause, we must examine the authorities under it. But because there appears to be some uncertainty as to why those cases did present political questions, and specifically as to whether this apportionment case is like those cases, we deem it necessary first to consider the contours of the "political question" doctrine.

Our discussion, even at the price of extending this opinion, requires review of a number of political question cases, in order to expose the attributes of the doctrine—attributes which, in various settings, diverge, combine, appear, and disappear in seeming disorderliness. . . . That review reveals that in the Guaranty Clause cases and in the other "political question" cases, it is the relationship between the judiciary and the coordinate branches of the Federal Government, and not the federal judiciary's relationship to the States, which gives rise to the "political question."

. . . The nonjusticiability of a political question is primarily a function of the separation of powers. Much confusion results from the capacity of the "political question" label to obscure the need for case-by-case inquiry. Deciding whether a matter has in any measure been committed by the Constitution to another branch of government, or whether the action of that branch exceeds whatever authority has been committed, is itself a delicate exercise in constitutional interpretation, and is a responsibility of this Court as ultimate interpreter of the Constitution. . . .

* * *

It is apparent that several formulations which vary slightly according to the settings in which the questions arise may describe a political question, although each has one or more elements which identify it as essentially a function of the separation of powers. Prominent on the surface of any case held to involve a political question is found a textually demonstrable constitutional commitment of the issue to a coordinate political department; or a lack of judicially discoverable and manageable standards for resolving it; or the impossibility of deciding without an initial policy determination of a kind clearly for nonjudicial discretion; or the impossibility of a court's undertaking independent resolution without expressing lack of the respect due coordinate branches of government; or an unusual need for unquestioning adherence to a political decision already made; or the potentially of embarrassment from multifarious pronouncements by various departments on one question.

Unless one of these formulations is inextricable from the case at bar, there should be no dismissal for non-justiciability on the ground of a political question's presence. The doctrine of which we treat is one of "political questions," not one of "political cases." The courts cannot reject as "no law suit" a bona fide controversy as to whether some action denominated "political" exceeds constitutional authority. The cases we have reviewed show the necessity for discriminating inquiry into the precise facts and posture of the particular case, and the impossibility of resolution by any semantic cataloguing.

But it is argued that this case shares the characteristics of decisions that constitute a category not yet considered, cases concerning the Constitution's guaranty, in Art. IV, Section 4, of a republican form of government. A conclusion as to whether the case at bar does present a political question cannot be confidently reached until we have considered those cases with special care. We shall discover that Guaranty Clause claims involve those elements which define a "political question," and for that reason and no other, they are nonjusticiable. In particular, we shall discover that the nonjusticiability of such claims has nothing to do with their touching upon matters of state governmental organization.

* * *

[Re *Luther v. Bordon:*] Clearly, several factors were thought by the Court in *Luther* to make the question there "political": the commitment to the other branches of the decision as to which is the lawful state government; the unambiguous action by the President, in recognizing the charter government as the lawful authority; the need for finality in the executive's decision; and the lack of criteria by which a court could determine which form of government was republican.

But the only significance that *Luther* could have for our immediate purposes is in its holding that the Guaranty Clause is not a repository of judicially manageable standards which a court could utilize independently in order to identify a State's lawful government. The Court has since refused to resort to the Guaranty Clause—which alone had been invoked for the purpose—as the source of a constitutional standard for invalidating state action. . . .

Just as the Court has consistently held that a challenge to state action based on the Guaranty Clause presents no justiciable question so has it held, and for the same reasons, that challenges to congressional action on the ground of inconsistency with the clause present no justiciable question. . . .

We come, finally, to the ultimate inquiry whether our precedents as to what constitute a nonjusticiable "political question" bring the case before us under the umbrella of that doctrine. A natural beginning is to note whether any of the common characteristics which we have been able to identify and label descriptively are present. We find none: The question here is the consistency of state action with the Federal Constitution. We have no question decided, or to be decided, by a political branch of government coequal with this Court. Nor do we risk embarrassment of our government abroad, or grave disturbance at home if we take issue with Tennessee as to the constitutionality of her action here challenged. Nor need the appellants, in order to succeed in this action, ask the Court to enter upon policy determinations for which judicially manageable standards are lacking. Judicial standards under the Equal Protection Clause are well developed and familiar, and it has been open to courts since the enactment of the Fourteenth Amendment to determine, if on the particular facts they must, that a discrimination reflects no policy, but simply arbitrary and capricious action.

This case does, in one sense, involve the allocation of political power within a State, and the appellants might conceivably have added a claim under the Guaranty Clause. Of course, as we have seen, any reliance on that clause would be futile. But because any reliance on the Guaranty Clause could not have succeeded it does not follow that appellants may not be heard on the equal protection claim which in fact they tender. True, it must be clear that the Fourteenth Amendment claim is not so enmeshed with those political question elements which render Guaranty Clause claims nonjusticiable as actually to present a political question itself. But we have found that not to be the case here.

In this connection special attention is due *Pacific States Tel. & T. Co. v. Oregon*. . . . In that case a corporation tax statute enacted by the initiative was attacked ostensibly on three grounds: (1) due process; (2) equal protection; and (3) the Guaranty Clause. But it was clear that the first two grounds were invoked solely in aid of the contention that the tax was invalid by reason of its passage.

* * *

The due process and equal protection claims were held nonjusticiable in *Pacific States* . . . because the Court believed that they were invoked merely in verbal aid of the resolution of issues which, in its view, entailed political questions. . . .

We conclude then that the non-justiciability of claims resting on the Guaranty Clause which arises from their embodiment of questions that were thought "political," can have no bearing upon the justiciability of the equal protection claim presented in this case. Finally, we emphasize that it is the involvement in Guaranty Clause claims of the elements thought to define "political questions," and no other feature, which could render them nonjusticiable. Specifically, we have said that such claims are not held nonjusticiable because they touch matters of state governmental organization. . . .

* * *

We conclude that the complaint's allegations of a denial of equal protection present a justiciable constitutional cause of action upon which appellants are entitled to a trial and a decision. The right asserted is within the reach of judicial protection under the Fourteenth Amendment.

The judgment of the District Court is reversed and the cause is remanded for further proceedings consistent with this opinion.

Reversed and remanded.

Source:
Supreme Court Reporter, Vol. 82, pp. 691–720.

Engle v. Vitale, 1962

U.S. Supreme Court decision issued June 25, 1962, declaring that religious observances in the public schools were unconstitutional. This and other decisions regarding state and religion were based on the "establishment" clause of the First Amendment as well as decisions applying the Bill of Rights to the states.

Previously, the Supreme Court had ruled in *Everson v. Board of Education of Ewing Township*, (330 U.S. 1), decided February 10, 1947, that religious institutions could benefit from government programs that are religiously neutral. A taxpayer had sued the Board of Education in Ewing, New Jersey, for using tax money to provide free transportation for all students attending parochial as well as public schools. In its 5-4 decision, the Supreme Court upheld the Board of Education, arguing that the state must be neutral, not adversarial, in its relations with religious groups. It reaffirmed, however, that the "wall between church and state . . . must be kept high and impregnable." (The phrase "wall of separation" is from commentary on the establishment clause by Thomas Jefferson in a letter to the Danbury, Connecticut, Baptist Association, January 1, 1802.)

The *Engle* case arose when a group of parents and taxpayers in North Hempstead, New York, objected to the daily recitation in the public schools of a nonsectarian prayer written by the New York State Board of Regents. Although the prayer was voluntary, the Supreme Court, in a 6-1 decision, barred the continuation of the daily recital, declaring that it violated constitutional prohibitions on the establishment of religion. The Court stated: "It is no part of the business of government to compose official prayers for any group of American people to recite as a part of a religious program carried on by government."

Neither Justice Frankfurter nor White participated in the decision.

Mr. Justice Black delivered the opinion of the Court.

The respondent Board of Education of Union Free School District No. 9, New Hyde Park, New York, acting in its official capacity under state law, directed the School District's principal to cause the following prayer to be said aloud by each class in the presence of a teacher at the beginning of each school day:

"Almighty God, we acknowledge our dependence upon Thee, and we beg Thy blessings upon us, our parents, our teachers and our Country."

This daily procedure was adopted on the recommendation of the State Board of Regents, a governmental agency created by the State Constitution to which the New York Legislature has granted broad supervisory, executive, and legislative powers over the State's public school system. These state officials composed the prayer which they recommended and published as a part of their "Statement on Moral and Spiritual Training in the Schools," saying: "We believe that this Statement will be subscribed to by all men and women of good will, and we call upon all of them to aid in giving life to our program."

Shortly after the practice of reciting the Regent's prayer was adopted by the School District, the parents of ten pupils brought this action in a New York State Court insisting that use of this official prayer in the public schools was contrary to the beliefs, religions, or religious practices of both themselves and their children. Among other things, these parents challenged the constitutionality of both the state law authorizing the School District to direct the use of prayer in public schools and the School District's regulation ordering the recitation of this particular prayer on the ground that these actions of official governmental agencies violate that part of the First Amendment of the Federal Constitution which commands that "Congress shall make no law respecting an establishment of religion"—a command which was "made applicable to the State of New York by the Fourteenth Amendment of the said Constitution." The New York Court of Appeals, over the dissents of Judges Dye and Fuld, sustained an order of the lower state courts which had upheld the power of New York to use the Regent's prayer as a part of the daily procedures of its public schools so long as the schools did not compel any pupil to join in the prayer over his or his parents' objection. We granted certiorari to review this important decision involving rights protected by the First and Fourteenth Amendments.

We think by using its public school system to encourage recitation of the Regents' prayer, the State of New York has adopted a practice wholly inconsistent with the Establishment Clause. There can, of course, be no doubt that New York's program of daily classroom invocation of God's blessings as prescribed in the Regents' prayer is a religious activity. It is a solemn avowal of divine faith and supplication for the blessings of the Almighty. The nature of such prayer has always been religious, none of the respondents has denied this and the trial court expressly so found:

"The religious nature of prayer was recognized by Jefferson and has been concurred in by theological writers, the United States Supreme Court and state courts and administrative officials, including New York's Commissioner of Education. A committee of the New York Legislature has agreed.

"The Board of Regents as amicus curiae, the respondents and intervenors all concede the religious nature of prayer, but seek to distinguish this prayer because it is based on our spiritual heritage. . . . "

The petitioners contend among other things that the state laws requiring or permitting use of the Regents' prayer must be struck down as a violation of the Establishment Clause because that prayer was composed by governmental officials as a part of a governmental program to further religious beliefs. For this reason, petitioners argue, the State's use of the Regents' prayer in its public school system breaches the constitutional wall of separation between Church and State. We agree with that contention since we think that the constitutional prohibition against laws respecting an establishment of religion must at least mean that in this country it is no part of the business of government to compose official prayers for any group of the American people to recite as a part of a religious program carried on by government.

It is a matter of history that this very practice of establishing governmentally composed prayers for religious services was one of the reasons which caused many of our early colonists to leave England and seek religious freedom in America. The Book of Common Prayer, which was created under governmental direction and which was approved by Acts of Parliament in 1548 and 1549, set out in minute detail the accepted form and content of prayer and other religious ceremonies to be used in the established, tax- supported Church of England. The controversies over the Book and what should be its content repeatedly threatened to disrupt the peace of that country as the accepted forms of prayer in the established church changed with the views of the particular ruler that happened to be in control at the time. Powerful groups representing some of the varying religious views of the people struggled among themselves to impress their particular views upon the Government and obtain amendments of the Book more suitable to their respective notions of how religious services should be conducted in order that the official religious establishment would advance their particular religious beliefs. Other groups, lacking the necessary political power to influence the Government on the matter, decided to leave England and its established church and seek freedom in America from England's governmentally ordained and supported religion.

It is an unfortunate fact of history that when some of the very groups which had most strenuously opposed the established Church of England found themselves sufficiently in control of colonial governments in this country to write their own prayers into law, they passed laws making their own religion the official religion of their respective colonies. Indeed, as late as the time of the Revolutionary War, there were established churches in at least eight of the thirteen former colonies and established religions in at least four of the other five. But the successful Revolution against English political domination was shortly followed by intense opposition to the practice of establishing religion by law. This opposition crystallized rapidly into an effective political force in Virginia where the minority religious groups such as Presbyterians, Lutherans, Quakers and Baptists had gained such strength that the adherents to the established Episcopal Church were actually a minority themselves. In 1785-1786, those opposed to the established Church, led by James Madison and Thomas Jefferson, who, though themselves not members of any of these dissenting religious groups, opposed all religious establishments by law on grounds of principle, obtained the enactment of the famous "Virginia Bill for Religious Liberty" by which all religious groups were placed on an equal footing so far as the State was concerned. Similar though less far-reaching legislation was being considered and passed in other States.

By the time of the adoption of the Constitution, our history shows that there was a widespread awareness among many Americans of the dangers of a union of Church and State. These people knew, some of them from bitter personal experience, that one of the greatest dangers to the freedom of the individual to worship in his own way lay in the Government's placing its official stamp of approval upon one particular kind of prayer or one particular form of religious services. They knew the anguish, hardship and bitter strife that could come when zealous religious groups struggled with one another to obtain the Government's stamp of approval from each King, Queen, or Protector that come to temporary power. The Constitution was intended to avert a part of this danger by leaving the government of this country in the hands of the people rather than in the hands of any monarch. But this safeguard was not enough. Our Founders were nor more willing to let the content of their prayers and their privilege of praying whenever they pleased be influenced by the ballot box than they were to let these vital matters of personal conscience depend upon the succession of monarchs. The First Amendment was added to the Constitution to stand as a guarantee that neither the power nor the prestige of the Federal Government would be used to control, support or influence the kinds of prayer the American people can say—that the people's religions must not be subjected to the pressures of government for change each time a new political administration is elected to office. Under that Amendment's prohibition against governmental establishment of religion, as reinforced by the provisions of the Fourteenth Amendment, government in this country, be it state or federal, is without power to prescribe by law any particular form of prayer which is to be used as an official prayer in carrying on any program of governmentally sponsored religious activity.

There can be no doubt that New York's state prayer program officially establishes the religious beliefs embodied in the Regents' prayer. The respondents' argument to the contrary, which is largely based upon the contention that the Regents' prayer is "non-denominational" and the fact that the program, as modified and approved by state courts, does not require all pupils to recite the prayer but permits those who wish to do so to remain silent or be excused from the room, ignores the essential nature of the program's constitutional defects. Neither the fact that the prayer may be denominationally neutral nor the fact that its observance on the part of the students is voluntary can serve to free it from the limitations of the Establishment Clause, as it might from the Free Exercise Clause, of the First Amendment, both of which are operative against the States by virtue of the Fourteenth Amendment. Although these two clauses may in certain instances overlap, they forbid two quite different kinds of governmental encroachment upon religious freedom. The Establishment Clause, unlike the Free Exercise Clause, does not depend upon any showing of direct governmental compulsion and is violated by the enactment of laws which establish an official religion whether those laws operate directly to coerce nonobserving individuals or not. This is not to say, of course, that laws officially prescribing a particular form of religious worship do not involve coercion of such individuals. When the power, prestige and financial support of government is placed behind a particular religious belief, the indirect coercive pressure upon religious minorities to conform to the prevailing officially approved religion is plain. But the purposes underlying the Establishment Clause go much further than that. Its first and most immediate purpose rested on the belief that a union of government and religion tends to destroy government and to degrade religion. The history of governmentally established religion, both in England and in this country, showed that whenever government had allied itself with one particular form of religion, the inevitable result had been that it had incurred the hatred, disrespect and even contempt of those who held contrary beliefs. That same history showed that many people had lost their respect for any religion that had relied upon the support of government to spread its faith. The Establishment Clause thus stands as an expression of principle on the part of the Founders of our Constitution that religion is too personal, too sacred, too holy, to permit its "unhallowed perversion" by a civil magistrate. Another purpose of the Establishment Clause rested upon an awareness of the historical fact that governmentally established religions and religious persecutions go hand in hand. The Founders knew that only a few years after the Book of Common Prayer became the only accepted form or religious services in the established Church of England, an Act of Uniformity was passed to compel all Englishmen to attend those services and to make it a criminal offense to conduct or attend religious gatherings of any other kind—a law which was consistently flouted by dissenting religious groups in England and which contributed to widespread persecutions of people like John Bunyan who persisted in holding "unlawful [religious' meetings . . . to the great disturbance and distraction of the good subjects of this kingdom. . . ." And they knew that similar persecutions had received the sanction of law in several of the colonies in this country soon after the establishment of official religions in those colonies. It was in large part to get completely away from this sort of systematic religious persecution that the Founders brought into being our Nation, our Constitution, and our Bill or Rights with its prohibition against any governmental establishment of religion. The New York laws officially prescribing the Regents' prayer are inconsistent both with the purposes of the Establishment Clause and with the Establishment itself.

It has been argued that to apply the Constitution in such a way as to prohibit state laws respecting an establishment of religious services in public schools is to indicate a hostility toward religion or toward prayer. Nothing, of course, could be more wrong. The history of man is inseparable from the history of religion. And perhaps it is too much to say that since the beginning of that history many people have devoutly believed that "More things are wrought by prayer than this world dreams of." It was doubtless largely due to men who believed this that there grew up a sentiment that caused men to leave the cross-currents of officially established state religions and religious persecution in Europe and come to this country filled with the hope that they could find a place in which they could pray when they pleased to the God of their faith in the language the chose. And there were men of this same faith in the power of prayer who led the fight for adoption of our Constitution and also for our Bill of Rights with the very guarantees of religious freedom that forbid the sort of governmental activity which New York has attempted here. These men know that the First Amendment, which tried to put an end to governmental control of religion and of prayer, was not written to destroy either. They knew rather that it was written to quiet well-justified fears which nearly all of them felt arising out of an awareness that governments of the past had shackled men's tongues to make them speak only the religious thoughts that government wanted them to speak and to pray only to the God that government wanted them to pray to. It is neither sacrilegious nor antireligious to say that each separate government in this country should stay out of the business of writing or sanctioning official prayers and leave that purely religious function to the people themselves and to those the people choose to look to for religious guidance.

It is true that New York's establishment of its Regent's prayer as an officially approved religious doctrine of that State does not amount to a total establishment of one particular religious sect to the exclusion of all other—that, indeed, the governmental endorsement of that prayer seems relatively insignificant when compared to the governmental encroachments upon religion which were commonplace 200 years ago. To these who may subscribe to the view that because the Regent's official prayer is so brief and general there can be no danger to religious freedom in its governmental establishment, however, it may be appropriate to say in the words of James Madison, the author of the First Amendment:

"[I]t is proper to take alarm at the first experiment on our liberties. . . . Who does not see that the same authority which can establish Christianity, in exclusion of all other

Religions, may establish with the same ease any particular sect of Christians, in exclusion of all other Sects? That the same authority which can force a citizen to contribute three pence only of his property for the support of any one establishment, may force him to conform to any other establishment in all cases whatsoever?"

The judgment of the Court of Appeals of New York is reversed and the cause remanded for further proceedings not inconsistent with this opinion.

Reversed and remanded.

Mr. Justice Douglas, concurring.

It is customary in deciding a constitutional question to treat it in its narrowest form. Yet at times the setting of the question gives it a form and content which no abstract treatment could give. The point for decision is whether the Government can constitutionally finance a religious exercise. Our system at the federal and state levels is presently honeycombed with such financing. Nevertheless, I think it is an unconstitutional undertaking whatever form it takes.

First, a word as to what this case does not involve.

Plainly, our Bill of Rights would not permit a State or the Federal Government to adopt an official prayer and penalize anyone who would not utter it. This, however, is not that case, for there is no element of compulsion or coercion in New York's regulation requiring that public schools be opened each day with the following prayer:

"Almighty God, we acknowledge our dependence upon Thee, and we beg Thy blessings upon us, our parents, our teachers and our Country."

The prayer is said upon the commencement of the school day, immediately following the pledge of allegiance to the flag. The prayer is said aloud in the presence of a teacher, who either leads the recitation or selects a student to do so. No student, however, is compelled to take part. The respondents have adopted a regulation which provides that "Neither teachers nor any school authority shall comment on participation or nonparticipation . . . nor suggest or request that any posture or language be used or dress be worn or be not used or not worn." Provision is also made for excusing children, upon written request of a parent or guardian, from the saying of the prayer or from the room in which the prayer is said. A letter implementing and explaining this regulation has been sent to each taxpayer and parent in the school district. As I read this regulation, a child is free to stand or not stand, to recite or not recite, without fear of reprisal or even comment by the teacher or any other school official.

In short, the only one who need utter the prayer is the teacher; and no teacher is complaining of it. Students can stand mute or even leave the classroom, if they desire.

McCollum, etc. v. Board of Education, 333 U.S. 203, 68 S.Ct. 461, 92 L.Ed. 649, does not decide this case. It involved the use of public school facilities for religious education of students. Students either had to attend religious instruction or "go to some other place in the school building for pursuit of their secular studies. . . . Reports of their presence or absence were to be made to their secular teachers." Id., at 209, 68 S.Ct., at 464. The influence of the teaching staff was therefore brought to bear on the student body, to support the instilling of religious principles. In the present case, school facilities are used to say the prayer and the teaching staff is employed to lead the pupils in it. There is, however, no effort at indoctrination and no attempt at exposition. Prayers of course may be so long and of such a character as to amount to an attempt at the religious instruction that was denied the public schools by the *McCollum* case. But New York's prayer is of a character that does not involve any element of proselytizing as in the *McCollum* case.

The question presented by this case is therefore an extremely narrow one. It is whether New York oversteps the bounds when it finances a religious exercise.

What New York does on the opening of its public schools is what we do when we open court. Our Crier has from the beginning announced the convening of the Court and then added "God save the United States and this Honorable Court." That utterance is a supplication, a prayer in which we, the judges, are free to join, but which we need not recite any more than the students need recite the New York prayer.

What New York does on the opening of its public schools is what each House of Congress does at the opening of each day's business. Reverend Frederick B. Harris is Chaplain of the Senate; Reverend Bernard Braskamp is Chaplain of the House. Guest chaplains of various denominations also officiate.

In New York the teacher who leads in prayer is on the public payroll; and the time she takes seems minuscule as compared with the salaries appropriated by state legislatures and Congress for chaplains to conduct prayers in the legislative halls. Only a bare fraction of the teacher's time is given to reciting this short 22-word prayer, about the same amount of time that our Crier spends announcing the opening of our sessions and offering a prayer for this Court. Yet for me the principle is the same, no matter how briefly the prayer is said, for in each of the instances given the person praying is a public official on the public payroll, performing a religious exercise in a governmental institution. It is said that the element of coercion is inherent in the giving of this prayer. If that is true here, it is also true of the prayer with which this Court is convened, and of those that open the Congress. Few adults, let alone children, would leave our courtroom or the Senate or the House while those prayers are being given. Every such audience is in a sense a "captive" audience.

At the same time I cannot say that to authorize this prayer is to establish a religion in the strictly historic meaning of those words? A religion is not established in the usual sense merely be letting those who choose to do so say the prayer that the public school teacher leads. Yet once government finances a religious exercise it insert a divisive influence into our communities. The New York Court said that the prayer given does not conform to all of the tenets of the Jewish, Unitarian, and Ethical Culture groups. One of the petitioners is an agnostic.

"We are a religious people whose institutions presuppose a Supreme Being." . . . Under our Bill of Rights free play is given for making religion an active force in our lives. But "if a religious leaven is to be worked into the affairs of our people, it is to be done by individuals and groups, not by the Government." . . . By reason of the First Amendment government is commanded "to have no interest in theology or ritual". . . for on those matters "government must be neutral." Ibid. The First Amendment leaves the Government in a position not of hostility to religion but of neutrality. The philosophy is that the atheist or agnostic—the non-believer—is entitled to go his own way. The philosophy is that if government interferes in matters spiritual, it will be a divisive force. The First Amendment teaches that a government neutral in the field of religion better serves all religious interests.

My problem today would be uncomplicated but for *Everson v. Board of Education*, . . .which allowed taxpayers' money to be used to pay "the bus fares of parochial school pupils as a part of a general program under which" the fares of pupils attending public and other schools were also paid. The *Everson* case seems in retrospect to be out of line with the First Amendment. Its result is appealing, as it allows aid to be given to needy children. Yet by the same token, public funds could be used to satisfy other needs of children in parochial schools—lunches, books, and tuition being obvious examples. Mr. Justice Rutledge stated in dissent what I think is durable First Amendment philosophy:

"The reasons underlying the Amendment's policy have not vanished with time or diminished in force. Now as when it was adopted the price of religious freedom is double. It is that the church and religion shall live both within and upon that freedom. There cannot be freedom of religion, safeguarded by the state, and intervention by the church or its agencies in the state's domain or dependency on its largesse. Madison's Remonstrance, Par. 6, 8. The great condition of religious liberty is that it be maintained free from sustenance, as also from other interferences, by the state. For when it comes to rest upon that secular foundation it vanishes with the resting. Id., Par. 7, 8. Public money devoted to payment of religious costs, educational or other, brings the quest for more. It brings too the struggle of sect against sect for the larger share or for any. Here one by numbers alone will benefit most, there another. That is precisely the history of societies which have had an established religion and dissident groups. . . . It is the very thing Jefferson and Madison experienced and sought to guard against, whether in its blunt or in its more screened forms. Ibid. The end of such strife cannot be other than to destroy the cherished liberty. The dominating group will achieve the dominate benefit; or all will embroil the state in their dissensions. . . .

What New York does with this prayer is a break with that tradition. I therefore join the Court in reversing the judgment below.

Mr. Justice Stewart, dissenting.

A local school board in New York has provided that those pupils who wish to do so may join in a brief prayer at the beginning of each school day, acknowledging their dependence upon God and asking His blessing upon them and upon their parents, their teachers, and their country. The Court today decides that in permitting this brief non-denominational prayer the school board has violated the Constitutional of the United States. I think this decision is wrong.

The Court does not hold, nor could it, that New York has interfered with the free exercise of anybody's religion. For the state courts have made clear that those who object to reciting the prayer must be entirely free of any compulsion to do so, including any "embarrassments and pressures." . . . But the Court says that in permitting school children to say this simple prayer, the New York authorities have established "an official religion."

With all respect, I think the Court has misapplied a great constitutional principle. I cannot see how an "official religion" is established by letting those who want to say a prayer say it. On the contrary, I think that to deny the wish of these school children to join in reciting this prayer is to deny them the opportunity of sharing in the spiritual heritage of our Nation.

The Court's historical review of the quarrels over the Book of Common Prayer in England throws no light for me on the issue before us in this case. England had then and has now an established church. Equally unenlightening, I think, is the history of the early establishment and later rejection of an official church in our own States. For we deal here not with the establishment of a state church, which would, of course, be constitutionally impermissible, but with whether school children who want to begin their day by joining in prayer must be prohibited from doing so. Moreover, I think that the Court's task, in this as in all areas of constitutional adjudication, is not responsibly aided by the uncritical invocation of metaphors like the "wall of separation," a phrase nowhere to be found in the Constitution. What is relevant to the issue here is not the history of an established church is sixteenth century England or in eighteenth century America, but the history of the religious traditions of our people, reflected in countless practices of the institutions and officials of our government.

At the opening of each day's Session of this Court we stand, while one of our officials invokes the protection of God. Since the days of John Marshall our Crier has said, "God save the United States and this Honorable Court." Both the Senate and the House of Representatives open their daily Sessions with prayer. Each of our Presidents, from George Washington to John F. Kennedy, has upon assuming his Office asked the protection and help of God.

The Court today says that the state and federal governments are without constitutional power to prescribe any particular form of words to be recited by any group of the American people on any subject touching religion. One of the stanzas of "The Star-Spangled Banner," made our National Anthem by Act of Congress in 1931, contains these verses:

"Blest with victory and peace, may the heav'n rescued land

Praise the Pow'r that hath made and preserved us a nation!

Then conquer we must, when our cause it is just,

And this be our motto 'In God is our Trust.'"

In 1954 Congress added a phrase to the Pledge of Allegiance to the Flag so that it now contains the words "one Nation under God, indivisible, with liberty and justice for all." In 1952 Congress enacted legislation calling upon the President each year to proclaim a National Day of Prayer. Since 1865 the words "In God we Trust" have been impressed on our coins.

Countless similar examples could be listed, but there is no need to belabor the obvious. It was all summed up by this Court just ten years ago in a single sentence: "We are a religious people whose institution presuppose a Supreme Being." . . .

I do not believe that this Court, or the Congress, or the President has by the actions and practices I have mentioned established an "official religion" in violation of the Constitution. And I do not believe the State of New York has done so in this case. What each has done has been to recognize and to follow the deeply entrenched and highly cherished spiritual traditions of our Nation—traditions which come down to us from those who almost two hundred years ago avowed their "firm Reliance on the Protection of divine Providence" when they proclaimed the freedom and independence of this brave new world.

I dissent.

Source:

Court Reporter, Vol. 82, pp. 1,261–1,277.

Martin Luther King, Jr., "I Have a Dream Speech," 1963

Address delivered by the Reverend Dr. Martin Luther King, Jr., August 28, 1963, at the Lincoln Memorial in ceremonies connected with the March on Washington for Jobs and Freedom, which attracted some 250,000 demonstrators. In this eloquent, emotionally charged speech, the black civil rights leader described his vision of freedom and equality for all Americans. "It is a dream deeply rooted in the American dream." It was a dream that the descendants of slaves and slave owners would live in brotherhood, that freedom and justice would replace oppression and injustice, that people would be judged on the basis of character not skin color. King looked forward to the day when all Americans could join in the spiritual refrain: "Free at last. Free at last; thank God Almighty, we are free at last." Excerpts from this speech, have been quoted by both proponents of affirmative action for blacks and opponents (especially "the content of their character," phrase).

After the march ended, President John F. Kennedy met with 10 of the civil rights leaders. He then issued a statement hailing the demonstration as an advance in the cause of civil rights and said he had been impressed by the "deep fervor and the quiet dignity" that the marchers had displayed. He did not, however, sufficiently promote the civil rights act then in Congress to achieve its passage before his assassination November 22, 1963.

I am happy to join with you today in what will go down in history as the greatest demonstration for freedom in the history of our nation.

Five score years ago, a great American, in whose symbolic shadow we stand today, signed the Emancipation Proclamation. This momentous decree came as a great beacon light of hope to millions of Negro slaves who had been seared in the flames of withering injustice. It came as a joyous daybreak to end the long night of their captivity.

But one hundred years later, the Negro still is not free; one hundred years later, the life of the Negro is still sadly crippled by the manacles of segregation and the chains of discrimination; one hundred years later, the Negro lives on a lonely island of poverty in the midst of a vast ocean of material prosperity; one hundred years later, the Negro is still languished in the corners of American society and finds himself in exile in his own land.

So we've come here today to dramatize a shameful condition. In a sense we've come to our nation's capital to cash a check. When the architects of our republic wrote the magnificent words of the Constitution and the Declaration of Independence, they were signing a promissory note to which every American was to fall heir. This note was the promise that all men, yes, black men as well as white men, would be guaranteed the unalienable rights of life, liberty, and the pursuit of happiness.

It is obvious today that America has defaulted on this promissory note in so far as her citizens of color are concerned. Instead of honoring this sacred obligation, America has given the Negro people a bad check; a check which has come back marked "insufficient funds." But we refuse to believe that the bank of justice is bankrupt. We refuse to believe that there are insufficient funds in the great vaults of opportunity of this nation. And so we've come to cash this check, a check that will give us upon demand the riches of freedom and the security of justice."

We have also come to this hallowed spot to remind America of the fierce urgency of now. This is no time to engage in the luxury of cooling off or to take the tranquilizing drug of gradualism. Now is the time to make real the promises of democracy; now is the time to rise from the dark and desolate valley of segregation to the sunlit path of racial justice; now is the time to lift our nation from the quicksands of racial injustice to the solid rock of brotherhood; now is the time to make justice a reality for all God's children. It would be fatal for the nation to overlook the urgency of the moment. This sweltering summer of the Negro's legitimate discontent will not pass until there is an invigorating autumn of freedom and equality.

Nineteen sixty-three is not an end, but a beginning. And those who hope that the Negro needed to blow off steam and will now be content, will have a rude awakening if the nation returns to business as usual. There will be neither rest nor tranquillity in America until the Negro is granted his citizenship rights. The whirlwinds of revolt will continue to shake the foundations of our nation until the bright day of justice emerges.

But there is something that I must say to my people, who stand on the worn threshold which leads into the palace of justice. In the process of gaining our rightful place, we must not be guilty of wrongful deeds. Let us not seek to satisfy our thirst for freedom by drinking from the cup of bitterness and hatred. We must forever conduct our struggle on the high plain of dignity and discipline. We must not allow our creative protests to degenerate into physical violence. Again and again we must rise to the majestic heights of meeting physical force with soul force. The marvelous new militancy, which has engulfed the Negro community, must not lead us to a distrust of all white people. For many of our white brothers, as evidenced by their presence here today, have come to realize that their destiny is tied up with out destiny. And they have come to realize that their freedom is inextricably bound to our freedom. We cannot walk alone. And as we walk, we must make the pledge that we shall always march ahead. We cannot turn back.

There are those who are asking the devotees of Civil Rights: "When will you be satisfied?" We can never be satisfied as long as the Negro is the victim of the unspeakable horrors of police brutality; we can never be satisfied as long as our bodies, heavy with the fatigue of travel cannot gain lodging in the motels of the highways and the hotels of the cities; we cannot be satisfied as long as the Negro's basic mobility is from a smaller ghetto to a larger one; we can never be satisfied as long as our children are stripped of their selfhood and robbed of their dignity by signs stating. "For White Only;" we cannot be satisfied as long as the Negro in Mississippi cannot vote and a Negro in New York believes he has nothing for which to vote. No! No, we are not satisfied, and we will not be satisfied until "justice rolls down like waters and righteousness like a mighty stream."

I am not unmindful that some of you have come here out of great trials and tribulations. Some of you have come fresh from narrow jail cells. Some of you have come from areas where your quest for freedom left you battered by the storms of persecution and staggered by the winds of police brutality. You have been the veterans of creative suffering. Continue to work with the faith that unearned suffering is redemptive. Go back to Mississippi: Go back to Alabama: Go back to South Carolina: Go back to Georgia: Go back to Louisiana: Go back to the slums and ghettos of our Northern cities, knowing that somehow this situation can and will be changed. Let us not wallow in the valley of despair.

So I say to you, my friends, that even though we face the difficulties of today and tomorrow, I still have a dream. It is a dream deeply rooted in the American dream, that one day this nation will rise up and live out the true meaning of its creed, "we hold these truths to be self-evident, that all men are created equal." I have a dream that one day on the red hills of Georgia, sons of former slaves and the sons of former slave owners will be able to sit down together at the table of brotherhood. I have a dream that one day even the state of Mississippi, a state sweltering with the heat of injustice, sweltering with the heat of oppression, will be transformed into an oasis of freedom and justice. I have a dream my four little children will one day live in a nation where they will not be judged by the color of their skin, but by the content of their character.

I Have a Dream Today!

I have a dream that one day in Alabama—with its vicious racists, with its Governor having his lips dripping with the words of interposition and nullification—one day right there in Alabama, little black boys and black girls will be able to join hands with little white boys and white girls as sisters and brothers.

I Have a Dream Today!

I have a dream that one day every valley shall be exalted, every hill and mountain shall be made low. The rough places will be plain and the crooked places will be made straight "and the glory of the Lord shall be revealed, and all flesh shall see it together."

This is our hope. This is the faith that I go back to the South with. With this faith we will be able to hew out of the mountain of despair, a stone of hope. With this faith we will be able to transform the jangling discords of our nation into a beautiful symphony of brotherhood. With this faith we will be able to work together, to pray together, to struggle together, to go to jail together, to stand up for freedom together, knowing that we will be free one day. And this will be the day. This will be the day when all of God's children will be able to sing with new meaning, "My country 'tis of thee, sweet land of liberty, of thee I sing. Land where my father died, land of the pilgrim's pride, from every mountain side, let freedom ring." And if America is to be a great nation, this must become true.

So let freedom ring from the prodigious hilltops of New Hampshire; let freedom ring from the mighty mountains of New York; let freedom ring from the heightening Alleghenies of Pennsylvania; let freedom ring from the snow-capped Rockies of Colorado; let freedom ring from the curvaceous slopes of California. But not only that. Let freedom ring from Stone Mountain of Georgia; let freedom ring from Lookout Mountain of Tennessee; let freedom ring from every hill and mole hill of Mississippi. "From every mountainside, let freedom ring." And when this happens, and when we allow freedom to ring, when we let it ring from every village and every hamlet from every state and every city, we will be able to speed up that day when all God's children, black men and white men, Jews and Gentiles, Protestants and Catholics, will be able to join hands and sing in the words of the old Negro spiritual: "Free at last; thank God Almighty, we are free at last."

Source:
The King Center, Atlanta, Ga.

John F. Kennedy, Telegram to George Wallace, 1963

Message sent by President John F. Kennedy to Alabama governor George C. Wallace on May 13, 1963, in response to Wallace's telegram. It had questioned the need to send federal troops to his state to quell rioting by whites who were protesting an agreement to desegregate public facilities in Birmingham. Kennedy replied that he would have been derelict in his duty if he had not taken steps to ensure that his government was able to meet its obligations. He noted that among those obligations, as detailed in the federal legal code, was the president's authority to determine whether a state was able to offer adequate protection to all its citizens. Kennedy expressed hope that Wallace would cooperate with his efforts.

Governor Wallace continued to resist. On June 11, 1963, President Kennedy broadcast a speech to the nation to report on the enforcement of a court order admitting two black students to the University of Alabama. He used the opportunity to outline his opposition to racism, declaring that the heirs of slaves are "not yet freed from the bonds of injustice." Calling for the Congress to pass civil rights legislation, Kennedy stated that every child "should have the equal right to develop their talent and their ability and their motivation, to make something of themselves."

So many racially motivated explosions occurred in Birmingham that year that the place was nicknamed "Bombingham." The worst white terrorist attack occurred in September when the Sixteenth Street Baptist Church, used for civil rights gatherings, was bombed, killing four black girls aged 11 to 14. The FBI had jurisdiction for racially motivated bombings, but Governor Wallace intervened, using information acquired by his anti-integration investigators who were supposed to be cooperating with the bureau. Three of the alleged perpetrators were convicted of minor offenses, pre-empting the establishment of a federal case. In 1977 the case was reopened, and one perpetrator was convicted. The state indicted two additional suspects in 2001, using conversation taped by an informant during the 1960s. Because the tapes were presumed inadmissible at that time, the information collected was not used in court. One suspect was convicted in 2001 and the second in a separate trial in 2002.

In response to the question raised in your telegram of last night, Federal troops would be sent into Birmingham, if necessary, under the authority of Title 10, Section 333, Paragraph 1 of the United States Code relating to the suppression of domestic violence. Under this section, which has been invoked by my immediate predecessor and other Presidents as well as myself on previous occasions, the Congress entrusts to the President all determinations as to (1) the necessity for action; (2) the means to be employed; and (3) the adequacy or inadequacy of the protection afforded by State authorities to the citizens of that State.

As yet, no final action has been taken under this section with respect to Birmingham inasmuch as it continues to be my hope, as stated last night, "that the citizens of Birmingham themselves will maintain standards of responsible conduct that will make outside intervention unnecessary. "Also, as I said last Thursday, in the absence of any violation of Federal statutes or court orders or other grounds for Federal intervention, our efforts will continue to be focused on helping local citizens to achieve and maintain a peaceful, reasonable settlement. The community leaders who worked out this agreement with a great sense of justice and foresight deserve to see it implemented in an atmosphere of law and order. I trust that we can count on your constructive cooperation in maintaining such an atmosphere; but I would be derelict in my duty if I did not take the preliminary steps announced last night that will enable this Government, if required, to meet its obligations without delay.

John F. Kennedy

Source:

Public Papers of the Presidents of the United States: John F. Kennedy, 1963. Washington, D.C.: Government Printing Office, 1961–63. p. 298.

Malcolm X (El Hajj Malik Shabazz), "Ballot or the Bullet" Symposium, 1964

Born Malcolm Little in Detroit, Malcolm, while in jail, became a follower of Elijah Mohammed, head of the Nation of Islam, or Black Muslims. This off-shoot of traditional Islam held that white Christians are inherently evil and black people must separate themselves from them. Malcolm caught Elijah Mohamed's attention and soon headed mosques, eventually becoming a major spokesman for the religion. Malcolm X delivered this speech April 3, 1964, at a symposium entitled "The Ballot or the Bullet" in Cleveland, Ohio. In it, Malcolm X outlined his emerging vision and philosophy for a black nationalist movement.

In 1964 Malcolm X traveled through several Islamic nations in North Africa and the Middle East, including a pilgrimage to Mecca. Although he made important contacts with religious and political leaders, the major impact of the tour was upon Malcolm X himself. After the trip, he converted to orthodox Islam and began voicing the belief that there could be a brotherhood among people of all races, including whites. This change caused a rift between him and the Nation of Islam, resulting in his assassination in 1965. His wife, Betty Shabazz, carried on his work.

Malcolm's writings and speeches continue to influence, but he also became a cult figure, identified with the phrase "by any means necessary," especially after the Spike Lee movie *Malcolm X* was released in 1992.

Mr. Moderator, Brother Lomax, brothers and sisters, friends and enemies: I just can't believe everyone in here is a friend and I don't want to leave anybody out. The question tonight, as I understand it, is "The Negro Revolt, and Where Do We Go From Here?" or "What Next?" In my little humble way of understanding it, it points toward either the ballot or the bullet.

Before we try and explain what is meant by the ballot or the bullet, I would like to clarify something concerning myself. I'm still a Muslim, my religion is still Islam. That's my personal belief. Just as Adam Clayton Powell is a Christian minister who heads the Abyssinian Baptist Church in New York, but at the same time takes part in the political struggles to try and bring about rights to the black people in this country; and Dr. Martin Luther King is a Christian minister down in Atlanta, Georgia, who heads another organization fighting for the civil rights of black people in this country; and Rev. Galamison, I guess you've heard of him, is another Christian minister in New York who has been deeply involved in the school boycotts to eliminate segregated education; well, I myself am a minister, not a Christian minister, but a Muslim minister; and I believe in action on all fronts by whatever means necessary.

Although I'm still a Muslim, I'm not here tonight to discuss my religion. I'm not here to try and change your religion. I'm not here to argue or discuss anything that we differ about, because it's time for us to submerge our differences and realize that it is best for us to first see that we have the same problem, a common problem—a problem that will make you catch hell whether you're a Baptist, or a Methodist, or a Muslim, or a nationalist. Whether you're educated or illiterate, whether you live on the boulevard or in the alley, you're going to catch hell just like I am. We're all in the same boat and we all are going to catch the same hell from the same man. He just happens to be a white man. All of us have suffered here, in this country, political oppression at the hands of the white man, economic exploitation at the hands of the white man, and social degradation at the hands of the white man.

Now in speaking like this, it doesn't mean that we're anti-white, but it does mean we're anti- exploitation, we're anti-degradation, we're anti-oppression. And if the white man doesn't want us to be anti-him, let him stop oppressing and exploiting and degrading us. Whether we are Christians or Muslims or nationalists or agnostics or atheists, we must first learn to forget our differences. If we have differences, let us differ in the closet; when we come out in front, let us not have anything to argue about until we get finished arguing with the man. If the late President Kennedy could get together with Khrushchev and exchange some wheat, we certainly have more in common with each other than Kennedy and Khrushchev had with each other.

If we don't do something real soon, I think you'll have to agree that we're going to be forced either to use the ballot or the bullet. It's one or the other in 1964. It isn't that time is running out—time has run out! 1964 threatens to be the most explosive year America has ever witnessed. The most explosive year. Why? It's also a political year. It's the year when all of the white politicians will be back in the so-called Negro community jiving you and me for some votes. The year when all of the white political crooks will be right back in your and my community with their false promises, building up our hopes for a letdown, with their trickery and their treachery, with their false promises which they don't intend to keep. As they nourish these dissatisfactions, it can only lead to one thing, an explosion; and now we have the type of black man on the scene in America today—I'm sorry, Brother Lomax—who just doesn't intend to turn the other cheek any longer.

Don't let anybody tell you anything about the odds are against you. If they draft you, they send you to Korea and make you face 800 million Chinese. If you can be brave over there, you can be brave right here. These odds aren't as great as those odds. And if you fight here, you will at least know what you're fighting for.

I'm not a politician, not even a student of politics; in fact, I'm not a student of much of anything. I'm not a Democrat, I'm not a Republican, and I don't even consider myself an American. If you and I were Americans, there'd be no problem. Those Hunkies that just got off the boat, they're already Americans; Polacks are already Americans; the Italian refugees are already Americans. Everything that came out of Europe, every blue-eyed thing, is already an American. And as long as you and I have been over here, we aren't Americans yet.

Well, I am one who doesn't believe in deluding myself. I'm not going to sit at your table and watch you eat, with nothing on my plate, and call myself a diner. Sitting at the table doesn't make you a diner, unless you eat some of what's on that plate. Being here in America doesn't make you an American. Being born here in America doesn't make you an American. Why, if birth made you American, you wouldn't need any legislation, you wouldn't need any amendments to the Constitution, you wouldn't be faced with civil-rights filibustering in Washington, D.C., right now. They don't have to pass civil-rights legislation to make a Polack an American.

No, I'm not an American. I'm one of the 22 million black people who are the victims of Americanism. One of the 22 million black people are the victims of democracy, nothing but disguised hypocrisy. So, I'm not standing here speaking to you as an American, or a patriot, or a flag-saluter, or a flag-waver—no, not I. I'm speaking as a victim of this American system. And I see America through the eyes of the victim. I don't see any American dream; I see an American nightmare.

These 22 million victims are waking up. Their eyes are coming open. They're beginning to see what they used to only look at. They're becoming politically mature. They are realizing that there are new political trends from coast to coast. As they see these new political trends, it's possible for them to see that every time there's an election the races are so close that they have to have a recount. They had to recount in Massachusetts to see who was going to be governor, it was so close. It was the same way in Rhode Island, in Minnesota, and in many other parts of the country. And the same with Kennedy and Nixon when they ran for president. It was so close they had to count all over again. Well, what does this mean? It means that when white people are evenly divided, and black people have a bloc of votes of their own, it is left up to them to determine who's going to sit in the White House and who's going to be in the dog house.

It was the black man's vote that put the present administration in Washington, D.C. Your vote, your dumb vote, your ignorant vote, your wasted vote put in an administration in Washington, D.C., that has seen fit to pass every kind of legislation imaginable, saving you until last, then filibustering on top of that. And your and my leaders have the audacity to run around clapping their hands and talk about how much progress we're making. And what a good president we have. If he wasn't good in Texas, he sure can't be good in Washington, D.C. Because Texas is a lynch state. It is in the same breath as Mississippi, no different; only they lynch you in Texas with a Texas accent and lynch you in Mississippi with a Mississippi accent. And these Negro leaders have the audacity to go and have some coffee in the White House with a Texan, a Southern cracker—that's all he is—and then come out and tell you and me that he's going to be better for us because, since he's from the South, he knows how to deal with the Southerners. What kind of logic is that? Let Eastland be president, he's from the South too. He should be better able to deal with them than Johnson.

In this present administration they have in the House of Representative 257 Democrats to only 177 Republicans. They control two-thirds of the House vote. Why can't they pass something that will help you and me? In the Senate, there are 67 senators who are of the Democrat Party. Only 33 of them are Republicans. Why, the Democrats have got the government sewed up, and you're the one who sewed it up for them. And what have they given you for it? Four years in office, and just now getting around to some civil-rights legislation. Just now, after everything else is gone, out of the way, they're going to sit down now and play with you all summer long—the same old giant con game that they call filibuster. All those are in cahoots together. Don't you ever think they're not in cahoots together, for the man that is heading the civil-rights filibuster is a man from Georgia named Richard Russell. When Johnson became president, the first man he asked for when he got back to Washington D.C., was "Dicky"—that's how tight they are. That's his boy, that's his pal, that's his buddy. But they're playing that old con game. One of them makes believe he's for you, and he's got it fixed where the other one is so tight against you, he never has to keep his promise.

So it's time in 1964 to wake up. And when you see them coming up with that kind of conspiracy, let them know your eyes are open. And let them know you got something else that's wide open too. It's got to be the ballot or the bullet. The ballot or the bullet. If you're afraid to use an expression like that, you should get on out of the country, you should get back in the cotton patch, you should get back in the alley. They get all the Negro vote, and after they get it, the Negro gets nothing in return. All they did when they got to Washington was give a few big Negroes big jobs. Those big Negroes didn't need big jobs, they already had jobs. That's camouflage, that's trickery, that's treachery, window-dressing. I'm not trying to knock out the Democrats for the Republicans, we'll get to them in a minute. But it is true—you put the Democrats first and the Democrats put you last.

Look at it the way it is. What alibis do they use, since they control Congress and the Senate? What alibi do they use when you and I ask, "Well, when are you going to keep your promise?" They blame the Dixiecrats. What is a Dixiecrat? A Democrat. A Dixiecrat is nothing but a Democrat in disguise. The titular head of the Democrats is also the head of the Dixiecrats, because the Dixiecrats are a part of the Democratic Party. The Democrats have never kicked the Dixiecrats out of the party. The Dixiecrats bolted themselves once, but the Democrats didn't put them out. Imagine, these lowdown Southern segregationists put the Northern Democrats down. But the Northern Democrats have never put the Dixiecrats down. No, look at that thing the way it is. They have got a con game going on, a political con game, and you and I are in the middle. It's time for you and me to wake up and start looking at it like it is, and trying to understand it like it is; and then we can deal with it like it is.

The Dixiecrats is Washington, D.C., control the key committees that run the government. The only reason the Dixiecrats control these committees is because they have seniority. The only reason they have seniority is because they come from states where Negroes can't vote. This is not even a government that's based on democracy. It is not a government that is made up of representatives of the people. Half of the people in the South can't even vote. Eastland is not even supposed to be in Washington. Half of the senators and congressmen who occupy these key positions in Washington, D.C., are there illegally, are there unconstitutionally.

I was in Washington, D.C., a week ago Thursday, when they were debating whether or not they should let the bill come onto the floor. And in the back of the room where the Senate meets, there's a huge map of the United States, and on that map it shows the location of Negroes throughout the country. And it shows that the Southern section of the country, the states that are most heavily concentrated with Negroes, are the ones that have senators and congressmen standing up filibustering and doing all other kinds of trickery to keep the Negro from being able to vote. This is pitiful. But it's not pitiful for us any longer; it's actually pitiful for the white man, because soon now, as the Negro awakens a little more and sees the vise that he's in, sees the bag that he's in, sees the real game that he's in, then the Negro's going to develop a new tactic.

These senators and congressmen actually violate the constitutional amendments that guarantee the people of that particular state or county the right to vote. And the Constitution itself has within it the machinery to expel any representative from a state where the voting rights of the people are violated. You don't even need new legislation. Any person in Congress right now, who is there from a state or a district where the voting rights of the people are violated, that particular person should be expelled from Congress. And when you expel him, you've removed one of the obstacles in the path of any real meaningful legislation in this country. In fact, when you expel them, you don't need new legislation, because they will be replaced by black representatives from countries and districts where the black man is in the majority, not in the minority.

If the black man in these Southern states had his full voting rights, the key Dixiecrats in Washington, D.C., which means the key Democrats in Washington, D.C., would lose their seats. The Democratic Party itself would lose its power. It would cease to be powerful as a party. When you see the amount of power that would be lost by the Democratic Party if it were to lose the Dixiecrat wing, or branch, or element, you can see where it's against the interests of the Democrats to give voting rights to Negroes in states where the Democrats have been in complete power and authority ever since the Civil War. You just can't belong to that party without analyzing it.

I say again, I'm not anti-Democrat, I'm not anti-Republican, I'm not anti-anything. I'm just questioning their sincerity, and some of the strategy that they've been using on our people by promising them promises that they don't intend to keep. When you keep the Democrats in power, you're keeping the Dixiecrats in power. I doubt that my good Brother Lomax will deny that. A vote for a Democrat is a vote for a Dixiecrat. That's why, in 1964, it's time now for you and me to become fore politically mature and realize what the ballot is for; what we're supposed to get when we cast a ballot; and that if we don't cast a ballot, it's going to end up in a situation where we're going to have to cast a bullet. It's either a ballot or a bullet.

In the North, they do it a different way. They have a system that's known as gerrymandering, whatever that means. It means when Negroes become too heavily concentrated in a certain area, and begin to gain too much political power, the white man comes along and changes the district lines. You may say, "Why do you keep saying white man?" Because it's the white man who does it. I haven't ever seen any Negro changing any lines. They don't let him get near the line. It's the white man who does this. And usually, it's the white man who grins at you the most, and pats you on the back, and is supposed to be your friend. He may be friendly, but he's not your friend

So, what I'm trying to impress upon you, in essence, is this: You and I in America are faced not with a segregationist conspiracy, we're faced with a government conspiracy. Everyone who's filibustering is a senator—that's the government. Everyone who's finagling in Washington, D.C., is a congressman—that's the government. You don't have anybody putting blocks in your path but people who are a part of the government. The same government that you go abroad to fight for and die for is the government that is in a conspiracy to deprive you of your voting rights, deprive you of your economic opportunities, deprive you of decent housing, deprive you of decent education. You don't need to go to the employer alone, it is the government itself, the government of America, that is responsible for the oppression and exploitation and degradation of black people in this country. And you should drop it in their lap. This government has failed the Negro. This so-called democracy has failed the Negro. And all these white liberals have definitely failed the Negro.

So, where do we go from here? First, we need some friends. We need some new allies. The entire civil-rights struggle needs a new interpretation, a broader interpretation. We need to look at this civil-rights thing from another angle—from the inside as well as from the outside. To those of us whose philosophy is black nationalism, the only way you can get involved in the civil-rights struggle is give it a new interpretation. That old interpretation excluded us. It kept us out. So, we're giving a new interpretation to the civil-rights struggle, an interpretation that will enable us to come into it, take part in it. And these handkerchief-heads who have been dillydallying and pussy-footing and compromising—we don't intend to let them pussyfoot and dillydally and compromise any longer.

How can you thank a man for giving you what's already yours? How then can you thank him for giving you only part of what's already yours? You haven't even made progress, if what's being given to you, you should have had already. That's not progress. And I love my Brother Lomax, the way he pointed out we're right back where we were in 1954. We're not even as far up as we were in 1954. We're behind where we were in 1954. There's more segregation now than there was in 1954. There's more racial animosity, more racial hatred, more racial violence today in 1964, than there was in 1954. Where is the progress?

And now you're facing a situation where the young Negro's coming up. They don't want to hear that turn-the-other-cheek" stuff, no. In Jacksonville, those were teenagers, they were throwing Molotov cocktails. Negroes have never done that before. But it shows you there's a new deal coming in. There's new thinking coming in. There's new strategy coming in. It'll be Molotov cocktails this month, hand grenades next month, and something else next month. It'll be ballots, or it'll be bullets. It'll be liberty, or it will be death. The only difference about this kind of death—it'll be reciprocal. You know what is meant by "reciprocal"? That's one of Brother Lomax's words, I stole it from him. I don't usually deal with those big words because I don't usually deal with big people. I deal with small people. I find you can get a whole lot of small people and whip hell out of a whole lot of big people. They haven't got anything to lose, and they've got everything to gain. And they'll let you know in a minute: "It takes two to tango; when I go, you go."

The black nationalists, those whose philosophy is black nationalism, in bringing about this new interpretation of the entire meaning of civil rights, look upon it as meaning, as Brother Lomax has pointed out, equality of opportunity. Well, we're justified in seeking civil rights, if it means equality of opportunity, because all we're doing there is trying to collect for our investment. Our mothers and fathers invested sweat and blood. Three hundred and ten years we worked in this country without a dime in return—I mean without a *dime* in return. You let the white man walk around here talking about how rich this country is, but you never stop to think how it got rich so quick. It got rich because you made it rich.

You take the people who are in this audience right now. They're poor, we're all poor as individuals. Our weekly salary individually amounts to hardly anything. But if you take the salary of everyone in here collectively it'll fill up a whole lot of baskets. It's a lot of wealth. If you can collect the wages of just these people right here for a year, you'll be rich—richer than rich. When you look at it like that, think how rich Uncle Sam had to become, not with this handful, but millions of black people. Your and my mother and father, who didn't work an eight-hour shift, but worked from "can't see" in the morning until "can't see" at night, and worked for nothing, making the white man rich, making Uncle Sam rich.

This is our investment. This is our contribution—our blood. Not only did we give our free labor, we gave of our blood. Every time he had a call to arms, we were the first ones in uniform. We died on every battlefield the white man had. We have made a greater sacrifice than anybody who's standing up in America today. We have made a greater contribution and have collected less. Civil rights, for those of us whose philosophy is black nationalism, means: "Give it to us now. Don't wait for next year. Give it to us yesterday, and that's not fast enough."

I might stop right here to point out one thing. Whenever you're going after something that belongs to you, anyone who's depriving you of the right to have it is a criminal. Understand that. Whenever you are going after something that is yours, you are within your legal rights to lay claim to it. And anyone who puts forth any effort to deprive you of that which is yours, is breaking the law, is a criminal. And this way pointed out by the Supreme Court decision. It outlawed segregation. Which means segregation is against the law. Which means a segregationist is breaking the law. A segregationist is a criminal. You can't label him as anything other than that. And when you demonstrate against segregation, the law is on your side. The Supreme Court is on your side.

Now, who is it that opposes you in carrying out the law? The police department itself. With police dogs and clubs. Whenever you demonstrate against segregation, whether it is segregated education, segregated housing, or anything else, the law is on your side, and anyone who stands in the way is not the law any longer. They are breaking the law, they are not representatives of the law. Any time you demonstrate against segregation and a man has the audacity to put a police dog on you, kill that dog, kill him, I'm telling you, kill that dog. I say it, if they put me in jail tomorrow, kill—that—dog. Then you'll put a stop to it. Now, if these white people in here don't want to see that kind of action, get down and tell the mayor to tell the police department to pull the dogs in. That's all you have to do. If you don't do it, someone else will.

If you don't take this kind of stand, your little children will grow up and look at you and think "shame." If you don't take an uncompromising stand—I don't mean go out and get violent; but at the same time you should never be nonviolent unless you run into some nonviolence. I'm nonviolent with those who are nonviolent with me. But when you drop that violence on me, then you've made me go insane, and I'm not responsible for what I do. And that's the way every Negro should get. Any time you know you're within the law, within your legal rights, within your moral rights, in accord with justice, then die for what you believe in. But don't die alone. Let your dying be reciprocal. This is what is meant by equality. What's good for the goose is good for the gander.

When we begin to get in this area, we need new friends, we need new allies. We need to expand the civil-rights struggle to a higher level—to the level of human rights. Whenever you are in a civil-rights struggle, whether you know it or not, you are confining yourself to the jurisdiction of Uncle Sam. No one from the outside world can speak out in your behalf as long as your struggle is a civil-rights struggle. Civil rights comes within the domestic affairs of this country. All of our African brothers and our Asian brothers and our Latin-American brothers cannot open their mouths and interfere in the domestic affairs of the United States. And as long as it's civil rights, this comes under the jurisdiction of Uncle Sam.

But the United Nations has what's known as the charter of human rights, it has a committee that deals in human rights. You may wonder why all of the atrocities that have been committed in Africa and in Hungary and in Asia and in Latin America are brought before the UN, and the Negro problem is never brought before the UN. This is part of the conspiracy. This old, tricky, blue-eyed liberal who is supposed to be your and my friend, supposed to be in our corner, supposed to be subsidizing our struggle, and supposed to be acting in the capacity of an adviser, never tells you anything about human rights. They keep you wrapped up in civil rights. And you spend so much time barking up the civil-rights tree, you don't even know there's a human-rights tree on the same floor.

When you expand the civil-rights struggle to the level of human rights, you can then take the case of the black man in this country before the nations in the UN. You can take it before the General Assembly. You can take Uncle Sam before a world court. But the only level you can do it on is the level of human rights. Civil rights keeps you under his restrictions, under his jurisdiction. Civil rights keeps you in his pocket. Civil rights means you're asking Uncle Sam to treat you right. Human rights are something you were born with. Human rights are you God-given rights. Human rights are the rights that are recognized by all nations of this earth. And any time any one violates your human rights, you can take them to the world court. Uncle Sam's hands are dripping with blood, dripping with the blood of the black man in this country. He's the earth's number-one hypocrite. He has the audacity—yes, he has—imagine him posing as the leader of the free world. The free world!—and you over here singing

"We Shall Overcome." Expand the civil-rights struggle to the level of human rights, take it into the United Nations, where our African brothers can throw their weight on our side, where our Asian brothers can throw their weight on our side, where our Latin-American brothers can throw their weight on our side, and where 800 million Chinamen are sitting there waiting to throw their weight on our side.

Let the world know how bloody his hands are. Let the world know the hypocrisy that's practiced over here. Let it be the ballot or the bullet. Let him know that it must be the ballot or the bullet.

When you take your case to Washington, D.C., you're taking it to the criminal who's responsible; it's like running from the wolf to the fox. They're all in cahoots together. They all work political chicanery and make you look like a chump before the eyes of the world. Here you are walking around in America, getting ready to be drafted and sent abroad, like a tin soldier, and when you get over there, people ask you what are you fighting for, and you have to stick your tongue in your cheek. No, take Uncle Sam to court, take him before the world.

By ballot I only mean freedom. Don't you know—I disagree with Lomax on this issue—that the ballot is more important than the dollar? Can I prove it? Yes. Look in the UN. There are poor nations in the UN; yet those poor nations can get together with their voting power and keep the rich nations from making a move. They have one nation—one vote, everyone has an equal vote. And when those brothers from Asia, and Africa and the darker parts of this earth get together, their voting power is sufficient to hold Sam in check. Or Russia in check. Or some other section of the earth in check. So, the ballot is most important.

Right now, in this country, if you and I, 22 million African-Americans—that's what we are—Africans who are in America. You're nothing but Africans. Nothing but Africans. In fact, you'd get farther calling yourself African instead of Negro. Africans don't catch hell. You're the only one catching hell. They don't have to pass civil-rights bills for Africans. An African can go anywhere he wants right now. All you've got to do is tie your head up. That's right, go anywhere you want. Just stop being a Negro. Change your name to Hoogagagooba. That'll show you how silly the white man is. You're dealing with a silly man. A friend of mine who's very dark put a turban on his head and went into a restaurant in Atlanta before they called themselves desegregated. He went into a white restaurant, he sat down, they served him, and he said, "What would happen if a Negro came in here?" And there he's sitting, black as night, but because he had his head wrapped up the waitress looked back at him and says, "Why, there wouldn't no nigger dare come in here."

So, you're dealing with a man whose bias and prejudice are making him lose his mind, his intelligence, every day. He's frightened. He looks around and sees what's taking place on this earth, and he sees that the pendulum of time is swinging in your direction. The dark people are waking up. They're losing their fear of the white man. No place where he's fighting right now is he winning. Everywhere he's fighting, he's fighting someone your and my complexion. And they're beating him. He can't win any more. He's won his last battle. He failed to win the Korean War. He couldn't win it. He had to sign a truce. That's a loss. Any time Uncle Sam, with all his machinery for warfare, is held to a draw by some rice-eaters, he's lost the battle. He had to sign a truce. America's not supposed to sign a truce. She's supposed to be bad. But she's not bad any more. She's bad as long as she can use her hydrogen bomb, but she can't use hers for fear Russia might use hers. Russia can't use hers, for fear that Sam might use his. So, both of them are weaponless. They can't use the weapon because each's weapon nullifies the other's. So the only place where action can take place is on the ground. And the white man can't win another war fighting on the ground. Those days are over. The black man knows it, the brown man knows it, the red man knows it, and the yellow man knows it. So they engage him in guerrilla warfare. That's not his style. You've got to have heart to be a guerrilla warrior, and he hasn't got any heart. I'm telling you now.

I just want to give you a little briefing on guerrilla warfare because, before you know it, before you know it—It takes heart to be a guerrilla warrior because you're on your own. In conventional warfare you have tanks and a whole lot of other people with you to back you up, planes over your head and all that kind of stuff. But a guerrilla is on his own. All you have is a rifle, some sneakers and a bowl of rice, and that's all you need—and a lot of heart. The Japanese on some of those islands in the Pacific, when the American soldiers landed, one Japanese sometimes could hold the whole army off. He'd just wait until the sun went down, and when the sun went down they were all equal. He would take his little blade and slip from bush to bush, and from American to American. The white soldiers couldn't cope with that. Whenever you see a white soldier that fought in the Pacific, he has the shakes, he has a nervous condition, because they scared him to death.

The same thing happened to the French up in French Indochina. People who just a few years previously were rice farmers got together and ran the heavily-mechanized French army out of Indochina. You don't need it—modern warfare today won't work. This is the day of the guerrilla. They did the same thing in Algeria. Algerians, who were nothing but Bedouins, took a rifle and sneaked off to the hills, and de Gaulle and all of his highfalutin' war machinery couldn't defeat those guerrillas. Nowhere on this earth does the white man win in a guerrilla warfare. It's not his speed. Just as guerrilla warfare is prevailing in Asia and in parts of Africa and in parts of Latin America, you've got to be mighty naive, or you've got to play the black man cheap, if you don't think some day he's going to wake up and find that it's got to be the ballot or the bullet.

I would like to say, in closing, a few things concerning the Muslim Mosque, Inc., which we established recently in New York City. It's true we're Muslims and our religion is Islam, but we don't mix our religion with our politics and our economics and our social and civil activities—not any more. We keep our religion in our mosque. After our religious services are over, then as Muslims we become involved in political action, economic action and social and civic action. We become involved with anybody, anywhere, any time and in any manner that's designed to eliminate the evils, the political, economic and social evils that are afflicting the people of our community.

The political philosophy of black nationalism means that the black man should control the politics and the politicians in his own community; no more. The black man in the black community has to be re- educated into the science of politics so he will know what politics is supposed to bring him in return. Don't be throwing out any ballots. A ballot is like a bullet. You don't throw your ballots until you see a target, and if that target is not within your reach, keep your ballot in your pocket. The political philosophy of black nationalism is being taught in the Christian church. It's being taught in the NAACP. It's being taught in CORE meetings. It's being taught in SNCC [Student Nonviolent Coordinating Committee] meetings. It's being taught in Muslim meetings. It's being taught where nothing but atheists and agnostics come together. It's being taught everywhere. Black people are fed up with the dillydallying, pussyfooting, compromising approach that we've been using toward getting our freedom. We want freedom *now*, but we're not going to get it saying "We Shall Overcome." We've got to fight until we overcome.

The economic philosophy of black nationalism is pure and simple. It only means that we should control the economy of our community. Why should white people be running all the stores in our community? Why should white people be running the banks of our community? Why should the economy of our community be in the hands of the white man? Why? If a black man can't move his store into a white community, you tell me why a white man should move his store into a black community. The philosophy of black nationalism involves a re-education program in the black community in regards to economics. Our people have to be made to see that any time you take your dollar out of your community and spend it in a community where you don't live, the community where you live will get poorer and poorer, and the community where you spend your money will get richer and richer. Then you wonder why where you live is always a ghetto or a slum area. And where you and I are concerned, not only do we lose it when we spend it out of the community, but the white man has got all our stores in the community tied up; so that though we spend it in the community, at sundown the man who runs the store takes it over across town somewhere. He's got us in a vise.

So the economic philosophy of black nationalism means in every church, in every civic organization, in every fraternal order, it's time now for our people to become conscious of the importance of controlling the economy of our community. If we own the stores, if we operate the businesses, if we try and establish some industry in our own community, then we're developing to the position where we are creating employment for our own kind. Once you gain control of the economy of your own community, then you don't have to picket and boycott and beg some cracker downtown for a job in his business.

The social philosophy of black nationalism only means that we have to get together and remove the evils, the vices, alcoholism, drug addiction, and other evils that are destroying the moral fiber of our community. We ourselves have to lift the level of our community, the standard of our community to a higher level, make our own society beautiful so that we will be satisfied in our own social circles and won't be running around here trying to knock our way into a social circle where we're not wanted.

So I say, in spreading a gospel such as black nationalism, it is not designed to make the black man re-evaluate the white man—you know him already—but to make the black man re-evaluate himself. Don't change the white man's mind—you can't change his mind, and that whole thing about appealing to the moral conscience of America—America's conscience is bankrupt. She lost all conscience a long time ago. Uncle Sam has no conscience. They don't know what morals are. They don't try and eliminate an evil because it's evil, or because it's illegal, or because it's immoral; they eliminate it only when it threatens their existence. So you're wasting your time appealing to the moral conscience of a bankrupt man like Uncle Sam. If he had a conscience, he'd straighten this thing out with no more pressure being put upon him. So it is not necessary to change the white man's mind. We have to change our own mind. You can't change his mind about us. We've got to change our own minds about each other. We have to see each other with new eyes. We have to see each other as brothers and sisters. We have to come together with warmth so we can develop unity and harmony that's necessary to get this problem solved ourselves. How can we do this? How can we avoid jealousy? How can we avoid the suspicion and the divisions that exist in the community? I'll tell you how.

I have watched how Billy Graham comes into a city, spreading what he calls the gospel of Christ, which is only white nationalism. That's what he is. Billy Graham is a white nationalist; I'm a black nationalist. But since it's the natural tendency for leaders to be jealous and look upon a powerful figure like Graham with suspicion and envy, how is it possible for him to come into a city and get all the cooperation of the church leaders? Don't think because they're church leaders that they don't have weaknesses that make them envious and jealous—no, everybody's got it. It's not an accident that when they want to choose a cardinal [as Pope] over there in Rome, they get in a closet so you can't hear them cussing and fighting and carrying on.

Billy Graham comes in preaching the gospel of Christ, he evangelizes the gospel, he stirs everybody up, but he never tries to start a church. If he came in trying to start a church, all the churches would be against him. So, he just comes in talking about Christ and tells everybody who gets Christ to go to any church where Christ is; and in this way the church cooperates with him. So we're going to take a page from his book.

Our gospel is black nationalism. We're not trying to threaten the existence of any organization, but we're spreading the gospel of black nationalism. Anywhere there's a church that is also preaching and practicing the gospel of black nationalism, join that church. If the NAACP is preaching and practicing the gospel of black nationalism, join the NAACP. If CORE is spreading and practicing the gospel of black nationalism, joint CORE. Join any organization that has a gospel that's for the uplift of the black man. And when you get into it and see them pussyfooting or compromising, pull out of it because that's not black nationalism. We'll find another one.

And in this manner, the organizations will increase in number and in quantity and in quality, and by August, it is then our intention to have a black nationalist convention which will consist of delegates from all over the country who are interested in the political, economic and social philosophy of black nationalism. After these delegates convene, we will hold a seminar, we still hold discussions, we will listen to everyone. We want to hear new ideas and new solutions and new answers. And at that time, if we see fit then to form a black nationalist party, we'll form a black nationalist party. If it's necessary to form a black nationalist army, we'll form a black nationalist army. It'll be the ballot or the bullet. It'll be liberty or it'll be death.

It's time for you and me to stop sitting in this country, letting some cracker senators, Northern crackers and Southern crackers, sit there in Washington, D.C., and come to a conclusion in their mind that you and I are supposed to have civil rights. There's no white man going to tell me anything about *my* rights. Brothers and sisters, always remember, if it doesn't take senators and congressmen and presidential proclamations to give freedom to the white man, it is not necessary for legislation or proclamation or Supreme Court decisions to give freedom to the black man. You let that white man know, if this is a country of freedom, let it be a country of freedom; and if it's not a country of freedom, change it.

We will work with anybody, anywhere, at any time, who is genuinely interested in tackling the problem head-on, nonviolently as long as the enemy is nonviolent, but violent when the enemy gets violent. We'll work with you on the voter-registration drive, we'll work with you on rent strikes, we'll work with you on school boycotts—I don't believe in any kind of integration; I'm not even worried about it because I know you're not going to get it anyway; you're not going to get it because you're afraid to die; you've got to be ready to die if you try and force yourself on the white man, because he'll get just as violent as those crackers in Mississippi, right here in Cleveland. But we will still work with you on the school boycotts because we're against a segregated school system. A segregated school system produces children who, when they graduate, graduate with crippled minds. But this does not mean that a school is segregated because it's all black. A segregated school means a school that is controlled by people who have no real interest in it whatsoever.

Let me explain what I mean. A segregated district or community is a community in which people live, but outsiders control the politics and the economy of that community. They never refer to the white section as a segregated community. It's the all-Negro section that's a segregated community. Why? The white man controls his own school, his own bank, his own economy, his own politics, his own everything, his own community—but he also controls yours. When you're under someone else's control, you're segregated. They'll always give you the lowest or the worst that there is to offer, but it doesn't mean you're segregated just because you have your own. You've got to *control* your own. Just like the white man has control of his, you need to control yours.

You know the best way to get rid of segregation? The white man is more afraid of separation than he is of integration. Segregation means that he puts you away from him, but not far enough for you to be out of his jurisdiction; separation means you're gone. And the white man will integrate faster than he'll let you separate. So we will work with you against the segregated school system because it's criminal, because it is absolutely destructive, in every way imaginable, to the minds of the children who have to be exposed to that type of crippling education.

Last but not least, I must say this concerning the great controversy over rifles and shotguns. The only thing that I've ever said is that in areas where the government has proven itself either unwilling or unable to defend the lives and the property of Negroes, it's time for Negroes to defend themselves. Article number two of the constitutional amendments provides you and me the right to own a rifle or a shotgun. It is constitutionally legal to own a shotgun or a rifle. This doesn't mean you're going to get a rifle and form battalions and go out looking for white folks, although you'd be within your rights—I mean, you'd be justified; but that would be illegal and we don't do anything illegal. If the white man doesn't want the black man buying rifles and shotguns, then let the government do its job. That's all. And don't let the white man come to you and ask you what you think about what Malcolm says—why, you old Uncle Tom. He would never ask you if he thought you were going to say, "Amen!" No, he is making a Tom out of you.

So, this doesn't mean forming rifle clubs and going out looking for people, but it is time, in 1964, if you are a man, to let that man know. If he's not going to do his job in running the government and providing you and me with the protection that our taxes are supposed to be for, since he spends all those billions for his defense budget, he certainly can't begrudge you and me spending $12 or $15 for a single-shot, or double-action. I hope you understand. Don't go out shooting people, but any time, brothers and sisters, and especially the men in this audience—some of you wearing Congressional Medals of Honor, with shoulders this wide, chests this big, muscles that big—any time you and I sit around and read where they bomb a church and murder in cold blood, not some grownups, but four little girls while they were praying to the same god the white man taught them to pray to, and you and I see the government go down and can't find who did it.

Why, this man—he can find Eichmann hiding down in Argentina somewhere. Let two or three American soldiers, who are minding somebody else's business way over in South Vietnam, get killed, and he'll send battleships, sticking his nose in their business. He wanted to send troops down to Cuba and make them have what he calls free elections—this old cracker who doesn't have free elections in his own country. No, if you never see me another time in your life, if I die in the morning, I'll die saying one thing: the ballot or the bullet, the ballot or the bullet.

If a Negro in 1964 has to sit around and wait for some cracker senator to filibuster when it comes to the rights of black people, why, you and I should hang our heads in shame. You talk about a march on Washington in 1963, you haven't seen anything. There's some more going down in '64. And this time they're not going like they went last year. They're not going to singing "We Shall Overcome." They're not going with white friends. They're not going with placards already painted for them. They're not going with round-trip tickets. They're going with oneway tickets.

And if they don't want that non-nonviolent army going down there, tell them to bring the filibuster to a halt. The black nationalists aren't going to wait. Lyndon B. Johnson is the head of the Democratic Party. If he's for civil rights, let him go into the Senate next week and declare himself. Let him go in there right now and declare himself. Let him go in there and denounce the Southern branch of his party. Let him go in there right now and take a moral stand—right now, not later. Tell him, don't wait until election time. If he waits too long, brothers and sisters, he will be responsible for letting a condition develop in this country which will create a climate that will bring seeds up out of the ground with vegetation on the end of them looking like something these people never dreamed of. In 1964, it's the ballot or the bullet. Thank you.

Source:

George Breitman, ed., *Malcolm X Speaks: Selected Speeches and Statements*, New York: Merit Publishers, 1965.

Lyndon B. Johnson, Voting Rights Bill Address to Congress, 1965

Speech delivered by President Lyndon Baines Johnson to a special joint session of Congress on March 15, 1965, a week after "Bloody Sunday," in which state troopers, some on horseback, using night sticks and tear gas, attacked unarmed demonstrators in Selma, Alabama, who were preparing to march to Montgomery, the Alabama state capital, to protest their denial of the franchise. The brutal beatings were televised, and the resulting public revulsion helped ensure the act's passage.

In his address, Johnson announced that he would send legislation to Congress that would strike down all state or local laws restricting the right of any U.S. citizen to vote in all federal, state, and local elections. He expressed his profound solidarity with the Civil Rights movement, repeatedly quoting the movement's hymn "We Shall Overcome" in referring to such evils as bigotry, injustice, and poverty. He insisted that the problem of racial injustice was not one that affected only African Americans or southerners, but all Americans. He also expressed his support for demonstrators, saying, "Peace cannot be purchased at the cost of liberty."

The Voting Rights Act of 1965 extended the Civil Rights Act of 1964 that had expanded other civil rights, especially regarding public accommodations and jobs, although court decisions and subsequent acts were necessary for its enforcement. The Voting Rights Act suspended the use of literacy, educational, moral, and other tests in areas where they had been used to deny the right to vote on account of race or color; authorized the appointment of federal examiners in such areas to register voters. It also provided criminal penalties for intimidating, threatening, or coercing any person for voting or attempting to vote and abolished the poll tax. The U.S. Supreme Court upheld the constitutionality of the act in *South Carolina v. Katzenbach* (383 U.S. 301 [1966]) and in *Katzenbach v. Morgan* (384 U.S. 641[1966]).

To the Congress of the United States:

In this same month ninety-five years ago—on March 30, 1870—the Constitution of the United States was amended for the fifteenth time to guarantee that no citizen of our land should be denied the right to vote because of race or color.

The command of the Fifteenth Amendment is unequivocal and its equal force upon State Governments and the Federal Government is unarguable.

Section I of this Amendment provides: The right of citizens of the United States to vote shall not be denied or abridged by the United States or by any State on account of race, color, or previous condition of servitude.

By the oath I have taken "to preserve, protect and defend the Constitution of the United States," duty directs—and strong personal conviction impels—that I advise the Congress that action is necessary, and necessary now, if the Constitution is to be upheld and the rights of all citizens are not to be mocked, abused and denied.

I must regretfully report to the Congress the following facts:

1. That the Fifteenth Amendment of our Constitution is today being systematically and willfully circumvented in certain State and local jurisdictions of our Nation.

2. That representatives of such State and local governments acting "under the color of law," are denying American citizens the right to vote on the sole basis of race or color.

3. That, as a result of these practices, in some areas of our country today no significant number of American citizens of the Negro race can be registered to vote except upon the intervention and order of a Federal Court.

4. That the remedies available under law to citizens thus denied their Constitutional rights—and the authority presently available to the Federal Government to act in their behalf—are clearly inadequate.

5. That the denial of these rights and the frustration of efforts to obtain meaningful relief from such denial without undue delay is contributing to the creation of conditions which are both inimical to our domestic order and tranquillity and incompatible with the standards of equal justice and individual dignity on which our society stands.

I am, therefore, calling upon the Congress to discharge the duty authorized in Section 2 of the Fifteenth Amendment "to enforce this Article by appropriate legislation."

I.

It could never be a welcome duty for any President to place before Congress such a report of the willful failure and refusal of public officials to honor, respect and abide by any provision of the Constitution of the United States. It is especially repugnant to report such disregard directed against the Fifteenth Amendment by officials at the State and local levels.

The essence of our American tradition of State and local governments is the belief expressed by Thomas Jefferson that Government is best which is closest to the people. Yet that belief is betrayed by those State and local officials who engage in denying the right of citizens to vote. Their actions serve only to assure that their State governments and local governments shall be remote from the people, least representative of the people's will and least responsive to the people's wishes.

If there were no other reasons, the strengthening and protection of the vital role of State and local governments would be reasons enough to act against the denial of the right to vote for any of our citizens.

But there are other reasons to act—clear, compelling and present reasons.

1. The challenge now presented is more than a challenge to our Constitution—it is a blatant affront to the conscience of this generation of Americans. Discrimination based on race or color is reprehensible and intolerable to the great American majority. In every national forum, where they have chosen to test popular sentiment, defenders of discrimination have met resounding rejection. Americans now are not willing that the acid of the few shall be allowed to corrode the souls of the many.

The Congress, the Courts, and the Executive, acting together in clear response to the will of the people and the mandate of the Constitution, have achieved more progress toward equality of rights in recent years than in all the years gone before. This tide will not be turned. The purposeful many need not and will not bow to the willful few.

2. In our system, the first right and most vital of all our rights is the right to vote. Jefferson described the elective franchise as "the ark of our safety." It is from the exercise of this rights that the guarantee of all our other rights flows.

Unless the right to vote be secure and undenied, all other rights are insecure and subject to denial for all our citizens. The challenge to this right is a challenge to America itself. We must meet this challenge as decisively as we would meet a challenge mounted against our land from enemies abroad.

3. In the world, America stands for—and works for—the right of all men to govern themselves through free, uninhibited elections. An ink bottle broken against an American Embassy, a fire set in an American library, an insult committed against our American flag, anywhere in the world, does far less injury to our country and our cause than the discriminatory denial of the right of any American citizen at home to vote on the basis of race or color.

The issue presented by the present challenge to our Constitution and our conscience transcends legalism, although it does not transcend the law itself. We are challenged to demonstrate that there are no sanctuaries within our law for those who flaunt it. We are challenged, also, to demonstrate by our prompt, fitting and adequate response now that the hope of our system is not force, not arms, not the might of militia or marshals—but the law itself.

II.

The problem of discriminatory denial of the right to vote has been with us ever since colonial times.

The test of real property ownership was universal among the colonies and religious qualifications were numerous. Race, color, sex, age, employment and residence were all used as the basis for qualifying voters. Such restrictions continued to flourish among the States even after formation of the Union.

The first literacy tests were legislated in Northern States in an effort to exclude immigrants—especially Irish—from the franchise. When the Fifteenth Amendment was adopted, there were only six States which had never discriminated against voting by Negroes.

If discrimination has been a prevalent practice in our history of voting rights, the struggle against discrimination has been our consistent purpose generation after generation.

Since the adoption of the Bill of Rights, no other right has been strengthened and fortified so often by Constitutional Amendment as the right to vote. As early as 1804—and as recently as 1964—the Constitution of the United States has been amended on at least six occasions to prohibit discrimination against the right to vote, to enlarge the franchise, and to assure the expression of the people's will as registered by them at the polls.

The challenge facing us today is not a challenge of what the Constitution of the United States shall say—but of what it shall mean.

What the Fifteenth Amendment says is unmistakable. What the Fifteenth Amendment actually means for some Americans in some jurisdictions is diametrically opposite to the clear intent of the language.

By the device of equal laws, unequally applied, Negro Americans are being denied the right and opportunity to vote and discrimination is given sanction under color of law. Varieties of techniques are infinite. Three are most commonplace.

1. *The technique of technical "error."*

Negro applicants for registration are disqualified on grounds of technical "errors" in their registration forms. Instances of record show Negroes disqualified for "errors" such as failure to write out middle names, abbreviating the words "street" and "avenue" in addresses, or failing to compute age exactly to the day. Where this technique is employed, "errors" are found in substantially all applications filed by Negroes, but few or none in applications filed by whites.

2. *The technique of non-cooperation.*

A technique commonly used in conjunction with the "error" technique involves simple non-cooperation by the registrar. Thus, he may be "out" for most of the day during registration periods. Registration may be possible only on certain days each month. Limits may be imposed upon the number of applicants processed each registration day. The variety of circumventions possible by this device is endless.

3. *The technique of subjective tests.*

By far the most common technique by which Negro citizens are prevented from exercising their right to register and to vote is the use of subjective tests, unfairly administered literacy tests, tests of "understanding," and tests of "character." The only standard used in the whim of the registrar. Such devices are used as vehicles for the rejection of untold thousands of voters—solely on the basis of race and color.

Whatever the technique, the intended purpose of such devices is effectively served.

—In one State ten years ago, 59.6 percent of voting age White persons were registered to vote. Only 4.3 percent of eligible Negroes were registered to vote. The changes since then are negligible.

—In several States, there are counties with sizeable Negro populations where not a single Negro is registered to vote.

—In scores of other counties where discrimination is not so blatant, it remains far more difficult for Negroes to register than for whites.

Too frequently discrimination is the aim and intent of such devices—and discrimination is the result.

III.

The Congress and the Executive Branch of the Federal Government have recognized—and sought to meet—these challenges to the authority of the Constitution of the United States. I am proud to have been closely associated with the succession of Federal enactments, beginning in

1957 with the first Civil Rights Law in more than eighty years.

The major steps taken have been these:

1. *The Civil Rights Act of 1957:* The approach of this statute was to challenge through litigation the discriminatory use of vote tests.

2. *The Civil Rights Act of 1960:* This statute, pursuing the same approach, sought to simplify such litigation.

3. *The Civil Rights Act of 1964:* Still following the same approach, sought to expedite litigation.

In some areas litigation has been effective. But eight years of litigation has made it clear that the prompt and fair registration of qualified Negro citizens cannot be achieved under present legislation in the face of consistent defiance of the laws of Congress or the command of the Constitution.

IV.

The challenge facing us is clear and immediate—it is also profound.

The Constitution is being flouted.

The intent of Congress expressed three times in the last seven years is being frustrated.

The national will is being denied.

The integrity of our Federal system is in contest.

Unless we act anew, with dispatch and resolution, we shall sanction a sad and sorrowful course for the future. For if the Fifteenth Amendment is successfully flouted today, tomorrow the First Amendment, the Fourth Amendment, the Fifth Amendment—the Sixth, the Eighth, indeed, all the provisions of the Constitution on which our system stands—will be subject to disregard and erosion. Our essential strength as a society governed by the rule of law will be crippled and corrupted and the unity of our system hollowed out and left meaningless.

For these reasons, therefore, I ask the Congress under the power clearly granted by the Fifteenth Amendment to enact legislation which would:

1. Strike down restrictions to voting in all elections—Federal, State, and local—which have been used to deny Negroes the right to vote.

2. Establish in all States and counties where the right to vote has been denied on account of race a simple standard of voter registration which will make it impossible to thwart the Fifteenth Amendment.

3. Prohibit the use of new tests and devices wherever they may be used for discriminatory purposes.

4. Provide adequate power to insure, if necessary, that Federal officials can perform functions essential to the right to vote whenever State officials deny that right.

5. Eliminate the opportunity to delay the right to vote by resort to tedious and unnecessary lawsuits.

6. Provide authority to insure that properly registered individuals will not be prohibited from voting.

Our purpose is not—and shall never be—either the quest for power or the desire to punish. We seek to increase the power of the people over all their governments, not to enhance the power of the Federal Government over any of the people.

For the life of this Republic, our people have zealously guarded their liberty against abuses of power by their governments. The one weapon they have used is the mightiest weapon in the arsenal of democracy—the vote. This has been enough, for as Woodrow Wilson said, "The instrument of all reform in America is the ballot."

Yet today, in areas of America, segments of our populace must live in just that involuntary condition—policed by forces they have no voice in choosing and forced to abide by laws they have no vote in adopting.

A people divided over the right to vote can never build a Nation united.

I am determined that these years shall be devoted to perfecting our unity so that we may pursue more successfully the fulfillment of our high purposes at home and in the world. While I have proposed to you other measures to serve the strengthening of our free society and the happiness of our free people, I regard action on the measures proposed in this Message to be first in priority. We cannot have government for all the people until we first make certain it is government of and by all the people.

Lyndon B. Johnson
The White House March 15, 1965

Source:

Public Papers of the Presidents of the United States, Lyndon B. Johnson, 1965. Washington, D.C.: Government Printing Office, 1963–68, pp. 287–291.

United States v. Price, 1966

This case, along with *United States v. Guest* (383 U.S. 745), decided the same day, overturned earlier Supreme Court decisions that had severely limited the ability of the Department of Justice to prosecute perpetrators of violence against people trying to exercise civil rights such as voting or freedom of expression. The case had particular significance for African Americans in the Deep South where local juries usually refused to convict whites who assaulted or even murdered blacks. Several notorious trials brought this situation to public attention. For example, a 1955 jury acquitted the men who murdered a teenaged black northerner, Emmett Till, for whistling at a white woman. (Till's supporters later claimed he lisped and that the whistle was the result, not an expression toward the woman.) However, that case did not result in any legal changes. Under President Lyndon Johnson, however, the murder of three civil rights workers in Philadelphia, Mississippi, in June 1964, and of African-American Col. Lemuel Penn several days later, spurred passage of the Civil Rights Act and helped change the climate for southern juries, who more frequently dealt guilty pleas.

The civil rights workers, two white northerners, Michael Schwerner and Andrew Goodman, and black Mississippian James Chaney were arrested by Deputy Sheriff Cecil Price while investigating a church burning, one of many such Klan-perpetrated actions against civil rights efforts, which often used churches for meetings. Hence the FBI's code name for the case, *MIBURN*, for "Mississippi burning." After conspiring with local Klansmen, Price released them, but their car was overtaken where the terrorists murdered them. Many, mostly white, northern college students had come to Mississippi to participate in education and voting rights projects (Freedom Summer) and the disappearance received substantial media coverage. Although a clear federal case could not be made, Johnson ordered the FBI to investigate. Eventually an informant revealed that the bodies were buried in a dam, where they were found August 4. On December 4, 19 people, Sheriff Price among them, were arrested and charged with violating the civil rights of the three murdered men. It took several trials and the Supreme Court decision, but in 1967, seven of the 19 conspirators, including Sheriff Price, were convicted.

The *Guest* case involved Penn's death, and was more clearly a federal case because Penn was returning from his army reserve duty. Because southern juries began including African Americans and even white jurors were willing to convict whites who harmed blacks, there has been less need to resort to federal courts. Nevertheless, the *Price* and *Guest* decisions allowed federal agents to investigate a much wider range of civil rights violations than before 1966.

MR. JUSTICE FORTAS delivered the opinion of the Court.

These are direct appeals from the dismissal in part of two indictments returned by the United States Grand Jury for the Southern District of Mississippi. The indictments allege assaults by the accused persons upon the rights of the asserted victims to due process of law under the Fourteenth Amendment. The indictment in No. 59 charges 18 persons with violations of 18 U. S. C. § 241. In No. 60, the same 18 persons are charged with offenses based upon 18 U. S. C. § 242. These are among the so-called civil rights statutes which have come to us from Reconstruction days, the period in our history which also produced the Thirteenth, Fourteenth, and Fifteenth Amendments to the Constitution.

The sole question presented in these appeals is whether the specified statutes make criminal the conduct for which the individuals were indicted. It is an issue of construction, not of constitutional power. We have no doubt of "the power of Congress to enforce by appropriate criminal sanction every right guaranteed by the Due Process Clause of the Fourteenth Amendment."

[The indictment alleges that] on June 21, 1964, Cecil Ray Price, the Deputy Sheriff of Neshoba County, Mississippi, detained Michael Henry Schwerner, James Earl Chaney and Andrew Goodman in the Neshoba County jail located in Philadelphia, Mississippi. He released them in the dark of that night. He then proceeded by automobile on Highway 19 to intercept his erstwhile wards. He removed the three men from their automobile, placed them in an official automobile of the Neshoba County Sheriff's office, and transported them to a place on an unpaved road.

These acts, it is alleged, were part of a plan and conspiracy whereby the three men were intercepted by the 18 defendants, including Deputy Sheriff Price, Sheriff Rainey and Patrolman Willis of the Philadelphia, Mississippi, Police Department. The purpose and intent of the release from custody and the interception, according to the charge, were to "punish" the three men. The defendants, it is alleged, "did wilfully assault, shoot and kill" each of the three. And, the charge continues, the bodies of the three victims were transported by one of the defendants from the rendezvous on the unpaved road to the vicinity of the construction site of an earthen dam approximately five miles southwest of Philadelphia, Mississippi.

These are federal and not state indictments. They do not charge as crimes the alleged assaults or murders. The indictments are framed to fit the stated federal statutes, and the question before us is whether the attempt of the draftsman for the Grand Jury in Mississippi has been successful: whether the indictments charge offenses against the various defendants which may be prosecuted under the designated federal statutes.

We shall deal first with the indictment in No. 60, based on § 242 of the Criminal Code, and then with the indictment in No. 59, under § 241. We do this for ease of exposition and because § 242 was enacted by the Congress about four years prior to § 241. Section 242 was enacted in 1866; § 241 in 1870.

I. No. 60.

Section 242 defines a misdemeanor, punishable by fine of not more than $ 1,000 or imprisonment for not more than one year, or both. So far as here significant, it provides punishment for "Whoever, under color of any law, statute, ordinance, regulation, or custom, willfully subjects any inhabitant of any State . . . to the deprivation of any rights, privileges, or immunities secured or protected by the Constitution or laws of the United States. . . ."

The indictment in No. 60 contains four counts, each of which names as defendants the three officials and 15 nonofficial persons. The First Count charges, on the basis of allegations substantially as set forth above, that all of the defendants conspired "to wilfully subject" Schwerner, Chaney and Goodman "to the deprivation of their right, privilege and immunity secured and protected by the Fourteenth Amendment to the Constitution of the United States not to be summarily punished without due process of law by persons acting under color of the laws of the State of Mississippi." This is said to constitute a conspiracy to violate § 242, and therefore an offense under 18 U. S. C. § 371. The latter section, the general conspiracy statute, makes it a crime to conspire to commit any offense against the United States. The penalty for violation is the same as for direct violation of § 242—that is, it is a misdemeanor.

On a motion to dismiss, the District Court sustained this First Count as to all defendants. As to the sheriff, deputy sheriff and patrolman, the court recognized that each was clearly alleged to have been acting "under color of law" as required by § 242. As to the private persons, the District Court held that "It is immaterial to the conspiracy that these private individuals were not acting under color of law" because the count charges that they were conspiring with persons who were so acting. The court necessarily was satisfied that the indictment, in alleging the arrest, detention, release, interception and killing of Schwerner, Chaney and Goodman, adequately stated as the purpose of the conspiracy, a violation of § 242, and that this section could be violated by "wilfully subject[ing the victims] . . . to the deprivation of their right, privilege and immunity" under the Due Process Clause of the Fourteenth Amendment.

No appeal was taken by the defendants from the decision of the trial court with respect to the First Count and it is not before us for adjudication.

The Second, Third and Fourth Counts of the indictment in No. 60 charge all of the defendants, not with conspiracy, but with substantive violations of § 242. Each of these counts charges that the defendants, acting "under color of the laws of the State of Mississippi," "did wilfully assault, shoot and kill" Schwerner, Chaney and Goodman, respectively, "for the purpose and with the intent" of punishing each of the three and that the defendants "did thereby wilfully deprive" each "of rights, privileges and immunities secured and protected by the Constitution and the laws of the United States"—namely, due process of law.

The District Court held these counts of the indictment valid as to the sheriff, deputy sheriff and patrolman. But it dismissed them as against the nonofficial defendants because the counts do not charge that the latter were "officers in fact, or de facto in anything allegedly done by them 'under color of law.'"

We note that by sustaining these counts against the three officers, the court again necessarily concluded that an offense under § 242 is properly stated by allegations of willful deprivation, under color of law, of life and liberty without due process of law. We agree. No other result would be permissible under the decisions of this Court.

But we cannot agree that the Second, Third or Fourth Counts may be dismissed as against the nonofficial defendants. Section 242 applies only where a person indicted has acted "under color" of law. Private persons, jointly engaged with state officials in the prohibited action, are acting "under color" of law for purposes of the statute. To act "under color" of law does not require that the accused be an officer of the State. It is enough that he is a willful participant in joint activity with the State or its agents. In the present case, according to the indictment, the brutal joint adventure was made possible by state detention and calculated release of the prisoners by an officer of the State. This action, clearly attributable to the State, was part of the monstrous design described by the indictment. State officers participated in every phase of the alleged venture: the release from jail, the interception, assault and murder. It was a joint activity, from start to finish. Those who took advantage of participation by state officers in accomplishment of the foul purpose alleged must suffer the consequences of that participation. In effect, if the allegations are true, they were participants in official lawlessness, acting in willful concert with state officers and hence under color of law.

Appellees urge that the decision of the District Court was based upon a construction of the indictment to the effect that it did not charge the private individuals with acting "under color" of law. Consequently, they urge us to affirm in No. 60. In any event, they submit, since the trial court's decision was based on the inadequacy of the indictment and not on construction of the statute, we have no jurisdiction to review it on direct appeal. *United States v. Swift & Co.*, 318 U.S. 442. We do not agree. Each count of the indictment specifically alleges that all of the defendants were acting "under color of the laws of the State of Mississippi." The fault lies not in the indictment, but in the District Court's view that the statute requires that each offender be an official or that he act in an official capacity. We have jurisdiction to consider this statutory question on direct appeal and, as we have shown, the trial court's determination of it is in error. Since each of the private individuals is indictable as a principal acting under color of law, we need not consider whether he might be held to answer as an "aider or abettor" under 18 U. S. C. § 2 (1964 ed.), despite omission to include such a charge in the indictment.

Accordingly, we reverse the dismissal of the Second, Third and Fourth Counts of the indictment in No. 60 and remand for trial.

II. No. 59.

No. 59 charges each of the 18 defendants with a felony—a violation of § 241. This indictment is in one count. It charges that the defendants "conspired together . . . to injure, oppress, threaten and intimidate" Schwerner, Chaney and Goodman "in the free exercise and enjoyment of the right and privilege secured to them by the Fourteenth Amendment to the Constitution of the United States not to be deprived of life or liberty without due process of law by persons acting under color of the laws of Mississippi." The indictment alleges that it was the purpose of the conspiracy that Deputy Sheriff Price would release Schwerner, Chaney and Goodman from custody in the Neshoba County jail at such time that Price and the other 17 defendants "could and would intercept" them "and threaten, assault, shoot and kill them." The penalty under § 241 is a fine of not more than $ 5,000, or imprisonment for not more than 10 years, or both.

Section 241 is a conspiracy statute. It reads as follows: *"If two or more persons conspire to injure, oppress, threaten, or intimidate any citizen in the free exercise or enjoyment of any right or privilege secured to him by the Constitution or laws of the United States, or because of his having so exercised the same; or "If two or more persons go in disguise on the highway, or on the premises of another, with intent to prevent or hinder his free exercise or enjoyment of any right or privilege so secured—"They shall be fined not more than $ 5,000 or imprisoned not more than ten years, or both."*

The District Court dismissed the indictment as to all defendants. In effect, although § 241 includes rights or privileges secured by the Constitution or laws of the United States without qualification or limitation, the court held that it does not include rights protected by the Fourteenth Amendment. It will be recalled that in No. 60 the District Court held that § 242 included the denial of Fourteenth Amendment rights—the same right to due process involved in the indictment under § 241. Both include rights or privileges secured by the Constitution or laws of the United States. Neither is qualified or limited. Each includes, presumably, *all* of the Constitution and laws of the United States. To the reader of the two sections, versed only in the English language, it may seem bewildering that the two sections could be so differently read.

But the District Court purported to read the statutes with the gloss of *Williams* I. In that case, the only case in which this Court has squarely confronted the point at issue, the Court did in fact sustain dismissal of an indictment under § 241. But it did not, as the District Court incorrectly assumed, hold that § 241 is inapplicable to Fourteenth Amendment rights. The Court divided equally on the issue. Four Justices, in an opinion by Mr. Justice Frankfurter, were of the view that § 241 "only covers conduct which interferes with rights arising from the substantive powers of the Federal Government"—rights "which Congress can beyond doubt constitutionally secure against interference by private individuals." 341 U.S., at 73, 77. Four other Justices, in an opinion by MR. JUSTICE DOUGLAS, found no support for Mr. Justice Frankfurter's view in the language of the section, its legislative history, or its judicial interpretation up to that time. They read the statute as plainly covering conspiracies to injure others in the exercise of Fourteenth Amendment rights. They could see no obstacle to using it to punish deprivations of such rights. Dismissal of the indictment was affirmed because MR. JUSTICE BLACK voted with those who joined Mr. Justice Frankfurter. He did so, however, for an entirely different reason—that the prosecution was barred by *res judicata*—and he expressed no view on the issue whether "§ 241, as applied, is too vague and uncertain in scope to be consistent with the Fifth Amendment." *Williams* I thus left the proper construction of § 241, as regards its applicability to protect Fourteenth Amendment rights, an open question.

In view of the detailed opinions in *Williams* I, it would be supererogation to track the arguments in all of their intricacy. On the basis of an extensive re-examination of the question, we conclude that the District Court erred; that § 241 must be read as it is written—to reach conspiracies "to injure . . . any citizen in the free exercise or enjoyment of any right or privilege secured to him by the Constitution or laws of the United States . . ."; that this language includes rights or privileges protected by the Fourteenth Amendment; that whatever the ultimate coverage of the section may be, it extends to conspiracies otherwise within the scope of the section, participated in by officials alone or in collaboration with private persons; and that the indictment in No. 59 properly charges such a conspiracy in violation of § 241. We shall confine ourselves to a review of the major considerations which induce our conclusion.

There is no doubt that the indictment in No. 59 sets forth a conspiracy within the ambit of the Fourteenth Amendment. Like the indictment in No. 60, *supra*, it alleges that the defendants acted "under color of law" and that the conspiracy included action by the State through its law enforcement officers to punish the alleged victims without due process of law in violation of the Fourteenth Amendment's direct admonition to the States.

1. The indictment specifically alleges that the sheriff, deputy sheriff and a patrolman participated in the conspiracy; that it was a part of the "plan and purpose of the conspiracy" that Deputy Sheriff Price, "while having [the three victims] . . . in his custody in the Neshoba County Jail . . . would release them from custody at such time that he [and others of the defendants] . . . could and would intercept [the three victims] . . . and threaten, assault, shoot and kill them."

This is an allegation of state action which, beyond dispute, brings the conspiracy within the ambit of the Fourteenth Amendment. It is an allegation of official, state participation in murder, accomplished by and through its officers with the participation of others. It is an allegation that the State, without the semblance of due process of law as required of it by the Fourteenth Amendment, used its sovereign power and office to release the victims from jail so that they were not charged and tried as required by law, but instead could be intercepted and killed. If the Fourteenth Amendment forbids denial of counsel, it clearly denounces denial of any trial at all. As we have consistently held "The Fourteenth Amendment protects the individual against *state action*, not against wrongs done by *individuals*." In the present case, the participation by law enforcement officers, as alleged in the indictment, is clearly state action, as we have discussed, and it is therefore within the scope of the Fourteenth Amendment.

2. The argument, however, of Mr. Justice Frankfurter's opinion in *Williams* I, upon which the District Court rests its decision, cuts beneath this. It does not deny that the accused conduct is within the scope of the Fourteenth Amendment, but it contends that in enacting § 241, the Congress intended to include only the rights and privileges conferred on the citizen by reason of the "substantive" powers of the Federal Government—that is, by reason of federal power operating directly upon the citizen and not merely by means of prohibitions of state action. As the Court of Appeals for the Fifth Circuit in *Williams* I, relied upon in the opinion below, put it, "the Congress had in mind the federal rights and privileges which appertain to citizens as such and not the general rights extended to all persons by the . . . Fourteenth Amendment." We do not agree.

The language of § 241 is plain and unlimited. As we have discussed, its language embraces *all* of the rights and privileges secured to citizens by *all* of the Constitution and *all* of the laws of the United States. There is no indication in the language that the sweep of the section is confined to rights that are conferred by or "flow from" the Federal Government, as distinguished from those secured or confirmed or guaranteed by the Constitution. We agree with the observation of Mr. Justice Holmes in *United States v. Mosley*, 238 U.S. 383, 387-388, that

"The source of this section in the doings of the Ku Klux and the like is obvious and acts of violence obviously were in the mind of Congress. Naturally Congress put forth all its powers. . . . This section dealt with Federal rights and with all Federal rights, and protected them in the lump . . . . [It should not be construed so] as to deprive citizens of the United States of the general protection which on its face § 19 [now § 241] most reasonably affords."

We believe, with Mr. Justice Holmes, that the history of the events from which § 241 emerged illuminates the purpose and means of the statute with an unmistakable light. We think that history leaves no doubt that, if we are to give § 241 the scope that its origins dictate, we must accord it a sweep as broad as its language. We are not at liberty to seek ingenious analytical instruments for excluding from its general language the Due Process Clause of the Fourteenth Amendment—particularly since the violent denial of legal process was one of the reasons motivating enactment of the section.

Section 241 was enacted as part of what came to be known as the Enforcement Act of 1870, 16 Stat. 140. n10 The Act was passed on May 31, 1870, only a few months after ratification of the Fifteenth Amendment. In addition to the new § 241, it included a re-enactment of a provision of the Civil Rights Act of 1866 which is now § 242. The intended breadth of § 241 is emphasized by contrast with the narrowness of § 242 as it then was. n11 Section 242 forbade the deprivation, "under color of any law," of "any right secured or protected by this act." The rights protected by the Act were narrow and specific: "to make and enforce contracts, to sue, be parties, give evidence, and to the full and equal benefit of all laws and proceedings for the security of person and property as is enjoyed by white citizens [and to] be subject to like punishment, pains, penalties, taxes, licenses, and exactions of every kind, and none other." Act of May 31, 1870, § 16, 16 Stat. 144, re-enacting with minor changes Act of April 9, 1866, § 1, 14 Stat. 27. Between 1866 and 1870 there was much agitated criticism in the Congress and in the Nation because of the continued denial of rights to Negroes, sometimes accompanied by violent assaults. In response to the demands for more stringent legislation Congress enacted the Enforcement Act of 1870. Congress had before it and re-enacted § 242 which was explicitly limited as we have described. At the same time, it included § 241 in the Act using broad language to cover not just the rights enumerated in § 242, but all rights and privileges under the Constitution and laws of the United States.

It was not until the statutory revision of 1874 that the specific enumeration of protected rights was eliminated from § 242. The section was then broadened to include as wide a range of rights as § 241 already did: "any rights, privileges, or immunities, secured or protected by the Constitution and laws of the United States." The substantial change thus effected was made with the customary stout assertions of the codifiers that they had merely clarified and reorganized without changing substance. n12 Section 241 was left essentially unchanged, and neither in the 1874 revision nor in any subsequent re-enactment has there been the slightest indication of a congressional intent to narrow or limit the original broad scope of § 241. It is clear, therefore, that § 241, from original enactment through subsequent codifications, was intended to deal, as Mr. Justice Holmes put it, with conspiracies to interfere with "Federal rights and with all Federal rights." We find no basis whatsoever for a judgment of Solomon which would give to the statute less than its words command.

The purpose and scope of the 1866 and 1870 enactments must be viewed against the events and passions of the time.The Civil War had ended in April 1865. Relations between Negroes and whites were increasingly turbulent. Congress had taken control of the entire governmental process in former Confederate States. It had declared the governments in 10 "unreconstructed" States to be illegal and had set up federal military administrations in their place. Congress refused to seat representatives from these States until they had adopted constitutions guaranteeing Negro suffrage, and had ratified the Fourteenth Amendment. Constitutional conventions were called in 1868. Six of the 10 States fulfilled Congress' requirements in 1868, the other four by 1870.

For a few years "radical" Republicans dominated the governments of the Southern States and Negroes played a substantial political role. But countermeasures were swift and violent. The Ku Klux Klan was organized by southern whites in 1866 and a similar organization appeared with the romantic title of the Knights of the White Camellia. In 1868 a wave of murders and assaults was launched including assassinations designed to keep Negroes from the polls. The States themselves were helpless, despite the resort by some of them to extreme measures such as making it legal to hunt down and shoot any disguised man.

Within the Congress pressures mounted in the period between the end of the war and 1870 for drastic measures. A few months after the ratification of the Thirteenth Amendment on December 6, 1865. Congress, on April 9, 1866, enacted the Civil Rights Act of 1866, which, as we have described, included § 242 in its originally narrow form. On June 13, 1866, the Fourteenth Amendment was proposed, and it was ratified in July 1868. In February 1869 the Fifteenth Amendment was proposed, and it was ratified in February 1870. On May 31, 1870, the Enforcement Act of 1870 was enacted.

In this context, it is hardly conceivable that Congress intended § 241 to apply only to a narrow and relatively unimportant category of rights. We cannot doubt that the purpose and effect of § 241 was to reach assaults upon rights under the entire Constitution, including the Thirteenth, Fourteenth and Fifteenth Amendments, and not merely under part of it.

This is fully attested by the only statement explanatory of § 241 in the recorded congressional proceedings relative to its enactment. We refer to the speech of Senator Pool of North Carolina who introduced the provisions as an amendment to the Enforcement Act of 1870. The Senator's remarks are printed in full in the Appendix to this opinion. He urged that the section was needed in order to punish invasions of the newly adopted Fourteenth and Fifteenth Amendments to the Constitution. He acknowledged that the States as such were beyond the reach of the punitive process, and that the legislation must therefore operate upon individuals. He made it clear that "It matters not whether those individuals be officers or whether they are acting upon their own responsibility." We find no evidence whatever that Senator Pool intended that § 241 should not cover violations of Fourteenth Amendment rights, or that it should not include state action or actions by state officials.

We conclude, therefore, that it is incumbent upon us to read § 241 with full credit to its language. Nothing in the prior decisions of this Court or of other courts which have considered the matter stands in the way of that conclusion.

The present application of the statutes at issue does not raise fundamental questions of federal-state relationships. We are here concerned with allegations which squarely and indisputably involve state action in direct violation of the mandate of the Fourteenth Amendment—that no State shall deprive any person of life or liberty without due process of law. This is a direct, traditional concern of the Federal Government. It is an area in which the federal interest has existed for at least a century, and in which federal participation has intensified as part of a renewed emphasis upon civil rights. Even as recently as 1951, when *Williams* I was decided, the federal role in the establishment and vindication of fundamental rights—such as the freedom to travel, nondiscriminatory access to public areas and nondiscriminatory educational facilities—was neither as pervasive nor as intense as it is today. Today, a decision interpreting a federal law in accordance with its historical design, to punish denials by state action of constitutional rights of the person can hardly be regarded as adversely affecting "the wise adjustment between State responsibility and national control. . . ." In any event, the problem, being statutory and not constitutional, is ultimately, as it was in the beginning, susceptible of congressional disposition.

Reversed and remanded.

Source:

University of Missouri Kansas City (UMKC) Law School. Available on-line. URL: http//www.law.umkc.edu/faculty/projects/ftrials/price&bowers/sctdecision.html. Accessed January 2004.

Miranda v. Arizona, 1966

Landmark U.S. Supreme Court decision issued on June 13, 1966, that extended federal constitutional protections to defendants in state criminal trials. The decision reversed the conviction of accused rapist Ernesto Miranda, who had been questioned by law enforcement officers without being advised of his rights. Citing Fifth Amendment protection against self-incrimination and Sixth Amendment right to counsel, the Supreme Court, in a 5-4 decision, ruled that as soon as suspects are seized by police, they must be informed of their rights. The phrases, familiar from TV programs, do not appear exactly the same way in the opinions, but they are summarized as: "you have the right to remain silent, anything you say can be used against you, you have the right to consult with an attorney before questioning and to have counsel present during questioning, and, if you are indigent, an attorney will be appointed for you." Many law enforcement agencies have the "Miranda rights" printed out and the suspects must sign that they have heard and understand them.

Miranda has been termed, depending on one's perspective, either the high or the low point for confession cases. For civil libertarians and defense lawyers, the decision meant that the poorest or most despicable criminal still had rights that must be respected. Others criticized the case as contributing to rising crime rates. Like other cases enforcing defendant's rights, it also contributed to better police work, more thorough investigations, and possibly more convictions, because cases could not be overturned because of coerced confessions. The decision permitted general questioning before the rights are read.

Many subjects actually waive their rights and speak directly to law enforcement without requesting an attorney, and many make incriminating statements which then become admissible in court. As expressed in oral arguments and in Chief Justice Earl Warren's majority opinion, the Federal Bureau of Investigation had been reading these rights to suspects for many years without any adverse impact on successful prosecutions.

Previously, in *Gideon v. Wainwright* (372 U.S. 375), issued March 18, 1963, the U.S. Supreme Court declared that accused persons have a constitutional right to representation by counsel in all state criminal trials. Clarence Earl Gideon, a poor, uneducated Florida drifter, wrote his own petition to the Supreme Court appealing a conviction for petit larceny after a trial in which he had been denied the assistance of a lawyer. Twenty-two states filed briefs supporting his position. The Court ruled unanimously that the Sixth Amendment made the right to counsel fundamental and essential to a fair trial, and that the Fourteenth Amendment extended this protection to state matters. The decision led to the creation of programs to supply counsel to indigent defendants throughout the United States.

In addition, on June 22, 1964, the U.S. Supreme Court established in *Escobedo v. Illinois* (378 U.S. 438) that under the Sixth Amendment a suspect in police custody has a right to consult counsel during an interrogation. Danny Escobedo had been convicted of murder on the basis of a confession he made prior to his formal indictment during an interrogation in which he had been denied access to his attorney and had not been advised of his constitutional right to refuse to answer police questions. As a result, the Supreme Court ruled that this confession could not be used as evidence against him. The success of a system of criminal justice, the Court said, should not depend on citizens' unawareness of their constitutional rights.

Two years after *Miranda*, Congress enacted a law (18 U.S.C. § 3501) that omitted the need of a warning and stated that any voluntary admission by the suspect was permissible in court. In *Dickerson v. United States* (530 U.S. 428 [2000]), Chief Justice Rehnquist, writing for the majority, concluded that the intent of that law was to overrule *Miranda*. His decision held that Congress cannot override a Supreme Court decision if the Court is interpreting the Constitution. Because, according to Rehnquist, *Miranda* is "constitutionally based," Congress could not use legislation to overturn it.

Mr. Chief Justice Warren delivered the opinion of the Court.

The cases before us raise questions which go to the roots of our concepts of American criminal jurisprudence: the restraints society must observe consistent with the Federal Constitution in prosecuting individuals for crime. More specifically, we deal with the admissibility of statements obtained from an individual who is subjected to custodial police interrogation and the necessity for procedures which assure that the individual is accorded his privilege under the Fifth Amendment to the Constitution not to be compelled to incriminate himself.

We dealt with certain phases of this problem recently in *Escobedo v. State of Illinois*, 378 U.S. 478 (1964). There, as in the four cases before us, law enforcement officials took the defendant into custody and interrogated him in a police station for the purpose of obtaining a confession. The police did not effectively advise him of his right to remain silent or of his right to consult with his attorney. Rather, they confronted him with an alleged accomplice who accused him of having perpetrated a murder. When the defendant denied the accusation and said "I didn't shoot Manuel, you did it," they handcuffed him and took him to an interrogation room. There, while handcuffed and standing, he was questioned for four hours until he confessed. During this interrogation, the police denied his request to speak to his attorney, and they prevented his retained attorney, who had come to the police station, from consulting with him. At his trial, the State, over his objection, introduced the confession against him. We held that the statements thus made were constitutionally inadmissible.

This case has been the subject of judicial interpretation and spirited legal debate. . . . We granted certiorari in these cases . . . in order further to explore some facets of the problems, thus exposed, of applying the privilege against self-incrimination to in-custody interrogation, and to give concrete constitutional guidelines for law enforcement agencies and courts to follow.

We start here . . . with the premise that our holding . . . is an application of principles long recognized and applied in other settings. . . . Escobedo . . . was but an explication of basic rights that are enshrined in our Constitution—that "No person . . . shall be compelled in any criminal case to be a witness against himself," and that "the accused shall . . . have the Assistance of Counsel"—rights which were put in jeopardy in that case through official overbearing. These precious rights were fixed in our Constitution only after centuries of persecution and struggle. And in the words of Chief Justice Marshall, they were secured "for ages to come, and . . . designed to approach immortality as nearly as human institutions can approach it,"

* * *

This was the spirit in which we delineated, in meaningful language, the manner in which the constitutional rights of the individual could be enforced against overzealous police practices. . . .

Our holding . . . briefly state[d] is this: the prosecution may not use statements, whether exculpatory or inculpatory, stemming from custodial interrogation of the defendant unless it demonstrates the use of procedural safeguards effective to secure the privilege against self-incrimination. By custodial interrogation, we mean questioning initiated by law enforcement officers after a person has been taken into custody or otherwise deprived of his freedom of action in any significant way. As for the procedural safeguards to be employed, unless other fully effective means are devised to inform accused persons of their right of silence and to assure a continuous opportunity to exercise it, the following measures are required. Prior to any questioning, the person must be warned that he has a right to remain silent, that any statement he does make may be used as evidence against him, and that he has a right to the presence of an attorney, either retained or appointed. The defendant may waive effectuation of these rights, provided the waiver is made voluntarily, knowingly and intelligently. If, however, he indicates in any manner and at any stage of the process that he wishes to consult with an attorney before speaking there can be no questioning. Likewise, if the individual is alone and indicates in any manner that he does not wish to be interrogated, the police may not question him. The mere fact that he may have answered some questions or volunteered some statements on his own does not deprive him of the right to refrain from answering any further inquiries until he has consulted with an attorney and thereafter consents to be questioned.

I.

The constitutional issue we decide . . . is the admissibility of statements obtained from a defendant questioned while in custody or otherwise deprived of his freedom of action in any significant way. . . . The defendant was questioned by police officers, detectives, or a prosecuting attorney in a room in which he was cut off from the outside world . . . . The defendant [was not] given a full and effective warning of his rights at the outset of the interrogation process. . . . The questioning elicited [confessions that] were admitted at . . . trial. . . .

An understanding of the nature and setting of this in-custody interrogation is essential to our decisions today. The difficulty in depicting what transpires at such interrogations stems from the fact that in this country they have largely taken place incommunicado. . . . The Commission on Civil Rights in 1961 found much evidence to indicate that "some policemen still resort to physical force to obtain confessions." . . .

. . .Unless a proper limitation upon custodial interrogation is achieved—such as these decisions will advance—there can be no assurance that practices of this nature will be eradicated in the foreseeable future. . . .

Again we stress that the modern practice of in-custody interrogation is psychologically rather than physically oriented. . . .This Court has recognized that coercion can be mental as well as physical, and that the blood of the accused is not the only hallmark of an unconstitutional inquisition." . . .

The officers are told by the manuals that the "principal psychological factor contributing to a successful interrogation is privacy—being alone with the person under interrogation." . . . In his office, the investigator possesses all the advantages. The atmosphere suggests the invincibility of the forces of the law."

To highlight the isolation and unfamiliar surroundings, the manuals instruct the police to display an air of confidence in the suspect's guilt and form outward appearance to maintain only an interest in confirming certain details. The guilt of the subject is to be posited as a fact. The interrogator should direct his comments toward the reasons why the subject committed the act. . . . The officers are instructed to minimize the moral seriousness of the offense, to cast blame on the victim or on society. These tactics are designed to put the subject in a psychological state where his story is but an elaboration of what the police purport to know already—that he is guilty. Explanations to the contrary are dismissed and discouraged.

. . .The manuals suggest that the suspect be offered legal excuses for his actions in order to obtain an initial admission of guilt. . . .

Having then obtained the admission of shooting, the interrogator is advised to refer to circumstantial evidence which negates the self-defense explanation. This should enable him to secure the entire story. . . .

When the techniques described above prove unavailing, the texts recommend they be alternated with a show of some hostility. One ploy often used has been termed the "friendly- unfriendly" or the "Mutt and Jeff" act. . . .

The interrogators sometimes are instructed to induce a confession out of trickery. . . .

The manuals also contain instructions for police on how to handle the individual who refuses to discuss the matter entirely, or who asks for an attorney or relatives. The examiner is to concede him the right to remain silent. . . . After this psychological conditioning, however, the officer is told to point out the incriminating significance of the suspect's refusal to talk. . . .

Few will persist in their initial refusal to talk. . .[if it is pointed out that a refusal implies guilt].

* * *

From these representative samples of interrogation techniques, the setting prescribed by the manuals and observed in practice becomes clear. In essence, it is this: To be alone with the subject is essential to prevent distraction and to deprive him of any outside support. The aura of confidence in his guilt undermines his will to resist. He merely confirms the preconceived story the police seek to have him describe. . . . When normal procedures fail to produce the needed result, the police may resort to deceptive stratagems such as giving false legal advice. It is important to keep the subject off balance, for example, by trading on his insecurity about himself or his surroundings. The police then persuade, trick, or cajole him out of exercising his constitutional rights.

* * *

In . . . *Miranda v. Arizona,* the police arrested the defendant and took him to a special interrogation room where they secured a confession. . . . The officers [did not] undertake to afford appropriate safeguards at the outset of the interrogation to insure that the statements were truly the product of free choice.

* * *

From the foregoing, we can readily perceive an intimate connection between the privilege against self-incrimination and police custodial questioning. It is fitting to turn to history and precedent underlying the Self-Incrimination Clause to determine its applicability in this situation.

II.

We sometimes forget how long it has taken to establish the privilege against self-incrimination, the sources from which it came and the fervor with which it was defended. Its roots go back into ancient times. . . . These sentiments worked their way over to the Colonies and were implanted after great struggle into the Bill of Rights. . . . We cannot depart from this noble heritage.

* * *

The question in these cases is whether the privilege is fully applicable during a period of custodial interrogation. In this Court, the privilege has consistently been accorded a liberal construction. . . . We are satisfied that all the principles embodied in the privilege apply to informal compulsion exerted by law-enforcement officers during in-custody questioning. An individual swept from familiar surroundings into police custody, surrounded by antagonistic forces, and subjected to the techniques of persuasion described above cannot be otherwise than under compulsion to speak. As a practical matter, the compulsion to speak in the isolated setting of the police station may well be greater than in courts or other official investigations, where there are often impartial observers to guard against intimidation or trickery.

* * *

. . . We have had little occasion in the past quarter century to reach the constitutional issues in dealing with federal interrogations. . . . Supervisory rules, requiring production of an arrested person before a commissioner "without unnecessary delay" and excluding evidence obtained in default of that statutory obligation, were nonetheless responsive to the same considerations of

Fifth Amendment policy that unavoidably face us now as to the States. . . .

* * *

Without the protections flowing from adequate warning and the rights of counsel, "all the careful safeguards erected around the giving of testimony, whether by an accused or any other witness, would become empty formalities in a procedure where the most compelling possible evidence of guilt, a confession, would have already been obtained at the unsupervised pleasure of the police."

III.

Today, then, there can be no doubt that the Fifth Amendment privilege is available outside of criminal court proceedings and serves to protect persons in all settings in which their freedom of action is curtailed in any significant way from being compelled to incriminate themselves. We have concluded that without proper safeguards the process of in-custody interrogation of persons suspected or accused of crime contains inherently compelling pressures which work to undermine the individual's will to resist and to compel him to speak where he would not otherwise do so freely. In order to combat these pressures and to permit a full opportunity to exercise the privilege against self-incrimination, the accused must be adequately and effectively apprised of his rights and the exercise of those rights must be fully honored.

. . .We encourage Congress and the States to continue their laudable search for increasingly effective ways of protecting the rights of the individual while promoting efficient enforcement of our criminal laws. However, unless we are shown other procedures which are at least as effective in apprising accused persons of their right of silence and in assuring a continuous opportunity to exercise it, the following safeguards must be observed.

At the outset, if a person in custody is to be subjected to interrogation, he must first be informed in clear and unequivocal terms that he has the right to remain silent. For those unaware of the privilege, the warning is needed simply to make them aware of it—the threshold requirement for an intelligent decision as to its exercise. More important, such a warning is an absolute prerequisite in overcoming the inherent pressures of the interrogation atmosphere. . . .

* * *

The warning of the right to remain silent must be accompanied by the explanation that anything said can and will be used against the individual in court. This warning is needed in order to make him aware not only of the privilege, but also of the consequences of forgoing it. It is only through an awareness of these consequences that there can be any assurance of real understanding and intelligent exercise of the privilege. Moreover, this warning may serve to make the individual more acutely aware that he is faced with a phase of the adversary system—that he is not in the presence of persons acting solely in his interest.

. . .The right to have counsel present at the interrogation is indispensable to the protection of the Fifth Amendment privilege under the system we delineate today. Our aim is to assure that the individual's right to choose between silence and speech remains unfettered throughout the interrogation process. . . . Thus, the need for counsel to protect the Fifth Amendment privilege comprehends not merely a right to consult with counsel prior to questioning, but also to have counsel present during any questioning if the defendant so desires.

The presence of counsel at the interrogation may serve several significant subsidiary functions as well. If the accused decides to talk to his interrogators, the assistance of counsel can mitigate the dangers of untrustworthiness. With a lawyer present the likelihood that the police will practice coercion is reduced, and if coercion is nevertheless exercised the lawyer can testify to it in court. The presence of a lawyer can also help to guarantee that the accused gives a fully accurate statement to the police and that the statement is rightly reported by the prosecution at trial. . . .

Accordingly we hold that an individual held for interrogation must be clearly informed that he has the right to consult with a lawyer and to have the lawyer with him during interrogation under the system for protecting the privilege we delineate today. . . .

If an individual indicates that he wishes the assistance of counsel before any interrogation occurs, the authorities cannot rationally ignore or deny his request on the basis that the individual does not have or cannot afford a retained attorney. . . . The need for counsel in order to protect the privilege exists for the indigent as well as the affluent. . . . The cases before us as well as the vast majority of confession cases with which we have dealt in the past involve those unable to retain counsel. . . .

In order fully to apprise a person interrogated of the extent of his rights under this system then, it is necessary to warn him not only that he has the right to consult with an attorney, but also that if he is indigent a lawyer will be appointed to represent him. . . .

* * *

If the interrogation continues without the presence of an attorney and a statement is taken, a heavy burden rests on the government to demonstrate that the defendant knowingly and intelligently waived his privilege against self-incrimination and his right to retained or appointed counsel. . . . Since the State is responsible for establishing the isolated circumstances under which the interrogation takes place and has the only means of making available corroborated evidence of warnings given during incommunicado interrogation, the burden is rightly on its shoulders.

". . .The record must show, or there must be an allegation and evidence which show, that an accused was offered counsel but intelligently and understandingly rejected the offer. Anything less is not waiver." . . .Moreover, where in-custody interrogation is involved, there is no room for the contention that the privilege is waived if the individual answers some questions or gives some information on his own prior to invoking his right to remain silent when interrogated. Whatever the testimony of the authorities as to waiver of rights by an accused, the fact of lengthy interrogation or incommunicado incarceration before a statement is made is strong evidence that the accused did not validly waive his rights. In these circumstances the fact that the individual eventually made a statement is consistent with the conclusion that the compelling influence of the interrogation finally forced him to do so. It is inconsistent with any notion of a voluntary relinquishment of the privilege. Moreover, any evidence that the accused was threatened, tricked, or cajoled into a waiver will, of course, show that the defendant did not voluntarily waive his privilege. The requirement of warnings and waiver of rights is a fundamental with respect to the Fifth Amendment privilege and not simply a preliminary ritual to existing methods of interrogation.

* * *

The principles announced today deal with the protection which must be given to the privilege against self-incrimination when the individual is first subjected to police interrogation while in custody at the station or otherwise deprived of his freedom of action in any different way, It is at this point that our adversary system of criminal proceedings commences, distinguishing itself at the outset from the inquisitorial system recognized in some countries. Under the system of warnings we delineate today or under any other system which may be devised and found effective, the safeguards to be erected about the privilege must come into play at this point.

Our decision is not intended to hamper the traditional function of police officers in investigating crime. . . .When an individual in custody or probable cause, the police may, of course, seek out evidence in the field to be used at trial against him. Such investigation may include inquiry of persons not under restraint. General on-the-scene questioning as to facts surrounding a crime or other general questioning of citizens in the fact-finding process is not affected by our holding. It is an act of responsible citizenship for individuals to give whatever information they may have to aid in law enforcement. In such situations the compelling atmosphere inherent in the process of in-custody interrogation is not necessarily present.

Confession remain[s] a proper element in law enforcement. Any statement given freely and voluntarily without any compelling influences is, of course, admissible in evidence. . . . There is no requirement that police stop a person who enters a police station and states and that he wishes to confess to a crime, or a person who calls the police to offer a confession or any other statement he desires to make. Volunteered statements of any kind are not barred by the Fifth Amendment and their admissibility is not affected by our holding today.

To summarize, we hold that when an individual is taken into custody or otherwise deprived of his freedom by the authorities in any significant way and is subjected to questioning, the privilege against self-incrimination is jeopardized. Procedural safeguards must be employed to protect the privilege and unless other full effective means are adopted to notify the person of his right of silence and to assure that the exercise of the right will be scrupulously honored, the following measures are required. He must be warned prior to any questioning that he has the right to remain silent, that anything he says can be used against him in a court of law, that he has the right to the presence of an attorney, and that if he cannot afford an attorney one will be appointed for him prior to any questioning if he so desires. Opportunity to exercise these rights must be afforded to him throughout the interrogation. After such warnings have been given, and such opportunity afforded him, the individual may knowingly and intelligently waive these rights and agree to answer questions or make a statement. But unless and until such warnings and waiver are demonstrated by the prosecution at trial, no evidence obtained as a result of interrogation can be used against him.

IV.

In announcing these principles, we are not unmindful of the burdens which law enforcement officials must bear, often under trying circumstances. We also fully recognize the obligation of all citizens to aid in enforcing the criminal laws. This Court, while protecting individual rights, has always given ample latitude to law enforcement agencies in the legitimate exercise of their duties. The limits we have placed on the interrogation process should not constitute an undue interference with a proper system of law enforcement. . . .

Custodial interrogation, by contrast, does not necessarily afford the innocent an opportunity to clear themselves. A serious consequence of the present practice of the interrogation alleged to be beneficial for the innocent is that many arrests "for investigation" subject large numbers of innocent persons to detention and interrogation. . . .

Over the years the Federal Bureau of Investigation has compiled an exemplary record of effective law enforcement while advising any suspect or arrested person, at the outset of an interview, that he is not required to make a statement, that any statement may be used against him in court, that the individual may obtain the services of an attorney of his own choice and, more recently, that he has a right to free counsel if he is unable to pay. . . .

"'The standard warning long given by Special Agents of the FBI to both suspects and persons under arrest is that the person has a right to say nothing and a right to counsel, and that any statement he does make may be used against him in court. . . .

"'After passage of the Criminal Justice Act of 1964, which provides free counsel for Federal defendants unable to pay, we added to our instructions to Special Agents the requirement that any person who is under arrest for an offense under FBI jurisdiction, or whose arrest is contemplated following the interview, must also be advised of his right to free counsel if he is unable to pay, and the fact that such counsel will be assigned by the Judge. At the same time, we broadened the right to counsel warning to read counsel of his own choice, or anyone else with whom he might wish to speak.

* * *

"'The FBI warning is given to a suspect at the very outset of the interview. . . . The warning may be given to a person arrested as soon as practicable after the arrest . . . but in any event it must precede the interview with the person for a confession or admission of his own guilt.

* * *

"'When the person who has been warned of his right to counsel decides that he wishes to consult with counsel before making a statement, the interview is terminated at that point. . . . It may be continued, however, as to all matters other than the person's own guilt or innocence. . . .

* * *

"'If any person being interviewed after warning of counsel decides that he wishes to consult with counsel before proceeding further the interview is terminated, as shown above. FBI Agents do not pass judgment on the ability of the person to pay for counsel. They do, however, advise those who have been arrested for an offense under FBI jurisdiction, or whose arrest is contemplated following the interview, of a right to free counsel if they are unable to pay, and the availability of such counsel from the Judge.'"

* * *

No. 759. *Miranda v. Arizona.*

On March 13, 1963, petitioner, Ernesto Miranda, was arrested at his home and taken in custody to a Phoenix police station. He was there identified by the complaining witness. The police then took him to "Interrogation Room No. 2" of the detective bureau. There he was questioned by two police officers. The officers admitted at trial that Miranda was not advised that he had a right to have an attorney present. Two hours later, the officers emerged from the interrogation room with a written confession signed by Miranda. At the top of the statement was a typed paragraph stating that the confession was made voluntarily, without threats or promises of immunity and "with full knowledge of my legal rights, understanding any statement I make may be used against me."

At his trial before a jury, the written confession was admitted into evidence over the objection of defense counsel, and the officers testified to the prior oral confession made by Miranda during the interrogation. Miranda was found guilty of kidnapping and rape. He was sentenced to 20 to 30 years' imprisonment on each count, the sentences to run concurrently. On appeal, the Supreme Court of Arizona held that Miranda's constitutional rights were not violated in obtaining the confession and affirmed the conviction. . . .

We reverse. From the testimony of the officers and by the admission of respondent, it is clear that Miranda was not in any way apprised of his right to consult with an attorney and to have one present during the interrogation, nor was his right not to be compelled to incriminate himself effectively protected in any other manner. Without these warnings the statements were inadmissible.

Source:

Supreme Court Reporter, Vol. 86, pp. 1,602–1,665.

Freedom of Information Act of 1966

Federal U.S. legislation enacted July 3, 1966, designed to make federal agencies disclose more information to the public. It stated that all records in the possession of the executive branch, except those specifically exempted by law, must be provided to any person who requests them. Exempted materials included national defense or foreign policy secrets, personnel or medical files, trade secrets or confidential financial information, certain law enforcement investigatory files, and information concerning private gas or oil wells. The act was amended in 1974 to make information easier, quicker, and cheaper to obtain by requiring agencies to publish uniform fees for providing documents; empowering federal courts to order agencies to comply with the act; setting time limits for agency responses to requests; and requiring annual reports to Congress from agencies and the attorney general on freedom of information matters. It was further amended in 1975 to include sensitive agencies, such as the FBI and the CIA, although later amendments and regulations put additional curbs on information coming out of these agencies in order to better protect sources and methods. Nevertheless, the Freedom of Information Act (FOIA) served to bring to light some of the more nefarious actions of government agencies as well as serving as a boon to journalists and historians. On the other hand, the prospect of seeing one's memos end up featured in the media has inhibited advisers from putting certain information on paper or in e-mails, thus affecting internal institutional history as well as the work of future historians. Various administrations have promulgated regulations effecting the release of information. Under Presidents Carter and Clinton, FOIA analysts were to give the benefit of the doubt to the requester, allowing more information to be released; under Republican administrations, decisions favored withholding information. The 2002 Homeland Security Act exempted certain previously public information concerning commerce and infrastructure from release because of the possibility it could aid terrorists.

An Act

To amend section 3 of the Administrative Procedure Act, chapter 324, of the Act of June 11, 1946 (60 Stat. 238), to clarify and protect the right of the public to information, and for other purposes.

Be it enacted by the Senate and House of Representatives of the United States of America in Congress assembled, That section 3, chapter 324, of the Act of June 11, 1946 (60 Stat. 238), is amended to read as follows:

"Sec. 3. Every agency shall make available to the public the following information:

"(a) Publication in the Federal Register.—Every agency shall separately state and currently publish in the Federal Register for the guidance of the public (A) descriptions of its central and field organization and the established places at which, the officers from whom, and the methods whereby, the public may secure information, make submittals or requests, or obtain decisions; (B) statements of the general course and method by which its functions are channeled and determined, including the nature and requirements of all formal and informal procedures available; (C) rules of procedure, descriptions of forms available or the places at which forms may be obtained, and instructions as to the scope and contents of all papers, reports, or examinations; (D) substantive rules of general applicability adopted as authorized by law, and statements of general policy or interpretations of general applicability formulated and adopted by the agency; and (E) every amendment, revision, or repeal of the foregoing. Except to the extent that a person has actual and timely notice of the terms thereof, no person shall in any manner be required to resort to, or be adversely affected by any matter required to be published in the Federal Register and not so published. For purposes of this subsection, matter which is reasonably available to the class of persons affected thereby shall be deemed published in the Federal Register when incorporated by reference therein with the approval of the Director of the Federal Register.

"(b) Agency Opinions and Orders.—Every agency shall, in accordance with published rules, make available for public inspection and copying (A) all final opinions (including concurring and dissenting opinions) and all orders made in the adjudication of cases, (B) those statements of policy and interpretations which have been adopted by the agency and are not published in the Federal Register, and (C) administrative staff manuals and instructions to staff that affect any member of the public, unless such materials are promptly published and copies offered for sale. To the extent required to prevent a clearly unwarranted invasion of personal privacy, an agency may delete identifying details when it makes available or publishes an opinion, statement of policy, interpretation, or staff manual or instruction: *Provided,* That in every case the justification for the deletion must be fully explained in writing. Every agency also shall maintain and make available for public inspection and copying a current index providing identifying information for the public as to any matter which is issued, adopted, or promulgated after the effective date of this Act and which is required by this subsection to be made available or published. No final order, opinion, statement of policy, interpretation, or staff manual or instruction that affects any member of the public may be relied upon, used or cited as precedent by an agency against any private party unless it has been indexed and either made available or published as provided by this subsection or unless that private party shall have actual and timely notice of the terms thereof.

"(c) Agency Records.—Except with respect to the records made available pursuant to subsections (a) and (b), every agency shall, upon request for identifiable records made in accordance with published rules stating the time, place, fees to the extent authorized by statute and procedure to be followed, make such records promptly available to any person. Upon complaint, the district court of the United States in the district in which the complainant resides, or has his principal place of business, or in which the agency records are situated shall have jurisdiction to enjoin the agency from the withholding of agency records and to order the production of any agency records improperly withheld from the complainant. In such cases the court shall determine the matter de novo and the burden shall be upon the agency to sustain its action. In the event of noncompliance with the court's order, the district court may punish the responsible officers for contempt. Except as to those causes which the court deems of greater importance, proceedings before the district court as authorized by this subsection shall take precedence on the docket over all other causes and shall be assigned for hearing and trial at the earliest practicable date and expedited in every way.

"(d) Agency Proceedings.—Every agency having more than one member shall keep a record of the final votes of each member in every agency proceeding and such record shall be available for public inspection.

"(e) Exemptions.—The provisions of this section shall not be applicable to matters that are (1) specifically required by Executive order to be kept secret in the interest of the national defense or foreign policy; (2) related solely to the internal personnel rules and practices of any agency; (3) specifically exempted from disclosure by statute; (4) trade secrets and commercial or financial information obtained from any person and privileged or confidential; (5) inter-agency or intra-agency memorandums or letters which would not be available by law to a private party in litigation with the agency; (6) personnel and medical files and similar files the disclosure of which would constitute a clearly unwarranted invasion of personal privacy; (7) investigatory files compiled for law enforcement purposes except to the extent available by law to a private party; (8) contained or related to examination, operating, or condition reports prepared by, on behalf of, or for the use of any agency responsible for the regulation or supervision of financial institutions; and (9) geological and geophysical information and data (including maps) concerning wells.

"(f) Limitation of Exemptions.—Nothing in this section authorizes withholding of information or limiting the availability of records to the public except as specifically stated in this section, nor shall this section be authority to withhold information from Congress.

"(g) Private Party.—As used in this section, 'private party' means any party other than an agency.

"(h) Effective Date.—This amendment shall become effective one year following the date of the enactment of this Act."

Approved July 4, 1966.

Source:

Statutes at Large, Vol. 80, pp. 250–251.

The Black Panther Party, The Black Panther Party Platform and Program, 1966

Platform of the Black Panther Party (BPP), a militant black political rights organization, founded by Bobby Seale and Huey Newton in October 1966 in Oakland, California. This 10-point platform made a number of demands for African Americans. Marxist influences infuse the platform, as in the assertion that if "white American businessmen" deny African Americans meaningful employment then the "means of production should be taken from the businessmen and placed in the community so that the people of the community can organize and employ all of its people." The party closed its platform by quoting the Declaration of Independence.

The Panthers were a highly controversial organization and remain so in historical treatments of them. Early Panthers asserted their Second Amendment right to bear arms and took advantage of a California law that outlawed only concealed weapons. Their open flaunting of guns gave them a frightening public image. Some of their literature also advocated violence. In addition, some Panthers, using the movie *Battle of Algiers* to teach them terrorist techniques, were responsible for assassinating police and other law enforcement officials and killing a California judge.

On the other hand, the Panthers assisted former convicts to better themselves and instituted free breakfast programs for needy children (although they sometimes resorted to extortion to acquire food for the breakfasts). The Federal Bureau of Investigation mounted a Counterintelligence Program to discredit Panther leaders and disrupt their programs, including the free breakfasts and their Marxist-oriented "Liberation schools."

After a Panther allegedly murdered a Chicago policeman, an FBI informant who was close to Chicago leader Fred Hampton gave his handler a map of Hampton's apartment. Supposedly the map ended up with the Chicago police, who raided the apartment, killing Hampton, who was in bed at the time, and an associate. The FBI and Chicago police eventually settled with the survivors.

WHAT WE WANT
WHAT WE BELIEVE

WE WANT freedom. We want power to determine the destiny of our Black Community.

WE BELIEVE that black people will not be free until we are able to determine our destiny.

WE WANT full employment for our people.

WE BELIEVE that the federal government is responsible and obligated to give every man employment or a guaranteed income. We believe that if the white American businessmen will not give full employment, then the means of production should be taken from the businessmen and placed in the community so that the people of the community can organize and employ all of its people and give a high standard of living.

WE WANT an end to the robbery by the CAPITALIST of our Black Community.

WE BELIEVE that this racist government has robbed us and now we are demanding the overdue debt of forty acres and two mules. Forty acres and two mules was promised 100 years ago as restitution for slave labor and mass murder of black people. We will accept the payment in currency which will be distributed to our many communities. The Germans are now aiding the Jews in Israel for the genocide of the Jewish people. The Germans murdered six million Jews. The American racist has taken part in the slaughter of over fifty million black people; therefore, we feel that this is a modest demand that we make.

WE WANT decent housing, fit for the shelter of human beings.

WE BELIEVE that if the white landlords will not give decent housing to our black community, then the housing and the land should be made into cooperatives so that our community, with government aid, can build and make decent housing for its people.

WE WANT education for our people that exposes the true nature of this decadent American society. We want education that teaches us our true history and our role in the present-day society.

WE BELIEVE in an educational system that will give to our people a knowledge of self. If a man does not have knowledge of himself and his position in society and the world, then he has little chance to relate to anything else.

WE WANT all black men to be exempt from military service.

WE BELIEVE that Black people should not be forced to fight in the military service to defend a racist government that does not protect us. We will not fight and kill other people of color in the world who, like black people, are being victimized by the white racist government of America. We will protect ourselves from the force and violence of the racist police and the racist military, by whatever means necessary.

WE WANT an immediate end to POLICE BRUTALITY and MURDER of black people.

WE BELIEVE we can end police brutality in our black community by organizing black self-defense groups that are dedicated to defending our black community from racist police oppression and brutality. The Second Amendment to the Constitution of the United States gives a right to bear arms. We therefore believe that all black people should arm themselves for self- defense.

WE WANT freedom for all black men held in federal, state, county and city prisons and jails.

WE BELIEVE that all black people should be released from the many jails and prisons because they have not received a fair and impartial trial.

WE WANT all black people when brought to trial to be tried in court by a jury of their peer group or people from their black communities, as defined by the Constitution of the United States.

WE BELIEVE that the courts should follow the United States Constitution so that black people will receive fair trials. The 14th Amendment of the U.S. Constitution gives a man a right to be tried by his peer group. A peer is a person from a similar economic, social, religious, geographical, environmental, historical and racial background. To do this the court will be forced to select a jury from the black community from which the black defendant came. We have been, and are being tried by all-white juries that have no understanding of the "average reasoning man" of the black community.

WE WANT land, bread, housing, education, clothing, justice and peace. And as our major political objective, a United Nations supervised plebiscite to be held throughout the black colony in which only black colonial subjects will be allowed to participate, for the purpose of determining the will of black people as to their national destiny.

WHEN, in the course of human events, it becomes necessary for one people to dissolve the political bonds which have connected them with another, and to assume, among the powers of the earth, the separate and equal station to which the laws of nature and nature's God entitle them, a decent respect to the opinions of mankind requires that they should declare the causes which impel them to the separation.

WE HOLD these truths to be self-evident, that all men are created equal; that they are endowed by their Creator with certain inalienable rights; that among these are life, liberty, and the pursuit of happiness. . . That, to secure these rights, governments are instituted among men, deriving their just powers from the consent of the governed; that, whenever any form of government becomes destructive of these ends, it is the right of the people to alter or abolish it, and to institute a new government, laying its foundation on such principles, and organizing its powers in such form, as to them shall seem most likely to effect their safety and happiness. . . Prudence, indeed, will dictate that governments long established should not be changed for light and transient causes; and, accordingly, all experience hath shown, that mankind are more disposed to suffer, while evils are sufferable, than to right themselves by abolishing the forms to which they are accustomed. . . But, when a long train of abuses and usurpations, pursuing invariably the same object, evinces a design to reduce them under absolute despotism, it is their right, it is their duty, to throw off such government, and to provide new guards for their future security. . .

Source:

The Maoist International Movement. "The Black Panther Party Platform and Program." Available on-line. URL: www.

etext.org/Politics/MIM/bpp/bpprog/htm. Accessed November 2003.

Omnibus Crime Control and Safe Streets Act, 1968

Federal legislation signed into law on June 19, 1968, to provide federal assistance to state and local law enforcement agencies in order to reduce street crime. The act created the Law Enforcement Assistance Administration to aid state and local agencies in funding programs for police, courts, corrections, control of organized crime, civil disorders, and related crime problems; it authorized $400 million in grants to develop programs over a two-year period. It prohibited interstate traffic in handguns and their sale to minors.

Its most controversial provisions sanctioned eavesdropping and wiretapping by federal, state, and local officials, specifying when and how they may be authorized (Title III). These provisions have been criticized as violations of rights to privacy. However, prior to the passage of this act, government agents conducted wiretaps but did not use this intelligence in court because they were prohibited by section 605 of the 1934 Federal Communications Act from "divulging" the fruits of those taps. The Department of Justice had for years appealed to Congress to allow overhears in court. Under the 1968 Act, a judicial official had to find probable cause and issue a warrant, but these Title III wiretaps can be used in court and have aided crimesolving, promoted guilty pleas (saving court costs) and produced successful prosecutions. However, the Act pointedly did not touch national security overhears.

Two years later the Organized Crime Control Act reinforced federal power against organized crime by strengthening legal tools for gathering evidence, by establishing new penal prohibitions, and by providing stronger sanctions in dealing with unlawful activities. It provided for special grand juries to report to federal courts, issuance of general immunity to compel witnesses to testify, and increased sentences for dangerous special offenders. Its provisions covered a wide range of offenses besides organized crime, including passing bad checks, burglary, and conspiracy. However, it is best known for Title IX, the Racketeer Influenced and Corrupt Organization (RICO) Act, which, among other provisions applied triple damages to organizations convicted of violating it. It took over 10 years, but its use brought down major organized crime families nationwide. However, it was also used effectively against white supremacist and antiabortion groups as well as small businesses sued by individuals, which may not have been intended by Congress, but were upheld on appeal in the courts.

An Act

To assist State and local governments in reducing the incidence of crime, to increase the effectiveness, fairness, and coordination of law enforcement and criminal justice systems at all levels of government, and for other purposes. . . . This Act may be cited as the "Omnibus Crime Control and Safe Streets Act of 1968".

Title I—Law Enforcement Assistance

Declarations and Purpose

Congress finds that the high incidence of crime in the United States threatens the peace, security, and general welfare of the Nation and its citizens. To prevent crime and to insure the greater safety of the people, law enforcement efforts must be better coordinated, intensified, and made more effective at all levels of government.

Congress finds further that crime is essentially a local problem that must be dealt with by State and local governments if it is to be controlled effectively.

It is therefore the declared policy of the Congress to assist State and local governments in strengthening and improving law enforcement at every level by national assistance. It is the purpose of this title to (1) encourage States and units of general local government to prepare and adopt comprehensive plans based upon their evaluation of State and local problems of law enforcement; (2) authorize grants to States and units of local government in order to improve and strengthen law enforcement; and (3) encourage research and development directed toward the improvement of law enforcement and the development of new methods for the prevention and reduction of crime and the detection and apprehension of criminals.

Part A—Law Enforcement Assistance Administration

Sec. 101. (a) There is hereby established within the Department of Justice, under the general authority of the Attorney General, a Law Enforcement Assistance Administration (hereafter referred to in this title as "Administration").

(b) The Administration shall be composed of an Administrator of Law Enforcement Assistance and two Associate Administrators of Law Enforcement Assistance, who shall be appointed by the President, by and with the advice and consent of the Senate. . . .

Part B—Planning Grants

Sec. 201. It is the purpose of this part to encourage States and units of general local government to prepare and adopt comprehensive law enforcement plans based on their evaluation of State and local problems of law enforcement.

Sec. 202. The Administration shall make grants to the States for the establishment and operation of State law enforcement planning agencies. . .for the preparation, development, and revision of the State plans required under section 303 of this title. . . .

Sec. 203. (a) A grant made under this part to a State shall be utilized by the State to establish and maintain a State planning agency. . . .

(b) The State planning agency shall—

(1) develop . . . a comprehensive statewide plan for the improvement of law enforcement throughout the State;

(2) define, develop, and correlate programs and projects for the State and the units of general local government in the State or combinations of States or units for improvement in law enforcement. . . .

* * *

Part C—Grants for Law Enforcement Purposes

Sec. 301. (a) It is the purpose of this part to encourage States and units of general local government to carry out programs and projects to improve and strengthen law enforcement.

(b) The Administration is authorized to make grants to States having comprehensive State plans approved by it under this part, for—

(1) Public protection . . . to improve and strengthen law enforcement and reduce crime in public and private places.

(2) The recruiting of law enforcement personnel and the training of personnel in law enforcement.

(3) Public education relating to crime prevention and encouraging respect for law and order. . . .

(4) Construction of . . . physical facilities which would fulfill or implement the purposes of this section.

(5) The organization, education, and training of special law enforcement units to combat organized crime. . . .

(6) The organization, education, and training of regular law enforcement officers, special law enforcement units, and law enforcement reserve units for the prevention, detection, and control of riots and other violent civil disorders, including the acquisition of riot control equipment.

(7) The recruiting, organization, training and education of community service officers to serve with and assist local and State law enforcement agencies in the discharge of their duties through such activities as recruiting; improvement of police-community relations and grievance resolution mechanisms; community patrol activities; encouragement of neighborhood participation in crime prevention and public safety efforts; and other activities designed to improve police capabilities, public safety and the objectives of this section. . . .

[A State Planning Administration will coordinate the grant program.]

Part D—Training, Education, Research, Demonstration, and Special Grants

Sec. 401. It is the purpose of this part to provide for and encourage training, education, research, and development for the purpose of improving law enforcement and developing new methods for the prevention and reduction of crime, and the detection and apprehension of criminals.

Sec. 402. (a) There is established within the Department of Justice a National Institute of Law Enforcement and Criminal Justice.

(b) The Institute is authorized—

(1) to make grants to, or enter into contracts with, public agencies, institutions of higher education, or private organizations to conduct research, demonstrations, or special projects pertaining to the purposes described in this title, including the development of new or improved approaches, techniques, systems, equipment, and devices to improve and strengthen law enforcement;

(2) to make continuing studies and undertake programs of research to develop new or improved approaches, techniques, systems, equipment, and devices to improve and strengthen law enforcement, including, but not limited to, the effectiveness of projects or programs carried out under this title;

(3) to carry out programs of behavioral research designed to provide more accurate information on the causes of crime and the effectiveness of various means of preventing crime, and to evaluate the success of correctional procedures;

(4) to make recommendations for action which can be taken by Federal, State, and local governments and by private persons and organizations to improve and strengthen law enforcement;

(5) to carry out programs of instructional assistance. . . .

* * *

(7) to establish a research center. . . .

* * *

Sec. 404. (a) The Director of the Federal Bureau of Investigation is authorized to—

(1) establish and conduct training programs at the Federal Bureau of Investigation National Academy at Quantico, Virginia, to provide, at the request of a State or unit of local government, training for State and local law enforcement personnel;

(2) develop new or improved approaches, techniques, systems, equipment, and devices to improve and strengthen law enforcement; and

(3) assist in conducting, at the request of a State or unit of local government, local and regional training programs for the training of State and local law enforcement personnel. . . .

(b) In the exercise of the functions, powers, and duties established under this section the Director of the Federal Bureau of Investigation shall be under the general authority of the Attorney General.

Part E—Administrative Provisions

* * *

Sec. 515. The Administration is authorized—

(a) to conduct evaluation studies of the programs and activities assisted under this title;

(b) to collect, evaluate, publish, and disseminate statistics and other information on the condition and progress of law enforcement in the several States; and

(c) to cooperate with and render technical assistance to States, units of general local government, combinations of such States or units, or other public or private agencies, organizations, or institutions in matters relating to law enforcement.

* * *

Sec. 518. (a) Nothing contained in this title or any other Act shall be construed to authorize any department, agency, officer, or employee of the United States to exercise any direction, supervision, or control over any police force or any other law enforcement agency of any State or any political subdivision thereof. . . .

Part F—Definitions

Sec. 601. As used in this title—

(a) "Law enforcement" means all activities pertaining to crime prevention or reduction and enforcement of the criminal law.

(b) "Organized crime" means the unlawful activities of the members of a highly organized, disciplined association engaged in supplying illegal goods and services, including but not limited to gambling, prostitution, loan sharking, narcotics, labor racketeering, and other unlawful activities of members of such organizations.

(c) "State" means any State of the United States, the District of Columbia, the Commonwealth of Puerto Rico, and any territory or possession of the United States.

(d) "Unit of general local government" means any city, county, township, town, borough, parish, village, or other general purpose political subdivision of a State, or an Indian tribe which performs law enforcement functions as determined by the Secretary of the Interior.

* * *

(i) "Public agency" means any State, unit of local government, combination of such States or units, or any department, agency, or instrumentality of any of the foregoing.

* * *

(k) "Community service officer" means any citizen with the capacity, motivation, integrity, and stability to assist in or perform police work but who may not meet ordinary standards for employment as a regular police officer selected from the immediate locality of the police department of which he is to be a part, and meeting such other qualifications promulgated in regulations.

Title II—Admissibility of Confessions, Reviewability of Admission in Evidence of Confessions in State Cases, Admissibility in Evidence of Eye Witness Testimony, and Procedures in Obtaining Writs of Habeas Corpus

* * *

"Section 3501. Admissibility of confessions

"(a) In any criminal prosecution brought by the United States or by the District of Columbia, a confession, as defined in subsection (e) hereof, shall be admissible in evidence if it is voluntarily given. Before such confession is received in evidence, the trial judge shall, out of the presence of the jury, determine any issue as to voluntariness. If the trial judge determines that the confession was voluntarily made it shall be admitted in evidence and the trial judge shall permit the jury to hear relevant evidence on the issue of voluntariness and shall instruct the jury to give such weight to the confession as the jury feels it deserves under all the circumstances.

"(b) The trial judge in determining the issue of voluntariness shall take into consideration all the circumstances surrounding the giving of the confession, including (1) the time elapsing between arrest and arraignment of the defendant making the confession, if it was made after arrest and before arraignment, (2) whether such defendant knew the nature of the offense with which he was charged or of which he was suspected at the time of making the confession, (3) whether or not such defendant was advised or knew that he was not required to make any statement and that any such statement could be used against him, (4) whether or not such defendant had been advised prior to questioning of his right to the assistance of counsel; and (5) whether or not such defendant was without the assistance of counsel when questioned and when giving such confession.

* * *

"Section 3502. Admissibility in Evidence of Eye Witness Testimony

"The testimony of a witness that he saw the accused commit or participate in the commission of the crime for which the accused is being tried shall be admissible in evidence in a criminal prosecution in any trial court ordained and established under article III of the Constitution of the United States."

Title III—Wiretapping and Electronic Surveillance
Findings. . . .

(a) Wire communications are normally conducted through the use of facilities which form part of an interstate network. The same facilities are used for interstate and intrastate communications. There has been extensive wiretapping carried on without legal sanctions, and without the consent of any of the parties to the conversation. Electronic, mechanical, and other intercepting devices are being used to overhear oral conversations made in private, without the consent of any of the parties to such communications. The contents of these communications and evidence derived therefrom are being used by public and private parties as evidence in court and administrative proceedings, and by persons whose activities affect interstate commerce. The possession, manufacture, distribution, advertising, and use of these devices are facilitated by interstate commerce.

* * *

(c) Organized criminals make extensive use of wire and oral communications in their criminal activities. The interception of such communications to obtain evidence of the commission of crimes or to prevent their commission is an indispensable aid to law enforcement and the administration of justice.

(d) To safeguard the privacy of innocent persons, the interception of wire or oral communications where none of the parties to the communication has consented to the interception should be allowed only when authorized by a court of competent jurisdiction and should remain under the control and supervision of the authorizing court. Interception of wire and oral communications should further be limited to certain major types of offenses and specific categories of crime with assurances that the interception is justified and that the information obtained thereby will not be misused.

"Chapter 119. Wire Interception and Interception of Oral Communications

* * *

"Section 2510. Definitions. . .

"(1) 'wire communication' means any communication made in whole or in part through the use of facilities for the transmission of communications by the aid of wire, cable, or other like connection between the point of origin and the point of reception furnished or operated by any person engaged as a common carrier in providing or operating such facilities for the transmission of interstate or foreign communications;

"(2) 'oral communication' means any oral communication uttered by a person exhibiting an expectation that such communication is not subject to interception under circumstances justifying such expectation;

* * *

"(4) 'intercept' means the aural acquisition of the contents of any wire or oral communication through the use of any electronic, mechanical, or other device.

"(5) 'electronic, mechanical, or other device' means any device or apparatus which can be used to intercept a wire or oral communication [with specified exceptions].

"(6) 'person' means any employee, or agent of the United States or any State or political subdivision thereof, and any individual, partnership, association, joint stock company, trust, or corporation;

"(7) 'Investigative or law enforcement officer' means any officer of the United States or of a State or political subdivision thereof, who is empowered by law to conduct investigations of or to make arrests for offenses enumerated in this chapter, and any attorney authorized by law to prosecute or participate in the prosecution of such offenses;

"(8) 'contents', when used with respect to any wire or oral communication, includes any information concerning the identity of the parties to such communication or the existence, substance, purport, or meaning of that communication;

* * *

"Section 2511. Interception and disclosure of wire or oral communications prohibited

"(1) Except as otherwise specially provided in this chapter any person who—

"(a) willfully intercepts, endeavors to intercept, or procures any other person to intercept or endeavor to intercept, any wire or oral communication;

"(b) willfully uses, endeavors to use, or procures any other person to use or endeavor to use any electronic, mechanical or other device to intercept any oral communication

"(iv) such use or endeavor to use (A) takes place on the premises of any business or other commercial establishment the operations of which affect interstate or foreign commerce; or (B) obtains or is for the purpose of obtaining information relating to the operations of any business or other commercial establishment the operations of which affect interstate or foreign commerce. . .

"(c) willfully discloses, or endeavors to disclose, to any other person the contents of any wire or oral communication, knowing or having reason to know that the information was obtained through the interception of a wire or oral communication in violation of this subsection; or "(d) willfully uses, or endeavors to use, the contents of any wire or oral communication, knowing or having reason to know that the information was obtained through the interception of a wire or oral communication in violation of this subsection; shall be fined . . . or imprisoned. . . .

* * *

"(c) It shall not be unlawful under this chapter for a person acting under color of law to intercept a wire or oral communication, where such person is a party to the communication or one of the parties to the communication has given prior consent to such interception.

"(d) It shall not be unlawful under this chapter for a person not acting under color of law to intercept a wire or oral communication where such person is a party to the communication or where one of the parties to the communication has given prior consent to such interception unless such communication is intercepted for the purpose of committing any criminal or tortuous act in violation of the Constitution or laws of the United States or of any State or for the purpose of committing any other injurious act.

"(3) Nothing contained in this chapter or in section 605 of the Communications Act of 1934 (48 Stat. 1143; 47 U.S.C. 605) shall limit the constitutional power of the President to take such measures as he deems necessary to protect the Nation against actual or potential attack or other hostile acts of a foreign power, to obtain foreign intelligence information deemed essential to the security of the United States, or to protect national security information against foreign intelligence activities. Nor shall anything contained in this chapter be deemed to limit the constitutional power of the President to take such measures as he deems necessary to protect the United States against the overthrow of the Government by force or other unlawful means, or against any other clear and present danger to the structure or existence of the Government. The contents of any wire or oral communication intercepted by authority of the President in the exercise of the foregoing powers may be received in evidence in any trial hearing, or other proceeding only where such interception was reasonable, and shall not be otherwise used or disclosed except as is necessary to implement that power.

"Section 2512. Manufacture, distribution, possession, and advertising of wire or oral communication intercepting devices prohibited [with exceptions].

* * *

"Section 2514. Immunity of witnesses

"Whenever in the judgment of a United States attorney the testimony of any witness. . .involving any violation of this chapter or any of the offenses enumerated in section 2516, or any conspiracy to violate this chapter or any of the offenses enumerated in section 2516 is necessary to the public interest, such United States attorney, upon the approval of the Attorney General, shall make application to the court that the witness shall be instructed to testify or produce evidence subject to the provisions of this section, and upon order of the court such witness shall not be excused from testifying or from producing . . . evidence on the ground that the testimony or evidence required of him may tend to incriminate him or subject him to a penalty or forfeiture. No such witness shall be prosecuted or subjected to any penalty or forfeiture for or on account of any transaction, matter or thing concerning which he is compelled, after having claimed his privilege against self-incrimination, to testify or produce evidence. . . . No witness shall be exempt under this section from prosecution for perjury or contempt committed while giving testimony or producing evidence under compulsion as provided in this section.

"Section 2515. Prohibition of use as evidence of intercepted wire or oral communications

"Whenever any wire or oral communication has been intercepted, no part of the contents of such communication and no evidence derived therefrom may be received in evidence in any trial, hearing, or other proceeding in or before any court, grand jury, department, officer, agency, regulatory body, legislative committee, or other authority of the United States, a State, or a political subdivision thereof. . . .

"Section 2516. Authorization for interception of wire or oral communications

"(1) The Attorney General, or any Assistant Attorney General specially designated by the Attorney General, may authorize an application to a Federal judge of competent jurisdiction for, and such judge may grant. . .an order authorizing or approving the interception of wire or oral communications by the Federal Bureau of Investigation, or a Federal agency having responsibility for the investigation of the offense as to which the application is made, when such interception may provide or has provided evidence of—

"(a) any offense punishable by death or by imprisonment for more than one year . . . relating to the enforcement of the Atomic Energy Act of 1954 or . . . relating to espionage, . . . sabotage, . . . treason . . . or . . . riots;

"(b) . . . restrictions on payments and loans to labor organizations, or any offense which involves murder, kidnapping, robbery, or extortion. . . .

"(c) bribery. . . , transmission of wagering information. . . . influencing or injuring an officer, juror, or witness. . . , obstruction of criminal investigations . . . , Presidential assassinations, kidnapping, and assault . . . , interference with commerce by threats or violence . . . , travel or transportation in aid of racketeering enterprises

. . . , influence operations of employee benefit plan . . . , theft from interstate shipment . . . , embezzlement from pension and welfare funds . . . , interstate transportation of stolen property);

"(d) any offense involving counterfeiting . . . ;

involving bankruptcy fraud or the manufacture, importation, receiving, concealment, buying, selling, or otherwise dealing in narcotic drugs, marihuana, or other dangerous drugs. . . .

"(f) any offense including extortionate credit transactions. . . .

"(g) any conspiracy to commit any of the foregoing offenses. . . .

* * *

"Section 2517. Authorization for disclosure and use of intercepted wire or oral communications

"(1) Any investigative or law enforcement officer who, by any means authorized by this chapter, has obtained knowledge of the contents of any wire or oral communication, or evidence derived therefrom, may disclose such contents to another investigative or law enforcement officer to the extent that such disclosure is appropriate to the proper performance of the official duties of the officer making or receiving the disclosure.

"(2) Any investigative or law enforcement officer who, by any means authorized by this chapter, has obtained knowledge of the contents of any wire or oral communication or evidence derived therefrom may use such contents to the extent such use is appropriate to the proper performance of his official duties.

"(3) Any person who has received, by any means authorized by this chapter, any information concerning a wire or oral communication, or evidence derived therefrom intercepted in accordance with the provisions of this chapter may disclose the contents of that communication. . . while giving testimony . . . in any criminal proceeding in any court of the United States or of any State or in any Federal or State grand jury proceeding.

* * *

"(5) When an investigative or law enforcement officer, while engaged in intercepting wire or oral communications in the manner authorized herein, intercepts wire or oral communications relating to offenses other than those specified in the order of authorization or approval, the contents thereof, and evidence derived therefrom, may be disclosed or used . . . when authorized or approved by a judge of competent jurisdiction. . . . [if] . . .

"(a) there is probable cause for belief that an individual is committing, has committed, or is about to commit a particular offense enumerated in section 2516 of this chapter;

"(b) there is probable cause for belief that particular communications concerning that offense will be obtained through such interception;

"(c) normal investigative procedures have been tried and have failed or reasonably appear to be unlikely to succeed if tried or to be too dangerous;

"(d) there is probable cause for belief that the facilities from which, or the place where, the wire or oral communications are to be intercepted are being used, or are about to be used, in connection with the commission of such offense. . . .

"(5) No order entered under this section may authorize or approve the interception of any wire or oral communication for any period longer than is necessary to achieve the objective of the authorization, nor in any event than thirty days. Extensions of an order may be granted. . . .

"(7) . . . Any investigative or law enforcement officer, specially designated by the Attorney General or by the principal prosecuting attorney of any State or subdivision thereof . . . who reasonably determines that—

"(a) an emergency situation exists with respect to conspiratorial activities threatening the national security interest or to conspiratorial activities characteristic of organized crime. . . .

* * *

"Sec. 605. Except as authorized by chapter 119, title 18, United States Code, no person receiving, assisting in receiving, transmitting, or assisting in transmitting, any interstate or foreign communication by wire or radio shall divulge or publish the existence, contents, substance, purport, effect, or meaning thereof, except through authorized channels of transmission or reception. . . .

* * *

Sec. 804. (a) There is hereby established a National Commission for the Review of Federal and State Laws Relating to Wiretapping and Electronic Surveillance. . . .

* * *

(d) It shall be the duty of the Commission to conduct a comprehensive study and review of the operation of the provisions of this title. . .to determine the effectiveness of such provisions during the six-year period immediately following the date of their enactment.

* * *

Title IV—State Firearms Control Assistance

Findings and Declaration

Sec. 901. (a) The Congress hereby finds and declares—

(1) that there is a widespread traffic in firearms moving in or otherwise affecting interstate or foreign commerce, and that the existing Federal controls over such traffic do not adequately enable the States to control this traffic within their own borders through the exercise of their police power;

(2) that the ease with which any person can acquire firearms other than a rifle or shotgun (including criminals, juveniles without the knowledge or consent of their parents or guardians, narcotics addicts, mental defectives, armed groups who would supplant the functions of duly constituted public authorities, and others whose possession of such weapons is similarly contrary to the public interest) is a significant factor in the prevalence of lawlessness and violent crime in the United States;

(3) that only through adequate Federal control over interstate and foreign commerce in these weapons, and over all persons engaging in the businesses of importing, manufacturing, or dealing in them, can this grave problem be properly dealt with, and effective State and local regulation of this traffic be made possible;

(4) that the acquisition on a mail-order basis of firearms other than a rifle or shotgun by nonlicensed individuals, from a place other than their State of residence, has materially tended to thwart the effectiveness of State laws and regulations, and local ordinances;

(5) that the sale or other disposition of concealable weapons by importers, manufacturers, and dealers holding Federal licenses, to nonresidents of the State in which the licensees' places of business are located, has tended to make ineffective the laws, regulations, and ordinances in the several States and local jurisdictions regarding such firearms;

(6) that there is a causal relationship between the easy availability of firearms other than a rifle or shotgun and juvenile and youthful criminal behavior, and that such firearms have been widely sold by federally licensed importers and dealers to emotionally immature, or thrill-bent juveniles and minors prone to criminal behavior;

(7) that the United States has become the dumping ground of the castoff surplus military weapons of other nations, and that such weapons, and the large volume of relatively inexpensive pistols and revolvers (largely worthless for sporting purposes), imported into the United States in recent years, has contributed greatly to lawlessness and to the Nation's law enforcement problems;

(8) that the lack of adequate Federal control over interstate and foreign commerce in highly destructive weapons (such as bazookas, mortars, antitank guns, and so forth, and destructive devices such as explosive or incendiary grenades, bombs, missiles, and so forth) has allowed such weapons and devices to fall into the hands of lawless persons, including armed groups who would supplant lawful authority, thus creating a problem of national concern. . . .

Chapter 44.—Firearms

"(a) As used in this chapter—

"(1) The term 'person' and the term 'whoever' includes any individual, corporation, company, association, firm, partnership, society, or joint stock company.

* * *

"(3) The term 'firearm' means any weapon (including a starter gun) which will or is designed to or may readily be converted to expel a projectile by the action of an explosive; the frame or receiver of any such weapon; or any firearm muffler or firearm silencer; or any destructive device.

"(4) The term 'destructive device' means any explosive, incendiary, or poison gas bomb, grenade, mine, rocket, missile, or similar device; and includes any type of weapon which will or is designed to or may readily be converted to expel a projectile by the action of any explosive and having any barrel with a bore of one-half inch or more in diameter.

"Section 922. Unlawful acts

"(a) It shall be unlawful—

"(1) for any person, except a licensed importer, licensed manufacturer, or licensed dealer, to engage in the business of importing, manufacturing, or dealing in firearms, or ammunition, or in the course of such business to ship, transport, or receive any firearm or ammunition in interstate or foreign commerce.

"(2) for any importer, manufacturer, or dealer licensed under the provisions of this chapter to ship or transport in interstate or foreign commerce, any firearm other than a rifle or shotgun, or ammunition to any person other than a licensed importer, licensed manufacturer, or licensed dealer. . . .

* * *

Title V—Disqualification for Engaging in Riots and Civil Disorders

"Section 7313. Riots and civil disorders

"(a) An individual convicted by any. . .competent jurisdiction of—

"(1) inciting a riot or civil disorder;

"(2) organizing, promoting, encouraging, or participating in a riot or civil disorder;

"(3) aiding or abetting any person in committing any offense specified in clause (1) or (2); or

"(4) any offense determined by the head of the employing agency to have been committed in furtherance of, or while participating in, a riot or civil disorder; shall, if the offense for which he is convicted is a felony, be ineligible to accept or hold any position in the Government of the United States or in the government of the District of

Columbia for the five years immediately following the date upon which his conviction becomes final. . . .

* * *

Title VI—Confirmation of the Director of the Federal Bureau of Investigation

Sec. 1101. Effective as of the day following the date on which the present incumbent in the office of Director ceases to serve as such, the Director of the Federal Bureau of Investigation shall be appointed by the President, by and with the advice and consent of the Senate, and shall receive compensation at the rate prescribed for level II of the Federal Executive Salary Schedule.

Title VII—Unlawful Possession or Receipt of Firearms

Sec. 1202. (a) Any person who—

(1) has been convicted by a court of the United States or of a State or any political subdivision thereof of a felony, or

(2) has been discharged from the Armed Forces under other than honorable conditions, or

(3) has been adjudged by a court of the United States or of a State or any political subdivision thereof of being mentally incompetent, or

(4) having been a citizen of the United States has renounced his citizenship, or

(5) being an alien is illegally or unlawfully in the United States. . . .

* * *

Title IX—Additional Grounds for Issuing Warrant

* * *

"Section 3103a. Additional grounds for issuing warrant

"In addition to the grounds for issuing a warrant in section 3103 of this title, a warrant may be issued to search for and seize any property that constitutes evidence of a criminal offense in violation of the laws of the United States."

* * *

Approved June 19, 1968, 7:14 p.m.

Source:
Statutes at Large, Vol. 82, pp 197–239.

Brandenburg v. Ohio, 1969

U.S. Supreme Court decision issued on June 9, 1969, protecting free speech unless such speech represented a clear threat of violence. It overturned an Ohio criminal syndicalism act under which the defendant had been convicted of leading a gathering of 12 hooded and armed figures who burned a cross and denounced blacks and Jews. The Supreme Court ruled that the constitutional guarantees of free speech and free press prevented a state from forbidding the advocacy of the use of force or of law violation "except where such advocacy is directed to inciting or producing imminent lawless action and is likely to incite or produce such action."

Argued Feb. 27, 1969.
Decided June 9, 1969.
Per Curiam.

The appellant, a leader of a Ku Klux Klan group, was convicted under the Ohio Criminal Syndicalism statute for "advocat[ing] . . . the duty, necessity, or propriety of crime, sabotage, violence, or unlawful methods of terrorism as a means of accomplishing industrial or political reform" and for "voluntarily assembl[ing] with any society, group, or assemblage of persons formed to teach or advocate the doctrines of criminal syndicalism." Ohio Rev. Code Ann. SectionSection 2923.13. He was fined $1,000 and sentenced to one to 10 years' imprisonment. The appellant challenged the constitutionality of the criminal syndicalism statute under the First and Fourteenth Amendments to the United States Constitution, but the intermediate appellate court of Ohio affirmed his conviction without opinion. The Supreme Court of Ohio dismissed his appeal, *sua sponte,* "for the reason that no substantial constitutional question exists herein." It did not file an opinion or explain its conclusions. Appeal was taken to this Court, and we noted probable jurisdiction. 393 U.S. 948, 89 S.Ct. 377, 21 L.Ed.2d 360 (1968). We reverse.

The record shows that a man, identified at trial as the appellant, telephoned an announcer-reporter on the staff of a Cincinnati television station and invited him to come to a Ku Klux Klan "rally" to be held at a farm in Hamilton County. With the cooperation of the organizers, the reporter and a cameraman attended the meeting and filmed the events. Portions of the films were later broadcast on the local station and on a national network.

The prosecution's case rested on the films and on testimony identifying the appellant as the person who communicated with the reporter and who spoke at the rally. The State also introduced into evidence several articles appearing in the film, including a pistol, a rifle, a shotgun, ammunition, a Bible, and a red hood worn by the speaker in the films.

One film showed 12 hooded figures, some of whom carried firearms. They were gathered around a large wooden cross, which they burned. No one was present other than the participants and the newsmen who made the film. Most of the words uttered during the scene were incomprehensible when the film was projected, but scattered phrases could be understood that were derogatory of Negroes and, in one instance, of Jews. Another scene on the same film showed the appellant, in Klan regalia, making a speech. The speech, in full, was as follows:

"This is an organizers' meeting. We have had quite a few members here today which are—we have hundreds, hundreds of members throughout the State of Ohio. I can quote from a newspaper clipping from the *Columbus, Ohio Dispatch*, five weeks ago Sunday morning. The Klan has more members in the State of Ohio than does any other organization. We're not a revengent organization, but if our President, our Congress, our Supreme Court, continues to suppress the white, Caucasian race, it's possible that there might have to be some revengeance taken.

"We are marching on Congress July the Fourth, four hundred thousand strong. From there we are dividing into two groups, one group to march on St. Augustine, Florida, the other group to march into Mississippi. Thank you."

The second film showed six hooded figures one of whom, later identified as the appellant, repeated a speech very similar to that recorded on the first film. The reference to the possibility of "revengeance" was omitted, and one sentence was added: "Personally, I believe the nigger should be returned to Africa, the Jew returned to Israel." Though some of the figures in the films carried weapons, the speaker did not.

[1] The Ohio Criminal Syndicalism Statute was enacted in 1919. From 1917 to 1920, identical or quite similar laws were adopted by 20 States and two territories. E. Dowell, A History of Criminal Syndicalism Legislation in the United States 21 (1939). In 1927, this Court sustained the constitutionality of California's Criminal Syndicalism Act. Cal. Penal Code SectionSection 11400-11402, the text of which is quite similar to that of the laws of Ohio. *Whitney v. California*, 274 U.S. 357, 47 S.Ct. 641, 71 L.Ed. 1095 (1927). The Court upheld the statute on the ground that, without more, "advocating" violent means to effect political and economic change involves such danger to the security of the State that the State may outlaw it. Cf. *Fiske v. Kansas*, 274 U.S. 380, 47 S.Ct. 655, 71 L.Ed. 1108 (1927). But *Whitney* has been thoroughly discredited by later decisions. See *Dennis v. United States*, 341 U.S. 494, at 507, 71 S.Ct. 857, at 866, 95 L.Ed. 1137 (1951). These later decisions have fashioned the principle that the constitutional guarantees of free speech and free press do not permit a State to forbid or proscribe advocacy of the use of force or of law violation except where such advocacy is directed to inciting or producing imminent lawless action and is likely to incite or produce such action. As we said in *Noto v. United States*, 367 U.S. 290, 297-298, 81 S.Ct. 1517, 1520-1521, 6 L.Ed.2d 836 (1961), "the mere abstract teaching . . . of the moral propriety or even moral necessity for a resort to force and violence, is not the same as preparing a group for violent action and steeling it to such action." See also *Herndon v. Lowry*, 301 U.S. 242, 259-261, 57 S.Ct. 732, 739- 740, 81 L.Ed. 1066 (1937); *Bond v. Floyd*, 385 U.S. 116, 134, 87 S.Ct. 339, 348, 17 L.Ed.2d 235 (1966). A statute which fails to draw this distinction impermissibly intrudes upon the freedoms guaranteed by the First and Fourteenth Amendments. It sweeps within its condemnation speech which our Constitution has immunized from governmental control. Cf. *Yates v. United States*, 354 U.S. 298, 77 S.Ct. 1064, 1 L.Ed.2d 1356 (1957); *De Jonge v. Oregon*, 299 U.S. 353, 57 S.Ct. 255, 81 L.Ed. 278 (1937); *Stromberg v. California*, 283 U.S. 359, 51 S.Ct. 532, 75 L.Ed. 1117 (1931). See also *United States v. Robel*, 389 U.S. 258, 88 S.Ct. 419, 19 L.Ed.2d 508 (1967); *Keyishian v. Board of Regents*, 385 U.S. 589, 87 S.Ct. 675, 17 L.Ed.2d 629 (1967); *Elfbrandt v. Russell*, 384 U.S. 11, 86 S.Ct. 1238, 16 L.Ed.2d 321 (1966); *Aptheker v. Secretary of State*, 378 U.S. 500, 84 S.Ct. 1659, 12 L.Ed.2d 992 (1964); *Baggett v. Bullitt*, 377 U.S. 360, 84 S.Ct. 1316, 12 L.Ed.2d 377 (1964).

[2, 3] Measured by this test, Ohio's Criminal Syndicalism Act cannot be sustained. The Act punishes persons who "advocate or teach the duty, necessity, or propriety" of violence "as a means of accomplishing industrial or political reform"; or who publish or circulate or display any book or paper containing such advocacy; or who "justify" the commission of violent acts "with intent to exemplify, spread or advocate the propriety of the doctrines of criminal syndicalism"; or who "voluntarily assemble" with a group formed "to teach or advocate the doctrines of criminal syndicalism." Neither the indictment nor the trial judge's instructions to the jury in any way refined the statute's bald definition of the crime in terms of mere advocacy not distinguished from incitement to imminent lawless action.

Accordingly, we are here confronted with a statute which, by its own words and as applied, purports to punish mere advocacy and to forbid, on pain of criminal punishment, assembly with others merely to advocate the described type of action. Such a statute falls within the condemnation of the First and Fourteenth Amendments. The contrary teaching of *Whitney v. California*, *supra*, cannot be supported, and that decision is therefore overruled.

Reversed.

Mr. Justice Black, concurring.

I agree with the views expressed by Mr. Justice Douglas in his concurring opinion in this case that the "clear and present danger" doctrine should have no place in the interpretation of the First Amendment. I join the Court's opinion, which, as I understand it, simply cites *Dennis v. United States*, 341 U.S. 494, 71 S.Ct. 857, 95 L.Ed. 1137 (1951), but does not indicate any agreement on the Court's part with the "clear and present danger" doctrine on which *Dennis* purported to rely.

Mr. Justice Douglas, concurring.

While I join the opinion of the Court, I desire to enter a *caveat.*

The "clear and present danger" test was adumbrated by Mr. Justice Holmes in a case arising during World War I—a war "declared" by the Congress, not by the Chief Executive. The case was *Schenck v. United States,* 249 U.S. 47, 52, 39 S.Ct. 247, 249, 63 L.Ed. 470, where the defendant was charged with attempts to cause insubordination in the military and obstruction of enlistment. The pamphlets that were distributed urged resistance to the draft, denounced conscription, and impugned the motives of those backing the war effort. The First Amendment was tendered as a defense. Mr. Justice Holmes in rejecting that defense said:

"The question in every case is whether the words used are used in such circumstances and are of such a nature as to create a clear and present danger that they will bring about the substantive evils that Congress has a right to prevent. It is a question of proximity and degree."

Frohwerk v. United States, 249 U.S. 204, 39 S.Ct. 249, 63 L.Ed. 561, also authored by Mr. Justice Holmes, involved prosecution and punishment for publication of articles very critical of the war effort in World War I. *Schenck* was referred to a conviction for obstructing security "by words of persuasion." *Id.,* at 206, 39 S.Ct. at 250. And the conviction in *Frohwerk* was sustained because "the circulation of the paper was in quarters where a little breath would be enough to kindle a flame." *Id.,* at 209, 39 S.Ct., at 251.

Debs v. United States, 249 U.S. 211, S.Ct. 252, 63 L.Ed. 566, was the third of the trilogy of the 1918 Term. Debs was convicted of speaking in opposition to the war where his "opposition was so expressed that its natural and intended effect would be to obstruct recruiting." *Id.,* at 215, 39 S.Ct. at 253.

"If that was intended and if, in all the circumstances, that would be its probable effect, it would not be protected by reason of its being part of a general program in expressions of a general and conscientious belief." *Ibid.*

In the 1919 Term, the Court applied the *Schenck* doctrine to affirm the convictions of other dissidents in World War I. *Abrams v. United States,* 250 U.S. 616, 40 S.Ct. 17, 63 L.Ed. 1173, was one instance. Mr. Justice Holmes, with whom Mr. Justice Brandeis concurred, dissented. While adhering to *Schenck,* he did not think that on the facts a case for overriding the First Amendment had been made out:

"It is only the present danger of immediate evil or an intent to bring it about that warrants Congress in setting a limit to the expression of opinion where private rights are not concerned. Congress certainly cannot forbid all effort to change the mind of the country." 250 U.S., at 628, 40 S.Ct., at 21.

Another instance was *Schaefer v. United States,* 251 U.S. 466, 40 S.Ct. 259, 64 L.Ed. 360, in which Mr. Justice Brandeis, joined by Mr. Justice Holmes, dissented. A third was *Pierce v. United States,* 252 U.S. 239, 40 S.Ct. 205, 64 L.Ed. 542, in which again Mr. Justice Brandeis, joined by Mr. Justice Holmes, dissented.

Those, then, were the World War I cases that put the gloss of "clear and present danger" on the First Amendment. Whether the war power—the greatest leveler of them all—is adequate to sustain that doctrine is debatable. The dissents in *Abrams, Schaefer,* and *Pierce* show how easily "clear and present danger" is manipulated to crush what Brandeis called "[t]he fundamental right of free men to strive for better conditions through new legislation and new institutions" by argument and discourse (*Pierce v. United States, supra,* at 273, 40 S.Ct. at 217) even in time of war. Though I doubt if the "clear and present danger" test is congenial to the First Amendment in time of a declared war, I am certain it is not reconcilable with the First Amendment in days of peace.

The Court quite properly overrules *Whitney v. California,* 274 U.S. 357, 47 S.Ct. 641, 71 L.Ed. 1095, which involved advocacy of ideas which the majority of the Court deemed unsound and dangerous.

Mr. Justice Holmes, though never formally abandoning the "clear and present danger" test, moved closer to the First Amendment ideal when he said in dissent in *Gitlow* [*Gitlow v. People of State of New York,* 268 U.S. 652, 45 S.Ct. 626, 69 L.Ed. 1138]:

"Every idea is an incitement. It offers itself for belief and it believed it is acted on unless some other belief outweighs it or some failure of energy stifles the movement at its birth. The only difference between the expression of an opinion and an incitement in the narrower sense is the speaker's enthusiasm for the result. Eloquence may set fire to reason. But whatever may be thought to the redundant discourse before us it had no chance of starting a present conflagration. If in the long run the beliefs expressed in proletarian dictatorship are destined to be accepted by the dominant forces of the community, the only meaning of free speech is that they should be given their chance and have their way."

We have never been faithful to the philosophy of that dissent.

The Court in *Herndon v. Lowry,* 301 U.S. 242, 57 S.Ct. 732, 81 L.Ed. 1066, overturned a conviction for exercising First Amendment rights to incite insurrection because of lack of evidence of incitement. *Id.,* at 259-261, 57 S.Ct., at 739-740. And see *Hartzel v. United States,* 322 U.S. 680, 64 S.Ct. 1233, 88 L.Ed. 1534. In Bridges v. California, 314, U.S. 252, 261-263, 62 S.Ct. 190, 192- 194, 86 L.Ed. 192, we approved the "clear and present danger" test in an elaborate dictum that tightened it and confined it to a narrow category. But in *Dennis v. United States,* 341 U.S. 494, 71 S.Ct. 857, 95 L.Ed. 1137, we opened wide the door, distorting the "clear and present danger" test beyond recognition.

In that case the prosecution dubbed an agreement to teach the Marxist creed a "conspiracy." The case was submitted to a jury on a charge that the jury could not convict unless it found that the defendants "intended to overthrow the Government as speedily as circumstances would permit."' *Id.,* at 509-511, 71 S.Ct., at 867. The Court sustained convictions under that charge, construing it to mean a determination of "whether the gravity of the "evil," discounted by its improbability, justifies such invasion of free speech as is necessary to avoid the danger."' *Id.,* at 510, 71 S.Ct., at 868, quoting from *United States v. Dennis,* 183 F.2d 201, 212.

Out of the "clear and present danger" test came other offspring. Advocacy and teaching of forcible overthrow of government as an abstract principle is immune from prosecution. *Yates v. United States,* 354 U.S. 298, 318, 77 S.Ct. 1064, 1076, 1 L.Ed.2d 1356. But an "active" member, who has a guilty knowledge and intent of the aim to overthrow the Government by violence, *Noto v. United States,* 367 U.S. 290, 81 S.Ct. 1517, 6 L.Ed.2d 836, may be prosecuted. *Scales v. United States,* 367 U.S. 203, 228, 81 S.Ct. 1469, 1485, 6 L.Ed.2d 782. And the power to investigate, backed by the powerful sanction of contempt, includes the power to determine which of the two categories fits the particular witness. *Barenblatt v. United States,* 360 U.S. 109, 130, 79 S.Ct. 1081, 1094, 3 L.Ed.2d 1115. And so the investigator roams at will through all of the beliefs of the witness, ransacking his conscience and his innermost thoughts.

Judge Learned Hand, who wrote for the Court of Appeals in affirming the judgment in *Dennis,* coined the "not improbable" test, *United States v. Dennis,* 2 Cir., 183 F.2d 201, 214, which this Court adopted and which Judge Hand preferred over the "clear and present danger" test. Indeed, in his book, *The Bill of Rights* 59 (1958), in referring to Holmes' creation of the "clear and present danger" test, he said, "I cannot help thinking that for once Homer nodded."

My own view is quite different. I see no place in the regime of the First Amendment for any "clear and present danger" test, whether strict and tight as some would make it, or free- wheeling as the Court in *Dennis* rephrased it.

When one reads the opinions closely and sees when and how the "clear and present danger" test has been applied, great misgivings are aroused. First, the threats were often loud but always puny and made serious only by judges so wedded to the *status quo* that critical analysis made them nervous. Second, the test was so twisted and perverted in *Dennis* as to make the trial of those teachers of Marxism an all-out political trial which was part and parcel of the cold war that has eroded substantial parts of the First Amendment.

Action is often a method of expression and within the protection of the First Amendment.

Suppose one tears up his own copy of the Constitution in eloquent protest to a decision of this Court. May he be indicted?

Suppose one rips his own Bible to shreds to celebrate his departure from one "faith" and his embrace of atheism. May he be indicted?

Last Term the Court held in *United States v. O'Brien,* 391 U.S. 367, 382, 88 S.Ct. 1673, 1682, 20 L.Ed.2d 672, that a registrant under Selective Service who burned his draft card in protest of the war in Vietnam could be prosecuted. The First Amendment was tendered as a defense and rejected, the Court saying:

"The issuance of certificates indicating the registration and eligibility classification of individuals is a legitimate and substantial administrative aid in the functioning of this system. And legislation to insure the continuing availability of issued certificates serves a legitimate and substantial purpose in the system's administration." 391 U.S., at 377-378, 88 S.Ct. at 1679.

But O'Brien was not prosecuted for not having his draft card available when asked for by a federal agent. He was indicted, tried and convicted for burning the card. And this Court's affirmance of that conviction was not, with all respect, consistent with the First Amendment.

The act of praying often involves body posture and movement as well as utterances. It is nonetheless protected by the Free Exercise Clause. Picketing, as we have said on numerous occasions, as "free speech plus." See *Bakery and Pastry Drivers and Helpers Local 802 of International Brotherhood of Teamsters v. Wohl,* 315 U.S. 769, 775, 62 S.Ct. 816, 819, 86 L.Ed. 1178 (Douglas, J., concurring); *Giboney v. Empire Storage Co.,* 336 U.S. 490, 501, 69 S.Ct. 684, 690, 93 L.Ed. 834; *Hughes v. Superior Court,* 339 U.S. 460, 465, 70 S.Ct. 718, 721, 94 L.Ed. 985; National Labor Relations Board v. Fruit and Vegetable *Packers,* 377 U.S. 58, 77, 84 S.Ct. 1063, 1073, 12 L.Ed.2d 129 (Black, J., concurring), and *id.,* at 93, 84 S.Ct. at 1081 (Harlan, J., dissenting); *Cox v. Louisiana,* 379 U.S. 559, 578, 85 S.Ct. 466, 468, 476, 13 L.Ed.2d 487 (opinion of Black, J.); *Amalgamated Food Employees v. Logan Plaza,* 391 U.S. 308, 326, 88 S.Ct. 1601, 1612, 29 L.Ed.2d 603 (Douglas, J., concurring). That means that it can be regulated when it comes to the "plus" or "action" side of the protest. It can be regulated as to the number of pickets and the place and hours (see *Cox v. Louisiana, supra*), because traffic and other community problems would otherwise suffer.

But none of these considerations are implicated in the symbolic protest of the Vietnam war in the burning of a draft card.

One's beliefs have long been thought to be sanctuaries which government could not invade. *Barenblatt* is one example of the ease with which that sanctuary can be violated. The lines drawn by the Court between the criminal act of being an "active" Communist and the innocent act of being a nominal or inactive Communist mark the difference only between deep and abiding belief and casual or uncertain belief. But I think that all matters of belief are beyond the reach of subpoenas or the probings of investigators. That is why the invasions of privacy made by investigating committees were notoriously unconstitutional. That is the deep-seated fault in the infamous loyalty-security hearings which, since 1947 when President Truman launched them, have processed 20,000,000 men and women. Those hearings were primarily concerned with one's thoughts, ideas, beliefs, and convictions. They were the most blatant violations of the First Amendment we have ever known.

The line between what is permissible and not subject to control and what may be made impermissible and subject to regulation is the line between ideas and overt acts.

The example usually given by those who would punish speech is the case of one who falsely shouts fire in a crowded theatre.

This is, however, a classic case where speech is brigaded with action. See *Speiser v. Randall,* 357 U.S. 513, 536-537, 78 S.Ct. 1332, 1346, 2 L.Ed.2d 1460 (Douglas, J., concurring.) They are indeed inseparable and a prosecution can be launched for the overt acts actually caused. Apart from rare instances of that kind, speech is, I think, immune from prosecution. Certainly there is no constitutional line between advocacy of abstract ideas as in *Yates* and advocacy of political action as in *Scales.* The quality of advocacy turns on the depth of the conviction; and government has no power to invade that sanctuary of belief and conscience.

Source:
Supreme Court Reporter, Vol. 89, pp. 1,827–1,834.

Furman v. Georgia, 1972

U.S. Supreme Court per curium decision issued on June 29, 1972, in which the death penalty as administered in three cases was held 5-4, with nine separate concurring and dissenting opinions, to constitute "cruel and unusual punishment" in violation of the Eighth and Fourteenth Amendments. (Only Justices William Brennan and Thurgood Marshall declared the death penalty per se unconstitutional.) The decision overturned the death sentences of three black petitioners from Georgia and Texas who had been convicted of capital crimes (murder and rape). Both states allowed juries at their discretion but without any specific guides or limits to impose the death penalty. *Furman* halted all executions in the 39 states with death penalties involving more than 600 prisoners. In *Gregg v. Georgia* (428 U.S. 153 [1976]) the Court permitted jury discretion if guidelines were provided. Inconsistencies remain, and the death penalty continues to be served against minority criminals more than whites, but the Court has allowed it to stand.

After DNA testing became widely available, in the late 1990s, a number of death row and life sentence subjects have been found to be innocent of the crimes of which they were convicted.

On June 21, 2002, the Supreme Court in *Atkins v. Virginia* (536 U.S. 304), citing a national consensus, decided that executing mentally retarded criminals violated the Eighth Amendment against cruel and unusual punishment. Thirteen years earlier, in *Penry v. Lynaugh* (492 U.S. 302), the Court held differently because a national consensus was not evident at that time. Four days after *Adkins,* the Supreme Court ruled 7-2 in *Ring v. Arizona* (No. 01-488) that juries, not judges, must determine whether a convicted murderer is subject to the death penalty.

Justices Douglas, Brennan, Stewart, White, and Marshall filed separate opinions in support of the judgments; Chief Justice Burger, Blackmun, Powell, and Rehnquist filed separate dissenting opinions. Only the per curiam and Justice Douglas's opinion are reproduced here.

Per Curiam.

Petitioner in No. 69-5003 was convicted of murder in Georgia and was sentenced to death. . . . Petitioner in No. 69-5030 was convicted of rape in Georgia and was sentenced to death. . . . Petitioner in Nos. 69-5031 was convicted of rape in Texas and was sentenced to death. . . . Certiorari was granted limited to the following question: "Does the imposition and carrying out of the death penalty in [these cases] constitute cruel and unusual punishment in violation of the Eighth and Fourteenth Amendments?" . . .The Court holds that the imposition and carrying out of the death penalty in these cases constitute cruel and unusual punishment in violation of the Eighth and Fourteenth Amendments. The judgment in each case is therefore reversed insofar as it leaves undisturbed the death sentence imposed, and the cases are remanded for further proceedings. So ordered.

Mr. Justice Douglas, concurring.

In these three cases the death penalty was imposed, one of them for murder, and two for rape. In each the determination of whether the penalty should be death or a lighter punishment was left by the State to the discretion of the judge or of the jury. In each of the three cases the trial was to a jury. They are here on petitions for certiorari which we granted limited to the question whether the imposition and execution of the death penalty constitute "cruel and unusual punishment" within the meaning of the Eighth Amendment as applied to the States by the Fourteenth. I vote to vacate each judgment, believing that the exaction of the death penalty does violate the Eighth and Fourteenth Amendments.

That the requirements of due process ban cruel and unusual punishment is now settled. . . . It is also settled that the proscription of cruel and unusual punishments forbids the judicial imposition of them as well as their imposition by the legislature

Congressman Bingham, in proposing the Fourteenth Amendment, maintained that "the privileges or immunities of citizens of the United States" as protected by the Fourteenth Amendment included protection against "cruel and unusual punishments:"

* * *

Whether the privileges and immunities route is followed, or the due process route, the result is the same.

It has been assumed in our decisions that punishment by death is not cruel, unless the manner of execution can be said to be inhuman and barbarous. . . . It is also said in our opinions that the proscription of cruel and unusual punishments "is not fastened to the obsolete, but may acquire meaning as public opinion becomes enlightened by a humane justice." . . . A like statement was made in Trop v. Dulles. . .that the Eighth Amendment "must draw its meaning from the evolving standards of decency that mark the progress of a maturing society."

The generality of a law inflicting capital punishment is one thing. What may be said of the validity of a law on the books and what may be done with the law in its application do, or may, lead to quite different conclusions.

It would seem to be incontestable that the death penalty inflicted on one defendant is "unusual" if it discriminates against him by reason of his race, religion, wealth, social position, or class, or if it is imposed under a procedure that gives room for the play of such prejudices.

There is evidence that the provision of the English Bill of Rights of 1689, from which the language of the Eighth Amendment was taken, was concerned primarily with selective or irregular application of harsh penalties and that its aim was to forbid arbitrary and discriminatory penalties of a severe nature:

* * *

The English Bill of Rights, enacted December 16, 1689, stated that "excessive bail ought not to be required, nor excessive fines imposed, nor cruel and unusual punishments inflicted." These were the words chosen for our Eighth Amendment. A like provision had been in Virginia's Constitution of 1776 and in the constitutions of seven other States. The Northwest Ordinance, enacted under the Articles of Confederation, included a prohibition cruel and unusual punishments. But the debates of the First Congress on the Bill of Rights throw little light on its intended meaning. All that appears is the following:

"Mr. Smith, of South Carolina, objected to the words 'nor cruel and unusual punishments;' the import of them being too indefinite.

"Mr. Livermore: The clause seems to express a great deal of humanity, on which account I have no objection to it; but as it seems to have no meaning in it, I do not think it necessary. What is meant by the terms excessive bail? Who are to be the judges? What is understood by excessive fines? It lies with the court to determine. No cruel and unusual punishment is to be inflicted; it is sometimes necessary to hang a man, villains often deserve whipping, and perhaps having their ears cut off; but are we in future to be prevented from inflicting these punishments because they are cruel? If a more lenient mode of correcting vice and deterring others from the commission of it could be invented, it would be very prudent in the Legislature to adopt it; but until we have some security that this will be done, we ought not to be restrained from making necessary laws by any declaration of this kind."

The words "cruel and unusual" certainly include penalties that are barbaric. But the words, at least when read in light of the English proscription against selective and irregular use of penalties, suggest that it is "cruel and unusual" to apply the death penalty—or any other penalty—selectively to minorities whose numbers are few, who are outcasts of society, and who are unpopular, but whom society is willing to see suffer though it would not countenance general application of the same penalty across the board. . . .

The Court in *McGautha v. California* . . . noted that in this country there was almost from the beginning a "rebellion against the common-law rule imposing a mandatory death sentence on all convicted murderers." The first attempted remedy was to restrict the death penalty to defined offenses such as "premeditated" murder. . . . But juries "took the law into their own hands" and refused to convict on the capital offense.

"In order to meet the problem of jury nullification, legislatures did not try, as before, to refine further the definition of capital homicides. Instead they adopted the method of forthrightly granting juries the discretion which they had been exercising in fact."

The Court concluded: "In light of history, experience, and the present limitations of human knowledge, we find it quite impossible to say that committing to the untrammeled discretion of the jury the power to pronounce life or death in capital cases is offensive to anything in the Constitution." . . .

The Court refused to find constitutional dimensions in the argument that those who exercise their discretion to send a person to death should be given standards by which that discretion should be exercised. . . .

But those who advance that argument overlook *McGautha,* supra.

We are now imprisoned in the *McGautha* holding. Indeed the seeds of the present cases are in *McGautha* Juries (or judges, as the case may be) have practically untrammeled discretion to let an accused live or insist that he die.

* * *

There is increasing recognition of the fact that the basic theme of equal protection is implicit in "cruel and unusual" punishments. "A penalty . . .*should be considered 'unusually' imposed if it is administered arbitrarily or discriminatorily." The same authors add that "[t]he extreme rarity with which applicable death penalty provisions are put to use raises a strong inference of arbitrariness," The President's Commission on Law Enforcement and Administration of Justice recently concluded:

"Finally there is evidence that the imposition of the death sentence and the exercise of dispensing power by the courts and the executive follow discriminatory patterns. The death sentence is disproportionately imposed and carried out on the poor, the Negro, and the members of unpopular groups."

A study of capital cases in Texas from 1924 to 1968 reached the following conclusions:

"Application of the death penalty is unequal: most of those executed were poor, young, and ignorant.

"Seventy-five of the 460 cases involved codefendants, who, under Texas law, were given separate trials. In several instances where a white and a Negro were co-defendants, the white was sentenced to life imprisonment or a term of years, and the Negro was given the death penalty.

"Another ethnic disparity is found in the type of sentence imposed for rape. The Negro convicted of rape is far more likely to get the death penalty than a term sentence, whereas whites and Latins are far more likely to get a term sentence than the death penalty."

Warden Lewis E. Lawes of Sing Sing said:

"Not only does capital punishment fail in its justification, but no punishment could be invented with so many inherent defects. It is an unequal punishment in the way it is applied to the rich and to the poor. The defendant of wealth and position never goes to the electric chair or to the gallows. Juries do not intentionally favor the rich, the law is theoretically impartial, but the defendant with ample means is able to have his case presented with every favorable aspect, while the poor defendant often has a lawyer assigned by the court. Sometimes such assignment is considered part of political patronage; usually the lawyer assigned has had no experience whatever in a capital case."

Former Attorney General Ramsey Clark has said, "It is the poor, the sick, the ignorant, the powerless and the hated who are executed." One searches our chronicles in vain for the execution of any member of the affluent strata of this society. The Leopolds and Loebs are given prison terms, not sentenced to death.

Jackson, a black, convicted of the rape of a white woman, was 21 years old. A court-appointed psychiatrist said that Jackson was of average education and average intelligence, that he was not an imbecile, or schizophrenic, or psychotic, that his traits were the product of environmental influences, and that he was competent to stand trial. Jackson had entered the house after the husband left for work. He held scissors against the neck of the wife, demanding money. She could find none and a struggle ensued for the scissors, a battle which she lost; and she was then raped, Jackson keeping the scissors pressed against her neck. While there did not appear to be any long-term traumatic impact on the victim, she was bruised and abrased in the struggle but was not hospitalized. Jackson was a convict who had escaped from a work gang in the area, a result of a three-year sentence for auto theft. He was at large for three days and during that time had committed several other offenses—burglary, auto theft, and assault and battery.

Furman, a black, killed a householder while seeking to enter the home at night. Furman shot the deceased through a closed door. He was 26 years old and had finished the sixth grade in school. Pending trial, he was committed to the Georgia Central State Hospital for a psychiatric examination on his plea of insanity tendered by court-appointed counsel. The superintendent reported that a unanimous staff diagnostic conference had concluded "that this patient should retain his present diagnosis of Mental Deficiency, Mild to Moderate, with Psychotic Episodes associated with Convulsive Disorder." The physicians agreed that "at present the patient is not psychotic, but he is not capable of cooperating with his counsel in the preparation of his defense"; and the staff believed "that he is in need of further psychiatric hospitalization and treatment."

Later, the superintendent reported that the staff diagnosis was Mental Deficiency, Mild to Moderate, with Psychotic, Episodes associated with Convulsive Disorder. He concluded, however, that Furman was "not psychotic at present, knows right from wrong and is able to cooperate with his counsel in preparing his defense."

Branch, a black, entered the rural home of a 65-year-old widow, a white, while she slept and raped her, holding his arm against her throat. Thereupon he demanded money and for 30 minutes or more the widow searched for money, finding little. As he left, Jackson said if the widow told anyone what happened, he would return and kill her. The record is barren of any medical or psychiatric evidence showing injury to her as a result of Branch's attack.

He had previously been convicted of felony theft and found to be a borderline mental deficient and well below the average IQ of Texas prison inmates. He had the equivalent of five and a half years of grade school education. He had a "dull intelligence" and was in the lowest fourth percentile of his class.

We cannot say from facts disclosed in these records that these defendants were sentenced to death because they were black. Yet our task in not restricted to an effort to divine what motives impelled these death penalties. Rather, we deal with a system of law and of justice that leaves to the uncontrolled discretion of judges or juries the determination whether defendants committing these crimes should die or be imprisoned. Under these laws no standards govern the selection of the penalty. People live or die, dependent on the whim of on man or of 12.

* * *

Those who wrote the Eighth Amendment knew what price their forebears had paid for a system based, not on equal justice, but on discrimination. In those days the target was not the blacks or the poor, but the dissenters, those who opposed absolutism in government, who struggled for a parliamentary regime, and who opposed governments' recurring efforts to foist a particular religion on the people. . . . But the tool of capital punishment was used with vengeance against the opposition and those unpopular with the regime. One cannot read this history without realizing that the desire for equality was reflected in the ban against "cruel and unusual punishments" contained in the Eighth Amendment.

In a Nation committed to equal protection of the laws there is no permissible "caste" aspect of law enforcement. Yet we know that the discretion of judges and juries in imposing the death penalty enables the penalty to be selectively applied, feeding prejudices against the accused if he is poor and despised, and lacking political clout, or if he is a member of a suspect or unpopular minority, and saving those who by social position may be in a more protected position. In ancient Hindu law a Brahman was exempt from capital punishment, and under that law, "[g]enerally, in the law books, punishment increased in severity as social status diminished." We have, I fear, taken in practice the same position, partially as a result of making the death penalty discretionary and partially as a result of the ability of the rich to purchase the services of the most respected and most resourceful legal talent in the Nation.

The high service rendered by the "cruel and unusual" punishment clause of the Eighth Amendment is to require legislatures to write penal laws that are evenhanded, nonselective, and nonarbitrary, and to require judges to see to it that general laws are not applied sparsely, selectively, and spottily to unpopular groups.

A law that stated that anyone making more than $50,000 would be exempt from the death penalty would plainly fall, as would a law that in terms said that blacks, those who never went beyond the fifth grade in school, those who made less than $3,000 a year, or those who were unpopular or unstable should be the only people executed. A law which in the overall view reaches that result in practice has no more sanctity than a law which in terms provides the same.

Thus, these discretionary statutes are unconstitutional in their operation. They are pregnant with discrimination and discrimination is an ingredient not compatible with the idea of equal protection of the laws that is implicit in the ban on "cruel and unusual" punishments.

Any law which is nondiscriminatory on its face may be applied in such a way as to violate the Equal Protection Clause of the Fourteenth Amendment. *Yick Wo v. Hopkins*, 118 U.S. 356, 6 S.Ct. 1064, 30 L.Ed. 220. Such conceivably might be the fate of a mandatory death penalty, where equal or lesser sentences were imposed on the elite, a harsher one on the minorities or members of the lower castes. Whether a mandatory death penalty would otherwise by constitutional is a question I do not reach.

I concur in the judgments of the Court.

Source:

Supreme Court Reporter, Vol. 92, pp. 2,726–2,736.

Shirley Chisholm, Speech on the Equal Rights Amendment (ERA), 1972

Speech about the Equal Rights Amendment (ERA) to the Constitution given by Representative Shirley Chisholm (D, N.Y.), the first African-American woman elected to Congress and the first to be nominated for U.S. president by a major political party. The amendment, initially proposed in 1923, would have prohibited discrimination on the basis of gender. Addressing the Speaker of the House in 1970, Chisholm strongly advocated the amendment's passage. She cited federal agencies and institutions designed to prevent gender discrimination, pronouncing them ineffective without "the authority of a constitutional amendment."

The original ERA was proposed by suffragist and feminist Alice Paul of the National Woman's Party on the 75th anniversary of the Seneca Falls Convention. It simply stated that "Men and women shall have equal rights throughout the United States and every place subject to its jurisdiction." The amendment was introduced in Congress in 1923 but failed to pass. While some women's groups favored it, many opposed it on the grounds that it would outlaw special legislation that protected women by keeping them from night-shift hours and dangerous working conditions. However, the Fair Labor Standards Act, enacted in 1938, granted many protections previously applied only to women—such as a minimum wage and a limitation on the number of hours required to be worked—to men. Women's organizations remained divided on the issue into the 1970s. From 1940 to 1960, both the Democratic and Republican parties included an endorsement of the ERA in their party platforms. However, until 1972 it was unable to gain enough support to get out of committee. In that year, enough signatures were collected to bring the ERA to the House floor under a discharge petition, and the ERA was passed by Congress.

It read:

> SEC. 1. Equality of rights under the law shall not be denied or abridged by the United States or any State on account of sex.
>
> SEC. 2. The Congress shall have the power to enforce, by appropriate legislation, the provisions of this article.
>
> SEC. 3. This amendment shall take effect two years after the date of ratification.

The brevity of the amendment is significant because its opponents implied that it made mandatory such "horrors"as unisex bathrooms and putting women into combat. Before the end of 1973, 30 of the required 38 states ratified the amendment. However, the preamble to the law required its ratification within seven years from the date of its submission by the Congress. Soon a well-organized and effective antifeminist opposition developed that claimed, in addition to specific "horrors," that granting equal rights to women would destroy American families. Although Congress extended the deadline for ratification for three years, to June 30, 1982, it remained three states short of ratification on the day of its demise. Since 1985, the Equal Rights Amendment has been reintroduced during each session of Congress and held in committee.

Both before and after the ERA left Congress, legislation has attempted to prevent discrimination against at least some women. For example, President John F. Kennedy signed the Equal Pay Act June 10, 1963, requiring equal pay for women, but applying it only to companies engaged in interstate business that employed more than 25 workers. It also barred labor unions from forcing employers to discriminate in wages on the basis of sex. A provision to prohibit firms from lowering the wages of men in order to equalize wages was eliminated before final passage. The failure of this provision, as well as various affirmative measures helping women overcome past discrimination, enabled employers to blame any policy that appeared to hurt men collectively or individually on equal rights for women. This perception fed a backlash that helped defeat the Equal Rights Amendment and that has continued into the 21st century. For example, universities have used the excuse of equalizing men's and women's sports as a way of eliminating the cost of men's sports that do not produce revenue, such as gymnastics or wrestling. (Court decisions have favored parity even where far fewer women than men pursue varsity athletics.)

Beginning in the mid-1960s, the National Organization for Women (NOW), not only advocated overturning legislation but instituted a cultural change that would bring them not only legal but social, political, and economic equality with men. NOW's statement of purpose, proclaimed at its founding convention October 29, 1966, declared that its members would seek to end discrimination against women wherever it occurred as well as eliminate outdated stereotypes of women. The statement asserted that NOW would not align itself with any political party but would seek to ensure that only those politicians and officials who supported full equality for women would be elected or appointed to public office. Building on the black Civil Rights movement, as well as the tactics of the suffragists of the early 20th century, NOW used demonstrations, parades, and civil disobedience to promote its cause.

By the late 1960s and early 1970s more radical groups developed that considered NOW too "establishment." Loosely organized, they advocated Marxist principles and some promoted lesbianism. Although they occupied the fringes of the women's movement, they appeared to confirm the stereotypes with which antifeminists tainted ERA promoters, leading to negative connotations to *feminist* and helping bring down the Equal Rights Amendment.

As late as 1974, lending institutions continued to discriminate against single women and to insist that husbands must sign or cosign loans to married women. The Equal Credit Opportunity Act sought to rectify this by outlawing credit discrimination due to sex or martial status.

Mr. Speaker, House Joint Resolution 264, before us today, which provides for equality under the law for both men and women, represents one of the most clear-cut opportunities we are likely to have to declare our faith in the principles that shaped our Constitution. It provides a legal basis for attack on the most subtle, most pervasive and most institutionalized form of prejudice that exists. Discrimination against women, solely on the basis of their sex, is so widespread that it seems to many persons normal, natural and right. Legal expression of prejudice on the grounds of religious or political belief has become a minor problem in our society. Prejudice on the basis of race is, at least, under systematic attack. There is reason for optimism that it will start to die with the present older generation. It is time we act to assure full equality of opportunity to those citizens who, although in a majority, suffer the restrictions that are commonly imposed on minorities, to women.

The argument that this amendment will not solve the problem of sex discrimination is not relevant. If the argument were used against a civil rights bill—as it has been used in the past—the prejudice that lies behind it would be embarrassing. Of course laws will not eliminate prejudice from the hearts of human beings. But that is no reason to allow prejudice to continue to be enshrined in our laws—to perpetuate injustice through inaction.

The amendment is necessary to clarify countless ambiguities and inconsistencies in our legal system. For instance, the Constitution guarantees due process of law, in the Fifth and Fourteenth amendments. But the applicability of due process of sex distinctions is not clear: Women are excluded from some state colleges and universities. In some states, restrictions are placed on a married woman who engages in an independent business. Women may not be chosen for some juries. Women even receive heavier criminal penalties than men who commit the same crime.

What would the legal effects of the equal rights amendment really be? The equal rights amendment would govern only the relationship between the State and its citizens—not relationships between private citizens.

The amendment would be largely self-executing, that is, any Federal or State laws in conflict would be ineffective one year after date of ratification without further action by the Congress or State legislatures.

Opponents of the amendment claim its ratification would throw the law into a state of confusion and would result in much litigation to establish its meaning. This objection overlooks the influence of legislative history in determining intent and the recent activities of many groups preparing for legislative changes in this direction.

State labor laws applying only to women, such as those limiting hours of work and weights to be lifted would become inoperative unless the legislature amended them to apply to men. As of early 1970 most States would have some laws that would be affected. However, changes are being made so rapidly as a result of Title VII of the Civil Rights Act of 1964, it is likely that by the time the equal rights amendment would become effective, no conflicting State laws would remain.

In any event, there has for years been great controversy as to the usefulness to women of these State labor laws. There has never been any doubt that they worked a hardship on women who need or want to work overtime and on women who need or want better paying jobs, and there has been no persuasive evidence as to how many women benefit from the archaic policy of the laws. After the Delaware hours law was repealed in 1966, there were no complaints from women to any of the State agencies that might have been approached.

Jury service laws not making women equally liable for jury service would have to be revised.

The selective service law would have to include women, but women would not be required to serve in the Armed Forces where they are not fitted any more than men are required to serve. Military service, while a great responsibility, is not without benefits, particularly for young men with limited education or training. Since October 1966, 246,000 young men who did not meet the normal mental or physical requirements have been given opportunities for training and correcting physical problems. This opportunity is not open to their sisters. Only girls who have completed high school and meet high standards on the educational test can volunteer. Ratification of the amendment would not permit application of higher standards to women.

Survivorship benefits would be available to husbands of female workers on the same basis as to wives of male workers. The Social Security Act and the civil service and military service retirement acts are in conflict.

Public schools and universities could not be limited to one sex and could not apply different admission standards to men and women. Laws requiring longer prison sentences for women than men would be invalid, and equal opportunities for rehabilitation and vocational training would have to be provided in public correctional institutions.

Different ages of majority based on sex would have to be harmonized.

Federal, State, and other governmental bodies would be obligated to follow nondiscriminatory practices in all aspects of employment, including public school teachers and State university and college faculties.

What would be the economic effects of the equal rights amendment? Direct economic effects would be minor. If any labor laws applying only to women still remained, their amendment or appeal would provide opportunity for women in better-paying jobs in manufacturing. More opportunities in public vocational and graduate schools for women would also tend to open up opportunities in better jobs for women.

Indirect effects could be much greater. The focusing of public attention on the gross legal, economic, and social discrimination against women by hearings and debates in the Federal and State legislatures would result in changes in attitude of parents, educators, and employers that would bring about substantial economic changes in the long run.

Sex prejudice cuts both ways. Men are oppressed by the requirements of the Selective Service Act, by enforced legal guardianship of minors, and by alimony laws. Each sex, I believe, should be liable when necessary to serve and defend this country.

Each has a responsibility for the support of children.

There are objections raised to wiping out laws protecting women workers. No one would condone exploitation. But what does sex have to do with it? Working conditions and hours that are harmful to women are harmful to men; wages that are unfair for women are unfair for men. Laws setting employment limitations on the basis of sex are irrational, and the proof of this is their inconsistency from State to State. The physical characteristics of men and women are not fixed, but cover two wide spans that have a great deal of overlap. It is obvious, I think, that a robust woman could be more fit for physical labor than a weak man. The choice of occupation would be determined by individual capabilities, and the rewards for equal work should be equal.

This is what it comes down to: artificial distinctions between persons must be wiped out of the law. Legal discrimination between the sexes is, in almost every instance, founded on outmoded views of society and the prescientific beliefs about psychology and physiology. It is time to sweep away these relics of the past and set future generations free of them.

Federal agencies and institutions responsible for the enforcement of equal opportunity laws need the authority of a Constitutional amendment. The 1964 Civil Rights Act and the 1963 Equal Pay Act are not enough; they are limited in their coverage—for instance, one excludes teachers, and the other leaves out administrative and professional women. The Equal Employment Opportunity Commission has not proven to be an adequate device, with its powers limited to investigation, conciliation and recommendation to the Justice Department. In its cases involving sexual discrimination, it has failed in more than one-half. The Justice Department has been even less effective. It has intervened in only one case involving discrimination on the basis of sex, and this was on a procedural point. In a second case, in which both sexual and racial discrimination were alleged, the racial bias charge was given far greater weight.

Evidence of discrimination on the basis of sex should hardly have to be cited here. It is in the Labor Department's employment and salary figures for anyone who is still in doubt. Its elimination will involve so many changes in our State and Federal laws that, without the authority and impetus of this proposed amendment, it will perhaps take another 194 years. We cannot be parties to continuing a delay. The time is clearly now to put this House on record for the fullest expression of that equality of opportunity which our founding fathers professed.

They professed it, but they did not assure it to their daughters, as they tried to do for their sons.

The Constitution they wrote was designed to protect the rights of white, male citizens. As there were no black Founding Fathers, there were no founding mothers—a great pity, on both counts. It is not too late to complete the work they left undone. Today, here, we should start to do so.

In closing I would like to make one point. Social and psychological effects will be initially more important than legal or economic results. As Leo Kanowitz has pointed out:

Rules of law that treat of the sexes per se inevitably produce far-reaching effects upon social, psychological and economic aspects of male-female relations beyond the limited confines of legislative chambers and courtrooms. As long as organized legal systems, at once the most respected and most feared of social institutions, continue to differentiate sharply, in treatment or in words, between men and women on the basis of irrelevant and artificially created distinctions, the likelihood of men and women coming to regard one another primarily as fellow human beings and only secondarily as representatives of another sex will continue to be remote. When men and women are prevented from recognizing one another's essential humanity by sexual prejudices, nourished by legal as well as social institutions, society as a whole remains less than it could otherwise become.

Source:

African-American History and Culture. CD-ROM. Facts On File, Inc., 1999.

Roe v. Wade, 1973

Controversial, U.S. Supreme Court decision issued January 22, 1973, ruling that the Fourteenth Amendment gave an adult woman the right to terminate her pregnancy during the first trimester without any government interference, and that during the second trimester the state may limit that right only to safeguard a woman's health.

The way was cleared for *Roe* in 1965 in *Griswold v. Connecticut* (381 U.S. 479), issued June 7, 1965, in which the U.S. Supreme Court for the first time referred to the right of privacy. Writing for the majority, Justice William O. Douglas overturned a Connecticut statute forbidding the use of contraceptives and the dissemination of medical advice on their use. The seven-person majority agreed that the statute infringed on a constitutionally protected right to privacy by married persons, even though the constitution did not explicitly include such a right.

The case involved "Jane Roe" (a pseudonym), an impoverished Texas woman who wished to terminate a pregnancy resulting from a rape. In its 7-2 decision, the Supreme Court declared a Texas antiabortion statute to be unconstitutional, as a violation of a woman's right to personal privacy. It stated that the fetus was not a person within the meaning of the Fourteenth Amendment and said that the state had no "compelling interest" in protecting prenatal life until viability. The decision did not decide the question of when life actually begins. The ruling aroused a storm of controversy and led to proposals for a constitutional amendment to prohibit abortions. Despite yearly marches by antiabortion foes every January 22, and a strong antiabortion movement, the decision remained in effect in the early 21st century. However, the Court majority approved such limitations as parental consent for minors and a waiting period before an abortion could take place—a hardship on wage earners who had to travel long distances to have an abortion. Republican administrations prevented federal funds from going to international programs that might conduct abortion, even if the funds went to other purposes.

Antiabortion foes became so vociferous that Congress passed, and the Court upheld, a law limiting how close they could come to an abortion clinic. Nevertheless, abortion foes resorted to civil disobedience to obstruct abortion clinics, and some engaged in terrorism by burning clinics down and wounding and even assassinating abortion clinic workers. Both abortion foes and advocates of a woman's right to choose in the Senate used the position on abortion by judicial nominees (among other things) as a litmus test as to whether or not they would be approved. As a result, a large number of vacancies have gone unfulfilled halfway through the George W. Bush administration.

Along with Roe, Dr. James Hubert Hallford, under criminal prosecution in Texas for performing abortions, sought standing to participate in the case on the grounds that the statute was too vague to permit him to know whether the abortions he performed were legal (saving the life of the mother) or illegal. His part in the case was dismissed. Another couple, Mr. and Mrs. "Doe" also wanted the law overturned. They were married, but Mrs. Doe had been warned that a pregnancy could endanger her health. Therefore, they claimed that the possibility of either carrying an unwanted pregnancy to term or seeking an illegal abortion affected their marital relations. The Court upheld a lower court's dismissal of their claim.

A companion case, *Doe v. Bolton*, 410 U.S. 179, was also decided. It concerned Georgia legislation that, to an extent at least, obviously reflects the influences of recent attitudinal change, of advancing medical knowledge and techniques, and of new thinking about an old issue.

Mr. Justice Blackmun delivered the opinion of the Court.

This Texas federal appeal and its Georgia companion, present constitutional challenges to state criminal abortion legislation. The Texas statutes under attack here are typical of those that have been in effect in many States for approximately a century. We forthwith acknowledge our awareness of the sensitive and emotional nature of the abortion controversy, of the vigorous opposing views, even among physicians, and of the deep and seemingly absolute convictions that the subject inspires. One's philosophy, one's experiences, one's exposure to the raw edges of human existence, one's religious training, one's attitudes toward life and family and their values, and the moral standards one establishes and seeks to observe, are all likely to influence and to color one's thinking and conclusions about abortion.

In addition, population growth, pollution, poverty, and racial overtones tend to complicate and not to simplify the problem.

Our task, of course, is to resolve the issue by constitutional measurement, free of emotion and of predilection. We seek earnestly to do this, and, because we do, we have inquired into, and in this opinion place some emphasis upon, medical and medical-legal history and what that history reveals about man's attitudes toward the abortion procedure over the centuries. We bear in mind, too, Mr. Justice Holmes' admonition in his now vindicated dissent in *Lochner v. New York* . . . (1905):

"[The Constitution] is made for people of fundamentally differing views, and the accident of our finding certain opinions natural and familiar, or novel, and even shocking, ought not to conclude or judgment upon the question whether statutes embodying them conflict with the Constitution of the United States."

I

The Texas statutes that concern us here are Arts. 1191-1194 and 1196 of the State's Penal Code. . . . These make it a crime to "procure an abortion" as therein defined, or to attempt one, except with respect to "an abortion procured or attempted by medical advice for the purpose of saving the life of the mother." Similar statutes are in existence in a majority of the States.

Texas first enacted a criminal abortion statute in 1854. This was soon modified into language that has remained substantially unchanged to the present time. . . . The final article in each of these compilations provided the same exception, as does the present Article 1196, for an abortion by "medical advice for the purpose of saving the life of the mother."

II

Jane Roe, a single woman who was residing in Dallas County, Texas, instituted this federal action in March 1970 against the District Attorney of the county. She sought a declaratory judgment that the Texas criminal abortion statutes were unconstitutional on their face, and an injunction restraining the defendant from enforcing the statutes.

Roe alleged that she was unmarried and pregnant; that she wished to terminate her pregnancy by an abortion "performed by a competent, licensed physician, under safe, clinical conditions"; that she was unable to get a "legal" abortion in Texas because her life did not appear to be threatened by the continuation of her pregnancy; and that she could not afford to travel to another jurisdiction in order to secure a legal abortion under safe conditions. She claimed that the Texas statutes were unconstitutionally vague and that they abridged her right of personal privacy, protected by the First, Fourth, Fifth, Ninth, and Fourteenth Amendments. By an amendment to her complaint Roe purported to sue "on behalf of herself and all other women: similarly situated. . . .

* * *

V

The principal thrust of appellant's attack on the Texas statutes is that they improperly invade a right, said to be possessed by the pregnant woman, to choose to terminate her pregnancy. Appellant would discover this right in the concept of personal "liberty" embodied in the Fourteenth Amendment's Due Process Clause; or in personal, marital, familial, and sexual privacy said to be protected by the Bill of Rights or its penumbras. . .or among those rights reserved to the people by the Ninth Amendment. Before addressing this claim, we feel it desirable briefly to survey, in several aspects, the history of abortion, for such insight as that history may afford us, and then to examine the state purposes and interests behind the criminal abortion laws.

It perhaps is not generally appreciated that the restrictive criminal abortion laws in effect in a majority of States today are of relatively recent vintage. Those laws, generally proscribing abortion or its attempt at any time during pregnancy except when necessary to preserve the pregnant woman's life, are not of ancient or even of common-law origin. Instead, they derive from statutory changes effected, for the most part, in the latter half of the 19th century.

* * *

5. The American law. In this country, the law in effect in all but a few States until mid-19th century was the pre-existing English common law. Connecticut, the first State to enact abortion legislation, adopted in 1821 that part of Lord Ellenborough's Act that related to a woman "quick with child." The death penalty was not imposed. Abortion before quickening was made a crime in that State only in 1860. In 1828, New York enacted legislation that, in two respects, was to serve as a model for early anti-abortion statutes. First, while barring destruction of an unquickened fetus as well as a quick fetus, it made the former only a misdemeanor, but the latter second-degree manslaughter. Second, it incorporated a concept of therapeutic abortion by providing that an abortion was excused if it "shall have been necessary to preserve the life of such mother, or shall have been advised by two physicians to be necessary for such purpose." By 1840, when Texas had received the common law, only eight American States had statutes dealing with abortion. It was not until after the War Between the States that legislation began generally to replace the common law. Most of these initial statutes dealt severely with abortion after quickening but were lenient with it before quickening. Most punished attempts equally with completed abortions. While many statutes included the exception for an abortion thought by one or more physicians to be necessary to save the mother's life, that provision soon disappeared and the typical law required that the procedure actually be necessary for that purpose.

Gradually, in the middle and late 19th century the quickening distinction disappeared from the statutory law of most States and the degree of the offense and the penalties were increased. By the end of the 1950's a large majority of the jurisdictions banned abortion, however and whenever performed, unless done to save or preserve the life of the mother. The exceptions, Alabama and the District of Columbia, permitted abortion to preserve the mother's health. Three States permitted abortions that were not "unlawfully" performed or that were not "without lawful justification," leaving interpretation of those standards to the courts. In the past several years, however, a trend toward liberalization of abortion statutes has resulted in adoption, by about one-third of the States, of less stringent laws. . .

It is thus apparent that at common law, at the time of the adoption of our Constitution, and throughout the major portion of the 19th century, abortion was viewed with less disfavor than under most American statutes currently in effect. Phrasing it another way, a woman enjoyed a substantially broader right to terminate a pregnancy than she does in most States today. At least with respect to the early stage of pregnancy, and very possibly without such a limitation, the opportunity to make this choice was present in this country well into the 19th century. Even later, the law continued for some time to treat less punitively an abortion procured in early pregnancy.

* * *

VII

Three reasons have been advanced to explain historically the enactment of criminal abortion laws in the 19th century and to justify their continued existence.

It has been argued occasionally that these laws were the product of a Victorian an social concern to discourage illicit sexual conduct. Texas, however, does not advance this justification in the present case, and it appears that no court or commentator has taken the argument seriously. The appellants and amici contend, moreover, that this is not a proper state purpose at all and suggest that, if it were, the Texas statutes are overbroad in protecting it since the law fails to distinguish between married and unwed mothers.

A second reason is concerned with abortion as a medical procedure. When most criminal abortion laws were first enacted, the procedure was a hazardous one for the woman. This was particularly true prior to the development of antisepsis. Antiseptic techniques, of course, were based on discoveries by Lister, Pasteur, and others first announced in 1867, but were not generally accepted and employed until about the turn of the century. Abortion mortality was high. Even after 1900, and perhaps until as late as the development of antibiotics in the 1940's, standard modern techniques such as dilation and curettage were not nearly so safe as they are today. Thus, it has been argued that a State's real concern in enacting a criminal abortion law was to protect the pregnant woman, that is, to restrain her from submitting to a procedure that placed her life in serious jeopardy.

Modern medical techniques altered this situation. Appellants and various amici refer to medical data indicating that abortion in early pregnancy, that is, prior to the end of the first trimester, although not without its risk, is now relatively safe. Mortality rates for women undergoing early abortions, where the procedure is legal, appear to be as low as or lower than the rates for normal childbirth. Consequently, any interest of the State in protecting the woman from an inherently hazardous procedure, except when it would be equally dangerous for her to forgo it, has largely disappeared. Of course, important state interests in the areas of health and medical standards do remain. The State has a legitimate interest in seeing to it that abortion, like any other medical procedure, is performed under circumstances that insure maximum safety for the patient. This interest obviously extends at least to the performing physician and his staff, to the facilities involved, to the availability of after-care, and to adequate provision for any complication or emergency that might arise. The prevalence of high mortality rates at illegal "abortion mills" strengthens, rather than weakens, the State's interest in regulating the conditions under which abortions are performed. Moreover, the risk to the woman increases as her pregnancy continues. Thus, the State retains a definite interest in protecting the woman's own health and safety when an abortion is proposed at a late stage of pregnancy.

The third reason is the State's interest—some phrase it in terms of duty—in protecting prenatal life. Some of the argument for this justification rests on the theory that a new human life is present from the moment of conception. The State's interest and general obligation to protect life then extends, it is argued, to prenatal life. Only when the life of the pregnant mother herself is at stake, balanced against the life she carries with her, should the interest of the embryo or fetus not prevail. Logically, of course, a legitimate state interest in this area need not stand or fall on acceptance of the belief that life begins at conception or at some other point prior to live birth. In assessing the State's interest, recognition may be given to the less rigid claim that as long as at least potential life is involved, the State may assert interests beyond the protection of the pregnant woman alone.

Parties challenging state abortion laws have sharply disputed in some courts the contention that a purpose of these laws, when enacted, was to protect prenatal life. Pointing to the absence of legislative history to support the contention, they claim that most state laws were designed solely to protect the woman. Because medical advances have lessened this concern, at least with respect to abortion in early pregnancy, they argue that with respect to such abortions the laws can no longer be justified by any state interest. There is some scholarly support for this view of original purpose. The few state courts called upon to interpret their laws in the late 19th and early 20th centuries did focus on the State's interest in protecting the woman's health rather than in preserving the embryo and fetus. Proponents of this view point out that in many States, including Texas, by statute or judicial interpretation, the pregnant woman herself could not be prosecuted for self-abortion or for cooperating in an abortion performed upon her by another. They claim that adoption of the "quickening" distinction through received common law and state statutes tacitly recognizes the greater health hazards inherent in late abortion and impliedly repudiates the theory that life begins at conception.

It is with these interests, and the weight to be attached to them, that this case is concerned.

VIII

The Constitution does not explicitly mention any right of privacy. In a line of decisions, however, going back perhaps as far as *Union Pacific R. Co. v. Botsford* . . . (1891), the Court has recognized that a right of personal privacy, or a guarantee of certain areas or zones of privacy, does exist under the Constitution. In varying contexts, the Court or individual Justices have, indeed, found at least the roots of that right in the First Amendment . . . ; in the Fourth and Fifth Amendments . . . ; in the penumbras of the Bill of Rights . . . ; in the Ninth Amendment . . . ; or in the concept of liberty guaranteed by the first section of the Fourteenth Amendment. . . . These decisions make it clear that only personal rights that can be deemed "fundamental" or "implicit in the concept of ordered liberty" . . . are included in this guarantee of personal privacy. They also make it clear that the right has some extension to activities relating to marriage . . . ; procreation . . . ; contraception, . . . ; family relationships . . . ; and child rearing and education. . . .

This right of privacy, whether it be founded in the Fourteenth Amendment's concept of personal liberty and restrictions upon state action, as we feel it is, or, as the District Court determined, in the Ninth Amendment's reservation of rights to the people, is broad enough to encompass a woman's decision whether or not to terminate her pregnancy. The detriment that the State would impose upon the pregnant woman by denying this choice altogether is apparent. Specific and direct harm medically diagnosable even in early pregnancy may be involved. Maternity, or additional offspring, may force upon the woman a distressful life and future. Psychological harm may be imminent. Mental and physical health may be taxed by child care. There is also the distress, for all concerned, associated with the unwanted child, and there is the problem of bringing a child into a family already unable, psychologically and otherwise, to care for it. In other cases, as in this one, the additional difficulties and continuing stigma of unwed motherhood may be involved. All these are factors the woman and her responsible physician necessarily will consider in consultation.

On the basis of elements such as these, appellant and some amici argue that the woman's right is absolute and that she is entitled to terminate her pregnancy at whatever time, in whatever way, and for whatever reason she alone chooses. With this we do not agree. Appellant's arguments that Texas either has no valid interest at all in regulating the abortion decision, or no interest strong enough to support any limitation upon the woman's sole determination, are unpersuasive. The Court's decisions recognizing a right of privacy also acknowledge that some state regulation in areas protected by that right is appropriate. As noted above, a State may properly assert important interests in safeguarding health, in maintaining medical standards, and in protecting potential life. At some point in pregnancy, these respective interests become sufficiently compelling to sustain regulation of the factors that govern the abortion decision. The privacy right involved, therefore, cannot be said to be absolute. In fact, it is not clear to us that the claim asserted by some amici that one has an unlimited right to do with one's body as one pleases bears a close relationship to the right of privacy previously articulated in the Court's decisions. The court has refused to recognize an unlimited right of this kind in the past. . . .

We, therefore, conclude that the right of personal privacy includes the abortion decision, but that this right is not unqualified and must be considered against important state interests in regulation.

We note that those federal and state courts that have recently considered abortion law challenges have reached the same conclusion. A majority, in addition to the District Court in the present case, have held state laws unconstitutional, at least in part, because of vagueness or because of overbreadth and abridgment of rights. . . .

Others have sustained state statutes. . . .

Although the result are divided, most of these courts have agreed that the right of privacy, however based, is broad enough to cover the abortion decision; that the right, nonetheless, is not absolute and is subject to some limitations; and that at some point the state interests as to protection of health, medical standards, and parental life, become dominant. We agree with this approach.

Where certain "fundamental rights" are involved, the Court has held that regulation limiting these rights may be justified only by a "compelling state interest," . . . and that legislative enactments must be narrowly drawn to express only the legitimate state interests at stake. . . .

In the recent abortion cases, cited above, courts have recognized these principles. Those striking down state laws have generally scrutinized the State's interests in protecting health and potential life, and have concluded that neither interest justified broad limitations on the reasons for which a physician and his pregnant patient might decide that she should have an abortion in the early stages of pregnancy. Courts sustaining state laws have held that the State's determinations to protect health or prenatal life are dominant and constitutionally justifiable.

IX

The district Court held that the appellee failed to meet his burden of demonstrating that the Texas statute's infringement upon Roe's rights was necessary to support a compelling state interest, and that, although the appellee presented "several compelling justifications for state presence in the area of abortions," the statutes outstripped these justifications and swept "far beyond any areas of compelling state interest." . . . Appellant and appellee both contest that holding. Appellant, as has been indicated, claims as absolute right that bars any state imposition of criminal penalties in the area. Appellee argues that the State's determination to recognize and protect prenatal life from and after conception constitutes a compelling state interest. As noted above, we do not agree fully with either formulation. . . .

The appellee and certain amici argue that the fetus is a "person" within the language and meaning of the Fourteenth Amendment. In support of this, they outline at length and in detail the well-known facts of fetal development. If this suggestion of personhood is established, the appellant's case, of course, collapses, for the fetus' right to life would then be guaranteed specifically by the Amendment. The appellant conceded as much on reargument. On the other hand, the appellee conceded on reargument that no case could be cited that holds that a fetus is a person within the meaning of the Fourteenth Amendment.

The Constitution does not define "person" in so many words. Section 1 of the Fourteenth Amendment contains three references to "person." The first, in defining "citizens," speaks of "persons born or naturalized in the United States." The word also appears both in the Due Process Clause and in the Equal Protection Clause. "Person" is used in other places in the Constitution: in the listing of qualifications for Representatives and Senators, Art.I, Section 2, cl. 2, and Section 3, cl. 3; in the Apportionment Clause, Art. I, Section 2, cl. 3; in the Migration and Importation provision, Art I, Section 9, cl. 1; in the Emolument Clause, Art. I, Section 9, cl. 8; in the Electors provisions Art. II, Section 1, cl. 2, and the superseded cl. 3; in the provision outlining qualifications for the office of the President, Art, II, Section 1, cl. 5; in the Extradition provisions, Art, IV, Section 2, cl. 2, and the superseded Fugitive Slave Clause 3; and in the Fifth, Twelfth, and Twenty-second Amendments, as well as in SectionSection 2 and 3 of the Fourteenth Amendment. But in nearly all these instances, the use of the word is such that it has application only postnatally. None indicates, with any assurance, that it has any possible prenatal application.

All this, together with our observation, supra, that throughout the major portion of the 19th century prevailing legal abortion practices were far freer than they are today, persuades us that the word "person," as used in the Fourteenth Amendment, does not include the unborn. This is in accord with the results reached in those few cases where the issue has been squarely presented. . . . Indeed, our decision in *United States v. Vuitch* . . . (1971), inferentially is to the same effect, for we there would not have indulged in statutory interpretation favorable to abortion in specified circumstances if the necessary consequence was the termination of life entitled to Fourteenth Amendment protection.

This conclusion, however, does not of itself fully answer the contentions raised by Texas, and we pass on to other considerations. . . .

The pregnant woman cannot be isolated in her privacy. She carried an embryo and, later, a fetus, if one accepts the medical definitions of the developing young in the human uterus. . . . The situation therefore is inherently different from marital intimacy, or bedroom possession of obscene material, or marriage, or procreation, or education, with which Eisenstadt and Grisworld, Stanley, Loving, Skinner and Pierce and Meyer were respectively concerned. As we have intimated above, it is reasonable and appropriate for a State to decide that at some point in time another interest, that of health of the mother or that of potential human life, becomes significantly involved. The woman's privacy is no longer sole and any right of privacy she possesses must be measured accordingly.

Texas urges that, apart from the Fourteenth Amendment, life begins at conception and is present throughout pregnancy, and that, therefore, the State has a compelling interest in protecting that life from and after conception. We need not resolve the difficult question of when life begins. When those trained in the respective disciplines of medicine, philosophy, and theology are unable to arrive at any consensus, the judiciary, at this point in the development of man's knowledge, is not in a position to speculate as to the answer.

It should be sufficient to note briefly the wide divergence of thinking on this most sensitive and difficult question. There has always been strong support for the view that life does not begin until live birth. This was the belief of the Stoics. It appears to be the predominant, though not the unanimous, attitude of the Jewish faith. It may be taken to represent also the position of a large segment of the Protestant community, insofar at that can be ascertained; organized groups that have taken a formal position on the abortion issue have generally regarded abortion as a matter for the conscience of the individual and her family. As we have noted, the common law found greater significance in quickening. Physicians and their scientific colleagues have regarded that event with less interest and have tended to focus either upon conception, upon live birth, or upon the interim point at which the fetus becomes "viable," that is, potentially able to live outside the mother's womb, albeit with artificial aid. Viability is usually placed at about seven months (28 weeks) but may occur earlier, even at 24 weeks. The Aristotelian theory of "mediate animation," that held sway throughout the Middle Ages and the Renaissance in Europe, continued to be official Roman Catholic dogma until the 19th century, despite opposition to this "ensoulment" theory from those in the Church who would recognize the existence of life from the moment of conception. The latter is now, of course, the official belief of the Catholic Church. As one brief amicus discloses, this is a view strongly held by many non- Catholics as well, and by many physicians. Substantial problems for precise definition of this view are posed, however, by new embryological data that purport to indicate that conception is a "process" over time, rather than an event, and by new medical techniques such as menstrual extraction, the "morning-after" pill, implantation of embryos, artificial insemination, and even artificial wombs

In areas other than criminal abortion, the law has been reluctant to endorse any theory that life, as we recognize it, begins before live birth or to accord legal rights to the unborn except in narrowly defined situations and except when the rights are contingent upon live birth. For example, the traditional rule of tort law denied recovery for prenatal injuries even though the child was born alive. That rule has been changed in almost every jurisdiction. In most States, recovery is said to be permitted only if the fetus was viable, or at least quick, when the injuries were sustained, though few courts have squarely so held. In a recent development, generally opposed by the commentators, some States permit the parents of a stillborn child to maintain an action for wrongful death because of prenatal injuries. Such an action, however, would appear to be one to vindicate the parents' interest and is thus consistent with the view that the fetus, at most, represents only the potentiality of life. Similarly, unborn children have been recognized as acquiring rights of interests by way of inheritance or other devolution of property, and have been represented by guardians ad litem. Perfection of the interests involved, again, has generally been contingent upon live birth. In short, the unborn have never been recognized in the law as persons in the whole sense.

X

In view of all this, we do not agree that, by adopting one theory of life, Texas may override the rights of the pregnant woman that are at stake. We repeat, however, that the State does have an important and legitimate interest in preserving and protecting the health of the pregnant woman, whether she be a resident of the State or a nonresident who seeks medical consultation and treatment there, and that it has still another important and legitimate interest in protecting the potentiality of human life. These interests are separate and distinct. Each grows in substantiality as the woman approaches term and, at a point during pregnancy, each becomes "compelling." With respect to the State's important and legitimate interest in the health of the mother, the "compelling" point, in the light of present medical knowledge, is at approximately the end of the first trimester. This is so because of the now-established medical fact . . . that until the end of the first trimester mortality in abortion may be less than mortality in normal childbirth. It follows that, from and after this point, a State may regulate the abortion procedure to the extent that the regulation reasonably relates to the preservation and protection of maternal health. Examples of permissible state regulation in this area are requirement as to the qualifications of the person who is to perform the abortion; as to the licensure of that person; as to the facility in which the procedure is to be performed, that is, whether it must be a hospital or may be a clinic or some other place of less-than-hospital status; as to the licensing of the facility; and the like.

This means, on the other hand, that, for the period of pregnancy prior to this "compelling" point, the attending physician, in consultation with his patient, is free to determine, without regulation by the State, that, in his medical judgment, the patient's pregnancy should be terminated. If that decision is reached, the judgment may be effectuated by an abortion free of interference by the State.

With respect to the State's important and legitimate interest in potential life, the "compelling" point is at viability. This is so because the fetus then presumably has the capability of meaningful life outside the mother's womb. State regulation protective of fetal life after viability thus has both logical and biological justifications. If the State is interested in protecting fetal life after viability, it may go so far as to proscribe abortion during that period, except when it is necessary to preserve the life or health of the mother.

Measured against these standards, Art. 1196 of the Texas Penal Code, in restricting legal abortions to those "procured or attempted by medical advice for the purpose of saving the life of the mother," sweeps too broadly. The statute makes no distinction between abortions performed early in pregnancy and those performed later, and it limits to a single reason, "saving" the mother's life, the legal justification for the procedure. The statute, therefore, cannot survive the constitutional attack made upon it here.

This conclusion makes it unnecessary for us to consider the additional challenge to the Texas statute asserted on grounds of vagueness.

XI

To summarize and to repeat:

1. A state criminal abortion statute of the current Texas type, that excepts from criminality only a life-saving procedure on behalf of the mother, without regard to preg-

nancy stage and without recognition of the other interests involved, is violative of the Due Process Clause of the Fourteenth Amendment.

(a) For the stage prior to approximately the end of the first trimester, the abortion decision and its effectuation must be left to the medical judgment of the pregnant woman's attending physician.

(b) For the stage subsequent to approximately the end of the first trimester, the State, in promoting its interest in the health of the mother, may, if it chooses, regulate the abortion procedure in ways that are reasonably related to maternal health.

(c) For the stage subsequent to viability, the State in promoting its interest in the potentiality of human life may, if it chooses, regulate, and even proscribe, abortion except where it is necessary, in appropriate medical judgment, for the preservation of the life or health of the mother.

2. The State may define the term "physician," as it has been employed in the preceding paragraphs of this Part XI of this opinion, to mean only a physician currently licensed by the State, and may proscribe any abortion by a person who is not a physician as so defined.

* * *

This holding, we feel, is consistent with the relative weights of the respective interests involved, with the lessons and examples of medical and legal history, with the lenity of the common law, and with the demands of the profound problems of the present day. The decision leaves the State free to place increasing restrictions on abortion as the period of pregnancy lengthens, so long as those restrictions are tailored to the recognized state interests. The decision vindicates the rights of the physician to administer medical treatment according to his professional judgment up to the points where important state interests provide compelling justifications for intervention. Up to those points, the abortion decision in all its aspects is inherently, and primarily, a medical decision, and basic responsibility for it must rest with the physician. If an individual practitioner abuses the privilege of exercising proper medical judgment, the usual remedies, judicial and intra-professional, are available.

XII

Our conclusion that Art. 1196 is unconstitutional means, of course, that the Texas abortion statutes, as a unit, must fall. . . .

We find it unnecessary to decide whether the District Court erred in withholding injunctive relief, for we assume the Texas prosecutorial authorities will give full credence to this decision that the present criminal abortion statutes of that State are unconstitutional.

It is so ordered.

Affirmed in part and reversed in part.

Source:
Supreme Court Reporter, Vol. 93, pp. 705–763.

Indian Self-Determination and Education Assistance Act, 1975

Heralded as the most important Indian legislation since the Indian New Deal of 1934, the Indian Self-Determination and Education Assistance Act was signed into law by President Gerald Ford in January 1975. Acknowledging that the federal government's overseeing Indian education and policy had hurt Indians more than it had helped them, the act paved the way for tribal self-rule. The government also pledged to improve the quality of Indian education.

The act stressed that programs for and services to American Indians previously operated by the Bureau of Indian Affairs (BIA) would continue, although they would now be contracted to and run by Indian organizations. The act ensured, however, that these programs would still be funded and monitored by the government. In his statement upon signing the bill, President Ford said that the government sought to alter the nature of its relationship to Indian tribes from a paternalistic into a more cooperative one.

Between 1984 and 1996, the act was amended 13 times. Many of the amendments dealt with programs that fostered and increased tribal self-governance. By 1994, 28 tribes had an annual funding agreement with the government that allowed them to administer their own programs, services, and activities. A 1996 amendment allowed for the selection of an additional 50 tribes per year to participate in self-governance programs.

(excerpt)

Sec. 450a. Congressional declaration of policy

(a) Recognition of obligation of United States

The Congress hereby recognizes the obligation of the United States to respond to the strong expression of the Indian people for self-determination by assuring maximum Indian participation in the direction of educational as well as other Federal services to Indian communities so as to render such services more responsive to the needs and desires of those communities.

(b) Declaration of commitment

The Congress declares its commitment to the maintenance of the Federal Government's unique and continuing relationship with, and responsibility to, individual Indian tribes and to the Indian people as a whole through the establishment of a meaningful Indian self-determination policy which will permit an orderly transition from the Federal domination of programs for, and services to, Indians to effective and meaningful participation by the Indian people in the planning, conduct, and administration of those programs and services. In accordance with this policy, the United States is committed to supporting and assisting Indian tribes in the development of strong and stable tribal governments, capable of administering quality programs and developing the economies of their respective communities.

(c) Declaration of national goal

The Congress declares that a major national goal of the United States is to provide the quantity and quality of educational services and opportunities which will permit Indian children to compete and excel in the life areas of their choice, and to achieve the measure of self-determination essential to their social and economic well-being.

Source:

Cornell Law School. The Legal Information Institute. U.S. Code Collection. Available on-line. URL: www4.law.cornell.edu/uscode/25/450a.html. Accessed November 2003.

Suggested Reading

Economic Boom and Social Transformation

Edward Berkowitz, *Losing Ground: American Social Policy, 1950–1980*. New York: Basic Books, 1984.

Melvin Dubovsky, *The State and Labor in Modern America*. Chapel Hill: University of North Carolina Press, 1994.

Walter A. McDougall, *The Heavens and the Earth: A Political History of the Space Age*. New York: Basic Books, 1985.

Robert Zeiger, *American Workers, American Unions, 1920–1985*. Baltimore: Johns Hopkins University Press, 1986.

Cold War: U.S. International Relations

Christian Appy, *Working Class War: American Combat Soldiers and Vietnam*. Chapel Hill: University of North Carolina Press, 1993.

Carol Gallagher, *American Ground Zero*. Cambridge, Mass.: MIT Press, 1993.

George Herring, *America's Longest War: the United States and Vietnam, 1950–1975*, 3rd ed. New York: McGraw-Hill, 1996.

Andrew Krepenevich, *The Army and Vietnam*. Baltimore: Johns Hopkins University Press, 1989

Katheryn Marshall, *In the Combat Zone: An Oral History of American Women in Vietnam, 1966–1975*. Boston: Little, Brown, 1987.

Thomas Paterson, *Contesting Castro: The United States and the Triumph of the Cuban Revolution*. New York: Oxford University Press, 1994.

Stephen G. Rabe, *Eisenhower and Latin America*. Chapel Hill: University of North Carolina Press, 1988.

Michael Schaller, *The American Occupation of Japan: The Origins of the Cold War in Asia*. New York: Oxford University Press, 1985.

Domestic Policies after World War II

David Caute, *The Great Fear: The Anti-Communist Purge under Truman and Eisenhower*. New York: Simon & Schuster, 1978.

Charles Debenedetti, with Charles Chatfield, *An American Ordeal: The Antiwar Movement of the Vietnam Era*. Syracuse, N.Y.: Syracuse University Press, 1990.

David Farber, *Chicago '68*. Chicago: University of Chicago Press, 1988.

———, *The Age of Great Dreams: America in the 1960s*. New York: Hill & Wang, 1994.

Raymond L. Garthoff, *Detente and Confrontation: American-Soviet Relations from Nixon to Reagan*, 1994

Todd Gitlin, *The Sixties: Years of Hope, Days of Rage*. New York: Bantam Books, 1987

Alonzo L. Hamby, *Man of the People: A Life of Harry S. Truman*. New York: Oxford University Press, 1995.

John Earl Haynes and Harvey Klehr, *Venona: Decoding Soviet Espionage in America*. New Haven, Conn.: Yale University Press, 1999.

Joan Hoff, *Nixon Reconsidered*. New York: Basic Books, 1994

Maurice Isserman and Michael Kazin, *America Divided: The Civil War of the 1960s*. New York: Oxford University Press, 2000.

J. Anthony Lukas, *Nightmare: The Underside of the Nixon Years*. Athens: Ohio University Press, 1999.

David McCullough. *Truman*. New York: Simon & Schuster, 1992.

Kenneth O'Reilly, *Hoover and the Un-Americans: The FBI, HUAC, and the Red Menace*. Philadelphia: Temple University Press, 1983.

Richard Gid Powers, *Secrecy and Power: The Life of J. Edgar Hoover*. New York: Free Press, 1987, Chapters 11 ff.

Ronald Radosh, with Joyce Milton, *The Rosenberg File*. New Haven, Conn.: Yale University Press, 1997.

Ellen W. Schrecker, *Many Are the Crimes: McCarthyism in America*. New York: Little, Brown, 1998.

Melvin Small, *The Presidency of Richard Nixon*. Lawrence: University Press of Kansas, 1999.

Athan G. Theoharis, *Spying on Americans: Political Surveillance from Hoover to the Huston Plan*. Philadelphia: Temple University Press, 1978.

Irwin Unger, *The Best of Intentions: The Triumph and Failure of the Great Society under Kennedy, Johnson, and Nixon*. New York: Doubleday, 1996.

Tom Wells, *The War Within: America's Battle over Vietnam*. Berkeley: University of California Press, 1994.

Struggle for Racial and Gender Equality and for the Extension of Civil Liberties

Michal Belknap, *Federal Law and Southern Justice: Racial Violence and Constitutional Conflict in the Post-*Brown *South*. Athens: The University of Georgia Press, 1987.

Kathleen C. Berkeley, *The Women's Liberation Movement in America*. Westport, Conn.: Greenwood Publishing Group, 1999.

Taylor Branch, *Parting the Waters: America in the King Years, 1954–1963*. New York: Simon & Schuster, 1988.

Seth Cagin and Philip Dray, *We are Not Afraid: The Story of Goodman, Schwerner, and Chaney and the Civil Rights Campaign for Mississippi*. New York: MacMillan, 1988.

Clayborn Carson, *In Struggle? SNCC and the Black Awakening of the 1960s*. Cambridge, Mass.: Harvard University Press, 1981.

Danny O. Coulson and Elaine Shannon, *No Heroes: Inside the FBI's Secret Counter-Terror Force*. Book One, "A New Kind of Killer." New York: Pocket Books, 1999.

Flora Davis, *Moving the Mountain: The Women's Movement in America since 1960*. New York: Simon & Schuster, 1991.

Mario Garcia, *Mexican Americans: Leadership, Ideology, and Identity*. New Haven, Conn.: Yale University Press, 1991.

Henry Hampton and Steve Fayer, with Sarah Flynn, *Voices of Freedom: An Oral History of the Civil Rights Movement*. New York: Bantam, 1990.

Charles Colcock Jones, *The Black Panther Party Reconsidered*. Baltimore: Black Classic Press, 1998.

Richard Kluger, *Simple Justice*. New York: Knopf, 1975.

Nicholas Lemann, *The Promised Land: The Great Black Migration and How It Changed America*. New York: Knopf, 1991.

Elaine Tyler May, *Homeward Bound: American Families in the Cold War Era*. New York: Basic Books, 1988.

Kenneth O'Reilly, *"Racial Matters": The FBI's Secret File on Black America*. New York: Free Press, 1989

Juan Williams, *Thurgood Marshall: American Revolutionary*. New York: Times Books, 1998.

ERA 10
Contemporary United States (1970s–Present)

Even more than in Era 9, Era 10 must be approached with the caveat that "presentism" and memory interfere with objectivity. In addition, no benefit of hindsight exists for the most recent occurrences, particularly those after the September 11, 2001, terrorist attacks (9/11). That event and the subsequent anthrax scare caused profound shifts in foreign relations, domestic affairs, politics, and the way Americans pursue such everyday activities as opening mail, shopping, and traveling. The editor can only guess what 21st century documents might be perceived as "landmark" a decade hence. She also imposes the further caveat that her perspective will infuse the introductions to recent documents to a greater extent than with those for which significance has been established by time.

Some trends are unmistakable. The post-Watergate nation has become more conservative politically, economically, and socially. "Liberals" seen on television talk shows would have occupied the center during the 1960s and 1970s. Bill Clinton, the only Democratic president to win two terms since Roosevelt, came into office as a "new" Democrat who successfully presided over welfare cutbacks and a balanced budget at the same time that his administration promoted environmental awareness and (unsuccessfully) health care reform. Conservatism became truly entrenched with the election of Ronald Reagan. He, in turn, has become the model for the current president, George W. Bush. Especially because of the cost of television advertising, politics became much more expensive, and by the 1990s, politicians had found ways to skirt the reforms enacted after Watergate. The congressional response correcting those changes will not take effect until after this volume goes to press.

Changes in society are evident in many ways. Affirmative action for women and minorities, originally proposed in the 1960s and 1970s to redress past discrimination, became by the 1980s an acceptable way to promote "diversity" in education and the workplace. However, the courts began to find government-sponsored affirmative action programs unconstitutional, producing a noticeable cutback in minority enrollments in state universities and the inclusion of minority businesses in government projects. At the beginning of the 21st century, minority proportions of the poor, unemployed, and undereducated are increasing, as are the number of minorities incarcerated. The growth of what one commentator calls the "prison-industrial complex" is also a characteristic of this period.

Conservative religion has increased its influence in this era, also bolstered by the Supreme Court. The "wall of separation" between church and state became substantially eroded by the courts as religion itself has become stronger politically and culturally. Immigration, legal and illegal, has changed the face of many American cities and spread to the suburbs and countryside as well. As one example, Americans no longer speak of a Judeo-Christian culture, but are more likely to refer to a "Judeo-Christian-Islamic" tradition. The inclusion of Muslims as a mainstream part of the American society predated 9/11, but it has become stronger in reaction to the minority of Americans who have attempted to demonize all Muslims because of the terrorism preached and practiced by Islamic extremists.

Technology and medicine continue their revolutionary advances. In medicine this period encompasses unexpected increases in some diseases, often attributed to environmental changes, while others have been eradicated. AIDs, which became epidemic among some sectors of the American population in the 1980s, can now be controlled, but with very expensive drug-taking regimes. Because of the cost and the stigma attached to the disease, it continues to spread throughout the rest of the world.

Technologically, the computer has revolutionized every segment of American life, from the cars people drive to methods of communication. Unfortunately, security has not kept up with the ubiquity of Internet use, leaving individuals vulnerable to "identity theft" and corporations and the government potentially subject to terrorism.

Prosperity flourished in the 1990s, increasing employment, reducing the number of Americans living in poverty, and leaving the federal and state government with budget surpluses. The prosperity began to end either in 2000 or with the economic policies of President George W. Bush. (The date depends on whether the analyst supports the Democrats or Republicans.) Regardless, according to the *New York Times Magazine* of October 20, 2002, the United States now has the greatest disparity between the well-to-do and the poor since the Gilded Age of the late 19th century. Moreover, the article claims the middle class, supposedly the hallmark of American society, is disappearing.

This era ends with the events surrounding 9/11, when the United States lost "forever" its sense of security. After previous "changing us forever" terrorism—the bombing of the Murragh Federal Building in Oklahoma City in 1995 by an American terrorist and the first World Trade Center bombing by Islamist extremists—the nation quickly returned to normalcy. When reactive legislation finally came, over a year after Oklahoma City, it affected mainly alien terrorists and Americans on death row. Not so after 9/11. Those events created immediate and profound changes in politics and the ways in which Americans travel or spend their leisure time. Not only did air travel plummet, Americans turned their shelter and entertainment dollars into new houses, renovating present residences, and enhancing their home amusement centers.

President George W. Bush declared a "war on terrorism." The documents selected here represent efforts to increase security at the expense of civil liberties, always a product of wartime. American troops were sent to Afghanistan, home to Osama bin Laden, the head of al-Qaeda and the mastermind of 9/11 and other terrorist actions. Although to date, bin Laden has not been captured, Americans and Afghan rebels were successful in routing the Afghan government, the Taliban, that harbored bin Laden and al-Qaeda's training camps. Even before the year's end, the bipartisanship that characterized the first reaction to 9/11 began to dissipate. A one-vote majority Democratic Senate and a slim-Republican-majority House left few major bills as Congress broke for the 2002 elections. At the same time, al-Qaeda was regrouping, terrorist incidents were occurring throughout the world, and Congress approved a possible war with Iraq. Congress and the press, meanwhile, were subjecting American intelligence agencies to the same kind of scrutiny and criticism they received after Watergate. Among the actions receiving the heaviest criticism were those put into place to correct the perceived "excesses" of the intelligence agencies uncovered at the beginning of this era in the mid-1970s.

Domestic Politics

Jimmy Carter, Pardon for Vietnam Draft Evaders, 1977

Edict and executive order issued by President Jimmy Carter January 21, 1977, his first full day in office, granting "a full, complete and unconditional pardon" for Vietnam War draft evaders. This followed President Gerald Ford's Vietnam Era Clemency Plan for any draft evaders who turned themselves in, a controversial and often condemned action. Those few who took advantage of the clemency, some 19 percent of those eligible, had to take an oath of allegiance and agree to a period of alternative service.

About 10,000 people were immediately affected by President Carter's action, including 1,600 draft resisters living in foreign countries, who were now allowed to return home to the United States. It was a compromise plan that gave far more help to those who evaded military services than to those who deserted or resisted while in the military. Only draft evaders received a full pardon, provided that they were nonviolent. Also pardoned were another 3,000 who had been indicted for draft evasion but were never caught, and a quarter of a million young men who never registered for the draft. However, the significant number of American soldiers who resisted the war while in service were excluded from Carter's pardon. Strong opposition to Carter's proclamation arose in Congress. The Senate, by a vote of 48 to 46, on January 24, barely defeated a resolution that would have condemned the pardon.

Proclamation 4483
Granting Pardon for Violations of the Selective Service Act, August 4, 1964 to March 28, 1973
By the President of the United States of America

A Proclamation

Acting pursuant to the grant of authority in Article II, Section 2, of the Constitution of the United States, I, Jimmy Carter, President of the United States, do hereby grant a full, complete and unconditional pardon to: (1) all persons who may have committed any offense between August 4, 1964 and March 28, 1973 in violation of the Military Selective Service Act or any rule or regulation promulgated thereunder; and (2) all persons heretofore convicted, irrespective of the date of conviction, of any offense committed between August 4, 1964 and March 28, 1973 in violation of the Military Selective Service Act, or any rule or regulation promulgated thereunder, restoring to them full political, civil and other rights.

This pardon does not apply to the following who are specifically excluded therefrom:

(1) All persons convicted of or who may have committed any offense in violation of the Military Selective Service Act, or any rule or regulation promulgated thereunder, involving force or violence; and

(2) All persons convicted of or who may have committed any offense in violation of the Military Selective Service Act, or any rule or regulation promulgated thereunder, in connection with duties or responsibilities arising out of employment as agents, officers or employees of the Military Selective Service system.

In Witness Whereof, I have hereunto set my hand this 21st day of January, in the year of our Lord nineteen hundred and seventy-seven, and of the Independence of the United States of America the two hundred and first.

Jimmy Carter

Source:

Public Papers of the Presidents of the United States: Jimmy Carter, 1977. Washington D.C.: Government Printing Office, 1981–1988, pp. 5, 6.

Ethics in Government Act, 1978

Federal legislation enacted October 26, 1978, that was designed to prevent top government officials from abusing their official position for private financial gain. For the first time, all three branches of government, including the Supreme Court, were covered by such legislation. The top 14,000 federal officials were required to submit annual financial statements detailing the sources of their income. Those who failed to file a disclosure form were subject to civil penalties. An Office of Government Ethics would monitor the disclosure statements as well as any conflicts of interest within the executive branch. Standby authority was granted for the appointment of a special prosecutor to investigate alleged wrongdoing by the president, vice president, cabinet members, or other high executive branch officials. In addition, new restrictions were placed on former officials doing business on behalf of private firms with the federal agency for which they had once worked. This act has been amended several times.

In *Morrison v. Olson* (478 U.S. 464), decided June 29, 1988, the U.S. Supreme Court upheld the authority of Congress in the 1978 act to investigate alleged criminal actions by designated officials in the executive branch of government. In this case, Congress claimed to have received false and misleading testimony from some officials of the Justice Department and wanted a special prosecutor to look into the matter and gain information that had been withheld. The Court ruled against the Justice Department contention that Congress had assumed authority that properly belonged to the executive branch.

(excerpt)

To establish certain Federal agencies, effect certain reorganization of the Federal Government, to implement certain reforms in the operation of the Federal Government and to preserve and promote the integrity of public officials and institutions, and for other purposes.

Be it enacted by the Senate and House of Representatives of the United States of America in Congress assembled, That this Act may be cited as the "Ethics in Government Act of 1978."

Title I—Legislative Personnel Financial Disclosure Requirements

Coverage

Sec. 101. (a) Each Member in office on May 15 of a calendar year shall file on or before May 15 of that calendar year a report containing the information as described in section 102(a).

(b) Any individual who is an officer or employee of the legislative branch designated in subsection (e) during any calendar year and performs the duties of his position or office for a period in excess of sixty days in that calendar year shall file on or before May 15 of the succeeding year a report containing the information as described in section 102(a).

(c) Within thirty days of assuming the position of an officer or employee designated in subsection (e), an individual other than an individual employed in the legislative branch upon assuming such position shall file a report containing the information as described in section 102(b) unless the individual has left another position designated in subsection (e) within thirty days prior to assuming his new position. This subsection shall take effect on January 1, 1979.

(d) Within thirty days of becoming a candidate in a calendar year for any election for the office of Member, or on or before May 15 of that calendar year, which ever is later, but in no event later than seven days prior to the election, and on or before May 15 of each successive year the individual continues to be a candidate, an individual shall file a report containing the information as described in section 102(b).

(e) The officers and employees referred to in subsections (b) and (c) are—

(1) each officer or employees of the legislative branch who is compensated at a rate equal to or in excess of the annual rate of basic pay in effect for grade GS-16 of the General Schedule; and

(2) at least one principal assistant designated for purposes of this section by each Member who does not have an employee compensated at a rate equal to or in excess of the annual rate of basic pay in effect for grade GS-16 of the General Schedule.

For the purposes of this title, the legislative branch includes the Architect of the Capitol, the Botanic Gardens, the Congressional Budget Office, the Cost Accounting Standards Board, the General Accounting Office, the Government Printing Office, the Library of Congress, the Office of the Attending Physician, and the Office of Technology Assessment.

(f) Reasonable extensions of time for filing any report may be granted by the designated committee of the Senate with respect to those filing with the Secretary and by the designated committee of the House of Representatives with respect to those filing with the Clerk but in no event may the extension granted to a Member or candidate result in a required report being filed later than seven days prior to an election involving the Member or candidate. If the day on which a report is required to be filed falls on a weekend or holiday, the report may be filed on the next business day.

(g) Notwithstanding the dates specified in subsection (d) of this section, an individual who is a candidate in calendar year 1978 shall file the report required by such subsection not later than November 1, 1978, except that a candidate for the Senate who has filed a report as of such date pursuant to the Rules of the Senate need not file the report required by subsection (d) of this section.

Contents of Reports

Sec. 102. (a) Each report filed pursuant to subsections (a) and (b) of section 101 shall include a full and complete statement with respect to the following:

(1)(A) The source, type, and amount or value of income (other than income referred to in subparagraph (B)) from any source (other than from current employment by the United States Government), and the source, date, and amount of honoraria from any source, received during the preceding calendar year, aggregating $100 or more in value.

(B) The source and type of income which consists of dividends, interest, rent, and capital gains, received during the preceding calendar year which exceeds $100 in amount or value, and an indication of which of the following categories the amount or value of such item of income is within:

(i) not more than $1,000,

(ii) greater than $1,000 but not more than $2,500,

(iii) greater than $2,500 but not more than $5,000,

(iv) greater than $5,000 but not more than $15,000,

(v) greater than $15,000 but not more than $50,000,

(vi) greater than $50,000 but not more than $100,000, or

(vii) greater than $100,000.

(2)(A) The identity of the source and a brief description of any gifts of transportation, lodging, food, or entertainment aggregating $250 or more in value received from any source other than a relative of the reporting individual during the preceding calendar year, except that any food, lodging, or entertainment received as personal hospitality of any individual need not be reported, and any gift a fair market value of $35 or less need not be aggregated for purposes of this subparagraph.

(B) The identity of the source, a brief description, and the value of all gifts other than transportation, lodging food, or entertainment aggregating $100 or more in value received from any source other than a relative of the reporting individual during the preceding calendar year, except that any gift with a fair market value of $35 or less need not be aggregated for purposes of this subparagraph. A gift need not be so aggregated if in an unusual case, a publicly available request for a waiver is granted.

(C) The identity of the source and a brief description of reimbursements received from any source aggregating $250 or more in value and received during the preceding calendar year.

(3) The identity and category of value of any interest in property held during the preceding calendar year in a trade or business, or for investment or the production of income, which has a fair market value which exceeds $1,000 as of the close of the preceding calendar year, excluding any personal liability owed to the reporting individual by a relative or any deposits aggregating $5,000 or less in a personal savings account. For purposes of this paragraph, a personal savings account shall include any certificate of deposit or any other form of deposit in a bank, savings and loan association, credit union, or similar financial institution.

(4) The identity and category of value of the total liabilities owed to any creditor other than a relative which exceed $10,000 at any time during the preceding calendar year, excluding—

(A) any mortgage secured by real property which is a personal residence of the reporting individual or his spouse;

(B) any loan secured by a personal motor vehicle, house hold furniture, or appliances, which loan does not exceed the purchase price of the item which secures it.

With respect to revolving charge accounts, only those with an outstanding liability which exceeds $10,000 ad of the close of the preceding calendar year need be reported under this paragraph.

(5) Except as provided in this paragraph, a brief description, the date, and category of value of any purchase, sale, or exchange during the preceding calendar year which exceeds $1,000—

(A) in real property, other than property used solely as a personal residence of the reporting individual or his spouse; or

(B) in stocks, bonds, commodities futures, and other forms of securities.

Reporting is not required under this paragraph of any transaction solely by and between the reporting individual, his spouse, or dependent children.

(6) The identity of all positions on or before the date of filing during the current calendar year as an officer, director, trustee, partner, proprietor, representative, employee, or consultant of any corporation, company, firm, partnership, or other business enterprise, any nonprofit organization, any labor organization, or any educational or other institution other than the United States. This paragraph shall not require the reporting of positions held in any religious, social, fraternal, or political entity and positions solely of an honorary nature.

(7) A description of the date, parties to, and terms of any agreement or arrangement with respect to: (A) future employment; (B) a leave of absence during the period of the reporting individual's Government service; (C) continuation of payments by a former employer other than the United States Government; and (D) continuing participation in an employee welfare or benefit plan maintained by a former employer.

(b) Each report filed pursuant to subsections (c) and (d) of section 101 shall include a full and complete statement with respect to the information required by paragraphs (3), (4), (6), and (in the case of reports filed pursuant to subsection (c) of section 101) (7) of subsection (a), as of a date, specified in such report, which shall be not more than thirty-one days prior to the date of filing, and the information required by paragraph (1) of subsection (a) for the year of filing and the preceding calendar year.

* * *

Source:
Statutes at Large, Vol. 92, pp. 1,824–1,885.

Ronald Reagan, First Inaugural Address, 1981

Politically, the United States voter had become more conservative since the days of Lyndon B. Johnson's Great Society. Ronald Reagan entered office with a strong conservative mandate. In his inaugural address, January 20, 1981, he set out the program that his administration, backed by a Republican Senate, would follow. Stressing his belief that big government was the cause of America's economic problems, Reagan announced his intention to "curb the size and influence of the federal establishment." He stated, "Government must provide opportunity, not smother it; foster productivity, not stifle it." His administration then dismantled social and economic programs like the Comprehensive Employment and Training Act (CETA), declaring them unworkable and a failure, which in CETA's case, at least, was not true. This legislation, enacted December 28, 1973, provided funding for employment and training for unemployed and underemployed people, creating a national manpower services program for these purposes. Programs were instituted to supply training for public-service jobs in an effort to aid the unemployed and also make federal, state, and local services more flexible. The act put some 300,000 people to work, accomplishing jobs with federal money that otherwise might have gone unfunded, such as work with state historical societies.

To create a healthy economy, Reagan sought to lighten the tax burden. Congress passed his tax reduction plan July 29, 1981. It rested on a theory called supply side economics: more money in private hands would "trickle down" and generate income for all segments of society. Despite significant cuts in federal programs, the tax reduction resulted in huge federal deficits not overcome until the last years of the Clinton administration.

In his inaugural address Reagan also demanded recognition of the distinction between the powers granted by the U.S. Constitution to the federal government and those reserved to the states. Indeed, with the concurrence of the Democratic House of Representatives, his program of reduction in federal programs was enacted, which meant more responsibilities fell to the states.

Senator Hatfield, Mr. Chief Justice, Mr. President, Vice President Bush, Vice President Mondale, Senator Baker, Speaker O'Neill, Reverend Moomaw, and my fellow citizens:

To a few of us here today this is a solemn and most momentous occasion, and yet in the history of our nation it is a common-place occurrence. The orderly transfer of authority as called for in the Constitution routinely takes place, as it has for almost two centuries, and few of us stop to think how unique we really are. In the eyes of many in the world, this every-four-year ceremony we accept as normal is nothing less than a miracle.

Mr. President, I want our fellow citizens to know how much you did to carry on this tradition. By your gracious cooperation in the transition process, you have shown a watching world that we are a united people pledged to maintaining a political system which guarantees individual liberty to a greater degree than any other, and I thank you and your people for all your help in maintaining the continuity which is the bulwark of our Republic.

The business of our nation goes forward. These United States are confronted with an economic affliction of great proportions. We suffer from the longest and one of the worst sustained inflations in our national history. It distorts our economic decisions, penalizes thrift, and crushes the struggling young and the fixed-income elderly alike. It threatens to shatter the lives of millions of our people.

Idle industries have cast workers into unemployment, human misery, and personal indignity. Those who do work are denied a fair return for their labor by a tax system which penalizes successful achievement and keeps us from maintaining full productivity.

But great as our tax burden is, it has not kept pace with public spending. For decades we have piled deficit upon deficit, mortgaging our future and our children's future for the temporary convenience of the present. To continue this long trend is to guarantee tremendous social, cultural, political, and economic upheavals.

You and I, as individuals, can, by borrowing, live beyond our means, but for only a limited period of time. Why, then, should we think that collectively, as a nation, we're not bound by that same limitation? We must act today in order to preserve tomorrow. And let there be no misunderstanding: We are going to begin to act, beginning today.

The economic ills we suffer have come upon us over several decades. They will not go away in days, weeks, or months, but they will go away. They will go away because we as Americans have the capacity now, as we've had in the past, to do whatever needs to be done to preserve this last and greatest bastion of freedom.

In this present crisis, government is not the solution to our problem; government is the problem. From time to time we've been tempted to believe that society has become too complex to be managed by self-rule, that government by an elite group is superior to government for, by, and of the people. Well, if no one among us is capable of governing himself, then who among us has the capacity to govern someone else? All of us together, in and out of government, must bear the burden. The solutions we seek must be equitable, with no one group singled out to pay a higher price.

We hear much of special interest groups. Well, our concern must be for a special interest group that has been too long neglected. It knows no sectional boundaries or ethnic and racial divisions, and it crosses-political party lines. It is made up of men and women who raise our food, patrol our streets, man our mines and factories, teach our children, keep our homes, and heal us when we're sick—professionals, industrialists, shopkeepers, clerks, cabbies, and truckdrivers. They are, in short, "We the people," this breed called Americans.

Well, this administration's objective will be a healthy, vigorous, growing economy that provides equal opportunities for all Americans, with no barriers born of bigotry or discrimination. Putting America back to work means putting all Americans back to work. Ending inflation means freeing all Americans from the terror of runaway living costs. All must share in the productive work of this "new beginning," and all must share in the bounty of a revived economy. With the idealism and fair play which are the core of our system and our strength, we can have a strong and prosperous America, at peace with itself and the world.

So, as we begin, let us take inventory. We are a nation that has a government—not the other way around. And this makes us special among the nations of the Earth. Our government has no power except that granted it by the people. It is time to check and reverse the growth of government, which shows signs of having grown beyond the consent of the governed.

It is my intention to curb the size and influence of the Federal establishment and to demand recognition of the distinction between the powers granted to the Federal Government and those reserved to the States or to the people. All of us need to be reminded that the Federal Government did not create the States; the States created the Federal Government.

Now, so there will be no misunderstanding, it's not my intention to do away with government. It is rather to make it work—work with us, not over us; to stand by our side, not ride on our back. Government can and must provide opportunity, not smother it; foster productivity, not stifle it.

If we look to the answer as to why for so many years we achieved so much, prospered as no other people on Earth, it was because here in this land we unleashed the energy and individual genius of man to a greater extent than has ever been done before. Freedom and the dignity of the individual have been more available and assured here than in any other place on Earth. The price for this freedom at times has been high, but we have never been unwilling to pay that price.

It is no coincidence that our present troubles parallel and are proportionate to the intervention and intrusion in our lives that result from unnecessary and excessive growth of government. It is time for us to realize that we're too great a nation to limit ourselves to small dreams. We're not, as some would have us believe, doomed to an inevitable decline. I do not believe in a fate that will fall on us no matter what we do. I do believe in a fate that will fall on us if we do nothing. So, with all the creative energy at our command, let us begin an era of national renewal. Let us renew our determination, our courage, and our strength. And let us renew our faith and our hope.

We have every right to dream heroic dreams. Those who say that we're in a time when there are not heroes, they just don't know where to look. You can see heroes every day going in and out of factory gates. Others, a handful in number, produce enough food to feed all of us then the world beyond. You meet heroes across a counter, and they're on both sides of that counter. There are entrepreneurs with faith in themselves and faith in an idea who create new jobs, new wealth and opportunity. They're individuals and families whose taxes support the government and whose voluntary gifts support church, charity, culture, art, and education. Their patriotism is quiet, but deep. Their values sustain our national life.

Now, I have used the words "they" and "their" in speaking of these heroes. I could say "you" and "your," because I'm addressing the heroes of whom I speak—you, the citizens of this blessed land. Your dreams, your hopes, your goals are going to be the dreams, the hopes, and the goals of this administration, so help me God.

We shall reflect the compassion that is so much a part of your makeup. How can we love our country and not love our countrymen; and loving them, reach out a hand when they fall, heal them when they're sick, and provide opportunity to make them self-sufficient so they will be equal in fact and not just in theory?

Can we solve the problems confronting us? Well, the answer is an unequivocal and emphatic "yes." To paraphrase Winston Churchill, I did not take the oath I've just taken with the intention of presiding over the dissolution of the world's strongest economy.

In the days ahead I will propose removing the roadblocks that have slowed our economy and reduced productivity. Steps will be taken aimed at restoring the balance between the various levels of government. Progress may be slow, measured in inches and feet, not miles, but we will progress. It is time to reawaken this industrial giant, to get government back within its means, and to lighten our punitive tax burden. And these will be our first priorities, and on these principles there will be no compromise.

On the eve of our struggle for independence a man who might have been one of the greatest among the Founding Fathers, Dr. Joseph Warren, president of the Massachusetts Congress, said to his fellow Americans, "Our country is in danger, but not to be despaired of. . .On you depend the fortunes of America. You are to decide the important questions upon which rests the happiness and the liberty of millions yet unborn. Act worthy of yourselves."

Well, I believe we, the Americans of today, are ready to act worthy of ourselves, ready to do what must be done to ensure happiness and liberty for ourselves, our children, and our children's children. And as we renew ourselves here in our own land, we will be seen as having greater strength throughout the world. We will again be the exemplar of freedom and a beacon of hope for those who do not now have freedom.

To those neighbors and allies who share our freedom, we will strengthen our historic ties and assure them of our support and firm commitment. We will match loyalty with loyalty. We will strive for mutually beneficial relations. We will not use our friendship to impose on their sovereignty, for our own sovereignty is not for sale.

As for the enemies of freedom, those who are potential adversaries, they will be reminded that peace is the highest aspiration of the American people. We will negotiate for it, sacrifice for it; we will not surrender for it, now or ever.

Our forbearance should never be misunderstood. Our reluctance for conflict should not be misjudged as a failure of will. When action is required to preserve our national security, we will act. We will maintain sufficient strength to prevail if need be, knowing that if we do so we have the best chance of never having to use that strength.

Above all, we must realize that no arsenal or no weapon in the arsenals of the world is so formidable as the will and moral courage of free men and women. It is a weapon our adversaries in today's world do not have. It is a weapon that we as Americans do have. Let that be understood by those who practice terrorism and prey upon their neighbors.

I'm told that tens of thousands of prayer meetings are being held on this day, and for that I'm deeply grateful. We are a nation under God, and I believe God intended for us to be free. It would be fitting and good, I think, if on each Inaugural Day in future years it should be declared a day of prayer.

This is the first time in our history that this ceremony has been held, as you've been told, on this West Front of the Capitol. Standing here, one faces a magnificent vista, opening up on this city's special beauty and history. At the end of this open mall are those shrines to the giants on whose shoulders we stand.

Directly in front of me, the monument to a monumental man, George Washington, father of our country. A man of humility who came to greatness reluctantly. He led America out of revolutionary victory into infant nationhood. Off to one side, the stately memorial to Thomas Jefferson. The Declaration of Independence flames with his eloquence. And then, beyond the Reflecting Pool, the dignified columns of the Lincoln Memorial. Whoever would understand in his heart the meaning of America will find it in the life of Abraham Lincoln.

Beyond those monuments to heroism is the Potomac River, and on the far shore the sloping hills of Arlington National Cemetery, with its row upon row of simple white markers bearing crosses or Stars of David. They add up to only a tiny fraction of the price that has been paid for our freedom.

Each one of those markers is a monument to the kind of hero I spoke of either. Their lives ended in places called Belleau Wood, The Argonne, Omaha Beach, Salerno, and halfway around the world on Guadalcanal, Tarawa, Pork Chop Hill, the Chosin Reservoir, and in a hundred rice paddies and jungles of a place called Vietnam.

Under one such marker lies a young man, Martin Treptow, who left his job in a small town barbershop in 1917 to go to France with the famed Rainbow Division. There, on the western front, he was killed trying to carry a message between battalions under heavy artillery fire.

We're told that on his body was found a diary. On the flyleaf under the heading, "My Pledge," he had written these words: "America must win this war. Therefore I will work, I will save, I will sacrifice, I will endure, I will fight cheerfully and do my utmost, as if the issue of the whole struggle depended on me alone."

The crisis we are facing today does not require of us the kind of sacrifice that Martin Treptow and so many thousands of others were called upon to make. It does require, however, our best effort and our willingness to believe in ourselves and to believe in our capacity to perform great deeds, to believe that together with God's help we can and will resolve the problems which now confront us.

And after all, why shouldn't we believe that? We are Americans.

God bless you, and thank you.

Source:

Public Papers of the Presidents of the United States: Ronald Reagan, 1981–1988. Washington, D.C.: Government Printing Office, 1982–91.

Immigration and Naturalization Service v. Chadha, 1983

This case dealt with a device, first used in 1932, called a congressional or legislative veto. Usually applied to domestic questions, it was a way for Congress to control executive authority. When placed in a law, it required certain presidential decisions to be subject to congressional disapproval, either by one or both houses. In some instances, Congress further delegated the veto to a committee or even a subcommittee so as not to burden the entire house. This process allowed Congress to respond to changing circumstances and make adjustments. Although legislative veto cases had come before the Supreme Court before, *Chadha* was the first time it dealt with its merits.

Chadha, a foreign national, was admitted to the United States on a student visa, and, after his visa had expired, an immigration judge suspended his deportation. By the terms of the Immigration and Nationality Act, which authorized either house of Congress to invalidate the decision of the executive branch allowing a particular deportable alien to remain in the United States, the House of Representatives vetoed this suspension. Chadha subsequently challenged the constitutionality of the act. The Supreme Court ruled 7-2, with Associate Justices White and Rehnquist dissenting, that the congressional veto provision of the act was unconstitutional. Chief Justice Burger, writing for the majority, reasoned that this action was legislative and subject to the procedural requirements for legislative action. A one-house veto, he held, is inherently unconstitutional, and by implication, so was a two-house veto. Congress continued to insert legislative veto provisions in statutes, but *Chadha* was cited when the Court, in *Clinton v. New York* (524 U.S. 681 [1998]), struck down the president's line-item veto in budget bills.

(excerpt)

Chief Justice Burger delivered the opinion of the Court.

We granted certiorari. Each [case] presents a challenge to the constitutionality of the provision in Section 244(c)(2) of the Immigration, 66 Stat. 216, as amended, 8 U.S.C. Section 1254(c)(2), authorizing one House of Congress by resolution, to invalidate the decision of the Executive Branch, pursuant to authority delegated by Congress to the Attorney General of the United States, to allow a particular deportable alien to remain in the United States.

I

Chadha is an East Indian who was born in Kenya and holds a British passport. He was lawfully admitted to the United States in 1966 on a nonimmigrant student visa. His visa expired on June 30, 1972. On October 11, 1973, the District Director of the Immigration and Naturalization Service ordered Chadha to show cause why he should not be deported for having "remained in the United States for a longer time than permitted." . . . A deportation hearing was held before an Immigration Judge on January 11, 1974. Chadha conceded that he was deportable for overstaying his visa and the hearing was adjourned to enable him to file an application for suspension of deportation. [The section of the Immigration and Nationality Act] at the time in question, provided:

". . . the Attorney General may, in his discretion, suspend deportation and adjust the status to that of an alien lawfully admitted for permanent residence, in the case of an alien who applies to the Attorney General for suspension of deportation and—

"(1) is deportable . . . ; has been physically present in the United States for a continuous period of not less than seven years immediately preceding the date of such application, and proves that during all of such period he was and is a person of good moral character; and is a person whose deportation would, in the opinion of the Attorney General, result in extreme hardship to the alien or to his spouse, parent, or child, who is a citizen of the United States or an alien lawfully admitted for permanent residence."

After Chadha submitted his application for suspension of deportation, the deportation hearing was resumed on February 7, 1974. On the basis of evidence adduced at the hearing . . . the Immigration Judge, on June 25, 1974, ordered that Chadha's deportation be suspended. . .and a report of the suspension was transmitted to Congress.

Once the Attorney General's recommendation for suspension of Chadha's deportation was conveyed to Congress, Congress had the power . . . to veto the Attorney General's determination that Chadha should not be deported. . . .

* * *

On December 12, 1975, Representative Eilberg, Chairman of the Judiciary Subcommittee on Immigration, Citizenship, and International Law, introduced a resolution opposing "the granting of permanent residence in the United States to [six] aliens," including Chadha. The resolution was referred to the House Committee on the Judiciary. On December 16, 1975, the resolution was discharged from further consideration by the House Committee on the Judiciary and submitted to the House of Representatives for a vote. The resolution had not been printed and was not made available to other Members of the House prior to or at the time it was voted on. So far, as the record before us shows, the House consideration of the resolution was based on Representative Eilberg's statement from the floor that

[i]t was the feeling of the committee, after reviewing 340 cases, that the aliens contained in the resolution [Chadha and five others] did not meet these statutory requirements, particularly as it relates to hardship; and it is the opinion of the committee that their deportation should not be suspended.

The resolution was passed without debate or recorded vote. Since the House action was pursuant to Section 244(c)(2), the resolution was not treated as an Art. I legislative act; it was not submitted to the Senate or presented to the President for his action.

After the House veto of the Attorney General's decision to allow Chadha to remain in the United States, the Immigration Judge reopened the deportation proceedings to implement the House order deporting Chadha. Chadha moved to terminate the proceedings on the ground that Section 244(c)(2) is unconstitutional. The Immigration Judge held that he had no authority to rule on the constitutional validity of Section 244(c)(2). On November 8, 1976, Chadha was ordered deported pursuant to the House action.

Chadha appealed the deportation order to the Board of Immigration Appeals, again contending that Section 244(c)(2) is unconstitutional. The Board held that it had "no power to declare unconstitutional an act of Congress" and Chadha's appeal was dismissed.

. . .Chadha filed a petition for review of the deportation order in the United States Court of Appeals for the Ninth Circuit. The Immigration and Naturalization Service agreed with Chadha's position before the Court of Appeals and joined him in arguing that Section 244(c)(2) is unconstitutional. In light of the importance of the question, the Court of Appeals invited both the Senate and the House of Representatives to file briefs amici curiae.

. . .The Court of Appeals held that the House was without constitutional authority to order Chadha's deportation; accordingly it directed the Attorney General "to cease and desist from taking any steps to deport this alien based upon the resolution enacted by the House of Representatives." The essence of its holding was that Section 244(c)(2) violates the constitutional doctrine of separation of powers.

We . . . now affirm.

II

Before we address the important question of the constitutionality of the one-House veto provision of Section 244(c)(2), we first consider several challenges to the authority of this Court to resolve the issue raised.

A

Appellate Jurisdiction

[1] Both Houses of Congress contend that we are without jurisdiction under 28 U.S.C. Section 1252 to entertain the INS appeal. . .:

"Any party may appeal to the Supreme Court from an interlocutory or final judgment, decree or order of any court of the United States, the United States District Court for the District of the Canal Zone, the District Court of Guam and the District Court of the Virgin Islands and any court of record of Puerto Rico, holding an Act of Congress unconstitutional in any civil action, suit, or proceeding to which the United States or any of its agencies, or any officer or employee thereof, as such officer or employee, is a party."

. . .The express requisites for an appeal under Section 1252, therefore, have been met.

. . .Both Houses contend that the INS has already received what it sought from the Court of Appeals, is not an aggrieved party, and therefore cannot appeal from the decision of the Court of Appeals. We cannot agree.

. . .The INS brief to the Court of Appeals did not alter the agency's decision to comply with the House action ordering deportation of Chadha. The Court of Appeals set aside the deportation proceedings and ordered the Attorney General to cease and desist from taking any steps to deport Chadha; steps that the Attorney General would have taken were it not for that decision.

[2] . . .We hold that the INS was sufficiently aggrieved by the Court of Appeals decision prohibiting it from taking action it would otherwise take. . . . When an agency of the United States is a party to a case in which the Act of Congress it administers is held unconstitutional, it is an aggrieved party for purposes of taking an appeal under Section 1252. The appeal . . . is therefore properly before us.

B

Severability

Congress also contends that the provision for the one-House veto in Section 244(c)(2) cannot be severed from Section 244. Congress argues that if the provision for the one-House veto is held unconstitutional, all of Section 244 must fall. If Section 244 in its entirety is violative of the Constitution, it follows that the Attorney General has no authority to suspend Chadha's deportation under Section 244(a)(1) and Chadha would be deported. From this, Congress argues that Chadha lacks standing to challenge the constitutionality of the one-House veto provision because he could receive no relief even if his constitutional challenge proves successful.

Only recently this Court reaffirmed that the invalid portions of a statute are to be severed "'[u]nless it is evident that the Legislature would not have enacted those provisions which are within its power, independently of that which is not.'" . . . Congress itself has provided the answer to the question of severability in Section 406 of the Immigration and Nationality Act, note following 8 U.S.C. Section 1101, which provides:

"If any particular provision of this Act, or the application thereof to any person or circumstance, is held invalid, the remainder of the Act and the application of such provision to other persons or circumstances shall not be affected thereby."

* * *

Standing

We must also reject the contention that Chadha lacks standing because a consequence of his prevailing will advance the interests of the Executive Branch in a separation-of-powers dispute with Congress, rather than simply Chadha's private interests. Chadha has demonstrated "injury in fact and a substantial likelihood that the judicial relief requested will prevent or redress the claimed injury . . . ." If the veto provision violates the Constitution, and is severable, the deportation order against Chadha will be canceled. Chadha therefore has standing to challenge the order of the Executive mandated by the House veto.

D

Alternative Relief

It is contended that the Court should decline to decide the constitutional question presented by these cases because Chadha may have other statutory relief available to him. It is argued that since Chadha married a United States citizen on August 10, 1980, it is possible that other avenues of relief may be open under [other sections]. It is true that Chadha may be eligible for classification as an "immediate relative" and, as such, could lawfully be accorded permanent residence. Moreover, in March 1980, just prior to the decision of the Court of Appeals in this case, Congress enacted the Refugee Act of 1980, under which the Attorney General is authorized to grant asylum, and then permanent residence, to any alien who is unable to return to his country of nationality because of "a well-founded fear of persecution on account of race."

It is urged that these two intervening factors constitute a prudential bar to our consideration of the constitutional question presented in this case. If we could perceive merit in this contention we might well seek to avoid deciding the constitutional claim advanced. But at most these other avenues of relief are speculative. It is by no means certain, for example, that Chadha's classification as an immediate relative would result in the adjustment of Chadha's status from nonimmigrant to permanent resident. If Chadha is successful in his present challenge he will not be deported and will automatically become eligible to apply for citizenship. A person threatened with deportation cannot be denied the right to challenge the constitutional validity of the process which led to his status merely on the basis of speculation over the availability of other forms of relief.

E

Jurisdiction

It is contended that the Court of Appeals lacked jurisdiction. . . . Congress argues that the one-House veto . . . takes place outside the administrative proceedings . . . and that the jurisdiction grant contained in Section 106(a) does not encompass Chadha's constitutional challenge. . . . Here, Chadha's deportation stands or falls on the validity of the challenged veto; the final order of deportation was entered against Chadha only to implement the action of the House of Representatives. Although the Attorney General was satisfied that the House action was invalid and that it should not have any effect on his decision to suspend deportation, he appropriately let controversy take its course through the courts.

. . . Chadha directly attacks the deportation order itself, and the relief he seeks—cancellation of deportation—is plainly inconsistent with the deportation order. Accordingly, the Court of Appeals had jurisdiction. . . .

F

Case or Controversy

[9] It is also contended that this is not a genuine controversy but "a friendly, nonadversary, proceeding" upon which the Court should not pass. This argument rests on the fact that Chadha and the INS take the same position on the constitutionality of the one-House veto. But it would be a curious result if, in the administration of justice, a person could be denied access to the courts because the Attorney General of the United States agreed with the legal arguments asserted by the individual.

A case or controversy is presented by these cases. . . . Congress is both a proper party to defend the constitutionality of Section 244(c)(2) and a proper petitioner under 28 U.S.C. Section 1254(1). Second, prior to Congress' intervention, there was adequate Art. III adverseness even though the only parties were the INS and Chadha. . . . We agree with the Court of Appeals that "Chadha has asserted a concrete controversy, and our decision will have real meaning: if we rule for Chadha, he will not be deported; if we uphold Section 244(c)(2), the INS will execute its order and deport him."

. . . We have long held that Congress is the proper party to defend the validity of a statute when an agency of government, as a defendant charged with enforcing the statute, agrees with plaintiffs that the statute is inapplicable or unconstitutional.

G

Political Question

It is also argued that these cases present a nonjusticiable political question because Chadha is merely challenging Congress' authority under the Naturalization Clause, U.S. Const., Art. I, Section 8, cl. 4, and the Necessary and Proper Clause, U.S.Const., Art. I, Section 8, cl. 18. It is argued that Congress' Art. I power "To establish an uniform Rule of Naturalization," combined with the Necessary and Proper Clause, grants it unreviewable authority over the regulation of aliens. The plenary authority of Congress over aliens under Art. I, Section 8, cl. 4, is not open to question, but what is challenged here is whether Congress has chosen a constitutionally permissible means of implementing that power. ". . . Congress has plenary authority in all cases in which it has substantive legislative jurisdiction so long as the exercise of that authority does not offend some other constitutional restriction."

* * *

It is correct that this controversy may, in a sense, be termed "political." But the presence of constitutional issues with significant political overtones does not automatically invoke the political question doctrine. Resolution of litigation challenging the constitutional authority of one of the three branches cannot be evaded by courts because the issues have political implications in the sense urged by Congress.

* * *

III A

We turn now to the question whether action of one House of Congress under Section 244(c)(2) violates strictures of the Constitution. We begin, of course, with the presumption that the challenged statute is valid. Its wisdom is not the concern of the courts; if a challenged action does not violate the Constitution, it must be sustained. . . .

* * *

By the same token, the fact that a given law or procedure is efficient, convenient, and useful in facilitating functions of government, standing alone, will not save it if it is contrary to the Constitution. Convenience and efficiency are not the primary objectives—or the hallmarks—of democratic government and our inquiry is sharpened rather than blunted by the fact that congressional veto provisions are appearing with increasing frequency in statutes which delegate authority to executive and independent agencies. . . .

* * *

Justice White undertakes to make a case for the proposition that the one-House veto is a useful "political invention," and we need not challenge that assertion. . . . But policy arguments supporting even useful "political inventions" are subject to the demands of the Constitution which defines powers and, with respect to this subject, sets out just how those powers are to be exercised.

Explicit and unambiguous provisions of the Constitution prescribe and define the respective functions of the Congress and of the Executive in the legislative process. Since the precise terms of those familiar provisions are critical to the resolution of these cases, we set them out verbatim. Article I provides:

"All legislative Powers herein granted shall be vested in a Congress of the United States, which shall consist of a Senate and House of Representatives." Art. I, Section 1. (Emphasis added.)

"Every Bill which shall have passed the House of Representatives and the Senate, shall, before it becomes a law, be presented to the President of the United States . . . ."

"Every Order, Resolution, or Vote to which the Concurrence of the Senate and House of Representatives may be necessary (except on a question of Adjournment) shall be presented to the President of the United States; and before the Same shall take Effect, shall be approved by him, or being disapproved by him, shall be repassed by two thirds of the Senate and House of Representatives, according to the Rules and Limitations prescribed in the Case of a Bill."

These provisions of Art. I are integral parts of the constitutional design for the separation of powers. . . . The very structure of the Articles delegating and separating powers under Arts. I, II, and III exemplifies the concept of separation of powers. . . .

* * *

IV

The Constitution sought to divide the delegated powers of the new Federal Government into three defined categories, Legislative, Executive, and Judicial, to assure, as nearly as possible, that each Branch of government would confine itself to its assigned responsibility. The hydraulic pressure inherent within each of the separate Branches to exceed the outer limits of its power, even to accomplish desirable objectives, must be resisted.

Although not "hermetically" sealed from one another, the powers delegated to the three Branches are functionally identifiable. When any Branch acts, it is presumptively exercising the power the Constitution has delegated to it. When the Executive acts, he presumptively acts in an executive or administrative capacity as defined in Art. II. And when, as here, one House of Congress purports to act, it is presumptively acting within its assigned sphere.

Beginning with this presumption, we must nevertheless establish that the challenged action under Section 244(c)(2) is of the kind to which the procedural requirement of Art. I, Section 7, apply. . . .Whether actions taken by either House are, in law and fact, an exercise of legislative power depends not on their form but upon "whether they contain matter which is properly to be regarded as legislative in its character and effect."

Examination of the action taken here by one House pursuant to Section 244(c)(2) reveals that it was essentially legislative in purpose and effect. In purporting to exercise power defined in Art. I, Section 8, cl. 4, to "establish an uniform Rule of Naturalization," the House took action that had the purpose and effect of altering the legal rights, duties, and relations of persons, including the Attorney General, Executive Branch officials and Chadha, all outside the Legislative Branch. Section 244(c)(2) purports to authorize one House of Congress to require the Attorney General to deport an individual alien whose deportation otherwise would be canceled under Section 244. The one-House veto operated in these cases to overrule the Attorney General and mandate Chadha's deportation; absent the House action, Chadha would remain in the United States. Congress has acted and its action has altered Chadha's status.

The legislative character of the one-House veto in these cases is confirmed by the character of the congressional action it supplants. Neither the House of Representatives nor the Senate contends that, absent the veto provision in Section 244(c)(2), either of them, or both of them acting together, could effectively require the Attorney General to deport an alien once the Attorney General, in the exercise of legislatively delegated authority, had determined the alien should remain in the United States. Without the challenged provision in Section 244(c)(2), this could have been achieved, if at all, only by legislation requiring deportation. Similarly, a veto by one House of Congress under Section 244(c)(2) cannot be justified as an attempt at amending the standards set out in Section 244(a)(1), or as a repeal of Section 244 as applied to Chadha. Amendment and repeal of statutes, no less than enactment, must conform with Art. I.

The nature of the decision implemented by the one-House veto in these cases further manifests its legislative character. After long experience with the clumsy, time-consuming private bill procedure, Congress made a deliberate choice to delegate to the Executive Branch, and specifically to the Attorney General, the authority to allow deportable aliens to remain in this country in certain specified circumstances. It is not disputed that this choice to delegate authority is precisely the kind of decision that can be implemented only in accordance with the procedures set out in Art. 1. Disagreement with the Attorney General's decision on Chadha's deportation—that is, Congress' decision to deport Chadha—no less than Congress' original choice to delegate to the Attorney General the authority to make that decision, involves determinations of policy that Congress can implement in only one way; bicameral passage followed by presentment to the President. Congress must abide by its delegation of authority until that delegation is legislatively altered or revoked.

Finally, we see that when the Framers intended to authorize either House of Congress to act alone and outside of its prescribed bicameral legislative role, they narrowly and precisely defined the procedure for such action. There are four provisions in the Constitution, explicit and unambiguous, by which one House may act alone with the unreviewable force of law, not subject to the President's veto:

(a) The House of Representatives alone was given the power to initiate impeachment's.

(b) The Senate alone was given the power to conduct trials following impeachment on charges initiated by the House and to convict following trial.

(c) The Senate alone was given final unreviewable power to approve or to disapprove Presidential appointments.

(d) The Senate alone was given unreviewable power to ratify treaties negotiated by the President.

Clearly, when the Draftsmen sought to confer special powers on one House, independent of the other House, or of the President, they did so in explicit, unambiguous terms. These carefully defined exceptions from presentment and bicameralism underscore the difference between the legislative functions of Congress and other unilateral but important and binding one-House acts provided for in the Constitution. These exceptions are narrow, explicit, and separately justified; none of them authorize the action challenged here. On the contrary, they provide further support for the conclusion that congressional authority is not to be implied and for the conclusion that the veto provided for in Section 244(c)(2) is not authorized by the Constitutional design of the powers of the Legislative Branch.

Since it is clear that the action by the House under Section 244(c)(2) was not within any of the express constitutional exceptions authorizing one House to act alone, and equally clear that it was an exercise of legislative power, that action was subject to the standards prescribed in Art. I. The bicameral requirement, the Presentment Clauses, the President's veto, and Congress' power to override a veto were intended to erect enduring checks on each

Branch and to protect the people from the improvident exercise of power by mandating certain prescribed steps. To preserve those checks, and maintain the separation of powers, the carefully defined limits on the power of each Branch must not be eroded. To accomplish what has been attempted by one House of Congress in this case requires action in conformity with the express procedures of the Constitution's prescription for legislative action: passage by a majority of both Houses and presentment to the President.

The veto authorized by Section 244(c)(2) doubtless has been in many respects a convenient shortcut; the "sharing" with the Executive by Congress of its authority over aliens in this manner is, on its face, an appealing compromise. In purely practical terms, it is obviously easier for action to be taken by one House without submission to the President; but it is crystal clear from the records of the Convention, contemporaneous writings and debates, that the Framers ranked other values higher than efficiency. The records of the Convention and debates in the states preceding ratification underscore the common desire to define and limit the exercise of the newly created federal powers affecting the states and the people. There is unmistakable expression of a determination that legislation by the national Congress be a step-by-step, deliberate and deliberative process.

The choices we discern as having been made in the Constitutional Convention impose burdens on governmental processes that often seem clumsy, inefficient, even unworkable, but those hard choices were consciously made by men who had lived under a form of government that permitted arbitrary governmental acts to go unchecked. There is no support in the Constitution or decisions of this Court for the proposition that the cumbersomeness and delays often encountered in complying with explicit constitutional standards may be avoided, either by the Congress or by the President. With all the obvious flaws of delay, untidiness, and potential for abuse, we have not yet found a better way to preserve freedom than by making the exercise of power subject to the carefully crafted restrains spelled out in the Constitution.

V

We hold that the congressional veto provision in Section 244(c)(2) is severable from the Act and that it is unconstitutional. Accordingly, the judgment of the Court of Appeals is

Affirmed.

Source:

Supreme Court Reporter, Vol. 103, pp. 2,764–2,817.

Texas v. Johnson, 1989

U.S. Supreme Court decision issued June 21, 1989, declaring that burning the American flag as a form of symbolic speech was an action protected by First Amendment guarantee of free expression. In its 5-4 decision, the Court ruled that the government "may not prohibit the expression of an idea simply because society finds the idea itself offensive or disagreeable." The case involved Gregory Johnson, a member of a Communist Party youth organization, who was convicted of defiling the flag after he burned one during the 1984 Republican National Convention in Dallas, Texas. The ruling invalidated state and federal laws against desecrating the flag and led to proposals for a U.S. constitutional amendment to prohibit flag burning.

Citations have been removed.

Justice Brennan delivered the opinion of the Court.

After publicly burning an American flag as a means of political protest, Gregory Lee Johnson was convicted of desecrating a flag in violation of Texas law. This case presents the question whether his conviction is consistent with the First Amendment. We hold that it is not.

I

While the Republican National Convention was taking place in Dallas in 1984, respondent Johnson participated in a political demonstrations dubbed the "Republican War Chest Tour." As explained in literature distributed by the demonstrators and in speeches made by them, the purpose of this event was to protest the policies of the Reagan administration and of certain Dallas-based corporations. The demonstrators marched through the Dallas streets, chanting political slogans and stopping at several corporate locations to stage "die-ins" intended to dramatize the consequences of nuclear war. On several occasions they spray-painted the walls of buildings and overturned potted plants, but Johnson himself took no part in such activities. He did, however, accept an American flag handed to him by a fellow protester who had taken it from a flagpole outside one of the targeted buildings.

The demonstration ended in front of Dallas City Hall, where Johnson unfurled the American flag, doused it with kerosene, and set it on fire. While the flag burned, the protester chanted: "America, the red, white, and blue, we spit on you." After the demonstrators dispersed, a witness to the flag burning collected the flag's remains and buried them in his backyard. No one was physically injured or threatened with injury, though several witnesses testified that they had been seriously offended by the flag burning.

Of the approximately 100 demonstrators, Johnson alone was charged with a crime. The only criminal offense with which he was charged was the desecration of a venerated object in violation of Tex.Penal Code. After a trial, he was convicted, sentenced to one year in prison, and fined $2,000. The Court of Appeals for the Fifth District of Texas at Dallas affirmed Johnson's conviction, but the Texas Court of Criminal Appeals reversed, holding that the State could not, consistent with the First Amendment, punish Johnson for burning the flag in these circumstances.

The Court of Criminal Appeals began by recognizing that Johnson's conduct was symbolic speech protected by the First Amendment: "Given the context of an organized demonstration, speeches, slogans, and the distribution of literature, anyone who observed appellant's act would have understood the message that appellant intended to convey. The act for which appellant was convicted was clearly 'speech' contemplated by the First Amendment." To justify Johnson's conviction for engaging in symbolic speech, the State asserted two interests: preserving the flag as a symbol of national unity and preventing breaches of the peace. The Court of Criminal Appeals held that neither interest supported his conviction.

Acknowledging that this Court had not yet decided whether the Government may criminally sanction flag desecration in order to preserve the flag's symbolic value, the Texas court nevertheless concluded that our decision in *West Virginia Board of Education v. Barnette* suggested that furthering this interest by curtailing speech was impermissible. "Recognizing that the right to differ is the centerpiece of our First Amendment freedoms," the court explained, "a government cannot mandate by fiat a feeling of unity in its citizens. Therefore, that very same government cannot carve out a symbol of unity and prescribed a set of approved messages to be associated with that symbol when it cannot mandate the status or feeling the symbol purports to represent." Noting that the State had not shown that the flag was in "grave and immediate danger" of being stripped of its symbolic value, the Texas court also decided that the flag's special status was not endangered by Johnson's conduct.

As to the State's goal of preventing breaches of the peace, the court concluded that the flag-desecration statute was not drawn narrowly enough to encompass only those flag burnings that were likely to result in a serious disturbance of the peace. And in fact, the court emphasized, the flag burning in this particular case did not threaten such a reaction. "Serious offense' occurred," the court admitted, "but there was no breach of peace nor does the record reflect that the situation was potentially explosive. One cannot equate 'serious offense' with incitement to breach the peace." The court also stressed that another Texas statute prohibited breaches of the peace. Citing *Boos v. Barry*, the court decided that Section 42.01 demonstrated Texas' ability to prevent disturbances of the peace without punishing this flag desecration.

Because it reversed Johnson's conviction on the ground that Section 42.09 was unconstitutional as applied to him, the state court did not address Johnson's argument that the statute was, on its face, unconstitutionally vague and overbroad. We granted certiorari and now affirm.

II

Johnson was convicted of flag desecration for burning the flag rather than for uttering insulting words. This fact somewhat complicates our consideration of his conviction under the First Amendment. We must first determine whether Johnson's burning of the flag constituted expressive conduct, permitting him to invoke the First Amendment in challenging his conviction. If his conduct was expressive, we next decide whether the State's regulation is related to the suppression of free expression. If the State's regulation is not related to expression, then the less stringent standard we announced in *United States v. O'Brien* for regulations of noncommunicative conduct controls. If it is, then we are outside of *O'Brien*' s test, and we must ask whether this interest justifies Johnson's conviction under a more demanding standard. A third possibility is that the State's asserted interest is simply not implicated on these facts, and in that event the interest drops out of the picture.

The First Amendment literally forbids the abridgment only of "speech," but we have long recognized that its protection does not end at the spoken or written word. While we have rejected "the view that an apparently limitless variety of conduct can be labeled 'speech' whenever the person engaging in the conduct intends thereby to express an idea," we have acknowledged that conduct may be "sufficiently imbued with elements of communication to fall within the scope of the First and Fourteenth Amendments. . . ."

In deciding whether particular conduct possesses sufficient communicative elements to bring the First Amendment into play, we have asked whether "[a]n intent to convey a particularized message was present, and [whether] the likelihood was great that the message would be understood by those who viewed it." Hence, we have recognized the expressive nature of students' wearing of black armbands to protest American military involvement in Vietnam; of a sit-in by blacks in a "whites only" area to protest segregation; of the wearing of American military uniforms in a dramatic presentation criticizing American involvement in Vietnam; and of picketing about a wide variety of causes.

Especially pertinent to this case are our decisions recognizing the communicative nature of conduct relating to flags. Attaching a peace sign to the flag, refusing to salute the flag, and displaying a red flag, we have held, all may find shelter under the First Amendment. That we have had little difficulty identifying an expressive element in conduct relating to flags should not be surprising. The very purpose of a national flag is to serve as a symbol of our country; it is, one might say, "the one visible manifestation of two hundred years of nationhood. Thus, we have observed:

"[T]he flag salute is a form of utterance. Symbolism is a primitive but effective way of communicating ideas. The use of an emblem or flag to symbolize some system, idea, institution, or personality, is a short cut from mind to mind. Causes and nations, political parties, lodges and ecclesiastical groups seek to knit the loyalty of their followings to a flag or banner, a color or design."

Pregnant with expressive content, the flag as readily signifies this Nation as does the combination of letters found in "America."

We have not automatically concluded, however, that any action taken with respect to our flag is expressive. Instead, in characterizing such action for First Amendment purposes, we have considered the context in which it occurred. . . .

The State of Texas conceded for purposes of its oral argument in this case that Johnson's conduct was expressive conduct, and this concession seems to us . . . prudent . . . . Johnson burned an American flag as part—indeed, as the culmination—of a political demonstration that coincided with the convening of the Republican Party and its renomination of Ronald Reagan for President. The expressive, overtly political nature of this conduct was both intentional and overwhelmingly apparent. At his trial, Johnson explained his reasons for burning the flag as follows: "The American Flag was burned as Ronald Reagan was being renominated as President. And a more powerful statement of symbolic speech, whether you agree with it or not, couldn't have been made at that time. It's quite a [juxtaposition]. We had new patriotism and no patriotism." In these circumstances, Johnson's burning of the flag was conduct "sufficiently imbued with elements of communication" to implicate the First Amendment.

III

The government generally has a freer hand in restricting expressive conduct than it has in restricting the written or spoken word. It may not, however, proscribe particular conduct because it has expressive elements. "[W]hat might be termed the more generalized guarantee of freedom of expression makes the communicative nature of conduct an inadequate basis for singling out that conduct for proscription. A law directed at the communicative nature of conduct must, like a law directed at speech itself, be justified by the substantial showing of need that the First Amendment requires." It is, in short, not simply the verbal or nonverbal nature of the expression, but the governmental interest at stake, that helps to determine whether a restriction on that expression is valid.

Thus, although we have recognized that where "'speech' and 'nonspeech' elements are combined in the same course of conduct, a sufficiently important governmental interest in regulating the nonspeech element can justify incidental limitations on First Amendment freedoms," we have limited the applicability of *O'Brien*'s relatively lenient standard to those cases in which "the governmental interest is unrelated to the suppression of free expression." In stating, moreover, that *O'Brien*'s test "in the last analysis is little, if any, different from the standard applied to time, place, or manner restrictions," we have highlighted the requirement that the governmental interest in question be unconnected to expression in order to come under *O'Brien*'s less demanding rule.

In order to decide whether *O'Brien*'s test applies here, therefore, we must decide whether Texas has asserted an interest in support of Johnson's conviction that is unrelated to the suppression of expression. If we find that an interest asserted by the State is simply not implicated on the facts before us, we need not ask whether *O'Brien*'s test applies. The State offers two separate interests to justify this conviction: preventing breaches of the peace and preserving the flag as a symbol of nationhood and national unity. We hold that the first interest is not implicated on this record and that the second is related to the suppression of expression.

A

Texas claims that its interest in preventing breaches of the peace justifies Johnson's conviction for flag desecration. However, no disturbance of the peace actually occurred or threatened to occur because of Johnson's burning of the flag. Although the State stresses the disruptive behavior of the protesters during their march toward City Hall, Brief for Petitioner 34-36, it admits that "no actual breach of the peace occurred at the time of the flagburning or in response to the flagburning."The State's emphasis on the protesters' disorderly actions prior to arriving at City Hall is not only somewhat surprising given that no charges were brought on the basis of this conduct, but it also fails to show that a disturbance of the peace was a likely reaction to Johnson's conduct. The only evidence offered by the State at trial to show the reaction to Johnson's actions was the testimony of several persons who had been seriously offended by the flag burning.

The State's position, therefore, amounts to a claim that an audience that takes serious offense at particular expression is necessarily likely to disturb the peace and that the expression may be prohibited on this basis. Our precedents do not countenance such a presumption. On the contrary, they recognize that a principal "function of free speech under our system of government is to invite dispute. It may indeed best serve its high purpose when it induces a condition of unrest, creates dissatisfaction with conditions as they are, or even stirs people to anger." It would be odd indeed to conclude both that "if it is the speaker's opinion that gives offense, that consequence is a reason for according its constitutional protection," and that the government may ban the expression of certain disagreeable ideas on the unsupported presumption that their very disagreeableness will provoke violence.

Thus, we have not permitted the government to assume that every expression of a provocative idea will incite a riot, but have instead required careful consideration of the actual circumstances surrounding such expression, asking whether the expression "is directed to inciting or producing imminent lawless action and is likely to incite or produce such action." To accept Texas' arguments that it need only demonstrate "the potential for a breach of the peace," and that every flag burning necessarily possesses that potential, would be to eviscerate our holding in *Brandenburg*. This we decline to do.

Nor does Johnson's expressive conduct fall within that small class of "fighting words" that are "likely to provoke the average person to retaliation, and thereby cause a breach of the peace." No reasonable onlooker would have regarded Johnson's generalized expression of dissatisfaction with the policies of the Federal Government as a direct personal insult or invitation to exchange fisticuffs.

We thus conclude that the State's interest in maintaining order is not implicated on these facts. The State need not worry that our holding will disable it from preserving the peace. We do not suggest that the First Amendment forbids a State to prevent "imminent lawless action." *Brandenburg.* And, in fact, Texas already has a statute specifically prohibiting breaches of the peace, which tends to confirm that Texas need not punish this flag desecration in order to keep the peace.

B

The State also asserts an interest in preserving the flag as a symbol of nationhood and national unity. In *Spence,* we acknowledged that the government's interest in preserving the flag's special symbolic value "is directly related to expression in the context of activity" such as affixing a peace symbol to a flag. We are equally persuaded that this interest is related to expression in the case of Johnson's burning of the flag. The State, apparently, is concerned that such conduct will lead people to believe either that the flag does not stand for nationhood and national unity, but instead reflects other, less positive concepts, or that the concepts reflected in the flag do not in fact exist, that is, that we do not enjoy unit as a Nation. These concerns blossom only when a person's treatment of the flag communicates some message, and thus are related "to the suppression of free expression" within the meaning of *O'Brien*. We are thus outside of *O'Brien*'s test altogether.

IV

It remains to consider whether the State's interest in preserving the flag as a symbol of nationhood and national unity justifies Johnson's conviction.

As in *Spence,* "[w]e are confronted with a case of prosecution for the expression of an idea through activity," and "[a]ccordingly, we must examine with particular care the interests advanced by [petitioner] to support its prosecution." Johnson was not, we add, prosecuted for the expression of just any idea; he was prosecuted for his expression of dissatisfaction with the policies of this country, expression situated at the core of our First Amendment values.

Moreover, Johnson was prosecuted because he knew that his politically charged expression would cause "serious offense." If he had burned the flag as a means of disposing of it because it was dirty or torn, he would not have been convicted of flag desecration under this Texas law: federal law designates burning as the preferred means of disposing of a flag "when it is in such condition that it is no longer a fitting emblem for display," and Texas has no quarrel with this means of disposal. The Texas law is thus not aimed at protecting the physical integrity of the flag in all circumstances, but is designed instead to protect it only against impairments that would cause serious offense to others. Texas concedes as much: "Section 42.09(b) reaches only those severe acts of physical abuse of the flag carried out in a way likely to be offensive. The statute mandates intentional or knowing abuse, that is, the kind of mistreatment that is not innocent, but rather is intentionally designed to seriously offend other individuals."

Whether Johnson's treatment of the flag violated Texas law thus depended on the likely communicative impact of his expressive conduct. Our decision in *Boos v. Barry* tells us that this restriction on Johnson's expression is content based. . . .

According to the principles announced in *Boos*, Johnson's political expression was restricted because of the content of the message he conveyed. We must therefore subject the State's asserted interest in preserving the special symbolic character of the flag to "the most exacting scrutiny."

Texas argues that its interest in preserving the flag as a symbol of nationhood and national unity survives this close analysis. Quoting extensively from the writings of this Court chronicling the flag's historic and symbolic role in our society, the State emphasizes the "'special place'" reserved for the flag in our Nation. The State's argument is not that it has an interest simply in maintaining the flag as a symbol of something, no matter what it symbolizes; indeed, if that were the State's position, it would be difficult to see how that interest in endangered by highly symbolic conduct such as Johnson's. Rather, the State's claim is that it has an interest in preserving the flag as a symbol of nationhood and national unity, a symbol with a determinate range of meanings. According to Texas, if one physically treats the flag in a way that would tend to cast doubt on either the idea that nationhood and national unity are the flag's referents or that national unity actually exists, the message conveyed thereby is a harmful one and therefore may be prohibited.

If there is a bedrock principle underlying the First Amendment, it is that the government may not prohibit the expression of an idea simply because society finds the idea offensive or disagreeable.

We have not recognized an exception to this principle even where out flag has been involved. In *Street v. New York*, we held that a State may not criminally punish a person for uttering words critical of the flag. Rejecting the argument that the conviction could be sustained on the ground that Street had "failed to show the respect for our national symbol which may properly be demanded of every citizen," we concluded that "the constitutionally guaranteed 'freedom to be intellectually . . . diverse or even contrary,' and the 'right to differ as to things that touch the heart of the existing order,' encompass the freedom to express publicly one's opinions about our flag, including those opinions which are defiant or contemptuous." Now may the government, we have held, compel conduct that would evince respect for the flag. "To sustain the compulsory flag salute we are required to say that a Bill of Rights which guards the individual's right to speak his own mind, left it open to public authorities to compel him to utter what is not in his mind."

In holding in *Barnette* that the Constitution did not leave this course open to the government, Justice Jackson described one of our society's defining principles in words deserving of their frequent repetition: "If there is any fixed star in our constitutional constellation, it is that no official, high or petty, can prescribe what shall be orthodox in politics, nationalism, religion, or other matters of opinion or force citizens to confess by word or act their faith therein." In *Spence*, we held that the same interest asserted by Texas here was insufficient to support a criminal conviction under a flag-misuse statute for the taping of a peace sign to an American flag. "Given the protected character Of [Spence's] expression and in light of the fact that no interest the State may have in preserving the physical integrity of a privately owned flag was significantly impaired on these facts." we held, "the conviction must be validated. . . ."

In short, nothing in our precedents suggests that a State may foster its own view of the flag by prohibiting expressive conduct relating to it. To bring its argument outside our precedents, Texas attempts to convince us that even if its interest in preserving the flag's symbolic role does not allow it to prohibit words or some expressive conduct critical of the flag, it does permit it to forbid the outright destruction of the flag. The State's argument cannot depend here on the distinction between written or spoken words and nonverbal conduct. That distinction, we have shown, is of no moment where the nonverbal conduct is expressive, as it is here, and where the regulation of that conduct is related to expression, as it is here. In addition, both *Barnette* and *Spence* involved expressive conduct, not only verbal communication, and both found that conduct protected.

Texas' focus on the precise nature of Johnson's expression, moreover, misses the point of our prior decisions: their enduring lesson, that the government may not prohibit expression simply because it disagrees with its message, is not dependent on the particular mode in which one chooses to express an idea. If we were to hold that a State may forbid flag burning wherever it is likely to endanger the flag's symbolic role, but allow it wherever burning a flag promotes that role—as where, for example, a person ceremoniously burns a dirty flag—we would be saying that when it comes to impairing the flag's physical integrity, the flag itself may be used as a symbol—as a substitute for the written or spoken word or a "short cut from mind to mind"—only in one direction. We would be permitting a State to "prescribe what shall be orthodox" by saying that one may burn the flag to convey one's attitude toward it and its referents only if one does not endanger the flag's representation of notion-hood and national unity.

We never before have held that the Government may ensure that a symbol be used to express only one view of that symbol or its referents. Indeed, in *Schacht v. United States*, we invalidated a federal statute permitting an actor portraying a member of one of our Armed Forces to "wear the uniform of that armed force if that portrayal does not tend to discredit that armed force." This proviso, we held, "which leaves Americans free to praise the war in Vietnam but can send persons like Schacht to prison for opposing it, cannot survive in a country which has the First Amendment."

We perceive no basis on which to hold that the principle underlying our decision in *Schacht* does not apply to this case. To conclude that the government may permit designated symbols to be used to communicate only a limited set of messages would be to enter territory having no discernible or defensible boundaries. Could the government, on this theory, prohibit the burning of state flags? Of copies of the Presidential seal? Of the Constitution? In evaluating these choices under the First Amendment, how would we decide which symbols were sufficiently special to warrant this unique status? To do so, we would be forced to consult our own political preferences, and impose them on the citizenry, in the very way that the First Amendment forbids us to do.

There is, moreover, no indication—either in the text of the Constitution or in our cases interpreting it—that a separate juridical category exists for the American flag alone. Indeed, we would not be surprised to learn that the persons who framed our Constitution and wrote the Amendment that we now construe were not known for their reverence for the Union Jack. The First Amendment does not guarantee that other concepts virtually sacred to our Nation as a whole—such as the principle that discrimination on the basis of race is odious and destructive—will go unquestioned in the marketplace of ideas. We decline, therefore, to create for the flag an exception to the joust of principles protected by the First Amendment.

It is not the State's ends, but its means, to which we object. It cannot be gainsaid that there is a special place reserved for the flag in this Nation, and thus we do not doubt that the government has a legitimate interest in making efforts to "preserv[e] the national flag as an unalloyed symbol of our country." We reject the suggestion, urged at oral argument by counsel for Johnson, that the government lacks "any state interest whatsoever" in regulating the manner in which the flag may be displayed. Congress has, for example, enacted precatory regulations describing the proper treatment of the flag, and we cast no doubt on the legitimacy of its interest in making such recommendations. To say that the government has an interest in encouraging proper treatment of the flag, however, is not to say that it may criminally punish a person for burning a flag as a means of political protest. "National unity as an end which officials may foster by persuasion and example is not in question. The problem is whether under our Constitution compulsion as here employed is a permissible means for its achievement."

We are fortified in today's conclusion by our conviction that forbidding criminal punishment for conduct such as Johnson's will not endanger the special role played by our flag or the feelings it inspires. To paraphrase Justice Holmes, we submit that nobody can suppose that this one gesture of an unknown man will change our Nation's attitude towards its flag. Indeed, Texas' argument that the burning of an American flag "'is an act having a high likelihood to cause a breach of the peace,'" and its statute's implicit assumption that physical mistreatment of the flag will lead to "serious offense," tend to confirm that the flag's special role is not in danger; if it were, no one would riot or take offense because a flag had been burned.

We are tempted to say, in fact, that the flag's deservedly cherished place in our community will be strengthened, not weakened, by our holding today. Our decision is a reaffirmation of the principles of freedom and inclusiveness that the flag best reflects, and of the conviction that our toleration of criticism such as Johnson's is a sign and source of our strength. Indeed, one of the proudest images of our flag, the one immortalized in our own national anthem, is of the bombardment it survived at Fort McHenry. It is the Nation's resilience, not its rigidity, that Texas sees reflected in the flag—and it is that resilience that we reassert today.

The way to preserve the flag's special role is not to punish those who feel differently about these matters. It is to persuade them that they are wrong. "To courageous, self-reliant men, with confidence in the power of free and fearless reasoning applied through the processes of popular government, no danger flowing from speech can be deemed clear and present, unless the incidence of the evil apprehended is so imminent that it may befall before there is opportunity for full discussion. If there be time to expose through discussion the falsehood and fallacies, to avert the evil by the processes of education, the remedy to be applied is more speech, not enforced silence." And, precisely because it is our flag that is involved, one's response to the flag burner may exploit the uniquely persuasive power of the flag itself. We can imagine no more appropriate response to burning a flag than waving one's own, no better way to counter a flag burner's message than by saluting the flag that burns, no surer means of preserving the dignity even of the flag that burned than by—as one witness here did—according its remains a respectful burial. We do not consecrate the flag by punishing it desecration, for in doing so we dilute the freedom that this cherished emblem represents.

V

Johnson was convicted for engaging in expressive conduct. The State's interest in preventing breaches of the peace does not support his conviction because Johnson's conduct did not threaten to disturb the peace. Nor does the State's interest in preserving the flag as a symbol of nationhood and national unity justify his criminal conviction for engaging in political expression. The judgment of the Texas Court of Criminal Appeals is therefore

Affirmed.

Source:

Supreme Court Reporter, Vol. 109, pp. 2,533–2,558.

Contract with America, 1994

At a rally on the grounds of the Capitol building in Washington, D.C., September 27, 1994, more than 300 Republican House candidates, including about 150 incumbents, signed a "Contract with America" crafted by House minority leader Newt Gingrich (R-Ga.). Focusing primarily on budget issues, the "contract" represented a platform of policies that Republican lawmakers would seek to pass if their party won a majority in the House in congressional elections in November. Signatories pledged a variety of tax cuts, an increase in defense spending, and a constitutional amendment requiring a balanced federal budget. In the November elections, the Republicans gained control of the House for the first time in 40 years, and Gingrich became speaker.

During the "first hundred days" (a phrase going back to congressional passage of F. D. Roosevelt's New Deal in that time), Congress became "subject to the same laws as everyone else," concerning such things as racial or sex discrimination; the House cut congressional committee staffs and budgets by 30 percent and . . . voted on every item in the Contract."

In part because of President Clinton's vetoes, a number of items in the contract did not succeed. The impasse between the Republican House and the Democratic president came to a head over approving the 1995 budget. Gingrich held his ground, and the government, except for "essential personnel," was shut down. Instead of convincing the country that the Republicans were saving the nation's checkbook from profligate Democrats, Gingrich's plan backfired. The public, a good proportion of whom depended in some way on federal largesse, blamed the Republicans. In 1996 Clinton retained the presidency, the Democrats held the Senate, and they gained some seats in the Republican-majority House.

As Republican Members of the House of Representatives and as citizens seeking to join that body we propose not just to change its policies, but even more important, to restore the bonds of trust between the people and their elected representatives. That is why, in this era of official evasion and posturing, we offer instead a detailed agenda for national renewal, a written commitment with no fine print.

This year's election offers the chance, after four decades of one-party control, to bring to the House a new majority that will transform the way Congress works. That historic change would be the end of government that is too big, too intrusive, and too easy with the public's money. It can be the beginning of a Congress that respects the values and shares the faith of the American family.

Like Lincoln, our first Republican president, we intend to act "with firmness in the right, as God gives us to see the right." To restore accountability to Congress. To end its cycle of scandal and disgrace. To make us all proud again of the way free people govern themselves.

On the first day of the 104th Congress, the new Republican majority will immediately pass the following major reforms, aimed at restoring the faith and trust of the American people in their government:

First, require all laws that apply to the rest of the country also apply equally to the Congress;

Second, select a major independent auditing firm to conduct a comprehensive audit of Congress for waste, fraud, or abuse;

Third, cut the number of House committees, and cut committee staff by one-third;

Fourth, limit the terms of all committee chairs;

Fifth, ban the casting of proxy votes in committee;

Sixth, require committee meetings to be open to the public;

Seventh, require a three-fifths majority vote to pass a tax increase;

Eighth, guarantee an honest accounting of our federal budget by implementing zero baseline budgeting.

Thereafter, within the first hundred days of the 104th Congress, we shall bring to the House Floor the following bills, each to be given full and open debate, each to be given a clear and fair vote, and each to be immediately available this day for public inspection and scrutiny.

The Fiscal Responsibility Act

—A balanced budget/tax limitation amendment and a legislative line-item veto to restore fiscal responsibility to an out-of-control Congress, requiring them to live under the same budget constraints as families and businesses.

The Taking Back Our Streets Act

—An anti-crime package including stronger truth in sentencing, "good faith" exclusionary rule exemptions, effective death penalty provisions, and cuts in social spending from this summer's crime bill to fund prison construction and additional law enforcement to keep people secure in their neighborhoods and kids safe in their schools.

The Personal Responsibility Act

—Discourage illegitimacy and teen pregnancy by prohibiting welfare to minor mothers and denying increased AFDC for additional children while on welfare, cut spending for welfare programs, and enact a tough two-years-and-out provision with work requirements to promote individual responsibility.

The Family Reinforcement Act

—Child support enforcement, tax incentives for adoption, strengthening rights of parents in their children's education, stronger child pornography laws, and an elderly dependent care tax credit to reinforce the central role of families in American society.

The American Dream Restoration Act
—A $500-per-child tax credit, begin repeal of the marriage tax penalty, and creation of American Dream Savings Accounts to provide middle-class tax relief.

The National Security Restoration Act
—No U.S. troops under UN command and restoration of the essential parts of our national security funding to strengthen our national defense and maintain our credibility around the world.

The Senior Citizens Fairness Act
—Raise the Social Security earnings limit, which currently forces seniors out of the workforce, repeal the 1993 tax hikes on Social Security benefits, and provide tax incentives for private long-term care insurance to let older Americans keep more of what they have earned over the years.

The Job Creation and Wage Enhancement Act
—Small business incentives, capital gains cut and indexation, neutral cost recovery, risk assessment/cost benefit analysis, strengthening of the Regulatory Flexibility Act and unfunded mandate reform to create jobs and raise worker wages.

The Common Sense Legal Reforms Act
—"Loser pays" laws, reasonable limits on punitive damages, and reform of product liability laws to stem the endless tide of litigation.

The Citizen Legislature Act
—A first-ever vote on term limits to replace career politicians with citizen legislators.

Further, we will instruct the House Budget Committee to report to the floor and we will work to enact additional budget savings, beyond the budget cuts specifically included in the legislation described above, to ensure that the federal budget deficit will be less than it would have been without the enactment of these bills.

Respecting the judgment of our fellow citizens as we seek their mandate for reform, we hereby pledge our names to this *Contract with America*.

Source:

National Center for Public Policy Research. "Contract with America." Available on-line. URL: www.nationalcenter.org/ContractwithAmerica.html. Accessed November 2003.

Clinton v. Jones, 1997

In a decision that, among other things, demonstrated how far removed the Supreme Court could get from political realities, the justices ruled unanimously that a sitting president could be sued for actions outside of his official duties.

The ruling came from a sexual harassment grievance pending against President Bill Clinton for alleged behavior while he was governor of Arkansas. In 1994 Paula C. Jones sued Clinton in federal court for violating her civil rights. Jones, a former Arkansas state employee, accused Clinton of having sexually propositioned her in a Little Rock hotel room in 1991. In her suit, Jones claimed that she was subjected to a hostile work environment after she rebuffed Clinton's unwelcome sexual advances. Jones sought damages for both emotional distress and defamation of character regarding the alleged hotel episode. President Clinton, who denied her accusations, argued that he should not be subject to a civil suit while in office. His lawyers invoked the principle of executive privilege in asking the federal courts to postpone Jones's complaint until Clinton left office. On May 27, 1997, the high court denied Clinton's request, rejecting his executive privilege claim. The justices held that nothing in the Constitution exempted the president from facing a valid civil complaint in a timely manner. At the same time, the Court said proper respect for the presidency obligated trial courts to accommodate the president's schedule as much as possible in civil actions.

On January 17, 1998, during the discovery process, Clinton, under oath, was interviewed in private by Jones's lawyers. It marked the first time that a sitting president had to submit as a defendant in a civil court challenge.

Susan Webber Wright, the federal judge presiding over the case, dismissed Jones's lawsuit April 1. Ruling that "there are no genuine issues for trial in this case," she found that Jones had not proved that she had been a victim of sexual harassment even if the encounter with Clinton had taken place. According to the judge, Jones had provided no evidence that she had been hurt, personally or professionally, by Clinton's alleged behavior. Jones initially intended to seek an appeal of Judge Wright's decision, but later reached a settlement with President Clinton for $850,000.

However, during the suit, Jones's lawyers questioned Clinton about a rumored affair with intern Monica Lewinsky. He denied it under oath. This opened the way for special prosecutor Kenneth Starr, who was looking into alleged misconduct by the Clintons in connection with a failed Arkansas resort named Whitewater, to question him about Lewinsky. Starr's findings led to Clinton's impeachment.

Note: Where it is feasible, a syllabus (headnote) will be released, as is being done in connection with this case, at the time the opinion is issued. The syllabus constitutes no part of the opinion of the Court but has been prepared by the Reporter of Decisions for the convenience of the reader. See United States v. Detroit Timber & Lumber Co., 200 U.S. 321, 337.

SUPREME COURT OF THE UNITED STATES

SYLLABUS

Clinton v. Jones, 1997

CERTIORARI TO THE UNITED STATES COURT OF APPEALS FOR THE EIGHTH CIRCUIT

No. 95-1853. Argued January 13, 1997—
Decided May 27, 1997

Respondent sued under 42 U.S.C. §§ 1983 and 1985 and Arkansas law to recover damages from petitioner, the current President of the United States, alleging, *inter alia*, that while he was Governor of Arkansas, petitioner made "abhorrent" sexual advances to her, and that her rejection of those advances led to punishment by her supervisors in the state job she held at the time. Petitioner promptly advised the Federal District Court that he would file a motion to dismiss on Presidential immunity grounds, and requested that all other pleadings and motions be deferred until the immunity issue was resolved. After the court granted that request, petitioner filed a motion to dismiss without prejudice and to toll any applicable statutes of limitation during his Presidency. The District Judge denied dismissal on immunity grounds and ruled that discovery could go forward, but ordered any trial stayed until petitioner's Presidency ended. The Eighth Circuit affirmed the dismissal denial, but reversed the trial postponement as the "functional equivalent" of a grant of temporary immunity to which petitioner was not constitutionally entitled. The court explained that the President, like other officials, is subject to the same laws that apply to all citizens, that no case had been found in which an official was granted immunity from suit for his unofficial acts, and that the rationale for official immunity is inapposite where only personal, private conduct by a President is at issue. The court also rejected the argument that, unless immunity is available, the threat of judicial interference with the Executive Branch would violate separation of powers.

Held:

1. This Court need not address two important constitutional issues not encompassed within the questions presented by the certiorari petition: (1) whether a claim comparable to petitioner's assertion of immunity might succeed in a state tribunal, and (2) whether a court may compel the President's attendance at any specific time or place. Pp. 7–9.

2. Deferral of this litigation until petitioner's Presidency ends is not constitutionally required. Pp. 7–28.

(a) Petitioner's principal submission—that in all but the most exceptional cases, the Constitution affords the President temporary immunity from civil damages litigation arising out of events that occurred before he took office—cannot be sustained on the basis of precedent. The principal rationale for affording Presidents immunity from damages actions based on their official acts—*i.e.*, to enable them to perform their designated functions effectively without fear that a particular decision may give rise to personal liability, see, *e.g.*, *Nixon v. Fitzgerald*, 457 U.S. 731, 749, 752, and n. 32—provides no support for an immunity for *unofficial* conduct. Moreover, immunities for acts clearly *within* official capacity are grounded in the nature of the function performed, not the identity of the actor who performed it. *Forrester v. White*, 484 U.S. 219, 229. The Court is also unpersuaded by petitioner's historical evidence, which sheds little light on the question at issue, and is largely canceled by conflicting evidence that is itself consistent with both the doctrine of presidential immunity as set forth in *Fitzgerald*, and rejection of the immunity claim in this case. Pp. 9-15.

(b) The separation of powers doctrine does not require federal courts to stay all private actions against the President until he leaves office. Even accepting the unique importance of the Presidency in the constitutional scheme, it does not follow that that doctrine would be violated by allowing this action to proceed. The doctrine provides a self executing safeguard against the encroachment or aggrandizement of one of the three co equal branches of Government at the expense of another. *Buckley v. Valeo*, 424 U.S. 1, 122. But in this case there is no suggestion that the Federal Judiciary is being asked to perform any function that might in some way be described as "executive." Respondent is merely asking the courts to exercise their core Article III jurisdiction to decide cases and controversies, and, whatever the outcome, there is no possibility that the decision here will curtail the scope of the Executive Branch's official powers. The Court rejects petitioner's contention that this case—as well as the potential additional litigation that an affirmance of the Eighth Circuit's judgment might spawn—may place unacceptable burdens on the President that will hamper the performance of his official duties. That assertion finds little support either in history, as evidenced by the paucity of suits against sitting Presidents for their private actions, or in the relatively narrow compass of the issues raised in this particular case. Of greater significance, it is settled that the Judiciary may severely burden the Executive Branch by reviewing the legality of the President's official conduct, see *e.g.*, *Youngstown Sheet & Tube Co. v. Sawyer*, 343 U.S. 579, and may direct appropriate process to the President himself, see *e.g.*, *United States v. Nixon*, 418 U.S. 683. It must follow that the federal courts have power to determine the legality of the President's unofficial conduct. The reasons for rejecting a categorical rule requiring federal courts to stay private actions during the President's term apply as well to a rule that would, in petitioner's words, require a stay "in all but the most exceptional cases." Pp. 15-24.

(c) Contrary to the Eighth Circuit's ruling, the District Court's stay order was not the "functional equivalent" of an unconstitutional grant of temporary immunity. Rather, the District Court has broad discretion to stay proceedings as an incident to its power to control its own docket. See, *e.g.*, *Landis v. North American Co.*, 299 U.S. 248, 254. Moreover, the potential burdens on the President posed by this litigation are appropriate matters for that court to evaluate in its management of the case, and the high respect owed the Presidency is a matter that should inform the conduct of the entire proceeding. Nevertheless, the District Court's stay decision was an abuse of discretion because it took no account of the importance of respondent's interest in bringing the case to trial, and because it was premature in that there was nothing in the record to enable a judge to assess whether postponement of trial after the completion of discovery would be warranted. Pp. 25-27.

(d) The Court is not persuaded of the seriousness of the alleged risks that this decision will generate a large volume of politically motivated harassing and frivolous litigation and that national security concerns might prevent the President from explaining a legitimate need for a continuance, and has confidence in the ability of federal judges to deal with both concerns. If Congress deems it appropriate to afford the President stronger protection, it may respond with legislation. Pp. 27–28

Source:

Cornell Law School, Legal Information Institute. Available online. URL: http://supct.law.cornell.edu/supct/html/95-1853.ZS.html. Accessed November 2003.

Printz v. United States, 1997

Major decision on state versus federal powers in which the U.S. Supreme Court ruled that the Brady gun control law intruded unconstitutionally on states' rights. It has a dual significance, both regarding the Rehnquist court's elevation of states' rights and the nation's conflict over gun control.

Problems of federalism, namely, the allocation of power between the national and state governments, has long been a subject for federal litigation. *National League of Cities v. Usery*, 426 U.S. 833), focused on the Tenth Amendment provision that reserves powers to the states that are not specifically granted to the federal government. Because of this 1976 ruling, a federal district court in Texas ruled that San Antonio's mass transit workers were not covered by federal wage and price regulations. The federal government joined the transit workers in appealing this decision to the Supreme Court in *Garcia v. San Antonio Metropolitan* (469 U.S. 528). On February 19, 1985, the high court ordered arguments regarding whether or not the Tenth Amendment as applied in *Usery* also applied in the San Antonio situation. In a 5-4 decision written by Associate Justice Blackmun, the Court ruled that the federal minimum wage regulations and hour standards applied to employees of public mass transit systems and, by extension, to other public employees as well, thereby restoring the protection of the Fair Labor Standards Act to most state workers: "state sovereign interests are more properly protected by procedural safeguards inherent in the structure of the Federal system than by judicially created limitations on Federal power." Dissenting, Justice Powell asserted that this ruling "rejects almost two hundred years of the understanding of the constitutional status of Federalism," an opinion shared by Associate Justices Rehnquist and O'Connor and Chief Justice Burger.

After Rehnquist became Chief Justice and Anthony Scalia and Clarence Thomas were added to the Court, the minority elevation of state sovereignty became the majority opinion. For example, in *Federal Maritime Commission v. South Carolina Ports Authority* (No. 01-46), decided May 29, 2002, the Supreme Court, 5-4, further extended the concept of state sovereignty by removing private complaints against states from federal jurisdiction. The decision was called the term's most important federalism case.

Printz also concerned federalism and state sovereignty. The 1993 federal law, named for James S. Brady, the former White House press secretary who was shot and gravely wounded in the assassination attempt on President Ronald Reagan in 1981, required state officials to conduct background checks on prospective handgun buyers and imposed a five-day precautionary waiting period on handgun sales. County Sheriff Jay Printz of Montana, who argued that the Brady law improperly imposed federal authority on state law enforcement, successfully challenged the statute in federal district court. In 1995 a federal appeals court overturned the district court's decision and upheld the law. On June 27, 1997, ruling on Printz's final appeal, the Supreme Court voted 5-4 to strike down the legislation's background check requirement. Such a federal requirement, the Court held, violated the principle of separate state sovereignty. The Court did not address the Brady law's five-day waiting period, leaving that provision intact for the time being. The sharply divided ruling revealed profoundly divergent views among the justices on the essential nature of the nation's system of shared authority between the federal government and the states. The *Printz* decision furthered the recent trend on the Court toward readjusting the state-federal balance of powers in favor of the states.

Note: Where it is feasible, a syllabus (headnote) will be released, as is being done in connection with this case, at the time the opinion is issued. The syllabus constitutes no part of the opinion of the Court but has been prepared by the Reporter of Decisions for the convenience of the reader. See United States v. Detroit Timber & Lumber Co., 200 U.S. 321, 337.

Brady Handgun Violence Prevention Act provisions require the Attorney General to establish a national system for instantly checking prospective handgun purchasers' backgrounds, note following 18 U.S.C. § 922 and command the "chief law enforcement officer" (CLEO) of each local jurisdiction to conduct such checks and perform related tasks on an interim basis until the national system becomes operative, §922(s). Petitioners, the CLEOs for counties in Montana and Arizona, filed separate actions challenging the interim provisions' constitutionality. In each case, the District Court held that the background check provision was unconstitutional, but concluded that it was severable from the remainder of the Act, effectively leaving a voluntary background check system in place. The Ninth Circuit reversed, finding none of the interim provisions unconstitutional.

Held:

1. The Brady Act's interim provision commanding CLEOs to conduct background checks, §922(s)(2), is unconstitutional. Extinguished with it is the duty implicit in the background check requirement that the CLEO accept completed handgun applicant statements (Brady Forms) from firearms dealers, §§922(s)(1)(A)(i)(III) and (IV). Pp. 4–34.

(a) Because there is no constitutional text speaking to the precise question whether congressional action compelling state officers to execute federal laws is unconstitutional, the answer to the CLEOs' challenge must be sought in historical understanding and practice, in the Constitution's structure, and in this Court's jurisprudence. P. 4.

(b) Relevant constitutional practice tends to negate the existence of the congressional power asserted here, but is not conclusive. Enactments of the early Congresses seem to contain no evidence of an assumption that the Federal Government may command the States' executive power in the absence of a particularized constitutional authorization. The early enactments establish, at most, that the Constitution was originally understood to permit imposition of an obligation on state judges to enforce federal prescriptions related to matters appropriate for the judicial power. The Government misplaces its reliance on portions of The Federalist suggesting that federal responsibilities could be imposed on state officers. None of these statements necessarily implies—what is the critical point here—that Congress could impose these responsibilities without the States' consent. They appear to rest on the natural assumption that the States would consent, see *FERC v. Mississippi,* 456 U.S. 742, 796, n. 35 (O'Connor, J., concurring in judgment and dissenting in part). Finally, there is an absence of executive commandeering federal statutes in the country's later history, at least until very recent years. Even assuming that newer laws represent an assertion of the congressional power challenged here, they are of such recent vintage that they are not probative of a constitutional tradition. Pp. 4-18.

(c) The Constitution's structure reveals a principle that controls these cases: the system of "dual sovereignty." See, e.g., *Gregory v. Ashcroft,* 501 U.S. 452, 457. Although the States surrendered many of their powers to the new Federal Government, they retained a residuary and inviolable sovereignty that is reflected throughout the Constitution's text. See, e.g., *Lane County v. Oregon,* 7 Wall. 71, 76. The Framers rejected the concept of a central government that would act upon and through the States, and instead designed a system in which the State and Federal Governments would exercise concurrent authority over the people. The Federal Government's power would be augmented immeasurably and impermissibly if it were able to impress into its service—and at no cost to itself—the police officers of the 50 States. Pp. 18–22.

(d) Federal control of state officers would also have an effect upon the separation and equilibration of powers between the three branches of the Federal Government itself. The Brady Act effectively transfers the President's responsibility to administer the laws enacted by Congress, Art. II, §§2 and 3, to thousands of CLEOs in the 50 States, who are left to implement the program without meaningful Presidential control. The Federal Executive's unity would be shattered, and the power of the President would be subject to reduction, if Congress could simply require state officers to execute its laws. Pp. 22–23.

(e) Contrary to the dissent's contention, the Brady Act's direction of the actions of state executive officials is not constitutionally valid under Art. I, §8, as a law "necessary and proper" to the execution of Congress's Commerce Clause power to regulate handgun sales. Where, as here, a law violates the state sovereignty principle, it is not a law "proper for carrying into Execution" delegated powers within the Necessary and Proper Clause's meaning. Cf. *New York v. United States,* 505 U.S. 144, 166. The Supremacy Clause does not help the dissent, since it makes "Law of the Land" only "Laws of the United States which shall be made in Pursuance [of the Constitution.]" Art. VI, cl. 2. Pp. 24–25.

(f) Finally, and most conclusively in these cases, the Court's jurisprudence makes clear that the Federal Government may not compel the States to enact or administer a federal regulatory program. See, e.g., *New York,* supra, at

188. The attempts of the Government and the dissent to distinguish New York—on grounds that the Brady Act's background check provision does not require state legislative or executive officials to make policy; that requiring state officers to perform discrete, ministerial federal tasks does not diminish the state or federal officials' accountability; and that the Brady Act is addressed to individual CLEOs while the provisions invalidated in *New York* were directed to the State itself—are not persuasive. A "balancing" analysis is inappropriate here, since the whole object of the law is to direct the functioning of the state executive, and hence to compromise the structural framework of dual sovereignty; it is the very principle of separate state sovereignty that such a law offends. See e.g., *New York*, supra, at 187. Pp. 25–34.

2. With the Act's background check and implicit receipt of forms requirements invalidated, the Brady Act requirements that CLEOs destroy all Brady Forms and related records, §922(s)(6)(B)(i), and give would be purchasers written statements of the reasons for determining their ineligibility to receive handguns, §922(s)(6)(C), require no action whatsoever on the part of CLEOs such as petitioners, who are not voluntary participants in administration of the federal scheme. As to them, these provisions are not unconstitutional, but simply inoperative. Pp. 34–36.

Source:

Cornell Law School. The Legal Information Institute. Available on-line. URL: http://supct.law.cornell.edu/supct/html/95-1853.ZS.html. Accessed November 2003.

Articles of Impeachment for President Clinton, 1998

Articles drafted December 11–12, 1998, by the House Judiciary Committee, which indicted President William Jefferson Clinton for charges of "high crimes and misdemeanors." The four articles were based on accusations made by independent counsel Kenneth Starr in a report submitted to Congress in September 1998. Starr had been originally appointed in 1994 under the 1978 independent counsel law to investigate the president and first lady's involvement in a failed real estate deal for Arkansas resort property called Whitewater. His powers were later extended to investigate the White House travel office scandal in which former staff were fired and a Clinton friend was substituted, the White House's acquisition of FBI files on George H. W. Bush administration White House personnel, and the president's relationship with intern Monica Lewinsky and state employee Paula Jones. Some members of Congress attempted to find an alternative to impeachment, such as censure, to punish the president. However, Republican Speaker of the House Robert Livingston did not schedule a censure vote as it was "not envisioned in the Constitution." In his opinion the House had the responsibility "to charge or not charge, impeach or not impeach." On December 19, 1998, the House voted to impeach President Clinton for obstruction of justice and perjury.

Because of the sexual ramifications of Clinton and Lewinsky's relationship and his alleged relationship with Paula Jones, the Starr Report, which was widely published and discussed in the media, contained information normally left off the network television and the mainstream journals.

Resolution impeaching William Jefferson Clinton, President of the United States, for high crimes and misdeameanors.

Resolved, that William Jefferson Clinton, President of the United States, is impeached for high crimes and misdemeanors, and that the following articles of impeachment be exhibited to the United States Senate:

Articles of impeachment exhibited by the House of Representatives of the United States of America in the name of itself and of the people of the United States of America, against William Jefferson Clinton, President of the United States of America, in maintenance and support of its impeachment against him for high crimes and misdemeanors.

Article I

In his conduct while President of the United States, William Jefferson Clinton, in violation of his constitutional oath faithfully to execute the office of President of the United States and, to the best of his ability, preserve, protect, and defend the Constitution of the United States, and in violation of his constitutional duty to take care that the laws be faithfully executed, has willfully corrupted and manipulated the judicial process of the United States for his personal gain and exoneration, impeding the administration of justice, in that:

On August 17, 1998, William Jefferson Clinton swore to tell the truth, the whole truth, and nothing but the truth before a Federal grand jury of the United States. Contrary to that oath, William Jefferson Clinton willfully provided perjurious, false and misleading testimony to the grand jury concerning one or more of the following: (1) the nature and details of his relationship with a subordinate Government employee; (2) prior perjurious, false and misleading testimony he gave in a Federal civil rights action brought against him; (3) prior false and misleading statements he allowed his attorney to make to a Federal judge in that civil rights action; and (4) his corrupt efforts to influence the testimony of witnesses and to impede the discovery of evidence in that civil rights action.

In doing this, William Jefferson Clinton has undermined the integrity of his office, has brought disrepute on the Presidency, has betrayed his trust as President, and has acted in a manner subversive of the rule of law and justice, to the manifest injury of the people of the United States.

Wherefore, William Jefferson Clinton, by such conduct, warrants impeachment and trial, and removal from office and disqualification to hold and enjoy any office of honor, trust or profit under the United States.

Article II

In his conduct while President of the United States, William Jefferson Clinton, in violation of his constitutional oath faithfully to execute the office of President of the United States and, to the best of his ability, preserve, protect, and defend the Constitution of the United States, and in violation of his constitutional duty to take care that the laws be faithfully executed, has willfully corrupted and manipulated the judicial process of the United States for his personal gain and exoneration, impeding the administration of justice, in that:

(1) On December 23, 1997, William Jefferson Clinton, in sworn answers to written questions asked as part of a Federal civil rights action brought against him, willfully provided perjurious, false and misleading testimony in response to questions deemed relevant by a Federal judge concerning conduct and proposed conduct with subordinate employees.

(2) On January 17, 1998, William Jefferson Clinton swore under oath to tell the truth, the whole truth, and nothing but the truth in a deposition given as part of a Federal civil rights action brought against him. Contrary to that oath, William Jefferson Clinton willfully provided perjurious, false and misleading testimony in response to questions deemed relevant by a Federal judge concerning the nature and details of his relationship with a subordinate Government employee, his knowledge of that employee's involvement and participation in the civil rights action brought against him, and his corrupt efforts to influence the testimony of that employee.

In all of this, William Jefferson Clinton has undermined the integrity of his office, has brought disrepute on the Presidency, has betrayed his trust as President, and has acted in a manner subversive of the rule of law and justice, to the manifest injury of the people of the United States.

Wherefore, William Jefferson Clinton, by such conduct, warrants impeachment and trial, and removal from office and disqualification to hold and enjoy any office of honor, trust or profit under the United States.

Article III

In his conduct while President of the United States, William Jefferson Clinton, in violation of his constitutional oath faithfully to execute the office of President of the United States and, to the best of his ability, preserve, protect, and defend the Constitution of the United States, and in violation of his constitutional duty to take care that the laws be faithfully executed, has prevented, obstructed, and impeded the administration of justice, and has to that end engaged personally, and through his subordinates and agents, in a course of conduct or scheme designed to delay, impede, cover up, and conceal the existence of evidence and testimony related to a Federal civil rights action brought against him in a duly instituted judicial proceeding.

The means used to implement this course of conduct or scheme included one or more of the following acts:

(1) On or about December 17, 1997, William Jefferson Clinton corruptly encouraged a witness in a Federal civil rights action brought against him to execute a sworn affidavit in that proceeding that he knew to be perjurious, false and misleading.

(2) On or about December 17, 1997, William Jefferson Clinton corruptly encouraged a witness in a Federal civil rights action brought against him to give perjurious, false and misleading testimony if and when called to testify personally in that proceeding.

(3) On or about December 28, 1997, William Jefferson Clinton corruptly engaged in, encouraged, or supported a scheme to conceal evidence that had been subpoenaed in a Federal civil rights action brought against him.

(4) Beginning on or about December 7, 1997, and continuing through and including January 14, 1998, William Jefferson Clinton intensified and succeeded in an effort to secure job assistance to a witness in a Federal civil rights action brought against him in order to corruptly prevent the truthful testimony of that witness in that proceeding at a time when the truthful testimony of that witness would have been harmful to him.

(5) On January 17, 1998, at his deposition in a Federal civil rights action brought against him, William Jefferson Clinton corruptly allowed his attorney to make false and misleading statements to a Federal judge characterizing an affidavit, in order to prevent questioning deemed relevant by the judge. Such false and misleading statements were subsequently acknowledged by his attorney in a communication to that judge.

(6) On or about January 18 and January 20-21, 1998, William Jefferson Clinton related a false and misleading account of events relevant to a Federal civil rights action brought against him to a potential witness in that proceeding, in order to corruptly influence the testimony of that witness.

(7) On or about January 21, 23 and 26, 1998, William Jefferson Clinton made false and misleading statements to potential witnesses in a Federal grand jury proceeding in order to corruptly influence the testimony of those witnesses. The false and misleading statements made by William Jefferson Clinton were repeated by the witnesses to the grand jury, causing the grand jury to receive false and misleading information.

In all of this, William Jefferson Clinton has undermined the integrity of his office, has brought disrepute on the Presidency, has betrayed his trust as President, and has acted in a manner subversive of the rule of law and justice, to the manifest injury of the people of the United States.

Wherefore, William Jefferson Clinton, by such conduct, warrants impeachment and trial, and removal from office and disqualification to hold and enjoy any office of honor, trust or profit under the United States.

Article IV

Using the powers and influence of the office of President of the United States, William Jefferson Clinton, in violation of his constitutional oath faithfully to execute the office of President of the United States and, to the best of his ability, preserve, protect, and defend the Constitution of the United States, and in disregard of his constitutional duty to take care that the laws be faithfully executed, has engaged in conduct that resulted in misuse and abuse of his high office, impaired the due and proper administration of justice and the conduct of lawful inquiries, and contravened the authority of the legislative branch and the truth-seeking purpose of a coordinate investigative proceeding in that, as President, William Jefferson Clinton, refused and failed to respond to certain written requests for admission and willfully made perjurious, false and misleading sworn statements in response to certain written requests for admission propounded to him as part of the impeachment inquiry authorized by the House of Representatives of the Congress of the United States.

William Jefferson Clinton, in refusing and failing to respond, and in making perjurious, false and misleading statements, assumed to himself functions and judgments necessary to the exercise of the sole power of impeachment vested by the Constitution in the House of Representatives and exhibited contempt for the inquiry.

In doing this, William Jefferson Clinton has undermined the integrity of his office, has brought disrepute on the Presidency, has betrayed his trust as President, and has acted in a manner subversive of the rule of law and justice, to the manifest injury of the people of the United States.

Wherefore, William Jefferson Clinton, by such conduct, warrants impeachment and trial, and removal from office and disqualification to hold and enjoy any office of honor, trust or profit under the United States.

See also INITIAL RESPONSE TO THE REFERRAL OF THE OFFICE OF INDEPENDENT COUNSEL, 1998; KENNETH STARR, STARR REPORT, 1998; IMPEACHMENT DEFENSE, 1999*; BILL CLINTON, STATEMENT FOLLOWING IMPEACHMENT ACQUITTAL, 1999.

Source:

Landmark Documents in American History, Facts On File, Inc.

Bush v. Gore, 2000

More than a month after voters cast their ballots in one of the closest elections in U.S. history, the presidential election of 2000 was finally decided by a 5-4 vote of the Supreme Court in *Bush v. Gore*. The case pitted Republican Texas Governor George W. Bush against Vice President Al Gore, the Democratic nominee. No one disputes that Gore won the popular vote by nearly 350,000 votes. However, the electoral vote was a tie with the Florida count in contention.

A number of factors compromised the legitimacy of any decision favoring Bush. First, George W. Bush's brother Jeb was Florida governor; the Secretary of State, who made decisions regarding elections, was a Republican partisan. Many black voters, a majority of whom were likely to have voted for Gore, were turned away because they were told their names were on lists of felons (the lists were later found to be full of errors, and provisional ballots were not accepted for those who claimed they were entitled to vote.) Moreover a number of places where minorities normally voted were changed without notice. Many Jewish voters, a majority of whom were presumed Democratic, accidentally voted for Reform candidate Patrick Buchanan because of a confusing ballot; even if voters realized the mistake, they were not permitted to make a correction. Republicans in the military filing absentee ballots were assisted by the party. Possibly hurting Republicans, initial results in favor of Gore were announced when the polls closed in the Eastern Time zone, although part of the largely Republican Florida panhandle was in the Central Time Zone and its polls were still open. Many military absentee ballots were not properly postmarked.

A number of court fights ensued, in which a Democratic majority state court found for Gore; the Supreme Court majority, which normally deferred to the state, instead found for Bush. The deadline to choose and certify state electors was December 12. About two hours before midnight on December 11, the U.S. Supreme Court issued its decision. In an unsigned 5-4 opinion, the Court supported Bush. However, it engendered acrimonious dissenting opinions. The majority held that the lack of standardization in the recount process violated the equal protection clause of the Fourteenth Amendment to the Constitution. The Court further determined that there was not enough time to complete the recounts. The Florida legislature voted to appoint electors for Bush, making him the 43rd president. Shortly thereafter Gore made a concession speech, and an hour later Bush made a victory speech. Both men stressed the importance of unity and national healing.

The decision prompted an election reform bill that would give states federal money to upgrade and reform their voting systems. While the Court retained its legitimacy—something that dissenters feared might be lost—it divided not only the country but the Court itself.

In the decision, the Court made clear in the majority opinion that its ruling applied only to *Bush v. Gore*. When asked to intervene in a 2002 New Jersey senate race in which a losing Democrat dropped out only weeks before the election and a former senator took his place, it refused to take the case.

On December 8, 2000, the Supreme Court of Florida ordered that the Circuit Court of Leon County tabulate by hand 9,000 ballots in Miami-Dade County. It also ordered the inclusion in the certified vote totals of 215 votes identified in Palm Beach County and 168 votes identified in Miami-Dade County for Vice President Albert Gore, Jr., and Senator Joseph Lieberman, Democratic Candidates for President and Vice President. The Supreme Court noted that petitioner, Governor George W. Bush asserted that the net gain for Vice President Gore in Palm Beach County was 176 votes, and directed the Circuit Court to resolve that dispute on remand. The court further held that relief would require manual recounts in all Florida counties where so-called "undervotes" had not been subject to manual tabulation. The court ordered all manual recounts to begin at once. Governor Bush and Richard Cheney, Republican Candidates for the Presidency and Vice Presidency, filed an emergency application for a stay of this mandate. On December 9, we granted the application, treated the application as a petition for a writ of certiorari, and granted certiorari.

The proceedings leading to the present controversy are discussed in some detail in our opinion in *Bush v. Palm Beach County Canvassing Bd.* (Bush I). On November 8, 2000, the day following the Presidential election, the Florida Division of Elections reported that petitioner, Governor Bush, had received 2,909,135 votes, and respondent, Vice President Gore, had received 2,907,351 votes, a margin of 1,784 for Governor Bush. Because Governor Bush's margin of victory was less than "one-half of a percent . . . of the votes cast," an automatic machine recount was conducted . . . , the results of which showed Governor Bush still winning the race but by a diminished margin. Vice President Gore then sought manual recounts in Volusia, Palm Beach, Broward, and Miami-Dade Counties, pursuant to Florida's election protest provisions. Fla. Stat. §102.166 (2000). A dispute arose concerning the deadline for local county canvassing boards to submit their returns to the Secretary of State (Secretary). The Secretary declined to waive the November 14 deadline imposed by statute. The Florida Supreme Court, however, set the deadline at November 26. We granted certiorari and vacated the Florida Supreme Court's decision, finding considerable uncertainty as to the grounds on which it was based. On December 11, the Florida Supreme Court issued a decision on remand reinstating that date. ___

On November 26, the Florida Elections Canvassing Commission certified the results of the election and declared Governor Bush the winner of Florida's 25 electoral votes. On November 27, Vice President Gore, pursuant to Florida's contest provisions, filed a complaint in Leon County Circuit Court contesting the certification. He sought relief pursuant to §102.168(3)(c), which provides that "[r]eceipt of a number of illegal votes or rejection of a number of legal votes sufficient to change or place in doubt the result of the election" shall be grounds for a contest. The Circuit Court denied relief, stating that Vice President Gore failed to meet his burden of proof. He appealed to the First District Court of Appeal, which certified the matter to the Florida Supreme Court.

Accepting jurisdiction, the Florida Supreme Court affirmed in part and reversed in part. The court held that the Circuit Court had been correct to reject Vice President Gore's challenge to the results certified in Nassau County and his challenge to the Palm Beach County Canvassing Board's determination that 3,300 ballots cast in that county were not, in the statutory phrase, "legal votes."

The Supreme Court held that Vice President Gore had satisfied his burden of proof under §102.168(3)(c) with respect to his challenge to Miami-Dade County's failure to tabulate, by manual count, 9,000 ballots on which the machines had failed to detect a vote for President ("undervotes"). Noting the closeness of the election, the Court explained that "[o]n this record, there can be no question that there are legal votes within the 9,000 uncounted votes sufficient to place the results of this election in doubt." A "legal vote," as determined by the Supreme Court, is "one in which there is a 'clear indication of the intent of the voter. '" The court therefore ordered a hand recount of the 9,000 ballots in Miami-Dade County. Observing that the contest provisions vest broad discretion in the circuit judge to "provide any relief appropriate under such circumstances," the Supreme Court further held that the Circuit Court could order "the Supervisor of Elections and the Canvassing Boards, as well as the necessary public officials, in all counties that have not conducted a manual recount or tabulation of the undervotes . . . to do so forthwith, said tabulation to take place in the individual counties where the ballots are located."

The Supreme Court also determined that both Palm Beach County and Miami-Dade County, in their earlier manual recounts, had identified a net gain of 215 and 168 legal votes for Vice President Gore. Rejecting the Circuit Court's conclusion that Palm Beach County lacked the authority to include the 215 net votes submitted past the November 26 deadline, the Supreme Court explained that the deadline was not intended to exclude votes identified after that date through ongoing manual recounts. As to Miami-Dade County, the Court concluded that although the 168 votes identified were the result of a partial recount, they were "legal votes [that] could change the outcome of the election. "The Supreme Court therefore directed the Circuit Court to include those totals in the certified results, subject to resolution of the actual vote total from the Miami-Dade partial recount.

The petition presents the following questions: whether the Florida Supreme Court established new standards for resolving Presidential election contests, thereby violating Art. II, §1, cl. 2, of the United States Constitution and failing to comply with 3 U.S.C. § 5 and whether the use of standardless manual recounts violates the Equal Protection and Due Process Clauses. With respect to the equal protection question, we find a violation of the Equal Protection Clause.

II A

The closeness of this election, and the multitude of legal challenges which have followed in its wake, have brought into sharp focus a common, if heretofore unnoticed, phenomenon. Nationwide statistics reveal that an estimated 2% of ballots cast do not register a vote for President for whatever reason, including deliberately choosing no candidate at all or some voter error, such as voting for two candidates or insufficiently marking a ballot. In certifying election results, the votes eligible for inclusion in the certification are the votes meeting the properly established legal requirements.

This case has shown that punch card balloting machines can produce an unfortunate number of ballots which are not punched in a clean, complete way by the voter. After the current counting, it is likely legislative bodies nationwide will examine ways to improve the mechanisms and machinery for voting.

B

The individual citizen has no federal constitutional right to vote for electors for the President of the United States unless and until the state legislature chooses a statewide election as the means to implement its power to appoint members of the Electoral College. This is the source for the statement . . .(1892) that the State legislature's power to select the manner for appointing electors is plenary; it may, if it so chooses, select the electors itself, which indeed was the manner used by State legislatures in several States for many years after the Framing of our Constitution. History has now favored the voter, and in each of the several States the citizens themselves vote for Presidential electors. When the state legislature vests the right to vote for President in its people, the right to vote as the legislature has prescribed is fundamental; and one source of its fundamental nature lies in the equal weight accorded to each vote and the equal dignity owed to each voter. The State, of course, after granting the franchise in the special context of Article II, can take back the power to appoint electors. ("[T]here is no doubt of the right of the legislature to resume the power at any time, for it can neither be taken away nor abdicated") (quoting Cong., 1st Sess. [1789-90]).

The right to vote is protected in more than the initial allocation of the franchise. Equal protection applies as well to the manner of its exercise. Having once granted the right to vote on equal terms, the State may not, by later arbitrary and disparate treatment, value one person's vote over that of another. . . .

There is no difference between the two sides of the present controversy on these basic propositions. Respondents say that the very purpose of vindicating the right to vote justifies the recount procedures now at issue. The question before us, however, is whether the recount procedures the Florida Supreme Court has adopted are consistent with its obligation to avoid arbitrary and disparate treatment of the members of its electorate.

Much of the controversy seems to revolve around ballot cards designed to be perforated by a stylus but which, either through error or deliberate omission, have not been perforated with sufficient precision for a machine to count them. In some cases a piece of the card—a chad—is hanging, say by two corners. In other cases there is no separation at all, just an indentation.

The Florida Supreme Court has ordered that the intent of the voter be discerned from such ballots. For purposes of resolving the equal protection challenge, it is not necessary to decide whether the Florida Supreme Court had the authority under the legislative scheme for resolving election disputes to define what a legal vote is and to mandate a manual recount implementing that definition. The recount mechanisms implemented in response to the decisions of the Florida Supreme Court do not satisfy the minimum requirement for non-arbitrary treatment of voters necessary to secure the fundamental right. Florida's basic command for the count of legally cast votes is to consider the "intent of the voter." This is unobjectionable as an abstract proposition and a starting principle. The problem inheres in the absence of specific standards to ensure its equal application. The formulation of uniform rules to determine intent based on these recurring circumstances is practicable and, we conclude, necessary.

The law does not refrain from searching for the intent of the actor in a multitude of circumstances. . . . In this instance, however, the question is . . . how to interpret the marks or holes or scratches on an inanimate object, a piece of cardboard or paper which, it is said, might not have registered as a vote during the machine count. The factfinder confronts a thing, not a person. The search for intent can be confined by specific rules designed to ensure uniform treatment.

The want of those rules here has led to unequal evaluation of ballots in various respects. . . . As seems to have been acknowledged at oral argument, the standards for accepting or rejecting contested ballots might vary not only from county to county but indeed within a single county from one recount team to another.

The record provides some examples. A monitor in Miami-Dade County testified at trial that he observed that three members of the county canvassing board applied different standards in defining a legal vote. And testimony at trial also revealed that at least one county changed its evaluative standards during the counting process. . . . This is not a process with sufficient guarantees of equal treatment.

* * *

The State Supreme Court ratified this uneven treatment. It mandated that the recount totals from two counties, Miami-Dade and Palm Beach, be included in the certified total. The court also appeared to hold sub silentio that the recount totals from Broward County, which were not completed until after the original November 14 certification by the Secretary of State, were to be considered part of the new certified vote totals even though the county certification was not contested by Vice President Gore. Yet each of the counties used varying standards to determine what was a legal vote. Broward County used a more forgiving standard than Palm Beach County, and uncovered almost three times as many new votes, a result markedly disproportionate to the difference in population between the counties.

In addition, the recounts in these three counties were not limited to so-called undervotes but extended to all of the ballots. The distinction has real consequences. A manual recount of all ballots identifies not only those ballots which show no vote but also those which contain more than one, the so-called overvotes. Neither category will be counted by the machine. This is not a trivial concern. At oral argument, respondents estimated there are as many as 110,000 overvotes statewide. As a result, the citizen whose ballot was not read by a machine because he failed to vote for a candidate in a way readable by a machine may still have his vote counted in a manual recount; on the other hand, the citizen who marks two candidates in a way discernable by the machine will not have the same opportunity to have his vote count, even if a manual examination of the ballot would reveal the requisite indicia of intent. Furthermore, the citizen who marks two candidates, only one of which is discernable by the machine, will have his vote counted even though it should have been read as an invalid ballot. The State Supreme Court's inclusion of vote counts based on these variant standards exemplifies concerns with the remedial processes that were under way.

That brings the analysis to yet a further equal protection problem. The votes certified by the court included a partial total from one county, Miami-Dade. The Florida Supreme Court's decision thus gives no assurance that the recounts included in a final certification must be complete. Indeed, it is respondent's submission that it would be consistent with the rules of the recount procedures to include whatever partial counts are done by the time of final certification, and we interpret the Florida Supreme Court's decision to permit this. This accommodation no doubt results from the truncated contest period established by the Florida Supreme Court in Bush I, at respondents' own urging. The press of time does not diminish the constitutional concern. A desire for speed is not a general excuse for ignoring equal protection guarantees.

In addition to these difficulties the actual process by which the votes were to be counted under the Florida Supreme Court's decision raises further concerns. That order did not specify who would recount the ballots. The county canvassing boards were forced to pull together ad hoc teams comprised of judges from various Circuits who had no previous training in handling and interpreting ballots. Furthermore, while others were permitted to observe, they were prohibited from objecting during the recount.

The recount process, in its features here described, is inconsistent with the minimum procedures necessary to protect the fundamental right of each voter in the special instance of a statewide recount under the authority of a single state judicial officer. Our consideration is limited to the present circumstances, for the problem of equal protection in election processes generally presents many complexities.

. . . We are presented with a situation where a state court with the power to assure uniformity has ordered a statewide recount with minimal procedural safeguards. When a court orders a statewide remedy, there must be at least some assurance that the rudimentary requirements of equal treatment and fundamental fairness are satisfied.

Given the Court's assessment that the recount process underway was probably being conducted in an unconstitutional manner, the Court stayed the order directing the recount so it could hear this case and render an expedited decision. The contest provision, as it was mandated by the State Supreme Court, is not well calculated to sustain the confidence that all citizens must have in the outcome of elections. The State has not shown that its procedures include the necessary safeguards. The problem, for instance, of the estimated 110,000 overvotes has not been addressed. . . .

Upon due consideration of the difficulties identified to this point, it is obvious that the recount cannot be conducted in compliance with the requirements of equal protection and due process without substantial additional work. It would require not only the adoption (after opportunity for argument) of adequate statewide standards for determining what is a legal vote, and practicable procedures to implement them, but also orderly judicial review of any disputed matters that might arise. In addition, the Secretary of State has advised that the recount of only a portion of the ballots requires that the vote tabulation equipment be used to screen out undervotes, a function for which the machines were not designed. If a recount of overvotes were also required, perhaps even a second screening would be necessary. Use of the equipment for this purpose, and any new software developed for it, would have to be evaluated for accuracy by the Secretary of State.

The Supreme Court of Florida has said that the legislature intended the State's electors to "participat[e] fully in the federal electoral process,". . . . That statute, in turn, requires that any controversy or contest that is designed to lead to a conclusive selection of electors be completed by December 12. That date is upon us, and there is no recount procedure in place under the State Supreme Court's order that comports with minimal constitutional standards. Because it is evident that any recount seeking to meet the December 12 date will be unconstitutional for the reasons we have discussed, we reverse the judgment of the Supreme Court of Florida ordering a recount to proceed.

Seven Justices of the Court agree that there are constitutional problems with the recount ordered by the Florida Supreme Court that demand a remedy. . . . The only disagreement is as to the remedy. Because the Florida Supreme Court has said that the Florida Legislature intended to obtain the safe-harbor benefits of 3 U.S.C. § 5 Justice Breyer's proposed remedy–remanding to the Florida Supreme Court for its ordering of a constitutionally proper contest until December 18-contemplates action in violation of the Florida election code, and hence could not be part of an "appropriate" order authorized by Fla. Stat. §102.168(8) (2000).

* * *

None are more conscious of the vital limits on judicial authority than are the members of this Court, and none stand more in admiration of the Constitution's design to leave the selection of the President to the people, through their legislatures, and to the political sphere. When contending parties invoke the process of the courts, however, it becomes our unsought responsibility to resolve the federal and constitutional issues the judicial system has been forced to confront.

The judgment of the Supreme Court of Florida is reversed, and the case is remanded for further proceedings not inconsistent with this opinion.

Pursuant to this Court's Rule 45.2, the Clerk is directed to issue the mandate in this case forthwith.

It is so ordered.

Source:

Cornell University, Legal Information Institute. Available online. URL: http://supct.law.cornell.edu/supct/search/display.html?terms=bush%20v.%20gore&url=/supct/html/00-949.ZPC.html. Accessed November 2003.

Bipartisan Campaign Reform Act, 2002

Also known as the McCain-Feingold/Shays-Meehan Act after its sponsors, Senators John McCain (R-Ariz.) and Russell Feingold (D.-Wis.) and Congressmen Christ Shays (R.-Conn.) and Martin T. Meehan.(D.-Mass.), this act was signed by President George W. Bush March 27, 2002. This act represented "the most sweeping campaign finance measure in a generation," according to the *New York Times*. The law prohibited national political parties and candidates in federal races from raising or spending "soft money." "Soft money" represented a loophole in the finance reforms passed after the Watergate scandals in the mid-1970s. It permitted interest groups to spend as much as they wished to promote their agenda through Election Day as long as they did not directly mention a candidate. Soft money contributions were often in the hundreds of thousands of dollars, coming from unions, corporations, trade associations, and wealthy individuals. Because the law did not go into effect until the day after the 2002 mid-term elections, commentators estimated that twice as much would be raised in that election than in the 1998 mid-term campaign. The Republicans received far more than the Democrats.

For the complete act, see thomas.loc.gov.

(a) SHORT TITLE- This Act may be cited as the 'Bipartisan Campaign Reform Act of 2002,'

* * *

SEC. 323. SOFT MONEY OF POLITICAL PARTIES.

(a) NATIONAL COMMITTEES-

(1) IN GENERAL- A national committee of a political party (including a national congressional campaign committee of a political party) may not solicit, receive, or direct to another person a contribution, donation, or transfer of funds or any other thing of value, or spend any funds, that are not subject to the limitations, prohibitions, and reporting requirements of this Act.

(2) APPLICABILITY- The prohibition established by paragraph (1) applies to any such national committee, any officer or agent acting on behalf of such a national committee, and any entity that is directly or indirectly established, financed, maintained, or controlled by such a national committee.

(b) STATE, DISTRICT, AND LOCAL COMMITTEES-

(1) IN GENERAL- Except as provided in paragraph (2), an amount that is expended or disbursed for Federal election activity by a State, district, or local committee of a political party (including an entity that is directly or indirectly established, financed, maintained, or controlled by a State, district, or local committee of a political party and an officer or agent acting on behalf of such committee or entity), or by an association or similar group of candidates for State or local office or of individuals holding State or local office, shall be made from funds subject to the limitations, prohibitions, and reporting requirements of this Act.

(2) APPLICABILITY-

(A) IN GENERAL- . . .Shall not apply to any amount expended or disbursed by a State, district, or local committee of a political party for an activity . . . to the extent the amounts expended or disbursed for such activity are allocated (under regulations prescribed by the Commission) among amounts—

(i) which consist solely of contributions subject to the limitations, prohibitions, and reporting requirements of this Act and

(ii) other amounts which are not subject to the limitations, prohibitions, and reporting requirements of this Act (other than any requirements of this subsection).

(B) CONDITIONS- Subparagraph (A) shall only apply if—

(i) the activity does not refer to a clearly identified candidate for Federal office;

(ii) the amounts expended or disbursed are not for the costs of any broadcasting, cable, or satellite communication, other than a communication which refers solely to a clearly identified candidate for State or local office;

(iii) the amounts expended or disbursed which are described in subparagraph (A)(ii) are paid from amounts which are donated in accordance with State law and which meet the requirements of subparagraph (C), except that no person (including any person established, financed, maintained, or controlled by such person) may donate more than $10,000 to a State, district, or local committee of a political party in a calendar year for such expenditures or disbursements; and

(iv) the amounts expended or disbursed are made solely from funds raised by the State, local, or district committee which makes such expenditure or disbursement, and do not include any funds provided to such committee from—

(I) any other State, local, or district committee of any State party,

(II) the national committee of a political party (including a national congressional campaign committee of a political party),

(III) any officer or agent acting on behalf of any committee described in subclause (I) or (II), or

(V) any entity directly or indirectly established, financed, maintained, or controlled by any committee described in subclause (I) or (II).

(C) PROHIBITING INVOLVEMENT OF NATIONAL PARTIES, FEDERAL CANDIDATES AND OFFICEHOLDERS, AND STATE PARTIES ACTING JOINTLY- Amounts specifically authorized to be spent under subparagraph (B)(iii) meet the requirements of this subparagraph only if the amounts—

(i) are not solicited, received, directed, transferred, or spent by or in the name of any person described in subsection (a) or (e); and

(ii) are not solicited, received, or directed through fundraising activities conducted jointly by 2 or more State, local, or district committees of any political party or their agents, or by a State, local, or district committee of a political party on behalf of the State, local, or district committee of a political party or its agent in one or more other States.

* * *

(d) TAX-EXEMPT ORGANIZATIONS- A national, State, district, or local committee of a political party (including a national congressional campaign committee of a political party), an entity that is directly or indirectly established, financed, maintained, or controlled by any such national, State, district, or local committee or its agent, and an officer or agent acting on behalf of any such party committee or entity, shall not solicit any funds for, or make or direct any donations to—

(1) a [tax-exempt] organization. . .or has submitted an application for determination of tax exempt status. . .and that makes expenditures or disbursements in connection with an election for Federal office (including expenditures or disbursements for Federal election activity); or

* * *

(e) FEDERAL CANDIDATES-

(1) IN GENERAL- A candidate, individual holding Federal office, agent of a candidate or an individual holding Federal office, or an entity directly or indirectly established, financed, maintained or controlled by or acting on behalf of 1 or more candidates or individuals holding Federal office, shall not—

(A) solicit, receive, direct, transfer, or spend funds in connection with an election for Federal office, including funds for any Federal election activity, unless the funds are subject to the limitations, prohibitions, and reporting requirements of this Act; or

(B) solicit, receive, direct, transfer, or spend funds in connection with any election other than an election for Federal office or disburse funds in connection with such an election unless the funds—

(i) are not in excess of the amounts permitted with respect to contributions to candidates and political committees. . .; and

(ii) are not from sources prohibited by this Act from making contributions in connection with an election for Federal office.

* * *

(20) FEDERAL ELECTION ACTIVITY-

(A) IN GENERAL- The term 'Federal election activity' means—

(i) voter registration activity during the period that begins on the date that is 120 days before the date a regularly scheduled Federal election is held and ends on the date of the election.

(ii) voter identification, get-out-the-vote activity, or generic campaign activity conducted in connection with an election in which a candidate for Federal office appears on the ballot (regardless of whether a candidate for State or local office also appears on the ballot);

(iii) a public communication that refers to a clearly identified candidate for Federal office (regardless of whether a candidate for State or local office is also mentioned or identified) and that promotes or supports a candidate for that office, or attacks or opposes a candidate for that office (regardless of whether the communication expressly advocates a vote for or against a candidate); or

(iv) services provided during any month by an employee of a State, district, or local committee of a political party who spends more than 25 percent of that individual's compensated time during that month on activities in connection with a Federal election.

(B) EXCLUDED ACTIVITY- The term Federal election activity' does not include an amount expended or disbursed by a State, district, or local committee of a political party for—

(i) a public communication that refers solely to a clearly identified candidate for State or local office, if the communication is not a Federal election activity. . .;

(ii) a contribution to a candidate for State or local office, provided the contribution is not designated to pay for a Federal election activity;

(iii) the costs of a State, district, or local political convention; and

(iv) the costs of grassroots campaign materials, including buttons, bumper stickers, and yard signs, that name or depict only a candidate for State or local office.

(21) GENERIC CAMPAIGN ACTIVITY- The term generic campaign activity' means a campaign activity that promotes a political party and does not promote a candidate or non-Federal candidate.

* * *

SEC. 313. USE OF CONTRIBUTED AMOUNTS FOR CERTAIN PURPOSES.

(a) PERMITTED USES- A contribution accepted by a candidate, and any other donation received by an individual as support for activities of the individual as a holder of Federal office, may be used by the candidate or individual—

(1) for otherwise authorized expenditures in connection with the campaign for Federal office of the candidate or individual;

(2) for ordinary and necessary expenses incurred in connection with duties of the individual as a holder of Federal office;

(3) for contributions to an organization described in section 170(c) of the Internal Revenue Code of 1986; or

(4) for transfers, without limitation, to a national, State, or local committee of a political party.

(b) PROHIBITED USE-

(1) IN GENERAL- A contribution or donation described in subsection (a) shall not be converted by any person to personal use.

(2) CONVERSION- For the purposes of paragraph (1), a contribution or donation shall be considered to be converted to personal use if the contribution or amount is used to fulfill any commitment, obligation, or expense of a person that would exist irrespective of the candidate's election campaign or individual's duties as a holder of Federal office. . . .

SEC. 302. PROHIBITION OF FUNDRAISING ON FEDERAL PROPERTY.

* * *

(1) IN GENERAL- It shall be unlawful for any person to solicit or receive a donation of money or other thing of

value in connection with a Federal, State, or local election from a person who is located in a room or building occupied in the discharge of official duties by an officer or employee of the United States. It shall be unlawful for an individual who is an officer or employee of the Federal Government, including the President, Vice President, and Members of Congress, to solicit or receive a donation of money or other thing of value in connection with a Federal, State, or local election, while in any room or building occupied in the discharge of official duties by an officer or employee of the United States, from any person.

(2) PENALTY- A person who violates this section shall be fined not more than $5,000, imprisoned not more than 3 years, or both. . . .

SEC. 303. STRENGTHENING FOREIGN MONEY BAN.

* * *

(a) PROHIBITION- It shall be unlawful for—

(1) a foreign national, directly or indirectly, to make—

(A) a contribution or donation of money or other thing of value, or to make an express or implied promise to make a contribution or donation, in connection with a Federal, State, or local election;

(B) a contribution or donation to a committee of a political party; or

(C) an expenditure, independent expenditure, or disbursement for an electioneering communication . . . or

(2) a person to solicit, accept, or receive a contribution or donation. . .from a foreign national.

SEC. 304. MODIFICATION OF INDIVIDUAL CONTRIBUTION LIMITS IN RESPONSE TO EXPENDITURES FROM PERSONAL FUNDS.

(1) INCREASE-

(A) IN GENERAL- if the opposition personal funds amount with respect to a candidate for election to the office of Senator exceeds the threshold amount, the limit . . .with respect to that candidate shall be the increased limit.

. . .

(j) LIMITATION ON REPAYMENT OF PERSONAL LOANS- Any candidate who incurs personal loans made after the effective date of the Bipartisan Campaign Reform Act of 2002 in connection with the candidate's campaign for election shall not repay (directly or indirectly), to the extent such loans exceed $250,000, such loans from any contributions made to such candidate or any authorized committee of such candidate after the date of such election.

* * *

(B) NOTIFICATION OF EXPENDITURE FROM PERSONAL FUNDS-

* * *

(i) DEFINITION OF EXPENDITURE FROM PERSONAL FUNDS–. . .

(I) an expenditure made by a candidate using personal funds; and

(II) a contribution or loan made by a candidate using personal funds or a loan secured using such funds to the candidate's authorized committee.

(ii) DECLARATION OF INTENT- Not later than the date that is 15 days after the date on which an individual becomes a candidate for the office of Senator, the candidate shall file a declaration stating the total amount of expenditures from personal funds that the candidate intends to make, or to obligate to make, with respect to the election that will exceed the State-by-State competitive and fair campaign formula with—

(I) the Commission; and

(II) each candidate in the same election.

* * *

(25) ELECTION CYCLE- . . .The term election cycle' means the period beginning on the day after the date of the most recent election for the specific office or seat that a candidate is seeking and ending on the date of the next election for that office or seat. For purposes of the preceding sentence, a primary election and a general election shall be considered to be separate elections.

(26) PERSONAL FUNDS- The term personal funds' means an amount that is derived from—

(A) any asset that, under applicable State law, at the time the individual became a candidate, the candidate had legal right of access to or control over, and with respect to which the candidate had—

(i) legal and rightful title; or

(ii) an equitable interest;

(B) income received during the current election cycle of the candidate, including—

(i) a salary and other earned income from bona fide employment;

(ii) dividends and proceeds from the sale of the candidate's stocks or other investments;

(iii) bequests to the candidate;

(iv) income from trusts established before the beginning of the election cycle;

(v) income from trusts established by bequest after the beginning of the election cycle of which the candidate is the beneficiary;

(vi) gifts of a personal nature that had been customarily received by the candidate prior to the beginning of the election cycle; and

(vii) proceeds from lotteries and similar legal games of chance; and

(C) a portion of assets that are jointly owned by the candidate and the candidate's spouse equal to the candidate's share of the asset under the instrument of conveyance or ownership, but if no specific share is indicated by an instrument of conveyance or ownership, the value of 1/2 of the property.

* * *

(2) CONTENT OF BROADCASTS-

(A) IN GENERAL- In the case of a candidate for Federal office, such candidate shall not be entitled to receive the rate under paragraph (1)(A) for the use of any broadcasting station unless the candidate provides written certification to the broadcast station that the candidate (and any authorized committee of the candidate) shall not make any direct reference to another candidate for the same office, in any broadcast using the rights and conditions of access under this Act, unless such reference meets the requirements of subparagraph (C) or (D).

(B) LIMITATION ON CHARGES- If a candidate for Federal office (or any authorized committee of such candidate) makes a reference described in subparagraph (A) in any broadcast that does not meet the requirements of subparagraph (C) or (D), such candidate shall not be entitled to receive the rate under paragraph (1)(A) for such broadcast or any other broadcast during any portion of the 45-day and 60-day periods described in paragraph (1)(A), that occur on or after the date of such broadcast, for election to such office.

(C) TELEVISION BROADCASTS- A candidate meets the requirements of this subparagraph if, in the case of a television broadcast, at the end of such broadcast there appears simultaneously, for a period no less than 4 seconds—

(i) a clearly identifiable photographic or similar image of the candidate; and

(ii) a clearly readable printed statement, identifying the candidate and stating that the candidate has approved the broadcast and that the candidate's authorized committee paid for the broadcast.

* * *

Source:

Thomas Legislative Information on the Internet. H. R. 2356. Available on-line. URL: thomas.loc.gov/. Accessed November 2003.

Foreign Policy Issues

Gerald R. Ford, Letter to Congress on the Recovery of the SS *Mayaguez*, 1975

Letter from President Gerald R. Ford, informing Congress, pursuant to the War Powers Act, that U.S. military forces had recaptured the American merchant ship, *Mayaguez,* which had been seized by troops of the new communist Khmer Rouge government in Cambodia. In the letter he stated that all 39 crew members of the ship were safe after a rescue mission that began on the evening of May 14. In the letter, he saluted the sailors and marines who took part in the operation.

The marines had stormed Tang Island where the ship was located, and suffered only light causalities. Later, three helicopters were reported missing. U.S. aircraft bombed Ream airfield and the naval base in Sihanoukville. Ford waited 11 hours before telling the American people about the *Mayaguez* rescue operation and that U.S. bomber forces were hitting Cambodian gunboats.

The rescue effort ultimately included fatalities. Twenty-three deaths occurred when a helicopter carrying security personnel crashed, and 15 participants died in the actual rescue mission. The 15 were among the last names placed on the Vietnam War Memorial wall in Washington , D.C. Eighteen additional personnel were listed as missing in action (MIA) at the time. The remains of nine of these MIAs were returned to the United States in 2000. Despite the casualties, many Americans accepted the incident as a badly needed U.S. victory after the fall of Saigon.

On 12 May 1975, I was advised that the SS *Mayaguez,* a merchant vessel of United States registry en route from Hong Kong to Thailand with a U.S. citizen crew, was fired upon, stopped, boarded, and seized by Cambodian naval patrol boats of the Armed Forces of Cambodia in international waters in the vicinity of Poulo Wai Island. The seized vessel was then forced to proceed to Koh Tang Island where it was required to anchor. This hostile act was in clear violation of international law.

In view of this illegal and dangerous act, I ordered, as you have been previously advised, United States military forces to conduct the necessary reconnaissance and to be ready to respond if diplomatic efforts to secure the return of the vessel and its personnel were not successful. Two United States reconnaissance aircraft in the course of locating the *Mayaguez* sustained minimal damage from small firearms. Appropriate demands for the return of the *Mayaguez* and its crew were made, both publicly and privately, without success.

In accordance with my desire that the Congress be informed on this matter and taking note of Section 4(a)(1) of the War Powers Resolution, I wish to report to you that at about 6:20 a.m., 13 May, pursuant to my instructions to prevent the movement of the *Mayaguez* into a mainland port, U.S. aircraft fired warning shots across the bow of the ship and gave visual signals to small craft approaching the ship. Subsequently, in order to stabilize the situation and in an attempt to preclude removal of the American crew of the *Mayaguez* to the mainland, where their rescue would be more difficult, I directed the United States Armed Forces to isolate the island and interdict any movement between the ship or the island and the mainland, and to prevent movement of the ship itself, while still taking all possible care to prevent loss of life or injury to the U.S. captives. During the evening of 13 May, a Cambodian patrol boat attempting to leave the island disregarded aircraft warnings and was sunk. Thereafter, two other Cambodian patrol craft were destroyed and four others were damaged and immobilized. One boat, suspected of having some U.S. captives aboard, succeeded in reaching Kompong Som after efforts to turn it around without injury to the passengers failed.

Our continued objective in this operation was the rescue of the captured American crew along with the retaking of the ship *Mayaguez*. For that purpose, I ordered late this afternoon [May 14] an assault by United States Marines on the island of Koh Tang to search out and rescue such Americans as might still be held there, and I ordered retaking of the *Mayaguez* by other marines boarding from the destroyer escort *Holt*. In addition to continued fighter and gunship coverage of the Koh Tang area, these Marine activities were supported by tactical aircraft from the *Coral Sea*, striking the military airfield at Ream and other military targets in the area of Kompong Som in order to prevent reinforcement or support from the mainland of the Cambodian forces detaining the American vessel and crew.

At approximately 9:00 p.m. EDT on 14 May, the *Mayaguez* was retaken by United States forces. At approximately 11:30 p.m., the entire crew of the *Mayaguez* was taken aboard the *Wilson*. U.S. forces have begun the process of disengagement and withdrawal.

This operation was ordered and conducted pursuant to the President's constitutional Executive power and his authority as Commander-in-Chief of the United States Armed Forces.

Sincerely,
Gerald R. Ford

Source:

Public Papers of the Presidents of the United States: Gerald R. Ford, 1975. Washington, D.C.: Government Printing Office, 1978. pp. 669–670.

Helsinki Accord, 1975

Accord signed on August 1, 1975, by 33 European countries, Canada, and the United States during the Helsinki Conference, held to ratify the agreements of the Conferences on Security and Cooperation in Europe (CSCE). The accord's signatories pledged respect for national sovereignty, territorial integrity, human rights, and civil liberties; recognition of a country's international obligations; peaceful settlement of disputes between nations; and a policy of international cooperation on technical, scientific, economic, and environmental issues. An offshoot of the policy of détente adopted by the superpowers, the Helsinki Accord was not a treaty and had no legal authority. Nevertheless, it was a landmark document at the time, and was generally accepted as a standard by which the human rights records of the Eastern bloc countries were judged.

(British spelling has been retained)

The Conference on Security and Co-operation in Europe, which opened at Helsinki on 3 July 1973 and continued at Geneva from 18 September 1973 to 21 July 1975, was concluded at Helsinki on 1 August 1975 by the High Representatives of Austria, Belgium, Bulgaria, Canada, Cyprus, Czechoslovakia, Denmark, Finland, France, the German Democratic Republic, the Federal Republic of Germany, Greece, the Holy See, Hungary, Iceland, Ireland, Italy, Liechtenstein, Luxembourg, Malta, Monaco, the Netherlands, Norway, Poland, Portugal, Romania, San Marino, Spain, Sweden, Switzerland, Turkey, the Union of Soviet Socialist Republics, the United Kingdom, the United States of America and Yugoslavia,

* * *

Motivated by the political will, in the interest of peoples, to improve and intensify their relations and to contribute in

Europe to peace, security, justice and co-operation as well as to rapprochement among themselves and with the other States of the world,

Determined, in consequence, to give full effect to the results of the Conference and to assure, among their States and throughout Europe, the benefits deriving from those results and thus to broaden, deepen and make continuing and lasting the process of detente,

The High Representatives of the participating States have solemnly adopted the following:

QUESTIONS RELATING TO SECURITY IN EUROPE

The States participating in the Conference on Security and Co-operation in Europe,

Reaffirming their objective of promoting better relations among themselves and ensuring conditions in which their people can live in true and lasting peace free from any threat to or attempt against their security;

Convinced of the need to exert efforts to make detente both a continuing and an increasingly viable and comprehensive process, universal in scope, and that the implementation of the results of the Conference of Security and Co-operation in Europe will be a major contribution to this process;

Considering that solidarity among peoples, as well as the common purpose of the participating States in achieving the aims as set forth by the Conference on Security and Co-operation in Europe, should lead to the development of better and closer relations among them in all fields and thus to overcoming the confrontation stemming from the character of their past relations, and to better mutual understanding;

Mindful of their common history and recognizing that the existence of elements common to their traditions and values can assist them in developing their relations, and desiring to search, fully taking into account the individuality and diversity of their positions and views, for possibilities of joining their efforts with a view to overcoming distrust and increasing confidence, solving the problems that separate them and cooperating in the interest of mankind;

Recognizing the indivisibility of security in Europe as well as their common interest in the development of co-operation throughout Europe and among themselves and expressing their intention to pursue efforts accordingly;

Recognizing the close link between peace and security in Europe and in the world as a whole and conscious of the need for each of them to make its contribution to the strengthening of world peace and security and to the promotion of fundamental rights, economic and social progress and well-being for all peoples;

Have adopted the following:

1. (a) Declaration on Principles Guiding Relations between Participating States

The participating States,

Reaffirming their commitment to peace, security and justice and the continuing development of friendly relations and co-operation;

Recognizing that this commitment, which reflects the interest and aspirations of peoples, constitutes for each participating State a present and future responsibility, heightened by experience of the past;

Reaffirming, in conformity with their membership in the United Nations and in accordance with the purposes and principles of the United Nations, their full and active support for the United Nations and for the enhancement of its role and effectiveness in strengthening international peace, security and justice, and in promoting the solution of international problems, as well as the development of friendly relations and co-operation among States;

Expressing their common adherence to the principles which are set forth below and are in conformity with the Charter of the United Nations, as well as their common will to act, in the application of these principles, in conformity with the purposes and principles of the Charter of the United Nations;

Declare their determination to respect and put into practice, each of them in its relations with all other participating States, irrespective of their political, economic or social systems as well as of their size, geographical location or level of economic development, the following principles, which all are primary significance, guiding their mutual relations:

I Sovereign equality, respect for the rights inherent in sovereignty

The participating States will respect each other's sovereign equality and individuality as well as all the rights inherent in and encompassed by its sovereignty, including in particular the right of every State to juridical equality, to territorial integrity and to freedom and political independence. They will also respect each other's right freely to choose and develop its political, social, economic and cultural systems as well as its right to determine its laws and regulations.

Within the framework of international law, all the participating States have equal rights and duties. They will respect each other's right to define and conduct as it wishes its relations with other States in accordance with international law and in the spirit of the present Declaration. They consider that their frontiers can be changed, in accordance with international law, by peaceful means and by agreement. They also have the right to belong or not to belong to international organizations, to be or not to be a party to bilateral or multilateral treaties including the right to be or not to be a party to treaties of alliance; they also have the right to neutrality.

II Refraining from the threat of use of force

The participating States will refrain in their mutual relations, as well as in their international relations in general, from the threat or use of force against the territorial integrity or political independence of any State, or in any other manner inconsistent with the purposes of the United Nations and with the present Declaration. No consideration may be invoked to serve to warrant resort to the threat or use of force in contravention of this principle.

* * *

III Inviolability of frontiers

The participating States regard as inviolable all one another's frontiers as well as the frontiers of all States in Europe and therefore they will refrain now and in the future from assaulting these frontiers.

* * *

V Peaceful settlement of disputes

The participating States will settle disputes among them by peaceful means in such a manner as not to endanger international peace and security, and justice.

They will endeavour in good faith and a spirit of cooperation to reach a rapid and equitable solution on the basis of international law.

For this purpose the will use such means as negotiation, enquiry, mediation, conciliation, arbitration, judicial settlement or other peaceful means of their own choice including any settlement procedure agreed to in advance of disputes to which they are parties.

In the event of failure to reach a solution by any of the above peaceful means, the parties to a dispute will continue to seek a mutually agreed way to settle the dispute peacefully.

Participating States, parties to a dispute among them, as well as other participating States, will refrain from any action which might aggravate the situation to such a degree as to endanger the maintenance of international peace and security and thereby make a peaceful settlement of the dispute more difficult.

VI Non-intervention in internal affairs

The participating States will refrain from any intervention, direct or indirect, individual or collective, in the internal or external affairs falling within the domestic jurisdiction of another participating State, regardless of their mutual relations.

* * *

Source:

John J. Maresca, *To Helsinki: The Conference on Security and Cooperation in Europe.* Durham, N.C.: Duke University Press, 1985, pp. 227–283.

Jimmy Carter, Human Rights Speech at Notre Dame, 1977

Address delivered by President Jimmy Carter at Notre Dame University on May 22, 1977. His speech was a major statement outlining the administration's central foreign policy theme of championing the cause of human rights around the world. He spelled out five "cardinal premises" that would determine U.S. "global involvement." They were advocating human rights, establishing closer cooperation among the industrial democracies, pursuing détente with the Soviet Union and China, supporting the developing nations against poverty and hunger, and working with every country "to rise above narrow national interest and work together" in order to "solve" the major problems facing all humankind. Carter asserted that in his presidency, "we have reaffirmed America's commitment to human rights as a fundamental tenet of our foreign policy." The address became most noted for Carter's assertion that "being confident of our own future we are now free of that inordinate fear of communism which once led us to embrace any dictator who joined our fear."

Carter continued to advocate human rights throughout the world after his defeat for a second term in 1980. As a result of his mediation in a number of international disputes, Carter was awarded the Nobel Peace Prize in 2002.

To Father Hesburgh and the great faculty of Notre Dame, to those who have been honored this afternoon with the degree from your great university, to the graduate and undergraduate group who, I understand, is the largest in the history of this great institution, friends and parents:

Thank you for that welcome. I'm very glad to be with you. You may have started a new graduation trend which I don't deplore, that is, throwing peanuts on graduation day. [*Laughter*] The more that are used or consumed the higher the price goes. [*Laughter*]

I really did appreciate the great honor bestowed upon me this afternoon. My other degree is blue and gold from the Navy, and I want to let you know that I do feel a kinship with those who are assembled here this afternoon. I was a little taken aback by the comment that I had brought a new accent to the White House. In the minds of many people in our country, for the first time in almost 150 years, there is no accent. [*Laughter*]

I tried to think of a story that would illustrate two points simultaneously and also be brief, which is kind of a difficult assignment. I was sitting on the Truman Balcony the other night with my good friend, Charles Kirbo, who told me about a man who was arrested and taken in to court for being drunk and for setting a bed on fire. When the judge asked him how he pled, he said, "not guilty." He said, "I was drunk but the bed was on fire when I got in it." [*Laughter*]

I think most of the graduates can draw the parallel between that statement and what you are approaching after this graduation exercise. But there are two points to that, and I'll come to the other one in just a few minutes.

In his 25 years as president of Notre Dame, Father Hesburgh has spoken more consistently and more effectively in the support of the rights of human beings than any other person I know. His interest in the Notre Dame Center for Civil Rights has never wavered. And he played an important role in broadening the scope of the center's work—and I visited there last fall—to see this work include, now, all people in the world, as shown by last month's conference here on human rights and American foreign policy.

And that concern has been demonstrated again today in a vivid fashion by the selection of Bishop Donal Lamont, Paul Cardinal Arns, and Stephen Cardinal Kim to receive honorary degrees. In their fight for human freedoms in Rhodesia, Brazil, and South Korea, these three religious leaders typify all that is best in their countries and in our church. I'm honored to join you in recognizing their dedication, their personal sacrifice, and their supreme courage.

Quite often, brave men like these are castigated and sometimes punished, sometimes even put to death, because they enter the realm where human rights is a struggle. And sometimes they are blamed for the very circumstance which they helped to dramatize, but it's been there for a long time. And the flames which they seek to extinguish concern us all and are increasingly visible around the world.

Last week, I spoke in California about the domestic agenda for our Nation: to provide more efficiently for the needs of our people, to demonstrate—against the dark faith of our times—that our Government can be both competent and more humane.

But I want to speak to you today about the strands that connect our actions overseas with our essential character as a nation. I believe we can have a foreign policy that is democratic, that is based on fundamental values, and that uses power and influence, which we have, for humane purposes. We can also have a foreign policy that the American people both support and, for a change, know about and understand.

I have a quiet confidence in our political system. Because we know that democracy works, we can reject the arguments of those rulers who deny human rights to their people.

We are confident that democracy's example will be compelling, and so we seek to bring that example closer to those from whom in the past few years we have been separated and who are not yet convinced about the advantages of our kind of life.

We are confident that the democratic methods are the most effective, and so we are not tempted to employ improper tactics here at home or abroad.

We are confident of our own strength, so we can seek substantial mutual reductions in the nuclear arms race.

And we are confident of the good sense of the American people, and so we let them share in the process of making foreign policy decisions. We can thus speak with the voices of 215 million, and not just of an isolated handful.

Democracy's great recent successes—in India, Portugal, Spain, Greece—show that our confidence in this system is not misplaced. Being confident of our own future, we are now free of that inordinate fear of communism which once led us to embrace any dictator who joined us in that fear. I'm glad that that's being changed.

For too many years, we've been willing to adopt the flawed and erroneous principles and tactics of our adversaries, sometimes abandoning our own values for theirs. We've fought fire with fire, never thinking that fire is better quenched with water. This approach failed, with Vietnam the best example of its intellectual and moral poverty. But through failure we have now found our way back to our own principles and values, and we have regained our lost confidence.

By the measure of history, our Nation's 200 years are very brief, and our rise to world eminence is briefer still. It dates from 1945, when Europe and the old international order lay in ruins. Before then, America was largely on the periphery of world affairs. But since then, we have inescapably been at the center of world affairs.

Our policy during this period was guided by two principles: a belief that Soviet expansion was almost inevitable but that it must be contained, and the corresponding belief in the importance of an almost exclusive alliance among non-Communist nations on both sides of the Atlantic. That system could not last forever unchanged. Historical trends have weakened its foundation. The unifying threat of conflict with the Soviet Union has become less intensive, even though the competition has become more extensive.

The Vietnamese war produced a profound moral crisis, sapping worldwide faith in our own policy and our system of life, a crisis of confidence made even more grave by the covert pessimism of some of our leaders.

In less than a generation, we've seen the world change dramatically. The daily lives and aspirations of most human beings have been transformed. Colonialism is nearly gone. A new sense of national identity now exists in almost 100 new countries that have been formed in the last generation. Knowledge has become more widespread. Aspirations are higher. As more people have been freed from traditional constraints, more have been determined to achieve, for the first time in their lives, social justice.

The world is still divided by ideological disputes, dominated by regional conflicts, and threatened by danger that we will not resolve the differences of race and wealth without violence or without drawing into combat the major military powers. We can no longer separate the traditional issues of war and peace from the new global questions of justice, equity, and human rights.

It is a new world, but America should not fear it. It is a new world, and we should help to shape it. It is a new world that calls for a new American foreign policy—a policy based on constant decency in its values and on optimism in our historical vision.

We can no longer have a policy solely for the industrial nations as the foundation of global stability, but we must respond to the new reality of a politically awakening world.

We can no longer expect that the other 150 nations will follow the dictates of the powerful, but we must continue—confidently—our efforts to inspire, to persuade, and to lead.

Our policy must reflect our belief that the world can hope for more than simple survival and our belief that dignity and freedom are fundamental spiritual requirements. Our policy must shape an international system that will last longer than secret deals.

We cannot make this kind of policy by manipulation. Our policy must be open; it must be candid; it must be one of constructive global involvement, resting on five cardinal principles.

I've tried to make these premises clear to the American people since last January. Let me review what we have been doing and discuss what we intend to do.

First, we have reaffirmed America's commitment to human rights as a fundamental tenet of our foreign policy. In ancestry, religion, color, place of origin, and cultural background, we Americans are as diverse a nation as the world has even seen. No common mystique of blood or soil unites us. What draws us together, perhaps more than anything else, is a belief in human freedom. We want the world to know that our Nation stands for more than financial prosperity.

This does not mean that we can conduct our foreign policy by rigid moral maxims. We live in a world that is imperfect and which will always be imperfect—a world that is complex and confused and which will always be complex and confused.

I understand fully the limits of moral suasion. We have no illusion that changes will come easily or soon. But I also believe that it is a mistake to undervalue the power of words and of the ideas that words embody. In our own history, that power has ranged from Thomas Paine's "Common Sense" to Martin Luther King, Jr.'s "I Have a Dream."

In the life of the human spirit, words *are* action, much more so than many of us may realize who live in countries where freedom of expression is taken for granted. The leaders of totalitarian nations understand this very well. The proof is that words are precisely the action for which dissidents in those countries are being persecuted.

Nonetheless, we can already see dramatic, worldwide advances in the protection of the individual from the arbitrary power of the state. For us to ignore this trend would be to lose influence and moral authority in the world. To lead it will be to regain the moral stature that we once had.

The great democracies are not free because we are strong and prosperous. I believe we are strong and influential and prosperous because we are free.

Throughout the world today, in free nations and in totalitarian countries as well, there is a preoccupation with the subject of human freedom, human rights. And I believe it is incumbent on us in this country to keep that discussion, that debate, that contention alive. No other country is as well-qualified as we to set an example. We have our own shortcomings and faults, and we should strive constantly and with courage to make sure that we are legitimately proud of what we have.

Second, we've moved deliberately to reinforce the bonds among our democracies. In our recent meetings in London, we agreed to widen our economic cooperation, to promote free trade, to strengthen the world's monetary system, to seek ways of avoiding nuclear proliferation. We prepared constructive proposals for the forthcoming meetings on North-South problems of poverty, development, and global well-being. And we agreed on joint efforts to reinforce and to modernize our common defense.

You may be interested in knowing that at this NATO meeting, for the first time in more than 25 years, all members are democracies. Even more important, all of us reaffirmed our basic optimism in the future of the democratic system. Our spirit of confidence is spreading. Together, our democracies can help to shape the wider architecture of global cooperation.

Third, we've moved to engage the Soviet Union in a joint effort to halt the strategic arms race. This race is not only dangerous, it's morally deplorable. We must put an end to it.

I know it will not be easy to reach agreements. Our goal is to be fair to both sides, to produce reciprocal stability, parity, and security. We desire a freeze on further modernization and production of weapons and a continuing, substantial reduction of strategic nuclear weapons as well. We want a comprehensive ban on all nuclear testing, a prohibition against all chemical warfare, no attack capability against space satellites, and arms limitations in the Indian Ocean.

We hope that we can take joint steps with all nations toward a final agreement eliminating nuclear weapons completely from our arsenals of death. We will persist in this effort.

Now, I believe in detente with the Soviet Union. To me it means progress toward peace. But the effects of detente should not be limited to our own two countries alone. We hope to persuade the Soviet Union that one country cannot impose its system of society upon another, either through direct military intervention or through the use of a client state's military force, as was the case with Cuban intervention in Angola.

Cooperation also implies obligation. We hope that the Soviet Union will join with us and other nations in playing a larger role in aiding the developing world, for common aid efforts will help us build a bridge of mutual confidence in one another.

Fourth, we are taking deliberate steps to improve the chances of lasting peace in the Middle East. Through wide-ranging consultation with leaders of the countries involved—Israel, Syria, Jordan, and Egypt—we have found some areas of agreement and some movement toward consensus. The negotiations must continue.

Through my own public comments, I've also tried to suggest a more flexible framework for the discussion of the three key issues which have so far been so intractable: the nature of a comprehensive peace—what is peace; what does it mean to the Israelis; what does it mean to their Arab neighbors; secondly, the relationship between security and borders—how can the dispute over border delineations be established and settled with a feeling of security on both sides; and the issue of the Palestinian homeland.

The historic friendship that the United States has with Israel is not dependent on domestic politics in either nation; it's derived from our common respect for human freedom and from a common search for permanent peace.

We will continue to promote a settlement which all of us need. Our own policy will not be affected by changes in leadership in any of the countries in the Middle East. Therefore, we expect Israel and her neighbors to continue to be bound by United Nations Resolutions 242 and 338, which they have previously accepted.

This may be the most propitious time for a genuine settlement since the beginning of the Arab- Israeli conflict almost 30 years ago. To let this opportunity pass could mean disaster not only for the Middle East but, perhaps, for the international political and economic order as well.

And fifth, we are attempting, even at the risk of some friction with our friends, to reduce the danger of nuclear proliferation and the worldwide spread of conventional weapons.

At the recent summit, we set in motion an international effort to determine the best ways of harnessing nuclear energy for peaceful use while reducing the risks that its products will be diverted to the making of explosives.

We've already completed a comprehensive review of our own policy on arms transfers. Competition in arms sales is inimical to peace and destructive of the economic development of the poorer countries.

We will, as a matter of national policy now in our country, seek to reduce the annual dollar volume of arms sales, to restrict the transfer of advanced weapons, and to reduce the extent of our coproduction arrangements about weapons with foreign states. And just as important, we are trying to get other nations, both free and otherwise, to join us in this effort.

But all of this that I've described is just the beginning. It's a beginning aimed towards a clear goal: to create a wider framework of international cooperation suited to the new and rapidly changing historical circumstances.

We will cooperate more closely with the newly influential countries in Latin America, Africa, and Asia. We need their friendship and cooperation in a common effort as the structure of world power changes.

More than 100 years ago, Abraham Lincoln said that our Nation could not exist half slave and half free. We know a peaceful world cannot long exist one-third rich and two-thirds hungry.

Most nations share our faith that, in the long run, expanded and equitable trade will best help the developing countries to help themselves. But the immediate problems of hunger, disease, illiteracy, and repression are here now.

The Western democracies, the OPEC nations, and the developed Communist countries can cooperate through existing international institutions in providing more effective aid. This is an excellent alternative to war.

We have a special need for cooperation and consultation with other nations in this hemisphere—to the north and to the south. We do not need another slogan. Although these are our close friends and neighbors, our links with them are the same links of equality that we forge for the rest of the world. We will be dealing with them as part of a new, worldwide mosaic of global, regional, and bilateral relations.

It's important that we make progress toward normalizing relations with the People's Republic of China. We see the American and Chinese relationship as a central element of our global policy and China as a key force for global peace. We wish to cooperate closely with the creative Chinese people on the problems that confront all mankind. And we hope to find a formula which can bridge some of the difficulties that still separate us.

Finally, let me say that we are committed to a peaceful resolution of the crisis in southern Africa. The time has come for the principle of majority rule to be the basis for political order, recognizing that in a democratic system the rights of the minority must also be protected.

To be peaceful, change must come promptly. The United States is determined to work together with our European allies and with the concerned African States to shape a congenial international framework for the rapid and progressive transformation of southern African society and to help protect it from unwarranted outside interference.

Let me conclude by summarizing: Our policy is based on an historical vision of America's role. Our policy is derived from a larger view of global change. Our policy is rooted in our moral values, which never change. Our policy is reinforced by our material wealth and by our military power. Our policy is designed to serve mankind. And it is a policy that I hope will make you proud to be Americans.

Thank you.

Source:

Public Papers of the Presidents of the United States: Jimmy Carter, 1977. Washington, D.C.: Government Printing Office, 1981–88. pp. 954– 962.

Panama Neutrality Treaty, 1977

Signed in Washington, D.C., by U.S. president Jimmy Carter and Panama's chief of government Brigadier General Omar Torrijos, September 7, 1977, at the same time as the Panama Canal Treaty, the Neutrality Treaty granted Panama control of the Panama Canal at the end of 1999 and guaranteed the permanent neutrality of the canal. In addition, the Panama Canal Treaty provided that the United States and Panama would control the operation and oversee the security of the canal jointly until 1999, with increasing control being given to the Panamanians. The Neutrality Treaty further provided that both the United States and Panama were responsible for defending the canal, maintaining its neutrality, and keeping it open. Shipping of all countries was to be guaranteed passage on a nondiscriminatory basis. U.S. forces would have the right to act after 2000 to ensure that the canal remains open and secure. The treaties were concluded after 14 years of negotiation, and they replaced the Hay–Bunau-Varilla Treaty of 1903.

The United States of America and the Republic of Panama have agreed upon the following:

Article I

The Republic of Panama declares that the Canal, as an international transit waterway, shall be permanently neutral in accordance with the regime established in this Treaty. The same regime of neutrality shall apply to any other international waterway that may be built either partially or wholly in the territory of the Republic of Panama.

Article II

The Republic of Panama declares the neutrality of the Canal in order that both in time of peace and in time of war it shall remain secure and open to peaceful transit by the vessels of all nations on terms of entire equality, so that there will be no discrimination against any nation, or its citizens or subjects, concerning the conditions or charges of transit, or for any other reason, and so that the Canal, and therefore the Isthmus of Panama, shall not be the target of reprisals in any armed conflict between other nations of the world. The foregoing shall be subject to the following requirements:

(a) Payment of tolls and other charges for transit and ancillary services, provided they have been fixed in conformity with the provisions of Article III(c);

(b) Compliance with applicable rules and regulations, provided such rules and regulations are applied in conformity with the provisions of Article III;

(c) The requirement that transiting vessel commit no acts of hostility while in the Canal; and

(d) Such other conditions and restrictions as are established by this Treaty.

Article III

1. For purposes of the security, efficiency and proper maintenance of the Canal the following rules shall apply:

(a) The canal shall be operated efficiently in accordance with conditions of transit through the Canal, and rules and regulations that shall be just, equitable and reasonable, and limited to those necessary for safe navigation and efficient, sanitary operation of the Canal;

(b) Ancillary services necessary for transit through the Canal shall be provided;

(c) Tolls and other charges for transit and ancillary services shall be just, reasonable, equitable and consistent with the principles of international law;

(d) As a pre-condition of transit, vessels may be required to establish clearly the financial responsibility and guarantees for payment of reasonable and adequate indemnification, consistent with international practice and standards, for damages resulting from acts or omissions of such vessels when passing through the Canal. In the case of vessels owned or operated by a State or for which it has acknowledged responsibility, a certification by that State that it shall observe its obligations under international law to pay for damages resulting from the act or omission of such vessels when passing through the Canal shall be deemed sufficient to establish such financial responsibility;

(e) Vessels of war and auxiliary vessels of all nations shall at all times be entitled to transit the Canal, irrespective of their internal operation, means of propulsion, origin, destination or armament, without being subjected, as a condition of transit, to inspection, search or surveillance. However, such vessels may be required to certify that they have complied with all applicable health, sanitation and quarantine regulations. In addition, such vessels shall be entitled to refuse to disclose their internal operation, origin, armament, cargo or destination. However, auxiliary vessels may be required to present written assurances, certified by an official at a high level of the government of the State requesting the exemption, that they are owned or operated by that government and in this case are being used only on government non-commercial service.

2. For the purposes of this Treaty, the terms "Canal," "vessel of war," "auxiliary vessel," "internal operation," "armament" and "inspection" shall have the meanings assigned them in Annex A to this Treaty.

Article IV

The United States of America and the Republic of Panama agree to maintain the regime of neutrality established in this Treaty, which shall be maintained in order that the Canal shall remain permanently neutral, notwithstanding the termination of any other treaties entered into by the two Contracting Parties.

Article V

After the termination of the Panama Canal Treaty, only the Republic of Panama shall operate the Canal and maintain military forces, defense sites and military installations within its national territory.

Article VI

1. In recognition of the important contributions of the United States of America and of the Republic of Panama to the construction, operation, maintenance, and protection and defense of the Canal, vessels of war and auxiliary vessels of those nations shall, notwithstanding any other provisions of this Treaty, be entitled to transit the Canal irrespective of their internal operation, means of propulsion, origin, destination, armament or cargo carried. Such vessels of war and auxiliary vessels will be entitled to transit the Canal expeditiously.

2. The United States of America, so long as it has responsibility for the operation of the Canal, may continue to provide the Republic of Colombia toll-free transit through the Canal for its troops, vessels and materials of war. Thereafter, the Republic of Panama may provide the Republic of Colombia and the Republic of Costa Rica with the right of toll-free transit.

Article VII

1. The United States of America and the Republic of Panama shall jointly sponsor a resolution in the Organization of American States opening to accession by all States of the world the Protocol to this Treaty whereby all the signatories will adhere to the objectives of this Treaty, agreeing to respect the regime of neutrality set forth herein.

2. The Organization of American States shall act as the depositary for this Treaty and related instruments.

Article VIII

This Treaty shall be subject to ratification in accordance with the constitutional procedures of the two Parties. The instruments of ratification of this Treaty shall be exchanged at Panama at the same time as the instruments of ratification of the Panama Canal Treaty, signed this date, are exchanged. This Treaty shall enter into force, simultaneously with the Panama Canal Treaty, six calendar months from the date of the exchange of the instruments of ratification. Done at Washington, this 7th day of September, 1977, in duplicate, in the English and Spanish languages, both texts being equally authentic.

Firmado en Washington, a los 7 dias de septiembre de 1977, en los idiomas ingles y espanol, siendo ambos textos igualmente autenticos.

For the United States of America: Por Los Estados Unidos De America:

For the Republic of Panama: Por La Republica De Panama:

SIGNED
President of the United States of America
Presidente de los Estados de America
SIGNED
Head of government of the Republic of Panama
Jefe de Gobierno de la Republica de Panama

Source:

United States Treaties and Other International Agreements, Vol. 33, part 1, 1979–81, pp. 11– 34.

Camp David Accords, 1978

Two agreements (a so-called framework for peace) signed by President Anwar Sadat of Egypt and Prime Minister Menachem Begin of Israel September 17, 1978, after a 13-day conference at the U.S. presidential retreat in Camp David, Maryland. U.S. president Jimmy Carter engineered and led the long, intense negotiations between Sadat and Begin, who agreed to work for a full peace treaty within three months to end 30 years' hostility between their two countries. In keeping with the accords, Israel returned the Sinai Peninsula, taken in the Arab-

Israeli "Six-Day" War in 1967, to Egypt. Interestingly, the Sinai, which was several times as large as Israel prior to the war, provided that nation for the first and last time with land containing oil. Israel removed its settlements from the Sinai before returning it to Egypt. Israel also temporarily halted building new Jewish settlements in the West Bank, the area west of the Jordan River, formerly belonging to Jordan and occupied by Israel after the 1967 war. The Palestine Liberation Organization (PLO), hard-line Arab states, and the Soviet Union denounced the accords. Nevertheless, Israel and Egypt signed a formal peace treaty in March 1979. However, the economic benefits that Egypt expected to derive from the accords never materialized, and Begin increased the Israeli presence in the West Bank instead of granting additional autonomy. Sadat was assassinated in 1981 by fellow Egyptians who advocated the complete destruction of Israel.

CAMP DAVID AGREEMENT A FRAMEWORK FOR PEACE IN THE MIDDLE EAST AGREED AT CAMP DAVID

Muhammad Anwar al-Sadat, President of the Arab Republic of Egypt, and Menachem Begin, Prime Minister of Israel, met with Jimmy Carter, President of the United States of America, at Camp David from September 5 to September 17, 1978, and have agreed on the following framework for peace in the Middle East. They invite other parties to the Arab-Israeli conflict to adhere to it.

Preamble

The search for peace in the Middle East must be guided by the following:

—The agreed basis for a peaceful settlement of the conflict between Israel and its neighbors is United Nations Security Council Resolution 242, in all its parts.

—After four wars during thirty years, despite intensive human efforts, the Middle East, which is the cradle of civilization and the birthplace of three great religions, does not yet enjoy the blessings of peace. The people of the Middle East yearn for peace so that the vast human and natural resources of the region can be turned to the pursuits of peace and so that this area can become a model for coexistence and cooperation among nations.

—The historic initiative of President Sadat in visiting Jerusalem and the reception accorded to him by the Parliament, Government and people of Israel, and the reciprocal visit of Prime Minister Begin to Ismailia, the peace proposals made by both leaders, as well as the warm reception of these missions by the peoples of both countries, have created an unprecedented opportunity for peace which must not be lost if this generation and future generations are to be spared the tragedies of war.

—The provisions of the Charter of the United Nations and the other accepted norms of international law and legitimacy now provide accepted standards for the conduct of relations among all States.

—To achieve a relationship of peace, in the spirit of Article 2 of the United Nations Charter, future negotiations between Israel and any neighbor prepared to negotiate peace and security with it, are necessary for the purpose of carrying out all the provisions and principles of Resolutions 242 and 338.

—Peace requires respect for the sovereignty, territorial integrity and political independence of every State in the area and their right to live in peace within secure and recognized boundaries free from threats or acts of force. Progress toward that goal can accelerate movement toward a new era of reconciliation in the Middle East marked by cooperation in promoting economic development, in maintaining stability, and in assuring security.

—Security is enhanced by a relationship of peace and by cooperation between nations which enjoy normal relations. In addition, under the terms of peace treaties, the parties can, on the basis of reciprocity, agree to special security arrangements such as demilitarized zones, limited armaments areas, early warning stations, the presence of international forces, liaison, agreed measures for monitoring, and other arrangements that they agree are useful.

Framework

Taking these factors into account, the parties are determined to reach a just, comprehensive, and durable settlement of the Middle East conflict through the conclusion of peace treaties based on Security Council Resolutions 242 and 338 in all their parts. Their purpose is to achieve peace and good neighborly relations. They recognize that, for peace to endure, it must involve all those who have been most deeply affected by the conflict. They therefore agree that this framework as appropriate is intended by them to constitute a basis for peace not only between Egypt and Israel, but also between Israel and each of its other neighbors which is prepared to negotiate peace with Israel on this basis. With that objective in mind, they have agreed to proceed as follows:

A. West Bank and Gaza

1. Egypt, Israel, Jordan and the representatives of the Palestinian people should participate in negotiations on the resolution of the Palestinian problem in all its aspects. To achieve that objective, negotiations relating to the West Bank and Gaza should proceed in three stages:

(a) Egypt and Israel agree that, in order to ensure a peaceful and orderly transfer of authority, and taking into account the security concerns of all the parties, there should be transitional arrangements for the West Bank and Gaza for a period not exceeding five years. In order to provide full autonomy to the inhabitants, under these arrangements the Israeli military government and its civilian administration will be withdrawn as soon as a self-governing authority has been freely elected by the inhabitants of these areas to replace the existing military government. To negotiate the details of a transitional arrangement, the Government of Jordan will be invited to join the negotiations on the basis of this framework. These new arrangements should give due consideration both to the principle of self-government by the inhabitants of these territories and to the legitimate security concerns of the parties involved.

(b) Egypt, Israel, and Jordan will agree on the modalities for establishing the elected self-governing authority in the West Bank and Gaza. The delegations of Egypt and Jordan may include Palestinians from the West Bank and Gaza or other Palestinians as mutually agreed. The parties will negotiate an agreement which will define the powers and responsibilities of the self-governing authority to be exercised in the West Bank and Gaza. A withdrawal of Israeli armed forces will take place and there will be a redeployment of the remaining Israeli forces into specified security locations. The agreement will also include arrangements for assuring internal and external security and public order. A strong local police force will be established, which may include Jordanian citizens. In addition, Israeli and Jordanian forces will participate in joint patrols and in the manning of control posts to assure the security of the borders.

(c) When the self-governing authority (administrative council) in the West Bank and Gaza is established and inaugurated, the transitional period of five years will begin. As soon as possible, but not later than the third year after the beginning of the transitional period, negotiations will take place to determine the final status of the West Bank and Gaza and its relationship with its neighbors, and to conclude a peace treaty between Israel and Jordan by the end of the transitional period. These negotiations will be conducted among Egypt, Israel, Jordan, and the elected representatives of the inhabitants of the West Bank and Gaza. Two separate but related committees will be convened, one committee, consisting of representatives of the four parties which will negotiate and agree on the final status of the West Bank and Gaza, and its relationship with its neighbors, and the second committee, consisting of representatives of Israel and representatives of Jordan to be joined by the elected representatives of the inhabitants of the West Bank and Gaza, to negotiate the peace treaty between Israel and Jordan, taking into account the agreement reached on the final status of the West Bank and Gaza. The negotiations shall be based on all the provisions and principles of U.N. Security Council Resolution 242. The negotiations will resolve, among other matters, the location of the boundaries and the nature of the security arrangements. The solution from the negotiations must also recognize the legitimate rights of the Palestinian people and their just requirements. In this way, the Palestinians will participate in the determination of their own future through:

(i) The negotiations among Egypt, Israel, Jordan and the representatives of the inhabitants of the West Bank and Gaza to agree on the final status of the West Bank and Gaza and other outstanding issues by the end of the transitional period.

(ii) Submitting their agreement to a vote by the elected representatives of the inhabitants of the West Bank and Gaza.

(iii) Providing for the elected representatives of the inhabitants of the West Bank and Gaza to decide how they shall govern themselves consistent with the provisions of their agreements.

(iv) Participating as stated above in the work of the committee negotiating the peace treaty between Israel and Jordan.

2. All necessary measures will be taken and provisions made to assure the security of Israel and its neighbors during the transitional period and beyond. To assist in providing such security, a strong local police force will be constituted by the self-governing authority. It will be composed of inhabitants of the West Bank and Gaza. The police will maintain continuing liaison on internal security matters with the designated Israeli, Jordanian and Egyptian officers.

3. During the transitional period, representatives of Egypt, Israel, Jordan, and the self-governing authority will constitute a continuing committee to decide by agreement on the modalities of admission of persons displaced from the West Bank and Gaza in 1967, together with necessary measures to prevent disruption and disorder. Other matters of common concern may also be dealt with by this committee.

4. Egypt and Israel will work with each other and with other interested parties to establish agreed procedures for a prompt, just and permanent implementation of the resolution of the refugee problem.

B. Egypt—Israel

1. Egypt and Israel undertake not to resort to the threat or the use of force to settle disputes. Any disputes shall be settled by peaceful means in accordance with the provisions of Article 33 of the Charter of the United Nations.

2. In order to achieve peace between them, the parties agree to negotiate in good faith with a goal of concluding within three months from the signing of this Framework a peace treaty between them, while inviting the other parties

to the conflict to proceed simultaneously to negotiate and conclude similar peace treaties with a view of achieving a comprehensive peace in the area. The Framework for the Conclusion of a Peace Treaty between Egypt and Israel will govern the peace negotiations between them. The parties will agree on the modalities and the timetable for the implementation of their obligations under the treaty.

C. Associated Principles

1. Egypt and Israel state that the principles and provisions described below should apply to peace treaties between Israel and each of its neighbors—Egypt, Jordan, Syria and Lebanon.

2. Signatories shall establish among themselves relationships normal to States at peace with one another. To this end, they should undertake to abide by all the provisions of the Charter of the United Nations. Steps to be taken in this respect include:

(a) Full recognition;

(b) Abolishing economic boycotts;

(c) Guaranteeing that under their jurisdiction the citizens of the other parties shall enjoy the protection of the due process of law.

3. Signatories should explore possibilities for economic development in the context of final peace treaties, with the objective of contributing to the atmosphere of peace, cooperation and friendship which is their common goal.

4. Claims Commissions may be established for the mutual settlement of all financial claims.

5. The United States shall be invited to participate in the talks on matters related to the modalities of the implementation of the agreements and working out the timetable for the carrying out of the obligations of the parties.

6. The United Nations Security Council shall be requested to endorse the peace treaties and ensure that their provisions shall not be violated. The permanent members of the Security Council shall be requested to underwrite the peace treaties and ensure respect for their provisions. They shall also be requested to conform their policies and actions which the undertakings contained in this Framework.

For the Government of the Arab Republic of Egypt: A. Sadat

For the Government of Israel: M. Begin

Witnessed by: Jimmy Carter President of the United States of America

Source:

A. S. Grenville and Bernard Wasserstein. *The Major International Treaties since 1945: A History and Guide with Texts.* London: Methuen, 1987.

U.S.-Iran Agreement on Release of the American Hostages, 1981

Agreement signed by the United States and Iran on January 19, 1981, the final day of Jimmy Carter's presidency. The document, signed by U.S. deputy secretary of state Warren Christopher and Iranian executive state minister Behzad Nabavi, called for the release of the 52 American hostages who had been held in Iran since November 4, 1979. The takeover of the American embassy by Iranian "students" came after an Islamic government overthrew Shah Mohammed Reza Pahlavi who had been trying to modernize his state. He had been put in power in 1953 with the help of the United States. The agreement called for the return of $8 billion in assets frozen by the United States following the seizure of the hostages and the U.S. embassy in Teheran in November 1979. In addition to spelling out details of the asset transfer, the accord also called for the establishment of an international tribunal to mediate claims by American and Iranian nationals against the other government. In addition, the United States agreed to lift trade sanctions against Iran, promised to identify assets belonging to the late Shah of Iran so that the Iranian government could lay claim to them, and vowed not to interfere in Iran's internal affairs.

To the Congress of the United States:

Pursuant to Section 204(b) of the International Emergency Economic Powers Act, 50 U.S.C. 1703, I hereby report to the Congress that I have today exercised the authority granted by this Act to take certain measures with respect to property of the Government of Iran and its controlled entities and instrumentalities.

1. On November 14, 1979, I took the step of blocking certain property and interests in property of the Government of Iran and its controlled entities and instrumentalities. This action was taken in response to a series of aggressive actions by Iran, including the attack on the United States Embassy in Tehran, the holding of U.S. citizens and diplomats as hostages, and threats to withdraw assets from United States banks, and otherwise seek to harm the economic and political interests of the United States. Subsequently, on April 7, 1980, and April 17, 1980, I took further action restricting various kinds of transactions with Iran by persons subject to the jurisdiction of the United States.

2. Agreement has now been reached with Iran concerning the release of the hostages and the settlement of claims of U.S. nationals against Iran. Among other things this agreement involves the payment by Iran of approximately $3.67 billion to pay off principal and interest outstanding on syndicated loan agreements in which a U.S.

bank is a party. This includes making all necessary payments to the foreign members of these syndicates. An additional $1.418 billion shall remain available to pay all other loans as soon as any disputes as to the amounts involved are settled and to pay additional interest to banks upon agreement or arbitration with Iran. In addition, there will be established an international tribunal to adjudicate various disputed claims by U.S. nationals against Iran; and the deposit of $1 billion by Iran from previously blocked assets as released, which will be available for payments of awards against Iran. Iran has committed itself to replenish this fund as necessary. This tribunal, among other things, will also hear certain disputes between Iranian nationals and the United States Government and contractual disputes between Iran and the United States.

In connection with this agreement, and to begin the process of normalization of relations between the two countries, I have issued and will issue, a series of Orders.

3. First, I have signed an Executive Order authorizing the Secretary of the Treasury to enter into or to direct the Federal Reserve Bank of New York to enter into escrow and depository agreements with the Bank of England.

Under these agreements, assets in the escrow account will be returned to the control of Iran upon the safe departure of the United States hostages from Iran. I have also by this Order instructed the Federal Reserve Bank of New York, as fiscal agent of the United States, to receive other blocked Iranian assets, and, as further directed by the Secretary of the Treasury, to transfer these assets to the escrow account.

4. Second, I have signed an Executive Order directing the Federal Reserve Bank of New York to transfer to its account at the Bank of England and then to the escrow account referred to in the preceding paragraph, the assets of the Government of Iran, both transfers to take place as and when directed by the Secretary of the Treasury.

In order to assure that this transaction can be executed, and having considered the claims settlement agreement described above, I have exercised my authority to nullify, and barred the exercise of, all rights, powers or privileges acquired by anyone; I have revoked all licenses and authorizations of acquiring any rights, powers, or privileges; and I have prohibited anyone from acquiring or exercising any right, power, or privileges, all with respect to these properties of Iran. These prohibitions and nullifications apply to rights, powers, or privileges whether acquired by court order, attachment, or otherwise. I have also prohibited any attachment or other like proceeding or process affecting these properties.

5. Third, I have signed an Executive Order which directs branches and offices of United States banks located outside the United States to transfer all Iranian government funds, deposits and securities held by them on their books on or after November 14, 1979 at 8:10 a.m. EST to the account of the Federal Reserve Bank of New York at the Bank of England in London. These assets will be transferred to the account of the Central Bank of Algeria, as escrow agent. The transfer is to include interest from the date of the blocking order at commercially reasonable rates. In addition, any banking institution that has executed a set-off subsequent to the date of the blocking order against Iranian deposits covered by this order is directed to cancel the set-off and to transfer the funds that had been subject to the set-off in the same manner as the other overseas deposits.

This Order also provides for the revocation of licenses and the nullifications and bars described in paragraph 4 of this report.

6. Fourth, I will have signed an Executive Order directing American banks located within the United States which hold Iranian deposits to transfer those deposits, including interest from the date of entry of the blocking order at commercially reasonable rates, to the Federal Reserve Bank of New York, to be held or transferred as directed by the Secretary of the Treasury. Half of these funds will be transferred to Iran and the other half (up to a maximum of $1 billion) will be placed in a security account as provided in the Declaration and the Claims Settlement Agreement that are part of the agreement we have reached with Iran. This fund will be maintained at a $500 million level until the claims program is concluded. While these transfers should take place as soon as possible, I have been advised that court actions may delay it. This Order also provides for the revocation of licenses and the nullifications and bars described in paragraph 4 of this report.

7. Fifth, I have signed an Executive Order directing the transfer to the Federal Reserve Bank of New York by non-banking institutions of funds and securities held by them for the Government of Iran, to be held or transferred as directed by the Secretary of the Treasury. This transfer will be accomplished at approximately the same time as that described in paragraph 6.

This Order also provides for the revocation of licenses and the nullifications and bars described in paragraph 4 of this report.

8. Sixth, I will sign, upon release of the hostages, an Executive Order directing any person subject to the jurisdiction of the United States who is in possession or control of properties owned by Iran, not including funds and securities, to transfer the property as directed by the Government of Iran acting through its authorized agent. The Order recites that it does not relieve persons subject to it from existing legal requirements other than those based on the International Emergency Economic Powers Act. This Order does not apply to contingent liabilities. This Order

also provides for the revocation of licenses and the nullifications and bars described in paragraph 4 of this report.

9. Seventh, I will sign, upon release of the hostages, an Executive Order revoking prohibitions previously imposed against transactions involving Iran. The Executive Order revokes prohibitions contained in Executive Order No. 12205 of April 7, 1980; and Executive Order No. 12211 of April 17, 1980; and the amendments contained in Proclamation No. 4702 of November 12, 1979. The two Executive Orders limited trade and financial transactions involving Iran and travel to Iran. The proclamation restricted oil imports. In revoking these sanctions I have no intention of superseding other existing controls relating to exports including the Arms Export Control Act and the Export Administration Act.

10. Eighth, I will sign, upon release of the hostages, an Executive Order providing for the waiver of certain claims against Iran. The Order directs that the Secretary of the Treasury shall promulgate regulations: (a) prohibiting any person subject to U.S. jurisdiction from prosecuting in any court within the United States or elsewhere any claim against the Government of Iran arising out of events occurring before the date of this Order arising out: (1) the seizure of the hostages on November 4, 1979; (2) their subsequent detention; (3) injury of the United States property or property of the United States nationals within the United States Embassy compound in Tehran after November 1979; (4) or injury to United States nationals or their property as a result of popular movements in the course of the Islamic Revolution in Iran which were not an act of the Government of Iran; (b) prohibiting any person not a U.S. national from prosecuting any such claim in any court within the United States; (c) ordering the termination of any previously instituted judicial proceedings based upon such claims; and (d) prohibiting the enforcement of any judicial order issued in the course of such proceedings.

The Order also authorizes and directs the Attorney General of the United States immediately upon the issuance of such a Treasury regulation to notify all appropriate courts of the existence of the Executive Order and implementing regulations and the resulting termination of relevant litigation. At the same time, I will create a commission to make recommendations on the issue of compensation for those who have been held as hostages.

11. Finally, I will sign, upon the release of the hostages, an Executive Order invoking the blocking powers of the International Emergency Economic Powers Act to prevent the transfer of property located in the United States and controlled by the estate of Mohammed Reza Pahlavi, the former Shah of Iran, or by any close relative of the former Shah served as a defendant in litigation in United States courts brought by Iran seeking the return of property alleged to belong to Iran. This Order will remain effective as to each person until litigation concerning such person or estate is terminated. The Order also requires reports from private citizens and Federal agencies concerning this property so that information can be made available to the Government of Iran about this property.

The Order would further direct the Attorney General to assert in appropriate courts that claims of Iran for recovery of this property are not barred by principles of sovereign immunity or the act of state doctrine.

12. In addition to these actions taken pursuant to the International Economic Emergency Powers Act, other relevant statutes, and my powers under the Constitution, I will take the steps necessary to withdraw all claims now pending against Iran before the International Court of Justice. Copies of the Executive Orders are attached.

Jimmy Carter
The White House, January 19, 1981.

Source:

Public Papers of the Presidents of the United States, Jimmy Carter, 1980–81. Washington, D.C.: Government Printing Office, 1981–88. pp. 3,040–3,043.

Ronald Reagan, Address to the Nation on Events in Lebanon and Grenada, 1983

Broadcast speech given by President Ronald Reagan on October 27, 1983, in which he defended the deployment of U.S. forces in Lebanon and Grenada. He discussed the October 23 killing of more than 200 U.S. marines by a suicide bomber in Lebanon and reminded Americans that the marines were in Lebanon as part of a multinational force designed to help end factional violence in Lebanon and promote peace in the Middle East.

He then defended the U.S. invasion of the Caribbean island nation of Grenada following a coup in which a Marxist government was replaced by one even more radical. He described Grenada's recent political history, the coup, and the invasion. He stated that the United States had acted principally to ensure the safety of American students attending medical school in Grenada and that it had acted only at the request of the Organization of Eastern Caribbean States. In his address, Reagan emphatically defended the invasion, describing Grenada as a "Soviet-Cuban colony being readied as a major military bastion to export terror and undermine democracy." A pro-American government took over after the invasion.

Reagan blamed the Soviet Union for encouraging and providing support for violence in both Grenada and Lebanon.

My fellow Americans:

Some 2 months ago we were shocked by the brutal massacre of 269 men, women, and children, more than 60 of them Americans, in the shooting down of a Korean airliner. Now, in these past several days, violence has erupted again, in Lebanon and Grenada.

In Lebanon, we have some 1,600 marines, part of a multinational force that's trying to help the people of Lebanon restore order and stability to that troubled land. Our marines are assigned to the south of the city of Beirut, near the only airport operating in Lebanon. Just a mile or so to the north is the Italian contingent and not far from them, the French and a company of British soldiers.

This past Sunday, at 22 minutes after 6 Beirut time, with dawn just breaking, a truck, looking like a lot of other vehicles in the city, approached the airport on a busy, main road. There was nothing in its appearance to suggest it was any different than the trucks or cars that were normally seen on and around the airport. But this one was different. At the wheel was a young man on a suicide mission.

The truck carried some 2,000 pounds of explosives, but there was no way our marine guards could know this. Their first warning that something was wrong came when the truck crashed through a series of barriers, including a chain-link fence and barbed wire entanglements. The guards opened fire, but it was too late. The truck smashed through the doors of the headquarters building in which our marines were sleeping and instantly exploded. The four-story concrete building collapsed in a pile of rubble.

More than 200 of the sleeping men were killed in that one hideous, insane attack. Many others suffered injury and are hospitalized here or in Europe.

This was not the end of the horror. At almost the same instant, another vehicle on a suicide and murder mission crashed into the headquarters of the French peacekeeping force, an eight-story building, destroying it and killing more than 50 French soldiers.

Prior to this day of horror, there had been several tragedies for our men in the multinational force. Attacks by snipers and mortar fire had taken their toll.

I called bereaved parents and/or widows of the victims to express on behalf of all of us our sorrow and sympathy. Sometimes there were questions. And now many of you are asking: Why should our young men be dying in Lebanon? Why is Lebanon important to us?

Well, it's true, Lebanon is a small country, more than five-and-a-half thousand miles from our shores on the edge of what we call the Middle East. But every President who has occupied this office in recent years has recognized that peace in the Middle East is of vital concern to our nation and, indeed, to our allies in Western Europe and Japan. We've been concerned because the Middle East is a powderkeg; four times in the last 30 years, the Arabs and Israelis have gone to war. And each time, the world has teetered near the edge of catastrophe.

The area is key to the economic and political life of the West. Its strategic importance, its energy resources, the Suez Canal, and the well-being of the nearly 200 million people living there—all are vital to us and to world peace. If that key should fall into the hands of a power or powers hostile to the free world, there would be a direct threat to the United States and to our allies.

We have another reason to be involved. Since 1948 our Nation has recognized and accepted a moral obligation to assure the continued existence of Israel as a nation. Israel shares our democratic values and is a formidable force an invader of the Middle East would have to reckon with.

For several years, Lebanon has been torn by internal strife. Once a prosperous, peaceful nation, its government had become ineffective in controlling the militias that warred on each other. Sixteen months ago, we were watching on our TV screens the shelling and bombing of Beirut which was being used as a fortress by PLO bands. Hundreds and hundreds of civilians were being killed and wounded in the daily battles.

Syria, which makes no secret of its claim that Lebanon should be a part of a Greater Syria, was occupying a large part of Lebanon. Today, Syria has become a home for 7,000 Soviet advisers and technicians who man a massive amount of Soviet weaponry, including SS-21 ground-to-ground missiles capable of reaching vital areas of Israel.

A little over a year ago, hoping to build on the Camp David accords, which had led to peace between Israel and Egypt, I proposed a peace plan for the Middle East to end the wars between the Arab States and Israel. It was based on U.N. resolutions 242 and 338 and called for a fair and just solution to the Palestinian problem, as well as a fair and just settlement of issues between the Arab States and Israel.

Before the necessary negotiations could begin, it was essential to get all foreign forces out of Lebanon and to end the fighting there. So, why are we there? Well, the answer is straightforward: to help bring peace to Lebanon and stability to the vital Middle East. To that end, the multinational force was created to help stabilize the situation in Lebanon until a government could be established and a Lebanese army mobilized to restore Lebanese sovereignty over its own soil as the foreign forces withdrew. Israel agreed to withdraw as did Syria, but Syria then reneged on its promise. Over 10,000 Palestinians who had been bringing ruin down on Beirut, however, did leave the country.

Lebanon has formed a government under the leadership of President Gemayal, and that government, with our assistance and training, has set up its own army. In only a year's time, that army has been rebuilt. It's a good army, composed of Lebanese of all factions.

A few weeks ago, the Israeli army pulled back to the Awali River in southern Lebanon. Despite fierce resistance by Syrian-backed forces, the Lebanese army was able to hold the line and maintain the defensive perimeter around Beirut.

In the year that our marines have been there, Lebanon has made important steps toward stability and order. The physical presence of the marines lends support to both the Lebanese Government and its army. It allows the hard work of diplomacy to go forward. Indeed, without the peacekeepers from the U.S., France, Italy, and Britain, the efforts to find a peaceful solution in Lebanon would collapse.

As to that narrower question—what exactly is the operational mission of the marines—the answer is, to secure a piece of Beirut, to keep order in their sector, and to prevent the area from becoming a battlefield. Our marines are not just sitting in an airport. Part of their task is to guard that airport. Because of their presence, the airport has remained operational. In addition, they patrol the surrounding area. This is their part—a limited, but essential part—in the larger effort that I've described.

If our marines must be there, I'm asked, why can't we make them safer? Who committed this latest atrocity against them and why?

Well, we'll do everything, we can to ensure that our men are as safe as possible. We ordered the battleship *New Jersey* to join our naval forces offshore. Without even firing them, the threat of its 16-inch guns silenced those who once fired down on our marines from the hills, and they're a good part of the reason we suddenly had a ceasefire. We're doing our best to make our forces less vulnerable to those who want to snipe at them or send in future suicide missions.

Secretary Shultz called me today from Europe, where he was meeting with the Foreign Ministers of our allies in the multinational force. They remain committed to our task. And plans were made to share information as to how we can improve security for all our men.

We have strong circumstantial evidence that the attack on the marines was directed by terrorists who used the same method to destroy our Embassy in Beirut. Those who directed this atrocity must be dealt justice, and they will be. The obvious purpose behind the sniping and, now, this attack was to weaken American will and force the withdrawal of U.S. and French forces from Lebanon. The clear intent of the terrorists was to eliminate our support of the Lebanese Government and to destroy the ability of the Lebanese people to determine their own destiny.

To answer those who ask if we're serving any purpose in being there, let me answer a question with a question. Would the terrorists have launched their suicide attacks against the multinational force if it were not doing its job? The multinational force was attacked precisely because it is doing the job it was sent to do in Beirut. It is accomplishing its mission.

Now then, where do we go from here? What can we do now to help Lebanon gain greater stability so that our marines can come home? Well, I believe we can take three steps now that will make a difference.

First, we will accelerate the search for peace and stability in that region. Little attention has been paid to the fact that we've had special envoys there working, literally, around the clock to bring the warring factions together. This coming Monday in Geneva, President Gemayel of Lebanon will sit down with other factions from his country to see if national reconciliation can be achieved. He has our firm support. I will soon be announcing a replacement for Bud McFarlane, who was preceded by Phil Habib. Both worked tirelessly and must be credited for much if not most of the progress we've made.

Second, we'll work even more closely with our allies in providing support for the Government of Lebanon and for the rebuilding of a national consensus.

Third, we will ensure that the multinational peacekeeping forces, our marines, are given the greatest possible protection. Our Commandant of the Marine Corps, General Kelley, returned from Lebanon today and will be advising us on steps we can take to improve security. Vice President Bush returned just last night from Beirut and gave me a full report of his brief visit.

Beyond our progress in Lebanon, let us remember that our main goal and purpose is to achieve a broader peace in all of the Middle East. The factions and bitterness that we see in Lebanon are just a microcosm of the difficulties that are spread across much of that region. A peace initiative for the entire Middle East, consistent with the Camp David accords and U.N. resolutions 242 and 338, still offers the best hope for bringing peace to the region.

Let me ask those who say we should get out of Lebanon: If we were to leave Lebanon now, what message would that send to those who foment instability and terrorism? If America were to walk away from Lebanon, what chance would there be for a negotiated settlement, producing a unified democratic Lebanon?

If we turned our backs on Lebanon now, what would be the future of Israel? At stake is the fate of only the second Arab country to negotiate a major agreement with Israel. That's another accomplishment of this past year, the May 17th accord signed by Lebanon and Israel.

If terrorism and intimidation succeed, it'll be a devastating blow to the peace process and to Israel's search for genuine security. It won't just be Lebanon sentenced to a future of chaos. Can the United States, or the free world, for that matter, stand by and see the Middle East incorporated into the Soviet bloc? What of Western Europe and Japan's dependence on Middle East oil for the energy to fuel their industries? The Middle East is, as I've said, vital to our national security and economic well-being.

Brave young men have been taken from us. Many others have been grievously wounded. Are we to tell them their sacrifice was wasted? They gave their lives in defense of our national security every bit as much as any man who ever died fighting in a war. We must not strip every ounce of meaning and purpose from their courageous sacrifice.

We're nation with global responsibilities. We're not somewhere else in the world protecting someone else's interests; we're there protecting our own.

I received a message from the father of a marine in Lebanon. He told me, "In a world where we speak of human rights, there is a sad lack of acceptance of responsibility. My son has chosen the acceptance of responsibility for the privilege of living in this country. Certainly in this country one does not inherently have rights unless the responsibility for these rights is accepted." Dr. Kenneth Morrison said that while he was waiting to learn if his son was one of the dead. I was thrilled for him to learn today that his son Ross is alive and well and carrying on his duties in Lebanon.

Let us meet our responsibilities. For longer than any of us can remember, the people of the Middle East have lived from war to war with no prospect for any other future. That dreadful cycle must be broken. Why are we there? Well, a Lebanese mother told one of our Ambassadors that her little girl had only attended school 2 of the last 8 years. Now, because of our presence there, she said her daughter could live a normal life.

With patience and firmness, we can help bring peace to that strifetorn region—and make our own lives more secure. Our role is to help the Lebanese put their country together, not to do it for them.

Now, I know another part of the world is very much on our minds, a place much closer to our shores: Grenada. The island is only twice the size of the District of Columbia, with a total population of about 110,000 people.

Grenada and a half dozen other Caribbean islands here were, until recently, British colonies. They're now independent states and members of the British Commonwealth. While they respect each other's independence, they also feel a kinship with each other and think of themselves as one people.

In 1979 trouble came to Grenada. Maurice Bishop, a protege of Fidel Castro, stage a military coup and overthrew the government which had been elected under the constitution left to the people by the British. He sought the help of Cuba in building an airport, which he claimed was for tourist trade, but which looked suspiciously suitable for military aircraft, including Soviet-built long-range bombers.

The six sovereign countries and one remaining colony are joined together in what they call the Organization of Eastern Caribbean States. The six became increasingly alarmed as Bishop built an army greater than all of theirs combined. Obviously, it was not purely for defense.

In this last year or so, Prime Minister Bishop gave indications that he might like better relations with the United States. He even made a trip to our country and met with senior officials of the White House and the State Department. Whether he was serious or not, we'll never know. On October 12th, a small group in his militia seized him and put him under arrest. They were, if anything, more radical and more devoted to Castro's Cuba than he had been.

Several days later, a crowd of citizens appeared before Bishop's home, freed him, and escorted him toward the headquarters of the military council. They were fired upon. A number, including some children, were killed, and Bishop was seized. He and several members of his cabinet were subsequently executed, and a 24-hour shoot-to-kill curfew was put in effect. Grenada was without a government, its only authority exercised by a self-proclaimed band of military men.

There were then about 1,000 of our citizens on Grenada, 800 of them students in St. George's University Medical School. Concerned that they'd be harmed or held as hostages, I ordered a flotilla of ships, then on its way to Lebanon with marines, part of our regular rotation program, to circle south on a course that would put them somewhere in the vicinity of Grenada in case there should be a need to evacuate our people.

Last weekend, I was awakened in the early morning hours and told that six members of the Organization of Eastern Caribbean States, joined by Jamaica and Barbados, had sent an urgent request that we join them in a military operation to restore order and democracy to Grenada. They were proposing this action under the terms of a treaty, a mutual assistance pact that existed among them.

These small, peaceful nations needed our help. Three of them don't have armies at all, and the others have very limited forces. The legitimacy of their request, plus my own concern for our citizens, dictated my decision. I believe our government has a responsibility to go to the aid of its citizens, if their right to life and liberty is threatened. The nightmare of our hostages in Iran must never be repeated.

We knew we had little time and that complete secrecy was vital to ensure both the safety of the young men who would undertake this mission and the Americans they were about to rescue. The Joint Chiefs worked around the clock to come up with a plan. They had little intelligence information about conditions on the island.

We had to assume that several hundred Cubans working on the airport could be military reserves. Well, as it turned out, the number was much larger, and they were a military force. Six hundred of them have been taken prisoner, and we have discovered a complete base with weapons and communications equipment, which makes it clear a Cuban occupation of the island had been planned.

Two hours ago we released the first photos from Grenada. They included pictures of a warehouse of military equipment—one of three we've uncovered so far. This warehouse contained weapons and ammunition stacked almost to the ceiling, enough to supply thousands of terrorists. Grenada, we were told, was a friendly island paradise for tourism. Well, it wasn't. It was a Soviet-Cuban colony, being readied as a major military bastion to export terror and undermine democracy. We got there just in time.

I can't say enough in praise of our military—Army rangers and paratroopers, Navy, Marine, and Air Force personnel—those who planned a brilliant campaign and those who carried it out. Almost instantly, our military seized the two airports, secured the campus where most of our students were, and are now in the mopping-up phase.

It should be noted that in all the planning, a top priority was to minimize risk, to avoid casualties to our own men and also the Grenadian forces as much as humanly possible. But there were casualties, and we all owe a debt to those who lost their lives or were wounded. They were few in number, but even one is a tragic price to pay.

It's our intention to get our men out as soon as possible. Prime Minister Eugenia Charles of Dominica—I called that wrong; she pronounces it Dominica—she is Chairman of OECS. She's calling for help from Commonwealth nations in giving the people their right to establish a constitutional government on Grenada. We anticipate that the Governor General, a Grenadian, will participate in setting up a provisional government in the interim.

The events in Lebanon and Grenada, though oceans apart, are closely related. Not only has Moscow assisted and encouraged the violence in both countries, but it provides direct support through a network of surrogates and terrorists. It is no coincidence that when the thugs tried to wrest control over Grenada, there were 30 Soviet advisers and hundreds of Cuban military and paramilitary forces on the island. At the moment of our landing, we communicated with the Governments of Cuba and the Soviet Union and told them we would offer shelter and security to their people on Grenada. Regrettably, Castro ordered his men to fight to the death, and some did. The others will be sent to their homelands.

You know, there was a time when our national security was based on a standing army here within our own borders and shore batteries of artillery along our coasts, and, of course, a navy to keep the sealanes open for the shipping of things necessary to our well-being. The world has changed. Today, our national security can be threatened in faraway places. It's up to all of us to be aware of the strategic importance of such places and to be able to identify them.

Sam Rayburn once said that freedom is not something a nation can work for once and win forever. He said it's like an insurance policy; its premiums must be kept up to date. In order to keep it, we have to keep working for it and sacrificing for it just as long as we live. If we do not, our children may not know the pleasure of working to keep it, for it may not be theirs to keep.

In these last few days, I've been more sure than I've ever been that we Americans of today will keep freedom and maintain peace. I've been made to feel that by the magnificent spirit of our young men and women in uniform and by something here in our Nation's Capital. In this city, where political strife is so much a part of our lives, I've seen Democratic leaders in the Congress join their Republican colleagues, send a message to the world that we're all Americans before we're anything else, and when our country is threatened, we stand shoulder to shoulder in support of our men and women in the Armed Forces.

May I share something with you I think you'd like to know? It's something that happened to the Commandant of our Marine Corps, General Paul Kelley, while he was visiting our critically injured marines in an Air Force hospital. It says more than any of us could ever hope to say about the gallantry and heroism of these young men, young men who serve so willingly so that others might have a chance at peace and freedom in their own lives and in the life of their country.

I'll let General Kelley's words describe the incident. He spoke of a "young marine with more tubes going in and out of his body than I have ever seen in one body."

"He couldn't see very well. He reached up and grabbed my four stars, just to make sure I was who I said I was. He held my hand with a firm grip. He was making signals, and we realized he wanted to tell me something. We put a pad of paper in his hand—and he wrote 'Semper Fi.'"

Well, if you've been a marine or if, like myself, you're an admirer of the marines, you know those words are a battlecry, a greeting, and a legend in the Marine Corps. They're marine shorthand for the motto of the Corps—"Semper Fidelis"—"always faithful."

General Kelley has a reputation for being a very sophisticated general and a very tough marine. But he cried when he saw those words, and who can blame him?

That marine and all those others like him, living and dead, have been faithful to their ideals. They've given willingly of themselves so that a nearly defenseless people in a region of great strategic importance to the free world will have a chance someday to live lives free of murder and mayhem and terrorism. I think that young marine and all of his comrades have given every one of us something to live up to.

They were not afraid to stand up for their country or, no matter how difficult and slow the journey might be, to give to others that last, best hope of a better future. We cannot and will not dishonor them now and the sacrifices they've made by failing to remain as faithful to the cause of freedom and the pursuit of peace as they have been.

I will not ask you to pray for the dead, because they're safe in God's loving arms and beyond need of our prayers. I would like to ask you all—wherever you may be in this blessed land—to pray for these wounded young men and to pray for the bereaved families of those who gave their lives for our freedom.

God bless you, and God bless America.

Source:

Public Papers of the Presidents of the United States: Ronald Reagan, 1983. Washington, D.C.: Government Printing Office, 1952–92. pp. 1,517–1,522.

Iran-Contra Affair, 1986–1987

The Iran-Contra affair, which surfaced in November 1986, created a constitutional crisis. At issue was the charge that the Ronald Reagan administration had illegally sold arms to Iran in exchange for the release of American hostages in Lebanon, and had illegally diverted profits from the sale to the rightist contra rebels fighting to overthrow Nicaragua's communist Sandinista government. Such a diversion of government funds allegedly violated the Boland amendment, introduced by Senator Edward P. Boland of Massachusetts, passed by Congress December 20, 1982, and signed the next day by President Reagan. The amendment specifically prohibited the U.S. government from using defense funds to support the military and paramilitary forces (the contras) fighting against Nicaragua's leftist Sandinista government. The law, part of an emergency spending bill, barred the Central Intelligence Agency (CIA) and the Defense Department (DOD) from furnishing equipment, training, advice, or support "for military activities for the purpose of overthrowing the government of Nicaragua or provoking a military exchange between Nicaragua and Honduras." The amendment expired August 8, 1985, and afterward any U.S. agency apart from the CIA and DOD could legally aid the Nicaraguan contras.

Following the congressional hearings, on August 12, 1987, President Reagan broadcast a speech defending his administration's actions, saying his government had initially sought purely diplomatic contact with Iran, but that the diplomatic talks "rapidly got all tangled up in the sale of arms, and the sale of arms got tangled up with hostages." He blamed his preoccupation with the hostages for influencing his decision to go ahead with the sale, which he called a mistake. He insisted that he had known nothing of the diversion of profits to the contras. The speech incorporated several other issues, including the recent Supreme Court nomination of Judge Robert Bork, arms control, a balanced-budget amendment to the Constitution, and Nicaragua.

Two congressional reports, both issued November 18, 1987, emerged from the Joint House Select Committee to Investigate Covert Arms Transaction with Iran and the Senate Select Committee on Secret Military Assistance to Iran and the Nicaragua. The 472-page majority report was signed by three Republican senators and all 15 Democrats of both committees. It said that "the common ingredients of the Iran and contra policies were secrecy, deception, and disdain for the law." Reagan was blamed for failing to "take care that the laws be faithfully executed," as required by the Constitution. Moreover, the White House violated the Boland amendment banning military aid to the contras. This majority report stated that while the president did not know about the diversion of funds, "he should have." A minority report, issued by two Republican senators and all six Republicans on the House committee, condemned the majority's charges as "hysterical." Reagan may have made "some mistakes," it said, but there was "no administration-wide dishonesty and cover-up."

Boland Amendment, 1982

Joint Resolution

Making further continuing appropriations and providing for productive employment for the fiscal year 1983, and for other purposes.

Resolved by the Senate and House of Representatives of the United States of America in Congress assembled, That the following sums are appropriated, out of any money in the Treasury not otherwise appropriated, and out of applicable corporate or other revenues, receipts, and funds, for the several departments, agencies, corporations, and other organizational units of the Government for the fiscal year 1983, and for other purposes, namely:

Sec. 793. None of the funds provided in this Act may be used by the Central Intelligence Agency or the Department of Defense to furnish military equipment, military training or advice, or other support for military activities, to any group or individual, not part of a country's armed forces, for the purpose of overthrowing the Government of Nicaragua or provoking a military exchange between Nicaragua and Honduras.

Source:

Statutes at Large, Vol. 96, pp. 1,831.

Ronald Reagan,
Address on Iran-Contra, 1987

My fellow Americans:

I've spoken to you from this historic office on many occasions and about many things. The power of the Presidency is often thought to reside within this Oval Office. Yet it doesn't rest here, it rests in you, the American people, and in your trust. Your trust is what gives a President his powers of leadership and his personal strength, and it's what I want to talk to you about this evening.

For the past 3 months, I've been silent on the revelations about Iran. And you must have been thinking: "Well, why doesn't he tell us what's happening? Why doesn't he just speak to us as he has in the past when we've faced troubles or tragedies?" Others of you, I guess, were thinking: "What's he doing hiding out in the White House?" Well, the reason I haven't spoken to you before now is this: You deserve the truth. And as frustrating as the waiting has been, I felt it was improper to come to you with sketchy reports, or possibly even erroneous statements, which would then have to be corrected, creating even more doubt and confusion. There's been enough of that. I've paid a price for my silence in terms of your trust and confidence. But I've had to wait, as you have, for the complete story. That's why I appointed Ambassador David Abshire as my Special Counselor to help get out the thousands of documents to the various investigations. And I appointed a Special Review Board, the Tower board, which took on the chore of pulling the truth together for me and getting to the bottom of things. It has now issued its findings.

I'm often accused of being an optimist, and it's true I had to hunt pretty hard to find any good news in the Board's report. As you know, it's well-stocked with criticisms, which I'll discuss in a moment; but I was very relieved to read this sentence: " . . . the Board is convinced that the President does indeed want the full story to be told." And that will continue to be my pledge to you as the other investigations go forward. I want to thank the members of the panel: former Senator John Tower, former Secretary of State Edmund Muskie, and former national security adviser Brent Scowcroft. They have done the Nation, as well as me personally, a great service by submitting a report of such integrity and depth. They have my genuine and enduring gratitude.

I've studied the Board's report. Its findings are honest, convincing, and highly critical; and I accept them. And tonight I want to share with you my thoughts on these findings and report to you on the actions I'm taking to implement the Board's recommendations. First, let me say I take full responsibility for my own actions and for those of my administration. As angry as I may be about activities undertaken without my knowledge, I am still accountable for those activities. As disappointed as I may be in some who served me, I'm still the one who must answer to the American people for this behavior. And as personally distasteful as I find secret bank accounts and diverted funds—well, as the Navy would say, this happened on my watch.

Let's start with the part that is the most controversial. A few months ago I told the American people I did not trade arms for hostages. My heart and my best intentions still tell me that's true, but the facts and the evidence tell me it is not. As the Tower board reported, what began as a strategic opening to Iran deteriorated, in its implementation, into trading arms for hostages. This runs counter to my own beliefs, to administration policy, and to the original strategy we had in mind. There are reasons why it happened, but no excuses. It was a mistake. I undertook the original Iran initiative in order to develop relations with those who might assume leadership in a post-Khomeini government.

It's clear from the Board's report, however, that I let my personal concern for the hostages spill over into the geopolitical strategy of reaching out to Iran. I asked so many questions about the hostages welfare that I didn't ask enough about the specifics of the total Iran plan. Let me say to the hostage families: We have not given up. We never will. And I promise you we'll use every legitimate means to free your loved ones from captivity. But I must also caution that those Americans who freely remain in such dangerous areas must know that they're responsible for their own safety.

Now, another major aspect of the Board's findings regards the transfer of funds to the Nicaraguan *contras*. The Tower board wasn't able to find out what happened to this money, so the facts here will be left to the continuing investigations of the court-appointed Independent Counsel and the two congressional investigating committees. I'm confident the truth will come out about this matter, as well. As I told the Tower board, I didn't know about any diversion of funds to the *contras*. But as President, I cannot escape responsibility.

Much has been said about my management style, a style that's worked successfully for me during 8 years as Governor of California and for most of my Presidency. The way I work is to identify the problem, find the right individuals to do the job, and then let them go to it. I've found this invariably brings out the best in people. They seem to rise to their full capability, and in the long run you get more done. When it came to managing the NSC staff, let's face it, my style didn't match its previous track record. I've already begun correcting this. As a start, yesterday I met with the entire professional staff of the National Security Council. I defined for them the values I want to guide the national security policies of this country. I told them that I wanted a policy that was as justifiable and understandable in public as it was in secret. I wanted a policy that reflected the will of the Congress as well as of the White House. And I told them that there'll be no more freelancing by individuals when it comes to our national security.

You've heard a lot about the staff of the National Security Council in recent months. Well, I can tell you, they are good and dedicated government employees, who put in long hours for the Nation's benefit. They are eager and anxious to serve their country. One thing still upsetting me, however, is that no one kept proper records of meetings or decisions. This led to my failure to recollect whether I approved an arms shipment before or after the fact. I did approve it; I just can't say specifically when. Well, rest assured, there's plenty of recordkeeping now going on at 1600 Pennsylvania Avenue.

For nearly a week now, I've been studying the Board's report. I want the American people to know that this wrenching ordeal of recent months has not been in vain. I endorse every one of the Tower board's recommendations. In fact, I'm going beyond its recommendations so as to put the house in even better order. I'm taking action in three basic areas: personnel, national security policy, and the process for making sure that the system works.

First, personnel—I've brought in an accomplished and highly respected new team here at the White House. They bring new blood, new energy, and new credibility and experience. Former Senator Howard Baker, my new Chief of Staff, possesses a breadth of legislative and foreign affairs skills that's impossible to match. I'm hopeful that his experience as minority and majority leader of the Senate can help us forge a new partnership with the Congress, especially on foreign and national security policies. I'm genuinely honored that he's given up his own Presidential aspirations to serve the country as my Chief of Staff. Frank Carlucci, my new national security adviser, is respected for his experience in government and trusted for his judgment and counsel. Under him, the NSC staff is being rebuilt with proper management discipline. Already, almost half the NSC professional staff is comprised of new people.

Yesterday I nominated William Webster, a man of sterling reputation, to be Director of the Central Intelligence Agency. Mr. Webster has served as Director of the FBI and as a U.S. District Court judge. He understands the meaning of "rule of law." So that his knowledge of national security matters can be available to me on a continuing basis, I will also appoint John Tower to serve as member of my Foreign Intelligence Advisory Board. I am considering other changes in personnel, and I'll move more furniture, as I see fit, in the weeks and months ahead.

Second, in the area of national security policy, I have ordered the NSC to begin a comprehensive review of all covert operations. I have also directed that any covert activity be in support of clear policy objectives and in compliance with American values. I except a covert policy that, if Americans saw it on the front page of their newspaper, they'd say, "That makes sense." I have had issued a directive prohibiting the NSC staff itself from undertaking covert operations—no ifs, ands, and buts. I have asked Vice President Bush to reconvene his task force on terrorism to review our terrorist policy in light of the events that have occurred.

Third, in terms of the process of reaching national security decisions, I am adopting in total the Tower report's model of how the NSC process and staff should work. I am directing Mr. Carlucci to take the necessary steps to make that happen. He will report back to me on further reforms that might be needed. I've created the post of NSC legal adviser to assure a greater sensitivity to matters of law. I am also determined to make the congressional oversight process work. Proper procedures for consultation with the Congress will be followed, not only in letter but in spirit. Before the end of March, I will report to the Congress on all the steps I've taken in line with the Tower board's conclusions.

Now, what should happen when you make a mistake is this: You take your knocks, you learn your lessons, and then you move on. That's the healthiest way to deal with a problem. This in no way diminishes the importance of the other continuing investigations, but the business of our country and our people must proceed. I've gotten this message from Republicans and Democrats in Congress, from allies around the world, and—if we're reading the signals right—even from the Soviets. And of course, I've heard the message from you, the American people. You know, by the time you reach my age, you've made plenty of mistakes. And if you've lived your life properly—so, you learn. You put things in perspective. You pull your energies together. You change. You go forward.

My fellow Americans, I have a great deal that I want to accomplish with you and for you over the next 2 years. And the Lord willing, that's exactly what I intend to do.

Good night, and God bless you.

Source:

Public Papers of the Presidents of the United States: Ronald Reagan, 1983. Washington, D.C.: Government Printing Office, 1952–92. pp. 208–211.

George Bush, Panama Invasion Address, 1989

On the evening of December 20, 1989, President George Bush gave a nationally televised speech announcing that he had ordered U.S. troops to Panama that morning in an effort to overthrow the government of General Manuel Antonio Noriega. Bush said he had acted in response to Panama's December 15 declaration that it was "in a state of war" with the United States because of economic sanctions imposed by the U.S. government in 1988. The move capped months of nonmilitary efforts by the Bush administration to force Noriega from power. In his speech, Bush said that his goals were to safeguard the lives of Americans living in Panama, to defend democracy in Panama, and to protect the integrity of the Panama Canal Treaty. Once this "Operation Just Cause" was launched it took only 24 hours to succeed but at the cost of 23 American fatalities and 394 wounded. Noriega was tried in the United States in 1992 and convicted on charges that included drug trafficking, money laundering, and racketeering. As of fall 2002 he remains in prison.

The American invasion of Panama also marked the first time American women engaged in direct combat as women—previous female combatants had dressed as men. Captain Linda Bray became the first American woman to command troops in battle. Because federal law forbade women from combat units, they were actually from the military police helping to secure the areas that the combat troops had captured, including dangerous outposts. Approximately 10 percent of these companies were female and many of them, like Bray, were officers.

Despite Bray's actions and lobbying on the part of women's organizations, Congress, through 2002, has continued to exclude women from combat.

My fellow citizens, last night I ordered U.S. military forces to Panama. No President takes such action lightly. This morning, I want to tell you what I did and why I did it.

For nearly 2 years, the United States, nations of Latin America and the Caribbean have worked together to resolve the crisis in Panama. The goals of the United States have been to safeguard the lives of Americans, to defend democracy in Panama, to combat drug trafficking, and to protect the integrity of the Panama Canal treaty. Many attempts have been made to resolve this crisis through diplomacy and negotiations. All were rejected by the dictator of Panama, General Manuel Noriega, an indicted drug trafficker.

Last Friday, Noriega declared his military dictatorship to be in a state of war with the United States and publicly threatened the lives of Americans in Panama. The very next day, forces under his command shot and killed an unarmed American serviceman; wounded another; arrested and brutally beat a third American serviceman; and then brutally interrogated his wife, threatening her with sexual abuse. That was enough.

General Noriega's reckless threats and attacks upon Americans in Panama created an imminent danger to the 35,000 American citizens in Panama. As President, I have no higher obligation than to safeguard the lives of American citizens. And that is why I directed our Armed Forces to protect the lives of American citizens in Panama and to bring General Noriega to justice in the United States. I contacted the bipartisan leadership of Congress last night and informed them of this decision, and after taking this action, I also talked with leaders in Latin America, the Caribbean, and those of other U.S. allies.

At this moment, U.S. forces, including forces deployed from the United States last night, are engaged in action in Panama. The United States intends to withdraw the forces newly deployed to Panama as quickly as possible. Our forces have conducted themselves courageously and selflessly. And as Commander in Chief, I salute every one of them and thank them on behalf of our country.

Tragically, some Americans have lost their lives in defense of their fellow citizens, in defense of democracy. And my heart goes out to their families. We also regret and mourn the loss of innocent Panamanians.

The brave Panamanians elected by the people of Panama in the elections last May, President Guillermo Endara and Vice Presidents Calderon and Ford, have assumed the rightful leadership of their country. You remember those horrible pictures of newly elected Vice President Ford, covered head to toe with blood, beaten mercilessly by so-called, "dignity battalions." Well, the United States today recognizes the democratically elected government of President Endara. I will send our Ambassador back to Panama immediately.

Key military objectives have been achieved. Most organized resistance has been eliminated. But the operation is not over yet. General Noriega is in hiding. And nevertheless, yesterday a dictator ruled Panama, and today constitutionally elected leaders govern.

I have today directed the Secretary of the Treasury and the Secretary of State to lift the economic sanctions with respect to the democratically elected government of Panama and, in cooperation with that government, to take steps to effect an orderly unlocking of Panamanian Government assets in the United States. I'm fully committed to implement the Panama Canal treaties and turn over the Canal to Panama in the year 2000. The actions we have taken and the cooperation of a new, democratic government in Panama will permit us to honor these commitments. As soon as the new government recommends a qualified candidate, Panamanian, to be Administrator of the Canal, as called for in the treaties, I will submit this nominee to the Senate for expedited consideration.

I am committed to strengthening our relationship with the democratic nations in this hemisphere. I will continue to seek solutions to the problems of this region through dialog and multilateral diplomacy. I took this action only after reaching the conclusion that every other avenue was closed and the lives of American citizens were in grave danger. I hope that the people of Panama will put this dark chapter of dictatorship behind them and move forward together as citizens of a democratic Panama with this government that they themselves have elected.

The United States is eager to work with the Panamanian people in partnership and friendship to rebuild their economy. The Panamanian people want democracy, peace, and the chance for a better life in dignity and freedom. The people of the United States seek only to support them in pursuit of these noble goals. Thank you very much.

Source:

Public Papers of the Presidents of the United States: George H. W. Bush, 1989. Washington, D.C.: Government Printing Office, 1992.

Persian Gulf War Resolution, 1991

Joint resolution passed by both houses of Congress on January 12, 1991, authorizing President George Bush to use U.S. military power to force Iraq to withdraw from Kuwait. After lengthy debate, the resolution passed the House of Representatives by a vote of 250 to 183 and the Senate by a vote of 52 to 47. The declaration stated that the United States was acting because of Iraq's invasion of Kuwait on August 2, 1990; its refusal to comply with a United Nations Security Council resolution ordering it to withdraw from Kuwait; and because of the threat posed by Iraq's military arsenal. The congressional resolution authorized the president to use U.S. military troops in order to force Iraq to comply with the UN resolution. This was the first time Congress had authorized the use of offensive military action since the controversial Gulf of Tonkin Resolution in 1964.

Whereas the President of the United States, with the authorization of Congress, has ordered military action against Iraq in an effort to force Iraqi Armed Forces from occupied Kuwait;

Whereas 415,000 men and women of the United States Armed Forces are now involved in armed conflict;

Whereas 158,000 members of the Reserves and National Guard have been called to active duty since August 22 and may become involved in armed conflict; and

Whereas Congress and the American people have the greatest pride in the men and women of the United States Armed Forces and support them in their efforts: Now, therefore, be it

Resolved by the Senate (the House of Representatives concurring), That (a) the Congress commends and supports the efforts and leadership of the President as Commander in Chief in the Persian Gulf hostilities.

(b) The Congress unequivocally supports the men and women of our Armed Forces who are carrying out their missions with professional excellence, dedicated patriotism and exemplary bravery.

Agreed to January 18, 1991.

Source:

Statutes at Large, Vol. 105, p. 2,409.

George H. W. Bush, Address on the End of the Persian Gulf War, 1991

Speech given by President George Bush to a joint session of Congress on March 6, 1991, announcing that after nine days of military action (February 23–March 3) the U.S.-dominated allied effort had achieved its goal of forcing Iraq to withdraw from Kuwait. "The war is over," Bush declared. He expressed his thanks to the many nations and individuals who had contributed to the success of Operation Desert Storm, as the mission was known. Expanding on the theme of peace, Bush spoke about his desire to create "a new world order" in which strong nations joined together to protect weaker ones, all under United Nations auspices.

It soon became apparent that by not invading Baghdad, crushing Saddam Hussein's palace guard and ousting Saddam as leader, the threat the Iraqi leader posed would continue. Inspectors were allowed into Iraq under UN resolutions and destroyed large caches of weapons. They also concluded that Iraq had been within a year of producing a nuclear weapon and that Iraq still contained many hidden sites for producing and storing biological and chemical weapons. Most other UN members agreed to Iraqi restrictions on inspectors (who were removed completely in 1998). Saddam blamed the suffering of his citizens (while he, his family, and cronies enjoyed enormous wealth) on sanctions placed on Iraq by the United Nations.

In 2002 President George W. Bush (George H. W.'s son) vowed to make sure that Iraq was disarmed and to end Saddam's reign as the only way to ensure that Iraq would not use biological, chemical, or nuclear weapons.

In his 1991 speech, the president also addressed a number of domestic issues, expressing his desire to "get this economy rolling again," and urged the public to support his domestic programs, including legislation on transportation, energy, and crime.

Speaker Foley. Mr. President, it is customary at joint sessions for the Chair to present the President to the Members of Congress directly and without further comment. But I wish to depart from tradition tonight and express to you on behalf of the Congress and the country, and through you to the members of our Armed Forces, our warmest congratulations on the brilliant victory of the Desert Storm Operation.

Members of the Congress, I now have the high privilege and distinct honor of presenting to you the President of the United States.

The President. Mr. President. And Mr. Speaker, thank you, sir, for those very generous words spoken from the heart about the wonderful performance of our military.

Members of Congress, 5 short weeks ago I came to this House to speak to you about the state of the Union. We met then in time of war. Tonight, we meet in a world blessed by the promise of peace.

From the moment Operation Desert Storm commenced on January 16th until the time the guns fell silent at midnight 1 week ago, this nation has watched its sons and daughters with pride—watched over them with prayer. As Commander in Chief, I can report to you our armed forces fought with honor and valor. And as President, I can report to the Nation aggression is defeated. The war is over.

This is a victory for every country in the coalition, for the United Nations. A victory for unprecedented international cooperation and diplomacy, so well led by our Secretary of State, James Baker. It is a victory for the rule of law and for what is right.

Desert Storm's success belongs to the team that so ably leads our Armed Forces: our Secretary of Defense and our Chairman of the Joint Chiefs, Dick Cheney and Colin Powell. And while you're standing—laughter!—this military victory also belongs to the one the British call the "Man of the Match"—the tower of calm at the eye of Desert Storm—General Norman Schwarzkopf.

And recognizing this was a coalition effort, let us not forget Saudi General Khalid, Britain's General de la Billiere, or General Roquejoffre of France—and all the others whose leadership played such a vital role. And most importantly, most importantly of all, all those who served in the field.

I thank the Members of this Congress—support here for our troops in battle was overwhelming. And above all, I thank those whose unfailing love and support sustained our courageous men and women—I thank the American people.

Tonight, I come to this House to speak about the world—the world after war. The recent challenge could not have been clearer. Saddam Hussein was the villain; Kuwait, the victim. To the aid of this small country came nations from North America and Europe, from Asia and South America, from Africa and the Arab world—all united against aggression. Our uncommon coalition must now work in common purpose: to forge a future that should never again be held hostage to the darker side of human nature.

Tonight in Iraq, Saddam walks amidst ruin. His war machine is crushed. His ability to threaten mass destruction is itself destroyed. His people have been lied to—denied the truth. And when his defeated legions come home, all Iraqis will see and feel the havoc he has wrought. And this I promise you: For all that Saddam has done to his own people, to the Kuwaitis, and to the entire world, Saddam and those around him are accountable.

All of us grieve for the victims of war, for the people of Kuwait and the suffering that scars the soul of that proud nation. We grieve for all our fallen soldiers and their families, for all the innocents caught up in this conflict. And, yes, we grieve for the people of Iraq—a people who have never been our enemy. My hope is that one day we will once again welcome them as friends into the community of nations. Our commitment to peace in the Middle East does not end with the liberation of Kuwait. So tonight, let me outline four key challenges to be met.

First, we must work together to create shared security arrangements in the region. Our friends and allies in the Middle East recognize that they will bear the bulk of the responsibility for regional security. But we want them to know that just as we stood with them to repel aggression, so now America stands ready to work with them to secure the peace. This does not mean stationing U.S. ground forces in the Arabian Peninsula, but it does mean American participation in joint exercises involving both air and ground forces. It means maintaining a capable U.S. naval presence in the region—just as we have for over 40 years. Let it be clear: Our vital national interests depend on a stable and secure Gulf.

Second, we must act to control the proliferation of weapons of mass destruction and the missiles used to deliver them. It would be tragic if the nations of the Middle East and Persian Gulf were now, in the wake of war, to embark on a new arms race. Iraq requires special vigilance. Until Iraq convinces the world of its peaceful intentions—that its leaders will not use new revenues to rearm and rebuild its menacing war machine—Iraq must not have access to the instruments of war.

And third, we must work to create new opportunities for peace and stability in the Middle East. On the night I announced Operation Desert Storm, I expressed my hope that out of the horrors of war might come new momentum for peace. "We've learned in the modern age geography cannot guarantee security and security does not come from military power alone.

All of us know the depth of bitterness that has made the dispute between Israel and its neighbors so painful and intractable. Yet, in the conflict just concluded, Israel and many of the Arab States have for the first time found themselves confronting the same aggressor. By now, it should be plain to all parties that peacemaking in the Middle East requires compromise. At the same time, peace brings real benefits to everyone. We must do all that we can to close the gap between Israel and the Arab states—and between Israelis and Palestinians. The tactics of terror lead absolutely nowhere. There can be no substitute for diplomacy.

A comprehensive peace must be grounded in United Nations Security Council Resolutions 242 and 338 and the principle of territory for peace. This principle must be elaborated to provide for Israel's security and recognition and at the same time for legitimate Palestinian political rights. Anything else would fail the twin test of fairness and security. The time has come to put an end to Arab- Israeli conflict.

The war with Iraq is over. The quest for solutions to the problems in Lebanon, in the Arab-Israeli dispute, and in the Gulf must go forward with new vigor and determination. And I guarantee you: No one will work harder for a stable peace in the region than we will.

Fourth, we must foster economic development for the sake of peace and progress. The Persian Gulf and Middle East form a region rich in natural resources—with a wealth of untapped human potential. Resources once squandered on military might must be redirected to more peaceful ends. We are already addressing the immediate economic consequences of Iraq's aggression. Now, the challenge is to reach higher—to foster economic freedom and prosperity for all the people of the region.

By meeting these four challenges we can build a framework for peace. I've asked Secretary of State Baker to go to the Middle East to begin the process. He will go to listen, to probe, to offer suggestions—to advance the search for peace and stability. I've also asked him to raise the plight of the hostages held in Lebanon. We have not forgotten them, and we will not forget them.

To all the challenges that confront this region of the world there is no single solution—no solely American answer. But we can make a difference. America will work tirelessly as a catalyst for positive change.

But we cannot lead a new world abroad if, at home, it's politics as usual on American defense and diplomacy. It's time to turn away from the temptation to protect unneeded weapons systems and obsolete bases. It's time to put an end to micromanagement of foreign and security assistance programs—micromanagement that humiliates our friends and allies and hamstrings our diplomacy. It's time to rise above the parochial and the pork barrel, to do what is necessary, what's right, and what will enable this nation to play the leadership role required of us.

The consequences of the conflict in the Gulf reach far beyond the confines of the Middle East. Twice before in this century, an entire world was convulsed by war. Twice this century, out of the horrors of war hope emerged for enduring peace. Twice before, those hopes proved to be a distant dream, beyond the grasp of man. Until now, the world we've known has been a world divided—a world of barbed wire and concrete block, conflict, and cold war.

Now, we can see a new world coming into view. A world in which there is the very real prospect of a new world order. In the words of Winston Churchill, a world order in which "the principles of justice and fair play protect the weak against the strong. . ." A world where the United Nations—freed from cold war stalemate—is poised to fulfill the historic vision of its founders. A world in which freedom and respect for human rights find a home among all nations. The Gulf war put this new world to its first test. And my fellow Americans, we passed that test.

For the sake of our principles—for the sake of the Kuwaiti people—we stood our ground. Because the world would not look the other way, Ambassador al-Sabah, tonight, Kuwait is free. And we're very happy about that.

Tonight, as our troops begin to come home, let us recognize that the hard work of freedom still calls us forward. We've learned the hard lessons of history. The victory over Iraq was not waged as "a war to end all wars." Even the new world order cannot guarantee an era of perpetual peace. But enduring peace must be our mission. Our success in the Gulf will shape not only the world order we seek, but our mission here at home.

In the war just ended, there were clear-cut objectives—timetables—and, above all, an overriding imperative to achieve results. We must bring that same sense of self-discipline, that same sense of urgency, to the way we meet challenges here at home. In my State of the Union Address and in my budget, I defined a comprehensive agenda to prepare for the next American century.

Our first priority is to get this economy rolling again. The fear and uncertainty caused by the Gulf crisis were understandable. But now that the war is over, oil prices are down, interest rates are down, and confidence is rightly coming back. Americans can move forward to lend, spend, and invest in this, the strongest economy on Earth.

We must also enact the legislation that is key to building a better America. For example, in 1990, we enacted an historic Clean Air Act. And now we've proposed a national energy strategy. We passed a child care bill that put power in the hands of parents. And today, we're ready to do the same thing with our schools and expand choice in education. We passed a crime bill that made a useful start in fighting crime and drugs. This year, we're sending to Congress our comprehensive crime package to finish the job. We passed the landmark Americans with Disabilities Act. And now we've sent forward our civil rights bill. We also passed the aviation bill. This year, we've sent up our new highway bill. And these are just a few of our pending proposals for reform and renewal.

So, tonight I call on Congress to move forward aggressively on our domestic front. Let's begin with two initiatives we should be able to agree or quickly—transportation and crime. And then, let's build on success with those and enact the rest of our agenda. If our forces could win the ground war in 100 hours, then surely the Congress can pass this legislation in 100 days. Let that be a promise we make tonight to the American people.

When I spoke in this House about the state of our Union, I asked all of you: If we can selflessly confront evil for the sake of good in a land so far away, then surely we can make this land all that it should be. In the time since then, the brave men and women of Desert Storm accomplishment more than even they may realize. They set out to confront an enemy abroad, and in the process, they transformed a nation at home. Think of the way they went about their mission—with confidence and quiet pride. Think about their sense of duty, about all they taught us about our values, about ourselves.

We hear so often about our young people in turmoil—how our children fall short, how our schools fail us, how American products and American workers are second-class. Well, don't you believe it. The America we saw in Desert Storm was first-class talent. And they did it using America's state- of-the-art technology. We saw the excellence embodied in the Patriot missile and the patriots who made it work. And we saw soldiers who know about honor and bravery and duty and country and the world- shaking power of these simple words. There is something noble and majestic about the pride, about the patriotism that we feel tonight.

So, to everyone here—and everyone watching at home—think about the men and women of Desert Storm. Let us honor them with our gratitude. Let us comfort the families of the fallen and remember each precious life lost.

Let us learn from them as well. Let us honor those who have served us by serving others. Let us honor them as individuals—men and women of every race, all creeds and colors—by setting the face of this nation against discrimination, bigotry, and hate. Eliminate them.

I'm sure that many of you saw on the television the unforgettable scene of four terrified Iraqi soldiers surrendering. They emerged from their bunker—broker, tears streaming from their eyes, fearing the worst. And then there was an American soldier. Remember what he said? He said: It's okay. You're all right now. You're all right now." That scene says a lot about America, a lot about who we are. Americans are a caring people. We are a good people, a generous people. Let us always be caring and good and generous in all we do.

Soon, very soon, our troops will begin the march we've all been waiting for—their march home. And I have directed Secretary Cheney to begin the immediate return of American combat units from the Gulf. Less than 2 hours from now, the first planeload of American soldiers will lift off from Saudi Arabia, headed for the U.S.A. It will carry men and women of the 24th Mechanized Infantry Division bound for Fort Stewart, Georgia. This is just the beginning of a steady flow of American troops coming home. Let their return remind us that all those who have gone before are linked with us in the long line of freedom's march.

Americans have always tried to serve, to sacrifice nobly for what we believe to be right. Tonight, I ask every community in this country to make this coming Fourth of July a day of special celebration for our returning troops. They may have missed Thanksgiving and Christmas, but I can tell you this: For them and for their families, we can make this a holiday they'll never forget.

In a very real sense, this victory belongs to them—to the privates and the pilots, to the sergeants and the supply officers, to the men and women in the machines, and the men and women who made them work. It belongs to the regulars, to the reserves, to the National Guard. This victory belongs to the finest fighting force this nation has ever known in its history.

We went halfway around the world to do what is moral and just and right. We fought hard and, with others, we won the war. We lifted the yoke of aggression and tyranny from a small country that many Americans had never even heard of, and we shall ask nothing in return.

We're coming home now—proud, confident, heads high. There is much that we must do, at home and abroad. And we will do it. We are Americans.

May God bless this great nation, the United States of America. Thank you all very, very much.

Source:

Public Papers of the presidents of the United States: George H. W. Bush, 1989. Washington, D.C.: Government Printing Office, 1952–92.

Bill Clinton and George W. Bush, The Mexico City Policy: Repeal, 1993, and Restoration, 2001

In 1984, President Ronald Reagan initiated the Mexico City Policy, named for the city in which he signed the memorandum. The policy prevented the Agency for International Development (AID) from offering any funding to nongovernmental organizations (NGOs) that provided abortions, abortion counseling, or recommendations to abortion providers. As a result, the Mexico City Policy is often known as the "Global Gag Rule."

In one of his first acts as president, Bill Clinton repealed the Mexico City Policy. He wrote that the use of government funds for abortion-related activities was already illegal, and that the policy's "excessively broad anti-abortion conditions . . . have undermined efforts to promote safe and efficacious family planning programs in foreign nations."

George W. Bush reinstated the Mexico City Policy as his first presidential act. In his memorandum, he wrote, "It is my conviction that taxpayer funds should not be used to pay for abortions or advocate or actively promote abortion, either here or abroad." The restoration was approved by Congress in May of 2001. This act demonstrated how the Republican majority Congress and President Bush rewarded the religious right, which was responsible for both funds and turning out Republican voters in the 2000 election. The withdrawal of funds from reproductive clinics worldwide, even though the money did not specifically pay for abortion or abortion-counseling, was expected to hurt women and families in developing countries.

January 22, 1993
MEMORANDUM FOR THE ACTING ADMINISTRATOR OF THE AGENCY FOR INTERNATIONAL DEVELOPMENT
SUBJECT: AID Family Planning Grants/Mexico City Policy

The Foreign Assistance Act of 1961 prohibits nongovernmental organizations ("NGO's") that receive Federal funds from using those funds "to pay for the performance of abortions as a method of family planning, or to motivate or coerce any person to practice abortions." (22 U.S.C. 2151b(f)(1)). The August 1984 announcement by President Reagan of what has become known as the "Mexico City Policy" directed the Agency for International Development ("AID") to expand this limitation and withhold AID funds from NGO's that engage in a wide range of activities, including providing advice, counseling, or information regarding abortion, or lobbying a foreign government to legalize or make abortion available. These conditions have been imposed even where an NGO uses non-AID funds for abortion-related activities.

These excessively broad anti-abortion conditions are unwarranted. I am informed that the conditions are not mandated by the Foreign Assistance Act or any other law. Moreover, they have undermined efforts to promote safe and efficacious family planning programs in foreign nations. Accordingly, I hereby direct that AID remove the conditions not explicitly mandated by the Foreign Assistance Act or any other law from all current AID grants to NGO's and exclude them from future grants.

WILLIAM J. CLINTON

Source:

National Archives and Records Administration. Clinton Presidential Materials Project. Available on-line. URL: http://clinton6nara.gov/1993/01/1993-01-22-1id-family-planning-grants-Mexico-city-policy.html. Accessed November 2003.

Memorandum January 22, 2001
MEMORANDUM FOR THE ADMINISTRATOR OF THE UNITED STATES AGENCY FOR INTERNATIONAL DEVELOPMENT
SUBJECT: Restoration of the Mexico City Policy

The Mexico City Policy announced by President Reagan in 1984 required nongovernmental organizations to agree as a condition of their receipt of Federal funds that such organizations would neither perform nor actively promote abortion as a method of family planning in other nations. This policy was in effect until it was rescinded on January 22, 1993.

It is my conviction that taxpayer funds should not be used to pay for abortions or advocate or actively promote abortion, either here or abroad. It is therefore my belief that the Mexico City Policy should be restored. Accordingly, I hereby rescind the "Memorandum for the Acting Administrator of the Agency for International Development, Subject: AID Family Planning Grants/ Mexico City Policy," dated January 22, 1993, and I direct the Administrator of the United States Agency for International Development to reinstate in full all of the requirements of the Mexico City Policy in effect on January 19, 1993.

George W. Bush

Source:

The White House Office of the Press Secretary. Available on-line. URL: www.whitehouse.gov/news/releases/20010123-5html. Accessed November 2003.

Economic and Technological Developments

Ronald Reagan, Tax Reduction Address, 1981

Broadcast speech given by President Ronald Reagan on July 27, 1981, to generate support for his tax reduction plan (which passed both houses of Congress two days later). Reagan urged members of Congress to vote for his proposal rather than a Democratic-sponsored alternative. His proposal rested on a theory called supply side economics in which more money in private hands would "trickle down" and generate income for all segments of society. Comparing the two bills using charts and graphs, Reagan claimed that the Democratic plan would actually result in a tax increase for the average family over the long term. (In a televised rebuttal, however, leading Democrats took issue with Reagan's interpretation.) He sought to reassure voters that he would not cut Social Security benefits. And he asked voters to contact their representatives to let them "know your feelings" on the tax plan. Despite significant cuts in federal programs, the tax reduction resulted in huge federal deficits not overcome until the last years of the Clinton administration.

Good evening.

I'd intended to make some remarks about the problem of social security tonight, but the immediacy of congressional action on the tax program, a key component of our economic package, has to take priority. Let me just say, however, I've been deeply disturbed by the way those of you who are dependent on social security have been needlessly frightened by some of the inaccuracies which have been given wide circulation. It's true that the social security system has financial problems. It's also true that these financial problems have been building for more than 20 years, and nothing has been done. I hope to address you on this entire subject in the near future.

In the meantime, let me just say this: I stated during the campaign and I repeat now, I will not stand by and see those of you who are dependent on social security deprived of the benefits you've worked so hard to earn. I make that pledge to you as your President. You have no reason to be frightened. You will continue to receive your checks in the full amount due you. In any plan to restore fiscal integrity of social security, I personally will see that the plan will not be at the expense of you who are now dependent on your monthly social security checks.

Now, let us turn to the business at hand. It's been nearly 6 months since I first reported to you on the state of the nation's economy. I'm afraid my message that night was grim and disturbing. I remember telling you we were in the worst economic mess since the Great Depression. Prices were continuing to spiral upward, unemployment was reaching intolerable levels, and all because government was too big and spent too much of our money.

We're still not out of the woods, but we've made a start. And we've certainly surprised those longtime and somewhat cynical observers of the Washington scene, who looked, listened, and said, "It can never be done; Washington will never change its spending habits." Well, something very exciting has been happening here in Washington, and you're responsible.

Your voices have been heard—millions of you, Democrats, Republicans, and Independents, from every profession, trade and line of work, and from every part of this land. You sent a message that you wanted a new beginning. You wanted to change one little, two little word—two letter word, I should say. It doesn't sound like much, but it sure can make a difference changing "by government," "control *by* government" to "control *of* government."

In that earlier broadcast, you'll recall I proposed a program to drastically cut back government spending in the 1982 budget, which begins October 1st, and to continue cutting in the '83 and '84 budgets. Along with this I suggested an across-the-board tax cut, spread over those same 3 years, and the elimination of unnecessary regulations which were adding billions to the cost of things we buy.

All the lobbying, the organized demonstrations, and the cries of protest by those whose way of life depends on maintaining government's wasteful ways were no match for your voices, which were heard loud and clear in these marble halls of government. And you made history with your telegrams, your letters, your phone calls and, yes, personal visits to talk to your elected representatives. You reaffirmed the mandate you delivered in the election last November—a mandate that called for an end to government policies that sent prices and mortgage rates skyrocketing while millions of Americans went jobless.

Because of what you did, Republicans and Democrats in the Congress came together and passed the most sweeping cutbacks in the history of the Federal budget. Right now, Members of the House and Senate are meeting in a conference committee to reconcile the differences between the two budget-cutting bills passed by the House and Senate. When they finish, all Americans will benefit from savings of approximately $140 billion in reduced government costs over just the next 3 years. And that doesn't include the additional savings from the hundreds of burdensome regulations already canceled or facing cancellation.

For 19 out of the last 20 years, the Federal Government has spent more than it took in. There will be another large deficit in this present year which ends September 30th, but with our program in place, it won't be quite as big as it might have been. And starting next year, the deficits will get smaller until in just a few years the budget can be balanced. And we hope we can begin whittling at that almost $1 trillion debt that hangs over the future of our children.

Now, so far, I've been talking about only one part of our program for economic recovery—the budget-cutting part. I don't minimize its importance. Just the fact that Democrats and Republicans could work together as they have, proving the strength of our system, has created an optimism in our land. The rate of inflation is no longer in double-digit figures. The dollar has regained strength in the international money markets, and businessmen and investors are making decisions with regard to industrial development, modernization and expansion—all of this based on anticipation of our program being adopted and put into operation.

A recent poll shows that where a year and a half ago only 24 percent of our people believed things would get better, today 46 percent believe they will. To justify their faith, we must deliver the other part of our program. Our economic package is a closely knit, carefully constructed plan to restore America's economic strength and put our nation back on the road to prosperity.

Each part of this package is vital. It cannot be considered piecemeal. It was proposed as a package, and it has been supported as such by the American people. Only if the Congress passes all of its major components does it have any real chance of success. This is absolutely essential if we are to provide incentives and make capital available for the increased productivity required to provide real, permanent jobs for our people.

And let us not forget that the rest of the world is watching America carefully to see how we'll act at this critical moment.

I have recently returned from a summit meeting with world leaders in Ottawa, Canada, and the message I heard from them was quite clear. Our allies depend on a strong and economically sound America. And they're watching events in this country, particularly those surrounding our program for economic recovery, with close attention and great hopes. In short, the best way to have a strong foreign policy abroad is to have a strong economy at home.

The day after tomorrow, Wednesday, the House of Representatives will begin debate on two tax bills. And once again, they need to hear from you. I know that doesn't give you much time, but a great deal is at stake. A few days ago I was visited here in the office by a Democratic Congressman from one of our southern States. He'd been back in his district. And one day one of his constituents asked him where he stood on our economic recovery program—I outlined that program in an earlier broadcast—particularly the tax cut. Well, the Congressman, who happens to be a strong leader in support of our program, replied at some length with a discussion of the technical points involved, but he also mentioned a few reservations he had on certain points. The constituent, a farmer, listened politely until he'd finished, and then he said, "Don't give me an essay. What I want to know is are you for 'im or agin 'im?

Well, I appreciate the gentleman's support and suggest his question is a message your own representatives should hear. Let me add, those representatives honestly and sincerely want to know your feelings. They get plenty of input from the special interest groups. They'd like to hear from their home folks.

Now, let me explain what the situation is and what's at issue. With our budget cuts, we've presented a complete program of reduction in tax rates. Again, our purpose was to provide incentive for the individual, incentives for business to encourage production and hiring of the unemployed, and to free up money for investment. Our bill calls for a 5-percent reduction in the income tax rates by October 1st, a 10-percent reduction beginning July 1st, 1982, and another 10-percent cut a year later, a 25-percent total reduction over 3 years.

But then to ensure the tax cut is permanent, we call for indexing the tax rates in 1985, which means adjusting them for inflation. As it is now, if you get a cost-of-living raise that's intended to keep you even with inflation, you find that the increase in the number of dollars you get may very likely move you into a higher tax bracket, and you wind up poorer than you would. This is called bracket creep.

Bracket creep is an insidious tax. Let me give an example. If you earned $10,000 a year in 1972, by 1980 you had to earn $19,700 just to stay even with inflation. But that's before taxes. Come April 15th, you'll find your tax rates have increased 30 percent. Now, if you've been wondering why you don't seem as well-off as you were a few years back, it's because government makes a profit on inflation. It gets an automatic tax increase without having to vote on it. We intend to stop that.

Time won't allow me to explain every detail. But our bill includes just about everything to help the economy. We reduce the marriage penalty, that unfair tax that has a working husband and wife pay more tax than if they were single. We increase the exemption on the inheritance or estate tax to $600,000, so that farmers and family-owned businesses don't have to sell the farm or store in the event of death just to pay the taxes. Most important, we wipe out the tax entirely for a surviving spouse. No longer, for example, will a widow have to sell the family source of income to pay a tax on her husband's death.

There are deductions to encourage investment and savings. Business gets realistic depreciation on equipment and machinery. And there are tax breaks for small and independent businesses which create 80 percent of all our new jobs.

This bill also provides major credits to the research and development industry. These credits will help spark the high technology breakthroughs that are so critical to America's economic leadership in the world. There are also added incentives for small businesses, including a provision that will lift much of the burden of costly paperwork that government has imposed on small business.

In addition, there's short-term but substantial assistance for the hard pressed thrift industry, as well as reductions in oil taxes that will benefit new or independent oil producers and move our nation a step closer to energy self-sufficiency. Our bill is, in short, the first real tax cut for everyone in almost 20 years.

Now, when I first proposed this—incidentally, it has now become a bipartisan measure co-authored by Republican Barber Conable and Democrat Kent Hance—the Democratic leadership said a tax cut was out of the question. It would be wildly inflationary. And that was before my inauguration. And then your voices began to be heard and suddenly, in February, the leadership discovered that, well, a 1-year tax cut was feasible. Well, we kept on pushing our 3-year tax cut and by June, the opposition found that a 2-year tax cut might work. Now it's July, and they find they could even go for a third year cut provided there was a trigger arrangement that would only allow it to go into effect if certain economic goals had been met by 1983.

But by holding the people's tax reduction hostage to future economic events, they will eliminate the people's ability to plan ahead. Shopkeepers, farmers, and individuals will be denied the certainty they must have to begin saving or investing more of their money. And encouraging more savings and investment is precisely what we need now to rebuild our economy.

There's also a little sleight of hand in that trigger mechanism. You see, their bill, the committee bill, ensures that the 1983 deficit will be $6 1/2 billion greater than their own trigger requires. As it stands now, the design of their own bill will not meet the trigger they've put in; therefore, the third year tax cut will automatically never take place.

If I could paraphrase a well-known statement by Will Rogers that he had never met a man he didn't like, I'm afraid we have some people around here who never met a tax they didn't hike. Their tax proposal, similar in a number of ways to ours but differing in some very vital parts, was passed out of the House Ways and Means Committee, and from now on I'll refer to it as the committee bill and ours as the bipartisan bill. They'll be the bills taken up Wednesday.

The majority leadership claims theirs gives a greater break to the worker than ours, and it does—that is, if you're only planning to live 2 more years. The plain truth is, our choice is not between two plans to reduce taxes; it's between a tax cut or a tax increase. There is now built into our present system, including payroll social security taxes and the bracket creep I've mentioned, a 22-percent tax increase over the next 3 years. The committee bill offers a 15-percent cut over 2 years; our bipartisan bill gives a 25-percent reduction over 3 years.

Now, as you can see by this chart, there is the 22-percent tax increase. Their cut is below that line. But ours wipes out that increase and with a little to spare. And there it is, as you can see. The red column—that is the 15-percent tax cut, and it still leaves you with an increase. The green column is our bipartisan bill which wipes out the tax increase and gives you an ongoing cut.

Incidentally, their claim that cutting taxes for individuals for as much as 3 years ahead is risky, rings a little hollow when you realize that their bill calls for business tax cuts each year for 7 years ahead. It rings even more hollow when you consider the fact the majority leadership routinely endorses Federal spending bills that project years into the future, but objects to a tax bill that will return your money over a 3-year period.

Now, here is another chart which illustrates what I said about their giving a better break if you only intend to live for 2 more years. Their tax cut, so called, is the dotted line. Ours is the solid line. As you can see, in an earning bracket of $20,000, their tax cut is slightly more generous than ours for the first 2 years. Then, as you can see, their tax bill, the dotted line, starts going up and up and up. On the other hand, in our bipartisan tax bill, the solid line, our tax cut keeps on going down, and then stays down permanently. This is true of all earning brackets—not just the $20,000 level that I've used as an example—from the lowest to the highest. This red space between the two lines is the tax money that will remain in your pockets if our bill passes; and it's the amount that will leave your pockets if their tax bill is passed.

Now, I take no pleasure in saying this, but those who will seek to defeat our Conable-Hance bipartisan bill as debate begins Wednesday are the ones who have given us five "tax cuts" in the last 10 years. But, our taxes went up $400 billion in those same 10 years. The lines on these charts say a lot about who's really fighting for whom. On the one hand, you see a genuine and lasting commitment to the future of working Americans; on the other, just another empty promise.

Those of us in the bipartisan coalition want to give this economy and the future of this Nation back to the people, because putting people first has always been America's secret weapon. The House majority leadership seems less concerned about protecting your family budget than with spending more on the Federal budget.

Our bipartisan tax bill targets three-quarters of its tax relief to middle-income wage earners who presently pay almost three-quarters of the total income tax. It also then indexes the tax brackets to ensure that you can keep that tax reduction in the years ahead. There also is, as I said, estate tax relief that will keep family farms and family-owned businesses in the family, and there are provisions for personal retirement plans and individual savings accounts.

Because our bipartisan bill is so clearly drawn and broadly based, it provides the kind of predictability and certainty that the financial segments of our society need to make investment decisions that stimulate productivity and make our economy grow. Even more important, if the tax cut goes to you, the American people, in the third year, that money returned to you won't be available to the Congress to spend, and that, in my view, is what this whole controversy comes down to. Are you entitled to the fruits of your own labor or does government have some presumptive right to spend and spend and spend?

I'm also convinced our business tax cut is superior to theirs because it's more equitable, and it will do a much better job promoting the surge in investment we so badly need to rebuild our industrial base.

There's something else I want to tell you. Our bipartisan coalition worked out a tax bill we felt would provide incentive and stimulate productivity, thus reducing inflation and providing jobs for the unemployed. That was our only goal. Our opponents in the beginning didn't want a tax bill at all. So what is the purpose behind their change of heart? They've put a tax program together for one reason only: to provide themselves with a political victory. Never mind that it won't solve the economic problems confronting our country. Never mind that it won't get the wheels of industry turning again or eliminate the inflation which is eating us alive.

This is not the time for political fun and games. This is the time for a new beginning. I ask you now to put aside any feelings of frustration or helplessness about our political institutions and join me in this dramatic but responsible plan to reduce the enormous burden of Federal taxation on you and your family.

During recent months many of you have asked what can you do to help make America strong again. I urge you again to contact your Senators and Congressmen. Tell them of your support for this bipartisan proposal. Tell them you believe this is an unequaled opportunity to help return America to prosperity and make government again the servant of the people.

In a few days the Congress will stand at the fork of two roads. One road is all too familiar to us. It leads ultimately to higher taxes. It merely brings us full circle back to the source of our economic problems, where the government decides that it knows better than you what should be done with your earnings and, in fact, how you should conduct your life. The other road promises to renew the American spirit. It's a road of hope and opportunity. It places the direction of your life back in your hands where it belongs.

I've not taken your time this evening merely to ask you to trust me. Instead, I ask you to trust yourselves. That's what America is all about. Our struggle for nationhood, our unrelenting fight for freedom, our very existence—these have all rested on the assurance that you must be free to shape your life as you are best able to, that no one can stop you from reaching higher or take from you the creativity that has made America the envy of mankind.

One road is timid and fearful; the other bold and hopeful.

In these 6 months, we've done so much and have come so far. It's been the power of millions of people like you who have determined that we will make America great again. You have made the difference up to now. You will make the difference again. Let us not stop now.

Thank you. God bless you, and good night.

Source:

Public Papers of the Presidents of the United States: Ronald Reagan, 1981. Washington, D.C.: Government Printing Office, 1982–91. pp. 664–668.

Gramm-Rudman-Hollings Act, 1985

Also known as the Balanced Budget and Emergency Deficit Control Act, this legislation, sponsored by Senators Phil Gramm (R.-Tex.), Warren Rudman (R.-N.H.), and Ernest Hollings (D.-S.C.) was passed by both houses of Congress on December 11, 1985. It required the president and Congress to work together to eliminate the budget deficit by 1991. The bill stipulated that the president's administration and Congress agree each year on budget cuts that would meet successively lower targets, which were also specified by the bill. If the cuts were made accordingly, the deficit was to reach zero by 1991. The law also stipulated that, if agreement was not reached, automatic reductions would be implemented. The legislation also set the national debt ceiling at more than $2 trillion.

The legislation worked. Not only was the Clinton administration able to balance the budget, but by the end of his years in office, the government was running a surplus. However, this condition was attributable to the unprecedented economic growth (partly attributable to the balanced federal budget) that occurred during the Clinton years. By the time Bush took office, however, those conditions were already changing, due in part to overproduction in the telecommunications and technology sectors. A combination of tax cuts and additional expenditures necessitated by security concerns at home and war abroad once again put the government in the red.

Please note that the "Federal Old-Age and Survivors Insurance Trust Fund and the Federal Disability Insurance Trust Fund" are what is commonly known as "Social Security."

(excerpt)

Title II—Deficit Reduction Procedures

Sec. 200. Short Title. . .

(a) Short Title.—This title may be cited as the Balanced Budget and Emergency Deficit Control Act of 1985.

* * *

Part A—Congressional Budget Process

Subpart I-Sec. 201. Congressional Budget.

a) Definitions.—

* * *

(6) The term 'deficit' means, with respect to any fiscal year, the amount by which total budget outlays for such fiscal year exceed total revenues for such fiscal year. In calculating the deficit for purposes of comparison with the maximum deficit amount under the Balanced Budget and Emergency Deficit Control Act of 1985 and in calculating the excess deficit . . . for any fiscal year, the receipts of the for such fiscal year and the taxes payable under sections 140(a), 3101(a), and 3111(a) of the Internal Revenue Code of 1954 during such fiscal year shall be included in total revenues for such fiscal year, and the disbursements of each such Trust Fund for such fiscal year shall be included in total budget outlays for such fiscal year. . . . Amounts paid by the Federal Financing Bank for the purchase of loans made or guaranteed by a department, agency, or instrumentality of the Government of the United States shall be treated as outlays of such department, agency, or instrumentality.

* * *

Sec. 301. (a) Content of Concurrent Resolution on the Budget.—On or before April 15 of each year, the Congress shall complete action on a concurrent resolution on the budget for the fiscal year beginning on October 1 of such year. The concurrent resolution shall set forth appropriate levels for the fiscal year beginning on October 1 of such year, and planning levels for each of the two ensuing fiscal years, for the following—

(1) totals for new budget authority, budget outlays, direct loan obligations, and primary loan guarantee commitments;

(2) total Federal revenues and the amount, if any, by which the aggregate level of Federal revenues should be increased or decreased by bills and resolutions to be reported by the appropriate committees;

(3) the surplus or deficit in the budget;

(4) new budget authority, budget outlays, direct loan obligations, and primary loan guarantee commitments for each major functional category, based on allocations of the total levels set forth pursuant to paragraph (1); and

(5) the public debt.

(b) Additional Matters in Concurrent Resolution

* * *

(3) require a procedure under which all or certain bills or resolutions providing new budget authority or new entitlement authority for such fiscal year shall not be enrolled until the Congress has completed action on any reconciliation bill or reconciliation resolution or both required by such concurrent resolution to be reported in accordance with section 310(b); and

(4) set forth such other matters, and require such other procedures, relating to the budget, as may be appropriate to carry out the purposes of this Act.

(c) Consideration of Procedures or Matters Which Have the Effect of Changing any Rule of the House of Representatives.—If the Committee on the Budget of the House of Representatives reports any concurrent resolution on the budget which includes any procedure or matter which has the effect of changing any rule of the House of Representatives, such concurrent resolution shall then be referred to the Committee on Rules with instructions to report it within five calendar days (not counting any day on which the House is not in session). The Committee on Rules shall have jurisdiction to report any concurrent resolution referred to it under this paragraph with an amendment or amendments changing or striking out any such procedure or matter.

(d) Views and Estimates of Other Committees.—On or before February 25 of each year, each committee of the House of Representatives having legislative jurisdiction shall submit to the Committee on the Budget of the House and each committee of the Senate having legislative jurisdiction shall submit to the Committee on the Budget of the Senate its views and estimates (as determined by the committee making such submission) with respect to all matters . . . which relate to matters within the jurisdiction or functions of such committee. The Joint Economic Committee shall submit to the Committees on the Budget of both Houses its recommendations as to the fiscal policy appropriate to the goals of the Employment Act of 1946. Any other committee of the House of Representatives or the Senate may submit to the Committee on the Budget of its House, and any joint committee of the Congress may submit to the Committees on the Budget of both Houses, its views and estimates with respect to all matters. . .which relate to matters within its jurisdiction or functions.

(e) Hearings and Report.—In developing of the concurrent resolution on the budget referred to in subsection (a) for each fiscal year, the Committee on the Budget of each House shall hold hearings and shall receive testimony from Members of Congress and such appropriate representatives of Federal departments and agencies, the general public, and national organizations as the committee deems desirable. Each of the recommendations as to short-term and medium-term goals set forth in the report submitted by the members of the Joint Economic Committee . . . may be considered by the Committee on the Budget of each House as part of its consideration of such concurrent resolution, and its report may reflect its views thereon, including its views on how the estimates of revenues and levels of budget authority and outlays set forth in such concurrent resolution are designed to achieve any goals it is recommending. The report accompanying such concurrent resolution shall include, but not be limited to—

(1) a comparison of revenues estimated by the committee with those estimated in the budget submitted by the President;

(2) a comparison of the appropriate levels of total budget outlays and total new budget authority, total direct loan obligations, total primary loan guarantee commitments, as set forth in such concurrent resolution, with those estimated or requested in the budget submitted by the President;

(3) with respect to each major functional category, an estimate of budget outlays and an appropriate level of new budget authority for all proposed programs and for all existing programs (including renewals thereof), with the estimate and level for existing programs being divided between permanent authority and funds provided in appropriation Acts, and with each such division being subdivided between controllable amounts and all other amounts;

(4) an allocation of the level of Federal revenues recommended in the concurrent resolution among the major sources of such revenues;

(5) the economic assumptions and objectives which underlie each of the matters set forth in such concurrent resolution and any alternative economic assumptions and objectives which the committee considered;

(6) projections (not limited to the following), for the period of five fiscal years beginning with such fiscal year, of the estimated levels of total budget outlays and total new budget authority, the estimated revenues to be received, and the estimated surplus or deficit, if any, for each fiscal year in such period, and the estimated levels of tax expenditures (the tax expenditures budget) by major functional categories;

(7) a statement of any significant changes in the proposed levels of Federal assistance to State and local governments;

(8) information, data, and comparisons indicating the manner in which, and the basis on which, the committee determined each of the matters set forth in the concurrent resolution; and

* * *

(g) Common Economic Assumptions.—The joint explanatory statement accompanying a conference report on a concurrent resolution on the budget shall set forth the common economic assumptions upon which such joint statement and conference report are based, or upon which any amendment contained in the joint explanatory statement to be proposed by the conferees in the case of technical disagreement is based.

(h) Budget Committees Consultation With Committees.—The Committee on the Budget of the House of

Representatives shall consult with the committees of its House having legislative jurisdiction during the preparation, consideration, and enforcement of the concurrent resolution on the budget with respect to all matters which relate to the jurisdiction or functions of such committees.

(i) Maximum Deficit Amount May Not Be Exceeded.—

(1)(A) Except as provided in paragraph (2), it shall not be in order in either the House of Representatives or the Senate to consider any concurrent resolution on the budget for a fiscal year under this section, or to consider any amendment to such a concurrent resolution, or to consider a conference report on such a concurrent resolution, if the level of total budget outlays for such fiscal year that is set forth in such concurrent resolution or conference report exceeds the recommended level of Federal revenues set forth for that year by an amount that is greater than the maximum deficit amount for such fiscal year . . ., or if the adoption of such amendment would result in a level of total budget outlays for that fiscal year which exceeds the recommended level of Federal revenues for that fiscal year, by an amount that is greater than the maximum deficit amount for such fiscal year. . . .

* * *

Concurrent Resolution on the Budget Must be Adopted before Legislation Providing New Budget Authority, New Spending Authority, New Credit Authority, or Changes in Revenues or the Public Debt Limit is Considered

Sec. 303. (a) In General.—It shall not be in order in either the House of Representatives or the Senate to consider any bill or resolution (or amendment thereto) as reported to the House or Senate which provides—

(1) new budget authority for a fiscal year;

(2) an increase or decrease in revenues to become effective during a fiscal year;

(3) an increase or decrease in the public debt limit to become effective during a fiscal year;

(4) new entitlement authority to become effective during a fiscal year; or

(5) new credit authority for a fiscal year,

until the concurrent resolution on the budget for such fiscal year has been agreed to,. . .

See also RONALD REAGAN, TAX REDUCTION ADDRESS, 1981; TAX REFORM ACT, 1986.

Source:

Statutes at Large, Vol. 99, pp. 1,038–1,101.

Ronald Reagan, *Challenger* Disaster Address, 1986

President Ronald Reagan was known as the Great Communicator. In this address following the January 28, 1986, explosion that destroyed the space shuttle *Challenger* he comforted the nation after this tragedy. The first space shuttle took off in 1981. By 1986, space shuttle lift-offs had become so routine that only one national channel gave it live coverage. The *Challenger*'s seven-member crew included New Hampshire schoolteacher S. Christa McAuliffe, who had won a national competition to ride aboard the shuttle and broadcast lessons to America's children. Her class was watching on television when the explosion occurred, shortly after takeoff.

Reagan announced that he was postponing his annual State of the Union message, which had been scheduled for that evening, out of respect and mourning for the astronauts who had been killed in the explosion. He reminded Americans that they had grown accustomed to the space program and had perhaps forgotten the dangers associated with it. He told the schoolchildren that exploration required bravery, and he restated his commitment to the continuance of America's space program. His concluding quotation came from a poem written by an American airman killed in World War II.

Lift-off had been postponed several times because Florida, where the shuttle was housed, was experiencing unusually frigid weather. The explosion was later blamed on an o-ring that had hardened in the cold. Despite engineers' objections, National Aeronautic and Space Administration (NASA) officials had decided that the danger posed by the temperature was not firmly established and authorized lift-off despite the objections of some NASA engineers. The disaster halted the space shuttle program for over two years. It resumed September 29, 1988, with the flight of the Space Shuttle *Discovery*. Compounded by a number of other setbacks, NASA never regained the reputation (or the appropriations) it garnered with its successful moon program.

Ladies and gentlemen, I'd planned to speak to you tonight to report on the state of the Union, but the events of earlier today have led me to change those plans. Today is a day for mourning and remembering. Nancy and I are pained to the core by the tragedy of the shuttle *Challenger*. We know we share this pain with all of the people of our country. This is truly a national loss.

Nineteen years ago, almost to the day, we lost three astronauts in a terrible accident on the ground. But we've never lost an astronaut in flight; we've never had a tragedy like this. And perhaps we've forgotten the courage it took for the crew of the shuttle. But they, the *Challenger* Seven, were aware of the dangers, but overcame them and did their jobs brilliantly. We mourn seven heroes: Michael Smith, Dick Scobee, Judith Resnik, Ronald McNair, Ellison Onizuka, Gregory Jarvis, and Christa McAuliffe. We mourn their loss as a nation together.

For the families of the seven, we cannot bear, as you do, the full impact of this tragedy. But we feel the loss, and we're thinking about you so very much. Your loved ones were daring and brave, and they had that special grace, that special spirit that says, "Give me a challenge, and I'll meet it with joy." They had a hunger to explore the universe and discover its truths. They wished to serve, and they did. They served all of us. We've grown used to wonders in this century. It's hard to dazzle us. But for 25 years the United States space program has been doing just that. We've grown used to the idea of space, and perhaps we forget that we've only just begun. We're still pioneers. They, the members of the *Challenger* crew, were pioneers.

And I want to say something to the schoolchildren of America who were watching the live coverage of the shuttle's take-off. I know it is hard to understand, but sometimes painful things like this happen. It's all part of the process of exploration and discovery. It's all part of taking a chance and expanding man's horizons. The future doesn't belong to the fainthearted; it belongs to the brave. The *Challenger* crew was pulling us into the future, and we'll continue to follow them.

I've always had great faith in and respect for our space program, and what happened today does nothing to diminish it. We don't hide our space program. We don't keep secrets and cover things up. We do it all up front and in public. That's the way freedom is, and we wouldn't change it for a minute. We'll continue our quest in space. There will be more shuttle flights and more shuttle crews and, yes, more volunteers, more civilians, more teachers in space. Nothing ends here; our hopes and our journeys continue. I want to add that I wish I could talk to every man and woman who works for NASA or who worked on this mission and tell them: "Your dedication and professionalism have moved and impressed us for decades. And we know of your anguish. We share it."

There's a coincidence today. On this day 390 years ago, the great explorer Sir Francis Drake died aboard ship off the coast of Panama. In his lifetime the great frontiers were the oceans, and an historian later said, "He lived by the sea, died on it, and was buried in it." Well, today we can say of the *Challenger* crew: Their dedication was, like Drake's, complete.

The crew of the space shuttle *Challenger* honored us by the manner in which they lived their lives. We will never forget them, nor the last time we saw them, this morning, as they prepared for their journey and waved good-bye and "slipped the surly bonds of earth" to "touch the face of God."

Source:

Public Papers of the Presidents of the United States: Ronald Reagan, 1981. Washington, D.C.: Government Printing Office, 1982–91. pp. 664–668.

Communications Decency Act of 1996

Federal law devised to regulate the distribution of pornographic material over the Internet. It was enacted February 8, 1996, as part of the comprehensive Telecommunications Act, a legislative overhaul of the nation's telecommunications laws.

The Decency Act criminalized transmission of indecent material via computer on-line services that could be accessed by children. Under its terms, the distribution over the Internet of indecent material to minors would be a felony punishable by up to two years in prison and a $100,000 fine. The measure was a controversial item in the congressional debate over the telecommunications overhaul. Its supporters argued that the law was needed to protect children from the rapidly growing volume of indecent material on the unregulated Internet. Opponents denounced the act as government-sanctioned censorship and a blow to free expression. Deciding on a legal challenge to the law, a three-judge federal panel ruled in June 1996 that the Decency Act violated free speech rights protected under the Constitution's First Amendment. The panel, which defended Internet communications as a form of free speech, blocked enforcement of the law. In June 1997 the U.S. Supreme Court, deciding on a Clinton administration appeal of the federal panel's ruling, struck down the act as an unconstitutional infringement on First Amendment rights to freedom of expression.

SEC. 502. OBSCENE OR HARASSING USE OF TELECOMMUNICATIONS FACILITIES UNDER THE COMMUNICATIONS ACT OF 1934.

Section 223 (47 U.S.C. 223) is amended—

(1) by striking subsection (a) and inserting in lieu thereof:

'(a) Whoever—

'(1) in interstate or foreign communications—

'(A) by means of a telecommunications device knowingly—

'(i) makes, creates, or solicits, and

'(ii) initiates the transmission of, any comment, request, suggestion, proposal, image, or other communication which is obscene, lewd, lascivious, filthy, or indecent, with intent to annoy, abuse, threaten, or harass another person;

'(B) by means of a telecommunications device knowingly—

'(i) makes, creates, or solicits, and

'(ii) initiates the transmission of, any comment, request, suggestion, proposal, image, or other communication which is obscene or indecent, knowing that the recipient of the communication is under 18 years of age, regardless of whether the maker of such communication placed the call or initiated the communication;

'(C) makes a telephone call or utilizes a telecommunications device, whether or not conversation or communication ensues, without disclosing his identity and with intent to annoy, abuse, threaten, or harass any person at the called number or who receives the communications;

'(D) makes or causes the telephone of another repeatedly or continuously to ring, with intent to harass any person at the called number; or

'(E) makes repeated telephone calls or repeatedly initiates communication with a telecommunications device, during which conversation or communication ensues, solely to harass any person at the called number or who receives the communication; or

'(2) knowingly permits any telecommunications facility under his control to be used for any activity prohibited by paragraph (1) with the intent that it be used for such activity, shall be fined under title 18, United States Code, or imprisoned not more than two years, or both.'; and (2) by adding at the end the following new subsections:

'(d) Whoever—

'(1) in interstate or foreign communications knowingly—

'(A) uses an interactive computer service to send to a specific person or persons under 18 years of age, or

'(B) uses any interactive computer service to display in a manner available to a person under 18 years of age, any comment, request, suggestion, proposal, image, or other communication that, in context, depicts or describes, in terms patently offensive as measured by contemporary community standards, sexual or excretory activities or organs, regardless of whether the user of such service placed the call or initiated the communication; or

'(2) knowingly permits any telecommunications facility under such person's control to be used for an activity prohibited by paragraph (1) with the intent that it be used for such activity, shall be fined under title 18, United States Code, or imprisoned not more than two years, or both.

'(e) In addition to any other defenses available by law:

'(1) No person shall be held to have violated subsection (a) or (d) solely for providing access or connection to or from a facility, system, or network not under that person's control, including transmission, downloading, intermediate storage, access software, or other related capabilities that are incidental to providing such access or connection that does not include the creation of the content of the communication.

'(2) The defenses provided by paragraph (1) of this subsection shall not be applicable to a person who is a conspirator with an entity actively involved in the creation or knowing distribution of communications that violate this section, or who knowingly advertises the availability of such communications.

'(3) The defenses provided in paragraph (1) of this subsection shall not be applicable to a person who provides access or connection to a facility, system, or network engaged in the violation of this section that is owned or controlled by such person.

'(4) No employer shall be held liable under this section for the actions of an employee or agent unless the employee's or agent's conduct is within the scope of his or her employment or agency and the employer (A) having knowledge of such conduct, authorizes or ratifies such conduct, or (B) recklessly disregards such conduct.

'(5) It is a defense to a prosecution under subsection (a)(1)(B) or (d), or under subsection (a)(2) with respect to the use of a facility for an activity under subsection (a)(1)(B) that a person—

'(A) has taken, in good faith, reasonable, effective, and appropriate actions under the circumstances to restrict or prevent access by minors to a communication specified in such subsections, which may involve any appropriate measures to restrict minors from such communications, including any method which is feasible under available technology; or

'(B) has restricted access to such communication by requiring use of a verified credit card, debit account, adult access code, or adult personal identification number.

'(6) The Commission may describe measures which are reasonable, effective, and appropriate to restrict access to prohibited communications under subsection (d). Nothing in this section authorizes the Commission to enforce, or is intended to provide the Commission with the authority to approve, sanction, or permit, the use of such measures. The Commission shall have no enforcement authority over the failure to utilize such measures. The Commission shall not endorse specific products relating to such measures. The use of such measures shall be admitted as evidence of good faith efforts for purposes of paragraph (5) in any action arising under subsection (d). Nothing in this section shall be construed to treat interactive computer services as common carriers or telecommunications carriers.

'(f)

(1) No cause of action may be brought in any court or administrative agency against any person on account of any activity that is not in violation of any law punishable by criminal or civil penalty, and that the person has taken in good faith to implement a defense authorized under

this section or otherwise to restrict or prevent the transmission of, or access to, a communication specified in this section.

'(2) No State or local government may impose any liability for commercial activities or actions by commercial entities, nonprofit libraries, or institutions of higher education in connection with an activity or action described in subsection (a)(2) or (d) that is inconsistent with the treatment of those activities or actions under this section: *Provided, however* , That nothing herein shall preclude any State or local government from enacting and enforcing complementary oversight, liability, and regulatory systems, procedures, and requirements, so long as such systems, procedures, and requirements govern only intrastate services and do not result in the imposition of inconsistent rights, duties or obligations on the provision of interstate services. Nothing in this subsection shall preclude any State or local government from governing conduct not covered by this section.

'(g) Nothing in subsection (a), (d), (e), or (f) or in the defenses to prosecution under subsection (a) or (d) shall be construed to affect or limit the application or enforcement of any other Federal law.

'(h) For purposes of this section—

'(1) The use of the term 'telecommunications device' in this section—

'(A) shall not impose new obligations on broadcasting station licensees and cable operators covered by obscenity and indecency provisions elsewhere in this Act; and

'(B) does not include an interactive computer service.

'(2) The term 'interactive computer service' has the meaning provided in section 230(e)(2).

'(3) The term 'access software' means software (including client or server software) or enabling tools that do not create or provide the content of the communication but that allow a user to do any one or more of the following:

'(A) filter, screen, allow, or disallow content;

'(B) pick, choose, analyze, or digest content; or

'(C) transmit, receive, display, forward, cache, search, subset, organize, reorganize, or translate content.

'(4) The term 'institution of higher education' has the meaning provided in section 1201 of the Higher Education Act of 1965 (20 U.S.C. 1141).

'(5) The term 'library' means a library eligible for participation in State-based plans for funds under title III of the Library Services and Construction Act (20 U.S.C. 355e et seq.).'.

Source:

Landmark Documents in American History, Facts On File, Inc.

President Clinton's Remarks at Announcement of Cloning Legislation, 1997

Remarks delivered by President Bill Clinton February 24, 1997, expressing concern about the possibility of creating genetic clones of humans. His comments came a day after researchers in Scotland announced that they had created the first clone of an adult animal, a sheep. The cloned lamb, named Dolly, had a genetic makeup identical to her mother's. This cloning success marked a major scientific breakthrough but also raised apprehensions worldwide about the potential for cloning human beings. In his comments, Clinton applauded the achievement of the Scottish researchers but called on the U.S. National Bioethics Advisory Commission to evaluate the discovery's full ethical and legal implications.

In follow-up remarks March 4, the president imposed a ban on federal funding of human cloning research. He called on America's privately sponsored scientists to refrain voluntarily from any work on human cloning until the federal bioethics advisory panel issued its findings. This appeal was necessary because human cloning was not declared illegal in the United States, as it has been in Britain. After considering the Commission's report, Clinton announced June 9, 1997, that he would seek the approval of Congress on new legislation that would "prohibit anyone in either public or private sectors from using these techniques to create a child." Stating that the new bill would "reaffirm our most cherished belief about the miracle of human life and the God-given individuality each person possesses," Clinton targeted human cloning as unethical. However, he emphasized his support for other scientific uses of cloning that would not be prohibited, such as cloning DNA in cells or the cloning of animals, since both techniques may aid in preventing diseases and in improving crop cultivation.

Another controversial issue that arose during the late 1990s and early 21st century involved the research use of stem cells. These cells are created in the earliest stages of cell division just after an egg has been fertilized. They are non-specific and therefore show great promise in developing into new organs or other parts of the body that could fight spinal cord injuries and diseases such as Alzheimer's and Parkinson's. Based on the idea that life begins when an egg is fertilized, the religious right objected to any use of any stem cells. The religious right formed an important constituency for President George W. Bush. On August 9, 2001, he announced highly limited criteria for federal funding of stem cell research: to qualify, the research had to be on stem cell "lines" created prior to his announcement and the embryo from which the stem cell line was derived no longer had the possibility of development as a human being. Moreover, the stem cells must have been derived from an embryo that was created for reproductive purposes; the embryo was no longer needed for these purposes; informed consent must have been obtained for the donation of the embryo; and no financial inducements could have been provided for donation of the embryo.

The President: Good morning. I'm glad to be joined this morning by the Vice President, Secretary Shalala, Dr. Harold Varmus, the head of NIH; Dr. Harold Shapiro, the President of Princeton and the Chairman of our Bioethics Advisory Commission; and Dr. Jack Gibbons, the President's Advisor on Science and Technology, all of whom know a lot about and care a lot about this issue we are discussing today.

The recent breakthrough in animal cloning is one that could yield enormous benefits, enabling us to reproduce the most productive strains of crop and livestock, holding out the promise of revolutionary new medical treatments and cures, helping to unlock the greatest secrets of the genetic code. But like the splitting of the atom, this is a discovery that carries burdens as well as benefits.

Science often moves faster than our ability to understand its implications. That is why we have a responsibility to move with caution and care to harness the powerful forces of science and technology so that we can reap the benefit while minimizing the potential danger.

This new discovery raises the troubling prospect that it might someday be possible to clone human beings from our own genetic material. There is much about cloning that we still do not know. But this much we do know: any discovery that touches upon human creation is not simply a matter of scientific inquiry, it is a matter of morality and spirituality as well.

My own view is that human cloning would have to raise deep concerns, given our most cherished concepts of faith and humanity. Each human life is unique, born of a miracle that reaches beyond laboratory science. I believe we must respect this profound gift and resist the temptation to replicate ourselves.

At the very least, however, we should all agree that we need a better understanding of the scope and implications of this most recent breakthrough. Last week, I asked our National Bioethics Advisory Commission, headed by President Harold Shapiro of Princeton, to conduct a thorough review of the legal and the ethical issues raised by this new cloning discovery, and to recommend possible actions to prevent its abuse, reporting back to me by the end of May.

In the meantime, I am taking further steps to prevent human cloning. The federal government currently restricts the use of federal funds for research involving human embryos. After reviewing these restrictions, our administration believes that there are loopholes that could allow the cloning of human beings if the technology were developed. Therefore, today I am issuing a directive that bans the use of any federal funds for any cloning of human beings.

Effective immediately, no federal agency may support, fund, or undertake such activity. Of course, a great deal of research and activity in this area is supported by private funds. That is why I am urging the entire scientific and medical community, every foundation, every university, every industry that supports work in this area to heed the federal government's example. I'm asking for a voluntary moratorium on the cloning of human beings until our Bioethics Advisory Commission and our entire nation have had a real chance to understand and debate the profound ethical implications of the latest advances.

As we gain a fuller understanding of this technology, we must proceed not just with caution, but also with a conscience, by insisting that not a single taxpayer dollar supports human cloning. And by urging a moratorium on all private research in this area, we can ensure that as we move forward on this issue, we weigh the concerns of faith and family and philosophy and values, not merely of science alone. Thank you very much.

Source:

Public Papers of the Presidents of the United States, William J. Clinton, 1997. Washington, D.C.: Government Printing Office, 1993–2001.

Social Developments

Lemon v. Kurtzman, 1971

The unanimous decision in this case of June 28, 1971, by the Burger Court (Brennan and White concurring in part and dissenting in part; Marshall not participating) set the stage for breaking down the wall of separation between church and state raised by Thomas Jefferson in 1802 and continued under the Rehnquist Court. Burger held that the establishment clause of the First Amendment "far from being a wall," was instead "blurred, indistinct, and a variable barrier depending on all the circumstances of a particular relationship."

The decision involved the constitutionality of Rhode Island and Pennsylvania acts allowing the state to support the salaries of teachers of secular subjects in parochial schools. In his opinion for the Court, Chief Justice Warren Burger established the "Lemon Test": "The cumulative criteria developed by the Court over many years," to determine the constitutionality of statutes under the First Amendment. Earlier Supreme Court cases determined that to be constitutional, laws involving religious matters must serve a secular legislative purpose and that in their primary effect they neither advance nor inhibit religion. To this Burger added an "excessive entanglement" provision: that unlike secular textbooks paid for by the state, instructors could "improperly involve faith and morals" while teaching secular subjects.

Another Rhode Island case, *Lynch v. Donnelly* (465 U.S. 668), decided March 5, 1984, instituted what has been called the "plastic reindeer" test. Pawtucket, like many cities across the United States, sponsored and funded a Christmas Nativity display. The 5-4 majority ruled that it did not violate the First Amendment doctrine of separation of church and state. The Christmas display also included the less sectarian reindeer, a Santa Claus house, and a Christmas tree. Because it did not have a strictly religious focus, it did not, according to the majority, represent a "real danger of establishment of a state church" through government recognition and support of religion in general. For the future, the courts would decide, on a case-by-case basis, whether practices or actions constitute establishment of a religion or mean to do so. In *Allegheny County v. American Civil Liberties Union* (492 U.S. 573 [1989]) the Court ruled that a creche by itself without other more secular symbols did violate the clause, hence the "plastic reindeer" test.

A 1992 5-4 decision, *Lee v. Weisman* (505 U.S. 577), ruled that even a nonsectarian prayer by the clergy at a public school ceremony, in this case, at a graduation, represented state action and therefore violated the establishment clause.

On June 23, 1997, the U.S. Supreme Court in *Agostini et al. v. Felton et al.* (521 U.S. 203) permitted public school teachers to tutor in religious schools. In its ruling, the Court held 5-4 that the establishment clause did not bar public school teachers from entering parochial schools to provide remedial education to underprivileged children. The decision overturned the precedent the Court had set in a 1985 case, *Aguilar v. Felton* (473 U.S. 402), in which the justices cited the establishment clause in prohibiting public employees from working in religious schools. At issue in *Agostini v. Felton* was New York City's efforts to spend a percentage of federal education monies they received on remedial instruction for poor children, including those in parochial schools. The *Aguilar* decision actually allowed public school teachers to instruct parochial school students but not on parochial school grounds. New York City then implemented a costly system of mobile classrooms parked outside parochial schools. In *Agostini,* the city sought a reversal of *Aguilar,* arguing that the 1985 ruling had forced it to divert money and time counterproductively from classroom teaching to the cumbersome logistics of the off-site tutoring program.

Two days after *Agostini,* the U.S. Supreme Court in *City of Boerne v. Flores, Archbishop of San Antonio, et al.* (117 S. Court 2197) overturned the Religious Freedom Restoration Act (RFRA), passed by Congress in 1993 in response to the Supreme Court's 1990 ruling in *Employment Div., Dept. of Human Resources of Ore. v. Smith* (494 U.S. 872) permitting Oregon to prohibit peyote use even for religious purposes. In that decision, the Court gave states greater leeway to restrict religious expression where it conflicted with public laws or other state prerogatives. The Court did so by relaxing the "compelling interest" standard that states previously had been required to apply when considering a limit on religion's free exercise. The RFRA required government at all levels to show compelling need before enforcing laws that "substantially burdened" religious practices. Congress claimed constitutional authority under the Fourteenth Amendment for defining religious liberty protections. The Court held that Congress exceeded its authority in RFRA and encroached on that of the judiciary by attempting to define the level of protection that the Constitution gave to religious expression. The majority asserted that such power to interpret the Constitution belonged exclusively to the judicial branch.

In a decision called the most important regarding religion in the schools in the last 40 years, the Court ruled 5-4, June 28, 2002, in *Zelman v. Simmons-Harris* (No. 00-1751), that Cleveland could use its vouchers for students to attend parochial schools. School vouchers had been offered as a way for the state to help pay tuition for students from substandard and failing public schools so that they could attend private schools, including those sponsored by a church. Because most students eligible for the vouchers could not afford independent school tuition even with the subsidies, over 90 percent of the Cleveland students used their vouchers for parochial schools.

MR. CHIEF JUSTICE BURGER delivered the opinion of the Court.

These two appeals raise questions as to Pennsylvania and Rhode Island statutes providing state aid to church-related elementary and secondary schools. Both statutes are challenged as violative of the Establishment and Free Exercise Clauses of the First Amendment and the Due Process Clause of the Fourteenth Amendment.

Pennsylvania has adopted a statutory program that provides financial support to nonpublic elementary and secondary schools by way of reimbursement for the cost of teachers' salaries, textbooks, and instructional materials in specified secular subjects. Rhode Island has adopted a statute under which the State pays directly to teachers in nonpublic elementary schools a supplement of 15% of their annual salary. Under each statute state aid has been given to church-related educational institutions. We hold that both statutes are unconstitutional.

I

The Rhode Island Statute

The Rhode Island Salary Supplement Act was enacted in 1969. It rests on the legislative finding that the quality of education available in nonpublic elementary schools has been jeopardized by the rapidly rising salaries needed to attract competent and dedicated teachers. The Act authorizes state officials to supplement the salaries of teachers of secular subjects in nonpublic elementary schools by paying directly to a teacher an amount not in excess of 15% of his current annual salary. As supplemented, however, a nonpublic school teacher's salary cannot exceed the maximum paid to teachers in the State's public schools, and the recipient must be certified by the state board of education in substantially the same manner as public school teachers.

In order to be eligible for the Rhode Island salary supplement, the recipient must teach in a nonpublic school at which the average per-pupil expenditure on secular education is less than the average in the State's public schools during a specified period. Appellant State Commissioner of Education also requires eligible schools to submit financial data. If this information indicates a per-pupil expenditure in excess of the statutory limitation, the records of the school in question must be examined in order to assess how much of the expenditure is attributable to secular education and how much to religious activity.

The Act also requires that teachers eligible for salary supplements must teach only those subjects that are offered in the State's public schools. They must use "only teaching materials which are used in the public schools." Finally, any teacher applying for a salary supplement must first agree in writing "not to teach a course in religion for so long as or during such time as he or she receives any salary supplements" under the Act.

Appellees are citizens and taxpayers of Rhode Island. They brought this suit to have the Rhode Island Salary Supplement Act declared unconstitutional and its operation enjoined on the ground that it violates the Establishment and Free Exercise Clauses of the First Amendment. Appellants are state officials charged with administration of the Act, teachers eligible for salary supplements under the Act, and parents of children in church-related elementary schools whose teachers would receive state salary assistance.

A three-judge federal court was convened pursuant to 28 U.S.C. 2281, 2284. It found that Rhode Island's nonpublic elementary schools accommodated approximately 25% of the State's pupils. About 95% of these pupils attended schools affiliated with the Roman Catholic church. To date some 250 teachers have applied for benefits under the Act. All of them are employed by Roman Catholic schools.

The court held a hearing at which extensive evidence was introduced concerning the nature of the secular instruction offered in the Roman Catholic schools whose teachers would be eligible for salary assistance under the Act. Although the court found that concern for religious values does not necessarily affect the content of secular subjects, it also found that the parochial school system was "an integral part of the religious mission of the Catholic Church."

The District Court concluded that the Act violated the Establishment Clause, holding that it fostered "excessive entanglement" between government and religion. In addition two judges thought that the Act had the impermissible effect of giving "significant aid to a religious enterprise." 316 F. Supp. 112. We affirm.

The Pennsylvania Statute

Pennsylvania has adopted a program that has some but not all of the features of the Rhode Island program. The Pennsylvania Nonpublic Elementary and Secondary Education Act was passed in 1968 in response to a crisis that the Pennsylvania Legislature found existed in the State's nonpublic schools due to rapidly rising costs. The statute affirmatively reflects the legislative conclusion that the State's educational goals could appropriately be fulfilled by government support of "those purely secular educational objectives achieved through nonpublic education. . . ."

The statute authorizes appellee state Superintendent of Public Instruction to "purchase" specified "secular educational services" from nonpublic schools. Under the "contracts" authorized by the statute, the State directly reimburses nonpublic schools solely for their actual expenditures for teachers' salaries, textbooks, and instructional materials. A school seeking reimbursement must maintain prescribed accounting procedures that identify the "separate" cost of the "secular educational service." These accounts are subject to state audit. The funds for this program were originally derived from a new tax on horse and harness racing, but the Act is now financed by a portion of the state tax on cigarettes.

There are several significant statutory restrictions on state aid. Reimbursement is limited to courses "presented in the curricula of the public schools." It is further limited "solely" to courses in the following "secular" subjects: mathematics, modern foreign languages, physical science, and physical education. Textbooks and instructional materials included in the program must be approved by the state Superintendent of Public Instruction. Finally, the statute prohibits reimbursement for any course that contains "any subject matter expressing religious teaching, or the morals or forms of worship of any sect."

The Act went into effect on July 1, 1968, and the first reimbursement payments to schools were made on September 2, 1969. It appears that some $5 million has been expended annually under the Act. The State has now entered into contracts with some 1,181 nonpublic elementary and secondary schools with a student population of some 535,215 pupils—more than 20% of the total number of students in the State. More than 96% of these pupils attend church-related schools, and most of these schools are affiliated with the Roman Catholic church.

Appellants brought this action in the District Court to challenge the constitutionality of the Pennsylvania statute. The organizational plaintiffs-appellants are associations of persons resident in Pennsylvania declaring belief in the separation of church and state; individual plaintiffs-appellants are citizens and taxpayers of Pennsylvania. Appellant Lemon, in addition to being a citizen and a taxpayer, is a parent of a child attending public school in Pennsylvania. Lemon also alleges that he purchased a ticket at a race track and thus had paid the specific tax that supports the expenditures under the Act. Appellees are state officials who have the responsibility for administering the Act. In addition seven church-related schools are defendants-appellees.

A three-judge federal court was convened pursuant to 28 U.S.C. 2281, 2284. The District Court held that the individual plaintiffs-appellants had standing to challenge the Act, 310 F. Supp. 42. The organizational plaintiffs-appellants were denied standing under Flast v. Cohen, 392 U.S. 83, 99, 101 (1968).

The court granted appellees' motion to dismiss the complaint for failure to state a claim for relief. 310 F. Supp. 35. It held that the Act violated neither the Establishment nor the Free Exercise Clause, Chief Judge Hastie dissenting. We reverse.

II

In *Everson v. Board of Education,* 330 U.S. 1 (1947), this Court upheld a state statute that reimbursed the parents of parochial school children for bus transportation expenses. There MR. JUSTICE BLACK, writing for the majority, suggested that the decision carried to "the verge" of forbidden territory under the Religion Clauses. Id., at 16. Candor compels acknowledgment, moreover, that we can only dimly perceive the lines of demarcation in this extraordinarily sensitive area of constitutional law.

The language of the Religion Clauses of the First Amendment is at best opaque, particularly when compared with other portions of the Amendment. Its authors did not simply prohibit the establishment of a state church or a state religion, an area history shows they regarded as very important and fraught with great dangers. Instead they commanded that there should be "no law respecting an establishment of religion." A law may be one "respecting" the forbidden objective while falling short of its total realization. A law "respecting" the proscribed result, that is, the establishment of religion, is not always easily identifiable as one violative of the Clause. A given law might not establish a state religion but nevertheless be one "respecting" that end in the sense of being a step that could lead to such establishment and hence offend the First Amendment.

In the absence of precisely stated constitutional prohibitions, we must draw lines with reference to the three main evils against which the Establishment Clause was intended to afford protection: "sponsorship, financial support, and active involvement of the sovereign in religious activity." *Walz v. Tax Commission,* 397 U.S. 664, 668 (1970).

Every analysis in this area must begin with consideration of the cumulative criteria developed by the Court over many years. Three such tests may be gleaned from our cases. First, the statute must have a secular legislative purpose; second, its principal or primary effect must be one that neither advances nor inhibits religion, *Board of Education v. Allen,* 392 U.S. 236, 243 (1968); finally, the statute must not foster "an excessive government entanglement with religion." *Walz,* supra, at 674.

Inquiry into the legislative purposes of the Pennsylvania and Rhode Island statutes affords no basis for a conclusion that the legislative intent was to advance religion. On the contrary, the statutes themselves clearly state that they are intended to enhance the quality of the secular education in all schools covered by the compulsory attendance laws. There is no reason to believe the legislatures meant anything else. A State always has a legitimate concern for maintaining minimum standards in all schools it allows to operate. As in Allen, we find nothing here that undermines the stated legislative intent; it must therefore be accorded appropriate deference.

In Allen the Court acknowledged that secular and religious teachings were not necessarily so intertwined that secular textbooks furnished to students by the State were in fact instrumental in the teaching of religion. 392 U.S., at 248. The legislatures of Rhode Island and Pennsylvania have concluded that secular and religious education are identifiable and separable. In the abstract we have no quarrel with this conclusion.

The two legislatures, however, have also recognized that church-related elementary and secondary schools have a significant religious mission and that a substantial portion of their activities is religiously oriented. They have therefore sought to create statutory restrictions designed to guarantee the separation between secular and religious educational functions and to ensure that State financial aid supports only the former. All these provisions are precautions taken in candid recognition that these programs approached, even if they did not intrude upon, the forbidden areas under the Religion Clauses. We need not decide whether these legislative precautions restrict the principal or primary effect of the programs to the point where they do not offend the Religion Clauses, for we conclude that the cumulative impact of the entire relationship arising under the statutes in each State involves excessive entanglement between government and religion.

III

In *Walz v. Tax Commission*, supra, the Court upheld state tax exemptions for real property owned by religious organizations and used for religious worship. That holding, however, tended to confine rather than enlarge the area of permissible state involvement with religious institutions by calling for close scrutiny of the degree of entanglement involved in the relationship. The objective is to prevent, as far as possible, the intrusion of either into the precincts of the other.

Our prior holdings do not call for total separation between church and state; total separation is not possible in an absolute sense. Some relationship between government and religious organizations is inevitable. *Zorach v. Clauson*, 343 U.S. 306, 312 (1952); *Sherbert v. Verner*, 374 U.S. 398, 422 (1963) (HARLAN, J., dissenting). Fire inspections, building and zoning regulations, and state requirements under compulsory school-attendance laws are examples of necessary and permissible contacts. Indeed, under the statutory exemption before us in *Walz*, the State had a continuing burden to ascertain that the exempt property was in fact being used for religious worship. Judicial caveats against entanglement must recognize that the line of separation, far from being a "wall," is a blurred, indistinct, and variable barrier depending on all the circumstances of a particular relationship.

This is not to suggest, however, that we are to engage in a legalistic minuet in which precise rules and forms must govern. A true minuet is a matter of pure form and style, the observance of which is itself the substantive end. Here we examine the form of the relationship for the light that it casts on the substance.

In order to determine whether the government entanglement with religion is excessive, we must examine the character and purposes of the institutions that are benefited, the nature of the aid that the State provides, and the resulting relationship between the government and the religious authority. MR. JUSTICE HARLAN, in a separate opinion in *Walz*, supra, echoed the classic warning as to "programs, whose very nature is apt to entangle the state in details of administration. . . ." Id., at 695. Here we find that both statutes foster an impermissible degree of entanglement.

(A) Rhode Island Program

The District Court made extensive findings on the grave potential for excessive entanglement that inheres in the religious character and purpose of the Roman Catholic elementary schools of Rhode Island, to date the sole beneficiaries of the Rhode Island Salary Supplement Act.

The church schools involved in the program are located close to parish churches. This understandably permits convenient access for religious exercises since instruction in faith and morals is part of the total educational process. The school buildings contain identifying religious symbols such as crosses on the exterior and crucifixes, and religious paintings and statues either in the classrooms or hallways. Although only approximately 30 minutes a day are devoted to direct religious instruction, there are religiously oriented extracurricular activities. Approximately two-thirds of the teachers in these schools are nuns of various religious orders. Their dedicated efforts provide an atmosphere in which religious instruction and religious vocations are natural and proper parts of life in such schools. Indeed, as the District Court found, the role of teaching nuns in enhancing the religious atmosphere has led the parochial school authorities to attempt to maintain a one-to-one ratio between nuns and lay teachers in all schools rather than to permit some to be staffed almost entirely by lay teachers.

On the basis of these findings the District Court concluded that the parochial schools constituted "an integral part of the religious mission of the Catholic Church." The various characteristics of the schools make them "a powerful vehicle for transmitting the Catholic faith to the next generation." This process of inculcating religious doctrine is, of course, enhanced by the impressionable age of the pupils, in primary schools particularly. In short, parochial schools involve substantial religious activity and purpose.

The substantial religious character of these church-related schools gives rise to entangling church-state relationships of the kind the Religion Clauses sought to avoid. Although the District Court found that concern for religious values did not inevitably or necessarily intrude into the content of secular subjects, the considerable religious activities of these schools led the legislature to provide for careful governmental controls and surveillance by state authorities in order to ensure that state aid supports only secular education.

The dangers and corresponding entanglements are enhanced by the particular form of aid that the Rhode Island Act provides. Our decisions from *Everson* to *Allen* have permitted the States to provide church-related schools with secular, neutral, or nonideological services, facilities, or materials. Bus transportation, school lunches, public health services, and secular textbooks supplied in common to all students were not thought to offend the Establishment Clause. We note that the dissenters in *Allen* seemed chiefly concerned with the pragmatic difficulties involved in ensuring the truly secular content of the textbooks provided at state expense.

In *Allen* the Court refused to make assumptions, on a meager record, about the religious content of the textbooks that the State would be asked to provide. We cannot, however, refuse here to recognize that teachers have a substantially different ideological character from books. In terms of potential for involving some aspect of faith or morals in secular subjects, a textbook's content is ascertainable, but a teacher's handling of a subject is not. We cannot ignore the danger that a teacher under religious control and discipline poses to the separation of the religious from the purely secular aspects of pre-college education. The conflict of functions inheres in the situation.

In our view the record shows these dangers are present to a substantial degree. The Rhode Island Roman Catholic elementary schools are under the general supervision of the Bishop of Providence and his appointed representative, the Diocesan Superintendent of Schools. In most cases, each individual parish, however, assumes the ultimate financial responsibility for the school, with the parish priest authorizing the allocation of parish funds. With only two exceptions, school principals are nuns appointed either by the Superintendent or the Mother Provincial of the order whose members staff the school. By 1969 lay teachers constituted more than a third of all teachers in the parochial elementary schools, and their number is growing. They are first interviewed by the superintendent's office and then by the school principal. The contracts are signed by the parish priest, and he retains some discretion in negotiating salary levels. Religious authority necessarily pervades the school system.

The schools are governed by the standards set forth in a "Handbook of School Regulations," which has the force of synodal law in the diocese. It emphasizes the role and importance of the teacher in parochial schools: "The prime factor for the success or the failure of the school is the spirit and personality, as well as the professional competency, of the teacher. . . ." The Handbook also states that: "Religious formation is not confined to formal courses; nor is it restricted to a single subject area." Finally, the Handbook advises teachers to stimulate interest in religious vocations and missionary work. Given the mission of the church school, these instructions are consistent and logical.

Several teachers testified, however, that they did not inject religion into their secular classes. And the District Court found that religious values did not necessarily affect the content of the secular instruction. But what has been recounted suggests the potential if not actual hazards of this form of state aid. The teacher is employed by a religious organization, subject to the direction and discipline of religious authorities, and works in a system dedicated to rearing children in a particular faith. These controls are not lessened by the fact that most of the lay teachers are of the Catholic faith. Inevitably some of a teacher's responsibilities hover on the border between secular and religious orientation.

We need not and do not assume that teachers in parochial schools will be guilty of bad faith or any conscious design to evade the limitations imposed by the statute and the First Amendment. We simply recognize that a dedicated religious person, teaching in a school affiliated with his or her faith and operated to inculcate its tenets, will inevitably experience great difficulty in remaining religiously neutral. Doctrines and faith are not inculcated or advanced by neutrals. With the best of intentions such a teacher would find it hard to make a total separation between secular teaching and religious doctrine. What would appear to some to be essential to good citizenship might well for others border on or constitute instruction in religion. Further difficulties are inherent in the combination of religious discipline and the possibility of disagreement between teacher and religious authorities over the meaning of the statutory restrictions.

We do not assume, however, that parochial school teachers will be unsuccessful in their attempts to segregate their religious beliefs from their secular educational responsibilities. But the potential for impermissible fostering of religion is present. The Rhode Island Legislature has not, and could not, provide state aid on the basis of a mere assumption that secular teachers under religious discipline can avoid conflicts. The State must be certain, given the Religion Clauses, that subsidized teachers do not inculcate religion—indeed the State here has undertaken to do so. To ensure that no trespass occurs, the State has therefore carefully conditioned its aid with pervasive restrictions. An eligible recipient must teach only those courses that are offered in the public schools and use only those texts and materials that are found in the public schools. In addition the teacher must not engage in teaching any course in religion.

A comprehensive, discriminating, and continuing state surveillance will inevitably be required to ensure that these restrictions are obeyed and the First Amendment otherwise respected. Unlike a book, a teacher cannot be inspected once so as to determine the extent and intent of his or her personal beliefs and subjective acceptance of the limitations imposed by the First Amendment. These prophylactic contacts will involve excessive and enduring entanglement between state and church.

There is another area of entanglement in the Rhode Island program that gives concern. The statute excludes teachers employed by nonpublic schools whose average per-pupil expenditures on secular education equal or exceed the comparable figures for public schools. In the event that the total expenditures of an otherwise eligible school exceed this norm, the program requires the government to examine the school's records in order to determine how much of the total expenditures is attributable to secular education and how much to religious activity. This kind of state inspection and evaluation of the religious content of a religious organization is fraught with the sort of entanglement that the Constitution forbids. It is a relationship pregnant with dangers of excessive government direction of church schools and hence of churches. The Court noted "the hazards of government supporting churches" in *Walz v. Tax Commission,* supra, at 675, and we cannot ignore here the danger that pervasive modern governmental power will ultimately intrude on religion and thus conflict with the Religion Clauses.

(B) Pennsylvania Program

The Pennsylvania statute also provides state aid to church-related schools for teachers' salaries. The complaint describes an educational system that is very similar to the one existing in Rhode Island. According to the allegations, the church-related elementary and secondary schools are controlled by religious organizations, have the purpose of propagating and promoting a particular religious faith, and conduct their operations to fulfill that purpose. Since this complaint was dismissed for failure to state a claim for relief, we must accept these allegations as true for purposes of our review.

As we noted earlier, the very restrictions and surveillance necessary to ensure that teachers play a strictly nonideological role give rise to entanglements between church and state. The Pennsylvania statute, like that of Rhode Island, fosters this kind of relationship. Reimbursement is not only limited to courses offered in the public schools and materials approved by state officials, but the statute excludes "any subject matter expressing religious teaching, or the morals or forms of worship of any sect." In addition, schools seeking reimbursement must maintain accounting procedures that require the State to establish the cost of the secular as distinguished from the religious instruction.

The Pennsylvania statute, moreover, has the further defect of providing state financial aid directly to the church-related school. This factor distinguishes both *Everson* and *Allen,* for in both those cases the Court was careful to point out that state aid was provided to the student and his parents—not to the church-related school. *Board of Education v. Allen,* supra, at 243–244; *Everson v. Board of Education,* supra, at 18. In Walz v. Tax Commission, supra, at 675, the Court warned of the dangers of direct payments to religious organizations:

> "Obviously a direct money subsidy would be a relationship pregnant with involvement and, as with most governmental grant programs, could encompass sustained and detailed administrative relationships for enforcement of statutory or administrative standards. . . ."

The history of government grants of a continuing cash subsidy indicates that such programs have almost always been accompanied by varying measures of control and surveillance. The government cash grants before us now provide no basis for predicting that comprehensive measures of surveillance and controls will not follow. In particular the government's post-audit power to inspect and evaluate a church-related school's financial records and to determine which expenditures are religious and which are secular creates an intimate and continuing relationship between church and state.

IV

A broader base of entanglement of yet a different character is presented by the divisive political potential of these state programs. In a community where such a large number of pupils are served by church-related schools, it can be assumed that state assistance will entail considerable political activity. Partisans of parochial schools, understandably concerned with rising costs and sincerely dedicated to both the religious and secular educational missions of their schools, will inevitably champion this cause and promote political action to achieve their goals. Those who oppose state aid, whether for constitutional, religious, or fiscal reasons, will inevitably respond and employ all of the usual political campaign techniques to prevail. Candidates will be forced to declare and voters to choose. It would be unrealistic to ignore the fact that many people confronted with issues of this kind will find their votes aligned with their faith.

Ordinarily political debate and division, however vigorous or even partisan, are normal and healthy manifestations of our democratic system of government, but political division along religious lines was one of the principal evils against which the First Amendment was intended to protect. Freund, Comment, Public Aid to Parochial Schools, 82 Harv. L. Rev. 1680, 1692 (1969). The potential divisiveness of such conflict is a threat to the normal political process. *Walz v. Tax Commission*, supra, at 695 (separate opinion of HARLAN, J.). See also *Board of Education v. Allen*, 392 U.S., at 249 (HARLAN, J., concurring); *Abington School District v. Schempp*, 374 U.S. 203, 307 (1963) (Goldberg, J., concurring). To have States or communities divide on the issues presented by state aid to parochial schools would tend to confuse and obscure other issues of great urgency. We have an expanding array of vexing issues, local and national, domestic and international, to debate and divide on. It conflicts with our whole history and tradition to permit questions of the Religion Clauses to assume such importance in our legislatures and in our elections that they could divert attention from the myriad issues and problems that confront every level of government. The highways of church and state relationships are not likely to be one-way streets, and the Constitution's authors sought to protect religious worship from the pervasive power of government. The history of many countries attests to the hazards of religion's intruding into the political arena or of political power intruding into the legitimate and free exercise of religious belief.

Of course, as the Court noted in *Walz*, "[a]dherents of particular faiths and individual churches frequently take strong positions on public issues." *Walz v. Tax Commission*, supra, at 670. We could not expect otherwise, for religious values pervade the fabric of our national life. But in *Walz* we dealt with a status under state tax laws for the benefit of all religious groups. Here we are confronted with successive and very likely permanent annual appropriations that benefit relatively few religious groups. Political fragmentation and divisiveness on religious lines are thus likely to be intensified.

The potential for political divisiveness related to religious belief and practice is aggravated in these two statutory programs by the need for continuing annual appropriations and the likelihood of larger and larger demands as costs and populations grow. The Rhode Island District Court found that the parochial school system's "monumental and deepening financial crisis" would "inescapably" require larger annual appropriations subsidizing greater percentages of the salaries of lay teachers. Although no facts have been developed in this respect in the Pennsylvania case, it appears that such pressures for expanding aid have already required the state legislature to include a portion of the state revenues from cigarette taxes in the program.

V

In *Walz* it was argued that a tax exemption for places of religious worship would prove to be the first step in an inevitable progression leading to the establishment of state churches and state religion. That claim could not stand up against more than 200 years of virtually universal practice imbedded in our colonial experience and continuing into the present.

The progression argument, however, is more persuasive here. We have no long history of state aid to church-related educational institutions comparable to 200 years of tax exemption for churches. Indeed, the state programs before us today represent something of an innovation. We have already noted that modern governmental programs have self-perpetuating and self-expanding propensities. These internal pressures are only enhanced when the schemes involve institutions whose legitimate needs are growing and whose interests have substantial political support. Nor can we fail to see that in constitutional adjudication some steps, which when taken were thought to approach "the verge," have become the platform for yet further steps. A certain momentum develops in constitutional theory and it can be a "downhill thrust" easily set in motion but difficult to retard or stop. Development by momentum is not invariably bad; indeed, it is the way the common law has grown, but it is a force to be recognized and reckoned with. The dangers are increased by the difficulty of perceiving in advance exactly where the "verge" of the precipice lies. As well as constituting an independent evil against which the Religion Clauses were intended to protect, involvement or entanglement between government and religion serves as a warning signal.

Finally, nothing we have said can be construed to disparage the role of church-related elementary and secondary schools in our national life. Their contribution has been and is enormous. Nor do we ignore their economic plight in a period of rising costs and expanding need. Taxpayers generally have been spared vast sums by the maintenance of these educational institutions by religious organizations, largely by the gifts of faithful adherents.

The merit and benefits of these schools, however, are not the issue before us in these cases. The sole question is whether state aid to these schools can be squared with the dictates of the Religion Clauses. Under our system the choice has been made that government is to be entirely excluded from the area of religious instruction and churches excluded from the affairs of government. The Constitution decrees that religion must be a private matter for the individual, the family, and the institutions of private choice, and that while some involvement and entanglement are inevitable, lines must be drawn.

The judgment of the Rhode Island District Court in No. 569 and No. 570 is affirmed. The judgment of the Pennsylvania District Court in No. 89 is reversed, and the case is remanded for further proceedings consistent with this opinion.

Source:

Supreme Court Reporter, Vol. 91, pp. 2,105–2,111.

University of California Regents v. Allan P. Bakke, 1978

U.S. Supreme Court decision, issued June 28, 1978, that by 5-4 ordered Allan P. Bakke to be admitted to the University of California Medical School at Davis because the school's racial quota plan was inflexibly and unjustifiably biased against white applicants like him. At the same time, in another 5-4 decision, the Court upheld the constitutionality of college admissions' affirmative actions to give advantage to blacks and other minorities to redress past discrimination against them. Bakke had sued the university, claiming "reverse discrimination" after being rejected for admission twice, though his grade average exceeded that of some "disadvantaged students" who had been admitted. *Bakke* was, in many ways, indecisive. The majority supported consideration of race in an admissions process as long as no quota was involved. But the justices filed six separate opinions. Four upheld Bakke's admission based on Title VI, which prohibited the exclusion of individuals from public programs on racial grounds; four agreed that "heightened" scrutiny was in order concerning racial discrimination. Justice Powell agreed with both positions and wrote the opinion for the Court.

Mr. Justice Powell announced the judgment of the Court.

This case presents a challenge to the special admissions program of the petitioner, the Medical School of the University of California at Davis, which is designed to assure the admission of a specified number of students from certain minority groups. The Superior Court of California sustained respondent's challenge, holding that petitioner's program violated the California Constitution, Title VI of the Civil Rights Act of 1964, and the Equal Protection Clause of the Fourteenth Amendment. The Court enjoined petitioner from considering respondent's race or the race of any other applicant in making admissions decisions. It refused, however, to order respondent's admission to the Medical School, holding that he had not carried his burden of proving that he would have been admitted but for the constitutional and statutory violations. The Supreme Court of California affirmed those portions of the trial court's judgment declaring the special admissions program unlawful and enjoining petitioner from considering the race of any applicant. It modified that portion of the judgment denying respondent's requested injunction and directed the trial court to order his admission.

For the reasons stated in the following opinion, I believe that so much of the judgment of the California court as holds petitioner's special admissions program unlawful and directs that respondent be admitted to the Medical School must be affirmed. For the reasons expressed in a separate opinion, my Brothers The Chief Justice, Mr. Justice Stewart, Mr. Justice Rehnquist and Mr. Justice Stevens concur in this judgment.

I also conclude for the reasons stated in the following opinion that the portion of the court's judgment enjoining petitioner from according any consideration to race in its admissions process must be reversed. For reasons expressed in separate opinions, my Brothers Mr. Justice Brennan, Mr. Justice White, Mr. Justice Marshall, and Mr. Justice Blackmun concur in this judgment.

Affirmed in part and reversed in part.

I

The Medical School of the University of California at Davis opened in 1968 with an entering class of 50 students. In 1971, the size of the entering class was increased to 100 students, a level at which it remains. No admissions program for disadvantaged or minority students existed when the school opened, and the first class contained three Asians but no blacks, no Mexican-Americans, and no American Indians. Over the next two years, the faculty devised a special admissions program to increase the representation of "disadvantaged" students in each Medical School class. The special program consisted of a separate admissions system operating in coordination with the regular admissions process.

Under the regular admissions procedure, a candidate could submit his application to the Medical School beginning in July of the year preceding the academic year for which admission was sought. Because of the large number of applications, the admissions committee screened each one to select candidates for further consideration. Candidates whose overall undergraduate grade point average fell below 2.5 on a scale of 4.0 were summarily rejected. About one out of six applicants was invited for a personal interview. Following the interviews, each candidate was rated on a scale of 1 to 100 by his interviewers and four other members of the admissions committee. The rating embraced the interviewers' summaries, the candidate's overall grade point average, grade point average in science courses, scores on the Medical College Admissions Test (MCAT), letters of recommendation, extracurricular activities, and other biographical data. The ratings were added together to arrive at each candidate's "benchmark" score. In 1973, five members rated each candidate, so that a perfect score was 500; in 1974, six members rated each candidate, so that a perfect score was 600. The full committee then reviewed the file and scores of each applicant and made offers of admission on a "rolling" basis. The chairman was responsible for placing names on the waiting list. They were not placed in strict numerical order; instead, the chairman had discretion to include persons with "special skills."

The special admissions program operated with a separate committee, a majority of whom were members of minority groups. On the 1973 application form, candidates were asked to indicate whether they wished to be considered as "economically and/or educationally disadvantaged" applicants; on the 1974 form the question was whether they wished to be considered as members of a "minority group," which the Medical School apparently viewed as "Blacks," "Chicanos," "Asians," and "American Indians." If these questions were answered affirmatively, the application was forwarded to the special admissions committee. No formal definition of "disadvantaged" was ever produced, but the chairman of the special committee screened each application to see whether it reflected economic or educational deprivation. Having passed this initial hurdle, the applications them were rated by the special committee in a fashion similar to that used by the general admissions committee, except that special candidates did not have to meet the 2.5 grade point average cutoff applied to regular applicants. About one-fifth of the total number of special applicants were invited for interviews in 1973 and 1974. Following each interview, the special committee assigned each special applicant a benchmark score. The special committee then presented its top choices to the general admissions committee. The latter did not rate or compare the special candidates against the general applicants, but could reject recommended special candidates for failure to meet course requirements for other specific deficiencies. The special committee continued to recommend special applicants until a number prescribed by faculty vote were admitted. While the overall class size was still 50, the prescribed number was 8; in 1973 and 1974, when the class size had doubled to 100, the prescribed number of special admissions also doubled, to 16.

From the year of the increase in class size—1971—through 1974, the special program resulted in the admission of 21 black students, 30 Mexican-Americans, and 12 Asians, for a total of 63 minority students. Over the same period, the regular admissions program produced 1 black, 6 Mexican-Americans, and 37 Asians, for a total of 44 minority students. Although disadvantaged whites applied to the special program in large numbers . . . none received an offer of admission through that process. Indeed, in 1974, at least, the special committee explicitly considered only "disadvantaged" special applicants who were members of one of the designated minority groups.

Allan Bakke is a white male who applied to the Davis Medical School in both 1973 and 1974. In both years Bakke's application was considered under the general admissions program, and he received an interview. His 1973 interview was with Dr. Theodore C. West, who considered Bakke "a very desirable applicant to [the] medical school." Despite a strong benchmark score of 468 out of 500, Bakke was rejected. His application had come late in the year, and no applicants in the general admissions process with scores below 470 were accepted after Bakke's application was completed. There were four special admissions slots unfilled at that time however, for which Bakke was not considered. After his 1973 rejection, Bakke wrote to Dr. George H. Lowrey, Associate Dean and Chairman of the Admissions Committee, protesting that the special admissions program operated as a racial and ethnic quota.

Bakke's 1974 application was completed early in the year. His student interviewer gave him an overall rating of 94, finding him "friendly, well tempered, conscientious and delightful to speak with." His faculty interviewer was, by coincidence. the same Dr. Lowrey to whom he had written in protest of the special admissions program. Dr. Lowrey found Bakke "rather limited in this approach" to the problems of the medical profession and found disturbing Bakke's "very definite opinions which were based more on his personal viewpoints than upon a study of the total problem." Dr. Lowrey gave Bakke the lowest of his six ratings, an 86; his total was 549 out of 600. Again, Bakke's application was rejected. In neither year did the chairman of the admissions committee, Dr. Lowrey, exercise his discretion to place Bakke on the waiting list. In both years, applicants were admitted under the special program with grade point averages, MCAT scores, and benchmark scores significantly lower than Bakke's.

After the second rejection, Bakke filed the instant suit in the Superior Court of California. He sought mandatory, injunctive, and declaratory relief compelling his admission to the Medical School. He alleged that the Medical

School's special admissions program operated to exclude him from the school on the basis of his race, in violation of his rights under the Equal Protection Clause of the Fourteenth Amendment, Art. I, Section 21, of the California Constitution, and Section 601 of Title VI of the Civil Rights Act of 1964. . . . The University cross-complained for a declaration that its special admissions program was lawful. The trial court found that the special program operated as a racial quota, because minority applicants in the special program were rated only against one other and 16 places in the class of 100 were reserved for them. Declaring that the University could not take race into account in making admissions decisions, the trial court held the challenged program violative of the Federal Constitution, the State Constitution, and Title VI. The court refused to order Bakke's admission, however, holding that he had failed to carry his burden of proving that he would have been admitted but for the existence of the special program.

Bakke appealed from the portion of the trial court judgment denying him admission, and the University appealed from the decision that its special admissions program was unlawful and the order enjoining it from considering race in the processing of applications. The Supreme Court of California transferred the case directly from the trial court, "because of the importance of the issues involved." The California court accepted the findings of the trial court with respect to the University's program. Because the special admissions program involved a racial classification, the Supreme Court held itself bound to apply strict scrutiny. It then turned to the goals the University presented as justifying the special program. Although the court agreed that the goals of integrating the medical profession and increasing the number of physicians willing to serve members of minority groups were compelling state interests, it concluded that the special admissions program was not the least intrusive means of achieving those goals. Without passing on the state constitutional or the federal statutory grounds cited in the trial court's judgment, the California court held that the Equal Protection Clause of the Fourteenth Amendment required that "no applicant may be rejected because of his race, in favor of another who is less qualified, as measured by standards applied without regard to race."

Turning to Bakke's appeal, the court ruled that since Bakke had established that the University had discriminated against him on the basis of his race, the burden of proof shifted to the University to demonstrate that he would not have been admitted even in the absence of the special admissions program. The court analogized Bakke's situation to that of a plaintiff under Title VII of the Civil Rights Act of 1964. On this basis, the court initially ordered a remand for the purpose of determining whether, under the newly allocated burden of proof, Bakke would have been admitted to either the 1973 or the 1974 entering class in the absence of the special admissions program. In its petition for rehearing . . . however, the University conceded its inability to carry that burden. The California court thereupon amended its opinion to direct that the trial court enter judgment ordering Bakke's admission to the Medical School. That order was stayed pending review in this Court. We granted certiorari to consider the important constitutional issue.

II

In this Court the parties . . . focused exclusively upon the validity of the special admissions program under the Equal Protection Clause. Because it was possible, however, that a decision on Title VI might obviate resort to constitutional interpretation, we requested supplementary briefing on the statutory issue.

A

At the outset we face the question whether a right of action for private parties exists under Title VI. Respondent argues that there is a private right of action. . . . We find its unnecessary to resolve this question in the instant case. The question of respondent's right to bring an action under Title VI was neither argued nor decided in either of the courts below, and this Court has been hesitant to review questions not addressed below. . . . Similarly, we need not pass upon petitioner's claim that private plaintiffs under Title VI must exhaust administrative remedies. We assume, only for the purposes of this case, that respondent has a right of action under Title VI.

B

The language of Section 601, 78 Stat. 252, like that of the Equal Protection Clause, is majestic in its sweep:

"No person in the United States shall, on the ground of race, color, or national origin, be excluded from participation in, be denied in the benefits of, or be subjected to discrimination under any program or activity receiving Federal financial assistance."

The concept of "discrimination," like the phrase "equal protection of the laws," is susceptible of varying interpretations. . . . Examination of the voluminous legislative history of Title VI reveals a congressional intent to halt federal funding of entities that violate a prohibition of racial discrimination similar to that of the Constitution. Although isolated statements of various legislators taken out of context, can be marshaled in support of the proposition that Section 601 enacted a purely color-blind scheme, without regard to the reach of the Equal Protection Clause, these comments must be read against the background of both the problem that Congress was addressing and the broader view of the statute that emerges from a full examination of the legislative debates.

The problem confronting Congress was discrimination against Negro citizens at the hands of recipients of federal moneys. . . . Over and over again, proponents of the bill detailed the plight of Negroes seeking equal treatment in such programs. . . .The legislators were dealing with the real and pressing problem of how to guarantee those citizens equal treatment.

In addressing that problem, supporters of Title VI repeatedly declared that the bill enacted constitutional principles.

* * *

Further evidence of the incorporation of a constitutional standard into Title VI appears in the repeated refusals of the legislation's supporters precisely to define the term "discrimination." Opponents sharply criticized this failure, but proponents of the bill merely replied that the meaning of "discrimination" would be made clear by reference to the Constitution or other existing law. . . .

In view of the clear legislative intent, Title VI must be held to proscribe only those racial classifications that would violate the Equal Protection Clause or the Fifth Amendment.

III A

Petitioner does not deny that decisions based on race or ethnic origin by faculties and administrations of state universities are reviewable under the Fourteenth Amendment. For his part, respondent does not argue that all racial or ethnic classifications are per se invalid. The parties do disagree as to the level of judicial scrutiny to be applied to the special admissions program. Petitioner argues that the court below erred in applying strict scrutiny, as this inexact term has been applied in our cases. That level of review, petitioner asserts, should be reserved for classifications that disadvantage "discrete and insular minorities." Respondent, on the other hand, contends that the California court correctly rejected the notion that the degree of judicial scrutiny accorded a particular racial or ethnic classification hinges upon membership in a discrete and insular minority and duly recognized that the "rights established [by the Fourteenth Amendment] are personal rights."

En route to this actual battle over the scope of judicial review, the parties fight a sharp preliminary action over the proper characterization of the special admissions program. Petitioner prefers to view it as establishing a "goal" of minority representation in the Medical School. Respondent, echoing the courts below, labels it a racial quota.

This semantic distinction is beside the point: The special admissions program is undeniably a classification based on race and ethnic background. To the extent that there existed a pool of at least minimally qualified minority applicants to fill the 16 special admissions seats, white applicants could compete only for 84 seats in the entering class, rather than the 100 open to minority applicants. Whether this limitation is described as a quota or a goal, it is a line drawn on the basis of race and ethnic status.

The guarantees of the Fourteenth Amendment extend to all persons. Its language is explicit: "No State shall . . . deny to any person within its jurisdiction the equal protection of the laws." It is settled beyond question that the "rights created by the first section of the Fourteenth Amendment are, by its terms, guaranteed to the individual. The rights established are personal rights." The guarantee of equal protection cannot mean one thing when applied to one individual and something else when applied to a person of another color. If both are not accorded the same protection, then it is not equal.

Nevertheless, petitioner argues that the court below erred in applying strict scrutiny to the special admissions program because white males, such as respondent, are not a "discrete and insular minority" requiring extraordinary protection from the majoritarian political process. This rationale, however, has never been invoked in our decisions as a prerequisite to subjecting racial or ethnic distinctions to strict scrutiny. Nor has this Court held that discreteness and insularity constituted necessary preconditions to a holding that a particular classification is invidious. These characteristics may be relevant in deciding whether or not to add new types of classifications to the list of "suspect" categories or whether a particular classification survives close examination. Racial and ethnic classifications, however, are subject to stringent examination without regard to these additional characteristics. We declared as much in the first cases explicitly to recognize racial distinctions as suspect.

* * *

The Court has never questioned the validity of those pronouncements. Racial and ethnic distinctions of any sort are inherently suspect and thus call for the most exacting judicial examination.

B

This perception of racial and ethnic distinctions is rooted in our Nation's constitutional and demographic history. The Court's initial view of the Fourteenth Amendment was that its "one pervading purpose" was the "the freedom of the slave race, the security and firm establishment of that freedom, and the protection of the newly-made freeman and citizen from the oppressions of those who had formerly exercised dominion over him." The Equal Protection Clause, however, was "[v]irtually strangled in infancy by post-civil-war judicial reactionism." It was relegated to decades of relative desuetude while the Due Process Clause of the Fourteenth Amendment, after a short germinal period, flourished as a cornerstone in the Court's defense of property and liberty of contract. In that cause, the Fourteenth Amendment's "one pervading purpose" was displaced. It was only as the era of substantive due process came to a close that the Equal Protection Clause began to attain a genuine measure of vitality.

By that time it was no longer possible to peg the guarantees of the Fourteenth Amendment to the struggle for equality of one racial minority. During the dormancy of the Equal Protection Clause, the United States had become a Nation of minorities. Each had to struggle—and to some extent struggles still—to overcome the prejudices not of a monolithic majority, but of a "majority" composed of various minority groups of whom it was said—perhaps unfairly in many cases—that a shared characteristic was a willingness to disadvantage other groups. As the Nation filed with the stock of many lands, the reach of the Clause was gradually extended to all ethnic groups seeking protection from official discrimination. . . .

Although many of the Framers of the Fourteenth Amendment conceived of its primary function as bridging the vast distance between members of the Negro race and the white "majority," the Amendment itself was framed in universal terms, without reference to color, ethnic origin, or condition of prior servitude. As this Court recently remarked in interpreting the 1866 Civil Rights Act to extend to claims of racial discrimination against white persons, "the 39th Congress was intent upon establishing in the federal law a broader principle than would have been necessary simply to meet the particular and immediate plight of the newly freed Negro slaves." And that legislation was specifically broadened in 1870 to ensure that "all persons," not merely "citizens," would enjoy equal rights under the law. Indeed, it is not unlikely that among the Framers were many who would have applauded a reading of the Equal Protection Clause that states a principle of universal application and is responsive to the racial, ethnic, and cultural diversity of the Nation.

Over the past 30 years, this Court has embarked upon the crucial mission of interpreting the Equal Protection Clause with the view of assuring to all persons "the protection of equal laws. . . ." Because the landmark decisions in this area arose in response to the continued exclusion of Negroes from the mainstream of American society, they could be characterized as involving discrimination by the "majority" white race against the Negro minority. But they need not be read as depending upon that characterization for their results. It suffices to say that "[o]ver the years, this Court has consistently repudiated '[d]istinctions between citizens solely because of their ancestry' as being 'odious to a free people whose institutions are founded upon the doctrine of equality.'"

Petitioner urges us to adopt for the first time a more restrictive view of the Equal Protection Clause and hold that discrimination against members of the white "majority" cannot be suspect if its purpose can be characterized as "benign." The clock of our liberties, however, cannot be turned back to 1868. It is far too late to argue that the guarantee of equal protection to all persons permits the recognition of special wards entitled to a degree of protection greater than that accorded others. . . .

Once the artificial line of a "two-class theory" of the Fourteenth Amendment is put aside, the difficulties entailed in varying the level of judicial review according to a perceived "preferred" status of a particular racial or ethnic minority are intractable. The concepts of "majority" and "minority" necessarily reflect temporary arrangements and political judgments. As observed above, the white "majority" itself is composed of various minority groups, most of which can lay claim to a history of prior discrimination at the hands of the State and private individuals. Not all of these groups can receive preferential treatment and corresponding judicial tolerance of distinctions drawn in terms of race and nationality, for then the only "majority" left would be a new minority of white Anglo-Saxon Protestants. There is no principled basis for deciding which groups would merit "heightened judicial solicitude" and which would not. Courts would be asked to evaluate the extent of the prejudice and consequent harm suffered by various minority groups. Those whose societal injury is thought to exceed some arbitrary level of tolerability then would be entitled to preferential classifications at the expense of individuals belonging to other groups. Those classifications would be free from exacting judicial scrutiny. As these preferences began to have their desired effect, and the consequences of past discrimination were undone, new judicial rankings would be necessary. The kind of variable sociological and political analysis necessary to produce such rankings simply does not lie within the judicial competence—even if they otherwise were politically feasible and socially desirable.

Moreover, there are serious problems of justice connected with the idea of preference itself. First, it may not always be clear that a so-called preference is in fact benign. Courts may be asked to validate burdens imposed upon individual members of a particular group in order to advance the group's general interest. Nothing in the Constitution supports the notion that individuals may be asked to suffer otherwise impermissible burdens in order to enhance the societal standing of their ethnic groups. Second, preferential programs may only reinforce common stereotypes holding that certain groups are unable to achieve success without special protection based on a factor having no relationship to individual worth. Third, there is a measure of inequity in forcing innocent persons in respondent's position to bear the burdens of redressing grievances not of their making.

By hitching the meaning of the Equal Protection Clause to these transitory considerations, we would be holding, as a constitutional principle, that judicial scrutiny of classifications touching on racial and ethnic background may vary with the ebb and flow of political forces. Disparate constitutional tolerance of such classifications well may serve to exacerbate racial and ethnic antagonisms rather than alleviate them. . . . Also, the mutability of a constitutional principle, based upon shifting political and social judgments, undermines the chances for consistent application of the Constitution from one generation to the next, a critical feature of its coherent interpretation. In expounding the Constitution, the Court's role is to discern "principles sufficiently absolute to give them roots throughout the community and continuity over significant periods of time, and to lift them above the level of the pragmatic political judgments of a particular time and place."

If it is the individual who is entitled to judicial protection against classifications based upon his racial or ethnic background because such distinctions impinge upon personal rights, rather than the individual only because of his membership in a particular group, then constitutional standards may be applied consistently. Political judgments regarding the necessity for the particular classification may be weighed in the constitutional balance, but the standard of justification will remain constant. This is as it should be, since those political judgments are the product of rough compromise struck by contending groups within the democratic process. When they touch upon an individual's race or ethnic background, he is entitled to a judicial determination that the burden he is asked to bear on that basis is precisely tailored to serve a compelling governmental interest. The Constitution guarantees that right to every person regardless of his background.

C

Petitioner contends that on several occasions this Court has approved preferential classifications without applying the most exacting scrutiny. Most of the cases upon which petitioner relies are drawn from three areas: school desegregation, employment discrimination, and sex discrimination. Each of the cases cited presented a situation materially different from the facts of this case.

The school desegregation cases are inapposite. Each involved remedies for clearly determined constitutional violations. Racial classifications thus were designed as remedies for the vindication of constitutional entitlement. Moreover, the scope of the remedies was not permitted to exceed the extent of the violations. Here, there was no judicial determination of constitutional violation as a predicate for the formulation of a remedial classification.

The employment discrimination cases also do not advance petitioner's cause. For example, in *Franks v. Bowman Transportation Co.* we approved a retroactive award of seniority to a class of Negro truckdrivers who had been the victims of discrimination—not just by society at large, but by the respondent in that case. While this relief imposed some burdens on other employees, it was held necessary "'to make [the victims] whole for injuries suffered on account of unlawful employment discrimination.'" The Courts of Appeals have fashioned various types of racial preferences as remedies for constitutional or statutory violations resulting in identified, race-based injuries to individuals held entitled to the preference. Such preferences also have been upheld where a legislative or administrative body charged with the responsibility made determinations of past discrimination by the industries affected, and fashioned remedies deemed appropriate to rectify the discrimination. But we have never approved preferential classifications in the absence of proved constitutional or statutory violations.

Nor is petitioner's view as to the applicable standard supported by the fact that gender- based classifications are not subjected to this level of scrutiny. Gender-based distinctions are less likely to create the analytical and practical problems present in preferential programs premised on racial or ethnic criteria. With respect to gender there are only two possible classifications. The incidence of the burdens imposed by preferential classifications is clear. There are no rival groups which can claim that they, too, are entitled to preferential treatment. Class-wide questions as to the group suffering previous injury and groups which fairly can be burdened are relatively manageable for reviewing courts. The resolution of these same questions in the context of racial and ethnic preferences presents far more complex and intractable problems than gender-based classifications. More importantly, the perception of racial classifications as inherently odious stems from a lengthy and tragic history that gender- based classifications do not share. In sum, the court has never viewed such classification as inherently suspect or as comparable to racial or ethnic classifications for the purpose of equal protection analysis.

* * *

In this case . . . there has been no determination by the legislature or a responsible administrative agency that the University engaged in a discriminatory practice requiring remedial efforts. . . .

IV

We have held that in "order to justify the use of a suspect classification, a State must show that its purpose or interest is both constitutionally permissible and substantial, and that its use of the classification is 'necessary . . . to the accomplishment' of its purpose or the safeguarding of its interests." The special admissions program purports to serve the purposes of; (i) "reducing the historic deficit of traditionally disfavored minorities in medical schools and in the medical profession"; (ii) countering the effects of societal discrimination; (iii) increasing the number of physicians who will practice in communities currently underserved; and (iv) obtaining the educational benefits that flow from an ethnically diverse student body. It is necessary to decide which, if any, of these purposes is substantial enough to support the use of a suspect classification.

A

If petitioner's purpose is to assure within its student body some specified percentage of a particular group merely because of its race or ethnic origin, such a preferential purpose must be rejected not as insubstantial but as facially invalid. Preferring members of any one group for no reason other than race or ethnic origin is discrimination for its own sake. This the Constitution forbids.

B

The State certainly has a legitimate and substantial interest in ameliorating, or eliminating where feasible, the disabling effects of identified discrimination. The line of school desegregation cases, commencing with *Brown,* attests to the importance of this state goal and the commitment of the judiciary to affirm all lawful means toward its attainment. In the school cases, the States were required by court order to redress the wrongs worked by specific instances of racial discrimination. That goal was far more focused than the remedying of the effects of "societal discrimination," an amorphous concept of injury that may be ageless in its reach into the past.

We have never approved a classification that aids persons perceived as members of relatively victimized groups at the expense of other innocent individuals in the absence of judicial, legislative, or administrative findings of constitutional or statutory violations. After such findings have been made, the governmental interest in preferring members of the injured groups at the expense of others is substantial, since the legal rights of the victims must be vindicated. In such a case, the extent of the injury and the consequent remedy will have been judicially, legislatively, or administratively defined. Also, the remedial action usually remains subject to continuing oversight to assure that it will work the least harm possible to other innocent persons competing for the benefit. Without such findings of constitutional or statutory violations, it cannot be said that the government has any greater interest in helping one individual than in refraining from harming another. Thus, the government has no compelling justification for inflicting such harm.

Petitioner does not purport to have made, and is in no position to make, such findings. Its broad mission is education, not the formulation of any legislative policy or the adjudication of particular claims of illegality. . . .

Hence, the purpose of helping certain groups whom the faculty of the Davis Medical School perceived as victims of "societal discrimination" does not justify a classification that imposes disadvantages upon persons like respondent, who bear no responsibility for whatever harm the beneficiaries of the special admissions program are thought to have suffered. To hold otherwise would be to convert a remedy heretofore reserved for violations of legal rights into a privilege that all institutions throughout the Nation could grant at their pleasure to whatever groups are perceived as victims of societal discrimination. That is a step we have never approved.

C

Petitioner identifies, as another purpose of its program, improving the delivery of health-care services to communities currently underserved. It may be assumed that in some situations a State's interest in facilitating the health care of its citizens is sufficiently compelling to support the use of a suspect classification. But there is virtually no evidence in the record indicating that petitioner's special admissions program is either needed or geared to promote that goal.

* * *

D

The fourth goal asserted by petitioner is the attainment of a diverse student body. This clearly is a constitutionally permissible goal for an institution of higher education. Academic freedom, though not a specifically enumerated constitutional right, long has been viewed as a special concern of the First Amendment. The freedom of a university to make its own judgments as to education includes the selection of its student body. . . .

* * *

The atmosphere of "speculation, experiment and creation"—so essential to the quality of higher education—is widely believed to be promoted by a diverse student body. . . .

Thus, in arguing that its universities must be accorded the right to select those students who will contribute the most to the "robust exchange of ideas," petitioner invokes a countervailing constitutional interest, that of the First Amendment. In this light, petitioner must be viewed as seeking to achieve a goal that is of paramount importance in the fulfillment of its mission.

It may be argued that there is greater force to these views at the undergraduate level than in a medical school where the training is centered primarily on professional competency. But even at the graduate level, our tradition and experience lend support to the view that the contribution of diversity is substantial . . .

* * *

Physicians serve a heterogeneous population. An otherwise qualified medical student with a particular background—whether it be ethnic, geographic, culturally advantaged or disadvantaged—may bring to a professional school of medicine experiences, outlooks, and ideas that enrich the training of its student body and better equip its graduates to render with understanding their vital service to humanity.

Ethnic diversity, however, is only one element in a range of factors a university properly may consider in attaining the goal of a heterogeneous student body. Although a university must have wide discretion in making the sensitive judgments as to who should be admitted, constitutional limitations protecting individual rights may not be disregarded. . . . As the interest of diversity is compelling in the context of a university's admissions program, the question remains whether the program's racial classification is necessary to promote this interest.

V.

A

It may be assumed that the reservation of a specified number of seats in each class for individuals from the preferred ethnic groups would contribute to the attainment of considerable ethnic diversity in the student body. But petitioner's argument that this is the only effective means of serving the interest of diversity is seriously flawed. . . . The diversity that furthers a compelling state interest encompasses a far broader array of qualifications and characteristics of which racial or ethnic origin is but a single though important element. Petitioner's special admissions program, focused solely on ethnic diversity, would hinder rather than further attainment of genuine diversity.

Nor would the state interest in genuine diversity be served by expanding petitioner's two-track system into a multitrack program with a prescribed number of seats set aside for each identifiable category of applicants. Indeed, it is inconceivable that a university would thus pursue the logic of petitioner's two-track program to the illogical end of insulating each category of applicants with certain desired qualifications from competition with all other applicants.

The experience of other university admissions programs, which take race into account in achieving the educational diversity valued by the First Amendment, demonstrates that the assignment of a fixed number of places to a minority group is not a necessary means toward that end. An illuminating example is found in the Harvard College program:

"In recent years Harvard College has expanded the concept of diversity to include students from disadvantaged economic, racial and ethnic groups. ". . .When the Committee on Admissions reviews the large middle group of applicants who are 'admissible' and deemed capable of doing good work in their courses, the race of an applicant may tip the balance in his favor just as geographic origin or a life spent on a farm may tip the balance in other candidates' cases. . . .

"In Harvard College admissions the Committee has not set target-quotas for the number of blacks, or of musicians, football players, physicists or Californians to be admitted in a given year. . . . But that awareness . . . means only that in choosing among thousands of applicants who are not only 'admissible' academically but have other strong qualities, the Committee, with a number of criteria in mind, pays some attention to distribution among many types and categories of students."

In such an admissions program, race or ethnic background may be deemed a "plus" in a particular applicant's file, yet it does not insulate the individual from comparison with all other candidates for the available seats. The file of a particular black applicant may be examined for his potential contribution to diversity without the factor of race being decisive. . . . Such qualities could include exceptional personal talents, unique work or service experience, leadership potential, maturity, demonstrated compassion, a history of overcoming disadvantage, ability to communicate with the poor, or other qualifications deemed important. In short, an admissions program operated in this way is flexible enough to consider all pertinent elements of diversity in light of the particular qualifications of each applicant, and to place them on the same footing for consideration, although not necessarily according them the same weight. Indeed, the weight attributed to a particular quality may vary from year to year depending upon the "mix" both of the student body and the applicants for the incoming class.

This kind of program treats each applicant as an individual in the admissions process. . . .

It has been suggested that an admissions program which considers race only as one factor is simply a subtle and more sophisticated—but no less effective—means of according racial preference than the Davis program. A facial intent to discriminate, however, is evident in petitioner's preference program and not denied in this case. No such facial infirmity exists in an admissions program where race or ethnic background is simply one element—to be weighed fairly against other elements—in the selection process. . . . In short, good faith would be presumed in the absence of a showing to the contrary in the manner permitted by our cases.

B

In summary, it is evident that the Davis special admissions program involves the use of an explicit racial classification never before countenanced by this Court. It tells applicants who are not Negro, Asian, or Chicano that they are totally excluded from a specific percentage of the seats in an entering class. . . . They are never afforded the chance to compete with applicants from the preferred groups for the special admissions seats. At the same time, the preferred applicants have the opportunity to compete for every seat in the class.

The fatal flaw in petitioner's preferential program is its disregard of individual rights as guaranteed by the Fourteenth Amendment. Such rights are not absolute. But when a State's distribution of benefits or imposition of burdens hinges on ancestry or the color of a person's skin, that individual is entitled to a demonstration that the challenged classification is necessary to promote a substantial state interest. Petitioner has failed to carry this burden. For this reason, that portion of the California court's judgment holding petitioner's special admissions program invalid under the Fourteenth Amendment must be affirmed.

C

In enjoining petitioner from ever considering the race of any applicant, however, the courts below failed to recognize that the State has a substantial interest that legitimate may be served by a properly devised admissions program involving the competitive consideration of race and ethnic origin. For this reason, so much of the California court's judgment as enjoins petitioner from any consideration of the race of any applicant must be reversed.

VI

With respect to respondent's entitlement to an injunction directing his admission to the Medical School, petitioner has conceded that it could not carry its burden of proving that, but for the existence of its unlawful special admissions program, respondent still would not have been admitted. Hence, respondent is entitled to the injunction, and that portion of the judgment must be affirmed.

Source:

Supreme Court Reporter, Vol. 98, pp. 2,733–2,815.

National Conference of Catholic Bishops, Pastoral Letter on War and Peace, 1983

Document issued by the National Conference of Catholic Bishops May 3, 1983, in which they condemned the nuclear arms race and called for a halt to the development, production, and deployment of nuclear weapons. The document, formally titled "The Challenge of Peace: God's Promise and Our Responsibility," was intended to provide guidance for Roman Catholic clergy on the subject of nuclear arms. The statement distinguished between moral principles, which represented a binding authority, and practical application of those principles, which might differ based on legitimate differences of interpretation. The letter expressed "profound skepticism" about the moral acceptability of any use of nuclear weapons. It opposed the "first use" of nuclear weapons in a conflict, and it permitted the concept of nuclear deterrence only on condition that the United States engage in arms reduction talks. The letter called on Catholics in the military to work for peace by promoting the concept of self-defense. It also asked Catholics to abstain from eating meat on Fridays and to increase penance and prayer as an expression of concern for peace.

The Second Vatican Council opened its evaluation of modern warfare with the statement: "The whole human race faces a moment of supreme crisis in its advance toward maturity." We agree with the council's assessment; the crisis of the moment is embodied in the threat which nuclear weapons pose for the world and much that we hold dear in the world. We have seen and felt the effects of the crisis of the nuclear age in the lives of people we serve. Nuclear weaponry has drastically changed the nature of warfare, and the arms race poses a threat to human life and human civilization which is without precedent.

We write this letter from the perspective of Catholic faith. Faith does not insulate us from the daily challenges of life but intensifies our desire to address them precisely in light of the gospel which has come to us in the person of the risen Christ. Through the resources of faith and reason we desire in this letter to provide hope for people in our day and direction toward a world freed of the nuclear threat.

As Catholic bishops we write this letter as an exercise of our teaching ministry. The Catholic tradition on war and peace is a long and complex one; it stretches from the Sermon on the Mount to the statements of Pope John Paul II. We wish to explore and explain the resources of the moral-religious teaching and to apply it to specific questions of our day. In doing this we realize, and we want readers of this letter to recognize, that not all statements in this letter have the same moral authority. At times we state universally binding moral principles found in the teaching of the Church; at other times the pastoral letter makes specific applications, observations and recommendations which allow for diversity of opinion on the part of those who assess the factual data of situations differently. However, we expect Catholics to give our moral judgments serious consideration when they are forming their own views on specific problems.

The experience of preparing this letter has manifested to us the range of strongly held opinion in the Catholic community on questions of fact and judgment concerning issues of war and peace. We urge mutual respect among individuals and groups in the Church as this letter is analyzed and discussed. Obviously, as bishops, we believe that such differences should be expressed within the framework of Catholic moral teaching. We need in the Church not only conviction and commitment but also civility and charity.

While this letter is addressed principally to the Catholic community, we want it to make a contribution to the wider public debate in our country on the dangers and dilemmas of the nuclear age. Our contribution will not be primarily technical or political, but we are convinced that there is no satisfactory answer to the human problems of the nuclear age which fails to consider the moral and religious dimensions of the questions we face.

Although we speak in our own name, as Catholic bishops of the Church in the United States, we have been conscious in the preparations of this letter of the consequences our teaching will have not only for the United States but for other nations as well. One important expression of this awareness has been the consultation we have had, by correspondence and in an important meeting held at the Vatican (January 18–19, 1983), with representatives of European bishop's conferences. This consultation with bishops of other countries, and, of course, with the Holy See, has been very helpful to us.

Catholic teaching has always understood peace in positive terms. In the words of Pope John Paul II: "Peace is not just the absence of war. . . . Like a cathedral, peace must be constructed patiently and with unshakable faith" (Coventry, England, 1982). Peace is the fruit of order. Order in human society must be shaped on the basis of respect for the transcendence of God and the unique dignity of each person, understood in terms of freedom, justice, truth and love. To avoid war in our day we must be intent on building peace in an increasingly interdependent world. In Part III of this letter we set forth a positive vision of peace and the demands such a vision makes on diplomacy, national policy, and personal choices.

While pursuing peace incessantly, it is also necessary to limit the use of force in a world comprised of nation states, faced with common problems but devoid of an adequate international political authority. Keeping the peace in the nuclear age is a moral and political imperative. In Parts I and II of this letter we set forth both the principles of Catholic teaching on war and a series of judgments, based in these principles, about concrete policies. In making these judgments we speak as moral teachers, not as technical experts.

I. Some Principles, Norms, and Premises of Catholic Teaching

A. On War

1. Catholic teaching begins in every case with a presumption against war and for peaceful settlement of disputes. In exceptional cases, determined by the moral principles of the just-war tradition, some uses of force are permitted.

2. Every nation has a right and duty to defend itself against unjust aggression.

3. Offensive war of any kind is not morally justifiable.

4. It is never permitted to direct nuclear or conventional weapons to "the indiscriminate destruction of whole cities or vast areas with their populations . . . " (*Pastoral Constitution,* #80). The intentional killing of innocent civilians or noncombatants is always wrong.

5. Even defensive response to unjust attack can cause destruction which violates the principle of proportionality, going far beyond the limits of legitimate defense. This judgment is particularly important when assessing planned use of nuclear weapons. No defensive strategy, nuclear or conventional, which exceeds the limits of proportionality is morally permissible.

B. On Deterrence

1. "In current conditions 'deterrence' based on balance, certainly not as an end in itself but as a step on the way toward a progressive disarmament, may still be judged morally acceptable. Nonetheless, in order to ensure peace, it is indispensable not to be satisfied with this minimum which is always susceptible to the real danger of explosion" (Pope John Paul II, *Message to U.N. Special Session on Disarmament,* #8, June 1982).

2. No *use* of nuclear weapons which would violate the principles of discrimination or proportionality may be *intended* in a strategy of deterrence. The moral demands of Catholic teaching require resolute willingness not to intend or to do moral evil even to save our own lives or the lives of those we love.

3. Deterrence is not an adequate strategy as a long-term basis for peace; it is a transitional strategy justifiable

only in conjunction with resolute determination to pursue arms control and disarmament. We are convinced that "the fundamental principle on which our present peace depends must be replaced by another, which declares that the true and solid peace of nations consists not in equality of arms but in mutual trust alone" (Pope John XXIII, *Peace on Earth,* #113).

C. The Arms Race and Disarmament

1. The arms race is one of the greatest curses on the human race; it is to be condemned as a danger, an act of aggression against the poor, and a folly which does not provide the security it promises. (Cf: *Pastoral Constitution,* #81; *Statement of the Holy See to the United Nations,* 1976.)

2. Negotiations must be pursued in every reasonable form possible; they should be governed by the "demand that the arms race should cease; that the stockpiles which exist in various countries should be reduced equally and simultaneously by the parties concerned; that nuclear weapons should be banned; and that a general agreement should eventually be reached about progressive disarmament and an effective method of control" (Pope John XXIII, *Peace On Earth,* #112).

D. On Personal Conscience

1. ***Military Service:*** "All those who enter the military service in loyalty to their country should look upon themselves as the custodians of the security and freedom of their fellow countrymen; and when they carry out their duty properly, they are contributing to the maintenance of peace" *(Pastoral Constitution,* #79).

2. ***Conscientious Objection:*** "Moreover, it seems just that laws should make humane provision for the case of conscientious objectors who refuse to carry arms, provided they accept some other form of community service" (*Pastoral Constitution.* #79).

3. ***Nonviolence:*** "In this same spirit we cannot but express our admiration for all who forego the use of violence to vindicate their rights and resort to other means of defense which are available to weaker parties, provided it can be done without harm to the rights and duties of others and of the community" (*Pastoral Constitution,* #78).

4. ***Citizens and Conscience:*** "Once again we deem it opportune to remind our children of their duty to take an active part in public life, and to contribute towards the attainment of the common good of the entire human family as well as to that of their own political community . . . . In other words, it is necessary that human beings, in the intimacy of their own consciences, should so live and act in their temporal lives as to create a synthesis between scientific, technical and professional elements on the one hand, and spiritual values on the other" (Pope John XXIII, *Peace on Earth,* #146, 150).

II. Moral Principles and Policy Choices

As bishops in the United States, assessing the concrete circumstances of our society, we have made a number of observations and recommendations in the process of applying moral principles to specific policy choices.

A. On the Use of Nuclear Weapons

1. ***Counter Population Use:*** Under no circumstances may nuclear weapons or other instruments of mass slaughter be used for the purpose of destroying population centers or other predominantly civilian targets. Retaliatory action which would indiscriminately and disproportionately take many wholly innocent lives, lives of people who are in no way responsible for reckless actions of their government, must also be condemned.

2. ***The Initiation of Nuclear War:*** We do not perceive any situation in which the deliberate initiation of nuclear war, on however restricted a scale, can be morally justified. Nonnuclear attacks by another state must be resisted by other than nuclear means. Therefore, a serious moral obligation exists to develop nonnuclear defensive strategies as rapidly as possible. In this letter we urge NATO to move rapidly toward the adoption of a "no first use" policy, but we recognize this will take time to implement and will require the development of an adequate alternative defense posture.

3. ***Limited Nuclear War:*** Our examination of the various arguments on this question makes us highly skeptical about the real meaning of "limited." One of the criteria of the just-war teaching is that there must be a reasonable hope of success in bringing about justice and peace. We must ask whether such a reasonable hope can exist once nuclear weapons have been exchanged. The burden of proof remains on those who assert that meaningful limitation is possible. In our view the first imperative is to prevent any use of nuclear weapons and we hope that leaders will resist the notion that nuclear conflict can be limited, contained or won in any traditional sense.

B. On Deterrence

In concert with the evaluation provided by Pope John Paul II, we have arrived at a strictly conditional moral acceptance of deterrence. In this letter we have outlined criteria and recommendations which indicate the meaning of conditional acceptance of deterrence policy. We cannot consider such a policy adequate as a long-term basis for peace.

C. On Promoting Peace

1. We support immediate, bilateral verifiable agreements to halt the testing, production and deployment of new

nuclear weapons systems. This recommendation is not to be identified with any specific political initiative.

2. We support efforts to achieve deep cuts in the arsenals of both superpowers; efforts should concentrate first on systems which threaten the retaliatory forces of either major power.

3. We support early and successful conclusion of negotiations of a comprehensive test ban treaty.

4. We urge new efforts to prevent the spread of nuclear weapons in the world, and to control the conventional arms race, particularly the conventional arms trade.

5. We support, in an increasingly interdependent world, political and economic policies designed to protect human dignity and to promote the human rights of every person, especially the least among us. In this regard, we call for the establishment of some form of global authority adequate to the needs of the international common good.

This letter includes many judgments from the perspective of ethics, politics and strategy needed to speak concretely and correctly to the "moment of supreme crisis" identified by Vatican II. We stress again that readers should be aware, as we have been, of the distinction between our statement of moral principles and of official church teaching and our application of these to concrete issues. We urge that special care be taken not to use passages out of context; neither should brief portions of this document be cited to support positions it does not intend to convey or which are not truly in accord with the spirit of its teaching.

In concluding this summary we respond to two key questions often asked about this pastoral letter:

Why do we address these matters fraught with such complexity, controversy and passion? We speak as pastors, not politicians. We are teachers, not technicians. We cannot avoid our responsibility to lift up the moral dimensions of the choices before our world and nation. The nuclear age is an era of moral as well as physical danger. We are the first generation since Genesis with the power to threaten the created order. We cannot remain silent in the face of such danger. Why do we address these issues? We are simply trying to live up to the call of Jesus to be peacemakers in our own time and situation.

What are we saying? Fundamentally, we are saying that the decisions about nuclear weapons are among the most pressing moral questions of our age. While these decisions have obvious military and political aspects, they involve fundamental moral choices. In simple terms, we are saying that good ends (defending one's country, protecting freedom, etc.) cannot justify immoral means (the use of weapons which kill indiscriminately and threaten whole societies). We fear that our world and nation are headed in the wrong direction. More weapons with greater destructive potential are produced every day. More and more nations are seeking to become nuclear powers. In our quest for more and more security we fear we are actually becoming less and less secure.

In the words of our Holy Father, we need a "moral about-face." The whole world must summon the moral courage and technical means to say no to nuclear conflict; no to weapons of mass destruction; no to an arms race which robs the poor and the vulnerable; and no to the moral danger of a nuclear age which places before humankind indefensible choices of constant terror or surrender. Peacemaking is not an optional commitment. It is a requirement of our faith. We are called to be peacemakers, not by some movement of the moment, but by our Lord Jesus. The content and context of our peacemaking is set not by some political agenda or ideological program, but by the teaching of his Church.

Ultimately, this letter is intended as an expression of Christian faith, affirming the confidence we have that the risen Lord remains with us precisely in moments of crisis. It is our belief in his presence and power among us which sustain us in confronting the awesome challenge of the nuclear age. We speak from faith to provide hope for all who recognize the challenge and are working to confront it with the resources of faith and reason.

To approach the nuclear issue in faith is to recognize our absolute need for prayer: we urge and invite all to unceasing prayer for peace with justice for all people. In a spirit of prayerful hope we present this message of peace.

Introduction

1. "The whole human race faces a moment of supreme crisis in its advance toward maturity." Thus the Second Vatican Council opened its treatment of modern warfare. Since the Council, dynamic of the nuclear arms race has intensified. Apprehension about nuclear war is almost tangible and visible today. As Pope John Paul II said in his message to the United Nations concerning disarmament: "Currently, the fear and preoccupation of so many groups in various parts of the world reveal that people are more frightened about what would happen if irresponsible parties unleash some nuclear war."

2. As bishops and pastors ministering in one of the major nuclear nations, we have encountered this terror in the minds and hearts of our people—indeed, we share it. We write this letter because we agree that the world is at a moment of crisis, the effects of which are evident in people's lives. It is not our intent to play on fears, however, but to speak words of hope and encouragement in time of fear. Faith does not insulate us from the challenges of life; rather, it intensifies our desire to help solve them precisely in light of the Good News which has come to us in the person of Jesus, the Lord of history. From the resources of our faith we wish to provide hope and strength to all who seek a world free of the nuclear threat. Hope sustains one's capacity to live with danger without being overwhelmed by it; hope is the will to struggle against obstacles even when they appear insuperable. Ultimately our hope rests in the God who gave us life, sustains the world by his power, and has called us to revere the lives of every person and all peoples.

3. The crisis of which we speak arises from this fact: nuclear war threatens the existence of our planet; this is a more menacing threat than any the world has known. It is neither tolerable nor necessary that human beings live under this threat. But removing it will require a major effort of intelligence, courage, and faith. As Pope John Paul II said at Hiroshima: "From now on it is only through a conscious choice and through a deliberate policy that humanity can survive."

4. As Americans, citizens of the nation which was first to produce atomic weapons, which has been the only one to use them, and which today is one of the handful of nations capable of decisively influencing the course of the nuclear age, we gave grave human, moral, and political responsibilities to see that a "conscious choice" is made to save humanity. This letter is therefore both an invitation and a challenge to Catholics in the United States to join with others in shaping the conscious choices and deliberate policies required in this "moment of supreme crisis."

Conclusion

330. As we close this lengthy letter, we try to answer two key questions as directly as we can.

331. Why do we address these matters fraught with such complexity, controversy, and passion? We speak as pastors, not politicians. We are teachers, not technicians. We cannot avoid our responsibility to lift up the moral dimensions of the choices before our world and nation. The nuclear age is an era of moral as well as physical danger. We are the first generation since Genesis with the power to virtually destroy God's creation. We cannot remain silent in the face of such danger. Why do we address these issues? We are simply trying to live up to the call of Jesus to be peacemakers in our own time and situation.

332. What are we saying? Fundamentally, we are saying that the decisions about nuclear weapons are among the most pressing moral questions of our age. While these decisions have obvious military and political aspects, they involve fundamental moral choices. In simple terms, we are saying that good ends (defending one's country, protecting freedom, etc.) cannot justify immoral means (the use of weapons which kill indiscriminately and threaten whole societies). We fear that our world and nation are headed in the wrong direction. More weapons with greater destructive potential are produced every day. More and more nations are seeking to become nuclear powers. In our quest for more and more security, we fear we are actually becoming less and less secure.

333. In the words of our Holy Father, we need a "moral about-face." The whole world must summon the moral courage and technical means to say "no" to nuclear conflict; "no" to weapons of mass destruction; "no" to an arms race which robs the poor and the vulnerable; and "no" to the moral danger of a nuclear age which places before humankind indefensible choices of constant terror or surrender. Peacemaking is not an optional commitment. It is a requirement of our faith. We are called to be peacemakers, not by some movement of the moment, but by our Lord Jesus. The content and context of our peacemaking is set, not by some political agenda or ideological program, but by the teaching of his Church.

334. Thus far in this Pastoral Letter we have made suggestions we hope will be helpful in the present world crisis. Looking ahead to the long and productive future of humanity for which we all hope, we feel that a more all-inclusive and final solution is needed. We speak here of the truly effective international authority for which Pope John XXIII ardently longed in *Peace on Earth,* and of which Pope Paul VI spoke to the United Nations on his visit there in 1965. The hope for such a structure is not unrealistic, because the point has been reached where public opinion sees clearly that, with the massive weaponry of the present, war is no longer viable. There *is* a substitute for war. There is negotiation under the supervision of a global body realistically fashioned to do its job. It must be given the equipment to keep constant surveillance on the entire earth. Present technology makes this possible. It must have the authority, freely conferred upon it by all the nations, to investigate what seem to be preparations for war by any one of them. It must be empowered by all the nations to enforce its commands on every nation. It must be so constituted as to pose no threat to any nation's sovereignty. Obviously the creation of such a sophisticated instrumentality is a gigantic task, but is it hoping for too much to believe that the genius of humanity, aided by the grace and guidance of God, is able to accomplish it? To create it may take decades of unrelenting daily toll by the world's best minds and most devoted hearts, but it shall never come into existence unless we make a beginning now.

335. As we come to the end of our Pastoral Letter we boldly propose the beginning of this work. The evil of the proliferation of nuclear arms becomes more evident every day to all people. No one is exempt from their danger. If ridding the world of the weapons of war could be done easily, the whole human race would gladly do it tomorrow. Shall we shrink from the task because it is hard?

336. We turn to our own government and we beg it to propose to the United Nations that it begin this work immediately; that it create an international task force for peace; that this task force, with membership open to every nation, meet daily through the years ahead with one sole agenda: the creation of a world that will one day be safe from war. Freed from the bondage of war that holds it captive in its threat, the world would at last be able to address its problems and to make genuine human progress, so that every day there may be more freedom, more food, and more opportunity for every human being who walks the face of the earth.

337. Let us have the courage to believe in the bright future and in a God who wills it for us—not a perfect world, but a better one. The perfect world, we Christians believe, is beyond the horizon, in an endless eternity where God will be all in all. But a better world is here for human hands and hearts and minds to make.

338. For the community of faith the risen Christ is the beginning and end of all things. For all things were created through him and all things will return to the Father through him.

339. It is our belief in the risen Christ which sustains us in confronting the awesome challenge of the nuclear arms race. Present in the beginning as the word of the Father, present in history as the word incarnate, and with us today in his word, sacraments, and spirit, he is the reason for our hope and faith. Respecting our freedom, he does not solve our problems but sustains us as we take responsibility for his work of creation and try to shape it in the ways of the Kingdom. We believe his grace will never fail us. We offer this letter to the Church and to all who can draw strength and wisdom from it in the conviction that we must not fail him. We must subordinate the power of the nuclear age to human control and direct it to human benefit. As we do this we are conscious of God's continuing work among us, which will one day issue forth in the beautiful final Kingdom prophesied by the seer of the Book of Revelation:

Then I saw a new heaven and a new earth; for the first heaven and the first earth had passed away and the sea was no more. And I saw the holy city, new Jerusalem, coming down out of heaven from God, prepared as a bride adorned for her husband; and I heard a great voice from the throne saying, "Behold, the dwelling of God is with men. He will dwell with them, and they shall be his people, and God himself will be with them, he will wipe away every tear from their eyes, and death shall be no more, neither shall there be mourning nor crying nor pain any more, for the former things have passed away." And he who sat upon the throne said, "Behold, I make all things new" (Rv. 21:1–5).

Source:
United States Catholic Conference, Inc., Washington, D.C.

Bowers v. Hardwick, 1986

U.S. Supreme Court decision issued June 30, 1986, ruling that an 1816 Georgia state law, which made sodomy a crime even if committed in the privacy of one's home, did not violate an individual's constitutional right to privacy. The case involved Michael Hardwick, a gay man who had been arrested in his home in Georgia for engaging in homosexual activity. Although Hardwick was not prosecuted, he subsequently challenged the law's constitutionality. The majority decision was made despite the fact that married couples had gained the right of sexual privacy in *Griswold v. Connecticut* (381 U.S. 479 [1965]). The Court based its decision primarily on the precedent set by a number of state laws against sodomy dating from the 17th century to the present day.

Ten years later, in *Romer, Governor of Colorado v. Evans et al.* (116 S. Ct. 1620 [1996]), the Court struck down, 6-3, a Colorado law that excluded homosexuals from civil rights protections. However, in *Boy Scouts of America v. Dale* (530 U.S. 640 [2000]), the Supreme Court in a 5-4 decision declared that a private organization, including the Boy Scouts, could discriminate against anyone in opposition to the group's values, in this case homosexuals.

All citations were removed from decisions below.

Justice White delivered the opinion of the Court.

In August 1982, respondent Hardwick (hereafter respondent) was charged with violating the Georgia statute criminalizing sodomy by committing that act with another adult male in the bedroom of respondent's home. After a preliminary hearing, the District Attorney decided not to present the matter to the grand jury unless further evidence developed.

Respondent then brought suit in the Federal District Court, challenging the constitutionality of the statute insofar as it criminalized consensual sodomy. He asserted that he was a practicing homosexual, that the Georgia sodomy statute, as administered by the defendants, placed him in imminent danger of arrest, and that the statute for several reasons violates the Federal Constitution. The District Court granted the defendants' motion to dismiss for failure to state a claim, relying on *Doe v. Commonwealth's Attorney for the City of Richmond* (1975), which this Court summarily affirmed (1976).

A divided panel of the Court of Appeals for the Eleventh Circuit reversed. The court first held that, because Doe was distinguishable and in any event had been undermined by later decisions, our summary affirmance in that case did not require affirmance of the District Court. Relying on our decisions in *Griswold v. Connecticut* (1965); *Roe v. Wade* (1973), [and others] the court went on to hold that the Georgia statute violated respondent's fundamental rights because his homosexual activity is a private and intimate association that is beyond the reach of state regulation by reason of the Ninth Amendment and the Due Process Clause of the Fourteenth Amendment. The case was remanded for trial, at which, to prevail, the State would have to prove that the statute is supported by a compelling interest and is the most narrowly drawn means of achieving that end.

Because other Courts of Appeals have arrived at judgments contrary to that of the Eleventh Circuit in this case, we granted the Attorney General's petition for certiorari questioning the holding that the sodomy statute violates the fundamental rights of homosexuals. We agree with petitioner that the Court of Appeals erred, and hence reverse its judgment.

This case does not require a judgment on whether laws against sodomy between consenting adults in general, or between homosexuals in particular, are wise or desirable. It raises no question about the right or propriety of state legislative decisions to repeal their laws that criminalize homosexual sodomy, or of state-court decisions invalidating those laws on state constitutional grounds. The issue presented is whether the Federal Constitution confers a fundamental right upon homosexuals to engage in sodomy and hence invalidates the laws of the many States that still make such conduct illegal and have done so for a very long time. The case also calls for some judgment about the limits of the Court's role in carrying out its constitutional mandate.

We first register our disagreement with the Court of Appeals and with respondent that the Court's prior cases have construed the Constitution to confer a right of privacy that extends to homosexual sodomy and for all intents and purposes have decided this case. The reach of this line of cases was sketched in *Carey v. Population Services International* (1977), *Pierce v. Society of Sisters* (1925), and *Meyer v. Nebraska,* [and] were described as dealing with child rearing and education; *Prince v. Massachusetts,* (1944), with family relationships; *Skinner v. Oklahoma ex rel. Williamson,* (1942), with procreation; *Loving v. Virginia,* (1967), with marriage; *Griswold v. Connecticut,* and *Eisenstadt v. Baird,* with contraception; and *Roe v. Wade,* (1973), with abortion. The latter three cases were interpreted as construing the Due Process Clause of the Fourteenth Amendment to confer a fundamental individual right to decide whether or not to beget or bear a child.

Accepting the decisions in these cases and the above description of them we think it evident that none of the rights announced in those cases bears any resemblance to the claimed constitutional right of homosexuals to engage in acts of sodomy that is asserted in this case. No connection between family, marriage, or procreation on the one hand and homosexual activity on the other has been demonstrated, either by the Court of Appeals or by respondent. Moreover, any claim that these cases nevertheless stand for the proposition that any kind of private sexual conduct between consenting adults is constitutionally insulated from state proscription is insupportable. Indeed, the Court's opinion in Carey twice asserted that the privacy right, which the Griswold line of cases found to be one of the protections provided by the Due Process Clause, did not reach so far.

Precedent aside, however, respondent would have us announce, as the Court of Appeals did, a fundamental right to engage in homosexual sodomy. This we are quite unwilling to do. It is true that despite the language of the Due Process Clauses of the Fifth and Fourteenth Amendments, which appears to focus only on the processes by which life, liberty, or property is taken, the cases are legion in which those Clauses have been interpreted to have substantive content, subsuming rights that to a great extent are immune from federal or state regulation or proscription. Among such cases are those recognizing rights that have little or no textual support in the constitutional language. *Meyer, Prince,* and *Pierce* fall in this category, as do the privacy cases from *Griswold* to *Carey.*

Striving to assure itself and the public that announcing rights not readily identifiable in the Constitution's text involves much more than the imposition of the Justice's own choice of values on the States and the Federal Government, the Court has sought to identify the nature of the rights qualifying for heightened judicial protection. In *Palko v. Connecticut,* (1937), it was said that this category includes those fundamental liberties that are "implicit in the concept of ordered liberty," such that "neither liberty nor justice would exist if [they] were sacrificed." A different description of fundamental liberties appeared in *Moore v. East Cleveland* (1977), where they are characterized as those liberties that are "deeply rooted in this Nation's history and tradition."

It is obvious to us that neither of these formulations would extend a fundamental right to homosexuals to engage in acts of consensual sodomy. Proscriptions against that conduct have ancient roots. See generally, Survey on the Constitutional Right to Privacy in the Context of Homosexual Activity, (1986). Sodomy was a criminal offense at common law and was forbidden by the laws of the original thirteen States when they ratified the Bill of

Rights. In 1868, when the Fourteenth Amendment was ratified, all but 5 of the 37 States in the Union had criminal sodomy laws. In fact, until 1961, all 50 States outlawed sodomy, and today, 24 States and the District of Columbia continue to provide criminal penalties for sodomy performed in private and between consenting adults. Against this background, to claim that a right to engage in such conduct is "deeply rooted in this Nation's history and tradition" or "implicit in the concept of ordered liberty" is, at best, facetious.

Nor are we inclined to take a more expansive view of our authority to discover new fundamental rights imbedded in the Due Process Clause. The Court is most vulnerable and comes nearest to illegitimacy when it deals with judge-made constitutional law having little or no cognizable roots in the language or design of the Constitution. That this is so was painfully demonstrated by the face-off between the Executive and the Court in the 1930's, which resulted in the repudiation of much of the substantive gloss that the Court had placed on the Due Process Clauses of the Fifth and Fourteenth Amendments. There should be, therefore, great resistance to expand the substantive reach of those Clauses, particularly if it requires redefining the category of rights deemed to be fundamental. Otherwise, the Judiciary necessarily takes to itself further authority to govern the country without express constitutional authority. The claimed right pressed on us today falls far short of overcoming this resistance.

Respondent, however, asserts that the result should be different where the homosexual conduct occurs in the privacy of the home. He relies on *Stanley v. Georgia,* (1969), where the Court held that the First Amendment prevents conviction for possessing and reading obscene material in the privacy of one's home. "If the First Amendment means anything, it means that a State has no business telling a man, sitting alone in his house, what books he may read or what films he may watch."

Stanley did protect conduct that would not have been protected outside the home, and it partially prevented the enforcement of state obscenity laws; but the decision was firmly grounded in the First Amendment. The right pressed upon us here has no similar support in the text of the Constitution, and it does not qualify for recognition under the prevailing principles for construing the Fourteenth Amendment. Its limits are also difficult to discern. Plainly enough, otherwise illegal conduct is not always immunized whenever it occurs in the home. Victimless crimes, such as the possession and use of illegal drugs, do not escape the law where they are committed at home. *Stanley* itself recognized that its holding offered no protection for the possession in the home of drugs, firearms, or stolen goods. And if respondent's submission is limited to the voluntary sexual conduct between consenting adults, it would be difficult, except by fiat, to limit the claimed right to homosexual conduct while leaving exposed to prosecution adultery, incest, and other sexual crimes even though they are committed in the home. We are unwilling to start down that road.

Even if the conduct at issue here is not a fundamental right, respondent asserts that there must be a rational basis for the law and that there is none in this case other than the presumed belief of a majority of the electorate in Georgia that homosexual sodomy is immoral and unacceptable. This is said to be an inadequate rationale to support the law. The law, however, is constantly based on notions of morality, and if all laws representing essentially moral choices are to be invalidated under the Due Process Clause, the courts will be very busy indeed. Even respondent makes no such claim, but insists that majority sentiments about the morality of homosexuality should be declared inadequate. We do not agree, and are unpersuaded that the sodomy laws of some States should be invalidated on this basis.

Accordingly, the judgment of the Court of Appeal is Reserved.

Justice Blackmun, with whom Justice Brennan, Justice Marshall, and Justice Stevens join, dissenting.

This case is no more about "a fundamental right to engage in homosexual sodomy," as the Court purports to declare than *Stanley v. Georgia* (1969), was about a fundamental right to watch obscene movies, or *Katz v. United States* (1967), was about a fundamental right to place interstate bets from a telephone booth. Rather, this case is about "the most comprehensive of rights and the right most valued by civilized men," namely "the right to be let alone."

The statute at issue, Ga. Code Ann. Section 16-6-2 (1984), denies individuals the right to decide for themselves whether to engage in particular forms of private, consensual sexual activity. The Court concludes that Section 16-6-2 is valid essentially because "the laws of . . . many States . . . still make such conduct illegal and have done so for a very long time." But the fact that the moral judgments expressed by statutes like Section 16-6-2 may be "'natural and familiar . . . ought not to conclude our judgment upon the question whether statutes embodying them conflict with the Constitution of the United States.'" Like Justice Holmes, I believe that "[i]t is revolting to have no better reason for a rule of law than that so it was laid down in the time of Henry IV. It is still more revolting if the grounds upon which it was laid down have vanished long since, and the rule simply persists from blind imitation of the past." I believe we must analyze Hardwick's claim in the light of the values that underlie the constitutional right to privacy. If that right means anything, it means that, before Georgia can prosecute its citizens for making choices about the most intimate aspects of their lives, it must do more than assert that the choice they have made is an "abominable crime not fit to be named among Christians.'"

I

In its haste to reverse the Court of Appeals and hold that the Constitution does not "confe[r] a fundamental right upon homosexuals to engage in sodomy," the Court relegates the actual statute being challenged to a footnote and ignores the procedural posture of the case before it. A fair reading of the statute and of the complaint clearly reveals that the majority has distorted the question this case presents.

First, the Court's almost obsessive focus on homosexuals is particularly hard to justify in light of the broad language Georgia has used. Unlike the Court, the Georgia Legislature has not proceeded on the assumption that homosexuals are so different from other citizens that their lives may be controlled in a way that would not be tolerated if it limited the choices of those other citizens. Rather, Georgia has provided that "[a] person commits the offense of sodomy when he performs or submits to any sexual act involving the sex organs of one person and the mouth or anus of another." The sex or status of the persons who engage in the act is irrelevant as a matter of state law. In fact, to the extent I can discern a legislative purpose for Georgia's 1968 enactment of Section 16-6-2, that purpose seems to have been to broaden the coverage of the law to reach heterosexual as well as homosexual activity. I therefore see no basis for the Court's decision to treat this case as an "as applied" challenge to Section 16-6-2 or for Georgia's attempt, both in its brief and at oral argument, to defend Section 16-6-2 solely on the grounds that it prohibits homosexual activity. Michael Hardwick's standing may rest in significant part on Georgia's apparent willingness to enforce against homosexuals a law it seems not to have any desire to enforce against heterosexuals. But his claim that Section 16-6-2 involves an unconstitutional intrusion into his privacy and his right or intimate association does not depend in any way on his sexual orientation.

Second, I disagree with the Court's refusal to consider whether Section 16-6-2 runs afoul of the Eighth or Ninth Amendments or the Equal Protection Clause of the Fourteenth Amendment. Respondent's complaint expressly invoked the Ninth Amendment, and he relied heavily before this Court on *Griswold v. Connecticut* (1965) which identifies that Amendment as one of the specific constitutional provisions giving "life and substance" to our understanding of privacy. More importantly, the procedural posture of the case requires that we affirm the Court of Appeals' judgment if there is any ground on which respondent may be entitled to relief. This case is before us on petitioner's motion to dismiss for failure to state a claim. It is a well-settled principle of law that "a complaint should not be dismissed merely because a plaintiff's allegations do not support the particular legal theory he advances, for the court is under a duty to examine the complaint to determine if the allegations provide for relief on any possible theory." Thus, even if respondent did not advance claims based on the Eighth or Ninth Amendments, or on the Equal Protection Clause, his complaint should not be dismissed if any of those provisions could entitle him to relief. I need not reach either the Eighth Amendment or the Equal Protection Clause issues because I believe that Hardwick has stated a cognizable claim that Section 16-6-2 interferes with constitutionally protected interests in privacy and freedom of intimate association. But neither the Eighth Amendment nor the Equal Protection Clause is so clearly irrelevant that a claim resting on either provision should be peremptorily dismissed. The Court's cramped reading of the issue before it makes for a short opinion, but it does little to make for a persuasive one.

II

"Our cases long have recognized that the Constitution embodies a promise that a certain private sphere of individual liberty will be kept largely beyond the reach of government." In construing the right to privacy, the Court has proceeded along two somewhat distinct, albeit complementary, lines. First, it has recognized a privacy interests with reference to certain decisions that are properly for the individual to make. Second, it has recognized a privacy interest with reference to certain places without regard for the particular activities in which the individuals who occupy them are engaged. The case before us implicates both the decisional and the spatial aspects of the right to privacy.

A

The Court concludes today that none of our prior cases dealing with various decisions that individuals are entitled to make free of governmental interference "bears any resemblance to the claimed constitutional right of homosexuals to engage in acts of sodomy that is asserted in this case." While it is true that these cases may be characterized by their connection to protection of the family, the Court's conclusion that they extend no further than this boundary ignores the warning in *Moore v. East Cleveland* (1977) against "clos[ing] our eyes to the basic reasons why certain rights associated with the family have been accorded shelter under the Fourteenth Amendment's Due Process Clause." We protect those rights not because they contribute, in some direct and material way, to the general public welfare, but because they form so central a part of an individual's life. "[T]he concept of privacy embodies the 'moral fact that a person belongs to himself and not others nor to society as a whole.'" And so we protect the decision whether to marry precisely because marriage "is an association that promotes a way of life, not causes; a harmony in living, not political faiths; a bilateral loyalty, not commercial or social projects." We protect the decision whether to have a child because parenthood alters so dramatically an individual's self-definition, not because of demographic considerations or the Bible's command to be fruitful and multiply. And we protect the family because it contributes so powerfully to the happiness of individuals, not because of a preference for stereotypical households. The Court recognized in *Roberts,* 468 U.S., at 619, 104 S.Ct., at 3250, that the "ability independently to define one's identity that is central to any concept of liberty" cannot truly be exercised in a vacuum; we all depend on the "emotional enrichment from close ties with others."

Only the most willful blindness could obscure the fact that sexual intimacy is "a sensitive, key relationship of human existence, central to family life, community welfare, and the development of human personality." The fact that individuals define themselves in a significant way through their intimate sexual relationships with others suggests, in a Nation as diverse as ours, that there may be many "right" ways of conducting those relationships, and that much of the richness of a relationship will come from the freedom an individual has to choose the form and nature of these intensely personal bonds.

In a variety of circumstances we have recognized that a necessary corollary of giving individuals freedom to choose how to conduct their lives is acceptance of the fact that different individuals will make different choices. For example, in holding that the clearly important state interest in public education should give way to a competing claim by the Amish to the effect that extended formal schooling threatened their way of life, the Court declared: "There can be no assumption that today's majority is 'right' and the Amish and others like them are 'wrong.' A way of life that is odd or even erratic but interferes no rights or interests of others is not to be condemned because it is different." The Court claims that its decision today merely refuses to recognize a fundamental right to engage in homosexual sodomy; what the Court really has refused to recognize is the fundamental interest all individuals have in controlling the nature of their intimate associations with others.

B

The behavior for which Hardwick faces prosecution occurred in his own home, a place to which the Fourth Amendment attaches special significance. The Court's treatment of this aspect of the case is symptomatic of its overall refusal to consider the broad principles that have informed our treatment of privacy in specific cases. Just as the right to privacy is more than the mere aggregation of a number of entitlements to engage in specific behavior, so too, protecting the physical integrity of the home is more than merely a means of protecting specific activities that often take place there. Even when our understanding of the contours of the right to privacy depends on "reference to a 'place,'" "the essence of a Fourth Amendment violation is 'not the breaking of [a person's] doors, and the rummaging of his drawers,' but rather is 'the invasion of his indefeasible right of personal security, personal liberty and private property.'"

The Court's interpretation of the pivotal case of *Stanley v. Georgia* (1969), is entirely unconvincing. *Stanley* held that Georgia's undoubted power to punish the public distribution of constitutionally unprotected, obscene material did not permit the State to punish the private possession of such material. According to the majority here, *Stanley* relied entirely on the First Amendment, and thus, it is claimed, sheds no light on cases not involving printed materials. Ante, at 2846. But that is not what *Stanley* said. Rather, the *Stanley* Court anchored its holding in the Fourth Amendment's special protection for the individual in his home:

"The makers of our Constitution undertook to secure conditions favorable to the pursuit of happiness. They recognized the significance of man's spiritual nature, of his feelings and of his intellect. They knew that only a part of the pain, pleasure and satisfactions of life are to be found in material things. They sought to protect Americans in their beliefs, their thoughts, their emotions and their sensations.'

"These are the rights that appellant is asserting in the case before us. He is asserting the right to read or observe what he pleases—the right to satisfy his intellectual and emotional needs in the privacy of his own home."

The central place that *Stanley* gives Justice Brandeis' dissent in *Olmstead,* a case raising no First Amendment claim, shows that *Stanley* rested as much on the Court's understanding of the Fourth Amendment as it did on the First. Indeed, in *Paris Adult Theater I v. Slaton* (1973) the Court suggested that reliance on the Fourth Amendment not only supported the Court's outcome in *Stanley* but actually was necessary to it: "If obscene material unprotected by the First Amendment in itself carried with it a 'penumbra' of constitutionally protected privacy, this Court would not have found it necessary to decide *Stanley* on the narrow basis of the 'privacy of the home,' which was hardly more than a reaffirmation that 'a man's home is his castle.'" "The right of the people to be secure in their . . . houses," expressly guaranteed by the Fourth Amendment, is perhaps the most "textual" of the various constitutional provisions that inform our understanding of the right to privacy, and thus I cannot agree with the Court's statement that "[t]he right pressed upon us here has no . . . support in the text of the Constitution," ante, at 2846. Indeed, the right of an individual to conduct intimate relationships in the intimacy of his or her own home seems to me to be the heart of the Constitution's protection of privacy.

III

The Court's failure to comprehend the magnitude of the liberty interests at stake in this case leads it to slight the question whether petitioner, on behalf of the State, has justified Georgia's infringement on these interests. I believe that neither of the two general justifications for Section 16-6-2 that petitioner has advanced warrants dismissing respondent's challenge for failure to state a claim.

First, petitioner asserts that the acts made criminal by the statute may have serious adverse consequences for "the general public health and welfare," such as spreading communicable diseases or fostering other criminal activity. Brief for Petitioner 37. Inasmuch as this case was dismissed by the District Court on the pleadings, it is not surprising that the record before us is barren of any evidence to support petitioner's claim. In light of the state of the record, I see no justification for the Court's attempt to equate the private, consensual sexual activity at issue here with the "possession in the home of drugs, firearms, or stolen goods," ante, at 2846, to which *Stanley* refused to extend its protection. None of the behavior so mentioned in *Stanley* can properly be viewed as "[v]ictimless," drugs and weapons are inherently dangerous and for property to be "stolen," someone must have been wrongfully deprived of it. Nothing in the record before the Court provides any justification for finding the activity forbidden by Section 16-6-2 to be physically dangerous, either to the persons engaged in it or to others.

The core of petitioner's defense of Section 16-6-2, however, is that respondent and others who engage in the conduct prohibited by Section 16-6-2 interfere with Georgia's exercise of the "right of the Nation and of the States to maintain a decent society." Essentially, petitioner argues, and the Court agrees, that the fact that the acts described in Section 16-6-2 "for hundreds of years, it not thousands, have been uniformly condemned as immoral" is a sufficient reason to permit a State to ban them today.

I cannot agree that either the length of time a majority has held its convictions or the passions with which it defends them can withdraw legislation from this Court's scrutiny. As Justice Jackson wrote so eloquently for the Court in *West Virginia Board of Education v. Barnette* (1943), "we apply the limitations of the Constitution with no fear that freedom to be intellectually and spiritually diverse or even contrary will disintegrate the social organization . . . [F]reedom to differ is not limited to things that do not matter much. That would be a mere shadow of freedom. The test of its substance is the right to differ as to things that touch the heart of the existing order." It is precisely because the issue raised by this case touches the heart of what makes individuals what they are that we should be especially sensitive to the rights of those whose choices upset the majority.

The assertion that "traditional Judeo-Christian values proscribe" the conduct involved, Brief for Petitioner 20, cannot provide an adequate justification for Section 16-6-2. That certain, but by no means all, religious groups condemn the behavior at issue gives the State no license to impose their judgments on the entire citizenry. The legitimacy of secular legislation depends instead on whether the State can advance some justification for its law beyond its conformity to religious doctrine. Thus, far from buttressing his case, petitioner's invocation of Leviticus, Romans, St. Thomas Aquinas, and sodomy's heretical status during the Middle Ages undermines his suggestion that Section 16-6-2 represents a legitimate use of secular coercive power. A State can no more punish private behavior because of religious intolerance than it can punish such behavior because of racial animus. "The Constitution cannot control such prejudices, but neither can it tolerate them. Private biases may be outside the reach of the law, but the law cannot, directly or indirectly, give them effect." No matter how uncomfortable a certain group may make the majority of this court, we have held that "[m]ere public intolerance or animosity cannot constitutionally justify the deprivation of a person's physical liberty."

Nor can Section 16-6-2 be justified as a "morally neutral" exercise of Georgia's power to "protect the public environment," Certainly, some private behavior can affect the fabric of society as a whole. Reasonable people may differ about whether particular sexual acts are moral or immoral, but "we have ample evidence for believing that people will not abandon morality, will not think any better of murder, cruelty and dishonesty, merely because some private sexual practice which they abominate is not punished by the law." Petitioner and the Court fail to see the difference between laws that protect public sensibilities and those that enforce private morality. Statutes banning public sexual activity are entirely consistent with protecting the individual's liberty interest in decisions concerning sexual relations: the same recognition that those decisions are intensely private which justifies protecting them from governmental interference can justify protecting individuals from unwilling exposure to the sexual activities of others. But the mere fact that intimate behavior may be punished when it takes place in public cannot dictate how States can regulate intimate behavior that occurs in intimate places.

This case involves no real interference with the rights of others, for the mere knowledge that other individuals do not adhere to one's value system cannot be a legally cognizable interest let alone an interest that can justify invading the houses, hearts, and minds of citizens who choose to live their lives differently.

IV

It took but three years for the Court to see the error in its analysis in *Minersville School District v. Gobitis* (1940), and to recognize that the threat to national cohesion posed by a refusal to salute the flag was vastly outweighed by the threat to those same values posed by compelling such a salute. See *West Virginia Board of Education v. Barnette* (1943). I can only hope that here, too, the Court soon will reconsider its analysis and conclude that depriving individuals of the right to choose for themselves how to conduct their intimate relationships poses a far greater threat to the values most deeply rooted in our Nation's history than tolerance of nonconformity could ever do. Because I think the Court today betrays those values, I dissent.

Source:

Supreme Court Reporter, Vol. 106, pp. 2,841–2,859.

Immigration Reform and Control Act, 1986

Legislation signed into law November 6, 1986, liberalizing regulations for persons residing illegally in the United States and seeking amnesty. It provided a process for legalizing the status of many illegal aliens who entered the United States before January 1, 1982. Under the new law, qualified alien applicants could receive temporary resident status and then, after residing in the United States for 18 months, apply for permanent resident status. The act also imposed civil and criminal penalties on employers who knowingly hire or help aliens not allowed to work in the United States. Among the many other provisions of the act were the categorization of temporary workers into two groups (agricultural laborers and all others), antidiscrimination rules, and some increases in emigration from colonies of foreign nations.

An Act

To amend the Immigration and Nationality Act to revise and reform the immigration laws, and for other purposes.

Be it enacted by the Senate and House of Representatives of the United States of America in Congress assembled,

Section 1. Short Title; References in Act.

(a) Short Title.—This Act may be cited as the "Immigration Reform and Control Act of 1986."

(b) Amendments to Immigration and Nationality Act.—Except as otherwise specifically provided in this Act, whenever in this Act an amendment or repeal is expressed as an amendment to, or repeal of, a provision, the reference shall be deemed to be made to the Immigration and Nationality Act.

* * *

Title I—Control of Illegal Immigration

Part A—Employment

Sec. 101. Control of Unlawful Employment of Aliens.

(a) In General.—

* * *

"Unlawful Employment of Aliens

"Sec. 274A. (a) Making Employment of Unauthorized Aliens Unlawful.—

"(1) In general.—It is unlawful for a person or other entity to hire, or to recruit or refer for a fee, for employment in the United States—

"(A) an alien knowing the alien is an unauthorized alien . . . with respect to such employment. . . .

* * *

"(2) Continuing employment.—It is unlawful for a person or other entity, after hiring an alien for employment in accordance with paragraph (1), to continue to employ the alien in the United States knowing the alien is (or has become) an unauthorized alien with respect to such employment.

"(3) Defense.—A person or entity that establishes that it has complied in good faith with the requirements of subsection (b) with respect to the hiring, recruiting, or referral for employment of an alien in the United States has established an affirmative defense that the person or entity has not violated paragraph (1)(A) with respect to such hiring, recruiting, or referral.

"(4) Use of labor through contract.—For purposes of this section, a person or other entity who uses a contract, subcontract, or exchange, entered into, renegotiated, or extended after the date of the enactment of this section, to obtain the labor of an alien in the United States knowing that the alien is an unauthorized alien . . . with respect to performing such labor, shall be considered to have hired the alien for employment in the United States in violation of paragraph (1)(A).

"(5) Use of state employment agency documentation—. . . a person or entity shall be deemed to have complied with the requirements . . . with respect to the hiring of an individual who was referred for such employment by a State employment agency (as defined by the Attorney

General), if the person or entity has and . . . appropriate documentation of such referral by that agency, which documentation certifies that the agency has complied with the procedures . . . with respect to the individual's referral.

"(b) Employment Verification System.—The requirements . . . are, in the case of a person or other entity hiring, recruiting, or referring an individual for employment in the United States, the requirements specified in the following three paragraphs:

"(1)Attestation after examination of documentation.

* * *

"Unfair Immigration-Related Employment Practices

"Sec. 274B. (a) Prohibition of Discrimination Based on National Origin or Citizenship Status.—

"(1) General rule.—It is an unfair immigration-related employment practice for a person or other entity to discriminate against any individual (other than an unauthorized alien) with respect to the hiring, or recruitment or referral for a fee, of the individual for employment or the discharging of the individual from employment—

"(A) because of such individual's national origin, or

"(B) in the case of a citizen or intending citizen . . . because of such individual's citizenship status.

"(2) Exceptions.—Paragraph (1) shall not apply to—

"(A) a person or other entity that employs three or fewer employees,

"(B) a person's or entity's discrimination because of an individual's national origin if the discrimination with respect to that person or entity and that individual is covered under section 703 of the Civil Rights Act of 1964, or

"(C) discrimination because of citizenship status which is otherwise required in order to comply with law, regulation, or executive order, or required by Federal, State, or local government contract, or which the Attorney General determines to be essential for an employer to do business with an agency or department of the Federal, State, or local government.

"(3) Definition of citizen or intending citizen.— . . . the term 'citizen or intending citizen' means an individual who—

"(A) is a citizen or national of the United States, or

"(B) is an alien who.—

"(i) is lawfully admitted for permanent residence, is granted the status of an alien lawfully admitted for temporary residence . . . , is admitted as a refugee under section 207, or is granted asylum under section 208, and

"(ii) evidence an intention to become a citizen of the United States through completing a declaration of intention to become a citizen;

but does not include (I) an alien who fails to apply for naturalization within six months of the date the alien first becomes eligible (by virtue of period of lawful permanent residence) to apply for naturalization or, if later, within six months after the date of the enactment of this section and (II) an alien who has applied on a timely basis, but has not been naturalized as a citizen within 2 years after the date of the application, unless the alien can establish that the alien is actively pursuing naturalization, except that time consumed in the Service's processing the application shall not be counted toward the 2-year period.

"(4) Additional exception providing right to prefer equally qualified citizens.—Notwithstanding any other provision of this section, it is not an unfair immigration-related employment practice for a person or other entity to prefer to hire, recruit, or refer an individual who is a citizen or national of the United States over another individual who is an alien if the two individuals are equally qualified.

"(b) Charges of Violations.—

"(1) In general.—Except as provided in paragraph (2), any person alleging that the person is adversely affected directly by an unfair immigration-related employment practice (or a person on that person's behalf) or an officer of the Service alleging that an unfair immigration-related employment practice has occurred or is occurring may file a charge respecting such practice or violation with the Special Counsel (appointed under subsection (c)). Charges shall be in writing under oath or affirmation and shall contain such information as the Attorney General requires. The Special Counsel by certified mail shall serve a notice of the charge (including the date. . . .

* * *

Sec. 1546. Fraud and misuse of visas, permits, and other documents";

* * *

"(b) Whoever uses—

"(1) an identification document, knowing (or having reason to know) that the document was not issued lawfully for the use of the possessor,

"(2) an identification document knowing (or having reason to know) that the document is false, or

"(3) a false attestation,

for the purpose of satisfying a requirement . . . of the Immigration and Nationality Act, shall be fined in accordance with this title, or imprisoned. . . .

"(c) This section does not prohibit any lawfully authorized investigative, protective, or intelligence activity of a law enforcement agency of the United States, a State, or a subdivision of a State, or of an intelligence agency of the United States, or any activity authorized under title V of the Organized Crime Control Act of 1970.

* * *

Part B—Improvement of Enforcement and Services

Sec. 111. Authorization of Appropriations for Enforcement and Service Activities of the Immigration and Naturalization Service.

(a) Two Essential Elements.—It is the sense of Congress that two essential elements of the program of immigration control established by this Act are—

(1) an increase in the border patrol and other inspection and enforcement activities of the Immigration and Naturalization Service and of other appropriate Federal agencies in order to prevent and deter the illegal entry of aliens into the United States and the violation of the terms of their entry, and

(2) an increase in examinations and other service activities of the Immigration and Naturalization Service and other appropriate Federal agencies in order to ensure prompt and efficient adjudication of petitions and applications provided for under the Immigration and Nationality Act.

(b) Increased Authorization of Appropriations for INS and EOIR.—In addition to any other amounts authorized to be appropriated, in order to carry out this Act there are authorized to be appropriated to the Department of Justice

* * *

Sec. 112. Unlawful Transportation of Aliens to the United States.

(a) Criminal Penalties.—Subsection (a) of section 274 (8 U.S.C. 1324) is amended to read as follows:

"(a) Criminal Penalties.—(1) Any person who—

"(A) knowing that a person is an alien, brings to or attempts to bring to the United States in any manner whatsoever such person at a place other than a designated port of entry, or place other than as designated by the Commissioner, regardless of whether such alien has received prior official authorization to come to, enter, or reside in the United States and regardless of any future official action which may be taken with respect to such alien;

"(B) knowing or in reckless disregard of the fact that an alien has come to, entered, or remains in the United States in violation of law, transports, or moves or attempts to transport or move such alien within the United States by means of transportation or otherwise, in furtherance of such violation of law;

"(C) knowing or in reckless disregard of the fact that an alien has come to, entered, or remains in the United States in violation of law, conceals, harbors, or shields from detection, or attempts to conceal, harbor, or shield from detection, such alien in any place, including any building or any means of transportation; or

"(D) encourages or induces an alien to come to, enter, or reside in the United States, knowing or in reckless disregard of the fact that such coming to, entry, or residence is or will be in violation of law,

shall be fined in accordance with title 18, United States Code, imprisoned not more than five years, or both, for each alien in respect to whom any violation of this subsection occurs.

"(2) Any person who, knowing or in reckless disregard of the fact that an alien has not received prior official authorization to come to, enter, or reside in the United States, brings to or attempts to bring to the United States in any manner whatsoever, such alien, regardless of any official action which may later be taken with respect to such alien shall, for each transaction constituting a violation of this paragraph, regardless of the number of aliens involved—

"(A) be fined in accordance with title 18, United States Code, or imprisoned not more than one year, or both; or

"(B) in the case of—

"(i) a second or subsequent offense,

"(ii) an offense done for the purpose of commercial advantage or private financial gain, or

"(iii) an offense in which the alien is not upon arrival immediately brought and presented to an appropriate immigration officer at a designated port of entry, be fined in accordance with title 18, United States Code, or imprisoned not more than five years, or both."

* * *

Sec. 115. Enforcement of the Immigration Laws of the United States.

It is the sense of the Congress that—

(1) the immigration laws of the United States should be enforced vigorously and uniformly, and

(2) in the enforcement of such laws, the Attorney General shall take due and deliberate actions necessary to safeguard the constitutional rights, personal safety, and human dignity of United States citizens and aliens.

Sec. 116. Restricting Warrantless Entry in the Case of Outdoor Agricultural Operations.

* * *

(a), an officer or employee of the Service may not enter without the consent of the owner (or agent thereof) or a properly executed warrant onto the premises of a farm or other outdoor agricultural operation for the purpose of interrogating a person believed to be an alien as to the person's right to be or to remain in the United States."

* * *

Approved November 6, 1986.

Source:
Statutes at Large, 1986, Vol. 100, pp. 3,359–3,445.

Equal Employment Opportunity Commission, Guidelines on Discrimination Because of Sex, 1990

In a 1990 update of its guidelines, the Equal Employment Opportunity Commission defined sexual harassment as "unwelcome sexual advances, requests for sexual favors, and other verbal or physical conduct of a sexual nature." Behavior is considered harassment when submission to sexual advances is made a condition of employment, or when job decisions, such as promotion or demotion, are based on the acceptance or rejection of such advances. Harassment may also result from behavior that "unreasonably" interferes with work performance, or creates a "hostile working environment."

The guidelines held that employers are responsible for the actions of any of their agents or supervisors, as well as non-employees, who come into contact with employees on a regular basis. Regardless of whether employers allow or forbid the behavior, or if "the employer knew or should have known" about the offending behavior, those employers are held responsible unless they can prove that they took "immediate" steps to correct the offense. In addition, if other employees have been passed over for benefits or promotions in favor of an individual who granted sexual favors to an employer, those employees denied benefits may hold the employer responsible.

The Commission urged employers to educate their workers about what constitutes sexual harassment and what to do if they are confronted with such behavior. This last directive led to the establishment of training programs and the implementation of grievance procedures across the country.

These guidelines reached the Supreme Court in two 1998 cases, *Burlington Industries v. Ellerth* (524 U.S. 722) and *Faragher v. City of Boca Raton* (524 U.S. 775). On June 26, 1998 the U.S. Supreme Court in *Burlington Industries v. Ellerth* (524 U.S. 722) and *Faragher v. City of Boca Raton* (524 U.S. 775) clarified the conditions for sexual harassment liability in the workplace. Kimberly Ellerth, a former employee of Burlington Industries, had allegedly received unsolicited sexual advances from her supervisor. In October 1994 Ellerth filed a sexual harassment suit against Burlington Industries that led the Court to address the issue of "whether . . . an employee who refuses the unwelcome and threatening sexual advances of a supervisor, yet suffers no adverse, tangible job consequences, can recover against the employer." The majority opinion ruled in favor of the plaintiff, stating that the harassment Ellerth experienced amounted to gender discrimination as defined by Title VII of the Civil Rights Act of 1964.

Faragher also dealt with inadequate supervision regarding sexual harassment. Beth Ann Faragher, a former lifeguard employed by the Boca Raton Parks and Recreation Department, was sexually harassed by her supervisor. Faragher's case forced the Court to examine the specific question of whether an employer may be held liable "for the acts of a supervisory employee whose sexual harassment of subordinates has created a hostile work environment amounting to employment discrimination." In his majority opinion, Justice David Souter stated that, under Title VII of the Civil Rights Act of 1964, sexual harassment amounts to discrimination and that the city had not done an adequate job disseminating its sexual harassment policy among its employees. Furthermore, the city had failed to sufficiently monitor the conduct of its supervisors. Souter summarized the ruling by saying, "We hold that an employer is vicariously liable for actionable discrimination caused by a supervisor, but subject to an affirmative defense looking to the reasonableness of the employer's conduct as well as that of a plaintiff victim." Title VII would not apply if the defense could prove that the employer had addressed an employee's sexual harassment accusation.

a) Harassment on the basis of sex is a violation of Sec. 703 of Title VII.[1] Unwelcome sexual advances, requests for sexual favors, and other verbal or physical conduct of a sexual nature constitute sexual harassment when (1) submission to such conduct is made either explicitly or implicitly a term or condition of an individual's employment, (2) submission to or rejection of such conduct by an individual is used as the basis for employment decisions affecting such individual, or (3) such conduct has the purpose or effect of unreasonably interfering with an individual's work performance or creating an intimidating, hostile, or offensive working environment.

(b) In determining whether alleged conduct constitutes sexual harassment, the Commission will look at the record as a whole and at the totality of the circumstances, such as the nature of the sexual advances and the context in which the alleged incidents occurred. The determination of the legality of a particular action will be made from the facts, on a case by case basis.

(c) Applying general Rule VII principles, an employer, employment agency, joint apprenticeship committee or labor organization (hereinafter collectively referred to as "employer") is responsible for its acts and those of its agents and supervisory employees with respect to sexual harassment regardless of whether the specific acts complained of were authorized or even forbidden by the employer and regardless of whether the employer knew or should have known of their occurrence. The Commission will examine the circumstances of the particular employment relationship and the job functions performed by the individual in determining whether an individual acts in either a supervisory or agency capacity.

(d) With respect to conduct between fellow employees, an employer is responsible for acts of sexual harassment in the workplace where the employer (or its agents or supervisory employees) knows or should have known of the conduct, unless it can show that it took immediate corrective action.

(e) An employer may also be responsible for the acts of nonemployees, with respect to sexual harassment of employees in the workplace, where the employer (or its agents or supervisory employees) knows or should have known of the conduct and fails to take immediately and appropriate corrective action. In reviewing these cases the Commission will consider the extent of the employer's control and any other legal responsibility which the employer may have with respect to the conduct of such non-employees.

(f) Prevention is the best tool for the elimination of sexual harassment. An employer should take all steps necessary to prevent sexual harassment from occurring, such as affirmatively raising the subject, expressing strong disapproval, developing appropriate sanctions, informing employees of their right to raise and how to raise the issue of harassment under Title VII, and developing methods to sensitize all concerned.

(g) Other related practices: Where employment opportunities or benefits are granted because of an individual's submission to the employer's sexual advances or request for sexual favors, the employer may be held liable for unlawful sex discrimination against other persons who were qualified for but denied that employment opportunity or benefit.

[1]The principles involved here continue to apply to race, color, religion or national origin.

Source:

U.S. Equal Employment Opportunity Commission. Available online. URL: www.eeoc.gov/policy/index.html. Accessed December 2003.

President George H. W. Bush's Remarks on the Americans with Disabilities Act, 1990

The Americans with Disabilities Act (ADA), prohibiting discrimination in employment, public accommodations, or transportation against people with a physical or mental disability, was enacted July 26, 1990. It defined disability as any condition that "substantially limits" a major life activity such as seeing or walking. It applied to alcoholics and drug users who were undergoing treatment for their addictions and by a 1998 Supreme Court decision, it included AIDS. Employers were forbidden to refuse to hire or promote a disabled job applicant or worker and were required to make "reasonable accommodations" for all disabled employees. Exemptions would be permitted only if an employer could show that the requirements would impose an "undue hardship." Telecommunications companies and all transit carriers—railroads, bus lines, mass transit systems, and school buses—were required to make their services accessible to the disabled. Newly constructed or renovated buildings were also required to be accessible by the disabled. Existing buildings were exempt from making any modifications that were not "readily achievable."

In *Albertson v. Kirkingburg* (527 U.S. 555), one of three June 1999 decisions limiting the scope of ADA, the U.S. Supreme Court ruled unanimously in favor of the employer of a truck driver, Hallie Kirkingburg, who was dismissed from his job because he had limited vision in one eye but had been certified erroneously as meeting federal requirements for commercial driving. When his employer discovered Kirkingburg's true visual capacity, he was fired. The Court's decision narrowed the circumstances in which an employee's dismissal could be called discriminatory, subject to protection under the ADA. Moreover, it outlined the Court's definition of disability. In his majority opinion, Justice David Souter asserted that the ADA did not require the company to relax its adherence to federal safety standards in order to employ Kirkingburg as a driver.

* * *

This is an immensely important day, a day that belongs to all of you. Everywhere I look, I see people who have dedicated themselves to making sure that this day would come to pass: my friends from Congress, as I say, who worked so diligently with the best interest of all at heart, Democrats and Republicans; members of this administration—and I'm pleased to see so many top officials and members of my Cabinet here today who brought their caring and expertise to this fight; and then, the organizations—so many dedicated organizations for people with disabilities, who gave their time and their strength; and perhaps most of all, everyone out there and others—across the breadth of this nation are 43 million Americans with disabilities. You have made this happen. All of you have made this happen. To all of you, I just want to say your triumph is that your bill will now be law, and that this day belongs to you. On behalf of our nation, thank you very, very much.

Three weeks ago we celebrated our nation's Independence Day. Today we're here to rejoice in and celebrate another "Independence Day," one that is long overdue. With today's signing of the landmark Americans for Disabilities Act, every man, woman, and child with a disability can now pass through once-closed doors into a bright new era of equality, independence and freedom. As I look around at all these joyous faces, I remember clearly how many years of dedicated commitment have gone into making this historic new civil rights act a reality. It's been the work of a true coalition, a strong and inspiring coalition of people who have shared both a dream and a passionate determination to make that dream come true. It's been a coalition in the finest spirit: a joining of Democrats and Republicans, of the legislative and the executive branches, of Federal and State agencies, of public officials and private citizens, of people with disabilities and without.

This historic act is the world's first comprehensive declaration of equality for people with disabilities—the first. Its passage has made the United States the international leader on this human rights issue. Already, leaders of several other countries, including Sweden, Japan, the Soviet Union, and all 12 members of the EEC (European Economic Community), have announced that they hope to enact now similar legislation.

Our success with this act proves that we are keeping faith with the spirit of our courageous forefathers who wrote in the Declaration of Independence: "We hold these truths to be self-evident, that all men are created equal, that they are endowed by their Creator with certain unalienable rights." These words have been our guide for more than two centuries as we've labored to form our more perfect union. But tragically, for too many Americans, the blessings of liberty have been limited or even denied. The Civil Rights Act of '64 took a bold step towards righting that wrong. But the stark fact remained that people with disabilities were still victims of segregation and discrimination, and this was intolerable. Today's legislation brings us closer to that day when no Americans will ever again be deprived of their basic guarantee of life, liberty, and the pursuit of happiness.

This act is powerful in its simplicity. It will ensure that people with disabilities are given the basic guarantees for which they have worked so long and so hard: independence, freedom of choice, control of their lives, the opportunity to blend fully and equally into the rich mosaic of the American mainstream. Legally, it will provide our disabled community with a powerful expansion of protections and then basic civil rights. It will guarantee fair and just access to the fruits of American life which we all must be able to enjoy. And then, specifically, first the ADA ensures that employers covered by the act cannot discriminate against qualified individuals with disabilities. Second, the ADA ensures access to public accommodations such as restaurants, hotels, shopping centers and offices. And third, the ADA ensures expanded access to transportation services. And fourth, the ADA ensures equivalent telephone services for people with speech or hearing impediments.

These provisions mean so much to so many. To one brave girl in particular, they will mean the world. Lisa Carl, a young Washington State woman with cerebral palsy, who I'm told is with us today, now will always be admitted to her hometown theater. Lisa, you might not have been welcome at your theater, but I'll tell you—welcome to the White House. We're glad you're here. The ADA is a dramatic renewal not only for those with disabilities but for all of us, because along with the precious privilege of being an American comes a sacred duty to ensure that every other American's rights are also guaranteed.

Together, we must remove the physical barriers we have created and the social barriers that we have accepted. For ours will never be a truly prosperous nation until all within it prosper. For inspiration, we need look no further than our own neighbors. With us in that wonderful crowd out there are people representing 18 of the daily Points of Light that I've named for their extraordinary involvement with the disabled community. We applaud you and your shining example. Thank you for your leadership for all that are here today.

Now, let me just tell you a wonderful story, a story about children already working in the spirit of the ADA—a story that really touched me. Across the Nation, some 10,000 youngsters with disabilities are part of Little League's Challenger Division. Their teams play just like others, but—and this is the most remarkable part—as they play, at their sides are volunteer buddies from conventional Little League teams. All of these players work together. They team up to wheel around the bases and to field grounders together and, most of all, just to play and become friends. We must let these children be our guides and inspiration.

I also want to say a special word to our friends in the business community. You have in your hands the key to the success of this act, for you can unlock a splendid resource of untapped human potential that, when freed, will enrich us all. I know there have been concerns that the ADA may be vague or costly, or may lead endlessly to litigation. But I want to reassure you right now that my administration and the United States Congress have carefully crafted this Act. We've all been determined to ensure that it gives flexibility, particularly in terms of the timetable of implementation, and we've been committed to containing the costs that may be incurred.

This act does something important for American business, though—and remember this: You've called for new sources of workers. Well, many of our fellow citizens with disabilities are unemployed. They want to work, and they can work, and this is a tremendous pool of people. And remember, this is a tremendous pool of people who will bring to jobs diversity, loyalty, proven low turnover rate, and only one request: the chance to prove themselves. And when you add together Federal, State, local, and private funds, it costs almost $200 billion annually to support Americans with disabilities—in effect, to keep them independent. Well, when given the opportunity to be independent, they will move proudly into the economic mainstream of American life, and that's what this legislation is all about.

Our problems are large, but our unified heart is larger. Our challenges are great, but our will is greater. And in our America, the most generous, optimistic nation on the face of the Earth, we must not and will not rest until every man and woman with a dream has the means to achieve it.

And today, America welcomes into the mainstream of life all of our fellow citizens with disabilities. We embrace you for your abilities and for your disabilities, for our similarities and indeed for our differences, for your past courage and your future dreams. Last year, we celebrated a victory of international freedom. Even the strongest person couldn't scale the Berlin Wall to gain the elusive promise of independence that lay just beyond. And so, together we rejoiced when that barrier fell.

And now I sign legislation which takes a sledgehammer to another wall, one which has for too many generations separated Americans with disabilities from the freedom they could glimpse, but not grasp. Once again, we rejoice as this barrier falls for claiming together we will not accept, we will not excuse, we will not tolerate discrimination in America.

With, again, great thanks to the Members of the United States Senate, leaders of whom are here today, and those who worked so tirelessly for this legislation on both sides of the aisles. And to those Members of the House of Representatives with us here today, Democrats and Republicans as well, I salute you. And on your behalf, as well as the behalf of this entire country, I now lift my pen to sign this Americans with Disabilities Act and say: Let the shameful wall of exclusion finally come tumbling down. God bless you all.

Source:

Public Papers of the Presidents of the United States: George H. W. Bush, 1990. Washington, D.C.: Government Printing Office, 1992.

Family and Medical Leave Act, 1993

Most industrial countries give regular paid leave for months, even years, to handle such events as the birth of a child. Congress objected to such provisions as socialistic. However, on February 5, 1993, President Bill Clinton signed this law requiring businesses that employ 50 or more people to grant their employees up to 12 weeks of unpaid leave annually for family and medical emergencies. The family leave issue had gained momentum during the 1992 presidential election season, when Democrat Bill Clinton reminded voters that President George H. W. Bush had vetoed Democrat-sponsored family leave bills. An employer would have to continue to furnish health care coverage during the leave. Moreover, the company must guarantee an employee the same job or an equivalent position when he or she returned to work. The legislation included a section on "Findings and Purposes," in which lawmakers outlined the rationale for federal action to balance workplace demands with the needs of families.

AN ACT

To grant family and temporary medical leave under certain circumstances.

Title I—General Requirements for Leave

Sec. 102. Leave Requirement.

(a) In General.—

(1) Entitlement to leave. . . . An eligible employee shall be entitled to a total of 12 workweeks of leave during any 12-month period for one or more of the following:

(A) Because of the birth of a son or daughter of the employee and in order to care for such son or daughter.

(B) Because of the placement of a son or daughter with the employee for adoption or foster care.

(C) In order to care for the spouse, or a son, daughter, or parent, of the employee, if such spouse, son, daughter, or parent has a serious health condition.

(D) Because of a serious health condition that makes the employee unable to perform the functions of the position of such employee.

(2) Expiration of entitlement. The entitlement to leave under subparagraphs (A) and (B) of paragraph (1) for a birth or placement of a son or daughter shall expire at the end of the 12-month period beginning on the date of such birth or placement.

(b) Leave Taken Intermittently or on a Reduced Leave Schedule.—

(1) In general. Leave under subparagraph (A) and (B) of subsection (a)(1) shall not be taken by an employee intermittently or on a reduced leave schedule unless the employee and the employer of the employee agree otherwise. Subject to paragraph (2), subsection (e)(2), and section

103(b)(5), leave under subparagraph (C) or (D) of subsection (a)(1) may be taken intermittently or on a reduced leave schedule when medically necessary. The taking of leave intermittently or on a reduced leave schedule pursuant to this paragraph shall not result in a reduction in the total amount of leave to which the employee is entitled under subsection (a) beyond the amount of leave actually taken.

(2) Alternative position. If an employee requests intermittent leave, or leave on a reduced leave schedule, under subparagraph (C) and (D) of subsection (a)(1), that is foreseeable based on planned medical treatment, the employer may require such employee to transfer temporarily to an available alternative position offered by the employer for which the employee is qualified and that—

(A) has equivalent pay and benefits; and

(B) better accommodates recurring periods of leave than the regular employment position of the employee.

(c) Unpaid Leave Permitted. Except as provided in subsection (d), leave granted under subsection (a) may consist of unpaid leave. Where an employee is otherwise exempt under regulations issued by the Secretary pursuant to section 13(a)(1) of the Fair Labor Standards Act of 1938 (29 U.S.C. 213(a)(1)), the compliance of an employer with this title by providing unpaid leave shall not affect the exempt status of the employee under such section.

(d) Relationship to Paid Leave.—

(1) Unpaid leave. If an employer provides paid leave for fewer than 12 workweeks, the additional weeks of leave necessary to attain the 12 workweeks of leave required under this title may be provided without compensation.

(2) Substitution of paid leave.—

(A) In general. An eligible employee may elect, or an employer may require the employee, to substitute any of the accrued paid vacation leave, personal leave, or family leave of the employee for leave provided under subparagraph (A), (B), or (C) of subsection (a)(1) for any part of the 12-week period of such leave under such subsection.

(B) Serious health condition. An eligible employee may elect, or an employer may require the employee, to substitute any of the accrued paid vacation leave, personal leave, or medical or sick leave of the employee for leave provided under subparagraph (C) or (D) of subsection (a)(1) for any part of the 12-week period of such leave under such subsection, except that nothing in this title shall require an employer to provide paid sick leave or paid medical leave in any situation in which such employer would not normally provide any such paid leave.

(e) Foreseeable Leave.—

(1) Requirement of notice. In any case in which the necessity for leave under subparagraph (A) or (B) of subsection (a)(1) is foreseeable based on an expected birth or placement, the employee shall provide the employer with not less than 30 days' notice, before the date the leave is to begin, of the employee's intention to take leave under such subparagraph, except that if the date of the birth or placement requires leave to begin in less than 30 days, the employee shall provide such notice as is practicable.

(2) Duties of employee. In any case in which the necessity for leave under subparagraph (C) or (D) of subsection (a)(1) is foreseeable based on planned medical treatment, the employee—

(A) shall make a reasonable effort to schedule the treatment so as not to disrupt unduly the operations of the employer, subject to the approval of the health care provider of the employee or the health care provider of the son, daughter, spouse, or parent of the employee, as appropriate; and

(B) shall provide the employer with not less than 30 days' notice, before the date the leave is to begin, of the employee's intention to take leave under such subparagraph, except that if the date of the treatment requires leave to begin in less than 30 days, the employee shall provide such notice as is practicable.

(f) Spouses Employed by the Same Employer. In any case in which a husband and wife entitled to leave under subsection (a) are employed by the same employer, the aggregate number of workweeks of leave to which both may be entitled may be limited to 12 workweeks during any 12-month period, if such leave is taken—

(1) under subparagraph (A) or (B) of subsection (a)(1); or

(2) to care for a sick parent under subparagraph (C) of such subsection.

* * *

Sec. 104. Employment and Benefits Protection.

(a) Restoration to Position.—

(1) In general. Except as provided in subsection (b), any eligible employee who takes leave under section 102 for the intended purpose of the leave shall be entitled, on return from such leave—

(A) to be restored by the employer to the position of employment held by the employee when the leave commenced; or

(B) to be restored to an equivalent position with equivalent employment benefits, pay, and other terms and conditions of employment.

(2) Loss of benefits. The taking of leave under section 102 shall not result in the loss of any employment benefit accrued prior to the date on which the leave commenced.

(3) Limitations. Nothing in this section shall be construed to entitle any restored employee to—

(A) the accrual of any seniority or employment benefits during any period of leave; or

(B) any right, benefit, or position of employment other than any right, benefit, or position to which the employee would have been entitled had the employee not taken the leave.

* * *

(5) Construction. Nothing in this subsection shall be construed to prohibit an employer from requiring an employee on leave under section 102 to report periodically to the employer on the status and intention of the employee to return to work.

(b) Exemption Concerning Certain Highly Compensated Employee—

(1) Denial of restoration. An employer may deny restoration under subsection

(a) to any eligible employee described in paragraph (2) if—

(A) such denial is necessary to prevent substantial and grievous economic injury to the operations of the employer;

(B) the employer notifies the employee of the intent of the employer to deny restoration on such basis at the time the employer determines that such injury would occur; and

(C) in any case in which the leave has commenced, the employee elects not to return to employment after receiving such notice.

(2) Affected employees. An eligible employee described in paragraph (1) is a salaried eligible employee who is among the highest paid 10 percent of the employees employed by the employer within 75 miles of the facility at which the employee is employed.

(c) Maintenance of Health Benefits—

(1) Coverage. Except as provided in paragraph (2), during any period that an eligible employee takes leave under section 102, the employer shall maintain coverage under any "group health plan" (as defined in section 5000(b)(1) of the Internal Revenue Code of 1986) for the duration of such leave at the level and under the conditions coverage would have been provided if the employee had continued in employment continuously for the duration of such leave.

(2) Failure to return from leave. The employer may recover the premium that under such group the employer paid for maintaining coverage for the employee under such group health plan during any period of unpaid leave under section 102 if—

(A) the employee fails to return from leave under section 102 after the period of leave to which the employee is entitled has expired; and

(B) the employee fails to return to work for a reason other than—

(i) the continuation, recurrence, or onset of a serious health condition that entitles the employee to leave under subparagraph (C) or (D) of section 102(a)(1); or

(ii) other circumstances beyond the control of the employee.

* * *

Sec. 105. Prohibited Acts.

(a) Interference With Rights.—

(1) Exercise of rights. It shall be unlawful for any employer to interfere with, restrain, or deny the exercise of or the attempt to exercise, any right provided under this title.

(2) Discrimination. It shall be unlawful for any employer to discharge or in any other manner discriminate against any individual for opposing any practice made unlawful by this title.

(b) Interference With Proceedings or Inquiries. It shall be unlawful for any person to discharge or in any other manner discriminate against any individual because such individual—

(1) has filed any charge, or has instituted or caused to be instituted any proceeding, under or related to this title;

(2) has given, or is about to give, any information in connection with any inquiry or proceeding relating to any right provided under this title; or

(3) has testified, or is about to testify, in any inquiry or proceeding relating to any right provided under this title.

Source:
Congressional Record. 103rd Cong., 1st Sess., 1993, Vol. 139.

Violence Against Women Act, 1994

Two subtitles of law signed by President Bill Clinton September 13, 1994. The Violence Against Women Act (VAWA) mandates a unified judicial response to sexual crimes committed against women and provides funding ($1.6 billion over six years) for programs intended to decrease the incidence of such crimes. Joseph Biden (D-Del.) proposed the act and introduced it in the Senate; Patricia Schroeder was its sponsor in the House of Representatives.

The act's provisions include: the creation of a national domestic violence hotline; more severe penalties for sex crimes; federal criminal penalties for anyone who crosses a state line to injure a spouse; mandatory arrest policies in cases of domestic violence; domestic violence education for police officers, prosecutors and judges; increased funding for battered women's shelters; the creation of a federal civil rights cause of action for victims of gender-motivated crimes of violence; new policies permitting battered immigrant spouses to petition for legal resident status; interstate enforcement of restraining orders; and prohibitions against gun ownership by anyone subject to a restraining order.

By the end of 1999, 12 federal courts had upheld VAWA as constitutional, and one—the Fourth Circuit Court in Richmond, Virginia—had ruled it unconstitutional. The Virginia case, *Brzonkala v. Virginia Polytechnic Institute & State University*, involved a female college student who brought a civil lawsuit against two students she claimed had raped her. Judge J. Michael Luttig ruled that the Violence Against Women Act, which permits rape victims to bring civil lawsuits whether or not the government presses criminal charges, was an impermissible federal intrusion into states' rights. (Criminal charges were not pressed because the college refused to refer the matter to the police.) In May 2000, the Supreme Court, in the appeal of the Virginia case, *United States v. Morrison* (529 U.S. 598 [2000]), supported the 4th Circuit opinion and invalidated the VAWA provision that had permitted women to sue rapists in federal court.

Subtitle B. National Stalker and Domestic Violence Reduction

SEC. 40601. AUTHORIZING ACCESS TO FEDERAL CRIMINAL INFORMATION DATABASES.

(a) ACCESS AND ENTRY- Section 534 of title 28, United States Code, is amended by adding at the end the following:

`(e)(1) Information from national crime information databases consisting of identification records, criminal history records, protection orders, and wanted person records may be disseminated to civil or criminal courts for use in domestic violence or stalking cases. Nothing in this subsection shall be construed to permit access to such records for any other purpose.

`(2) Federal and State criminal justice agencies authorized to enter information into criminal information databases may include—

`(A) arrests, convictions, and arrest warrants for stalking or domestic violence or for violations of protection orders for the protection of parties from stalking or domestic violence; and

`(B) protection orders for the protection of persons from stalking or domestic violence, provided such orders are subject to periodic verification.

`(3) As used in this subsection—

`(A) the term 'national crime information databases' means the National Crime Information Center and its incorporated criminal history databases, including the Interstate Identification Index; and

`(B) the term 'protection order' includes an injunction or any other order issued for the purpose of preventing violent or threatening acts or harassment against, or contact or communication with or physical proximity to, another person, including temporary and final orders issued by civil or criminal courts (other than support or child custody orders) whether obtained by filing an independent action or as a pendente lite order in another proceeding so long as any civil order was issued in response to a complaint, petition, or motion filed by or on behalf of a person seeking protection.'

(b) RULEMAKING- The Attorney General may make rules to carry out the subsection added to section 534 of title 28, United States Code, by subsection (a), after consultation with the officials charged with managing the National Crime Information Center and the Criminal Justice Information Services Advisory Policy Board.

SEC. 40602. GRANT PROGRAM.

(a) IN GENERAL- The Attorney General is authorized to provide grants to States and units of local government to improve processes for entering data regarding stalking and domestic violence into local, State, and national crime information databases.

(b) ELIGIBILITY- To be eligible to receive a grant under subsection (a), a State or unit of local government shall certify that it has or intends to establish a program that enters into the National Crime Information Center records of—

(1) warrants for the arrest of persons violating protection orders intended to protect victims from stalking or domestic violence;

(2) arrests or convictions of persons violating protection or domestic violence; and

(3) protection orders for the protection of persons from stalking or domestic violence.

SEC. 40603. AUTHORIZATION OF APPROPRIATIONS.

There are authorized to be appropriated to carry out this subtitle—

(1) $1,500,000 for fiscal year 1996;

(2) $1,750,000 for fiscal year 1997; and

(3) $2,750,000 for fiscal year 1998.

SEC. 40604. APPLICATION REQUIREMENTS.

An application for a grant under this subtitle shall be submitted in such form and manner, and contain such information, as the Attorney General may prescribe. In addition, applications shall include documentation showing—

(1) the need for grant funds and that State or local funding, as the case may be, does not already cover these operations;

(2) intended use of the grant funds, including a plan of action to increase record input; and

(3) an estimate of expected results from the use of the grant funds.

SEC. 40605. DISBURSEMENT.

Not later than 90 days after the receipt of an application under this subtitle, the Attorney General shall either provide grant funds or shall inform the applicant why grant funds are not being provided.

SEC. 40606. TECHNICAL ASSISTANCE, TRAINING, AND EVALUATIONS.

The Attorney General may provide technical assistance and training in furtherance of the purposes of this subtitle, and may provide for the evaluation of programs that receive funds under this subtitle, in addition to any evaluation requirements that the Attorney General may prescribe for grantees. The technical assistance, training, and evaluations authorized by this section may be carried out directly by the Attorney General, or through contracts or other arrangements with other entities.

SEC. 40607. TRAINING PROGRAMS FOR JUDGES.

The State Justice Institute, after consultation with nationally recognized nonprofit organizations with expertise in stalking and domestic violence cases, shall conduct training programs for State (as defined in section 202 of the State Justice Institute Authorization Act of 1984 (42 U.S.C. 10701)) and Indian tribal judges to ensure that a judge issuing an order in a stalking or domestic violence case has all available criminal history and other information, whether from State or Federal sources.

SEC. 40608. RECOMMENDATIONS ON INTRASTATE COMMUNICATION.

The State Justice Institute, after consultation with nationally recognized nonprofit associations with expertise in data sharing among criminal justice agencies and familiarity with the issues raised in stalking and domestic violence cases, shall recommend proposals regarding how State courts may increase intrastate communication between civil and criminal courts.

SEC. 40609. INCLUSION IN NATIONAL INCIDENT-BASED REPORTING SYSTEM.

Not later than 2 years after the date of enactment of this Act, the Attorney General, in accordance with the States, shall compile data regarding domestic violence and intimidation (including stalking) as part of the National Incident-Based Reporting System (NIBRS).

SEC. 40610. REPORT TO CONGRESS.

The Attorney General shall submit to the Congress an annual report, beginning one year after the date of the enactment of this Act, that provides information concerning the incidence of stalking and domestic violence, and evaluates the effectiveness of State antistalking efforts and legislation.

SEC. 40611. DEFINITIONS.

As used in this subtitle—

(1) the term `national crime information databases' refers to the National Crime Information Center and its incorporated criminal history databases, including the Interstate Identification Index; and

(2) the term `protection order' includes an injunction or any other order issued for the purpose of preventing violent or threatening acts or harassment against, or contact or communication with or physical proximity to, another person, including temporary and final orders issued by civil or criminal courts (other than support or child custody orders) whether obtained by filing an independent action or as a pendente lite order in another proceeding so long as any civil order was issued in response to a complaint, petition, or motion filed by or on behalf of a person seeking protection.

Source:

U.S. Department of Justice. Available on-lin. URL: www.usdoj.gov/. Accessed December 2003.

Amendments to the American Indian Religious Freedom Act (AIRFA), 1994

These amendments passed in 1994 provided for the traditional use of peyote by Indians for religious purposes. In 1990, the U.S. Supreme Court ruled in the case of *Smith v. Oregon* (494 U.S. 1990) that it was constitutionally permissible for a state to prohibit the use of peyote if a state felt a compelling reason to do so. In 1994, only 28 states had laws protecting the sacramental use of peyote. In response to this lack of uniformity, Congress enacted AIRFA to do away with the "hardship for Indian people who participate in such religious ceremonies." In some states, members of the Native American Church could be arrested and brought to trial on narcotics charges for peyote use, although most practitioners so charged were acquitted on the grounds of freedom of religion. Even so, many peyotists were subject to felony arrest and prosecution and carried criminal records for practicing their faith. These amendments sought to decriminalize activities surrounding peyotism.

Also boosting protection for traditional Indian practices, President George H. W. Bush signed the Native American Graves Protection and Repatriation Act (NAGPRA) into law. This initiative required federal agencies and museums that received federal funding to consult various Native American authorities regarding the care of human remains, funerary objects, sacred objects, and objects of enduring cultural value. Although the Smithsonian Institution is exempt from this law, it is required to repatriate cultural objects under the National Museum of the American Indian Act. In addition to the various artifacts mentioned, NAGPRA also protects burial sites located on tribal and federal lands. NAGPRA is enforced by the Secretary of the Interior, a review committee of seven members, and an Interior Department archeologist.

On May 24, 1996, the Clinton administration further protected Native American interests in Executive Order 13007, calling for the protection of indigenous sacred sites. The executive order, which has no enforceable power, requires each executive branch agency to accommodate access to and ceremonial use of Indian sacred sites by Indian religious practitioners and to avoid adversely affecting the physical integrity of such sacred sites.

January 25, 1994
An act to amend the American Indian Religious Freedom Act to provide for the traditional use of peyote by Indians for religious purposes, and for other purposes.

Be it enacted by the Senate and House of Representatives of the United States of America in Congress assembled,

SECTION 1. SHORT TITLE.

This Act may be cited as the 'American Indian Religious Freedom Act Amendments of 1994'.

SECTION 2. TRADITIONAL INDIAN RELIGIOUS USE OF THE PEYOTE SACRAMENT. The Act of August 11, 1978 (42 U.S.C. 1996), commonly referred to as the 'American Indian Religious Freedom Act,' is amended by adding at the end thereof the following new section:

SECTION 3.

(a) The Congress finds and declares that—

(1) for many Indian people, the traditional ceremonial use of the peyote cactus as a religious sacrament has for centuries been integral to a way of life, and significant in perpetuating Indian tribes and cultures;

(2) since 1965, this ceremonial use of peyote by Indians has been protected by Federal regulation;

(3) while at least 28 States have enacted laws which are similar to, or are in conformance with, the Federal regulation which protects the ceremonial use of peyote by Indian religious practitioners, 22 States have not done so, and this lack of uniformity has created hardship for Indian people who participate in such religious ceremonies;

(4) the Supreme Court of the United States, in the case of *Employment Division v. Smith*, 494 U.S. 872 (1990), held that the First Amendment does not protect Indian practitioners who use peyote in Indian religious ceremonies, and also raised uncertainty whether this religious practice would be protected under the compelling State interest standard; and

(5) the lack of adequate and clear legal protection for the religious use of peyote by Indians may serve to stigmatize and marginalize Indian tribes and cultures, and increase the risk that they will be exposed to discriminatory treatment.

(b)

(1) Notwithstanding any other provision of law, the use, possession, or transportation of peyote by an Indian for bona fide traditional ceremonial purposes in connection with the practice of a traditional Indian religion is lawful, and shall not be prohibited by the United States or any State. No Indian shall be penalized or discriminated against on the basis of such use, possession or transportation, including, but not limited to, denial of otherwise applicable benefits under public assistance programs.

(2) This section does not prohibit such reasonable regulation and registration by the Drug Enforcement Administration of those persons who cultivate, harvest, or distribute peyote as may be consistent with the purposes of this Act.

(3) This section does not prohibit application of the provisions of section 481.111(a) of Vernon's Texas Health and Safety Code Annotated, in effect on the date of enactment of this section, insofar as those provisions pertain to the cultivation, harvest, and distribution of peyote.

(4) Nothing in this section shall prohibit any Federal department or agency, in carrying out its statutory responsibilities and functions, from promulgating regulations establishing reasonable limitations on the use or ingestion of peyote prior to or during the performance of duties by sworn law enforcement officers or personnel directly involved in public transportation or any other safety-sensitive positions where the performance of such duties may be adversely affected by such use or ingestion. Such regulations shall be adopted only after consultation with representatives of traditional Indian religions for which the sacramental use of peyote is integral to their practice. Any regulation promulgated pursuant to this section shall be subject to the balancing test set forth in section 3 of the Religious Freedom Restoration Act (Public Law 103-141; 42 U.S.C. 2000bb-1).

(5) This section shall not be construed as requiring prison authorities to permit, nor shall it be construed to prohibit prison authorities from permitting, access to peyote by Indians while incarcerated within Federal or State prison facilities.

(6) Subject to the provisions of the Religious Freedom Restoration Act (Public Law 103-141; 42 U.S.C. 2000bb-1), this section shall not be construed to prohibit States from enacting or enforcing reasonable traffic safety laws or regulations.

(7) Subject to the provisions of the <B>Religious Freedom Restoration Act (Public Law 103-141; 42 U.S.C. 2000bb-1), this section does not prohibit the Secretary of Defense from promulgating regulations establishing rea-

sonable limitations on the use, possession, transportation, or distribution of peyote to promote military readiness, safety, or compliance with international law or laws of other countries. Such regulations shall be adopted only after consultation with representatives of traditional Indian religions for which the sacramental use of peyote is integral to their practice.

(c) For purposes of this section__

(1) the term 'Indian' means a member of an Indian tribe;

(2) the term 'Indian tribe' means any tribe, band, nation, pueblo, or other organized group or community of Indians, including any Alaska Native village (as defined in, or established pursuant to, the Alaska Native Claims Settlement Act (43 U.S.C. 1601 et seq.)), which is recognized as eligible for the special programs and services provided by the United States to Indians because of their status as Indians;

(3) the term 'Indian religion' means any religion—

(A) which is practiced by Indians, and

(B) the origin and interpretation of which is from within a traditional Indian culture or community; and

(4) the term 'State' means any State of the United States, and any political subdivision thereof.

(d) Nothing in this section shall be construed as abrogating, diminishing, or otherwise affecting—

(1) the inherent rights of any Indian tribe;

(2) the rights, express or implicit, of any Indian tribe which exist under treaties, Executive orders, and laws of the United States;

(3) the inherent right of Indians to practice their religions; and

(4) the right of Indians to practice their religions under any Federal or State law.'

Speaker of the House of Representatives.
Vice President of the United States and
President of the Senate.

Source:

Statutes at Large, Vol. 108, p. 3,126.

Glass Ceiling Commission Report, 1995

The Glass Ceiling Commission, a bipartisan federal panel established in 1991 to study the demography of the U.S. workplace, issued its report March 15, 1995. Entitled "Good for Business: Making Full Use of the Nation's Human Capital," the report revealed that women and minorities were extremely underrepresented in senior management posts. According to the commission's report, the so-called glass ceiling and other discriminatory barriers that stymied the careers of women and minorities were still firmly in place, despite three decades of affirmative-action efforts to eradicate them.

(excerpt)

Highlights of the Research

Federal Glass Ceiling Commission research papers, as well as testimony presented at the public hearings, clearly document that today's American labor force is gender and race segregated—white men fill most top management positions in corporations.

According to surveys of Fortune 1500 companies conducted by Korn/Ferry International and Catalyst over the last decade, 95 to 97 percent of senior managers —vice presidents and above—were men. A 1989 Korn/ Ferry survey found that 97 percent of male executives are white. A 1992 survey of Fortune 1500 companies found that 95 percent of the three to five percent of the top managers who were women were white non-Hispanic women. In 1994, two women were CEOs of Fortune 1000 companies.

The representation of women and minorities on Fortune 1500 boards of directors is also limited. Cox and Smolinski point out that less than 10 percent of the largest employers have women on their board of directors. According to a 1992 Heidrick & Struggles survey, *Minorities and Women on Corporate Boards,* non-U.S. citizens held 2.85 percent of the board seats of 806 Fortune companies, slightly less than the 3.11 percent combined total held by all racial and ethnic minorities.

Conversely, the American workforce is increasingly diverse. In 1950, white men comprised 65 percent of the labor force; in 1990 white male representation has dropped to 43 percent. During the same period, presentation of white women in the labor force increased from 24.2 percent to 35.3 percent. At the same time, minority representation in the labor force doubled, to 15.2 percent. Over the last decade, the size of the Asian and Pacific Islander American population has doubled, becoming the fastest growing of minority groups in the United States.

A larger proportion of women and minorities are locked into low-wage, low prestige, and dead- end jobs, which according to Harlan and Bertheide, are not connected to any career ladder . . .

Source:

U.S. Department of Labor. Glass Ceiling Final Report. Available on-line. URL: www.dol.gov/asp/programs/history/reich/reports/ceiling2.pdf. Accessed November 2003.

The Personal Responsibility and Work Opportunity Reconciliation Act, 1996

Better known as the Welfare Reform Act, this legislation (P.L. 104–193) overhauled the federal welfare system. The political debate over welfare revision intensified with the 1994 national congressional elections. One of the pledges made in the "Contract with America," the conservative campaign manifesto endorsed by many Republican candidates for the House of Representatives, was sweeping welfare reform. The Republican victories in the House spurred a legislative showdown on welfare. Defying traditional Democratic precepts, President Bill Clinton moved to the political center on this issue and signed the law August 22, 1996. Liberal fellow Democrats objected and accused him of selling out America's poor. The legislation shifted responsibility for administering welfare from Washington to the states, which would receive federal welfare funds in lump-sum payments ("block grants"). It ended the federal guarantee of cash assistance to poor families and introduced nationwide work requirements for welfare recipients and placed time limits on recipients' eligibility for assistance. The law effectively ended welfare as a federal entitlement. One of the ironies in this law, which disproportionately affected mothers with children, was that Republicans, who touted family values, required even the mothers of small children to go to work. While welfare roles shrank substantially in the five years after the passage of the act, the United States was also undergoing unprecedented prosperity, with low unemployment generally making the statistics somewhat difficult to interpret.

An Act To provide for reconciliation pursuant to section 201(a)(1) of the concurrent resolution on the budget for fiscal year 1997.

Be it enacted by the Senate and House of Representatives of the United States of America in Congress

SECTION 1. SHORT TITLE.

This Act may be cited as the "Personal Responsibility and Work Opportunity Reconciliation Act of 1996."

* * *

Title I—Block Grants for Temporary Assistance for Needy Families Sec. 101. Findings.

The Congress makes the following findings:

(1) Marriage is the foundation of a successful society.

(2) Marriage is an essential institution of a successful society which promotes the interests of children.

(3) Promotion of responsible fatherhood and motherhood is integral to successful child rearing and the well-being of children.

(4) In 1992, only 54 percent of single-parent families with children had a child support order established and, of that 54 percent, only about one-half received the full amount due. Of the cases enforced through the public child support enforcement system, only 18 percent of the caseload has a collection.

(5) The number of individuals receiving aid to families with dependent children (. . . AFDC) has more than tripled since 1965. More than two-thirds of these recipients are children. Eighty-nine percent of children receiving AFDC benefits now live in homes in which no father is present.

(A)

(i) The average monthly number of children receiving AFDC benefits—

(I) was 3,300,000 in 1965;

(II) was 6,200,000 in 1970;

(III) was 7,400,000 in 1980; and

(IV) was 9,300,000 in 1992.

(ii) While the number of children receiving AFDC benefits increased nearly threefold between 1965 and 1992, the total number of children in the United States aged 0 to 18 has declined by 5.5 percent.

(B) The Department of Health and Human Services has estimated that 12,000,000 children will receive AFDC benefits within 10 years.

(C) The increase in the number of children receiving public assistance is closely related to the increase in births to unmarried women. Between 1970 and 1991, the percentage of live births to unmarried women increased nearly threefold, from 10.7 percent to 29.5 percent.

(6) The increase of out-of-wedlock pregnancies and births is well documented as follows:

(A) It is estimated that the rate of nonmarital teen pregnancy rose 23 percent from 54 pregnancies per 1,000 unmarried teenagers in 1976 to 66.7 pregnancies in 1991. The overall rate of nonmarital pregnancy rose 14 percent from 90.8 pregnancies per 1,000 unmarried women in 1980 to 103 in both 1991 and 1992. In contrast, the overall pregnancy rate for married couples decreased 7.3 percent between 1980 and 1991, from 126.9 pregnancies per 1,000 married women in 1980 to 117.6 pregnancies in 1991.

(B) The total of all out-of-wedlock births between 1970 and 1991 has risen from 10.7 percent to 29.5 percent and if the current trend continues, 50 percent of all births by the year 2015 will be out-of-wedlock.

(7) An effective strategy to combat teenage pregnancy must address the issue of male responsibility, including statutory rape culpability and prevention. The increase of teenage pregnancies among the youngest girls is particularly severe and is linked to predatory sexual practices by men who are significantly older.

(A) It is estimated that in the late 1980's, the rate for girls age 14 and under giving birth increased 26 percent.

(B) Data indicates that at least half of the children born to teenage mothers are fathered by adult men. Available data suggests that almost 70 percent of births to teenage girls are fathered by men over age 20.

(C) Surveys of teen mothers have revealed that a majority of such mothers have histories of sexual and physical abuse, primarily with older adult men.

(8) The negative consequences of an out-of-wedlock birth on the mother, the child, the family, and society are well documented as follows:

(A) Young women 17 and under who give birth outside of marriage are more likely to go on public assistance and to spend more years on welfare once enrolled. These combined effects of "younger and longer" increase total AFDC costs per household by 25 percent to 30 percent for 17-year-olds.

(B) Children born out-of-wedlock have a substantially higher risk of being born at a very low or moderately low birth weight.

(C) Children born out-of-wedlock are more likely to experience low verbal cognitive attainment, as well as more child abuse, and neglect.

(D) Children born out-of-wedlock were more likely to have lower cognitive scores, lower educational aspirations, and a greater likelihood of becoming teenage parents themselves.

(E) Being born out-of-wedlock significantly reduces the chances of the child growing up to have an intact marriage.

(F) Children born out-of-wedlock are 3 times more likely to be on welfare when they grow up.

(9) Currently 35 percent of children in single-parent homes were born out-of-wedlock, nearly the same percentage as that of children in single-parent homes whose parents are divorced (37 percent). While many parents find themselves, through divorce or tragic circumstances beyond their control, facing the difficult task of raising children alone, nevertheless, the negative consequences of raising children in single-parent homes are well documented as follows:

(A) Only 9 percent of married-couple families with children under 18 years of age have income below the national poverty level. In contrast, 46 percent of female-headed households with children under 18 years of age are below the national poverty level.

(B) Among single-parent families, nearly \1/2\ of the mothers who never married received AFDC while only \1/5\ of divorced mothers received AFDC.

(C) Children born into families receiving welfare assistance are 3 times more likely to be on welfare when they reach adulthood than children not born into families receiving welfare.

(D) Mothers under 20 years of age are at the greatest risk of bearing low birth weight babies.

(E) The younger the single-parent mother, the less likely she is to finish high school.

(F) Young women who have children before finishing high school are more likely to receive welfare assistance for a longer period of time.

(G) Between 1985 and 1990, the public cost of births to teenage mothers under the aid to families with dependent children program, the food stamp program, and the medicaid program has been estimated at $120,000,000,000.

(H) The absence of a father in the life of a child has a negative effect on school performance and peer adjustment.

(I) Children of teenage single parents have lower cognitive scores, lower educational aspirations, and a greater likelihood of becoming teenage parents themselves.

(J) Children of single-parent homes are 3 times more likely to fail and repeat a year in grade school than are children from intact 2-parent families.

(K) Children from single-parent homes are almost 4 times more likely to be expelled or suspended from school.

(L) Neighborhoods with larger percentages of youth aged 12 through 20 and areas with higher percentages of single-parent households have higher rates of violent crime.

(M) Of those youth held for criminal offenses within the State juvenile justice system, only 29.8 percent lived primarily in a home with both parents. In contrast to these incarcerated youth, 73.9 percent of the 62,800,000 children in the Nation's resident population were living with both parents.

(10) Therefore, in light of this demonstration of the crisis in our Nation, it is the sense of the Congress that prevention of out-of-wedlock pregnancy and reduction in out-of-wedlock birth are very important Government interests and the policy contained in part A of title IV of the Social Security Act (as amended by section 103(a) of this Act) is intended to address the crisis.

* * *

PART A—BLOCK GRANTS TO STATES FOR TEMPORARY ASSISTANCE FOR NEEDY FAMILIES

SEC. 401. PURPOSE.

(a) In General.—The purpose of this part is to increase the flexibility of States in operating a program designed to— "(1) provide assistance to needy families so that children may be cared for in their own homes or in the homes of relatives; "(2) end the dependence of needy parents on government benefits by promoting job preparation, work, and marriage; "(3) prevent and reduce the incidence of out-of-wedlock pregnancies and establish annual numerical goals for preventing and reducing the incidence of these pregnancies; and "(4) encourage the formation and maintenance of two-parent families. "(b) No Individual Entitlement.—This part shall not be interpreted to entitle any individual or family to assistance under any State program funded under this part.

SEC. 402. ELIGIBLE STATES; STATE PLAN.

(a) In General.—As used in this part, the term 'eligible State' means, with respect to a fiscal year, a State that, during the 2-year period immediately preceding the fiscal year, has submitted to the Secretary a plan that the Secretary has found includes the following: "(1) Outline of family assistance program.— "(A) General provisions.—A written document that outlines how the State intends to do the following: "(i) Conduct a program, designed to serve all political subdivisions in the State (not necessarily in a uniform manner), that provides assistance to needy families with (or expecting) children and provides parents with job preparation, work, and support services to enable them to leave the program and become self-sufficient. "(ii) Require a parent or caretaker receiving assistance under the program to engage in work (as defined by the State) once the State determines the parent or caretaker is ready to engage in work, or once the parent or caretaker has received assistance under the program for 24 months (whether or not consecutive), whichever is earlier. "(iii) Ensure that parents and caretakers receiving assistance under the program engage in work activities in accordance with section 407. "(iv) Take such reasonable steps as the State deems necessary to restrict the use and disclosure of information about individuals and families receiving assistance under the program attributable to funds provided by the Federal Government. "(v) Establish goals and take action to prevent and reduce the incidence of out-of-wedlock pregnancies, with special emphasis on teenage pregnancies, and establish numerical goals for reducing the illegitimacy ratio of the State . . . for calendar years 1996 through 2005. "(vi) Conduct a program, designed to reach State and local law enforcement officials, the education system, and relevant counseling services, that provides education and training on the problem of statutory rape so that teenage pregnancy prevention programs may be expanded in scope to include men. "(B) Special provisions.— "(i) The document shall indicate whether the State intends to treat families moving into the State from another State differently than other families under the program, and if so, how the State intends to treat such families under the program. "(ii) The document shall indicate whether the State intends to provide assistance under the program to individuals who are not citizens of the United States, and if so, shall include an overview of such assistance. "(iii) The document shall set forth objective criteria for the delivery of benefits and the determination of eligibility and for fair and equitable treatment, including an explanation of how the State will provide opportunities for recipients who have been adversely affected to be heard in a State administrative or appeal process. "(iv) Not later than 1 year after the date of enactment of this Act, unless the chief executive officer of the State opts out of this provision by notifying the Secretary, a State shall, consistent with the exception provided in section 407(e)(2), require a parent or caretaker receiving assistance under the program who, after receiving such assistance for 2 months is not exempt from work requirements and is not engaged in work, as determined under section 407(c), to participate in community service employment, with minimum hours per week and tasks to be determined by the State. "(2) Certification that the state will operate a child support enforcement program.—A certification by the chief executive officer of the State that, during the fiscal year, the State will operate a child support enforcement program under the State plan approved under part D. "(3) Certification that the state will operate a foster care and adoption assistance program. . . . "(4) Certification of the administration of the program. . . . "(5) Certification that the state will provide [I]ndians with equitable access to assistance. . . . "(6) Certification of standards and procedures to ensure against program fraud and abuse. . . . "(7) Optional certification of standards and procedures to ensure that the state will screen for and identify domestic violence.— "(A) In general.—At the option of the State, a certification by the chief executive officer of the State that the State has established and is enforcing standards and procedures to— "(i) screen and identify individuals receiving assistance under this part with a history of domestic violence while maintaining the confidentiality of such individuals; "(ii) refer such individuals to counseling and supportive services; and "(iii) waive, pursuant to a determination of good cause, other program requirements such as time limits (for so long as necessary) for individuals receiving assistance, residency requirements, child support cooperation requirements, and family cap provisions, in cases where compliance with such requirements would make it more difficult for individuals receiving assistance under this part to escape domestic violence or unfairly penalize such individuals who are or have been victimized by such violence, or individuals who are at risk of further domestic violence. . . .

* * *

Provisions.—The following provisions of law shall apply to any program or activity which receives funds provided under this part: "(1) The Age Discrimination Act of 1975,

"(2) Section 504 of the Rehabilitation Act of 1973, "(3) The Americans with Disabilities Act of 1990,"

(4) Title VI of the Civil Rights Act of 1964, "(d) Aliens.—For special rules relating to the treatment of aliens, see section 402 of the Personal Responsibility and Work Opportunity Reconciliation Act of 1996.

* * *

SEC. 412. DIRECT FUNDING AND ADMINISTRATION BY INDIAN TRIBES.

"(a) Grants for Indian Tribes.— "(1) Tribal family assistance grant.— "(A) In general.—For each of fiscal years 1997, 1998, 1999, 2000, 2001, and 2002, the Secretary shall pay to each Indian tribe that has an approved tribal family assistance plan a tribal family assistance grant for the fiscal year. . . .

"(B) Eligible indian tribe.-. . .The term 'eligible Indian tribe' means an Indian tribe or Alaska Native organization that conducted a job opportunities and basic skills training program in fiscal year 1995. . . . '(C) Use of grant.—Each Indian tribe to which a grant is made under this paragraph shall use the grant for the purpose of operating a program to make work activities available to members of the Indian tribe. . . .

"SEC. 413. RESEARCH, EVALUATIONS, AND NATIONAL STUDIES.

"(a) Research.—The Secretary shall conduct research on the benefits, effects, and costs of operating different State programs funded under this part, including time limits relating to eligibility for assistance. The research shall include studies on the effects of different programs and the operation of such programs on welfare dependency, illegitimacy, teen pregnancy, employment rates, child well-being, and any other area the Secretary deems appropriate. The Secretary shall also conduct research on the costs and benefits of State activities under section 409. "(b) Development and Evaluation of Innovative Approaches To Reducing Welfare Dependency and Increasing Child Well-Being.— "(1) In general.—The Secretary may assist States in developing, and shall evaluate, innovative approaches for reducing welfare dependency and increasing the well-being of minor children living at home with respect to recipients of assistance under programs funded under this part. The Secretary may provide funds for training and technical assistance to carry out the approaches developed pursuant to this paragraph. "(2) Evaluations.—In performing the evaluations under paragraph (1), the Secretary shall, to the maximum extent feasible, use random assignment as an evaluation methodology. "(c) Dissemination of Information.—The Secretary shall develop innovative methods of disseminating information on any research, evaluations, and studies conducted under this section, including the facilitation of the sharing of information and best practices among States and localities through the use of computers and other technologies. . . . (g) Report on Circumstances of Certain Children and Families.— "(1) In general.—Beginning 3 years after the date of the enactment of this Act, the Secretary of Health and Human Services shall prepare and submit to the Committees on Ways and Means and on Economic and Educational Opportunities of the House of Representatives and to the Committees on Finance and on Labor and Resources of the Senate annual reports that examine in detail. . .: "(A) Individuals who were children in families that have become ineligible for assistance under a State program funded under this part by reason of having reached a time limit on the provision of such assistance. "(B) Children born after such date of enactment to parents who, at the time of such birth, had not attained 20 years of age. "(C) Individuals who, after such date of enactment, became parents before attaining 20 years of age. "(2) Matters described.—The matters described in this paragraph are the following: "(A) The percentage of each group that has dropped out of secondary school (or the equivalent), and the percentage of each group at each level of educational attainment. "(B) The percentage of each group that is employed. "(C) The percentage of each group that has been convicted of a crime or has been adjudicated as a delinquent. "(D) The rate at which the members of each group are born, or have children, out-of-wedlock, and the percentage of each group that is married. "(E) The percentage of each group that continues to participate in State programs funded under this part. "(F) The percentage of each group that has health insurance provided by a private entity (broken down by whether the insurance is provided through an employer or otherwise), the percentage that has health insurance provided by an agency of government, and the percentage that does not have health insurance. "(G) The average income of the families of the members of each group. "(H) Such other matters as the Secretary deems appropriate. . . .

SEC. 414. STUDY BY THE CENSUS BUREAU.

"(a) In General.—The Bureau of the Census shall continue to collect data on the 1992 and 1993 panels of the Survey of Income and Program Participation as necessary to obtain such information as will enable interested persons to evaluate the impact of the amendments made by title I of the Personal Responsibility and Work Opportunity Reconciliation Act of 1996 on a random national sample of recipients of assistance under State programs funded under this part and (as appropriate) other low-income families, and in doing so, shall pay particular attention to the issues of out-of-wedlock birth, welfare dependency, the beginning and end of welfare spells, and the causes of repeat welfare spells, and shall obtain information about the status of children participating in such panels.

* * *

SEC. 104. SERVICES PROVIDED BY CHARITABLE, RELIGIOUS, OR PRIVATE ORGANIZATIONS.

* * *

(b) Religious Organizations—The purpose of this section is to allow States to contract with religious organizations, or to allow religious organizations to accept certificates, vouchers, or other forms of disbursement . . . on the same basis as any other nongovernmental provider without impairing the religious character of such organizations, and without diminishing the religious freedom of beneficiaries of assistance funded under such program.

(c) Nondiscrimination Against Religious Organizations.—In the event a State exercises its authority . . . religious organizations are eligible, on the same basis as any other private organization, as contractors to provide assistance, or to accept certificates, vouchers, or other forms of disbursement . . . so long as the programs are implemented consistent with the Establishment Clause of the United States Constitution. Except as provided in subsection (k), neither the Federal Government nor a State receiving funds under such programs shall discriminate against an organization . . . on the basis that the organization has a religious character.

(d) Religious Character and Freedom.—

(1) Religious organizations.—A religious organization with a contract. . .or which accepts certificates, vouchers, or other forms of disbursement. . .shall retain its independence from Federal, State, and local governments, including such organization's control over the definition, development, practice, and expression of its religious beliefs.

(2) Additional safeguards.—Neither the Federal Government nor a State shall require a religious organization to—

(A) alter its form of internal governance; or

(B) remove religious art, icons, scripture, or other symbols; in order to be eligible. . .

(e) Rights of Beneficiaries of Assistance.—

(1) In general.—If an individual described in paragraph (2) has an objection to the religious character of the organization or institution from which the individual receives, or would receive, assistance . . . the State in which the individual resides shall provide such individual (if otherwise eligible for such assistance) within a reasonable period of time after the date of such objection with assistance from an alternative provider that is accessible to the individual and the value of which is not less than the value of the assistance which the individual would have received from such organization.

* * *

(f) Employment Practices.—A religious organization's exemption provided under section 702 of the Civil Rights Act of 1964 regarding employment practices shall not be affected by its participation in, or receipt of funds from [these] programs.

(g) Nondiscrimination Against Beneficiaries.—Except as otherwise provided in law, a religious organization shall not discriminate against an individual in regard to rendering assistance . . . on the basis of religion, a religious belief, or refusal to actively participate in a religious practice.

(h) Fiscal Accountability.—

(1) In general . . . any religious organization contracting to provide assistance . . . shall be subject to the same regulations as other contractors to account in accord with generally accepted auditing principles for the use of such funds provided under such programs.

(j) Limitations on Use of Funds for Certain Purposes.—No funds provided directly to institutions or organizations to provide services and administer programs. . .shall be expended for sectarian worship, instruction, or proselytization.

(k) Preemption.—Nothing in this section shall be construed to preempt any provision of a State constitution or State statute that prohibits or restricts the expenditure of State funds in or by religious organizations.

* * *

SEC. 107. ((NOTE: 42 USC 613 note.)) STUDY ON ALTERNATIVE OUTCOMES MEASURES.

(a) Study.—The Secretary shall, in cooperation with the States, study and analyze outcomes measures for evaluating the success of the States in moving individuals out of the welfare system through employment as an alternative to the minimum participation rates described in section 407 of the Social Security Act. The study shall include a determination as to whether such alternative outcomes measures should be applied on a national or a State-by-State basis. . . .

* * *

SEC. 115. ((NOTE: 42 USC 862a.)) DENIAL OF ASSISTANCE AND BENEFITS FOR CERTAIN DRUG-RELATED CONVICTIONS.

(a) In General.—An individual convicted (under Federal or State law) of any offense which is classified as a felony by the law of the jurisdiction involved and which has as an element the possession, use, or distribution of a controlled substance . . . shall not be eligible for—

(1) assistance under any State program funded under part A of title IV of the Social Security Act, or (2) benefits under the food stamp program. . .or any State program carried out under the Food Stamp Act of 1977.

See also CONTRACT WITH AMERICA, 1994.

Source:

Congressional Record. 104th Cong., 2d sess., 1996. Vol. 142.

Proposition 215, 1996

A California state proposition passed by a statewide vote on November 5, 1996, that legalized the prescription of marijuana for medicinal purposes. The law exempts from criminal laws patients and defined caregivers who possess or cultivate marijuana for medical treatment recommended by a physician and guarantees that those physicians shall not be punished or denied any right or privilege. Prior to the November vote, opponents of the hotly debated Proposition 215 had argued that it would create legal loopholes that drug dealers and cultivators would use to protect themselves from criminal prosecution. Detractors also stressed that marijuana had never been approved by the Federal Drug Administration (there would thus be no regulation of the substance or its quality), and, moreover, that there was no undisputed clinical proof of marijuana's medicinal value. Supporters of the proposition emphasized the advantages of marijuana, pointing out that it had indeed been shown to be effective in treating side effects of chemotherapy such as nausea; in lowering internal eye pressure associated with glaucoma, thus slowing the onset of blindness; in reducing the prolonged suffering and increasing the appetites of AIDS patients; and in alleviating muscle spasticity and chronic pain due to multiple sclerosis, epilepsy, and spinal cord injuries. The proposition, passed with the support of 55.6 percent of the Californians voting in the November election, contradicted the definition of marijuana in the Controlled Substance Act of 1970. In that act, which established the legal foundation of a federal strategy aimed at reducing the consumption of illicit drugs, marijuana was defined as a Schedule I drug, i.e., with no known medical use. Proposition 215, by challenging such a definition, complemented recent rulings in state supreme courts in Washington, Illinois, and Michigan that found marijuana penalties to be unconstitutional due to the incorrect identification of the substance as a Schedule I drug.

The act has been challenged on both sides, both by the federal government in its attempts to enforce the Controlled Substances Act and by civil disobedience of local California clinics and officials claiming that the California law takes precedence. The Supreme Court upheld the federal government unanimously in May 2001, in *United States v. Oakland Cannabis Buyers Cooperative* (121 S. Cr. 1711), by concluding that the Oakland Cannabis Buyers' Cooperative and similar groups cannot legally distribute marijuana, even if they claim that recipients have medical need for it. The most flagrant example of civil disobedience took place September 17, 2002, when members from a clinic raided by the Drug Enforcement Agency handed out prescription marijuana on the steps of the Santa Cruz city hall with the blessing of the city council.

Initiative Measure to be Submitted Directly to the Voters Medical Use of Marijuana. Initiative Statute. Provides that patients or defined caregivers, who possess or cultivate marijuana for medical treatment recommended by a physician, are exempt from general provisions of law which otherwise prohibit possession or cultivation of marijuana. Provides physicians shall not be punished or denied any right or privilege for recommending marijuana to a patient for medical purposes. Declares that the measure not be construed to supersede prohibitions of conduct endangering others nor to condone diversion of marijuana for nonmedical purposes. Contains severability clause. Summary of estimate by Legislative Analyst and Director of Finance of fiscal impact on state and local government: Because this measure restricts the use of marijuana to only those persons for whom it is prescribed by a licensed physician, it would probably have no significant state or local fiscal impact.

To The Honorable Secretary Of State Of California: We, the undersigned, registered, qualified voters of California, residents of ________________________ County (or City and County), hereby propose an addition to the Health and Safety Code, relating to the compassionate use of marijuana, and petition the Secretary of State to submit the same to the voters of California for their adoption or rejection at the next succeeding general election or at any special statewide election held prior to that general election or otherwise provided by law. The proposed addition to the Health and Safety code shall read as follows: Section 1. Section 11362.5 is added to the Health and Safety Code, to read:

11362.5. (a) This section shall be known and may be cited as the Compassionate Use Act of 1996.

(b) (l) The people of the State of California hereby find and declare that the purposes of the Compassionate Use Act of 1996 are as follows:

(A) To ensure that seriously ill Californians have the right to obtain and use marijuana for medical purposes where that medical use is deemed appropriate and has been recommended by a physician who has determined that the person's health would benefit from the use of marijuana in the treatment of cancer, anorexia, AIDS, chronic pain, spasticity, glaucoma, arthritis, migraine, or any other illness for which marijuana provides relief.

(B) To ensure that patients and their primary caregivers who obtain and use marijuana for medical purposes upon the recommendation of a physician are not subject to criminal prosecution or sanction.

(C) To encourage the federal and state governments to implement a plan to provide for the safe and affordable distribution of marijuana to all patients in medical need of marijuana.

(2) Nothing in this act shall be construed to supersede legislation prohibiting persons from engaging in conduct that endangers others, nor to condone the diversion of marijuana for nonmedical purposes.

(c) Notwithstanding any other provision of law, no physician in this state shall be punished, or denied any right or privilege, for having recommended marijuana to a patient for medical purposes.

(d) Section 11357, relating to the possession of marijuana, and Section 11358, relating to the cultivation of marijuana, shall not apply to a patient, or to a patient's primary caregiver, who possesses or cultivates marijuana for the personal medical purposes of the patient upon the written or oral recommendation or approval of a physician.

(e) For the purposes of this section, "primary caregiver" means the individual designated by the person exempted under this act who has consistently assumed responsibility for the housing, health, or safety of that person.

Sec. 2. If any provision of this measure or the application thereof to any person or circumstance is held invalid, that invalidity shall not affect other provisions or applications of the measure which can be given effect without the invalid provision or application, and to this end the provisions of this measure are severable.

Source:

Landmark Documents in American History, Facts On File, Inc.

United States v. Virginia et al., 1996

U.S. Supreme Court decision ordering the Virginia Military Institute (VMI), a state-funded, all-male military academy, to admit women. In 1995 a federal appeals court ruled that VMI's exclusion of female applicants violated the Constitution by denying women equal protection under the Fourteenth Amendment. At the same time, the appellate court held that Virginia had adequately remedied that violation by establishing a women's leadership program at the all-female Mary Baldwin College. On challenge, the Supreme Court considered both aspects of the lower court's decision. On June 26, 1996, the high court ruled 7-1 that VMI's admissions policy was unconstitutional. The justices found that a state-funded institution that treated the genders differently violated the Fourteenth Amendment's equal protection clause. Applying a "skeptical scrutiny" standard in evaluating Virginia's sponsorship of VMI, the majority concluded that the state had shown no compelling justification for offering different educational opportunities to men and women. The Court also deemed the separate state-funded women's leadership program at Mary Baldwin an inadequate alternative to females seeking admission to VMI. The decision in *United States v. Virginia et al.* would force state-sponsored military academies such as VMI and the Citadel in South Carolina to go private if they wanted to remain all-male.

Note: Where it is feasible, a syllabus (headnote) will be released, as is being done in connection with this case, at the time the opinion is issued. The syllabus constitutes no part of the opinion of the Court but has been prepared by the Reporter of Decisions for the convenience of the reader. See United States v. Detroit Lumber Co., *200 U.S. 321, 337.*

Virginia Military Institute (VMI) is the sole single sex school among Virginia's public institutions of higher learning. VMI's distinctive mission is to produce "citizen soldiers," men prepared for leadership in civilian life and in military service. Using an "adversative method" of training not available elsewhere in Virginia, VMI endeavors to instill physical and mental discipline in its cadets and impart to them a strong moral code. Reflecting the high value alumni place on their VMI training, VMI has the largest per student endowment of all undergraduate institutions in the Nation. The United States sued Virginia and VMI, alleging that VMI's exclusively male admission policy violated the Fourteenth Amendment's Equal Protection Clause. The District Court ruled in VMI's favor. The Fourth Circuit reversed and ordered Virginia to remedy the constitutional violation. In response, Virginia proposed a parallel program for women: Virginia Women's Institute for Leadership (VWIL), located at Mary Baldwin College, a private liberal arts school for women. The District Court found that Virginia's proposal satisfied the Constitution's equal protection requirement, and the Fourth Circuit affirmed. The appeals court deferentially reviewed Virginia's plan and determined that provision of single gender educational options was a legitimate objective. Maintenance of single sex programs, the court concluded, was essential to that objective. The court recognized, however, that its analysis risked bypassing equal protection scrutiny, so it fashioned an additional test, asking whether VMI and VWIL students would receive "substantively comparable" benefits. Although the Court of Appeals acknowledged that the VWIL degree lacked the historical benefit and prestige of a VMI degree, the court nevertheless found the educational opportunities at the two schools sufficiently comparable.

Held:

1. Parties who seek to defend gender based government action must demonstrate an "exceedingly persuasive justification" for that action. *E.g., Mississippi Univ. for Women v. Hogan,* 458 U.S. 718, 724. Neither federal nor state government acts compatibly with equal protection when a law or official policy denies to women, simply because they are women, full citizenship stature—equal opportunity to aspire, achieve, participate in and contribute to society based on their individual talents and capacities. To meet the burden of justification, a State must show "at least that the [challenged] classification serves 'important governmental objectives and that the discriminatory means employed' are 'substantially related to the achievement of those objectives.'" *Ibid.,* quoting *Wengler v. Druggists Mutual Ins. Co.,* 446 U.S. 142, 150. The justification must be genuine, not hypothesized or invented *post hoc* in response to litigation. And it must not rely on overbroad generalizations about the different talents, capacities, or preferences of males and females. See, *e.g., Weinberger v. Wiesenfeld,* 420 U.S. 636, 643, 648. The heightened review standard applicable to sex based classifications does not make sex a proscribed classification, but it does mean that categorization by sex may not be used to create or perpetuate the legal, social, and economic inferiority of women. Pp. 13–16.

2. Virginia's categorical exclusion of women from the educational opportunities VMI provides denies equal protection to women. Pp. 17–29.

(a) Virginia contends that single sex education yields important educational benefits and that provision of an option for such education fosters diversity in educational approaches. Benign justifications proffered in defense of categorical exclusions, however, must describe actual state purposes, not rationalizations for actions in fact differently grounded. Virginia has not shown that VMI was established, or has been maintained, with a view to diversifying, by its categorical exclusion of women, educational opportunities within the State. A purpose genuinely to advance an array of educational options is not served by VMI's historic and constant plan to afford a unique educational benefit only to males. However well this plan serves Virginia's sons, it makes no provision whatever for her daughters. Pp. 17–22.

(b) Virginia also argues that VMI's adversative method of training provides educational benefits that cannot be made available, unmodified, to women, and that alterations to accommodate women would necessarily be so drastic as to destroy VMI's program. It is uncontested that women's admission to VMI would require accommodations, primarily in arranging housing assignments and physical training programs for female cadets. It is also undisputed, however, that neither the goal of producing citizen soldiers, VMI's *raison d'être,* nor VMI's implementing methodology is inherently unsuitable to women. The District Court made "findings" on "gender based developmental differences" that restate the opinions of Virginia's expert witnesses about typically male or typically female "tendencies." Courts, however, must take "a hard look" at generalizations or tendencies of the kind Virginia pressed, for state actors controlling gates to opportunity have no warrant to exclude qualified individuals based on "fixed notions concerning the roles and abilities of males and females." *Mississippi Univ. for Women,* 458 U. S., at 725. The notion that admission of women would downgrade VMI's stature, destroy the adversative system and, with it, even the school, is a judgment hardly proved, a prediction hardly different from other "self fulfilling prophec[ies], see *id.,* at 730, once routinely used to deny rights or opportunities. Women's successful entry into the federal military academies, and their participation in the Nation's military forces, indicate that Virginia's fears for VMI's future may not be solidly grounded. The State's justification for excluding all women from "citizen soldier" training for which some are qualified, in any event, does not rank as "exceedingly persuasive." Pp. 22–29.

3. The remedy proffered by Virginia—maintain VMI as a male only college and create VWIL as a separate program for women—does not cure the constitutional violation. Pp. 29–41.

(a) A remedial decree must closely fit the constitutional violation; it must be shaped to place persons unconstitutionally denied an opportunity or advantage in the position they would have occupied in the absence of discrimination. See *Milliken v. Bradley,* 433 U.S. 267, 280. The constitutional violation in this case is the categorical exclusion of women, in disregard of their individual merit, from an extraordinary educational opportunity afforded men. Virginia chose to leave untouched VMI's exclusionary policy, and proposed for women only a separate program, different in kind from VMI and unequal in tangible and intangible facilities. VWIL affords women no opportunity to experience the rigorous military training for which VMI is famed. Kept away from the pressures, hazards, and psychological bonding characteristic of VMI's adversative training, VWIL students will not know the feeling of tremendous accomplishment commonly experienced by VMI's successful cadets. Virginia maintains that methodological differences are justified by the important differences between men and women in learning and developmental needs, but generalizations about "the way women are," estimates of what is appropriate for *most women,* no longer justify denying opportunity to women whose talent and capacity place them outside the average description. In myriad respects other than military training, VWIL does not qualify as VMI's equal. The VWIL program is a pale shadow of VMI in terms of the range of curricular choices and faculty stature, funding, prestige, alumni support and influence. Virginia has not shown substantial equality in the separate educational opportunities the State supports at VWIL and VMI. Cf. *Sweatt* v. *Painter,* 339 U.S. 629. Pp. 30–37

Source:

Cornell Law School. The Legal Information Institute. Available on-line. URL: http://supct.lawcornell.edu/supct/html/94-1941.ZS.html. Accessed November 2003.

Bill Clinton, Remarks in Apology for Tuskegee Study, 1997

Formal apology made by President Bill Clinton for an infamous medical experiment conducted by the federal government in Tuskegee, Alabama, in which some 400 African-American male syphilis sufferers were denied treatment for 40 years. From 1932 to 1972, the U.S. Public Health Service observed those men in Macon County, Alabama, as part of a study to determine how the disease spread and how it killed. Those afflicted with syphilis, which in its advanced stages causes grave mental deterioration and can lead to death, were not informed that they had the disease. Nor did they receive any therapeutic care—not even after penicillin in 1947 became the standard and highly effective treatment for the sexually transmitted disease. Public disclosure of the Tuskegee Study in 1972 triggered widespread outrage in the black community and brought demands for just redress. Since 1973 the federal government has paid approximately $10 million in restitution to the men and their heirs. On May 16, 1997, President Clinton hosted survivors of the Tuskegee experiment and their families at a White House ceremony in which he belatedly apologized on behalf of the American people for the shameful wrong perpetrated against them by the U.S. government.

The President: Ladies and gentlemen, on Sunday, Mr. Shaw will celebrate his 95th birthday. (Applause.) I would like to recognize the other survivors who are here today and their families: Mr. Charlie Pollard is here. (Applause.) Mr. Carter Howard. (Applause.) Mr. Fred Simmons. (Applause.) Mr. Simmons just took his first airplane ride, and he reckons he's about 110 years old, so I think it's time for him to take a chance or two. (Laughter.) I'm glad he did. And Mr. Frederick Moss, thank you, sir. (Applause.)

I would also like to ask three family representatives who are here — Sam Doner is represented by his daughter, Gwendolyn Cox. Thank you, Gwendolyn. (Applause.) Ernest Hendon, who is watching in Tuskegee, is represented by his brother, North Hendon. Thank you, sir, for being here. (Applause.) And George Key is represented by his grandson, Christopher Monroe. Thank you, Chris. (Applause.)

I also acknowledge the families, community leaders, teachers and students watching today by satellite from Tuskegee. The White House is the people's house; we are glad to have all of you here today. I thank Dr. David Satcher for his role in this. I thank Congresswoman Waters and Congressman Hilliard, Congressman Stokes, the entire Congressional Black Caucus. Dr. Satcher, members of the Cabinet who are here, Secretary Herman, Secretary Slater, members of the Cabinet who are here, Secretary Herman, Secretary Slater. A great friend of freedom, Fred Gray, thank you for fighting this long battle all these long years.

The eight men who are survivors of the syphilis study at Tuskegee are a living link to a time not so very long ago that many Americans would prefer not to remember, but we dare not forget. It was a time when our nation failed to live up to its ideals, when our nation broke the trust with our people that is the very foundation of our democracy. It is not only in remembering that shameful past that we can make amends and repair our nation, but it is in remembering that past that we can build a better present and a better future. And without remembering it, we cannot make amends and we cannot go forward.

So today America does remember the hundreds of men used in research without their knowledge and consent. We remember them and their family members. Men who were poor and African American, without resources and with few alternatives, they believed they had found hope when they were offered free medical care by the United States Public Health Service. They were betrayed.

Medical people are supposed to help when we need care, but even once a cure was discovered, they were denied help, and they were lied to by their government. Our government is supposed to protect the rights of its citizens; their rights were trampled upon. Forty years, hundreds of men betrayed, along with their wives and children, along with the community in Macon County, Alabama, the City of Tuskegee, the fine university there, and the larger African American community.

The United States government did something that was wrong—deeply, profoundly, morally wrong. It was an outrage to our commitment to integrity and equality for all our citizens.

To the survivors, to the wives and family members, the children and the grandchildren, I say what you know: No power on Earth can give you back the lives lost, the pain suffered, the years of internal torment and anguish. What was done cannot be undone. But we can end the silence. We can stop turning our heads away. We can look at you in the eye and finally say on behalf of the American people, what the United States government did was shameful, and I am sorry. (Applause.)

The American people are sorry — for the loss, for the years of hurt. You did nothing wrong, but you were grievously wronged. I apologize and I am sorry that this apology has been so long in coming. (Applause.)

To Macon County, to Tuskegee, to the doctors who have been wrongly associated with the events there, you have our apology, as well. To our African American citizens, I am sorry that your federal government orchestrated a study so clearly racist. That can never be allowed to happen again. It is against everything our country stands for and what we must stand against is what it was.

So let us resolve to hold forever in our hearts and minds the memory of a time not long ago in Macon County, Alabama, so that we can always see how adrift we can become when the rights of any citizens are neglected, ignored and betrayed. And let us resolve here and now to move forward together.

The legacy of the study at Tuskegee has reached far and deep, in ways that hurt our progress and divide our nation. We cannot be one America when a whole segment of our nation has no trust in America. An apology is the first step, and we take it with a commitment to rebuild that broken trust. We can begin by making sure there is never again another episode like this one. We need to do more to ensure that medical research practices are sound and ethical, and that researchers work more closely with communities.

Today I would like to announce several steps to help us achieve these goals. First, we will help to build that lasting memorial at Tuskegee. (Applause.) The school founded by Booker T. Washington, distinguished by the renowned scientist George Washington Carver and so many others who advanced the health and well-being of African Americans and all Americans, is a fitting site. The Department of Health and Human Services will award a planning grant so the school can pursue establishing a center for bioethics in research and health care. The center will serve as a museum of the study and support efforts to address its legacy and strengthen bioethics training.

Second, we commit to increase our community involvement so that we may begin restoring lost trust. The study at Tuskegee served to sow distrust of our medical institutions, especially where research is involved. Since the study was halted, abuses have been checked by making informed consent and local review mandatory in federally-funded and mandated research.

Still, 25 years later, many medical studies have little African American participation and African American organ donors are few. This impedes efforts to conduct promising research and to provide the best health care to all our people, including African Americans. So today, I'm directing the Secretary of Health and Human Services, Donna Shalala, to issue a report in 180 days about how we can best involve communities, especially minority communities, in research and health care. You must—every American group must be involved in medical research in ways that are positive. We have put the curse behind us; now we must bring the benefits to all Americans. (Applause.)

Third, we commit to strengthen researchers' training in bioethics. We are constantly working on making breakthroughs in protecting the health of our people and in vanquishing diseases. But all our people must be assured that their rights and dignity will be respected as new drugs, treatments and therapies are tested and used. So I am directing Secretary Shalala to work in partnership with higher education to prepare training materials for medical researchers. They will be available in a year. They will help researchers build on core ethical principles of respect for individuals, justice and informed consent, and advise them on how to use these principles effectively in diverse populations.

Fourth, to increase and broaden our understanding of ethical issues and clinical research, we commit to providing postgraduate fellowships to train bioethicists especially among African Americans and other minority groups. HHS will offer these fellowships beginning in September of 1998 to promising students enrolled in bioethics graduate programs.

And, finally, by executive order I am also today extending the charter of the National Bioethics Advisory Commission to October of 1999. The need for this commission is clear. We must be able to call on the thoughtful, collective wisdom of experts and community representatives to find ways to further strengthen our protections for subjects in human research.

We face a challenge in our time. Science and technology are rapidly changing our lives with the promise of making us much healthier, much more productive and more prosperous. But with these changes we must work harder to see that as we advance we don't leave behind our conscience. No ground is gained and, indeed, much is lost if we lose our moral bearings in the name of progress.

The people who ran the study at Tuskegee diminished the stature of man by abandoning the most basic ethical precepts. They forgot their pledge to heal and repair. They had the power to heal the survivors and all the others and they did not. Today, all we can do is **apologize**. But you have the power, for only you—Mr. Shaw, the others who are here, the family members who are with us in

Tuskegee—only you have the power to forgive. Your presence here shows us that you have chosen a better path than your government did so long ago. You have not withheld the power to forgive. I hope today and tomorrow every American will remember your lesson and live by it.

Thank you, and God bless you.

Source:

National Archives and Records Administration. Clinton Presidential Materials Project. Available on-line. URL: http://clinton5.nara.gov/New/Remarks/19970516-898.html. Accessed November 2003.

Baker v. State of Vermont, 1998

Vermont Supreme Court ruling that the state's marriage laws as they stood were unconstitutional because they granted benefits and protections to heterosexual couples, who could marry and therefore reap the legal benefits of marriage, and not to same-sex couples. The suit was brought by three same-sex couples who had been in committed relationships for between four and 25 years. Two of the couples had raised children together. Each of the couples applied for marriage licenses but were denied the licenses in accordance with the commonly held definition of marriage as the union of a man and a woman as husband and wife.

The ruling hinged on Article 7 of the Vermont Constitution, which provided "[t]hat government is, or ought to be, instituted for the common benefit, protection, and security of the people, nation, or community, and not for the particular emolument or advantage of any single person, family or set of persons, who are a part only of that community; and that the community hath an indubitable, unalienable, and indefeasible right, to reform or alter government, in such a manner as shall be, by that community, judged most conducive to the public weal." As Judge Amestoy wrote for the majority, the "common benefits" clause of the Vermont Constitution prohibited "the conferral of advantages or emoluments upon the privileged." The majority discounted the state's argument that the purpose of marriage law was to "further the link between procreation and child-rearing." The court pointed out that many married couples had no intention of raising children, while many same-sex couples, through artificial insemination or adoption, do raise children together. "In short," the court wrote, "the marital exclusion treats persons who are similarly situated for purposes of the law, differently." The majority concluded that the legislature should change the law either by legalizing gay marriage or offering an alternative form of same-sex union that conferred the same benefits and protections as heterosexual marriage.

The legislature chose the latter by enacting Vermont's Civil Union Law of 2000. Marriage itself continued to be confined to heterosexual unions. However, two people over 18 of the same sex who are not related could form a civil union under the new law and receive all the same rights as a married couple. These rights include joint adoption, survivor benefits, family leave benefits, and spousal abuse programs. Couples who met the requirements for a civil union could obtain a license that the clerk must issue to all couples who qualify. Civil unions must then be certified within 60 days of the issuance of the license. If a couple wished to dissolve their civil union, they followed the same procedure as married couples seeking divorce.

Legal recognition of these civil unions did not stretch beyond Vermont's borders. The Defense of Marriage Act, signed by President Clinton in 1996, explicitly stated that the federal government did not recognize same-sex unions that are treated like marriage and that other states would not be forced to recognize them either. As this goes to press, the courts have not dealt with the 1996 act's constitutionality.

Opinion by Chief Justice Amestoy

May the State of Vermont exclude same-sex couples from the benefits and protections that its laws provide to opposite-sex married couples? That is the fundamental question we address in this appeal, a question that the Court well knows arouses deeply-felt religious, moral, and political beliefs. Our constitutional responsibility to consider the legal merits of issues properly before us provides no exception for the controversial case. The issue before the Court, moreover, does not turn on the religious or moral debate over intimate same-sex relationships, but rather on the statutory and constitutional basis for the exclusion of same-sex couples from the secular benefits and protections offered married couples.

We conclude that under the Common Benefits Clause of the Vermont Constitution, which, in pertinent part, reads, "That government is, or ought to be, instituted for the common benefit, protection, and security of the people, nation, or community, and not for the particular emolument or advantage of any single person, family, or set of persons, who are a part only of that community," Vt. Const., ch. I, art 7., plaintiffs may not be deprived of the statutory benefits and protections afforded persons of the opposite sex who choose to marry. We hold that the State is constitutionally required to extend to same-sex couples the common benefits and protections that flow from marriage under Vermont law. Whether this ultimately takes the form of inclusion within the marriage laws themselves or a parallel "domestic partnership" system or some equivalent statutory alternative, rests with the Legislature. Whatever system is chosen, however, must conform with the constitutional imperative to afford all Vermonters the common benefit, protection, and security of the law.

Plaintiffs are three same-sex couples who have lived together in committed relationships for periods ranging from four to twenty-five years. Two of the couples have raised children together. Each couple applied for a marriage license from their respective town clerk, and each was refused a license as ineligible under the applicable state marriage laws. Plaintiffs thereupon filed this lawsuit against defendants—the State of Vermont, the Towns of Milton and Shelburne, and the City of South Burlington—seeking a declaratory judgment that the refusal to issue them a license violated the marriage statutes and the Vermont Constitution. . . .

Assuming that the marriage statutes preclude their eligibility for a marriage license, plaintiffs contend that the exclusion violates their right to the common benefit and protection of the law guaranteed by Chapter I, Article 7 of the Vermont Constitution. They note that in denying them access to a civil marriage license, the law effectively excludes them from a broad array of legal benefits and protections incident to the marital relation, including access to a spouse's medical, life, and disability insurance, hospital visitation and other medical decision-making privileges, spousal support, intestate succession, homestead protections, and many other statutory protections. They claim the trial court erred in upholding the law on the basis that it reasonably served the State's interest in promoting the "link between procreation and child rearing." They argue that the large number of married couples without children, and the increasing incidence of same-sex couples with children, undermines the State's rationale. They note that Vermont law affirmatively guarantees the right to adopt and raise children regardless of the sex of the parents, and challenge the logic of a legislative scheme that recognizes the rights of same-sex partners as parents, yet denies them—and their children—the same security as spouses.

In considering this issue, it is important to emphasize at the outset that it is the Common Benefits Clause of the Vermont Constitution we are construing, rather than its counterpart, the Equal Protection Clause of the Fourteenth Amendment to the United States Constitution. . . .

In understanding the import of the Common Benefits Clause, this Court has often referred to principles developed by the federal courts in applying the Equal Protection Clause. At the same time, however, we have recognized that "[a]lthough the provisions have some similarity of purpose, they are not identical." Indeed, recent Vermont decisions reflect a very different approach from current federal jurisprudence. That approach may be described as broadly deferential to the legislative prerogative to define and advance governmental ends, while vigorously ensuring that the means chosen bear a just and reasonable relation to the governmental objective.

Although our decisions over the last few decades have routinely invoked the rhetoric of suspect class favored by the federal courts, there are notable exceptions. . . . Vermont courts—having "access to specific legislative history and all other proper resources" to evaluate the object and effect of State laws—would engage in a meaningful, case-specific analysis to ensure that any exclusion from the general benefit and protection of the law would bear a just and reasonable relation to the legislative goals.

Although it is accurate to point out that our decisions have consistently recited the federal rational-basis/strict-scrutiny tests, it is equally fair to observe that we have been less than consistent in their application. Just as commentators have noted the United States Supreme Court's obvious yet unstated deviations from the rational-basis standard, so have this Court's holdings often departed from the federal test. . . .

"Labels aside," Vermont case law has consistently demanded in practice that statutory exclusions from publicly-conferred benefits and protections must be "premised on an appropriate and overriding public interest." The rigid categories utilized by the federal courts under the Fourteenth Amendment find no support in our early case law and, while routinely cited, are often effectively ignored in our more recent decisions. . . .

The words of the Common Benefits Clause are revealing. While they do not, to be sure, set forth a fully-formed standard of analysis for determining the constitutionality of a given statute, they do express broad principles which usefully inform that analysis. Chief among these is the principle of inclusion. As explained more fully in the discussion that follows, the specific proscription against governmental favoritism toward not only groups or "set[s] of men," but also toward any particular "family" or "single man," underscores the framers' resentment of political preference of any kind. The affirmative right to the "common benefits and protections" of government and the corollary proscription of favoritism in the distribution of public "emoluments and advantages" reflect the framers' overarching objective "not only that everyone enjoy equality before the law or have an equal voice in government but also that everyone have an equal share in the fruits of the common enterprise." Thus, at its core the Common Benefits Clause expressed a vision of government that afforded every Vermonter its benefit and protection and provided no Vermonter particular advantage. . . .

These and other provisions have led one historian to observe that Vermont's first charter was the "most democratic constitution produced by any of the American states." The historical origins of the Vermont Constitution thus reveal that the framers, although enlightened for their day, were not principally concerned with civil rights for African-Americans and other minorities, but with equal access to public benefits and protections for the community as a whole. The concept of equality at the core of the Common Benefits Clause was not the eradication of racial or class distinctions, but rather the elimination of artificial governmental preferments and advantages. The Vermont Constitution would ensure that the law uniformly afforded every Vermonter its benefit, protection, and security so that social and political preeminence would reflect differences of capacity, disposition, and virtue, rather than governmental favor and privilege.

The language and history of the Common Benefits Clause thus reinforce the conclusion that a relatively uniform standard, reflective of the inclusionary principle at its core, must govern our analysis of laws challenged under the Clause. Accordingly, we conclude that this approach, rather than the rigid, multi-tiered analysis evolved by the federal courts under the Fourteenth Amendment, shall direct our inquiry under Article 7. . . . Our concern here is with delineating, not with labelling the excluded class as "suspect," "quasi-suspect," or "non-suspect" for purposes of determining different levels of judicial scrutiny.

We look next to the government's purpose in drawing a classification that includes some members of the community within the scope of the challenged law but excludes others. Consistent with Article 7's guiding principle of affording the protection and benefit of the law to all members of the Vermont community, we examine the nature of the classification to determine whether it is reasonably necessary to accomplish the State's claimed objectives. . . .

With these general precepts in mind, we turn to the question of whether the exclusion of same-sex couples from the benefits and protections incident to marriage under Vermont law contravenes Article 7. The first step in our analysis is to identify the nature of the statutory classification. As noted, the marriage statutes apply expressly to opposite-sex couples. Thus, the statutes exclude anyone who wishes to marry someone of the same sex. Next, we must identify the governmental purpose or purposes to be served by the statutory classification. The principal purpose the State advances in support of the excluding same-sex couples from the legal benefits of marriage is the government's interest in "furthering the link between procreation and child rearing." The State has a strong interest, it argues, in promoting a permanent commitment between couples who have children to ensure that their offspring are considered legitimate and receive ongoing parental support. The State contends, further, that the Legislature could reasonably believe that sanctioning same-sex unions "would diminish society's perception of the link between procreation and child rearing . . . [and] advance the notion that fathers or mothers . . are mere surplusage to the functions of procreation and child rearing." The State argues that since same-sex couples cannot conceive a child on their own, state-sanctioned same-sex unions "could be seen by the Legislature to separate further the connection between procreation and parental responsibilities for raising children." Hence, the Legislature is justified, the State concludes, "in using the marriage statutes to send a public message that procreation and child rearing are intertwined."

Do these concerns represent valid public interests that are reasonably furthered by the exclusion of same-sex couples from the benefits and protections that flow from the marital relation? It is beyond dispute that the State has a legitimate and long-standing interest in promoting a permanent commitment between couples for the security of their children. It is equally undeniable that the State's interest has been advanced by extending formal public sanction and protection to the union, or marriage, of those couples considered capable of having children, i.e., men and women. And there is no doubt that the overwhelming majority of births today continue to result from natural conception between one man and one woman.

It is equally undisputed that many opposite-sex couples marry for reasons unrelated to procreation, that some of these couples never intend to have children, and that others are incapable of having children. Therefore, if the purpose of the statutory exclusion of same-sex couples is to "further[] the link between procreation and child rearing," it is significantly under-inclusive. The law extends the benefits and protections of marriage to many persons with no logical connection to the stated governmental goal.

Furthermore, while accurate statistics are difficult to obtain, there is no dispute that a significant number of children today are actually being raised by same-sex parents, and that increasing numbers of children are being conceived by such parents through a variety of assisted-reproductive techniques.

Thus, with or without the marriage sanction, the reality today is that increasing numbers of same-sex couples are employing increasingly efficient assisted-reproductive techniques to conceive and raise children. The Vermont Legislature has not only recognized this reality, but has acted affirmatively to remove legal barriers so that same-sex couples may legally adopt and rear the children conceived through such efforts.

Therefore, to the extent that the State's purpose in licensing civil marriage was, and is, to legitimize children and provide for their security, the statutes plainly exclude many same-sex couples who are no different from opposite-sex couples with respect to these objectives. If anything, the exclusion of same-sex couples from the legal protections incident to marriage exposes their children to the precise risks that the State argues the marriage laws are designed to secure against. In short, the marital exclusion treats persons who are similarly situated for purposes of the law, differently. . . .

The question thus becomes whether the exclusion of a relatively small but significant number of otherwise qualified same-sex couples from the same legal benefits and protections afforded their opposite-sex counterparts contravenes the mandates of Article 7. It is, of course, well settled that statutes are not necessarily unconstitutional because they fail to extend legal protection to all who are similarly situated. . . . We turn, accordingly, from the principal justifications advanced by the State to the interests asserted by plaintiffs.

As noted, in determining whether a statutory exclusion reasonably relates to the governmental purpose it is appropriate to consider the history and significance of the benefits denied. What do these considerations reveal about the benefits and protections at issue here? In Loving v. Virginia (1967), the United States Supreme Court, striking down Virginia's anti-miscegenation law, observed that "[t]he freedom to marry has long been recognized as one of the vital personal rights." The Court's point was clear; access to a civil marriage license and the multitude of legal benefits, protections, and obligations that flow from it significantly enhance the quality of life in our society.

The Supreme Court's observations in Loving merely acknowledged what many states, including Vermont, had long recognized. One hundred thirty-seven years before Loving, this Court characterized the reciprocal rights and responsibilities flowing from the marriage laws as "the natural rights of human nature." Early decisions recognized that a marriage contract, although similar to other civil agreements, represents much more because once formed, the law imposes a variety of obligations, protections, and benefits. In short, the marriage laws transform a private agreement into a source of significant public benefits and protections.

While the laws relating to marriage have undergone many changes during the last century, largely toward the goal of equalizing the status of husbands and wives, the benefits of marriage have not diminished in value. On the contrary, the benefits and protections incident to a marriage license under Vermont law have never been greater. They include, for example, the right to receive a portion of the estate of a spouse who dies intestate and protection against disinheritance through elective share provisions; preference in being appointed as the personal representative of a spouse who dies intestate; the right to bring a lawsuit for the wrongful death of a spouse; the right to bring an action for loss of consortium; the right to workers' compensation survivor benefits; the right to spousal benefits statutorily guaranteed to public employees, including health, life,disability, and accident insurance; the opportunity to be covered as a spouse under group life insurance policies issued to an employee; the opportunity to be covered as the insured's spouse under an individual health insurance policy; the right to claim an evidentiary privilege for marital communications; homestead rights and protections; the presumption of joint ownership of property and the concomitant right of survivorship; hospital visitation and other rights incident to the medical treatment of a family member; and the right to receive, and the obligation to provide, spousal support, maintenance, and property division in the event of separation or divorce.

While other statutes could be added to this list, the point is clear. The legal benefits and protections flowing from a marriage license are of such significance that any statutory exclusion must necessarily be grounded on public concerns of sufficient weight, cogency, and authority that the justice of the deprivation cannot seriously be questioned. Considered in light of the extreme logical disjunction between the classification and the stated purposes of the law — protecting children and "furthering the link between procreation and child rearing" — the exclusion falls substantially short of this standard. The laudable governmental goal of promoting a commitment between married couples to promote the security of their children and the community as a whole provides no reasonable basis for denying the legal benefits and protections of marriage to same-sex couples, who are no differently situated with respect to this goal than their opposite-sex counterparts. Promoting a link between procreation and childrearing similarly fails to support the exclusion. We turn, accordingly, to the remaining interests identified by the State in support of the statutory exclusion.

The State asserts that a number of additional rationales could support a legislative decision to exclude same-sex partners from the statutory benefits and protections of marriage. Among these are the State's purported interests in "promoting child rearing in a setting that provides both male and female role models," minimizing the legal complications of surrogacy contracts and sperm donors, "bridging differences" between the sexes, discouraging marriages of convenience for tax, housing or other benefits, maintaining uniformity with marriage laws in other states, and generally protecting marriage from "destabilizing changes." The most substantive of the State's remaining claims relates to the issue of childrearing. It is conceivable that the Legislature could conclude that opposite-sex partners offer advantages in this area, although we note that child-development experts disagree and the answer is decidedly uncertain. The argument, however, contains a more fundamental flaw, and that is the Legislature's endorsement of a policy diametrically at odds with the State's claim. In 1996, the Vermont General Assembly enacted, and the Governor signed, a law removing all prior legal barriers to the adoption of children by same-sex couples. In light of these express policy choices, the State's arguments that Vermont public policy favors opposite-sex over same-sex parents or disfavors the use of artificial reproductive technologies, are patently without substance.

Similarly, the State's argument that Vermont's marriage laws serve a substantial governmental interest in maintaining uniformity with other jurisdictions cannot be reconciled with Vermont's recognition of unions, such as first-cousin marriages, not uniformly sanctioned in other states. Thus, the State's claim that Vermont's marriage laws were adopted because the Legislature sought to conform to those of the other forty-nine states is not only speculative, but refuted by two relevant legislative choices which demonstrate that uniformity with other jurisdictions has not been a governmental purpose. . . .

Finally, it is suggested that the long history of official intolerance of intimate same-sex relationships cannot be reconciled with an interpretation of Article 7 that would give state-sanctioned benefits and protection to individuals of the same sex who commit to a permanent domestic relationship. We find the argument to be unpersuasive for several reasons. First, to the extent that state action historically has been motivated by an animus against a class, that history cannot provide a legitimate basis for continued unequal application of the law. Second, whatever claim may be made in light of the undeniable fact that federal and state statutes — including those in Vermont — have historically disfavored same-sex relationships, more recent legislation plainly undermines the contention. See, e.g., Laws of Vermont, 1977, No. 51, § 2, 3 (repealing former § 2603 of Title 13, which criminalized fellatio). In 1991, Vermont was one of the first states to enact statewide legislation prohibiting discrimination in employment, housing, and other services based on sexual orientation. Furthermore, as noted earlier, recent enactments of the General Assembly have removed barriers to adoption by same-sex couples, and have extended legal rights and protections to such couples who dissolve their "domestic relationship."

Thus, viewed in the light of history, logic, and experience, we conclude that none of the interests asserted by the State provides a reasonable and just basis for the continued exclusion of same-sex couples from the benefits incident to a civil marriage license under Vermont law. Accordingly, in the faith that a case beyond the imagining of the framers of our Constitution may, nevertheless, be safely anchored in the values that infused it, we find a constitutional obligation to extend to plaintiffs the common benefit, protection, and security that Vermont law provides opposite-sex married couples.It remains only to determine the appropriate means and scope of relief compelled by this constitutional mandate. . . .

DOOLEY, J., concurring.

Vermont's legal climate differs considerably from that in other jurisdictions where courts have held that lesbians and gay men are not a suspect classification. . . .In this concurrence, I do not detail a suspect-classification analysis, but I can summarize my opinion by saying that I agree with the general framework adopted by the Oregon courts. . .

More importantly, I cannot endorse, in this vitally important area of constitutional review, a standard that relies wholly on factors and balancing, with no mooring in any criteria or guidelines, however imperfect they may be. . . . For the above reasons, I concur in the mandate, but respectfully disagree with Part II of the Court's decision, the majority's rationale for reaching this mandate.

JOHNSON, J., concurring in part and dissenting in part.

Plaintiffs come before this Court claiming that the State has unconstitutionally deprived them of the benefits of marriage based solely upon a discriminatory classification that violates their civil rights. They ask the Court to remedy the unlawful discrimination by enjoining the State and its municipalities from denying them the license that serves to identify the persons entitled to those benefits. The majority agrees that the Common Benefits Clause of the Vermont Constitution entitles plaintiffs to obtain the same benefits and protections as those bestowed upon married opposite-sex couples, yet it declines to give them any relief other than an exhortation to the Legislature to deal with the problem. I concur with the majority's holding, but I respectfully dissent from its novel and truncated remedy, which in my view abdicates this Court's constitutional duty to redress violations of constitutional rights. I would grant the requested relief and enjoin defendants from denying plaintiffs a marriage license based solely on the sex of the applicants. . . .

The majority declares that the issue before this Court does not turn on the heated moral debate over intimate same-sex relationships, and further, that this Court has a constitutional responsibility to consider the legal merits of even controversial cases. Yet, notwithstanding these pronouncements, the majority elects to send plaintiffs to an uncertain fate in the political caldron of that very same moral debate. And to what end? Passing this case on to the Legislature will not alleviate the instability and uncertainty that the majority seeks to avoid, and will unnecessarily entangle this Court in the Legislature's efforts to accommodate the majority's mandate within a "reasonable period of time. . . ."

Source:

Stan Baker, et al. v. State of Vermont, et al., 170 Vt. 194, 744 A.2d 864 (1999).

National Endowment for the Arts v. Finley, 1998

U.S. Supreme Court decision delivered June 25, 1998, that upheld a 1990 congressional mandate requiring the National Endowment for the Arts (NEA) to consider "general standards of decency" and "values of the American public" when deciding which projects to fund. Performance artist Karen Finley and three other plaintiffs in the case called the mandate unconstitutional and claimed that they had been denied funding from the NEA because of the content of their work. The Court's majority opinion rebuffed their claim contending that the congressional mandate "stops well short of an absolute restriction" and that "it does not preclude awards to projects that might be declared 'indecent' or 'disrespectful.'" In his dissenting opinion, Justice David Souter stated that Congress's mandate was a violation of the First Amendment because it amounted to "viewpoint discrimination" and because "Congress's purpose in imposing the decency and respect criteria was to prevent funding of art that conveys an offensive message."

JUSTICE O'CONNOR delivered the opinion of the Court.

The National Foundation on the Arts and Humanities Act, as amended in 1990, requires the Chairperson of the National Endowment for the Arts (NEA) to ensure that "artistic excellence and artistic merit are the criteria by which [grant] applications are judged, taking into consideration general standards of decency and respect for the diverse beliefs and values of the American public." 20 U.S.C. § 954(d)(1). In this case, we review the Court of Appeals' determination that §954(d)(1), on its face, impermissibly discriminates on the basis of viewpoint and is void for vagueness under the First and Fifth Amendments. We conclude that §954(d)(1) is facially valid, as it neither inherently interferes with First Amendment rights nor violates constitutional vagueness principles.

I

A

With the establishment of the NEA in 1965, Congress embarked on a "broadly conceived national policy of support for the . . . arts in the United States," see §953(b), pledging federal funds to "help create and sustain not only a climate encouraging freedom of thought, imagination, and inquiry but also the material conditions facilitating the release of . . . creative talent." §951(7). The enabling statute vests the NEA with substantial discretion to award grants; it identifies only the broadest funding priorities, including "artistic and cultural significance, giving emphasis to American creativity and cultural diversity," "professional excellence," and the encouragement of "public knowledge, education, understanding, and appreciation of the arts." See §§954(c)(1)–(10). Applications for NEA funding are initially reviewed by advisory panels composed of experts in the relevant field of the arts. Under the 1990 Amendments to the enabling statute, those panels must reflect "diverse artistic and cultural points of view" and include "wide geographic, ethnic, and minority representation," as well as "lay individuals who are knowledgeable about the arts." §§959(c)(1)–(2). The panels report to the 26-member National Council on the Arts (Council), which, in turn, advises the NEA Chairperson. The Chairperson has the ultimate authority to award grants but may not approve an application as to which the Council has made a negative recommendation. §955(f).

Since 1965, the NEA has distributed over three billion dollars in grants to individuals and organizations, funding that has served as a catalyst for increased state, corporate, and foundation support for the arts. Congress has recently restricted the availability of federal funding for individual artists, confining grants primarily to qualifying organizations and state arts agencies, and constraining sub-granting. See Department of the Interior and Related Agencies Appropriations Act, 1998, Pub. L. 105-83, §329, 111 Stat. 1600. By far the largest portion of the grants distributed in fiscal year 1998 were awarded directly to state arts agencies. In the remaining categories, the most substantial grants were allocated to symphony orchestras, fine arts museums, dance theater foundations, and opera associations. See National Endowment for the Arts, FY 1998 Grants, Creation & Presentation 5–8, 21, 20, 27.

Throughout the NEA's history, only a handful of the agency's roughly 100,000 awards have generated formal complaints about misapplied funds or abuse of the public's trust. Two provocative works, however, prompted public controversy in 1989 and led to congressional revaluation of the NEA's funding priorities and efforts to increase oversight of its grant-making procedures. The Institute of Contemporary Art at the University of Pennsylvania had used $30,000 of a visual arts grant it received from the NEA to fund a 1989 retrospective of photographer Robert Mapplethorpe's work. The exhibit, entitled The Perfect Moment, included homoerotic photographs that several Members of Congress condemned as pornographic. See, e.g., 135 Cong. Rec. 22372 (1989). Members also denounced artist Andres Serrano's work Piss Christ, a photograph of a crucifix immersed in urine. See, e.g., id., at 9789. Serrano had been awarded a $15,000 grant from the Southeast Center for Contemporary Art, an organization that received NEA support.

When considering the NEA's appropriations for fiscal year 1990, Congress reacted to the controversy surrounding the Mapplethorpe and Serrano photographs by eliminating $45,000 from the agency's budget, the precise amount contributed to the two exhibits by NEA grant recipients. Congress also enacted an amendment providing that no NEA funds "may be used to promote, disseminate, or produce materials which in the judgment of [the NEA] may be considered obscene, including but not limited to, depictions of sadomasochism, homoeroticism, the sexual exploitation of children, or individuals engaged in sex acts and which, when taken as a whole, do not have serious literary, artistic, political, or scientific value." D of the Interior and Related Agencies Appropriations Act, 1990, Pub. L. 101-121, 103 Stat. 738, 738–742. The NEA implemented Congress' mandate by instituting a requirement that all grantees certify in writing that they would not utilize federal funding to engage in projects inconsistent with the criteria in the 1990 appropriations bill. That certification requirement was subsequently invalidated as unconstitutionally vague by a Federal District Court, see *Bella Lewitzky Dance Foundation v. Frohnmayer,* 754 F. Supp. 774 (CD Cal. 1991), and the NEA did not appeal the decision.

In the 1990 appropriations bill, Congress also agreed to create an Independent Commission of constitutional law scholars to review the NEA's grant-making procedures and assess the possibility of more focused standards for public arts funding. The Commission's report, issued in September 1990, concluded that there is no constitutional obligation to provide arts funding, but also recommended that the NEA rescind the certification requirement and cautioned against legislation setting forth any content restrictions. Instead, the Commission suggested procedural changes to enhance the role of advisory panels and a statutory reaffirmation of "the high place the nation accords to the fostering of mutual respect for the disparate beliefs and values among us." See Independent Commission, Report to Congress on the National Endowment for the Arts 83–91 (Sept. 1990), 3 Record, Doc. No. 151, Exh. K (hereinafter Report to Congress).

Informed by the Commission's recommendations, and cognizant of pending judicial challenges to the funding limitations in the 1990 appropriations bill, Congress debated several proposals to reform the NEA's grant-making process when it considered the agency's reauthorization in the fall of 1990. The House rejected the Crane Amendment, which would have virtually eliminated the NEA, see 136 Cong. Rec. 28656–28657 (1990), and the Rohrabacher Amendment, which would have introduced a prohibition on awarding any grants that could be used to "promote, distribute, disseminate, or produce matter that has the purpose or effect of denigrating the beliefs, tenets, or objects of a particular religion" or "of denigrating an individual, or group of individuals, on the basis of race, sex, handicap, or national origin," id., at 28657–28664. Ultimately, Congress adopted the Williams/Coleman Amendment, a bipartisan compromise between Members opposing any funding restrictions and those favoring some guidance to the agency. In relevant part, the Amendment became §954(d)(1), which directs the Chairperson, in establishing procedures to judge the artistic merit of grant applications, to "tak[e] into consideration general standards of decency and respect for the diverse beliefs and values of the American public."

The NEA has not promulgated any official interpretation of the provision, but in December 1990, the Council unanimously adopted a resolution to implement §954(d)(1) merely by ensuring that the members of the advisory panels that conduct the initial review of grant applications represent geographic, ethnic, and aesthetic diversity. See Minutes of the Dec. 1990 Retreat of the National Council on the Arts, reprinted in App. 12-13; Transcript of the Dec. 1990 Retreat of the National Council on the Arts, reprinted in id., 32–33. John Frohnmayer, then Chairperson of the NEA, also declared that he would "count on [the] procedures" ensuring diverse membership on the peer review panels to fulfill Congress' mandate . . .

Section 954(d)(1) merely adds some imprecise considerations to an already subjective selection process. It does not, on its face, impermissibly infringe on First or Fifth Amendment rights. Accordingly, the judgment of the Court of Appeals is reversed and the case is remanded for further proceedings consistent with this opinion . . .

Source:

Landmark Documents in American History, Facts On File, Inc.

George W. Bush, Executive Order Establishing White House Office of Faith-Based Initiatives, 2001

In the early 21st century many social issues, including teenaged pregnancies, alcoholism and drug abuse, and domestic violence, continue to plague American communities. Government-sponsored programs and private charities had limited success in curbing these problems. George W. Bush pointed to the success of religious (i.e., faith-based) groups in turning around at-risk individuals. Early in his presidency he sought to find a way to help these organizations without infringing on the First Amendment. To achieve this goal he created the Office of Faith-Based Initiatives in the White House and designated five Executive Department Centers for Faith-Based and Community Initiatives in the Departments of Justice, Education, Labor, Health and Human Services, and Housing and Urban Development. The program met with resistance from civil liberties groups as well as religious organizations, which were concerned about the restrictions imposed on them in order to receive federal funds. Nevertheless, in 2002 the various centers were administering grants and the White House was sponsoring activities implementing the program.

By the authority vested in me as President of the United States by the Constitution and the laws of the United States of America, and in order to help the Federal Government coordinate a national effort to expand opportunities for faith-based and other community organizations and to strengthen their capacity to better meet social needs in America's communities, it is hereby ordered as follows:

Section 1. Policy. Faith-based and other community organizations are indispensable in meeting the needs of poor Americans and distressed neighborhoods. Government cannot be replaced by such organizations, but it can and should welcome them as partners. The paramount goal is compassionate results, and private and charitable community groups, including religious ones, should have the fullest opportunity permitted by law to compete on a level playing field, so long as they achieve valid public purposes, such as curbing crime, conquering addiction, strengthening families and neighborhoods, and overcoming poverty. This delivery of social services must be results oriented and should value the bedrock principles of pluralism, nondiscrimination, evenhandedness, and neutrality.

Sec. 2. Establishment. There is established a White House Office of Faith-Based and Community Initiatives (White House OFBCI) within the Executive Office of the President that will have lead responsibility in the executive branch to establish policies, priorities, and objectives for the Federal Government's comprehensive effort to enlist, equip, enable, empower, and expand the work of faith-based and other community organizations to the extent permitted by law.

Sec. 3. Functions. The principal functions of the White House OFBCI are, to the extent permitted by law: (a) to develop, lead, and coordinate the Administration's policy agenda affecting faith-based and other community programs and initiatives, expand the role of such efforts in communities, and increase their capacity through executive action, legislation, Federal and private funding, and regulatory relief;

(b) to ensure that Administration and Federal Government policy decisions and programs are consistent with the President's stated goals with respect to faith-based and other community initiatives;

(c) to help integrate the President's policy agenda affecting faith-based and other community organizations across the Federal Government;

(d) to coordinate public education activities designed to mobilize public support for faith-based and community nonprofit initiatives through volunteerism, special projects, demonstration pilots, and public-private partnerships;

(e) to encourage private charitable giving to support faith-based and community initiatives;

(f) to bring concerns, ideas, and policy options to the President for assisting, strengthening, and replicating successful faith-based and other community programs;

(g) to provide policy and legal education to State, local, and community policymakers and public officials seeking ways to empower faith-based and other community organizations and to improve the opportunities, capacity, and expertise of such groups;

(h) to develop and implement strategic initiatives under the President's agenda to strengthen the institutions of civil society and America's families and communities;

(i) to showcase and herald innovative grassroots nonprofit organizations and civic initiatives;

(j) to eliminate unnecessary legislative, regulatory, and other bureaucratic barriers that impede effective faith-based and other community efforts to solve social problems;

(k) to monitor implementation of the President's agenda affecting faith-based and other community organizations; and

(l) to ensure that the efforts of faith-based and other community organizations meet high standards of excellence and accountability.

Sec. 4. Administration. (a) The White House OFBCI may function through established or ad hoc committees, task forces, or interagency groups.

(b) The White House OFBCI shall have a staff to be headed by the Assistant to the President for Faith-Based and Community Initiatives. The White House OFBCI shall have such staff and other assistance, to the extent permitted by law, as may be necessary to carry out the provisions of this order. The White House OFBCI operations shall begin no later than 30 days from the date of this order.

(c) The White House OFBCI shall coordinate with the liaison and point of contact designated by each executive department and agency with respect to this initiative.

(d) All executive departments and agencies (agencies) shall cooperate with the White House OFBCI and provide such information, support, and assistance to the White House OFBCI as it may request, to the extent permitted by law.

(e) The agencies? actions directed by this Executive Order shall be carried out subject to the availability of appropriations and to the extent permitted by law.

Sec. 5. Judicial Review. This order does not create any right or benefit, substantive or procedural, enforceable at law or equity by a party against the United States, its agencies or instrumentalities, its officers or employees, or any other person.

GEORGE W. BUSH
THE WHITE HOUSE, January 29, 2001

Source:
The White House. Available on-line. URL: www.whitehouse.gov/news/releases/2002/01/20010129-2.html. Accessed November 2003.

September 11, 2001, and Aftermath

George W. Bush, Presidential Address following the September 11th Terrorist Attacks, 2001

On the morning of September 11, 2002, two hijacked planes crashed into each of the twin towers of the World Trade Center in New York City. Within less than two hours, both buildings collapsed, killing almost 2,749 people (as of February 2004; the exact number may never be known), including more than 300 firefighters and police who had come to the rescue. Another hijacked plane hit the Pentagon in Washington, D.C., killing 184 individuals. Hearing over cell and airphones about the first three crashes, passengers in a fourth hijacked plane attacked the four perpetrators, and that plane, carrying 44 people, crashed into a Pennsylvania field. A prisoner who claimed knowledge of the plot later said that plane was aiming for the U.S. Capitol.

President George W. Bush was reading a story to schoolchildren when he was told of the attack. He spent the rest of the day flying to different cities around the country. Vice President Richard Cheney and other high-level officials were evacuated to a secret hideout, where the vice president remained off and on for weeks. This was the worst terrorist attack in terms of lives lost to occur anywhere, and the president treated it as a real—not a metaphorical—war against terrorism generally, and against the alleged perpetrators, followers of Osama bin Laden (al-Qaeda) in particular. Visibly shaken earlier in the day, Bush regained his composure to deliver this message of condolence and encouragement to a country in shock and mourning.

Four days later, in response to the September 11 terrorist attacks, Bush declared a national emergency, a condition not defined in any of the pertinent federal regulations, that gives the president enhanced power. His proclamation listed the relevant sections of the U.S. Code and his intent to suspend the laws that limit his ability to keep more troops available. In addition, he claimed the authority to call the reserves to active duty and to increase military funding beyond what had been allowed in the year's budget. Essentially, this declaration prepared the armed forces and Coast Guard for war.

Good evening. Today, our fellow citizens, our way of life, our very freedom came under attack in a series of deliberate and deadly terrorist acts. The victims were in airplanes, or in their offices; secretaries, businessmen and women, military and federal workers; moms and dads, friends and neighbors. Thousands of lives were suddenly ended by evil, despicable acts of terror.

The pictures of airplanes flying into buildings, fires burning, huge structures collapsing, have filled us with disbelief, terrible sadness, and a quiet, unyielding anger. These acts of mass murder were intended to frighten our nation into chaos and retreat. But they have failed; our country is strong.

A great people has been moved to defend a great nation. Terrorist attacks can shake the foundations of our biggest buildings, but they cannot touch the foundation of America. These acts shattered steel, but they cannot dent the steel of American resolve.

America was targeted for attack because we're the brightest beacon for freedom and opportunity in the world. And no one will keep that light from shining.

Today, our nation saw evil, the very worst of human nature. And we responded with the best of America — with the daring of our rescue workers, with the caring for strangers and neighbors who came to give blood and help in any way they could.

Immediately following the first attack, I implemented our government's emergency response plans. Our military is powerful, and it's prepared. Our emergency teams are working in New York City and Washington, D.C. to help with local rescue efforts.

Our first priority is to get help to those who have been injured, and to take every precaution to protect our citizens at home and around the world from further attacks.

The functions of our government continue without interruption. Federal agencies in Washington which had to be evacuated today are reopening for essential personnel tonight, and will be open for business tomorrow. Our financial institutions remain strong, and the American economy will be open for business, as well.

The search is underway for those who are behind these evil acts. I've directed the full resources of our intelligence and law enforcement communities to find those responsible and to bring them to justice. We will make no distinction between the terrorists who committed these acts and those who harbor them.

I appreciate so very much the members of Congress who have joined me in strongly condemning these attacks. And on behalf of the American people, I thank the many world leaders who have called to offer their condolences and assistance.

America and our friends and allies join with all those who want peace and security in the world, and we stand together to win the war against terrorism. Tonight, I ask for your prayers for all those who grieve, for the children whose worlds have been shattered, for all whose sense of safety and security has been threatened. And I pray they will be comforted by a power greater than any of us, spoken through the ages in Psalm 23: "Even though I walk through the valley of the shadow of death, I fear no evil, for You are with me."

This is a day when all Americans from every walk of life unite in our resolve for justice and peace. America has stood down enemies before, and we will do so this time. None of us will ever forget this day. Yet, we go forward to defend freedom and all that is good and just in our world.

Thank you. Good night, and God bless America.

Source:

The White House. Available on-line. URL: www.whitehouse.gov/news/releases/2001/09/20010911-16.html. Accessed November 2003.

George W. Bush, Military Order, 2001

President George W. Bush authorized this Military Order, also known as the Detention, Treatment, and Trial of Certain Non-Citizens in the War against Terrorism, November 13, 2001, as part of his ongoing war on terrorism in the aftermath of the September 11 attacks. The order made it easier for noncitizens who are suspected terrorists to be arrested, tried, convicted, and punished.

Bush considered the order as protecting the United States against possible future attacks. But critics of the order, such as the American Civil Liberties Union, considered it as a dangerous assault on due process. The order allows suspected terrorists to be tried in military, rather than civilian, courts, in secret proceedings that, according to Bush and Attorney General John Ashcroft, protect against the possibility of retaliatory attacks from other terrorists. In these military courts, only two-thirds of the military commission members present need to vote for conviction in order for the accused to be convicted; in jury trials, the decision must be unanimous. In addition, sentencing is based upon a two-thirds vote, meaning that the death penalty could be imposed on a suspected terrorist with one-third of the military commission dissenting. The convicted could not appeal to any other court, either in the United States or in a foreign country. The secretary of defense was given almost full authority to expand the provisions of the order as he saw fit. As a result of the criticism, Secretary of Defense Donald Rumsfeld made some changes when he issued the guidelines for using the order in 2002.

More than 1,000 people were detained under the order in less than a month. The names of only a handful of these were released, and not until several weeks after the initial arrests, in response to intense media criticism after one detainee died of heart failure while in custody. A number of detainees were found to have no associations with terrorism and were released, many after weeks and months incommunicado. As of winter 2004, many still remain in custody. In addition, prisoners taken in Afghanistan are being held at the U.S. naval base in Guantánamo Bay, Cuba. The United States considers them "unlawful combatants" rather than prisoners of war, and, therefore, they do not fall under the safeguards of the Geneva Convention. At press time two indictments were announced and the treatment of detainees has had mixed results in the lower courts.

Detention, Treatment, and Trial of Certain Non-Citizens in the War against Terrorism

By the authority vested in me as President and as Commander in Chief of the Armed Forces of the United States by the Constitution and the laws of the United States of America, including the Authorization for Use of Military

Force Joint Resolution (Public Law 107-40, 115 Stat. 224) and sections 821 and 836 of title 10, United States Code, it is hereby ordered as follows:

Section 1. Findings.

(a) International terrorists, including members of al Qaida, have carried out attacks on United States diplomatic and military personnel and facilities abroad and on citizens and property within the United States on a scale that has created a state of armed conflict that requires the use of the United States Armed Forces.

(b) In light of grave acts of terrorism and threats of terrorism, including the terrorist attacks on September 11, 2001, on the headquarters of the United States Department of Defense in the national capital region, on the World Trade Center in New York, and on civilian aircraft such as in Pennsylvania, I proclaimed a national emergency on September 14, 2001 (Proc. 7463, Declaration of National Emergency by Reason of Certain Terrorist Attacks).

(c) Individuals acting alone and in concert involved in international terrorism possess both the capability and the intention to undertake further terrorist attacks against the United States that, if not detected and prevented, will cause mass deaths, mass injuries, and massive destruction of property, and may place at risk the continuity of the operations of the United States Government.

(d) The ability of the United States to protect the United States and its citizens, and to help its allies and other cooperating nations protect their nations and their citizens, from such further terrorist attacks depends in significant part upon using the United States Armed Forces to identify terrorists and those who support them, to disrupt their activities, and to eliminate their ability to conduct or support such attacks.

(e) To protect the United States and its citizens, and for the effective conduct of military operations and prevention of terrorist attacks, it is necessary for individuals subject to this order pursuant to section 2 hereof to be detained, and, when tried, to be tried for violations of the laws of war and other applicable laws by military tribunals.

(f) Given the danger to the safety of the United States and the nature of international terrorism, and to the extent provided by and under this order, I find consistent with section 836 of title 10, United States Code, that it is not practicable to apply in military commissions under this order the principles of law and the rules of evidence generally recognized in the trial of criminal cases in the United States district courts.

(g) Having fully considered the magnitude of the potential deaths, injuries, and property destruction that would result from potential acts of terrorism against the United States, and the probability that such acts will occur, I have determined that an extraordinary emergency exists for national defense purposes, that this emergency constitutes an urgent and compelling government interest, and that issuance of this order is necessary to meet the emergency.

Sec. 2. Definition and Policy.

(a) The term "individual subject to this order" shall mean any individual who is not a United States citizen with respect to whom I determine from time to time in writing that:

(1) there is reason to believe that such individual, at the relevant times,

(i) is or was a member of the organization known as al Qaida;

(ii) has engaged in, aided or abetted, or conspired to commit, acts of international terrorism, or acts in preparation therefor, that have caused, threaten to cause, or have as their aim to cause, injury to or adverse effects on the United States, its citizens, national security, foreign policy, or economy; or

(iii) has knowingly harbored one or more individuals described in subparagraphs (i) or (ii) of subsection 2(a)(1) of this order; and

(2) it is in the interest of the United States that such individual be subject to this order.

(b) It is the policy of the United States that the Secretary of Defense shall take all necessary measures to ensure that any individual subject to this order is detained in accordance with section 3, and, if the individual is to be tried, that such individual is tried only in accordance with section 4.

(c) It is further the policy of the United States that any individual subject to this order who is not already under the control of the Secretary of Defense but who is under the control of any other officer or agent of the United States or any State shall, upon delivery of a copy of such written determination to such officer or agent, forthwith be placed under the control of the Secretary of Defense.

Sec. 3. Detention Authority of the Secretary of Defense. Any individual subject to this order shall be —

(a) detained at an appropriate location designated by the Secretary of Defense outside or within the United States;

(b) treated humanely, without any adverse distinction based on race, color, religion, gender, birth, wealth, or any similar criteria;

(c) afforded adequate food, drinking water, shelter, clothing, and medical treatment;

(d) allowed the free exercise of religion consistent with the requirements of such detention; and

(e) detained in accordance with such other conditions as the Secretary of Defense may prescribe.

Sec. 4. Authority of the Secretary of Defense Regarding Trials of Individuals Subject to this Order.

(a) Any individual subject to this order shall, when tried, be tried by military commission for any and all offenses triable by military commission that such individual is alleged to have committed, and may be punished in accordance with the penalties provided under applicable law, including life imprisonment or death.

(b) As a military function and in light of the findings in section 1, including subsection (f) thereof, the Secretary of Defense shall issue such orders and regulations, including orders for the appointment of one or more military commissions, as may be necessary to carry out subsection (a) of this section.

(c) Orders and regulations issued under subsection (b) of this section shall include, but not be limited to, rules for the conduct of the proceedings of military commissions, including pretrial, trial, and post-trial procedures, modes of proof, issuance of process, and qualifications of attorneys, which shall at a minimum provide for —

(1) military commissions to sit at any time and any place, consistent with such guidance regarding time and place as the Secretary of Defense may provide;

(2) a full and fair trial, with the military commission sitting as the triers of both fact and law;

(3) admission of such evidence as would, in the opinion of the presiding officer of the military commission (or instead, if any other member of the commission so requests at the time the presiding officer renders that opinion, the opinion of the commission rendered at that time by a majority of the commission), have probative value to a reasonable person;

(4) in a manner consistent with the protection of information classified or classifiable under Executive Order 12958 of April 17, 1995, as amended, or any successor Executive Order, protected by statute or rule from unauthorized disclosure, or otherwise protected by law, (A) the handling of, admission into evidence of, and access to materials and information, and (B) the conduct, closure of, and access to proceedings;

(5) conduct of the prosecution by one or more attorneys designated by the Secretary of Defense and conduct of the defense by attorneys for the individual subject to this order;

(6) conviction only upon the concurrence of two-thirds of the members of the commission present at the time of the vote, a majority being present;

(7) sentencing only upon the concurrence of two-thirds of the members of the commission present at the time of the vote, a majority being present; and

(8) submission of the record of the trial, including any conviction or sentence, for review and final decision by me or by the Secretary of Defense if so designated by me for that purpose.

Sec. 5. Obligation of Other Agencies to Assist the Secretary of Defense.

Departments, agencies, entities, and officers of the United States shall, to the maximum extent permitted by law, provide to the Secretary of Defense such assistance as he may request to implement this order.

Sec. 6. Additional Authorities of the Secretary of Defense.

(a) As a military function and in light of the findings in section 1, the Secretary of Defense shall issue such orders and regulations as may be necessary to carry out any of the provisions of this order.

(b) The Secretary of Defense may perform any of his functions or duties, and may exercise any of the powers provided to him under this order (other than under section 4(c)(8) hereof) in accordance with section 113(d) of title 10, United States Code.

Sec. 7. Relationship to Other Law and Forums.

(a) Nothing in this order shall be construed to —

(1) authorize the disclosure of state secrets to any person not otherwise authorized to have access to them;

(2) limit the authority of the President as Commander in Chief of the Armed Forces or the power of the President to grant reprieves and pardons; or

(3) limit the lawful authority of the Secretary of Defense, any military commander, or any other officer or agent of the United States or of any State to detain or try any person who is not an individual subject to this order.

(b) With respect to any individual subject to this order —

(1) military tribunals shall have exclusive jurisdiction with respect to offenses by the individual; and

(2) the individual shall not be privileged to seek any remedy or maintain any proceeding, directly or indirectly, or to have any such remedy or proceeding sought on the individual's behalf, in (i) any court of the United States, or any State thereof, (ii) any court of any foreign nation, or (iii) any international tribunal.

(c) This order is not intended to and does not create any right, benefit, or privilege, substantive or procedural, enforceable at law or equity by any party, against the United States, its departments, agencies, or other entities, its officers or employees, or any other person.

(d) For purposes of this order, the term "State" includes any State, district, territory, or possession of the United States.

(e) I reserve the authority to direct the Secretary of Defense, at any time hereafter, to transfer to a governmental authority control of any individual subject to this order. Nothing in this order shall be construed to limit the authority of any such governmental authority to prosecute any individual for whom control is transferred.

Sec. 8. Publication.

This order shall be published in the Federal Register.

GEORGE W. BUSH
THE WHITE HOUSE,
November 13, 2001.

Source:

The White House. Available on-line. URL: www.whitehouse.gov/news/releases/2001/11/20011113-27.html. Accessed November 2003.

George W. Bush, Address to a Joint Session of Congress and the American People, 2001

In his September 20, 2001, speech to a joint session of Congress, President George W. Bush outlined America's response to the September 11, 2001, terrorist attacks on the World Trade Center and the Pentagon.

In the September 20 speech, which some consider the finest he made, Bush accused the Taliban, Afghanistan's Islamic fundamentalist rulers, of "sponsoring and sheltering and supplying" al-Qaeda, the terrorist network believed by the United States to have orchestrated the attacks. President Bush also demanded that the Taliban turn over all al-Qaeda leaders to the United States and that they shut down terrorist training camps within their borders. "Any nation that continues to harbor or support terrorism," he said, "will be regarded by the United States as a hostile regime." In addition, Bush announced the creation of the Office of Homeland Security. This new cabinet-level organization would coordinate all domestic counterterrorism efforts. On several occasions in the speech, Bush emphasized the distinction between Islam and terrorism. Calling the terrorists "traitors to their own faith," he pointed out that their "pretenses to piety" masked the terrorists' "murderous" ideology.

On October 7, 2001, President Bush announced the first American and British military strikes against Taliban military installations and alleged al-Qaeda training camps in Afghanistan. The much-anticipated bomb-and-missile strikes commenced after a three-week diplomatic effort to build an international coalition of support. After the 9/11 attacks, the United States had demanded that the Taliban shut down al-Qaeda operations and surrender its leaders to the United States. In his address, Bush cited the Taliban's failure to meet these demands as the reason for the strikes. He also emphasized that these strikes represented only one facet of a complex conflict: "today we focus on Afghanistan, but the battle is broader." Although the Taliban government fell and was replaced by a coalition government, as of winter 2004, several al-Qaeda leaders, including bin Laden, remained at large.

On October 8, 2001, almost four weeks after the attacks on the World Trade Center and the Pentagon, President Bush issued an executive order creating a new office devoted to the domestic protection of the United States. Many critics ascribed the U.S. government's failure to anticipate the attacks to a lack of coordination among the nation's intelligence-gathering agencies. Turf wars between the Central Intelligence Agency (CIA) and the Federal Bureau of Investigation (FBI) were seen as particularly detrimental to America's ability to thwart terrorist attacks at home. This lack of coordination, coupled with the realization that, contrary to conventional wisdom, the United States was vulnerable to enemy attacks on its own soil, prompted President Bush to create the Office of Homeland Security. According to the order, its mission, "shall be to develop and coordinate the implementation of a comprehensive national strategy to secure the United States from terrorist threats or attacks." Bush appointed Pennsylvania governor Tom Ridge to lead the office, a cabinet-level position answerable only to the president. Many congressional and media critics argued that without secretary status and departmental budget and authority, Ridge would command little clout among the many agencies with homeland security responsibilities. When these fears turned out to be accurate, President Bush agreed to support the creation of a full Department of Homeland Security. He signed the new department into law November 25, 2002.

Mr. Speaker, Mr. President pro tempore, Members of Congress, and fellow Americans:

In the normal course of events, Presidents come to this chamber to report on the state of the Union. Tonight, no such report is needed. It has already been delivered by the American people.

We have seen it in the courage of passengers, who rushed terrorists to save others on the ground—passengers like an exceptional man named Todd Beamer. Please help me to welcome his wife, Lisa Beamer, here tonight.

We have seen the state of our Union in the endurance of rescuers, working past exhaustion. We have seen the unfurling of flags, the lighting of candles, the giving of blood, the saying of prayers—in English, Hebrew, and Arabic. We have seen the decency of a loving and giving people, who have made the grief of strangers their own.

My fellow citizens, for the last nine days, the entire world has seen for itself the state of our Union—and it is strong.

Tonight we are a country awakened to danger and called to defend freedom. Our grief has turned to anger, and anger to resolution. Whether we bring our enemies to justice, or bring justice to our enemies, justice will be done.

I thank the Congress for its leadership at such an important time. All of America was touched on the evening of the tragedy to see Republicans and Democrats, joined together on the steps of this Capitol, singing "God Bless America." And you did more than sing, you acted, by delivering forty billion dollars to rebuild our communities and meet the needs of our military.

Speaker Hastert and Minority Leader Gephardt—Majority Leader Daschle and Senator Lott—I thank you for your friendship and your leadership and your service to our country.

And on behalf of the American people, I thank the world for its outpouring of support. America will never forget the sounds of our National Anthem playing at Buckingham Palace, and on the streets of Paris, and at Berlin's Brandenburg Gate. We will not forget South Korean children gathering to pray outside our embassy in Seoul, or the prayers of sympathy offered at a mosque in Cairo. We will not forget moments of silence and days of mourning in Australia and Africa and Latin America.

Nor will we forget the citizens of eighty other nations who died with our own. Dozens of Pakistanis. More than 130 Israelis. More than 250 citizens of India. Men and women from El Salvador, Iran, Mexico, and Japan. And hundreds of British citizens. America has no truer friend than Great Britain. Once again, we are joined together in a great cause. The British Prime Minister has crossed an ocean to show his unity of purpose with America, and tonight we welcome Tony Blair.

On September the eleventh, enemies of freedom committed an act of war against our country. Americans have known wars—but for the past 136 years, they have been wars on foreign soil, except for one Sunday in 1941. Americans have known the casualties of war—but not at the center of a great city on a peaceful morning. Americans have known surprise attacks—but never before on thousands of civilians. All of this was brought upon us in a single day—and night fell on a different world, a world where freedom itself is under attack.

Americans have many questions tonight. Americans are asking: Who attacked our country?

The evidence we have gathered all points to a collection of loosely affiliated terrorist organizations known as al-Qaida. They are the same murderers indicted for bombing American embassies in Tanzania and Kenya, and responsible for the bombing of the U.S.S. *Cole*.

Al-Qaida is to terror what the mafia is to crime. But its goal is not making money; its goal is remaking the world—and imposing its radical beliefs on people everywhere.

The terrorists practice a fringe form of Islamic extremism that has been rejected by Muslim scholars and the vast majority of Muslim clerics—a fringe movement that perverts the peaceful teachings of Islam. The terrorists' directive commands them to kill Christians and Jews, to kill all Americans, and make no distinctions among military and civilians, including women and children.

This group and its leader—a person named Usama bin Ladin—are linked to many other organizations in different countries, including the Egyptian Islamic Jihad and the Islamic Movement of Uzbekistan.

There are thousands of these terrorists in more than sixty countries. They are recruited from their own nations and neighborhoods, and brought to camps in places like Afghanistan where they are trained in the tactics of terror. They are sent back to their homes or sent to hide in countries around the world to plot evil and destruction.

The leadership of al-Qaida has great influence in Afghanistan, and supports the Taliban regime in controlling most of that country. In Afghanistan, we see al-Qaida's vision for the world.

Afghanistan's people have been brutalized—many are starving and many have fled. Women are not allowed to attend school. You can be jailed for owning a television. Religion can be practiced only as their leaders dictate. A man can be jailed in Afghanistan if his beard is not long enough.

The United States respects the people of Afghanistan —after all, we are currently its largest source of humanitarian aid—but we condemn the Taliban regime. It is not only repressing its own people, it is threatening people everywhere by sponsoring and sheltering and supplying terrorists. By aiding and abetting murder, the Taliban regime is committing murder. And tonight, the United States of America makes the following demands on the Taliban:

Deliver to United States authorities all the leaders of al-Qaida who hide in your land.

Release all foreign nationals—including American citizens—you have unjustly imprisoned, and protect foreign journalists, diplomats, and aid workers in your country.

Close immediately and permanently every terrorist training camp in Afghanistan and hand over every terrorist, and every person in their support structure, to appropriate authorities.

Give the United States full access to terrorist training camps, so we can make sure they are no longer operating.

These demands are not open to negotiation or discussion. The Taliban must act and act immediately. They will hand over the terrorists, or they will share in their fate.

I also want to speak tonight directly to Muslims throughout the world: We respect your faith. It is practiced freely by many millions of Americans, and by millions more in countries that America counts as friends. Its teachings are good and peaceful, and those who commit evil in the name of Allah blaspheme the name of Allah. The terrorists are traitors to their own faith, trying, in effect, to hijack Islam itself. The enemy of America is not our many Muslim friends; it is not our many Arab friends.

Our enemy is a radical network of terrorists, and every government that supports them.

Our war on terror begins with al-Qaida, but it does not end there. It will not end until every terrorist group of global reach has been found, stopped, and defeated.

Americans are asking: Why do they hate us?

They hate what we see right here in this chamber—a democratically elected government. Their leaders are self-appointed. They hate our freedoms—our freedom of religion, our freedom of speech, our freedom to vote and assemble and disagree with each other.

They want to overthrow existing governments in many Muslim countries, such as Egypt, Saudi Arabia, and Jordan. They want to drive Israel out of the Middle East. They want to drive Christians and Jews out of vast regions of Asia and Africa.

These terrorists kill not merely to end lives, but to disrupt and end a way of life. With every atrocity, they hope that America grows fearful, retreating from the world and forsaking our friends. They stand against us, because we stand in their way.

We are not deceived by their pretenses to piety. We have seen their kind before. They are the heirs of all the murderous ideologies of the twentieth century. By sacrificing human life to serve their radical visions—by abandoning every value except the will to power—they follow in the path of fascism, and Nazism, and totalitarianism. And they will follow that path all the way, to where it ends: in history's unmarked grave of discarded lies.

Americans are asking: How will we fight and win this war?

We will direct every resource at our command—every means of diplomacy, every tool of intelligence, every instrument of law enforcement, every financial influence, and every necessary weapon of war—to the disruption and defeat of the global terror network.

This war will not be like the war against Iraq a decade ago, with its decisive liberation of territory and its swift conclusion. It will not look like the air war above Kosovo two years ago, where no ground troops were used and not a single American was lost in combat.

Our response involves far more than instant retaliation and isolated strikes. Americans should not expect one battle, but a lengthy campaign, unlike any other we have seen. It may include dramatic strikes, visible on television, and covert operations, secret even in success. We will starve terrorists of funding, turn them one against another, drive them from place to place, until there is no refuge or rest. And we will pursue nations that provide aid or safe haven to terrorism. Every nation, in every region, now has a decision to make. Either you are with us, or you are with the terrorists. From this day forward, any nation that continues to harbor or support terrorism will be regarded by the United States as a hostile regime.

Our Nation has been put on notice: We are not immune from attack. We will take defensive measures against terrorism to protect Americans.

Today, dozens of federal departments and agencies, as well as state and local governments, have responsibilities affecting homeland security. These efforts must be coordinated at the highest level. So tonight I announce the creation of a Cabinet-level position reporting directly to me—the Office of Homeland Security.

These measures are essential. But the only way to defeat terrorism as a threat to our way of life is to stop it, eliminate it, and destroy it where it grows.

Many will be involved in this effort, from FBI agents to intelligence operatives to the reservists we have called to active duty. All deserve our thanks, and all have our prayers. And tonight, a few miles from the damaged Pentagon, I have a message for our military: Be ready. I have called the armed forces to alert, and there is a reason. The hour is coming when America will act, and you will make us proud.

This is not, however, just America's fight. And what is at stake is not just America's freedom. This is the world's fight. This is civilization's fight. This is the fight of all who believe in progress and pluralism, tolerance and freedom.

We ask every nation to join us. We will ask, and we will need, the help of police forces, intelligence services, and banking systems around the world. The United States is grateful that many nations and many international organizations have already responded—with sympathy and with support. Nations from Latin America, to Asia, to Africa, to Europe, to the Islamic world. Perhaps the NATO Charter reflects best the attitude of the world: an attack on one is an attack on all.

The civilized world is rallying to America's side. They understand that if this terror goes unpunished, their own cities, their own citizens may be next. Terror, unanswered, can not only bring down buildings, it can threaten the stability of legitimate governments. And we will not allow it.

Americans are asking: What is expected of us?

I ask you to live your lives and hug your children. I know many citizens have fears tonight, and I ask you to be calm and resolute, even in the face of a continuing threat.

I ask you to uphold the values of America, and remember why so many have come here. We are in a fight for our principles, and our first responsibility is to live by them. No one should be singled out for unfair treatment or unkind words because of their ethnic background or religious faith.

I ask you to continue to support the victims of this tragedy with your contributions. Those who want to give can go to a central source of information, libertyunites.org, to find the names of groups providing direct help in New York, Pennsylvania, and Virginia.

The thousands of FBI agents who are now at work in this investigation may need your cooperation, and I ask you to give it.

I ask for your patience, with the delays and inconveniences that may accompany tighter security—and for your patience in what will be a long struggle.

I ask your continued participation and confidence in the American economy. Terrorists attacked a symbol of American prosperity. They did not touch its source. America is successful because of the hard work, and creativity, and enterprise of our people. These were the true strengths of our economy before September eleventh, and they are our strengths today.

Finally, please continue praying for the victims of terror and their families, for those in uniform, and for our great country. Prayer has comforted us in sorrow, and will help strengthen us for the journey ahead.

Tonight I thank my fellow Americans for what you have already done and for what you will do. And ladies and gentlemen of the Congress, I thank you, their representatives, for what you have already done, and for what we will do together.

Tonight, we face new and sudden national challenges. We will come together to improve air safety, to dramatically expand the number of air marshals on domestic flights, and take new measures to prevent hijacking. We will come together to promote stability and keep our airlines flying with direct assistance during this emergency.

We will come together to give law enforcement the additional tools it needs to track down terror here at home. We will come together to strengthen our intelligence capabilities to know the plans of terrorists before they act, and find them before they strike.

We will come together to take active steps that strengthen America's economy, and put our people back to work. Tonight we welcome here two leaders who embody the extraordinary spirit of all New Yorkers: Governor George Pataki, and Mayor Rudy Giuliani. As a symbol of America's resolve, my Administration will work with the Congress, and these two leaders, to show the world that we will rebuild New York City.

After all that has just passed, all the lives taken, and all the possibilities and hopes that died with them, it is natural to wonder if America's future is one of fear. Some speak of an age of terror. I know there are struggles ahead, and dangers to face. But this country will define our times, not be defined by them. As long as the United States of America is determined and strong, this will not be an age of terror; this will be an age of liberty, here and across the world.

Great harm has been done to us. We have suffered great loss. And in our grief and anger we have found our mission and our moment. Freedom and fear are at war. The advance of human freedom—the great achievement of our time, and the great hope of every time—now depends on us. Our Nation—this generation—will lift a dark threat of violence from our people and our future. We will rally the world to this cause, by our efforts and by our courage. We will not tire, we will not falter, and we will not fail.

It is my hope that in the months and years ahead, life will return almost to normal. We'll go back to our lives and routines, and that is good. Even grief recedes with time and grace. But our resolve must not pass. Each of us will remember what happened that day, and to whom it happened. We will remember the moment the news came—where we were and what we were doing. Some will remember an image of fire, or a story of rescue. Some will carry memories of a face and a voice gone forever.

And I will carry this. It is the police shield of a man named George Howard, who died at the World Trade Center trying to save others. It was given to me by his mom, Arlene, as a proud memorial to her son. This is my reminder of lives that ended, and a task that does not end.

I will not forget this wound to our country, or those who inflicted it. I will not yield. I will not rest. I will not relent in waging this struggle for the freedom and security of the American people.

The course of this conflict is not known, yet its outcome is certain. Freedom and fear, justice and cruelty, have always been at war, and we know that God is not neutral between them.

Fellow citizens, we will meet violence with patient justice—assured of the rightness of our cause, and confident of the victories to come. In all that lies before us, may God grant us wisdom, and may He watch over the United States of America.

Thank you.

Source:

The White House. Available on-line. URL: www.whitehouse.gov/news/releases/2001/09/20010920-8.html. Accessed November 2003.

The USA PATRIOT Act, 2001 (Official Summary)

Excerpts from an official summary of the major statute passed in the wake of the September 11 terrorism. The title is an acronym for *Uniting and Strengthening America by Providing Appropriate Tools Required to Intercept and Obstruct Terrorism.* The bill, which was signed into law by President George W. Bush October 27, 2001, was designed to provide for both the surveillance and tracking of terrorists. It incorporated a number of reforms law enforcement and intelligence policy makers had been requesting for years. However, many of those same "reforms" and additional powers granted to the executive branch disturbed both civil libertarians and members of Congress (who nonetheless passed the bill unanimously in the Senate and with one dissent in the House). President George W. Bush and Attorney General John Ashcroft pressured Congress to move swiftly despite the statute's substantial constitutional and fiscal challenges. Each house developed a version, and while both curbed civil liberties to some extent, neither gave the president all the power he requested. The House and Senate conferees worked together to reach a compromise. Instead of voting on this version, however, Congress substituted an administration bill that contained only a sunset provision regarding detention as a concession to civil liberties concerns.

Most of the act's provisions affect noncitizens. However, the act stresses that the federal government would protect the rights of any ethnic group that might as a whole be identified with terrorists. Other major points of the bill include increased penalties for terrorist activity, allowing roving wiretaps without the necessity of granting a separate warrant for each one, and nationwide search warrants. The bill explicitly outlawed possession of substances that can be used for biological weapons. In addition, it updates legislation to cover technologies such as e-mail that did not exist when earlier statutes were passed.

Title I: Enhancing Domestic Security Against Terrorism - Establishes in the Treasury the Counterterrorism Fund

(Sec. 102) Expresses the sense of Congress that: (1) the civil rights and liberties of all Americans, including Arab Americans, must be protected, and that every effort must be taken to preserve their safety; (2) any acts of violence or discrimination against any Americans be condemned; and (3) the Nation is called upon to recognize the patriotism of fellow citizens from all ethnic, racial, and religious backgrounds.

(Sec. 104) Authorizes the Attorney General to request the Secretary of Defense to provide assistance in support of Department of Justice (DOJ) activities relating to the enforcement of Federal criminal code (code) provisions regarding the use of weapons of mass destruction during an emergency situation involving a weapon (currently, chemical weapon) of mass destruction.

(Sec. 105) Requires the Director of the U.S. Secret Service to take actions to develop a national network of electronic crime task forces throughout the United States to prevent, detect, and investigate various forms of electronic crimes, including potential terrorist attacks against critical infrastructure and financial payment systems

(Sec. 106) Modifies provisions relating to presidential authority under the International Emergency Powers Act to: (1) authorize the President, when the United States is engaged in armed hostilities or has been attacked by a foreign country or foreign nationals, to confiscate any property subject to U.S. jurisdiction of a foreign person, organization, or country that he determines has planned, authorized, aided, or engaged in such hostilities or attacks (the rights to which shall vest in such agency or person as the President may designate); and (2) provide that, in any judicial review of a determination made under such provisions, if the determination was based on classified information such information may be submitted to the reviewing court ex parte and in camera.

Title II: Enhanced Surveillance Procedures - Amends the Federal criminal code to authorize the interception of wire, oral, and electronic communications for the production of evidence of: (1) specified chemical weapons or terrorism offenses; and (2) computer fraud and abuse.

(Sec. 203) . . .Permits the sharing of grand jury information that involves foreign intelligence or counterintelligence with Federal law enforcement, intelligence, protective, immigration, national defense, or national security officials (such officials), subject to specified requirements.

Authorizes an investigative or law enforcement officer, or an attorney for the Government, who, by authorized means, has obtained knowledge of the contents of any wire, oral, or electronic communication or evidence derived therefrom to disclose such contents to such officials to the extent that such contents include foreign intelligence or counterintelligence.

Directs the Attorney General to establish procedures for the disclosure of information . . . that identifies a United States person, as defined in the Foreign Intelligence Surveillance Act of 1978 (FISA)

(Sec. 204) Clarifies that nothing in code provisions regarding pen registers shall be deemed to affect the acquisition by the Government of specified foreign intelligence information, and that procedures under FISA shall be the exclusive means by which electronic surveillance and the interception of domestic wire and oral (current law) and electronic communications may be conducted

(Sec. 206) Grants roving surveillance authority under FISA after requiring a court order approving an electronic surveillance to direct any person to furnish necessary information, facilities, or technical assistance in circumstances where the Court finds that the actions of the surveillance target may have the effect of thwarting the identification of a specified person.

(Sec. 207) Increases the duration of FISA surveillance permitted for non-U.S. persons who are agents of a foreign power.

(Sec. 209) Permits the seizure of voice-mail messages under a warrant.

(Sec. 211) Amends the Communications Act of 1934 to permit specified disclosures to Government entities, except for records revealing cable subscriber selection of video programming from a cable operator.

(Sec. 212) Permit electronic communication and remote computing service providers to make emergency disclosures to a governmental entity of customer electronic communications to protect life and limb.

(Sec. 213) Authorizes Federal district courts to allow a delay of required notices of the execution of a warrant if immediate notice may have an adverse result and under other specified circumstances.

(Sec. 214) Prohibits use of a pen register or trap and trace devices [methods of capturing telephone call information] in any investigation to protect against international terrorism or clandestine intelligence activities that is conducted solely on the basis of activities protected by the first amendment to the U.S. Constitution

(Sec. 215) Authorizes the Director of the FBI (or designee) to apply for a court order requiring production of certain business records for foreign intelligence and international terrorism investigations. . . .

(Sec. 216) Amends the code to: (1) require a trap and trace device to restrict recoding or decoding so as not to include the contents of a wire or electronic communication; (2) apply a court order for a pen register or trap and trace devices to any person or entity providing wire or electronic communication service in the United States whose assistance may facilitate execution of the order; (3) require specified records kept on any pen register or trap and trace device on a packet-switched data network of a provider of electronic communication service to the public; and (4) allow a trap and trace device to identify the source (but not the contents) of a wire or electronic communication.

(Sec. 217) Makes it lawful to intercept the wire or electronic communication of a computer trespasser in certain circumstances.

(Sec. 218) Amends FISA to require an application for an electronic surveillance order or search warrant to certify that a significant purpose (currently, the sole or main purpose) of the surveillance is to obtain foreign intelligence information

(Sec. 219) Amends rule 41 of the FRCrP [Federal Rules of Criminal Procedure] to permit Federal magistrate judges in any district in which terrorism-related activities may have occurred to issue search warrants for searches within or outside the district.

(Sec. 220) Provides for nationwide service of search warrants for electronic evidence.

(Sec. 223) Amends the Federal criminal code to provide for administrative discipline of Federal officers or employees who violate prohibitions against unauthorized disclosures of information gathered under this Act. Provides for civil actions against the United States for damages by any person aggrieved by such violations. [Sec. 225 exempts service providers, landlords, or others or assist government agents acting under the act from civil suits.]

(224) Terminates this title on December 31, 2005, except with respect to any particular foreign intelligence investigation beginning before that date, or any particular offense or potential offense that began or occurred before it.

Title IV: Protecting the Border

Subtitle B: Enhanced Immigration Provisions

Amends the Immigration and Nationality Act to broaden the scope of aliens ineligible for admission or deportable due to terrorist activities to include an alien who: (1) is a representative of a political, social, or similar group whose political endorsement of terrorist acts undermines U.S. antiterrorist efforts; (2) has used a position of prominence to endorse terrorist activity, or to persuade others to support such activity in a way that undermines U.S. antiterrorist efforts (or the child or spouse of such an alien under specified circumstances); or (3) has been associated with a terrorist organization and intends to engage in threatening activities while in the United States.

Title IV, B (Sec. 411); Title VIII, (Sec. 802)

"Title IV. B (Sec. 411) Includes within the definition of "terrorist activity" the use of any weapon or dangerous device.

Redefines "engage in terrorist activity" to mean, in an individual capacity or as a member of an organization, to: (1) commit or to incite to commit, under circumstances indicating an intention to cause death or serious bodily injury, a terrorist activity; (2) prepare or plan a terrorist activity; (3) gather information on potential targets for terrorist activity; (4) solicit funds or other

things of value for a terrorist activity or a terrorist organization (with an exception for lack of knowledge); (5) solicit any individual to engage in prohibited conduct or for terrorist organization membership (with an exception for lack of knowledge); or (6) commit an act that the actor knows, or reasonably should know, affords material support, including a safe house, transportation, communications, funds, transfer of funds or other material financial benefit, false documentation or identification, weapons (including chemical, biological, or radiological weapons), explosives, or training for the commission of a terrorist activity; to any individual who the actor knows or reasonably should know has committed or plans to commit a terrorist activity; or to a terrorist organization (with an exception for lack of knowledge).

"[Title IV. B (Sec. 411)] defines "terrorist organization" as a group: (1) designated under the Immigration and Nationality Act or by the Secretary of State; or (2) a group of two or more individuals, whether related or not, which engages in terrorist-related activities.

"Title VIII. (Sec. 802) Amends the Federal criminal code to: (1) revise the definition of "international terrorism" to include activities that appear to be intended to affect the conduct of government by mass destruction; and (2) defines 'domestic terrorism' as activities that occur primarily within U.S. jurisdiction, that involve criminal acts dangerous to human life, and that appear to be intended to intimidate or coerce a civilian population, to influence government policy by intimidation or coercion, or to affect government conduct by mass destruction, assassination, or kidnapping.

(Sec. 412) Provides for mandatory detention until removal from the United States (regardless of any relief from removal) of an alien certified by the Attorney General as a suspected terrorist or threat to national security. Requires release of such alien after seven days if removal proceedings have not commenced, or the alien has not been charged with a criminal offense. Authorizes detention for additional periods of up to six months of an alien not likely to be deported in the reasonably foreseeable future only if release will threaten U.S. national security or the safety of the community or any person. Limits judicial review to habeas corpus proceedings in the U.S. Supreme Court, the U.S. Court of Appeals for the District of Columbia, or any district court with jurisdiction to entertain a habeas corpus petition. Restricts to the U.S. Court of Appeals for the District of Columbia the right of appeal of any final order by a circuit or district judge.

(Sec. 413) Authorizes the Secretary of State, on a reciprocal basis, to share criminal- and terrorist-related visa lookout information with foreign governments.

(Sec. 414) Declares the sense of Congress that the Attorney General should: (1) fully implement the integrated entry and exit data system for airports, seaports, and land border ports of entry with all deliberate speed. . . .

(Sec. 416) Directs the Attorney General to implement fully and expand the foreign student monitoring program to include other approved educational institutions like air flight, language training, or vocational schools.

(Sec. 427) Prohibits benefits to terrorists or their family members.

V: Removing Obstacles to Investigating Terrorism

Authorizes the Attorney General to pay rewards from available funds pursuant to public advertisements for assistance to DOJ to combat terrorism and defend the Nation against terrorist acts. . . .

(Sec. 503) Amends the DNA Analysis Backlog Elimination Act of 2000 to qualify a Federal terrorism offense for collection of DNA for identification.

(Sec. 504) Amends FISA to authorize consultation among Federal law enforcement officers regarding information acquired from an electronic surveillance or physical search in terrorism and related investigations or protective measures

(Sec. 505) Allows the FBI to request telephone toll and transactional records, financial records, and consumer reports in any investigation to protect against international terrorism or clandestine intelligence activities only if the investigation is not conducted solely on the basis of activities protected by the first amendment to the U.S. Constitution

(Sec. 506) Revises U.S. Secret Service jurisdiction with respect to fraud and related activity in connection with computers. Grants the FBI primary authority to investigate specified fraud and computer related activity for cases involving espionage, foreign counter-intelligence,

information protected against unauthorized disclosure for reasons of national defense or foreign relations, or restricted data, except for offenses affecting Secret Service duties.

(Sec. 507) Provide[s] for disclosure of educational records to the Attorney General in a terrorism investigation or prosecution.

Title VIII: Strengthening the Criminal Laws Against Terrorism

Amends the Federal criminal code to prohibit specific terrorist acts or otherwise destructive, disruptive, or violent acts against mass transportation vehicles, ferries, providers, employees, passengers, or operating systems.

(Sec. 803) Prohibits harboring any person knowing or having reasonable grounds to believe that such person has committed or to be about to commit a terrorism offense.

(Sec. 804) Establishes Federal jurisdiction over crimes committed at U.S. facilities abroad.

(Sec. 805) Applies the prohibitions against providing material support for terrorism to offenses outside of the United States.

(Sec. 806) Subjects to civil forfeiture all assets, foreign or domestic, of terrorist organizations.

(Sec. 808) Expands: (1) the offenses over which the Attorney General shall have primary investigative jurisdiction under provisions governing acts of terrorism transcending national boundaries; and (2) the offenses included within the definition of the Federal crime of terrorism.

(Sec. 809) Provides that there shall be no statute of limitations for certain terrorism offenses if the commission of such an offense resulted in, or created a foreseeable risk of, death or serious bodily injury to another person

(Sec. 811) Makes: (1) the penalties for attempts and conspiracies the same as those for terrorism offenses. . . .

(Sec. 814) Revises prohibitions and penalties regarding fraud and related activity in connection with computers to include specified cyber-terrorism offenses.

(Sec. 817) Prescribes penalties for knowing possession in certain circumstances of biological agents, toxins, or delivery systems, especially by certain restricted persons.

Title IX: Improved Intelligence

Require[s] the Director of Central Intelligence. . .to establish requirements and priorities for foreign intelligence collected under [FISA] and to provide assistance to the Attorney General . . . to ensure that information derived from electronic surveillance or physical searches is disseminated for efficient and effective foreign intelligence purposes. Requires the inclusion of international terrorist activities within the scope of foreign intelligence under such Act

(Sec. 903) Expresses the sense of Congress that officers and employees of the intelligence community should establish and maintain intelligence relationships to acquire information on terrorists and terrorist organizations.

Title X: Miscellaneous

(Sec. 1002) Expresses the sense of Congress condemning acts of violence or discrimination against any American, including Sikh-Americans. Calls upon local and Federal law enforcement authorities to prosecute to the fullest extent of the law all those who commit crimes.

(Sec. 1009) Directs the FBI to study and report to Congress on the feasibility of providing to airlines access via computer to the names of passengers who are suspected of terrorist activity by Federal officials. . . .

(Sec. 1012) Amends the Federal transportation code to prohibit States from licensing any individual to operate a motor vehicle transporting hazardous material unless the Secretary of Transportation determines that such individual does not pose a security risk warranting denial of the license. Requires background checks of such license applicants by the Attorney General upon State request.

(Sec. 1016) Critical Infrastructures Protection Act of 2001. Defines critical infrastructure as systems and assets, whether physical or virtual, so vital to the United States that their incapacity or destruction would have a debilitating impact on security, national economic security, national public health or safety, or any combination of those matters.

Source:

Official Summary of the USA PATRIOT Act, 2001. Also available on-line from the American Library Association. URL: www.ala.org.

Aviation and Transportation Security Act, 2001

This bill was passed by Congress November 16, 2001, and signed by President Bush on November 19. It came in response to increased concerns over airline security following the September 11, 2001, attacks. The Aviation and Transportation Security Act attempted to prevent such hijackings in the future by increasing airport security. The bill required that within a year most airport security screeners would be federal employees, a goal met on November 19, 2002. Five airports were to test alternative security arrangements involving private contractors. After three years, airports could request that private contractors handle screening. Background checks were required for all screeners, and all screeners must be U.S. citizens. Although these federal screeners were allowed to unionize, they could not strike. To pay the new workers' salaries, airlines could collect the amount they would normally spend per year on screeners—about $700 million—and charge passengers $2.50 for each leg of their trip, with a maximum charge of $5.00 per trip. The bill also required closer inspection of checked baggage, screening of all passengers, and more air marshals. In addition, flight schools were required to conduct background checks on noncitizens seeking instruction in the operation of aircraft over 12,500 pounds, and flight school employees would be trained to recognize suspicious behavior.

The Transportation Security Administration began February 19, 2002. Within the following year a number of the components of the act that proved impossible within the prescribed time frame were modified.

(excerpt)

An Act

To improve aviation security, and for other purposes.

Be it enacted by the Senate and House of Representatives of the United States of America in Congress assembled,

This Act may be cited as the Aviation and Transportation Security Act.'

Title I—Aviation Security

SEC. 101. TRANSPORTATION SECURITY ADMINISTRATION.

(a) IN GENERAL- The Transportation Security Administration shall be an administration of the Department of Transportation.

* * *

(1) APPOINTMENT- The head of the Administration shall be the Under Secretary of Transportation for Secu-

rity. The Under Secretary shall be appointed by the President, by and with the advice and consent of the Senate.

(2) QUALIFICATIONS- The Under Secretary must—

(A) be a citizen of the United States; and

(B) have experience in a field directly related to transportation or security.

(3) TERM- The term of office of an individual appointed as the Under Secretary shall be 5 years.

(c) LIMITATION ON OWNERSHIP OF STOCKS AND BONDS- The Under Secretary may not own stock in or bonds of a transportation or security enterprise or an enterprise that makes equipment that could be used for security purposes.

(d) FUNCTIONS- The Under Secretary shall be responsible for security in all modes of transportation, including—

(1) civil aviation security, and related research and development activities; and

(2) security responsibilities over other modes of transportation that are exercised by the Department of Transportation.

(e) SCREENING OPERATIONS- The Under Secretary shall—

(1) be responsible for day-to-day Federal security screening operations for passenger air transportation and intrastate air transportation. . .;

(2) develop standards for the hiring and retention of security screening personnel;

(3) train and test security screening personnel; and

(4) be responsible for hiring and training personnel to provide security screening at all airports in the United States where screening is required. . .in consultation with the Secretary of Transportation and the heads of other appropriate Federal agencies and departments.

(f) ADDITIONAL DUTIES AND POWERS-

* * *

(1) receive, assess, and distribute intelligence information related to transportation security;

(2) assess threats to transportation;

(3) develop policies, strategies, and plans for dealing with threats to transportation security;

(4) make other plans related to transportation security, including coordinating countermeasures with appropriate departments, agencies, and instrumentalities of the United States Government;

(5) serve as the primary liaison for transportation security to the intelligence and law enforcement communities;

(6) on a day-to-day basis, manage and provide operational guidance to the field security resources of the Administration, including Federal Security Managers. . .;

(7) enforce security-related regulations and requirements;

(8) identify and undertake research and development activities necessary to enhance transportation security;

(9) inspect, maintain, and test security facilities, equipment, and systems;

(10) ensure the adequacy of security measures for the transportation of cargo;

(11) oversee the implementation, and ensure the adequacy, of security measures at airports and other transportation facilities;

(12) require background checks for airport security screening personnel, individuals with access to secure areas of airports, and other transportation security personnel;

(13) work in conjunction with the Administrator of the Federal Aviation Administration with respect to any actions or activities that may affect aviation safety or air carrier operations;

(14) work with the International Civil Aviation Organization and appropriate aeronautic authorities of foreign governments under section 44907 to address security concerns on passenger flights by foreign air carriers in foreign air transportation; and

(15) carry out such other duties, and exercise such other powers, relating to transportation security as the Under Secretary considers appropriate, to the extent authorized by law.

(g) NATIONAL EMERGENCY RESPONSIBILITIES-

(1) IN GENERAL- Subject to the direction and control of the Secretary, the Under Secretary, during a national emergency, shall have the following responsibilities:

(A) To coordinate domestic transportation, including aviation, rail, and other surface transportation, and maritime transportation (including port security).

(B) To coordinate and oversee the transportation-related responsibilities of other departments and agencies of the Federal Government other than the Department of Defense and the military departments.

(C) To coordinate and provide notice to other departments and agencies of the Federal Government, and appropriate agencies of State and local governments, including departments and agencies for transportation, law enforcement, and border control, about threats to transportation.

(D) To carry out such other duties, and exercise such other powers, relating to transportation during a national emergency as the Secretary shall prescribe.

(2) AUTHORITY OF OTHER DEPARTMENTS AND AGENCIES- The authority of the Under Secretary under this subsection shall not supersede the authority of any other department or agency of the Federal Govern-

ment under law with respect to transportation or transportation-related matters, whether or not during a national emergency.

(3) CIRCUMSTANCES- The Secretary shall prescribe the circumstances constituting a national emergency for purposes of this subsection.

(h) MANAGEMENT OF SECURITY INFORMATION- In consultation with the Transportation Security Oversight Board, the Under Secretary shall—

(1) enter into memoranda of understanding with Federal agencies or other entities to share or otherwise cross-check as necessary data on individuals identified on Federal agency databases who may pose a risk to transportation or national security;

(2) establish procedures for notifying the Administrator of the Federal Aviation Administration, appropriate State and local law enforcement officials, and airport or airline security officers of the identity of individuals known to pose, or suspected of posing, a risk of air piracy or terrorism or a threat to airline or passenger safety;

(3) in consultation with other appropriate Federal agencies and air carriers, establish policies and procedures requiring air carriers—

(A) to use information from government agencies to identify individuals on passenger lists who may be a threat to civil aviation or national security; and

(B) if such an individual is identified, notify appropriate law enforcement agencies, prevent the individual from boarding an aircraft, or take other appropriate action with respect to that individual; and

(4) consider requiring passenger air carriers to share passenger lists with appropriate Federal agencies for the purpose of identifying individuals who may pose a threat to aviation safety or national security.

(i) VIEW OF NTSB- In taking any action under this section that could affect safety, the Under Secretary shall give great weight to the timely views of the National Transportation Safety Board.

* * *

Source:

Thomas Legislative Information on the Internet. S. 1447. Available on-line. URL: http://thomas.loc.gov/cgi-bin/bdquery/z?d107:s.00147:. Accessed November 2003.

Joint Resolution to Authorize the Use of U.S. Armed Forces against Iraq, 2002

On October 16, 2002, President Bush signed a congressional resolution giving him the authority to use military force, if necessary, to destroy the biological and chemical weapons that, according to the White House, are being stored by Saddam Hussein's government in Iraq, and to shut down Baghdad's alleged nuclear weapons program. The president called the Iraqi regime "a serious and growing threat to peace." The president and congressional supporters of the resolution considered the resolution a way to influence the United Nations Security Council and General Assembly to pass an additional resolution or resolutions requiring Iraq to submit to unconditional weapons inspections or risk military action. The White House had insisted that as commander in chief Mr. Bush already had the power to order a military strike against Iraq in defense of the United States. But he had lobbied hard for congressional support so that he could argue to the United Nations that the country was behind him. In order to garner Democratic support, the White House agreed to accept attempting to work through the United Nations, but if the UN was not forthcoming, he made it clear he would act alone.

Iraq condemned the draft resolution as "an insult to the international community."

October 11, 2002

Joint Congressional Resolution

Whereas the Iraq Liberation Act (Public Law 105-338) expressed the sense of Congress that it should be the policy of the United States to support efforts to remove from power the current Iraqi regime and promote the emergence of a democratic government to replace that regime;

Whereas on September 12, 2002, President Bush committed the United States to 'work with the United Nations Security Council to meet our common challenge' posed by Iraq and to 'work for the necessary resolutions,' while also making clear that 'the Security Council resolutions will be enforced, and the just demands of peace and security will be met, or action will be unavoidable';

Whereas the United States is determined to prosecute the war on terrorism and Iraq's ongoing support for international terrorist groups combined with its development of weapons of mass destruction in direct violation of its obligations under the 1991 cease-fire and other United Nations Security Council resolutions make clear that it is in the national security interests of the United States and in furtherance of the war on terrorism that all relevant United Nations Security Council resolutions be enforced, including through the use of force if necessary;

Whereas Congress has taken steps to pursue vigorously the war on terrorism through the provision of authorities and funding requested by the President to take the necessary actions against international terrorists and terrorist organizations, including those nations, organizations or persons who planned, authorized, committed or aided the terrorist attacks that occurred on September 11, 2001, or harbored such persons or organizations;

Whereas the President and Congress are determined to continue to take all appropriate actions against international terrorists and terrorist organizations, including those nations, organizations or persons who planned, authorized, committed or aided the terrorist attacks that occurred on September 11, 2001, or harbored such persons or organizations;

Whereas the President has authority under the Constitution to take action in order to deter and prevent acts of international terrorism against the United States, as Congress recognized in the joint resolution on Authorization for Use of Military Force (Public Law 107-40); and

Whereas it is in the national security of the United States to restore international peace and security to the Persian Gulf region: Now, therefore, be it

Resolved by the Senate and House of Representatives of the United States of America in Congress assembled,

SECTION 1. SHORT TITLE.

This joint resolution may be cited as the `Authorization for the Use of Military Force Against Iraq'.

SEC. 2. SUPPORT FOR UNITED STATES DIPLOMATIC EFFORTS.

The Congress of the United States supports the efforts by the President to — (1) strictly enforce through the United Nations Security Council all relevant Security Council resolutions applicable to Iraq and encourages him in those efforts; and (2) obtain prompt and decisive action by the Security Council to ensure that Iraq abandons its strategy of delay, evasion and noncompliance and promptly and strictly complies with all relevant Security Council resolutions.

SEC. 3. AUTHORIZATION FOR USE OF UNITED STATES ARMED FORCES.

(a) AUTHORIZATION- The President is authorized to use the Armed Forces of the United States as he determines to be necessary and appropriate in order to —

(1) defend the national security of the United States against the continuing threat posed by Iraq; and

(2) enforce all relevant United Nations Security Council resolutions regarding Iraq.

(b) PRESIDENTIAL DETERMINATION- In connection with the exercise of the authority granted in subsection (a) to use force the President shall, prior to such exercise or as soon thereafter as may be feasible, but no later than 48 hours after exercising such authority, make available to the Speaker of the House of Representatives and the President pro tempore of the Senate his determination that —

(1) reliance by the United States on further diplomatic or other peaceful means alone either (A) will not adequately protect the national security of the United States against the continuing threat posed by Iraq or (B) is not likely to lead to enforcement of all relevant United Nations Security Council resolutions regarding Iraq; and

(2) acting pursuant to this resolution is consistent with the United States and other countries continuing to take the necessary actions against international terrorists and terrorist organizations, including those nations, organizations or persons who planned, authorized, committed or aided the terrorists attacks that occurred on September 11, 2001.

(c) WAR POWERS RESOLUTION REQUIREMENTS-

(1) SPECIFIC STATUTORY AUTHORIZATION- Consistent with section 8(a)(1) of the War Powers Resolution, the Congress declares that this section is intended to constitute specific statutory authorization within the meaning of section 5(b) of the War Powers Resolution.

(2) APPLICABILITY OF OTHER REQUIREMENTS- Nothing in this resolution supersedes any requirement of the War Powers Resolution.

SEC. 4. REPORTS TO CONGRESS.

(a) The President shall, at least once every 60 days, submit to the Congress a report on matters relevant to this joint resolution, including actions taken pursuant to the exercise of authority granted in section 3 and the status of planning for efforts that are expected to be required after such actions are completed, including those actions described in section 7 of Public Law 105-338 (the Iraq Liberation Act of 1998).

(b) To the extent that the submission of any report described in subsection (a) coincides with the submission of any other report on matters relevant to this joint resolution otherwise required to be submitted to Congress pursuant to the reporting requirements of Public Law 93-148 (the War Powers Resolution), all such reports may be submitted as a single consolidated report to the Congress.

(c) To the extent that the information required by section 3 of Public Law 102-1 is included in the report required by this section, such report shall be considered as meeting the requirements of section 3 of Public Law 102-1.

Source:

The New York Times on the Web. URL: www.nytimes.com.

Organization of the Homeland Security Department, 2002

President George W. Bush signed legislation creating a Department of Homeland Security November 25, 2002. Shortly after the terrorist attacks of 9/11, President Bush named Thomas Ridge, then governor of Pennsylvania, to head the White House Office of Homeland Security. He now nominated Ridge to head the new agency. Its purpose was to coordinate all activities related to domestic security and counterterrorism except the intelligence collecting of the Federal Bureau of Investigation, the Central Intelligence Agency, and the intelligence units of the Department of Defense. However, the new department would conduct intelligence analysis. Ridge would head what had been 22 formerly independent agencies or components of other departments, including the Federal Emergency Management Agency (FEMA), the Coast Guard and Transportation Security Administration from the Department of Transportation, the Secret Service and Customs Service from Treasury, the Immigration and Naturalization Service and National Domestic Preparedness Office (FBI) from Justice, and the Animal and Plant Health Inspection Service from the Department of Agriculture. When fully staffed, the new department was expected to have approximately 170,000 employees. The Homeland Security Act also established a commission to study intelligence.

101. EXECUTIVE DEPARTMENT; MISSION.

(a) ESTABLISHMENT- There is established a Department of Homeland Security, as an executive department of the United States within the meaning of title 5, United States Code.

(b) MISSION-

(1) IN GENERAL- The primary mission of the Department is to—

(A) prevent terrorist attacks within the United States;

(B) reduce the vulnerability of the United States to terrorism;

(C) minimize the damage, and assist in the recovery, from terrorist attacks that do occur within the United States;

(D) carry out all functions of entities transferred to the Department, including by acting as a focal point regarding natural and manmade crises and emergency planning;

(E) ensure that the functions of the agencies and subdivisions within the Department that are not related directly to securing the homeland are not diminished or neglected except by a specific explicit Act of Congress;

(F) ensure that the overall economic security of the United States is not diminished by efforts, activities, and programs aimed at securing the homeland; and

(G) monitor connections between illegal drug trafficking and terrorism, coordinate efforts to sever such connections, and otherwise contribute to efforts to interdict illegal drug trafficking.

(2) RESPONSIBILITY FOR INVESTIGATING AND PROSECUTING TERRORISM- Except as specifically provided by law with respect to entities transferred to the Department under this Act, primary responsibility for investigating and prosecuting acts of terrorism shall be vested not in the Department, but rather in Federal, State, and local law enforcement agencies with jurisdiction over the acts in question…

Source:

Thomas Legislative Information on the Internet. http://thomas.loc.gov/cgi-bin/query/z?c107:h.r.5005.enr: , or in pdf format at http://news.findlaw.com/nytimes/docs/terrorism/hsa2002.pdf. Accessed November 2003.

Suggested Reading

Domestic Politics

Lou Cannon. *President Reagan: The Role of a Lifetime*. 2d ed. New York: Public Affairs, 2000.

Danny O. Coulson, with Eileen Shannon. *No Heroes: Inside the FBI's Secret Counter-Terror Force*. New York: Pocket Books, 1999.

Jim Dwyer, David Kocienieski, Deidre Murphy, and Peg Tyre. *Two Seconds Under the World: The Conspiracy Behind the World Trade Center Bombing*. New York: Crown, 1994

John Robert Greene. *The Presidency of Gerald Ford*. Lawrence: University Press of Kansas, 1995.

Haynes Johnson. *Best of Times: America in the Clinton Years*. New York: Harcourt, 1999.

Haynes Johnson. *Sleepwalking Through History: America in the Reagan Years*. New York: W.W. Norton, 1991.

Kevin Phillips. *The Politics of Rich and Poor*. New York: Random House, 1990.

Richard Posner. *An Affair of State: The Investigation, Impeachment, and Trial of President Clinton*. Cambridge, Mass.: Harvard University Press, 1999.

Foreign Policy Issues

Michael Beschloss and Strobe Talbott. *At the Highest Levels: The Inside Story of the End of the Cold War*. Boston: Little Brown, 1993.

Tom Clancy, with Frederick M. Franks. *Into the Storm: A Study in Command*. New York: G.P. Putnam, 1997.

Theodore Draper. *A Very Thin Line: The Iran-Contra Affairs*. New York: Hill & Wang, 1991.

John L. Gaddis. *The United States and the End of the Cold War*. New York: Oxford University Press, 1992.

Raymond L. Garthoff. *Detente and Confrontation: American-Soviet Relations from Nixon to Reagan*. Washington, D.C.: Brookings Institution, 1994.

Rhodri Jeffreys-Jones. *The CIA & American Democracy*. New Haven, Conn.: Yale University Press, 1989, 1998.

Michael Schaller. *Altered States: The U.S. and Japan since the Occupation*. 1996.

Gaddis Smith. *Morality, Reason and Power: American Diplomacy in the Carter Years*. New York: Hill & Wang, 1986.

Washington Post Political Staff. *Deadlock: The Inside Story of America's Closest Election*. New York: Public Affairs, 2001.

Economic and Technological Developments

Janet Abbate. *Inventing the Internet*. Cambridge, Mass.: MIT Press, 1999.

Michael J. Boskin *Reagan and the Economy: The Successes, Failures, and Unfinished Agenda*. San Francisco: Institute for Contemporary Studies Press, 1989.

Paul E. Cerruzi. *A History of Modern Computing*. Cambridge, Mass.: MIT Press, 1998

Daniel Quinn Mills. *Buy, Lie, and Sell High: How Investors Lost Out on Enron and the Internet Bubble*. New York: Wiley, 2002.

Social Developments

Carl Abbott. *The Metropolitan Frontier: Cities in the Modern American West*. Tucson: University of Arizona Press, 1994.

Elliott Currie. *Confronting Crime: An American Challenge*. New York: Pantheon Books, 1986.

Elliott Robert Barkan. *And Still They Came: Immigrants and American Society, 1920 to the 1990s*. Wheeling, Ill.: H. Davidson, 1996.

Alma M. Garcia, and Mario T. Garcia. *Chicana Feminist Thought: The Basic Historical Writings*. London and New York: Routledge, 1997.

Charles R. Morris. *The AARP: America's Most Powerful Lobby and the Clash of Generations*. New York: Times Books, 1996.

Bruce J. Shulman. *The Seventies: The Great Shift in American Culture, Society, and Politics*. New York: Free Press, 2001.

Randy Shilts. *And the Band Played On: Politics, People, and the Aids Epidemic*. New York: St. Martin's Press, 1987.

Cornel West. *Race Matters*. New York: Vintage Books, 1994.

Roberto Suro. *Strangers Among Us: How Latino Immigration Is Transforming America*. New York: Knopf, 1998.

William Julius Wilson. *Poverty, Inequality, and the Future of Social Policy*. New York: Russell Sage Foundation, 1995.

Cultural Developments

Louis Gates, Jr. *Loose Canons: Notes on the Culture Wars*. New York: Oxford University Press, 1992.

James D. Hunter. *Culture Wars: The Struggle to Define America*. New York: Basic Books, 1991.

Mark Silk. *Spiritual Politics: Religion and America since World War II*. New York: Simon & Schuster, 1988.

September 11, 2001, and Aftermath

Thomas L. Friedman. *Longitudes and Attitudes: Exploring the World After September 11*. New York: Farrar, Straus and Giroux, 2002.

Strobe Talbot and Nayan Chand, eds. *The Age of Terror: America and the World after September 11*. New York: Basic Books, 2001.

Bob Woodward. *Bush at War*. New York: Simon & Schuster, 2002.

Index

Boldface page numbers denote extensive treatment of a topic.

B

G

H

I

J

K

L

N

O

P

S

T

U

V

Y

Z